Introduction to

ABNORMAL
CHILD *and*
ADOLESCENT
PSYCHOLOGY

This book is dedicated to my wonderful wife, Jennifer, and my three darling children: Thomas, Marie, and Anne Catherine.

Introduction to

ABNORMAL CHILD *and* ADOLESCENT PSYCHOLOGY

ROBERT WEIS
DENISON UNIVERSITY

SAGE Publications
Los Angeles • London • New Delhi • Singapore

For information:

Sage Publications, Inc.
2455 Teller Road
Thousand Oaks, California 91320
E-mail: order@sagepub.com

Sage Publications India Pvt. Ltd.
B 1/I 1 Mohan Cooperative Industrial Area
Mathura Road, New Delhi 110 044
India

Sage Publications Ltd.
1 Oliver's Yard
55 City Road
London EC1Y 1SP
United Kingdom

Sage Publications Asia-Pacific Pte. Ltd.
33 Pekin Street #02-01
Far East Square
Singapore 048763

Printed in the United States of America

Library of Congress Cataloging-in-Publication Data

Weis, Robert, 1973-
Introduction to abnormal child and adolescent psychology / Robert Weis.
    p. cm.
Includes bibliographical references and index.
ISBN 978-1-4129-2657-7 (cloth)
    1. Child psychopathology. 2. Adolescent psychopathology. I. Title.

RJ499.W3925 2008
618.92′89—dc22   2007021784

This book is printed on acid-free paper.

07   08   09   10   11   10 9 8 7 6 5 4 3 2 1

Acquisitions Editor:	Cheri Dellelo
Editorial Assistant:	Lara Grambling
Associate Editor:	Deya Saoud
Production Editor:	Catherine M. Chilton
Copy Editor:	Diana Breti
Typesetter:	C&M Digitals (P) Ltd.
Proofreader:	William H. Stoddard
Indexer:	Diggs Publication Services
Cover Designer:	Glenn Vogel
Marketing Manager:	Amberlyn Erzinger

Brief Contents

Contents

Preface

Now is an exciting time to study abnormal child psychology. The field of child psychopathology is relatively new and rapidly changing. The study and practice of abnormal child psychology began when Lightner Witmer established the first psychological clinic for children in 1896. However, some of the most exciting developments in the field have emerged only in the past 25 years. For example, the theoretical perspective of developmental psychopathology has changed the way professionals view children's development (and maldevelopment) across time and from multiple perspectives. Technical advances in neuroimaging and clinical neuroscience have allowed us to better appreciate the genetic and biological underpinnings of children's behavior. The past decade has also seen greater importance placed on empirically supported treatments and the dramatically increased use of psychotropic medications for youth. Finally, changes in the demographic and socioeconomic makeup of the United States have required us to view children's development within broader social and cultural contexts.

Now is a particularly exciting time for newcomers to the field. In most of the more established sciences, such as physics and chemistry, students must spend years mastering fundamental principles and research techniques before they can contribute meaningfully to the discipline. However, in the field of abnormal child psychology, there is so much new ground to explore! Students can ask relevant, novel questions almost immediately. Important questions such as "Why is autism more commonly diagnosed today compared to 20 years ago? Why are adolescent girls more likely than boys to become depressed? What's the best way to help physically abused children?" need answers. The field needs bright and motivated individuals who are willing to devote their professional lives to understanding and helping children and adolescents in need.

Goals of This Book

This book was written as an introductory text. I adopted a developmental psychopathology approach to understanding youths with behavioral, social-emotional, and cognitive disorders. The developmental psychopathology perspective examines the emergence of child and adolescent disorders over time, pays special attention to risk and protective factors that influence developmental processes and trajectories, and examines child psychopathology in the context of normal child development.

Introduction to Developmental Psychopathology

I have four main goals for this book. First, I want to introduce students to the developmental psychopathology paradigm and show how this perspective can help organize our understanding of various childhood disorders. Examining patterns of development and maldevelopment over time adds a level of complexity that, I hope, will spark students' curiosity about child development and the emergence of behavior and learning problems.

In the book, I hope to go beyond merely describing each disorder; I also want to introduce students to the multitude of factors that cause child psychopathology. Potential etiologies are numerous and complex. To help students organize the research literature, I examine each disorder across five broad levels of analysis:

Genetics (e.g., behavioral and molecular genetics research)

Biology (e.g., brain structure and functioning, hormones, neuroimaging studies)

Psychological Processes (e.g., the interplay between children's thoughts, feelings, and actions)

Interpersonal Relations (e.g., parent-child attachment, family functioning, peer relationships)

Social-Cultural Context (e.g., children's race, ethnicity, SES, neighborhood)

The causes of child psychopathology can be analyzed at each of these levels. However, the most complete accounts of child psychopathology usually involve interactions across multiple levels of analysis and across time. In reading this book, I hope students will see that the field of abnormal child psychology is interdisciplinary and complex.

The Integration of Science and Practice

Second, I want to convey the value and interdependence of psychological research and human service. I want to challenge the notion that psychological research and clinical practice are separate professional endeavors. Instead, I hope to illustrate that competent, ethical clinical work draws upon existing psychological research, while the most meaningful psychological research is often inspired by clinical practice.

Perhaps the most salient feature of this text is that it introduces students to the scientist-practitioner approach to abnormal child psychology. The scientist-practitioner perspective assumes that the field of abnormal child psychology is foremost a science. The field needs to be founded in scientific theory and supported by empirical data. Students must appreciate the methods and findings of psychological research in order to accurately understand children's social, emotional, and behavioral problems. At the same time, the scientist-practitioner perspective assumes that the best psychological research is relevant to the day-to-day lives of children, families, and society. Research allows us to accurately understand children in need, to help alleviate children's problems, and to find ways to promote the welfare of children in society.

Greater Attention to Empirically Supported Treatment

My third goal is to provide students with an understanding of empirically supported treatments. These treatments include psychosocial and pharmacological interventions as well as primary (universal) and secondary (indicated) prevention techniques. To the extent possible, I try to provide a detailed description of each treatment so that students can appreciate both the theory behind the intervention and how the treatment plays out in clinics, hospitals, and schools. Then, I briefly review the efficacy and effectiveness of each form of treatment and (more often) the limitations in the research literature.

I try to supplement the text with interesting case studies. I hope that these case studies bring to life my descriptions of the various disorders, their causes, and treatments. I also hope these case studies allow students to focus their attention on children and families, rather than on disorders per se. Although names and other identifying information have been changed, the case studies describe real clients. Whenever possible, I provide information about children's outcomes after treatment.

Relevance to Life

Finally, I want to show students *why* an understanding of child psychopathology and its treatment might be important to them. Most students will not become psychologists or counselors. However, all students will have multiple opportunities to influence the lives and developmental outcomes of children and adolescents in the future (if not already). Some students will become physicians, nurses, teachers, librarians, daycare providers, occupational or recreational therapists, or other professionals who have immediate, frequent contact with children. Other students will volunteer as coaches, tutors, or mentors in schools and in the community. Nearly all students will become parents and have the primary responsibility of raising the next generation of youth. Although few students will become mental health professionals, all can rely on psychological science and critical thinking to make informed decisions about the welfare of our families, schools, neighborhoods, and society.

A Final Word to Instructors

To accompany this text, I have created ancillary material for instructors and students. Instructor material is designed to facilitate lectures, class discussion, and the creation of exams. I hope that this material will allow instructors greater time and flexibility to engage students in the classroom rather than manage the "nuts and bolts" of their courses. The ancillary instructor material includes the following:

- Sample syllabi, chapter outlines, and chapter summaries
- PowerPoint slides for each chapter, including tables and figures from the text

- Supplemental lectures on topics relevant to child/adolescent psychopathology
- Supplemental tables and figures in digital format
- Discussion questions and classroom exercises
- Suggested movie and Web site resources
- Multiple choice, short answer, and essay questions drawn from the book

I am especially happy to offer instructors a wide variety of exam questions from which to build their tests. The exam questions are organized according to Bloom's (1956) taxonomy of educational objectives. Consequently, questions are grouped according to the level of abstraction, creativity, and critical thinking needed to adequately answer them. I have grouped these questions into five general categories:

1. Knowledge: Students must recall facts or define important terms.

2. Comprehension: Students must summarize, explain, or give examples of key ideas.

3. Analysis: Students must compare and contrast two or more ideas, theories, or therapies.

4. Application: Students must use information in the text to solve a problem or apply their understanding to a case study.

5. Synthesis: Students must critically examine the strengths and weaknesses of a theory, idea, or therapy and judge its merits.

Multiple-choice questions in the test bank tend to focus on students' (1) knowledge and (2) comprehension of information presented in the text. Short-answer and essay questions in the instructor's material cover all five categories, with emphasis on (3) analysis, (4) application, and (5) synthesis. Although many instructors will write their own exam questions, I hope that these questions will serve as a springboard for exam preparation or class discussion and help instructors develop their students' critical thinking skills.

Finally, I hope instructors will encourage students to visit the Web site for this course. The Web site includes flashcards and other study aids, links of interest to students, links to video clips, and recommendations for feature films dealing with child and adolescent psychopathology. I hope that the Web site, like this book, will initiate an interest in child development and psychological science that will continue for years to come.

Acknowledgments

I am grateful to many people for their support and encouragement. First, I am thankful for the professional training and mentorship of Dr. Chris Lovejoy and the clinical faculty at Northern Illinois University, who embody the spirit of the scientist-practitioner tradition. Second, I want to acknowledge three clinician-scholars who have greatly influenced my view of developmental psychopathology and the delivery of psychological services to children, adolescents, and families: Dr. Thomas Linscheid and Dr. Joseph Hatcher of Columbus Children's Hospital and Dr. Terry Kaddatz of St. Michael Hospital in Stevens Point, Wisconsin. Third, I would like to thank my colleagues at Denison University, especially Drs. Cody Brooks, Frank Hassebrock, and Sarah Hutson-Comeaux, for their collegiality and support. Fourth, I must thank the reviewers of this manuscript, who offered many helpful suggestions in its preparation. They are David L. Carlston, Midwestern State University; Robert Devasch, University of South Carolina; Christie Karpiak, University of Scranton; Rich Milich, University of Kentucky; Martin Murphy, University of Akron; Wendy J. Nilsen, University of Rochester; Jill Norvilitis, SUNY College at Buffalo; Elizabeth Soliday, Washington State University, Vancouver; Ric Steele, University of Kansas; and Margaret Wright, Miami University of Ohio. Finally, I am most indebted to my wonderful wife and three children, who have taught me more about child development than anything I have read thus far. I hope that this text, in some small way, reflects their love and support for me over the years.

—Robert Weis
Granville, Ohio

CHAPTER 1

The Science and Practice of Abnormal Child Psychology

Welcome to the Study of Abnormal Child Psychology

Childhood is a time of physical maturation, intellectual development, and social-emotional growth. Ideally, children are provided with ample opportunities for play and exploration within the safety and security of a loving family and supportive social network. However, for a significant number of youth, childhood is marked by biological, behavioral, or social-contextual challenges that can adversely affect their development.

The study of child psychopathology is complex and diverse. The sheer number of psychological disorders that can afflict children and adolescents is daunting, to say nothing of the multitude of causal factors and treatments. However, the last 20 years have witnessed a marked increase in the scientific study of abnormal child and adolescent psychology. Theory and empirical research have helped to advance the field, enabling researchers to identify some of the causes of childhood disorders and guiding clinicians toward the most promising forms of treatment.

There is, perhaps, no more exciting time to be studying abnormal child psychology than now. Students interested in psychological research will discover many areas of child psychopathology that deserve their attention. Each disorder can be explored from multiple perspectives, ranging from its genetic and biological underpinnings to the behavioral and social-cultural factors that cause and maintain it. At the same time, students interested in helping at-risk youth will discover new developments in the application of psychological research to prevent and treat childhood disorders.

The field of abnormal child psychology is broad and constantly changing. There is much work to be done. Geneticists, neuroscientists, physicians, psychologists, counselors, teachers, parents, and all other individuals who interact with youth can play a role in the prevention and alleviation of childhood disorders and the promotion of children's mental health. This text is intended to introduce you to this intellectually exciting and personally rewarding discipline. Welcome!

Prevalence of Childhood Disorders

Epidemiologists are scientists who study the prevalence of medical and psychological disorders in the general population. **Prevalence** refers to the percentage of individuals in a given population who have a medical or psychological condition.[1] To estimate prevalence, epidemiologists collect data from thousands of individuals in the population, asking them to comment on their current physical or psychological health. To estimate the prevalence of psychological disorders among children and adolescents, epidemiologists usually rely on information gathered from parents, other caregivers, and (sometimes) children themselves.

Conducting epidemiological research is difficult for several reasons. First, researchers are challenged by the task of collecting data from thousands of people in the population. Many people do not want to participate in lengthy surveys, others do not understand questions asked of them, and still others provide inaccurate information. Second, the information collected depends greatly on *who* answers the researchers' questions. For example, parents may be able to comment on children's disruptive behavior, but they may be less accurate in estimating children's difficulties with depression or use of alcohol (Loeber, Green, & Lahey, 1990). Third, conducting a large-scale epidemiological survey is costly and time consuming. For these reasons, determining the exact prevalence of childhood disorders has been challenging.

Despite these methodological obstacles, at least seven large epidemiological studies designed to estimate the prevalence of child and adolescent disorders have been conducted in English-speaking countries. Collectively, these studies include data from tens of thousands of youths and their caregivers, using a variety of research strategies. Results indicate that approximately 15% of youths aged 6 to 16 have a diagnosable mental disorder at any given point in time (Breton et al., 1999; British Medical Association, 2006; Costello et al., 1996; Meltzer, Gatward, Goodman, & Ford, 2003; Offord et al., 1987; Shaffer et al., 1996; Simonoff et al., 1997).

A prevalence of 15% indicates that as many as 11,100,000 youths in the United States are experiencing significant psychological distress and impairment (U.S. Census Bureau, 2006). Furthermore, by the time they reach age 16, as many as 30% will have experienced a psychological disorder at some point in their lives (British Medical Association, 2006). The most common category of mental disorders among youth is anxiety disorders (e.g., phobias, fears of separation), followed by conduct problems (e.g., oppositional and aggressive behaviors) and Attention-Deficit/Hyperactivity Disorder (ADHD; see Table 1.1).

---

[1]Boldface type indicates a new or key term.

Table 1.1   Prevalence of Psychological Disorders in Children and Adolescents

Problem	Prevalence (%)
Any anxiety disorder	6.5
Attention-deficit/hyperactivity disorder	3.3
Conduct problems	3.3
Any depressive disorder	2.1
Any substance use disorder	0.8
Autism and other pervasive developmental disorders	0.3
Any eating disorder	0.1
Any bipolar disorder	0.1
Schizophrenia	0.1

Source: Based on the Ontario Child Health Study (Offord et al., 1987), the National Institutes of Mental Health Methodology for Epidemiology of Mental Disorders in Children and Adolescents Study (Shaffer et al., 1996), the Great Smoky Mountains Study (Costello et al.,1996), the Virginia Twin Study of Adolescent Behavioral Development (Simonoff et al., 1997), the Quebec Child Mental Health Survey (Breton et al., 1999), the British Child Mental Health Survey (Meltzer et al., 2003), and the British Medical Association Board of Science Survey (British Medical Association, 2006).

Psychological disorders have direct, deleterious consequences on the quality of life of children and their families. The direct cost of child and adolescent mental health care in the United States is approximately $12 million annually (Ringel & Sturm, 2001). Youths who experience mental disorders are at risk for lower academic achievement, which can adversely affect their ability to reach their earning potential as adults. Furthermore, the parents of children and adolescents with mental disorders often show reduced productivity at work because of the demands associated with caring for these youths.

The cost to society of child and adolescent psychological disorders is also enormous. Society must not only pay for the direct cost of mental health treatment, but must also cover expenses associated with child and adolescent mental illness. These associated costs include incarceration and rehabilitation for youths with conduct problems, drug and alcohol counseling for youths with substance abuse and dependence, and family supervision and reunification services for youths who experience childhood maltreatment. School districts must pay for special educational services for children with cognitive, learning, and behavioral problems that interfere with their ability to benefit from traditional public education. Although the prevention of childhood mental disorders would spare families considerable suffering and spare society enormous expense, prevention remains an underutilized approach to dealing with child and adolescent psychopathology in the United States (Tolan & Dodge, 2005).

Although approximately 15% of youth experience full-blown psychological *disorders*, the percentage of youth who encounter significant mental health *problems* is even greater (see Table 1.2). To be classified with a mental disorder, youths must show both significant symptoms and marked distressed or impairment in day-to-day functioning. However, many youths experience serious problems in their family relationships, educational attainment, and social functioning but fall short of meeting

Table 1.2   Prevalence of Mental Health Problems Among Youth in the United States

Problem	Prevalence (%)
Anxiety problems	13.0
Disruptive behavior problems	10.3
Mood problems	6.2
Substance use problems	2.0
Any mental health problem	20.9

Source: Based on the Methodology for Epidemiology of Mental Disorders in Children and Adolescents (MECA) Study (Shaffer et al., 1996).

diagnostic criteria for a mental disorder. For example, many children experience considerable feelings of sadness and symptoms of social withdrawal, but they do not meet diagnostic criteria for Major Depressive Disorder. Similarly, many adolescent girls show poor body image and unhealthy eating habits, but they do not qualify for a diagnosis of Anorexia or Bulimia Nervosa. Youths with subthreshold emotional or behavioral problems are clearly not reaching their social and emotional potentials and deserve the attention of parents, teachers, and mental health practitioners. Indeed, as many as 21% of youth in the United States have *either* a diagnosable mental disorder *or* a subthreshold behavioral or emotional problem that significantly interferes with their general functioning and quality of life (Shaffer, Fisher, Lucas, Dulcan, & Schwab-Stone, 2000). Consequently, approximately one in five youths are in need of psychological treatment or support.

Sociodemographics and Children's Mental Health

Mental health problems are not equally distributed across the population (British Medical Association, 2006; Shaffer et al., 1996). First, mental and behavioral disorders are more common among adolescents than among children. Although the prevalence of some disorders, like ADHD, gradually decreases from childhood to adolescence, the prevalence of most disorders, especially conduct problems, depression, and anxiety, increases dramatically during the early teenage years. Although mental health problems can emerge at any age, early adolescence appears to be a time in development that places youths at particular risk.

Second, boys and girls are at different risk for developing psychological disorders across development. Specifically, young boys are more likely than young girls to develop most early childhood disorders, especially developmental disorders (e.g., Autism, Mental Retardation) and disruptive behavior problems (e.g., ADHD, conduct problems). However, by early adolescence, these differences between genders narrow. By late adolescence, girls show a greater likelihood of emotional disorders, especially depression and anxiety, than do boys.

Third, youths from socially and economically impoverished families and neighborhoods are at increased risk for developing most psychological disorders. Across English-speaking countries, youths from low-income families, single-parent families, parents of low educational attainment, and high-crime neighborhoods show increased prevalence for almost all child and adolescent disorders. In the United States, African American and other ethnic minority children show increased risk for many mental health problems. Researchers are actively searching for the causes of child psychopathology among low-income minority youth, as well as ways to reduce the risks they face.

The Rise of Pharmacotherapy

One of the greatest changes in the field of abnormal child psychology in the last two decades has been the dramatic increase in the use of medication by children and adolescents. The use of psychotropic medication has increased approximately three-fold in the past 15 years (Olfson, Marcus, Weissman, & Jensen, 2002). Recent data indicate that approximately 1 in 10 adolescent boys and 1 in 14 adolescent girls who visit a physician are prescribed a psychotropic medication (Thomas, Conrad, Casler, & Goodman, 2006). Indeed, psychotropic medication prescriptions for adolescents increased 191% from 1994 to 2001, compared to an increase of only 6% for nonpsychotropic medications (Thomas et al., 2006; see Figure 1.1).

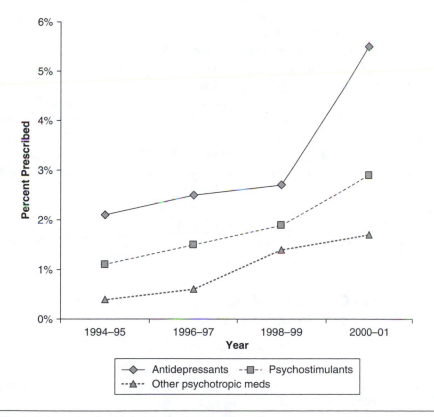

Figure 1.1   Psychotropic Medication Use Over Time

Source: Based on Thomas et al. (2006).

Note: Prescriptions for adolescents have increased 191% since 1994. Approximately 20% of adolescents prescribed psychotropic medications were not diagnosed with a mental disorder.

Table 1.3   Psychotropic Medication Use Among Youth in the United States

Medication	Prevalence (%)
Any psychotropic medication	5.2
Psychostimulants (Ritalin, Adderall)	3.4
Antidepressants (Paxil, Prozac)	1.5
Antianxiety medications (BuSpar)	0.4
Antipsychotics (Risperdal)	0.4

Source: Based on Bonati and Clavenna (2005).

Note: Table shows prevalence of medication use among youth with and without psychiatric problems.

Estimates of the prevalence of psychotropic medication among youth vary (Bonati & Clavenna, 2005; see Table 1.3). Overall, approximately 5.2% of children and adolescents in the United States have been prescribed at least one psychotropic medication. The most frequently prescribed class of medications for youth are psychostimulants, like methylphenidate (i.e., Ritalin), which are often used to treat ADHD. The second most frequently prescribed medications for youth are antidepressants, especially serotonin reuptake inhibitors like paroxetine (i.e., Paxil) and fluoxetine (i.e., Prozac). In most cases, these medications are prescribed by pediatricians and family practice physicians, rather than psychiatrists.

The use of prescription medications is even higher among youths referred for psychiatric treatment. In one epidemiological study of youths referred to mental health professionals in the United States, approximately 29% were prescribed at least one psychotropic medication (Warner, Pottick, & Mukherjee, 2004). Medication was most frequently used to treat children with ADHD, depression, and psychotic disorders. Youths who show two or more psychiatric disorders are especially likely to be prescribed medication. More than 40% of youths with multiple psychiatric disorders receive medication. Youths receiving inpatient psychiatric treatment are most likely to use prescription medication. Indeed, approximately 70%–75% of psychiatrically hospitalized youths are prescribed at least one psychotropic medication during the course of their inpatient stay (Dean, McDermott, & Marshall, 2006; Lekhwani, Nair, Nikhinson, & Ambrosini, 2004; Najjar, Welch, Grapentine, Sachs, Siniscalchi, & Price, 2004).

Barriers to Child Mental Health Services in the United States

Some experts have argued that the child mental health system in the United States is in a state of crisis (President's New Freedom Commission on Mental Health, 2003). Available data indicate that the prevalence of child and adolescent mental health problems has increased over the past two decades. However, families' access to high-quality mental health services remains grossly inadequate. Only about one-third of youths who need mental health services receive treatment (Burns et al., 1995). Families who are able to obtain mental health services often find treatment inadequate or outdated.

Tolan and Dodge (2005) have identified several barriers to children's access to high-quality, empirically based mental health services. First, financial hardship often interferes with children's access to comprehensive treatment. In the United States, mental health treatment and medical treatment do not receive equal coverage from insurance companies, despite evidence that mental health problems cost families and society considerable financial expense. Families may find themselves unable to pay for high-quality treatment for their children and adolescents. Families who are uninsured or underinsured face the additional challenge of obtaining treatment from a public social service system that is often overburdened and underfunded.

Second, even if families can pay for high-quality mental health services, they may be unable to find these services. As we will see, many of the empirically supported, high-quality mental health treatments that have been identified by researchers are not available in most communities. For example, Multisystemic Therapy (MST) is an empirically supported treatment for older adolescents with serious conduct problems. Many well-designed studies have shown MST to reduce adolescents' disruptive behavior problems, improve their social and academic functioning, reduce their likelihood of arrest and incarceration, and save money (Henggeler & Lee, 2003). However, few clinicians are trained in providing MST, and MST is available in only a small number of communities. Consequently, many clinicians rely on other, less well-supported interventions.

Third, there are simply not enough experts in child and adolescent mental health to satisfy the need for services. Jenkins (1998) estimated that the current mental health care system is able to address the needs of only about 10% of all youths with psychological problems. Youths who receive treatment are typically those who show the most serious distress or impairment. Youths with less severe problems, such as moderate depression, mild learning problems, or unhealthy eating habits, often remain unrecognized and untreated until their condition worsens. Inadequate mental health services are especially pronounced among poor and ethnic minority youth (Ringel & Sturm, 2001).

Finally, stigma can interfere with children's access to mental health treatment. Many caregivers are reluctant to refer their children for therapy because of the negative connotations associated with diagnosis and treatment. Approximately 25% of pediatrician visits involve behavioral or emotional problems that could be better addressed by child and adolescent mental health professionals (Horwitz et al., 2002). Stigma associated with the diagnosis and treatment of childhood disorders causes many at-risk youths to be denied treatment.

What Is *Abnormal* Child Psychology?

Differentiating Normal From Abnormal Child Behavior

Defining Abnormal Behavior in Children

There is no consensus on how to define abnormal behavior in children and adolescents and no agreement on how to best differentiate abnormality from normal functioning. However, mental health practitioners and researchers have proposed several criteria to identify children with behavioral and social-emotional problems.

One approach to defining abnormality is based on **statistical deviancy**. In this approach, abnormal behaviors are defined by their relative infrequency in the general population. For example, thoughts about death are fairly common among adolescents. However, recurrent thoughts about killing oneself are statistically infrequent and could indicate a mood disturbance such as depression. Advocates of the statistical infrequency approach might administer a rating scale to clients and identify youths who show symptoms well beyond the range of normality, compared to other children and adolescents of the same age and gender.

The chief limitation of the statistical deviancy approach to defining abnormality is that not all infrequent behaviors are indicative of mental disorders. Imagine a child who is tearful, prefers to stay in her room, does not want to play with friends, and is having problems completing schoolwork. From the statistical deviancy perspective, we might diagnose this girl with depression because she shows mood problems that are rare among children her age. However, if we learn that her grandfather died a few days before her assessment, we would likely interpret her behavior as a normal grief reaction, not as an indicator of Major Depressive Disorder. Although statistical infrequency may be an important component of a definition of abnormality, it is insufficient. Statistical deviancy does not take into account the context of children's behavior.

Another approach to defining abnormality is based on **degree of impairment**. From this perspective, abnormal behavior is defined by thoughts, feelings, or actions that interfere with the individual's social, academic, or occupational functioning. For example, an adolescent who feels sad because she broke up with her boyfriend would not be diagnosed with depression, as long as she is able to maintain relationships with friends, get along with parents, and perform adequately in school. However, her behavior might be considered abnormal if her functioning deteriorates in any of these areas.

Defining abnormality by level of impairment has a serious drawback: Many people with mental disorders do not show overt impairment in functioning. For example, an adolescent who carefully plans his suicide may show so few overt problems at home or in school that parents and friends are surprised when he attempts self-harm. By most accounts, Eric Harris and Dylan Klebold, the adolescents who killed 12 classmates and a teacher in Columbine High School in April, 1999, showed few symptoms of impairment before they committed their heinous crimes (see Image 1.1).

Yet another definition of abnormality might incorporate the individual's degree of **psychological distress**. People can show psychological distress through depressed mood, irritability, anxiety, worry, panic, confusion, frustration, anger, or any other feeling of dysphoria. Psychological distress is one of the central features of most anxiety and mood disorders.

One limitation of defining abnormality in terms of psychological distress is that distress is often subjective. Some signs of distress can be observed by others, such as sweaty palms and flushed face. However, distress is usually assessed by asking clients

Eric Harris
12/10/97

Guns in School

〆   In the past few weeks there has been news of several shootings in high schools. A student

in Texas killed three fellow classmates and injured many more when he fired at a prayer group

before school. This student had several other weapons with him when he was apprehended,

showing how easy it was to bring so many weapons to school and not be noticed. Students who

bring guns to school are hardly ever detected. This is shocking to most parents and even other

students since it is just as easy to bring a loaded handgun to school as it is to bring a calculator.   *ouch!*

The problem of guns in school is a major one faced by many parents, teachers, and citizens these

days. Solutions are hard to come by in such a situation because of how widespread the problem is

and how different each school in each town can be. Students can get weapons into school too

easily and they have to much access to weapons outside of school.

I.

   A. Weapons in school are hard to detect and students have ways of getting out of

      searches or other ways of detection.

       1. One example of students avoiding detection is a 1990 survey conducted by the

          Centers For Disease Control (CDC) which found that one in 20 high school

          students carried a gun in school during the past month (CDC).

       2. Students can use their backpacks, purses, or even projects to bring weapons

          into school.

       3. Metal detectors can be avoided by using other school entrances.

   B. Students have access to many weapons and can obtain a gun from many places.

       1. The low price of junk guns (as low as 69 dollars) brings these guns within the

          economic reach of children (Gun Digest, 288).

JC-001-026352

Image 1.1   Guns in School. A paper submitted by Eric Harris approximately one year before he and Dylan Klebold shot 12 classmates and one teacher in Columbine High School. His teacher commented on the paper: "Thorough and logical. A few formatting problems, however. Nice job!"

Source: Released to public domain by the Jefferson County Sheriff's Office, July 6, 2006.

to report their feelings. Subjective assessment of distress in children is problematic for at least two reasons. First, not all children are equally aware of their mood states or able to differentiate among various emotions. For example, some children express dysphoria by crying while others develop physical symptoms, like upset stomach. Furthermore, young children often confuse negative emotions such as "fear" and "anger." Second, children's ratings of distress often cannot be compared against an objective criterion. For example, a child who reports feeling "bad" might be experiencing more distress than another child who reports feeling "terrible."

A second limitation to defining abnormality based on distress is that many youths with serious behavior problems do not experience negative emotions. For example, adolescents with conduct problems often show no signs of anxiety or depression. They may only express remorse when they are caught and punished. Similarly, younger children with oppositional and defiant behavior toward adults rarely express psychological distress. Instead, their disruptive behavior causes distress to their parents and teachers.

Abnormal behavior might also be defined by actions that violate society's standards or rules. Put another way, abnormality may be defined in terms of **cultural deviancy**. For example, Conduct Disorder is characterized by a persistent pattern of behavior that violates the rights of others or the rules of society. Adolescents with Conduct Disorder often have histories of disruptive behavior problems that clearly go against cultural norms and mores: shoplifting, robbery, violence toward others, truancy.

The chief limitation of defining abnormal behavior exclusively by the degree to which it violates social or cultural norms is that these norms can vary considerably from culture to culture. For example, in Western industrialized societies, parents often require young children to sleep in their own beds, usually in separate rooms. Children who refuse to sleep in their own beds may be classified as having a sleep disorder. However, in many nonwestern societies, requiring young children to sleep alone is considered cruel and detrimental to their social and emotional development.

Some experts define abnormality in terms of **behavioral rigidity**. From this perspective, abnormal behavior is characterized by the repeated and inflexible display of certain actions, thoughts, or emotional reactions, especially in response to psychosocial stressors. For example, a child who shows fear at the prospect of separating from his mother may be displaying abnormal behavior if he shows this fear in almost all situations. Under some circumstances, clinginess to parents is adaptive, for example, when the child is in an unfamiliar and potentially dangerous setting, such as a crowded airport. Under other circumstances, separation anxiety is clearly maladaptive, such as when a child is unwilling to leave his parents to attend school. Whereas mental health is characterized by flexibility in responding to changes in situational demands, abnormal behavior may be marked by the persistent use of a limited number of behaviors that are clearly not adaptive in all situations. The chief drawback to defining abnormal behavior in terms of rigidity is that terms like "inflexibility" and "maladaptive" are, themselves, vague.

A final way to differentiate abnormality from normal functioning is based on the notion of **harmful dysfunction**. According to Jerome Wakefield (1992), a behavior is considered abnormal if it meets two criteria. First, the behavior must be harmful; that is, it must be associated with a significant impairment in daily functioning. Second, the behavior must reflect an underlying biological dysfunction; that is, it must have an underlying medical or biological cause.

The harmful dysfunction approach to defining abnormality has two limitations. First, the requirement that a behavior be "harmful" may be too stringent. As we have seen, many youths with depression, anxiety, and other emotional problems show no impairment in functioning. Furthermore, the definition of "harmful" is somewhat vague and subjective. For example, Wakefield's (1992) definition does not tell clinicians how severe an adolescent's depressive symptoms must be to be considered "harmful." Must an adolescent be actively contemplating suicide to have a mental disorder?

Second, Wakefield's (1992) requirement that people show underlying biological dysfunction is also problematic. Most people with mental disorders do not show a clear biological cause for their disorder. Even children with disorders that have strong genetic and biological underpinnings, such as autism and ADHD, do not consistently show structural or functional brain abnormalities. There is no blood test or "chemical imbalance" that can be used to diagnose these childhood disorders.

The Psychiatric Definition of Abnormality

Most mental health practitioners and researchers use the *Diagnostic and Statistical Manual of Mental Disorders, Fourth Edition, Text Revision (DSM-IV-TR;* American Psychiatric Association, 2000) to diagnose mental disorders. *DSM-IV-TR* is published by the American Psychiatric Association and reflects the current psychiatric conceptualization of mental illness. *DSM-IV-TR* defines **mental disorder** as follows:

> A clinically significant behavioral or psychological syndrome or pattern that occurs in an individual and that is associated with present distress or disability or with a significantly increased risk of suffering, death, pain, disability, or an important loss of freedom. (p. xxxi)

According to the *DSM-IV-TR*, a person might be classified as having a mental disorder if she shows thoughts, feelings, or actions that are associated with (1) psychological distress, such as anxiety, depression, or discomfort; (2) impaired functioning, such as problems with social relationships, school, or work; or (3) risk of harm to self or others.

It is worth noting that people experiencing mental disorders must show at least one of these features—distress, impairment, *or* risk—they need not show all three characteristics. Some seriously depressed adolescents experience tremendous emotional pain and frequently think about killing themselves, but they do not show marked impairment in their social or academic functioning. Other youths who show serious conduct problems have been arrested and have dropped out of school, but they report no problems with anxiety, depression, or low self-esteem.

Abnormality, Ethnicity, and Culture

According to the *DSM-IV-TR*, clinicians must carefully differentiate symptoms of a mental disorder from behaviors and psychological states that are sanctioned in a given culture. Differentiating abnormal symptoms from culturally sanctioned behavior is especially challenging when clinicians are asked to assess youths from other cultures.

Julia

Julia was a 16-year-old Asian American girl who was referred to our clinic by her oncologist after she was diagnosed with a rare form of cancer. Julia refused to participate in radiation therapy or take medications for her illness. Her physician suspected that Julia was paranoid because she attempted to attack him when he tried to examine her in his office.

With the help of a translator, Julia's therapist learned that she was a second-generation Hmong immigrant from Southeast Asia who lived with her parents and extended family. Julia and her family had limited contact with individuals outside the Hmong community and refused to participate in Western medicine. Instead, Julia and her parents practiced traditional Eastern folk medicine.

Because Julia's therapist doubted that folk medicine alone would help her cancer, she suggested that Julia's community shaman talk with her physician to identify which aspects of medical treatment might be acceptable to Julia and her family. Over time, Julia was able to successfully participate in Western medical treatment by having the shaman attend all of the radiation therapy sessions, bless the medications prescribed by the oncologist, and perform other folk remedies important to Julia and her family.

Faul and Gross (2006) have identified four ways ethnicity and culture can affect the diagnostic process. First, ethnic minority groups living in the United States often have different cultural values that affect their views of children, beliefs about child rearing, and behaviors they consider problematic. For example, white, middle-class parents often place great value on fostering children's social-emotional development and encouraging child autonomy. These parents often provide high levels of warm and responsive behavior during parent-child interactions. In contrast, many African American parents place relatively greater value on children's compliance; consequently, they may adopt less permissive and more authoritarian socialization tactics. Clinicians need to be aware of cultural differences in socialization goals and parents' ideas about appropriate and inappropriate child behavior.

Second, ethnic minorities living in the United States, especially immigrants, encounter psychosocial stressors associated with acculturation. Acculturation stressors can include assimilation into the mainstream culture, separation from extended family and friends, language differences, limited educational and employment opportunities, and prejudice. Many ethnic minorities also face the additional stress of low social and economic status. Many immigrants to the United States, especially those from Latin America, do not share the same legal status as members of the dominant culture. For these reasons, the sheer number of psychosocial stressors encountered by ethnic minority families is greater than those encountered by families who are members of the dominant culture.

Third, language differences can cause problems in the assessment and diagnosis of non-native speakers. The assessment and diagnostic process was designed predominantly for English-speaking individuals living in the United States. The words that describe some psychological symptoms are not easily translated into other languages. Furthermore, many symptoms reported by individuals from other cultures do not readily map onto *DSM-IV-TR* diagnostic criteria. Psychological tests are almost always developed with English-speaking children and adolescents in mind. For example, white children raised in Columbus, Ohio will likely find the following question on an intelligence test fairly easy: "Who was Christopher Columbus?" However, Cambodian immigrant children who recently moved to the city might find the question extremely challenging. Psychologists must be aware of differences in language and cultural knowledge when interpreting test results.

Fourth, ethnic minorities are often underrepresented in mental health research. Over the past two decades, researchers have made considerable gains in understanding the causes and treatment for a wide range of child and adolescent disorders. However, researchers know relatively little about how differences in children's ethnicity and cultural backgrounds might place them at greater risk for certain disorders or affect treatment. For example, emerging data suggest that the prevalence of alcohol and drug abuse among adolescents differs, depending on adolescents' ethnicities. Researchers have only recently begun to create treatment programs designed specifically for minority youth. For example, the TEMAS program was created to help Spanish-speaking children and adolescents overcome mood and anxiety problems using culturally relevant storytelling (Costantino, Malgady, & Cardalda, 2005). Clearly, more research needs to be done to investigate the interplay between psychopathology and culture among ethnic minority youth.

What Is *Child* Psychology?

Understanding the Development of Psychopathology

Developmental psychopathology is a broad approach to studying normal and abnormal development across the lifespan. Developmental psychopathologists believe that development is shaped by the complex interaction of biological, psychological, and social-cultural factors over time. An adequate understanding of development, therefore, depends on the appreciation of each of these domains, how they interact, and how they affect the person from infancy through adulthood (Rutter & Sroufe, 2000).

Developmental psychopathologists study human development across several levels of analysis. These levels include the person's genetics, brain structure and functioning, psychological development (i.e., actions, thoughts, emotions), family interactions and peer relationships, and the broader social-cultural context in which the person lives. Factors on each of these levels can individually affect development. More frequently, however, factors across levels interact over time to shape children's developmental outcomes (Cicchetti & Toth, 1998).

Probabilistic Epigenesis

Developmental psychopathologists use the term **epigenesis** to describe the way biological, psychological, and social-cultural factors interact with each other to influence development over time (see Figure 1.2). Development unfolds as genetic and biological factors guide and direct psychological, familial, and social functioning (Gottlieb & Willoughby, 2006).

Consider Nina, a child with Down syndrome. Nina's syndrome was caused by a genetic mutation on chromosome 21, probably acquired through an abnormality in her mother's egg cell. This genetic mutation caused Nina's brain and central nervous system to develop in an abnormal fashion. Her neurological development, in turn, shaped her psychological functioning during early childhood. Nina's parents reported delays in her motor development (e.g., sitting up, walking), use of language, and acquisition of daily living skills (e.g., toilet training, dressing). In school, she showed problems learning to read, write, and count. These psychological characteristics affected the type of care she received from parents and teachers. Nina's mother was understandably very protective, and her teachers often offered Nina extra attention in school. Nina's cognitive functioning also affected her relationships with peers. Nina preferred to play with younger children rather than her classmates. By the time Nina reached junior high school, she was well below her peers academically. However, Nina was able to spend half the school day

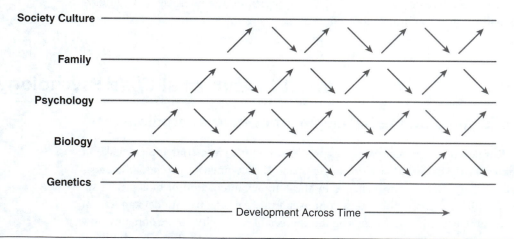

Figure 1.2   Developmental Epigenesis

Source: Based on Gottlieb and Willoughby (2006).

Note: Development unfolds over time. Genetic, biological, psychological, familial, and social-cultural factors interact with each other—across time—to shape children's outcomes. Because of the complex interplay of factors affecting development, children's outcomes are "probabilistic," not predetermined.

in a regular sixth-grade classroom, assisted by an aide. She spent the remainder of the day in a special education class. These extra services offered by her school district (a social-cultural factor) enabled Nina to begin a part-time job during high school.

Nina's story illustrates the unfolding of development over time. Each level of development affects the one beyond it. However, epigenesis is a bidirectional process. Genetic and biological factors certainly affect psychological and social functioning; however, psychological and social factors can also determine the effects of genes and biology on development. Arnold Sameroff (2000) used the term **transactional** to refer to the way factors across levels affect each other over time.

To understand the transactional nature of development, consider Anthony, another child with Down syndrome. Anthony's mother, Anita, was heartbroken when her obstetrician told her that Anthony had Down syndrome. Rather than despair, Anita decided that she was going to maximize her son's cognitive, social, and behavioral potential by giving him the most enriching early environment that she could provide. After Anthony's birth, Anita spent countless hours talking with Anthony, reading him books, listening to music, playing games, and going on outings. Although Anthony acquired language and daily living skills slowly, Anita had high expectations for him. She remained patient and tried to provide structure and help so that Anthony might learn these skills independently. Anita enrolled Anthony in a special needs preschool and was heavily involved throughout his education. Anthony developed fairly good language and daily living skills and was able to graduate with his high school class. Today, Anthony is employed full time in the mailroom of a large company and lives independently.

Understanding and predicting child development is extremely difficult for two reasons. First, development is influenced by many factors across multiple levels: genes, biology, psychology, family, society. Second, these factors are constantly changing over time, each interacting with the others. Consequently, the unfolding of development is not predetermined by one's genes, biology, or any other factor. Instead, the unfolding of development is **probabilistic**; a person's developmental outcome can vary depending on the interplay of many biological and environmental factors. Developmental psychopathologists use the term "probabilistic epigenesis" to refer to the complex transaction of biogenetic, psychological, familial, and social-cultural factors that shape development over time (Cicchetti & Sroufe, 2000; Gottlieb & Willoughby, 2006).

Developmental Pathways

Developmental psychopathologists often liken child development to a journey along a path. Indeed, they often refer to children as following certain **developmental pathways,** or trajectories, toward either healthy or unhealthy outcomes (Pickles & Hill, 2006).

As children grow, they face certain developmental tasks or challenges along their paths (see Table 1.4). These tasks depend largely on the age and developmental level of the child. Erik Erikson (1963) outlined some of the most important developmental tasks facing individuals as they progress from infancy through old age. For

Table 1.4   Developmental Tasks in Childhood and Adolescence

Infants, toddlers, and preschool-age children

- Attachment (basic trust) to one or more specific caregivers
- Learning to sit, stand, walk, and jump
- Acquiring functional language
- Obedience to simple commands and instructions of adults
- Toilet training
- Appropriate play with toys and other people
- Achieving a sense of autonomy from parents

School-age children

- Learning reading, writing, mathematics
- Attending and behaving appropriately at school
- Following rules for behavior at home, at school, and in public places
- Getting along with peers at school
- Making friends with peers

Younger adolescents

- Attending and behaving appropriately at school
- Learning to solve advanced problems with numbers, algebra
- Learning required language, history, and other subjects
- Completing secondary schooling
- Getting along with peers in school
- Making and maintaining close friendships
- Obeying the laws of society

Older adolescents

- Working or preparing for future higher education
- If working, behaving appropriately in the workplace
- If in school, meeting academic standards for courses or degrees
- Forming and maintaining romantic relationships
- Obeying the laws of society
- Transitioning from parents, living independently

Source: Based on Masten, Burt, & Coatsworth (2006).

example, the primary developmental task facing infants is to establish a sense of trust in a loving and responsive caregiver. Infants must expect their caregivers to be sensitive and responsive to their physical, social, and emotional needs and to see themselves as worthy of receiving this care and attention from others. The primary developmental task of adolescence is to establish a sense of identity. Adolescents must develop a coherent sense of self that links childhood experiences with goals for adulthood. They usually accomplish this task by trying out different social roles and behaviors during the teenage years.

Developmental tasks present forks in the developmental path. The child can either successfully master the developmental task or have problems with its success-ful resolution. Mastery of developmental tasks leads to social, emotional, and behavior **competence**, placing children on course for optimal development. For example, infants who establish a sense of basic trust in caregivers may have greater ability to make and keep friends in later childhood. Unsuccessful resolution of developmental tasks, however, can lead to problems in later development. For example, failure to establish a sense of trust in caregivers during infancy may interfere with children's abilities to develop close peer relationships later in childhood (Masten et al., 2006).

Progress along developmental pathways, therefore, builds upon itself over time. Early developmental experiences set the groundwork for later developmental experiences. If children show early social, emotional, and behavioral competence, they can use these early skills to master later developmental tasks. However, failure to master early developmental tasks can interfere with the development of later skills and abilities. For example, a preschool child who learns to control his behavior and emotions during play will likely have an easier time making friends when he enters first grade. However, a preschooler who continues to tantrum or act aggressively when he does not get his way may be ostracized by peers in the first-grade classroom.

To understand the hierarchical nature of development, consider another analogy: Development is like a building. Our genetic endowment might form the foundation of the building, providing us with our physical attributes, raw neurobiological potential, and behavioral predispositions. The ground floor might consist of early environmental experiences, such as our prenatal surroundings or the conditions of our birth and delivery. Subsequent floors might consist of postnatal experiences, such as our nutrition and health care, the relationships we develop with our parents, the quality of our education, and the friends we make in school. The integrity of the upper levels of our "building" is partially determined by the strength of the lower levels. For example, problems with the foundation will place additional challenges on the formation of higher levels. However, especially well-developed higher levels can, partially, compensate for difficulties in the foundation.

The building does not exist in a vacuum, however. The context in which the structure is created is also important. Just as temperature, wind, and rain can affect the construction of a building, so, too, can the child's social-cultural climate affect his development. Certain social and cultural conditions can promote the child's psychological integrity: high-quality schools, safe neighborhoods, and communities that protect and value children and families. Other social and cultural factors, such as exposure to poverty and crime, can compromise child development.

Distinguishing Normality From Abnormality

From the perspective of developmental psychopathology, normal and abnormal behavior is determined by the degree to which it promotes children's competence. Behaviors that allow children to develop social, emotional, and behavioral competence over time and meet the changing demands of the environment are regarded as **adaptive**. Examples of adaptive behavior include toddlers learning to understand other people's emotional states, school-age children learning to think before acting, and adolescents using complex moral reasoning to solve interpersonal problems.

These behaviors are adaptive because they allow children to understand and interact with their environment in effective and flexible ways (Sroufe, 1997).

Behaviors that interfere with children's social, emotional, and behavioral competence or do not meet the changing demands of the environment are regarded as **maladaptive**. Examples of maladaptive behavior include toddlers who do not understand others' emotional expressions and withdraw from social interactions, school-age children who impulsively hit others when they are angry, and adolescents who fail to show respect to peers. These behaviors are considered maladaptive because they indicate a failure to develop social competencies and they interfere with children's social-emotional well-being (Sroufe, 1997).

From the perspective of developmental psychopathology, normal behavior is determined by the degree to which the child's actions are adaptive, given her developmental tasks. Consequently, normality and abnormality are dependent on children's **developmental context**. Consider a two-year-old child who stubbornly refuses to dress in the morning and tantrums when told that he cannot have cookies for breakfast. Although these oppositional behaviors cause parents grief, they are usually not considered abnormal in two year olds. In fact, defiance and stubbornness can reflect toddlers' developmentally appropriate bids for autonomy. However, the same behaviors shown by a six-year-old child would likely be considered maladaptive and abnormal. In the context of his age and level of development, these behaviors likely reflect problems balancing needs for autonomy with respect for parental authority (Cicchetti & Aber, 1998).

From the perspective of developmental psychopathology, normal and abnormal behavior are also determined by the degree to which a behavior is adaptive, given the child's environment. Consequently, normality and abnormality are dependent on children's **environmental context**. Consider Xavier, a 13-year-old boy who has a history of running away from home, staying out all night, skipping school, and earning low grades. Clearly, Xavier's behavior is problematic. However, if we discover that Xavier is also experiencing physical abuse at home, we might see how his problematic behavior reflects an attempt to cope with this psychosocial stressor. Specifically, Xavier stays out at night and runs away from home to escape physical maltreatment. Furthermore, he likely has difficulty completing assignments and attending school because of his stressful home environment. Although Xavier's behavior deserves the attention of caring professionals, his actions are best understood in terms of the environmental context.

The Importance of Understanding Normal Development

From the perspective of developmental psychopathology, abnormal development reflects a deviation from normality. Therefore, our ability to recognize, understand, and treat childhood disorders depends on our knowledge of normal child development. Consider George, a 14-year-old boy who begins drinking with friends at parties. Approximately once every month for the past six months, George has drunk at least five or more alcoholic beverages while partying with friends. He drinks in order to "have fun with friends" and has never gotten into trouble or put himself in dangerous situations while intoxicated. Consider also a 12-year-old girl, Maria, who is dieting to lose weight. Although Maria's weight is average for a girl her age and height, she is very dissatisfied with her body and feels like she needs to lose at least 15 lbs. Whether we regard George and Maria's actions as abnormal depends partially on whether their behaviors are atypical of adolescents their age or inconsistent with the environmental demands they face.

Developmental psychopathologists also believe that abnormal behavior can shed light on normal child and adolescent development. Youths who clearly show delays in mastering developmental tasks or failures in meeting environmental demands can teach us about how development typically proceeds. For example, children with autism show unusual deficits in perceiving and interpreting other people's social behavior. By studying these deficits, researchers are beginning to understand how the ability to process social information develops in typically developing infants and children.

Focus on Individual Differences in Development

Developmental psychopathologists are very interested in individual differences in child and adolescent development; that is, they want to discover what leads to differences in the way some children develop compared to others. Predicting individual differences in development is extremely difficult because, as we have seen, many factors interact over time to affect children's developmental outcomes. The complex interactions between biogenetic, psychological, familial, and social factors over time produce two phenomena: equifinality and multifinality (Cicchetti, 1990; Sroufe, 1989b).

Equifinality occurs when children with different developmental histories show similar developmental outcomes. For example, imagine that you are a psychologist who conducts psychological evaluations for a juvenile court. As part of your duties, you assess adolescent boys who have been arrested and convicted of illegal activities, such as theft, assault, and drug use, in order to make recommendations to the court regarding probation and treatment. All of the boys that you assess have similar developmental outcomes; that is, they all show conduct problems. However, after interviewing many of the boys, you discover that their developmental histories are quite different. Some boys have long histories of antisocial behavior, beginning in early childhood. Other boys have no histories of conduct problems until their recent arrest. Still other boys' conduct problems are limited to times when they were using drugs and alcohol. Your discovery illustrates the principle of equifinality in child development: There are many different paths to the same developmental outcomes.

The principle of **multifinality** refers to the tendency of children with similar early experiences to show different social, emotional, and behavioral outcomes. For example, imagine that you are a clinical social worker who evaluates children who have been physically abused. During the course of your career, you have assessed a number of children who have been abused by their caregivers. You notice, however, that some of these children show long-term emotional and behavioral problems while others seem to show few adverse effects. Your observation reflects the principle of multifinality: Children with similar early experiences show different outcomes.

The principle of equifinality makes definitive statements about the *causes* of psychopathology extremely difficult. Because of equifinality, we usually cannot infer the causes of children's behavior problems based on their current symptoms. For example, many people incorrectly believe that all adolescents who sexually abuse younger children were, themselves, sexually abused in the past. In actuality, adolescents engage in sexual abuse for many reasons, not only because they were victimized themselves.

The principle of multifinality limits the statements we can make about children's *prognosis*. For example, many people erroneously believe that if a child has been sexually abused, she is likely to exhibit a host of emotional and behavior problems later in life, ranging from sexual deviancy and aggression to depression and anxiety. In fact, the developmental outcomes of boys and girls who have been sexually abused vary considerably. Some children show significant maladjustment while others show few long-term effects. Their diversity of outcomes illustrates the difficulty in making predictions regarding development.

Risk and Resilience

What explains equifinality and multifinality? Why is there such great diversity in children's developmental pathways? The answer is that child development is multiply determined by the complex interplay of genetic, biological, psychological, familial, and social-cultural factors. Some of these factors promote healthy, adaptive development, whereas other factors increase the likelihood that children will follow less-than-optimal, more maladaptive developmental trajectories.

Developmental psychopathologists use the term **risk factors** to describe influences on development that interfere with the acquisition of children's competencies or compromise children's ability to adapt to their environments. In contrast, psychologists use the term **protective factors** to refer to influences on development that buffer the negative effects of risks on children's development and promote adaptive functioning (see Table 1.5). Risk and protective factors occur across levels of functioning: They can be genetic, biological, psychological, familial, or social-cultural (Cicchetti, 2006; Luthar, 2006).

The salience of a risk factor depends on the child's age, gender, level of development, and environmental context. For example, child sexual abuse is a risk factor for later psychosocial problems. However, the effects of sexual abuse depend on the gender of the child and the age at which the abuse occurs. For example, boys often show the greatest adverse effects of sexual victimization when they are abused in early childhood, whereas girls often show the poorest developmental outcomes when abuse occurs during early adolescence (Richters & Cicchetti, 1993).

Similarly, the ability of protective factors to buffer children from the harmful effects of risk depends on context (see Image 1.2). For example, many children who experience sexual abuse at the hands of a family member (e.g., stepfather) experience considerable psychological distress and behavioral impairment. However, children who are able to rely on a caring, nonoffending parent are often able to cope with this stressor more effectively than youths without the presence of a supportive parent (Heflin & Deblinger, 2003).

Table 1.5   Some Risk and Protective Factors Across Childhood and Adolescence

Domain	Possible Risk Factors	Possible Protective Factors
Genetic	• Inherited genetic disorders • Genetic mutations	• Genetic screening • Early identification
Biological	• Inadequate prenatal health care • Complications during pregnancy or delivery • Inadequate postnatal health care, immunizations • Malnutrition • Exposure to environmental toxins, teratogens • Childhood illness or injury • Abnormalities in brain development • Speech, language, vision, hearing problems	• Good access to prenatal and postnatal care • High quality nutrition • Early recognition of medical and developmental delays or deficits • Early intensive treatment for medical problems and developmental delays
Psychological	• Cognitive delays or deficits • Hyperactivity, inattention, learning problems • Problems regulating emotions • Problems in social interactions	• Enriched learning, environmental experiences • High-quality special educational services • Help from therapist, school counselor, parents to remedy problems in emotional control or social functioning
Familial	• Parental death, separation, or abandonment • Parental divorce, marital conflict • Cold, distant, intrusive, or harsh parenting • Child abuse or neglect • Placement into foster care, group home • Parental substance abuse or mental illness • Parental antisocial behaviors	• Close relationship with at least one caregiver • Sensitive, responsive parenting behavior • Consistent use of parental discipline • Adequate parental monitoring • Good relationships with peers, extended kin • Adoption by loving, responsive parents
Social-Cultural	• Low socioeconomic status (SES) • Dangerous, high-crime neighborhood • Inadequate educational opportunities • Rejected by peers or association with deviant peers • Discrimination	• Peer acceptance, close friends • Involvement in prosocial activities (e.g., sports, clubs) • Relationships with adult mentors (e.g., coaches) • Adequate educational opportunities

Protective factors are believed to promote resilience in youths at risk for maladaptive development. **Resilience** refers to the tendency of some children to develop social, emotional, and behavioral competence despite the presence of multiple risk factors. Consider the following stories about two brothers growing up in the same impoverished, high-crime neighborhood.

Image 1.2   A Portrait of Resilience: Karol Wojtyla. Karol's mother died when he was eight; his two older siblings were dead by the time this photo was taken at the age of 12. His family had little money. During adolescence, he experienced the Great Depression and the destruction of World War II. However, Karol's close relationship to his father may have protected him from these childhood stressors. He became a champion for human rights and a major figure of the 20th century: Pope John Paul II.

Source: AP Photo. Used with permission.

Ramon and Rafael

Ramon, the older brother, begins showing disruptive behavior at a young age. He is disrespectful to his mother, defiant toward his teachers, and disinterested in school. By late elementary school, he has been suspended a number of times for fighting and chronic truancy. In junior high school, Ramon begins associating with peers who introduce him to other antisocial behaviors, such as shoplifting and breaking into cars. By adolescence, Ramon rarely attends school and earns money selling drugs. At 15, Ramon is removed from his mother's custody because of his antisocial behavior and truancy.

Rafael, the younger brother, also shows early problems with defiance and aggression. However, these problems do not persist beyond the early elementary school years. Although Rafael does not enjoy school, he befriends an art teacher who recognizes his talent for drawing. The teacher offers to tutor him in art and help him show his work. Rafael also takes art classes at a local community center to learn new mediums. Through these classes, he meets other adolescents interested in drawing and painting. Rafael's grades in high school are generally low; however, he excels in art, music, and draftsmanship. He graduates with his class and studies interior design at community college.

What accounts for Ramon's struggles and Rafael's resilience? Although there is no easy answer, a partial explanation might be the presence of protective factors at just the right time in Rafael's development. Ramon's path to antisocial behavior was probably facilitated by antisocial peers who introduced him to criminal activities. In contrast, Rafael's peer group encouraged prosocial activities and the development of artistic competence. If Rafael's teacher did not encourage the development of his art talents until later in Rafael's development, perhaps after he developed friendships with deviant peers, would he have followed the same developmental pathway as Ramon? Although we do not know for sure, we can speculate that these protective factors played an important role in his ability to achieve despite multiple risks (Cicchetti & Toth, 1991; Sroufe & Rutter, 1984).

Most protective factors occur spontaneously: a teacher nurtures a special talent in an at-risk youth, a coach encourages a boy with depression to join a team, or a girl who has been abused is adopted by loving parents. Sometimes, however, protective factors are planned to prevent the emergence of disorders. For example, communities may offer free infant and toddler screenings to identify children with developmental disabilities at an early age. Identification of developmental delays in infancy or toddlerhood can lead to early intensive intervention and better prognosis. Similarly, schools may offer prevention programs for girls who might develop eating disorders. Volunteers might teach girls about healthy eating, risks of dieting, and stress management. Even psychotherapy can be seen as a protective factor. Therapy helps children and adolescents alter developmental trajectories away from maladaption and toward adaptation (Quinton & Rutter, 1998; Toth & Cicchetti, 1999).

As we have seen, developmental psychopathology is an emerging approach to understanding abnormal child behavior in the context of normal child development, in relation to the environment, and across time. Developmental psychopathology offers a rich and multifaceted perspective on abnormal child psychology across a number of different levels: genetic, biological, psychological, familial, and social-cultural. Throughout this book, the principles of developmental psychopathology will be used to explore the causes and treatment of child and adolescent disorders across these levels and within various developmental contexts.

The *Science* of Abnormal Child Psychology

The Scientist-Practitioner Approach

Integrating Science and Practice

The **scientist-practitioner approach** to abnormal psychology assumes that psychological research and clinical practice are interdependent and equally important facets of psychological training. Psychologists trained in the scientist-practitioner tradition are first and foremost scientists. They are committed to understanding human behavior through careful and systematic empirical investigation. Psychological science is concerned primarily with understanding behavior, with the goal of explaining, predicting, and/or influencing aspects of behavior that are relevant to people's lives. Psychological scientists, whether they work in research labs or mental health clinics, rely on scientific principles to inform their work, and they try to base their professional activities on knowledge gained through systematic data collection.

Most scientist-practitioners are clinicians who use scientific knowledge to alleviate distress and promote the welfare of their clients. Clinicians are called to apply information gained through research to help children, adults, and families. Furthermore, they may be asked to consult with other professionals, evaluate the effectiveness of social programs, and teach or supervise new generations of mental health experts. These individuals often work in mental health clinics, hospitals, schools, counseling centers, and other places where psychological services are delivered to individuals or groups.

Other scientist-practitioners are primarily engaged in research. Although they may also see clients on a limited basis, these professionals are devoted to understanding the prevalence, causes, and treatment of mental disorders. Researchers might be employed at a college or university, a medical school, a hospital, or an independent research center.

From the scientist-practitioner perspective, both the science and practice of psychology are important to the discipline. Psychological science informs clinical practice by helping psychologists use the most accurate assessment techniques and effective therapeutic methods possible. At the same time, the practice of assessment and therapy guides research by helping scientists focus their efforts on discovering principles and practices that have real-world applications.

The scientist-practitioner approach has its roots in a 1941 report to the American Association for Applied Psychology written by David Shakow (Baker & Benjamin, 2000). In the report, Shakow outlined the importance of research and clinical training in the education and development of clinical psychologists. He argued that psychologists must be able to integrate scientific principles and knowledge with their expertise as clinicians. Shakow recognized that psychologists could not balance their time equally between research and clinical practice; most would consider themselves either chiefly researchers or primarily practitioners. However, he asserted that an appreciation for science and practice was necessary for all psychologists, regardless of their professional role. As Drabick and Goldfried (2000) explain,

> The scientist practitioner model sought to encourage the development of practitioners who are both consumers of assessment and treatment research findings and evaluators of their own interventions using empirical methods, as well as researchers who are capable of producing and reporting clinically relevant data to the scientific community. Indeed, graduates would be well-trained clinicians who combined practice with an awareness of scientific research; or, conversely, . . . competent researchers with sensitivity to clinical issues. (p. 330)

Shakow's report was used by the American Psychological Association (1947) to formulate the first guidelines for the training of clinical psychologists. Today, most university-based clinical training programs identify themselves in the scientist-practitioner tradition.

Scientifically Informed Practice

The core tenets of the scientist-practitioner approach are outlined by Richard McFall's (1991) now-classic paper, "Manifesto for a Science of Clinical Psychology." McFall's cardinal principle is that scientifically based psychology is the only legitimate and acceptable form of understanding and alleviating psychological disorders. Stated another way, psychology is a science that must have its roots in empiricism and objective evaluation. According to McFall, "all forms of legitimate clinical psychology must be grounded in science . . . all competent clinical psychologists must be scientists first and foremost, and . . . all clinicians must ensure that their practice is scientifically valid" (p. 76).

From McFall's (1991) perspective, the distinction between psychological science and clinical practice is artificial. The only way clinicians can help their clients in a competent and ethical manner is to base their interventions on the research literature and on empirical investigation. Before practicing any form of assessment or treatment, clinicians must ask, "What is the empirical evidence supporting my practice?" Whenever possible, clinicians must rely on assessment strategies and therapy techniques that have received empirical support.

Unfortunately, many clinicians do not ground their interventions in the research literature or empirical data (Garb & Boyle, 2004). Instead, they may base their clinical practice on other factors, including theory, clinical experience, and anecdotal information provided by others. Although theories, experience, and anecdotes can be useful when combined with empirical evidence, they are insufficient guides for clinical practice by themselves. Psychological scientists believe that empirical data provide the best evidence either for or against a specific clinical intervention.

Without empirical data, clinicians might intervene in ways that are not effective. Ineffective interventions can harm clients and their families in at least three ways. First, ineffective interventions can cost significant time and money—resources that might be better spent participating in treatment with more empirical support. For example, available treatments for childhood disorders include listening to certain types of music, wearing special glasses, taking large doses of vitamins, avoiding certain textured foods, riding on horseback, swimming with dolphins, re-enacting the birth experience, and a host of other therapies with little systematic support. Although most of these interventions do not cause physical or psychological harm to clients, they can cost significant time, energy, and money. Furthermore, when insurance companies compensate individuals for participating in these therapies, resources available for more empirically supported interventions are diminished.

Second, families who participate in ineffective treatment can lose hope in the therapeutic process and in psychological treatment more generally. For example, many parents of oppositional and defiant children seek help to manage their children's behavior. Although a number of well-supported interventions exist to treat children's disruptive behavior, many families are given therapy that lacks empirical support. Consequently, they meet with limited success. As a result, many parents come to believe that psychological interventions will not help their children. Some parents simply give up on treatment; others decide to use medication.

Third, interventions that lack empirical support can be harmful to clients, families, and society. The history of psychology is marked by examples of clinicians harming individuals and society by practicing without empirical basis. Perhaps nowhere is this more obvious than in the treatment of autism. In the 1960s, Bruno Bettelheim suggested that autism was caused by parents who were cold and rejecting toward their children. Bettelheim's erroneous theory for the etiology of autism placed unnecessary blame on parents and resulted in a host of interventions that were completely ineffective at alleviating autistic symptoms.

Later, sociologist Douglas Biklen (1993) recommended that individuals with autism and severe mental retardation who were mute might be able to communicate with others if facilitated by a trained therapist. The subsequent practice of "facilitated communication" involved the therapist guiding the client's hand as the client supposedly typed messages on a keyboard. In one case, a client participating in facilitated communication supposedly reported that he had been abused by his family. As a result, the client was removed from his family's custody, despite no corroborating evidence of maltreatment. Later, the technique of facilitated communication was discredited by showing that the messages typed by clients actually reflected knowledge and information provided by facilitators, not by the individuals with developmental disabilities.

Even more recently, physician Andrew Wakefield and colleagues (1998) incorrectly suggested that the measles-mumps-rubella (MMR) vaccine caused autism in some children susceptible to the disorder. Consequently, many conscientious parents refused to immunize their infants, resulting in an unnecessary and sometimes dangerous increase in these childhood illnesses.

Clinicians also harm clients in more subtle ways when they provide information that lacks empirical support. For example, some clinicians erroneously perpetuate the myth that most sexually abused children victimize other children in the future. This incorrect belief can unnecessarily worry parents and stigmatize young victims. Similarly, other clinicians convey the notion that certain childhood disorders, like ADHD, do not exist; rather, problems with hyperactivity and inattention are caused by inadequate parenting. Such unsupported beliefs can distract parents from empirically supported interventions and cause parents to feel unnecessarily guilty and ineffective.

Scientist-practitioners engaged in full-time clinical practice try to approach their daily activities using the principles of psychological science. From the scientist-practitioner perspective, clinical work is analogous to a research study in which the practitioner's sample size consists of one individual (i.e., the client). The clinician generates hypotheses about the source of the client's problem and the best form of treatment, based on data gathered from the client and information presented in the research literature. Then, the clinician administers treatment and evaluates the client's outcomes using objective criteria. Finally, the clinician might modify her intervention based on information from the client, in order to improve effectiveness.

Clinically Informed Research

Most professionals have focused on the importance of clinicians applying principles of psychological science to their practice. Somewhat less attention has been directed at the importance of researchers conducting studies that are meaningful to therapists. A scientist-practitioner approach to psychopathology implies that psychological research must be relevant to clinical practice.

A number of researchers have recognized the considerable gap between psychological research and clinical practice (Antony, 2005). Unfortunately, many researchers eschew the lack of scientific rigor that characterizes most clinical interventions, while therapists often find psychological research to be inaccessible and detached from their daily practice. From the scientist-practitioner perspective, researchers can take at least three steps to bridge this gap between research and practice.

First, psychological research must address practical problems that have relevance to clinicians. Although research in basic psychological structure and functioning is extremely important, research that has direct application to clinicians' day-to-day work is most likely to be used by therapists in the community.

Second, researchers must disseminate their findings in a manner that clinicians can understand and use. As psychology students know, reading an empirical study from a peer-reviewed journal can be challenging. It is extremely tempting to read the article's abstract, introduction, and discussion and omit the method and results section, in order to avoid the often complex and confusing description of research design and statistics. Furthermore, relatively few research articles are written with clinicians as the primary audience. Often, readers who want to apply findings to their clinical work must determine the implications of research to their practice on their own. Researchers must be more mindful of clinicians when disseminating their research, to maximize the likelihood that clinicians will understand and apply their findings.

Third, the intervention techniques that are developed by researchers must translate to the real world. New therapies are usually evaluated in university clinics and research hospitals, and they are evaluated under ideal circumstances. For example, when evaluating a new therapy, researchers carefully select clients with only certain disorders, provide therapists with considerable training in delivering the interventions, and carefully monitor clients' participation in treatment and clinicians' adherence to the treatment program. However, when therapies are used outside research settings, they may not be as feasible to administer or as effective at reducing clients' symptoms. For example, behavioral treatments have been shown to reduce children's disruptive behavior problems in carefully controlled research studies. However, when these programs are administered in real-world clinics, as many as 50% of families drop out of treatment before completion.

From the scientist-practitioner perspective, researchers must be mindful of the needs of clinicians when designing, conducting, and reporting their studies. A closer connection is needed between psychological science and clinical practice if applied psychology is to flourish.

Students as Emerging Scientists and Practitioners

Psychology students often find themselves providing services to children and adolescents in distress. Students sometimes act as aides for individuals with mental retardation and developmental delays; behavior therapists for youths with autism;

tutors for children with learning disabilities; and psychological technicians in residential treatment facilities, juvenile detention centers, and hospitals. Students can also provide paraprofessional services through volunteer experiences. For example, many students mentor at-risk youth, provide in-services to grade school and high school students, monitor telephone crisis hotlines, and help local community mental health centers.

Because students often provide frontline psychological services, they have enormous potential for improving the functioning of children, adolescents, and families. However, students can also contribute to the propagation of inaccurate information and the dissemination of ineffective and unsupported treatments. Although psychology students are not in a position to direct interventions, they can approach treatment from the perspective of psychological science. Specifically, students can ask the following questions:

1. What is the evidence for the intervention or service that I am providing? Is there a theoretical and empirical basis for my work? Are there alternative services that might provide greater benefits to the people I serve?

2. Am I effective? Am I monitoring the effectiveness of the services I provide to determine whether I am helping my clients? Is there any possibility that I might be harming them?

3. Am I providing ethical, time-effective, and cost-effective services? During my work, do I respect the rights and dignity of others, conduct myself in a responsible and professional manner, and represent the field of psychology with integrity? Are my activities being supervised by someone who practices in an ethical and scientifically mindful manner?

As you read this book, consider how you might use the empirical literature to inform your own understanding of child and adolescent disorders. A scientific approach to child psychopathology is not reserved for licensed psychologists or university professors. Instead, all students, parents, teachers, and individuals who work with youth are called upon to use empirical data to help improve the functioning of others.

Critical Thinking Exercises

1. Some experts believe that the child mental health system is in a state of crisis. Why? What might state governments and/or private social services do to provide high-quality mental health services to children?

2. According to the *DSM-IV-TR,* a mental disorder is a pattern of behavior characterized by distress, disability (impairment), or risk. What might be some limitations to this definition of "mental disorder," especially when it is applied to children and adolescents?

3. Sigmund Freud wrote about the difficulty of predicting children's development:

    So long as we trace development from its final outcome backwards, the chain of events appears continuous. . . . But if we proceed the reverse way, if we start from the premises and try to follow these up to the final result . . . we notice at once that there might have been another result and we might have been just as well able to understand and explain the latter. Hence the chain of causation can always be recognized with certainty if we follow the line of analysis backwards, whereas to predict it is impossible. (from Sroufe & Rutter, 1984)

    Apply this passage to the concept of "probabilistic epigenesis."

4. In his "Manifesto for a Science of Clinical Psychology," Richard McFall (1991) argues that the only legitimate form of psychology is *scientific* psychology. How can psychological research guide the practice of psychotherapy? How can the clinical experiences of therapists inform psychological research? In what ways can students think of themselves as scientists and practitioners?

CHAPTER 2

The Causes of Child Psychopathology

Research Methods and Theories

The Scientific Study of Behavior

Science is the systematic search for order in the natural world. Scientists seek to identify meaningful relationships between observable events, in order to describe, predict, explain, and/or control these events. Physical scientists focus chiefly on the principles of physical matter and movement. Biological scientists concentrate on relationships within and between living systems. Behavioral scientists direct their attention to the structure and functioning of behavior, that is, to people's thoughts, feelings, and actions.

Three Features of Scientific Inquiry

There is no universally accepted method of scientific inquiry. However, science can be differentiated from nonscientific approaches to understanding the world in at least three ways (Newsom & Hovanitz, 2005).

First, to help organize their understanding of nature, scientists generate hypotheses about natural phenomena. **Hypotheses** are initial explanations or accounts about the natural world that typically are based on observation and previous research. Hypotheses are stated clearly and unambiguously, using either mathematical formulas or verbal statements. When scientists express hypotheses verbally, they **operationally define** the terms they use; that is, they carefully describe how phenomena can be measured. For example, a behavioral scientist might operationally define the term "aggressive" as "getting into physical fights at least three times per month."

Operational definitions translate hypotheses into clear, observable terms and allow scientists to communicate with one another precisely and consistently.

Second, scientists generate testable hypotheses. The statements that scientists make about the natural world must be open to evaluation by others. Specifically, hypotheses must be **falsifiable**, that is, capable of being disconfirmed.

Technically speaking, scientists do not seek to prove their hypotheses. Instead, they seek to examine the possibility that their hypotheses might be wrong. Once scientists generate a hypothesis, they re-word the hypothesis as a statement that can be disconfirmed. This falsifiable hypothesis is often called the **null hypothesis**. For example, if a psychologist's hypothesis is "Disruptive adolescents will show higher levels of depression than nondisruptive adolescents," his null hypothesis might be "Disruptive adolescents will show levels of depression *equal* to nondisruptive adolescents." Then, the psychologist examines whether the null hypothesis can be rejected. Rejecting the null hypothesis can provide support for the psychologist's ideas, but it does not *prove* the ideas to be correct.

A third facet of science is that scientists systematically evaluate hypotheses using empirical data. One goal of hypothesis testing is to determine **causal relationships** between two or more events. To establish that variable A causes variable B, three conditions must be met (Alloy, Abramson, Raniere, & Dyller, 1999):

1. *Variable A and variable B must show covariation;* that is, a change in the presence or strength of variable A must be associated with a corresponding change in the presence or strength of variable B. For example, if we say that child physical abuse causes depression, then children who experience abuse should also show greater likelihood of becoming depressed.

2. *Variable A must precede variable B.* For example, if child abuse causes depression, then we would expect children who experience abuse to subsequently show depression. We would not expect depression to exist before the onset of abuse.

3. *Alternative causes for the covariation of variables A and B must be ruled out.* For example, children who have experienced abuse may become depressed, but this covariation does not necessarily imply that abuse *causes* depression. Other variables may account for both abuse and children's depressive symptoms. One alternative explanation is that mothers who are depressed may be more likely to mistreat their children. Furthermore, mothers with depression may pass on genes that predispose their children to problems with depression.

Hypothesis Testing: Determining Causes

Experimental Research

Behavioral scientists typically rely on two research methods to test hypotheses about child psychopathology: experimental studies and correlational studies. In an

experiment, researchers are usually interested in examining differences between two or more groups (Kendall, Flannery-Schroeder, & Ford, 1999). After randomly assigning participants to groups, researchers manipulate one variable (i.e., the independent variable) and notice the effects of this manipulation on a second variable (i.e., the dependent variable).

In the field of abnormal child psychology, experimental research is most frequently used to examine the efficacy of treatment. For example, a researcher might be interested in determining the efficacy of a new treatment designed to improve the verbal skills of children with autism. She might randomly assign children with autism to two groups. Children in the treatment group might receive 30 weeks of the new treatment (i.e., the independent variable), while children in the control group might be assigned to a waiting list. After 30 weeks, the researcher examines differences in children's language skills (i.e., the dependent variable) across groups. Differences between groups on the dependent variable might indicate that the new treatment has an effect on children's verbal skills.

Experimental studies allow researchers to infer causal relationships between independent and dependent variables. First, the researcher systematically manipulates the independent variable (i.e., the treatment) and notices a corresponding change in the dependent variable (i.e., children's outcomes). Second, the change in the independent variable precedes the change in the dependent variable. Third, because the researcher randomly assigned participants to treatment and control groups at the onset of the study, differences between groups at the end of the study can be attributable to manipulation of the independent variable, rather than to other factors.

Correlational Research

Scientists who study the causes of psychopathology are often unable to conduct experimental research. For example, it is unethical to expose children to abuse to see whether maltreatment causes emotional disorders. Consequently, most etiological research is correlational in nature. In a **correlational study**, researchers are chiefly interested in associations between two variables (Kazdin, 1999). For example, a researcher might examine whether children who have histories of abuse (i.e., variable A) show greater likelihood of depression (i.e., variable B). Similarly, researchers might examine whether the size of certain brain regions is associated with the severity of autistic symptoms.

Researchers usually quantify the magnitude of the association between variables using a correlation coefficient. The **Pearson product-moment correlation coefficient** (r) is the most commonly used statistic. Correlation coefficients range from 1.0 to −1.0. The *strength* of association is determined by the absolute value of the coefficient. Coefficients near 1.0 or −1.0 indicate strong covariation between variables, whereas coefficients near 0 indicate weak or absent covariation. The *direction* of the association is determined by the sign of the coefficient. Positive values indicate a direct association between variables (i.e., as one variable increases, the other increases), whereas negative values indicate an inverse association (i.e., as one variable increases, the other decreases).

Correlations and Causality

Correlational studies allow researchers to notice associations between variables, but they do not allow researchers to infer causal relationships between variables. Why?

First, a correlation between two variables does not tell us the temporal relationship between the variables. Imagine that researchers notice that the size of a certain brain area is negatively correlated with the severity of children's autistic symptoms: The smaller the brain region, the greater the child's symptoms. We might be tempted to infer a causal relationship between brain and behavior, specifically, that an underdevelopment of this brain region causes autism. However, it is also possible that autistic symptoms, over time, cause this part of the brain to atrophy. Correlations do not allow us to determine temporal relationships between variables. Consequently, they do not allow us to infer causality.

The second reason we cannot infer causal relationships from correlational data is that correlational studies do not rule out alternative explanations for covariation. If we notice a correlation between the size of a brain region and the severity of children's autistic symptoms, we might be tempted to conclude that brain structure influences behavior or behavior affects brain structure. However, an alternative possibility is that a third factor might account for both a reduction in brain size and an increase in autistic symptoms (see Figure 2.1). For example, children exposed to certain toxins during gestation might show both brain abnormalities and features

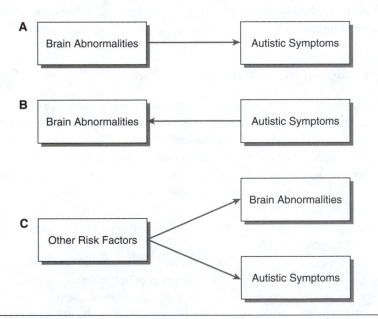

Figure 2.1   Correlation Does Not Imply Causality

Source: Based on Baron-Cohen (2005) and Lawrence, Lott, and Haier (2005).

Note: Although there is a correlation between brain structure and autistic symptoms, we do not know if (a) brain abnormalities cause autistic behaviors, (b) autistic behaviors lead to abnormal brain development, or (c) other risk factors, like exposure to toxins, cause both brain abnormalities and autism.

of autism. Correlational studies do not control for these alternative explanations for covariation; consequently, they cannot be used to infer causal relationships.

Types of Correlational Studies

There are two types of correlational research designs that are especially relevant to scientists who examine the causes of childhood disorders (Alloy et al., 1999). In a **cross-sectional study**, researchers examine the association between variables at the same point in time. For example, researchers might examine the brain structure of children with autism. At the same time, they might ask parents to complete a questionnaire regarding the severity of their children's autistic symptoms. Cross-sectional studies can be conducted relatively quickly. However, because data are collected at the same point in time, researchers cannot determine the temporal relationship between the variables.

In a longitudinal study, researchers specify the temporal relationship between variables by measuring variables at different times. In a **prospective longitudinal study**, researchers measure a hypothesized causal variable at time 1 and measure its expected outcome at time 2. For example, researchers might hypothesize that certain brain abnormalities lead to later autistic symptoms. To test this hypothesis, they might assess brain structure during toddlerhood and autistic symptoms one or two years later. Prospective longitudinal studies have the advantage over cross-sectional studies of testing temporal relationships between variables.

Prospective longitudinal studies are difficult to conduct because participants often drop out of studies before their completion and researchers must wait a long time to test their hypotheses. Consequently, some researchers use other types of longitudinal designs to test hypotheses about the etiology of disorders. In a **retrospective longitudinal study**, researchers examine individuals with known disorders and ask them (or their parents) to recall events in the past that might have caused the disorder. For example, researchers might ask the parents of children with autism to recall social and language deficits that their children showed during infancy and that might have preceded the emergence of the disorder. The chief limitation of retrospective longitudinal studies is that they depend on the accuracy of people's memories for events in the sometimes distant past.

In a **follow-back study**, researchers examine the case histories, school records, or medical records of individuals with known disorders to determine whether events in their past may have contributed to the emergence of the disorder. For example, Osterling and Dawson (1994) reviewed videotapes of the first birthday parties of children later diagnosed with autism. Compared to typically developing children, one-year-olds later diagnosed with autism showed deficits in social and language skills during their birthday parties. Although parents usually did not notice these deficits in social and language skills at the time, they were observable on the videotape to researchers. The researchers suggested that early deficits in social and language functioning, often not noticeable by others, may contribute to the development of autism later in development. Follow-back studies, like the one conducted by Osterling and Dawson (1994), do not rely on parents' memories of past events. However, obtaining high-quality records of children's developmental histories is often difficult.

Special Relationships Between Variables

Psychologists have long recognized the complexity of child development. Rarely is there a one-to-one correspondence between a single risk factor and a particular developmental outcome (Alloy et al., 1999).

Instead, researchers are often interested in identifying the conditions under which one variable is associated with another. A **moderator** is a variable that affects the nature of the relationship between two other variables (Baron & Kenny, 1986). For example, harsh physical discipline can contribute to the development of disruptive behavior problems in children. However, the relationship between harsh discipline and child behavior problems seems to be moderated by ethnicity (see Figure 2.2). White preschoolers who experience harsh discipline show increased risk for behavior problems as adolescents. However, African American preschoolers who experience harsh discipline do not show increased risk for later behavior problems; instead, physical discipline predicts fewer behavior problems among African American youth (Deater-Deckard, Dodge, Bates, & Pettit, 1996; Lansford, Deater-Deckard, Dodge, Bates, & Pettit, 2004). Although findings are preliminary, physical discipline may be a risk factor for behavior problems among white children and a possible protective factor among some African American children.

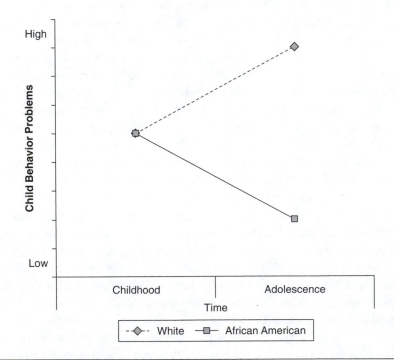

Figure 2.2   Moderation

Source: Based on Lansford et al. (2004).

Note: A moderator affects the direction or strength of the association between two variables. In this case, children's ethnicity moderated the effects of physical discipline on children's behavior problems.

Moderators affect the direction or strength of the association between two variables. In Figure 2.2, ethnicity moderated the relationship between physical discipline and children's disruptive behavior problems. Moderator variables tend to be categorical variables. Some frequently studied moderator variables in child psychopathology research are gender (i.e., boy, girl), age (e.g., child, adolescent, adult), socioeconomic status (e.g., low-income, middle class), and diagnostic status (e.g., diagnosis, no diagnosis).

In other studies, researchers test hypotheses regarding the mechanism by which one variable affects another variable. A **mediator** is a variable that may account for the relationship between two other variables (Baron & Kenny, 1986). Usually, mediators explain how one variable (e.g., a risk factor) might influence another variable (e.g., a disorder).

For example, researchers noticed that children of overly controlling and demanding parents are prone to depression later in development. Until recently, however, researchers did not know exactly how overly controlling parents contributed to children's depressive symptoms. Kenney-Benson and Pomerantz (2005) hypothesized that children's perfectionism mediated the relationship between their parents' use of control and their likelihood of developing depression (see Figure 2.3). The children of excessively controlling parents reported high levels of perfectionism. Perfectionism, in turn, predicted children's depressive symptoms (Flett, Hewitt, Oliver, & Macdonald, 2002).

Figure 2.3   Mediation

Source: Based on Kenney-Benson and Pomerantz (2005).

Note: A mediator accounts for the mechanism by which one variable affects another variable. In this case, maternal control was associated with perfectionism in children. Perfectionism, in turn, was associated with childhood depression.

Mediators tend to be continuous variables that explain the mechanism by which a risk factor (e.g., parental overcontrol) leads to a developmental outcome or disorder (e.g., depression). Mediators help researchers explain how risk factors contribute to the development of psychopathology.

The Causes of Child Psychopathology: Research Methods

Developmental psychopathologists study the potential causes of childhood disorders from multiple levels of analysis. These levels include children's genes, brain structure and functioning, psychological processes, family environment, and broader social-cultural experiences. Researchers obtain the most complete picture of children's development when they integrate data from multiple levels. However, the research methods used at each of these levels are diverse, making communication across levels difficult. Understanding the research methods across levels is especially challenging for students who are new to the field. In this section, we will examine some of the basic principles and methods used by researchers across these levels of analysis. An understanding of these methods is necessary to appreciate research on the various childhood disorders presented in subsequent chapters.

Genetic Influences on Development

Gene Structure and Functioning

Chromosomes are threadlike structures that are found in the nucleus of the cells in our body. Each chromosome consists of proteins and **deoxyribonucleic acid (DNA)**. DNA is shaped like a twisted ladder, or double helix. The ropes of the ladder are made up of sugars (deoxyribose) and phosphates. The rungs of the ladder consist of pairs of purine and pyrimidine bases held together by hydrogen bonds (see Image 2.1). Their structure only allows them to combine in certain ways (McClead, Menke, & Coury, 1996).

A **nucleotide** consists of one base pair "rung," a deoxyribose "rope," and a phosphate "rope." Three nucleotides arranged together in the ladder form a trinucleotide,

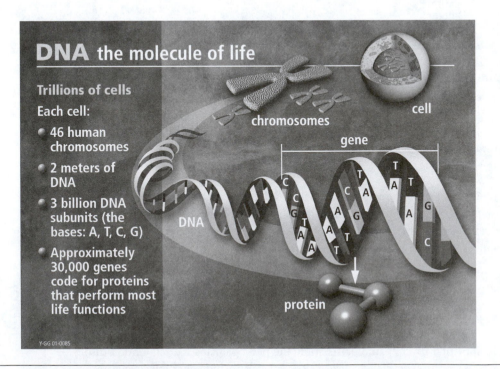

Image 2.1   From Cells to DNA

Source: Courtesy of the U.S. Department of Energy Human Genome Program.

sometimes called a codon. Each trinucleotide instructs the cell to build a specific amino acid. These amino acids are used to build proteins, which form the structure and characteristics of the person. Thousands of trinucleotides form a **gene**. A single human cell contains approximately 30,000 genes.

Most of the cells in your body contain 23 pairs of chromosomes. When a cell reproduces, each chromosome spits in two and duplicates itself, resulting in 46 pairs. The cell then divides, forming two daughter cells with 23 pairs each. This process is called **mitosis**. In another process, called **meiosis**, the cell divides before duplicating itself. As a result, the cells that are formed have half the number of chromosomes: 23 total instead of 23 pairs. These cells are sex cells, either sperm or ova. When they unite in fertilization, the resulting zygote has the usual 23 chromosome pairs.

Scientists use the term **genotype** to refer to the collection of genes that we inherit from our parents. Many people erroneously believe that genes determine behavior. For example, newscasters may incorrectly report that researchers have discovered a gene responsible for homosexuality or a gene that makes people behave aggressively. Nothing could be further from the truth. Genes merely form a blueprint for the body's creation of proteins. Some of these proteins partially determine our eye color or skin pigmentation. Others determine whether we have straight or curly hair. No gene directs behavior. However, genes can lead to certain structural and functional changes in our bodies that predispose us to behave in certain ways.

Behavioral Genetics

Behavioral geneticists study the relationship between genes and behavior. Behavioral geneticists use three approaches to identifying the relative contributions of genetic and environmental influences on child development. The first, and simplest, approach is by conducting a **family study**. In a family study, researchers determine whether a certain behavior or mental disorder is shared by members of the same family. If the disorder is partially genetically determined, relatives who are closely biologically related will be most likely to be affected.

For example, researchers have examined the heritability of children's intelligence using family studies. If we look at the light gray bars on Figure 2.4, we see that the correlation of children's IQ scores is higher among biological relatives than among non-biological relatives. The mean correlation between two biological siblings' IQ scores is approximately .45, whereas the mean correlation between two unrelated children's IQ scores is only about .27. These findings suggest that genetic factors play a role in children's intelligence.

The primary limitation of family studies is that they do not adequately control for environmental effects. Although it is true that biological relatives share similar genes, they also usually live in similar environments. Most family members share the same house, live in the same neighborhoods, enjoy similar pastimes, and come from similar socioeconomic and cultural backgrounds. Therefore, when family studies indicate that closely related relatives are more likely to have a disorder than more distant relatives, we cannot determine whether this similarity is due to common genes or similar environments.

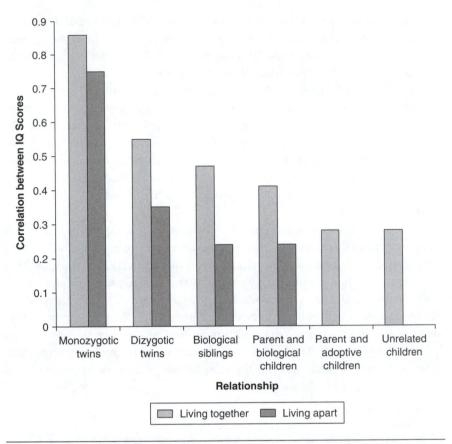

Figure 2.4   The Effects of Genotype and Environment on Children's Intelligence
Source: Based on Sattler (2001).

To tease apart the relative effects of genes and environment on behavior, behavioral geneticists conduct **adoption studies.** In an adoption study, researchers examine children who were separated from their biological families shortly after birth. If a behavioral attribute is greatly influenced by genetics, we would expect children to show greater similarity to their biological relatives than to their adoptive relatives.

For example, the mean correlation between parents and their biological children's IQ scores is approximately .40. In contrast, the mean correlation between parents and their adoptive children's IQ scores is only .25. Because children show greater similarity to their biological parents than their adoptive parents, we can conclude that genetic factors play unique roles in the development of children's intelligence.

The primary weakness of adoption studies is that parents who adopt children are often not typical of parents in the general population. Adoption agencies carefully screen prospective adoptive parents before placing a child in their custody. Consequently, adoptive parents are less likely to have mental health problems and are more likely to have higher income and educational backgrounds than other parents. Furthermore, parents who offer their children for adoption often have higher rates of mental illness and lower social and economic backgrounds than parents in the general population. These systemic differences between biological and adoptive families may partially account for the greater similarity between children and their biological parents compared to their adoptive parents.

A third way that behavioral geneticists identify the relative contributions of genes and environment to behavior is by conducting a **twin study**. In a twin study, researchers compare the behavioral similarity (i.e., concordance) between monozygotic and dizygotic twins. Monozygotic (MZ; identical) twins are the product of the same egg and sperm cell; consequently, they have 100% genetic similarity. Dizygotic (DZ; fraternal) twins are the products of different egg and sperm cells; consequently, they share only 50% of their genes, like biologically related siblings. **Behavioral concordance** is expressed as the correlation between twins, ranging from 1.0 (i.e., perfect behavioral similarity) to 0 (i.e., no behavioral similarity).

The correlation between IQ scores for MZ twins is .85, whereas the correlation for DZ twins is only .55. The higher concordance for MZ twins than DZ twins indicates that intelligence is at least partially genetically determined.

In some cases, twin and adoption studies are combined by examining twins who both live with their biological parents (e.g., the light bars in Figure 2.4) and twins separated at birth (e.g., the dark bars in Figure 2.4). For example, the mean correlation in IQ for MZ twins reared together is .85, whereas the mean correlation for MZ twins reared apart is .75. The high correlations for twins reared apart and reared together indicate that genetic factors play important roles in the development of intelligence. Even twins separated shortly after birth have remarkably similar IQs.

Behavioral geneticists often divide environmental influences on behavior into two types: shared environmental factors and nonshared environmental factors. **Shared environmental factors** are experiences common to siblings. For example, siblings usually are reared by the same parents, grow up in the same house, attend the same schools, and belong to the same church. Shared environmental experiences make siblings more alike. In contrast, **nonshared environmental factors** are experiences that differ between siblings. For example, siblings may have different friends, play different sports, or enjoy different subjects in school. Siblings may also have different types of relationships with their parents. For example, a girl and boy might have different relationships with their father. These nonshared environmental factors often account for more of the variance in children's behavior than do shared experiences. Nonshared environmental factors help to explain why siblings can be so different even though they grow up in the same home.

Molecular Genetics

Another way to study the effects of genes on behavior is to examine children's genes at the molecular (rather than the behavioral) level. Recent advances in our knowledge of the human genome and in gene research technology have allowed scientists to begin to search for specific genes that might be partially responsible for certain disorders (Rende & Waldman, 2006).

In typically developing individuals, genes show a natural amount of variation. For example, some genes code for blue eyes while others code for brown. These variations in the genetic code are called **alleles**. Molecular geneticists can attempt to link the presence of specific alleles (i.e., variations in the genetic code) with certain diseases or disorders.

One way to identify which alleles might be responsible for specific disorders is to conduct a molecular genetic **linkage study**. In a linkage study, researchers search the entire genetic structure of individuals (i.e., perform a "genome scan"), looking for associations between the presence of certain alleles and the existence of a specific disorder. If researchers find certain alleles in individuals with the disorder and do not find these alleles in people without the disorder, they hypothesize that the allele is partially responsible for the disorder (Dick & Todd, 2006).

Researchers tend to use linkage studies when they do not know exactly where to look for genes responsible for the disorder. Given the magnitude of the human genome, it is extremely difficult to identify links between certain alleles and specific disorders. However, researchers have successfully used linkage studies to identify alleles responsible for disorders cause by single genes, such as Huntington's Disease. Linkage approaches have been less successful in identifying the causes of disorders that depend on the presence or absence of multiple alleles.

An alternative technique is to conduct an association study. In an **association study**, researchers select a specific gene that they believe might play a role in the emergence of a disorder. Then, they examine whether there is an association between a particular allele of this "candidate" gene and the disorder (Dick & Todd, 2006).

For example, researchers hypothesized that a specific gene, which affects the neurotransmitter dopamine, might play a role in the development of ADHD. They suspected this particular gene because abnormalities in dopamine functioning have been identified as a specific cause for ADHD symptoms. Furthermore, medications that affect dopamine in the brain can reduce ADHD symptoms. The researchers identified a group of children with and without ADHD. Then, they examined whether the two groups of children had different alleles for the candidate gene. The researchers found that a certain allele for this gene was much more common among youths with ADHD compared to youths without the disorder. Consequently, they concluded that the gene may be partially responsible for ADHD (Rende & Waldman, 2006).

Of course, molecular genetics research is much more complicated than has been described here. Nearly all mental disorders are influenced by multiple genes; there is almost never a one-to-one relationship between the presence of a specific allele and the emergence of a given disorder. Furthermore, genes never affect behavior directly; their influence on behavior is always influenced by environmental experience (Rende & Waldman, 2006).

Gene-Environment Interactions

Genes guide our maturation, but they do not determine our development. Our **phenotype**, the observable expression of our genetic endowment, is determined by the interaction between our genes and the environment.

We should not think of genes and environment as independently influencing children's developmental outcomes. Rather, there is a correlation between children's genotype and the quality of their environmental experiences. Scarr and McCartney

(1983) have identified three ways genotypes and environments are related and how this relationship influences development.

1. *Passive Gene-Environment Correlation.* Although our biological parents determine our genotype, they also determine the quality of our early environmental experiences. Our genes and early experiences are related. For example, parents with high intelligence may pass on this genetic predisposition to their children. At the same time, because of their high intelligence and perhaps above-average salaries, these parents have access to higher quality medical care, more nutritious meals, excellent child care, and better schools. Intelligent parents speak and read to their children frequently, provide stimulating educational toys, and take their children on outings to museums and zoos. In this manner, their children passively receive genotypes and early environmental experiences conducive to high intelligence.

2. *Evocative Gene-Environment Correlation.* As children develop, their phenotype gradually emerges from the interaction between their genotype and early environment. Like their parents, they may begin to show signs of above-average intelligence. They show well-developed verbal skills, learn more quickly than their peers, perform more tasks independently, and are curious about a wide range of topics. These behaviors evoke certain responses in others. School personnel may identify them as "gifted" and provide them with more enriched educational experiences. They may be admitted into accelerated classes in junior and senior high school and gain academic scholarships to highly selective colleges.

3. *Active Gene-Environment Correlation.* As children continue to develop, they actively select environmental experiences conducive to their genotype. For example, they might develop friendships with other bright children with similar interests and hobbies; seek out clubs that satisfy their curiosity in science, music, or art; and select challenging but rewarding majors in college. Children's tendency to select environmental experiences conducive to their genotypes is sometimes called "niche-picking." As children gain more autonomy, niche-picking plays an increasingly important role in shaping development. In a sense, youths select their own environments based on the cumulative influence of their genes and early environmental experiences.

Biological Influences on Development

Neuroimaging

We have witnessed considerable advances in our understanding of brain development in the past 30 years. Beginning in the 1970s, clinicians and researchers used **computed tomography** (CT) to obtain more detailed images of the brain. In CT scanning, multiple images are taken using a movable X-ray device. These images are then integrated by computer to provide a clearer picture of the brain. However, CT scanning, like older X-ray imaging, exposed individuals to radiation. Consequently, it was used sparingly in children and only when medically necessary.

In the 1980s, a new tool was developed: **magnetic resonance imaging** (MRI). MRI technology is based on the fact that when body tissues are placed in a strong magnetic field and exposed to a brief pulse of radiofrequency energy, cells from the tissue give off a brief signal, called a "magnetic resonance." Different types of tissue give off slightly different signals. In the brain, neurons (i.e., grey matter), myelin (i.e., white matter), and cerebral spinal fluid give different signals. These signals, associated with a particular type of brain tissue (called a "voxel"), can be interpreted by a computer and used to generate a digital image (called a "pixel"). MRI machines generate two-dimensional images of brain tissue that can be integrated by the computer (i.e., "stacked" on top of one another) to create a three-dimensional image of the brain (Giedd, Shaw, Wallace, Gogtay, & Lenroot, 2006).

MRI has a number of advantages over CT and most other imaging techniques. First, MRI does not subject individuals to radiation; it is believed to be safe and has even been used to obtain images of the brains of developing fetuses. Second, because it is safe, MRI can be used with healthy children and administered repeatedly over time (see Image 2.2). Consequently, MRI technology allows us to study children's brains multiple times across development. Third, MRI yields clearer and more precise pictures of the brain than older neuroimaging methods. Today, MRI resolution is generally in the 1 to 2 mm range (Giedd et al., 2006).

Besides helping us understand normal brain development, MRI can also allow us to detect structural abnormalities in the brains of youths with mental disorders. In a typical MRI study, researchers scan the brains of youths with and without a specific disorder. For example, Castellanos and colleagues (2002) scanned the

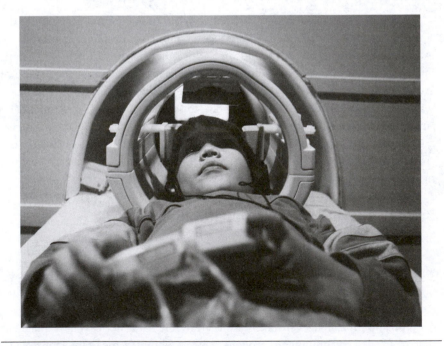

Image 2.2   Neuroimaging. Nine-year-old Patrick is shown participating in an MRI study of children with dyslexia.

Source: AP Photo/Manuel Balce Ceneta. Used with permission.

brains of children with and without ADHD. The researchers compared the volumes of the frontal cortex of children in the two groups. They found that children with ADHD showed an average 4% reduction in volume of the frontal cortex compared to children without ADHD. These results are important because underactivity in portions of the frontal cortex is believed to account for some ADHD symptoms.

Functional magnetic resonance imaging (fMRI) is a relatively new technique used to measure brain activity (Pine, 2006). The techniques used in fMRI greatly resemble MRI. However, the fMRI device measures changes in oxygenated hemoglobin concentrations in the brain. When the individual engages in mental activity, oxygenated hemoglobin concentrations increase in brain regions that become active. Consequently, fMRI yields a picture of the individual's brain showing regions most active during certain mental activities (Sadock & Sadock, 2003).

To perform fMRI, researchers typically obtain an image of the individual's brain using traditional MRI. Then researchers ask the individual to perform a series of mental activities while they collect fMRI data. For example, researchers might ask adolescents with autism to describe the emotional expression on pictures of people's faces, or ask children with learning disabilities to read or solve math problems. These fMRI images are then superimposed over the traditional MRI to show brain regions that are most active during the mental tasks.

Tamm, Menon, and Reiss (2006) used fMRI to determine which brain regions might be responsible for the deficits in attention shown by youths with ADHD. They asked 14 adolescents with ADHD and 12 adolescents without ADHD to perform a test of attention while they collected fMRI data. In this task, youths were presented with a series of either green circles or green triangles. They were asked to press one button when they saw a circle and a different button when they saw a triangle. As expected, youths with ADHD made significantly more errors in the task than youths without ADHD. Furthermore, youths with ADHD showed significantly less activity in certain brain areas (i.e., their parietal lobes) compared to their healthy peers. The researchers concluded that these brain regions may play a role in people's ability to direct and regulate attention.

Neuroimaging studies involving children and adolescents often yield inconsistent results. The primary reason for the inconsistent results of many neuroimaging studies is that children show enormous variability in their brain volumes and rates of brain development. For example, total brain volumes can differ by as much as 20% based on factors such as children's age, gender, and environment. Researchers wishing to identify structural abnormalities in the brains of children with specific disorders need to carefully control for these factors. A second reason for inconsistent findings is that many studies have been unable to detect structural abnormalities in children because of low image resolution. Even today, with better technology, many children find it uncomfortable to remain in MRI devices for long enough periods of time to obtain the clearest images possible (Giedd et al., 2006).

Perhaps the most important reason for the inconsistent findings is that mental and behavioral disorders in children and adolescents rarely have single causes that can be traced to specific brain regions. For example, ADHD appears to be caused by a complex relationship between biological, psychological, and environmental factors. It would be a mistake to think that a specific brain abnormality would account for all (or even most) cases of ADHD or any other disorder. Instead, it is likely that early differences in brain structure interact with environmental experiences to produce symptoms (Johnson & de Haan, 2006).

Brain Development

The development of the central nervous system begins shortly after conception and continues well into adulthood. During the first month after conception, the **neural tube** is formed. This tissue will later become the basis for the brain and spinal cord. During the second and third months of gestation, the brain gradually begins to take shape at the top of the neural tube, with the foremost part of the brain becoming most prominent. Shortly after the first trimester, there is a rapid proliferation of neurons and an increase in neural density. From month three to month five of gestation, these neurons gradually make their way from the center of the brain to the outmost areas, a process called migration. These neurons, which migrate to the outermost shell of the brain, will later form the cortex. At the beginning of the second trimester, the brain experiences a period of rapid cell death, called **apoptosis**. Approximately 50% of neurons will die during this process, presumably to make way for more important neural connections and increased brain organization (Giedd et al., 2006).

During the remainder of gestation, there is a dramatic increase in myelin, the white fatty coating that surrounds neurons and helps with their conductivity. Increased **myelinization** is believed to speed up neural activity and make brain processes occur more quickly and efficiently. This increase in myelinization continues at a rapid rate until age two years. Myelinization then slows, but continues until at least adolescence.

Also during the third trimester of gestation, there is a dramatic increase in the number of connections between neurons. This rapid increase in synaptic connections continues until approximately age two years. Indeed, the average two-year-old child has approximately 50% more synaptic connections than the average adult. After age two years, however, there is a gradual reduction in the number of synaptic connections. Developmental biologists believe that many of the connections that are not needed simply die off, in a process called **synaptic pruning**. Although pruning might seem like a waste of neural connections, it is actually a normal and healthy process. Pruning makes the brain process information more efficiently, by strengthening neural connections that are frequently used and discarding neural connections that are not necessary.

Approximately 15 years ago, most neuroscientists believed that the brain reached its mature size and structure around age 10 years. However, recent research suggests that the brain continues to change dramatically, at least through late adolescence or early adulthood. Certain brain structures seem to gradually increase in size during childhood and then decrease beginning sometime in adolescence (see Image 2.3).

One brain region, the cortex, follows this inverted U-shaped pattern of growth and deterioration. The **cortex** is divided into four regions or lobes. The occipital lobe, located near the back of the brain, is primarily responsible for visual processing. This

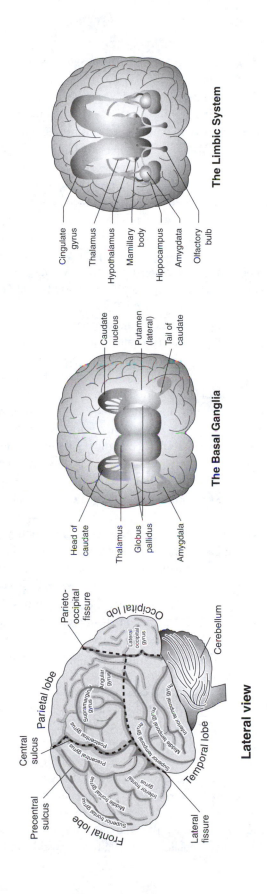

Image 2.3   Important Parts of the Developing Brain

Source: From Kempler (2005). Used with permission.

brain region appears to undergo the most change during early childhood. In contrast, the volume of the parietal lobe (located on the sides and top of the brain) peaks around age 10 or 11 years and then gradually decreases in size. The parietal lobe is primarily responsible for integrating visual, auditory, and tactile information. Pruning in this region may account for improved sensory and motor functioning that occurs during adolescence. The volume of the frontal lobe peaks shortly thereafter, around age 11 or 12 years. The frontal cortex plays an important role in organizing, planning, and prioritizing behavior. The pruning of the frontal cortex, which begins in early adolescence and continues until early adulthood, is believed to underlie adolescents' increased capacity for attention, inhibition, and overall behavioral control. The temporal lobe (located on the sides and bottom of the brain) shows peak volume around age 16 years. The temporal lobe has multiple functions, including the expression and regulation of emotions. Pruning of the temporal lobe, which usually begins during middle to late adolescence, may underlie adolescents' abilities to understand and regulate emotions (Giedd et al., 2006).

Another brain region that seems to change during childhood and adolescence is the basal ganglia. The **basal ganglia** are located under the cortex, between the brain stem and the higher-level cortical regions. They consist of a number of structures, including the caudate, putamen, globus pallidus, and substantia nigra. The basal ganglia perform many important functions. One of their primary roles is to help control movement. Another function is to filter incoming information from the senses and relay this information to other brain regions where it can be processed. The basal ganglia have also been implicated in the regulation of attention and emotions. Researchers believe that structural changes in the basal ganglia, especially the pruning that occurs during childhood and adolescence, might account for children's increased motor functioning, attention, and emotional processing across development (Giedd et al., 2006).

A third brain region that appears to change across childhood and adolescence is the **limbic system**. The limbic system is located deep inside the brain, behind the temporal lobes. The primary components of the limbic system are the amygdala and hippocampus. The amygdala aids in our understanding and expression of emotions, especially negative feelings such as fear and rage. The hippocampus also plays a role in emotional processing, especially the formation of emotion-laden memories. Although neuroimaging studies are just beginning to give us a better understanding of these elusive brain regions, some data indicate that the limbic system may continue to change well into adolescence (Giedd et al., 2006).

A fourth brain structure, the **corpus callosum**, seems to increase in volume from early childhood through adolescence. The corpus callosum is a heavily myelinated structure that connects the left and right hemispheres of the brain. Its primary job is to relay and integrate information across hemispheres. Damage to the corpus callosum is associated with impairments in a wide range of functions, including attention and arousal, memory storage and retrieval, hearing, and language.

A final area of the brain, the **cerebellum**, increases in volume during childhood and undergoes considerable pruning during early adolescence. The cerebellum, or "little brain," is located in the back of the brain, near the brain stem. Neuroscientists originally believed that the cerebellum was chiefly responsible for balance, posture, and coordination. Researchers now believe the cerebellum plays a role in mental gracefulness and efficiency in addition to adroitness in physical movement. Maturation of the cerebellum during adolescence might explain the increased physical gracefulness exhibited by older adolescents as well as a general increase in mental efficiency across development.

Neural Plasticity: How Experience Can Drive Brain Development

So far, we have examined some of the techniques used by neuroscientists to study brain structure and functioning. The notion of gene-environment correlation implies that genes influence brain structure, which, in turn, affects behavior. However, the relationship between brain structure and behavior is bidirectional. Some of the most exciting research in the past 20 years has shown that the brain can change in response to experience.

The structure and functioning of the brain is determined by the interaction of genes and environmental experiences. Specifically, genes and environment interact in three ways to shape the developing brain (Black, Jones, Nelson, & Greenough, 1998). First, certain aspects of brain development are **gene-driven**. These aspects are largely impervious to the effects of experience and almost entirely determined by the person's genetic code. For example, the development of the neural tube and migration of neurons from the center of the brain to the cortex is believed to be genetically preprogrammed and largely insensitive to experience. Developmental psychologists sometimes refer to this importance of genes over experience in embryonic development as *canalization*.

Other aspects of brain development are **experience-expectant**; that is, the formation of the brain region is partially dependent on information received from the environment. Infants have an overabundance of neural connections, many of which they do not need. Connections that are used are maintained and strengthened while connections that are not used atrophy and die. Whether a connection is maintained or pruned depends on experience. For example, an infant exposed to the Japanese language during the first few years of life may strengthen neural connections responsible for processing the sounds used in Japanese. However, infants not exposed to Japanese during this early period of development may lose neural connections that might play a role in processing the Japanese language. Consequently, children who are not exposed to Japanese in infancy and early childhood may find it relatively difficult to speak the language without an accent later in life. Developmental psychologists often refer to periods of development in which experience can greatly shape neural structure and functioning as developmentally sensitive periods.

Third, brain development can be **experience-dependent**; that is, environmental experiences in later life can actually lead to the formation of new neural connections or to changes in the brain's organization or structure. The ability of the brain to change after the first few years of life was unimaginable one generation ago. However, recent research points to the ways the brain can change in response to environmental conditions throughout the lifespan.

Neuroscientists use the term **plasticity** to refer to the brain's malleability, that is, its capacity to change its structure and/or functioning in response to environmental experiences. These environmental experiences can be either internal or external. Internal experiences alter the immediate environment of the brain and nervous system. For example, exposure to too much testosterone or stress hormone can lead to structural changes in various brain regions. In contrast, external experiences come from outside the organism. For example, an infant who ingests lead or other environmental toxins can experience brain damage.

Neuroscientists have discovered that the brain is remarkably adaptive to environmental stressors, especially when these stressors occur early in life. Perhaps the most striking example of brain plasticity is seen following a surgical procedure called a functional hemispherectomy. **Functional hemispherectomy** is performed on some children who have medically intractable epilepsy that arises in one hemisphere of the brain. These seizures cause severe impairment, occur very frequently, and are not responsive to medication. To perform a functional hemispherectomy, the surgeon removes the entire parietal lobe of the nonfunctional hemisphere (which is often the origin of the seizures) and severs the corpus callosum (which allows the seizure to travel from one hemisphere to the other; Pulsifer, Brandt, Salorio, Vining, Carson, & Freeman, 2004).

Despite removal or disconnection of several brain regions, children usually show remarkable recovery from the procedure. Children often experience motor deficits on the side of the body opposite the hemisphere that was removed. Furthermore, if the left hemisphere is removed, most children experience temporary disturbance in language. However, children usually recover much of this lost functioning within 6 to 12 months after surgery, as the remaining hemisphere gradually assumes many of these lost functions. Most children are able to return to school 6 to 8 weeks post-surgery (Jonas et al., 2004; van Empelen, Jennekens-Schinkel, Buskens, Helders, & Van Nieuwenhuizen, 2004).

Environmental experiences need not be as dramatic as a hemispherectomy to produce changes in the organization of the brain. Rats reared in isolation show dramatic increases in stress hormone. These chronic elevations in stress hormone seem to alter the rats' stress response. As a result, isolated rats often show long-term propensities toward aggression as adults. Similarly, some children who are repeatedly exposed to physical or sexual abuse show dysregulation of certain brain regions responsible for the body's stress response. This dysregulation, in turn, can cause problems with anxiety and mood later in life.

Environmental experiences also need not be negative to affect brain functioning. Positive environmental experiences can actually increase metabolic activity and lead to the formation of new neural connections. Long ago, the neuropsychologist D. O. Hebb (1949) proposed that the simultaneous activation of neurons can cause the neurons to form new synaptic connections. Hebb suggested that neurons that "fire together, wire together." Recently neuroscientists have been able to show **synaptogenesis**, that is, the formation of new neural connections due to experience. For example, rats reared in enriched living environments (e.g., given extra space and access to toys and mazes) show differences in brain structure and functioning compared to rats reared in typical cages. Humans who receive extensive training in Braille show increases in the size of brain regions responsible for processing the sense of touch. Even skilled musicians show a reorganization of brain regions responsible for controlling the finger positions of their instruments (Cicchetti & Curtis, 2006)!

Gottesman (1963) developed the concept of the **reaction range** to demonstrate the way genes and environment interact to influence development. From Gottesman's perspective, our genotype sets an upper and lower limit, or range, on our intellectual and behavioral potentials. Then the quality of our environment determines where, within this range, our actual abilities fall. If we are provided with enriched environmental experiences, we may develop toward the higher end of the range. If we encounter impoverished or harmful experiences, our development might be toward the lower end of our potential.

The notion of a reaction range helps to explain why children reared in the same environments can show different developmental trajectories. To take an extreme example, consider two children, one born with a genetic abnormality, Down syndrome, and another, healthy child. Both children may be raised in the same family and given the same early environmental experiences, but the genotype of the first child places an upper limit on his intellectual development. It is unlikely that he will develop intelligence within the normal range, regardless of the quality of environmental experiences. The second boy, raised in the same environment, would show a different developmental trajectory and much higher intellectual functioning.

Behavioral Influences on Development

Researchers who study the psychological causes of child psychopathology are interested in explaining maladaptation at the behavioral level. The term "behavior" encompasses three important facets of children's functioning: their thoughts, feelings, and actions. Psychologists recognize that thoughts, feelings, and actions are closely connected; each partially influences, and is influenced by, the others.

Psychologists often use learning theory to explain and predict children's behavior. From the perspective of learning theory, children's actions are chiefly determined by environmental factors. Learning occurs in three principal ways: (1) through classical conditioning, (2) through operant conditioning, and (3) through social imitation or modeling.

Classical Conditioning

In classical conditioning, learning occurs when the child associates two stimuli paired together in time. One stimulus is initially called the neutral stimulus (NS) because it does not elicit a response. The other stimulus is initially called an unconditioned stimulus (UCS) because it naturally elicits an unconditioned response (UCR). The organism may come to associate the NS with the UCS if the two stimuli are presented together. For example, Pavlov demonstrated that dogs would associate the sound of a metronome (NS) with the presentation of meat powder (UCS) if the two stimuli were presented contiguously. After repeated presentations, the metronome alone elicited salivation. After conditioning, the previously neutral stimulus (e.g., metronome) is referred to as the conditioned stimulus (CS), whereas the resulting response (e.g., salivation) is referred to as the conditioned response (CR).

Classical conditioning is often used to explain and to treat childhood disorders. For example, a girl who is bitten by a dog might associate the sight of a dog (NS) with the experience of being bitten (UCS). The dog bite, in turn, naturally causes a fear response (UCR). Later, the presence of any dog (CS) may elicit a similar fear response (CR).

One way of decreasing behaviors acquired through classical conditioning is to use **extinction**. Extinction involves repeatedly presenting the CS until it no longer elicits the CR. Extinction is usually accomplished gradually, in a process called graded exposure. For example, a therapist might recommend that a girl with a fear of dogs gradually expose herself to dogs, in order to extinguish this fear. Initially, the girl might simply look at pictures of dogs, then remain in a room with a dog on a leash, and finally pet a dog. After the girl is repeatedly exposed to the dog, the dog's presence no longer elicits a fear response.

Operant Conditioning

Whereas classical conditioning occurs when individuals associate two stimuli, operant conditioning occurs when individuals associate a behavior with a consequence in the environment. Operant conditioning is based on the notion that the consequences of our actions determine the likelihood that the actions will be repeated. If the consequences of our actions increase the likelihood that we will repeat the behavior in the future, these consequences have **reinforced** our behavior. If the consequences of our actions decrease the likelihood that we will repeat our behavior in the future, these consequences have **punished** our behavior. Reinforcement increases the likelihood of future behavior, whereas punishment decreases the likelihood of future behavior (see Figure 2.5).

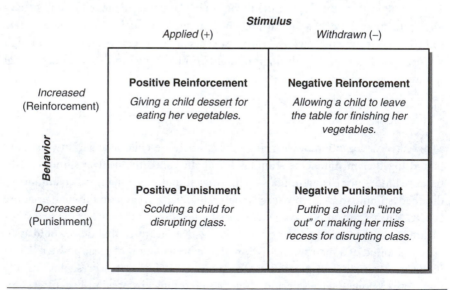

Figure 2.5   Operant Conditioning

Note: Reinforcement leads to an increase in behavior; punishment leads to a decrease in behavior.

Reinforcement can be positive or negative. **Positive reinforcement** occurs when an individual is presented with a stimulus that increases the likelihood of behavior. For example, a father might give his daughter ice cream after she eats her vegetables at dinner. If the presentation of ice cream following the meal increases the likelihood that the girl eats her vegetables in the future, we say that the ice cream positively reinforced the child's eating.

Many people mistakenly believe that the adjective "positive" in the term "positive reinforcement" refers to the pleasantness of the reinforcer. In fact, the term "positive" simply refers to the fact that the stimulus is *presented* to the individual. Some presumably pleasant stimuli are not positively reinforcing to all children. For example, providing a two-year-old with one M&M for using the toilet may increase the likelihood that he will use the toilet in the future. However, providing one M&M to a 10-year-old for completing his math homework will likely not increase the likelihood that he will complete his math homework. Additionally, some presumably unpleasant stimuli can be positively reinforcing. For example, a teacher may reprimand her student for disrupting class. If the teacher's reprimand results in an increase in the student's disruptive behavior, the teacher's behavior is positively reinforcing, no matter how aversive it appears.

Negative reinforcement occurs when the withdrawal or avoidance of a stimulus increases the likelihood of behavior. For example, a father might allow his daughter to leave the dinner table only after she finishes her vegetables. If escaping the dinner table by eating vegetables increases the likelihood that the girl eats her vegetables in the future, we say that the father's action negatively reinforced the child's eating.

Negative reinforcement often underlies childhood behavior problems. For example, a mother might ask her son to turn off the television and clean his room. The son might ignore his mother because he prefers to watch his favorite TV program. The mother might withdraw her request and clean her son's room herself. If the mother's behavior (i.e., withdrawal of her request) increases the likelihood that her son will ignore her requests in the future, we say that her actions are negatively reinforcing his disobedience.

In contrast to reinforcement, punishment always results in a *decrease* in the probability of future behavior. There are two types of punishment: positive and negative. **Positive punishment** involves a stimulus *presentation* that decreases the likelihood of behavior. For example, a mother might spank her son for his disobedience. If spanking results in a decrease in her child's defiance, then the mother's action was a form of positive punishment. **Negative punishment** involves a stimulus *removal* that decreases the likelihood of behavior. For example, a teacher might remove a child from a desirable classroom activity following his disruptive behavior in class. If the teacher's action results in a decrease in the student's disruptive behavior, then the teacher's behavior was a form a negative punishment.

Clinicians prefer to use reinforcement to correct child behavior problems. However, in some cases, punishment can be used therapeutically. For example, a therapist might teach a parent to use positive punishment to correct her son's bed wetting. Specifically, every time the boy wets the bed, the parent might require the boy to perform a series of actions designed to correct the problem behavior. These actions might include stripping the bed, taking the bedding to the washing machine, helping to start the wash, putting on new sheets, and sitting on the toilet. Similarly, a therapist might teach a parent to use "time out" as a form of negative punishment for her disruptive preschooler. "Time out" involves removing the child from all potentially reinforcing stimuli for a period of time, in an attempt to decrease the child's defiance. The child might be required to sit in a special chair for three minutes with no access to toys, television, or other potentially pleasurable stimuli.

Social Learning

Behaviors can also be acquired through the observation of others. Bandura, Ross, and Ross (1961) demonstrated that children who watched adults behaving aggressively toward an inflatable doll often imitated the adults' aggressive actions. Bandura believed that learning through imitation, or **modeling**, was a primary mechanism of behavioral acquisition. Social learning was especially likely when models were similar to children in age and gender and when models were reinforced for their actions.

Modeling is also used to explain and to treat child behavior problems. For example, parents who model anxiety to their children can increase their children's likelihood of developing an anxiety disorder. A mother who is afraid of social situations might model this fear to her daughter. Specifically, she might avoid attending social gatherings and overtly worry about appearing foolish in public. She might also convey to her daughter that other people are often critical and judgmental, thereby increasing her daughter's fears of social situations. As a result, the daughter might develop anxiety in social situations and a tendency toward social withdrawal.

A therapist might also use modeling as a means to reduce the daughter's social phobia. Specifically, the therapist might ask the child's teacher to pair the girl with a "classroom buddy"—a female classmate who shows well-developed social skills and is willing to model appropriate social behavior. By watching her "buddy," the girl might discover that social situations are often pleasant and are rarely catastrophic. Consequently, her social anxiety may decrease.

Familial Influences on Development

Parent-Infant Attachment

Attachment refers to the affective bond between parent and child that serves to protect and reassure the child in times of danger or uncertainty. According to John Bowlby (1969, 1973, 1980), the parent-child attachment relationship has three basic functions. Most important, the attachment relationship serves to protect the young child from danger. Infants and young children are biologically predisposed to seek contact and proximity to their parents when scared, upset, or unsure of their surroundings. At the same time, parents are predisposed to respond to their infant's bids for attention and care.

Second, the attachment relationship is designed to provide dyads with an avenue for sharing positive emotional experiences. Through interactions with parents, infants learn about the natural reciprocity of social interactions and the give-and-take of interpersonal relationships.

Third, the attachment relationship helps the infant learn to regulate negative emotions and behaviors. Initially, the infant controls anxiety and distress by directly relying on comfort from his parent. Over time, the child develops an **internal working model**, or mental representation of his parent, that helps him cope with psychosocial stress. Essentially, the infant learns to use this mental representation of his parent as a "secure base" from which to explore his surroundings and control his emotions and actions.

The quality of parent-child interactions over the first few years of life influences the initial quality of the attachment relationship. Parents who provide sensitive and responsive care to their children, by meeting their children's needs in a consistent and developmentally appropriate fashion, usually develop **secure attachment relationships** with their children. Their children, in turn, come to expect sensitive and responsive care from their parents. At the same time, these children come to view themselves as worthy of receiving sensitive and responsive care from others.

In contrast, parents who do not provide sensitive and responsive care in a consistent fashion are likely to foster **insecure attachment relationships** with their children. When scared or upset, these children do not expect their parents to effectively meet their needs and help them regulate their emotions. They adopt internal working models of their parents as unavailable or inconsistent. At the same time, they may view themselves as unworthy of receiving attention and care from others.

Ainsworth, Belhar, Waters, and Wall (1978) identified three patterns of attachment that develop over the first few months of life. These patterns can be observed in the behavior of 12-month-old infants using the **strange situation**, a laboratory-based test of infant-mother attachment. The strange situation occurs in a laboratory playroom and involves separating infants from their parents for short periods of time (see Table 2.1). In the strange situation, most infants experience distress when separated. However, researchers are primarily interested in how infants respond to their parents when they are reunited. Specifically, researchers observe whether infants are able to use their parents as a means to reduce distress and return to play.

Most children who participate in the strange situation show secure attachment relationships with their parents. These children use their parents as a secure base from which to regulate their emotions, control their behavior, and return to play. Although they usually show considerable distress during separation, they seek comfort and physical contact with their parents when they are reunited. After a little while, reassurance from caregivers soothes these infants and they can return to play and exploration.

In contrast, some infants develop **insecure-avoidant attachment** relationships with their parents. When reunited with their mothers, these infants show passivity and disinterest. In fact, many of these infants actively avoid their parents' bids for attention by turning away or ignoring them. Although these infants might be upset by separation, they appear uninterested or resentful of their parents when they return. Instead of using their parents as a secure base from which to regulate their behavior and return to play, these infants attempt to rely on themselves to cope with

Table 2.1   The Strange Situation

Episode	Persons Present	Duration	Description of Events
1	Mother, infant	30 secs	Parent and infant are introduced to the experimental room.
2	Mother, infant	3 min	Parent and infant are alone. Parent does not participate while infant explores.
3	Mother, infant, stranger	3 min	Stranger enters, converses with parent, then approaches infant. Parent leaves.
4	Stranger, infant	3 min	First separation episode. Stranger tries to play with infant.
5	**Mother, infant**	**3 min**	**First reunion episode. Parent greets and comforts infant, then leaves again.**
6	Infant alone	3 min	Second separation episode.
7	Stranger, infant	3 min	Stranger enters, tries to play with infant.
8	**Mother, infant**	**3 min**	**Second reunion episode. Parent enters, greets infant, and picks up infant; stranger leaves inconspicuously.**

Source: Based on Ainsworth et al. (1978).

the stress of separation. Attachment theorists reason that parents who consistently dismiss their children's bids for attention foster insecure-avoidant attachment relationships with their infants.

Other infants develop **insecure-ambivalent attachment** relationships with their parents. When separated, these infants usually respond with considerable distress. However, when reunited with their parents, these infants alternate between seeking and resisting their caregivers' support. For example, an infant might initially motion to be picked up by her mother and then immediately push away. The behavior of these infants conveys the notion that they desperately want comfort from their parents, but that they do not expect their parents to adequately provide for their needs. Attachment theorists reason that parents who alternate between providing care and ignoring their children foster this insecure-ambivalent pattern of attachment.

Longitudinal research indicates that the development of secure attachment relationships in infancy and early childhood is associated with later social-emotional competence. For example, infants who display secure patterns of attachment tend to show more flexible and adaptive behavior during childhood and early adolescence. These children show fewer behavior problems at school, are better liked by peers, evidence greater control over their actions and emotions, and have advanced social skills and capacity for empathy. In contrast, infants classified as insecure may be at risk for social-emotional problems later in development. Specifically, these children sometimes have difficulty with self-reliance and flexible problem solving, problems with peer relationships, and difficulty controlling emotions such as anger and anxiety (Main, Kaplan, & Cassidy, 1985; Sroufe, 1989a; Weinfield, Sroufe, & Egeland, 2000).

Parent-Child Interactions

Although parenting practices differ considerably across families and cultures, psychologists have identified at least two dimensions of parenting that are important to most children's cognitive and social-emotional development (Cowan & Cowan, 2006). The first dimension, **parental responsiveness,** refers to the degree to which parents display warmth and acceptance toward their children, orient their behavior to meet their children's needs in a sensitive and responsive fashion, and engage their children through shared activities and positive emotions. The second dimension, **parental demandingness,** refers to the degree to which parents have age-appropriate expectations for their children's behavior, clearly establish and consistently enforce rules governing their behavior, and supervise their children (Maccoby & Martin, 1983).

Diana Baumrind (1991) has classified parents into four parenting types, based on the degree to which they endorse responsiveness and demandingness in their usual interactions with their children (see Figure 2.6).

Authoritative parents are both responsive and demanding toward their children. These parents set high, but age-appropriate, expectations for their children's behavior and help their children meet these expectations by providing them with nurturance and support. They are assertive in their interactions with their children, but not intrusive. They use discipline to support their children and to teach them how to control their own behavior; they do not use discipline punitively. They value responsibility but also recognize children's needs for sensitive and responsive care.

Authoritarian parents show high levels of demandingness but low levels of responsiveness. These parents value obedience and achievement in their children.

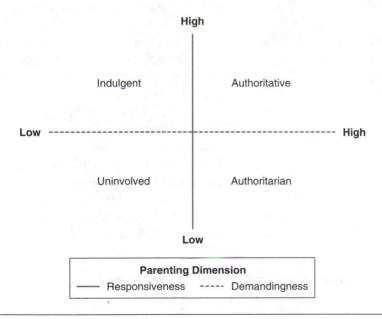

Figure 2.6   Baumrind's Parenting Typology

Note: In samples of predominantly white, middle-class families, children of authoritative parents showed the best developmental outcomes.

They set high standards for their children and firm limits on their children's behaviors. They establish clear rules and expect them to be obeyed without question. These parents are highly involved in their children's lives, providing them with organized, structured, and supervised educational, extracurricular, and social experiences. They strive to teach self-reliance and responsibility to their children, but they may give their children little support and encouragement to live up to these responsibilities.

Indulgent parents show high levels of responsiveness, but low levels of demandingness. These parents are described as lenient, nondirective, and permissive. They value autonomy and exploration in their children. They place few limits on their children's behaviors and are reticent to discipline.

Uninvolved parents show low levels of both responsiveness and demandingness. These parents display infrequent or inconsistent interactions toward their children, often because they are distracted by other psychosocial stressors (e.g., parents working multiple jobs, caring for an elderly relative). In extreme cases, these parents may reject or neglect their children.

Prospective longitudinal research has shown that children's social-emotional outcomes are related to parenting style (Baumrind, 1991; Weiss & Schwarz, 1996). Overall, children of authoritative parents display the best developmental outcomes. On average, these children show well-developed social skills, emotional competence, and capacity for self-regulation and self-direction. Children of authoritarian parents tend to perform well academically but are at risk for low self-esteem and peer problems, especially in late childhood and early adolescence. Children of indulgent parents often display high levels of self-esteem and well-developed social skills, but they are susceptible to behavior problems during childhood and substance use problems during adolescence. Children of uninvolved parents display the poorest developmental outcomes. These children are at particular risk for low academic achievement, behavior problems, and emotional difficulties across development.

Psychologists have also identified a third dimension of parenting, **parental hostility/coercion**, which is especially relevant to the development of children's behavior problems. Hostile/coercive parenting reflects parenting tactics that express negative affect or indifference toward children or involve the use of threat, harsh physical punishment, or psychological manipulation (Lovejoy, Weis, O'Hare, & Rubin, 1999). Examples of hostile/coercive parenting behavior include threatening to hurt or abandon a child, slapping or handling a child roughly, and using guilt or ridicule to control a child's behavior. Prospective longitudinal research indicates that hostile/coercive parenting behavior may contribute to the development of disruptive behavior problems in childhood and adolescence, especially problems with defiance and aggression (Barber, 2002; Patterson, Reid, & Dishion, 1992).

Social-Cultural Influences on Development

Proximal Versus Distal Risk Factors

Until now, we have focused chiefly on the immediate causes of child psychopathology. These causes include the child's genotype, biological structure and functioning, learning experiences, and familial context. These immediate determinants of children's functioning are often referred to as **proximal risk factors** because abnormalities in these areas can directly affect children's well-being. For example, a genetic disorder can lead to Mental Retardation, whereas exposure to hostile/coercive parenting can contribute to oppositional and defiant behavior. The overwhelming majority of research addressing the causes of child psychopathology focuses on proximal risk factors because they are typically the easiest to control and study (Wade & Cairney, 2006).

Researchers have increasingly turned their attention to other, distal risk factors for child behavior problems. **Distal risk factors** are social, cultural, and broader environmental influences on child development that do not directly affect children's functioning but can affect their social, emotional, and behavioral competence.

One important distal risk factor is socioeconomic status (SES), a construct that reflects parents' educational attainment, income, employment status, and living condition. Children from low-SES families are at increased risk for developing behavioral and emotional disorders compared to youths from middle- and high-SES backgrounds. Another frequently studied distal risk factor is ethnicity. For example, African American youth show greater likelihood of developing a mental or behavioral disorder than their white counterparts. Other distal risk factors include family structure (e.g., single-parent families), neighborhood quality (e.g., population density, crime), and broader social norms and mores (Wade & Cairney, 2006).

How do distal factors contribute to child psychopathology? According to Wade and Cairney (2006), risk factors like poverty and neighborhood disadvantage can affect child development in at least three ways. First, distal risk factors can directly influence child development. For example, infants and toddlers who ingest lead are at risk for developing behavioral and learning problems in early childhood. Typically, youths are exposed to lead from lead-based paint that flakes off the walls of older homes. Children from low-SES families are disproportionately exposed to lead-based paint because they often live in older, more deteriorated homes. Consequently, rates of lead poisoning, and subsequent neurological impairment, are much greater among low-SES ethnic minority youth than among middle-class white children (Dilworth-Bart & Moore, 2006).

Second, proximal factors can mediate the effects of distal risks on child development. In this case, distal risk factors undermine parents' abilities to provide optimal care to their children. This less-than-optimal care, in turn, can lead to children's behavioral or emotional problems. For example, Conger, Ge, Elder, Lorenz, and Simons (1994) discovered that the degree to which parents argued over financial concerns predicted the extent to which they showed hostile and coercive behaviors toward their children. Their hostile and coercive parenting behaviors, in turn, predicted the development of their children's behavior problems.

Third, distal risk factors can moderate the effects of proximal factors on children's outcomes. For example, the effects of parenting behavior (e.g., a proximal factor) on children's development might differ depending on whether the child is from a low- or high-SES background (e.g., a distal factor). Lundahl, Risser, and Lovejoy (2006) found that psychotherapy that involves teaching parents to reduce hostile/coercive behavior toward their children is often associated with a reduction of children's behavior problems. However, the effects of parental psychotherapy on children's behavior depend on parents' SES. Psychotherapy is more effective among middle-class parents than low-SES parents. Social and economic disadvantage might interfere with parents' abilities to participate in treatment and, consequently, reduce its benefits.

Bioecological Systems Theory

Perhaps the most influential and comprehensive account for the way social and contextual factors affect child development has been offered by the developmental psychologist Urie Bronfenbrenner. According to Bronfenbrenner's (1979, 2000) **bioecological systems theory**, children's environment can be viewed as a hierarchy of four nested social systems, each encompassing the others like Russian dolls.

The **microsystem** reflects children's immediate surroundings and proximal influences on their development. Factors within the microsystem include children's genetic inheritance, biological functioning, psychological processes, and interactions with parents and family. The microsystem also includes children's other significant relationships (e.g., with teachers, coaches, peers) and the various social roles they adopt (e.g., student, athlete, friend). The microsystem is the "primary engine of development," and children's interactions with caregivers and friends are typically the most important proximal determinants of development (Bronfenbrenner & Morris, 1998).

The **mesosystem** refers to the connections between microsystems. For example, children's relationships at home and school are important determinants of their overall functioning. However, the quality of interactions *between* home and school also influences children's well-being. Children whose parents take an active role in their educational and extracurricular activities will likely show different outcomes than children whose parents show disinterest in their academic and after-school activities.

The **exosystem** reflects contextual influences that affect microsystems but do not affect children directly. For example, a father might be required to change work schedules or to work longer hours to keep his job. These work-related changes might influence the amount of time he is able to spend with his child. Similarly, the school board might decide to reduce funding for certain extracurricular activities, causing a child to give up a favorite sport or club. The parent's change in work schedule and the school board's change in funding can alter children's daily experiences and, consequently, their development.

The **macrosystem** refers to broad social, economic, and cultural influences on children's development. Chief among these factors are socioeconomic disadvantage, neighborhood quality, and media exposure.

Bronfenbrenner recognized that the effects of all four systems on development change over time. First, the importance of various systems depends on children's age and developmental level. For example, the relative importance of peers to child development increases across childhood and early adolescence. Second, the nature of proximal and distal risk factors changes across generations. For example, the degree to which children are exposed to violent crime and other social-cultural risk factors has increased dramatically in recent decades (Bronfenbrenner, McClelland, Wethington, Moen, & Ceci, 1996). A full understanding of child development, therefore, depends on an appreciation for children's interactions with these environmental systems and how these interactions vary across time.

Critical Thinking Exercises

1. Why is random assignment essential for experimental research?

2. Imagine that you want to determine the long-term effects of stimulant medication (e.g., Ritalin) on children with Attention-Deficit/Hyperactivity Disorder. How might you conduct (a) a prospective longitudinal study, (b) a retrospective longitudinal study, or (c) a follow-back study to examine these effects? What are the strengths/weaknesses of each of these research designs?

3. As children develop, the relative importance of passive gene-environment effects gradually decreases while the relative importance of active gene-environment effects gradually increases. Why?

4. The American Academy of Pediatrics has urged parents to monitor young children's access to television and limit infants' exposure to electronic media altogether. Their recommendation is based on the understanding that the infant and toddler brain is developing rapidly. What is the evidence that brain development extends *beyond* early childhood? Should parents also monitor and limit their adolescents' media consumption?

5. Considerable research indicates that children whose parents display high levels of responsiveness and demandingness, but low levels of hostility/coercion, tend to have the best developmental outcomes. However, most of the research supporting this conclusion has been conducted with white, middle-class families. Why might it be important to consider ethnicity and socioeconomic status when making claims about optimal parenting behavior? How might culture affect the relationship between parenting and children's outcomes?

CHAPTER 3

Assessing and Diagnosing Children's Problems

Mental health practitioners spend most of their time engaging in three types of professional activities: assessment, diagnosis, and treatment. **Assessment** refers to the process of gathering information about children and families in order to gain an accurate understanding of their psychosocial functioning. **Diagnosis** refers to the task of describing the client's functioning, usually by matching the client's functioning to descriptions of psychiatric conditions recognized by other practitioners. **Treatment** involves the use of psychosocial and/or medicinal therapies to alleviate distress or impairment and promote children's well-being. In this chapter, we will examine how clinicians assess and diagnose child and adolescent problems. In the next chapter, we will focus on psychotherapy for children, adolescents, and families.

Psychological Assessment

Purposes of Assessment

Psychological assessment refers to the process of gathering data about children and families in order to reach valid conclusions about their current functioning and future well-being. The assessment of children and adolescents can have many purposes (Carter, Marakovitz, & Sparrow, 2006; Sattler, 2001). First, assessment can be conducted to screen children for possible behavior problems or developmental delays. For example, a pediatrician might ask a psychologist to screen a toddler who is showing delays in language acquisition and social skills despite normal sensory and motor functioning. The psychologist might conduct a brief evaluation in order to determine whether the child has a significant delay that needs greater attention. Early screening can prevent more severe problems later in development.

Second, assessment can be used to reach a diagnosis. For example, parents might refer their child to a psychologist because the child is showing a wide range of emotional and disruptive behavior problems. The psychologist would likely conduct a detailed evaluation of the child's strengths and weaknesses in order to identify the nature of the child's problems. The clinician would likely assign one or more diagnostic labels to describe the child's main problem areas. Diagnosis might help parents understand their child's functioning, allow the clinician to estimate the child's prognosis, and help the clinician plan treatment.

Third, some assessments are conducted to identify and treat a specific behavior problem. For example, a third-grade teacher might ask a school psychologist to assess a student who repeatedly bullies younger children during recess. In this case, the purpose of the assessment is not to assign a diagnosis. Instead, the purpose of assessment is to identify potential causes of the bullying and to plan an intervention. After careful observation of the bully's behavior, the school psychologist might notice that the boy initiates fights with younger children only in the presence of peers. She might recommend that the bully and his peers be separated during recess in order to avoid the problem in the future.

A fourth purpose of assessment is to monitor progress in treatment. For example, a pediatrician might prescribe methylphenidate (Ritalin) to a boy with ADHD. She might ask the child's teachers to rate the boy's ADHD symptoms for three weeks. During the first week, the boy might not take any medication. During the second week, the boy might take a low dose of the medication. During the third week, the boy might take a slightly higher dose. The pediatrician might use teachers' ratings over the three weeks to determine whether the medication reduced the boy's symptoms and which dose was more effective.

The purpose of psychological assessment is to obtain an informed understanding of the child and family. Psychological assessment involves much more than administering a test or assigning a diagnosis. Instead, assessment involves appreciating the strengths and weaknesses of clients within the context of their surroundings and drawing valid conclusions regarding how to help them improve their lives.

Psychological assessment is also a process. From the scientist-practitioner perspective, each assessment is analogous to a research study with a sample size of one (i.e., $N = 1$, the client). The clinician listens to the family's presenting problem and begins to formulate hypotheses about the child's functioning. For example, if a mother reports that her child is earning low grades at school, possible hypotheses might be (1) the child has ADHD or a learning disorder that interferes with his academic performance; (2) the child has an emotional problem, such as depression, that distracts him from his work; or (3) the child has high intelligence and is bored with traditional classroom instruction.

Then, the clinician systematically tests each of these hypotheses by gathering data from parents, teachers, and the child. Hypotheses that are supported by data are retained; hypotheses not supported by data are revised or discarded. For example, after careful testing, the clinician might find little evidence of ADHD, a learning problem, or above-average intelligence. However, while interviewing the child, the clinician might find evidence of mood problems, perhaps associated with difficulty making friends in school. The clinician might revise her hypothesis, asserting that the child's academic problems are due to symptoms of depression caused by a lack of peer acceptance.

The clinician's hypothesis can be supported or not supported by the effectiveness of treatment. In this example, the clinician decides to teach the child social skills in order to improve his social standing at school. She reasons that as the child's social functioning improves, so, too, will his mood and academic performance. She provides social skills training to the child and parent for 10 weeks. Each week, she elicits feedback from the child's teacher regarding his social functioning in the classroom and his academic performance. The clinician notices a modest increase in the child's social functioning over the course of treatment. More important, this increase in social skills is accompanied by improvement in grades and academic motivation.

The process of psychological assessment, therefore, involves generating and systematically evaluating clinical hypotheses using behavioral data. This process of assessment begins with the first therapy session and continues until the end of treatment.

The Four Pillars of Assessment

Jerome Sattler (2001) has identified four components of psychological assessment that are optimal for obtaining an accurate understanding of children and families. These four "pillars" of psychological assessment are (1) clinical interviews, (2) observations of children and families, (3) norm-referenced tests, and (4) informal data gathering. From Sattler's perspective, the process of psychological assessment is analogous to the process of erecting a building. The conclusions and treatment recommendations that clinicians make regarding child and family functioning are supported by the four primary assessment methods. Removal of any of these pillars can compromise the integrity of clinician's inferences, just as removal of one of the support beams of a building can adversely affect its stability.

The most accurate understanding of children's functioning is based on **multi-method assessment**. Multimethod assessment involves gathering data in a number of different ways in order to obtain a complete picture of children's functioning. Under ideal conditions, multimethod assessment involves all four assessment pillars: interviews, observations, norm-referenced testing, and informal data gathering.

To understand the importance of multimethod assessment, consider the following example. A probation officer refers a 14-year-old boy, Brian, for psychological assessment after the boy is arrested for shoplifting and fleeing from police. The clinician interviews the boy and his mother. Brian's mother tells the clinician that Brian is "a good kid" who has been showing an increase in disruptive behavior problems since his father's recent incarceration. Brian expresses remorse for shoplifting and attributes his misbehavior to "family problems" at home. He also begs the clinician for a "second chance" and states that he is willing to "turn over a new leaf." Based on interview data, the clinician erroneously concludes that Brian's behavior reflects problems adjusting to his father's incarceration. However, if the clinician had relied on other assessment methods, his conclusion likely would have differed. For example, informal data gathering from teachers might have revealed that Brian has a history of aggression, callousness, and deceit. Personality test data might have also shown that Brian has disruptive and antisocial behavior tendencies. Relying on a single method of assessment can yield a distorted picture of children's functioning.

Accurate assessment also relies on **multiple informants**. Data should be gathered from many different people knowledgeable about the child's functioning, especially parents, teachers, other caregivers, and the child.

Previous research has shown low correlations between parents, teachers, and children's ratings of child behavior. Specifically, correlations between informants tend to range from .30 to .40. In general, parents and teachers tend to report more child disruptive behavior problems than do children, whereas children tend to report more anxiety and mood problems than do parents and teachers. Consequently, a clinician who relies only on information provided by one informant will likely obtain an inaccurate picture of children's functioning (Achenbach, McConaughy, & Howell, 1987; Kamphaus & Frick, 2002).

Why do informants disagree so much in their reports of children's functioning? The answer is twofold. First, different informants are privy to different types of information about children's functioning. For example, parents have access to information about children's overt behavior at home, whereas teachers are usually better able to comment on children's academic and behavioral functioning at school. Children, themselves, are often more accurate than parents and teachers in reporting internal psychological symptoms, like anxiety and depression.

Second, children's behavior can vary dramatically across settings. For example, children may appear anxious at school but appear relaxed with family members. Similarly, children may be defiant and disrespectful toward parents but be courteous and compliant toward teachers. Disagreement between informants, therefore, often reflects differences in informants' knowledge of the child and variance in the child's behavior across settings.

The art of psychological assessment involves integrating information using multiple methods from multiple informants to obtain an accurate picture of children's functioning. Often, information is discrepant and clinicians must rely on their experience and knowledge of the child and family to make sense of the data. The science of psychological assessment involves using multimethod, multi-informant data to generate and systematically evaluate hypotheses regarding children's behavior.

Assessment Techniques

Clinical Interviews

Perhaps the most important component of psychological assessment is the clinical interview. The interview usually occurs during the first session, and it can sometimes extend across multiple sessions. The interview usually involves the child and his or her parents, and it can sometimes include extended family members, teachers, and other people knowledgeable about the child's functioning. Some clinicians prefer to interview children and parents together, whereas other clinicians separate adults and children.

The assessment interview has three purposes. One purpose of the interview is to identify the family's presenting problem and to begin to establish rapport. The presenting problem is the primary reason(s) the family is seeking treatment. Presenting problems might include a decrease in the child's academic functioning, an increase in disruptive behavior problems, or a referral from a teacher because of a suspected learning disability. The clinician pays special attention to the degree to which all family members, especially the child, want to participate in treatment. The clinician begins to establish rapport with the child and parents by empathically listening to their concerns, accurately reflecting their thoughts and feelings, and offering an initial plan to address their problems.

Another purpose of the interview is to gather data about the child's psychosocial history and current functioning. Typically, clinicians interview the child, parents, and teachers to gain a wide range of information about the history and current status of the presenting problem; the developmental history of the child; relationships between the child, family, and school; and the child's strengths and weaknesses (see Table 3.1).

During the course of the interview, some clinicians also conduct a **mental status examination** of the child (Groth-Marnat, 2003; Sadock & Sadock, 2003). The mental status examination is a brief assessment of the child's current functioning in three broad areas: (1) overt behavior, (2) emotions, and (3) cognitions (see Table 3.2). With respect to behavior, the clinician examines the child's actions and social behavior during the interview session. She is especially interested in the child's general appearance, posture, degree of eye contact, quality of interactions with parents, and attitude toward the therapist.

With respect to emotions, the clinician assesses the child's mood and affect. **Mood** refers to the child's long-term emotional disposition. Mood is usually assessed by asking the child and his parents about the child's overall emotional functioning. Moods can range from shy and inhibited, to touchy and argumentative, to sanguine and carefree. **Affect** refers to the child's short-term emotional expression. Affect is usually inferred by watching the child's facial expressions, posture, and body movements during the session. Affect can include tearfulness, expressions of anger, and social withdrawal. Some children show a normal range of affective displays whereas others show very little emotional expression. The clinician is especially interested in whether the child's affect is appropriate to the given situation. For example, a child who laughs while talking about a parent's death displays inappropriate affect.

The clinician assesses the child's cognition in several ways. One aspect of cognition is **thought content**, that is, the subject matter of the child's cognition. For example, some children are preoccupied with certain interests or hobbies, whereas other children's thoughts are plagued by persistent worries or fears. In severe instances, children have delusions or bizarre thoughts that do not correspond to reality. Another aspect of cognition is **thought process**, that is, the way in which the

Table 3.1   Psychosocial History for Children and Adolescents

Dimension	Possible Question(s)
Presenting problem	
Onset	When did the problem begin?
Course	Has the problem changed, become better, or become worse?
Duration	How long has the problem lasted?
Antecedents	Any psychosocial stressors before problem onset?
Consequences	Any factors that might reinforce or maintain the problem over time?
Attempts to solve	Is there anything that has alleviated the problem?
Family background	
Parents	Occupations? Educational backgrounds? Marital status?
Siblings	Living in household? Relationship to child?
Socioeconomic status	Family income and financial security? Housing situation?
Family psychiatric history	History of behavioral, emotional, cognitive, or substance use problems in the family?
Culture	Language spoken in home? Religious beliefs? Other relevant cultural or ethnic factors?
Child's developmental history	
Problems with pregnancy/delivery	Premature birth/low birth weight? Maternal substance use during gestation?
Early development	Attachment to parents? Achievement of developmental milestones (e.g., walking, talking)?
Medical history	Physical health of the child? Injuries/illnesses? Chronic conditions? Medications?
Current physical health	Appetite, energy level, sleep quality?
Child's academic history	
Academic achievement	Current grade in school? Academic performance? Adjustment to school?
Academic problems	Failed a grade? Received special education services?
Relationship with teachers	Family involvement in child's education? Behavior at school?
Academic/career goal	Will child graduate from high school or college? Are goals realistic?
Child's social history	
Relationship to parents	Amount of contact with mother, father? Quality of relationships?
Peer status	Friends at school? Rejected by peers?
Social skills	Ability to listen, take turns, develop friendships?

Dimension	Possible Question(s)
Child's behavioral history	
Interests, hobbies, activities	Sports, clubs, after-school activities?
Substance use	Cigarette, alcohol, and other drug use? Problems associated with use?
Sexual behavior	Sexually active? Problems with sexual identity?
Child's psychiatric history	
Previous problems	Previous psychiatric disorders?
History of treatment	Ever participated in therapy? Ever been psychiatrically hospitalized?
Medications	Ever prescribed medication for psychiatric diagnosis?

Table 3.2   Brief Mental Status Examination for Children and Adolescents

1. Overt behavior
   - General appearance
   - Posture, eye contact, body movements, activity level
   - Behavior toward clinician and caregivers

2. Emotions
   - Mood
   - Affect
   - Appropriateness

3. Cognitions
   - Thought content
   - Thought process
   - Intelligence
   - Attention
   - Memory
   - Orientation to person, place, and time
   - Insight
   - Judgment

child forms associations and solves problems. Thought process is usually inferred from the child's speech. For example, the clinician observes whether the child's speech is coherent, whether it is rapid and difficult to follow, or whether the child abruptly stops speaking in mid-conversation.

Other aspects of cognition include the child's overall intelligence, attention and memory, and orientation. **Orientation** refers to the child's awareness of himself, his surroundings, and current events. For example, a child involved in a car accident might become disoriented; lack of orientation to person, place, and time usually indicates serious impairment.

Finally, clinicians assess the child's insight and judgment. **Insight** refers to the degree to which the child recognizes that he might have a social, emotional, or behavioral disorder. Youths with eating disorders and conduct problems often show poor insight; they often deny having any problems whatsoever. **Judgment** refers to the child's understanding of the seriousness of his behavior problem and its impact on himself and others. Judgment also refers to the child's ability to consider the consequences of his behavior before acting. Disorders such as ADHD are usually characterized by poor judgment.

A third purpose of the interview is to arrive at a psychiatric diagnosis. Many clinicians review diagnostic criteria informally during the course of the interview. Other clinicians conduct structured diagnostic interviews to review criteria with children and parents. In a **structured diagnostic interview**, the clinician systematically reviews all of the major psychiatric diagnoses with children and/or parents to determine whether the child meets criteria for any diagnosis. For example, the Diagnostic Interview Schedule for Children (DISC; Shaffer et al., 2000) can be administered to children and parents to review the diagnostic criteria for anxiety, mood, behavior, substance use, and thought problems in children and adolescents. The interview takes about 1.5 to 2 hours to complete, but it provides a comprehensive assessment of the child's functioning.

Behavioral Observations

Methods of Observation

Behavioral observations are essential to child assessment. Although parental reports of child behavior are important, there is no substitute for the rich amount of information that can be gathered from watching children. Clinicians observe children in three ways (Groth-Marnat, 2003). First, most clinicians observe children as they participate in the **clinical interview**. Using this procedure, clinicians note children's activity level, speech and language, emotions, quality of interactions with parents, and a wide range of other overt actions. The shortcoming of informal clinic observation is that children's behavior in the clinic may not be representative of children's behavior at home and school.

Second, many clinicians observe children performing **analogue tasks** in the clinic. Analogue tasks are designed to mimic activities or situations in which children engage in daily life. For example, a clinician might want to observe the interactions between a mother and her preschool-age child. The clinician might ask the dyad to play in the clinic playroom for 20 minutes. At the end of the play session, the clinician might ask the mother to tell the child to stop playing and clean up the room. This analogue task allows the clinician to observe firsthand how the mother issues commands to her child, how the child responds to her commands, and how the mother responds to acts of defiance by her child. Information gathered from analogue observation can help the clinician understand how the pattern of interactions between parent and child might contribute to the child's behavior problems. Furthermore, observational data might be used to plan treatment.

A third approach involves **naturalistic observation**. Naturalistic observations are most frequently used by mental health professionals who work in schools. During math class, a school psychologist might monitor the activity level of a child suspected of having ADHD. The frequency of ADHD symptoms shown by the target child might be compared to the frequency of ADHD symptoms shown by another child in the class. The primary strength of naturalistic observation is that it permits clinicians to examine children's behavior in natural settings. The chief weakness of naturalistic observation is that it is time consuming. A second shortcoming of naturalistic observation is **reactivity**; that is, children might react to the fact that they are being observed and act in *un*natural ways.

Functional Analysis of Behavior

During their observations, clinicians often perform a functional analysis of children's behavior. **Functional analysis** is based on the notion that children's behavior is purposeful; that is, their behavior serves a function (Sattler, 2002). In most cases, behavior serves to maximize rewards and minimize punishment. By carefully observing events that occur immediately before and immediately after a behavior, clinicians can determine the behavior's purpose. The clinician can use information about the behavior's purpose to plan treatment (Kamphaus & Frick, 2002; Ramsay, Reynolds, & Kamphaus, 2002).

To perform a functional analysis of behavior, the clinician first defines the child's behavior problem in clear, observable terms. For example, a mother might complain that her preschool-age child is "defiant." However, terms like "defiant" are vague and not easily observed. Consequently, the clinician might operationally define the term "defiant" as the child's failure to comply with his mother's commands within 10 seconds. By defining the child's behavior in clear, observable terms, the clinician can more easily observe the child's problem behavior and identify its purpose.

Next, the clinician gathers data regarding the antecedents and consequences of the target behavior. **Antecedents** refer to environmental conditions that immediately precede the target behavior, whereas **consequences** refer to conditions that immediately follow the behavior. Clinicians conceptualize the behavior in the following terms: A (antecedent) → B (behavior) → C (consequence).

For example, the clinician might observe the parent-child dyad during an analogue play session. She might notice that the child refuses to obey his mother's commands when her commands are vague. Specifically, the child obeys his mother when she tells him to perform a single, clear action (e.g., "Pick up *that* toy"), but he often fails to comply when his mother issues a vague or complex command (e.g., "Clean up"). The clinician discovers that vague or complex commands often precede the child's noncompliance. Furthermore, the clinician might notice that the mother often backs down from her commands when her child ignores her or when he refuses to obey. Therefore, the consequence of the child's noncompliance is that the mother stops issuing her request and allows the child to continue playing.

The clinician can use information about the antecedents and consequences of the child's behavior to plan treatment. Because vague and complex commands often precede the child's noncompliance, the clinician might decide to help the mother issue clearer, more concrete commands to her child—commands that the child is more likely to obey. Similarly, because the child's noncompliance is often reinforced by the mother's backing down from her commands, the clinician might teach the mother to be more consistent and insist that her child obey her commands.

Norm-Referenced Testing

Standardization

Norm-referenced testing involves the administration of a standardized measure of children's behavior that allows comparisons of that child to other individuals her age. Examples of norm-referenced tests include intelligence tests, personality tests, and behavior rating scales.

All norm-referenced tests are administered, scored, and interpreted in a **standardized format**; that is, each administration of the test involves the same item content, the same administration procedure, and the same method of scoring and interpretation. For example, all seven-year-old children who take the Wechsler Intelligence Scale for Children–Fourth Edition (WISC-IV; Wechsler, 2003) are administered the same test items. Items are presented in the same way to all children according to specific rules described in the test manual. These rules include where participants must sit, how instructions must be presented, how much time is allowed, and what sort of help (if any) examiners can provide. Children's answers are scored in the same way, using specific guidelines presented in the manual.

Standardized test administration and scoring allow clinicians to compare children's test scores. Two children who obtain the same number of test items correct on an intelligence test are believed to have comparable levels of overall intellectual functioning *only* if they were administered the test in a standardized fashion. If one child was given extra time, additional help, or greater encouragement by the test administrator, comparisons would be inappropriate.

Children's scores on norm-referenced tests are always compared to the performance of other children, in order to make these scores more meaningful. For example, imagine that a nine-year-old girl correctly answers 45 questions on the WISC-IV. A clinician would record her "raw score" as 45. However, a raw score of 45 does not allow the clinician to determine whether the girl's performance indicates that she is intellectually gifted, average, or cognitively delayed. To interpret her raw score, the clinician needs to compare her score to a large representative sample of children who have already taken the WISC-IV; that is, he must compare the girl's score to the performance of a **norm group**.[2] If the mean raw score for nine-year-olds in the norm group was 45, and the girl's raw score was 45, the clinician might conclude that the girl's intellectual functioning is within the average range. However, if the mean raw score for nine-year-old children was 30, and the girl's raw score was 45, the clinician might conclude that the girl has above-average intellectual functioning.

The results of norm-referenced testing, therefore, depend greatly on comparison of the individual child with the norm group. At a minimum, comparisons are made based

---

[2]Because people in the norm group were administered the test using standardized procedures, the group is sometimes called the "standardization sample."

on children's age. For example, on measures of intelligence, nine-year-old children must be compared to other nine-year-old children, not to six-year-old children or 12-year-old children. On other psychological tests, especially tests of behavior and personality, comparisons are made based on age and gender. For example, boys tend to show more symptoms of hyperactivity than do girls. Consequently, when a clinician obtains parents' ratings of hyperactivity for a nine-year-old boy, he compares these ratings to the ratings for other nine-year-old boys in the norm group.

Standard Scores

Usually, clinicians want to quantify the degree to which children score above or below the mean for the norm group. To quantify children's deviation from the mean, clinicians transform the child's raw test score to a **standard score**. A standard score is simply a raw score that has been changed to a different scale with a designated mean and standard deviation. Examples of standard scores include IQ scores ($M = 100$, $SD = 15$), SAT scores ($M = 1000$, $SD = 200$), T scores ($M = 50$, $SD = 10$), and z scores ($M = 0$, $SD = 1$).

Standard scores are more meaningful than raw scores (see Figure 3.1). For example, knowing that Anne answered 61 questions correctly on an IQ test and 120 questions on the SAT tells us very little. However, knowing that she earned an IQ score of 130 and an SAT score of 1400 suggests that she is very intelligent.

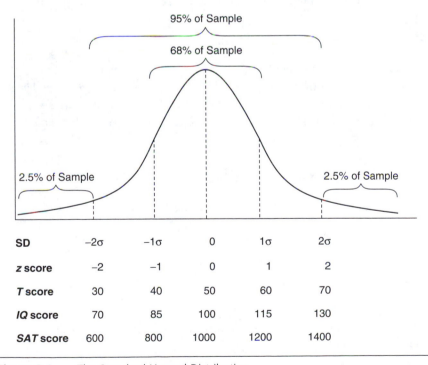

SD	-2σ	-1σ	0	1σ	2σ
z score	−2	−1	0	1	2
T score	30	40	50	60	70
IQ score	70	85	100	115	130
SAT score	600	800	1000	1200	1400

Figure 3.1   The Standard Normal Distribution

Note: Approximately 68% of people earn scores within one standard deviation from the mean. Approximately 95% of people earn scores within two standard deviations from the mean. Raw scores can be transformed into standard scores to make them easier to understand.

How do psychologists convert raw scores to standard scores? The answer requires a little bit of basic statistics. Calculation of raw scores to standard scores is based on the assumption that children's scores fall along a bell-shaped distribution called the **normal distribution**. Most people score very close to the mean of this distribution, while progressively fewer people earn scores at the extremes. Assuming a normal distribution, raw scores can be converted to standardized z scores using the following formula:

$$z = (\text{Person's raw score} - \text{Mean raw score for norm group}) / SD$$

For example, if nine-year-old Mary earns a raw score of 45 and the mean raw score for nine-year-old children in the norm group is 45 with a standard deviation of 5, then Mary's z score is:

$$z = (\text{Person's raw score} - \text{Mean raw score for norm group}) / SD$$
$$z = (45 - 45) / 5$$
$$z = 0$$

However, if nine-year-old Julia earns a raw score of 50 and the mean raw score for nine-year-old children in the norm group is 45 with a standard deviation of 5, then Julia's z score is:

$$z = (\text{Person's raw score} - \text{Mean raw score for norm group}) / SD$$
$$z = (50 - 45) / 5$$
$$z = 1$$

The z score tells us the number of standard deviations the person's score is above or below the mean of the norm group. Mary's z score is 0; her score is equivalent to the mean. Julia's z score is 1; her score is 1 standard deviation above the mean.

A z score can be transformed into any other standard score, such as an IQ score or a T score:

$$\text{New standard score} = M_{\text{new distribution}} + z(SD_{\text{new distribution}})$$

If we want to convert Mary's score into an IQ score with $M = 100$ and $SD = 15$, then

$$\text{New standard score} = M_{\text{new distribution}} + z(SD_{\text{new distribution}})$$
$$= 100 + 0(15)$$
$$= 100$$

If we want to convert Julia's score into an IQ score with $M = 100$ and $SD = 15$, then

$$\text{New standard score} = M_{\text{new distribution}} + z(SD_{\text{new distribution}})$$
$$= 100 + 1(15)$$
$$= 115$$

We can also convert Julia's score into any other standard score as long as we know the mean and standard deviation of the scale. For example, if we want to transform her score to a T score with $M = 50$ and $SD = 10$,

$$\text{New standard score} = M_{\text{new distribution}} + z(SD_{\text{new distribution}})$$
$$= 50 + 1(10)$$
$$= 60$$

Julia, therefore, earned a raw score of 45, a z score of 1, an IQ score of 115, and a T score of 60. Transforming raw scores to standard scores to other standard scores is analogous to translating one language into another. A z score of 1, an IQ score of 115, and a T score of 60 all represent the same level of performance, just as the words *house*, *casa*, and *maison* refer to the same object.

It is important to know that there are different types of standard scores. Nearly all IQ tests yield results in standardized IQ scores; however, most personality tests yield results using standardized T scores.

Intelligence Tests

Psychologists do not agree on a definition for intelligence. Over the past 100 years, considerable effort has gone into defining intelligence and developing tests to measure it. Nearly all theorists recognize that intelligence reflects some aspects of the person's mental functioning that has its origins in genetics and biology but is shaped by experience and education. Albert Binet and Theodore Simon (1916), the developers of the first intelligence test, defined intelligence as the ability "to judge well, to comprehend well, and to reason well" (pp. 42–43). Years later, another important figure in the history of intelligence testing, David Wechsler (1958), described intelligence as "the aggregate or global capacity of the individual to act purposefully, to think rationally, and to deal effectively with his environment" (p. 7). Even more recently, John Carroll (1997) claimed that intelligence is "the degree to which, and the rate at which, people are able to learn and retain in long-term memory the knowledge and skills that can be learned from the environment, that is, what is taught in the home and in school, as well as things learned from everyday experience" (p. 44).

Intelligence is a broad construct that is related to people's abilities to adapt to their environments, to solve problems, and to use information accurately and efficiently. According to a survey of experts, the most important components of intelligence include the capacity for reasoning and abstract thinking, problem solving, knowledge acquisition, memory, adaptation to one's surroundings, speed of processing information, adroitness with language and mathematics, general knowledge, and creativity (Snyderman & Rothman, 1987).

The WISC-IV (Wechsler, 2003) is the most frequently used measure of intellectual functioning for children and adolescents. Wechsler began developing tests in the 1930s in an attempt to measure facets of adults' intelligence and problem-solving abilities. His first intelligence test, the Wechsler-Bellevue Intelligence Scale, was designed for adults. Later, he created a simplified version of his adult scale to measure children's intellectual functioning (see Table 3.3). The first version of the WISC was created in 1949; subsequent revisions were published in 1974, 1991, and 2003.

Table 3.3   Items similar to those on the WISC-IV

Composite/Subtests	Examples

Verbal Comprehension:

Similarities	In what way are a shoe and a sock alike? In what way are a car and a train alike?
Vocabulary	What is a horse? What does *jumping* mean?
Comprehension	What should you do if you get lost in a store? Why should you look both ways before crossing the street?

Perceptual Reasoning:

Picture Concepts	Select one picture from each row so that the pictures have a characteristic in common:

Matrix Reasoning	Select one of the five choices below to complete the matrix:

1	2	3	4	5

Block Design	Reproduce a design using colored blocks:

Composite/Subtests	Examples

Working Memory:

Digit Span

Repeat a string of 2 to 9 numbers from memory.
Then, repeat a string of 2 to 8 numbers *backwards* from memory.

Letter-Number
Sequencing

Listen to a string of 2 to 8 letters and numbers. Then, repeat the string from memory with numbers first (in ascending order), then letters (in alphabetical order). For example, *w 7 b 2* would be repeated *2 7 b w*.

Processing Speed:

Coding

Copy as many symbols as possible from a key in two minutes

Key:

1	2	3	4	5	6
=	V	/	O	X	L

Problems:

3	6	1	2	6	4

Decide as fast as possible whether one of two symbols on the left appears in the group of symbols on the right.

Symbol Search

The WISC-IV provides five standard scores that psychologists use to form the basis of their evaluations regarding children's intelligence. First, the psychologist examines the child's Full Scale IQ. Full Scale IQ is a broad measure of the child's intellectual ability; it reflects children's performance across all of the components of the test. In most cases, the Full Scale IQ is used to estimate general intellectual functioning.

The WISC-IV also provides four composite scores, each reflecting a slightly different aspect of children's intelligence (Sattler & Dumont, 2004):

- *Verbal Comprehension* reflects knowledge gained through formal and informal educational experiences and reflects the application of verbal skills to new situations. Everyday tasks that require verbal comprehension include providing factual information, defining words, and understanding verbal analogies.
- *Perceptual Reasoning* reflects the ability to organize and interpret visually presented material and to engage in visual-spatial problem solving. Everyday tasks that require perceptual reasoning include solving puzzles and mazes, manipulating geometric shapes, and recognizing and understanding patterns.
- *Working Memory* reflects the ability to attend to information, retain and manipulate information in memory, and apply information when necessary. Everyday tasks that require working memory include remembering someone's telephone number and solving arithmetic problems in one's head.
- *Processing Speed* reflects the capacity to visually scan and process nonverbal information quickly and accurately. Tasks that require processing speed include scanning a supermarket aisle for a specific product or activities that require matching and sorting.

The psychologist examines the child's score on each composite and notes areas of relative strength and weakness. For example, Josh might show a Full Scale IQ within the average range, but his verbal comprehension score might be much lower than his perceptual reasoning score. The psychologist might predict that Josh will have difficulty with traditional verbal instruction in school. He might recommend that teachers use visual demonstrations and hands-on practice to help Josh learn.

Intelligence test scores are believed to be normally distributed, with a mean of 100 and a standard deviation of 15. The distribution of test scores in the general population is bell-shaped, with most people earning scores relatively close to 100 and fewer people earning scores at the extremes. Approximately 68% of all people earn IQ scores within one standard deviation about the mean (e.g., IQ = 85–115), which is generally considered the normal range. Furthermore, approximately 95% of people earn IQ scores within two standard deviations about the mean (e.g., IQ = 70–130). The remaining 5% of individuals earn IQ scores at the extremes. Approximately 2.5% have IQ scores less than 70, and they may qualify for the diagnosis of Mental Retardation. Approximately 2.5% earn IQ scores greater than 130, indicative of superior intellectual functioning (Cohen & Swerdlik, 2005).

Academic Achievement

Academic achievement refers to the knowledge and skills that children learn through academic instruction. Some clinicians distinguish between tests of intelligence, which measure a person's intellectual ability or capacity to learn, and tests of achievement, which measure information that the person has already learned and retained.

Tests of academic achievement generally measure three areas of academic functioning: reading, mathematics, and writing. These three areas reflect the main types of learning disorders recognized by mental health professionals: Reading Disorder (sometimes called dyslexia), Mathematics Disorder, and Disorder of Written

Table 3.4   Dimensions of the Woodcock-Johnson III Tests of Achievement

Domain/Specific Area	Examples
Reading	
Basic reading	Recognizing letters, reading words, reading fluency, sounding out novel words
Reading comprehension	Understanding the meaning of sentences and paragraphs
Mathematics	
Math calculation skills	Math skills ranging from arithmetic to geometry, math fluency
Math reasoning	Formulating and solving story problems
Written language	
Basic writing skills	Spelling, editing, grammar, and punctuation
Written expression	Writing sentences and paragraphs, writing fluency
Oral language	
Listening comprehension	Understanding directions, answering questions about stories
Oral expression	Recalling verbal stories, telling the names of objects

Note: "Fluency" refers to the ability to perform academic tasks quickly and accurately. In a test of academic fluency, the child is asked to correctly solve as many problems as possible in a given period of time (e.g., three minutes).

Expression. Some tests assess a fourth dimension of academic functioning, Oral Language, which reflects the child's listening and speaking skills.

The Woodcock-Johnson III Tests of Achievement (WJ-III; Woodcock, McGrew, & Mather, 2001) is an example of a comprehensive test of academic achievement. The WJ-III assesses academic achievement in four broad areas: reading, mathematics, written language, and oral language (see Table 3.4). The test also allows clinicians to assess children's academic skills and knowledge in specific areas, such as young children's pre-academic skills and older children's ability to sound out new words.

The WJ-III yields standardized scores on each of the four achievement domains with a mean of 100 and standard deviation of 15. Scores more than one standard deviation below the mean (i.e., < 85) can indicate delays in a particular area of achievement, while scores more than two standard deviations below the mean (i.e., < 70) might indicate a specific learning disability. Usually, clinicians examine children's IQ and achievement test scores together in order to obtain a more complete picture of children's cognitive strengths and weaknesses.

Adaptive Functioning

Adaptive functioning refers to "how effectively individuals cope with common life demands and how well they meet the standards of personal independence expected of someone in their particular age group, sociocultural background, and community setting" (*DSM-IV-TR*, p. 42). Stated another way, adaptive functioning refers to the child's ability to perform day-to-day activities in an age-appropriate manner and to meet the demands of parents, teachers, and other people with whom they interact. Adaptive functioning is often assessed in children suspected of Mental Retardation and other developmental delays, to determine their ability to meet the demands of daily life.

To measure adaptive functioning, most psychologists administer a rating scale to caregivers and teachers (see Table 3.5). Like tests of intelligence and academic achievement, adaptive behavior rating scales are norm-referenced measures. That is, the ratings of the parent or teacher can be compared to the ratings of parents or teachers in the norm group. The psychologist can convert the parent or teacher ratings into a standard score, just like an IQ score, that tells the child's standing relative to his or her peers.

Table 3.5   Adaptive Functioning in Young Children

Dimension	Example
Conceptual skills	
Communication	Follows simple commands, such as "Come here." Uses complete sentences. Begins and ends conversations appropriately.
Functional academics	Knows colors. Counts from 1 to 20. Writes first and last name.
Self-direction	Follows simple rules, such as "No yelling indoors." Controls temper when parent takes a toy away. Asks permission before playing with another child's toy.
Social skills	
Leisure	Asks to be read a favorite book. Waits turn during games and activities. Plays board games.
Social	Shares toys with others. Offers to help others. Greets others appropriately with "Hi" and a smile.
Practical skills	
Community use	Recognizes various public places, like the library and fire station. Looks both ways before crossing street. Finds restrooms in public places.
Home living	Gets own snacks from pantry. Places dirty clothes in laundry basket. Wipes dirty feet before entering house.
Health and safety	Avoids hot stove. Buckles seatbelt or car seat. Carries scissors appropriately.
Self-care	Washes hands with soap. Uses bathroom without help. Cuts meals into bite-size pieces.

Personality and Social-Emotional Functioning

Tests of children's personality and social-emotional functioning fall into three categories: (1) self-report personality tests, (2) projective personality tests, and (3) specific measures of social and emotional problems.

Self-Report Measures of Personality. The most frequently used self-report measure of adolescent personality is the **Minnesota Multiphasic Personality Inventory-Adolescent** (MMPI-A; Butcher et al., 1992). Despite its name, the MMPI-A is better viewed as a test of adolescent psychopathology and social-emotional functioning than adolescent personality per se. The MMPI-A consists of a series of true/false items that assess 10 domains of functioning. The names of these 10 clinical domains are somewhat archaic because they are based on the original version of the MMPI, developed in 1943 (see Table 3.6).

Adolescents' responses to test items on each clinical scale are compared to adolescents of the same gender in the norm group. Raw scores are converted to T scores with a mean of 50 and standard deviation of 10. T scores > 65 can indicate clinically significant problems on that dimension of social-emotional functioning. Clinicians usually plot the adolescent's T scores on a personality profile to graphically represent the most salient aspects of the adolescent's functioning (see Figure 3.2).

Projective Measures of Personality. The most well-known projective instrument is the **Rorschach**, a test that consists of 10 bilaterally symmetrical inkblots. The

Table 3.6   Clinical Scales of the MMPI-A

- **Hypochondriasis (Hs)** reflects excessive concern over physical illness and pain, a tendency to express psychological distress in terms of somatic complaints, and general preoccupation with oneself.
- **Depression (D)** reflects subjective feelings of psychological distress, brooding, apathy, physical slowness, and a general disinterest in other people or activities.
- **Hysteria (Hy)** reflects a tendency to deny psychological distress, to manipulate others, and to seek attention and sympathy from others.
- **Psychopathic Deviate (Pd)** reflects general problems in social functioning, alienation from parents and prosocial peers, resentment of authority, and a tendency toward delinquent behavior.
- **Masculinity-Femininity (Mf)** reflects the degree to which the adolescent endorses traditional masculine or feminine roles or interests.
- **Paranoia (Pa)** reflects suspiciousness, sensitivity to criticism, self-righteousness, and feelings of persecution.
- **Psychasthenia (Pt)** reflects anxiety, obsessive thoughts, compulsive behaviors, unreasonable fears, and excessive doubts.
- **Schizophrenia (Sc)** reflects thought problems, a tendency to withdraw into fantasy, eccentric behavior, and feelings of alienation from self or others.
- **Hypomania (Ma)** reflects feelings of euphoria, increased irritability, inflated mood, and general agitation.
- **Social Introversion (Si)** reflects shyness, lack of social skills, and a tendency to withdraw from social interactions.

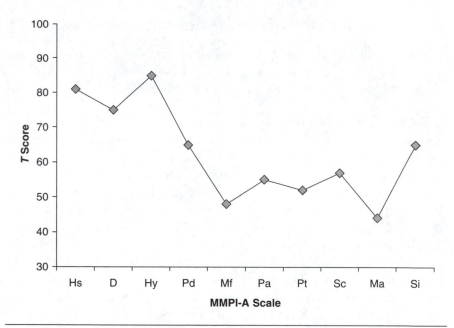

Figure 3.2   MMPI-A

Note: The MMPI-A yields *T* scores on 10 clinical scales, reflecting the adolescent's social-emotional functioning. Scores > 65 can indicate significant distress or impairment. This girl's scores suggest significant problems with depression, physical complaints, and acting out.

Rorschach is based on the projective hypothesis, the notion that people who take the test "project" or impose structure and organization on the inkblots in order to perceive them in meaningful ways (Beck, 1937). Individuals with social, emotional, or cognitive disturbance will show difficulty in the perceptual-cognitive process required to make sense of the inkblots. Consequently, uncharacteristic ways of responding to the inkblots can reflect distress or impairment.

John Exner (2003) developed a standardized method for administering, scoring, and interpreting the Rorschach inkblot test known as the **Comprehensive System**. Clinicians who use Exner's method administer the test in two parts. During the response phase, the clinician administers each inkblot, asking the client, "What might this be?" The clinician records responses verbatim for later coding. During the inquiry phase, the clinician reviews the client's responses in order to determine which aspects of the inkblots the client used to generate his or her response.

It is commonly assumed that clinicians are interested in what clients see in the inkblots. In Exner's method, however, scoring is based largely on *how* clients perceive the blots rather than *what* they see. For example, clinicians record whether clients use the shape, shading, color, or position of the blot to perceive the image. The clinician calculates the frequency with which clients use each feature of the inkblots in the perceptual process and compares this frequency with other individuals of the same age and gender in the norm group. Deviations can indicate problems in social, emotional, or cognitive functioning.

Specific Tests of Social-Emotional Problems. Clinicians can also administer a wide range of specific measures to youths suspected of particular disorders. For example, the Children's Depression Inventory and Reynolds Adolescent Depression Scale are self-report rating scales designed for children and adolescents, respectively, to assess depression and other mood problems. The Revised Children's Manifest Anxiety Scale is another child self-report measure designed to assess physiological arousal, worry, and social anxiety. The Social Skills Rating System can be completed by parents or teachers to measure children's social skills. Many more measures of specific areas of children's functioning exist—too many to account here. Selection is based largely on the clinician's hypotheses regarding the nature of children's problems.

Behavioral Functioning

Many clinicians ask parents and teachers to rate children's functioning using behavioral checklists or rating scales. Examples of behavioral rating scales include the Child Behavior Checklist, the Conners Rating Scales-Revised, and the Behavior Assessment System for Children-Second Edition (BASC-2; Reynolds & Kamphaus, 2004). For example, the BASC-2 Parent Rating Scale (PRS) can be completed by parents, whereas the BASC-2 Teacher Rating Scale (TRS) can be completed by teachers or other school personnel (see Figure 3.3). The TRS assesses four broad domains of children's behavior:

- *Externalizing problems* reflect children's disruptive behavior. Externalizing symptoms include hyperactivity, aggression, and conduct problems.
- *Internalizing problems* reflect disturbance in children's emotional functioning. Internalizing symptoms include anxiety, depression, and physical complaints such as headache or upset stomach.
- *School problems* reflect academic difficulties, including low motivation, inattention, and learning problems.
- *Adaptive skills* reflect behavioral and social-emotional competence, appropriate social and daily living skills, and children's prosocial behavior.

Ratings of children's behavior are compared to the ratings of other parents and teachers, respectively, in the norm group. Raw scores are converted to *T* scores, just like on the MMPI-A.

Behavior rating scales are a quick and relatively easy way for clinicians to obtain a wide range of data on children's functioning. Furthermore, norm-referenced comparisons allow the clinician to determine whether children's behavior significantly deviates from normality. Behavior rating scales, like the BASC-2, are frequently used in the assessment of disruptive behavior disorders like ADHD.

Evaluating Psychological Tests

Although there are many kinds of psychological tests, not all tests are created equal. Before administering a test, clinicians must examine the test's reliability and

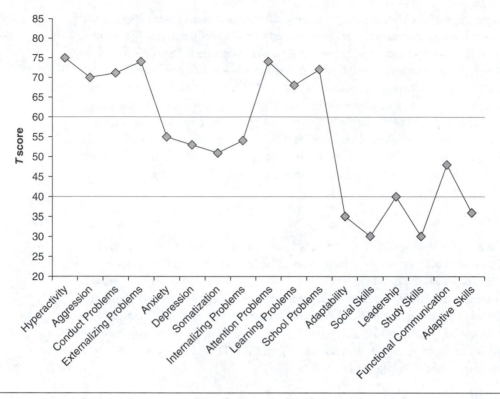

Figure 3.3   BASC-2

Note: The BASC-2 yields *T* scores on many dimensions of children's behavioral, social, and emotional functioning. A 10-year-old boy's teacher completed this BASC-2. The boy has significantly more externalizing symptoms and school-related problems than his peers. Also, the boy's adaptive skills are significantly lower than those of other boys his age.

validity. Reliability refers to the consistency of scores generated by the test; validity refers to the degree to which the test measures aspects of children's functioning that it was designed to measure. Tests must be reliable and valid in order for the clinician to appropriately use test data to understand clients and plan treatment.

Reliability

Reliability refers to the consistency of a psychological test (Anastasi & Urbina, 1997). Reliable tests yield consistent scores over time and across administrations. Although there are many types of test reliability, the two most common forms are test-retest reliability and internal consistency.

Test-retest reliability refers to the consistency of test scores over time. Imagine that you go to a shoe store and measure your feet. The foot-measuring device at the store indicates that you wear a size 10. Further imagine that you return to the shoe store one week later, and the same device now indicates that you wear a size 8. You would conclude that the foot-measuring instrument has poor test-retest reliability because it yields inconsistent scores across repeated administrations. Similarly, a psychological test should yield consistent results across repeated test administrations. For example, a child who earns a Full Scale IQ of 110 should earn a similar IQ score if she takes the test six months later.

Internal consistency refers to the degree to which test items yield consistent scores. Imagine that the shoe store clerk measured your right foot and the scale indicated that you wear a size 10. Then, imagine that the clerk measured your left foot and the scale indicated that you wear a size 5. You might conclude that the measuring device has poor internal consistency because it yields inconsistent results when administered to your right and left feet. Similarly, psychological tests must display internal consistency. For example, imagine that we construct a depression test in which children must rate 10 descriptors of mood on a scale of 1 (low) to 5 (high). These mood descriptors include symptoms of depression, such as feeling "blue," "sad," and "down." We would expect children with depression to rate all of these items highly and children without depression to rate all items low. The consistency with which children rate items reflects the internal consistency of the test.

Test-retest reliability and internal consistency are quantified by the reliability coefficient. Reliability coefficients are analogous to correlation coefficients, but they range from 0 to 1.0. A reliability coefficient of 1.0 indicates perfect consistency. Most tests that measure stable psychological traits have test-retest reliabilities of .80 or higher. Tests that measure more transient psychological states, such as short-term moods, tend to have lower test-retest reliability coefficients.

Validity

Validity refers to the degree to which a test measures what it was designed to measure. More specifically, the validity of a psychological test refers to the degree to which its users can have confidence in the inferences made from the test's results (Anastasi & Urbina, 1997; Sattler, 2001). Tests of intelligence should measure intelligence, tests of math achievement should measure math achievement, and so forth.

Reliability is a necessary, but not sufficient, condition for validity. Imagine that you measure your feet and the scale consistently indicates you wear a size 10. You try on a size 10 shoe and it fits perfectly. You conclude that the scale is a valid measure of shoe size. Now imagine that you measure your feet and the scale consistently indicates that you wear a size 10. However, when you try on a pair of size 10 shoes, you discover they fit poorly. Your discovery demonstrates that even though a test yields consistent results, the test may not measure what it is supposed to measure.

Technically speaking, validity is not a property of a test. Rather, validity refers to the ability to use test results for a specific purpose. Imagine that you measure your feet and the scale indicates that you wear a size 10. You subsequently try on a size 10 hat and discover it is much too large. The foot-measuring device is a valid test for shoe size; however, the device is not a valid indicator of hat size. Similarly, results of an IQ test can allow us to infer something about a child's intelligence; these results cannot be used to understand the child's personality.

The validity of psychological tests can be examined in at least three ways. First, psychologists examine the **content validity** of the test. Specifically, the content of test items should be relevant to the test's purpose. For example, a test designed to measure depression should have test items that ask people about various depressive symptoms. Symptoms of other mental disorders, such as anger and anxiety, might not be appropriate for the test. Psychologists often evaluate content validity by asking experts to rate the relevance of test items to the attribute they want to measure.

Psychologists also examine the **construct validity** of the test. Construct validity refers to the degree to which test scores reflect hypothesized behavioral attributes, or constructs. Most psychological variables are constructs: intelligence, depression, anxiety, aggression. Constructs cannot be measured directly; instead, they must be inferred from overt actions or people's self-reports. For example, intelligence might be inferred from superior reading ability, depression might be inferred from frequent crying, and aggression might be inferred from a history of physical fighting.

To investigate the construct validity of a test, psychologists examine the relationship of test scores to other measures of similar and dissimilar constructs. Evidence of *convergent validity* comes from significant relationships between test scores and theoretically similar constructs. Evidence of *discriminant validity* comes from non-significant relationships between test scores and theoretically dissimilar constructs. For example, children's scores on a depression test should correlate significantly with other measures of depression; however, their scores should not correlate significantly with measures of intelligence, anxiety, or aggression.

Finally, psychologists examine the test's **criterion-related validity**. Criterion-related validity refers to the degree to which test scores can be used to infer a probable standing on some external variable of interest (i.e., a criterion; Anastasi & Urbina, 1997). One measure of criterion-related validity is called *concurrent validity*, the degree to which test scores are related to theoretically similar constructs at the same point in time. For example, children's IQ scores should be associated with other external measures of intelligence, such as their grade-point average or the number of honors classes they have taken in high school. Similarly, children's scores on a test of aggression should relate to other indicators of aggression, such as the number of times the child has been disciplined for fighting at school.

Another aspect of criterion-related validity is called *predictive validity*. Predictive validity refers to the ability of test scores to predict theoretically expected outcomes. For example, IQ scores might be expected to predict children's likelihood of attending college or their college grade-point average. Similarly, scores on a childhood aggression test might be expected to predict the likelihood of arrest during adolescence or adulthood.

Clinical Decision Making

Once clinicians have gathered assessment information, how do they make decisions regarding case conceptualization, diagnosis, and treatment? Most clinicians follow one of two broad decision-making processes: clinical judgment or actuarial decision making.

Most clinicians rely on **clinical judgment**. Clinical judgment refers to the practice of combining information from interviews, behavioral observations, norm-referenced testing, and other sources in ways consistent with the clinician's training and experience. By definition, clinical decision making is unique to the individual practitioner. Some clinicians place great importance on information gathered during the interview, others emphasize observational data, while still others rely heavily on norm-referenced test data. The relative importance clinicians give to various sources of data is usually determined by the type of training they received; their implicit understanding of child development, personality, and psychopathology; and their areas of expertise.

In contrast, some clinicians practice **actuarial decision making**. These clinicians combine interview, observational, and norm-referenced test data using statistical formulas. These actuarial formulas are largely based on the results of empirical studies and the prevalence rates of disorders in the general population. After combining actuarial data, clinicians base diagnostic decisions and treatment recommendations on whether their clients exceed some empirically derived cutoff score. The actuarial process tends to place little emphasis on the clinician's impressions of his or her clients; rather, considerable weight is given to clients' developmental histories and standardized test data.

On average, actuarial decision making is about 10% more accurate than clinical judgment in explaining and predicting people's psychosocial functioning (Grove, Zald, Lebow, Snitz, & Nelson, 2000). Actuarial decision making tends to be greatly superior to clinical judgment when clinicians rely heavily on interview data to make decisions and to plan treatment. In contrast, actuarial decision making and clinical judgment demonstrate approximately equal accuracy when clinicians rely heavily on norm-referenced test data to draw their conclusions (Garb, 1989).

Why do practitioners make errors when they rely on clinical judgment? Nezu and Nezu (1993) identified four logical mistakes that clinicians often make in their clinical decision making that lead them astray. First, clinicians often rely heavily on the **availability heuristic** when making decisions. That is, they believe that the probability of an event occurring is directly related to the ease with which information about the event comes to mind. For example, suicide is extremely rare among children and adolescents who take antidepressant medication. However, the media have recently highlighted a number of deaths associated with the use of these medications. A clinician might overestimate the risk of suicide associated with taking antidepressant medication because accounts of these deaths easily come to mind.

Second, practitioners often rely excessively on the **representativeness heuristic** when formulating clinical decisions. After clinicians hear clients report a certain symptom that characterizes (i.e., is representative of) a specific disorder, they might neglect to explore the possibility of other disorders. For example, the symptoms of depressed mood, fatigue, sleep problems, and appetite disturbance are characteristic of depression. Consequently, a therapist whose client reports these symptoms might prematurely diagnose the client with depression, rather than explore the possibility of another disorder, like hypothyroidism, that might better explain these symptoms.

Third, clinicians make erroneous judgments when they rely heavily on the **anchoring heuristic**. During the course of the clinical interview, practitioners often place greatest emphasis on information presented early in the interview and relatively less importance on information presented later. For example, an adolescent might present for treatment because of academic and disruptive behavior problems. The clinician might focus on these disruptive behavior problems during the interview and neglect to assess the possibility that the adolescent might have under-lying mood problems, as well.

Fourth, clinicians often show **confirmatory biases** in their decision making. That is, clinicians often look for information that confirms their initial hypotheses and overlook or dismiss conflicting information. For example, a clinician who believes her client's academic problems are caused by ADHD might overlook other potential causes for his low grades, such as the presence of a visual impairment or a learning disability.

Characteristics of the client and the clinician can influence the accuracy of clinical judgments. Pottick, Kirk, Hsieh, and Tian (2007) asked mental health professionals to read a vignette about a boy with Conduct Disorder, a psychiatric condition charac-terized by serious disruptive and rule-breaking behavior. The researchers manipu-lated the ethnicity of the boy in the story. The researchers found that clinicians were more likely to diagnose the child when they believed he was white compared to when he was African American or Latino. The researchers speculated that mental health professionals might regard conduct problems in a white youth as a sign of "mental disorder" but regard the same symptoms in a nonwhite youth as a sign of environ-mental stress or "delinquency." Furthermore, clinicians' professional training influ-enced their diagnostic decisions: Psychiatrists were more likely than social workers and psychologists to diagnose the boy in the vignette with Conduct Disorder.

Clinicians gain the most accurate understanding of client functioning when they rely on multiple methods of data collection, especially norm-referenced test data. Interviews and clinic-based observations alone are often insufficient bases upon which to make diagnostic and treatment decisions. In fact, clinicians who base deci-sions on interview data alone often generate inaccurate impressions of their clients (Garb, 1996, 2000). Furthermore, the amount of experience that clinicians have in diagnostic interviewing is *not* strongly related to their diagnostic accuracy (Garb, 2000). Instead, accuracy in clinical judgment is greatly improved when practition-ers incorporate norm-referenced test data into the decision-making process and rely on empirical methods whenever possible (Garb, 1996, 2000).

Diagnosis

DSM-IV-TR

The *DSM-IV-TR* is a compendium of mental disorders published by the American Psychiatric Association and organized into 16 broad categories based on each dis-order's symptom presentation. Each disorder is defined using specific signs and symptoms. To be diagnosed with a given disorder, the individual must show the diagnostic features described in the manual.

DSM-IV-TR uses a categorical approach to diagnostic classification. **Categorical classification** involves dividing up mental disorders into types, or categories, based on sets of defining criteria. The categorical approach is also used predominantly in biology and medicine. For example, an animal is classified as a mammal if it (a) has vertebrae, (b) has hair, and (c) feeds its young with mother's milk. An animal that does not possess these features is not a mammal. Similarly, each mental disorder is defined by the presence of specific diagnostic criteria listed in the *DSM-IV-TR*. A person without those criteria would not be diagnosed with a given disorder.

Advantages of Diagnosis

Diagnosis has a number of benefits. Perhaps the most obvious benefit to diagnostic classification is parsimony. Imagine that you are a psychologist who has just completed a thorough assessment of a three-year-old child with suspected developmental delays. You discover that the child shows severe and pervasive problems with social interactions, communication, and repetitive behavior. Instead of describing each of these symptoms, you can simply use the appropriate diagnostic label: Autistic Disorder. Diagnostic classification is used for the sake of parsimony in medicine, too. Physicians do not describe children as having mild fever, upset stomach, sweaty palms, flushed face, gastrointestinal upset, vomiting, diarrhea, dizziness, and fatigue; instead, they simply say the child has influenza.

A second advantage to diagnosis is that it can aid in professional communication. Another mental health professional who sees your diagnosis knows that your client exhibits a cluster of symptoms described in *DSM-IV-TR*. The second professional does not need to conduct her own assessment of the child to arrive at an independent diagnosis to know something about the child's symptoms.

A third advantage of diagnostic classification is that it can aid in prediction. If you know that your client has Autistic Disorder, you can use the existing research literature to determine prognosis. For example, most children with autism show chronic impairment in social and communicative functioning; however, prognosis is best among children with higher intelligence and better language skills before age five. The research literature also indicates that children who participate in treatment before age four often have the best developmental outcomes. You might use this information to provide parents with realistic expectations regarding their child's future so that they can make more informed decisions regarding treatment.

A fourth and closely related benefit of diagnostic classification is that it can help plan treatment. If you know that your client has Autistic Disorder, you can also use the existing research literature to plan an intervention. For example, a number of studies have indicated that early, intensive behavioral interventions can be effective in improving the social and communication skills of young children with autism. However, other forms of treatment, such as art and music therapy, have far less empirical support. Consequently, you can use knowledge gained from research studies involving other children with autism to help your client.

Fifth, diagnostic classification can help individuals obtain social or educational services. For example, the Individuals With Disabilities Education Act (IDEA; U.S. Department of Education, 2006) is a federal law that entitles children with Autistic Disorder to special education because of their developmental disability. Special education might involve enrollment in a special needs preschool, early intensive behavioral training paid for by the school district, provision of a classroom aide or tutor, academic accommodations, life skills training, and a host of other services. Children may only be entitled to receive these services if they are diagnosed with autism or another developmental disorder. Consequently, diagnostic classification is sometimes a means to obtaining educational or social benefits.

A sixth benefit of diagnostic classification is that diagnosis can sometimes help parents. Although no parent is happy when his or her child has a psychiatric diagnosis, many parents feel relieved when their child's disorder is finally identified. After hearing that her three-year-old child had autism, one parent said, "Well, I finally know what's wrong. I always suspected it and now I know. I suppose we can finally move forward." Diagnostic labels can also help parents contact the parents of children with similar disorders in order to share information and gain social support.

Finally, diagnostic classification can facilitate scientific discovery. Researchers who conduct studies on the causes and treatment of autism can compare the results of their investigations with the findings of others. Indeed, many studies are conducted by teams of researchers in multiple locations. As long as researchers use the same diagnostic criteria and procedures to classify children, results can be combined to generate a more thorough understanding of the disorder.

Disadvantages of Diagnosis

The *DSM-IV-TR* classification system also has some inherent disadvantages and risks. The first main drawback of the *DSM-IV-TR* classification system is that it often gains parsimony at the expense of detailed information. Although a diagnostic label can convey considerable information to others, it cannot possibly convey the same amount of information as a thorough description of the individual. Of particular concern is the fact that *DSM-IV-TR* diagnoses do not take into account the individual's environment. Many so-called "maladaptive" behaviors exhibited by children and adolescents with mental disorders can be seen as attempts to adapt to stressful environments. For example, some physically abused children come to believe that other people have hostile motives and intentions. Although this sense of mistrust is problematic, it may be best understood in terms of the child's attempt to cope with a history of physical victimization.

A second drawback of the *DSM-IV-TR* lies in its exclusive focus on individuals. *DSM-IV-TR* conceptualizes psychopathology as something that exists within the person. However, childhood disorders are often relational in nature. For example, Oppositional Defiant Disorder (ODD) is diagnosed in children who show patterns of noncompliant and oppositional behavior toward others, especially adults in positions of authority. Similarly, Separation Anxiety Disorder (SAD) is displayed by children who show persistent fears of separation from caregivers. Considerable research indicates that the quality of parent-child interactions plays an important role in the development of both ODD and SAD. Furthermore, treatment for both disorders relies heavily on parental involvement. However, in the *DSM-IV-TR* system, both ODD and SAD are diagnosed in the child. The *DSM-IV-TR* approach to diagnosis can overlook the role caregivers, family members, and peers play in the development and maintenance of children's problems.

A third drawback in the *DSM-IV-TR* system is that distinctions between normality and abnormality are sometimes arbitrary. In the categorical approach used by *DSM-IV-TR*, individuals either have a given disorder or they do not. For example, to be diagnosed with ADHD, a child needs to show at least six symptoms of inattention or hyperactivity-impulsivity. If the child displays only five of the required six symptoms, he would not qualify for the ADHD diagnosis. However, as we will see, many youths who show subthreshold symptomatology experience significant distress and impairment and often do not differ appreciably from children who fully meet diagnostic criteria.

An alternative approach to categorical classification is **dimensional (continuous) classification.** Advocates of the dimensional approach to classification recognize that most psychological disorders fall along a continuum ranging from total symptom absence to severe symptom presentation. At any given time, a person can show all, some, or none of the symptoms for a given disorder. Rather than dichotomizing people into either having the disorder or not having the disorder, advocates of the dimensional approach prefer to describe individuals based on the number or severity of their symptoms (Achenbach, 1982; Kamphaus, Reynolds, & Imperato-McCammon, 1999).

For example, a clinician might ask parents to complete the BASC-2 rating scale about their child. Recall that the BASC-2 provides norm-referenced scores on a number of different dimensions, such as attention, aggressive behavior, anxiety, and depression. Instead of diagnosing a child with a single disorder, the psychologist might use BASC-2 ratings to describe the child's functioning on all relevant dimensions. For example, the clinician might notice that the child has average attention, moderately high levels of aggression, and extremely high levels of anxiety and depression compared to other children his age.

A fourth limitation of the *DSM-IV-TR* classification system is that there are often unclear boundaries between diagnostic categories. Categorical classification systems, like *DSM-IV-TR*, work best when all members of a diagnostic group are homogeneous, when there are clear boundaries between two different diagnoses, and when diagnostic categories are mutually exclusive. Unfortunately, these conditions are not always met.

There are often unclear boundaries between different mental disorders. For example, children with Bipolar Disorder, a serious mood disorder seen in approximately 1% to 2% of youth, often have ADHD. Indeed, some studies indicate that 90% of youths with Bipolar Disorder also meet diagnostic criteria for ADHD. The presence of multiple disorders in the same individual is called **comorbidity.** Comorbidity is actually very common among youths with psychiatric diagnoses; it is more likely that a child referred for treatment will have multiple disorders rather than only one. In some cases, comorbidity is caused by the child actually having two distinct disorders. For example, many children with Bipolar Disorder clearly show symptoms of ADHD, even when they are not having mood problems. Sometimes, however, high rates of comorbidity may be due to unclear boundaries between *DSM-IV-TR* diagnostic categories. Both Bipolar Disorder and ADHD are characterized by an increase in behavioral activity, short attention span, distractibility, talkativeness, and impulsive behavior. Some children with Bipolar Disorder may mistakenly be diagnosed with ADHD because of this overlap in symptoms.

A fifth criticism of the *DSM-IV-TR* system is that certain diagnostic criteria are subjective and value-laden (Jensen, Hoagwood, & Zitner, 2006). Many terms that are part of the diagnostic criteria are vague and subject to the interpretation of individual clinicians. For example, the *DSM-IV-TR* diagnostic criteria include terms like "subaverage," "failure," "distortion," and "deficit" without clear definitions of these terms. Almost every disorder in the *DSM-IV-TR* requires the individual to show "clinically significant impairment" in order to be diagnosed; however, the term "clinically significant impairment" is vague and tautological. After all, "clinically significant impairment" is the type of impairment that a clinician considers severe enough to need treatment (Fulford, 1994; Jensen et al., 2006).

Stigma

A final weakness of the *DSM-IV-TR* approach is that diagnostic classification can lead to stigmatization. **Stigmatization** occurs when people judge children, adolescents, or families because of the youth's diagnostic label. Stigmatization of mental illness comes in many forms. During casual conversation, people use terms like "crazy," "wacked," "nuts," and "psycho" without giving much thought to the implications these words have for people with mental illness. Children may use the derogatory term "retard" to describe peers who behave foolishly. Parents of children with psychological and behavioral disorders often report discrimination from school and medical personnel because of their child's illness. Some insurance companies discriminate against individuals with mental disorders by not providing equal coverage for mental and physical illnesses. Movies and television shows depict people with mental illness as violent, unpredictable, deranged, or devious. Even children with mental illness are portrayed in a negative light on film. Broadcasters disproportionately report individuals with mental illness behaving erratically or violently (Hinshaw, 2006).

Stigmatization can negatively affect youths and their families in several ways. First, it can cause a sense of shame or degradation that decreases self-esteem and lowers self-worth. The negative self-image generated by the social judgments of others, in turn, can exacerbate symptoms or hinder progress in therapy. Second, stigmatization can lead to **self-fulfilling prophecies**. Youths may eventually come to believe that they are deviant, "damaged," or "deranged" because of their diagnostic label. In some cases, children may alter their behavior to fit the diagnostic label or use the diagnosis to excuse disruptive behavior problems. For example, a child might explain the reason for a recent suspension from school: "I can't help it. It's not my fault. It's my ADHD." Third, stigmatization can decrease the likelihood that families will seek psychological services because they want to avoid the shame of the diagnostic label. Indeed, more than three-fourths of youth in the United States who show significant behavioral, emotional, and learning problems do not receive treatment, many because parents do not want their children assigned a diagnostic label (Hinshaw, 2005).

To avoid stigmatization, some mental health professionals do not diagnose children with disorders that have strong negative connotations. For example, between 1994 and 1997, the U.S. Department of Education showed a 38% decrease in the number of children diagnosed with Mental Retardation and a 202% increase in the number of children given the less stigmatizing classification of "learning disabled." Giving children inaccurate diagnoses or euphemistic labels in order to avoid stigmatization can cause harm. For example, children with Mental Retardation who are euphemistically labeled as having "learning problems" actually show reductions in self-esteem over time. Furthermore, older adolescents with Mental Retardation who are euphemistically classified as "learning disabled" are more likely to drop out of school and become unemployed than adolescents who are accurately diagnosed (Vig, 2005).

One way to reduce the negative effects of diagnostic labeling is to be careful with the way we describe people with psychiatric disorders. Diagnostic labels refer to people's thoughts, feelings, and actions; they do not refer to individuals themselves. Therefore, it is more appropriate to refer to a person as *experiencing* a specific disorder than it is to define the person *in terms of* the disorder. For example, we use the term "a child with autism" instead of "an autistic child" because the child shows a pattern of behavior defined by the diagnostic label "autism." We use the term "an adolescent with depression" instead of "a depressed adolescent" because the adolescent shows mood and behavioral symptoms consistent with a depressive disorder.

Avoiding diagnostic labels when describing people is not political correctness; it is precise use of language. Labeling children and adolescents as "autistic," "depressed," or "bipolar" implies that they *are* the diagnosis. It suggests that disorders are inherent parts of the person that are immutable to change and reflect some sort of moral weakness or personality flaw. In contrast, describing children as "having autism," "experiencing depression," or "showing bipolar disorder" reminds listeners that these disorders reflect only a constellation of behaviors, not the person. Although diagnostic symptoms may often overshadow children's abilities, strengths, and talents, correctly describing youth as "having a disorder" rather than "being a disorder" helps us differentiate the qualities of the person from the features of the disorder itself (Faul & Gross, 2006).

Multiaxial Diagnosis

DSM-IV-TR encourages clinicians to assess clients on five axes, or domains, each reflecting a different area of the person's functioning. The primary purpose of multiaxial assessment is to ensure a more comprehensive and systematic evaluation of the client; it increases the likelihood that the clinician will consider multiple domains of the individual's functioning and not focus exclusively on his or her primary diagnosis. A second purpose of multiaxial assessment is to convey more information than would be given if the clinician simply assigned one diagnostic label.

The five axes are as follows:

Axis I: Clinical disorders and other conditions that may be a focus of attention

Axis II: Personality disorders and mental retardation

Axis III: General medical conditions

Axis IV: Psychosocial and environmental problems

Axis V: Global assessment of functioning

On Axis I, the clinician lists all relevant mental and behavioral disorders except Personality Disorders and Mental Retardation. If the individual meets diagnostic criteria for multiple disorders, then all disorders are listed. The first diagnosis listed is usually considered the person's primary diagnosis. The **primary diagnosis** typically reflects the client's most salient disorder or the disorder that prompted a referral for mental health services. The clinician may also list "other conditions that may be a focus of clinical attention" on Axis I. These "other conditions" are problems in psychosocial functioning that are included in a special section of *DSM-IV-TR* but are not technically considered mental disorders. "Other conditions" that are relevant to children and adolescents include parent-child relationship problems, sibling rivalries, and bereavement (i.e., grieving the loss of a loved one).

On Axis II, the clinician indicates the presence of Personality Disorders and Mental Retardation. A **personality disorder** is an enduring pattern of thoughts, feelings, or actions that markedly deviates from the individual's cultural norm. This pattern emerges during adolescence, is pervasive and inflexible, and leads to chronic impairment in day-to-day functioning or to psychological distress. For example, Antisocial Personality Disorder is characterized by a pervasive pattern of disregard for the rights of others and the rules of society. Individuals with Antisocial Personality Disorder, usually men, often have extensive histories of aggression and legal problems. Another personality disorder, Borderline Personality Disorder, is characterized by a pervasive pattern of instability in interpersonal relationships, self-image, and mood. Individuals with Borderline Personality Disorder, usually women, show repeated problems with impulsivity, emotional lability, and relationship problems. Since personality disorders reflect atypical development of normal personality, they are usually not diagnosed until adulthood.

People with Mental Retardation show significant impairments in intellectual and adaptive functioning that emerge during childhood. Approximately 2% to 3% of the U.S. population has Mental Retardation. If Mental Retardation is present, it is listed on Axis II. Mental Retardation and Personality Disorders are assigned their own axis in the multiaxial system so that clinicians do not overlook them during the assessment process (*DSM-IV-TR*).

On Axis III, the clinician lists current medical conditions that might be relevant to understanding or treating the person's mental disorder. For example, some medical conditions can exacerbate psychological symptoms. For example, feelings of depression can be increased by hypothyroidism. In this case, the clinician would include the diagnosis Major Depressive Disorder on Axis I and the medical disorder hypothyroidism on Axis III. Other medical conditions can interfere with treatment. For example, significant vision problems (coded on Axis III) might interfere with the education and treatment of a child with autism (coded on Axis I).

Axis IV is used to report psychosocial and environmental stressors that may affect diagnosis, treatment, or prognosis. Typically, these psychosocial stressors are negative events and life experiences that exacerbate Axis I disorders. They tend to fall into nine broad categories (see Table 3.7).

For example, a child with Major Depressive Disorder (coded on Axis I) might also experience the divorce of her parents (coded on Axis IV). Parental divorce might exacerbate her symptoms of depression or interfere with her ability to participate in treatment. A child with autism (coded on Axis I) and Mental Retardation (coded on

Table 3.7   Psychosocial and Environmental Problems

Problem	Examples
Problems with primary support group	Health problems in family member; disruption of family by separation, divorce, or estrangement; removal from parent's home; remarriage of parent; birth of a sibling
Problems related to the social environment	Loss or separation from a friend; relocation to new neighborhood and peer group; inadequate social support; discrimination
Educational problems	Inadequate school environment; problems between school personnel and child/family; change in schools
Occupational problems	Parental unemployment; threat of job loss; parent's work schedule; job dissatisfaction
Housing problems	Homelessness; inadequate housing; unsafe neighborhood
Economic problems	Extreme poverty; inadequate finances; insufficient government assistance or child support
Problems with access to health care services	Inadequate health care services; transportation to services unavailable; inadequate health insurance
Problems related to interaction with the legal system	Arrest; incarceration; victim of crime
Other psychosocial and environmental problems	Exposure to disasters; unavailability of social service agencies

Source: Reprinted with permission from the *DSM-IV-TR*.

Axis II) might come from a single-parent, low-income family (coded on Axis IV). His mother might be unable to take time off work to participate in treatment.

On Axis V, clinicians provide an overall numerical rating of the person's functioning. The **Global Assessment of Functioning (GAF) scale** is a numerical rating system that reflects the individual's current psychological, social, and occupational well-being. The scale ranges from 1 (i.e., danger to self or others, inability to care for self) to 100 (i.e., superior functioning in a wide range of activities). The GAF scale is divided into 10-point increments. Each increment is characterized by a different level of symptom severity and psychosocial functioning (see Table 3.8). The clinician assigns a numerical rating based on her assessment of the patient's current symptom presentation. She might make repeated GAF ratings during the course of treatment to monitor treatment progress.

The *DSM-IV-TR* multiaxial assessment system adopts a **biopsychosocial perspective** on understanding psychopathology. Axes I and II reflect psychological disorders and processes, Axis III is used to reflect biological and medical conditions that are relevant to the person's functioning, while Axis IV reflects social and cultural influences on the person. Axis V provides a numerical summary of the individual's overall level of functioning. By separating biological, psychological, and social domains into separate axes, the *DSM-IV-TR* system does not imply that these aspects of people's functioning are distinct from one another. Rather, use of the multiaxial system is meant to suggest that all three domains are necessary to obtain the most complete understanding of the individual that is possible.

Table 3.8   Global Assessment of Functioning (GAF) Scale

100 91	Superior functioning in a wide range of activities, life's problems never seem to get out of hand, is sought out by others because of his or her many positive qualities. No symptoms.
90 81	Absent or minimal symptoms (e.g., mild anxiety before an exam), good functioning in all areas, interested and involved in a wide range of activities, socially effective, generally satisfied with life, no more than everyday problems and concerns (e.g., an occasional argument with family members).
80 71	If symptoms are present, they are transient and expectable reactions to psychosocial stressors (e.g., difficulty concentrating after a family argument); no more than slight impairment in social, occupational, or school functioning (e.g., temporarily falling behind in school work).
70 61	Some mild symptoms (e.g., depressed mood, mild insomnia) OR some difficulty in social, occupational, or school functioning (e.g., occasional truancy, theft within the household), but generally functioning pretty well, has some meaningful interpersonal relationships.
60 51	Moderate symptoms (e.g., flat affect, occasional panic attacks) OR moderate difficulty in social, occupational, or school functioning (e.g., few friends, conflicts with peers).
50 41	Serious symptoms (e.g., suicidal ideation, severe obsessions or rituals, frequent shoplifting) OR any serious impairment in social, occupational, or school functioning (e.g., no friends).
40 31	Some impairment in reality testing or communication (e.g., speech is at times illogical, obscure, or irrelevant) OR major impairment in several areas such as work or school, family relations, judgment, thinking, or mood (e.g., child frequently fights with younger children, is defiant at home, and is failing at school).
30 21	Behavior is considerably influenced by delusions or hallucinations OR serious impairment in communication or judgment (e.g., sometimes incoherent, grossly inappropriate actions, suicidal preoccupation) OR inability to function in most areas (e.g., stays in bed all day, no contact with peers).
20 11	Some danger of hurting self or others (e.g., suicide attempts without clear expectation of death, frequently violent, manic excitement) OR occasionally fails to maintain minimal personal hygiene (e.g., smears feces) OR gross impairment in communication (e.g., largely incoherent or mute).
10 1	Persistent danger of severely hurting self or others (e.g., recurrent violence) OR persistent inability to maintain minimal personal hygiene OR serious suicidal act with clear expectation of death.
0	Inadequate information.

Source: Reprinted with permission from the *DSM-IV-TR*.

Critical Thinking Exercises

1. Why is it important for psychologists to rely on multiple informants when assessing children? Who might be the best person to report (a) a preschool-age child's disruptive behavior at home, (b) a seven-year-old girl's difficulty with reading, (c) an adolescent suspected of depression?

2. Why is it important for psychologists to rely on multiple methods when assessing children? What assessment techniques might you use to assess (a) Attention-Deficit/Hyperactivity Disorder in a six-year-old boy, (b) reading disabilities in a seven-year-old girl, (c) depression in a 15-year-old adolescent?

3. Paully is an 11-year-old boy who bullies younger children during recess. How might you conduct a functional analysis of Paully's behavior to determine the antecedents and consequences of his bullying?

4. Can a psychological test be reliable but not valid? Can a test be valid but not reliable?

5. Terry is a nine-year-old boy diagnosed with a learning disability. His guidance counselor explained to his teacher, "Terry has trouble with reading because he has a learning disability." Is the guidance counselor correct? Does Terry's diagnosis actually *explain* his learning problems? What might be the benefit of this diagnostic label?

CHAPTER 4

The Practice and Ethics of Psychotherapy With Children

What Is Psychotherapy?

Most mental health professionals spend the majority of their time practicing psychotherapy. However, no one has provided a definition of psychotherapy that satisfies all practitioners. One influential definition of **psychotherapy** has been offered by Raymond Corsini (2005), an expert in clinical interventions:

> Psychotherapy is a formal process of interaction between two parties . . . for the purpose of amelioration of distress in one of the two parties relative to any or all of the following areas of disability or malfunction: cognitive functions (disorders of thinking), affective functions (suffering or emotional discomforts), or behavioral functions (inadequacy of behavior) . . . . The therapist [has] some theory of personality's origins, development, maintenance and change along with some method of treatment logically related to that theory and professional and legal approval to act as a therapist. (p. 1)

According to this definition, psychotherapy is an interpersonal process. Therapy must involve interactions between at least two individuals: a therapist and a client. The therapist can be any professional who has specialized training in the delivery of mental heath services. Therapists can include psychologists, psychiatrists, counselors, and social workers; however, therapists can also include teachers and other paraprofessionals who have received training and supervision in the use of psychosocial interventions. The therapist uses a theory about the causes of psychopathology to develop a means of alleviating the client's psychological distress.

The client is an individual experiencing some degree of distress or impairment who agrees to participate in the therapeutic interaction to bring about change.

Common Factors in Therapy

The purpose of psychotherapy is to alter the thoughts, feelings, or behaviors of the client. Change occurs primarily through interactions with the therapist. Specifically, the therapist provides certain conditions, consistent with his or her theory of psychopathology, to improve the functioning of the client. Jerome Frank (1973) has suggested that certain factors are common to all forms of psychotherapy. These factors include the presence of a trusting relationship between the client and therapist, a specific setting in which change is supposed to take place, a theory or explanation for the client's suffering, and a therapeutic ritual in which the client and therapist must engage to alleviate the client's suffering. Frank argues these common or "nonspecific" factors of psychotherapy have been primary components of psychological and spiritual healing since ancient times.

In his person-centered approach to counseling, Carl Rogers (1957) identified three **necessary and sufficient factors for therapeutic change.** First, the therapist must provide the client with unconditional positive regard; that is, the therapist must be supportive and nonjudgmental of the client's behavior and characteristics in order to establish a relationship built on trust and acceptance. Second, the therapist must respond to the client with congruence; that is, the therapist must show his or her genuine feelings toward the client and avoid remaining emotionally detached, distant, or disengaged. Rogers described the ideal therapeutic relationship as "transparent"; that is, the client should easily witness the clinician's genuine feelings during the therapy session. The therapist does not try to hide his or her feelings or put on airs. Third, the therapist must show empathy toward the client. Specifically, the therapist must strive to understand the world from the client's perspective and take a profound interest in the client's thoughts, feelings, and actions. Rogers believed that clients whose therapists provided them with these three conditions would experience the greatest benefits from treatment.

Few practitioners dispute the importance of the psychotherapeutic factors identified by Frank (1973) and Rogers (1957). However, most clinicians regard these common factors as necessary but *not* sufficient to bring about change. Most therapists supplement these common factors with specific strategies and techniques consistent with their theories of the origins of psychopathology. The specific therapeutic methods they use depend on the system of psychotherapy they practice and the presenting problem of the client (Frank & Frank, 2004).

Systems of Psychotherapy

There are hundreds of specific systems or "schools" of psychotherapy. However, they can be loosely categorized in terms of the level at which they approach clients' presenting problems. Specifically, the various systems of psychotherapy address different levels of the client's behavioral, cognitive, and social-emotional functioning.

These levels include (1) the client's overt behaviors and symptoms, (2) the client's patterns of thinking, (3) the client's family relationships, (4) the client's other interpersonal relationships, and (5) the client's knowledge of himself and his intrapersonal functioning (Prochaska & Norcross, 2003).

To understand the various systems of psychotherapy, consider a 16-year-old girl, Anna, who suffers from Bulimia Nervosa, an eating disorder usually characterized by recurrent binge eating and vomiting. The type of treatment that Anna receives will largely depend on the level(s) of functioning to which her therapist attends. Anna may be treated from the approach of behaviorism, cognitive therapy, family system therapy, interpersonal therapy, or psychodynamic psychotherapy.

Behavior Therapy

Behavior therapy focuses primarily on the client's overt actions and maladaptive patterns of behavior. Behavior therapy has its origins in the work of Joseph Wolpe (1958), Hans Eysenck (1959), and B. F. Skinner (1974). Behavior therapists address clients' problems at the symptom level. Behavior therapists do not assume that underlying personality traits or intrapsychic conflicts influence behavior. Instead, behavior is largely determined by **environmental contingencies**, that is, environmental conditions that either reinforce or punish certain behaviors. The goal of behavior therapy is usually to alter these environmental contingencies to increase the likelihood that clients will engage in more adaptive patterns of action.

A behavior therapist would carefully note the frequency of Anna's binge eating. Then, the therapist would likely perform a functional analysis of Anna's maladaptive eating behavior. Specifically, the therapist might find that the antecedents of Anna's bingeing often include being alone and feeling hungry. Furthermore, the consequences of Anna's bingeing might include a temporary reduction in hunger but more lasting feelings of guilt and shame.

Over the course of treatment, the therapist might teach Anna to monitor her binge eating, its antecedents, and its consequences. Then, the therapist might help Anna avoid antecedents that trigger binges. For example, the therapist might help Anna eat more regular, balanced meals to avoid feelings of intense hunger. Similarly, the therapist might help Anna identify ways to avoid the loneliness and boredom that often trigger her binges. The therapist might encourage Anna to become more involved in after-school activities or teach her to develop more satisfying peer relationships. By altering environmental factors that elicit or reinforce her binges, Anna should be able to decrease the frequency of her symptoms.

Cognitive Therapy

Cognitive therapy focuses primarily on the client's patterns of thinking about herself, others, and the future. One cognitive therapist, Aaron Beck (1976), argued that people experience psychological distress and impairment when they engage in systematic errors in thinking called **cognitive distortions**. Specifically, psychological distress occurs when people hold beliefs or perceptions that do not correspond to reality and cast themselves, others, and the world in a bleak, threatening, or dangerous light. For example, people who hold overly negative, pessimistic views of themselves, others, and the future can experience depression. Their beliefs lead them to anticipate failure and doubt their ability to reach their goals. Alternatively, individuals who believe that other people are hostile and critical, who view the world as a dangerous place, and who see themselves as largely unable to control external events may experience anxiety. According to Beck, cognitive therapists help clients identify cognitive distortions and adopt more realistic ways of thinking.

Another cognitive therapist, Albert Ellis, claimed that **irrational beliefs** often contribute to psychological distress and maladaptive ways of acting (Ellis, 2005; Ellis & Harper, 1961). When people engage in absolute, black-or-white thinking, they often place considerable pressure on themselves to achieve and predispose themselves to depression, anxiety, or anger. People who make dogmatic demands on themselves (e.g., "I *must* get into graduate school") often set themselves up for failure and increase their likelihood of low self-worth. Similarly, people who place rigid demands on others (e.g., "My teacher *should* have given me a higher grade on the exam") can experience anger and frustration. Accord to Ellis, cognitive therapists challenge clients' absolute, dogmatic, and rigid beliefs and teach clients to think more logically.

A cognitive therapist would focus her attention on the thoughts associated with Anna's bingeing and vomiting. A therapist adopting Beck's (1976) approach to cognitive therapy might help Anna identify cognitive distortions that occur before she vomits. Specifically, Anna might think, "I'm afraid of becoming fat. If I become fat, then no one will love me." The therapist might help Anna challenge this belief to determine whether it is true or whether it is a distortion of reality. For example, the therapist might ask Anna, "If you become fat, what's the likelihood that *no one* will love you?" Then the therapist might help Anna think more realistically about her eating behavior. For example, the therapist might encourage Anna to adopt a different thought, like, "I know I feel terrible right now, but if I don't throw up I'll feel OK in a little while."

A therapist adopting Ellis's (2005) perspective of cognitive therapy might help Anna identify irrational beliefs that contribute to her vomiting. For example, Anna might hold the irrational belief, "I need to be thin and beautiful so that people will love me." The therapist would likely challenge this belief, arguing that Anna does not necessarily *need* to be thin or beautiful in order to be loved. Furthermore, the therapist would help Anna identify more logical ways of thinking. For example, the therapist might encourage Anna to think, "I'd *like* to be thin and beautiful, but it wouldn't be terrible if I gained some weight."

Both Beck's (1976) and Ellis's (2005) approaches to cognitive therapy emphasize the connection between thoughts, feelings, and actions. As clients learn to think in more realistic, logical ways, they may experience fewer negative emotions and behave in a more adaptive manner. Often, cognitive therapists incorporate elements of behavior therapy into their treatments. **Cognitive-behavioral therapy** refers to the integrated use of cognitive and behavioral approaches to treatment.

Family Therapy

Family therapists focus on patterns of communication and interaction among family members. There are many different types of family therapy. Most have certain features in common. For example, all family therapists view the family as a **system**, that is, a network of connected individuals who influence and partially direct each other's behavior. Viewing the family as a system has several important implications for therapy. First, family therapists see the entire family as their "client," not just the person who is identified by certain family members as "the one with the problem." Second, a systems approach to treatment assumes that change in one member of the family will necessarily change all members of the family. Consequently, family therapists believe that helping one or two family members improve their functioning can often lead to symptom reduction in the family member with the identified problem.

One form of family therapy, developed by Salvador Minuchin (1974), is **structural family therapy**. Structural family therapists are chiefly concerned with the quality of relationships between family members. In healthy families, parents form strong social-emotional bonds, or alliances, with each other that are based on mutual respect and open lines of communication. Furthermore, in healthy families, parents form boundaries between themselves and their children. Specifically, parents respect children's developing autonomy and provide for their social-emotional needs, but they also remain figures of authority in the family.

In other families, however, alliances are formed between one parent and the children, leaving the other parent disconnected or estranged from the rest of the family. For example, mother and daughter might form an alliance against father because of father's excessive use of alcohol. Father might feel alienated from his family while mother and daughter might grow to resent father. Furthermore, in unhealthy families, boundaries between parents and children are often overly rigid or excessively diffuse. **Disengaged families** are characterized by overly rigid boundaries, in which open communication between family members is stifled and members feel disconnected from one another. In contrast, **enmeshed families** are characterized by diffuse boundaries where family members lack autonomy and constantly intrude into one another's lives.

Most family therapists would insist on seeing Anna and her parents together, for at least part of treatment. The therapist would likely pay attention to alliances and boundaries in Anna's family and the way Anna's eating disorder might help to maintain the family system in a maladaptive way. For example, the therapist might discover that Anna's parents frequently argue with one another and are considering a divorce. The therapist might notice that the onset of Anna's symptoms coincided with the onset of her parents' marital problems. The therapist might hypothesize that Anna's eating symptoms serve to maintain the family system by distracting her parents from their marital problems.

A family therapist might also notice that Anna's parents are overprotective and excessively demanding. The therapist might interpret Anna's desire to lose weight as a maladaptive attempt to gain the approval of her parents. The therapist might refer Anna's parents to a marital therapist to help them improve the quality of their relationship. At the same time, the therapist might work with Anna and her parents to help improve communication in the home. One goal of therapy might be to help Anna's parents give her more autonomy over her day-to-day behavior.

Interpersonal Therapy

Interpersonal therapy focuses primarily on the quality of clients' relationships with others. Interpersonal therapy is based on the theoretical writings of Harry Stack Sullivan (1953) and John Bowlby (1973). Sullivan believed that interpersonal relationships are essential for mental health. Friendships in childhood help youngsters develop a sense of identity and self-worth and form the basis for more intimate, romantic relationships later in life. Problems in interpersonal relationships can interfere with social-emotional functioning and self-concept. Bowlby (1969), the founder of attachment theory, believed that people form mental models of interpersonal relationships through their interaction with caregivers and other significant individuals in their lives. Mental models built on trust and expectations for care promote later social-emotional adjustment. However, mental models based on mistrust and inconsistent care can interfere with the development of social-emotional competence.

Interpersonal therapists conceptualize psychopathology as arising from disruptions or problems in interpersonal relationships (Klerman & Weissman, 1993). First, interpersonal relationships can be disrupted when a loved one dies or is separated from the family. Second, relationship problems can arise when the person experiences a major change in social roles (e.g., transitions from junior high to high school). Third, problems can occur when the person's social roles conflict with the expectations of others (e.g., parents and adolescents disagree about dating or the importance of attending college). Finally, interpersonal problems can occur when the individual has interpersonal deficits that interfere with his ability to make and keep friends (e.g., excessive shyness or lack of social skills). An interpersonal therapist attempts to identify and correct relationship problems that might contribute to the client's primary diagnosis.

An interpersonal therapist might notice that Anna's eating problems occurred shortly after her father changed jobs and the family moved to a new neighborhood and school district. The therapist might interpret Anna's eating disorder as a maladaptive attempt to lose weight, appear attractive to others, and gain acceptance by peers at her new school. Through a combination of support and suggestions, the therapist would help Anna grieve the loss of her old neighborhood and friends, cope with her move to a new school, and find more effective ways to make new friends.

Psychodynamic Therapy

Psychodynamic therapy focuses chiefly on intrapsychic conflict, that is, conflict within the self. Psychodynamic therapy is based on the theoretical and clinical work of Sigmund Freud (1923/1961), Anna Freud (1936), and a host of so-called neo-Freudian theorists. Although there are a vast number of psychodynamic approaches to therapy, almost all believe that unconscious thoughts, feelings, dreams, images, or wishes influence our behavior. According to the **topographic theory of mind**, the mind can be divided into two levels, the conscious and the unconscious. Although unconscious mental activity cannot be directly accessed, unconscious mental processes influence and direct day-to-day actions. The principle of psychic determinism holds that behavior is not random; actions are influenced by both conscious will and unconscious mental activity. From the psychodynamic perspective, psychological symptoms often reflect unconscious mental activity.

The primary goal of psychodynamic therapy is to provide **insight**, that is, to make the person aware of unconscious mental conflict that contributes to his psychological symptoms. Insight is believed to result in symptom alleviation and more adaptive behavior.

The technique that the therapist uses to help the client achieve insight depends on the type of psychodynamic therapy she uses. One way therapists help clients gain insight is by paying attention to the client's **transference**, the attitude and patterns of interaction that the client develops toward the therapist. Transference is believed to reflect the client's history of interpersonal relationships and unconscious fantasies projected onto the therapist. For example, an adolescent who has been physically abused or neglected by her parents might express mistrust and hostility toward the therapist in the transference relationship. The client might unconsciously expect the therapist to abandon, reject, or mistreat her in a way similar to her parents. The therapist can use transference to help the client gain awareness of mental conflict. For example, the therapist might interpret the client's transference by suggesting, "I notice that whenever we talk about ending treatment, you get very angry and resentful toward me. I wonder if you're afraid that I'm going to abandon you?" Over the course of therapy, as clients gain greater insight into the causes of their distress, they may experience symptom reduction, develop more effective means of coping with anxiety, and achieve more satisfying relationships with others.

A psychodynamic therapist might focus her attention on Anna's transference. For example, over the course of multiple sessions, the therapist might notice that Anna often acts helpless and childlike during therapy sessions, as if she wants the therapist to tell her what to do. Furthermore, Anna might become frustrated and angry toward the therapist when the therapist remains nondirective and insists that Anna solve problems for herself. The therapist might interpret Anna's transference as an unconscious desire to remain in a childlike state. The therapist might suggest that as long as Anna remains irresponsible and childlike, she does not have to assume adult responsibilities that cause her considerable distress: finding a boyfriend, going to college, leaving home. The therapist might suggest that Anna's eating disorder ensures that her parents will coddle her and provide her with attention and sympathy, rather than insist that she develop more autonomous, age-appropriate behavior.

Other Schools of Therapy

There are many other systems of psychotherapy designed for children, adolescents, and adults, besides the ones described above. For example, **play therapy** is a variant of psychodynamic therapy designed for young children. In play therapy, children are encouraged to express unconscious mental conflict through their use of toys, art, and other symbolic forms of expression. **Group therapy** is a modification of behavior, cognitive, or interpersonal therapy in which clients meet in small groups or classes that are facilitated by one or two therapists. In group therapy, clients develop interpersonal skills and a better understanding of the effect of their behavior on others. In practice, most therapists consider themselves to be eclectic; that is, they adopt a number of therapeutic approaches and attempt to tailor approaches to meet the needs of individual clients.

Child Psychotherapy

History

The American psychologist Lightner Witmer was the first professional to apply psychological methods to treat children and adolescents. Witmer was trained as a researcher. He received his doctorate in psychology under the direction of the experimental psychologist Wilhelm Wundt at the University of Leipzig. After graduation, he directed the psychology laboratory at the University of Pennsylvania. In 1896, Witmer was asked by a local schoolteacher to help one of her students who was "a chronic bad speller." After careful interview, observation, and testing, Witmer concluded that the boy had underlying reading problems that interfered with his school performance. Witmer suggested systematic tutoring to help the boy overcome his reading and spelling problems.

Witmer began receiving referrals from other teachers and parents. Most of these referrals concerned children with academic problems, mental retardation, speech delays, and other problems that interfered with their ability to perform well in school. In 1897, Witmer established a psychological clinic to treat these children— the first psychological clinic in the United States. By 1904, the University of Pennsylvania began offering the first courses in clinical psychology, with special emphasis on the assessment and treatment of childhood disorders.

Witmer's influence on child psychotherapy was short-lived. In 1909, psychiatrist William Healy established a child guidance clinic in Chicago, the Juvenile Psychopathic Institute. Healy's clinic differed from Witmer's clinic in two respects. First, Healy's clinic focused primarily on children with disruptive behavior problems and juvenile delinquency, rather than academic problems and mental retardation. Second, Healy's approach to treatment was based on psychodynamic theory, rather than behavioral and educational interventions.

For the next 50 years, psychodynamic treatments dominated the practice of clinical child psychology. One leading figure in the treatment of childhood disorders at this time was Anna Freud. From the 1920s to the 1960s, Freud provided training in London on the application of psychodynamic techniques to children and adolescents. Until the 1960s, therapy for children was largely a downward extension of psychodynamic approaches developed for adults. These approaches were often ineffective in reducing children's behavior problems (Kazdin & Weisz, 2003).

Beginning in the 1960s and continuing until today, behavioral and cognitive-behavioral interventions, initially developed for adults, were modified for use with children and adolescents. In the 1970s, research investigating the use of behavioral and cognitive-behavioral treatment increased dramatically. Today, cognitive-behavioral interventions have received considerable empirical support for the alleviation of a wide range of child and adolescent disorders.

Child Versus Adult Psychotherapy

Child psychotherapy and adult psychotherapy differ in many ways. First, there are often motivational differences between child and adolescent clients and their adult counterparts. Most adults refer themselves to therapy; by the time they make the initial appointment, they are at least partially motivated to change their behavior. Indeed, some evidence suggests that the very act of seeking treatment and making an initial appointment is itself therapeutic (Howard, Kopta, Krause, & Orlinsky, 1986; Kopta, 2003). In contrast, children and adolescents are almost always referred by others (e.g., parents and teachers). Youths seldom recognize their behavioral, emotional, and social problems and typically show low motivation to change. Indeed, many youths with psychiatric disorders show very little psychological distress; instead, distress is usually experienced by other people in the children's lives. Most therapists initially try to increase children's willingness to trust the therapist and participate in treatment.

Second, cognitive and social-emotional differences between children, adolescents, and adults can influence the therapeutic process. Recall that most forms of child and adolescent therapy are downward extensions of adult therapeutic techniques. However, by virtue of their youth, children and adolescents often lack many of the cognitive, social, and emotional skills necessary to fully benefit from these techniques. For example, cognitive therapy depends greatly on clients' ability to engage in metacognition, that is, to think about their own thinking. However, metacognitive skills develop across childhood and adolescence; some youths may find cognitive therapy too abstract and difficult. Similarly, cognitive and insight-oriented therapies often rely heavily on verbal exchanges between client and therapist. Young children, with underdeveloped verbal abilities, may not benefit from these types of "talk" therapy.

Third, the goals of therapy often differ for children compared to adults. In adult psychotherapy, the primary objective of treatment is usually symptom reduction. Most therapists and clients consider treatment to be successful when clients return to a previous state of functioning. In therapy with children and adolescents, return to previous functioning is often inadequate. Instead, the goal of child and adolescent therapy is to alleviate symptoms while simultaneously promoting children's development. For example, a child with ADHD might participate in behavior therapy and take medication to alleviate his hyperactivity and inattention. However, these behavior problems have likely alienated him from classmates. Consequently, the therapist might have an additional goal of helping the child gain peer status in the classroom and overcome a history of peer rejection.

Fourth, children and adolescents often have less control over their ability to change than do adults. Adults usually have greater autonomy over their behavior and environmental circumstances than do children. For example, a woman who is depressed might decide to exercise more, join a social support group, practice meditation, change jobs, or leave her boyfriend in order to alleviate her distress. However, a child who is depressed because of his parents' martial conflict has far less ability to alter his environment. Although he might decide to exercise or participate in extracurricular activities, he is unable to leave home or get new parents. Instead, the boy's social-emotional functioning is closely connected to the behavior of his parents. Consequently, the boy's capacity to change is directly associated with his parents' involvement in therapy.

Finally, children and adolescents are more likely to have multiple psychiatric conditions compared to adults. In fact, comorbidity is the rule rather than the exception among children and adolescents with psychiatric disorders. Among youths in the community, approximately 50% who have one disorder also have a second disorder. Among youths referred to clinics, rates of comorbidity range from 50% to 90%, depending on the age of the child and the specific problem. Clinicians who treat children and adolescents must address multiple disorders simultaneously, often without the zealous participation of their young clients (Kazdin & Weisz, 2003).

Does Child and Adolescent Psychotherapy Work?

Psychotherapy Research

Wherever possible, clinicians must rely on the empirical literature to guide their practice. Furthermore, clinicians must employ a scientific attitude, or empirical approach, in order to tailor treatments to meet the needs of their clients (Stricker & Trierweiler, 2006).

Randomized Controlled Studies

To show that a treatment is effective, the researcher or clinician must demonstrate that the intervention *causes* symptom reduction. In science, causal relationships are most clearly demonstrated through **experimental research** designs. The type of experimental research most frequently used by professionals who evaluate psychological treatment is called the randomized controlled study.

In a **randomized controlled study**, researchers identify a group of individuals with the same disorder. Typically, individuals are recruited from the community, mental health clinics, or hospitals. Then, participants are randomly assigned to at least two groups. One group, the treatment group, receives the intervention. The other group, the control group, is used for comparison. **Random assignment** implies that each participant has an equal chance of being assigned to the treatment or the control group. By randomly assigning participants, the researcher decreases the likelihood that groups differ in characteristic ways before the treatment. Random assignment is essential to experimental research. Without random assignment, differences between groups that emerge at the end of the study might be attributable to differences that existed before the study, rather than to the treatment itself.

Many randomized controlled studies are double-blind. In a **double-blind study**, neither researchers nor participants know to what group participants have been assigned. Double-blind studies reduce biases on the part of researchers and participants. For example, researchers might behave differently toward participants in the treatment versus the control group if they know the group status of participants. Differences in researchers' behaviors toward members of these groups might affect the results of the evaluation.

Participants might also behave differently if they know whether they have been assigned to the treatment or control group. The **placebo effect** refers to the tendency of people to show improvement when they believe they are receiving treatment. Typically, people who believe that they are receiving treatment pay greater attention to their health and behavior, take better care of themselves, and are more optimistic about their outcomes. Researchers must control for placebo effects; they need to be able to attribute symptom reduction to the treatment itself, not to participants' expectations for improvement.

A critical decision in randomized controlled studies is what to do with participants in the control group (Kazdin, 2003). Many researchers compare the treatment group to a **no-treatment control group**. In this type of study, participants in the control group receive no treatment whatsoever. The primary shortcoming of using a no-treatment control group is that participants assigned to this group will clearly know that they are not receiving treatment. Consequently, differences between controls and participants in the treatment group can be attributable to placebo effects rather than the treatment per se. A second problem with using a no-treatment control group is that it is often unethical to withhold treatment from people with mental health problems, even for the sake of testing the efficacy of a new therapy. For example, it would be unethical to assign children with learning disorders to a no-treatment control group. By denying children treatment, we would be contributing to their academic delays.

Other researchers compare participants in the treatment group to participants assigned to a **waitlist control group**. In this type of study, participants assigned to the control group are placed on a waiting list to receive treatment. Treatment is delayed but not altogether withheld from participants. Waitlist control groups are usually more ethically justifiable than no-treatment control groups. However, they also have the limitation that participants assigned to the waitlist clearly know that they are not receiving treatment.

A third type of control group used in many randomized controlled studies is the **attention-placebo control group**. In an attention-placebo controlled study, participants assigned to the control group receive a theoretically inert form of treatment that resembles the treatment received by participants in the treatment group. For example, participants in an attention-placebo group might have weekly meetings with a therapist who listens to their concerns and responds in an empathic manner. Participants in the control group would likely believe that they were receiving the active treatment, thereby controlling for placebo effects between groups. However, participants in the attention-placebo group would not receive any specific form of treatment. For example, they would not be taught specific behavioral or cognitive techniques designed to reduce symptoms.

Finally, some researchers compare participants who receive the experimental treatment with participants who receive a treatment that is already available. For example, if a researcher develops a new form of treatment for ADHD, this new treatment might be compared to a treatment that already exists. Use of a **standard treatment control group** is the most stringent test of a new form of therapy. The new treatment must show that it reduces symptoms *and* that its benefits match or exceed those offered by existing therapies. A variant of the use of standard treatment controls is to compare an experimental treatment with "treatment as usual" (TAU). In this case, participants assigned to the treatment group receive the new therapy while participants assigned to the control group are referred to clinicians in the community and receive whatever form of care these clinicians recommend (i.e., treatment as usual).

A recent study conducted by Ronald Rapee and colleagues illustrates a randomized controlled trial. Rapee, Abbott, and Lyneham (2006) recruited 267 children with anxiety disorders and randomly assigned them to one of three conditions. The first group received a cognitive-behavioral treatment program for youths with anxiety problems. The second group received bibliotherapy; that is, their parents were given a book that described ways to treat childhood anxiety problems and parents were encouraged to use the techniques described in the book with their children at home. Children in the third group were placed on a waiting list. Three months after the beginning of the study, researchers examined the percentage of children in each group who no longer met diagnostic criteria for an anxiety disorder (see Figure 4.1). Results showed that significantly more children who participated in bibliotherapy (25.9%) were free of an anxiety disorder than children assigned to the waitlist control condition (6.7%). However, children who received cognitive-behavioral therapy were more likely to be free of their anxiety problems (61.1%) than children assigned to either of the other two groups. Results indicate that bibliotherapy is effective in reducing childhood anxiety; however, cognitive-behavioral therapy is preferable to bibliotherapy as a primary form of treatment.

Quasi-Experimental Studies

In some cases, random assignment is not possible. For example, researchers might want to examine the effectiveness of a new form of therapy to treat adolescents with severe depression and suicidal thoughts. It would be inappropriate to randomly assign youths to a control group that did not receive the best treatment possible. When random assignment is not possible, the research design is said to be quasi-experimental.

Quasi-experimental research cannot be used to infer causal relationships between variables because improvement in symptoms can be attributable to other factors, not the treatment per se. For example, if adolescents with severe depression participate in a new treatment and they show significant symptom alleviation, we might say that the treatment was *associated with* symptom reduction; however, it would be inappropriate to infer that treatment *caused* the adolescents' improvement in functioning.

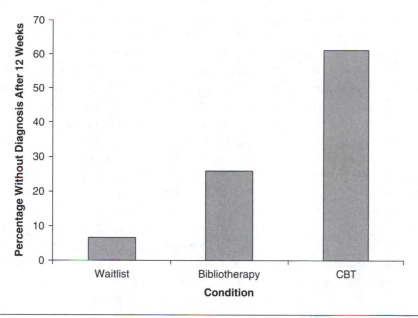

Figure 4.1   A Randomized Controlled Trial of Two Treatments for Childhood
Anxiety

Source: Based on Rapee et al. (2006).

Note: Youths with anxiety disorders were randomly assigned to one of three conditions: (1) waitlist,
(2) bibliotherapy, or (3) cognitive-behavioral therapy (CBT). Results showed that youths responded
best to CBT; however, bibliotherapy was superior to the waitlist control.

The **internal validity** of a research study refers to the degree to which we can
attribute changes in the dependent variable (e.g., symptom reduction) to manipulation of the independent variable (e.g., treatment). When other factors, besides
treatment, can explain symptom reduction, researchers say these factors threaten
the internal validity of the study.

What factors, besides treatment, might cause symptom reduction and threaten
the internal validity of a study? Kazdin (2003) identifies at least five **threats to internal validity** that limit the causal inferences we can make from quasi-experimental
research.

First, maturation can compromise the internal validity of a treatment study.
Maturation refers to changes in the child that occur as a result of the passage of time.
For example, in most adolescents, an episode of major depression lasts approximately two to nine months. Over time, depressive symptoms usually decrease even
if no treatment is provided. Consequently, a researcher who administers a new therapy to adolescents with severe depression over the course of six months might erroneously conclude the treatment is effective if adolescents' symptoms decrease over
time. Unless the researcher compares adolescents who received treatment with
adolescents in a control group, the effects of treatment cannot be distinguished
from maturation.

Second, events in the surrounding environment can threaten the internal validity of research. Events might include major news stories (e.g., terrorist attacks); natural disasters (e.g., hurricanes); changes in family environment or schools (e.g., a new teacher); or more subtle changes in temperature, weather, or the quality of the child's life. For example, a researcher might administer a new treatment for adolescent depression beginning in February and ending in May. The researcher might notice that adolescents' depression scores decrease over the course of treatment. She might erroneously attribute symptom reduction to her treatment. However, environmental changes across the duration of treatment might also be responsible for symptom alleviation. For example, adolescents might experience an improvement in mood simply because of more pleasant weather, greater opportunities for outdoor recreational activities, or anticipation of summer vacation.

A third threat to internal validity is repeated testing. The act of repeatedly assessing children can cause them to show improvement in their functioning over time. For example, a researcher might administer a 10-week treatment program to youths with math difficulties. To assess his treatment, he might ask the children to complete a math achievement test before the intervention, halfway through the treatment, and again upon completion. Children might show improvement in their math scores over time not because they benefited from the intervention but because they were exposed to the same math problems on three different occasions.

Fourth, in quasi-experimental studies, a lack of random assignment can lead to selection biases. Selection biases refer to systematic differences between treatment and control groups that emerge when groups are not randomly assigned at the beginning of the study. Imagine that a researcher investigates the efficacy of a new treatment for depression by recruiting adolescents with depression from hospitals and clinics. She assigns the first 25 adolescents who agree to participate in the study to the treatment group, and she places the remaining 25 adolescents on a waiting list to serve as controls. After 10 weeks of treatment, the researcher notices greater mood improvement among adolescents who received treatment. The researcher cannot attribute these differences to the treatment itself. Instead, selection biases before treatment might account for symptom differences after treatment. For example, the first 25 adolescents who agreed to participate in the study may have been more motivated to participate in treatment than the latter 25 assigned to the control group.

Finally, attrition can threaten the validity of all treatment outcome studies, especially studies that involve quasi-experimental designs. Attrition refers to the loss of participants over the course of the study. Attrition most often occurs because participants decide to withdraw from the study or simply stop attending follow-up appointments. When a large percentage of participants who receive treatment withdraw from a study, researchers may not be able to attribute symptom reduction to treatment. For example, a researcher might notice differences between treatment and control groups following a 10-week trial of a new therapy for depression. However, if 50% of participants assigned to the treatment group withdrew from the study before its completion, the researcher cannot be certain whether the 50% who remained in the study were representative of the treatment group as a whole. It is possible that the 50% who withdrew showed an *increase* in depression, prompting them to drop out.

A recent study illustrates how a lack of random assignment to a control group can threaten internal validity. Walker, Roffman, Stephens, Wakana, and Berghuis (2006) randomly assigned 97 high school students who frequently used marijuana to two conditions. The first group received a brief form of cognitive-behavioral treatment called Motivational Enhancement Therapy (MET). The second group was assigned to a waiting list. After three months, researchers assessed adolescents' marijuana use (see Figure 4.2). Youths who received MET showed significant reduction in marijuana use. However, youths in the control group, who did not receive treatment, showed a similar reduction in marijuana use. The researchers hypothesized that the act of repeatedly asking adolescents about their marijuana use may have caused a decrease in marijuana smoking across both groups. If the researchers had failed to include a control group in their study, they would have only noticed the decrease in marijuana use among adolescents who received MET and would have mistakenly attributed this decrease to the treatment itself.

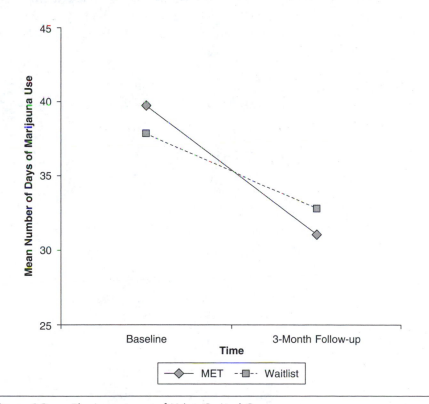

Figure 4.2   The Importance of Using Control Groups

Source: Based on Walker et al. (2006).

Note: Researchers randomly assigned adolescents who frequently used marijuana to one of two conditions: (1) motivational enhancement therapy (MET) or (2) a waiting list. Youths who participated in MET showed a reduction in marijuana use. However, youths assigned to the waiting list also showed a reduction in marijuana use, even though they did not receive treatment.

Single-Subject Studies

A third way to investigate the efficacy of treatment is to conduct a single-subject research study. In a single-subject study, the same individual's behavior is compared before and after treatment. Differences in behavior during or after treatment provide evidence for treatment efficacy. Single-subject studies are sometimes called time-series studies because the same individual's behavior is studied across time (Gaynor, Baird, & Nelson-Gray, 1999).

The simplest way to evaluate treatment effectiveness is to collect data regarding the frequency and/or severity of the child's problematic behavior before and after the intervention. This method is called an **AB design**. The "A" refers to the level of problematic behavior at baseline while the "B" refers to the level of problematic behavior after the intervention. For example, children with autism sometimes engage in high-rate, stereotyped behaviors, such as hand flapping or rocking back and forth, which can be distracting to teachers and classmates. To collect baseline data, a therapist might observe the number of times a child with autism flaps his hands during one hour of class on three consecutive days. Then, he instructs the child's classroom aide to reinforce the child with eye contact and a light touch each minute he keeps his hands in his pockets or on his lap. Finally, he observes the child's behavior in the classroom for another three consecutive days after treatment. A decrease in frequency of the child's hand flapping suggests improvement in functioning (see Figure 4.3).

The chief limitation of the AB design is that it suffers from the same threats to internal validity as quasi-experimental research. Without a control group for

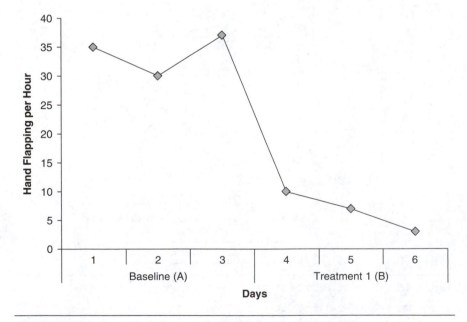

Figure 4.3   AB Single-Subject Research Study

Note: In this study, a child with autism is observed for three days to gather baseline data on the frequency of hand flapping (A). Then, the therapist reinforces the child for keeping his hands at his side (B). The reduction in hand flapping suggests that positive reinforcement is effective to treat this problem.

comparison, clinicians cannot be sure that changes in the child's behavior can be attributed to treatment.

To provide better evidence for a causal relationship between treatment and symptom reduction, many researchers use **ABAB designs**, also called "reversal designs." First, the therapist collects data at baseline and after the intervention, just as in an AB design. Then, she temporarily withdraws treatment and notices any change in the child's behavior (the second "A"). If the intervention is responsible for improvement in the child's behavior, then withdrawal of the intervention should result in the temporary return of the child's behavior problems. Finally, the therapist would reinstate the intervention (the second "B"). If the intervention works, the child's behavior problems should subsequently decrease (see Figure 4.4).

The chief limitation of the ABAB design is that it is sometimes unethical to withdraw treatment. Imagine that a therapist is treating a young child with severe Mental Retardation for head banging; the boy repeatedly bangs his head against the wall when he becomes frustrated, angry, or bored. First, the therapist monitors the rate of the child's head banging at baseline (A). Then, the therapist contingently interrupts the child's head banging by misting him with water from a spray bottle when he begins to engage in the behavior (B). To establish a causal connection between the water mist and the decrease in head banging, the clinician would need to withdraw use of the water mist and observe a subsequent increase in head banging. However, because head banging carries serious risks, withdrawal of treatment is unethical.

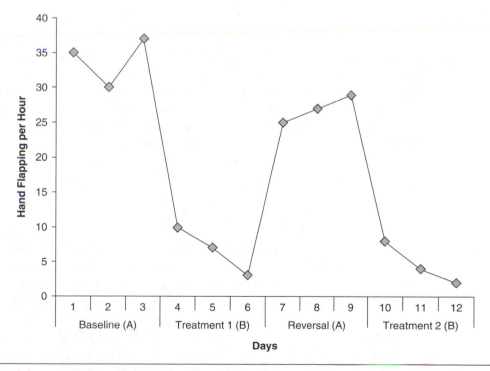

Figure 4.4   ABAB "Reversal" Single-Subject Study

Note: In this study, the therapist collects baseline data on the child's hand flapping (A) and then provides reinforcement contingent on keeping hands at side (B). In the reversal phase (second A), reinforcement is removed, resulting in an increase in hand flapping. Finally, reinforcement is re-applied (second B) to again reduce the behavior.

A third way to examine the effectiveness of treatment is to conduct a **multiple-baseline design**. Here, the therapist identifies two behavior problems and targets them one at a time. For example, a boy with autism might show both hand flapping and rocking in the classroom. First, the therapist collects baseline data regarding the frequency of both behaviors for one hour on three consecutive days (baseline). Then, he targets the child's hand flapping by instructing the classroom aide to reinforce the child for keeping his hands in his pockets. He observes the child for another three days. If the intervention is effective, he should notice a reduction in the child's hand flapping, but not a reduction in the child's rocking. Next, the therapist targets the child's rocking. As the teacher continues to reinforce the child for keeping his hands in his pockets, the therapist instructs the child's classroom aide to reinforce him with a light touch on the shoulders every minute he does not rock. The therapist subsequently observes behavior for an additional three days. If the second intervention is effective, the child should show a reduction in both behavior problems.

The chief limitation of all single-subject research designs is that causal inferences are based on data from only one client. Consequently, it is often unclear whether the results of a single-subject study are applicable to other individuals with similar problems. The **external validity** of a study refers to the degree to which results generalize to other people and situations. To establish the external validity of findings generated from single-subject research, results must be replicated, or repeated with other individuals and in other settings.

Psychotherapy Efficacy

One way to examine the efficacy of child psychotherapy is through meta-analysis. In a **meta-analysis**, researchers combine the results of several studies into a single analysis. To perform a meta-analysis, researchers locate all of the research examining the efficacy of child and adolescent psychotherapy. Each study typically compares at least one group of children who received treatment with another group of children who served as controls. Then, for each study, researchers calculate a numerical value that indicates the difference between the two groups' scores on some measure of functioning after treatment. Many researchers use the following formula:

$$\text{ES} = (M_{\text{treatment group}} - M_{\text{control group}})/SD_{\text{control group}}$$

In this formula, we subtract the mean score for the control group from the mean score for the treatment group to tell us the difference between groups after treatment. Positive scores indicate that the treatment group fared better than the control group after treatment; that is, the therapy worked. Negative scores indicate that the control group fared better than the treatment group; that is, the therapy was harmful.

Next, we take this difference between groups and divide it by the standard deviation of the control group.[3] This tells us how many standard deviations apart the two groups are after treatment. We call this value the **effect size (ES)**.

---

[3] Some researchers divide by the pooled standard deviation for both groups.

Since the ES is in standard units, we can combine the effect sizes of many studies, even if they used different measures to evaluate therapy outcomes. Specifically, we might calculate the average effect size across all studies that have investigated the efficacy of some form of psychotherapy. Most researchers consider effect sizes of 0.20 to be small, 0.50 to be medium, and 0.80 to be large (Cohen, 1988).

Four large meta-analyses have investigated the efficacy of child and adolescent psychotherapy (Casey & Berman, 1985; Kazdin, Bass, Ayers, & Rodgers, 1990; Weisz, Weiss, Alicke, & Klotz, 1987; Weisz, Weiss, Han, Granger, & Morton, 1995). Results of these four meta-analyses are quite consistent. Average effect sizes ranged between .71 and .88 and are considered moderate to large. These average effect sizes are similar to the average effect sizes obtained from studies involving psychotherapy for adults (Shapiro & Shapiro, 1982; Smith & Glass, 1977). These findings suggest that psychotherapy for children and adolescents works, that youngsters who participate in therapy often fare much better than youngsters in control groups, and that the efficacy of child and adolescent therapy is comparable to the efficacy of therapy for adults (see Figure 4.5).

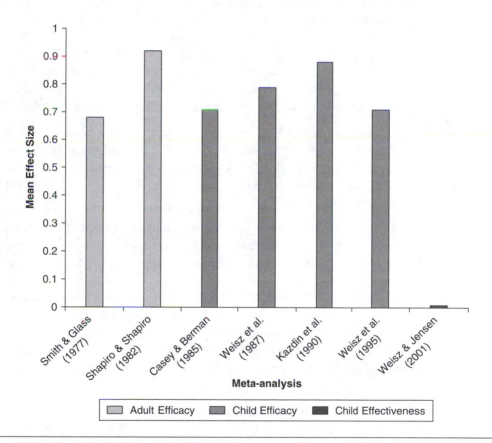

Figure 4.5   Does Psychotherapy Work?

Source: Based on Weisz, Jensen, & McLeod (2005).

Note: Large meta-analyses indicate that adults (light gray) and youths (medium gray) who receive psychotherapy show greater improvement than controls who do not receive therapy. These findings indicate that both adult and child therapy is efficacious. Studies investigating child therapy (dark gray; final bar only) have generally not demonstrated its effectiveness in real-life situations.

What Therapies Work Best?

Although it is encouraging to know that therapy for children and adolescents is efficacious, we probably want to know *which* system of therapy works best. Researchers who examine the efficacy of adult psychotherapy have generally concluded that all forms of therapy are approximately equally effective. No single system of psychotherapy works best under all circumstances (Lambert & Ogles, 2004). Some researchers have referred to this phenomenon as the **dodo verdict** (Parloff, 1984; Rosenzweig, 1936). In *Alice in Wonderland,* Alice watches a race in which each contestant starts in a different position, each races in a different direction, and all contestants win. One of the characters in the book, the dodo bird, concludes, "Everybody has won, and all must have prizes." So, too, in adult psychotherapy, there is little evidence that any form of therapy is superior to any other form of therapy, overall.

Weisz and colleagues (1995) performed a meta-analysis to investigate whether the dodo verdict applied to child and adolescent therapy. Their meta-analysis yielded three important results:

1. Behavioral therapies tended to yield greater effect sizes ($M = 0.76$) than nonbehavioral therapies ($M = 0.35$). Behavioral techniques, such as classical and operant conditioning, modeling, and skills training, yielded more beneficial outcomes than other, nonbehavioral techniques (e.g., psychodynamic treatments).

2. Children's age and gender predicted their response to therapy. Treatment tended to work better for adolescents than for children and was more efficacious for girls than boys. On the other hand, therapy was equally efficacious for both externalizing (e.g., disruptive behavior problems) and internalizing disorders (e.g., depression, anxiety).

3. Children show global and specific improvements in therapy. Previous research with adults showed that therapy often has global effects on clients. Adult clients often experience improvement in a wide range of thoughts, feelings, and behaviors, even if these behaviors were not the focus of therapy. Weisz and colleagues (1995) found that children, like adults, experience some global benefits from participating in therapy. However, the greatest improvement in children's functioning occurs in problem areas specifically targeted for treatment. The average effect size for problems specifically addressed in therapy was 0.60, whereas the average effect size for problems not a focus of treatment was 0.30.

Caveats in Efficacy Research

We might conclude from the results of the meta-analyses that psychotherapy usually improves the well-being of children and adolescents who are referred to treatment. However, we must keep in mind the source of the information used in these meta-analyses (Weisz, Doss, & Hawley, 2005). First, the researchers who conducted these meta-analyses tended to calculate the average effect size across all studies. If the effect sizes were 0.50, 0.70, and 0.90 in three studies, respectively, their average effect size would be 0.70. Calculating the average in this way ignores the number of children in each of the three studies. For example, if there were 100 children in the first study (ES = 0.50), 20 children in the second study (ES = .70), and only 10 students in the last study (ES = 0.90), the average effect size for the three studies, 0.70, would not accurately reflect the overall outcome for children who participated in the studies. Consequently, researchers now tend to weight the effect sizes of studies, assigning greater importance to studies with larger samples. If we look at the overall effect size of child and adolescent psychotherapy using the weighting method, we see that the average effect size is 0.54, much lower than 0.70 (Weisz et al., 1995). We can conclude that the effects of therapy on children and adolescents are probably "moderate" rather than "strong."

Second, the four meta-analyses were performed using only published research studies. Including only published research studies is a reasonable approach because published studies undergo review by experts in the field, ensuring their quality. However, many studies of child therapy are conducted and never published. Might unpublished studies yield a less optimistic picture of the efficacy of therapy? The answer appears to be "yes." McLeod and Weisz (2004) compared the effect sizes of published and unpublished studies of child psychotherapy. Most of the unpublished studies were students' doctoral dissertations. They found that the average effect size for the published studies was 0.63, whereas the average effect size for the unpublished studies was 0.27. This finding suggests that published research probably overestimates the efficacy of child and adolescent psychotherapy. This is probably because editors tend to publish only studies showing significant effects (i.e., publication bias), and students who do not see significant effects in their studies are reluctant to submit them for publication (i.e., called the "file drawer problem" because the researcher puts the manuscript in a file rather than submitting it for publication). If we examined both published and unpublished studies, we would probably see that the efficacy of child and adolescent psychotherapy is lower than previously thought.

Third, and perhaps most important, the meta-analyses reported above examined only psychotherapy efficacy studies. **Efficacy studies** examine the effects of therapy under optimal conditions. They are usually conducted by university-based research teams with well-trained and supervised clinicians administering the treatments. Clinicians tend to use only one form of treatment, which is carefully planned and followed using a therapy manual. Participants in efficacy studies are voluntary; they agree to participate in the research project. Participants are also carefully selected. They are screened to make sure they have the disorder or problem that the researcher is interested in studying, and they typically do not have comorbid disorders.

However, most child and adolescent psychotherapy is not administered under ideal conditions. Typically, therapy is conducted in clinics, hospitals, and schools. Clinicians are usually not trained in any one specific form of therapy; rather, they rely on an array of therapy techniques. Most often, these techniques include active and empathic listening, expressive and interpretive techniques such as play or art therapy, addressing children's or parents' weekly concerns, and providing a warm and responsive therapeutic alliance with the family (Weisz, Jensen, et al., 2005). These approaches tend to be based on the clinician's experience as a therapist.

Clinicians tend to have large caseloads with little time for careful review and preparation. They may also be limited by insurance companies in the number and kinds of therapies they provide. In most clinical settings, clients are not hand selected; clinicians treat almost anyone who seeks help. Furthermore, children and adolescents are often unwilling to participate in treatment; they are brought to therapy by their parents. Finally, clients tend to have multiple, often poorly defined problems that sometimes do not fit neatly into *DSM-IV-TR* diagnostic categories.

Does child and adolescent therapy work in these more ordinary conditions? Little research has been directed to answer this question. A handful of **effectiveness studies** have been conducted, investigating the ability of child and adolescent therapy to improve children's functioning under real-world conditions. The mean effect size for 14 effectiveness studies is $-.001$ (Weisz, Doss et al., 2005). This suggests that there is little evidence that child and adolescent therapy, as it is typically practiced, has any benefits to children and adolescents as a group. Therapy can and does help individual children; however, there is little research supporting its effectiveness overall. Clearly, more effectiveness studies need to be conducted to examine the usefulness of therapy under real-world conditions.

Empirically Supported Treatments

In 1993, the American Psychological Association (APA) organized a task force to identify treatments for psychiatric disorders that have demonstrated efficacy in research studies. The Task Force on Psychological Intervention Guidelines was convened for two reasons. First, members of the task force hoped that if they identified groups of empirically supported treatments, clinicians might have an easier time identifying and using the most efficacious and promising treatments that are available. Second, members of the task force wanted to justify the practice of psychotherapy to insurance companies and show that many forms of psychotherapy are, in fact, supported by empirical data showing that they work.

The APA task force identified a number of empirically supported psychotherapies for adults. These therapies were divided into three categories. **Well-established/ efficacious treatments** showed support from at least two randomized controlled studies demonstrating the therapy's efficacy over a placebo control group or another existing treatment. **Probably efficacious treatments** had empirical support for their efficacy, but only from one randomized controlled trial or a small number of single-subject studies. A third category of treatments, **promising treatments**, demonstrated effectiveness in quasi-experimental studies or one single-subject research study and merited further attention.

In 1998, a second task force provided a similar list of empirically supported therapies for child and adolescent disorders (Lonigan, Elbert, & Johnson, 1998). The task force committees identified treatments for ADHD (Pelham, Wheeler, & Chronis, 1998), child and adolescent conduct problems (Brestan & Eyberg, 1998), autism (Rogers, 1998), child and adolescent depression (Kaslow & Thompson, 1998), and child and adolescent anxiety disorders (Ollendick & King, 1998). Treatments for other disorders commonly experienced by youth, such as eating disorders and substance use disorders, were absent from the list because no empirically supported treatments had been identified that met the committee's criteria.

Since the time of the task force's initial identification of empirically supported treatments for child and adolescent disorders, many individuals and professional organizations have suggested modifications to the group's initial criteria for well-established and probably efficacious treatments (Nathan & Gorman, 2002). Many professionals praise the APA's focus on identifying and disseminating empirically supported treatments for specific disorders. Indeed, the focus on empirically supported treatments emphasizes the scientific basis upon which the practice of psychology is founded.

On the other hand, critics have stressed the dangers of overemphasizing the importance of empirically supported treatments in clinical practice (Beutler, Zetzer, & Williams, 1996). Some researchers have challenged the use of randomized, controlled experiments as a means of establishing the efficacy of treatment. These critics argue that randomized, controlled experiments are most sensitive to detecting short-term symptom reduction rather than long-term changes in personality and functioning; consequently, they are more likely to support short-term behavioral interventions rather than long-term therapies. Furthermore, the criteria for well-established treatments favor studies with high internal validity (i.e., efficacy studies performed in ideal research settings). However, most therapy is practiced under less-than-optimal conditions. Critics argue that the results of efficacy studies may not generalize to real-world practice (Westen, Novotney, & Thompson-Brenner, 2004).

Summary and Conclusions

What can we learn from research on the efficacy and effectiveness of child and adolescent psychotherapy? First, we can say that psychotherapy with children and adolescents is efficacious. Over the past 50 years, researchers have identified a number of therapy techniques that can be used to treat both externalizing and internalizing problems. These interventions produce meaningful improvements in the lives of families who participate in them. Second, for many childhood problems, professionals have limited knowledge of what works. For example, there is yet no consensus on how to treat serious child and adolescent disorders such as Anorexia Nervosa or Alcohol Abuse. Third, although child psychotherapy is efficacious, there is limited evidence for its effectiveness. The few studies examining the effects of child and adolescent therapy in ordinary clinical settings suggest that, on average, therapy yields few benefits. These discouraging findings are probably the result of high therapist workloads, a lack of training in empirically supported interventions, and the complexity and diversity of children's problems encountered in most clinics.

On a more positive note, scientist-practitioners seek to unite the two sometimes disparate factions of clinical child psychology: the researchers who conduct efficacy trials and the clinicians who must meet the mental health needs of families in the community. Some scientist-practitioners, especially those working in university settings, are trying to develop ways to make empirically supported treatments more user-friendly, so that clinicians can access them more easily and make them part of their clinical repertoire. Other scientist-practitioners, especially those working in hospitals, clinics, and schools, are trying to use as many empirically supported interventions as possible in their day-to-day practice, to maximize the effectiveness of their practice. Clearly, much more work needs to be done to bridge the gap between efficacy and effectiveness. However, if clinical psychology is going to remain a viable science in both academic and clinical settings, this bridge must be built.

Ethical Issues in Child and Adolescent Therapy

Clinicians are placed in positions of authority and trust. Clients usually come to therapists in varying states of emotional distress and impairment. Clients are often vulnerable and they need care that is sensitive and responsive to their needs. The provision of competent and ethically mindful services is especially important when clients are juveniles. Parents place their most valuable assets—their children—in the care of therapists, with expectations that clinicians will help their children overcome problems and achieve the highest levels of competence possible.

Ethics refers to the standard of behavior that is determined to be acceptable for a given profession. Ethics should not be confused with a person's morality, that is, his personal beliefs in the rightness or wrongness of a given behavior. Ethical behavior is determined by group consensus; morality is determined by personal determination and belief.

All mental health professionals adhere to a code of ethics that guides their professional practice. Different professional organizations have different ethics codes. These codes include the APA's (2002) *Ethical Principles of Psychologists and Code of Conduct,* the National Association of School Psychologists' *Professional Conduct Manual and Principles for Professional Ethics,* the American Counseling Association's *Code of Ethics,* and the American School Counselor Association's *Ethical Standards for School Counselors.* Because the APA Ethics Code is the most frequently used system, we will examine it in greater detail.

APA Ethics Code

The primary purpose of the APA Ethics Code is to protect the welfare of individuals with whom psychologists work (e.g., clients, research participants, students). The secondary purpose of the Ethics Code is to educate psychologists, students, and the general public about the ethical practice of psychology. Because the Ethics Code is endorsed by the APA, all APA members and student affiliates are required to be familiar with the code and adhere to its rules. Failure to adhere to the Ethics Code can result in sanctions from the APA, psychology licensing boards, and other professional organizations.

The APA Ethics Code consists of four parts: (1) an Introduction, (2) a Preamble, (3) five General Principles, and (4) specific Ethical Standards. The Introduction and Preamble describe the purpose, organization, and scope of the Ethics Code. The five **General Ethical Principles** are broad ideals for the professional behavior of psychologists. The General Principles are aspirational in nature; they are not enforceable rules. Instead, the General Principles describe the highest ideals of psychological practice toward which all psychologists should strive:

A. *Beneficence and Nonmaleficence*
   Psychologists strive to benefit those with whom they work and they take care to do no harm.

B. *Fidelity and Responsibility*
   Psychologists establish relationships of trust, . . . are aware of their professional and scientific responsibilities, . . . uphold professional standards of conduct, clarify their professional roles and obligations, [and] accept appropriate responsibility for their behavior.

C. *Integrity*
   Psychologists seek to promote accuracy, honesty, and truthfulness in science, teaching, and the practice of psychology.

D. *Justice*
   Psychologists recognize that fairness and justice entitle all persons to access to and benefit from the contributions of psychology.

E. *Respect for People's Rights and Dignity*
   Psychologists respect the dignity and worth of all people and the rights of individuals to privacy, confidentiality, and self-determination.

The bulk of the ethics code consists of the **Ethical Standards**: specific rules that guide professional practice. The ethical standards govern all professional activities including assessment, therapy, research, and teaching. Although there are too many Ethical Standards to describe here, we will examine some of the rules that are most relevant to the treatment of children and adolescents.

Competence

The Ethical Standards dictate that psychologists treat, teach, and conduct research only in areas in which they have received appropriate training, supervised experience, or advanced study. Psychologists must be aware of the boundaries of their competence and seek additional training, consultation, or supervision if they want to expand their area of expertise.

> Dr. Williams is a clinical psychologist who has 15 years of experience treating adults and couples with psychological problems, especially alcohol abuse. Dr. Williams decides that he wants to expand his practice in order to include adolescents with substance use problems. Should Dr. Williams accept adolescents into his practice?

Because Dr. Williams has not received specialized training or supervision in the treatment of adolescent substance use disorders, it would likely be unethical for him to offer services to adolescents without first receiving additional training.

Ideally, Dr. Williams would participate in some additional coursework on adolescent substance use disorders and receive supervision from a colleague who has expertise in this area.

Practicing within the boundaries of competence is important because it protects the welfare of children and families. Psychologists who practice outside their areas of training will likely be less effective than therapists who are more knowledgeable and skillful. Therapists who practice outside the boundaries of their competence also risk harming their clients.

Confidentiality

Confidentiality refers to the expectation that information that clients provide during the course of assessment and treatment will not be disclosed to others. The expectation of confidentiality serves at least two purposes. First, the expectation of confidentiality increases the likelihood that people in need of mental health services will seek treatment. Second, the expectation of confidentiality allows clients to disclose information more freely and, consequently, it facilitates the therapeutic process.

In most cases, confidentiality is an ethical and legal right of clients. Therapists who violate a client's right to confidentiality may be sanctioned by professional organizations and held legally liable. Most psychologists consider protection of clients' confidentiality to be one of the most important ethical standards.

Although clients have the right to expect confidentiality when discussing information with their therapists, clients should be aware that the information they disclose is not entirely private. There are certain **limitations to confidentiality** that therapists must make known to clients, preferably during the first therapy session. First, if the client is an imminent danger to self or others, the therapist is required to break confidentiality to protect the welfare of the client or someone he or she threatens. For example, if an adolescent tells his therapist that he plans on killing himself after he leaves the therapy session, the therapist has a duty to warn the adolescent's parents or the police, in order to protect the adolescent from self-harm. The psychologist's duty to protect the health of the adolescent supersedes the adolescent's right to confidentiality.

Second, if the therapist suspects child abuse or neglect, the therapist is usually required to break confidentiality to protect the maltreated child. For example, if during the course of therapy a 12-year-old girl admits to being physically and sexually maltreated by her stepfather, the psychologist would have a duty to inform the girl's mother and the authorities to protect the child from further victimization.

Third, in exceptional circumstances, a judge can issue a court order requiring the therapist to disclose information provided in therapy. For example, a judge might order a psychologist to provide information about an adolescent client who has been arrested for serious criminal activity. Sometimes, information about treatment is necessary for the court proceedings. Court orders to disclose information about treatment are rare; however, psychologists are legally obligated to comply with these orders.

Fourth, therapists can disclose limited information about clients in order to obtain payment for services. For example, therapists often need to provide information about clients to insurance companies. This information typically includes the client's name, demographic information, diagnosis, and a plan for treatment. Usually, insurance companies are the only parties who have access to this information.

Fifth, therapists can disclose limited information about clients to colleagues to obtain consultation or supervision. It is usually acceptable for psychologists to describe clients' problems in general terms in order to gain advice or recommendations from other professionals. However, therapists only provide information to colleagues that is absolutely necessary for them to receive help, and they avoid using names and other identifying information.

In most states, the right to confidentiality is held by children's parents, not by children themselves. From a legal standpoint, parents have the right to the information their children or adolescents disclose in therapy. Consider the following scenario:

> Samantha was a 14-year-old girl who was referred to Dr. Graham because of disruptive behavior problems. During the course of therapy, Samantha admitted that she frequently drinks alcohol, uses marijuana, and recently began experimenting with prescription pain medications she obtains from friends. Although Dr. Graham was concerned with Samantha's substance use, she decided not to disclose the information to Samantha's parents. Weeks later, Samantha's father called Dr. Graham and demanded to see her therapy notes regarding Samantha. Samantha's father suspected that Samantha was using drugs and wanted information from the therapist about his daughter's substance use.

Dr. Graham needs to balance the father's legal right to receive information about his daughter's treatment with Dr. Graham's ethical obligation to protect Samantha's confidentiality. The APA Ethics Code states that when a psychologist's ethical responsibilities conflict with the law, the psychologist should make known her commitment to the Ethics Code and take steps to resolve the conflict in a responsible manner. In this case, Dr. Graham might consult with a colleague to gain another professional's opinion. Then, she might explain to Samantha's father that disclosing therapy notes would likely violate Samantha's trust and destroy the quality of the therapeutic relationship. If Samantha's father still insists on receiving the information, Dr. Graham might try to reach a compromise between Samantha and her parents. For example, perhaps Samantha could disclose the information to her parents directly, with the therapist facilitating communication between the two parties.

Of course, the best way to deal with a situation like the one described above is to prevent it. Therapists usually discuss the limitations of confidentiality with youths and their parents, to clarify under what circumstances information will be shared with parents. Ideally, parents and children reach a confidentiality agreement during the first session. Sometimes, therapists create a written contract to avoid ambiguity and prevent future problems.

Informed Consent

Psychologists must obtain informed consent from individuals before they engage in assessment, treatment, or research. Informed consent protects people's right to self-determination. Individuals are entitled to make voluntary and knowledgeable decisions.

Informed consent to therapy includes a number of components. First, individuals are entitled to a description of treatment, its anticipated risks and benefits, and an estimate of its duration and cost. Second, the psychologist must discuss alternative treatments that might be available and review the strengths and weaknesses of the recommended treatment approach. Third, psychologists must remind clients that participation is voluntary and that they are free to refuse treatment or withdraw from therapy at any time. Finally, psychologists should review the limits of confidentiality with their clients.

Children and adolescents, by virtue of their age and legal status as minors, are not capable of providing consent. Consent implies that individuals both understand and freely agree to participate. Young children may not fully appreciate the risks and benefits of participation in treatment. Older children and adolescents may not freely agree to participate because they may be pressured by others (e.g., the psychologist, school personnel) to attend treatment. Instead, consent is obtained from parents or legal guardians. Psychologists are required to obtain the **assent** of children and adolescents before providing services. To obtain assent, psychologists typically describe the treatment or research using language that youth can understand. Then, psychologists provide opportunities for children to ask questions and ask children for their permission to participate.

Multiple Relationships

Psychologists must avoid multiple relationships. A multiple relationship occurs when a psychologist, who is in a professional role with a client, enters into another relationship with the same individual or a person closely associated with that individual. Multiple relationships can impair psychologists' objectivity, competence, and the effectiveness of the services that they provide. Consider the following scenario:

Dr. Jacoby is a respected psychologist at a child guidance clinic. Her neighbor, and good friend, asks her to provide therapy for her adolescent daughter, Mariah. Mariah has recently been exhibiting problems with anxiety and depression. Dr. Jacoby agrees to treat Mariah and, consequently, enters into a multiple relationship. Mariah is both Dr. Jacoby's client and the daughter of Dr. Jacoby's good friend. During the course of therapy, Mariah tells Dr. Jacoby that she is pregnant and does not want to tell her mother. Dr. Jacoby's objectivity might be compromised because of her dual relationship. Although the needs of her client should be paramount, she might sacrifice Mariah's expectation for confidentiality to maintain her friendship with Mariah's mother.

A related ethical issue is therapists' **duty to clarify their professional roles**. When psychologists provide services to multiple people who have a relationship with one another, they must clarify their relationship with each of these individuals.

Imagine that a mother and her adolescent daughter seek therapy because they frequently argue. At the onset of therapy, the therapist must clarify her relationship with both mother and daughter. One solution is that all parties agree that the clinician will assume the role of primary therapist for the daughter. Although the clinician might occasionally meet with mother and daughter together, the clinician's primary responsibility might be the interests of the daughter. If the mother seeks help with specific problems (e.g., depression), the clinician might refer her to another therapist. An alternative solution is that all parties agree that the parent-adolescent dyad will be the primary focus of therapy. In this case, the therapist might propose that mother and daughter always meet together for therapy sessions and that the therapist will not meet with either person alone.

Psychologists must carefully identify their relationship with all family members to avoid conflicting roles. When roles are unclear, family members can become estranged from the therapeutic process or feel like their trust has been violated by the therapist.

Critical Thinking Exercises

1. Maddy is a 14-year-old girl who is experiencing depression following the death of her father. How might her counselor use (a) behavior therapy, (b) cognitive therapy, and (c) interpersonal therapy to help Maddy?

2. Compare and contrast psychotherapy for adults with psychotherapy for children and adolescents. How is child and adolescent therapy particularly challenging?

3. When physicians want to show that a new medication is efficacious for treating a medical disorder, they compare the new medication to a placebo. Why? How might a psychologist use a placebo to investigate the efficacy of a new psychotherapy?

4. Child and adolescent psychotherapy has been shown to be efficacious; however, data supporting its effectiveness is limited. Why?

5. Dr. Maeryn, a child psychologist, promises her adolescent client, "It's important for you to be open and honest in therapy. Everything you say will be kept a secret and never shared with anyone else." What is problematic about Dr. Maeryn's statement?

CHAPTER 5

Mental Retardation and Intellectual Disabilities

Dontrell

Dontrell was a five-year-old African American boy referred to our clinic by his pediatrician. Dontrell showed delays in understanding language, speaking, and performing daily tasks. His mother had used alcohol and other drugs during pregnancy. She did not receive prenatal care because she was afraid that an obstetrician would report her drug use to the police. Dontrell was born with various drugs in his system and had respiratory and cardiovascular problems at birth. Shortly after delivery, Dontrell's mother disappeared, leaving him in his grandmother's care.

Dontrell was slow to reach many developmental milestones. Whereas most children learn to sit up by age six months and walk by their first birthday, Dontrell showed delays mastering each of these developmental tasks. Most striking were Dontrell's marked delays in language. Although he could understand and obey simple commands, he was able to speak only 15–20 words and many of these were difficult to understand. He could not identify colors, was unable to recite the alphabet, and could not count. He also had considerable problems performing day-to-day tasks typical of children his age. For example, he could not dress himself, wash his face, brush his teeth, or eat with utensils.

Dontrell also showed significant problems with his behavior. First, he was hyperactive and inattentive. Second, Dontrell showed serious problems with defiance and aggression. When he did not get his way, he would tantrum and throw objects. He would also hit, kick, and bite other children and adults when he became upset. Third, Dontrell's grandmother said that he had "an obsession for food." Dontrell apparently had an insatiable appetite and was even caught hoarding food under his bed and stealing food from relatives.

Dr. Valencia, the psychologist who performed the evaluation, was most struck by Dontrell's appearance. Although only five years old, Dontrell weighed approximately 100 lbs. He approached Dr. Valencia with a scowl and icy stare. Dr. Valencia extended her hand and said, "Hello." Dontrell grabbed Dr. Valencia's hand and kissed it! His grandmother quickly apologized, responding, "Sorry . . . he does that sometimes. He's showing that he likes you."

What Is Mental Retardation?

If you were asked to imagine a child with Mental Retardation, what picture would come to your mind? You might imagine a boy with very low intelligence. He might speak using simple sentences, or he might be unable to speak at all. Maybe he looks different from other boys: he has a flatter face, lower-set ears, a protruding tongue, and short stature. He might be clumsy, walk in an awkward manner, or need a wheelchair to move about. He might not interact much with other children, and when he does, he might appear unusual or act inappropriately. In school, he might have a classroom aide to help him, but he still might have trouble reading sentences, learning addition and subtraction, and writing. He might be friendly but still seem "different" from most other boys his age.

For most people, our image of children with Mental Retardation is formed by our personal experiences. We might have attended school with children who had Mental Retardation, tutored children with developmental delays, volunteered for the Special Olympics or other recreational programs for youths with disabilities, or seen children with Mental Retardation at the mall, where we work, or elsewhere in the community.

Although our image of Mental Retardation, generated from these experiences, might be accurate, it is probably not complete. Mental Retardation is a term that describes an extremely diverse group of people. They range from children with severe developmental disabilities who need constant care to youths with only mild delays who are usually indistinguishable from others (Hodapp, Zakemi, Rosner, & Dykens, 2006).

DSM-IV-TR Definition of Mental Retardation

Diagnostic Criteria

According to the *DSM-IV-TR*, Mental Retardation is characterized by significantly subaverage intellectual functioning, significant limitations in adaptive functioning, and symptom onset before age 18 years (see Table 5.1).

First, all individuals with Mental Retardation must show significantly low **intellectual functioning**. These individuals show problems perceiving and processing new information, learning quickly and efficiently, applying knowledge and skills to solve novel problems, thinking creatively and flexibly, and responding rapidly and accurately. In children and adults, intelligence is measured using a standardized, individually administered intelligence test. IQ scores are normally distributed with a mean of 100 and a standard deviation of 15. IQ scores approximately two standard deviations below the mean (i.e., IQ < 70) can indicate significant deficits in intellectual functioning. IQ scores less than 70 are seen in approximately 2.5% of the population (Durand & Christodulu, 2006).

Second, individuals with Mental Retardation show significant deficits in **adaptive functioning**. According to the *DSM-IV-TR*, adaptive functioning refers to "how

Table 5.1 Diagnostic Criteria for Mental Retardation

A. Significantly subaverage intellectual functioning: An IQ of approximately 70 or below on an individually administered IQ test (or for infants, a clinical judgment of significantly subaverage intellectual functioning)

B. Deficits or impairments in adaptive functioning (i.e., the person's effectiveness in meeting the standards expected for his or her age by his or her cultural group) in at least two of the following areas:

  1. Communication

  2. Self-care

  3. Home living

  4. Social/interpersonal skills

  5. Use of community resources

  6. Self-direction

  7. Functional academic skills

  8. Work

  9. Leisure

  10. Health

  11. Safety

C. Onset is before age 18 years

Type of Mental Retardation reflects level of intellectual impairment:

Mild Mental Retardation	IQ level 50–55 to approximately 70
Moderate Mental Retardation	IQ level 35–40 to 50–55
Severe Mental Retardation	IQ level 20–25 to 35–40
Profound Mental Retardation	IQ level below 20 or 25
Mental Retardation, severity unspecified	Strong presumption of Mental Retardation, but person's intelligence is untestable by standard tests

Source: Reprinted with permission from the *DSM-IV-TR*.

effectively individuals cope with common life demands and how well they meet the standards of personal independence expected of someone in their particular age group, sociocultural background, and community setting" (p. 42). Whereas intellectual functioning refers to people's ability to learn information and solve problems, adaptive functioning refers to their typical level of success in meeting the day-to-day demands of society in an age-appropriate manner. *DSM-IV-TR* specifies 11 areas of adaptive functioning: communication (understanding others, speaking), self-care (dressing, bathing), home living (cleaning, cooking), social/interpersonal skills (interacting with family, making friends), use of community resources (going to the library, shopping), self-direction (determining daily activities), functional academic skills (reading, writing, arithmetic skills), work (going to work on time, performing job correctly), leisure (taking interest in a hobby), health (proper nutrition), and safety (avoiding dangerous situations).

Adaptive functioning can be assessed by interviewing caregivers about children's usual behavior and comparing their reports to the behavior of typically developing children of the same age and cultural group. Often, psychologists administer a norm-referenced interview or rating scale to caregivers to collect information about children's functioning. These instruments provide standard scores much like IQ scores, which indicate children's adaptive functioning relative to their peers. Scores more than two standard deviations below the mean (i.e., < 70) on two or more domains could indicate significant impairment in adaptive functioning (Durand & Christodulu, 2006).

Finally, all individuals with Mental Retardation show limitations in intellectual and adaptive functioning early in life. Although some people are not identified as having Mental Retardation until they are adults, they must have histories of intellectual and daily living problems stemming from childhood. *DSM-IV-TR* specifies that onset must be before age 18 years. This requirement differentiates Mental Retardation from other disorders marked by cognitive problems, such as Alzheimer's Disease.

It is important to keep in mind that Mental Retardation is characterized by low intellectual functioning *and* problems in adaptive behavior. Many people believe that Mental Retardation is determined solely by IQ; however, deficits in adaptive functioning are equally necessary for the diagnosis. A child with an IQ of 65 but with no problems in adaptive functioning would not be diagnosed with Mental Retardation.

Subtypes of Mental Retardation

Mild Mental Retardation (IQ: 55–70)

As infants and toddlers, children with mild Mental Retardation usually appear no different than other children (Jacobson & Mulick, 1996). They achieve most developmental milestones at expected ages, learn basic language, and interact with family members and peers. Their intellectual deficits are usually first identified when they begin school. Teachers may notice that they require more time and practice to master academic skills, such as letter and number recognition, reading, and math. As they progress in school and their schoolwork becomes more challenging, these children fall further behind and may repeat a grade. Some children grow frustrated with traditional education and display behavior problems in class. By middle school, these children master basic reading and math but seldom make further academic progress. After school, they typically blend back into society, perform semiskilled jobs, and live independently in the community. They usually require only occasional support from others to overcome their intellectual deficits. For example, they may need help completing a job application, filing a tax return, or managing their finances.

Moderate Mental Retardation (IQ: 40–55)

Children with moderate Mental Retardation often show signs of their intellectual impairments as infants or toddlers (Jacobson & Mulick, 1996). Their motor skills usually develop in a typical fashion, but parents often notice delays in learning to speak and interacting with others. These children often seem less interested in their surroundings compared to their age mates. They are often first identified as having Mental Retardation as toddlers or preschoolers, when they show little or no language development. Instead, they rely mostly on gestures and single word utterances. By the time they begin school, these children usually speak in short, simple phrases and show self-care skills similar to typically developing toddlers. However, they display problems mastering basic reading, writing, and mathematics. By adolescence, these children are able to communicate effectively with others, have basic self-care skills, and have simple reading and writing abilities. They may continue to have trouble with reading a newspaper, performing arithmetic, or handling money. As adults, some may perform unskilled jobs if they are given training and supervision. They usually live with family members or in residential care facilities.

Severe Mental Retardation (IQ: 25–40)

Children with severe Mental Retardation are usually first identified in infancy (Jacobson & Mulick, 1996). They almost always show early delays in basic developmental milestones such as sitting up and walking. They also usually show one or more biological anomalies that are indicative of a genetic or medical disorder. These children often have health problems, are at risk for long-term motor disorders, or have seizures. They require ample supervision from parents and caregivers. By the time they begin school, they may be able to move on their own and perform some basic self-care skills such as feeding, dressing, and using the toilet. They may communicate using single words and gestures. As adults, their speech continues to be limited and difficult to understand, although their ability to understand others is often better developed. They are usually unable to read or write, but they may be able to perform simple daily living tasks under close supervision. They typically live with family or in residential care.

Profound Mental Retardation (IQ: <25)

Children with profound Mental Retardation are first identified in infancy (Jacobson & Mulick, 1996). They almost always show multiple biological anomalies and health problems indicative of neurological damage. By the time they reach school age, their skills are similar to those of typically developing one-year-olds. They may be able to sit up, imitate sounds, understand simple commands, and recognize familiar people. About half of the children with profound Mental Retardation will continue to require help from others throughout their lives. The other half will show slow development of adaptive skills. They may learn to walk, develop some communication skills, and be able to perform some self-care activities. As adults, they usually continue to require constant support and supervision from family and caregivers. They may also show chronic medical problems and sensory impairments.

Remember that the diagnosis of Mental Retardation is determined solely by the child's intelligence and adaptive functioning. Two people can show Mental Retardation but look and act very differently. For example, one person might be a child with Down syndrome. Another child with the same IQ might have acquired Mental Retardation after injuring her head in a bicycle accident. The label Mental

Retardation tells us only about a person's general intellectual and adaptive functioning; the diagnosis says nothing about etiology, symptoms, course, or outcomes (Baumeister & Bacharach, 2000).

The AAIDD Definition of Mental Retardation

The American Association on Intellectual and Developmental Disabilities (AAIDD),[4] an organization of professionals and laypersons who study, assist, and advocate for individuals with Mental Retardation, have rejected the classification system of the *DSM-IV-TR*. The AAIDD claims that categorizing individuals into mild, moderate, severe, and profound subtypes ignores the heterogeneity of individuals within each classification, is not helpful in planning treatment, and generally overlooks the person's strengths.

Instead of classifying individuals based on level of intellectual and adaptive impairment, members of the AAIDD describe individuals with Mental Retardation based on **needed supports** (Luckasson et al., 2002). Supports refer to a broad array of assistance that helps the individual function effectively in society. Supports can be formal assistance provided by health care providers, mental health professionals, teachers, educational specialists, professional caregivers, or human service agencies. Supports can also refer to informal help from parents, friends, or members of the community. The AAIDD designates four possible levels of supports, based on how much and how long assistance is needed: intermittent (i.e., occasional, in time of crisis), limited (i.e., short-term), extensive (i.e., long-term), and pervasive (i.e., constant).

Rather than categorize clients into mild, moderate, severe, and profound subtypes, the AAIDD recommends that professionals describe individuals' need for supports in at least nine areas of functioning. For example, a child with Mental Retardation might be described as needing "extensive" educational support, such as a full-time classroom aide, for all academic activities, but only "intermittent" support in areas of social functioning, such as one-time training to help him learn to make friends.

The AAIDD's approach to classifying individuals with Mental Retardation in terms of needed supports has two main advantages. First, this approach conveys more information about clients than simply classifying them into mild, moderate, severe, or profound subtypes. Second, it focuses on clients' abilities rather than on their impairments. The main drawback to the AAIDD approach is that it is complex. Describing clients on so many dimensions of functioning is cumbersome and can hinder communication among professionals. The AAIDD approach can also make research difficult; with so many combinations of needed supports and areas of functioning, it is difficult to identify homogenous groups of individuals for study. For these reasons, most clinicians and researchers rely on the *DSM-IV-TR* classification system.

---

[4] The AAIDD was formerly called the American Association on Mental Retardation.

Associated Characteristics

Stereotypies

Some children with mental retardation show stereotypies, behaviors that are performed in a consistent, rigid, and repetitive manner and that have no immediate, practical significance (Carcani-Rathwell, Rabe-Hasketh, & Santosh, 2006). Stereotypies often involve repeated movements of the hands, arms, or upper body. For example, some children flap their hands, repeatedly move their fingers, twirl, fidget with objects, or rock back and forth. The prevalence of stereotypies is related to the severity of children's intellectual impairments. For example, approximately 2% of children with mild Mental Retardation show stereotypies, compared to approximately 10% of children with profound Mental Retardation (Mink & Mandelbaum, 2006).

Self-Injurious Behaviors

Self-injurious behaviors (SIBs) usually involve repetitive movements of the hands, limbs, or head in a manner that can, or does, cause physical harm or damage to the person. Examples of SIBs include head banging, self-hitting, self-biting, hair pulling, severe skin picking, eye gouging, pica (eating inedible substances such as dirt), and chronic rumination (regurgitating food in the throat). Head banging and self-biting are the two most common SIBs (Kahng, Iwata, & Lewin, 2002). SIBs are problematic not only because they can cause physical injury, but also because they limit individuals' access to many activities, such as educational experiences and outings in the community (Kahng et al., 2002).

SIBs usually occur in episodes or "bouts," often occurring many times each day. Children with SIBs usually show the same behaviors in each episode. In some children, episodes only last for a few seconds. These episodes are usually triggered by the environment, such as when a child with Mental Retardation is reprimanded by a caregiver. In other children, episodes last for minutes or hours, more or less continuously. During these episodes, the child may not eat or sleep. Although these episodes may be triggered by environmental events, they are usually maintained over time by neurochemical or other biological factors (Holden & Gitlesen, 2006; Thompson & Caruso, 2002).

Approximately 5% to 16% of individuals with Mental Retardation show SIBs (Rojahn & Esbensen, 2002; Thompson & Caruso, 2002). In one of the largest studies to date, involving more than 130,000 people with Mental Retardation, researchers found the prevalence of SIBs to be approximately 8% of individuals with Mental Retardation. The prevalence of SIBs, like stereotypies, is directly related to the severity of children's intellectual and adaptive impairments. SIBs are most commonly seen in children with severe and profound Mental Retardation, children in institutional settings, and children with known neurodevelopmental disorders such as autism (Thompson & Caruso, 2002).

There are at least three possible explanations for SIBs in children with Mental Retardation (Thompson & Caruso, 2002). One explanation is that children show SIBs because these behaviors serve a certain purpose or function. Carr, Levin, McConnachie, Carlson, Kemp, and Smith (1994) have suggested that individuals engage in SIBs when they lack communication or social skills to effectively interact with others. Head banging may be a way of communicating "I don't like this!" or "I'm bored!" To test this hypothesis, Hanley, Iwata, and McCord (2003) reviewed 536 cases of self-injurious or problematic behavior among people with Mental Retardation. In 95.9% of cases, the SIBs served some identifiable purpose. These purposes included (1) gaining attention, food, or specific items; (2) escaping a chore, activity, or social interaction that they disliked; (3) providing stimulation or enjoyment; or (4) some combination of these three functions (see Figure 5.1).

A second explanation is that SIBs are caused by a hypersensitivity to the neurotransmitter dopamine. Three bodies of evidence support this hypothesis. First, destroying dopamine receptors in the brains of neonatal rats causes them to develop a hypersensitivity to dopamine. If these rats are then injected with drugs that activate dopamine in the brain (e.g., dopamine agonists like amphetamine or

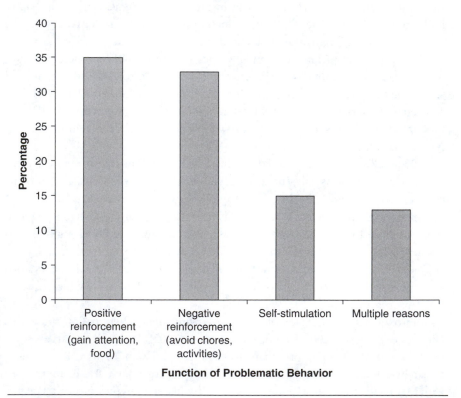

Figure 5.1   Functions of Self-Injurious and Problematic Behavior Shown by People With Mental Retardation

Source: Based on Hanley et al. (2003).

Note: More than 95% of cases of problematic behavior have some identifiable function, usually maintained by positive or negative reinforcement.

cocaine), they display severe self-injury. Second, healthy rats given chronic high dosages of dopamine agonists also show self-injury. Third, some antipsychotic drugs, which bind to dopamine receptors, decrease SIBs in humans.

A third possibility is that SIBs are maintained by high levels of endogenous opioids (i.e., endorphins; Schroeder et al., 2001). These naturally occurring chemicals bind to certain receptors in the brain and produce analgesia and feelings of pleasure. Children and adults who show SIBs may be better able to tolerate the pain associated with these behaviors because of these analgesic properties. Some individuals who show SIBs may actually derive pleasure from self-injury.

Evidence for the endorphin hypothesis comes from three sources. First, people with Mental Retardation who show SIBs display a dramatic increase in endorphins immediately after engaging in self-harm; this increase in naturally occurring opioids is much faster than in individuals who do not show SIBs (Sandman, Hetrick, & Taylor, 1997). Second, many people with Mental Retardation and SIBs have abnormalities in the functioning of opioid receptors and levels in their brains (Sandman, Spence, & Smith, 1999). Third, some studies indicate that SIBs can be reduced by administering drugs that block opioid receptors (i.e., opioid antagonists; Thompson & Caruso, 2002).

Comorbid Mental Health Problems

The term **dual diagnosis** refers to the presence of mental disorders among individuals with Mental Retardation. Until recently, many mental health professionals believed that people with Mental Retardation could not suffer from other psychiatric disorders. Some experts believed that low intellectual functioning somehow immunized these individuals against depression, anxiety, and psychological distress. Other professionals simply did not differentiate Mental Retardation from other mental illnesses. Gradually, professionals became aware that people with Mental Retardation could suffer from the full range of psychiatric disorders. In fact, the prevalence of psychopathology among individuals with Mental Retardation may be four to five times greater than the prevalence of mental disorders in the general population (Brereton, Tonge, & Einfeld, 2006; Wallander, Dekker, & Koot, 2006).

The exact prevalence of psychiatric disorders among individuals with Mental Retardation is unknown because their behavioral and emotional problems are often overlooked. **Diagnostic overshadowing** refers to the tendency of clinicians to attend to the features of Mental Retardation rather than to the symptoms of co-existing mental disorders. Why might clinicians miss anxiety, depression, and even psychotic symptoms in people with Mental Retardation? Some mental health professionals simply do not have much experience in assessing and treating people with intellectual disabilities. Others erroneously attribute psychiatric problems to the person's low intelligence or problems in adaptive functioning. Diagnostic overshadowing in individuals with Mental Retardation is ironic because *DSM-IV-TR* places Mental Retardation on Axis II so that clinicians will not overlook it in the diagnostic process. Instead, Mental Retardation often causes clinicians to overlook the presence of Axis I disorders (Einfeld et al., 2006; Koskentausta, Iivanainen, & Almqvist, 2007).

Epidemiology

Prevalence

Experts disagree about the prevalence of Mental Retardation. If we assume that IQ scores are normally distributed in the population, we would expect approximately 2.5% of individuals in the general population to earn IQ scores less than 70. Consequently, some people estimate the prevalence of Mental Retardation to be between 2.5% and 3% of the general population (Hodapp et al., 2006).

Other experts argue that the prevalence of Mental Retardation is lower, perhaps as low as 1% or 2% (*DSM-IV-TR*). There are several reasons for these low estimates. First, Mental Retardation is not determined by the individual's IQ score alone; the diagnosis also requires impairment in adaptive functioning. Many people with IQ scores in the 55–70 range do not show significant deficits in adaptive functioning. Consequently, they are not diagnosed with Mental Retardation.

Second, a person's IQ can fluctuate over time. Although IQ scores are quite stable for people with severe and profound Mental Retardation, IQs are less stable for individuals scoring on the higher end of the Mental Retardation continuum (i.e., IQ 55–70). Someone might earn an IQ score below 70 when assessed as a child but earn a score slightly above 70 in adolescence. Consequently, he or she would no longer qualify for the diagnosis (Keogh, Bernheimer, & Guthrie, 1997).

Third, the life expectancy of individuals with severe and profound Mental Retardation is less than the life expectancy of typically developing individuals. Severe and profound Mental Retardation is often associated with serious health problems that reduce longevity.

Age and Gender

The prevalence of Mental Retardation varies by age. Specifically, Mental Retardation is more frequently diagnosed among school-age children and adolescents than among adults (Hodapp & Dykens, 2006). If all the people in a town are screened for Mental Retardation, the prevalence is approximately 1.25% (McLaren & Bryson, 1987); if only school-age children are assessed, the prevalence increases to 2.5% (National Center for Educational Statistics, 2003). Why are more school-age children classified as having Mental Retardation than people in the general population? The answer seems to be that the cognitive impairments associated with Mental Retardation are more noticeable when people are in school. After a person leaves school, these impairments are less noticeable and less likely to be diagnosed.

Mental Retardation is slightly more common in males than in females. The gender ratio is approximately 1.3:1. Experts disagree why males are more likely to show Mental Retardation than females. Some people believe the male central nervous system is more susceptible to damage. Others believe that males are more likely to show Mental Retardation than females because some forms of Mental Retardation are caused by abnormalities on the X chromosome. Because boys have only one X chromosome, they may be more susceptible to disabilities caused by damage to this chromosome (Hodapp et al., 2006; Stromme & Hagberg, 2000).

Etiology

Organic Versus Cultural-Familial Mental Retardation

Edward Zigler (1969) attempted to classify children with Mental Retardation based on the causes of their impairments. Specifically, Zigler divided children with Mental Retardation into two groups. The first group consisted of children with identifiable causes for Mental Retardation. He classified these children with **organic Mental Retardation** because most of the known causes of Mental Retardation at that time involved genetic disorders or biological abnormalities, such as Down syndrome. As a group, children with organic Mental Retardation had IQ scores less than 50, physical features indicating neurological problems, and medical complications associated with the disorder. Children with organic Mental Retardation usually had parents and siblings with normal intellectual functioning and came from families of all socioeconomic backgrounds.

Children in the second group showed no clear cause for their cognitive and adaptive impairments. They tended to earn IQ scores in the 50 to 70 range, had normal physical appearances, and showed no other health or medical problems. They were more likely to have parents, siblings, and other biological relatives with low intellectual functioning or Mental Retardation. Furthermore, they often came from low-income families. Zigler referred to individuals in this second group as experiencing "familial" Mental Retardation because children and family members often had low levels of intellectual and adaptive functioning. Today, many experts refer to people in this category as experiencing **cultural-familial Mental Retardation** because children in this group are believed to experience Mental Retardation due to a combination of environmental deprivation (e.g., low levels of cognitive stimulation, poor schools) and genetic diathesis toward low intelligence.

The terms "organic" and "cultural-familial" can be misleading. A child with organic Mental Retardation does not necessarily have a genetic cause for his impairments. Similarly, the deficits shown by a child with familial Mental Retardation are not necessarily caused by environmental factors. The organic/familial distinction is based solely on whether we can identify the cause of the child's Mental Retardation. Some causes of organic Mental Retardation are environmental factors, such as mothers' consumption of alcohol during pregnancy or a child's ingestion of lead. Similarly, some types of familial Mental Retardation may be due to genetic anomalies that we have not yet identified. For example, the cause of fragile X syndrome, the second most common genetic cause of Mental Retardation, was not identified until 1991. Even today, as many as 80% of people with fragile X do not know they have the disorder (Dykens, Hodapp, & Finucane, 2000). As genetic and medical research progresses, it is likely that more causes of Mental Retardation will be uncovered (Hodapp et al., 2006).

Similar Sequence and Similar Structures

Typically developing children progress through a series of cognitive stages in a reliable order across their development. Infants learn to represent people in their minds and engage in pretend play, preschoolers show mastery of language, school-age children develop knowledge of conservation and concrete problem solving, and adolescents show higher-level abstract thinking. Zigler (1969) suggested that the sequence of cognitive development among children with Mental Retardation is similar to the sequence of cognitive development seen in typically developing children. His **similar sequence hypothesis** posits that children with Mental Retardation progress through the same cognitive stages as typically developing children, albeit at a slower pace.

Zigler (1969) also suggested that the cognitive structures of children with Mental Retardation are similar to the cognitive structures of typically developing children of the same mental age. His **similar structure hypothesis** indicates that two children of the same mental age (one with Mental Retardation and the other without Mental Retardation) will show similar abilities. According to the similar structure hypothesis, a 16-year-old with Mental Retardation whose intellectual functioning resembles that of a five-year-old child should show the same pattern of cognitive abilities as a typically developing five-year-old child.

Subsequent research on children with cultural-familial Mental Retardation has generally supported the similar sequence and similar structure hypotheses. Children with cultural-familial Mental Retardation show the expected sequence of cognitive development, although they reach stages at a slower rate than typically developing children (Zigler, Balla, & Hodapp, 1986). Furthermore, children with cultural-familial Mental Retardation generally show similar cognitive abilities as children without Mental Retardation of the same developmental age (Weisz, 1990).

Subsequent research involving children with organic Mental Retardation has yielded mixed results. The cognitive development of children with organic Mental Retardation does follow an expected sequence, similar to the development of typically developing children. However, children with organic Mental Retardation often show different cognitive abilities than typically developing children of the same mental age. Specifically, children with organic Mental Retardation often show characteristic strengths and weaknesses in their cognitive abilities; their cognitive abilities are not uniformly low. Furthermore, these cognitive strengths and weaknesses depend on the cause of the child's Mental Retardation. For example, children with Down syndrome often show one pattern of cognitive abilities, whereas children with fragile X syndrome show different cognitive profiles.

Behavioral Phenotypes

The finding that children with different types of organic Mental Retardation show characteristic patterns of cognitive abilities is important. If scientists could identify the cognitive and behavioral characteristics associated with each known cause for Mental Retardation, this information could be used to plan children's education and improve their adaptive functioning (Hodapp & DesJardin, 2002).

Gradually, researchers have moved away from lumping all children with known causes of Mental Retardation into one large "organic" category. Instead, researchers are beginning to study children with specific causes of Mental Retardation in separate groups, in order to better understand the strengths and weaknesses associated with each disorder. For example, some researchers study the abilities of children with Down syndrome while others focus their attention on understanding the strengths and weaknesses of children with fragile X syndrome (Hodapp et al., 2006).

Stated another way, researchers are interested in determining a **behavioral phenotype** for children with each known cause of Mental Retardation. According to Dykens (1995), a behavioral phenotype involves "the heightened probability or likelihood that people with a given syndrome will exhibit certain behavioral or developmental sequelae relative to those without the syndrome" (p. 523). Behavioral phenotypes include the appearance, overall intellectual and adaptive functioning, cognitive strengths and weaknesses, co-occurring psychiatric disorders, medical complications, and developmental outcomes of children with specific causes for their Mental Retardation. Behavioral phenotypes are probabilistic. Although not every child will show all of the features associated with the disorder, a general description might help organize and guide research and assist practitioners in developing empirically based interventions (Dykens, 2001; Hodapp & DesJardin, 2002). In the next section, we examine some of these known causes of organic Mental Retardation and the characteristic abilities and behaviors shown by children with each disorder.

Known Causes of Mental Retardation

More than 750 different causes of Mental Retardation have been identified. They can be loosely organized into five general categories: (1) chromosomal abnormalities, (2) genetic metabolic disorders, (3) embryonic teratogen exposure, (4) complications during delivery, and (5) childhood illness or injury.

Chromosomal Abnormalities

Down Syndrome. Down syndrome is a genetic disorder characterized by moderate to severe Mental Retardation, problems with language and academic functioning, and characteristic physical features. The disorder was first described by John Langdon Down in 1866. It occurs in approximately 1 per 1,000 live births. The likelihood of having a child with Down syndrome depends on maternal age (see Figure 5.2).

Approximately 95% of cases of Down syndrome are caused by an extra 21st chromosome. This form of the disorder is sometimes called "trisomy 21" because the child shows three chromosome 21s rather than the usual two. Trisomy 21 is not inherited. Instead, it is due to a **nondisjunction**, that is, a failure of the chromosome to separate during meiosis. In most cases, the mother contributes two chromosomes instead of one, but cases of paternal nondisjunction have also been reported.

Down syndrome can also occur when the child inherits one chromosome 21 from each parent and an abnormally fused chromosome (usually consisting of chromosome 21 and 15) from one of the parents. This abnormality, called a **translocation**, results in additional genetic material. It occurs in approximately 3% of youths with Down syndrome. Down syndrome caused by translocation is inherited. Usually, the parents are unaffected carriers of abnormally fused chromosomes, and they unknowingly pass them on to their children.

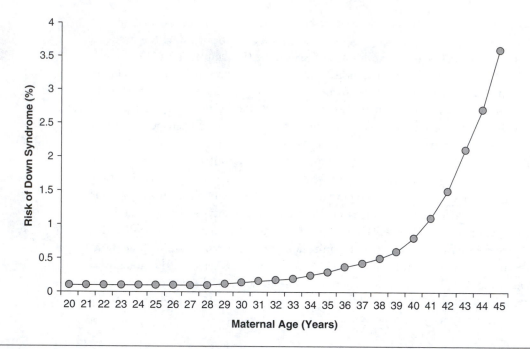

Figure 5.2   Risk of Down Syndrome Increases as a Function of Maternal Age

Source: Based on Cuckle, Wald, and Thompson (1987).

Note: After a woman reaches age 35, most physicians recommend prenatal screening due to increased risk.

Finally, Down syndrome can occur when some cells fail to separate during mitosis. This causes the child to have some normal cells and some cells with an abnormal amount of genetic information. This is called **chromosomal mosaicism**. Just as a mosaic is made up of different colored tiles, people with chromosomal mosaicism have cells of different genetic makeups. Chromosomal mosaicism accounts for approximately 2% of cases of Down syndrome.

Children with Down syndrome have characteristic facial features including flattened face, slanting eyes, wide nasal bridge, and low-set ears (see Image 5.1). Other physical features include short stature and poor muscle tone (hypotonia). In most typically developing children, the palms show two or more large, horizontal creases. In contrast, children with Down syndrome often show a single large crease, known as a simian crease, extending from the thumb across the palm. Children with Down syndrome show small overall brain size and fewer folds and convolutions than in brains of typically developing children. Fewer folds suggest reduced surface area of the cortex and may be partially responsible for low intelligence.

Children with Down syndrome are mentally retarded; few show IQs greater than 60. Cognitive development progresses in a typical fashion for the first few months of life. After the child's first birthday, however, intellectual development slows and falls further behind typically developing peers. As a result, the delays of children with Down syndrome become more pronounced as children age.

Children with Down syndrome show significant deficits in language (Dykens & Hodapp, 2001). They often have simplistic grammar, limited vocabulary, impoverished sentence structure, and impaired articulation. In fact, 95% of parents report difficulties understanding the speech of their children with Down syndrome (Kumin, 1994). These children also show problems with auditory learning and short-term memory. Consequently, they often struggle in traditional education settings where teachers present lessons verbally.

However, children with Down syndrome show relative strengths in visual-spatial reasoning (Dykens & Hodapp, 2001). For example, these children can repeat a series of hand movements presented visually more easily than they can repeat a series of numbers presented verbally (Dykens et al., 2006). Some experts have suggested that teachers should capitalize on these children's visual-spatial abilities in the classroom. For example, Buckley (1999) taught children with Down syndrome how to read by having children visually match printed words with pictures, play word-matching games with flashcards, and manipulate flashcards with words printed on them into sentences. These techniques, which relied heavily on their propensity toward visual learning, led to increased reading skills. Furthermore, their advances in reading spilled over into other areas. For example, Buckley noticed improvements in speech and language.

Young children with Down syndrome are usually described as happy, social, and friendly. It is extremely rewarding to volunteer as a tutor for a child with Down syndrome because these children are often socially outgoing and affectionate. Children with Down syndrome are less likely to develop psychiatric disorders than other children with Mental Retardation (Dykens, Hodapp, & Evans, 2006). However, in adolescence they may experience emotional and behavioral problems due to social isolation or increased recognition of their impairments (Reiss, 1990).

Medical complications associated with Down syndrome include congenital heart disease, thyroid abnormalities, respiratory problems, and leukemia (Chase, Osinowo, & Pary, 2002). After age 35, many adults with Down syndrome show early symptoms of Alzheimer's Disease (Coppus et al., 2006). Postmortem studies of their brains have shown a high incidence of neurofibrillary tangles and plaques, similar to those shown by older adults with Alzheimer's Disease. The life expectancy for individuals with Down syndrome is approximately 60 years.

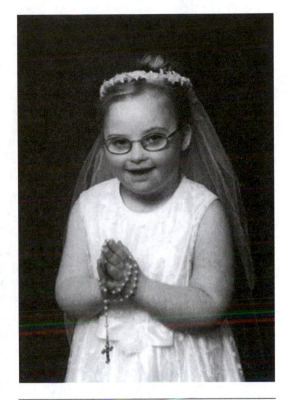

Image 5.1　　Michelle. Michelle is a seven-year-old girl with Down syndrome preparing for her first communion. She attended religious education classes with other children her age and received communion with her classmates.

Source: Photo is courtesy of the National Association for Down Syndrome, www.nads.org. Used with permission of her mother.

Fragile X Syndrome. Fragile X syndrome is an inherited genetic disorder that is associated with physical anomalies, moderate to severe Mental Retardation, and social and behavior problems. It occurs in 1 per 1,500 live births, about 1 per 1,000 males and 1 per 2,000 females (Sadock & Sadock, 2003).

Fragile X syndrome is caused by a mutation in a gene on the X chromosome, called the **fragile X mental retardation 1 (FMR1) gene**. In normal individuals, this gene contains a three-nucleotide sequence of cytosine-guanine-guanine (CGG) that repeats a small number of times. It produces fragile X mental retardation protein (FMRP), which assists in normal brain maturation and cognitive development (Comery, Harris, Willems, Oostra, & Greenough, 1997). Children with fragile X syndrome show an unusually high number of CGG repeats (Verkerk, Pieretti, Sutcliffe, Fu, Kuhl, & Pizzuti, 1991). Children who inherit 50 to 200 repeated sequences usually show no symptoms. They are typically unaware that they carry the genetic mutation, but they may pass this mutation on to their offspring. Children who inherit more than 200 repeated sequences usually show symptoms. The repeated sequences interfere with the functioning of the FMR1 gene and, consequently, decrease the amount of FMRP produced (Pieretti et al., 1991). In general, the less FMRP produced, the more severe children's cognitive impairments (Tassone, Hagerman, Ikle, Dyer, Lampe, & Willemsen, 1999). Brain scans of children with fragile X show abnormalities of the prefrontal cortex, caudate nucleus, and cerebellum, presumably from less FMRP production (Reiss, Eliez, Smith, Patwardhan, & Haberecht, 2000).

Boys and girls differ in their presentation of fragile X syndrome, with boys showing greater intellectual impairment, more severe behavior problems, and more physical anomalies. Boys show relatively greater impairment because they inherit only one affected X chromosome. Girls, on the other hand, inherit one affected X chromosome and a second X chromosome, which is typically unaffected. The additional unaffected X chromosome produces normal amounts of FMRP and contributes to higher cognitive functioning.

Boys with fragile X tend to have elongated heads, large ears, hyper-flexible joints, and large testicles after puberty (Sadock & Sadock, 2003). They also tend to be shorter than other boys. Medical problems sometimes associated with fragile X include heart murmur and crossed eyes (see Image 5.2).

Boys with fragile X syndrome tend to show moderate to severe Mental Retardation. Additionally, they show a curious pattern of strengths and weaknesses in the way they process information and solve problems (Alanay et al., 2007). They perform relatively well on tasks that require **simultaneous processing**, that is, perceiving, organizing, and interpreting information all at once. Solving puzzles or completing mazes demands simultaneous

Image 5.2   Blake. Blake is a preschool-age boy with fragile X syndrome. His parents describe him as "a sweet and spunky little guy."

Source: Used with permission from the National Fragile X Foundation, www.fragilex.org.

processing. Alternatively, boys with fragile X syndrome show relative deficits in **sequential processing,** that is, the capacity to arrange and process information in a certain order. Reading a sentence or following instructions on how to assemble a toy requires sequential processing. These boys also show weakness in planning and organizing activities in an efficient manner (Loesch et al., 2003).

Boys with fragile X also tend to show characteristic patterns of behavior. Most notably, many show autistic-like behavior, such as a reluctance to make eye contact or be touched by others. However, only about 25% of boys with fragile X meet diagnostic criteria for autism. The rest appear extremely shy in social situations. Many boys with fragile X also display hyperactivity and inattention. Perhaps as many as 90% have ADHD (Dykens & Hodapp, 2001; Sullivan, Hooper, & Hatton, 2007).

Girls with fragile X tend to show higher IQs, less noticeable physical anomalies, and less severe behavior problems than do boys with the disorder. Like boys, girls may have problems with visual-spatial abilities (Cornish, Munir, & Cross, 1998) and inattention (Mazzocco, Pennington, & Hagerman, 1993). They may also show excessive shyness, gaze aversion, and social anxiety (Hodapp & Dykens, 2006).

Prader-Willi Syndrome. Prader-Willi syndrome (PWS) is a noninherited genetic disorder characterized by mild Mental Retardation, overeating and obesity, oppositional behavior toward adults, and obsessive-compulsive behavior. PWS occurs in 1 per 20,000 live births (Dykens & Shah, 2003).

Prader-Willi syndrome is usually caused by the deletion of genetic information on portions of chromosome 15. In 70% of cases, the father's information is deleted, so the child inherits only one set of genetic information, from the mother. In most of the remaining cases, the mother contributes both pairs of chromosome 15 (called **maternal uniparental disomy;** UPD). In both instances, the father does not contribute the significant portion of chromosome 15, resulting in missing paternal genetic information.

Individuals with PWS show either mild Mental Retardation or borderline intellectual functioning. Average IQs range from 65–70 (Dykens & Shah, 2003). These children show characteristic strengths and weaknesses on various cognitive tasks. For example, children with PWS show relative strengths on visual-spatial skills. Indeed, some children with PWS may be able to solve jigsaw puzzles faster than the psychologists who test them (Dykens & Cassidy, 1999). On the other hand, these children show weaknesses in short-term memory. Their adaptive behavior is usually much lower than their IQ because their disruptive behavior often interferes with their acquisition of daily living skills.

The most striking feature of many children with PWS is their intense interest in food (Dykens, 2000; Dykens & Cassidy, 1999). Infants with the disorder show problems with sucking, feeding, and weight gain. However, between two and six years of age, children with PWS eat enormous amounts of food (i.e., show **hyperphagia**). Some evidence suggests that these children have abnormal neural functioning in the paraventricular nucleus of the hypothalamus, the area of the brain that controls satiety. Since these children never feel full, they eat to excess and are often preoccupied by food. Some children steal food, hoard food, or obtain food from the garbage in an attempt to satisfy themselves. If their diet is not monitored, they will eat to excess and become obese. Medical complications associated with obesity are a leading cause of death among adults with PWS (Dykens & Shah, 2003).

The onset of hyperphagia is also associated with changes in behavior. Many (70%–95%) children with PWS become argumentative, defiant, and throw temper tantrums (Dykens & Cassidy, 1999; Dykens & Kasari, 1997). Approximately 42% of children with PWS destroy property during their disruptive outbursts, while 34% physically attack others (Dykens, Cassidy, & King, 1999).

Most (71%–98%) children with PWS show obsessive thoughts or ritualistic, compulsive behaviors (Dykens & Cassidy, 1999). The most common obsessions concern food (Dykens & Cassidy, 1999). They may eat foods in a certain order or according to color, texture, type, or caloric content (Dykens, 2000). Children with PWS often show nonfood obsessions and compulsive behavior, too. They may hoard paper and pens; order and arrange toys and household objects by color, size, or shape; repeat information or questions; appear overly concerned with symmetry; and redo activities (e.g., untying and tying shoes, rewriting homework) until the behavior is done exactly right (Dimitropoulos, Feurer, Butler, & Thompson, 2001). Approximately 97% of individuals with PWS pick their skin, usually on their head or legs (Dykens & Cassidy, 1999).

In early adulthood, some individuals with PWS show psychotic symptoms, including distorted thinking and hallucinations. In one study, 12.1% of parents of children with PWS reported auditory or visual hallucinations in their children (Stein, Keating, Zar, & Hollander,1994). Life expectancy among adults with PWS is usually somewhat reduced because of obesity.

Angelman's Syndrome. Angelman's syndrome is a genetically based developmental disorder characterized by Mental Retardation, speech impairment, happy demeanor, and unusual motor behavior. The disorder was identified by the English physician Harry Angelman when three children (later diagnosed with the syndrome) were admitted to his hospital at the same time. All three children showed severe Mental Retardation, an inability to speak, and problems with gait and balance. Their movements were sporadic, jerky, and irregular. They tended to walk with arms uplifted, sometimes on their toes, lurching forward with abrupt starts and stops. Most strikingly, all three children frequently smiled and laughed (Clayton-Smith, 2001; Dykens & Shah, 2003).

Later, while visiting the Castelvecchio Museum in Verona, Angelman saw a painting titled *Boy with a Puppet* that reminded him of the happy disposition of his three young patients (see Image 5.3). Angelman subsequently wrote a scientific paper describing his three "Puppet Children," which slowly attracted the attention of clinicians throughout the world (Angelman, 1965). Today, professionals refer to the disorder as Angelman's syndrome. Approximately 1 per 15,0000–20,000 children have the disorder.

Both PWS and Angelman's syndrome are caused by abnormalities on portions of chromosome 15. Healthy children inherit two chromosome 15s, one from each parent. PWS occurs when children inherit genetic information on chromosome 15 only from the mother. In contrast, Angelman's syndrome occurs when children inherit genetic information on chromosome 15 only from the father. In 70% of cases of Angelman's syndrome, genetic information from the mother is deleted. In another 3%–5% of cases, the father contributes two chromosome 15s and the mother contributes none. In the remaining cases of Angelman's syndrome, the child shows other genetic mutations in chromosome 15 or the cause is unknown.

The most striking feature of Angelman's syndrome is the persistent social smile and happy demeanor shown by children with the disorder. Many infants with Angelman's syndrome begin this persistent smiling between 1 and 3 months of age. Later in development, it is accompanied by laughter, giggling, and happy grimacing. Facial features of children with Angelman's syndrome often include a wide smiling mouth, thin upper lip, and pointed chin (Williams, 2005).

Despite children's social smiling, Angelman's syndrome is usually not recognized until toddlerhood or the preschool years. Parents and physicians often suspect the disorder when children continue to show cognitive impairment, lack of spoken language, and movement problems. By childhood, children's intellectual functioning is generally in the range of severe or profound Mental Retardation. Youths with the disorder show levels of functioning similar to a 2½- to three-year-old child. Most children with Angelman's syndrome are unable to speak, although some can meaningfully use a few words. They usually can understand other people and are able to obey simple commands.

Image 5.3   *Boy With a Puppet*, Giovanni Francesco Caroto (1520). This oil painting prompted Angelman to write the first scientific account of children with the disorder that now bears his name. The smile of the boy in the painting reminded Angelman of his three patients.

Nearly all children with Angelman's syndrome show hyperactivity and inattention. Parents usually describe them as constantly "on the go." Children may flap their arms, fiddle with their hands, and become easily excitable. Hyperactivity often interferes with their ability to sleep. Children with Angelman's syndrome often have difficulty sustaining their attention on one person or task for long periods of time. Problems with hyperactivity and inattention continue throughout childhood but decrease somewhat with age.

Some children with Angelman's syndrome show skin and eye hypopigmentation; that is, they may appear pale and have light-colored eyes. Hypopigmentation occurs when the gene that codes for skin pigmentation is deleted along with the other information on chromosome 15 that causes Angelman's syndrome. Other children with Angelman's syndrome show feeding problems. They may thrust their tongues outward when fed, have difficulty sucking and swallowing, or drool. In most cases, these problems resolve over time.

Image 5.4   Mary. Mary is a preschool-age girl with Williams syndrome. She shows a persistent happy demeanor, characteristic of children with the disorder.

Source: Reprinted with permission of Mary's family.

More than 90% of children with Angelman's syndrome have seizures. Sometimes, seizures are difficult to notice because of these children's sporadic motor movements. In most cases, physicians prescribe anticonvulsant medications to reduce the number and severity of seizures. Adults with Angelman's syndrome have life expectancies approximately 10–15 years shorter than typically developing individuals. Life expectancy is dependent on the severity of comorbid medical problems, especially seizures.

Williams Syndrome. Williams syndrome (WS) is a genetic disorder characterized by low intellectual functioning, unusual strengths in spoken language and sociability, hyperactivity, impulsivity, and inattention. Children with WS can be identified by their facial features. They often show broad foreheads; full lips; widely spaced teeth; star-shaped patterns in their irises; and elfin-like noses, eyes, and ears (see Image 5.4). Their facial features suggest a mixture of joy and mischievousness. WS is caused by a small deletion in a portion of chromosome 7. The disorder occurs in approximately 1 per 20,000 live births.

Despite their low IQ scores, children with WS show curious strengths in certain areas of language. They have unusually well-developed lexicons (Hodapp & Dykens, 2006). They can tell relatively complex stories with advanced vocabulary and complex grammar (Reilly, Klima, & Bellugi, 1990). They may even use sound effects when telling stories to add emphasis. Some children with WS show relative strengths in auditory memory and music (Hodapp & DesJardin, 2002). Teachers sometimes alter their instructional methods to play to the strengths of children with WS. For example, children with WS might respond best to verbal instruction rather than to reading and may prefer to work with partners or in groups, rather than independently (Hodapp & DesJardin, 2002).

Children with WS do poorly on visual-spatial tasks. They have great difficulty copying pictures or figures. This relative deficit in visual-spatial abilities is likely due to the genetic deletion that causes WS. Specifically, the portion of chromosome 7 that is deleted contains a gene that codes for an enzyme called LIM kinase. This enzyme is necessary for brain development and functioning, especially in brain regions responsible for visual-spatial processing. Deficits in this enzyme likely underlie the visual-spatial problems shown by children with the disorder.

Children with WS are described as friendly and sociable (Rosner, Hodapp, Fidler, Sagun, & Dykens, 2004). They are especially good at remembering faces and inferring a person's mental state and emotions based on his or her affect (Tager-Flusberg,

Boshart, & Baron-Cohen, 1998). Sometimes, they are overly trusting of strangers, placing them at risk for exploitation by others.

Children with WS often show problems with high-rate behavior and are easily excitable. They display inattention, hyperactivity, and impulsivity; many are diagnosed with ADHD (Einfeld, 2005). Furthermore, children with WS show hyperacusis, that is, an unusual sensitivity to loud noises. Truck engines, fire alarms, and school bells can cause them considerable distress.

Most children with WS show problems with anxiety. Like typically developing children, young children with WS fear tangible and imposing images and events such as storms, vaccinations, and ghosts. However, unlike typically developing children, older children with WS continue to fear these stimuli and show a marked increase in generalized anxiety. In particular, older children with WS often fear that something bad is about to happen. Many are extremely sensitive to failure and criticism by others (Dykens, 2003). In a sample of 51 individuals with WS, 35% showed full-blown phobias for objects or social situations while 84% showed subthreshold problems with anxiety. In contrast, the prevalence of phobias among children with other types of Mental Retardation is only about 1%.

Dykens and Hodapp (2001) have suggested that the characteristic features of WS may place them at increased risk for developing anxiety problems. For example, their hyperacusis may make them especially sensitive to developing fears of loud noises. Early problems with balance and gait might contribute to fears of falling from high places. Their social sensitivity may place them at increased risk for social anxiety. Consequently, the fears of children with WS may stem from the interaction of genotype, early experiences, and the behavioral characteristics of WS (Dykens & Hodapp, 2001).

Children with WS are at risk for cardiovascular problems. The portion of chromosome 7 that is deleted in WS also contains a gene that codes for elastin. Elastin is used by the cardiovascular system to give connective tissue its elastic, flexible properties. Insufficient elastin can cause hypertension, other cardiovascular diseases, and early death.

Genetic Metabolism Disorders

Phenylketonuria. Phenylketonuria (PKU) is a metabolic disorder that is caused by a recessive gene inherited from both parents. In most cases, PKU is characterized by the body's inability to convert **phenylalanine**, an essential amino acid found in certain foods, to paratyrosine. In PKU, the enzyme that breaks down phenylalanine (phenylalanine hydroxylase) is not produced by the liver. As the child eats foods rich in phenylalanine, such as dairy, meats, cheeses, and certain breads, the substance builds up and becomes toxic. Phenylalanine toxicity eventually causes brain damage and Mental Retardation.

PKU is caused by a recessive gene. In order for a child to show PKU, he or she must inherit the gene from both the mother and father. Children who inherit the gene from only one parent are carriers of the disorder but do not display symptoms.

If a carrier mates with another carrier, each offspring has a 25% chance of showing PKU. The disorder occurs in approximately 1 per 11,500 children.

Newborns are routinely screened for PKU through a blood test conducted shortly after birth. If the disorder is detected, the child is placed on a diet consisting of foods that are low in phenylalanine. The diet decreases the chances of toxicity; consequently, adherence to the diet results in normal intellectual development. Most physicians suggest the diet should be continued indefinitely. Since phenylalanine is an essential amino acid, children on the diet must be monitored by their pediatricians. They are at risk for low red blood cell count (anemia) and low blood glucose levels (hypoglycemia).

Youths with PKU who do not diet show symptoms several months after birth. By childhood, they often develop severe Mental Retardation. Children with untreated PKU are often hyperactive, show erratic motor movements, and throw tantrums. They also may vomit and have convulsions. They usually cannot communicate with others. These impairments are irreversible, even if a phenyl-free diet is initiated later in childhood.

Embryonic Teratogen Exposure

Mental Retardation can also occur when children are exposed to certain environmental toxins during gestation. The placenta is a bag-like membrane that partially surrounds the fetus during gestation. It delivers oxygen and nutrients from the mother to the fetus and allows the fetus to excrete waste. The placenta is porous; substances ingested by the mother can pass directly to the fetal system. **Teratogens** are environmental substances that cause maldevelopment in the fetus, often resulting in Mental Retardation.

Maternal Illness. Viruses acquired by the mother during pregnancy used to be a leading cause of organic Mental Retardation. Exposure to the **rubella virus**, especially during the first few months of pregnancy, often caused severe Mental Retardation, cataracts, and deafness. Similarly, **maternal syphilis** was associated with fetal maldevelopment and Mental Retardation. Other diseases, such as measles, mumps, diphtheria, tetanus, and poliovirus can also cause Mental Retardation. Today, these illnesses are largely prevented by childhood immunizations and regular medical care.

Infants can acquire **human immunodeficiency virus** (HIV) from an infected mother either in utero or through breast feeding. HIV causes damage to the child's central nervous and immune systems. The risk of transmission from an infected mother is approximately 30%. However, zidovudine (Retrovir), taken prenatally by mothers, can reduce the likelihood of transmission to less than 5% (Sadock & Sadock, 2003). The progression of HIV in newborns is more rapid than in adults. Most infants born with HIV show progressive brain degeneration, Mental Retardation, and seizures during their first year of life. Most affected children die before age three.

Maternal Substance Use. Many drugs, if ingested by pregnant women, are associated with low birth weight, small head circumference, and increased risk for behavioral and learning problems in childhood. Interestingly, "hard" drugs, such as heroin and cocaine, are not as consistently associated with children's Mental Retardation as are more socially accepted drugs like alcohol.

Fetal alcohol syndrome (FAS) is caused by maternal alcohol consumption during pregnancy. FAS is characterized by Mental Retardation, hyperactivity, and slow physical growth. Facial features of FAS include wide-spaced eyes (hypertelorism), small head (microcephaly), small opening to the eye, low-set ears, and a short upturned nose. Children with FAS often have cardiac problems. By school age, they tend to show hyperactivity and learning problems.

The prevalence of FAS is approximately 1-3 per 1,000 live births. However, the prevalence among children of women who have Alcohol Dependence is approximately 1 in 3. Experts disagree on how much alcohol must be consumed to produce FAS. Some data indicate that FAS can result from only 2 to 3 oz. of alcohol per day during the course of gestation. Furthermore, binge drinking during pregnancy greatly increases the chance of FAS. Although occasional consumption of alcohol during pregnancy may not produce FAS, it may lead to subtle cognitive, behavioral, and physical abnormalities such as mild learning problems, reduced attention span, or short stature. Most physicians recommend abstaining from alcohol entirely during pregnancy.

The intellectual functioning of children with FAS varies considerably. Most children with FAS show mild to moderate Mental Retardation, although some earn IQ scores within the borderline to low-average range. These children usually have academic problems and may drop out of school. Many have learning disabilities. The most common behavioral problems associated with FAS are hyperactivity, impulsivity, and inattention. Young children with FAS are often diagnosed with ADHD. Older children and adolescents with FAS report feelings of restlessness and difficulty sustaining attention on reading and other homework.

Children with FAS are at risk for mood problems as they enter late childhood and adolescence. They may become depressed because of their academic deficits, behavior problems, or stigmatization associated with the disorder.

Andrew

Andrew was a 14-year-old boy with FAS who was referred to our clinic because of a marked increase in disruptive behavior at school. Andrew was a large boy, approximately 5'10" and more than 175 lbs. He displayed many of the physical features of youths with fetal alcohol syndrome, including wide-spaced eyes, upturned nose, low-set ears, and broad face.

Andrew's mother had an extensive history of alcohol and other drug dependence. She drank throughout her pregnancy with Andrew and was intoxicated at the time of his delivery. Andrew had longstanding academic problems. His IQ was approximately 67, whereas his reading and mathematics scores were

(Continued)

(Continued)

comparable to those of a second- or third-grade child. Andrew received special education services, including remedial tutoring; however, he felt humiliated about receiving these special services. Since beginning junior high school the previous year, Andrew's behavior became increasingly disruptive. He would often "clown around" in class, play pranks on teachers and other classmates, and get into fights on the playground. Andrew admitted to being teased by classmates because of his appearance, his academic problems, and his family history. "I know I'm slow," he said, "I don't need the other kids to tell me."

Andrew met with Dr. Onak for weekly therapy sessions. Andrew was initially clownish and disruptive during the sessions, but he gradually came to trust his therapist and share his feelings. During one session, Andrew commented, "You know, if it wasn't for my mom, I wouldn't have all of the problems that I'm having right now." Dr. Onak replied, "I guess you're right. Your mom makes you pretty upset when you visit her. That causes you to get into trouble." Andrew replied, hesitantly, "No. That's not what I mean. I mean, if it wasn't for my mom's drinking—when I was inside her—I wouldn't be so dumb. If only she could have loved me more than alcohol."

Complications During Pregnancy and Delivery

Complications that occur during gestation or delivery can contribute to Mental Retardation. Although these prenatal and perinatal experiences do not uniformly cause Mental Retardation, they present significant risk. Maternal hypertension or uncontrolled diabetes during pregnancy are sometimes associated with Mental Retardation in children. Delivery complications that interfere with the fetus's ability to obtain sufficient oxygen for extended periods of time (**anoxia**) can also lead to central nervous system damage and Mental Retardation. For example, anoxia can occur when the umbilical cord wraps around the fetus's throat, interfering with oxygen intake. Finally, very low birth weight infants (i.e., weight < 1,000 g) are also at risk for low intelligence. Approximately 20% of very low birth weight infants develop learning problems or mild Mental Retardation. These symptoms usually do not emerge until later in childhood.

Childhood Illness or Injury

The two childhood illnesses most associated with the development of Mental Retardation are encephalitis and meningitis. **Encephalitis** refers to the swelling of brain tissue, whereas **meningitis** refers to an inflammation of the meninges, the membrane that surrounds the brain and spinal cord. Both illnesses can be caused by bacteria or viral infections, although viral infections are more serious because they are often resistant to treatment.

All serious head injuries have the potential to cause Mental Retardation. An obvious source of injuries is car accidents; however, most childhood head injuries occur around the home. Falls from tables, open windows, and stairs account for many injury-related cognitive impairments. Similarly, children who almost drown in swimming pools or bathtubs can experience brain damage and corresponding cognitive problems. Finally, children who are physically abused can experience Mental Retardation because of environmental neglect or physical trauma (Appleton & Baldwin, 2006). Lead poisoning is a significant risk factor for Mental Retardation. Lead can be found in the paint of older buildings, in lead-soldered water pipes, and in industrial waste. Infants and toddlers may eat paint chips flaking off the walls of older homes. Older children may inhale dust containing lead-based paint from walls, porches, and window panes. Lead enters the child's bloodstream and produces widespread cerebral damage. Exposure can cause Mental Retardation, movement problems (ataxia), convulsions, and coma. If poisoning is detected early, children can be treated by flushing the lead from the bloodstream. Damage caused by prolonged exposure is irreversible.

The risk of lead poisoning varies by socioeconomic status and ethnicity. For example, 7% of middle-class white children are exposed to sufficient amounts of lead to cause poisoning. The risk of lead poisoning among low-income white and black children is much higher: 25% and 55%, respectively. Risk is particularly high among poor children living in urban settings (Dilworth-Bart & Moore, 2006; Phelps, 2005).

Cultural-Familial Mental Retardation

Cultural-familial Mental Retardation results from the interaction of the child's genes and environmental experiences over time. Children inherit a genetic propensity toward low intelligence. Furthermore, these children experience environmental deprivation that interferes with their ability to reach their cognitive potentials. Environmental deprivation might include poor access to health care, inadequate nutrition, lack of cognitive stimulation during early childhood (e.g., parents talking, playing, and reading with children), low-quality educational experiences, and lack of cultural experiences (e.g., listening to music, trips to the museum). Over time, the interaction between genes and environment contributes to children's low intellectual functioning.

Socioeconomic Status

Familial Mental Retardation is more prevalent among children from low-income families than middle-class families. The correlation between SES and children's intelligence is approximately .33. Furthermore, the relationship between SES and children's IQ increases when children experience extreme poverty or socioeconomic disadvantage (Turkheimer, Haley, Waldron, D'Onofrio, & Gottesman, 2003).

Both genetic and environmental factors explain this association between SES and children's intelligence. With respect to genetics, low-income parents tend to have lower IQ scores than middle-class parents. Individuals with higher IQs complete more years of schooling and assume more challenging and higher-paying jobs. The children of high-income parents inherit their parents' genotypes that predispose them to a higher range of intellectual and adaptive functioning (Stromme & Magnus, 2000).

Furthermore, children from low-income families are exposed to environments that may restrict their intellectual potential. For example, low-income children are more likely to experience gestational and birth complications, have limited access to high-quality health care and nutrition, have greater exposure to environmental toxins, receive less cognitive stimulation from their home environments, and attend less optimal schools (McLoyd, 1998). These environmental deficits or risk factors limit the child's cognitive and adaptive potential. Young children in poverty earn IQ scores approximately nine points lower than children from middle-class families (Brooks-Gunn & Duncan, 1997; Duncan & Brooks-Gunn, 2000).

Ethnicity

Familial Mental Retardation is also more frequently seen among ethnic minorities, especially African American children (Raghavan & Small, 2004). This association is partially due to the fact that many African American children live in low-income families and experience the same genetic and environmental risk factors as children from other low-income families. Whereas the average IQ score for middle-class whites is approximately 100, the average IQ score for low-income African Americans is approximately 90. Consequently, African Americans and individuals from low-income families are more frequently diagnosed with mild Mental Retardation than are white, middle-class children (McLoyd, Hill, & Dodge, 2005).

Home Environment

Many studies suggest a relationship between the quality of the home environment and children's intellectual development. After reviewing the data, Sattler (2002) identified two broad ways parents can enrich their children's home environment and help them achieve their intellectual potentials. First, families who provide their children with ample verbal stimulation, model and provide feedback regarding language, and give many opportunities for verbal learning appear to foster greater intellectual development in their children. Parents should take every opportunity to interact with their children through talking, playing, and reading. Second, encouraging academic achievement, curiosity, and independence in children is associated with increased intellectual functioning. Parents should encourage creative play, arts and crafts, and home-made games and activities, especially with young children, in order to help them develop novel and flexible problem-solving skills.

Treatment

Prenatal Screening

Shortly after birth, newborns are routinely administered a series of blood tests in order to determine the presence of genetic and other medical disorders that might cause Mental Retardation. For example, all infants are administered a genetic test to screen for PKU. If PKU is found, a genetic counselor and nutritionist will meet with parents to discuss feeding options for the child.

If parents are at risk for having children with Mental Retardation or other developmental delays, a physician may recommend genetic screening during gestation. Parents who may be carriers of specific genetic disorders, parents who have had other children with developmental delays, or mothers older than age 35 often participate in screening.

At 15 to 18 weeks' gestation, mothers can undergo **serum screening** (Newberger, 2000). This procedure is usually called the "triple test" or "triple screen" because it involves testing mother's blood for three serum markers: alpha-fetoprotein, unconjugated estriol, and human chorionic gonadotropin. These serums are naturally produced by the fetus's liver and the placenta. If the child has Down syndrome, alpha-fetoprotein and unconjugated estiol may be unusually low while human chorionic gonadotropin levels may be unusually high. Significant elevations can be a sign of a genetic disorder, but this test has a high rate of false positives. Consequently, if test results are positive, the physician will usually recommend that the mother participate in additional testing.

Amniocentesis is a more invasive screening technique that is usually conducted during weeks 15 to 20 of gestation. The procedure involves removing a small amount of amniotic fluid with a needle inserted into the abdomen of the mother. The amniotic fluid contains fetal cells, which can be cultured and examined for genetic abnormalities. Amniocentesis is invasive; it carries a 0.5% risk of fetal death. Amniocentesis can also be conducted before 15 weeks' gestation, at the beginning of the second trimester, but the risk of fetal death increases to 1%–2%.

Chorionic villus sampling (CVS) is another genetic screening technique that can be done earlier, usually between 8 and 12 weeks' gestation. In CVS, the physician takes a small amount of chorionic villi, the wisp-like tissue that connects the placenta to the wall of the uterus. This tissue usually has the same genetic and biochemical makeup as the developing fetus. The tissue can be analyzed to detect genetic or biological anomalies. CVS is usually only performed when there is greatly increased risk of the fetus having a developmental or medical disorder. The risk of miscarriage associated with CVS is 0.5% to 1.5%.

Recently, physicians have been using ultrasound to detect structural abnormalities in the fetus that might indicate the presence of a developmental disorder (Rissanen, Niemimaa, Suonpää, Ryynänen, & Heinonen, 2007). Ultrasound is believed to be a relatively safe procedure for both mother and fetus. Between 11 and 14 weeks' gestation, embryos with Down syndrome often show flatter facial profile and shorter (or absent) nasal bones than typically developing fetuses. The presence of these physical abnormalities, revealed by ultrasound, could indicate the presence of a genetic disorder. Based on the findings, mothers can decide whether they want to pursue more invasive testing.

Infant and Preschool Prevention

A number of state- and locally administered programs have been developed to prevent the emergence of Mental Retardation in children at risk for low IQ. One of the most recent and, perhaps, the best-designed prevention programs for at-risk children is the **Infant Health and Development Program** (IHDP). Participants in the IHDP were 985 premature infants who showed either low birth weight (weight 2,001 to 2,500 grams) or very low birth weight (weight < 2000 grams). Previous research indicated that these children were at increased risk for developmental delays, including Mental Retardation and learning problems (Baumeister & Bacharach, 1996). Infants were randomly assigned to either an early intervention group or a control group. The parents of children in the intervention group received regular home visits from program staff. During these visits, staff taught parents games and activities that they could play with their infants to promote cognitive, linguistic, and social development. Staff also served as references to parents, helping parents address problems associated with caring for a preterm, low birth weight infant. When infants turned one year old, parents were invited to place them in a high-quality preschool program. The program was free and transportation to and from the preschool program was provided. The preschool ran year round, five days per week, until children were three years old. Families assigned to the control group were not given home visits or offered the preschool program.

To evaluate the success of the intervention, children's cognitive development was assessed at the end of the preschool program (age three years), at age five years, and at age eight years. Children who participated in the program earned slightly higher IQs than children in the control group at age three. However, by age five, these differences in IQ disappeared.

The results of the IHDP indicate that early intervention programs can boost IQ scores among at-risk children, but increases in IQ are not maintained over time. The data are largely consistent with other early intervention programs designed to increase the cognitive functioning of low-income children (Farran, 2000).

Experts have disagreed on how to interpret the findings. Supporters of the IHDP concede that the results of the intervention were "largely negative" (Blair & Wahlsten, 2002, p. 130). However, advocates of the program believe the data speak to the importance of continuing educational enrichment for high-risk children beyond the preschool years. If the program had been extended through elementary school, children in the intervention group might have continued to show higher IQ scores than controls.

Critics of the IHDP argue that early intervention programs do not prevent Mental Retardation and developmental delays and they should be discontinued (Baumeister & Bacharach, 2000). Instead, the money and time used for early intervention programs could be spent on primary prevention, such as providing at-risk families with better access to health care and nutrition services. Critics argue that it is difficult to boost children's IQ scores because a person's genotype sets an upper limit on his or her intellectual potential (Baumeister & Bacharach, 2000). Furthermore, simply offering intervention services to high-risk families does not mean that they will take advantage of these services. In fact, 20% of children in the intervention group attended the preschool program less than 10 days in two years and 55 children never attended at all (Hill, Brooks-Gunn, & Waldfogel, 2003). Since gains in IQ are directly related to participation in treatment, getting families to participate in treatment seems to be a critical goal of any effective early intervention program.

Educational Interventions

In 1975, Congress passed the Education of All Handicapped Children Act (Public Law 94-142). This act mandated a free and appropriate public education for all children with disabilities aged 3 to 18 years. From its implementation in 1977 through the mid-1980s, the practice of mainstreaming became more common in public school systems across the United States. **Mainstreaming** involved placing children with Mental Retardation in classrooms with typically developing peers, to the maximum extent possible. At first, mainstreamed children with Mental Retardation were allowed to participate in nonacademic classes, such as gym, art, and music, with typically developing children. For other subjects, they attended self-contained special education classes for children with developmental delays (Verhoeven & Vermeer, 2006).

In the mid-1980s, many parents argued that children with Mental Retardation and other disabilities had the right to attend all classes with typically developing peers. This movement, sometimes called the "Regular Education Initiative," gradually led to the practice of inclusion. **Inclusion** involves the education of children with Mental Retardation alongside typically developing peers for all subjects, usually with the support of a classroom aide.

In 1997, Congress amended PL 94-142 by passing the Individuals With Disabilities Education Act (IDEA; PL 105-17). IDEA codified the practice of inclusion by demanding that children with disabilities be educated in the least restrictive environment possible:

> To the maximum extent appropriate, children with disabilities . . . are educated with children who are not disabled, and special classes, separate schooling, or other removal of children with disabilities from the regular educational environment occurs only when the nature or severity of the disability of a child is such that education in regular classes with the use of supplementary aids and services cannot be achieved satisfactorily. (p. 61)

In addition to providing services for children with disabilities, IDEA also requires local educational systems to identify all infants, toddlers, and children with disabilities living in the community, whether or not they attend school. Once children are identified, a team of educational professionals (e.g., regular education teachers, special education teachers, school psychologists) conducts a comprehensive evaluation of the child's strengths and limitations and designs a written plan for the child's education. Infants and toddlers, aged 0 to 3 years, are provided with an **Individualized Family Services Plan** (IFSP). For preschoolers and school-aged children, school personnel develop an **Individualized Education Program** (IEP) in consultation with parents. Typically, IEPs provide extra support to children while at school; children may be given special education services or a classroom aide. IEPs also usually specify accommodations for children with disabilities that help them achieve their cognitive, social, emotional, or behavioral potentials. IDEA was revised again in 2004 as the Individuals With Disabilities Education Improvement Act (PL 108-446; Williamson, McLeskey, Hoppey, & Rentz, 2006).

In general, inclusion improves the functioning of children with developmental disabilities, especially children with mild or moderate Mental Retardation. Inclusion seems to work best when (1) students with Mental Retardation can become active in the learning process, and (2) these children frequently interact and cooperate with typically developing classmates. Inclusion may also have benefits for typically developing peers. Specifically, inclusion may teach typically developing children greater tolerance and understanding of individuals with developmental delays and increase students' willingness to welcome children with delays into their peer groups.

The educational rights of children with Mental Retardation have increased greatly over the past 30 years. The trend toward inclusion has allowed these children to have access to educational experiences that their counterparts, a generation ago, were typically not afforded. Today, the focus of attention has shifted from *where* children are educated (e.g., regular versus special education classes) to *how* they are educated (e.g., the nature and quality of services they receive; Zigler, Hodapp, & Edison, 1990). Simply placing all children with disabilities in regular classrooms is not enough. Now, we must learn to tailor regular educational experiences to the needs of these children in order to allow them to benefit from these experiences. Tailoring might involve smaller class size, more classroom aides, greater access to behavioral or medical consultants, specialized teacher training, and more time for teachers to plan lessons for students with disabilities (Hocutt, 1996).

Behavioral Interventions

Positive Reinforcement

Problematic behaviors are the primary reason children with Mental Retardation are referred for treatment. Parents, teachers, and caregivers usually initiate the referral. Approximately 4% to 9% of children with Mental Retardation show disruptive behavior problems (Handen & Gilchrist, 2006a).

Applied behavior analysis (ABA) is a scientific approach to identifying an individual's problematic behavior, determining its cause, and changing it (Feeley & Jones, 2006). The principles of ABA are based largely on the work of B. F. Skinner (1974), who believed that the study of behavior should be based on observable, quantifiable data. Skinner believed that psychologists do not need to rely on latent (unobservable) constructs to explain and predict behavior. Instead, behavior can be understood in terms of overt actions and environmental contingencies. Instead of viewing behavior as originating from within the person, applied behavior analysts understand behavior primarily as a function of environmental antecedents and consequences (Holburn, 2005).

First, a behavior analyst tries to determine the behavior's purpose. To accomplish this task, the clinician conducts a functional analysis of the child's behavior. A **functional analysis** involves carefully specifying the child's undesirable behavior, identifying the environmental contingencies that immediately precede the behavior (i.e., the antecedents), and identifying the environmental events that occur immediately after the behavior (i.e., the consequences) that likely maintain it. A functional analysis of behavior, therefore, involves identifying A (antecedents),

B (the behavior), and C (its consequences). To change the child's behavior, the therapist can either alter the antecedents that prompt the undesirable behavior or change the consequences of the behavior so that it is no longer reinforced.

Whenever possible, therapists use positive reinforcement to strengthen desirable behavior while, at the same time, reduce undesirable behavior. In a technique called **differential reinforcement**, therapists provide positive reinforcement only for behaviors that are desirable while they ignore unwanted actions.

The two most common forms of differential reinforcement are (1) differential reinforcement of incompatible behaviors and (2) differential reinforcement of zero behavior. In **differential reinforcement of incompatible behaviors (DRI)**, the therapist provides positive reinforcement when the child engages in a behavior that is incompatible with the problematic behavior. For example, if a child engages in hand flapping or skin picking, the therapist might reinforce him for keeping his hands in his pockets or holding onto a special toy or blanket. Since the child cannot flap his hands and keep them in his pockets at the same time, the hand flapping should decrease. In **differential reinforcement of zero behavior (DR0)**, the therapist reinforces the child for not engaging in the problematic behavior for a certain period of time. For example, a therapist might give a child an M&M every 30 seconds he does not engage in hand flapping or skin picking.

Positive Punishment

Reinforcement increases behavioral frequency; punishment decreases it (Singh, Osborne, & Huguenin, 1996). Positive punishment involves the presentation of a stimulus that decreases the frequency of a behavior. A common form of positive punishment used by parents is spanking. However, behavior therapists do not use spanking as a means of reducing behavior. Instead, some behavior therapists rely on other forms of positive punishment. For example, some therapists use aversive tastes, water mists, or visual screens to decrease severe behavior problems (Singh et al., 1996).

Since positive punishment techniques are aversive, they are only used under certain conditions, such as when children's behaviors are dangerous or life-threatening and other methods of treatment have been ineffective at reducing the problematic behavior. Punishment is only used in combination with positive reinforcement, and its use is carefully reviewed and monitored by independent experts. Parents must consent to the use of punishment before it is used to correct their children's behavior problem (APA, 1996).

Salvy, Mulick, Butter, Bartlett, and Linscheid (2004) describe the use of **punishment by contingent stimulation** to reduce self-injurious behavior in a toddler with Mental Retardation. The girl, Johanna, would bang her head against her crib and other hard surfaces approximately 100 times each day. She had visible bruises on her forehead because of her behavior. Nonaversive interventions were not effective in reducing Johanna's head banging. The therapists and Johanna's mother decided to use punishment to reduce SIBs. The punisher was a brief electric shock that was administered by a device attached to Johanna's leg. The therapists could administer the shock remotely using a hand-held activator. The shock was unpleasant (like being snapped by a rubber band), but it did not cause injury.

Treatment involved two phases. In the first (experimental evaluation) phase, Johanna and her mother played in an observation room in the hospital. Observers counted the frequency of her head banging during the first 10 minutes. This provided a baseline of Johanna's behavior to evaluate the effectiveness of the punishment. Then, the shock device was attached to Johanna's leg but shocks were not administered. Observations continued for another 10 minutes to see whether Johanna's behavior would change merely because she wore the device. Next, therapists began administering a brief electrical shock contingent on Johanna's head banging. As before, observations were conducted for an additional 10 minutes. Finally, the shock device was removed and Johanna's behavior was observed for another 10 minutes. Results showed that the frequency of Johanna's head banging decreased from 30 times during baseline observation to 4 times after punishment.

During the second phase of treatment (home implementation), Johanna's mother was taught to punish Johanna's behavior at home. Therapists observed Johanna's behavior in the home for two days to obtain baseline data. On the third day, the shock device was attached to Johanna's leg. When Johanna began banging her head, her mother said "No hit, Johanna," retrieved the activator from her purse, and immediately issued a brief shock. The frequency of Johanna's behavior was recorded over the next month, at which time the shock device was removed from the home. Results showed that the frequency of Johanna's head banging at home decreased from 117 times per day at baseline to zero times per day after the contingent administration of shocks (see Figure 5.3). Johanna's mother discovered that the verbal prompt "No hit, Johanna" combined with the action of walking toward her purse was sufficient to stop

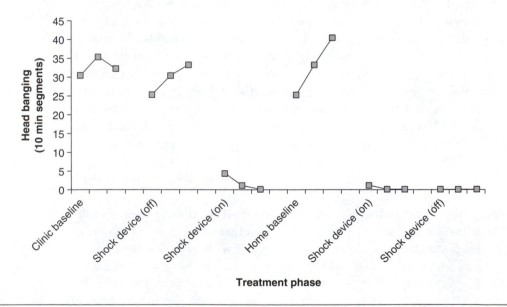

Figure 5.3   Use of Punishment by Contingent Stimulation to Treat Self-Injurious Behavior

Source: Based on Salvy, Mulick, Butter, Bartlett, and Linscheid (2004).

Note: Therapists administered brief, mild electric shocks to reduce head banging in a toddler with Mental Retardation. Punishment was only used after all other forms of treatment proved ineffective.

Johanna's head banging. At one-year follow-up, her mother reported no problems with Johanna's SIBs and no need to use the shock device.

Another form of positive punishment is called **overcorrection**. In overcorrection, the therapist requires the child to correct his problematic behavior by restoring his surroundings to the same (or better) condition than that which existed prior to his disruptive act. Overcorrection is often used when children show chronic problems using the toilet, wetting the bed, or destroying property. In the case of bedwetting, the therapist might require the child to strip his bedding, take his bedding and wet clothes to the laundry, help wash the clothes, and assist in making the new bed. For most children, this procedure is aversive because it is tedious and takes time away from sleep or enjoyable activities.

Overcorrection is often combined with a technique called **positive practice**. In positive practice, the therapist makes the child repeatedly practice an acceptable behavior immediately following his unacceptable act. In the case of bedwetting, the child might be required to sit on the toilet five times to practice the appropriate means of urinating. Positive practice can be aversive to children, but it also teaches children alternative, appropriate behavior.

Negative Punishment

Negative punishment occurs when the therapist withdraws a stimulus from the child, which decreases the recurrence of the child's behavior. Usually, the stimulus that is withdrawn is pleasant to the child. Consequently, the child experiences distress over its removal. Negative punishment is usually less aversive than positive punishment, so it is more often used to reduce problematic behavior.

The most benign form of negative punishment is **extinction**. In extinction, the therapist withdraws reinforcement from the child immediately following an unwanted behavior. Hanley and colleagues (2003) found that some children with developmental delays tantrum in order to obtain attention from caregivers. Caregivers would unknowingly reinforce their children's tantrums by looking at, talking to, and holding them. To extinguish these tantrums, caregivers can withdraw this reinforcement; that is, they can simply ignore their children's bids for attention. This strategy is sometimes called "planned ignoring."

When caregivers begin to extinguish behavior, the rate of children's behavior sometimes temporarily increases. This phenomenon is called an **extinction burst**. Children will usually escalate their problematic behavior in an attempt to gain the reinforcement that was previously provided. Over time, the behavior's frequency and intensity will decrease, as long as reinforcement is withheld. Extinction is a slow, but effective, means of reducing behavior problems. The primary drawback of extinction is that it cannot be used to reduce SIBs because these behaviors cannot be ignored.

A second form of negative punishment is **time out**. In time out, the therapist limits the child's access to reinforcement for a certain period of time. Time out can take a number of forms, but it must involve the complete absence of reinforcement. Children should not be allowed to play, avoid tasks, or gain attention from others while in time out. Time out is usually accomplished by physically removing the child from the reinforcing situation for several minutes.

A final form of negative punishment is **response cost**. In response cost, the therapist withdraws reinforcers from the child immediately following a problematic act. Each problematic behavior "costs" the child a number of tangible reinforcers, such as candy, points, tokens, or other desired objects or privileges. Response cost is analogous to receiving a fine. Response cost is similar to time out. In time out, reinforcement is withdrawn *for a specific amount of time.* In response cost, reinforcement is withdrawn *in a specific quantity.* Response cost is often used in combination with token economies. Children may be reinforced with tokens or points for each desirable behavior and required to give up a certain number of tokens or points for each problematic behavior.

Behavioral treatment for people with Mental Retardation has considerable empirical support. Kahng and colleagues (2002) reviewed 35 years of published research on the effectiveness of behavior therapy to treat SIBs. Data from 706 individuals showed an overall reduction in SIBs of 83.7%. The most effective treatments tended to involve punishment (e.g., overcorrection, shock, time out) with 83.2% effectiveness, followed by extinction (e.g., planned ignoring) with 82.6% effectiveness, and positive reinforcement (e.g., DRI, DR0) with 73.2% effectiveness. Combining behavioral interventions usually resulted in slightly higher effectiveness than the use of any single intervention alone.

Medication

Medication is frequently administered to children and adolescents with Mental Retardation. Approximately 19%–29% of people in the community with Mental Retardation and 30%–40% of individuals in residential facilities with Mental Retardation are prescribed at least one psychiatric medication (Singh, Ellis, & Wechsler, 1997). Little research has examined the efficacy of medication in youths with Mental Retardation, for at least three reasons. First, for a long time, mental health experts did not think that children with Mental Retardation suffered from psychiatric disorders, or they overlooked their psychiatric symptoms. The problem of dual diagnosis has only recently been recognized. Second, it is difficult to recruit large samples of children with both Mental Retardation and a psychiatric diagnosis. Consequently, most research has involved very small samples. Third, many research studies have not used adequate experimental designs. Typically, a double-blind, placebo-controlled study is necessary to infer a causal relationship between the use of a medication and symptom reduction, but this type of study has been rare in the research literature (Singh, Matson, Cooper, Dixon, & Sturmey, 2005).

Medications for Disruptive Behaviors

Risperidone (Risperdal) is an atypical antipsychotic medication that blocks certain dopamine and serotonin receptors. It was first released in the United States in 1994 as a medication to treat schizophrenia and other psychotic disorders in adults. Some psychiatrists began using risperidone with developmentally delayed children who showed disruptive behavior problems. Today, risperidone is frequently used to treat oppositional and defiant behavior, destructive behavior, aggression, and self-injurious behavior in children and adolescents with Mental Retardation (Handen & Gilchrist, 2006b; Singh et al., 2005).

Evidence supporting the use of risperidone to treat disruptive behavior problems comes from a series of double-blind, placebo-controlled studies of children and adolescents who showed behavior problems and low intelligence. For example, Aman, De Smedt, Derivan, Lyons, Findling, and the Risperidone Disruptive Behavior Study Group (2002) examined 118 children aged 5 to 12 years who showed both low intellectual functioning and significant behavior problems. Children were randomly assigned to either an experimental group whose members received a low dose of risperidone or to a control group whose members received a placebo. Six weeks later, 77% of the children in the experimental group showed significant improvement in their behavior, compared to only 33% of children in the control group (see Figure 5.4). Other studies have yielded similar results (Findling, Aman, Eerdekens, Derivan, Lyons, & Risperidone Behavior Study Group, 2004; Snyder et al., 2002).

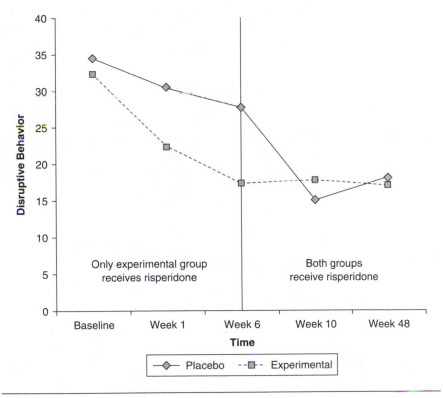

Figure 5.4   The Effects of Risperidone

Source: Based on Aman et al. (2002).

Note: Children who received risperidone showed a significant reduction in disruptive behavior after one week, compared to controls. When children in the control group began using risperidone, they also showed a reduction in disruptive behavior.

Medication for Stereotypies and Self-Injurious Behavior

Physicians often prescribe traditional antipsychotic medications to suppress SIBs. Most traditional antipsychotics block dopamine receptors. Interestingly, some individuals who show SIBs also display a hypersensitivity to dopamine. Consequently, there is reason to expect that medications that block certain dopamine receptors would be especially effective at reducing SIBs and stereotypies (Szymanski & Kaplan, 2006).

Research examining the effectiveness of dopamine blockers has been limited, however. Two antipsychotic medications, haloperidol and fluphenazine, appear to be effective in treating adults with SIBs; however, these medications have not been adequately studied with children (Aman, Collier-Crespin, & Lindsay, 2000). Critics argue that these drugs reduce problematic behavior mostly through sedation. Consequently, individuals taking traditional antipsychotics show a general decrease in *all* behaviors, not just problematic ones.

Some individuals who engage in self-injurious behavior show high secretions of endogenous opioids. Opioids may reduce pain sensitivity during the SIBs. Consequently, some physicians have used **naltrexone**, a drug that blocks opioid receptors, to curb SIBs. Research investigating the efficacy of naltrexone has been mixed. Unfortunately, some of the largest studies, including those involving children, have not shown naltrexone to be efficacious.

Medication for Anxiety and Mood Disorders

Antidepressants have been used to treat anxiety and mood disorders in adolescents with Mental Retardation. Unfortunately, research supporting their use has largely involved only case studies and anecdotal reports (Aman et al., 2000). Physicians have also used lithium and valporic acid for children with Mental Retardation and Bipolar Disorder. However, few large-scale studies have been conducted to investigate their efficacy (Aman et al., 2000).

Update: Dontrell and Andrew

After diagnosing Dontrell with Mental Retardation, Dr. Valencia provided a written report of her findings to his pediatrician. Dr. Valencia also recommended that Dontrell be screened for a possible genetic disorder that might underlie his impairments. Approximately one week later, she learned that Dontrell had PWS. Most infants are screened for genetic disorders like PWS shortly after birth. However, Dontrell may have been overlooked because of his mother's reluctance to receive medical attention during pregnancy.

Dontrell's pediatrician began administering growth hormone treatment to help him lose weight. Furthermore, his grandmother began meeting with a nutritionist to help Dontrell maintain a healthy diet and achieve sufficient exercise. Dr. Valencia referred Dontrell to a special needs preschool that offered early intensive behavioral training for children with developmental delays. She also continued to meet with Dontrell's grandmother on a weekly basis to teach her strategies to deal with Dontrell's disruptive behavior. These techniques involved (1) reinforcing Dontrell with praise and healthy treats for using language and playing quietly, (2) ignoring aversive behaviors like tantrums, and (3) responding to aggressive behaviors with time out. These techniques were effective in reducing, but not eliminating, Dontrell's behavior problems.

Six months later, Dontrell's grandmother called Dr. Valencia to say that Dontrell was making progress in language and adaptive skills at home and school. For example, he was able to make simple verbal requests (usually for food), respond to questions, and play with classmates. His physician also began administering medications to help him with his hyperactivity and sleep problems.

Andrew, the adolescent with FAS, continued to participate in therapy with Dr. Onak for several months. Most of the therapy was supportive in nature. Dr. Onak helped Andrew identify and cope with his feelings toward his mother, who made little progress in her own recovery from alcohol dependence. Dr. Onak acknowledged Andrew's mother's role in the development of his problems, but insisted that Andrew assume responsibility for his own life. He explained, "Your mom might have made it hard for you to learn at school and live a normal life, but now it's your decision. What are you going to do about it?" Over time, Andrew decided that he needed to learn from his mother's mistakes and avoid drinking. He also needed to "make something" of his life in order to be a good role model for his younger sister.

Andrew eventually decided that he no longer wanted to visit his mother on weekends. With Andrew's permission, Dr. Onak suggested to Andrew's aunt and social worker that a three-month moratorium be placed on visitation. During this moratorium, Andrew's mood and behavior at home improved. Furthermore, Andrew did not get into any fights at school. Andrew began an after-school job at a local grocery store, which also increased his self-esteem and self-concept. Andrew never resumed regular visitation with his mother, who bore a third child later that year.

Critical Thinking Exercises

1. When many people think of Mental Retardation, they think about a child with Down syndrome. To what extent is a child with Down syndrome an accurate portrayal of all children with Mental Retardation?

2. Until recently, people mistakenly believed that children and adolescents with Mental Retardation could not experience other psychiatric disorders. Why? Why might it be difficult for a psychologist or physician to assess anxiety and depression in a child with moderate Mental Retardation?

3. Many professionals classify Mental Retardation into two broad categories: organic Mental Retardation and cultural-familial Mental Retardation. How can these labels be misleading? Why might it be better to describe children with Mental Retardation based on their behavioral phenotype?

4. How does the treatment for PKU illustrate the interaction of genes and environment in child development?

5. Why are children of lower SES backgrounds at greater risk for certain types of Mental Retardation? Why might low-SES children with Mental Retardation have poorer prognoses than middle-class children with Mental Retardation?

CHAPTER 6

Autism and Other Pervasive Developmental Disorders

Kylie and Thomas

When I found out I was pregnant, Matt and I were over the moon. Then I had a scan which confirmed that we were having twins. At 37 weeks, I gave birth by C-section to Kylie, who weighed 5 lbs 9 oz, and then Thomas, who was 6 lbs 3 oz. It was hard at first, but then we learned to cope . . . with the lack of sleep at least!

By 14 months, Kylie was walking and talking. However, Thomas was a lot slower. Our doctor said he was just the slower twin and not to worry. At 18 months, Thomas finally began to walk, but he never played with his twin sister and wasn't talking. I asked the nurse who was also beginning to be concerned about him. She got in contact with a local child development center and a lady came to see us.

Image 6.1 Thomas

Source: Used with permission of his mother.

Image 6.2 Kylie

Source: Used with permission of her mother.

(Continued)

(Continued)

> Penny came to our house to watch Thomas. I remember he sat on the floor lining his bricks in a row and making unusual sounds. He was disinterested in the rest of us. Penny sat writing in her book. Then she looked at us and said, "I think Thomas may have autism." I actually had an idea that she might say that. I had looked on the Internet and came across a Web site which explained to me what the symptoms were. To be honest, the shock wasn't so bad when we were told. After his assessment, Thomas was diagnosed with severe Autistic Disorder.
>
> The twins are now eight. Thomas is still nonverbal and still in diapers. Kylie is his big sister and always will be. She sits with him and tries so hard to teach him words. I used to be really upset at the stares that Thomas would get from others. But now I just take no notice. I hate the word "normal." Thomas is normal to us.

Source: Reproduced with permission of Kylie and Thomas's mother.

What Are Pervasive Developmental Disorders?

Pervasive Developmental Disorders (PDDs) are serious conditions characterized by "severe and pervasive impairment" in at least one of three areas of functioning: (1) reciprocal social interaction; (2) communication; or (3) the presence of stereotyped behaviors, interests, or activities. In most cases, youths with pervasive developmental disorders show marked impairments in two or all three of these areas (Georgiades et al., 2007).

Reciprocal social interaction refers to the child's ability to interact with other people by maintaining eye contact, displaying appropriate emotions, understanding others' social behaviors, and participating in the natural give-and-take of social interactions. All children with PDDs show at least some problems in social interactions. Some children show an interest in other people, but their social interactions are awkward or one-sided. Other youths are almost completely socially withdrawn and unresponsive to others.

Communication skills include the child's ability to understand language, to gesture, to speak, to appropriately use language in dialogue with others, and to read and write. Almost all children with pervasive developmental disorders show at least some deficits in communication skills; however, there is a considerable range in their communicative abilities. Some children with PDDs can talk, read, and write, but their use of language in social situations is awkward or idiosyncratic. Other children with PDDs are completely mute.

Many youths with PDDs show **stereotyped behaviors, interests, or activities**. Some youths appear preoccupied with idiosyncratic topics, such as electrical circuits, train schedules, or sports statistics. These children and adolescents exhaust others' patience, attempting to talk about their interests at every opportunity. Other youths with PDDs show an extreme need for "sameness"; that is, they resent disruptions to their daily schedules, surroundings, or belongings. Still other children and adolescents show repetitive and socially isolated actions that appear to have no purpose. For example, some children with PDDs will fidget with their fingers, rock in place, spin, or wave their arms for long periods of time.

Most, but not all, children with PDDs have Mental Retardation. Some children and adolescents show severe or profound impairment in intellectual functioning. These youths often need constant supervision and care. Other youths with PDDs earn IQ scores within normal limits and may even have special talents, skills, or abilities. However, their social, communicative, and behavioral deficits interfere with their daily functioning.

As you can see, youths with PDDs show a wide range of impairments and abilities. To say that someone has PDD merely implies that he has marked problems in social, communicative, and/or behavioral functioning. The term PDD does not tell us much about the child's unique strengths and challenges. As we discuss children and adolescents with PDD in this chapter, we need to be mindful of their heterogeneity. There is no such thing as a "typical" child with PDD.

Autistic Disorder

Autism was first described by Leo Kanner (1943) more than 60 years ago. Kanner used the term "early infantile autism" to describe 11 children who showed difficulty relating to other people and adjusting to new situations. Kanner identified two features that he believed were especially salient in these children. First, the children showed "autistic aloneness" or a tendency toward extreme self-isolation and an apparent lack of interest in social interaction. Second, they displayed an "obsessive insistence on sameness" or a strong desire to avoid novelty or changes to their daily routine.

Kanner also noticed that his patients showed marked delays or deficits in language. All were slow in learning to speak and most showed unusual characteristics in their language use. For example, many of these children repeated words or phrases. Others reversed or misused pronouns in their speech. Still others spoke in an awkward, rigid manner.

Today, **Autistic Disorder** describes a persistent and pervasive deficit in three general areas: (1) social interaction; (2) communication; and (3) flexible, adaptive behavior (see Table 6.1). We will now examine each of these essential features.

Social Interaction

Perhaps the most salient feature of autism is the child's pervasive deficits in social interaction. Children with autism are often described as being "in their own world" and largely uninterested in social interactions. They may avoid eye contact with others and seem uninterested in others' activities or reactions to their behavior. They may not respond to the sound of their name, hand clapping and waving, or other bids for their attention. Young children with autism do not assume an anticipatory posture before being picked up. Indeed, they are often reluctant to let others touch them. They may not respond to hugs and other signs of affection from others, and they usually show little emotion. They seldom, if ever, initiate social interactions and usually do not participate in imitative games like "peek-a-boo" or "the itsy-bitsy spider" (Bregman, 2005).

Table 6.1   Diagnostic Criteria for Autistic Disorder

A. A total of six (or more) of the following symptoms from (1), (2), and (3) below, with at least two symptoms from (1), one symptom from (2), and one symptom from (3).

1. Qualitative impairment in social interaction (must have at least 2):
    a. Shows marked impairment in nonverbal behaviors (e.g., eye contact, facial expressions, body postures)
    b. Failure to develop peer relationships
    c. Does not spontaneously share enjoyment, interests, or achievements with others (e.g., showing a toy or drawing, pointing out an object of interest)
    d. Lacks social or emotional reciprocity

2. Qualitative impairment in communication (must have at least 1):
    a. Delay in the development of spoken language or lack of spoken language
    b. If child has adequate speech, child shows problems initiating or sustaining conversations with others
    c. Shows stereotyped and repetitive use of language or idiosyncratic language (e.g., echolalia, makes up words)
    d. Lack of varied, make-believe play or failure to imitate others during play

3. Restricted repetitive and stereotyped patterns of behavior, interests, and activities (must show at least 1):
    a. Preoccupation with one or more stereotyped or restricted patterns of interest that is abnormal in intensity or focus
    b. Inflexible adherence to specific routines or rituals that seem to have no purpose
    c. Stereotyped and repetitive motor mannerisms (e.g., hand or finger flapping or twisting, complex whole-body movements)
    d. Persistent preoccupation with parts of objects

B. The child showed delays or abnormal functioning in at least one of the following areas before age 3 years: (1) social interaction, (2) language as used in social communication, and (3) symbolic or imaginative play.

C. The symptoms are not better explained by Rett's Disorder or Childhood Disintegrative Disorder.

Source: Reprinted with permission from the *DSM-IV-TR*.

As children with autism develop, they begin to show greater tolerance for social interactions with family members. For example, they may allow parents to place them on their laps or let caregivers touch and cuddle with them. Some seem to enjoy being tickled or held in affectionate ways. Nevertheless, children with autism rarely initiate social interactions or engage in novel activities. They appear relatively uninterested in playing with other children and are generally unable to form friendships. They may interact with others, but their communication and social relationships seem artificial and one-sided.

Older children and adolescents with autism usually continue to show marked impairments in social functioning. They tend to have few friends and social interests, and they may be ostracized by peers. Some older children with autism are able to engage in rigid, scripted play in which they direct activities. For example, high-functioning adolescents with autism might enjoy playing the role of "banker" in *Monopoly*. These youths generally avoid unscripted activities such as "hanging out" with friends. Some of these children and adolescents develop narrow interests or become obsessed with specific hobbies, such as collecting trading cards or certain types of rocks. However, they infrequently join clubs or play spontaneously with peers (Bregman, 2005).

Communication

All children with autism show marked impairment in language. Approximately 50% of children with autism are mute. Those who are able to speak tend to show marked delays in language (Howlin, 2006).

Children with autism show five types of language problems. First, approximately 85% of children with autism who speak show **echolalia**; that is, they repeat words that they hear others speak or overhear on television and radio. Oftentimes, these words are taken out of context or repeated at inappropriate times, so they seem nonsensical to others.

Second, many children with autism show **pronoun reversal**. For example, a child with autism might state, "You are hungry" when he wants to say, "I am hungry." Other children with autism refer to themselves in the third person, saying, "He wants some water" when they mean to say, "I want some water."

Third, many children with autism show **abnormal prosody**; that is, their tone or manner of speech is atypical or awkward. For example, some children with autism speak mechanically. Other children speak with an unusual rhythm or intonation, using a sing-song voice. Still others talk loudly or stress the wrong syllables when speaking.

Fourth, almost all children with autism who are able to speak show **problems with pragmatics**; that is, they have difficulty using language in a given social context (Tager-Flusberg, Paul, & Lord, 2005). They may speak in grammatically correct sentences, but their sentences do not fit the social situation. For example, many children with autism do not provide appropriate context for their statements. A boy with autism might begin a conversation saying, "*We* enjoyed *that* yesterday. . . ." without explaining to his friend that he is referring to a movie that he saw with his family earlier in the week. Another example of poor pragmatics is tangential conversation. For example, a schoolmate might ask a girl with autism, "How are you today?" The girl might respond in an off-topic, tangential manner, saying, "I ate a hotdog for lunch." Still other children with autism inappropriately switch topics in the middle of conversations, often confusing and frustrating listeners.

Fifth, the communication style of children with autism is generally one-sided. These children communicate primarily to express their needs or to gain information. They seldom talk to others to share their thoughts, past experiences, or feelings. In general, children with autism do not show the natural reciprocity that characterizes most dialogue. They seem to be talking *to* others rather than talking *with* others (Bregman, 2005).

Repetitive Behaviors

Children with autism show repetitive behaviors that fall into two general categories: (1) stereotyped, repetitive motor movements and (2) insistence on following elaborate, ritualized routines (Klinger, Dawson, & Renner, 2003).

Image 6.3   Shaun. Shaun is a boy with autism. He is fascinated with the sound of water hitting the pavement outside his house.

Source: Used with permission of his family and photographer Lindsay Weekes.

The most common stereotyped behaviors include rocking, hand flapping, whirling, and unusual repetitive mannerisms with hands and fingers (Volkmar, Cohen, & Paul, 1986). Roughly one-half of children with autism show at least one of these repetitive behaviors. Stereotypes are most common among younger children with autism and among individuals with lower intellectual functioning.

Complex ritualistic behaviors are more common among older children with autism and among individuals with higher intellectual functioning. Some children spend hours each day sorting and arranging toys, clothes, or collectables. Other children have food rituals. For example, one child with autism insisted on eating his foods in a certain order, according to color and texture. Still other children with autism show compulsive behaviors such as ritualistic patterns of walking around the room or turning light switches on and off. Some children show intense preoc-cupation with specific topics such as the batting averages of baseball players, the birth and death dates of U.S. presidents, or the history of certain weather patterns (see Image 6.3).

A common feature of many children with autism is their strong desire for daily routines. Many of these children insist on the same day-to-day schedules and become extremely distressed when daily routines are altered or broken. For example, one boy with autism became argumentative and aggressive because he was unable to watch his favorite television program during a power outage.

Longitudinal studies indicate that stereotyped and ritualistic behaviors usually emerge *after* deficits in social functioning and communication (Klinger et al., 2003). Some experts have suggested that children develop these repetitive behaviors in response to their impairment in social and communicative functioning. For example, children with severe or profound Mental Retardation might use stereo-typed rocking or hand flapping to escape boredom or alleviate anxiety. Higher-functioning youths with autism might insist on daily rituals in order to gain a sense of control over their otherwise stressful daily lives. Other youths might develop circumscribed interests in response to ostracism by peers.

Asperger's Disorder

In 1944, the Viennese pediatrician Hans Asperger described four children with behavioral characteristics that resembled the children with autism described by Kanner one year earlier. Like Kanner's patients, Asperger's patients showed marked problems interacting with others. Asperger noticed that they had considerable problems approaching others and engaging them in conversation, looking others in the eye while speaking, and showing typical emotions. The children also tended to be preoccupied with singular topics about which they knew a great deal of information. Unlike the children described by Kanner, however, Asperger's patients showed good vocabularies and basic language skills. Indeed, many of these children were very talkative and would carry on lengthy discourses on their favorite, idiosyncratic subjects.

Today, **Asperger's Disorder** (AD) describes children with severe impairments in social functioning and marked preoccupation with idiosyncratic topics (see Table 6.2). Unlike children with autism, children with AD *do not* show delays in intellectual functioning or self-help skills in early childhood. In fact, some children with AD show average or above-average IQs. Also in contrast to children with autism, children with AD *do not* show delays in language acquisition in early childhood (Volkmar & Klin, 2000).

Table 6.2 Diagnostic Criteria for Asperger's Disorder

---

1. Qualitative impairment in social interaction (must have at least 2):
   a. Shows marked impairment in nonverbal behaviors (e.g., eye contact, facial expressions, body postures)
   b. Failure to develop peer relationships
   c. Does not spontaneously share enjoyment, interests, or achievements with others (e.g., showing a toy or drawing, pointing out an object of interest)
   d. Lacks social or emotional reciprocity

2. Restricted repetitive and stereotyped patterns of behavior, interests, and activities (must show at least 1):
   a. Preoccupation with one or more stereotyped or restricted patterns of interest that is abnormal in intensity or focus
   b. Inflexible adherence to specific routines or rituals that seem to have no purpose
   c. Stereotyped and repetitive motor mannerisms (e.g., hand or finger flapping or twisting, complex whole-body movements)
   d. Persistent preoccupation with parts of objects

3. Symptoms cause marked impairment in functioning

4. There is no clinically significant general delay in language (e.g., child speaks single words by age 2 years and meaningful phrases by age 3 years)

5. There is no clinically significant delay in cognitive development or in the development of age-appropriate self-help skills other than social interaction (e.g., child does not have Mental Retardation or problems with daily living skills)

6. Child does not meet diagnostic criteria for another specific Pervasive Developmental Disorder or Schizophrenia

---

Source: Reprinted with permission from the *DSM-IV-TR*.

Tyler

Tyler was a 10-year-old boy who was referred to our clinic by his pediatrician. His doctor said Tyler was having "social problems and issues with self-esteem." Tyler was a healthy child who lived with his father (a software developer), mother (a homemaker), and three-year-old sister. According to his mother, Tyler had difficulty interacting with children his own age. Tyler had ostracized himself from his classmates because of his unusual preoccupation with fantasy role-playing games. Instead of playing sports or talking about movies, Tyler seemed to bring up fantasy and role-playing games whenever he got the chance. Even his classmates, who initially found role-playing games interesting, had been put off by Tyler's persistent discussion of ogres, magic spells, and "hit points."

At first, Tyler didn't seem to notice that his preoccupation with role-playing games bored or annoyed his peers. Later, when classmates began to avoid him, Tyler started to retreat further into fantasy gaming and away from age-appropriate social play.

Tyler's psychologist, Dr. Nash, asked, "Don't you want to play with the other kids?" Tyler responded, "Of course I do, but they don't want to play with me. I try to get them to play Magic the Gathering or Dreamblade but they won't. So, I just play by myself. It's easier that way."

Social Awkwardness

The hallmark of AD, like the other PDDs, is social impairment. However, unlike children with autism, youths with AD often want to be around other people. They usually like to spend time with family and desire to be accepted by peers. Unfortunately, their social deficits interfere with their abilities to interact with others and make friends. Youths with AD usually appear awkward or insensitive to others during social interactions. For example, a child with AD who wants to join a game might simply intrude on the activity or insist on directing play activities around his or her own interests.

Over time, the awkward and inappropriate social behavior displayed by children with AD can cause peer rejection. Children with AD are prone to anxiety and depression because they usually want friends, but they are frequently ostracized by classmates and peers (Tsai, 2004b).

Idiosyncratic Language

By definition, children with AD do not show delays in language acquisition. They tend to speak in two-word phrases by their second birthdays and use simple sentences by age three years. By the time they reach preschool, their language is generally well-developed and complex. Some children with AD are even precocious with respect to language.

Although children with AD do not show marked language delays, their language is unusual in at least three respects. First, many individuals with AD show poor prosody. For example, they may speak too quickly, use jerky speech, or speak loudly

Table 6.3   Language Characteristics of Children With Asperger's Disorder

Language and Communication	Percentage
Not aware of social situation when talking	68
Talks in monologues, comments on own actions, or talks to self	56
Shows deviant modulation (e.g., monotonous) or articulation (e.g., over-exact)	54
Gets off topic or derailed when talking	33
Pedantic or long-winded speech	30
Verbosity or "endless talking"	28
Obsessive questioning, frequently debates with others, argumentative	26
Precocious, "know-it-all"	21
Neologisms (i.e., makes up or uses unusual words or phrases)	21
Common speech problems (e.g., stutters, lisps)	21
Echolalia (i.e., repeating words or phrases)	19

Source: Based on Hippler and Klicpera (2003).

Note: Speech characteristics of 43 children and adolescents initially seen by Hans Asperger and colleagues.

at inappropriate times. Second, their speech is usually tangential and circumstantial. For example, they may talk incessantly about an esoteric topic. Third, children with AD often talk constantly. Their discussions are usually described as pedantic ramblings that exhaust their listeners. Often, children with AD do not seem to care whether anyone is listening to them at all (Klin, McPartland, & Volkmar, 2005; see Table 6.3).

Circumscribed Interests

Perhaps the most interesting feature of children with AD is their fascination with idiosyncratic topics. As stated by Klinger and colleagues (2003), these highly specialized interests are often "appropriate in *content*, but always unusual in their *intensity*" (p. 421). For example, it is not uncommon to see a five-year-old fascinated by trains or a ten-year-old interested in baseball statistics. These idiosyncratic interests become problematic when they preoccupy the child's time to the extent they interfere with other activities or social relationships. For example, the five-year-old might spend hours each day playing with and talking about trains, exhausting his parents' patience. He might frequently tantrum if denied access to trains. Similarly, the ten-year-old may be ostracized by classmates and reprimanded by his teachers because of his obsessive interest in earned run averages.

Experts disagree as to whether AD is a separate disorder from autism. Many experts believe AD is simply a form of high-functioning autism (Mayes, Calhoun, & Grites, 2001). For example, it is extremely difficult to differentiate children with autism who have normal intellectual functioning from children with AD. Similarly, many children diagnosed with autism in early childhood show improvement in language abilities over time; by late childhood or adolescence, they sometimes show symptoms very similar to those displayed by children with AD (Gilchrist, Green, Cox, Burton, Rutter, & Le Couteur, 2001; Ozonoff, South, & Miller, 2000).

On the other hand, other experts maintain that the disorders are distinct (Szatmari, Archer, & Fisman, 1995). For example, most high-functioning individuals with autism do not show the same degree of circumscribed interests and preoccupations as do children with AD.

Rett's Disorder

Rett's Disorder is a severe neurological disorder first described by the Austrian physician Andreas Rett in 1966. By chance, Rett noticed two girls in his waiting room displaying similar patterns of unusual hand movements. After reviewing the medical records of these girls, he discovered that they had similar developmental histories. Both girls showed relatively normal social, cognitive, and motor development for the first few months of life and then displayed a dramatic loss of functioning in all three areas. They also displayed the stereotypical hand movements that he witnessed in his office.

Today, **Rett's Disorder** (RD) is characterized by a unique pattern of social, cognitive, and behavioral development resulting in severe or profound Mental Retardation (see Table 6.4). Infants with Rett's Disorder seem to develop normally, at least for a period of five or six months. In some cases, these infants display excessive hand movements or hand gesturing, but these signs are minimal and usually overlooked by parents and pediatricians.

Then, usually between 12 and 24 months of age, these children experience rapid deterioration in social, communicative, cognitive, and behavioral functioning. First, children with RD display rapid head growth deceleration. By age four years, head circumference is generally two to three standard deviations below the mean and roughly the weight of a typically developing one-year-old child (Armstrong, 2001; Tsai, 2004a).

Second, children with RD lose interest in social activities and develop a preoccupation with inanimate objects. By the time they reach the preschool years, these children show most of the same social deficits as children with autism.

Table 6.4   Diagnostic Criteria for Rett's Disorder

A. All of the following:
  1. Apparently normal prenatal and perinatal development
  2. Apparently normal psychomotor development through first 5 months after birth
  3. Normal head circumference at birth

B. Onset of all of the following after the period of normal development:
  1. Deceleration of head growth between ages 5 and 48 months
  2. Loss of previously acquired purposeful hand skills between ages 5 and 30 months with the later development of stereotyped hand movements (e.g., hand-wringing or "washing")
  3. Loss of social engagement
  4. Poorly coordinated walk or body movements
  5. Severely impaired receptive and expressive language development with severe psychomotor retardation (i.e., slowed or sluggish movements)

Source: Reprinted with permission from the *DSM-IV-TR*.

Third, these children display the loss of purposeful hand movements; that is, they can no longer gesture, grasp objects, or hold objects in meaningful ways. Purposeful hand movements are often replaced by stereotyped gestures or hand wringing. Children with RD may squeeze, clap, tap, or make rubbing or washing movements with their hands.

Fourth, youths with RD show serious impairments in language and cognition. By early childhood, these children usually earn IQ scores in the range of severe or profound Mental Retardation. Many become mute, although some retain the ability to speak in simple words or phrases.

Although many children with RD show problems with breathing, breathing irregularities are not required for the diagnosis. Some children with the disorder intermittently hyperventilate, while others spontaneously hold their breath or swallow gulps of air. Children with RD may also show problems with eating. Many of these children swallow infrequently. Consequently, they may drool profusely and have difficulty ingesting food. Others do not chew their food. Some exhibit a frequent tongue thrust, making oral ingestion difficult. Most suck or bite their fingers and hands. Others grimace or grind their teeth.

Children with RD tend to have certain physical abnormalities. First, they tend to be underweight and short in stature. Second, most have orthopedic problems, spinal deformities, or joint contractures. By age eight, the majority show scoliosis. Third, girls with RD typically have low bone mineral density. Consequently, they often develop osteoporosis later in life. Finally, seizures are common among children with RD. Approximately 80% develop some form of seizure, usually during early childhood.

Most cases of RD are caused by mutations in a specific gene that codes for the X-linked methyl-CpG-binding protein 2 (**MECP2**; Amir, Van den Veyver, Wan, Tran, Francke, & Zoghbi, 1999). MECP2 plays a role in the development of the brain and central nervous system. Mutations to the gene that codes for MECP2 cause abnormalities in brain development. Approximately 85% of individuals with RD show specific MECP2 mutations. Thirty different mutations on this gene have been identified so far, each leading to slightly different manifestation of the disorder (Tsai, 2004b; Van Acker, Loncola, & Van Acker, 2005).

The prognosis of RD is poor. After children show a loss of social, communicative, cognitive, and motor functioning in early childhood, they tend to enter a plateau stage that lasts until adolescence. During this plateau period, some children with RD show an increase in social interaction and language, especially if they are given intensive educational support. During adolescence, most individuals with RD show further physical deterioration, including severe scoliosis. Approximately 80% become wheelchair dependent.

Childhood Disintegrative Disorder

In 1908, the Viennese special education teacher Theodore Heller described six children with a severe developmental disorder that is now called Childhood Disintegrative Disorder (CDD). Heller used the term "infantile dementia" to describe the disorder because of the rapid cognitive, linguistic, and behavioral deterioration shown by the children (Volkmar, Koenig, & State, 2005; see Table 6.5).

Table 6.5   Diagnostic Criteria for Childhood Disintegrative Disorder

A. Apparently normal development for the first 2 years after birth (i.e., age-appropriate verbal and nonverbal communication, social relationships, play, and day-to-day behavior)

B. Significant loss of previously acquired skills, before age 10 years, in at least two of the following areas:
   1. Receptive or expressive language
   2. Social skills or adaptive behavior
   3. Bowel or bladder control
   4. Play
   5. Motor skills

C. Abnormal functioning in at least two of the following areas:
   1. Qualitative impairment in social interaction (e.g., problems in nonverbal behaviors, failure to develop peer relationships, lack of social or emotional reciprocity)
   2. Qualitative impairments in communication (e.g., delay or lack of spoken language, inability to sustain or initiate a conversation, stereotyped and repetitive use of language)
   3. Restricted, repetitive, and stereotyped patterns of behavior, interests, and activities including stereotyped motor movements and mannerisms

D. Symptoms are not better explained by another Pervasive Developmental Disorder or Schizophrenia.

Source: Reprinted with permission from the *DSM-IV-TR*.

Children with CDD show typical development from birth until at least age two years (see Figure 6.1). Most show adequate social development, learn to crawl and walk in an age-expected manner, and learn to speak in simple two-word sentences by their second birthday. Then, usually around age three, they experience a significant loss of functioning in at least two of the following areas: (1) social skills or adaptive behavior, (2) language, (3) bowel or bladder control, (4) play, or (5) motor skills. In most cases, children with CDD deteriorate in most or all of these areas. Deterioration is usually rapid, typically occurring over a matter of weeks or months. By the time children reach preschool age, they show little interest in social interactions, are largely unresponsive to others, have no meaningful use of language, and show very low cognitive functioning. Children with CDD also tend to show stereotyped behaviors and may overreact to changes in their daily routine.

By early childhood, the intellectual functioning of children with CDD is generally within the range of severe or profound Mental Retardation. They are often incontinent and need to be fed by others. Most are unable to communicate verbally and remain largely disinterested in other people and social stimuli. In approximately 25% of cases, however, children show limited recovery from the disorder. Specifically, they may show increased interest in caregivers and learn to speak in simple words or phrases.

The cause of CDD is unknown. In many cases, the onset of the disorder follows a stressful life event or medical illness, for example, the death of a grandparent, a surgery, or a childhood illness. However, researchers doubt that these stressors cause the disorder because they are fairly common experiences for young children.

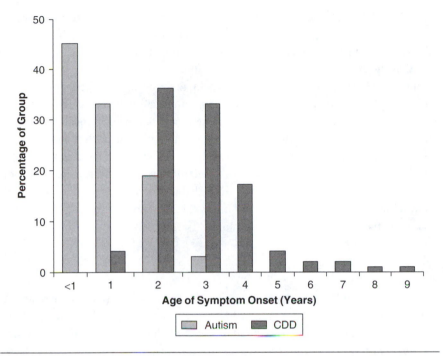

Figure 6.1   Onset of Autistic Disorder and Childhood Disintegrative Disorder

Source: From Volkmar et al. (2005). Used with permission.

Note: Autism is usually first recognized before age three years; in contrast, CDD is usually not seen until after age two or three years.

Researchers have been unable to find structural brain differences in children with and without CDD. Furthermore, CDD does not appear to run in families. Consequently, researchers have speculated that CDD may be due to a genetic mutation rather than genes inherited from parents (Volkmar et al., 2005).

The long-term prognosis for children with CDD is poor. Approximately 25% of children with CDD develop seizures, while an additional 25%–50% show other serious medical problems. Nearly all will be dependent on others for care (Tsai, 2004b).

Pervasive Developmental Disorder Not Otherwise Specified

Children can be diagnosed with Pervasive Developmental Disorder Not Otherwise Specified (PDD-NOS) when they display severe and pervasive impairment in social interactions, communication skills, or stereotyped interests and behaviors, but do not meet full diagnostic criteria for any other pervasive developmental disorder.

PDD-NOS is usually used to diagnose children who show **childhood-onset autism**. These children meet all diagnostic criteria for autism except the onset of the disorder is after age three years. Researchers have generally found few differences between children with autism whose onset is before versus after age three years.

PDD-NOS is also frequently used to describe individuals with **residual autism**. These individuals have met diagnostic criteria for autism in the past, but they have shown such improvement in their social, communicative, or behavioral functioning that they no longer meet the criteria for the disorder.

Finally, PDD-NOS is sometimes used to describe a heterogeneous group of children who show many features of autism but not enough characteristics to meet diagnostic criteria. These children are often said to have **atypical autism**. For example, some children show symptoms consistent with both autism and Asperger's Disorder, but symptoms are not severe enough to merit either diagnosis. Other children with severe or profound Mental Retardation show autistic-like behaviors, but the clinician is uncertain whether these behaviors reflect autism or simply the child's low cognitive functioning. Still other children show medical or neurological disorders that cause autistic-like symptoms (Tsai, 2004b).

The Autism Spectrum

DSM-IV-TR adopts a categorical approach to diagnosis: Children are diagnosed with either Autistic Disorder, AD, or PDD-NOS. However, Lorna Wing (1981) has proposed that pervasive developmental disorders should be viewed continuously, rather than categorically. At one end of the continuum are children with effective social functioning, expressive language, and flexible interests and behaviors. At the other end of the continuum are children who are completely socially withdrawn, mute, and preoccupied by stereotyped behaviors or rituals. In between these two extremes lie many children classified with pervasive developmental disorders. Some high-functioning children show only moderate impairments in one or two domains of functioning. These individuals might be diagnosed with high-functioning autism (i.e., PDD-NOS) or AD. Other children show severe deficits in all three areas and would be diagnosed with Autistic Disorder. Wing and others have suggested that these differences in functioning largely reflect children's levels of intelligence and verbal ability (Georgiades et al., 2007).

Today, many researchers and clinicians use the term **autism spectrum disorders** to describe the pervasive developmental disorders. The use of the term "spectrum" implies that differences between the three most common pervasive developmental disorders, Autistic Disorder, AD, and PDD-NOS, reflect a difference in *degree* of impairment rather than a difference in *kind* (Bregman, 2005; Wing, 2000).

Not all experts agree that pervasive developmental disorders should be viewed continuously. Klin and colleagues (2005) have argued that high-functioning autism and AD can be differentiated from one another based on the unique features of each disorder. For example, children with autism tend to isolate themselves from others and appear disinterested in social contact; in contrast, children with AD often seek out friendships with peers and interactions with adults. Another difference lies in language. Children with autism are likely to show severe and pervasive language problems, while children with AD often show language impairments predominantly in the area of pragmatics.

Associated Features and Disorders of the Autism Spectrum

Mental Retardation

Mental Retardation is not part of the diagnostic criteria for autism. However, approximately 70% of children and adolescents with Autistic Disorder also show Mental Retardation (Fombonne, 2005). Among youth with autism and Mental Retardation, approximately 40% show mild to moderate Mental Retardation and 60% show severe to profound Mental Retardation.

Anxiety and Depression

Most studies have shown relatively high rates of anxiety and mood disorders among youths with PDDs (Klinger et al., 2003). Prevalence estimates for anxiety disorders range from 7% to 84%. Anxiety is most common among individuals with high-functioning autism and AD. Obsessive-Compulsive Disorder (OCD) is the most common comorbid anxiety disorder. It is possible that autism and OCD have similar underlying genetic causes.

Rates of depression among individuals with PDDs vary from 4% to 58%. Depression is most common among older children and adolescents with autism and AD. It is possible that many high-functioning youths with autism and AD develop depression because they are aware of their social deficits or because they are rejected by peers (Kim, Szatmari, Bryson, Streiner, & Wilson, 2000). However, there is not enough research to draw this conclusion definitively (Howlin, 2005). Youths with autism and depression tend to show increased irritability and agitation, greater social withdrawal, and increased stereotyped behavior.

ADHD

The most common disruptive behavior problem among youths with PDDs is ADHD. Approximately 64% of children with autism show significant problems with attention and concentration, while 48% display hyperactive and impulsive tendencies (Tsai, 2004a). Some youths with PDDs show aggression and self-injurious behaviors; however, these behaviors are usually associated with comorbid Mental Retardation, rather than autism per se.

Tics and Tourette's Disorder

Tics are sudden, rapid, and recurrent motor movements or vocalizations that are beyond the individual's control. Motor tics are most common; they usually involve involuntary movements of the head, face, and neck. Examples include nose twitching, facial grimacing, eye blinks, and head tilting. Vocal tics are less common than motor tics. Examples of vocal tics include brief utterances such as chirps, grunts, or clicks. Motor and vocal tics usually occur multiple times per day in bouts. They may be triggered or exacerbated by stressful experiences or anxiety.

Tourette's Disorder is a psychological condition characterized by the presence of multiple motor tics and at least one vocal tic. Some people with Tourette's Disorder show coprolalia; that is, they involuntarily utter obscenities. However, coprolalia is seen in only 10% of people with Tourette's Disorder and is not necessary for the diagnosis (Spessot & Peterson, 2006).

Tics and Tourette's Disorder are more common among youths with autism than among typically developing children. Approximately 30% of youths with autism have tics, while 6.5% meet full diagnostic criteria for Tourette's Disorder (Baron-Cohen, Scahill, Izaguirre, Hornsey, & Robertson, 1999). Since autistic behaviors, OCD, and tics frequently co-occur, some researchers have speculated that these disorders have similar genetic or neurological underpinnings.

Epidemiology of Autism Spectrum Disorders

Prevalence

A number of large epidemiological studies have been conducted investigating the prevalence of Autistic Disorder in the general population (see Figure 6.2). Prevalence estimates vary, depending on the definition of autism used by the researchers, the size of the sample, and the year in which the study was conducted. Most studies indicate that 13 out of every 10,000 children will develop Autistic Disorder (Fombonne, 2005).

Less information is available about the prevalence of the other PDDs. The prevalence of AD is approximately 3 out of every 10,000 youth. Professionals used to think that Rett's Disorder was extremely rare. However, as medical and mental health professionals are become more familiar with the disorder, its prevalence has increased. Epidemiological studies estimate its prevalence to be 1 per 15,000 girls (Van Acker et al., 2005). The disorder is seen almost exclusively in girls.

PDD-NOS is the most frequently diagnosed PDD. Approximately 20 per 10,000 children meet criteria for PDD-NOS. The relatively high prevalence of PDD-NOS is probably due to the fact that this disorder reflects a large and heterogeneous mix of children (Fombonne, 2005).

Most epidemiological studies have estimated the prevalence of any autism spectrum disorder (i.e., autism, AD, or PDD-NOS) at approximately 3.6 per 1,000 youth (Fombonne, 2005). However, recent data collected by the Centers for Disease Control Autism and Developmental Disabilities Monitoring Network (CDC-ADDMN, 2007a, 2007b) indicate that the prevalence of autism spectrum disorders may be much higher, perhaps as high as 6.6 per 1,000 youth. Prevalence estimates for the PDDs have increased dramatically in recent years. The median prevalence for autism in studies conducted between 1966 and 1993 was 4.7 per 10,000. In contrast, the median prevalence in studies conducted between 1994 and 2004 was

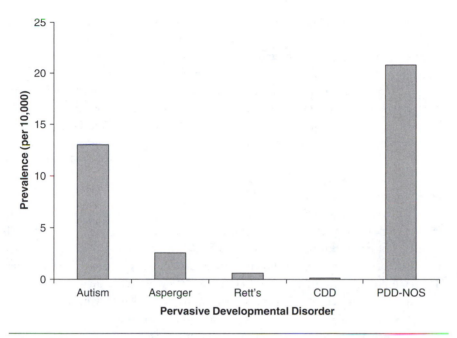

Figure 6.2   Prevalence of Pervasive Developmental Disorders in the General Population

Source: Based on Centers for Disease Control Autism and Developmental Disabilities Monitoring Network (2007a, 2007b) and Fombonne (2005).

Note: Most data indicate that autism spectrum disorders affect 3.6 per 1,000 youth. However, recent data indicate that the prevalence of autism spectrum disorders may be as high as 6.6 per 1,000 youth.

12.7 per 10,000. Some experts believe that more children are developing autism now than in recent years. However, most of the evidence suggests that autism is better recognized today than in the past; consequently, rates of diagnosis have increased (Gurney, Fritz, Ness, Sievers, Newschaffer, & Shapiro, 2003).

Gender and Ethnicity

Boys are more likely to be diagnosed with autism than are girls. Across studies, the gender ratio is approximately 4.3:1. On average, boys with autism are more likely than girls to have IQ scores within the normal range, whereas girls with autism are more likely to have IQ scores indicative of severe or profound Mental Retardation. Girls with autism are also more likely than boys to have seizures. Experts used to believe that girls with autism showed greater impairment in social and communicative functioning than did boys. However, emerging data indicate that these apparent differences were probably due to the fact that girls with autism often have lower IQ scores than boys. After controlling for IQ, girls and boys with autism show similar patterns of social behavior and language (CDC-ADDMN, 2007a, 2007b; Frombonne, 2005).

Experts are not sure why boys are more likely than girls to have autism. One explanation is that girls, in general, have an advantage in social and linguistic functioning compared to boys. Therefore, girls with autism would need to show greater levels of impairment before they would be diagnosed. Evidence for this explanation comes from studies showing that girls, on average, display superior social and communicative functioning at various times in development. For example, across the lifespan, girls are better than boys at interpreting other people's facial expressions, emotions, and nonverbal behavior. Similarly, girls show greater tendency to use language to convey emotions and share feelings than do boys. It is possible that these strengths in social and communicative functioning make autism less noticeable among girls (Koenig & Tsatsanis, 2005).

An alternative explanation is that male hormones lead to the development of autism disproportionately in boys. Considerable evidence suggests that high levels of male hormones during gestation can affect the developing brain. In particular, prenatal hormones have been shown to affect the limbic system and frontal cortex. This is important because the limbic system and frontal cortex are involved in perceiving, processing, and responding to social information. Furthermore, these brain regions may be underactive in youths with autism. It is possible that excessive exposure to male sex hormones in utero affects brain development, which, in turn, increases the likelihood of autistic behaviors (Koenig & Tsatsanis, 2005).

Most studies indicate that autism spectrum disorders are equally common among white and ethnic minority youth (CDC-ADDMN, 2007a). However, some evidence indicates that white children may be at slightly increased risk for pervasive developmental disorders over their African American counterparts. For example, the prevalence of autism spectrum disorders among white youth in Missouri and Pennsylvania is 7.7 and 7.6 per 1,000 youth, respectively. In contrast, the prevalence of autism spectrum disorders among their African American counterparts is 4.7 and 4.2 per 1,000 youth, respectively (CDC-ADDMN, 2007b). Experts do not know why white youth may be at increased risk for autism spectrum disorders in certain areas of the country.

Course

Parents of children with autism often report that their children's symptoms began during the first two years of life. Many parents remember feeling that something was "different" or unusual about their infant's social behavior. Some parents describe their infants as aloof, distant, or avoidant (Lord & Richler, 2006).

Prospective studies of infants later diagnosed with autism largely confirm parents' reports. Early signs of autism are sometimes present by age 18 months. For example, 18-month-olds later diagnosed with autism spend less time looking at others' faces and initiating social interactions with caregivers. They often do not respond when others call their names and do not share interesting toys with caregivers. Young children later diagnosed with autism seldom direct their attention when other people point to objects or events, and they show delays in make-believe social play (Klinger et al., 2003).

Most parents first seek professional advice shortly after their children's second birthday (Siklos & Kerns, 2007). They usually decide to seek the help of a pediatrician or psychologist because their child shows significant delays in language. Whereas typically developing children are able to speak in simple two-word phrases by their second birthday (e.g., "Give drink" or "Me cookie"), most children later diagnosed with autism speak few, if any, words by age two years.

On the other hand, one-third of children with autism do not show early signs of the disorder. Instead, this sizeable minority of children seems to show relatively normal social and linguistic development up to age two years. After age two, however, these children often display a lack of social initiative and social skills, a loss of language, and an increase in stereotyped behaviors (Davidovitch, Click, Holtzman, Tirosh, & Safir, 2000).

The course of autism is highly variable. Some individuals show a gradual improvement in autistic symptoms across childhood and adolescence (Piven et al., 1993). In one study, 13% of previously diagnosed children no longer met diagnostic criteria for autism five years later. An equal number of children with autism show continued impairment in social and communicative functioning and increases in ritualistic behavior, especially during adolescence (Klinger et al., 2003).

The long-term prognosis is generally poor (see Figure 6.3). Only a minority of children diagnosed with autism live independently as adults. Most live with their parents or in supervised communities. Their social outings are usually organized by others and not self-directed. Most adults with autism are unemployed or work unskilled jobs. Even the most high-functioning adults with autism usually assume semiskilled positions. Most have few friends. Fewer than 5% marry (Howlin, 2005).

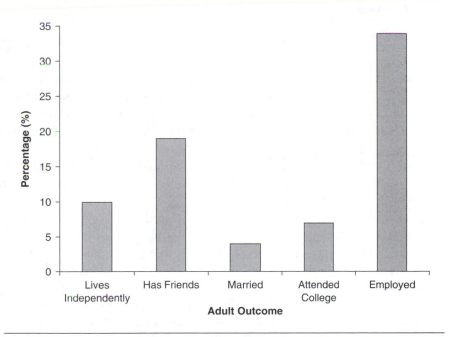

Figure 6.3   Adult Outcomes of People With Autism

Source: Based on Howlin (2005).

Note: Most individuals with autism have problems in social functioning throughout life.

Etiology of Autism Spectrum Disorders

The earliest hypotheses for the causes of autism placed considerable blame on families. Kanner (1943) believed that the parents of his patients were emotionally distant from their children. He described these parents as showing little interest in their children's behavior, as socially aloof, and as overly intellectual. Extending these observations, the philosopher and writer Bruno Bettelheim (1967) suggested that cold and rejecting parents *caused* their children to develop autistic behaviors. So-called "refrigerator mothers" caused children to retreat into themselves in response to their dismissive parenting practices. Bettelheim and others suggested that autism could be treated by helping parents become warmer and more accepting of their children.

Beginning in the 1960s and 1970s, researchers began challenging the theories of Bettelheim and others regarding the etiology of autism. Bernard Rimland (1964) first suggested that autism might have a neurological cause. Empirical data also showed that autism was not caused by cold or rejecting parenting. In fact, many parents of children with autism were extremely involved in their children's development and care. Unfortunately, many parents assumed that they were somehow responsible for having a child with autism. New theories, which implicated genetics and neurodevelopment, slowly alleviated some of this guilt.

Today, we still do not know exactly what causes autism. However, most of the evidence points to a combination of genetic, neurobiological, and early environmental factors. It is clear that there is no single cause for autism. Instead, autism spectrum disorders are caused by a complex interplay of biological and environmental factors.

Genetics

Research consistently indicates that autism has a strong genetic component (Rutter, 2005). Individuals who have a high degree of genetic similarity tend to show high rates of concordance for autism. If one monozygotic twin has autism, the other twin has a 31%–91% chance of also having the disorder. In contrast, concordance rates for dyzygotic twins are generally less than 5%. If the definition of autism is expanded to include broad social abnormalities, concordance rates for monozygotic twins increase to 92% while concordance rates for dizygotic twins are only about 10% (Tsai, 2005).

Autism also runs in families. The prevalence of autism in the general population is approximately 0.15%. However, if one child has autism, the likelihood of a sibling having autism ranges from 2.2% to 4.5%. Furthermore, the likelihood of a sibling having any autism spectrum disorder is approximately 6% (Klinger et al., 2003; Tsai, 2004a).

Despite twin and family data, there is probably not a single gene responsible for autism. It is more likely that multiple genes predispose individuals to a wide range of autism spectrum behaviors. For example, researchers have studied the behavioral characteristics of twins discordant for autism; that is, one of the twins has autism and the other twin does not. They found that the twins who did not have autism often displayed mild autism spectrum behaviors, such as social deficits, language delays, or excessively rigid and obsessive behavior. The severity of these behaviors may depend on the number of affected genes and certain environmental conditions (Freitag, 2007).

Behavioral geneticists have attempted to determine which genes might play a role in autism. In one of the largest studies so far, the **Autism Genome Project**, researchers in 19 different countries studied approximately 1,200 families in which two or more members had autism. By looking at family members' DNA, the researchers discovered that abnormalities in chromosome 11 were often associated with the presence of the disorder. Furthermore, some people with autism showed an absence of a particular gene called **neurexin 1**, a gene that produces proteins important to early brain maturation and neural connections. An abnormality or absence of the neurexin 1 gene might underlie some types of autism (Autism Genome Project Consortium, 2007).

Currently, there is no consensus regarding which chromosomes or genes play the greatest role in autism. Some experts believe 5 to 10 genes may be responsible for autism spectrum disorders (Klinger et al., 2003; Tsai, 2004a). Other researchers believe that the search for the genes responsible for autism has been elusive because autism itself is a heterogeneous disorder. Certain genes may contribute to certain autistic symptoms, but not others (Tager-Flusberg & Joseph, 2003). Despite these challenges, researchers are optimistic that the genes that make children susceptible to autism will be identified within the next decade (Rutter, 2005).

Biological Causes

Brain Structure and Synaptic Density

Neuroscientists have compared the brain structure of individuals with and without autism. Although results have been somewhat inconsistent, youths with autism tend to show abnormalities in brain size and synaptic density. Children with autism often have macrocephaly; that is, they have unusually large brains. At the same time, they display unusually low synaptic density in certain brain regions and very high synaptic density in other brain regions (Lawrence et al., 2005).

This atypical distribution in brain density might be due to the way the brains of individuals with autism develop. Before birth and during early infancy, the brain experiences considerable growth, with new neural connections forming and brain mass accumulating. In later infancy and across childhood, however, neural connections that are frequently used are strengthened while other connections that are seldom used atrophy. This process, called neural pruning, is normal and healthy. It allows our brains to perform more efficiently because we keep the neural connections that we need and discard those connections that we do not use. However, synaptic pruning may not occur properly among youths with autism. For these children, the brain might keep too many neural connections in areas where they are not needed and too few neural connections in areas that are frequently used (Klinger et al., 2003).

Abnormalities of the Limbic System

A second brain area that sometimes differs in individuals with and without autism is the limbic system. The **limbic system** is partially responsible for processing social information, such as our social actions, emotional expressions and reactions, and personally relevant memories.

One component of the limbic system, the **amygdala**, seems particularly important to our social and emotional functioning (Baron-Cohen, 2005; Lawrence et al., 2005). The amygdala is located deep in the temporal lobe of the brain. It becomes highly active when we watch other people's social behaviors and attempt to understand the motives for their actions or their emotional displays. Abnormalities in the structure or functioning of the amygdala might underlie some of the deficits shown by youths with autism. For example, Baron-Cohen and colleagues (1999) compared the brain activity of individuals with and without autism as they attempted to infer the mental states of others. Compared to typically developing individuals, people with autism showed significant reductions in amygdala activity. A second line of evidence comes from structural studies of the brains of individuals with autism. Individuals with autism often show reduced amygdala volume or neural density relative to healthy controls (Schumann & Amaral, 2006).

A third line of evidence suggesting the amygdala plays a role in the etiology of autism comes from studies of animals and humans with damage to this brain region. Humans with damage to the amygdala often show deficits in social understanding that resemble those deficits displayed by high-functioning individuals with autism. For example, they have problems recognizing and responding to others' facial expressions, detecting social faux pas, and understanding other people's intentions based on their overt behavior. Furthermore, intentional damage to the amygdala in monkeys causes autistic-like behaviors such as social isolation, lack of eye contact, and stereotyped behaviors (Schultz & Robins, 2005).

Fusiform Gyrus

A third brain region that may be important to the development of autism is the **right fusiform gyrus**. This brain region is located on the underside of the temporal lobe, near the occipital lobe. For a long time, this brain area was believed to play a specific role in processing human faces. When healthy adults are asked to view images of human faces, especially faces displaying negative emotions, they show strong activation of their right fusiform gyrus. In contrast, children and adolescents with autism who are asked to process facial expressions do not show increased activation in this brain region. Instead, people with autism use a different brain area, the inferior temporal gyri, to process facial information. Interestingly, the inferior temporal gyri are usually used to process information about objects, not people. These findings indicate that people with autism process facial information using parts of their brains that most people use to process information about objects. This abnormality in information processing may help explain the difficulty that people with autism have understanding other people's emotions and social behavior (Critchley et al., 2000; Pierce, Muller, Ambrose, Allen, & Courchesne, 2001; Schultz et al., 2003).

The fusiform gyrus does much more than process human faces. It also seems to be important in understanding human social behavior. In a clever experiment, Castelli, Happe, Frith, and Frith (2000) showed healthy individuals simple cartoons of geometric shapes engaging in human-like social behavior. For example, one cartoon showed a circle entering a schematic of a house and playing hide-and-seek with a triangle. Another cartoon showed two shapes "fighting" or "chasing" each other. People without autism almost always described these shapes as having human intentions that motivated their behavior. For example, they reported that the shapes were "playing," "chasing," or "fighting." In contrast, people with autism usually did not view the shapes as behaving in a social manner. Instead, they sometimes reported that the shapes were simply "bumping into" each other (Klin, 2000).

More important, people with and without autism showed different levels of activity in their fusiform gyri when watching the shapes. As you might expect, people without autism showed greater activity of the right fusiform gyrus compared to people with autism. These findings indicate that the right fusiform gyrus is important to understanding social interactions in general, not just faces. Hypoactivation of this brain region in people with autism might impair their understanding of social situations and contribute to their social deficits (Schultz et al., 2003).

Functioning of the Prefrontal Cortex

A fourth brain area that may play a role in autism is the prefrontal cortex. Considerable evidence suggests that this brain region is responsible for higher-order cognitive activities such as regulating attention, extracting information from the environment, organizing information, and using information to solve future problems. The prefrontal cortex acts like the chief executive officer of the brain, directing, organizing, and planning mental activity and behavior. For this reason, psychologists often say that the prefrontal cortex is responsible for **executive functioning** (Tsatsanis, 2005).

Emerging evidence indicates that children with autism show marked deficits in attention, organization, and planning—in short, the executive functions. Although their short-term, rote memory is intact (and sometimes exceptional), children with autism often have difficulty paying attention to important aspects of their environment. For example, when watching a television program, they may pay greater attention to objects in the background than to the activities of the main characters. Their lack of attention to salient social information could interfere with their ability to correctly perceive and respond to social situations (Klin, 2000; Klin, Jones, Schultz, & Volkmar, 2003).

Even high-functioning children with autism show deficits in organization and planning. Specifically, they tend to have difficulty processing information in flexible ways and solving problems on the spot. Ozonoff and colleagues (2004) have suggested that their rigid cognitive style might explain their strong desire for sameness and repetitive, stereotyped behaviors. Indeed, some people with damage to their prefrontal cortex show a desire for sameness and a propensity for stereotyped behaviors like individuals with autism (Tsatsanis, 2005).

Areas of the prefrontal cortex are also important in processing social information. Specifically, the **orbital** and **medial prefrontal cortex** become highly active when we engage in tasks that require social cognition, that is, when we watch social interactions and try to understand other people's thoughts, feelings, and intentions. In contrast, people with autism show underactivity of these brain regions, perhaps explaining their deficits in social understanding. Similarly, damage to these brain regions produces autistic-like symptoms in animals and problems in social cognition in humans (Boddaert et al., 2004; Schultz & Robins, 2005).

Summary of Structural and Functional Brain Differences

Brain imaging and neurological studies indicate that people with autism often show abnormalities in the structure and functioning of certain brain regions. Of particular interest are three brain areas: the amygdala, the fusiform gyrus, and portions of the prefrontal cortex. These areas play important roles in the perception of, processing of, and responses to social information. Interestingly, researchers have recently discovered neural pathways connecting portions of the prefrontal cortex, the amygdala, and the fusiform gyrus. Furthermore, neuroimaging studies indicate that when healthy individuals process social information, all three areas of this pathway become active. This has led some researchers to suggest that the prefrontal cortex, the amygdala (and other areas of the limbic system), and the fusiform gyrus form a **social brain** that is responsible for processing social information (Baron-Cohen, 2005; Frith & Frith, 1999; Schultz et al., 2003). Abnormal functioning of this social brain neural network might underlie many of the psychological and behavioral impairments shown by youths with autism and other PDDs.

Deficits in Social Cognition

Simon Baron-Cohen (2005) has suggested that dysfunction of the social brain leads to early problems in the development of children's **social cognition**. Specifically, social brain dysfunction causes children to perceive, interpret, and respond to social information in a manner qualitatively different from typically developing peers. Problems in social cognition emerge in infancy and lead to the development of serious social deficits and language delays. We will now examine how infants and young children later diagnosed with autism process social information differently than their typically developing peers.

Lack of Joint Attention

One of the chief ways infants learn about other people and the world around them is through joint attention (Mundy & Thorp, 2006). **Joint attention** refers to the infant's ability to share attention with his caregiver on a single object or event in the outside world. In typically developing infants, joint attention gradually emerges between 6 and 18 months of age.

To understand joint attention, consider the following example. Imagine that an eight-month-old child is sitting in her high chair. Her mother points to a bowl on the table and says, "Do you want some cereal?" The girl follows her mother's pointing finger, gazes in the direction of the cereal, and squeals. The infant shows **responding joint attention**; she is able to follow the gaze or gesture of her mother.

Imagine, also, a 10-month-old girl sitting on the floor inspecting some toys. By chance, the girl swipes at a toy frog and it "ribbits." The girl is surprised by the noise and momentarily shifts her gaze from the toy to her mother. The mother looks at the girl, smiles, and says reassuringly, "That's a frog!" The child smiles at her mother and turns her attention back to the toy. In this case, the child shows a more complex skill, **initiating joint attention**. Specifically, the infant spontaneously initiates a social interaction with her mother through their shared attention on the frog.

Through shared attention, infants learn about the world around them. At the very least, the 10-month-old girl learned the name "frog." Although this seems trivial, consider what might happen if the child did not have the capacity for joint attention. Without joint attention, the child would miss out on countless learning opportunities. As her parent tried to teach her about cereal, frogs, and other objects in her environment, she would not be focusing her attention on the same objects or events. As a result, the flow of information to the child would be greatly reduced. The lack of joint attention might cause problems with the acquisition of language, general knowledge, and intelligence (Mundy & Burnette, 2005).

Indeed, children diagnosed with autism spectrum disorders often show marked problems with joint attention (especially initiating joint attention) during the first two years of life. Psychologists have documented these early deficits in three different ways. First, researchers have asked parents of children with autism to recall their children's social functioning when they were infants. Most parents remembered that their children had marked problems with shared attention and eye contact between 12 and 18 months of age. Second, psychologists have reviewed home movies of infants later diagnosed with autism. Even during their first birthday parties, these children showed deficits in joint attention and social interaction compared to their typically developing peers. Third, a few prospective longitudinal studies have shown that deficits in joint attention during infancy are associated with problems with language acquisition and social functioning later in childhood (Charman, 2003; Mundy & Burnette, 2005).

Problems With Social Orientation

Brain abnormalities may also underlie problems with social orientation. Most typically developing infants show well-developed capacities for **social orientation**. For example, if we gave a 12-month-old child a new toy car, he might smile, play with the car briefly, and show the car to his mother. Although the child lacks language, he communicates his enjoyment to his mother by showing her the car and smiling. His mother might acknowledge her son's enjoyment by meeting his gaze, smiling, and enthusiastically saying, "What a great car!"

Early parent-child exchanges teach children about social interactions. Even at 12 months, the infant is learning that social communication occurs between people, that people take turns signaling and responding to one another, that the social exchange is usually centered on a common theme, and that effective communication involves eye contact and emotional expression (Carpenter, 2006; Rogers & Williams, 2006).

Image 6.4   Problems With Social Orientation. Researchers tracked the gaze of individuals without autism (black) and people with autism (white) as they watched films of social interactions. People without autism attended to actors' eyes and important objects in the environment. People with autism attended primarily to inanimate objects in the room and often missed important aspects of the social interaction.

Unfortunately, young children who are eventually diagnosed with autism show problems with social orientation. Although they might be extremely pleased with a new toy car, they are less likely to share this pleasure with another person. Instead, they would likely appear engrossed by the car and generally uninterested in other people around them. Similarly, these children often do not respond when family members call their names, clap their hands, or otherwise try to attract their attention. Instead, these children often appear distant or aloof (Nadel & Aouka, 2006).

A lack of social responsiveness causes these children to miss out on important social information, especially information from people's faces (see Image 6.4). When processing others' facial expressions, typically developing children attend primarily to others' eyes. The eyes provide a rich source of information regarding the emotional quality and intent of the other person's communication. In contrast, children with autism are more likely to attend to the other person's mouth. The mouth is believed to convey less important information about the social interaction. In one study, high-functioning adolescents and adults with autism focused twice as much on speakers' mouths and 2.5 times less on speakers' eyes than did individuals without autism (Klin, Jones, Schultz, Volkmar, & Cohen, 2002).

Delays in Symbolic Play

Between 18 and 24 months of age, children develop the capacity for symbolic play. *Symbolic play* refers to the child's ability to allow one object to represent (i.e., symbolize) another object. Children show symbolic play in two ways. First, they can pretend that one object (e.g., a blackboard eraser) represents another object (e.g., a telephone). Thus, a two-year-old can pretend to talk to her father on the telephone while holding the eraser up to her ear. Second, children can pretend that an inanimate object represents a living thing. For example, the child might decide to give his plastic toy dinosaur a drink of water and lay him down for a nap. Symbolic play is often called "pretend play" because children are able to pretend that one object represents another object.

Children who are eventually diagnosed with autism show marked delays in symbolic play. When children with autism begin to show symbolic play, it is usually simplistic and mechanical. For example, typically developing children often show elaborate pretend play involving creative and flexible scripts. My son routinely hosted dinner parties for his toy dinosaurs complete with appetizers, a main course, and dessert. The pretend play of children with autism tends to be more repetitive and without flexible, elaborative themes (Wolfberg & Schuler, 2006).

Why is it important that children with autism show deficits in pretend play? First, a lack of pretend play by 24 months of age can be an early sign of autism. Although parents and physicians often overlook other signs, such as delays in joint attention or social orientation, the absence of pretend play can be a useful indicator that there might be a problem in the child's development. Since the treatment for autism is most effective when it is initiated early, recognition and treatment of the disorder during the toddler years can lead to better prognosis (Yoder & McDuffie, 2006).

Second, pretend play is a precursor to children's language (Klinger et al., 2003). Jean Piaget believed that children begin to show pretend play when they develop the capacity for complex mental representations. In the case of pretend play, an object (e.g., an eraser) is allowed to mentally represent another object (e.g., a telephone). A similar process occurs in verbal language. The child learns that a certain utterance (e.g., the sound "cup") represents a particular object (e.g., a cup). Words are, after all, symbols that represent objects and events. Delays in the development of symbolic play, therefore, may be associated with the delays and deficits in language shown by people with autism.

Lack of Empathy

According to Baron-Cohen (2005), children with autism show deficits in a specific aspect of social cognition: **empathy**. Imagine that you are standing in the hallway of a building on campus and you notice another student suddenly leave a nearby classroom. She quickly exits the classroom, shuts the door behind her, leans her head against the wall, and begins to cry. What just happened? Based on your observations, you might infer that the student received a low grade on an important exam or that her professor chastised her in front of the class. In either case, you would likely feel sorry for her and maybe try to comfort her.

Our ability to react in an empathic manner, therefore, depends on two social abilities. First, we need to understand that the person's mental state (e.g., thoughts, beliefs, feelings) motivated her behavior. By understanding her mental state, we can infer that she either received a low grade on the exam or was humiliated in front of the class. Second, we need to have an appropriate emotional reaction to her crying. We would probably feel troubled by the incident and want to help her in some way. Our ability to empathize allows us to interpret social situations accurately and respond to people in sensitive and appropriate ways.

Sometime during the preschool years, most children begin to understand that people's thoughts, beliefs, intentions, and desires motivate their behaviors.

Furthermore, children appreciate that other people's thoughts and intentions can differ from their own. In short, children develop what cognitive psychologists call a **theory of mind**.

Developmental psychologists measure theory of mind using something called a **false belief task**. In one study, the psychologist introduced preschool-age children to a puppet named Sally who hid a toy in a basket and then left the room. While Sally was away, another puppet moved the toy to a different location (a box). The children were asked where Sally would look for her toy when she returned. Young children, without theory of mind, responded that Sally would search for the toy in the box because that is where the toy was moved. These children did not appreciate that Sally's behavior would be motivated by beliefs that differed from their own. Older children, with theory of mind, answered the false belief task correctly: They responded that Sally would search for the toy in the basket because Sally falsely believed the toy was still in its original location (Baron-Cohen, Leslie, & Frith, 1985).

In typically developing children, theory of mind emerges sometime between three and five years of age. However, children with autism show specific impairment in theory of mind. In one study, 85% of typically developing preschoolers successfully passed a false belief task compared to only 20% of preschoolers with autism (see Figure 6.4). Furthermore, the 20% of children with autism who passed the false belief task showed great difficulty on other tasks measuring theory of mind.

Why is this deficit in theory of mind important to understanding autism? The answer is that a well-developed theory of mind is necessary for most complex social interactions. Children with autism display what Baron-Cohen (1995) calls **mindblindness**; that is, they are often unable to appreciate that other people have mental states that motivate and direct their actions. If a child with autism witnessed a student abruptly leaving a classroom and crying, he would likely have difficulty understanding the student's behavior. Specifically, he would have trouble appreciating that some antecedent event and mental state (e.g., failing a test, feeling embarrassed) motivated the student's actions. Because he is unable to infer the student's mental state, he may not respond to the situation in an appropriate way.

Summary of Social Cognitive Deficits

Taken together, the available evidence indicates that autism is a neurodevelopmental disorder. Its primary causes are genetic, although the exact genes responsible for autism spectrum disorders remain elusive.

Genetic factors may predispose individuals to autism by affecting brain structure and functioning. Emerging data indicates that children with autism may have abnormalities in brain regions that play important roles in social and emotional behavior. For example, genetic factors may lead to abnormalities in the "social brain," which, in turn, affect the child's ability to perceive, process, interpret, and respond to social situations.

Deficits in social cognition can be seen as early as the first year of life. Infants later diagnosed with autism show problems with joint attention, social orientation, and (later) pretend play. These problems, in turn, likely interfere with the development of theory of mind, empathy, and language (see Figure 6.5). They also limit the quality of the child's learning experiences and lead to further problems with neurological development.

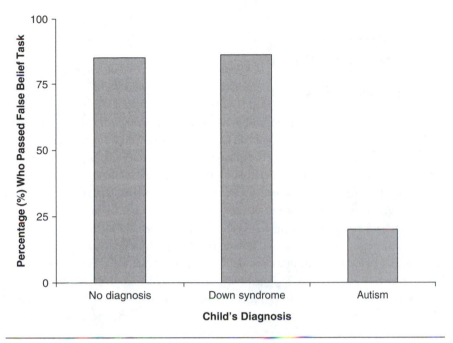

Figure 6.4   The False Belief Task

Source: Based on Baron-Cohen et al. (1985).

Note: Children with autism often fail the false belief task, but healthy children and children with Down syndrome usually pass this task. These results indicate that children with autism have problems with theory of mind; that is, understanding the intentions and motives of others.

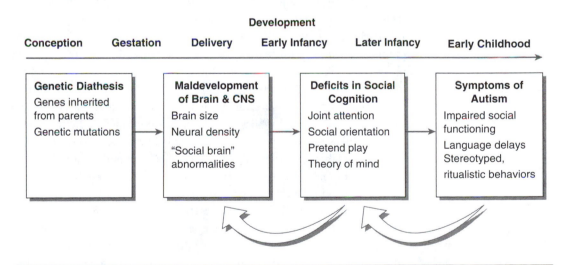

Figure 6.5   A Developmental Model for Autism

Note: In this general model, individuals show genetic risk for the disorder, which can lead to structural and/or functional differences in the developing brain. Brain abnormalities, in turn, can lead to problems in the development of social cognition during infancy. Social cognitive abnormalities also affect developing brain structure. By early childhood, deficits can be severe enough to merit the diagnosis of autism.

Treatment

Home-Based Treatments

Early Intensive Behavioral Intervention

Many experts regard **early intensive behavioral intervention** (EIBI) as the gold standard in the treatment of young children with autism. EIBI is a behavioral treatment in which children are taught skills on a one-on-one basis using principles of operant conditioning and observational learning. Although there are a number of different EIBI programs, they have several features on common (Crockett, Fleming, Doepke, & Stevens, 2007; Lovaas, Cross, & Revlin, 2006).

First, the focus of EIBI is on children's overt behavior. Behavior therapists view autism as consisting of a pattern of behavioral deficits and excesses. Deficits include problems in communication and social interaction. Excesses include stereotypies and tantrums. Treatment is designed to improve areas of deficit and reduce areas of excess. Behavior therapists do not focus primarily on constructs that are not readily observable, such as the parent-child attachment relationship or the way the child integrates or processes information. Instead, they focus predominantly on children's overt actions.

Second, behavior therapists rely on learning theory to guide their interventions. They use modeling, prompting, and positive reinforcement to teach children new skills and to shape appropriate behavior.

Third, behavior therapists structure the child's environment to maximize learning. Typically developing children are constantly learning from their surroundings through their observation and imitation of others, through dialogue, and through exploratory play. However, children with autism show deficits in all three areas, making it difficult for them to learn like other children. Put another way, there is a mismatch between the abilities of the child with autism and his or her environment. To compensate for this mismatch, learning experiences are structured so that there is a high probability that children will succeed at learning, rather than fail.

Therapists use **discrete trial training** to simplify the learning experience and increase the probability of skill acquisition. Skills are taught systematically. Behaviors are selected by the therapist and are designed to build upon one another to gradually improve the child's functioning. One of the first behaviors a child may learn is to sit when prompted by the therapist. Another behavior frequently taught in initial training sessions is to maintain eye contact with the therapist. These behaviors are essential for the acquisition of other, more complex behaviors.

Discrete trial training typically occurs in a distraction-free setting. First, the therapist gets the child's attention, usually with a verbal (e.g., calling the child's name) or physical (e.g., gently positioning the child's head) prompt. Then, the therapist issues a clear and succinct verbal command such as, "Sit down." The therapist structures the environment so that it is relatively easy for the child to comply: A chair might be located immediately behind the child. Additionally, the therapist might physically prompt (e.g., nudge) the child backward so that she sits. Immediately after the child complies, she is positively reinforced. The choice of reinforcer depends on the child.

Frequently used reinforcers include touching/hugging, verbal praise/smiling, or food/drink. The entire procedure is repeated multiple times and prompting is gradually faded. The learning trial ends when the child successfully displays the behavior 85%–90% of the time. Parents are then asked to practice the behavior at home.

The most well-known EIBI program is the **UCLA Young Autism Project**, developed by O. Ivar Lovaas. The program accepts children under four years of age who have autism but no other major medical problems. The children participate in intensive behavioral training, approximately 40 hours per week, for about three years. Each child is trained individually; four or five therapists are assigned to each child. Training is typically conducted in the child's home.

Lovaas's EIBI program consists of six stages. As children progress through the stages, they acquire greater capacity for social interaction, language, and behavioral regulation. The first goal of training (Stage 1) is to establish a teaching relationship between the therapist and child. Discrete trial training is used almost exclusively to teach children basic skills necessary for later learning, such as how to sit down and maintain eye contact. Once children are able to attend to the therapist, training focuses on increasing the child's receptive vocabulary and imitation skills (Stage 2). The child is taught how to obey simple commands (e.g., "Pick up the cup") and discriminate between two commands (e.g., "Pick up the cup" when presented with a cup and a crayon). The child is also taught to imitate the therapist's actions, such as waving or clapping. Imitation is one of the easiest ways for children to acquire new skills or combine behaviors in novel ways. In Stage 3, the therapist tries to increase the child's expressive vocabulary. Initially, the child is reinforced for imitating speech sounds (e.g., "aaahhh"), then words, then phrases, and finally simple sentences. The child is also reinforced for correctly labeling objects. Only about half of the children in the program are able to adequately imitate speech (Lovaas & Smith, 2003; Smith, Groen, & Wynn, 2000).

For those who show signs of emerging language, training focuses on expanding communication skills and using language during social interactions (Stage 4). At this stage, the child may begin preschool for typically developing children. The therapist focuses on improving the child's social skills. In Stage 5, the focus of training is on peer interactions. The therapist typically works with the child at home and at school, teaching skills such as initiating play with peers, asking for help in the classroom, and taking turns. Finally (Stage 6), children may be ready to enter a regular kindergarten classroom, and their training is discontinued. These children tend to have the best developmental outcomes. Other children will repeat preschool in order to acquire needed linguistic or social skills. Children who repeat preschool and continue to show marked delays usually need ongoing support services throughout their development (Lovaas, 1987; Lovaas & Smith, 2003).

A number of studies have examined the effectiveness of EIBI at improving the intellectual, linguistic, and behavioral functioning of children with autism (Anderson, Avery, DiPietro, Edwards, & Christian, 1987; Birnbrauer & Leach, 1993; Fenske, Zalenski, Krantz, & McClannahan, 1985; Harris, Handleman, Gordon, Kristoff, & Fuentes, 1991; Hoyson, Jamieson, & Strain, 1984). Lovaas (1987) evaluated 59 children with autism referred to the UCLA Young Autism Project. Children were assigned to three treatment groups, depending on the availability of therapists: (a) an experimental group that received 40 hours per week of training, (b) a control group that received less than 10 hours per week of training, and (c) a second control group that was referred to other professionals in the community for treatment. Most children referred to professionals in the community participated in special education. Results showed that children in the experimental group earned higher IQ scores than children in the control groups at age seven years. Furthermore, 47% of children in the experimental group were identified as "best outcome" because they showed IQ scores above 85 and were placed in classrooms with typically developing peers. In contrast, only 3% of children in the control groups were described as "best outcome." Follow-up testing showed that the gains children displayed during preschool were maintained at age 12 years (Lovaas, 1987; McEachin et al., 1993; see Table 6.6).

More recent research has attempted to replicate Lovaas's (1987) study using random assignment. For example, Smith, Groen, and Wynn (2000) examined 28 children with autism and other PDDs referred to the UCLA Young Autism Project. They randomly assigned children to two groups: (a) an experimental group that received 25 hours per week of EIBI training and (b) a control group whose parents were trained to use the EIBI principles at home, but whose children did not receive intensive services. Results showed that children in the experimental group earned higher IQ scores than children in the control group; however, the magnitude of the IQ gains was only about half of that observed in Lovaas's original study (i.e., 16 points, not 31 points). Additionally, only 13% of children in the EIBI group were described as "best outcome" in this study (see Table 6.7).

Table 6.6 EIBI Treatment for Autism

Group	Mean IQ Score			Best Outcome (%)	
	Pretreatment	Age 7	Age 12	Age 7	Age 12
EIBI (40 hrs/wk)	63	83	85	47	42
Minimal treatment (< 10 hrs/wk)	57	52	55	0	0
Special education	60	59	–	5	–

Source: Based on Lovaas and Smith (2003); Lovaas (1987); and McEachin, Smith, and Lovaas (1993).

Note: EIBI = Early intensive behavioral intervention. Best Outcome = IQ score > 85 and unassisted placement in regular education classroom.

Table 6.7 Randomized Evaluation of EIBI

Group	Mean IQ Score		Best Outcome (%)
	Pretreatment	Posttreatment	Posttreatment
EIBI (25 hrs/wk)	51	66	13
Parent training	51	50	8

Source: Based on Smith, Groen, and Wynn (2000).

Note: EIBI = Early intensive behavioral intervention. Best Outcome = IQ score > 85 and unassisted placement in regular education classroom. Note that two additional children who received EIBI were placed in regular education classrooms but did achieve IQ scores > 85 to meet "best outcome" status.

These findings suggest that EIBI can be efficacious in improving the intellectual functioning of children with autism. However, parents should not routinely expect the remarkable changes in IQ initially reported by Lovaas (1987). Programs that provide fewer hours of training per week are associated with more modest gains in IQ and perhaps no apparent gains in adaptive functioning (Smith, Groen, & Wynn, 2000).

Pivotal Response Training

Although discrete trial training can be effective at improving the intellectual, behavioral, and linguistic functioning of children with autism, it has some limitations. One limitation is that discrete trial training may not increase children's spontaneous social or linguistic behavior. For example, a child with autism might be taught to say, "Hello. How are you?" when introduced to a stranger, but she may not spontaneously ask questions or engage others unless prompted by caregivers. Put another way, children with autism often appear to have a low motivation to engage in spontaneous social or linguistic interactions, even after they have participated in extensive discrete trial training.

A second limitation of discrete trial training is that the skills that children acquire via this method do not automatically generalize to new situations or people. For example, a child with autism may be able to draw or color when prompted and monitored by her therapist, but she may have difficulty initiating and sustaining the behavior alone. Put another way, children who learn behaviors though discrete trial training may become overly dependent on others to guide and regulate their activities; they often have problems with self-management and self-direction.

Pivotal response training is designed to increase the motivation and self-regulation skills of children with autism (Schreibman & Koegel, 2005). In pivotal response training, *parents* are taught behavioral techniques to improve children's motivation and self-regulation. Then, parents use these techniques in the home and community. Ideally, parent-guided treatment leads to improvement in children's functioning and the generalization of skills outside the therapy setting (Lovaas, Koegel, Simmons, & Long, 1973).

Pivotal response training differs from discrete trial training in several ways. First, pivotal response training is conducted in naturalistic settings, like the home and community. The diversity of settings fosters generalization of skills. Second, the child, not the therapist, selects the focus of the social interaction. For example, if a child is playing with a certain toy, the therapist takes the child's lead and begins an interaction addressing aspects of the toy. This technique maximizes the child's interest in the learning experience. Third, the therapist uses reinforcers that are naturally tied to the learning experience or the child's behavior (i.e., **direct reinforcers**). For example, giving the child access to a toy car is a direct reinforcer for saying the word "car." In contrast, giving the child food or drink for saying the word "car" is not directly related to the child's behavior. The use of direct reinforcers strengthens the child's understanding of the behavior-consequence relationship and more closely resembles events in the real world. Finally, the therapist reinforces children for their *attempts* at social or linguistic interaction, rather than for successfully engaging in the behavior. If the therapist reinforces attempts, the child is more likely to initiate novel behaviors in the future.

Pivotal response training can also be used to increase children's *motivation* to verbally engage others (Koegel, Koegel, & Brookman, 2005). For example, parents teach children simple questions such as, "What is that?" "Where is it?" and "Whose is it?" Then, parents model, prompt, and reinforce children's use of the questions in naturalistic settings. As children gradually master the use of these questions, prompts can be faded and reinforcement comes from the child's interactions with the environment, not from the parents. Indeed, simple questions and verbal statements can replace functionally equivalent disruptive behaviors. For example, a child with autism might tantrum during a meal because his parents do not give him much attention. To correct these tantrums, the child might be taught to use functionally equivalent questions (e.g., "Am I being good?") or statements (e.g., "Talk to me") that attract the parents' attention in more appropriate ways.

Parents use a similar procedure to increase self-management and self-direction. First, they select a target behavior. For example, parents may want their children to be able to play independently for 30 minutes, so that they can perform household chores. Second, parents identify a direct reinforcer for the target behavior. If the child enjoys playing with toy cars, access to the cars can be contingent on independent play. Third, the parent demonstrates appropriate and inappropriate independent play to the child. For example, appropriate play might be sitting in the living room, playing with cars on the floor. Inappropriate play might be leaving the room, playing with the cars on the piano, or engaging in stereotypies or disruptive behavior. Fourth, the parent teaches the child to self-monitor the target behavior. Initially, parents can prompt children every few minutes by asking, "Are you playing quietly?" Appropriate play could be reinforced with access to an additional toy car. Eventually, the prompts are given less often, the schedule of reinforcement is decreased, and children are able to monitor and reinforce their own behavior.

Data supporting the use of pivotal response training comes primarily from studies employing single-subject designs; evidence from randomized clinical trials is limited. However, 85%–90% of children with autism show improved communication skills when treated with pivotal response training (Koegel, 1995, 2000). Teaching children to initiate verbal interactions using simple questions is also associated with increased language skills (Koegel, Carter, & Koegel, 2003; Koegel, Koegel, Shoshan, & McNerney, 1999) and a reduction in problem behavior (Carr & Durand, 1985).

School-Based Interventions

The TEACCH Method

The **Treatment and Education of Autistic and Related Communication-Handicapped Children (TEACCH)** approach to intervention was developed by Eric Schopler, a student of Bettelheim. Schopler disagreed with Bettelheim's assertion that cold and rejecting mothers caused autistic behavior in their children.

Schopler and colleagues developed a comprehensive program for youths with autism that stressed understanding and compassion for these children and their families (Mesibov, Shea, & Schopler, 2005).

TEACCH relies heavily on principles of operant conditioning and observational learning. It is administered in a specialized classroom environment. The focus of treatment is to help children with autism fit comfortably and effectively in the classroom. This is accomplished in two ways. First, therapists try to expand children's behavioral repertoire by teaching them new social, communicative, and daily living skills. Second, therapists attempt to structure the child's environment to increase the likelihood that the child can complete activities successfully and as independently as possible (Mesibov et al., 2005; Siegel & Ficcaglia, 2006).

TEACCH practitioners used a method of instruction called **structured teaching**. As its name implies, structured teaching involves a variety of structures and supports to help children understand and master the classroom environment. The technique capitalizes on the developmental principle of **scaffolding**. Just as a physical scaffold supports a building as it is being constructed, a behavioral scaffold guides and supports the developing child as he learns new skills through interactions with his environment (Vygotsky, 1978).

Scaffolding can be seen in the classroom setting. The classroom itself is highly organized and predictable. Activity stations are clearly partitioned, color-coded, and labeled so that children can understand what behavior is to be performed in each location. Stations are also structured to minimize distractions. Within each station, therapists use colors, pictures, shapes, and other prompts so that children can complete activities successfully. For example, in the bathroom area, the soap, water faucet, and towel might be assigned the same color to remind children to use all three objects when washing. In the closet, silhouettes of children's coats might be painted on the wall under pegs, to prompt children to hang up their coats when entering the classroom. Children's desks or work stations might be labeled with their pictures or names (Mesibov et al., 2005).

Scaffolding of daily activities can also be seen in the use of **visual schedules**. Since many young children with autism have limited language abilities, therapists rely heavily on pictures and other visual symbols to organize and direct children's behavior. A visual schedule might consist of a list of pictures outlining the child's activities for the day. Children can refer to visual schedules throughout the day to help them transition from one activity to the next with minimal instruction from staff. Children can also monitor their progress in daily activities by checking off tasks as they complete them.

Scaffolding is also used to help children perform individual activities. Imagine that the therapist wants to teach the child to brush his teeth. The therapist avoids using verbal instruction (i.e., telling the child what to do). Instead, the therapist teaches the skill by first breaking the activity into small, easy steps and labeling these steps using a visual prompt. The steps required to brush teeth might be presented in picture form on a card placed near the sink. Then, the therapist clearly and slowly demonstrates each step. Next, the therapist helps the child perform each step using **hand-over-hand assistance** (i.e., the therapist guides the child's hands with her own). The therapist gradually replaces her physical prompts with gestures (e.g., pointing to the water faucet) or simple verbal prompts (e.g., "turn off"). The activity is periodically repeated until the child can perform it independently.

Scaffolding is also used to teach communication. First, the therapist teaches the child to associate single objects with specific activities. For example, a spoon might represent "eating lunch," a roll of toilet paper "use of the bathroom," and a small plastic shovel "going outside for recess." Children learn to use these physical objects to communicate a desire to engage in their corresponding activities. A child who wants to use the bathroom might bring the roll of toilet paper to the teacher. Later, physical objects are gradually replaced by more abstract representations for these activities. For example, the child might communicate a desire to use the toilet by presenting the teacher with a photograph or drawing of the toilet.

Techniques used by therapists in the classroom are also taught to parents, so that skills can generalize to the home. Each family is assigned two therapists; one works primarily with the child while the other serves chiefly as a "parent consultant." The consultant helps parents learn about autism and the basic principles of learning and scaffolding. The therapist then teaches parents the techniques used in the classroom. In most cases, the therapist watches parents use these same techniques with their own children and coaches parents to help them use the techniques most effectively. Consultants may also conduct home visits to help parents structure the home environment in an organized, predictable way (Mesibov et al., 2005).

Most of the data supporting TEACCH come from older studies or research conducted by the developers of the program (Mesibov, 1997; Schopler, Mesibov, & Baker, 1982; Schopler, Mesibov, DeVellis, & Short, 1981). These studies indicate that the program is effective in improving socialization, communication, and daily living skills. More recent research conducted by independent teams supports these findings (Ozonoff & Cathcart, 1998). It appears that children who receive instruction at home, in addition to school, show greater improvement in functioning than do children who participate in school-based programs alone.

Academic Inclusion

Children with autism are educated in a wide range of settings, depending on their degree of impairment (Mandlawitz, 2004; U.S. Department of Education, 2006). Some children are "mainstreamed" into regular education classrooms. These children spend all or nearly all of their day with typically developing peers. Each mainstreamed child might be provided with a paraprofessional aide who attends classes and helps with activities. Other children are only partially mainstreamed. They may participate in certain regular education classes but be pulled out into special education classes for specific subjects (Handleman, Harris, & Martins, 2005). Children with greater impairments are placed in more restrictive settings. For example, some children with autism and Mental Retardation participate in integrated classrooms. These classrooms consist of a mixture of children with and without disabilities, but they are organized with the needs of children with disabilities in mind. Other children with autism and Mental Retardation are educated almost exclusively in special education classrooms. These classrooms have a high degree of structure and low student-to-teacher ratios. Young children with autism may also be educated in special preschools or at home.

Academic inclusion is based on the notion that children with developmental disabilities can benefit from interactions with other typically developing children. Classmates can model appropriate social and linguistic skills and provide academic tutoring and support. Children with autism also have the opportunity to practice and generalize social and communicative skills more easily when they spend time in regular education settings with typically developing peers. Furthermore, children with autism who are educated in classrooms with typically developing peers are likely to be held to higher standards than children placed exclusively in special education classrooms.

Unfortunately, research indicates that merely exposing children with autism to typically developing classmates is of limited benefit. Instead, typically developing classmates need to be systematically taught how to interact with a classmate who has autism. For example, typically developing peers might be taught how to use gestures to get the child's attention, how to use physical prompts to guide and direct his behavior, and how to issue praise to reinforce appropriate actions. Teachers can also structure group activities and lessons that encourage children with autism and typically developing children to work collaboratively. Some schools have even developed mentoring, tutoring, and "buddy" programs in which children with and without autism are paired during social activities (Durand, 2005).

The main criticism of academic inclusion is that it is technically not a treatment approach; it simply refers to the setting in which treatment takes place. The effectiveness of academic inclusion depends not so much on *where* the child is taught but *how* and *what* the child is taught. For example, inclusion might be highly effective for some youths with autism who are provided high-quality supportive services that enable them to participate in the academic curriculum. On the other hand, inclusion can be ineffective for children who are not provided adequate support services to participate in day-to-day classroom activities (Mesibov & Shea, 1996; Siegel & Ficcaglia, 2006).

Medication

Pharmacotherapy is frequently used to treat many of the co-occurring disorders and behavior problems shown by children and adolescents with autism. For example, Martin, Scahill, Klin, and Volkmar (1999) reported that 55% of youths with autism at their university-based treatment center were taking at least one psychiatric medication, and 29% were taking two or more medications.

Antipsychotic medications have been used to treat autism and other PDDs for some time. Although there are many different types of antipsychotic medications, almost all of them affect the neurotransmitter dopamine. Traditional antipsychotics have little or no impact on autistic symptoms. Some of the newer antipsychotic medications, however, have shown modest benefits. Haloperidol (Haldol) seems to be better than a placebo in reducing stereotyped behaviors. Furthermore, it may be useful in reducing agitation, aggression, and other disruptive behavior problems. Another atypical antipsychotic medication, risperidone (Risperdal), has also been shown to be effective in reducing symptoms of anxiety, depression, aggression, and SIBs that sometimes accompany autism. Risperidone may also increase the social functioning of youths with autism (Nagaraj, Singhi, & Malhi, 2006). A third antipsychotic medication, pimozide (Orap), may also be effective in treating agitation, disruptive behavior, and tics in youths with autism (Tsai, 2004b, 2005).

The primary drawback to haloperidol and other antipsychotic agents is their tendency to produce sedation if given in high doses. Long-term use of haloperidol can also produce a side effect known as **tardive diskinesia,** which is characterized by involuntary motor movements of the mouth and jaw. This condition is sometimes irreversible, so the medication is used sparingly with children. Risperidone is associated with weight gain and daydreaming.

In general, medication is not recommended as a first-line treatment for children and adolescents with autism. Medication is chiefly used to treat comorbid symptoms such as tics, disruptive behavior problems, hyperactivity, and anxiety. Given the limited number of studies investigating these medications with youths who have autism, and given their side effects, they are used very cautiously.

Autism: A Sibling's Perspective

Day by day I kept a mental journal of my brother's peculiar habits—those we have now come to know as typical characteristics of autism. I was 5; he was 6. He refused to make eye contact with me, or anyone else for that matter. I learned not to take offense at it. He was echolalic and would repeat TV commercials he heard for hours on end. I learned to appreciate his precision and even laughed at times. He broke anything and everything he could get his hands on. I learned to take better care in putting my things away. He had pica and ate Play-Doh, among other things. I learned to work with clay. He ate staples. I learned to berate him without guilt because I drew the line at his health and well-being. By the age of 8, he still refused to use the toilet. I learned to clean up after him. He feared strange surroundings. I learned to comfort and talk him through new experiences. I learned to challenge but also respect his little world. I did not realize it then, but my brother emerged as one of my greatest teachers—through whom I learned responsibility, accountability, patience, stamina, self-discipline, and unconditional love.

Source: From Konidaris (2005). Used with permission.

Interventions With Little Empirical Support

There are many treatments for autism that have limited empirical support (see Table 6.8). These treatments include interventions designed to increase children's social skills (e.g., "holding therapy" and "pet therapy"), communication skills (e.g., "facilitated communication"), emotional and behavioral functioning (e.g., "art/music therapy"), and sensorimotor functioning (e.g., "auditory integration training"; Simpson et al., 2005). Metz, Mulick, and Butter (2005) conducted a Google search

Table 6.8   Treatments for Autism With Limited Empirical Support

Therapy	Descriptifon
Holding therapy	Based on the incorrect notion that children with autism have disturbed attachment to their mothers and that autistic behaviors are the child's way of withdrawing from the mother's rejection; therapist encourages "mother-child holding" to repair the broken attachment bond
Pet therapy	Contact with animals such as cats, dogs, horses, and dolphins is believed to reduce children's anxiety, improve social and communicative skills, and teach decision making and responsibility; some advocates believe dolphins' use of sonar and echolocation causes physiological changes in children's bodies, leading to improvement in functioning
Facilitated communication	Based on the incorrect notion that individuals with autism who are unable to communicate verbally can communicate when assisted by trained professionals; professionals facilitate communication by guiding the patient's hand as he points to symbols/pictures or types messages; evaluations of facilitated communication indicate that "messages" from individuals with autism are likely sent by the professionals who assist them, not by the patients themselves
Auditory integration training	Based on the idea that children with autism have extremely sensitive hearing and that autistic signs are caused by auditory discomfort; children receive auditory training by listening to specialized recordings of music on headphones
Art/music therapy	Art therapy is believed to allow nonverbal expression through drawing, painting, and sculpting; music therapy involves listening to specific musical pieces or playing instruments to reduce anxiety, reinforce positive behavior, and permit self-expression
Megavitamin/diet therapies	Based on the notion that nutritional deficiencies underlie autism; some advocates recommend supplements of B6 and magnesium, other dietary supplements, or avoidance of certain foods
Irlen lenses	Based on the belief that autism is caused by a perceptual disturbance related to difficulties processing light, called scotopic sensitivity; children wear tinted glasses

Source: Based on Simpson et al. (2005).

using the terms "autism" and "treatment" and found 65 distinct treatments—most with no empirical basis. These treatments included the use of mental telepathy, the consumption of fish oil and thyme, and the injection of sheep stem cells!

Some unsupported treatments seem promising to families and are portrayed positively by the media; however, they are not recommended. Most of these treatment approaches have little or no evidence showing that they improve the social, communicative, or behavioral functioning of children with autism. Others have been evaluated and have been shown to be ineffective in helping children with autism and developmental disorders. Worse yet, some purported treatments for autism may even be harmful.

Why might parents select a treatment with limited empirical support? There are at least three reasons. First, many parents are not aware of the empirical data regarding the treatment for autism. Most parents do not have access to reputable journals and professional newsletters. Even if they did, published empirical studies are often difficult to read and evaluate. Consequently, most parents might rely on advice from therapists, paraprofessionals, or well-meaning friends—advice that might not be empirically based.

Second, many parents have tried one of the more traditional approaches to treatment and have met with limited success. Understandably, many of these parents turn to other, less supported therapies in the hope that these treatments might help their children.

Third, and perhaps most unfortunately, high-quality and empirically supported treatments for autism are unavailable to many families. For example, TEACCH programs are generally unavailable outside of North Carolina, and behavioral programs in the Lovaas tradition are generally found only in research hospitals and universities. Many local practitioners and well-intentioned volunteer organizations claim to provide "TEACCH" programming or applied behavioral interventions, but they usually do not provide the same high-quality and comprehensive services offered by university-based programs (Metz et al., 2005).

Best Practices

To help parents and practitioners identify interventions that tend to be most effective in the treatment of autism, the National Research Council commissioned a panel of experts to review the empirical literature. The Committee on Educational Interventions for Children with Autism subsequently identified six components of effective treatment (Lord & McGee, 2001; Scott & Baldwin, 2005).

First, effective treatment involves early identification and intervention. The panel recommended that treatment should begin as soon as the child is diagnosed with autism. The best outcomes occur when treatment begins before age three years. Infants, toddlers, and preschool-age children in the community should be periodically screened for autism to identify the disorder and intervene early (Charman & Baron-Cohen, 2006).

Second, treatment must be intensive. Children with the best outcomes participate in full-time educational treatment all year long. Some research suggests a dose-response effect for treatment. That is, children who received full-time treatment (i.e., 40 hours per week) showed significantly greater improvement than children who received less intensive treatment (e.g., 20 hours per week). The committee recommended a minimum of 25 hours of instruction per week, extended across the entire calendar year.

Third, treatment must involve repeated, planned, and structured learning opportunities. Examples of learning opportunities include discrete trial training, pivotal response training, or structured teaching. Regardless of the approach, training should be geared toward the needs of the child and repeated frequently.

Fourth, treatment programs should have low student-to-teacher ratios. Ideally, instruction occurs on a 1:1 basis. However, treatment programs for very young children should not have more than two children for each therapist. Ideally, each child should only have a limited number of therapists, to maintain consistency in treatment.

Fifth, parents must be active in their children's treatment. Parents' participation in treatment is strongly associated with their children's outcomes. Parents must not only be knowledgeable about the treatment program's strategy and tactics, they must also implement the program at home. Parental participation in the program increases generalization of children's skills from school to home and provides children with more opportunities to practice skills across contexts.

Finally, programs must constantly monitor children's progress in treatment and alter intervention strategies to meet children's needs and developing skills. No two children with autism are exactly alike. Consequently, not all children with autism will respond to any single intervention. Intervention strategies need to be tailored to individual children and modified during the course of treatment in order to produce the greatest benefits.

Critical Thinking Exercises

1. Compare and contrast Autistic Disorder and Asperger's Disorder. Why are both of these disorders considered PDDs? How might a clinician differentiate them?

2. What is the "autism spectrum?" Evaluate the assertion that PDDs should be viewed on a spectrum rather than as discrete disorders.

3. What is the evidence that genes and abnormal brain development underlie some autism spectrum disorders? Why don't all children with autism show the same brain anomalies?

4. How do infants and toddlers who are later diagnosed with autism show deficits in social cognition and "mind-blindness?"

5. Compare and contrast discrete trial training with pivotal response training for autism. What are the advantages and limitations of each approach to treatment?

CHAPTER 7

Learning Disorders and Academic Problems

Daniel

Daniel was a nine-year-old boy referred to our clinic because of low academic achievement. Daniel began struggling in school when he was in kindergarten. He had trouble recognizing and writing letters and numbers, answering questions about stories, and following instructions. A medical examination showed that he was healthy. Daniel repeated kindergarten the following year, but his academic problems continued.

In the first grade, Daniel was tested to determine whether he had a learning disability. Daniel's IQ score was 103, indicating average intellectual functioning. His standardized scores on tests of reading (75), writing (78), and mathematics (81) were significantly below most of his peers. However, Daniel's reading, writing, and math test scores were not low enough for him to receive special education services.

At the time of the evaluation, Daniel was attending a regular third-grade classroom. He showed significant trouble in reading. He often confused letters with similar appearances, like P, B, D, and C, and had trouble differentiating similar-looking words such as *that, this, those,* and *these.* Daniel could not sound out unknown words; instead, he usually guessed at the pronunciation of words that he did not know. Daniel showed problems with reading comprehension. He would often skip words or whole lines of text while reading and had problems answering questions about what he read.

Daniel hated school. He was especially embarrassed to read aloud in front of the class. He resented the teacher for correcting him when he misread a word. Daniel would often try to avoid schoolwork by averting his eyes in class, volunteering to do chores in the classroom (e.g., clean the blackboards), or "charming" the teacher. At home, Daniel would whine or tantrum when his mother asked him to do his homework.

Daniel explained, "It's not that I'm dumb or lazy, it's just that I have a hard time with reading. I look at the page and it's all jumbled up. If I read a sentence or two, I can't tell you about it later."

(Continued)

> Dr. Butler, a psychologist at the clinic, suggested that Daniel be tested to see whether he had a learning disorder. His mother responded, "OK. But didn't they already test him when he was in the first grade and find out that he wasn't dyslexic? Besides, can't Ritalin work for these sorts of problems?"

What Are Learning Disorders?

Learning Disorders (LDs) are serious conditions that can adversely affect children's academic functioning, career attainment, self-concept, and behavior. Although there is disagreement as to the exact definition of LD, most experts agree that LDs are characterized by the following (Loomis, 2006):

1. Children with LDs have marked difficulty learning to read, write, or perform mathematics. These academic skill problems are believed to be due to dysfunction in underlying psychological processes.

2. Genetics often plays a role in LDs. Learning problems run in families and monozygotic twins usually show strong concordance for LDs. Genes are believed to cause subtle abnormalities in brain structure, functioning, perception, memory, and information processing, which, in turn, interfere with learning.

3. Children with LDs show marked deficits in academic achievement. If untreated, these deficits usually persist over time; they do not simply reflect delays in the acquisition of academic skills. Children with LDs are not simply "slow learners" or academic "late bloomers."

4. Although children's intelligence and academic achievement are correlated, LDs are not caused by low intelligence or Mental Retardation.

5. LDs are not caused by emotional problems (e.g., test anxiety, depression), socioeconomic deprivation (e.g., malnutrition, poverty), or impoverished educational experiences (e.g., low-quality schools). Although these factors can exacerbate children's learning problems, they do not cause LDs.

Current Definition of Learning Disorders

DSM-IV-TR recognizes three main LDs: **Reading Disorder, Disorder of Written Expression,** and **Mathematics Disorder** (see Table 7.1). LD is diagnosed when the person's achievement in reading, mathematics, or written expression is "substantially below" the level of achievement expected based on her intelligence. The individual's learning problems must also interfere with her academic performance or her ability to perform tasks that require academic skills (e.g., reading a newspaper, calculating correct change for a dollar, writing a letter). Furthermore, the person's low academic performance cannot be attributed exclusively to Mental Retardation

Table 7.1   Diagnostic Criteria for Learning Disorders

A. Reading, writing, or mathematics achievement, as measured by individually administered standardized tests, is substantially below that expected given the person's chronological age, measured intelligence, and age-appropriate education.
B. The disturbance significantly interferes with academic achievement or activities of daily living that require reading, writing, or math.
C. If a sensory deficit is present (i.e., blindness, deafness), the academic difficulties are in excess of those usually associated with it.
    1. Reading Disorder is diagnosed in people with reading problems.
    2. Disorder of Written Expression is diagnosed in people with writing problems.
    3. Mathematics Disorder is diagnosed in people with math-related problems.

Source: Reprinted with permission from the *DSM-IV-TR.*

or pervasive developmental disorders, visual or hearing impairments, differences in language or cultural background, or impoverished educational experiences.

To diagnose LDs, most psychologists determine whether the individual shows a significant discrepancy between IQ and achievement. First, the clinician administers a norm-referenced IQ test to measure intelligence. Then, he administers a norm-referenced achievement test to measure reading, writing, and/or mathematics achievement. *DSM-IV-TR* considers a discrepancy of more than two standard deviations between IQ and achievement scores to constitute a significant discrepancy. For example, a person with an IQ score of 100 and a reading achievement score of 70 might quality for the diagnosis of Reading Disorder.

What Are Learning Disabilities?

The term "learning disabilities" is not used by *DSM-IV-TR.* The term was coined by Samuel Kirk (1962) to describe children who showed significant delays in the development of reading, writing, math, or oral language. Kirk suggested that these delays interfered with children's ability to learn and were likely caused by structural abnormalities of the brain. Kirk differentiated learning disabilities from other psychological conditions that often interfere with learning, such as Mental Retardation, blindness, and deafness (Hallahan & Mock, 2003).

In 1975, Congress enacted the Education for All Handicapped Children Act (Public Law 94-142). This law provided free special education services to school-age children with disabilities, including children with learning disabilities. The U.S. Office of Education proposed the following definition of **specific learning disabilities**, which borrows heavily from Kirk's conceptualization:

The term "specific learning disability" means a disorder in one or more of the psychological processes involved in understanding or in using language . . . which may manifest itself in an inability to listen, speak, read, write, spell, or do mathematical calculations. The term does not include children who have LDs which are primarily the result of visual, hearing, or motor handicaps, or mental retardation, or emotional disturbance, or of environmental, cultural, or economic disadvantage (U.S. Department of Education, 1977, p. 65083).

The current definition of learning disabilities is outlined by the Individuals With Disabilities Education Improvement Act (IDEA, 2004), an extension of the Education for All Handicapped Children Act. According to IDEA, children can be classified with learning disabilities if they show problems in any of the following areas:

1. Oral expression

2. Listening comprehension

3. Written expression

4. Basic reading skills

5. Reading fluency skills

6. Reading comprehension

7. Mathematics calculation

8. Mathematics problem solving

Furthermore, children's low achievement in these areas must not be due to Mental Retardation, emotional problems, other disabling conditions, language differences, or impoverished educational experiences (U.S. Department of Education, 2006).

Many experts have criticized the list of learning disabilities identified in IDEA. Specifically, Fletcher and colleagues (2002) have argued that problems with (1) oral expression and (2) listening comprehension do not reflect academic skill problems. Consequently, children with oral expression or listening comprehension problems should be classified as having speech/language disorders rather than learning disabilities. Indeed, these problems are usually treated by speech and language therapists and not psychologists, counselors, or teachers.

Most medical professionals use the *DSM-IV-TR* definition of LD to diagnose youths with significant learning problems. In contrast, school districts use the legal definition of "specific learning disability" to determine students' eligibility for special education services (Samms-Vaughn, 2006).

Identifying Children With Learning Disabilities

IDEA does not specify how professionals must identify youths with learning disabilities. Instead, IDEA gives state governments considerable freedom to determine the specific classification criteria they will use. Consequently, different states use different criteria: The stricter the criteria, the fewer children who qualify for special education services. For example, approximately 8% of youth in Rhode Island are classified as having learning disabilities, compared to 2.5% of youth in Kentucky (Reschly, 2006). This variation in classification criteria has caused some cynics to quip: "The best way to help a child overcome his learning disability is to move him to a different state!"

IDEA allows states to use three approaches to identify youths with learning disabilities: (1) IQ-achievement discrepancies, (2) intra-individual discrepancies, and (3) responsiveness to intervention.

IQ-Achievement Discrepancy

The IQ-achievement discrepancy method for identifying learning disabilities is the most widely used procedure in public schools. The IQ-achievement discrepancy method is also the procedure specified by *DSM-IV-TR* as a means to diagnose LDs. Professionals who use this procedure compare children's IQ and academic achievement using standardized tests. Significantly low achievement, relative to IQ, can indicate the presence of a learning disability (*DSM-IV-TR*; Reschly, 2004).

Most research indicates that the IQ-achievement discrepancy approach is *not* a valid method of identifying youths with learning disabilities. The IQ-achievement discrepancy method has at least three weaknesses. First, the IQ-achievement discrepancy approach is often not useful in differentiating youths with and without learning problems. Many young children who show marked delays in reading fall short of the discrepancy needed to be classified as having a learning disability. Although these children (like Daniel) display serious delays in reading, they are often denied special education because they do not meet the discrepancy cutoff identified by the state. Over time, these children often fall further behind their peers.

Second, children identified with learning disabilities using the IQ-achievement method do not show different patterns of cognitive abilities than youths with learning problems who fall short of the IQ-achievement cutoff. For example, youths with reading problems who do and do not show significant discrepancies display similar problems with sounding out words, recognizing letters and words, knowledge of vocabulary, short-term memory, speech and language, and classroom behavior. There is little evidence that youths who meet the IQ-achievement discrepancy process information differently than youths who fall short of this discrepancy (Fletcher et al., 2002; Fletcher, Morris, & Lyon, 2003; Francis, Fletcher, Stuebing, Lyon, Shaywitz, & Shaywitz, 2005).

Third, youths with reading problems who do and do not show significant IQ-achievement discrepancies display similar outcomes. Children in both groups display long-term problems with reading. Youths with reading problems who do and do not have significant IQ-achievement discrepancies respond similarly to treatment. There is little evidence that youths with IQ-achievement discrepancies need to be taught using different methods than other youths with reading problems (Hoskyn & Swanson, 2000; Stuebing, Fletcher, LeDoux, Lyon, Shaywitz, & Shaywitz, 2002; Vellutino, Scanlon, & Lyon, 2000).

Intra-Individual Discrepancy

A second approach to identifying children with learning disabilities is to examine the pattern of strengths and weaknesses that they show on norm-referenced tests of ability and achievement. Children who show significant weaknesses in one ability or achievement area might be classified as having a disability in this domain (Fletcher et al., 2003).

Table 7.2   Intra-Individual Achievement Approach to Identifying Youths With Learning Disabilities

Domain	Standard Score	Overall Score	Difference	Significant
Basic reading	**72**	**95**	**−23**	**Yes**
Reading comprehension	88	95	−7	No
Math calculation	98	95	3	No
Math reasoning	102	95	7	No
Basic writing	103	95	8	No
Written expression	105	95	10	No
Oral expression	106	95	11	No
Listening comprehension	102	95	7	No
Phoneme awareness	**71**	**95**	**−24**	**Yes**
Working memory	105	95	10	No

Note: This child shows significant relative weaknesses in basic reading and phoneme awareness (i.e., understanding the relationship between letters and sounds). He might have a specific learning disability in the area of basic reading skills.

For example, the Woodcock-Johnson III allows clinicians to measure children's performance in multiple domains of cognitive ability and academic achievement. The clinician obtains a standard score with a mean of 100 and standard deviation of 15 on each of these domains. Then, the clinician examines whether the child's score on any one of these domains differs significantly from the child's overall performance. For example, in Table 7.2, we see that the child displays significant relative weaknesses on tests measuring his basic reading skills and phoneme awareness (i.e., the ability to understand the relationship between letters and sounds). These findings indicate that the child might have a specific learning disability in the area of reading. The clinician might hypothesize that the child's problems with basic reading, such as his difficulty sounding out words, is due to underlying problems with phoneme awareness (Mather & Schrank, 2003; Volker, Lopata, & Cook-Cottone, 2006).

The intra-individual discrepancy approach has several advantages over the IQ-achievement approach. First, emerging data indicate that the intra-individual approach is better than the IQ-achievement approach at differentiating youths with and without learning problems. Consequently, the intra-individual method may possess greater validity as a means to identify children with learning disabilities.

Second, the intra-individual approach often conveys more information to clinicians than the IQ-achievement method. Clinicians who use the intra-individual approach focus on multiple areas of children's functioning, not just on the magnitude of the difference between their IQ and achievement scores. Indeed, researchers have begun to identify subgroups of children based on their pattern of academic strengths and weaknesses identified by the intra-individual approach (Fletcher et al., 2003; Grigorenko, 2001).

Third, the intra-individual approach can guide clinicians toward appropriate treatments more easily than the IQ-achievement approach. By identifying children based on specific patterns of strengths and weaknesses, clinicians can better understand children's skills and tailor remediation accordingly. For example, children who show problems in basic reading often respond well to treatments that teach phonics skills. Clinicians who use the intra-individual method can more precisely target areas of relative weakness that need remediation while capitalizing on areas of relative strength (Lovett & Barron, 2002).

Response to Intervention

A third way of conceptualizing learning disabilities is based on children's educational progress and outcomes (Reschly, 2006). Proponents of the **response to intervention** (**RTI**) approach believe that youths with learning disabilities can be identified based on their inability to respond to "scientific, research-based" teaching methods (U.S. Department of Education, 2006). Children who are provided with high-quality, empirically based instruction, but who fail to show academic progress, may be classified with learning disabilities.

School systems that use the RTI approach usually rely on a three-phase system to identify children with learning disabilities. In Phase I, all children in a class are evaluated to assess their basic academic skills. Data collected in Phase I are used to evaluate the overall effectiveness of instruction. If most children show adequate progress mastering reading, writing, and math, then the method of instruction is deemed adequate.

In Phase II, youths who showed significant academic deficits during Phase I are provided with additional instruction to help them catch up to their peers. Additional instruction is usually administered in small groups. For example, students who show specific deficits in reading might be provided with 20 minutes of group reading instruction.

In Phase III, students who do not respond to additional group instruction are given intensive individual intervention. For example, a student who continues to show reading deficits despite extra group instruction might receive one-on-one tutoring. Only students who continue to show academic deficits after intensive individual intervention (Phase III) are classified as having learning disabilities (Burns & Senesac, 2005; Gresham, 2006).

The RTI approach places less emphasis on standardized testing and greater focus on children's actual performance in the classroom. Because RTI is based on observations of children's performance in class, RTI allows teachers to identify youths' academic delays much earlier than more traditional discrepancy approaches. The RTI approach also lends itself to treatment. A youth who fails to respond to one scientifically based form of instruction can be provided with other evidence-based teaching methods until she shows improvement (Reschly, Tilly, & Grimes, 1999).

The RTI approach is relatively new. Emerging data indicate that it is effective in identifying young children's learning problems, preventing future academic skill deficits, and reducing the number of students referred for special education. Furthermore, the approach is beginning to be successfully implemented in school systems across the country (Ardoin, Witt, Connell, & Koenig, 2005; Vellutino, Scanlon, Small, & Fanuele, 2006).

Many experts rely on both standardized testing and RTI approaches to identify children with learning disabilities (Fiorello, Hale, & Snyder, 2006; J. B. Hale,

Kaufman, Naglieri, & Kavale, 2006; Holdnack & Weiss, 2006). For example, IQ testing can predict children's future academic performance and, possibly, the likelihood that they will respond to academic interventions (Fuchs & Young, 2006).

Epidemiology of Children's Learning Problems

Prevalence

Overall Prevalence

Approximately 4%–6% of U.S. schoolchildren receive special education services because of a learning disability. However, the actual prevalence of learning problems is probably much higher. Many children remain unidentified and untreated. Other children show marked academic problems but do not quite meet the threshold for LD. In one estimate, as many as 20% of school-age youth show either LDs or significant learning problems that interfere with their performance in school (Silver & Hagin, 2002).

The number of children and adolescents with learning disabilities has increased dramatically in recent years. In 1976, approximately 3.3 million children received special education services. Today, that number has increased to over 6.7 million. The increased prevalence of learning disabilities is largely due to two factors. First, teachers have increased awareness of learning problems in children, making it easier for them to identify at-risk students. Second, government legislation that mandates the identification and remediation of learning disabilities has increased over the past 30 years, causing a corresponding increase in youths classified with learning disabilities (Reschly, 2006).

Reading Disorder (sometimes called "dyslexia") is the most common LD; as many as 80% of children with LDs have reading problems. The prevalence of writing problems (8%–15%) and mathematics problems (5%–8%) is much lower. Many children with LDs experience trouble in two or more domains. For example, roughly half of all youths with math-related problems also show difficulty reading. Furthermore, children with both mathematics and reading problems show greater impairment in each of these areas than do children with mathematics or reading problems alone (Augustyniak, Murphy, & Phillips, 2006; Loomis, 2006).

Gender

Among children *in treatment*, learning disabilities are more common among boys than girls. In the areas of reading and writing, boys are two to three times more likely than girls to be classified as having a learning disability. In the domain of mathematics, the gender ratio is smaller, approximately 1.6:1 (McDermott, Goldberg, Watkins, Stanley, & Glutting, 2006).

Among youth *in the community*, gender ratios are approximately equal. It is likely that boys with learning disabilities are more likely to be referred for treatment than are girls with learning disabilities because boys often show other disruptive behavior problems that merit intervention. Furthermore, boys with LDs often show more severe academic deficits than do girls with LDs (Loomis, 2006; Young, 2005).

Ethnicity and Socioeconomic Factors

Ethnic minority youths are approximately two to three times more likely than non-minority youths to experience significant problems in reading and writing. For example, the prevalence of reading delays is higher among African American (63%) and Hispanic American (58%) children than among non-Hispanic white children (27%; Lyon, Fletcher, Fuchs, & Chhabra, 2006). Interestingly, studies show approximately equal prevalence across ethnicities for mathematics difficulties (McDermott, Goldberg et al., 2006). It is possible that the impoverished learning and educational opportunities often experienced by ethnic minority youth affect reading and writing achievement more than math.

Low-SES children are also at increased risk for LDs. Approximately one-half of youths living in poverty display significant learning problems. Low SES places children at risk for learning problems in at least three ways. First, low-SES parents may be unable to provide enriched early home environments to their children. Children living in poverty may not have the same access to high-quality medical care, nutritious meals, stimulating toys, and educational games as their middle-class counterparts. Second, low-SES parents may be less able to provide high-quality learning experiences to their children. These parents may talk and read to their children less often, place less value on their children's academic success, and show less involvement in their children's schooling. Finally, low-SES children often attend less-than-optimal schools. Because most children must attend local public schools, and because schools are largely funded by local taxes, children living in disadvantaged neighborhoods often receive inferior education (Pianta, 2006; Silver & Hagin, 2002).

Course

Children with LDs are at risk for long-term academic difficulties. Many youths begin to show learning problems in kindergarten but are not identified until their academic problems worsen. Approximately 70% of children with reading disabilities who are not identified until the third grade continue to show reading problems in adolescence and early adulthood.

Children's early learning problems place them at risk for academic failure later in life. Children with LDs are more likely than typical learners to earn low grades, to repeat a grade in school, and to drop out of school before graduation. The high school dropout rate for youths with learning disabilities is approximately 37%, compared to an average of 12% nationally (National Center for Educational Statistics, 2003).

The long-term outcomes for children with LDs depend on at least three factors: (1) early intervention, (2) familial support, and (3) the child's personal resiliency. First, youths who receive high-quality, empirically based interventions, especially before the third grade, tend to show marked improvement in their academic skills. Consequently, they are less likely to experience long-term achievement problems. Second, youths who receive support from their families are often better able to cope with their learning problems. Parents can emotionally support their children and advocate for their children's educational needs. Third, youths can rely on other, nonacademic skills to compensate for their academic problems. For example, some children develop competence in sports, art, music, or community service and derive self-esteem, motivation, and career interests from these nonacademic accomplishments (Loomis, 2006).

Comorbidity

Self-Concept and Mood

The impact of LDs on children's self-esteem is mixed. Some data indicate that youths with LDs are at risk for developing negative self-concepts because of their academic struggles. However, most recent research indicates that children with LDs show specific deficits in academic self-concept, but they do not show problems with low self-concept overall. Consequently, they may have a dim view of their academic skills but not a negative impression of themselves in general (Lackaye, Margalit, Ziv, & Ziman, 2006; Lipka & Siegel, 2006).

Research regarding the association between LDs and children's mood is also mixed. Some research indicates that youths with learning problems are at risk for a host of negative emotions. These feelings range from self-blame and anger to helplessness and despair (Loomis, 2006). However, other research indicates that depression is equally common among children with and without learning problems (Lipka & Siegel, 2006).

Peer Interactions

Children with LDs are at risk for peer rejection. At least three factors account for children's increased risk for rejection by classmates. First, children's academic skill deficits and low grades can make them less attractive to classmates. Peers might view them as unintelligent or lazy. Indeed, some data indicate that children with LDs show the same likelihood of peer rejection as children who earn low grades but do not have LDs (Nowicki, 2003).

Second, children with LDs often show other disruptive behavior problems such as hyperactivity and impulsivity. Classmates might find these disruptive behaviors aversive and avoid children with LDs who display them (Samms-Vaughn, 2006).

Third, children with LDs often show deficits in social skills. Children with LDs often prefer younger playmates and display less stable friendships. Some youths with LDs have difficulty understanding other people's emotional expressions and acting appropriately in social situations. They often have low social self-efficacy; that is, they lack confidence in their ability to get along with others. These social deficits and doubts can compromise their peer interactions and friendships (Lackaye et al., 2006; Lipka & Siegel, 2006).

Behavior Problems

ADHD and LDs frequently co-occur. Approximately 15%–40% of youths with LDs have ADHD whereas 25%–50% of youths with ADHD have LDs (Palacios & Semrud-Clikeman, 2005; Silver & Hagin, 2002).

The reason for the high comorbidity between ADHD and LD is not yet known. Some researchers have suggested that children with learning problems display inattention and hyperactivity in the classroom because they are frustrated or bored. However, subsequent research has generally failed to confirm this hypothesis. Instead, most research indicates that ADHD and LD have common genetic causes. For example, twin studies indicate that a common set of genes may predispose children to both disorders. Portions of chromosomes 6 and 16 have been implicated in the development of both ADHD and children's reading problems (Mayes & Calhoun, 2006; Willcutt, Pennington, Olson, Chhabildas, & Hulslander, 2005).

Several researchers have observed a connection between LDs and the development of children's conduct problems. Specifically, some youths with LDs show increased likelihood of oppositional-defiant behavior toward adults, aggression, theft, vandalism, robbery, and chronic truancy. Conduct problems are especially likely among children with significant reading problems and below-average intelligence (Palacios & Semrud-Clikeman, 2005).

Two hypotheses have been offered to explain the relationship between LDs and conduct problems. The **school failure hypothesis** suggests that academic failure mediates the relationship between children's learning problems and the development of conduct problems. Specifically, children and adolescents with learning problems struggle academically and show less involvement in school-related activities. Consequently, they may associate with deviant peers who model and reinforce delinquent behaviors. Alternatively, the **susceptibility hypothesis** posits that children with LDs often have other personality and behavioral attributes that place them at risk for conduct problems. For example, youths with LDs often display ADHD symptoms that compromise their decision making and judgment. Consequently, these youths may be prone to disruptive behaviors such as losing their temper, taking risks, and responding aggressively (Lipka & Siegel, 2006).

Genetic Bases for Learning Disorders

Reading and Writing

LDs are heritable conditions. Family studies indicate that 35%–40% of children with Reading or Writing Disorders, compared to only about 5% of the general population, have an immediate family member with at least one LD. Familial concordance seems to be stronger for boys than for girls. Approximately 40% of boys and 18% of girls who have a parent with LDs show serious learning problems themselves. Twin studies provide further evidence that LDs have a genetic component. Concordance rates for monozygotic and dizygotic twins are .85 and .35, respectively (Grigorenko, 2001; Hawke, Wadsworth, & Defries, 2006).

Molecular genetics research indicates that portions of chromosome 15 may contain genes responsible for some cases of Reading Disorder. For example, the DYX1C1 gene seems to underlie certain reading problems. Experts believe that other genes on chromosome 6 and 15 account for other types of reading and writing problems (LoTurco, Wang, & Paramasivam, 2006; Marino & Molteni, 2006).

Mathematics

Mathematics Disorder is also heritable. Mathematics Disorder runs in families; roughly 50% of children with Mathematics Disorder have a sibling with the disorder. Concordance rates for monozygotic and dizygotic twins are .73 and .56, respectively (Butterworth, 2005).

Children with certain X-linked genetic disorders, such as Turner syndrome or fragile X syndrome, often show marked impairment in their mathematical abilities. Turner syndrome is caused by the absence or inactivity of a portion of the X chromosome. Fragile X syndrome usually results from a genetic mutation of the X chromosome. Girls with these disorders display underlying deficits in behavioral inhibition, reasoning, short-term memory, and visual-spatial skills that seem to impair their math performance. The fact that girls with these X-linked disorders show specific deficits in mathematical abilities supports the notion that Mathematics Disorder is partially influenced by one's genotype (Mazzocco & McCloskey, 2005).

Although LDs are believed to have underlying genetic and neuropsychological causes, experience also plays a role in the development and maintenance of learning problems. Recall that the principle of passive gene-environment correlation asserts that parents provide not only their genotypes to their children, but also their early environmental experiences. Parents who have difficulty with reading, writing, and math may be less likely to model and reinforce these academic skills to their children. Indeed, Byrne and colleagues (2006) noticed that parents with reading problems had fewer books and magazines in their home, read to their children less often, and placed less emphasis on literacy than parents with average reading skills. Genetic risk, combined with impoverished early learning experiences, likely underlies many cases of LD.

Reading Disorder: Basic Reading Problems

Reading Disorder is the most common LD. Approximately 80% of children with LDs have Reading Disorder. *DSM-IV-TR* classifies all significant reading problems under the diagnosis of Reading Disorder. However, IDEA indicates that children can show problems in three separate areas of reading: (1) basic reading skills, (2) reading fluency, and (3) reading comprehension (Lyon et al., 2001, 2006).

Basic Reading Skills

Reading is a complex task that children do not acquire naturally. As children learn to read, they progress along a continuum of reading skills. First, children learn basic reading skills. These skills include (1) the ability to recognize letters, (2) the awareness of phonemes or the basic sounds of language, (3) an understanding of the connection between letters and the sounds they make, and (4) the capacity to sound out novel words. Consider Alex, a girl with basic reading skill deficits:

Alex

Alex was a 10-year-old girl with a history of low academic achievement, especially in the areas of reading. Alex displayed problems mastering basic phonics skills. Because she could not sound out words, she guessed at their meaning based on their initial letters, length, or context. She often confused words with similar appearance. For example, Alex sometimes read "what" instead of "that" and often mistook "thought" for "though" and "through." Alex was completely unable to sound out novel words or read stories at her grade level that did not contain pictures or other contextual cues.

Alex had difficulty understanding directions and completing tasks in a timely manner. In school, Alex frequently made mistakes because she did not understand written directions. Alex performed best when her teacher presented instructions orally, demonstrated tasks, and monitored Alex's progress as she completed her work. Alex admitted that she was frequently confused by assignments at school. "Sometimes, I just guess at what I'm supposed to do because I don't understand the directions. I also look at the other kids in the class to find out what to do. I have a lot of friends who are willing to help me, so I get by."

Letter Recognition

Children learn to recognize individual letters by their names and sounds. For example, preschool-age children learn to recognize the letter "s" from a list of printed letters, to name the letter "s," and to tell a parent that the "s" makes the /s/ sound. Letter recognition is essential to the development of all other reading skills.

After letter recognition, children must develop phoneme awareness. **Phonemes** are the smallest units of spoken language; they are the sounds that individual letters or combinations of letters make. Examples of phonemes include the /s/ sound, as in *sip*, or the /sh/ sound, as in *ship*. There are 41 phonemes in the English language. These phonemes can be combined in many ways to form the English spoken language. **Phoneme awareness** refers to children's recognition that spoken language can be broken down into phonemes and that phonemes can be combined to create spoken language (Samms-Vaughn, 2006).

Phoneme Awareness

Phoneme awareness does not come naturally to children. Spoken language is seamless. When we speak, we usually blend sounds together. We usually do not clearly articulate each sound of each word. For example, when we ask a friend, "What do you want to do today?" our question might sound like, "Waddayawanna do today?" Children must learn that these strings of spoken language can be segmented into discrete sounds.

Typically, children need systematic instruction to develop phoneme awareness. Indeed, a considerable percentage of time that children spend in early elementary school is devoted to learning phoneme awareness. Parents and teachers can foster children's phoneme awareness in several ways.

Methods to Teach Phoneme Awareness

1. Phoneme isolation: Recognizing individual sounds in words

   Tell me the first sound in "paste." Answer: /p/

2. Phoneme identity: Recognizing a common sound in different words

   Tell me the sound that is the same in "bike," "boy," and "bell." Answer: /b/

3. Phoneme categorization: Recognizing the phoneme that does not belong

   Which word does not belong: bus, bun, rug? Answer: rug

4. Phoneme blending: Listening to separately spoken phonemes and combining them to form a spoken word

   What word is /s/ /k/ /ü/ /l/? Answer: school

5. Phoneme segmentation: Breaking words into sounds by counting phonemes

   How many sounds are in "ship"? Answer: three (/sh/ /i/ /p/)

6. Phoneme deletion: Recognizing the word that remains when a phoneme is deleted

   What is "smile" without the /s/? Answer: mile

Source: From National Reading Panel (2000). Used with permission.

Phonics

Phoneme awareness is essential for the acquisition of the next basic reading skill: understanding the connection between printed letter combinations and the sounds they make. Specifically, children must learn to translate graphemes into phonemes. **Graphemes** are the units of written language that represent phonemes. For example, the grapheme *ship* represents the three phonemes /sh/ /i/ /p/. Children with adequate phoneme awareness are able to use their understanding of phonemes to decode written words into spoken language.

The ability to decode written words into phonemes depends on children's phonics skills. **Phonics instruction** emphasizes the correspondence between letters and sounds. Although there are many ways to teach phonics, all phonics-based teaching methods help children see the basic relationship between letter combinations and the sounds letters make (see Image 7.1).

The cat sat on Sam's lap.
The cat had a nap.
Sam will pat the cat.

Image 7.1   A Phonics-Based Reading Program. Texts emphasize the repetition of words with the same phonemes.

One of the most widely studied methods for teaching phonics is direct instruction. **Direct instruction** involves the systematic presentation and practice of basic skills in highly structured settings. Skills are broken down into simple steps. Then, each step is introduced, modeled, and practiced. In direct phonics instruction, children are initially taught to convert letters into sounds. Later, they are taught to combine or blend sounds into recognizable words.

Direct Instruction

Step 1: The teacher explicitly states the goals for the lesson.

Today, we are going to learn how to read words that contain the letters "st" and make the sound /st/. By the end of the lesson, you will be able to read words that have /st/ in them.

Step 2: The teacher breaks down material into small steps, giving students the chance to practice each step.

Here are the letters "st." What are the letters? (Child answers "st.")

They make the /st/ sound. What sound do they make? (Child answers /st/.)

(Continued)

(Continued)

Step 3: Teacher provides clear and detailed instructions.

Let's practice some words that start with /st/. All of these words begin with the /st/ sound. Ready? (Teacher gives examples.)

Step 4: Teacher provides guidance during initial practice.

Start with this word. (Teacher points to each part of the word as child reads it.)

Step 5: Teacher provides systematic feedback and corrects child's mistakes immediately.

Now read this word. (Child correctly reads the word *stop*.)

Good. Now this one. (Child incorrectly reads the word *stem*.)

No. The word is "stem." Read it again with me.

Step 6: Teacher gives additional practice, either during seatwork, homework, or during the next lesson.

During the last lesson, we learned about words that begin with /st/. Today, we're going to review and practice more /st/ words.

Almost any skill can be taught by breaking it down into component steps, providing clear instructions and ample practice, immediately correcting mistakes, and liberally reinforcing its appropriate use. Typically, children are first taught very basic tasks that have a high probability of being successfully completed. Then, teachers help children build upon early skills until they demonstrate mastery in more advanced tasks. Advocates of direct instruction believe that children who continue to show learning problems despite average cognitive ability lack adequate instruction; they do not have some underlying disorder that renders them unable to learn (Adams & Carnine, 2003).

Decoding Unfamiliar Words

The final basic reading skill is the ability to read unfamiliar words. New readers can approach novel words in at least two ways. The first method is called **phonemic mediation**. Readers with adequate phoneme awareness and phonics skills can sound out unfamiliar words, translating them into spoken language. Then they examine whether the word they decode is familiar and makes sense in the sentence.

Consider the following sentence: *Cat has a snack.* A beginning reader might know the first three words in the sentence but be unfamiliar with the word *snack*. He might use phonics skills to sound out the word by translating each letter into its corresponding phoneme: /s/ - /n/ - /ă/ - /k/. Then, he examines whether the resulting combination of phonemes corresponds to his existing spoken vocabulary. For example, he might think to himself, "The word sounds like *snack*. I know what a *snack* is. The word *snack* makes sense in the sentence, so the word must be *snack*."

A second method to decode unfamiliar words relies largely on children's memories and the use of **contextual cues**. If children lack phoneme awareness or phonics skills, they may try to infer words based on their appearance, other words in the sentence, or contextual cues (e.g., pictures).

In the sentence *Cat has a snack,* a beginning reader might attempt to guess at the meaning of the word *snack* based on its length or beginning letter. Then, he might use pictures to test whether his inference is correct. In many cases, use of appearance and contextual cues result in successful reading. However, in some cases, these strategies lead to reading errors. For example, a child might incorrectly read the sentence as *Cat has a sack* because he sees a picture of the cat holding a bag of candy.

Brain Areas Involved in Basic Reading

Three areas of the brain are important to reading (see Image 7.2). The first area is the **left occipito-temporal cortex,** a brain region located near the boundary of the occipital and temporal lobes. In this region, a small area known as the left fusiform gyrus seems to be critical to our ability to detect words. Functional MRI studies indicate that the left fusiform gyrus helps us recognize familiar printed words. It is likely that this brain region is especially involved in our ability to read rapidly and accurately. Damage to the left fusiform gyrus renders people unable to recognize familiar words. Instead, people with damage to this brain region must sound out even simple, frequently occurring words. Their reading is slow and laborious (L. Cohen, Lehericy, Chochon, Lemer, Rivaud, & Dehaene, 2002; McCandliss, Cohen, & Dehaene, 2003).

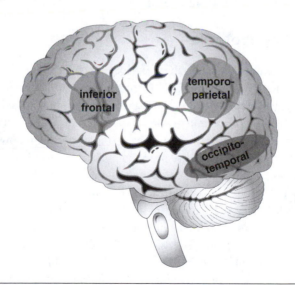

Image 7.2   Brain Areas Involved in Basic Reading

Source: From Rayner, Foorman, Perfetti, Pesetsky, and Seidenberg (2001).

Note: Printed words are first processed by the left occipito-temporal region, which allows us to recognize and read common words. Uncommon words are processed by the left temporo-parietal cortex, which allows us to sound out novel words. The left inferior frontal regions help us interpret the word's meaning and context within the sentence.

Two other brain regions are responsible for converting graphemes into phonemes. The first is the **left inferior frontal cortex**, located in a portion of the frontal lobe known as *Broca's area*. The second is the **left temporo-parietal cortex**. This brain region is located between the temporal and parietal lobes and roughly corresponds to *Wernicke's area*. These brain regions seem to be responsible for our ability to sound out novel words (Frackowiak, Friston, Frith, Dolan, Price, & Zeki, 2004; Shaywitz & Shaywitz, 2005)

Evidence implicating the left inferior frontal cortex and left temporo-parietal cortex in reading comes from two sources. First, damage to these regions renders people unable to sound out novel words. However, people with damage to these regions are often able to recognize and read familiar words based on their appearance. Second, electrical stimulation of these brain areas disrupts the ability to sound out novel words in healthy individuals. However, electrical stimulation to these regions does not interfere with the ability to recognize familiar words (Cao, Bitan, Chou, Burman, & Booth, 2006).

By measuring activity in the brain, researchers have identified a neurological pathway that underlies our ability to read. Approximately 200 milliseconds after a word is presented, it is processed by the left occipito-temporal regions. These regions are involved in detecting and processing familiar words. Words that require phonological decoding (i.e., unfamiliar words) are further processed by the left temporo-parietal area approximately 150 milliseconds later. This area allows us to sound out novel words. Complex words may also be processed by the left inferior frontal region approximately 100 milliseconds later. The left inferior frontal region helps us understand the word's meaning and its association with other words in the sentence (Rayner et al., 2001; Simos et al., 2005).

Basic Reading Problems

Most children with reading disabilities have underlying deficits in basic reading skills. Children with Reading Disorder often display a lack of phoneme awareness and a deficiency in phonics skills. Instead of using phonics principles to decode words, they often rely on memory, word appearance, and contextual cues to infer word meaning. When reading frequently occurring words, they show few problems. When reading novel words, they are prone to mistakes.

Children's lack of phoneme awareness and phonics skills are especially noticeable when they are asked to read **pseudowords**, that is, words that follow basic principles of the English language but have no meaning. Examples of pseudowords include *throught, plesh*, and *britter*. Children with adequate phoneme awareness and phonics skills are able to sound out these words. Children without adequate phoneme awareness are usually unable to correctly decode pseudowords. Instead, they may mistakenly "read" these words according to their appearance: *thought, flesh*, and *bitter*.

Brain Areas Involved in Reading Disorder

Abnormal functioning of the left inferior frontal cortex and left temporo-parietal cortex probably underlies Reading Disorder. Children with Reading Disorder show less activity in these brain regions when processing novel words or pseudowords, compared to youths without reading problems. Decreased activity of these left hemisphere brain regions might explain deficits in phonological awareness among youths with Reading Disorder (Shaywitz & Shaywitz, 2005; Simos et al., 2002).

Instead of relying on the left frontal and temporo-parietal areas to process language, children with Reading Disorder often use other brain areas in the right hemisphere (see Image 7.3). Specifically, many children with Reading Disorder rely on the **right frontal cortex**, a brain area believed to be responsible for processing visual information. Interestingly, older children with Reading Disorder show greater reliance on right hemisphere brain regions than younger children with Reading Disorder (Cao et al., 2006).

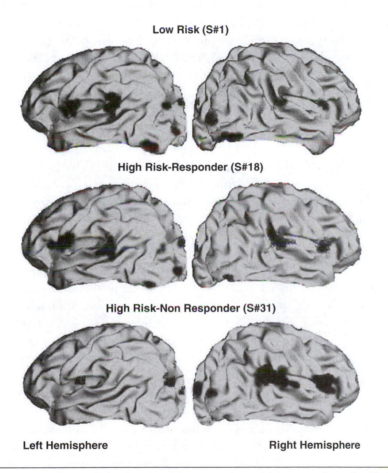

Image 7.3   Effects of Phonics Instruction on Brain Activity. Researchers classified kindergarteners into three groups: children who showed normal reading (top row), children who showed initial reading problems but improved following phonics instruction (middle row), and children who showed initial reading problems but did not improve following phonics instruction (bottom row). Normal readers and children who improved their reading learned to rely on left hemisphere brain regions responsible for language processing. Children who continued to have reading problems continued to rely on right hemisphere areas.

Source: From Simos et al. (2005). Used with permission.

These findings indicate that older children with Reading Disorder may learn to compensate for their poor phonics skills in three ways. First, they may rely on the appearance of the word to guess its meaning. Second, they may use the context of the sentence or the story to infer the word's meaning. Third, they may simply memorize words based on their appearance. Although these strategies can be effective for early readers, they are almost always inadequate to read complex material and to read with high comprehension (Shaywitz & Shaywitz, 2005; Simos et al., 2002).

Children with Reading Disorder who receive instruction in phonics show a significant increase in activity in the left frontal and temporo-parietal areas. In several studies, two to eight months of phonics instruction caused significant increases in left hemisphere activity. After instruction, the brain activity of children with and without Reading Disorder was indistinguishable. Phonics instruction may normalize brain activity among children with Reading Disorder, helping these children process words like normal readers (Aylward et al., 2003; Shaywitz et al., 2004).

Treatment of Basic Reading Problems

Explicit Instruction in Phoneme Awareness and Phonics

In 2000, the National Institute for Child Health and Human Development commissioned a group of experts to determine the most effective methods of reading instruction. The group, called the National Reading Panel (NRP), gathered data from numerous studies comparing different methods to teach reading. The panel concluded that methods that provided explicit instruction in letter recognition and phoneme awareness were most effective in helping children learn to read (NRP, 2000).

More recent research has confirmed the importance of systematic instruction in phoneme awareness and phonics skills. Children who receive direct instruction, in particular, show large gains in phoneme awareness, word recognition, and reading comprehension relative to children who do not receive direct instruction. Furthermore, direct instruction is effective in improving the reading skills of children with reading disabilities. The best outcomes are generally attained by children who begin receiving direct instruction in kindergarten and continue to participate in direct instruction through the second or third grade (Adams & Carnine, 2003; Carlson & Francis, 2002).

Figure 7.1 summarizes the NRP findings with respect to phoneme awareness. Explicitly teaching children to recognize and manipulate phonemes had a large and direct effect on their phoneme awareness skills. Explicit training in phoneme awareness was also associated with significant gains in reading and spelling.

Figure 7.2 summarizes the NRP's (2000) findings regarding the effects of explicit phonics instruction on children's reading. Overall, children who receive systematic instruction in phonics show significantly greater gains in reading than children who do not receive phonics instruction. Phonics programs that encourage children to convert letters (graphemes) into sounds (phonemes) and combine or blend sounds into recognizable words were associated with the greatest improvement in reading. Systematic phonics instruction is most effective when it is administered

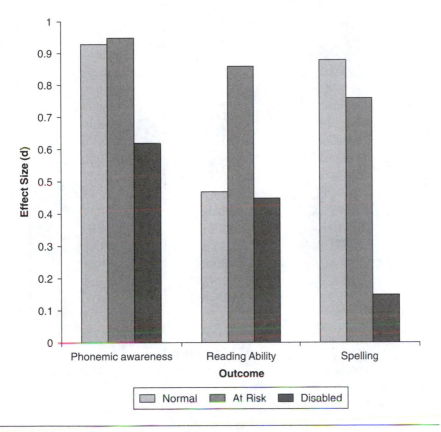

Figure 7.1   Effects of Phoneme Awareness Training

Source: Based on NRP (2000).

Note: Children who receive systematic instruction in phoneme awareness show greater gains in phoneme skills, reading, and spelling compared to children who do not receive training in phoneme awareness. Training can improve phoneme awareness and reading skills in normal children, at-risk children, and youths with reading disabilities.

individually or in small groups and when it is initiated before second grade. Phonics-based reading instruction is also associated with gains in children's reading comprehension (Kerins, 2006).

Whole Language Instruction

Whole language instruction is based on the belief that learning to read is a natural process that occurs through continued exposure to spoken and written language. Advocates of whole language instruction criticize systematic phonics instruction in which teachers carefully introduce, model, and reinforce the relationship between words and sounds. Instead, proponents of whole language argue that children will naturally discover the rules of reading on their own, as long as they are given opportunities to read and they are allowed to direct their own learning (Y. M. Goodman, 1989; K. S. Goodman, 1992).

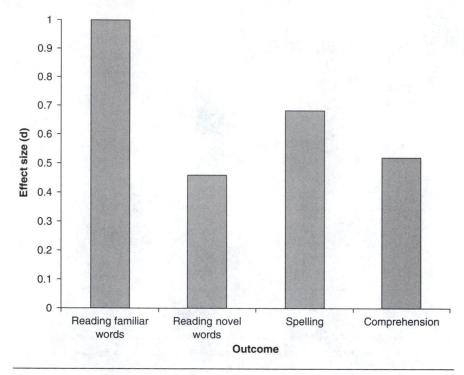

Figure 7.2   Effects of Systematic Phonics Instruction on Reading

Source: Based on NRP (2000).

Note: Children who receive systematic phonics training, especially training conducted before the second grade, show improvements in basic reading, spelling, and reading comprehension compared to children who do not receive systematic phonics instruction.

Whole language approaches to reading instruction are "learner-centered" and designed to increase children's interest in reading. Although instructional approaches vary, teachers who adopt the principles of whole language allow children to select their own reading materials in order to capitalize on their motivation to learn. In some cases, children might dictate stories to the teacher. After the teacher transcribes the stories, children are encouraged to read them. Teachers also encourage students to use contextual cues and pictures to interpret the meaning of the stories they read.

Little research supports the efficacy of whole language instruction. Stahl, McKenna, and Pagnucco (1994) found only 14 studies that included quantitative data investigating the efficacy of whole language approaches to teaching reading. These studies provided some evidence that whole language reading instruction increased children's reading comprehension. However, Stahl and colleagues concluded that there were too few studies to support the adoption of whole language techniques in the classroom.

Whole Word Instruction

Whole word instruction is an extension of the whole language approach. Both whole word and whole language approaches emphasize the meaning behind printed material rather than the ability to sound out words. In whole word instruction, teachers encourage children to process words as wholes, rather than break them down into phonemes. Initially, children learn to recognize a limited number of common words on sight. Then, their reading vocabulary is gradually expanded as teachers introduce new words during the course of reading practice.

In traditional whole word instruction, teachers usually do not provide explicit instruction in phonics. Advocates of the whole word approach believe that breaking words down into phonemes is artificial and not meaningful to students. Instead, teachers might present whole words on flashcards and encourage students to recognize words based on their appearance. This approach is believed to have two chief advantages over phonics-based instruction. First, by learning words as wholes, children may be less likely to be confused by irregular phonemes in the English language. For example, *pint* and *hint* have different pronunciations despite the fact they both end in *int* (Rayner et al., 2001). Second, practitioners of the whole word approach argue that this approach is more meaningful to children than phonics instruction and, consequently, improves children's motivation to read.

Whole word instruction often relies on **leveled texts** to increase children's reading vocabulary (see Image 7.4). Leveled texts are short books that are ordered according

On the Bed

The mouse sat on the bed.

The cat sat on the bed.

The dog sat on the bed.

The cow sat on the bed.

The elephant sat on the bed.

Image 7.4   Whole Word Instruction. Children read leveled texts, like this one. Each text introduces new words, such as "elephant." Children are encouraged to use pictures and other contextual cues to derive the meaning of words.

to the difficulty of vocabulary, repetition of words, inclusion of novel words, use of picture cues, and complexity of sentence structure. Children are initially assigned to low-leveled texts, based on the number of sight words they know. Then, teachers gradually present more difficult texts to expand the child's reading vocabulary.

Reading Recovery is one of the most frequently used whole word approaches to reading instruction. Some data indicate that Reading Recovery is effective at reducing reading problems among children with reading delays. Several studies indicate that as many as 81% of children with reading problems show marked improvement in their reading ability following participation in Reading Recovery (Zane, 2005).

On the other hand, much of the research supporting Reading Recovery is flawed (D'Agostino & Murphy, 2004; Zane, 2005). First, in several studies, attrition was very high among children who received Reading Recovery compared to children who received other forms of reading instruction. For example, in one study, more than one-third of youths who participated in Reading Recovery dropped out of the program before completion. Only those children who successfully completed the Reading Recovery program (and who presumably had the best outcomes) were used to evaluate the program's effectiveness.

Second, teachers who administered Reading Recovery were often better trained than teachers in the comparison groups. In one study, Reading Recovery teachers received two years of training in the program, whereas teachers who administered the comparison treatment received only two weeks of training. The efficacy of Reading Recovery, therefore, may be due to the expertise of teachers rather than the efficacy of treatment.

Finally, Reading Recovery is less efficacious when administered to children with reading disabilities compared to youths without serious reading problems (Elbaum, Vaughn, Hughes, & Moody, 2000). Chapman, Tunmer, and Prochnow (2001) showed that Reading Recovery improved the decoding skills of youths *without* Reading Disorder, but was largely ineffective for youths *with* serious reading problems. Reading Recovery, therefore, may be most efficacious for youths *least* in need of reading remediation.

Reading Disorder: Fluency and Comprehension Problems

The Development of Fluency and Comprehension

Fluency

Reading fluency refers to the ability to read rapidly, accurately, and with proper expression. Fluent readers recognize words quickly, attend to important words in sentences more than unimportant words, and emphasize critical words so that sentences make sense.

Reading fluency is important. Fluent readers spend less mental energy processing text. Instead, their cognitive resources can be directed at other tasks, like extracting meaning from what they read. Fluent readers also spend less time reading individual words and sentences. Therefore, they encounter more words and gain relatively greater practice with reading than do disfluent readers. Finally, fluent readers are able to determine where to place emphasis or where to pause so that sentences makes sense. Reading fluency, therefore, allows readers to better interpret and understand text.

Children become fluent readers through extensive practice with reading. Initially, children must sound out almost all words in order to gain familiarity with the irregularities of the English language. Over time, children begin to recognize frequently occurring words on sight. Consequently, their speed and accuracy increases. As children's reading experience accumulates, they encounter more novel words, which gradually become familiar sight words. Practice allows children to make reading automatic; that is, practice lets children "turn low-frequency words into high-frequency words" (Rayner et al., 2001, p. 40).

Comprehension

Reading comprehension refers to children's ability to read text for meaning, to remember information from the text, and to use information to solve problems or share with others. Reading comprehension is an active process in which children construct meaning from what they read. Reading comprehension, therefore, depends on the interaction between the reader and the text. The reader's understanding of the text will depend on her basic reading skills, reading fluency, and prior knowledge.

Reading comprehension depends principally on children's basic reading skills and reading fluency. In order to understand text, children must be able to recognize words. If children are unable to recognize familiar words or incorrectly decode novel words, their reading comprehension will suffer. Children's reading comprehension also depends on their ability to read quickly. To understand text, children must be able to combine information from the beginning and end of the passage. Consider the following sentence:

Matt has a fat cat that likes to wear a hat.

A child who must sound out individual words in the sentence might have difficulty remembering information presented early in the sentence by the time he reaches the end of the sentence. For example, a disfluent reader might be able to answer the question, "What does the cat like to wear?" but not "Whose cat likes to wear a hat?"

Reading comprehension also depends on children's general language skills. Indeed, the correlation between people's spoken language comprehension and reading comprehension is .90 (Rayner et al., 2001). Many of the same abilities important to reading comprehension are also important to the comprehension of spoken language. First, children must possess adequate information processing skills to comprehend passages. For example, when listening to or reading a passage, children must be able to attend to the most important information, ignore irrelevant information, notice the sequence of events, and pay attention to causal relationships in the story. Second, listening and reading comprehension depends greatly on children's working memory. Children must be able to remember information from passages long enough to answer questions. Third, children must also have adequate contextual knowledge about the story in order to make sense of the information that is presented. For example, children who read a story about Vikings will have difficulty comprehending the story if they have never been taught about Vikings before.

Reading comprehension is influenced by practice. Children with greater exposure to stories gain experience understanding passages. Reading experience also increases children's reading vocabulary, fluency, and general knowledge, which further promote reading comprehension. Ironically, children with adequate basic reading skills are more likely to practice reading and, therefore, develop high levels of reading fluency and comprehension. In contrast, children with basic reading skill deficits are less likely to practice and, consequently, are more likely to show problems with fluency and comprehension (Rayner et al., 2001; Shaywitz, Holford, Holahan, & Fletcher, 1995).

Fluency and Comprehension Problems

Children with reading fluency and comprehension problems often have histories of poor phoneme awareness and word-decoding skills. These children never developed the basic reading skills necessary to sound out novel words. Consequently, their exposure to novel words and practice with reading was limited. Problems reading novel words often leads to an overall reduction in the rate of reading (i.e., fluency) and accuracy with which children can answer questions about the passages they read (i.e., comprehension; Lyon, Fletcher, & Barnes, 2003).

Wolf and Bowers (1999) developed the **double-deficit model** to explain the relationship between basic reading skills, reading fluency, and reading comprehension. According to this model, children can be grouped into three categories based on the type of reading problems they show. First, some children show problems with basic reading skills. These children have difficulty sounding out words and, consequently, answering questions about what they have read. Lack of phoneme awareness and basic phonics skills often underlies these deficits. Second, some children show adequate basic reading skills but problems with reading fluency. These children have particular difficulty recognizing common words on sight. Consequently, their reading is slow and laborious. Their reading comprehension is also usually impaired. Because their rate of reading is slow, they often have difficulty remembering information from the beginning of the passage by the time they reach the end of the passage. Third, a small group of children show impairments in both basic reading skills and reading fluency. These children show the greatest level of reading problems overall.

It is rare for children to show specific problems with reading comprehension but no deficits in phoneme awareness, decoding, or fluency. Only about 6% of youths with reading problems show difficulty in comprehension alone. Youths with comprehension problems, but not basic reading or fluency problems, tend to have underlying difficulties with oral language and reasoning (Leach, Scarborough, & Rescorla, 2003; Ransby & Swanson, 2003).

Treatment of Fluency and Comprehension Problems

Fluency

Practice is critical to the development of reading fluency. Children who display fluency problems must be given more reading opportunities. Most teachers rely on one of two approaches to provide children with reading practice. One tactic is called **guided oral reading**. In guided oral reading, the child reads and re-reads a text aloud until she becomes proficient. Teachers or peers listen to the child, provide assistance sounding out words, and correct reading errors. Sometimes, children read along with audiotapes, videos, or computer programs.

A second strategy to improve fluency is **independent silent reading**. For example, teachers who use the Sustained Silent Reading (SSR) or Drop Everything and Read (DEAR) programs devote 15–30 minutes of class time each day to independent silent reading. Students are allowed to select their own reading material, and they do not receive systematic help and correction from teachers or peers.

The NRP (2000) reviewed the effect of guided oral reading and independent silent reading on children's reading fluency and comprehension (see Figure 7.3). Children who participated in guided oral reading showed increased reading accuracy, reading speed, and reading comprehension compared to children who did not

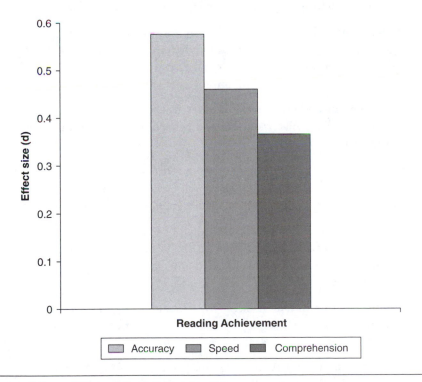

Figure 7.3   Effects of Guided Oral Reading

Source: Based on National Reading Panel (2000).

Note: Guided oral reading is associated with increases in children's fluency and comprehension.

receive opportunities for guided oral reading. Guided oral reading is effective for normal readers and children with reading disabilities (Chard, Vaughn, & Tyler, 2003; Kuhn & Stahl, 2003).

The NRP (2000) was unable to draw firm conclusions regarding the merits of independent silent reading. Too few studies were conducted to adequately evaluate these programs. However, most of the research that had been conducted indicated that these programs were not associated with increases in reading fluency.

Comprehension

Most teachers recognize that reading comprehension skills must be systematically introduced and modeled in the classroom. Children who are provided with systematic training in reading comprehension show significant improvements compared to youths who do not receive explicit instruction (Rosenshine, Meister, & Chapman, 1996).

At least seven techniques have been shown to improve children's reading comprehension (NRP, 2000):

1. **Cooperative learning:** Children read and discuss text with peers. Peers help each other understand material. This technique is associated with increased comprehension and more advanced strategies for analyzing text.

2. **Graphic organizers:** Children represent material from the text using charts, graphs, or pictures. Students might underline or highlight key terms or connect ideas with arrows. This strategy is often used in science and social studies classes. It is associated with improved memory for text.

3. **Question answering:** Children answer teachers' questions about the text. This technique is effective in improving children's recall of important ideas or themes.

4. **Question generation:** Children generate their own questions while reading. Readers might ask themselves *who*, *what*, *when*, *where*, and *why*. This method increases reading comprehension among youth in first through twelfth grades.

5. **Story structure:** Children learn to identify elements of stories, such as the main characters, the plot, and the timeline of events. This technique is particularly effective with younger readers and readers who have comprehension problems.

6. **Summarization:** Children identify the main idea of a passage and connect information in the text to the main idea. This technique is especially effective for older children.

7. **Multiple strategy instruction:** Teachers combine two or more of the above strategies in flexible ways. For example, a teacher might have students read a story, generate questions, summarize the main points, and draw a timeline of events. The use of multiple strategies is generally more effective than the use of single techniques.

Recent research has identified two other approaches that seem to increase reading comprehension (Kim, Vaughn, Wanzek, & Wei, 2004). These approaches are particularly relevant for children with Reading Disorder:

1. **Activating background knowledge:** Teachers encourage students to recall information relevant to the passage *before* reading. For example, before reading a passage about Vikings, teachers might ask students to tell all that they know about Vikings.

2. **Explicit teaching of vocabulary:** Teachers provide students with systematic instruction on word meaning to make sure they understand individual words in the text.

Systematic comprehension instruction is associated with increases in children's memory for information, speed of reading, understanding, and ability to apply information to answer questions or solve problems (NRP, 2000; Rosenshine et al., 1996; Therrien, Wickstrom, & Jones, 2006).

Disorder of Written Expression

Writing in Normal Children

Writing is a complex task that takes years to master. For most children, the writing process involves three steps: planning, translating, and reviewing (Hayes & Flower, 1980). First, children plan the writing task. Planning involves determining the purpose of the writing, generating a main topic and supporting ideas, and organizing these ideas so that they make sense.

Imagine that a teacher asks students to write a report on sharks. Most children would begin the writing process by identifying the purpose of the writing assignment and an appropriate format for the paper. An essay on shark behavior would be written differently than a creative story about a fictional shark. Then, children might gather information about sharks, identify the most important information that they want to include in their essays, and discard irrelevant information. Finally, children would likely spend time organizing their thoughts generated from the information they gathered. Some children might outline their essays, whereas others might use diagrams or flowcharts.

Second, children translate their ideas into written text. Translation depends on children's phoneme awareness, their knowledge of vocabulary and spelling, and the mechanics of writing (e.g., how they hold a pencil).

Third, children review their writing. Reviewing involves rereading their stories, identifying mistakes, and making changes. Mistakes can be at the level of individual words (e.g., illegible handwriting, misspellings), sentences (e.g., missing subject, predicate), or paragraphs (e.g., no topic sentence). Editing can also involve analyzing the composition's grammar and punctuation (e.g., Are singular and plural verbs used correctly?) or theme (e.g., Does the sentence make sense?).

Children With Writing Problems

Planning

Children with writing disabilities spend far less time and effort planning assignments than their classmates (Graham & Harris, 2000). Specifically, children with writing disabilities do not think about their goals for writing, do not generate much information about the topic, and do not organize their thoughts before sitting down to write. Instead, most youths with writing disabilities begin writing about the first relevant concept that comes into their minds. Then, they add information that is prompted by their first sentence. For example, a child without writing problems might write the following topic sentence:

Sharks are some of the most dangerous animals in the ocean.

Then, she might follow up with additional sentences supporting her topic:

Sharks have hundreds of teeth that are as sharp as knives.

An adult shark can eat 100 pounds of fish each day.

Sharks have been known to eat fish, seals, and even other sharks!

In contrast, a child with writing difficulties might begin his essay in the same way:

Sharks are some of the most dangerous animals in the ocean.

Sharks have hundreds of teeth that are as sharp as knives.

Then, he might follow up with a series of sentences that are prompted by the sentence that immediately precedes it. The result is a list of ideas that strays from the topic:

If one cuts you, you will be in a lot of trouble.

You will need to swim to shore and see a doctor.

The doctor will tell you not to go out into the ocean again.

You might swim in swimming pools.

This lack of planning, often shown by children with writing problems, has two adverse consequences. First, the stories of children with writing disabilities tend to be disjointed and difficult to follow. In the above example, the reader expects that the paragraph will be about shark's teeth or the fact that they are dangerous, but the actual text conveys a story about a swimmer. Second, the stories of children with disabilities tend to be brief. Indeed, children with writing disabilities tend to generate stories approximately two-thirds shorter than those of their classmates. Because children with disabilities do not plan and organize their writing before they begin, they run out of ideas earlier than their peers (Graham, Harris, MacArthur, & Schwartz, 1991).

Translation

Children with writing disabilities often show problems translating their thoughts onto paper. Spelling errors and poor handwriting are extremely common among children with writing problems. Indeed, spelling errors and illegible handwriting account for 41% and 66% of the variance in children's overall quality of writing, respectively (Graham, Harris, & MacArthur, 2004). Spelling problems and poor handwriting interfere with writing by slowing the writing process. Children who struggle with spelling devote cognitive resources to spelling individual words, rather than focusing on sentence quality or paragraph coherence. Children who have difficulty with mechanics may write too slowly to keep up with the thoughts they want to convey. Consequently, their writing may be disorganized or illogical.

Reviewing

Children with writing disabilities review and edit their work differently than their classmates. When most children review their writing, they attend to all aspects of the text, including whether individual sentences make sense and whether paragraphs are organized into a coherent story.

In contrast, children with writing disabilities focus primarily on low-level writing mistakes when editing. Low-level mistakes include errors in capitalization, mistakes in punctuation, and illegible handwriting. A child with writing disabilities might write, "The boy and the girl *is* going to the party." However, he might edit the sentence by changing the order of the boy and the girl in the sentence, altering the punctuation, or rewriting the sentence so that it is more legible. In one study, approximately 70% of the revisions made by youths with writing problems involved surface-level changes that did not correct substantive errors (De La Paz, Swanson, & Graham, 1998; MacArthur, Graham, & Schwartz, 1991).

Treatment of Writing Problems

Improving Planning and Reviewing

Self-Regulated Strategy Development (SRSD; Graham, 2006) is a method for systematically teaching children how to plan and review their writing. In SRSD, children are explicitly taught to think about the goals of their writing, to generate and organize ideas, and to elaborate on the sentences that they produce. In elementary school classes, teachers might use the POW acronym to help students recall the steps to effective pre-writing: (1) Pick my idea, (2) Organize my notes, and (3) Write and say more. First, teachers describe each of the POW steps. Then, they model the use of each step in front of the class while thinking aloud. Next, they encourage students to memorize and use the steps. Finally, teachers monitor their students as they use the steps on their own (Graham & Harris, 2003).

Teachers also encourage children to review their writing during the writing process (see Image 7.5). For example, young children are taught to analyze stories using the following questions:

- Who is the main character?
- When does the story take place?
- Where does the story take place?
- What does the main character (and other characters) do or want to do?
- What happens then?
- How does the story end?
- How does the main character (and other characters) feel?

Empirical studies have investigated the efficacy of SRSD for children with and without writing problems (see Figure 7.4). Four aspects of children's writing have been evaluated: (1) writing quality, the overall value of the composition; (2) writing elements, such as identification of main characters, location, time frame, and conclusion; (3) grammar; and (4) length.

Overall, children who participate in SRSD show increased writing skills in all four areas compared to youths who receive other forms of writing instruction. SRSD is associated with improvements in the writing skills of youths with writing disabilities and typically developing children. Furthermore, the benefits of SRSD are maintained

Albert the Fish

On a warm, sunny day two years ago **(When)**, there was a big gray fish named Albert **(Who)**. He lived in a big icy pond near the edge of town **(Where)**. Albert was swimming around the pond when he spotted a big juicy worm on top of the water. Albert knew how good worms tasted and wanted to eat this one for dinner **(What He Wanted To Do)**. So he swam very close to the worm and bit into him. Suddenly, Albert was pulled through the water into a boat **(What Happened)**. He had been caught by a fisherman **(Ending)**. Albert felt sad **(Feelings)** and wished he had been more careful.

Image 7.5   Improving Children's Writing. Students are taught to identify the parts of their story to determine whether it makes sense. Children focus chiefly on errors in grammar, sentence structure, and logical organization rather than on low-level mistakes.

Source: Based on the National Center on Accelerated Student Learning (http://kc.vanderbilt.edu).

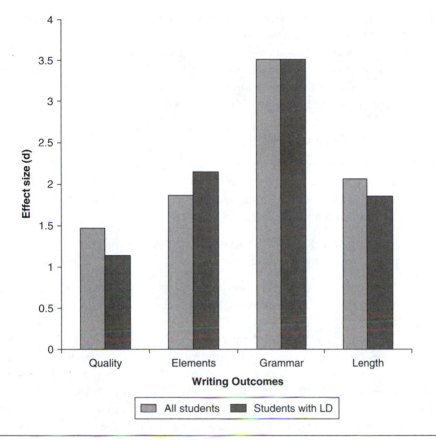

Figure 7.4   Effects of SRSD on Writing

Source: Based on Graham and Harris (2003).

Note: Children who participate in SRSD show improvements in four areas of writing compared to youths who receive traditional writing instruction. SRSD is associated with improvements in both typical readers and children with learning disabilities.

over time and generalize to other types of writing assignments. For example, children who are initially taught to write essays also show improvement in writing book reports or short stories. The benefits of SRSD are attributed to the fact that teachers systematically introduce and model planning and reviewing strategies and encourage students to actively participate in the writing process (Graham & Harris, 2003). Similar results have been obtained by other writing instruction techniques that explicitly teach planning, organizing, and editing (Graham, 2006; Wong, 1997).

Improving Translation: Handwriting and Spelling

Some children show writing problems because they have difficulty with mechanics (Monroe & Troia, 2006). Techniques that improve handwriting and spelling often lead to improvements in the overall quality and length of children's stories (Graham, Harris, & Fink, 2002).

The goal of *handwriting instruction* is to help students write legibly and quickly. Students must also be able to write automatically, so that they can direct their attention to the quality of their composition rather than to the mechanics of writing. One method of handwriting instruction consists of four steps:

1. Alphabet Warm-up: Students learn to name and identify letters.

2. Alphabet Practice: Three lower-case letters with similar shapes are presented (e.g., l, i, t). First, the teacher models how to write each letter. Students practice writing the letters with guidance from the teacher. Students practice writing words containing the letters.

3. Alphabet Rockets: Children rapidly copy sentences with words that contain the previously introduced letters.

4. Alphabet Fun: Children are taught to write the letters in a creative way (e.g., making the "t" into a tomahawk; Graham, Harris, & Fink, 2000).

Spelling instruction involves three components (Graham et al., 2004). First, teachers help students learn to spell frequently occurring words. Teachers might use "word banks" or flashcards to familiarize children with the correct spelling of common words. Repeated exposure to commonly misspelled words is important to help children learn about spelling irregularities in the English language. Graham and colleagues (2002) recommend using a word sorting activity in which children are asked to sort common words based on similar phonemes (e.g., *made*, *laid*, and *say* belong in the same group). Students might also engage in games designed to reward spelling improvement. For example, in a game called Spelling Road Race, students move tokens around a game board when they correctly spell words.

A second component of spelling instruction involves teaching children to spell novel words by analogy. For example, a child who is able to spell *ought* might be able to use this knowledge to spell words such as *bought*, *brought*, and *thought*. Students might also be taught word-building activities. For example, teachers might encourage students to generate as many words as they can that end with "oy."

A final component of spelling instruction involves proofreading. Children are taught to review their own writing and identify and correct spelling mistakes. In some cases, students review each other's compositions and correct misspellings.

Handwriting and spelling instruction is associated with improvements in the quality of children's overall writing. Effective instruction seems to have two components. First, effective instruction is explicit; teachers introduce, model, and reinforce children as they engage in each activity. Second, effective instruction is repeated. Children are given opportunities to practice new skills until they demonstrate proficiency.

Mathematics Disorder

Mathematics Development in Normal Children

Numerosity

Some experts have argued that children are biologically predisposed to understand and process mathematics information. Infants may have an appreciation for **numerosity**, that is, the understanding that a group of stimuli can be understood in terms of their number. Numerosity allows us to differentiate 12 pieces of candy from 6 pieces of candy or differentiate 12 chimes on a clock from 6 chimes on a clock.

Starkey and Cooper (1980) examined whether four- through seven-month-old infants could differentiate groups of dots presented in different numbers. First, infants were presented with a group of three dots. When infants became habituated, or no longer responded to the dots, the researchers changed the number of dots in the display. Infants who habituated to three dots showed renewed interest when presented with only two dots. Starkey and Cooper's findings indicate that young infants appreciate simple numerosities. More recent research has shown that young infants can also discriminate between sounds of different numbers (Lipton & Spelke, 2003).

Other data indicate that infants may have a basic appreciation for number. Karen Wynn (1992) examined whether five-month-olds could discriminate between a correct numerical expression (1 + 1 = 2) and an incorrect expression (1 + 1 = 1). First, infants saw a case containing a doll. Then, the case was obscured by a screen. Next, infants saw a hand apparently place a second doll behind the screen. Finally, the screen was removed and infants were shown either a correct display (i.e., two dolls) or an incorrect display (i.e., one doll). Infants looked at the incorrect display significantly longer than the correct display, suggesting that they had an appreciation for simple numerosities.

Recent research indicates that six-month-olds show activation of the middle-frontal areas of the brain when they encounter these unexpected mathematical events. This brain region also becomes active when adults observe mathematical irregularities (Berger, Tzur, & Posner, 2006). This finding indicates that the brain mechanisms involved in our appreciation for number may be present at birth and active from a very early age. Although not all researchers agree (Mix, Huttenlocher, & Levine, 2002), these data indicate that infants may be hard-wired to understand and process numbers.

Counting

Children's ability to count develops between the ages of two through five years. Young children seem to obey certain rules of counting that follow a fixed sequence (Gelman & Gallistel, 1978):

1. One-to-one correspondence: One number is assigned to each object.
2. Stable order: Numbers are counted in a specific order.

3. Cardinality: The last number stated reflects the quantity of the items counted.

4. Abstraction: Objects of any kind can be grouped and counted.

5. Order irrelevance: Objects can be counted in any order.

Children's counting skills increase with experience. However, children universally progress through similar stages of counting, suggesting that counting is mediated by brain maturation.

Arithmetic Computation

Beginning in elementary school, children's math skills become more complex, as children transition from simple counting to arithmetic. Addition depends greatly on children's counting abilities. For example, young children use fairly immature strategies to add numbers. Initially, they might count on their fingers to solve addition problems. Later, addition is performed verbally or mentally.

Young children also use less efficient strategies to add. For example, when young children are asked to add 7 + 4, they usually first count from 1 to 7 and then count four more numbers until they arrive at the correct answer. Later, children use the **counting-on strategy**; they begin with the largest number (i.e., 7) and then count four more digits until they arrive at the answer. Similar shortcuts are used for subtraction and other mathematical operations (Augustyniak et al., 2006).

With experience, children learn to store math facts in long-term memory. For example, children simply recall that 7 + 4 = 11; they no longer need to count to arrive at the correct answer. **Direct retrieval** from long-term memory permits more automatic math computations. Children can direct their attention to conceptualizing the arithmetic problems rather than to counting. Direct retrieval also frees short-term memory, allowing children to perform more complex calculations in their heads (Geary & Hoard, 2005).

Math Reasoning and Problem Solving

By late childhood, children begin to develop more complex math problem-solving skills. These skills include the ability to solve story problems, to draw information from charts and graphs, and to perform mathematical operations with complex sets of numbers (i.e., borrowing, long division, fractions). These higher-order math skills depend on a number of underlying cognitive abilities.

Children's ability to solve story problems depends on their verbal reasoning skills, attention, and concentration. First, children must be able to read and understand the story problem. Second, they must attend to important parts of the story problem and ignore irrelevant information.

Children's abilities to use charts and graphs depend on their visuospatial reasoning skills and attention/concentration. First, they must appreciate the relationship between visually presented information in the chart or graph and the quantities these illustrations represent. Second, they must identify important elements of the chart or graph and ignore extraneous details. Children's abilities to perform complex mathematical calculations, like adding three-digit numbers or performing long division, also depend on their visuospatial skills. Children must line up numbers properly to ensure that they perform calculations using the correct digits (Geary & Hoard, 2005).

Adolescents who have entered the stage of formal operations are able to think more abstractly and flexibly about mathematical concepts. Formal operational thinking allows adolescents to learn algebra, geometry, and other mathematical disciplines that are not directly tied to concrete objects. Adolescents' abilities to solve equations, geometric proofs, or rate-of-change problems depend on their foundational math skills as well as their ability to reason abstractly.

Development of Mathematics Disorder

Children with Mathematics Disorder develop math skills in the same progression as youths who do not show math problems. However, children with Mathematics Disorder often display difficulties mastering basic counting and computational skills that serve as the foundation for higher-order mathematical reasoning.

First, youths with Mathematics Disorder frequently have difficulty remembering math facts. Whereas most fourth graders can effortlessly recall $4 + 5 = 9$, children with Mathematics Disorder often need to perform this mathematical computation to recall the correct answer. Consequently, children with Mathematics Disorder spend greater cognitive resources performing basic calculations and fewer resources conceptualizing the problem itself (Geary & Hoard, 2001).

Second, youths with Mathematics Disorder often show problems remembering math procedures. For example, when presented with a problem such as $41 - 29 = ?$, children with Mathematics Disorder may forget how to "borrow" (Temple & Sherwood, 2002).

Because of their difficulty retrieving math facts and procedures, youths with Mathematics Disorder often rely on immature strategies to solve math problems. For example, many first graders count on their fingers to solve addition problems. However, children with Mathematics Disorder often continue to rely on this immature tactic into the third and fourth grades. Furthermore, when young children with Mathematics Disorder count, they often count all digits rather than rely on more advanced "add-on" strategies. These immature strategies result in slow, error-prone calculations (Butterworth, 1999; Geary & Hoard, 2005; Jordan, Hanich, & Kaplan, 2003).

Problems remembering math facts, difficulty performing math computations, and reliance on immature problem-solving strategies interfere with children's abilities to solve higher-order math problems. By the time they reach early adolescence, youths with Mathematics Disorder may have difficulty performing simple arithmetic problems quickly and accurately and not understand higher-level math procedures (e.g., graph interpretation, long division).

What explains the deficits shown by youths with Mathematics Disorder? Brian Butterworth (2005) has developed the **defective number module hypothesis** to explain the cause of certain Mathematics Disorders. According to this hypothesis, the neurological system that is believed to underlie infants' appreciation for numerosity does not develop properly. This neurological system involves many brain areas, especially portions of the parietal lobes known as the **right intraparietal sulci (IPS)**. The right IPS seems to play an important role in estimating numerosity for small sets of stimuli, a capacity displayed by infants and young children. The left IPS seems to be important for more complex numerical processing and arithmetic calculations shown by older children. Problems in the development of either right or left IPS would affect mathematical ability. Indeed, neuroimaging studies indicate that some youths with Mathematics Disorder show abnormalities in these brain regions (Dehaene, Piazza, Pinel, & Cohen, 2003; Piazza, Giacomini, Le Bihan, & Dehaene, 2003).

David Geary and Mary Hoard (2005) have suggested an alternative developmental model for Mathematics Disorder (see Figure 7.5). According to their **developmental model for Mathematics Disorder**, children's math skills depend on underlying neuropsychological abilities, including their (1) language abilities, (2) visuospatial abilities, and (3) executive functioning.

Children's language skills enable them to understand the correspondence between spoken numbers (e.g., "twenty-two") and written numbers (e.g., 22). Language skills also help children listen to and understand orally presented math problems and to read/formulate math story problems. Some youths with mathematics disabilities may have underlying verbal deficits that interfere with their math skills.

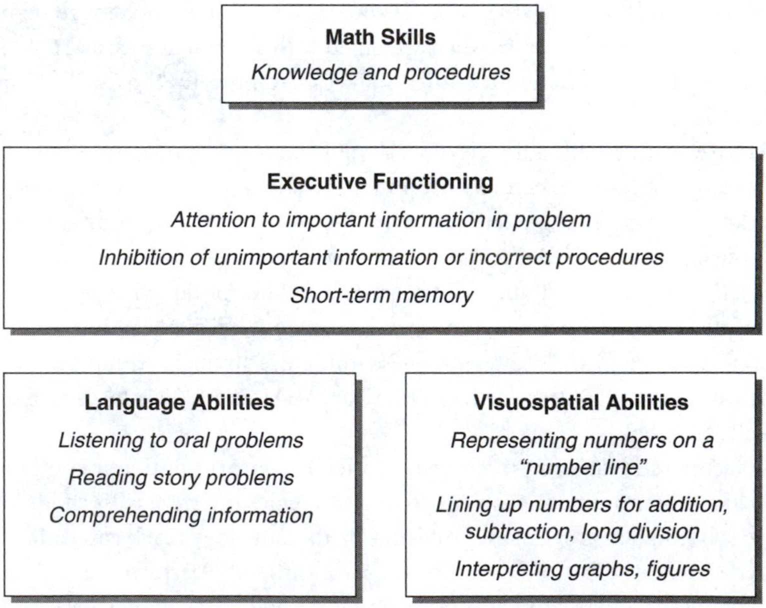

Math Skills

Knowledge and procedures

Executive Functioning

Attention to important information in problem

Inhibition of unimportant information or incorrect procedures

Short-term memory

Language Abilities

Listening to oral problems

Reading story problems

Comprehending information

Visuospatial Abilities

Representing numbers on a "number line"

Lining up numbers for addition, subtraction, long division

Interpreting graphs, figures

Figure 7.5   A Developmental Model for Mathematics Disorder

Note: According to Geary and Hoard (2005), problems in language, visuospatial abilities, and executive functioning underlie mathematics disabilities.

Children's visuospatial skills allow them to represent numerical values along a continuum (i.e., a "number line"), to organize and correctly line up numbers for multidigit calculation, and to draw information from charts and graphs. Some youths with Mathematics Disorder have visuospatial deficits that compromise these abilities. For example, many youths with Mathematics Disorder have difficulty representing digits on a number line; consequently, they often have trouble determining which values are "greater than" or "less than" other values. These children also misalign multidigit problems, causing computational errors (Zorzi, Priftis, & Umilta, 2002).

Children's executive functioning allows them to attend to important information in mathematics problems, ignore unimportant details, retrieve math facts from long-term memory, and perform mathematic operations in short-term memory. Some data indicate that youths with Mathematics Disorder have difficulty with all four tasks. Youths with Mathematics Disorder often have difficulty recognizing important elements of story problems and are easily distracted by extraneous information. They may also be unable to inhibit irrelevant mathematical operations when presented with math problems. For example, when they see the problem $6 \times 4 = ?$, children with Mathematics Disorder might answer "10" because of their failure to inhibit the use of addition. Children with Mathematics Disorder also have difficulty retrieving math facts and, consequently, rely on immature strategies (e.g., counting) to solve math problems. As a result, their short-term memories are often overly taxed, and they are unable to devote sufficient resources to understanding and effectively framing math problems (Barrouillet, Fayol, & Lathuliere, 1997; Geary & Hoard, 2005).

Luke

Luke was a 10-year-old African American boy who was referred to our clinic because of behavior and academic problems. Luke earned below-average grades in most subjects, but he performed poorest in math. As a fifth grader, Luke could add and subtract simple numbers, but he had great difficulty with multiplication, division, and computations involving "borrowing" or "remainders." His teacher recommended that he be "held back" next year so that he could get "extra practice" before progressing to junior high school.

Dr. Ideran observed Luke as he completed some math problems in her office. She noticed that Luke often arrived at the correct answer for addition, subtraction, and simple multiplication problems. However, he was largely unable to divide and his progress was extremely slow and effortful.

"You got a lot of them right," she said, "but it takes you a long time, doesn't it?" Luke replied, "Yeah. I'm not too fast." Dr. Ideran asked, "So, how do you go about solving a problem like 4 × 7?" Luke was reluctant to answer. After a long pause and sigh, tears rolled down his cheeks. Embarrassed, Luke said, "I just start with four . . . and keep counting up by fours . . . until I get to the answer." Dr. Ideran said, "Yes. That takes a lot of work and energy doesn't it? Do you want to learn a better way?"

Treatment of Mathematics Disorder

Targets of Instruction

To treat Mathematics Disorder, therapists can target three areas: (1) preparatory arithmetic skills, (2) basic math computation skills, and (3) math problem solving (Kroesbergen & VanLuit, 2003). Interventions designed to teach preparatory arithmetic skills are usually directed toward very young children and youths with developmental delays. These interventions help children develop an appreciation for numerosity, the ability to recognize numerals, and basic counting skills.

Interventions designed to teach basic computational skills are directed at elementary school-age children with Mathematics Disorder. These interventions focus primarily on addition, subtraction, multiplication, and division. Often, interventions address more complex mathematic operations, such as operations involving three-digit numbers, long division, fractions, and decimals. These interventions help children acquire and automatize math facts and procedures.

Interventions that focus on math problem solving are usually reserved for older children who show adequate computational skills. These interventions provide children with training in understanding story problems and applying math facts and procedures.

Methods of Instruction

Clinicians generally rely on one of three methods for math instruction: (1) direct instruction, (2) self-instruction, or (3) mediated/assisted instruction (Goldman, 1989). **Direct mathematics instruction** involves the systematic presentation of math knowledge and skills. In direct instruction, the teacher introduces and demonstrates the skill following a carefully designed script. Then the skill is broken down into specific steps, which children perform. Teachers provide help and feedback regarding children's performance, correcting children's mistakes (see Table 7.3). Gradually, teacher assistance is faded as children gain mastery of the skill. Children are given repeated opportunities to practice the skill and extend it to new problems.

Self-instruction is a second method to improve children's math skills. In self-instruction, teachers systematically present a series of verbal steps or "prompts" that children can use to solve math problems. Teachers model the use of these prompts as they complete problems on the blackboard in front of the class. Then, children are encouraged to use the prompts when solving their own problems, while the teacher monitors their use. Initially, teachers provide careful assistance to children in using the prompts. Eventually, teacher assistance is faded until children can use the prompts to solve problems on their own.

Teachers who use **mediated/assisted instruction** begin with the student's understanding of the mathematical problem. Then they offer assistance and guidance to the child to help him solve the problem correctly. Mediated/assisted instruction does not involve the use of a script (as direct instruction) or a series of steps (as self-instruction). Instead, the teacher offers increasingly detailed hints at solving the math problem until the child is able to complete the problem successfully. In this

Table 7.3   Three Methods for Teaching Mathematics Skills

Problem: Anne had 9 apples. She gave 4 apples to her friend. How many apples does Anne have left?

Direct Instruction[a]

Step A
Read the problem with me. *Teacher reads the problem.*
What kind of problem is it? *Answer: Subtraction*

Step B
Good. It's subtraction. Is the big number given? *Answer: Yes.*

Step C
Let's read the problem again. *Teacher reads the problem again.*
Is 9 the big number or the small number? *Answer: The big number.*
What kind of number is 4? Answer: *The small number.*

Step D
Good. Now let's take 9 and subtract 4. Watch me. Nine minus four is five.
Now you say "Nine minus four is five." *Child repeats.*
Good. What is the answer? *Answer: Five*

Step E
Good. Now let's read the next problem.

Self-Instruction[b]
Teacher introduces and demonstrates the following steps to solve story problems. Teacher encourages children to use the steps (first aloud, then silently) as she monitors.

What are you asked?	*How many apples does Anne have left?*
What numbers do you have?	*9 and 4*
What number(s) do you need to know?	*How many left?*
What must you do?	*Subtract, 9 − 4*
What is the answer?	*5*
Check your answer.	*4 + 5 = 9, so it checks out!*

Mediated/Assisted Instruction[c]
Teacher provides a structured sequence of hints to help the child complete the problem. Hints become gradually more specific and content-related until the child is able to arrive at the correct answer.

Hint Strategy	*Example*
Simple negative feedback: Teacher asks child to check answer.	Your answer is not quite right. Try again.
Working memory refresher: Teacher reminds child of important parts of the problem.	Remember, she has 9 and gives away 4.
Numerals as memory aids: Teacher asks child to write down important parts of problem.	Let's write it down in numbers: 9 − 4.
Enumeration: Teacher uses a series of verbal instructions and numbers to guide child.	Nine apples [points to nine] minus four apples [points to four] is what?
Complete demonstration: Teacher completes problems for child, giving rationale.	See. Nine minus four is five.

a. Based on DISTAR Arithmetic (Engelmann & Carnine, 1975).

b. Based on Fleischner and Manheimer (1997).

c. Based on Goldman (1989).

way, children are encouraged to derive their own way of solving math problems, rather than rely on a formal set of rules provided by the teacher.

Efficacy

Treatment techniques vary in their efficacy (see Figure 7.6). Interventions that use direct instruction tend to be most effective in improving children's basic computational skills. Self-instruction appears to be most effective at teaching higher-level math problem solving. Across all categories, mediated/assisted instruction is least effective. These results indicate that interventions that provide direct, systematic instruction should be incorporated into remediation programs for Mathematics Disorder (Kroesbergen & VanLuit, 2003).

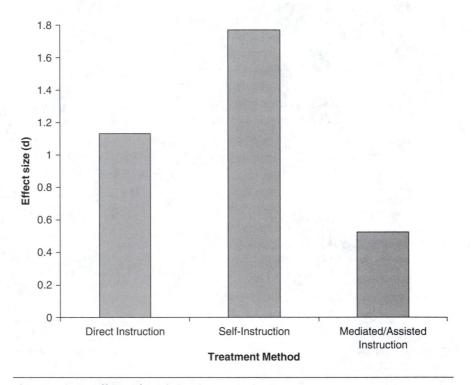

Figure 7.6   Effects of Mathematics Instruction

Source: Based on Kroesbergen and VanLuit (2003).

Note: Youths who receive self-instruction show the greatest improvement in math skills. However, direct instruction was particularly effective in improving children's computational skills.

Update: Daniel and Luke

Dr. Butler administered the WISC-IV and the Woodcock-Johnson III Tests of Achievement to Daniel. Daniel's intellectual functioning (IQ = 101) fell within the average range. However, his standard scores on measures of reading (64) indicated significant deficits. Dr. Butler also noticed that Daniel's reading problems were associated with a lack of phoneme awareness and deficient phonics skills. Dr. Butler diagnosed Daniel with Reading Disorder and forwarded a copy of her evaluation to Daniel's school.

Daniel received special education for his reading problems. He participated in small-group tutoring and instruction using a phonics-based curriculum. He also received help with oral reading and reading fluency. One year after the evaluation, Daniel's basic reading skills and reading comprehension had improved considerably. Daniel's mother was pleased with his progress. "He still doesn't like school," she explained, "but he doesn't hate it either."

Dr. Ideran believed that Luke's primary problem with mathematics was that he lacked basic math facts. Dr. Ideran referred Luke to a teacher in the school district who specialized in children with mathematics problems. The teacher helped Luke learn basic math facts and operations so that he could solve problems more quickly and efficiently. Luke seemed to enjoy activities that involved flashcards and computer-administered math "games." Gradually, Luke's math fluency increased until he mastered basic arithmetic skills. However, six months after the evaluation, Luke was still behind his peers and needed additional tutoring to catch up. Luke was allowed to progress to the sixth grade where he continued to receive systematic tutoring in mathematics.

Critical Thinking Exercises

1. What is the difference between Learning Disorders and learning disabilities?

2. Explain and critique the three main techniques used to identify children with learning disabilities.

3. Why might ethnic minority children or youth from low-income families be at increased risk for academic problems? How might state governments and local school districts prevent or alleviate learning disabilities among these at-risk children?

4. Compare and contrast phonics-based direct instruction with whole word approaches to treating reading disabilities. Which treatment strategy seems to have greater empirical support for young children with reading problems?

5. Develop an intervention program for (a) a 12-year-old boy with difficulty writing research papers in his seventh-grade history class and (b) a 10-year-old girl who has difficulty with math story problems.

CHAPTER 8

Attention-Deficit/ Hyperactivity Disorder

Corey

Corey was an eight-year-old boy who was referred to our clinic by his mother. His mother reported that Corey showed significant problems with hyperactivity and impulsiveness at home. "Most second-grade boys are active, but Corey is always on the go," she reported. "Watching him tires me out." According to his mother, Corey had difficulty remaining seated during meals, constantly fidgeted with objects around the house, talked incessantly, and engaged in high-rate, restless behavior. "He's very impulsive," she added. "As soon as I let him out of the car, I know he'll run right out into the parking lot. He's constantly doing dangerous stunts with his bike. He just doesn't think things through."

Corey also showed problems with inattention at home. Corey had difficulty sustaining his attention on any activity that required concentration or effort. "He can't focus on his homework for more than a few minutes at a time," his mother said. "I tried to reward him for completing his work, but then he rushes through it sloppily." Corey was also extremely forgetful. He often neglected his chores, forgot to complete school assignments, and lost belongings for school. His mother said, "This is the third schoolbag he's had this year. He'd forget to put on his underwear if I didn't remind him."

Corey showed similar problems with hyperactivity, impulsivity, and inattention at school. Corey completed assignments quickly, making careless mistakes. His work was often difficult to read. His grades were slightly below average because he often forgot to turn in assignments, lost his work, or rushed through tests without reading directions. "When I remind him to obey the class rules, he's always apologetic," his teacher said. "He wants to be good, but he just can't follow through."

Dr. Graves interviewed Corey in his office. "You have a hard time doing what you're supposed to do at home and in school?" she asked. "Yeah," admitted Corey, "I'm always getting into trouble because I'm so hyper. My mom calls me her 'Energizer Bunny.'"

What Is Attention-Deficit/Hyperactivity Disorder?

When most people think of children with Attention-Deficit/Hyperactivity Disorder (ADHD), they usually envision youths who have difficulty paying attention in class; are easily distractible; have trouble remaining seated; and are restless, talkative, and impulsive. In other words, most people view "typical" children with ADHD as having two general behavior problems: (1) inattention and (2) hyperactivity-impulsivity.

In fact, most people's impressions of ADHD are accurate. Many children and adolescents with ADHD show problems with both inattention and hyperactivity-impulsivity. *DSM-IV-TR* lists behavioral symptoms that define problems in each of these domains (see Table 8.1). Children with significant **attention problems** show persistent and developmentally unexpected difficulties with attention to detail, sustaining attention over time, listening to others and following through with assignments, organizing tasks, staying focused, and remembering information and where they placed objects. Children who have significant problems with **hyperactivity-impulsivity** fidget and squirm, have difficulty remaining seated and staying still, show problems playing quietly, are talkative and "on the go," blurt out answers in class, have trouble waiting, and intrude into others' conversations or activities.

Children can also be diagnosed with ADHD if they show significant symptoms of inattention *or* hyperactivity-impulsivity (see Table 8.2). By definition, children must show at least six out of a possible nine symptoms of *either* inattention *or* hyperactivity-impulsivity to be diagnosed with the disorder. If the child shows significant symptoms of inattention, but not significant symptoms of hyperactivity-impulsivity, he may be diagnosed with **ADHD, Predominantly Inattentive Type**. On the other hand, if a child shows significant symptoms of hyperactivity-impulsivity, but not significant symptoms of inattention, he might qualify for the diagnosis of **ADHD, Predominantly Hyperactive-Impulsive Type**. If the child shows significant symptoms of both inattention and hyperactivity-impulsivity, he would likely meet diagnostic criteria for **ADHD, Combined Type**.

The fact that children can be diagnosed with ADHD if they show *either* significant hyperactivity-impulsivity *or* significant inattention means that two children diagnosed with ADHD can have qualitatively different symptoms. A fourth grader with ADHD, Predominantly Hyperactive-Impulsive Type might wander about the classroom, talk excessively with peers, interrupt the teacher, and disrupt learning. In contrast, his classmate with ADHD, Predominantly Inattentive Type might sit quietly at her desk, look out the classroom window, think about events occurring in the hallway, and daydream (Bauermeister, Alegria, Bird, Rubio-Stipec, & Canino, 1992; Hudziak et al., 1998; Lahey, Carlson, & Frick, 1997; McBurnett, 1997).

It is also important to realize that symptoms of inattention and hyperactivity-impulsivity must be inconsistent with the child's developmental level. All children show problems with inattention and hyperactivity-impulsivity from time to time. Younger children generally have greater problems with inattention and hyperactivity-impulsivity than older children. To qualify for a diagnosis of ADHD, children must

Table 8.1   Diagnostic Criteria for Attention-Deficit/Hyperactivity Disorder

I. Either (A) or (B)

  A. Six (or more) of the following symptoms of inattention have persisted for at least 6 months to a degree that is maladaptive or inconsistent with developmental level

   1. Inattention

      a. Often fails to give close attention to details or makes careless mistakes in schoolwork or other activities
      b. Often has difficulty sustaining attention in tasks or play activities
      c. Often does not seem to listen when spoken to directly
      d. Often does not follow through on instructions and fails to finish schoolwork, chores, or other duties (not due to oppositional behavior or failure to understand instructions)
      e. Often has difficulty organizing tasks and activities
      f. Often avoids, dislikes, or is reluctant to engage in tasks that require sustained mental effort, such as schoolwork or homework
      g. Often loses things necessary for tasks and activities (e.g., toys, school assignments, pencils, books, or tools)
      h. Is often easily distracted by extraneous stimuli
      i. Is often forgetful in daily activities

  B. Six (or more) of the following symptoms of hyperactivity-impulsivity have persisted for at least 6 months to a degree that is maladaptive or inconsistent with developmental level

   1. Hyperactivity

      a. Often fidgets with hands or feet or squirms in seat
      b. Often leaves seat in classroom or in other situations in which remaining seated is expected
      c. Often runs about or climbs excessively in situations in which it is inappropriate (in adolescents, may be limited to subjective feelings of restlessness)
      d. Often has difficulty playing or engaging in leisure activities quietly
      e. Is often "on the go" or often acts as if "driven by a motor"
      f. Often talks excessively

   2. Impulsivity

      g. Often blurts out answers before questions have been completed
      h. Often has difficulty waiting turn
      i. Often interrupts or intrudes on others (e.g., butts into conversations or games)

II. Some inattentive or hyperactive-impulsive symptoms that caused impairment were present before age 7 years.

III. Some impairment from the symptoms is present in two or more settings (e.g., at home and at school)

IV. There must be evidence of clinically significant impairment in social or academic functioning

V. The symptoms are not better explained by a Pervasive Developmental Disorder, Schizophrenia, or another mental disorder

Source: Reprinted with permission from the *DSM-IV-TR.*

Table 8.2   Subtypes of Attention-Deficit/Hyperactivity Disorder

Diagnosis	Description
Attention-Deficit/Hyperactivity Disorder, Predominantly Inattentive Type	Person shows significant symptoms of inattention, but subthreshold symptoms of hyperactivity-impulsivity
Attention-Deficit/Hyperactivity Disorder, Predominantly Hyperactive-Impulsive Type	Person shows significant symptoms of hyperactivity-impulsivity, but subthreshold symptoms of inattention
Attention-Deficit/Hyperactivity Disorder, Combined Type	Person shows significant symptoms of inattention and hyperactivity-impulsivity

Source: Reprinted with permission from the *DSM-IV-TR.*

show symptoms that greatly exceed symptoms of inattention and/or hyperactivity-impulsivity shown by children of the same age. Psychologists can compare a child suspected of having ADHD with other children of the same age by using norm-referenced rating scales. If the parents' reports indicate that the child's symptoms exceed 95% or 97% of children his age in the standardization sample, the child might qualify for a diagnosis of ADHD.

To be diagnosed with ADHD, children's symptoms must be pervasive; they must exist in multiple contexts. *DSM-IV-TR* requires children to show symptoms in at least two settings, usually at home *and* at school. By definition, a child cannot be diagnosed with ADHD if he only shows symptoms with parents but never with teachers or adults outside the home.

Finally, *DSM-IV-TR* conceptualizes ADHD as a disorder that emerges in early childhood. In order to be diagnosed with ADHD, individuals must have at least some symptoms of inattention *or* hyperactivity-impulsivity before age seven.

Subtypes of ADHD

DSM-IV-TR specifies three subtypes of ADHD: (1) ADHD Combined Type, (2) ADHD Predominantly Hyperactive-Impulsive Type, and (3) ADHD Predominantly Inattentive Type.

ADHD Combined Type (ADHD/C)

Children with ADHD/C show significant inattentive and hyperactive-impulsive symptoms. Parents and teachers describe them as sloppy, impulsive, distractible, rushed, irresponsible, and high rate (Lahey et al., 1997). Most experts believe children with ADHD/C have underlying problems with behavioral inhibition. Disinhibition causes them to have difficulty with sustained attention and behavioral regulation at home, at school, and with peers.

ADHD Predominantly Hyperactive-Impulsive Type (ADHD/HI)

Children with ADHD/HI show significant hyperactive-impulsive symptoms but only subthreshold problems with inattention. They are usually described as "driven by a motor" or "constantly running and on the go." These children may have problems with attention and concentration, but their inattention is not severe enough to merit a diagnosis of ADHD/C (Frick et al., 1994; Owens & Hoza, 2003).

Children with ADHD/HI tend to be younger than children with ADHD/C. Approximately 76% of children with ADHD/HI are younger than seven years. Some experts believe ADHD/HI is an early manifestation of ADHD/C. These experts argue that many young children with ADHD/HI will eventually merit the ADHD/C diagnosis when they become older (Faraone, Biederman, Weber, & Russell, 1998; Lahey et al., 1998; Marsh & Williams, 2004).

ADHD Predominantly Inattentive Type (ADHD/I)

Children with ADHD/I represent a heterogeneous mix of youngsters who display significant inattentive symptoms but subthreshold hyperactive-impulsive symptoms. Although ADHD/I is the second most common subtype of ADHD in clinical settings, it is the most commonly seen subtype in community studies. This is probably because children with ADHD/C display hyperactive-impulsive symptoms, which prompt their referral to psychiatric clinics, whereas the inattentive symptoms of children with ADHD/I are often overlooked by parents and teachers (Carlson, Shin, & Booth, 1999).

ADHD/I is usually seen in older children and adolescents. Typically, children are not diagnosed until after they enter school. It is likely that inattentive symptoms exist at an earlier age, but they may not be recognized until they interfere with the child's academic functioning. Consider Brandy, a girl with ADHD/I:

Brandy

Brandy was a 10-year-old biracial girl with a history of low academic achievement. She was referred to our clinic for psychological testing by her pediatrician, who suggested that she might have a learning disability.

Brandy's academic problems emerged two years earlier, when she was in the third grade. She began making careless mistakes on homework and often asked teachers to repeat instructions on assignments. In class, Brandy had difficulty listening and often daydreamed. "Brandy always seems to be off in her own little world," said her teacher. "She seems more interested in doodling or in staring out the window than in listening to me. I called her mother to make sure that Brandy was getting enough sleep, but she assured me that wasn't the problem."

Brandy's mother reported similar problems with inattention at home: "She never seems to listen to me. It's not that she's being disrespectful; it's just that I have to remind her a thousand times to do something." Brandy's mother also remarked about her daughter's forgetfulness: "She's always asking, 'where's my shoes, where's my homework?'" Brandy was generally compliant, except during homework time. Her mother explained, "I'll tell her to go upstairs and to do her homework, but when I check on her, she's listening to music or drawing. She says she'll get to work, but she never does."

Dr. Kennedy administered an IQ and academic achievement test. Brandy's scores indicated average intelligence and academic skills. He shared his findings with Brandy's mother: "I don't think your daughter has a learning disability. I need a little more information, but I think that she might have ADHD." Her mother replied, "ADHD? That can't be. She's so quiet and well-behaved!"

Table 8.3   Behaviors of Children With "Sluggish Cognitive Tempo"

Forgetful	Drowsy/sleepy	Stares into space
Daydreams	Easily confused	Acts overtired
Sluggish/slow to respond	Seems to be "in a fog"	Underactive/lacks energy

Source: Based on McBurnett et al. (2001).

Recent research suggests there are two distinct types of children who are diagnosed with ADHD/I. The first type shows significant problems with inattention and moderate but subthreshold symptoms of hyperactivity-impulsivity. These children are typically described as "distractible and forgetful" and "having difficulty organizing tasks" (Owens & Hoza, 2003). They do not pay attention to teachers at school or parents at home and may get into trouble because of their distractibility and lack of focus.

Other youths with ADHD/I show significant problems with inattention but almost no symptoms of hyperactivity-impulsivity. Some of these children, like Brandy, are described as having a **sluggish cognitive tempo** (see Table 8.3). They often daydream, appear drowsy, and act confused. Interpersonally, they are described as lethargic, hypoactive, or passive. In school, they often appear spacey and disoriented, as if their minds were constantly wandering from topic to topic. They may not be aware of events around them (e.g., a teacher giving instructions) and take a long time to respond when asked a question. These children often do not get into trouble at school, but they may have problems making friends and getting along with classmates (Carlson & Mann, 2002; Gaub & Carlson, 1997; McBurnett, Pfiffner, & Frick, 2001).

Researchers examining large groups of children are able to differentiate ADHD/I children with and without sluggish cognitive tempo. In one study, 28% of children with ADHD/I showed sluggish cognitive tempo and low levels of hyperactivity-impulsivity (Gaub & Carlson, 1997). Some experts have argued that children diagnosed with ADHD/I and who show sluggish cognitive tempo should be placed in a separate diagnostic category than other children with ADHD/I (Barkley, DuPaul, & McMurray, 1990; Lahey, Schaughency, Hynd, Carlson, & Piacentini, 1987).

Associated Features and Disorders

Comorbid Disorders

Comorbid psychiatric disorders are common among children with ADHD. In one large epidemiological study, 44% of children with ADHD had at least one other psychiatric disorder, 32% had at least two other disorders, and 11% had at least three other disorders (Szatmari, Offord, & Boyle, 1989).

Conduct Problems

Many youths with ADHD develop significant conduct problems at some point in their lives. Approximately 54%–67% of children with ADHD show Oppositional Defiant Disorder (ODD), a psychiatric disorder characterized by persistent stubbornness and noncompliance toward adults. Children with ODD refuse to obey, talk back, throw tantrums, and are otherwise spiteful and argumentative toward caregivers.

Approximately 30%–56% of adolescents with ADHD show Conduct Disorder (CD), a more serious behavioral disturbance characterized by a persistent disregard for the rules of society. Youths with CD show a wide range of disruptive and destructive behaviors including physical fighting, theft, vandalism, and truancy (Whittinger, Langley, Fowler, Thomas, & Thapar, 2007).

Approximately 18%–24% of youths with ADHD develop Antisocial Personality Disorder (APD) as adults. APD is a serious personality disturbance defined by a persistent disregard for the rights of others. Adults with APD often have histories of aggression and illegal behavior. Overall, the presence of ADHD in childhood increases the likelihood of developing ODD, CD, and/or APD 10-fold (Angold, Costello, & Erkanli, 1999; Barkley, 1998; Fischer, Barkley, Smallish, & Fletcher, 2002).

Although ADHD and conduct problems frequently co-occur, they are considered separate disorders. Many children are hyperactive, impulsive, and/or inattentive but do not talk back to parents, fight with classmates, or skip school. Other children and adolescents show serious patterns of defiant and aggressive behavior toward family and peers but show no problems with hyperactivity or inattention (S. King et al., 2005).

Furthermore, ADHD and conduct problems in childhood and adolescence seem to have different underlying causes. ADHD is viewed predominantly as a neurodevelopmental disorder, characterized by problems with impulse control and information processing. ADHD shows high heritability and appears to be strongly influenced by genetics (Barkley, 1998). In contrast, conduct problems are viewed primarily as learned disorders, associated with problematic parent-child interactions, inadequate parental monitoring, association with deviant peers, and socioeconomic disadvantage. CD also has a somewhat lower heritability than ADHD (Loeber & Stouthamer-Loeber, 1986).

On the other hand, both ADHD and conduct problems are characterized by difficulties in **executive functioning**, that is, the ability to plan, prioritize, and regulate behavior. Indeed, some experts believe that the strong co-occurrence of ADHD and conduct problems in childhood and adolescence is due to abnormalities in the development of executive functioning (Coolidge, Thede, & Young, 2000).

Substance Use Problems

ADHD appears to place children at greater risk for substance use problems during adolescence (Biederman, Wilens, Mick, Spencer, & Faraone, 1999). Approximately 15% of children with ADHD develop at least one substance use disorder (Barkley, 1998), with prevalence being slightly higher for girls with ADHD than boys with ADHD (Biederman & Faraone, 2004; Biederman, Mick et al., 2002). The drug most frequently used by adolescents with ADHD is nicotine (Burke, Loeber, & Lahey, 2001; Milberger, Biederman, Faraone, Chen, & Jones, 1997). Adolescents with ADHD are also at risk for abusing alcohol, marijuana, inhalants, and stimulants (Barkley, Fischer, Edelbrock, & Smallish, 1990).

Why are adolescents with ADHD at increased risk for substance use problems? The available data are limited, but they suggest that the reasons depend on the type of substance that adolescents use. Adolescents with ADHD may use nicotine to help them focus and maintain their attention over time (Milberger et al., 1997). In contrast, adolescents with ADHD may use alcohol and marijuana because they are introduced to these substances by deviant peers (Marshal, Molina, & Pelham, 2003). Because adolescents with ADHD are often rejected by prosocial peers, they may form friendships with deviant peers who encourage or tolerate alcohol and drug use (Henker & Whalen, 1999). Indeed, Marshal and colleagues (2003) found that the relationship between ADHD and substance use was mediated by adolescents' association with deviant peers. Adolescents with ADHD may succumb to peer pressure in order to gain acceptance and to avoid further social rejection (Marshal et al., 2003).

Anxiety and Mood Disorders

Internalizing disorders are also fairly common among youths with ADHD (Bagwell, Molina, Kashdan, Pelham, & Hoza, 2006). Approximately 25% of children and adolescents with ADHD have at least one anxiety disorder while 20%–30% experience depression (Fischer et al., 2002; Tannock, 2000).

Most data indicate that anxiety and mood problems are more common among girls with ADHD than boys with ADHD. Girls who show the "sluggish cognitive tempo" pattern of ADHD/I are particularly prone to anxiety and mood problems (Carlson & Mann, 2002; Power, Costigan, Eiraldi, & Leff, 2004). These girls show a curious mixture of depressive, drowsy, passive, and withdrawn behavior that is usually not seen in other youths with ADHD.

The relationship between ADHD and Bipolar Disorder is unclear. Bipolar Disorder is a serious emotional disorder characterized by at least one episode of elevated, expansive, or irritable mood. Many children and adolescents with Bipolar Disorder show chronic problems with irritability and depressed mood. Early research indicated that children with ADHD were at increased risk for Bipolar Disorder, but later research did not replicate these findings (Barkley, 2004). The best data available suggest that the presence of Bipolar Disorder greatly increases a child's likelihood of developing ADHD; however, the presence of ADHD does not greatly increase a child's likelihood of developing Bipolar Disorder (Singh, DelBello, Kowatch, & Strakowski, 2006).

Associated Characteristics

Problems in Parent-Child Interactions

Children with ADHD often have problematic interactions with their parents. One way psychologists study parent-child interactions in young children is to observe dyads playing or performing a structured task (e.g., reading a book, cleaning up after play). During these interactions, mothers of children with ADHD are more negative and hostile and less sensitive and responsive to their children than are mothers of children without ADHD. Their children, in turn, engage in more aversive and noncompliant behavior (Barkley, 1988). Researchers believe that these parent-child behaviors are reciprocal: Parents engage in more hostile-intrusive parenting tactics because they are frustrated by their children's high-rate behavior; children engage in more disruptive behavior because of their parents' punitive discipline (Chronis, Lahey, Pelham, Kipp, Baumann, & Lee, 2003).

Mothers of children with both ADHD and conduct problems are at particular risk for mood disorders and substance use problems (Chronis et al., 2003). These mothers often blame themselves for their children's disruptive behavior and doubt their competency as parents (Mash & Johnston, 1990). Their feelings of low parenting efficacy may contribute to the development of depression. The relationship between children's disruptive behavior and parents' substance use is more complex. One possibility is that parental alcohol and drug abuse causes children to show high-rate, aversive behaviors. Another possibility is that similar genes (shared by both parents and children) account for both children's disruptive behavior problems and their parents' substance use disorder.

A third possibility is that children's disruptive behavior may increase parents' use of alcohol and other drugs. Pelham and colleagues (1998) asked the parents of disruptive children to interact with another child (i.e., not their own child) for a short period of time. The child, who was actually a confederate, engaged in either normal or disruptive behavior during the session. After the session, adult participants were offered alcoholic beverages while completing follow-up questionnaires. As expected, parents who interacted with children behaving disruptively reported greater feelings of inadequacy and more negative emotions than parents who interacted with children behaving normally. Furthermore, parents with family histories of substance use disorders consumed more alcohol after interacting with children behaving disruptively than with children acting compliantly. Pelham and colleagues (1998) suggested that some parents, particularly those with a genetic diathesis toward alcohol abuse, may cope with their children's disruptive behavior by drinking.

Problems With Peers

It is extremely important for school-age children to be accepted by peers and to develop friendships with children in their age group (Sullivan, 1953). These peer relationships are believed to contribute to children's self-esteem, to serve as models for adult interpersonal relationships, and to promote the development of children's identity and their capacity for intimacy in adolescence and adulthood. Indeed, the degree to which we are liked and accepted by peers in early elementary school is one of the best predictors of our social and emotional well-being in adolescence (Rubin, Bukowski, & Parker, 1998).

Unfortunately, children with ADHD are frequently disliked by peers. Their hyperactive and impulsive behavior often interferes with their ability to behave appropriately during peer interactions. Children's ADHD symptoms often cause peers to reject them quickly. In one study, unfamiliar children rated children with ADHD as less desirable play partners after only two brief play sessions (Pelham & Bender, 1982). In another study, children at a summer camp rejected children with ADHD after only three days (Erhardt & Hinshaw, 1994). After children are rejected by some of their peers, they often develop negative reputations among the rest of the peer group. Indeed, 60%–70% of children with ADHD may not have a single friend in their class.

Hoza and colleagues (2005) used **sociometric ratings** to determine the peer status of school-age children with and without ADHD. All children in a class were asked to privately identify the children with whom they most and least enjoyed playing. Then, researchers tallied children's nominations to determine the peer status of each child. Children were categorized into one of five groups based on their peer nominations. *Popular* children received the greatest number of positive nominations. *Rejected* children received the greatest number of negative nominations. *Controversial* children received a large number of both positive and negative nominations. *Neglected* children received few nominations altogether. *Average* children received an average number of nominations, both positive and negative.

Hoza and colleagues (2005) discovered that children with ADHD were not only unpopular, they were actively rejected by their classmates (see Figure 8.1). Indeed, 52% of children with ADHD were rejected. Although children with ADHD sought friendships with their classmates, especially popular children, these high-status popular children were *most* likely to reject and avoid them. The tendency for children with ADHD to be rejected was not merely due to comorbid problems, such as oppositional or defiant behavior. Children were rejected based on their ADHD symptoms alone. Peer rejection occurred to children with ADHD as young as seven years of age.

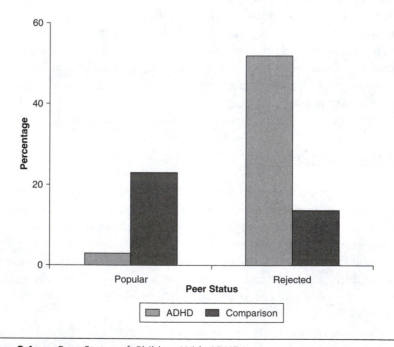

Figure 8.1   Peer Status of Children With ADHD

Source: Based on Hoza et al. (2005).

Note: Compared to healthy children, youths with ADHD are less popular and more frequently rejected by classmates. Peer rejection can lead to association with deviant peers and more severe behavior problems later in childhood.

Peer rejection can contribute to the development of conduct problems. Once children develop negative reputations, these reputations are difficult to change (Hoza, Mrug, Pelham, Greiner, & Gnagy, 2003; Price & Dodge, 1989a). Even if children's ADHD symptoms can be decreased (e.g., with medication), children may still be rejected by peers because of their history of hyperactivity and impulsivity. If children are unable to develop meaningful, prosocial peer relationships before middle childhood, they may seek friendships with other peer-rejected children. These peer-rejected friends may introduce them to more serious antisocial and disruptive acts (Dishion, Andrews, & Crosby, 1995; Dishion, Eddy, Haas, Li, & Spracklen, 1997).

Academic Difficulties

Children with ADHD often show difficulties across academic domains, with particular problems in reading and math (DeShazo Barry, Lyman, & Grofer Klinger, 2002; Rapport, Scanlan, & Denney, 1999). Compared to typically developing youth, children with ADHD are more likely to earn failing grades, to be retained in school, and to drop out before graduation (Mannuzza, Klein, Abikoff, & Moulton, 2004). Longitudinal studies show that symptoms of ADHD in early childhood predict academic problems into adolescence, with more severe early symptoms associated with greater academic impairment later in development (DeShazo Barry et al., 2002; Fergusson & Horwood, 1995; Fergusson, Lynskey, & Horwood, 1997). The prevalence of learning disabilities in children with ADHD may be as high as 38% (Snyder, 2000). Academic problems are specifically associated with children's ADHD symptoms, not just with their comorbid conduct problems (Rapport et al., 1999).

It is unclear exactly how ADHD interferes with children's academic performance. Some data suggest that ADHD symptoms interfere with children's access to information in school (Rapport et al., 1999). Children who are hyperactive or inattentive may miss information presented by teachers and opportunities to practice newly learned academic skills. Missed learning experiences may contribute to a generally lower fund of information (Buckley, Dodd, Burke, Guerin, McEvoy, & Hillery, 2006). Other data suggest that deficits in working memory underlie both ADHD and children's learning problems (Renz, Lorch, Milich, Lemberger, Bodner, & Welsh, 2003). Children with ADHD may have problems holding information in working memory long enough to use this information effectively to solve academic problems. They may also show difficulty organizing information and relaying information to others. These deficits interfere with their ability to learn new information and to perform adequately on academic tasks.

Epidemiology

Prevalence

Approximately 2%–9% of the general population meets diagnostic criteria for ADHD. Prevalence seems to be higher among school-age children compared to preschoolers, adolescents, and adults. For example, approximately 5%–9% of school-age children have ADHD while only about 4%–5% of adolescents and adults have the disorder (Murphy & Barkley, 1996; National Institutes of Health, 2000).

Among people diagnosed with ADHD, approximately 60% show ADHD/C, approximately 25% have ADHD/I, and approximately 15% have ADHD/HI (Biederman, Kwon et al., 2005). ADHD/I is seen most often in older children and adolescents while ADHD/HI is most common among preschoolers and young school-age children.

The prevalence of ADHD has increased dramatically over the last 15 years. Data from the U.S. Department of Health and Human Services indicate that approximately 1% of children aged 3–18 years were diagnosed with ADHD in the late 1980s (Olfson, Gameroff, Marcus, & Jensen, 2003). Today, 3.4% of youth have been officially diagnosed and are receiving some form of treatment for the disorder. Over that time, low-income children showed the greatest *increase* in receiving treatment, although black and Hispanic children with ADHD were far less likely to receive treatment than white children.

Olfson and colleagues (2003) offer four explanations for the apparent increase in the prevalence of ADHD. First, the U.S. Department of Education recognized ADHD as a disabling condition under the IDEA. Consequently, many parents sought diagnoses for their children in order to gain educational accommodations and special services. Second, the number of school-based health clinics increased during this time period, giving low-income children greater access to mental health services. Third, the 1990s witnessed advances in the assessment of ADHD, leading to better identification of children with the disorder. Fourth, there was a general increase in public awareness of the disorder and, perhaps, a decrease in stigma. Organizations such as Children and Adults With Attention-Deficit/Hyperactivity Disorder (CHADD) and the Attention Deficit Disorder Association (ADDA) advocated for the rights of individuals with ADHD and their families (Olfson et al., 2003).

Gender

ADHD is more common in boys than in girls. Among clinic-referred children, the gender ratio is approximately 10:1 in favor of boys. In community samples, the gender ratio favors boys 3:1 (Arnold, 1996; Gaub & Carlson, 1997). The large gender ratio among clinic-referred children may be partially due to referral bias, not actual differences in boys' and girls' behavior. Boys with ADHD are more likely to be referred to clinics because of their co-existing disruptive behavior problems. Girls with ADHD, who are less likely to show oppositional and defiant symptoms than boys with the disorder, may not be referred for treatment.

Overall, girls with ADHD usually show better functioning than boys (Arnold, 1996; Gaub & Carlson, 1997). Girls display fewer and less severe ADHD symptoms than boys (Abikoff et al., 2002; Biederman, Mick et al., 2002; Newcorn et al., 2001). They are less likely than boys to have other disruptive behavior problems and substance use disorders (Biederman, Mick et al., 2002; Levy, Hay, Bennett, & McStephen, 2005; Wilens, Spencer, & Biederman,1996). They are also less likely to have learning difficulties (Biederman, Mick et al., 2002; Doyle, Faraone, DuPre, & Biederman, 2001).

Girls with ADHD also show slightly different symptoms than boys. Girls are two times more likely to display inattentive symptoms and to be diagnosed with ADHD/I than boys (Biederman & Faraone, 2004; Biederman, Mick et al., 2002). Furthermore, girls with ADHD have slightly lower average IQ scores than boys with the disorder, although the magnitude of the difference is very small.

Course

Many parents of children with ADHD ask, "Will my child grow out of it?" Unfortunately, longitudinal studies indicate that ADHD symptoms are fairly stable across childhood and adolescence. Preschoolers with ADHD almost always continue to show symptoms into early childhood (Lahey et al., 2004). Furthermore, children with ADHD in early elementary school tend to continue to show symptoms in junior high school (Larsson, Larsson, & Lichtenstein, 2004). However, approximately 25%–35% of children diagnosed with ADHD no longer meet diagnostic criteria by the time they reach adolescence (Barkley, 1997a; Claude & Firestone, 1995). This discontinuity in ADHD during adolescence is probably due to changes in the adolescent brain that occur during puberty (Larsson et al., 2004; Willoughby, 2003). Developments in brain structure and functioning that are triggered by the onset of puberty may lead to greater capacity for attention and behavioral inhibition in some children, thus reducing the severity of ADHD symptoms.

For most youths, the severity of ADHD symptoms decreases with age (Biederman, Mick, & Faraone, 2000; Larsson et al., 2004). Approximately every five years, the prevalence of ADHD in a given age group decreases by 50%. However, a small number of children actually show an increase in symptom severity (Willoughby, Curran, Costello, & Angold, 2000).

The presentation of ADHD symptoms also changes with age. Symptoms of hyperactivity-impulsivity usually decrease during adolescence while symptoms of inattention often increase (Barkley, Fischer, Smallish, & Fletcher, 2002; Hart, Lahey, Loeber, Applegate, Green, & Frick, 1995). Instead of climbing on furniture and running around the classroom, adolescents with ADHD show low motivation to engage in tasks that require sustained effort (e.g., homework), difficulty organizing activities (e.g., long-term, multistep projects such as completing a term paper), poor self-control (e.g., reckless stunts), or problems with time management (e.g., submitting assignments late, forgetting appointments; Barkley, 2004a).

The persistence of ADHD into adulthood depends on how we measure ADHD symptoms and from whom we gather information (Barkley, Fischer et al., 2002). If we rely on young adults' reports of their own ADHD symptoms, we see that only 6% of adolescents with ADHD continue to show significant symptoms in adulthood (Barkley, Fischer et al., 2002). However, if we rely on parents' reports of young adults' symptoms, the persistence of ADHD into adulthood increases to 46% (Barkley, Fischer et al., 2002).

Do ADHD symptoms simply "go away" in late adolescence and early adulthood? Most researchers think the answer is "No." One reason for the relatively low persistence from adolescence to adulthood is that the *DSM-IV-TR* diagnostic criteria for ADHD may not adequately measure ADHD symptoms in adults. For example, very few adults with ADHD run around their workplace as if "driven by a motor." Instead, adults with ADHD might have subjective feelings of restlessness. When researchers use developmentally sensitive criteria to measure adult ADHD, the persistence of the disorder from adolescence to adulthood increases to 66% (Barkley, Fischer et al., 2002). Altogether, these data suggest that ADHD is a fairly stable disorder that emerges during early childhood and often persists into early adulthood (Fischer, Barkley, Smallish, & Fletcher, 2005).

Etiology

Genetics

Behavioral Genetics

ADHD is a neurodevelopmental disorder with a strong genetic basis. Although the exact genes that underlie ADHD have not been identified, genetic factors may explain as much as 80% of the variance in ADHD symptoms among children with the disorder (Brookes et al., 2006).

Twin studies suggest that ADHD is heritable. Concordance between monozygotic twins is 50%–80%, whereas concordance between dizygotic twins is only 33% (Bradley & Golden, 2001; Larsson et al., 2004). Concordance rates are higher for hyperactivity-impulsivity symptoms than for symptoms of inattention (Sherman, Iacono, & McGue, 1997).

ADHD runs in families. Family studies indicate that the children of parents with ADHD are two to eight times more likely than the children of parents without ADHD to develop ADHD themselves (Faraone et al., 1992; Frick, Lahey, Christ, Loeber, & Green, 1991). Siblings of children with ADHD are three to five times more likely to have the disorder compared to controls. Adoption studies indicate that children's ADHD symptoms correlate more strongly with symptoms of their biological parents than with their adoptive parents (Kutcher et al., 2004).

Although genetics accounts for the lion's share of the variance of ADHD symptoms, environmental factors also play important roles. Nonshared environmental factors—experiences unique to individual children—seem especially important in predicting ADHD symptoms (Larsson et al., 2004). Furthermore, the importance of nonshared environmental factors increases as children enter adolescence and assume more autonomy regarding their selection of friends, classes, sports, hobbies, and daily schedules. Shared environmental experiences, such as parents' disciplinary tactics and the family's diet, explain relatively little of the variance in children's ADHD symptoms.

Molecular Genetics

Genes associated with the dopamine neurotransmitter system probably play a primary role in the development of ADHD. Evidence for their involvement comes from four sources. First, dopamine receptors are especially prevalent in brain regions responsible for regulating attention and inhibiting behavior: the prefrontal cortex and striatum (Jackson & Westlind-Danielsson, 1994; Missale, Nash, Robinson, Jaber, & Caron, 1998). Second, people with lesions to these areas (and presumably damage to the dopamine neurotransmitter system) show ADHD symptoms (Misener et al., 2004). Third, medications used to treat ADHD stimulate the dopamine system (Seeman & Madras, 1998; Stein et al., 2005). Fourth, mice lacking genes that code for the dopamine system show hyperactivity and have difficulty controlling their behavior (Clifford, Tighe, Croke, Sibley, Drago, & Waddington, 1998). Family studies have implicated four genes in particular: dopamine receptor D1, D4, and D5 genes and the dopamine transporter gene (Grady et al., 2003; Maher, Marazita, Ferrell, & Vanyukov, 2002; Misener et al., 2004; Stein et al., 2005).

Brain Structure and Functioning

Prefrontal Cortex

MRI studies have compared the brains of youths with and without ADHD. Relative to controls, children with ADHD show an average 5% reduction in **cerebral volume.** This reduction includes both gray and white matter and tends to be more pronounced in the right hemisphere.

Other studies have investigated differences in specific brain regions. Some studies have found an overall reduction in the size of the prefrontal cortex among children with ADHD (Castellanos et al., 1994, 1996, 2001, 2002; Filipek, Semrud-Clikeman, Steingrad, Kennedy, & Biederman, 1997; D. E. Hill, Yeo, Campbell, Hart, Vigil, & Brooks, 2003; Kates et al., 2002; Mostofsky, Cooper, Kates, Denckla, & Kaufmann, 2002; Seidman, Valera, & Makris, 2005). The prefrontal cortex is largely responsible for executive functioning, a person's capacity to effectively perceive, process, and use information in order to solve problems and attain long-term goals (Riccio, Homack, Jarratt, & Wolfe, 2006). Just as an executive of a company is responsible for organizing and implementing the company's resources in order to meet its objectives, the executive functioning areas of the brain are responsible for organizing and utilizing one's cognitive resources in order to effectively meet the demands of the environment. The executive functions include the ability to attend to relevant information, to ignore distractions, to quickly shift from one task to another, to organize information, to plan and prioritize future actions, and to follow through with one's plans in a logical and efficient manner (Biederman, Monuteaux et al., 2004).

Children with ADHD often show deficits in executive functioning (Pennington & Ozonoff, 1996). Indeed, children with ADHD show more severe problems with executive functioning than do healthy controls (Seidman, Biederman, Faraone, Weber, & Ouellette, 1997) or clinic-referred children without ADHD (Seidman, Biederman, Monuteaux, Weber, & Faraone, 2000). Executive functioning deficits tend to be relatively stable over time. Children with ADHD who also have deficits in executive functioning usually continue to show executive functioning deficits during adolescence (Seidman et al., 1997) and into adulthood (Seidman, Biederman, Weber, Hatch, & Faraone, 1998).

Two subdivisions of the prefrontal cortex seem to underlie these deficits in executive functioning: the orbital frontal region and the dorsolateral prefrontal region. The **orbital frontal region** is responsible for inhibition and impulse control. The

dorsolateral prefrontal region plays a role in organization, planning, and attending. Both regions tend to be smaller in children with ADHD than in controls. Furthermore, children with ADHD show underactivity in both of these brain regions during tasks requiring behavioral inhibition and memory (Langleben, Austin, Krikorian, Ridlehuber, Goris, & Strauss, 2001; Lee et al., 2004; Seidman et al., 2005; Sowell, Thompson, Welcome, Henkenius, Toga, & Peterson, 2003).

Frontal-Striatal Neural Circuit

The **basal ganglia (striatum)** is another brain region that has been implicated in ADHD (Shafritz, Marchione, Gore, Shaywitz, & Shaywitz, 2004). The striatum consists of the caudate, putamen, and globus pallidus, although the caudate seems to be especially important in the development and maintenance of ADHD. Together, these brain structures are functionally connected to the prefrontal cortex through a series of neural connections. Collectively, they form the prefrontal-striatal circuit. This neural network is essential to the execution of the executive functions because it relays information between the prefrontal cortex and other areas of the brain related to attention, memory, and action.

Many experts believe that the symptoms of ADHD may be produced by dysfunction in the **frontal-striatal neural circuit** (Faraone & Biederman, 1998; Giedd, Blumenthal, Molloy, & Castellanos, 2001). Evidence for this claim comes from four sources. First, damage to the striatum in animals produces inattention and hyperactivity (Pliszka, Lancaster, Liotti, & Semrud-Clikeman, 2006).

Second, children with ADHD often show structural abnormalities in a portion of the striatum called the caudate (Pliszka et al., 2006), an area rich in dopamine receptors and responsible for regulating behavior and attention (Castellanos, 2003; Castellanos et al., 2001, 2002; Overmeyer et al., 2001; Wellington, Semrud-Clikeman, Gregory, Murphy, & Lancaster, 2006). In healthy children, the left caudate is usually larger than the right; however, children with ADHD sometimes show larger right caudate nuclei. However, not all studies show this reversed asymmetry (D. E. Hill et al., 2003; Semrud-Clikeman & Pliszka, 2005).

Third, children with ADHD sometimes show underactivity of the caudate. Caudate underactivity is most pronounced during tasks that require attention and behavioral inhibition (Vaidya et al., 1998). This reduced activity may account for children's high-rate behaviors and distractibility.

Fourth, stimulant medications, like methylphenidate (Ritalin), seem to affect dopamine activity in the striatum and cause an increase in caudate activity. This activity is associated with improvements in children's behavioral control and attention (Carrey, MacMaster, Sparkes, Khan, & Kusumakar, 2002; Ilgin, Senol, Gucuyener, Gokcora, & Sener, 2001; Lee et al., 2004; Seidman et al., 2005; Vaidya et al., 1998; Volkow et al., 2001).

Neuropsychological Systems

Gray (1982, 1987) hypothesized the existence of two neuropsychological systems that govern overt behavior. The **behavioral inhibition system (BIS)** is responsible for slowing or stopping behavior in response to punishment or a lack of reinforcement. Imagine a child who engages in high-rate behavior on the playground. At recess, boisterous behavior is appropriate; however, when recess ends, the child must reduce the frequency and intensity of his behavior to meet the expectations of the classroom. The BIS is responsible for inhibiting his behavior and making it conform to environmental expectations.

According to Gray (1987), children with ADHD show underactivity of the BIS. These children are unable to adjust their behavior to meet the demands of new situations, such as the transition from recess to the classroom. They may show difficulties inhibiting their boisterous play even when classmates no longer reciprocate (i.e., a lack of reinforcement) or the teacher becomes angry (i.e., punishment). Although children with ADHD know how they should behave in class, their underactive BIS interferes with their ability to follow classroom rules.

The **behavioral activation system (BAS)** is responsible for adjusting behavior to achieve reinforcement or to escape punishment. Imagine that a boy is playing on his school's basketball team. In order to be successful, the boy must follow the rules of the game, pass the ball to other players, and play defense. To win the game, the boy must delay immediate gratification in order to work with the team. If the boy is able to engage in these behaviors, he is likely to enjoy playing the game, to be praised by his teammates, and to be encouraged by his coach.

Children with ADHD, however, show overactivity of the BAS. Their behavior is governed primarily by a strong need for immediate reinforcement. Indeed, some theorists have argued that these children have a greater sensitivity to rewards than other children (Nigg, 2001). Consequently, a boy with ADHD might behave impulsively on the basketball court in order to achieve immediate gratification, rather than work with his teammates. For example, he might ignore the referee, refuse to share the ball with other players, and avoid parts of the game that are less exciting (e.g., defense).

Prenatal and Perinatal Risks

One of the leading environmental causes of ADHD is complications during gestation and delivery (Root & Resnick, 2003). Maternal cigarette (Linnet et al., 2003) and alcohol use (Mick, Biederman, Faraone, Sayer, & Kleinman, 2002) during gestation are associated with increased likelihood of ADHD in offspring. The exact mechanism by which these substances contribute to the development of ADHD is unknown; however, cigarettes and alcohol probably restrict the fetus's access to oxygen and nutrition. Furthermore, children with fetal alcohol syndrome frequently show hyperactivity-impulsivity and inattention (Biederman, Milberger, & Faraone, 1995).

Health problems before or after delivery are also associated with increased likelihood of ADHD (Amor et al., 2005). Medical conditions that deprive the fetus or neonate of oxygen for extended periods of time present the greatest risk. Areas of the brain responsible for behavioral inhibition and executive functioning (i.e., frontal-striatal regions) seem to be highly susceptible to damage caused by hypoxia. Indeed, animals deliberately deprived of oxygen during their neonatal period show increased hyperactivity later in life (Brake, Sullivan, & Gratton, 2000).

Certain environmental toxins have also been linked to the development of ADHD symptoms. Chief among these toxins is lead poisoning during infancy and early childhood (Goldstein & Goldstein, 1998).

Barkley's Neurodevelopmental Model for ADHD

So far, we have seen that genetic and biological factors are associated with the development of ADHD. Now, we will examine the mechanism by which these risk factors lead to the disorder. One of the most plausible explanations for the development of ADHD in children has been offered by Russell Barkley. According to Barkley's **neurodevelopmental model** (1997a, 1998), problems in neural development, caused primarily by genetic and early biological risks, lead to problems with behavior later in life. His model offers one explanation for how early neural development can contribute to the emergence of later ADHD.

At the heart of Barkley's model is the concept of **behavioral inhibition**. According to Barkley (1997a, 1998), the chief problem with ADHD is not inattention; instead, the fundamental deficit in ADHD is a lack of behavioral inhibition. Behavioral inhibition refers to the ability to inhibit immediate responses, especially responses that usually provide immediate gratification. Children show behavioral inhibition when they resist the impulse to act, when they stop responding in the middle of an action, or when they ignore a distracting stimulus in order to complete another behavior. Behavioral inhibition allows children time to consider other, more adaptive ways of responding.

For example, children show behavioral inhibition when they resist the urge to blurt out answers in class. Although blurting out answers might provide them with immediate reinforcement (e.g., teacher gives them attention, classmates laugh), it may not be the most beneficial way of responding. By inhibiting this behavior, children can consider alternative ways of responding (e.g., raising their hands) that could be more reinforcing in the long term (e.g., teacher provides praise for correct answer).

According to Barkley (1997a, 1998), children with ADHD show fundamental deficits in their capacity for behavioral inhibition (see Figure 8.2). These deficits arise primarily from genetics but also from early environmental experiences (e.g., prenatal distress, birth complications). In typically developing children, behavioral inhibition gives children time to develop more sophisticated cognitive processes that allow them to regulate behavior and solve complex problems.

Barkley (1997a, 1998) asserts that the capacity for behavioral inhibition permits the development of four basic executive functions. Each of these executive functions begins as an overt, observable behavior. Gradually, each function is internalized into mental representations or thoughts.

The executive functions serve three primary purposes. First, they allow children to determine their own behavior, rather than to be controlled by environmental stimuli. For example, the executive functions allow schoolchildren to ignore noises in the hallway and, instead, to focus on their teacher. Second, the executive functions allow children to be influenced by delayed reinforcers rather than by immediate gratification. For example, the executive functions allow children to resist the

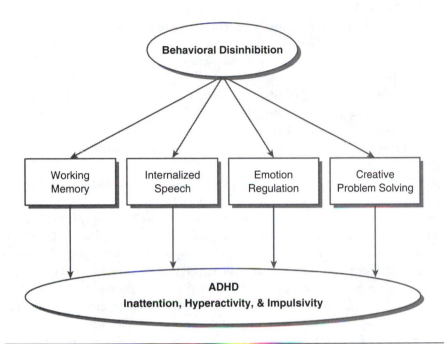

Figure 8.2   Barkley's Neurodevelopmental Model for ADHD

Note: Early problems with behavioral inhibition can adversely affect the development of the four executive functions. Executive functioning deficits underlie symptoms of ADHD.

temptation to play video games (i.e., an immediate reinforcer) and, instead, complete their homework to earn a high grade (i.e., a delayed reinforcer). Third, executive functions allow children to set long-term goals. For example, executive functions allow children to plan and organize their behaviors (e.g., setting sequential short-term tasks) to accomplish long-term goals (e.g., completing a class presentation).

The first executive function to emerge is **working memory**. Working memory involves holding information in short-term memory; analyzing this information to detect useful patterns, principles, or rules; and applying this information to solve future problems. Stated another way, working memory allows us to remember past experiences and use these experiences to plan for the future. Children with ADHD often have difficulty with working memory. They appear forgetful, do not seem to listen to others or learn from past experiences, and do not consider the consequences of their behaviors before they act. Instead, their behavior is tied largely to the here and now. They are influenced primarily by stimuli in their immediate environments rather than by past events or future consequences (Wu, Anderson, & Castiello, 2006).

The second executive function to emerge is **internalized speech**. Children's speech guides and directs their overt behavior, giving them increased control over their actions (Vygotsky, 1978). As toddlers, children use speech primarily to communicate with others. As preschoolers, children begin to speak to themselves while performing tasks. This "self-directed" speech helps organize their actions and regulate their behavior. By the early school years, self-directed speech becomes even less overt, perhaps only noticeable when the child learns new behaviors or when he is trying to solve particularly difficult problems. By middle childhood, self-directed speech is usually completely internalized. In essence, self-directed speech becomes thought. Thoughts, or private speech, allow children to guide their behavior in logical and organized ways.

A lack of behavioral inhibition interferes with the internalization of speech. Children with ADHD have difficulty organizing and directing their behavior, following rules, and obeying others' instructions. Instead of being motivated by internalized speech and thoughts, they rely on other people and their environment for direction.

The third executive function to develop is **emotion regulation**. As children become better at inhibiting immediate behaviors, they also gain greater capacity to control the emotions that would normally follow those behaviors. Consequently, they are less influenced by immediate, transitory emotions and more influenced by expectations for long-term rewards. For example, children become increasingly better at suffering through the short-term boredom of studying for a test in order to achieve future rewards associated with the studying (e.g., good grades, praise from parents). In short, children's motivation becomes less extrinsic and more intrinsic.

Children with ADHD, however, continue to show problems with emotion regulation. They have difficulty regulating their moods, show reduced ability to maintain their motivation on tasks that require sustained effort, and appear heavily dependent on immediate reinforcement from the environment to direct their behavior. Consequently, children with ADHD can spend two hours playing video games that provide immediate reinforcement, but they quickly lose interest in other activities that depend on intrinsic motivation (e.g., reading, drawing, collecting).

The fourth and most complicated executive function to develop is the capacity for **creative problem solving**. Initially, children learn about their surroundings by physically manipulating objects in their environment. During play, children discover the properties of objects by disassembling them, performing simple experiments, and combining objects in new and creative ways (e.g., a child playing with bristle blocks or Lego). Later in development, objects can be mentally manipulated, analyzed, and combined in novel ways in order to solve problems. Whereas younger children might build a "fort" in their living room out of pillows and blankets through trial and error, older children can mentally plan the "fort" before beginning actual construction.

By late childhood, children can also combine words, images, information, and ideas in novel ways. This allows them to organize information, plan strategies, and solve increasingly more complex problems before acting. For example, middle-school students arranging a Halloween party can plan the guest list, refreshments, entertainment, and each person's responsibilities for the party well in advance. Children with ADHD, however, show difficulty with organization, planning, and problem solving.

In summary, Barkley's (1997a, 1998) neurodevelopmental model posits that the underlying problem with ADHD is a deficit in behavioral inhibition. Problems with behavioral inhibition are primarily determined by genetics and early environmental risks. Difficulty with behavioral inhibition interferes with the development of the executive functions during infancy and early childhood. Children show impairments in working memory, internalized speech (thinking), emotional regulation, and creative problem solving. Over time, these impairments in executive functioning can interfere with subsequent brain development and lead to the emergence of ADHD.

Treatment

If we view ADHD as a neurodevelopmental disorder, we notice some important implications for its treatment. First, because we have little control over children's genes and early neurological development, we should not expect to cure ADHD (Barkley, 2004). Instead, ADHD should be viewed as a developmental disorder, analogous to Mental Retardation or Learning Disorder. Treatment primarily involves symptom alleviation. That is, clinicians focus mostly on reducing children's disruptive behavior problems and increasing their social functioning, rather than in eliminating the disorder, per se. Because the disorder often continues into adolescence and early adulthood, treatment requires long-term intervention.

Second, because ADHD is primarily a neurodevelopmental disorder, traditional psychosocial interventions will likely have limited effects (Barkley, 2004). Early treatments for ADHD involved social skills training; that is, teaching children skills to help them learn rules and obey others. Unfortunately, these interventions were largely ineffective. Children with ADHD know how they should behave at home and school; they simply have difficulty obeying rules and adjusting their behavior to meet the expectations of the situation. According to Barkley (2004), "ADHD can be viewed as a disorder of performance—of doing what one knows rather than knowing what to do" (p. 43). The most effective treatments for ADHD help children engage in appropriate behavior at the proper point in time.

Finally, because children with ADHD often show poor executive functioning, interventions must not rely on children's internal motivation to change (Barkley, 2004). The very nature of ADHD makes it difficult for children to organize and direct their behavior over sustained periods of time. Instead, children with ADHD are primarily motivated by immediate reinforcement from the environment. Consequently, interventions that provide children with immediate, tangible rewards will be most effective.

For example, if we want a child with ADHD to complete her math homework, we might offer her access to her favorite TV program contingent on the homework's completion. However, a more effective tactic might be to break the assignment into smaller steps (e.g., five math problems) and immediately reward completion of each step with a token that can be exchanged for five minutes of TV. A child without ADHD would use her executive functions to sustain her attention long enough to complete the entire homework assignment. However, a child with ADHD would need shorter-term reinforcement in order to sustain her attention over time.

Medication

Description

Pharmacotherapy is currently the first-line treatment for children with ADHD. The most common medications prescribed are the psychostimulants. These medications affect the neurotransmitters dopamine (DA) and norepinephrine (NE). They cause increased attention and behavioral inhibition (Greenhill, Pliszka, & Dulcan, 2002). There are two broad types of psychostimulants: amphetamines and methylphenidates. The most frequently prescribed amphetamines are Adderall and Dexedrine. The most frequently used methylphenidates are Ritalin, Focalin, Metadate, and Concerta. Approximately 3% of all school-age children and 1.2% of all preschoolers take one of these medications (Olfson et al., 2003; Zito, Safer, dos Reis, Gardner, Boles, & Lynch, 2000).

Amphetamine and methylphenidate have slightly different chemical structures and mechanisms of action (Faraone & Biederman, 1998; Greenhill & Ford, 2002; Pliszka, 2003a). Both medications stimulate the central nervous system by effectively increasing dopamine and norepinephrine levels in the synaptic cleft. **Amphetamine** works primarily by increasing the release of dopamine from presynaptic storage vesicles, resulting in more dopamine output to the cleft. **Methylphenidate** slows the dopamine transporter system that removes dopamine from the cleft, thereby allowing dopamine to remain in the cleft for longer periods of time. Both medications also block norepinephrine reuptake (Greenhill et al., 1996). The overall effect of both of these medications is a net increase in dopamine activity in brain regions that are typically underactive in children and adolescents with ADHD, particularly the frontal-striatal circuit. This increase in dopamine activates the regions that are responsible for executive control, behavioral inhibition, and working memory (Greenhill, 2005). Youths taking these medications experience increased ability to attend; ignore distractions; inhibit behavior; and engage in organization, planning, and problem solving.

What would happen if youths without ADHD took stimulant medication (see Figure 8.3)? Neuroimaging studies suggest that the same brain circuitry is used to regulate attention and achieve behavioral inhibition, regardless of a person's diagnostic status. Specifically, the frontal-striatal neural circuit seems to be largely responsible for attention and inhibition, with other brain regions (e.g., corpus callosum, cerebellum) playing important supportive roles. Stimulant medication seems to active frontal-striatal brain regions, especially by increasing dopamine in the striatum (Vaidya et al., 1998; Volkow et al., 2001).Consequently, low doses of stimulant medication reduce impulsivity and increase attention in individuals with and without ADHD (Shafritz et al., 2004; Solanto, 1998).

Efficacy

More than 200 placebo-controlled studies have demonstrated the effectiveness of stimulant medication in reducing ADHD symptoms in children older than five years of age (Joshi, 2004; Wilens & Spencer, 2000). For example, Biederman, Lopez,

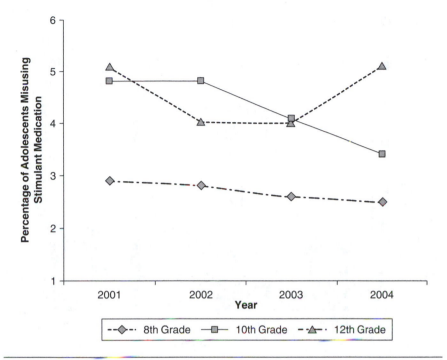

Figure 8.3   Misuse of Stimulant Medication Among Adolescents

Source: From Johnston, O'Malley, Bachman, and Schulenberg (2005). Used with permission.

Note: Approximately 5% of high school seniors have misused or abused stimulant medications like Ritalin.

Boellner, and Chandler (2002) investigated the long-term effects of Adderall on 509 children (aged 6–12 years) with ADHD (see Figure 8.4). Children were randomly assigned to either a placebo group or to a treatment group that received 10 mg, 20 mg, or 30 mg of Adderall for three weeks. Clinicians and parents, who were blind to children's group status, rated children's ADHD symptoms at the end of the three-week intervention. Results showed that all doses of medication were superior to the placebo. Furthermore, there was a dose-response relationship between children's improvement and dosage; children receiving more medication were more likely to improve (McGough et al., 2005).

Across studies, approximately 70% of children with ADHD respond to medication compared to only 13% taking a placebo (Greenhill & Ford, 2002). The response rate increases to 80%–90% if children try a second type of stimulant medication if they do not respond to the first type (Pliszka, 2003a). Medication seems to affect ADHD symptoms and reduce other disruptive behavior problems such as oppositional behavior, defiance, and some conduct problems (Joshi, 2004).

The most common side effects of stimulants are insomnia (59%), decreased appetite (56%), stomachache (34%), headache (30%), and dizziness (13%; Ahmann, Waltonen, Olson, Theye, Van Erem, & LaPlant, 1993). These side effects are usually minor and go away when dosage is reduced. Early research indicated that children who take stimulant medication may experience a slowdown in their physical development.

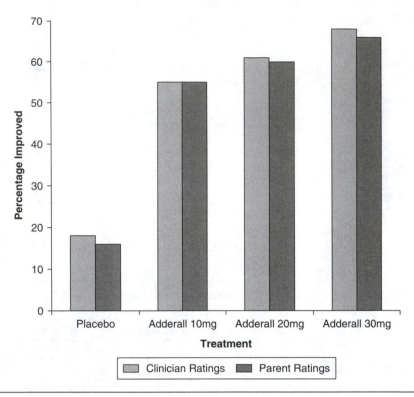

Figure 8.4   Stimulant Medication Is Efficacious in Reducing ADHD Symptoms

Source: Based on Biederman, Lopez et al. (2002).

However, more recent research suggests that children with ADHD who do not take stimulant medication also show slower growth rates, so the exact effects of stimulants on children's growth is still debated (Spencer, Biederman, Harding, Faraone, & Wilens, 1996).

The most widely used non-stimulant medication for ADHD is atomoxetine (Strattera; Pliszka, 2003b). Strattera is a selective norepinephrine reuptake inhibitor (SNRI). Like the stimulants, Strattera seems to affect the NE system; unlike the stimulants, it appears to have little effect on dopamine activity. A number of randomized clinical trials have shown Strattera to be superior to placebo and comparable to methylphenidate in reducing ADHD symptoms (Barkley, 2004; Michelson et al., 2001, 2002; Pliszka, 2003b). Furthermore, it is associated with fewer side effects than the stimulants.

Limitations

Medication therapy for ADHD has several limitations. First, not all children respond to medication. Even in carefully controlled research studies, as many as 15%–30% of children with ADHD do not show improvement. In the community, nonresponse rates may exceed 50% (MTA Cooperative Group, 1999). Clearly, medication is not a panacea for ADHD.

Second, discontinuation of the medication results in the return of ADHD symptoms. Most physicians view stimulant medication as a long-term treatment for ADHD. Longitudinal studies of the effects of stimulant medications have shown that they can be used effectively for at least two years (Joshi, 2004), but their efficacy and safety after that time is largely unknown.

Third, the effectiveness of medication with preschoolers and adolescents is not well-documented. Although there are a number of well-controlled studies showing the effectiveness of methylphenidate among school-age children, preschoolers and adolescents have received far less research attention (Greenhill et al., 2006). Less than 5% of studies investigating the efficacy of medication for ADHD have involved adolescents. Furthermore, stimulants seem to be less effective in preschool-age children than in school-age children (McGough et al., 2006; Wigal et al., 2006) and carry additional risk (Swanson et al., 2006).

Fourth, stimulant medications should be used cautiously in children with tics or Tourette's syndrome. High doses of stimulants can exacerbate tics, probably because of the medication's action on the dopamine system (Pidsosny & Virani, 2006; Stewart, Illmann, Geller, Leckman, King, & Pauls, 2006).

Finally, many families are reluctant to use medications to manage their children's ADHD symptoms. For these families, psychosocial interventions offer an alternative avenue of treatment.

Psychosocial Treatments

Clinical Behavior Therapy

Clinical behavior therapy is the most frequently used, empirically supported, non-pharmacological treatment for ADHD. This form of treatment is called "clinical" behavior therapy because clinicians typically administer treatment from hospitals and clinics, rather than in people's homes. The focus of therapy is on children's overt behavior. Clinical behavior therapy has three main components: (1) parent consultation, (2) school consultation, and (3) a combined home-school reward system.

Parent consultation, sometimes called "parent training," involves helping the caregivers of children with ADHD learn more effective ways to manage their children's behavior. Typically, the therapist meets with parents on a weekly basis, over the course of two to three months. Each week, the therapist introduces a new parenting principle or tactic designed to improve the quality of parents' interactions with their children or help parents manage their children's high-rate, aversive behaviors. Early sessions focus on teaching parents how to attend to children's positive behavior and reinforce children for obeying rules. These sessions help parents acknowledge and strengthen desirable aspects of their children's behavior—behaviors that are often overshadowed by children's ADHD symptoms.

Later sessions focus on setting clear expectations for children and administering consistent discipline for children's misbehavior. Clinicians usually teach parents of young children to use time out to address disruptive behavior problems. Parents of older children may be taught how to use tokens or points to reinforce appropriate behavior and penalize inappropriate actions. The purpose of these sessions is to help parents address their children's misbehavior without yelling, threatening, or resorting to hostile and coercive interactions.

In addition to meeting with parents, clinicians consult with teachers and other school personnel and implement a home-school reward system. Clinicians usually help teachers identify times or situations when the child is most often off task. Then, clinicians help teachers change the environment to reduce disruptive behavior and encourage on-task activities. Clinicians also encourage teachers to keep a daily report card of children's appropriate behavior at school, which can be monitored and rewarded by parents at home. Finally, clinicians may help teachers develop a classroom-wide token economy or point system to encourage students' attention and compliance. Tokens can be exchanged for privileges enjoyed by all students in the class.

Researchers have studied the efficacy of clinical behavior therapy for ADHD over the past 25 years. Overall, results suggest that parent training is effective at reducing core ADHD symptoms and other disruptive behavior problems in school-age children (Barkley, 1998; Hinshaw, Klein, & Abikoff, 2002).

However, parent training for ADHD has several limitations. First, the efficacy of parent training is strongly related to parents' involvement in the program. For example, in one study of kindergarten children with ADHD, clinical behavior therapy led to improvements in children's behavior at school, but not at home (Barkley et al., 2000). The failure of treatment to improve home behavior was probably due to the fact that most parents did not consistently attend the parent training program. When parents consistently attended training sessions, treatment was associated with improvements across home and school contexts (Anastopoulos, Shelton, & Barkley, 2005).

Second, parent training does not produce long-term behavior change. Although some children show reductions in symptoms immediately after their parents' completion of the training program, these benefits usually do not last more than 12 months. Indeed, in most follow-up studies, children whose parents receive training and those who do not are indistinguishable on measures of their children's ADHD symptoms several months after the completion of treatment (Hinshaw et al., 2002).

Third, parent training does not always normalize child behavior (Hinshaw et al., 2002). **Normalization** refers to whether children, at the end of treatment, cannot be distinguished from children without significant behavior problems. Even after parent training, children tend to show symptoms of ADHD and continue to merit the ADHD diagnosis. In fact, only about 25% of children whose parents participate in treatment show reductions in ADHD symptoms to normative levels (Anastopoulos et al., 2005; Hinshaw et al., 2002; Klein, Abikoff, Klass, Ganeles, Seese, & Pollack, 1997).

Fourth, parent training programs are less effective with adolescents than with children (Barkley, 2004). Parent training works best when parents have a high degree of control over their children's environmental contingencies. However, parents have much less control over adolescents than over school-age children. Consequently, some clinicians supplement traditional parent consultation with parent-adolescent problem-solving and communication training (Barkley, DuPaul, & Connor, 1999). Specifically, clinicians teach parent-adolescent dyads how to solve problems and handle disputes constructively, rather than by resorting to yelling, sarcasm, criticism, or "shutting down." Unfortunately, supplementing traditional parent training with communication training does not seem to be more effective than traditional parent training alone (Barkley, Edwards, Laneri, Fletcher, & Metevia, 2001). Only about 23% of adolescents show reliable improvement in their behavior, and 17% of dyads actually showed a worsening of family disputes, perhaps because they were encouraged to discuss conflicts openly rather than to avoid them.

Direct Contingency Management

A second form of behavioral treatment for ADHD is direct contingency management (Pfiffner & O'Leary, 1993). Direct contingency management is used in schools and specialized classroom settings in which therapists have a great deal of control over children's surroundings. In direct contingency management, therapists alter children's environments to maximize the frequency of desired actions. They rely heavily on systematic rewards and punishments to shape behavior. Usually, environmental contingencies are used to increase attention, reduce disruptive behavior in the classroom, and improve the quality of children's interactions with peers.

One of the best-known examples of a direct contingency management program for children with ADHD is the Summer Treatment Program (STP) developed by William Pelham (Pelham, Fabiano, Gnagy, Greiner, & Hoza, 2005). The STP provides comprehensive treatment for children with ADHD over the summer months, a time during which most children do not receive treatment for their ADHD symptoms. The STP is an eight-week program for children aged 5 through 15 years with ADHD and other disruptive behavior problems.

Children are divided into age-matched teams led by staff members, usually college students who are trained as behavior therapists. Teams stay together throughout the summer in order to foster friendships and improve the social functioning of members. Each group spends three hours per day in a modified classroom setting, led by special education teachers. Children participate in one hour of academic instruction, one hour of computer-assisted instruction, and one hour of art class. Children spend the rest of the day in recreational group activities that are highly structured, such as soccer, softball, and swimming. These activities are designed to improve children's social and motor skills.

STP differs from traditional summer camps; staff members use direct contingency management to modify children's behavior. The tactics used by staff members resemble the strategies taught to parents during clinical behavior therapy. The low staff-to-child ratio allows staff to closely monitor children's behavior throughout the day and provide immediate reinforcement contingent on children's appropriate behavior. The intervention is intensive and comprehensive.

First, staff members issue brief, clear, and specific commands to children and only when they are certain children are attending. Clear directions reduce the chance that children will not comply with the command because of inattention, ambiguity, or distraction. Second, staff members provide immediate and liberal reinforcement contingent on desirable behavior. Social reinforcers include eye contact and smiles, touch (e.g., a high-five), or recognition (e.g., buttons, stickers).

Third, staff members use tokens with younger children and a point system with older children to foster desirable behavior. Staff award tokens or points for appropriate behavior in the classroom (e.g., attending to the teacher, working quietly) and during recreation (e.g., listening to coaches, following pool safety rules). Tokens/points can be exchanged for privileges. Response cost is used to reduce inappropriate behavior. Staff take away tokens or deduct points contingent on unwanted behaviors (e.g., excessive talking in class, teasing peers on the soccer field). For more serious rule violations, staff use time out. For example, children who deliberately hurt others or destroy property are removed from positive reinforcement (e.g., no swim or computer time).

The behavioral interventions used by STP staff are supplemented by social skills training, parent training, and medication assessment and management. First, all children participate in 10 minutes of formal social skills training each day. Staff members initially introduce a social skill (such as raising your hand before speaking in class) by talking about it, demonstrating it, and breaking it down into steps. Then, children are encouraged to practice the skill during a role-play. Staff members remind children to use the new skill throughout the day and reward them liberally for its use. Second, caregivers participate in weekly group parent training sessions designed to teach them how to use behavioral principles in the home. Staff members give parents a daily report card and encourage them to reward their children for appropriate behavior at camp. Finally, children in the STP are assessed to determine the appropriateness of medication to treat their ADHD symptoms. If medication is warranted, the effectiveness of the medication is monitored during camp.

Direct contingency management appears to greatly improve children's behavior (DuPaul & Eckert, 1997; DuPaul & Stoner, 2003). Treatment programs using direct contingency management have been shown to increase attention and appropriate social behavior, reduce disruptive behavior and aggression, and improve children's self-esteem (Barkley et al., 2000; Pelham, Carlson, Sams, Dixon, & Hoza, 1993). Furthermore, parents report a high degree of satisfaction with intensive classroom or summer camp interventions (Pelham, Fabiano et al. 2005; Wells et al., 2000).

For example, Chronis and colleagues (2004) performed one of the first controlled studies of the effectiveness of STP for children with ADHD (see Figure 8.5). In their study, 44 children (90% Caucasian, 90% boys) aged 6 to 13 years participated in an eight-week STP modeled after the one developed by Pelham and Hoza (1996). All children had ADHD and 85% also showed either Oppositional Defiant Disorder or Conduct Disorder.

The researchers used a BAB within-subjects design to evaluate the effectiveness of the STP. For the first five weeks of camp (Phase B), staff used direct contingency management to modify children's behavior. For two days during week six (Phase A), staff refrained from using direct contingency management. For the final two weeks of the STP, direct contingency management procedures were reinitiated (Phase B). Independent observers rated children's behavior during all three phases of the evaluation. Children showed a significant increase in disruptive behavior when treatment was removed compared to when direct contingency management was used.

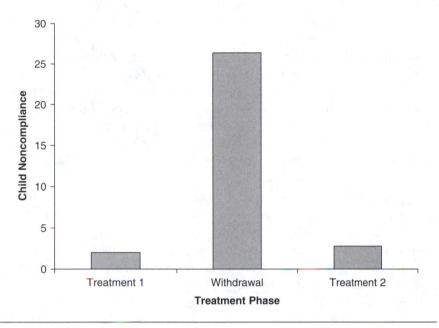

Figure 8.5   Summer Treatment Program for Youths With ADHD

Source: Based on Chronis et al. (2004).

Note: Chronis and colleagues (2004) used direct contingency management during treatment phases 1 and 2, but withdrew contingencies between treatment phases. Children's noncompliance increased during treatment withdrawal, indicating that treatment was efficacious.

Direct contingency management has some important limitations (Hinshaw et al., 2002). First, treatment gains acquired in the special classrooms or summer camps do not generalize to children's homes and are not well-maintained after the program ends (Pelham & Hinshaw, 1992). Second, direct contingency management procedures are not typically associated with better academic functioning (Pelham et al., 1993). Although children who participate in these special programs show improvements in behavior, their academic skills usually remain unimproved. Third, almost no studies have investigated the efficacy of direct contingency management with adolescents who have ADHD. Finally, summer treatment programs are not available in most communities. Parents who want their children to attend a summer camp program may be unable to find one near their home (Barkley, 2004).

Multimodal Psychosocial Therapy

Multimodal Psychosocial Therapy (MPT) is a broad-based treatment for children with ADHD that integrates psychosocial, educational, and behavioral treatment (Hechtman, Abikoff, & Jensen, 2005; Klein, Abikoff, Hechtman, & Weiss, 2004). MPT is designed to improve children's (1) home behavior, (2) academic skills, and (3) social functioning with peers and adults. MPT consists of a number of treatment components, each targeting one or more of these domains of functioning.

To improve behavior at home, parents participate in small-group parent training sessions (Hechtman et al., 2004a). This component of treatment is similar to the parent training provided in clinical behavior therapy. Parents are taught principles of operant conditioning and how these principles can be used to manage the behavior of children with ADHD. Key components of treatment involve learning how to give effective commands, to attend and reinforce appropriate child behavior, and to selectively ignore and punish inappropriate child behavior. Teachers provide feedback regarding children's behavior at school using a daily report card. Parents can reinforce appropriate behavior at school by rewarding children at home, based on these reports.

To improve academic functioning, children receive educational skills training, support, and tutoring (Hechtman et al., 2004a). For example, in one MPT program, children participated in a 16-week study skills program designed to teach time management, listening comprehension, organization of written work, and various study skills. They also received individualized academic plans and remedial tutoring in spelling, writing, and arithmetic.

To improve social functioning, children participate in social skills training (Abikoff et al., 2004a). In small groups, children are taught basic interaction skills, how to get along with peers, how to interact with adults, how to carry on a conversation, and how to deal with conflict situations. In each training session, the therapist introduces a specific skill, breaks it down into small steps, models it, and encourages children to practice the skill in a role-play. Sometimes, children are videotaped while practicing the skill and group members provide feedback after watching the tape. Outside the class, parents and teachers remind children to practice the skill in real-life situations and reinforce its appropriate use.

MPT is effective in reducing ADHD symptoms in school-age children (Abikoff et al., 2004a, 2004b; Hechtman et al., 2004a, 2004b, 2005). Specifically, treatment is associated with fewer disruptive behavior problems, better academic performance, improved social functioning, and more satisfying parent-child interactions. The effectiveness of MPT may be attributed to the fact that it is an intensive, comprehensive form of treatment.

MPT has two primary limitations. First, most communities do not offer MPT. The limited access to MPT is probably because there are few professionals trained in MPT and fewer clinics willing to devote the time and resources to develop MPT programs. The second drawback to MPT is that it may be less effective for younger children compared to older children (McGoey, DuPaul, Eckert, Volpe, & van Brakle, 2005). Its efficacy with adolescents has not been adequately examined.

Medication Versus Psychosocial Treatment

Both stimulant medication and certain psychosocial treatments can effectively reduce ADHD symptoms in children. Is one treatment better than the other? Should we combine treatments to produce the greatest effects? The American Academy of Pediatrics (2001) recommends that children with ADHD participate in both medication and behavioral treatment. Is there any evidence to support this recommendation?

Fortunately, there have been a few very well-conducted studies comparing the efficacy of pharmacological and psychosocial treatments. In one recent study, researchers examined 103 children with ADHD (93% boys; Abikoff et al., 2004a, 2004b; Hechtman et al., 2004a, 2004b). Children were randomly assigned to one of three treatment groups. The first group received only methylphenidate. The second group received methylphenidate plus MPT. The third group received methylphenidate plus an attention placebo. The children in this third condition worked on projects with staff members, received help with homework, and participated in nondirective therapy with a counselor about day-to-day problems. Their parents also attended a parent support group but did not receive parent training. Parents, teachers, psychiatrists, and independent observers rated children's behavior every six months for two years. The researchers were interested in whether children who received both medication and MPT would fare better than children in the other two groups.

Results were consistent across all outcome variables. First, all three groups of children showed improved functioning from the beginning of the study to the time the study ended. For example, children in all three treatment groups showed fewer disruptive behavior problems, improved academic functioning, better social functioning, and better quality parent-child interactions over the course of treatment. Most of the improvement in children's behavior occurred during the first six months of treatment. The second important finding of the study was that all three groups of children showed generally equivalent outcomes at one- and two-year follow-up. Contrary to the researchers' expectations, children who received methylphenidate plus MPT fared no better than children who received methylphenidate alone or methylphenidate plus placebo (see Figure 8.6).

A larger study comparing the pharmacological and psychosocial treatments for ADHD yielded similar results. In the Multimodal Treatment Study of Children With ADHD (MTA Study), 579 children with ADHD were randomly assigned to one of four treatment groups (MTA Cooperative Group, 1999; Swanson et al., 2001). The first group received medication for 14 months. Most of the children in this group were prescribed stimulant medication, usually methylphenidate. The second group participated in approximately eight months of behavioral treatment. Treatment included both clinical behavior therapy and the summer camp treatment program. Children in this group did not receive medication. The third group received a combination of medication and the behavioral treatments. The fourth group received community care; that is, they were not treated by the research team. Instead, they were referred to mental health professionals in their communities. Most (67%) children who received community care were eventually prescribed medication. Researchers assessed the functioning of children after 14 months of treatment to examine efficacy.

Results indicated that all four treatments were reasonably effective at reducing ADHD symptoms and other disruptive behaviors (Swanson et al., 2001). However, children who participated in either medication management or combined treatment were two times more likely to improve compared to children who received only behavioral treatment or community care (see Figure 8.7). The addition of behavioral treatment to medication alone produced a statistically significant but small improvement in children's behavior.

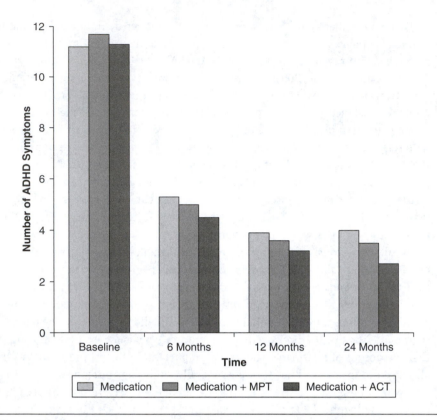

Figure 8.6   Should We Combine Medication and Behavior Therapy?

Source: Based on Abikoff et al. (2004b).

Note: Results of one large study indicated that combining medication with Multimodal Psychosocial Treatment (MPT) or Attention Control Treatment (ACT) did not lead to better improvement than using medication alone.

Taken together, the MTA study suggests that medication alone is superior to behavioral treatment alone for children's ADHD symptoms. Adding behavioral treatment to medication can lead to a slight improvement in children's functioning over medication alone.

Other data indicate that psychosocial treatment may be as efficacious as medication. Pelham and colleagues (2000) re-analyzed data from the MTA study. The researchers compared children's functioning while they were participating in the summer treatment program with the functioning of children who were receiving medication alone. They found that children actively participating in STP showed levels of functioning comparable to children receiving medication. By analyzing children's outcomes after the STP had ended, the MTA evaluation may have missed the program's benefits for children's functioning.

There are at least three additional reasons for using psychosocial treatments (Pelham, Fabiano et al., 2005). First, parents strongly prefer behavioral treatments

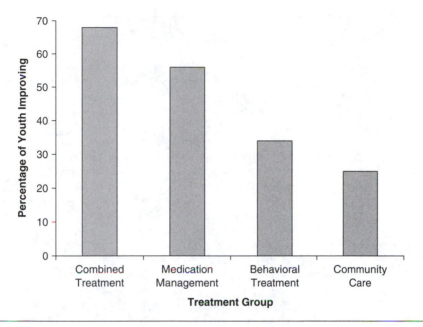

Figure 8.7   The MTA Study

Source: Based on Swanson et al. (2001).

Note: Combining medication with behavior therapy, or using medication alone, is superior to behavior therapy alone to treat ADHD.

over pharmacological ones. Parents are understandably wary of putting their children on stimulant medications, especially those for which we have limited data regarding their long-term impacts on health and behavior. Second, not all children respond to pharmacological treatments for ADHD. Psychosocial interventions offer an alternative form of treatment to non-responders. Third, there is some evidence that combining psychosocial interventions with medication leads to better outcomes than using medication alone (Pelham & Waschbusch, 1999). The evidence for this claim is mixed, but most practitioners argue that combined treatment is preferable to medication alone.

Before ending our discussion of the treatment of ADHD, we should keep in mind that most of us do not have access to well-designed medication management programs, intensive summer treatment programs, or multimodal interventions. Instead, most (92%) children with ADHD receive only medication prescribed by physicians in the community. Only 26% of children with ADHD participate in some form of psychosocial intervention. Sadly, as the MTA study shows, community care often yields only modest benefits. We must remember that the efficacy of medication and behavioral treatment lies not with the medication itself, but with the skill and scientific judgment of the scientist-practitioners who administer it (Olfson et al., 2003).

Update: Corey

After assessing Corey's behavior at school and at home, Dr. Graves diagnosed Corey with ADHD, Combined Type. She told Corey's parents, "Most of the data indicate that a combination of medication and behavior therapy works best for kids Corey's age. How do you feel about trying medication to see if it's useful in managing his symptoms?"

Corey's parents agreed to a two-week trial of medication administered by Corey's pediatrician. The pediatrician instructed Corey's parents, "During the first week, we're going to give him a placebo once in the morning before he goes to school. Then, we're going to ask his teacher to complete a brief rating scale to assess his classroom behavior. During the second week, we'll start him on a low dose of a stimulant medication each day before school. We'll continue to ask his teacher to assess Corey's classroom behavior. If the medication is helpful, the teacher should notice a reduction in Corey's hyperactivity, impulsivity, and inattention from the first to the second week."

In fact, Corey's teacher reported a marked decrease in symptoms even though she did not know Corey had begun taking medication. After several weeks, his pediatrician found the minimum dosage that was effective.

Dr. Graves continued to meet with Corey's parents to teach them about ADHD and behavioral techniques to manage Corey's symptoms. She explained, "Medication can help Corey sit still and pay attention. It provides a window of opportunity for you to teach social and academic skills that Corey otherwise might miss."

Dr. Graves also talked with Corey about his attitude toward taking medication. Corey commented, "I don't think about it much. I just know that it helps me do better in school and get along with Mom at home. I guess it works."

Critical Thinking Exercises

1. Can a child be diagnosed with ADHD and *not* have problems with hyperactivity?

2. What is meant by the term "sluggish cognitive tempo?" Why might children with sluggish cognitive tempo *not* receive treatment?

3. Why are children with ADHD at risk for problematic parent-child interactions? Why are children with ADHD at risk for peer rejection? If you were a clinician, how might you prevent these social problems among young children with ADHD?

4. Barkley claims that ADHD is not primarily a disorder of inattention; rather, it is a disorder caused by a lack of behavioral inhibition. How does behavioral inhibition play a critical role in Barkley's model for ADHD?

5. Philip is an eight-year-old boy recently diagnosed with ADHD, Combined Type. His mother is reluctant to use medication to manage his symptoms; instead, she wants Philip to participate in "talk therapy" with a counselor to help him "learn how to behave." What might you say to Philip's mother regarding (a) the merits and limitations of medication for ADHD, and (b) the benefits and drawbacks of psychosocial treatments?

CHAPTER 9

Conduct Problems in Children and Adolescents

Kyle

Kyle was a 14-year-old boy who was referred to our clinic by his caseworker from the department of juvenile justice. Kyle was arrested for vandalizing 17 school buses, causing several thousand dollars of damage.

Kyle had a history of disruptive behavior. His mother remembered, "As a toddler, he was a handful. He was always getting into mischief, disobeying me, and throwing tantrums." By the time Kyle was in second grade, he had been suspended twice for physical aggression. Once, he stuck a nail from the inside of his shoe through the toe and kicked classmates on the playground. On another occasion, he shoved a classmate down the stairs. Kyle got in trouble for playing pranks, such as "mooning" other children in gym class, spraying class-mates with a bottle of urine, and pulling the fire alarm.

By the time Kyle reached the sixth grade, he had few friends his own age. He preferred to spend time with older boys at the nearby junior high school who introduced him to more serious antisocial behaviors. Kyle began using alcohol and marijuana and skipping school.

At the time of the referral, Kyle was attending an eighth-grade classroom for youths with behavior problems. He had gotten into trouble earlier in the year for making sexually suggestive and racially offensive comments to two girls at the school. He also injured a classmate during a fight. One teacher said, "Kyle deliberately tries to provoke us—rocking in his chair, making offensive noises, talking back, swearing, and lying. He doesn't care about being punished."

Dr. Witek, the psychologist who interviewed Kyle, was most concerned about Kyle's fascination with fire and explosives. Kyle said proudly, "About two years ago, I began building bombs in my house. I use cigarette lighters, aerosols, gaso-line, fireworks, batteries, Styrofoam containers . . . whatever I can get my hands on. My friends and me build them and set them off in the field."

Kyle's mother said to Dr. Witek, "I know Kyle has made a lot of trouble, but he's really not a bad kid. I think if his father played a larger role in his life, he'd be OK."

What Are Child and Adolescent Conduct Problems?

Most children show conduct problems from time to time. After all, parents routinely describe children entering "the terrible twos" or "the horrible threes." Usually, children show a developmentally normative increase in oppositional and defiant behavior during the toddler and early preschool years. Two-year-olds may insist on selecting their own clothes in the morning, even though they prefer to wear shorts and a t-shirt in the middle of winter. Three-year-olds may tantrum when told to go to bed. Four-year-olds may stubbornly refuse to eat their vegetables and sit at the table for an hour to see whether their parents will acquiesce to their demands to be excused. In one study, 97% of toddlers initially ignored or refused to obey adults' requests to clean up after play (Klimes-Dougan & Kopp, 1999).

How can we distinguish normative child behavior from childhood behavior problems? Although there is no easy answer to this question, Lahey and Waldman (2003) suggest that differentiating normal from abnormal behavior must be determined in light of children's overall development context. First, behaviors often become problematic when they persist unchanged to an age at which they are not developmentally normative. For example, when a two-year-old refuses to obey his father's request to clean up his toys, we might consider his behavior developmentally normative. However, when the same behavior is shown by a five- or six-year-old child, we would likely consider the behavior atypically oppositional. Second, some behaviors become problematic when they become potentially destructive or dangerous. For example, when a three-year-old whines because he does not want to go to bed, we might consider his behavior mildly aversive but not developmentally unexpected. However, when a three-year-old hits, kicks, or bites his caregiver to avoid bedtime, we would consider his behavior problematic.

Oppositional Defiant Disorder

DSM-IV-TR identifies two disorders that describe children and adolescents with conduct problems: Oppositional Defiant Disorder (ODD) and Conduct Disorder. ODD is characterized by a "recurrent pattern of negativistic, defiant, disobedient, and hostile behavior toward authority figures that persists for at least 6 months" (p. 100). Children with ODD show at least four symptoms of noncompliant and defiant behavior toward adults, including losing their temper; arguing with authority figures; refusing to obey adults' requests; deliberately annoying or blaming others; and showing anger, resentment, or spitefulness (see Table 9.1). These symptoms must be atypical for the child's age and developmental level and significantly interfere with the child's relationships or academic functioning.

To some extent, ODD reflects a continuation and escalation of disruptive behavior shown by many toddlers and some preschoolers. However, children with ODD show more frequent and severe behavior problems than typical children their age. Keenan and Wakschlag (2004) compared the frequency of disruptive behaviors of young children referred for psychiatric treatment with the behavior of children in the community (see Figure 9.1). Among clinic-referred children, disruptive behavior was common. Approximately 70% of referred children repeatedly denied an

Table 9.1   Diagnostic Criteria for Oppositional Defiant Disorder

A. A pattern of negativistic, hostile, and defiant behavior lasting at least 6 months, during which four (or more) of the following are present (Note: consider the criterion met only if the behavior occurs more frequently than is typically observed in individuals of comparable age and developmental level):

1. Often loses temper

2. Often argues with adults

3. Often actively defies or refuses to comply with adults' requests or rules

4. Often deliberately annoys people

5. Often blames others for his or her mistakes or misbehavior

6. Is often touchy or easily annoyed by others

7. Is often angry and resentful

8. Is often spiteful or vindictive

B. The disturbance causes clinically significant impairment in social or academic functioning.

C. The behaviors do not occur exclusively during a Mood or Psychotic Disorder.

D. Criteria are not met for Conduct Disorder.

Source: Reprinted with permission from the *DSM-IV-TR*.

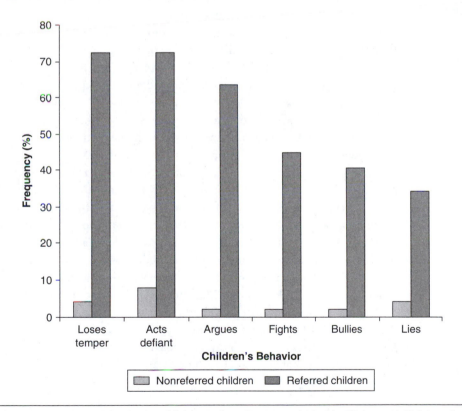

Figure 9.1   Disruptive Behavior in Children Referred to Mental Health Clinics and Children From the Community (Nonreferred)

Source: Based on Keenan and Wakschlag (2004).

Note: Although noncompliant behavior is fairly common among preschoolers, serious problems with temper, defiance, and aggression are rare.

adult's requests or threw tantrums. In contrast, such oppositional behavior was relatively rare among nonreferred children; only about 4%–8% showed these disruptive behaviors. Although strong-willed behavior is common among preschoolers, symptoms of ODD are not (Eyberg, 2006).

Many children with ODD show defiance toward parents but appear compliant and respectful toward teachers, coaches, and other adults. In fact, some children with ODD only show symptoms toward one parent but not the other. The fact that children with ODD can show symptoms in certain situations or with specific people suggests that environmental factors greatly influence the development and maintenance of the disorder. ODD differs from ADHD, in which, by definition, symptoms are present across multiple situations (Eyberg, 2006).

Conduct Disorder

Conduct Disorder (CD) is a more serious and persistent condition that usually manifests in late childhood or adolescence. CD is characterized by a "repetitive and persistent pattern of behavior in which the basic rights of others or major age-appropriate societal norms or rules are violated" (*DSM-IV-TR*, p. 93; see Table 9.2).

The symptoms of CD can be grouped into four broad categories: (1) aggression to people and animals, (2) destruction of property, (3) deceitfulness or theft, and (4) age-inappropriate rule violations. Aggression to people and animals involves initiating physical fights, physical cruelty to or assault of others, and robbery. Destruction of property involves intentionally damaging others' belongings through vandalism, arson, or other reckless acts. Deceitful behaviors include breaking and entering, stealing, or lying to earn a reward or to avoid a responsibility. Other serious rule violations include staying out all night, running away from home, or truancy.

Conduct problems exist along a continuum ranging from mild difficulties with oppositional and defiant behavior (e.g., tantrums, refusing to obey) to serious violations of the rights of others (e.g., assault, rape). Children with ODD and CD show the same pattern of oppositional, defiant, and disrespectful attitudes toward adults in authority. However, children with ODD typically do not show physical aggression to people or animals, deliberately destroy property, or frequently engage in theft and deceitfulness. On the other hand, almost all children with CD show the essential features of ODD (Frick, Lahey, Loeber, Stouthamer-Loeber, Christ, & Hanson, 1992). To avoid redundancy, children with CD are not given the additional diagnosis of ODD.

The symptoms of CD include 15 indicators of serious conduct problems. To be diagnosed with CD, youths must show at least three symptoms in the past 12 months. Because the criteria reflect such diverse behaviors, two children with CD can show dramatically different behavioral profiles. Consider the following 15-year-old boys, each of whom might be diagnosed with CD (Tremblay, 2003):

- Anthony has run away from home, is frequently truant from school, and stays out all night without his parents' permission.
- Brett initiates physical fights with peers, uses a knife to rob others, and forces girls into sexual activity.
- Charles deliberately vandalizes school property, sets fires, and tortures animals.
- Dean breaks into others' homes, shoplifts, and steals credit cards.

Table 9.2   Diagnostic Criteria for Conduct Disorder

I. A repetitive and persistent pattern of behavior in which the basic rights of others or major age-appropriate societal norms or rules are violated, as manifested by the presence of three (or more) of the following criteria in the past 12 months, with at least one criterion present in the last 6 months:

   A. Aggression to people and animals

      1. Often bullies, threatens, or intimidates others

      2. Often initiates physical fights

      3. Has used a weapon that can cause serious physical harm to others (e.g., a bat, brick, broken bottle, knife, gun)

      4. Has been physically cruel to people

      5. Has been physically cruel to animals

      6. Has stolen while confronting a victim (e.g., mugging, purse snatching, armed robbery)

      7. Has forced someone into sexual activity

   B. Destruction of property

      1. Has deliberately engaged in fire setting with the intention of causing serious damage

      2. Has deliberately destroyed others' property (other than by fire setting)

   C. Deceitfulness or theft

      1. Has broken into someone else's house, building, or car

      2. Often lies to obtain goods or favors or to avoid obligations (i.e., "cons" others)

      3. Has stolen items of nontrivial value without confronting victim (e.g., shoplifting without breaking and entering, forgery)

   D. Serious violations of rules

      1. Often stays out at night despite parental prohibitions, beginning before age 13 years

      2. Has run away from home overnight at least twice while living in parental or parental surrogate home (or once without returning for a lengthy period of time)

      3. Is often truant from school, beginning before age 13 years

II. The disturbance in behavior causes clinically significant impairment in social, academic, or occupational functioning.

III. If the individual is 18 years or older, criteria are not met for Antisocial Personality Disorder.

Diagnosis is based on age of onset:
Conduct Disorder, Childhood-Onset Type: Onset of at least one criterion before age 10 years
Conduct Disorder, Adolescent-Onset Type: Absence of any criteria before age 10 years

Source: Reprinted with permission from the *DSM-IV-TR*.

Although all of these boys might be diagnosed with CD, each shows a different pattern of symptoms. The diagnostic label "CD" reflects a large and heterogeneous group of children and adolescents.[5]

Because of the diverse symptoms of CD, researchers have been interested in differentiating children and adolescents into groups based on the pattern of symptoms they show. Researchers have attempted to classify youth in three general ways: (1) based on whether their symptoms are overt or covert, (2) based on whether they show proactive or reactive aggression, and (3) based on the age at which they first showed symptoms. We will now examine each of these three dimensions.

---

[5]Interestingly, a hypothetical 15-year-old boy ("Ernie") who repeatedly robs others at gunpoint but shows no other symptoms might not meet diagnostic criteria for CD.

Overt Versus Covert Conduct Problems

The diagnostic criteria for CD can be loosely divided into two broad clusters: overt symptoms and covert symptoms (see Table 9.3). **Overt symptoms** refer to observable and confrontational antisocial acts, especially acts of physical aggression. Examples of overt symptoms include physical assault, robbery, and bullying. In contrast, **covert symptoms** refer to secretive antisocial behaviors that usually do not involve physical aggression. Examples of covert symptoms include breaking into someone's home, burglary, lying, skipping school, and running away from home. Although most youths with CD show both overt and covert symptoms, these two symptom clusters can be differentiated. Some children, especially boys, tend to show mostly overt symptoms of CD, whereas other children, especially girls, are more likely to show covert symptoms (Achenbach, Howell, Quay, & Conners, 1991; Biederman, Mick et al., 2002; Frick et al., 1993; Loeber & Hay, 1997; Tackett, Krueger, Sawyer, & Graetz, 2003; Tackett, Krueger, Iacono, & McGue, 2005).

Frick and colleagues (1993) reviewed 60 published studies on youths with CD. The researchers discovered that children's conduct problems could be described in terms of two independent dimensions: (1) overt vs. covert and (2) destructive vs. nondestructive. Children's behavior could be overt-nondestructive (e.g., defiance, talking back), overt-destructive (e.g., fighting, bullying), covert-nondestructive (e.g., truancy, running away), or covert-destructive (e.g., vandalism, theft). Overt-nondestructive behaviors reflect ODD. The other types of behaviors reflect CD (Monuteaux, Fitzmaurice, Blacker, Buka, & Biederman, 2004; Tackett et al., 2005).

Table 9.3 Children's Conduct Problems

Overt Symptoms	Covert Symptoms
• Bullies, threatens, or intimidates others • Initiates physical fights • Physically cruel to people • Physically cruel to animals • Uses a weapon	• Steals without confrontation • Runs away from home • Breaks into a house, building, or car • Often truant from school

Source: Based on Tackett et al. (2003).

Reactive Versus Proactive Aggression

Overt conduct problems can further be differentiated into two types of aggression: reactive and proactive. Children show **reactive aggression** when they engage in physical violence in response to a threat, a frustrating event, or a provocation. For example, a child might shove a classmate because the classmate stole his pencil (Connor, Steingard, Cunningham, Anderson, & Melloni, 2004).

Reactive aggression usually occurs because children act impulsively and automatically (out of anger), without considering alternative, prosocial ways of responding (e.g., asking a teacher for help, finding another activity). Reactive aggression is most often seen in younger children and children with ADHD—children who have difficulty controlling their emotions or inhibiting their behavior. Children with a history of physical abuse and/or bullying by peers are also likely to show reactive aggression (Coie, Dodge, Terry, & Wright, 1991; Connor et al., 2004; Dodge & Coie, 1987; Dodge, Pettit, Bates, & Valente, 1995; Waschbusch, Willoughby, & Pelham, 1998).

Children show **proactive aggression** when they deliberately engage in an aggressive act in order to obtain a desired goal (Connor et al., 2004; Dodge, Pettit, & Bates, 1997). For example, a child might shove a classmate and steal his pencil because he wants it.

Most experts believe that children *learn* to use proactive aggression. Learning occurs through modeling and reinforcement. First, parents model proactive aggression when they use hostile behaviors in the home, such as yelling and harsh physical discipline, to force children to comply with their commands. By observing their parents, children learn that proactive aggression is a legitimate and effective way of achieving one's short-term objectives. Second, children's use of proactive aggression is strengthened through positive reinforcement. Children learn that they can acquire objects, money, and social status through fighting or bullying (Bandura, 1973).

Although occasional aggressive outbursts are common during childhood, repeated displays of reactive and proactive aggression are infrequent. Approximately 7% of children show recurrent problems with reactive aggression, 3% show patterns of proactive aggression, and 10% show a mixture of reactive and proactive aggression (Dodge et al., 1997; Waschbusch et al., 1998).

Childhood-Onset Versus Adolescent-Onset Conduct Problems

Most mental health practitioners and researchers distinguish between two types of childhood conduct problems, based on the age at which children begin showing symptoms and the persistence of the symptoms across development (Frick & Munoz, 2006; Moffitt, 2003). Indeed, *DSM-IV-TR* requires clinicians to specify the age of onset of children's CD symptoms.

The differentiation between childhood-onset and adolescent-onset conduct problems is based on a 30-year longitudinal study of 1,000 New Zealand youths called the Dunedin Multidisciplinary Health and Development Study (Moffitt, Caspi, Rutter, & Silva, 2001). In the Dunedin study, researchers identified two developmental pathways for childhood conduct problems: the life-course persistent path and the adolescence-limited path.

Individuals with life-course persistent conduct problems first show symptoms in preschool or early elementary school. Some children with life-course persistent symptoms can be identified as early as age 4½ years (Kim-Cohen, Arseneault, Caspi, Tomas, Taylor, & Moffitt, 2005). These youths display difficulties in emotional control in infancy and early childhood, neurological abnormalities and delayed motor development in preschool, lower IQ and reading problems in school, and later neuropsychological deficits, especially in the areas of decision making, judgment, and memory (Moffitt, 2003). More important, children with life-course persistent conduct problems show an increase in conduct problems throughout childhood and adolescence (Lahey & Loeber, 1994; Moffitt, 1993, 2003). As adults, they are at risk for antisocial behaviors, mental health and substance use problems, work and financial difficulties, domestic abuse and relationship problems, and incarceration (Frick, 2004; Moffitt & Caspi, 2001; Moffitt, Caspi, Harrington, & Milne, 2002).

Brandyn

Brandyn was a five-year-old boy who was referred to our clinic by his Head Start teacher because of defiant and aggressive behavior at school. According to his teacher, Mrs. Miller, Brandyn became angry and resentful whenever she placed limits on him. For example, he would often tantrum, throw objects, and hit her when she asked him to pick up his belongings. Brandyn also bullied and intimidated other children in the class in order to obtain toys and to get his way. His teacher explained, "Brandyn seeks out the younger kids and torments them until he gets what he wants. If they stand up to him, he pushes or pinches them. He even choked a classmate because she wouldn't give him a marker."

Brandyn engaged in other acts of aggression designed to get attention from others. For example, he cut a classmate's ponytail off and repeatedly destroyed other students' toys and artwork. Classmates often avoided playing with Brandyn because of his aggressive acts. Mrs. Miller commented, "I don't know what to do with him. He doesn't seem bothered when we reprimand him and we can't keep him in the time-out chair. He just gets up and runs down the hall. He thinks it's funny when we chase after him."

Brandyn's mother reported similar problems with aggression and defiance at home. "He doesn't listen to me at all," she explained. "He seems to enjoy making my life miserable." His mother discovered him cutting off the cat's whiskers and setting fire to the carpet in the living room. Brandyn was also caught breaking into the neighbor's apartment through a basement window.

Brandyn's mother was very frustrated with Brandyn's behavior. She explained, "It's hard enough being a single mother and working a crummy job. Then, I have to come home and deal with him. I love him, but I don't know what to do. It scares me sometimes because I see him heading down the same road as his father. I guess the apple doesn't fall too far from the tree."

Youth with adolescence-limited conduct problems show their first symptoms after puberty (Moffitt, 1993). They usually do not show psychosocial risk factors for the disorder (e.g., emotional control problems, cognitive/academic deficits). They tend to engage in covert, nonconfrontational antisocial acts (e.g., stealing, truancy, running away) rather than overt acts of aggression. Their behavior problems tend to persist into middle adolescence and then gradually taper off. Most individuals who show adolescence-limited conduct problems do not show serious symptoms in adulthood. However, a small percentage of these adolescents engage in petty crimes and experience financial problems into their middle 20s (Moffitt et al., 2002).

Associated Features and Disorders

Most youths with conduct problems show other cognitive, behavioral, or emotional disorders (Essau, 2003). In fact, it is more common to see a child with conduct problems and some other disorder than conduct problems alone (McMahon & Frick, 2005).

ADHD

Many children and adolescents with conduct problems have ADHD. Overall, approximately 36% of boys and 57% of girls with conduct problems also meet diagnostic criteria for ADHD (Waschbusch, 2002). Comorbid ADHD is more common among youths with CD (75%) than youths with ODD (27%; Whittinger et al., 2007).

Although there is little disagreement that ADHD and conduct problems co-occur, there is considerable debate regarding the nature of their association. Many experts believe the hyperactive-impulsive symptoms of ADHD act as the "motor" that drives youths to engage in aggression and other antisocial acts. Children's high-rate and impulsive behaviors in early childhood elicit negative reactions from caregivers and lead to problems in caregiver-child interactions. These problems, in turn, often contribute to the development of oppositional and defiant behaviors. Early problems with ODD, in turn, can lead to CD in adolescence (Lahey, McBurnett, & Loeber, 2000).

Other research suggests that the strong association between conduct problems and ADHD is due to shared genetic factors. In a large twin study, Nadder, Rutter, Silberg, Maes, and Eaves (2002) concluded that a common set of genes underlies both ADHD and ODD. The mechanism by which genes influence behavior is unknown. One possibility is that genes directly predispose children to both ADHD and ODD. Another possibility is that genes predispose children to show symptoms of ADHD, which, in turn, evoke hostile behavior by parents, teachers, and peers. These hostile behaviors can lead to the emergence of ODD.

Although they frequently co-occur, ADHD and conduct problems are probably caused by different underlying neural impairments (van Goozen, Cohen-Kettenis, Snoek, Matthys, Swaab-Barneveld, & van Engeland, 2004). According to Gray's (1994) neuropsychological theory, behavior is regulated by two neuropsychological systems: the behavioral activation system (BAS) and the behavioral inhibition system (BIS). The BAS is controlled by a neural pathway that connects the brain's pleasure center (in the hypothalamus) to other brain regions. The primary job of the BAS is to motivate behavior. The BAS is responsible for our desire for pleasure, excitement, satiety, and well-being. In contrast, the BIS is regulated primarily by the prefrontal cortex and neural pathways that connect the frontal lobe to other brain regions. The chief job of the BIS is to inhibit a person's activity when behavior might not be reinforced or when it might be punished. The BAS and BIS are competing neuropsychological systems that regulate behavior. The BAS might motivate us to drive fast because we derive pleasure from the exhilaration of going 90 mph; the BIS would cause us to slow down in order to avoid getting a speeding ticket.

Children with ADHD show deficits in BIS activity. These children display problems inhibiting behaviors, even when they know those behaviors will be punished. For example, children with ADHD are talkative and blurt out answers in class even when they know those behaviors will result in a detention.

In contrast, children with conduct problems (but not ADHD) do not consistently show problems with behavioral inhibition (van Goozen et al., 2004). Instead, they show a more general dysregulation of both BAS and BIS (Nigg, Hinshaw, &

Huang-Pollock, 2006). First, children with conduct problems become highly aroused by potential reinforcement. They tend to focus primarily on the pleasurable aspects of their misbehavior (e.g., stealing a candy bar), while they minimize or ignore the potentially negative aspects (e.g., getting caught). This high saliency of reward reflects an overactive BAS. Furthermore, once their BAS becomes active, these children show a general insensitivity to punishment. Despite threats of negative consequences, these children continue to misbehave. This perseveration, despite punishment, reflects an underactive BIS.

Anxiety

Children with conduct problems are more likely to have anxiety disorders than children without conduct problems. Furthermore, girls with conduct problems are more likely than boys with conduct problems to have anxiety disorders. Approximately 14% of boys and 22% of girls with ODD show significant anxiety, while 9% of boys and 16% of girls with CD have comorbid anxiety disorders (Maughan, Rowe, Messer, Goodman, & Meltzer, 2004).

The relationship between conduct problems and anxiety is unclear (McMahon & Frick, 2005). Some studies have shown that children with comorbid conduct and anxiety disorders are less impaired than children with conduct problems alone (Fergusson, Horwood, & Nagin, 2000). Other studies have shown the opposite effect, specifically, that children with both conduct and anxiety problems display more severe symptoms of both disorders (McMahon & Frick, 2005).

It is likely that the relationship between conduct problems and anxiety depends on the personality characteristics of the child. Moderate levels of anxiety allow children to benefit from parental discipline. Some children may display lower levels of conduct problems because they fear parental disapproval or punishment. For these children, comorbid anxiety problems decrease the severity of their conduct symptoms. However, certain children and adolescents have personality traits that make them slow to respond to punishment. These children may have underactive BIS, making them persist in misbehavior despite threats of discipline. For these children and adolescents, comorbid anxiety might be associated with an increase in conduct problems, especially hostile and aggressive behaviors (Frick & Loney, 2002).

Depression

Some children who show conduct problems also experience depression. Approximately 2%–4% of children with ODD and 11%–13% of youths with CD experience depression (Maughan et al., 2004).

Years ago, researchers thought that depression and feelings of low self-worth caused children's conduct problems. Some people believed that depressive symptoms were masked by children's disruptive and aggressive behavior. Subsequent research has not supported this theory of **masked depression** (Toolan, 1962).

Instead, longitudinal studies indicate that children's conduct problems usually precede their symptoms of depression. Today, most researchers believe that conduct problems can contribute to children's mood symptoms. Patterson and Capaldi

(1991) have offered the **dual failure model** to explain the association between conduct problems and depression. According to this model, conduct problems cause children to experience failure in two important areas of functioning: peer relationships and academics. Peer rejection and academic problems, in turn, can cause depression and feelings of low self-worth (Ezpeleta, Domenech, & Angold, 2006).

The relationship between conduct problems and depression is especially strong for girls (Ehrensaft, 2005). Disruption of family and peer social networks may be particularly stressful for girls, causing depressed mood and increased disruptive behaviors. These disrupted interpersonal relationships can lead to despair and feelings of hopelessness.

Adolescents with conduct problems often show problems with impulsivity and poor problem solving, putting them at increased risk for suicide (Ruchkin, Schwab-Stone, Koposov, Vermeiren, & King, 2003). In one study, two-thirds of adolescents who completed suicide had histories of antisocial behavior; about 50% were retrospectively diagnosed with CD (Ezpeleta et al., 2006).

Substance Use Problems

Youths with conduct problems are at increased risk for substance use disorders (Clark, Parker, & Lynch, 1999). Children and adolescents with conduct problems often begin using nicotine, alcohol, and other drugs at earlier ages than children without conduct problems (McGue, Iacono, Legrand, & Elkins, 2001; McGue, Iacono, Legrand, Malone, & Elkins, 2001). In one study, 41.9% of youths with conduct problems tried alcohol and 23.1% tried marijuana by their fourteenth birthday (see Figure 9.2). In contrast, only 26.9% and 6.9% of 14-year-olds without conduct problems had tried alcohol and marijuana, respectively (S. M. King, Iacono, & McGue, 2004). Conduct problems also place children and adolescents at increased risk for using alcohol and marijuana on a regular basis and using multiple substances simultaneously (Button, Hewitt, Rhee, Young, Corley, & Stalling, 2006; K. M. King & Chassin, 2004).

What causes adolescents with conduct problems to use alcohol and other drugs? First, there seems to be a common set of genes that predisposes individuals to both conduct problems and substance use disorders (McGue et al., 2001a, 2001b). Studies of twins and adopted children reared apart indicate a significant association between children's genes and the emergence of both conduct problems and substance use disorders (Clark, Vanyukov, & Cornelius, 2002). Some researchers have suggested that children inherit genes that cause overactivity in the BAS neurotransmitter system, making them highly sensitive to rewards and pleasure (Vanyukov & Tarter, 2000). This sensitivity might predispose them to both conduct problems (e.g., to obtain excitement) and substance use (e.g., to obtain pleasure from the drug).

Second, disruptive children are typically first introduced to alcohol and other drugs by older, deviant peers (Van Kammen, Loeber, & Stouthamer-Loeber, 1991). Deviant peers provide access to these substances, model their use, and reward adolescents with acceptance into the peer group. Substance use problems, therefore, are typically part of a larger spectrum of Conduct Disorder symptoms fostered by deviant peers.

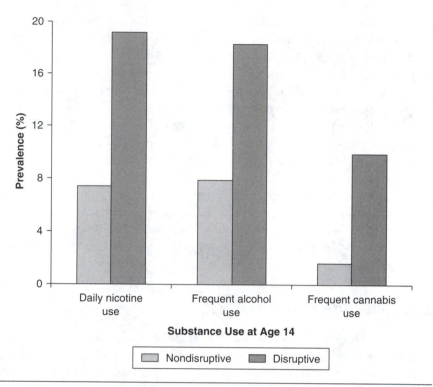

Figure 9.2   Substance Use Among Adolescents With and Without Conduct Problems

Source: Based on S. M. King et al. (2004).

Note: Fourteen-year-olds with behavior problems are more likely to use cigarettes, alcohol, and marijuana on a regular basis than are youths without behavior problems.

Learning Problems

Young children with conduct problems usually show considerable difficulties in school (Dishion, Capaldi, Spracklen, & Li, 1995). They are more likely to earn low grades, to repeat a grade, and to drop out of school before graduation than youths without conduct problems (Kazdin, 2005b). Disruptive youths usually show problems in critical areas of academic achievement, especially reading and mathematics. Approximately 25% of children with conduct problems show academic underachievement; that is, their academic performance is significantly lower than what might be predicted by their age and intelligence. Academic underachievement is especially likely when children have both ADHD and conduct problems (Finch, Nelson, & Hart, 2006).

By middle childhood, children's academic difficulties often lead to negative attitudes toward school and teachers (Sameroff, Peck, & Eccles, 2004). Youths with conduct problems often devalue education, put less effort and time into their school work, and show reduced confidence in their ability to perform. These negative attitudes can cause youths with conduct problems to distance themselves from school, teachers, and prosocial peers.

Schools, too, sometimes play a role in the development of conduct problems. Schools that place little emphasis on academic work, hold low expectations for students' academic achievement and classroom behavior, and provide students with poor working conditions can contribute to children's disruptive behavior problems. Unfortunately, these characteristics are often seen among schools in low-income, high-crime neighborhoods (Sameroff et al., 2004).

Epidemiology

Prevalence

The prevalence of conduct problems depends on gender (Maughan et al., 2004). With respect to ODD, prevalence for boys ranges from 1.9% to 13.3%, with most estimates being within the 3%–5% range. For girls, the prevalence of ODD ranges from 1.1% to 9.4%, with most estimates being approximately 3%. With respect to CD, prevalence estimates for boys range from 1.7% to 14%, with most estimates being within the 5%–10% range. For girls, prevalence ranges from approximately 1% to 8%, with most estimates being within the 2%–4% range.

The prevalence of conduct problems also varies by age. Across development, rates of ODD decrease and rates of CD increase. Approximately 3% of preschoolers have ODD compared to less than 1% of adolescents; conversely, less than 1% of preschoolers meet diagnostic criteria for CD, whereas approximately 5% of adolescents may have the disorder (Lahey et al., 2000; Maughan et al., 2004).

The apparent decrease in ODD with age is largely due to the fact that *DSM-IV-TR* does not permit ODD to be diagnosed when CD is present. Older children who meet diagnostic criteria for both ODD and CD are only given the CD diagnosis. If we simply look at the percentage of children who meet diagnostic criteria for ODD (regardless of whether they have CD), we see that the prevalence remains fairly stable across childhood and adolescence. These data suggest that ODD symptoms do not disappear; instead, they are overshadowed by more serious CD symptoms (Maughan et al., 2004).

Gender

Research investigating gender differences in children's conduct problems has yielded complex results. Overall, boys are more likely than girls to show conduct problems. For example, in one large community sample of twins, boys (13.9%) were about three times more likely than girls (4.9%) to meet diagnostic criteria for CD (Gelhorn, Stallings, Young, Corley, Rhee, & Hewitt, 2005).

However, the exact prevalence of conduct problems by gender depends on the age of the child. For example, conduct problems in boys typically emerge in preschool and are characterized by hyperactivity, destructive behavior, and physical aggression (Loeber & Stouthamer-Loeber, 1998). In contrast, conduct problems in girls usually do not emerge until adolescence and often involve more covert symptoms. Consequently, in early childhood, boys are approximately three times more likely than girls to show serious conduct problems (Biederman, Mick et al., 2002). However, by adolescence, the gender ratio for CD may be 2:1 (Finch et al., 2006).

Until recently, most experts believed that girls simply showed less aggression than boys. However, emerging data suggest that girls aggress in different ways than boys—ways that can be easily overlooked. Specifically, girls often use **relational aggression**; that is, they harm other people's mood, self-concept, or social status by damaging or manipulating interpersonal relationships (Crick & Grotpeter, 1995). Relational aggression can occur in a number of ways. Girls can spread rumors; ostracize another girl from a social network; share another girl's secrets without her consent; steal another girl's on-line identity; or make fun of another girl's weight, clothes, or general appearance. These tactics can be used either reactively (e.g., because the girl is angry at something another girl did) or proactively (e.g., because the girl wants to gain popularity or social status by harming a peer).

There are at least three reasons that girls are more likely to show relational aggression than physical aggression (Ehrensaft, 2005). First, parents socialize girls differently than boys. From an early age, girls are discouraged to show anger through physical aggression. They may learn to use relational aggression to express anger, frustration, and discontent. Whereas physical aggression by girls is usually punished, relational aggression is often overlooked. Second, relational aggression may be more effective than physical aggression at harming other girls. Because girls' moods and identities are so connected with their social relationships, damage to these relationships might be more hurtful than physical assault. In fact, girls view relational aggression as extremely distressing and comparable to physical bullying (Crick, 1995, 1997; Crick & Grotpeter, 1995). Third, girls' relatively more advanced language skills make relational aggression possible. Relational aggression does not typically emerge until late childhood and adolescence, when children's verbal skills are developed enough to engage in these complex, socially aggressive acts (Tiet, Wasserman, Loeber, McReynolds, & Miller, 2001). Since young girls' verbal skills are often better developed than those of boys, girls may be able to show relational aggression at younger ages than boys.

Course

Most children show an increase in disruptive behavior from late infancy through the preschool years. Beginning in early childhood, however, disruptive behavior problems typically decline. Some young children continue to show an increase in oppositional and defiant behavior during early childhood and merit the diagnosis of ODD (Gelhorn et al., 2005).

In samples of clinic-referred children, there is a strong relationship between ODD and CD. In one study, 80% of clinic-referred children with ODD eventually developed CD (Lahey, Waldman, & McBurnett, 1999). In samples of children from the community, only about 25%–33% of children with ODD develop CD (Keenan, Loeber, & Green, 1999; Rowe, Maughan, Pickles, Costello, & Angold, 2002).

Most experts view ODD and CD as distinct, but related, disorders. For example, Lahey, Loeber, Quay, Frick, and Grimm (1992) suggest that ODD is a precursor to CD in some children. Although most children with ODD do not develop CD, a certain percentage of children will show more severe conduct problems.

The developmental outcomes of children with conduct problems depend greatly on the age at which they first showed symptoms. Children with childhood-onset conduct problems have poorer prognoses. These youths are at risk for antisocial and criminal behavior (Caspi, 2000; Farrington, 1998), educational and employment problems (Caspi, Wright, Moffitt, & Silva, 1998), mental health problems (Darke, Ross, & Lynskey, 2003; Fergusson & Lynskey, 1998), and teenage pregnancy (Bardone, Moffitt, Caspi, Dickson, Stanton, & Silva, 1998; Woodward & Fergusson, 1999). In a 25-year longitudinal study of almost 1,000 children with early-onset conduct problems, Fergusson, Horwood, and Ridder (2005) found that children who showed the most serious conduct problems at age seven also showed the worst developmental outcomes in adulthood.

Boys with CD are at particular risk for developing Antisocial Personality Disorder (APD) as adults. APD is a serious character disturbance defined by a persistent disregard for the rights of others. Adults with APD repeatedly violate others' rights through unlawful behaviors, deceitfulness, aggression, recklessness, or irresponsible and potentially dangerous behavior. Furthermore, individuals with APD often show little remorse for their misdeeds (Dolan & Rennie, 2006).

Approximately 40%–70% of adolescent boys with CD will develop APD by early adulthood (Fombonne, Wostear, Cooper, Harrington, & Rutter, 2001; Lahey, Loeber, Burke, & Applegate, 2005). A boy's likelihood of developing APD depends on two factors. First, the sheer number of covert (but not overt) symptoms that the boy shows in adolescence predicts his likelihood of showing future antisocial behavior. Deceitfulness, property destruction, and theft are some of the best predictors of the development of APD. Second, adolescents with CD who come from low-income families are at particular risk for developing APD in adulthood. In one study, adolescents from low-SES backgrounds (65%) were much more likely to develop APD than adolescents from middle-class families (20%; Lahey et al., 2005).

Girls with CD are at risk for internalizing disorders in adolescence and adulthood. As young adults, 75% of girls previously diagnosed with CD show some type of internalizing disorder, including depression and anxiety. Some girls previously diagnosed with CD develop Borderline Personality Disorder (BPD) in adulthood. BPD is a serious personality disorder characterized by tumultuous interpersonal relationships, mood dysregulation, impulsive and reckless behavior, and self-harm. The symptoms of CD in adolescence may interfere with girls' development of identity and healthy relationships, thus leading to the emergence of BPD in later life (Bardone, Moffitt, Caspi, Dickson, & Silva, 1996; Ehrensaft, 2005; Moffitt et al., 2001; Woodward & Fergusson, 1999).

Youths with adolescence-limited CD have better developmental outcomes than children whose symptoms begin in childhood. Nevertheless, youths with adolescence-limited symptoms show considerable impairment during their teenage years. These youths are at risk for academic failure, suspension, expulsion, legal problems, and conflicts with parents and peers. Some of their antisocial behaviors during adolescence can have long-term consequences. For example, youths who drop out of high school or are arrested may have limited employment opportunities in adulthood. Longitudinal studies indicate that youths with adolescence-limited conduct problems often show residual effects of their disruptive behavior in early adulthood (Moffitt et al., 2002). Consequently, youths who begin to show disruptive behavior in adolescence merit the attention of parents, teachers, and mental health professionals as much as youths with childhood-onset conduct problems.

Etiology

Genetics

Conduct problems run in families. Youths with ODD or CD often have first-degree relatives with histories of conduct problems or antisocial behavior (Meyer et al., 2000). However, family studies do not tell us whether the transmission of conduct problems from parent to child is due to shared genes or common environmental experiences.

The results of twin studies have yielded inconsistent findings. Heritability estimates range from 6% to 71%. Across all studies, genetic factors account for approximately 40%–50% of the variance in children's conduct problems, broadly defined (Dick, Viken, Kaprio, Pulkkinen, & Rose, 2005; Gelhorn et al., 2005; Rhee & Waldman, 2002). Recent molecular genetics studies indicate that portions of chromosomes 2 and 19 may be partially responsible for this heritability (Dick et al., 2004).

If we assume that approximately 50% of the variance in children's conduct problems is attributable to genetics, then the remaining variance must be attributable to environmental causes (see Figure 9.3). Nonshared environmental factors account for the lion's share of the remaining variance in children's conduct problems, with estimates ranging from 31% to 86%. In contrast, shared environmental experiences typically account for very little of the variance in conduct problems, with estimates ranging from 0% to 37% (Tackett et al., 2005).

Temperament and Early Neurological Development

Youths with childhood-onset conduct problems often have certain temperamental characteristics that contribute to their disruptive behavior (Dodge & Pettit, 2003; Loeber & Farrington, 2000). **Temperament** refers to the physiological, emotional, and behavioral responses a child typically displays in response to environmental stimuli (Nigg, 2006). A child's temperament is chiefly determined by genetic factors; temperament can be observed at birth or shortly thereafter. Some newborns show "easy" temperaments: They display moderate levels of emotional activity, do not react negatively or fearfully to novel situations, readily engage their environment, and are able to cope with changes in their routine. Other infants show "difficult" temperaments: They display either extremely high or extremely low levels of emotional activity, are quick to cry and fuss at novel stimuli, are easily frustrated, and have difficulty adjusting to change. Children with early-onset conduct problems often show difficult temperaments in infancy and early childhood (Frick,

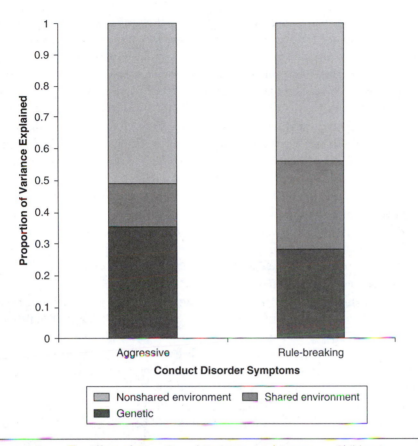

Figure 9.3   The Effect of Genetic and Environmental Factors on Children's Conduct Problems

Source: Based on Tackett et al. (2005).

Note: The type of disruptive behavior that children show determines how important genetic and environmental factors are in children's conduct problems. Genetic and nonshared environmental factors account for most of the variance in children's aggressive symptoms. However, non-aggressive conduct symptoms (e.g., stealing, lying, truancy) are explained by genetic, nonshared, *and* shared factors.

Cornell, Barry, Bodin, & Dane, 2003; Frick, Cornell, Bodin, Dane, Barry, & Loney, 2003; Loney, Frick, Clements, Ellis, & Kerlin, 2003).

Recently, researchers have begun examining *how* difficult temperament can contribute to the development of conduct problems (Frick, 2004; Frick & Morris, 2004). So far, two developmental pathways have been identified: (1) problems with emotion regulation and (2) problems with low emotional arousal.

Problems With Emotion Regulation

Some children with difficult temperament show problems with **excessive emotional reactivity** (Eisenberg et al., 2001; Eisenberg, Fabes, Guthrie, & Reiser, 2000; Frick, Cornell, Barry et al., 2003). When confronted with an environmental stressor, these children display intense, negative emotional reactions and take an unusually long time to soothe (Keenan, Gunthorpe, & Young, 2002). Keenan and Shaw (2003) believe this tendency is caused by an underlying problem with emotion regulation. These children have difficulty controlling negative emotions and responding to stressors in adaptive, flexible, and age-appropriate ways. When frustrated, these children often react with extreme emotional outbursts including anger and aggression. Problems with emotion regulation emerge between 6 and 24 months of life.

Difficulty with emotion regulation can lead to the development of conduct problems in several ways (Frick, 2004; Frick & Morris, 2004; Keenan & Shaw, 2003). First, young children's early emotional displays can interfere with the development of more effective emotion regulation skills. Most infants and toddlers learn to control negative emotions by relying on parents for comfort, support, and reassurance. However, the parents of these at-risk children may have difficulty responding sensitively and appropriately because of their children's outbursts. Consequently, their children may enter their preschool years with diminished capacity for emotional control (Keenan & Shaw, 2003).

Second, emotion regulation problems can compromise the quality of parent-child interactions during the preschool years (Kochanska & Aksan, 2006; Patterson et al., 1992). Crying, yelling, and aggression interfere with children's abilities to internalize rules and maintain appropriate behavior. These emotional displays also lead parents to adopt hostile and angry disciplinary tactics that can model aggression or inadvertently reinforce children's disruptive behaviors.

Third, excessive emotional reactivity can interfere with the development of social problem-solving skills in early childhood (Dodge & Pettit, 2003). Children with social problem-solving skills deficits have difficulties negotiating social disputes in logical and flexible ways. Instead, they rely on impulsive decision making and aggressive actions to resolve interpersonal dilemmas (Crick & Dodge, 1996).

Finally, intense displays of negative emotion can lead to peer rejection (Rubin et al., 1998). Peers avoid children with emotion regulation problems because of their tendency toward aversive emotional displays, high-rate behaviors, and aggression. Consequently, children with emotion regulation difficulties may associate with other peer-rejected children who introduce them to antisocial behaviors.

Low Emotional Arousal

Other children with difficult temperament show extremely low levels of emotional arousal (Frick & Morris, 2004). These youths have a reduction in overall autonomic activity: low resting heart rate, reduced brain activity, low galvanic skin response (Frick & Morris, 2004; Raine, 2002). Additionally, these children may have general underarousal of the **hypothalamus-pituitary-adrenal (HPA) axis**, the body's stress-response system (van Goozen & Fairchild, 2006). Underarousal of the HPA axis causes reduced secretion of epinephrine and cortisol, two hormones responsible for physiological activation in response to threat (McBurnett, Lahey, Rathouz, & Loeber, 2000; McBurnett et al., 2005). Low emotional arousal is believed to be largely determined by one's genes. Twin studies indicate high heritability for emotional arousal and reactivity (Lahey & Waldman, 2003; Viding, Blair, Moffitt, & Plomin, 2004).

Toddlers with low levels of emotional arousal are slow to react to pleasurable stimuli, appear less afraid of frightening or dangerous situations, and do not seem to adjust their behavior when punished (Shaw, Gilliom, Ingoldsby, & Nagin, 2003). By middle childhood, these children often show **callous-unemotional traits**: an inability to feel empathy for others' suffering or distress, a lack of remorse for misbehavior, a desire to use others for personal gain, and a lack of response to discipline or punishment (Frick, Bodin, & Barry, 2000; Pardini, Lochman, & Frick, 2003; Silverthorn, Frick, & Reynolds, 2001; van Goozen, Fairchild, Snoek, & Harold, 2007). Adolescents who show callous-unemotional traits often display a fascination with impulsive, dangerous, or delinquent behaviors (Dadds, Fraser, Frost, & Hawes, 2005).

Early problems with low emotional arousal can contribute to the development of conduct problems in at least three ways. First, children with low emotional arousal do not seem to experience typical patterns of fear and guilt when they engage in misbehavior and when they are reprimanded by parents (Essau, Sasagawa, & Frick, 2006). This impaired ability to experience fear and guilt interferes with their ability to internalize parental rules and prohibitions, the development of conscience, and the capacity for advanced moral reasoning (Essau et al., 2006; Pardini et al., 2003). Consequently, these children often show premeditative, aggressive behaviors without regard for the rights of others (Frick, Cornell, Bodin et al., 2003).

Second, children with low emotional arousal show an overall reduction in autonomic reactivity that renders them less sensitive to punishment (Frick, Cornell, Barry et al., 2003; Frick & Morris, 2004). Consequently, they do not correct their misbehavior when disciplined by adults. Indeed, discipline appears to have little effect on these children, making the process of socialization challenging (Dadds & Salmon, 2003).

Third, children's low autonomic arousal may render them less able to experience pleasure, excitement, and exhilaration (Frick, Cornell, Barry et al., 2003; Frick, Cornell, Bodin et al., 2003). Whereas typically developing children and adolescents derive pleasure from moderate levels of stimulation (e.g., playing sports, going to the movies), children with low autonomic activity need to engage in high-rate, novel, and sometimes dangerous activities to obtain the same pleasurable experience (e.g., reckless skateboarding, driving). Many people describe these youths as "unusually daring," prone to "sensation seeking," or "risk takers" (Essau et al., 2006).

Children who show callous-unemotional traits are at increased risk for showing serious aggressive behaviors by late childhood and adolescence (Frick, Cornell, Bodin et al., 2003; Frick, Stickle, Dandreaux, Farrell, & Kimonis, 2005). For example, childhood callous-unemotional traits predict future antisocial behavior, delinquency, and violent criminal offenses (Kruh, Frick, & Clements, 2005; van Goozen et al., 2007). The presence of low emotional reactivity and callous-unemotional traits may be a better predictor of future antisocial behavior than the presence of CD alone (Caputo, Frick, & Brodsky, 1999; Essau et al., 2006). Frick, Cornell, Barry et al. (2003) studied 98 school-age children, separated into four groups based on the presence or absence of (1) conduct problems (CP) and (2) callous-unemotional traits. As we might expect, children with CP at the beginning of the study were more likely than children without CP to show disruptive behaviors four years later. However, children who showed callous-unemotional traits at the beginning of the study, regardless of whether they also showed CP, displayed the greatest likelihood of aggressive and delinquent behavior at follow-up (see Figure 9.4).

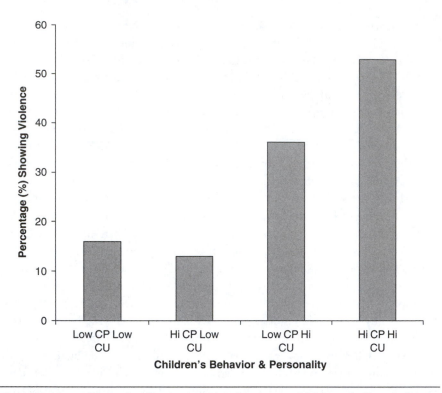

Figure 9.4   Effects of Callous-Unemotional Traits on Children's Likelihood of Aggression

Note: Frick, Cornell, Barry, and colleagues (2003) divided children into four groups based on the presence or absence of conduct problems (CP) and callous-unemotional traits (CU). Four years later, they assessed children's aggressive behavior. Children with CU showed more aggressive behavior, regardless of whether they also had histories of conduct problems.

Taken together, research indicates that the presence of difficult temperament in infancy can predispose children toward conduct problems in later childhood and adolescence. Problems with emotional reactivity or unusually low emotional arousal can independently contribute to later behavior problems. Although difficult temperament is largely determined by genetic factors, the emergence of later conduct problems is caused by a complex interplay of temperamental and environmental factors that are just beginning to be understood.

Parent-Child Interactions

Parenting Behavior

Although genetic and temperamental factors can predispose children to conduct problems, the development of ODD and CD depends greatly on early learning experiences. Chief among these experiences is the quality of early parent-child interactions (Constantino et al., 2006; Guttmann-Steinmetz & Crowell, 2006).

Hostile parenting behavior is associated with the development of children's conduct problems. **Hostile parenting behavior** includes harsh disciplinary tactics such as yelling, arguing, spanking, hitting, or criticizing children in response to their misbehavior. Hostile parenting can also involve using guilt and shame to correct children's misbehavior or relying on parental power to make children comply with requests or commands. Usually, hostile parenting is administered in an inconsistent fashion. Parents are often unwilling to hit or yell at their children for every misbehavior. Instead, parents tend to rely on hostile practices only when other tactics have proved ineffective or when they have become increasingly frustrated. Consequently, hostile parenting is almost always associated with parental anger and resentment (Baumrind, 1991).

Gerald Patterson and colleagues (1992) have identified a particularly problematic pattern of parent-child interactions known as **coercive family process**. In coercive interactions, parents inadvertently model hostile and aggressive behavior to their children and reinforce their children's noncompliant and defiant behavior. The coercive process typically begins when the parent issues a command and the child ignores the command or refuses to comply. If the parent withdraws the command, the child is negatively reinforced for ignoring the parent's request. Consequently, the child will be more likely to ignore parental commands in the future.

If the parent reissues the command, the child may engage in a more aversive refusal, perhaps by throwing a tantrum. Again, if the parent backs down from her command, the child is negatively reinforced for his defiance. The child will learn that tantrums result in the withdrawal of parental commands. Consequently, the child is more likely to tantrum in the future. At the same time, the parent is negatively reinforced for withdrawing her command. She learns that the act of giving in to her child's tantrum causes her child to stop crying.

In most coercive exchanges, parents inadvertently reinforce children for ignoring or defying their commands. In some instances, however, parents become angry and insist on compliance. In these cases, parents may engage in hostile behaviors such as yelling, threatening, or physically disciplining children in a state of anger. In these instances, parents model hostile-aggressive behaviors for their children. They also show their children that verbal and physical aggression are effective ways of dealing with problematic social situations.

Through coercive parent-child exchanges, parents reinforce children for oppositional-defiant behavior while children reinforce parents for lax discipline. Parents also model angry outbursts and aggressive displays to their children. Over time, these interactions can escalate into symptoms of ODD and physical aggression (Snyder, 2001).

Parents of disruptive children frequently alternate between overly permissive and hostile-coercive parenting behaviors (Cunningham & Boyle, 2002). Typically, parents are lax on discipline, perhaps because they want to avoid stress associated with correcting their children's misbehavior (McKee, Harvey, Danforth, Ulaszek, & Friedman, 2004). However, when parents become frustrated or threatened by children's misbehavior, they may respond in a hostile or aggressive fashion: yelling, threatening, grabbing, or hitting. Parents' reliance on overly permissive and hostile-coercive parenting behaviors is one of the best predictors of conduct problems in young children (Chamberlain, Reid, Ray, Capaldi, & Fisher, 1997; Patterson et al., 1992; Sameroff et al., 2004). Frequent use of these tactics also predicts conduct problems in elementary school and middle school (Ackerman, Brown, & Izard, 2003). Furthermore, harsh discipline is one of the best predictors in determining whether a child with ODD will develop CD as an adolescent (Rowe et al., 2002).

Parenting Cognition

Parents' thoughts about their children's misbehavior can affect both their parenting behavior and their children's developmental outcomes (Dix, 1993). Suppose that a mother notices that her preschool-age child often tantrums in the late afternoon. She could make two different **attributions** for her child's misbehavior. First, she might attribute her misbehavior to *external* and *unstable* causes, saying, "Oh, she just gets tired during that time of the day. She needs a longer nap." Alternatively, she might attribute the child's tantrum to *internal* and *stable* causes, saying, "Oh, she's such a bad girl. She seems to enjoy making me upset."

Parents of children with conduct problems are more likely to attribute behavior problems to internal and stable factors (Dix & Lochman, 1990; Johnston & Freeman, 1997). Internal and stable attributions increase the likelihood that parents will respond to misbehavior in hostile or coercive ways (Bugental, Johnston, New, & Silvester, 1998). If a parent believes that her child misbehaves because she is "a bad girl" or "deliberately being naughty," the parent is prone to anger and resentment. However, if a parent attributes her child's misbehavior to transient, situational factors (e.g., fatigue, hunger, boredom), the parent is more likely to respond in a more sympathetic way (Snyder, Cramer, Afrank, & Patterson, 2005).

The way parents think about their own parenting skills can also affect their disciplinary tactics (Johnston, 2005; Johnston & Freeman, 1997). The parents of disruptive children frequently feel powerless over their children, and they often report little confidence in their caregiving abilities (see Figure 9.5). Parents who feel powerless over their children's behavior may give up trying to discipline their children. In one study, the parents of disruptive preschoolers disciplined their children *less* often than the parents of nondisruptive preschoolers, despite the fact that children in the former group showed more behavior problems. These feelings of powerlessness can also cause parents to resent their children's misbehavior and increase the likelihood that parents will discipline in a hostile or coercive manner (Cunningham & Boyle, 2002).

We need to remember that the relationship between parenting behavior and child misbehavior is transactional; parents and children influence each other's behaviors over time. For example, a child who has difficulty regulating his emotions might engage in more crying, tantrums, and disruptive behavior than most children his age. His aversive emotional displays might cause his mother to adopt hostile-coercive strategies to manage his behavior. These less-than-optimal parenting behaviors might, in turn, contribute to more severe oppositional-defiant behaviors and future conduct problems. In fact, children with difficult temperaments and affect regulation problems seem to elicit hostile-coercive behaviors from their parents (Moffitt et al., 2001; Stoolmiller, 2001). These parenting behaviors, in turn, contribute to the development of conduct problems throughout childhood (Dodge, 2006; Patterson, DeGarmo, & Knutson, 2000; Shaw, Lacourse, & Nagin, 2005).

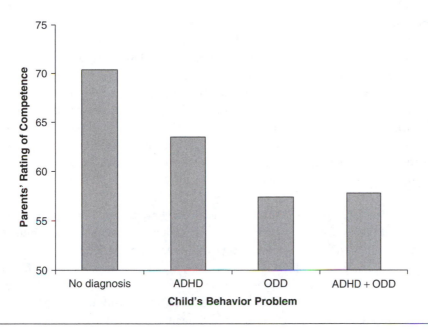

Figure 9.5   Parents of Children With ODD Report Low Competence

Source: Based on Cunningham and Boyle (2002).

Note: Parents' doubts and frustrations can cause them to respond in hostile ways, exacerbating their children's conduct problems.

Parents' Mental Health

Parental psychopathology also predicts children's conduct problems (Crnic & Low, 2002). Maternal depression, paternal antisocial behavior, and parental substance abuse are all associated with children's disruptive behavior problems. Marital conflict, too, is associated with children's conduct problems (Chronis et al., 2007). Parents' emotional and behavioral problems can contribute to children's disruptive behavior by interfering with the quality of parent-child interactions. For example, mothers with depression are often less supportive and more coercive toward their children than mothers without depression; their emotional distress and low energy interferes with the care and discipline they give their children (Lovejoy, Graczyk, O'Hare, & Neuman, 2000). Additionally, parents with disruptive behavior problems often model hostile and aggressive behaviors in the home (Calzada, Eyberg, Rich, & Querido, 2004; Frick & Loney, 2002; Querido, Eyberg, & Boggs, 2001).

Parental Monitoring

By late childhood and early adolescence, children assume greater autonomy over their behavior. They are given greater freedom to plan their day and they are able to participate in more activities without parental supervision. However, the increased autonomy that children enjoy also provides them with more opportunities to engage in disruptive and antisocial acts.

Low parental monitoring is strongly associated with the development of conduct problems in late childhood and adolescence (Loeber & Farrington, 2000; Rowe et al., 2002; Wasserman & Seracini, 2000; see Figure 9.6). **Parental monitoring** has three components. First, parents must know children's whereabouts, activities, and peers. Second, parents must set developmentally appropriate limits on children's activities. Third, parents must consistently discipline children when they fail to adhere to rules (Snyder, Reid, & Patterson, 2003). Children whose parents fail to monitor or supervise their activities show increased likelihood of conduct problems; however, children whose parents set firm limits on after-school activities show decreased rates of delinquency (Chronis et al., 2007; Galambos, Barker, & Almeida, 2003; Laird, Pettit, Dodge, & Bates, 2003).

Patterson and Yoerger (2002) have argued that low parental monitoring is one of the chief mechanisms by which children's disruptive behavior continues into adolescence. They encourage parents to set clear expectations on their children's behavior, to supervise their children's activities, and to administer consequences for their children's rule violations. Although these are wise suggestions, some data suggest that these tactics are more easily said than done. Adolescents are adroit at keeping parents in the dark about potentially delinquent activities. Furthermore, excessive parental supervision can actually lead to an *increase* in adolescent behavior problems if teens feel overcontrolled by parents (Kerr & Stattin, 2000).

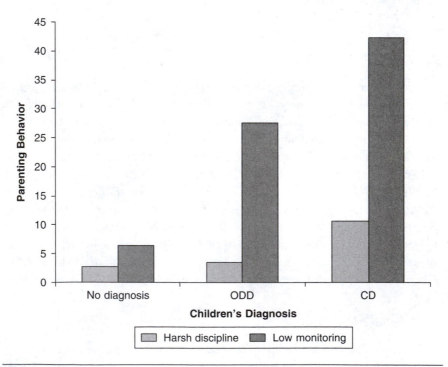

Figure 9.6   Low Parental Monitoring Predicts Children's Conduct Problems

Source: Based on Rowe et al. (2002).

Social Information Processing

Children with conduct problems often show characteristic biases in their social information processing, that is, the way they perceive, interpret, and solve social dilemmas and interpersonal disputes (Dodge, 2003; Reinecke, 2006). Crick and Dodge (1994) developed **social information processing theory** to explain how children solve interpersonal dilemmas. According to this theory, the way people think and feel about social situations influences their actions.

In social information processing theory, a child must perform five mental processes in order to solve an interpersonal problem. First, the child must *encode cues* about the social situation; that is, he or she must take in information about the situation in order to understand it. Cues can include external information about the situation itself or internal information about the child. Imagine that a 10-year-old boy is waiting in line in the school lunchroom. He is suddenly struck from behind and notices milk running down his back. He further notices that a larger, older boy is standing behind him, looking sheepish, while other children in the lunchroom are beginning to snicker. The younger boy feels embarrassed and confused.

In the second step of the information processing model, children must *interpret internal and external cues* so that they make sense. The boy in the story above might infer that his classmate spilled milk down his back by accident and that he wants to apologize. Alternatively, the boy might make a hostile attribution for the older boy's behavior, believing that he deliberately spilled the milk to humiliate him.

Third, the child must *clarify his goals* for the social situation. That is, the child must decide what he wants to accomplish. One goal might be to avoid further embarrassment and to get cleaned up. An alternative goal might be to take revenge on the older classmate.

Fourth, the child must *develop a plan of action*. The child can do this either by creating a new solution to the problem or by drawing upon past experiences in similar situations. Ideally, the child generates multiple possible solutions. For example, he might consider walking away from the situation, laughing over his misfortune with the rest of his peers, or punching the older boy in retaliation.

Fifth, the child must *evaluate his options* and select the best course of action. This step involves weighing the costs and benefits of each potential solution and reaching a decision about how to act. For example, if the child decides to hit the older boy, he might feel better in the short term. However, he will likely get in trouble and may even be suspended from school.

Finally, the child *enacts the solution* to the problem that he believes is the best. Then, the cycle begins anew, as the child begins to process others' reactions to his solution. According to Crick and Dodge (1994), the information-processing steps occur extremely rapidly, usually without children knowing that they are engaging in them.

Considerable research has shown that aggressive children tend to show biases in their social information processing. Furthermore, these deficits differ depending on whether children show reactive or proactive aggression (Kempes, Matthys, de Vries, & van Engeland, 2005). Children who show reactive aggression tend to have problems with the first two steps: encoding and interpreting cues (Crick & Dodge, 1996; Schwartz et al., 1998). Specifically, they take in less information about the situation. For example, they might attend to one or two salient features of the situation (e.g., the milk, the other children laughing) and ignore other potentially important cues (e.g., the boy behind saying, "I'm sorry"). These children also have difficulty understanding their own emotional reactions to the situation. For example, they might mistake feelings of embarrassment for feelings of anger. Consequently, children who engage in reactive aggression usually show a **hostile attribution bias** for others' behavior; they are likely to interpret others' benign behavior as hostile or threatening. Consequently, they often react in an aggressive manner (Dodge, 1993; Dodge et al., 1995).

Children with proactive aggression tend to have difficulty with the last three steps: clarifying goals and developing and evaluating possible solutions (Crick & Dodge, 1996). First, children who engage in proactive aggression tend to select instrumental goals rather than relational goals. That is, their objective is often to get something that they want rather than to make a friend or to maintain a relationship. Consequently, they often act out of self-interest rather than out of respect for the feelings of others. Second, when evaluating potential courses of action, children who show proactive aggression often emphasize the positive aspects of aggressive behavior (e.g., it will allow me to get what I want) and minimize the negative aspects of aggression (e.g., I might get in trouble). Indeed, these children seem to focus excessively on potential rewards (e.g., stealing a candy bar or a car) rather than on possible punishment (e.g., getting grounded or arrested; Barry, Frick, Grooms, McCoy, Ellis, & Loney, 2000; Frick, Cornell, Barry et al., 2003; Frick, Cornell, Bodin et al., 2003). Consequently, they frequently select solutions that allow them to get what they want with little forethought about the consequences of their actions.

Peers

Across childhood and adolescence, friends gradually assume greater importance to children's self-concepts and emotional well-being (Patterson et al., 2000; Patterson & Yoerger, 2002). Older children and adolescents develop identities through interactions with their friends; friends influence their thoughts, feelings, and actions. Prosocial peers can protect youths from stressors by providing them with a social support system independent of their families (Brendgen, Wanner, Morin, & Vitaro, 2005). Deviant peers, however, can contribute to children's behavior problems (Moffitt et al., 2001).

Boys who show academic and conduct problems in school are often rejected by prosocial peers (Dishion, Andrews et al., 1995; Dodge et al., 2003; Snyder et al., 2003). Children with low academic achievement are seldom selected for group projects and may be teased by classmates. Even in kindergarten, children avoid classmates who are hyperactive or highly disruptive (Lacourse, Nagin, Vitaro, Cote, Arseneault, & Tremblay, 2006). Youths who show problems with affect regulation, anger, or aggression are actively avoided because of their impulsive and aversive displays (Price & Dodge, 1989b; Schwartz et al., 1998). Interestingly, children who show angry reactive aggression are more likely to be rejected by peers than children who show proactive aggression (Dodge & Coie, 1987; Price & Dodge, 1989b). Some bullies are popular, especially among younger children (Price & Dodge, 1989b).

Socially ostracized boys may seek out other boys who are socially rejected, a tendency known as **selective affiliation** (Snyder et al., 2003). These deviant peers introduce boys to more serious antisocial behaviors such as physical aggression, vandalism, truancy, theft, and alcohol use (Haselager, Cillessen, Van Lieshout, Riksen-Walraven, & Hartup, 2002; Petras et al., 2004).

Boys learn to engage in antisocial behavior from peers through a process called **deviancy training** (Dishion, McCord, & Poulin, 1999). In deviancy training, deviant peers positively reinforce boys for talking about antisocial activities. In one study, researchers compared the conversations of disruptive and nondisruptive peer groups (Dishion, Spracklen, Andrews, & Patterson, 1996). Nondisruptive boys tended to reinforce each other for telling jokes and interesting stories. In contrast, disruptive boys reinforced each other for discussions about antisocial behavior, such as getting into trouble at school, shoplifting, or bullying.

Over time, boys engage in increasingly more severe antisocial behaviors in order to obtain further reinforcement from the deviant peer group. Deviant conversations among peer group members in late childhood predict delinquency, aggression, and substance use problems by early adolescence (Lacourse et al., 2006; Patterson et al., 2000). Deviant peers, therefore, amplify boys' emerging behavior problems, leading them to engage in more severe and problematic antisocial acts. The process of deviancy training seems to begin early. In fact, deviant discussions with peers predict future behavior in children as young as six years old (Snyder et al., 2003).

For girls, the emergence of conduct problems tends to coincide with puberty. Early menarche places girls at risk for later conduct problems (Burt, McGue, DeMarte, Krueger, & Iacono, 2006). Among girls who already show conduct problems before puberty, the stressors of puberty seem to exacerbate disruptive behavior symptoms, leading to a general increase in the severity and frequency of behavior problems (see Figure 9.7). However, even girls without pre-pubertal behavior problems are at risk for conduct problems following early menarche. The physical changes of puberty can attract older, deviant boys who introduce early-maturing girls to antisocial and sexually precocious behavior.

Neighborhoods

Children's neighborhoods may also affect their likelihood of conduct problems (Boyle & Lipman, 2002; Leventhal & Brooks-Gunn, 2000). Youths from disadvantaged, high-crime neighborhoods are more likely to develop ODD and CD than children from middle-class communities (Brooks-Gunn, Duncan, Klebanov, & Sealand, 1993; Chase-Lansdale & Gordon, 1996; Greenberg, Lengua, Coie, & Pinderhughes, 1999; Ingoldsby & Shaw, 2002).

Neighborhoods can influence child development in several ways (Kroneman, Loeber, & Hipwell, 2004). First, neighborhoods may lack institutional resources to meet the needs of children in the community. For example, poor neighborhoods

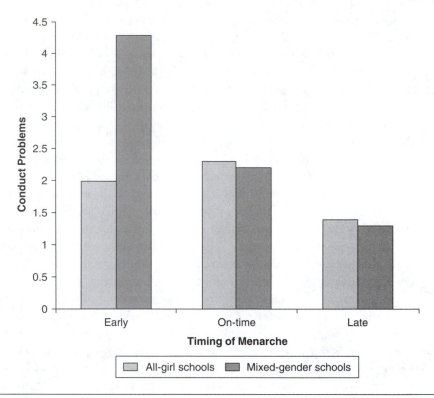

Figure 9.7   Girls Who Begin Puberty Early Are More Likely to Develop Conduct
Problems

Source: From Caspi, Lynam, Moffitt, and Silva (1993). Used with permission.

Note: Early-maturing girls may associate with older, deviant boys who introduce them to antisocial
behaviors. Early-maturing girls who attend all-girl schools do *not* show increased risk of conduct
problems.

often have lower-quality daycare centers and public schools. Children who attend
these schools may not receive optimal educational services, especially if they show
a developmental or learning disability. As a result, they may experience academic
difficulties, come to devalue learning, and begin to show problematic behavior in
and out of school.

Second, neighborhoods may provide inadequate supervision and monitoring of
children's activities, especially during after-school hours. For example, children living in low-income neighborhoods often have limited access to prosocial activities.
High-quality recreation centers, after-school programs, and organized athletics
tend to be disproportionately available in middle- and upper-class neighborhoods.
In the absence of prosocial programming, youths from disadvantaged neighborhoods may engage in unsupervised, antisocial activities after school (Brody et al.,
2001; Kim, Hetherington, & Reiss, 1999; Kupersmidt, Griesler, DeRosier, Patterson,
& Davis, 1995).

Third, low-income, high-crime neighborhoods often have weak social control networks; that is, these neighborhoods often lack organizations and community members that encourage prosocial behavior and limit antisocial activity (Kroneman et al., 2004). For example, in upper- and middle-class neighborhoods, children's disruptive behavior is kept in check by police, neighborhood watch groups, and concerned community members. Adolescents who wander the neighborhood at night or vandalize property are quickly brought to the attention of authorities. In contrast, community members living in poorer neighborhoods often tolerate higher levels of antisocial behavior among youth. After all, in high-crime neighborhoods, adolescents wandering the streets at night or engaging in petty acts of vandalism do not merit as much attention as people who engage in other, more serious criminal activities.

Of course, not all children who grow up in disadvantaged neighborhoods develop conduct problems. Certain factors can protect children from environmental risks posed by their surroundings. Chief among these protective factors is family cohesion and parental monitoring. Children whose parents set high expectations for their behavior, support their prosocial activities, and monitor their whereabouts are more likely to have positive developmental outcomes, regardless of neighborhood risks (Gorman-Smith, Tolan, & Henry, 2000; Plybon & Kliewer, 2001; Shaw, Ramirez, Trost, Randall, & Stice, 2004).

What About Adolescence-Limited Conduct Problems?

Up until now, we have examined the causes of conduct problems that emerge in early childhood and often persist into adolescence. However, we should remember that many youths display adolescence-limited conduct problems (Moffitt, 2003). These adolescents begin showing symptoms shortly after puberty and then display a pattern of antisocial behavior during early adolescence. Their delinquent acts are almost always rebellious but not aggressive (Piquero & Brezina, 2001). Behaviors include destruction of property (e.g., vandalism, joyriding), deceitfulness (e.g., lying, shoplifting), and other rule violations (e.g., staying out all night, running away from home, truancy). These children typically only engage in delinquent behavior when encouraged by deviant peers (Moffitt & Caspi, 2001). In middle or late adolescence, the frequency and severity of these behaviors begin to decrease.

Youths with adolescence-limited conduct problems usually do not show the same genetic, temperamental, and psychosocial risk factors as individuals with childhood-onset conduct problems. Adolescence-limited conduct problems are often viewed as an extreme, maladaptive form of adolescent rebellion (Frick, 2004). Moffitt (2003) asserts that adolescents often find themselves in a "maturity gap"; that is, they possess many of the cognitive and physical attributes of adults, yet they do not have access to the privileges and responsibilities of adulthood. Encouraged by antisocial peers, these adolescents engage in disruptive acts in order to develop a sense of autonomy and identity independent of parents and family (Moffitt, 1993). As these adolescents gradually assume more positive adult responsibilities, their disruptive behaviors usually decrease.

Treatment

Treatment for Younger Children

Parent Management Training

Parent management training (PMT) is the most widely used and best-supported treatment for conduct problems in children. PMT is based on the notion that children's disruptive behaviors often develop in the context of hostile-coercive parent-child interactions (Patterson et al., 1992). The clinician assesses the quality of parent-child interactions and notes how parents might inadvertently reinforce or model oppositional, defiant, or aggressive behavior. During the course of therapy, the clinician teaches parents how to interact with their children in more adaptive ways and how to avoid coercive parent-child exchanges (Schultz, 2006; Steiner & Remsing, 2007).

There are a number of different PMT programs designed for children of various ages (Harwood & Eyberg, 2006; Markie-Dadds & Sanders, 2006). In most cases, parents participate in weekly PMT sessions without their children. Parents learn new child management skills each week and practice these skills at home. Barkley's (1997b) Defiant Children parent training program is often used with disruptive preschool- or school-aged children. There are ten steps in the program; each step consists of a principle or skill that parents learn in the session and apply in their home during the course of the week (see Table 9.4). Some parents can complete one step each week, but most parents require multiple weeks to master some steps. The steps can be loosely categorized into four phases of treatment.

In the first phase (Step 1), parents learn about the causes of children's disruptive behavior problems. Although parents frequently blame themselves for their children's misbehavior, therapists show how children's misbehavior is influenced by parent, child, and environmental factors.

In phase two (Steps 2–4), parents are taught basic learning principles, with an emphasis on positive reinforcement. Parents who seek treatment for their disruptive children usually attend predominantly to their children's misbehavior. Consequently, therapists teach parents how to attend to and praise appropriate behavior. First, parents learn to attend to children's desirable behavior. Then, parents learn to use positive reinforcement to increase the frequency of children's compliance. Parents are taught that in order for reinforcement to be effective, it must be contingent on appropriate behavior; that is, it must occur *immediately* following the appropriate behavior and it must be *consistently* provided. Later, parents learn to extinguish many of their children's inappropriate behaviors through selective ignoring. That is, parents systematically ignore unwanted behaviors that are aversive but not dangerous (e.g., tantrums, interruptions while parents are on the phone). Finally, parents learn to establish either a token economy (for younger children) or a point system (for older children) in the home. Children earn tokens or points contingent on specific appropriate behaviors, such as compliance with parental requests or homework completion.

In phase three (Steps 5–7), parents learn how to reduce children's disruptive behavior using discipline and environmental structuring. First, parents learn how to use time out for serious rule violations. Time out is first practiced at home, with a single behavior problem. Later, time out is used for other behavior problems at

Table 9.4 Parent Management Training

Step	Topic/Description
1	**Why do children misbehave?**
	The therapist teaches parents the causes of child misbehavior, how these causes interact, and what parents can do to identify these causes in their own families.
2	**Pay attention!**
	Many parents of disruptive children focus primarily on their children's misbehavior. In this session, the therapist teaches parents to attend to and appreciate their children's appropriate actions.
3	**Increasing children's compliance**
	After parents learn to attend to their children's appropriate behavior, the therapist teaches them to contingently reinforce their children's appropriate actions using praise and attention. The therapist especially encourages parents to attend to and reward their children when they are not interrupting or bothering them, such as when they are playing quietly.
4	**Using token economies**
	Parents are taught how to implement a token economy in the home to increase child compliance with commands, rules, and chores.
5	**Using time out at home**
	The therapist teaches parents how to use the token system as a form of punishment using response cost; tokens are withdrawn for inappropriate actions. Parents also learn how to use time out in the home. Initially, time out is used for only one or two problem behaviors.
6	**Practicing time out**
	Parents gradually expand their use of time out to other behavior problems. During the session, the therapist and parents address problems using the time out procedure.
7	**Managing children in public places**
	Parents are taught how to use modified versions of time out to discipline children outside the home in stores, restaurants, church. Parents are also taught how to "think ahead" and plan for children's misbehavior in public.
8	**Using the daily school behavior report card**
	Teachers are asked to complete a daily report card regarding the child's behavior at school. Parents use the home token economy to reinforce appropriate behavior at school, based on teachers' reports on the card.
9	**Handling future behavior problems**
	The therapist and parents discuss how to deal with future behavior problems and challenging situations. Parents are shown how to use the skills they acquired in the parent training course to address future behavior problems.
10	**Booster session and follow-up meetings**
	The therapist asks parents to attend a follow-up "booster" session one month after the training ends to check on the family's progress. Parents can use this session to troubleshoot new problems or discuss ways to fade the token system. Follow-up visits may be scheduled every three months as needed.

Source: Based on Barkley (1997b).

home. Finally, parents extend time out to public settings (e.g., restaurants, shopping trips). Parents also learn how to avoid behavior problems by structuring the environment to help their children behave. For example, before going grocery shopping, a parent might decide to bring snacks and a few small toys for the child so that she does not fuss or tantrum during the trip.

The fourth phase (Steps 8-10) involves generalizing children's appropriate behavior to the school setting and maintaining behavioral gains in the future. Teachers are asked to complete a daily report card on children's behavior at school. Parents monitor children's school behavior using the daily report card and reward children for their compliance when they are at home. Later, parents and therapists work together to plan for other potential behavior problems. Many therapists encourage parents to attend a follow-up or "booster" session sometime after training has ended, in order for therapists to check in on the progress of families.

PMT has received considerable empirical support (Kazdin, 2005b). Children whose parents participate in PMT show decreased oppositional, defiant, and aggressive behavior at home and at school. They show more prosocial behavior at home, get into fewer disciplinary problems at school, and are less likely to show serious disruptive behavior problems in the future. After treatment, their functioning is similar to peers without conduct problems. Most longitudinal studies have shown that the effects of treatment last at least one to three years; however, some studies have shown that treatment gains are maintained 10 to 14 years after the end of treatment (Kazdin & Whitley, 2006).

PMT also has some limitations. First, PMT is less effective for parents under high stress. Single parents, low-income parents, parents experiencing marital conflict, and parents who have substance use or mental health problems tend to drop out of PMT or progress slowly (Dadds & McHugh, 1992; Kazdin, 2005b). Psychosocial stressors can interfere with parents' abilities to attend sessions, practice parenting skills, and persevere in the face of environmental challenges. Second, PMT has received less empirical support when used with adolescents (Kazdin, 2005b). Adolescents typically show more severe conduct problems than children, perhaps making them more resistant to treatment. Furthermore, parents tend to have less control over their adolescents' environments and, consequently, have less ability to change environmental contingencies to alter their adolescents' behavior. Third, most clinicians in the community have not received formal training in PMT (Kazdin, 2005b). Parents who want to participate in PMT may be unable to find skilled therapists in their communities.

Parent-Child Interaction Therapy

Parent-child interaction therapy (PCIT) is a variant of PMT designed for families with disruptive preschoolers and young school-age children (Nixon, 2002; Querido & Eyberg, 2005). As with PMT, the focus of PCIT is on the way parents interact with their children and address child misbehavior. Unlike PMT, parents and children attend therapy sessions together. Clinicians observe parent-child interactions and teach parents techniques for managing their children's behavior during the sessions.

PCIT is divided into two phases. In the first phase, **child-directed interaction**, the goal of treatment is to increase parents' sensitivity and responsiveness toward their children and to improve the quality of the parent-child relationship. These sessions resemble play; children select a play activity and parents follow their lead.

Table 9.5   Parent-Child Interaction Therapy: PRIDE Skills

Skill	Reason	Examples
PRAISE appropriate behavior	Causes your child's good behavior to increase	Parent: *Good job putting the toys away!*
REFLECT appropriate talk	Shows your child that you are listening	Child: *I drew a tree.* Parent: *Yes. It looks like an apple tree.*
IMITATE appropriate play	Lets your child lead; shows your child that you approve of his/her game	Child: *I put a nose on the potato head.* Parent: *I'm going to do that too.*
DESCRIBE appropriate behavior	Shows your child that you are interested in what he/she does	Parent: *You're making a tower with the block. You're drawing a square.*
Show **ENTHUSIASM**	Lets your child know that you are enjoying the time you are spending together	Parent: *You are a REALLY hard worker!*

Source: Based on T. Patterson and Kaslow (2002).

One component of this phase of treatment is to help parents develop a set of skills that spell the acronym PRIDE. While playing with their children, parents practice praising, reflecting, imitating, and describing their children's appropriate behavior in an enthusiastic way (see Table 9.5). Furthermore, parents are discouraged from assuming too much control over the play situation, from asking questions or making demands, and from being critical of their child's behavior. In this way, parents strengthen children's appropriate actions and convey acceptance and warmth (Eyberg, 2006).

In the second phase of PCIT, **parent-directed interaction**, the goal of treatment is to help parents create more realistic expectations for their children's behavior, to reduce hostile and coercive parent-child exchanges, and to promote fair and consistent use of discipline. An important component of this phase of therapy is learning how to give effective commands to children. Commands must be given when children are paying attention, they must be stated clearly and concretely, and they must be followed up immediately by consequences, either praise (for compliance) or discipline (for noncompliance). Another component of this phase is teaching parents how to use time out effectively (Eyberg, 2006).

In PCIT, the therapist meets with the parent and child together. The therapist acts as the parent's teacher and coach. The therapist demonstrates all of the skills to the parent in the therapy session. Then the therapist coaches the parent during the session until the parent has performed the skill adequately with her child. The therapist also troubleshoots specific behavior problems as they arise in the session and helps the parent tailor treatment to meet her child's specific needs. In general, PCIT is a hands-on approach to PMT.

Several studies have shown PCIT to be effective at reducing disruptive behavior in very young children, both at home and in the classroom (Herschell & McNeil, 2005; Nixon, Sweeney, Erickson, & Touyz, 2003; Schuhmann, Foote, Eyberg, Boggs, & Algina, 1998). Furthermore, PCIT seems to improve the sensitivity and care parents show to their children, decrease parental hostility and criticism toward their children, and reduce parenting stress (Eisenstadt, Eyberg, McNeil, Newcomb, & Funderburk, 1993; Werba, Eyberg, Boggs, & Algina, 2006). Improvements in children's behavior are maintained for at least one to two years after treatment (Boggs et al., 2004; Eisenstadt et al., 1993; Eyberg, Funderburk, Hembree-Kigin, McNeil, Querido, & Hood, 2001; Funderburk, Eyberg, Newcomb, McNeil, Hembree-Kigin, & Capage, 1998; Nixon, Sweeney, Erickson, & Touyz, 2004) and possibly up to six years after treatment (Hood & Eyberg, 2003). An abbreviated version of the PCIT has also been developed that seems to be equally efficacious (Nixon et al., 2003, 2004).

Videotaped Modeling and the Incredible Years Program

Carolyn Webster-Stratton (2005) has developed a comprehensive program for young children with emerging conduct problems. The Incredible Years program consists of separate modules for parents, teachers, and children. The program was designed especially for low-income, high-stress families—families most likely to drop out of traditional PMT (Webster-Stratton & Reid, 2007).

The **Incredible Years BASIC** parent training program resembles Barkley's Defiant Children program, with certain modifications made for children aged 2 to 10 years. The program consists of 14 parent training sessions, each approximately two hours long. Parents learn to attend to children's behavior, to reinforce appropriate actions, and to punish inappropriate actions using noncoercive methods. In the program, parents watch videotaped vignettes of parent-child interactions. These vignettes are designed to illustrate the problematic parent-child interactions that underlie children's conduct problems and to teach alternative, effective parenting behaviors. Parents watch the vignettes with other parents and then discuss the child management principles and parenting skills with each other and the therapist. The therapist acts as a collaborator and supporter rather than as a teacher. The therapist encourages parents to decide for themselves how to implement the parenting principles introduced by the program into their daily lives and to tailor the program to meet their individual needs.

The **Incredible Years ADVANCE** parent training program is offered to parents as a supplement to the BASIC program. Webster-Stratton (1990) realized that parents with high levels of stress and conflict in the home have difficulty implementing the BASIC program and avoiding hostile-coercive exchanges with their children (Webster-Stratton & Hammond, 1999). The ADVANCE program consists of 14 additional sessions that teach parents self-control and anger management strategies, communication skills, interpersonal problem-solving skills, and techniques to strengthen their social support network. These skills are designed to improve parents' mood states, to decrease family discord and tension, and to provide parents with the support they need to effectively implement the BASIC program.

The **Incredible Years Academic Skills Training (SCHOOL)** and **Teacher Training (TEACHER)** programs were developed as adjuncts to the BASIC and ADVANCE parent training programs. These programs were designed to improve the academic, behavioral, and social competence of children at school. The SCHOOL program consists of four to six sessions attended by groups of parents. It focuses on improving parents' involvement in their children's education, fostering parental collaboration with teachers, and increasing parents' monitoring of children's activities with peers. The TEACHER program is a workshop for teachers. Topics in this program include classroom management strategies, strengthening children's social skills and avoiding peer rejection, improving communication with parents, monitoring children's activities, and reducing physical aggression/bullying.

The **Incredible Years Child Training Program** was developed for four- to eight-year-old children with emerging conduct problems. This 22-week program is administered to small groups of children and uses a series of videotaped vignettes, puppets, and role-play activities to improve children's social functioning, especially at school. The program consists of empathy training, problem-solving skills training, anger control, friendship skills, and communication skills training. The overall goal is to teach children how to behave in class, how to make and keep friends, and how to play appropriately with peers (Webster-Stratton, 2005).

The efficacy of the Incredible Years BASIC and ADVANCE parent training programs have been investigated in a series of randomized, controlled studies (Webster-Stratton, 2005). Results show that the BASIC program is efficacious in improving parents' attitudes toward childrearing, their quality of parent-child interactions, and their children's behavior. Parents who participate in the program display fewer hostile-coercive behaviors toward their children; their children display fewer conduct problems over time. Parents who also participate in the ADVANCE program report improved interactions with their spouses, better communication and problem-solving skills, and greater satisfaction with treatment than parents who only participate in the BASIC program. These improvements in marital quality, communication, and problem solving are associated with improved parent-child interactions, especially for fathers.

The efficacy of the entire program has been evaluated on children with emerging conduct problems and low-income children at risk for developing conduct problems (Beauchaine, Webster-Stratton, & Reid, 2005; Webster-Stratton, Reid, & Hammond, 2001, 2004). Overall, children whose families participate in either parent-based, school-based, or child-based interventions show greater improvement in behavior than children whose families do not participate in treatment. Furthermore, children whose families participate in more of the treatment components (e.g., parent, teacher, *and* child training) fare better than families that participate in only one component. Across studies, the BASIC program tends to be the most effective component of the Incredible Years program. However, the ADVANCE program is especially efficacious for mothers with depression, fathers with histories of substance abuse, and families experiencing psychosocial stress (e.g., single-parent or low-income families).

Despite the success of the Incredible Years program, 25%–46% of parents report significant child behavior problems three years after completing treatment (Webster-Stratton, 1990; Webster-Stratton & Hammond, 1990). The best predictors of continued child behavior problems are high marital distress or spousal abuse, single-parent status, maternal depression, low socioeconomic status, high life stress, and a family history of substance abuse. These findings speak to the importance of programs like ADVANCE, which are designed to improve the socioemotional functioning of parents. Improvements in parents' mood and social functioning might help them respond to their children's needs and discipline in a consistent and noncoercive fashion.

Treatment for Older Children and Adolescents

Problem-Solving Skills Training

Problem-Solving Skills Training (PSST) is based on the notion that youths with disruptive behavior problems show characteristic biases in the way they perceive, interpret, and respond to interpersonal problems. These social information-processing biases interfere with their ability to respond to social dilemmas in prosocial ways and increase the likelihood that they will show hostile and aggressive behaviors (Reinecke, 2006).

Recall that social information processing consists of five steps: (1) encoding cues about the social situation, (2) interpreting these cues, (3) clarifying goals, (4) developing possible plans for action, and (5) evaluating and implementing the best plan to solve the problem. Children who show high levels of aggression often display biases in the ways they solve social problems. PSST attempts to correct the biased information-processing styles of aggressive children by teaching them how to systematically progress through these social problem-solving steps. In PSST, the child and therapist meet together for 12 to 20 sessions, each approximately 30 to 50 minutes in length.

The therapist initially teaches the child a simplified social problem-solving strategy (see Table 9.6). Each step prompts the child to attend to certain aspects of the interpersonal problem and helps the child solve the problem in prosocial ways. First, the child asks himself, "What am I supposed to do?" This requires the child to identify the problem and determine how he should act in the situation. Second, the child asks, "What are all my possibilities?" This step reminds the child to generate as many courses of action as possible. Third, the child says, "I'd better concentrate and focus in." This step encourages the child to evaluate the possible courses of action. Fourth, the child says, "I need to make a choice." This step requires the child to select the best response. Fifth, the child evaluates his actions and concludes either "I did a good job" or "I made a mistake." The steps slow the problem-solving process and help the child consider more information before acting.

In each session, the therapist usually begins by describing an interpersonal problem that the child might encounter in everyday life, for example, arguments during recess, on the bus, or in the hallways at school. The therapist then shows the child how to use the steps to solve the problem. Next, the therapist and child might role-play the situation. In the first few sessions, the child says each step aloud as he works through the problem. After the child becomes more familiar with the steps, he can solve the problem silently. Throughout each session, the therapist coaches the child in the use of the steps and provides praise and encouragement. Some therapists will also use a token economy during sessions. They reinforce the child's attention and participation in the session and withdraw tokens for inattentive, disruptive, or inappropriate behavior. If possible, parents are also taught the problem-solving steps. Parents are encouraged to prompt and reward the child for using the steps at home.

Table 9.6   Problem-Solving Steps and Self-Statements

Step	Self-Statement	Purpose
1.	What am I supposed to do?	This step requires the child to identify and define the problem.
2.	I have to look at all my possibilities.	This step asks the child to generate alternative solutions to the problem.
3.	I'd better concentrate and focus in.	This step instructs the child to concentrate and evaluate the solutions he has generated.
4.	I need to make a choice.	In this step, the child chooses the best action.
5.	I did a good job [or] I made a mistake	In the final step, the child verifies whether the solution was the best among those available, whether the problem-solving process was correctly followed, or whether a less-than-desirable solution was selected.

Source: Based on Kazdin and Weisz (2003).

Note: Problem-solving steps are taught through modeling and practiced during role play. The child and therapist alternate turns practicing the steps. The therapist prompts and shapes the child's use of the steps using reinforcement. As the child learns the steps, prompts are gradually faded. The child also progresses from saying the steps aloud (overt), to saying them silently (covert), to combining them.

PSST has been shown to be effective in reducing aggressive and disruptive behavior in school-aged children (Kazdin, 2005a). In several studies, children who participated in PSST showed greater symptom reduction than children who participated in an attention control group. Both inpatient and outpatient children showed improved functioning, relative to controls, and treatment gains were maintained one year later. Furthermore, children who participated in both PSST and PMT showed better outcomes than children who received either treatment alone (Kazdin, 2005a).

Multisystemic Therapy

Multisystemic therapy (MST) is an intensive form of family- and community-based treatment that has been shown to be effective in treating serious conduct problems in adolescents (Henggeler & Lee, 2003). Whereas PMT is frequently used for children and adolescents who show oppositional and defiant behaviors, MST is used most often used with adolescents who show more serious antisocial and violent behavior. In fact, MST has been used successfully with adolescents exhibiting chronic juvenile delinquency, violent crime, substance abuse, psychiatric crisis, and sexual offenses (Henggeler & Lee, 2003). In short, MST is one of the most successful interventions for adolescents with longstanding and serious behavior problems.

MST therapists target three systems essential to the adolescents' welfare: (1) family, (2) school, and (3) peers (Saldana & Henggeler, 2006). In the family, therapists might help parents develop more effective skills for interacting with their adolescents. For example, MST therapists might administer a parent training program, teach parents how to monitor their adolescents' whereabouts after school, or help parents learn to avoid conflict situations with their adolescents. MST therapists also try to remove obstacles that interfere with parents' abilities to provide supportive and consistent care. For example, therapists might address parents' marital discord, assist a parent in overcoming alcohol dependence, or increase the social support network of a single parent. In any case, MST therapists see themselves as resources and allies for parents. Therapists hope that by improving the skills and well-being of parents, these parents will more effectively manage their adolescents' behavior.

A second realm of intervention is the adolescent's school. Most MST therapists seek to increase parental involvement in their adolescents' education. Therapists might serve as liaisons between parents and teachers or help parents advocate for their children's educational needs. Therapists might teach parents to monitor their adolescents' attendance at school and behavior in the classroom. Again, therapists try to remove obstacles to the adolescents' academic achievement. For example, MST therapists might help to resolve any conflicts between parents and teachers or deal with practical problems, like helping parents find time to attend parent-teacher conferences.

A third avenue of intervention involves the adolescents' peers. Association with deviant peers is one of the best predictors of adolescent behavior problems. Consequently, MST therapists attempt to limit adolescents' opportunities for inter-actions with deviant peers and increase opportunities for interactions with proso-cial youth. At the very least, MST therapists encourage parents and other people involved in the adolescent's life (e.g., family members, teachers, police) to closely monitor his whereabouts, especially after school. At the same time, therapists might help the adolescent develop new peer networks. For example, a MST therapist might encourage an adolescent to try out for a sports team, join a club at school, or volunteer in the community. The therapist might also help the adolescent improve his social skills, in order to increase the likelihood that he will be accepted by proso-cial peers (Saldana & Henggeler, 2006).

MST is an intense, flexible, and family-friendly intervention. MST therapists usually work in teams of three to five and they are available 24 hours a day, seven days a week. Therapists usually meet with family members in their home or in the community, rather than in an office, in order to increase the family's attendance and involvement. MST usually lasts three to five months.

There is considerable evidence supporting the efficacy of MST for adolescents with conduct problems (Hart, Nelson, & Finch, 2006; Saldana & Henggeler, 2006). Across a number of randomized controlled trials, adolescents whose families par-ticipate in MST are 25% to 70% less likely to be rearrested and 47% to 64% less likely to be removed from their homes one to four years after treatment than families who do not participate in MST. Treatment appears to improve family func-tioning and parenting skills, which, in turn, decrease adolescents' association with deviant peers and their disruptive behavior (Huey, Henggeler, Brondino, & Pickrel, 2000; Saldana & Henggeler, 2006).

Recently, researchers examined the long-term outcomes of adolescents who par-ticipated in MST. In this study, 176 adolescents previously arrested for serious crimes were randomly assigned to receive either MST or traditional individual psychotherapy (Schaeffer & Borduin, 2005). The adolescents in the study averaged 3.9 arrests for felonies and 47.8% had at least one arrest for violent crime (e.g., sexual assault, assault and battery with intent to kill). Researchers examined arrest records approximately 13 years after treatment. Results showed that adolescents who participated in MST were less likely than adolescents who participated in individual therapy to be arrested for a future serious offense (see Figure 9.8). Furthermore, adolescents who participated in MST committed half as many offenses overall as adolescents who participated in individual therapy. These results suggest that MST is not only effective in reducing adolescent antisocial behavior, but it may have long-term effects on adolescents' developmental outcomes.

Unfortunately, MST programs are available to only about 1% of adolescents with serious conduct problems. Most therapists do not have formal training in MST. Although MST is intensive, it is less costly than out-of-home placement or incarceration. One study concluded a cost savings of approximately $60,000 per adolescent who participated in MST compared to adolescents who did not. Hopefully, continued research supporting MST will prompt individuals and agencies to develop programs in their communities (Henggeler & Lee, 2003).

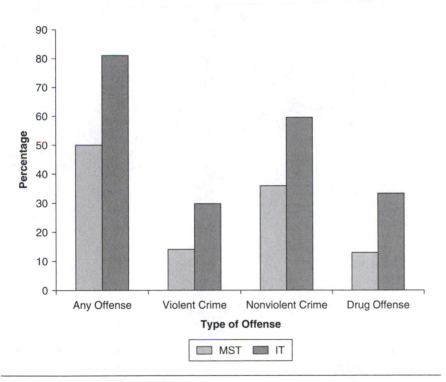

Figure 9.8   Efficacy of Multisystemic Therapy (MST)

Source: Based on Schaeffer and Borduin (2005).

Note: Researchers compared the behavioral outcomes of adolescents with conduct problems who participated in MST versus interpersonal therapy (IT), a non-behavioral form of treatment. Adolescents who participated in MST were less likely to show future antisocial behavior.

Update: Kyle and Brandyn

Kyle, the 14-year-old boy who was arrested for vandalizing school buses, met diagnostic criteria for Conduct Disorder. Although Kyle's mother attributed Kyle's misbehavior to a lack of paternal involvement, Dr. Witek thought that a wide range of interventions would be needed to reduce Kyle's antisocial behavior. Dr. Witek suggested that she initially meet with Kyle's mother alone to help her find ways to better monitor Kyle's behavior and to keep him away from situations that often led to his misbehavior. Unfortunately, Kyle was arrested for physically assaulting a classmate the following week and sent to a juvenile detention center. His long-term outcome is unknown.

Brandyn, the five-year-old boy who showed problems with aggression and defiance, had many features of Childhood-Onset Conduct Disorder. His therapist, Jim Reynolds, believed that Brandyn's mother and teacher needed help managing his behavior before it became more problematic.

Jim met individually with Brandyn's mother to help her find more effective ways to discipline Brandyn. First, Brandyn's mother read the book *Parenting the Strong-Willed Child,* to learn more about the causes of child noncompliance and how to deal with Brandyn's aggressive outbursts. Then, Jim met with Brandyn and his mother together so that he could observe the two interact in the clinic playroom (i.e., a variation of PCIT). He taught Brandyn's mother to reinforce Brandyn's appropriate behavior with praise and attention and to ignore Brandyn's tantrums. He also taught her how to give Brandyn clear commands and follow through with discipline. Finally, Jim helped her use time out more effectively when Brandyn became aggressive. Progress was slow, and Brandyn's mother missed several appointments because of her work schedule. However, the frequency and severity of Brandyn's outbursts decreased.

Jim recognized that Brandyn's mother's ability to correct Brandyn's defiant behavior was largely dependent on her own mental health. Jim suggested that she meet with her own therapist to help her cope with the social and emotional stress that she encountered in her daily life. She later reported that her participation in counseling was "most important" in helping her find the strength and patience to deal with her son.

Critical Thinking Exercises

1. What is the difference between ODD and CD? What is the evidence for and against viewing ODD as a developmental precursor for CD?

2. Why is CD much more commonly diagnosed among adolescent boys than adolescent girls? Are the diagnostic criteria for CD gender biased? Should they be changed?

3. Why might a clinician ask a parent *at what age* his child's conduct problems emerged? Will a young child with conduct problems "grow out of it"?

4. How might a child's temperament and early neurological development influence his likelihood of developing conduct problems later in life? Why don't all children with difficult temperaments develop CD?

5. Apply the concepts of (a) passive, (b) evocative, and (c) active gene-environment correlation to the development of CD.

6. Why are most interventions for conduct problems designed for *young* children? What psychosocial interventions, if any, can be efficacious with older children and adolescents? How are interventions for adolescents different from the treatments developed for young children?

CHAPTER 10

Substance Use Disorders in Adolescents

Erica

Erica was a 16-year-old girl who was referred to our clinic by the juvenile court after she was arrested for driving a car while intoxicated. Two weeks earlier, Erica had attended a party at her friend's house. She consumed approximately six or seven alcoholic beverages and drove home. A police officer noticed Erica driving erratically, pulled her over, and determined that her blood alcohol content was .09. Erica was arrested. Her father made her spend the night in jail "to teach her a lesson."

Erica resented having to meet with her substance abuse counselor, Randy Moore. She explained, "I don't know why I'm here. I'm not an addict, I don't use hard drugs, and I didn't do anything that a million other kids my age haven't done." Nevertheless, the judge ordered Erica to participate in a substance abuse evaluation, 12 sessions of counseling, and community service.

Erica began drinking alcohol, at parties and on weekends with friends, when she was 14 years old. She said that she hated beer but liked sweet drinks. "I mostly drink to relax and have fun with my friends," Erica said. "They call me 'Captain Cook' because that's the kind of champagne I like to drink. Drinking helps me unwind and have a good time." Erica admitted to also using marijuana at parties and other social gatherings, but denied using other drugs.

"Has your drinking ever gotten in the way of your daily life?" asked Randy. Erica replied, "Not really, although I have been hung over a few times this year." Randy asked, "What about school?" Erica responded, "I guess my grades are lower now than when I started high school. But I think that's because I hang around with different kids than I used to. I don't think it's the drinking."

"What's your relationship with your mom and dad like?" asked Randy. Erica replied, "It's fine. My mom's a doctor and my dad's an investment banker, so they're pretty busy. As long as I bring home good grades and stay out of trouble, they leave me alone. Now they're on my case because of the arrest."

After the initial session, Erica stated, "I know I have to be here, and I'm really sorry for what I did, but I obviously don't have a drinking problem. Besides, I'm sure you have people worse off than me who really need your help." Randy responded, "Let's schedule an appointment for next week and talk some more."

What Are Substance Use Disorders?

People are diagnosed with substance use disorders when they show a problematic pattern of alcohol or other drug use that interferes with their daily functioning or causes significant psychological distress. *DSM-IV-TR* uses the term "substance" to refer to drugs and medications that can be misused. It identifies 11 classes of substances including nicotine, alcohol, marijuana, cocaine, opioids (e.g., heroin), and hallucinogens. Most research on substance use disorders in adolescents has been directed at alcohol and marijuana use problems. Consequently, in this chapter, we will focus our attention on alcohol and marijuana use in adolescents as a model for understanding and treating substance use disorders more generally.

DSM-IV-TR distinguishes between two substance use disorders: Substance Abuse and Substance Dependence. Both disorders are characterized by repeated, problematic use of alcohol or other drugs; however, Substance Abuse indicates less severe impairment than Substance Dependence.

Substance Abuse

According to *DSM-IV-TR*, Substance Abuse is "a maladaptive pattern of substance use manifested by recurrent and significant adverse consequences related to the repeated use of substances" (p. 198). To be diagnosed with Substance Abuse, the adolescent's alcohol or other drug use must have adversely affected her social, academic, or occupational functioning repeatedly during a 12-month period (see Table 10.1).

DSM-IV-TR identifies four possible negative consequences of Substance Abuse. First, the adolescent might repeatedly fail to fulfill major role obligations at home, school, or work. For example, a high school student might repeatedly miss class because she oversleeps after drinking too much the previous evening. Second, the adolescent might repeatedly use substances in situations that are particularly

Table 10.1   Diagnostic Criteria for Substance Abuse

A. A maladaptive pattern of substance use leading to clinically significant impairment or distress, as manifested by one (or more) of the following, occurring within a 12-month period:

1. Recurrent substance use resulting in a failure to fulfill major role obligations at home, school, or work (e.g., repeated absences or poor performance related to substance use; substance-related absences, suspensions, or expulsions from school)

2. Recurrent substance use in situations in which it is physically hazardous (e.g., driving an automobile when impaired by substance use)

3. Recurrent substance-related legal problems (e.g., arrests for substance-related disorderly conduct)

4. Continued substance use despite having persistent or recurrent social or interpersonal problems caused or exacerbated by the effects of the substance (e.g., arguments with family members about consequences of intoxication, physical fights)

B. The symptoms have never met the criteria for Substance Dependence for this class of substance.

Source: Reprinted with permission from the *DSM-IV-TR*.

hazardous. For example, a 16-year-old might frequently drive while intoxicated after parties. Third, the adolescent might experience recurrent substance-related legal problems. For example, an adolescent might be arrested twice for disorderly conduct and criminal mischief after acting out while intoxicated. Fourth, the adolescent might continue to use substances despite recurrent social problems associated with substance use. For example, a junior high school student might continue to drink excessively at parties even though his drinking has led to arguments with his parents and a loss of his old friends.

Substance Abuse is only diagnosed when adolescents repeatedly use alcohol and other drugs in a manner that causes significant distress or impairment. The term "abuse" is not synonymous with the term "use." Many younger adolescents and most older adolescents occasionally use substances, especially nicotine and alcohol. Some youngsters use these substances repeatedly. However, repeated use does not constitute "abuse" until it leads to distress or impairment.

Substance Dependence

Substance Dependence is considered a more serious problem than Substance Abuse. Adolescents with Substance Dependence display a cluster of "cognitive, behavioral, and physiological symptoms" indicating that they use alcohol or other drugs despite multiple, significantly adverse effects (*DSM-IV-TR*, p. 192). Adolescents who show Substance Dependence display a number of serious impairments similar to those of adolescents with Substance Abuse. In addition, adolescents with Substance Dependence have a general loss of control over their substance use. The hallmarks of Substance Dependence are tolerance and withdrawal.

Table 10.2   *Diagnostic Criteria for Substance Dependence*

A. A maladaptive pattern of substance use leading to clinically significant impairment or distress, as manifested by three (or more) of the following, occurring within a 12-month period:

1. Tolerance, as defined by either of the following:
    a. A need for markedly increased amounts of the substance to achieve intoxication or desired effect
    b. Markedly diminished effect with continued use of the same amount of the substance

2. Withdrawal, as manifested by either of the following:
    a. Characteristic withdrawal syndrome for the substance
    b. The same (or a closely related) substance is taken to avoid withdrawal symptoms

3. The substance is often taken in larger amounts or over a longer period than was intended

4. There is a persistent desire or unsuccessful efforts to cut down or control substance use

5. A great deal of time is spent in activities necessary to obtain the substance, use the substance, or recover from its effects

6. Important social, occupational, or recreational activities are given up or reduced because of the substance use

7. The substance use is continued despite knowledge of having a persistent or recurrent physical or psychological problem that is likely to have been caused or exacerbated by the substance

---

Source: Reprinted with permission from the *DSM-IV-TR*.

Tolerance occurs when individuals need to take the substance more frequently or at higher doses to achieve the same subjective effects. Typically, the positive effects of most substances are strongest after their first use. With each subsequent administration, people need to take more of the substance to produce the same benefits. Physiologically, the body compensates for the recurrent presence of the drug by decreasing its response to the substance. The rate of tolerance depends on the substance. Some substances, such as cocaine and heroin, result in rapid tolerance. Other substances, such as marijuana, produce tolerance more slowly. The rate at which tolerance occurs partially determines the likelihood of dependence.

Withdrawal refers to the negative physiological and psychological symptoms caused by decreased use of the substance. Withdrawal symptoms most often occur when a person suddenly discontinues use. The symptoms of withdrawal depend on the nature of the substance; different drugs have different withdrawal symptoms. However, withdrawal symptoms are usually the opposite of the effects of ingesting the substance. For example, smoking marijuana produces relaxation and a state of emotional well-being in most people. After long-term marijuana use, discontinuation of the drug can cause the opposite effects: anxiety, agitation, and irritability.

To be diagnosed with Substance Dependence, the adolescent must show three or more dependence symptoms during a 12-month period. These symptoms include tolerance, withdrawal, and several other indicators of problematic use. Because the diagnosis of Substance Dependence indicates more problematic use of alcohol and/or other drugs than the diagnosis of Substance Abuse, an adolescent who meets diagnostic criteria for Substance Dependence is not assigned the additional diagnosis of Substance Abuse.

Problems Diagnosing Substance Use Disorders in Adolescents

Some researchers have claimed that the *DSM-IV-TR* substance use disorders do not apply well to adolescents (Chung, Martin, Armstrong, & Labouvie, 2002; Deas, Roberts, & Grindlinger, 2005; Martin, Chung, Kirisci, & Langenbucher, 2006). One criticism is that the *DSM-IV-TR* criteria are developmentally insensitive. The symptoms most commonly seen among adolescents who misuse alcohol and other drugs are absent from the *DSM-IV-TR* criteria. For example, two of the most frequently occurring signs of Alcohol Abuse and Dependence among adolescents are academic problems and truancy. However, neither problem is included in the current diagnostic criteria. Consequently, some researchers have developed more developmentally appropriate criteria for adolescent substance use problems. These criteria include (1) breaking curfew, (2) lying to parents, (3) showing a reduction in grades, and (4) engaging in truancy (E. F. Wagner & Austin, 2006).

A second criticism is that the *DSM-IV-TR* conceptualization of Alcohol Dependence does not differentiate adolescents with and without alcohol use problems. A hallmark of Alcohol Dependence is tolerance for alcohol. However, most adolescent drinkers show tolerance whether they use alcohol occasionally or daily. Another feature of Alcohol Dependence is withdrawal symptoms after the person stops regular use. However, most adolescents (even the heaviest drinkers) do not show symptoms of alcohol withdrawal, probably because adolescents usually have shorter histories of alcohol use than adults.

A third criticism is that adolescents often show different patterns of alcohol and other drug use than adults (E. F. Wagner & Austin, 2006). Adolescent substance use differs from adult substance use in several ways:

- Adolescent substance use, especially alcohol use, is more episodic than alcohol use by adults. Most adolescents tend to drink in binges, especially at parties. They usually do not drink every day.
- Adolescents often use a greater number of substances simultaneously than do adults. Indeed, it is more common for adolescents to misuse alcohol and marijuana together than to misuse either substance alone. In contrast, most adults who show substance use problems have a single substance of choice.
- Adolescents with substance use disorders are more likely to show comorbid behavior problems than are adults with substance use disorders. Furthermore, adolescents are more likely to show disruptive and antisocial behaviors, whereas adults are more likely to develop mood and anxiety disorders associated with their substance use.

Finally, adolescents are more likely than adults to "outgrow" their substance use problems. Because of the great number of physiological and psychosocial changes occurring during adolescence, many adolescents show a gradual reduction in substance use by the time they reach early adulthood. For example, many older adolescents use alcohol fairly regularly, especially during their late teens and early twenties. However, most young adults dramatically reduce their alcohol consumption after they assume more adult-like responsibilities (e.g., gain full-time employment, have children). Although all serious substance use problems merit treatment regardless of the person's age, adolescents usually show a different course of substance use than do adults.

Alcohol and Marijuana Use, Abuse, and Dependence

Alcohol

Alcohol is the drug most widely used by adolescents. Alcohol is often overlooked as a possible drug of abuse because of its widespread availability in the United States. Alcohol is legal in nearly all parts of the country, and it is heavily advertised on television and in magazines. Furthermore, many adolescents and parents regard alcohol consumption as part of adolescent culture. After all, most adolescents drink alcohol at least occasionally at some point during their high school years. For these reasons, adolescents and adults tend to minimize the risks associated with alcohol use (Johnston et al., 2005).

Psychological Effects of Alcohol

Alcohol is technically a **sedative**. It falls into the same class of drugs as benzodiazepines, barbiturates, and most sleeping pills. The effects of alcohol depend on the amount consumed. Experts usually describe its effects as **biphasic**. Mild to moderate alcohol use produces one set of (largely desirable) effects: increased arousal, sociability, euphoria, and reduced anxiety. Extended alcohol consumption produces a different cluster of (largely aversive) effects: sedation, cognitive and motor impairments, heart and respiratory problems, and other health risks (Perham, Moore, Shepherd, & Cusens, 2007).

Moderate alcohol consumption usually produces pleasurable effects. Consequently, many adolescents will continue to drink in order to maintain or enhance these subjective feelings of well-being. Unfortunately, excessive alcohol consumption produces less-than-desirable effects in most people. Excessive alcohol use can result in **binge drinking**, that is, consuming five or more alcoholic beverages in a single episode. Binge drinking can cause fatigue, dizziness, nausea, and blackout. Bingeing may also produce severe impairment in judgment and problem solving. Physiologically, binge drinking is associated with disturbances in balance and coordination, slurred speech, restlessness and irritability, and problems with heart rate and respiration. In rare cases, excessive alcohol consumption can cause coma and death.

Physiological Effects of Alcohol

Alcohol is rapidly absorbed by the gastrointestinal tract and quickly diffuses throughout the bloodstream. It is metabolized primarily by the liver. The enzymes **alcohol dehydrogenase** and **acetaldehyde dehydrogenase** are chiefly responsible for its metabolism. The exact mechanisms by which alcohol affects mood, cognition, and behavior are unknown. However, alcohol seems to affect the functioning of at least five major neurotransmitters: norepinephrine, glutamate, dopamine, opioids, and GABA (γ- aminobutyric acid; Kosten, George, & Kleber, 2005; Meyer & Quenzer, 2005; Nace, 2005).

First, low doses of alcohol stimulate the norepinephrine system, causing increased feelings of arousal and behavioral excitation. Alcohol seems to target a brain region known as the reticular formation, located near the base of the brain. The **reticular formation** is responsible for alerting us to important information in the environment and initiating attention and arousal. Increased norepinephrine activity in this brain area is probably responsible for the increase in alertness, sociability, and talkativeness shown by most people after one or two alcoholic beverages.

At the same time, alcohol affects glutamate functioning. Glutamate is a major excitatory neurotransmitter in the central nervous system. Alcohol acts to inhibit the neurotransmission of glutamate, thereby slowing neuronal activity. Specifically, alcohol interferes with certain glutamate receptor sites, especially the NMDA (N-methyl-D-aspartate) receptor. Consumption of one or two alcoholic beverages can begin to decrease glutamate activity, producing feelings of relaxation and stress reduction. Reduced glutamate activity might partially explain the negatively reinforcing properties of alcohol; alcohol can alleviate anxiety. Glutamate is also partially responsible for associative learning and memory. Excessive alcohol use, therefore, can lead to memory problems including difficulty forming new memories and periods of memory loss (i.e., "blackouts").

Moderate alcohol consumption affects dopamine activity. Researchers have identified a neural pathway that they believe is responsible for the pleasurable effects of most addictive drugs, including alcohol. This "reward pathway" extends from the ventral tegmental area (VTA) of the midbrain to the nucleus accumbens, amygdala, and hippocampus, located in the limbic system. This neural pathway responds primarily to dopamine, a neurotransmitter responsible for feelings of pleasure, positive affect (i.e., energy, sociability), and increased motor activity. Because this dopamine-rich pathway extends from the midbrain (VTA) to the limbic system, it is called the **dopaminergic mesolimbic pathway**.

How does the dopaminergic mesolimbic pathway operate? Alcohol stimulates dopaminergic neurons in the VTA. The VTA, in turn, increases dopamine levels in a nearby brain area, the nucleus accumbens, producing subjective feelings of euphoria, pleasure, and emotional well-being. These pleasant effects constitute the first phase of the "biphasic" response to alcohol, and they are the primary reason most people, especially adolescents, drink. Furthermore, these pleasurable feelings also positively reinforce alcohol use, making the person consume more of the drug. Alcohol also increases neuronal activity in the amygdala and hippocampus, brain areas responsible for processing emotions and forming new memories. The increased activity of these brain regions may account for the highly emotional memories associated with alcohol consumption and the "cravings" for alcohol experienced by chronic drinkers.

Alcohol produces other pleasurable effects through its activity on the body's production of natural opioids. Researchers have discovered opioid receptors throughout the brain. These receptors are primarily responsible for subjective feelings of satisfaction and alleviation of pain. Typically, the body makes natural opioids (i.e., endorphin, enkephalin) to cope with stressful or painful situations. These opioids are produced by the pituitary gland and released into the bloodstream to circulate throughout the body. Alcohol consumption increases the release of endogenous opioids, producing these pleasurable effects.

Finally, moderate alcohol consumption affects GABA, a major inhibitory neurotransmitter. GABA binds to receptor sites throughout the central nervous system, causing cells to rapidly take in negatively charged chloride ions. This increase in negatively charged particles makes cells less likely to fire. Alcohol enhances the effects of GABA, producing a rapid influx of chloride into cells and a general decrease in neuronal activity. This decrease in neuronal activity is partially responsible for many of the sedating effects of alcohol: relaxation, cognitive sluggishness, and slowed reaction time.

Most adolescents who use alcohol experience tolerance; that is, they report needing more alcohol to achieve previous levels of euphoria (Chung et al., 2002). Researchers distinguish between two types of tolerance (Meyer & Quenzer, 2005). First, adolescents can experience **acute tolerance** during a single drinking episode. Specifically, people experience the greatest effects of alcohol after only a few drinks, with diminishing effects after each successive drink. Many adolescents often try to "chase the high" by continuing their alcohol use after reaching this period of diminishing returns. Unfortunately, continued use results in increased sedation rather than increased pleasure.

Second, chronic alcohol use is associated with **pharmacodynamic tolerance** (Koob & LeMoal, 2006). Over sustained periods of time, the sensitivity of the neuroreceptors that respond to alcohol gradually decreases. For example, long-term alcohol use is associated with decreased sensitivity of GABA and dopamine receptors. Individuals who drink frequently may not exhibit the same sedating effects of alcohol due to this decrease in sensitivity to GABA. Frequent drinkers may also require more alcohol to achieve a state of euphoria due to decreased dopamine activity. Decreased receptor sensitivity is believed to be a homeostatic mechanism, that is, a way for the body to compensate for the individual's history of excessive alcohol use.

Because of this decrease in sensitivity, abrupt discontinuation of alcohol can produce withdrawal symptoms in chronic users. Without alcohol, the body's sensitivity to GABA and dopamine is diminished. Consequently, chronic drinkers who stop using alcohol may experience negative effects due to the relative underactivity of these neurotransmitters. Decreased GABA sensitivity can produce feelings of anxiety, excitability, irritability, restlessness, and excessive motor activity. Some adults experience delirium tremens, a cluster of symptoms that include tremors, seizures, confusion, and visual and tactile hallucinations. Decreased dopamine activity can cause low energy, fatigue, and depression.

Marijuana

Marijuana is the most commonly used illegal drug. Marijuana contains dozens of compounds known to affect brain chemistry. These compounds fall into a certain class called cannabinoids. The most powerful cannabinoid is **delta-9-tetrahydrocannabinol** (THC; O'Brien et al., 2005).

Psychological Effects of Marijuana

When someone smokes a marijuana cigarette, approximately half of the THC enters the lungs and is rapidly absorbed. Within seconds of the first puff, THC enters the brain and affects mood, cognition, and behavior.

Moderate doses of marijuana usually produce mild intoxication. Within seconds of use, people often feel lightheaded and dizzy. Some people report tingling sensations in their limbs. After a few minutes, most people experience feelings of euphoria, disinhibition, and increased energy and sociability. Continued use (10–30 minutes) produces reductions in anxiety, a general sense of relaxation, and a state of emotional well-being or contentment. Cognitive and motor processes are usually slowed. For example, marijuana users may show slowed movements, speech, or problem-solving ability. Slowed cognitive and motor responses can interfere with people's abilities to perform complex mental activities (e.g., complete homework) and motor activities (e.g., drive a car). Effects typically last a few hours. Larger doses of marijuana can cause paradoxical effects: increased anxiety and agitation, perceptual distortions or visual hallucinations, and paranoia.

Physiological Effects of Marijuana

THC is detected by cannabinoid receptors located throughout the brain. The largest concentrations of these receptors are in the basal ganglia, cerebellum, hippocampus, and cortex. When THC is detected by these receptors, it causes a reduction in the cell's metabolic activity and the activity of neurotransmitters. The specific effects of THC depend on *where* it is detected. For example, THC detected by the basal ganglia affects movement and coordination, whereas THC detected by receptors in the cortex affects thinking, judgment, and problem solving.

THC is known to affect a wide range of neurotransmitters, including norepinephrine, dopamine, glutamate, GABA, and serotonin. The multiple brain areas and neurotransmitters affected by THC likely account for the diverse effects of the substance on people's behavior.

Experts disagree about the long-term physiological risks of repeated marijuana use (O'Brien et al., 2005). People who frequently use marijuana often show impairments in attention, memory, and problem-solving ability relative to individuals who do not use the drug. Some researchers, but not all, have found that these cognitive impairments persist for weeks or months after discontinuing marijuana use (Pope & Yurgelun-Todd, 2004). Many chronic users show decreased motivation and goal-directed behavior, a phenomenon called **amotivational syndrome** (Meyer & Quenzer, 2005). However, experts are unsure whether this lack of motivation is caused by the physiological effects of the drug or by environmental factors associated with drug use. For example, people who frequently use marijuana may drop out of mainstream culture and adopt an unconventional lifestyle characterized by low achievement motivation.

Perhaps the most serious effect of chronic marijuana use is health impairment. Smoking marijuana is associated with the same health risks as smoking cigarettes: respiratory problems, circulatory problems, and cancer. Marijuana can also suppress immune functioning. Finally, the effects of marijuana can impair people's sensory and motor functioning, increasing their likelihood of injury.

Most people show acute tolerance to marijuana. During the course of a single marijuana episode, most people need to use more of the drug to achieve the initial state of intoxication. Animal studies demonstrate pharmacodynamic tolerance to marijuana. Long-term use causes reductions in the number and sensitivity of cannabinoid receptors in animals. There is less evidence for pharmacodynamic tolerance in humans; however, many people who frequently use marijuana report needing more of the drug after months or years of use.

Frequent marijuana use can cause dependence. Individuals who are dependent on marijuana report cravings for the drug and show a characteristic pattern of withdrawal symptoms associated with abstinence. Frequent users who are denied the drug can experience sleep and appetite disturbance, anxiety, agitation, restlessness, and general irritability. Sometimes, marijuana withdrawal is also associated with physical symptoms such as sweating, chills, and nausea. Chronic marijuana users show more severe withdrawal symptoms including intense cravings for the drug, depression, anger, bizarre dreams, and headaches. Withdrawal symptoms typically last only a few days.

Associated Psychiatric Disorders

Approximately 50% of adolescents in the community with Substance Abuse or Dependence show at least one other mental disorder. Among adolescents referred to treatment, comorbidity ranges from 50% to 90% (Rowe, Liddle, Greenbaum, & Henderson, 2004).

Adolescents who have both a substance use problem and a psychiatric diagnosis show greater impairment than adolescents with either substance use or psychiatric problems alone. Specifically, adolescents with dual diagnoses show more school-related difficulties, greater family conflict, more emotional distress, and more legal problems than adolescents with either substance use disorders or psychiatric disturbances alone (Grella, Hser, Joshi, & Rounds-Bryant, 2001). Adolescents with dual diagnoses also show poorer prognoses. They are more likely to have substance use problems during adulthood, experience long-term psychiatric illness, and develop personality disorders.

Adolescents with both substance use and mental health problems may be less responsive to treatment than adolescents with substance use or mental disorders alone. Adolescents with dual diagnoses are more likely to drop out of treatment or relapse within one year of treatment completion (Rowe et al., 2004; Wise, Cuffe, & Fischer, 2001).

Behavior Problems

ADHD is the most frequently occurring psychiatric disorder shown by adolescents with Substance Abuse (Dennis et al., 2002, 2004). Approximately 15%–30% of adolescents with ADHD eventually develop a substance use disorder. Conversely, most (50%–75%) adolescents with substance use disorders have ADHD. Adolescents with ADHD and substance use problems show more severe symptoms of both disorders and greater impairment in overall functioning. Their substance use tends to be longer and more resistant to treatment than that of individuals without ADHD. After treatment for substance use problems, youths with ADHD are more than twice as likely to relapse compared to adolescents without ADHD (Latimer, Ernst, Hennessey, Stinchfield, & Winters, 2004).

The relationship between ADHD and Substance Abuse is unclear (J. J. Wilson & Levin, 2005). At least three hypotheses have been offered to explain their high comorbidity. First, ADHD and substance use problems can have a common genetic or biological cause. For example, adolescents with both disorders display problems with executive functioning and behavioral inhibition that could stem from their genetic makeup. Second, both ADHD and substance use problems are correlated with other disruptive behavior disorders. For example, children with ADHD show increased likelihood of developing ODD and CD later in their development. ODD and CD, in turn, are associated with adolescent substance use problems. It is possible that ADHD, ODD/CD, and substance use problems are part of a spectrum of externalizing behavior that unfolds across development. Third, symptoms of ADHD could increase the probability of substance use problems. For example, individuals with ADHD often show problems with decision making, social problem solving, and peer relations. These problems can cause peer rejection, social isolation, and depression. Rejected children with ADHD might use substances to gain acceptance from peers or to cope with feelings of loneliness.

Approximately 35%–40% of adolescents with substance abuse also meet diagnostic criteria for CD (Henggeler, Pickrel, Brondino, & Crouch, 1996; Kaminer, Burleson, & Goldberger, 2002). Furthermore, nearly 90% of youths with substance use disorders show at least some problems with oppositional, defiant, or disruptive behavior (Waldron, Slesnick, Brody, Charles, & Thomas, 2001). Among adolescents with CD, alcohol and other drug abuse is usually part of a much larger problem with impulsive, disruptive, and destructive behavior.

Depression and Anxiety

Approximately 25%–50% of adolescents with substance use problems are depressed. Longitudinal data indicate that most adolescents do not use alcohol and other drugs primarily to cope with depression. Instead, mood disorders often develop after the onset of adolescents' substance use problems. Comorbid depression and substance use problems can sometimes be explained by shared genetic and psychosocial risk factors, as well (Goodwin, Fergusson, & Horwood, 2004).

Adolescents with substance use problems show greater likelihood of suicidal thoughts, suicide attempts, and suicide completion than their counterparts without substance use disorders (Kaminer & Bukstein, 2005). Mood problems, especially depression, associated with substance use partially account for the relationship between substance use and suicidal ideation. However, at least one study showed that the likelihood of suicide attempts remained elevated even after controlling for co-occurring depression (Wu, Hoven, Liu, Cohen, Fuller, & Shaffer, 2005). It is possible that alcohol and other drugs increase the likelihood of adolescent suicide by producing feelings of dysphoria, by lowering adolescents' inhibitions against self-harm, and by increasing impulsive and risky decision making.

Approximately 10%–40% of adolescents with substance use problems show comorbid anxiety (Kaminer & Bukstein, 2005; Waldron et al., 2001). The relationship between substance use and anxiety is complex. Some anxiety disorders usually precede the development of adolescents' substance use problems. For example, some adolescents use alcohol and other drugs to cope with social anxiety or unwanted memories of traumatic experiences. Alternatively, other anxiety disorders usually develop after the onset of substance use problems. For example, chronic use of alcohol can produce a gradual increase in worry and generalized anxiety.

Psychotic Disorders

Three large community based studies have demonstrated an association between adolescent marijuana use and the development of psychotic symptoms later in life (Crome & Bloor, 2005). Adolescents who regularly used marijuana were more likely to report psychotic symptoms (e.g., hallucinations, delusions) or develop

Schizophrenia in late adolescence or early adulthood compared to adolescents who did not use marijuana. The association between marijuana use and psychotic symptoms could not be explained by adolescents' levels of psychological distress. Therefore, it is unlikely that adolescents who eventually showed psychotic symptoms used marijuana to treat early symptoms of psychosis. Instead, the data suggest that repeated marijuana use may increase the likelihood of psychotic symptoms, especially among those adolescents who have a genetic predisposition toward Schizophrenia.

Epidemiology

Prevalence

Prevalence of Adolescent Substance Use

To estimate prevalence, scientists at the University of Michigan Institute for Social Research have annually assessed adolescent substance use in a project called Monitoring the Future (MTF; Johnston, O'Malley, Bachman, & Schulenberg, 2006). These researchers collect data regarding adolescents' attitudes and overt behavior regarding substance use. In recent years, approximately 50,000 youths in eighth, tenth, and twelfth grades have completed anonymous surveys. Their data allow us to determine normative substance use throughout adolescence and see trends in adolescents' substance use over the past 30 years.

Recent data indicate that adolescent alcohol use is common (Johnston et al., 2006). By their senior year in high school, nearly 75% of adolescents have used alcohol at some point in their lives, approximately 65% have used alcohol in the past year, and almost 50% have used alcohol in the past 30 days. A sizable minority of younger adolescents also report alcohol use. Approximately 40% of students in eighth grade report trying alcohol at some point in their lives, while 15% report alcohol use in the previous month (see Figure 10.1).

Marijuana use is also fairly widespread, especially among older adolescents. Approximately 45% of high school seniors have tried marijuana; almost 18% have used it within the past month. Marijuana use is less common among younger adolescents. Only about 15% of eighth-grade students report having tried the drug.

Although many adolescents report having tried alcohol and marijuana, most adolescents do not try other illicit drugs. Only about 25% of high school seniors have tried another illicit substance in their lifetime. Excluding alcohol and marijuana, the most commonly used drugs among twelfth-grade students were prescription medications, including Vicodin (10%), other medicinal narcotics (9%), medicinal amphetamines (9%), barbiturates (7%), tranquilizers (7%), and OxyContin (6%). Less than 6% of high school seniors reported trying other so-called "street" drugs like hallucinogens, crack cocaine, heroin, and methamphetamines (Feinberg, 2006).

In general, substance use has decreased over the past decade (Kuehn, 2006). The greatest reductions in substance use have been for drugs like marijuana, LSD,

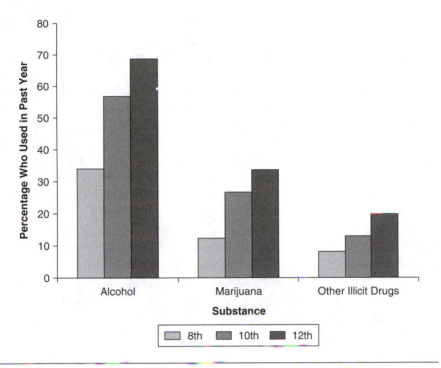

Figure 10.1   Percentage of Youth Who Have Used Various Substances in the Past Year

Source: From Johnston et al. (2006). Used with permission.

Note: Most tenth through twelfth graders have tried alcohol; approximately 25% have tried marijuana.

methamphetamine, and ecstasy. Although these drugs reached peak levels in the middle to late 1990s, their use has been decreasing ever since. In contrast, occasional alcohol use among adolescents has remained fairly steady over the years. Use of other drugs, especially prescription medications, seems to be on the rise among adolescents.

Data from MTF indicate that alcohol use during adolescence is developmentally normative. Furthermore, marijuana use by older adolescents is fairly common, with almost half of twelfth-grade students admitting to trying marijuana. Besides alcohol and marijuana, the illicit drugs most frequently used by adolescents appear to be prescription medications. Adolescent substance use is largely opportunistic. Most adolescents obtain alcohol, marijuana, and prescription drugs from friends, classmates, and family (e.g., stealing from parents). In contrast, use of "street drugs" like cocaine and methamphetamine is relatively uncommon.

Prevalence of Adolescent Substance Abuse and Dependence

What about substance use disorders? Studies assessing the prevalence of adolescent Substance Abuse and Dependence have yielded inconsistent findings. Results vary depending on the sample of adolescents studied, the method of questioning, and the researcher's definitions of "abuse" and "dependence."

One method of defining "abuse" and "dependence" is to use *DSM-IV-TR* definitions to identify youths with substance abuse problems. When researchers use *DSM-IV-TR* diagnostic criteria, the prevalence of Substance Abuse among adolescents in the community ranges from 1% to 9%, while the prevalence of Substance Dependence among adolescents in the community ranges from 1% to 5%.

A second method of classifying substance use problems is to base classification on the frequency of use. For example, many researchers believe that daily use of alcohol or marijuana for one month or longer indicates a significant substance use disorder. Using this criterion, almost 3% of high school seniors abuse alcohol while almost 5% abuse marijuana (Johnston et al., 2006; see Figure 10.2).

Yet a third technique involves classifying alcohol abuse in terms of binge drinking. Binge drinking is often associated with increased intoxication, risk-taking behavior, and many of the harmful effects of alcohol use. Unfortunately, binge drinking is fairly common among adolescents. Approximately 25% of high school seniors admit to binge drinking in the past two weeks, while less than 10% of eighth-grade students admit to bingeing (see Figure 10.3). Interestingly, there is a

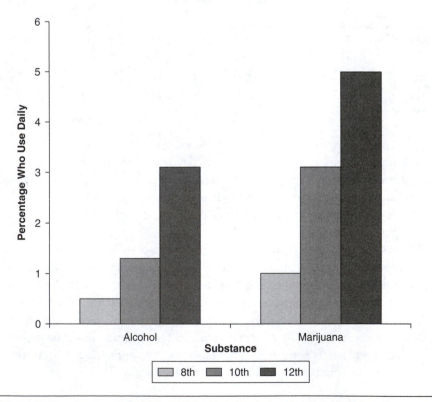

Figure 10.2 Percentage of Youth Who Use Alcohol or Marijuana Daily

Source: From Johnston et al. (2006). Used with permission.

Note: Most people regard daily use of alcohol and marijuana by adolescents as problematic. Using this criterion, approximately 3%–5% of youth have substance use problems.

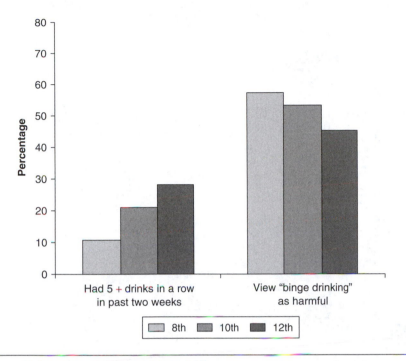

Figure 10.3   Binge Drinking Among Adolescents

Source: From Johnston et al. (2006). Used with permission.

Note: Approximately 25% of twelfth graders binge drink. Although binge drinking carries serious risk, most older adolescents do not regard it as harmful.

moderate, inverse relationship between binge drinking and perceived risk associated with bingeing. Adolescents who show the greatest rate of binge drinking are least likely to view their consumption as dangerous.

Gender Differences

Patterns of substance use differ slightly for boys and girls. Boys usually begin using cigarettes, alcohol, and marijuana at earlier ages than girls (Andrews, 2005). At any given age, the percentage of boys who have tried any of these substances is slightly higher than the percentage of girls (Johnston et al., 2005; see Figure 10.4). Boys are also more likely than girls to binge drink, to engage in dangerous activities as a result of their substance use, and to get into trouble at school because of alcohol or other drugs.

Gender differences in the rates of substance use disorders are less clear. Some research indicates that adolescent boys show greater prevalence of Substance Abuse and Dependence than girls. For example, approximately 30% of adolescent boys report binge drinking compared to only about 22% of adolescent girls. Other studies have not found gender differences in substance use disorders (Johnston et al., 2005).

The presentation of substance use problems is different for adolescent boys and girls (Andrews, 2005; Hsieh & Hollister, 2004). Boys with substance use problems

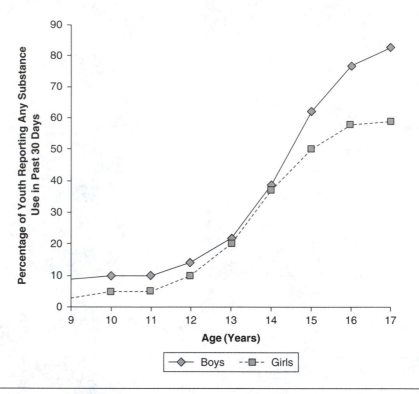

Figure 10.4   Gender Differences in Substance Use

Source: Based on Sambrano, Springer, Sale, Kasim, and Hermann (2005).

Note: Boys tend to use alcohol and other drugs at slightly earlier ages than girls.

are more likely than girls to show comorbid disruptive behavior. Boys with substance use disorders show high rates of impulsivity, aggression, and antisocial behaviors. They are also more likely than girls to experience legal problems associated with their substance use. For boys, Substance Abuse usually reflects a more general problem with conduct and antisocial behavior.

Girls with substance use problems often report greater emotional disturbance than boys. These girls often show comorbid problems with depression, anxiety, and physical complaints. Girls with substance use problems are also more likely than boys to have histories of family problems and sexual abuse.

Ethnicity

Substance use differs by ethnicity (Wagner & Austin, 2006). Native American youth show the highest rates of substance use, abuse, and dependence overall, followed by white and Hispanic adolescents. Native American and white adolescents also begin using alcohol and other drugs at earlier ages and may show greater comorbid psychiatric problems than most other ethnic minorities living in the United States (Abbott, 2007).

African American and Asian American adolescents show the lowest rates of substance use, abuse, and dependence. The low prevalence of substance use problems among African American adolescents is remarkable because African American adolescents are disproportionately exposed to risk factors associated with substance use disorders, such as low SES (Gil, Vega, & Turner, 2002). It is possible that certain aspects of African American culture somehow protect these youths from developing substance use problems. For example, involvement in extended family kinships or church activities may buffer African American youths against the potentially harmful effects of socioeconomic hardship.

Hispanic American adolescents usually show prevalence rates somewhere between those of white and African American adolescents (see Figure 10.5). However, Hispanic American adolescents show the greatest use of certain "hard" drugs such as cocaine and crack. Furthermore, Hispanic American adolescents born in the United States show greater rates of drug abuse and dependence than Hispanic American adolescents born in other countries (Vega, Gil, & Wagner, 1998). Among foreign-born adolescents, acculturation and ethnic identity seem to influence their likelihood of using alcohol and other drugs.

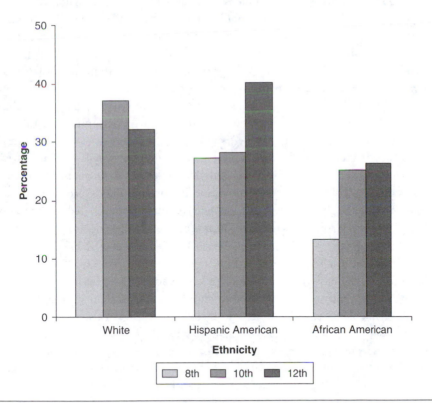

Figure 10.5   Ethnic Differences in Adolescent Substance Use

Source: From Johnston et al. (2006). Used with permission.

Note: White adolescents show the highest rates of problematic drinking and marijuana use, while African American adolescents show the lowest prevalence. Hispanic adolescents tend to show slightly higher use of so-called "hard" drugs like crack.

Course

Adolescents tend to use substances in an orderly, predictable fashion (Kandel, Yamaguchi, & Chen, 1992). Among adolescents who use alcohol and other drugs, a typical pattern of use begins in late childhood with cigarettes. Then, sometime during adolescence, youth may begin to use alcohol and try marijuana. Some individuals subsequently try other illicit drugs such as stimulants (e.g., cocaine) or opioids (e.g., heroin). This progression from "soft" to "hard" drugs has led some people to suggest that marijuana is a "gateway drug" that introduces youths to other illicit substances.

Evidence supporting the **gateway hypothesis** is limited. On the one hand, longitudinal data indicate that the vast majority of adolescents who abuse stimulants (e.g., cocaine) and opioids (e.g., heroin) have also used cigarettes, alcohol, and marijuana. On the other hand, most adolescents who use cigarettes, alcohol, and marijuana *do not* use other illicit substances. We might conclude, therefore, that the abuse of "hard" drugs is almost always dependent on the use of cigarettes, alcohol, and marijuana; however, use of these "softer" drugs does not imply an escalation to other illicit substances (Tucker, Ellickson, Orlando, Martino, & Klein, 2005).

Why do most youths stop at alcohol and marijuana while some youths progress to using cocaine, heroin, and other illicit substances? Recent longitudinal studies have shed some light on this question (Stice, Kirz, & Borbely, 2002; Wagner & Austin, 2006). At least three factors seem to predict escalation in substance use. First, adolescents with histories of impulsive and disruptive behavior are more likely to escalate their use of alcohol and other drugs and develop Substance Abuse. Their substance use may be part of a larger problem with disruptive and antisocial activity. Second, adolescents whose parents model excessive substance use in the home are at increased risk of developing substance use problems. Parents who drink or use other drugs to excess may provide adolescents with access to these substances and model their use. Third, and most important, friends' use of alcohol and other drugs strongly predicts the adolescents' likelihood of escalated substance use. Peers introduce adolescents to illicit substances, then model and reinforce their use (Kessler, Berglund, Dernier, Jin, & Walters, 2005; O'Brien et al., 2005).

Adolescents who develop Substance Abuse are at risk for a host of deleterious outcomes. First, substances carry direct risks to adolescents' health. For example, excessive use of alcohol can cause transient illness; impairment in cognitive functioning; and, in rare cases, coma and death. Substance use can also place adolescents in hazardous situations. For example, adolescents who binge drink may drive while intoxicated, practice risky sexual behavior, or engage in aggressive or antisocial activity. Substance use also carries psychosocial risks. Adolescents with substance use problems show increased conflict and decreased communication with parents, greater likelihood of school-related problems and academic difficulties, and poorer peer relationships. Certainly, problems with family, school, and peers are partly responsible for adolescents' substance use. However, adolescents who use alcohol and other drugs likely exacerbate these social difficulties and compound their substance use problems (Tucker et al., 2005).

What happens to adolescents who use alcohol and other drugs after they finish high school? Recent data indicate that the risk for developing chronic substance use problems increases dramatically after adolescents leave high school, regardless of whether they drop out of high school, graduate and enter the workforce, or graduate and attend college (White, Labouvie, & Papadaratsakis, 2005). Risk for problematic substance use peaks between the ages of 18 and 22 years. By age 25 years, there is usually a dramatic decline in substance use and misuse, especially among people who attended college. This decrease in substance use with age is probably caused by young adults entering the workforce, assuming more adult-like responsibilities, marrying, and having children (Rohrbach, Sussman, Dent, & Sun, 2005; White, McMorris, Catalano, Fleming, Haggerty, & Abbott, 2006).

Substance use problems during adolescence can have negative effects on psychosocial functioning in adulthood. Most adolescents who use alcohol and other drugs during adolescence *do not* continue to show substance use problems as adults, especially if the onset of their substance use was in later adolescence. However, some adolescents, especially those who begin using substances before age 14 years, show long-term substance use problems. These adolescents are also likely to display lower levels of social competence, decreased employment, and increased likelihood of depression and criminal behavior (S. A. Brown, Myers, & Stewart, 1998; Caspi, Harrington, Moffitt, & Milne, 2002; Chassin, Pitts, & DeLucia, 1999).

Etiology

The development of substance use disorders is complex. A model that explains the emergence of substance use problems must take into account a wide range of genetic, biological, psychological, and social-cultural factors. One biopsychosocial model has been offered by Sher (1991) to explain the development of alcohol abuse. Sher's model suggests that alcohol use disorders can emerge along three possible developmental pathways. First, alcohol abuse can develop when people inherit a genetic or biological sensitivity to the effects of alcohol and derive a great deal of pleasure from its use (the enhanced reinforcement pathway). Second, alcohol abuse can arise when people rely on alcohol to cope with depression or anxiety. In this case, alcohol use is negatively reinforced by the alleviation of psychological distress (the negative affect pathway). Third, alcohol abuse can emerge as part of a larger pattern of antisocial behavior. In this pathway, alcohol use problems emerge in the context of CD (the deviance-prone pathway).

These three pathways to substance use problems are not mutually exclusive; many people abuse alcohol and other drugs for multiple reasons. However, these pathways are useful for organizing our understanding of the etiology of substance use disorders (Chassin, Ritter, Trim, & King, 2003).

The Enhanced Reinforcement Pathway

Genetic Diathesis

At the beginning of all three pathways lies a biological diathesis toward developing Substance Abuse (see Figure 10.6). Considerable research has shown an association between problematic substance use in parents and the development of substance use

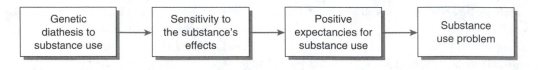

Figure 10.6 The Enhanced Reinforcement Model for Alcohol Use

Source: From Sher (1991). Used with permission.

disorders in their offspring. Approximately two-thirds of adolescents who show substance use problems have at least one biological parent with a history of Substance Abuse (Winters, Stinchfield, Opland, Weller, & Latimer, 2000). Substance Abuse is especially common among biological fathers (Henggeler et al., 1996).

Having a parent with a history of Alcohol Dependence increases one's likelihood of developing a substance use disorder two- to nine-fold (Chassin et al., 2003). Twin and family studies indicate that this association between parent and child substance use is at least partially heritable, with 60% of the variance of alcohol use and 33% of other drug use attributable to genetics (Han, McGue, & Iacono, 1999). Genetic factors predict the likelihood of using alcohol and other drugs, the age at which people first begin using substances, and the overall probability of a substance use disorder (McGue, Pickens, & Svikis, 1992).

Researchers have attempted to identify which genes are responsible for the heritability of substance use problems (O'Brien et al., 2005). It appears that no single gene is responsible; rather, a number of genes likely play important roles. Of particular importance are genes that code for dopamine, serotonin, and endogenous opioid receptors.

Positive Expectations and Pleasurable Effects

Although having a parent with a substance use disorder places the child at risk for future substance use problems, the mechanism by which biological diathesis leads to substance use disorders is not known. The enhanced reinforcement pathway assumes that biological diathesis makes offspring unusually sensitive to the pharmacological effects of the substance. For example, individuals who have this biological diathesis may respond more intensely to the effects of alcohol, may experience more pleasure from drinking, or may have fewer negative side effects from drinking excessively (Zuckerman, 2007).

At the same time, as adolescents experiment with alcohol and other drugs, they learn about the effects of these substances on their behavioral, social, and emotional functioning. Eventually, they come to expect substances to be beneficial. As use increases, the substances assume reinforcing properties by either bringing about pleasure (i.e., positive reinforcement) or alleviating distress or boredom (i.e., negative reinforcement).

A biological sensitivity to the effects of the substance and an expectation that the substance will have positive effects can lead to problematic use. For example, adolescents at risk for substance use disorders often have unusually positive expectations for substance use; that is, they expect substances to produce a great number of benefits with few drawbacks (Van Voorst & Quirk, 2003). Indeed, distorted beliefs in the positive effects of alcohol can increase the frequency or amount of drinking (Barnow, Schultz, Lucht, Ulrich, Preuss, & Freyberger, 2004; Kirisci, Tarter, Vanyukov, Reynolds, & Habeych, 2004). In contrast, adolescents who have negative experiences with alcohol and other drugs, or adolescents who are anxious about substance use, are less likely to develop substance use problems.

The Negative Affect Pathway

Individuals can also develop substance use problems in response to stress and negative affect (see Figure 10.7). Stress can arise from negative early childhood experiences, such as growing up in an abusive or neglectful home. Stress can also be caused by later environmental factors, such as witnessing marital conflict, experiencing disruptions in family and interpersonal relationships, or encountering school-related difficulties (Bond, Toumbourou, Thomas, Catalano, & Patton, 2005; A. M. Libby et al., 2004; A. M. Libby, Orton, Stover, & Riggs, 2005). These stressors, in turn, can cause anxiety, depression, and low self-worth. Adolescents who are unable to cope with these negative emotions may use alcohol and other drugs to alleviate psychological distress.[6] Substance use, therefore, is negatively reinforced by the reduction of anxiety and depression. Over time, substance use can increase and lead to abuse (K. G. Anderson, Ramo, & Brown, 2006).

The stress and negative affect pathway has not enjoyed widespread empirical support as an explanation for substance use problems among adolescents. Most cross-sectional studies show only moderate associations between adolescents' ratings of negative affect and their alcohol use. Furthermore, most longitudinal studies have shown that adolescents' symptoms of depression and anxiety usually *do not* precede the emergence of their substance use problems. Instead, some data indicate the opposite effect: Adolescent substance use often leads to social and academic problems that elicit depression and anxiety. When mood and anxiety problems predict later substance use, the relationship between mood and substance use is usually weak (S. M. King et al., 2004) or attributable to other factors, such as disruptive behavior problems (Bardone et al., 1998; Goodman & Capitman, 2000; Goodwin et al., 2004; Patton, Coffey, Carlin, Degenhardt, Lynskey, & Hall, 2002; Rao, Daley, & Hammen, 2000).

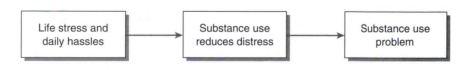

Figure 10.7   The Negative Affect Model for Alcohol Use

Source: From Sher (1991). Used with permission.

---

[6] Some people use the term "self-medication" to refer to the practice of using substances to alleviate distress.

On the other hand, recent data indicate that the stress and negative affect model might apply to a subset of adolescents who experienced child maltreatment (Libby et al., 2005; B. A. Miller & Mancuso, 2004). Physically abused boys and sexually abused girls show increased likelihood of developing mood problems associated with their victimization. They may rely on alcohol and other drugs to cope with these mood problems.

Furthermore, specific mood and anxiety disorders may place children at risk for substance use problems. For example, adolescents who experience extreme anxiety in social situations often use alcohol to cope with anticipatory anxiety. These adolescents might drink *before* going to a party, in order to relax. Their repeated alcohol use can lead to abuse (Merikangas, 2005). Adolescents with Bipolar Disorder also show greater likelihood of developing substance use problems (Wilens et al., 2004).

Finally, the stress and negative affect pathway might apply to youths from affluent families. Suburban children living in affluent households may use alcohol and other drugs to cope with depression and anxiety. Furthermore, affluent adolescent boys use alcohol to gain social standing with peers. Luthar and Latendresse (2005) suggest that affluent adolescents lead overly scheduled lives and experience considerable pressure to excel academically, athletically, and socially. At the same time, their parents are often less involved in their lives because of career and social demands. This combination of high stress and low parental supervision places affluent youths at risk.

The Deviance-Prone Pathway

The deviance-prone pathway offers a third explanation for the development of adolescent substance use problems (Chassin et al., 2003). According to this model, adolescent substance use is part of a much larger problem with general antisocial behavior (see Figure 10.8). Consequently, the causes of adolescent substance use problems are similar to the causes of other disruptive behavior problems. These causes include early problems with neurobehavioral inhibition, cognitive and academic delays, peer rejection, and low parental monitoring.

Neurobehavioral Disinhibition

Young children who show neurobehavioral disinhibition are at increased risk for developing substance use problems later in life (Tarter et al., 2003; Zuckerman, 2007). **Neurobehavioral disinhibition** is characterized by three features: (1) behavioral undercontrol, (2) emotional reactivity, and (3) deficits in executive functioning.

First, children with behavioral undercontrol show high-rate, risky, and impulsive behaviors (Elkins, King, McGue, & Iacono, 2006). These children have a strong need for excitement and are often described as "sensation-seekers" or "daredevils." The tendency toward behavioral undercontrol is likely inherited; twin and family studies show strong heritability for risk-taking and sensation-seeking behavior (Iacono, Carlson, Taylor, Elkins, & McGue, 1999; Young, Stallings, Corley, Krauter, & Hewitt, 2000). Adults with substance use disorders often display behavioral

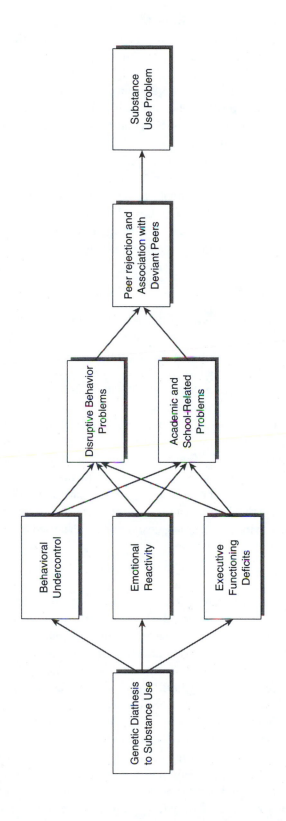

Figure 10.8 The Deviance-Prone Model for Alcohol Use

Source: From Sher (1991). Used with permission.

undercontrol, and they may genetically predispose their children to similar behaviors (King & Chassin, 2004). Indeed, behavioral undercontrol is a strong predictor of later disruptive behavior problems and substance use.

Second, children with neurobehavioral disinhibition display a high degree of emotional reactivity (Chassin et al., 1999). As young children, they display difficult temperaments. Their caregivers describe them as irritable and fussy. Later in childhood, these children often overreact to stress and display a tendency toward irritability, anger, and aggressive outbursts.

Third, children with neurobehavioral disinhibition show deficits in executive functioning (Kirisci, Vanyukov, & Tarter, 2005; Tarter, Kirisci, Habeych, Reynolds, & Vanyukov, 2004). Executive functioning refers to the cognitive processes that allow children to inhibit immediate impulses, plan and prioritize behavior, and achieve long-term goals. Children with deficits in executive functioning display problems with inattention, hyperactivity, and impulsivity.

Academic and Peer Problems

According to the deviance-prone model, problems with neurobehavioral disinhibition can interfere with children's academic performance. Specifically, children who show problems with behavioral undercontrol may have difficulty attending to teachers and adhering to classroom rules. They may also have trouble staying on task in class and completing exams. Deficits in executive functioning can also interfere with children's abilities to complete assignments in a timely fashion, to plan and organize academic activities, and to accomplish long-term projects. Children with neurobehavioral disinhibition often have negative views of school, earn low grades, and struggle academically (Gau, Chong, Yang, Yen, Liang, & Cheng, 2007).

Problems with disinhibition can also affect children's interactions with peers. Peers often find these children's high-rate, disruptive behavior aversive. They may avoid interacting with them in the classroom and during recess. Furthermore, children who display emotional reactivity, especially aggression, are often rejected by peers.

Association with Deviant Peers

Academic problems and peer rejection can cause children to distance themselves from classmates and mainstream peer groups. Instead of associating with prosocial peers, these disruptive children associate with other rejected youths. Typically, rejected peers display similar histories of academic and disruptive behavior problems (Pearson, Sweeting, West, Young, Gordon, & Turner, 2006).

Early substance use often occurs when deviant peers introduce children to alcohol and other drugs. Peers model substance use, encourage experimentation, and reinforce continued use over time. Rejected children might initially engage in substance use to gain acceptance into the deviant peer group. Over time, repeated use can lead to an exacerbation of social and academic problems and the development of substance use disorders (Barnes, Hoffman, Welte, Farrell, & Dintcheff, 2006).

The relationship between deviant peers and substance use may be different for boys and girls. Some girls associate with deviant peers for the same reasons as boys:

They are ostracized by prosocial peers because of their behavioral and academic problems. However, early pubertal maturation also increases the likelihood that girls will associate with deviant peers. Older boys, in particular, may introduce early-maturing girls to alcohol and other drugs, encourage antisocial behavior, and pressure them to engage in sexual activity. Despite their appearance, these early-developing girls may lack the maturity to resist social pressures. Indeed, early-developing girls show greater consumption of alcohol and other drugs than typically developing girls. Furthermore, they are more likely to develop substance use problems than their typically developing peers (Andrews, 2005).

Protective Factors

The association between academic/peer problems and children's substance use is moderated by parenting. Parents can affect their children's likelihood of developing substance use problems in two ways. First, children whose parents monitor their daily activities are less likely to develop substance use problems, regardless of their academic and peer status (Barnes et al., 2006). Parents who monitor their children provide fewer opportunities for their children to associate with deviant peers and experiment with alcohol and other drugs (Gau et al., 2007).

Second, parents who provide sensitive and responsive care to their children and discipline their children in a consistent and noncoercive manner can reduce the likelihood of their children's substance use (Parker & Benson, 2005). In contrast, parents who interact with their children in a hostile or coercive fashion can cause children to further distance themselves from the family and affiliate more strongly with deviant peers (Urberg, Luo, Pilgrim, & Degirmencioglu, 2003). King and Chassin (2004) found that parents' use of consistent, noncoercive discipline can protect some disruptive adolescents from developing substance use problems. However, they also found that adolescents with a strong genetic diathesis to behavioral undercontrol often developed substance use disorders regardless of the quality of parental care.

Treatment

Primary Prevention Programs

Primary prevention programs target all youths, regardless of their risk status for developing a psychological disorder. Primary prevention programs generally fall into two categories: school-based programs and community-based programs.

D.A.R.E.

D.A.R.E. is the best-known school-based program designed to prevent substance use problems. D.A.R.E. originated in Los Angeles in 1983. It was originally intended to increase contact between police and school-age children. The program consisted of weekly visits by uniformed police officers to fifth- and sixth-grade classrooms.

Officers discussed the dangers of substance use, ways to avoid peer pressure to use alcohol and other drugs, and techniques to promote abstinence. It has since been expanded to elementary and junior high school classrooms across the United States.

Despite its popularity, D.A.R.E. does not appear to be effective in reducing alcohol and other drug use. The first meta-analysis of D.A.R.E., funded by the National Institute of Justice, revealed that children who did and did not participate in D.A.R.E. had equal rates of substance use by early adolescence (Ennett, Tobler, Ringwalt, & Flewelling, 1994). Other randomized controlled studies showed that D.A.R.E. produced increases in children's knowledge of substance use problems but did not cause changes in children's substance use or abuse (Clayton, Cattarello, & Johnstone, 1996; Dukes, Stein, & Ullman, 1997; Rosenbaum, Gordon, & Hanson, 1998).

Media Campaigns

Two national media campaigns have also targeted alcohol and other drug use among children and adolescents (O'Brien et al., 2005). Beginning in 1987, the Partnership for a Drug Free America (PDFA) produced television ads designed to provide substance abuse education to youth and their parents. Evaluation of the campaign indicated that it was successful in reaching a large number of families across the United States. Furthermore, the media campaign coincided with an overall decrease in substance use among American youth. Proponents of the program concluded that it was effective in preventing substance use problems. However, critics argued that the general decrease in substance use actually *preceded* the onset of the media campaign; therefore, it may be inappropriate to attribute this reduction in substance use to the campaign.

In the late 1990s, a second media campaign was conducted by the White House Office of National Drug Control Policy. This campaign resembled the PDFA campaign and consisted largely of television ads directed toward parents and children. The ads were designed to (1) increase parent-child communication about alcohol and other drugs, (2) increase parental monitoring of children's peer groups and after-school activities, (3) decrease children's positive beliefs and expectations about substance use, and (4) decrease youths' actual use of alcohol and other drugs.

An evaluation of the campaign demonstrated that the program reached a large number of families. It also increased parent-child communication about substance use. However, the campaign was largely unable to increase parental monitoring or decrease children's subsequent substance use. In fact, exposure to the media campaign was actually associated with an *increase* in children's intentions to use marijuana! It is possible that youths who were told to abstain from certain drugs, like marijuana, strongly resented these prohibitions. To exert their autonomy, they may have decided to use the drug.

Overall, evaluations of school- and media-based prevention campaigns have not been encouraging. Nevertheless, policymakers will likely continue to implement these programs, despite limited evidence regarding their effectiveness. All too often, people form opinions and shape public policy based on anecdotal evidence rather than on carefully collected data (Birkeland, Murphy-Graham, & Weiss, 2005).

In the case of D.A.R.E., policy informed by anecdotal impressions and ideology alone seems to have resulted in a considerable loss of time and money. In the case of certain media campaigns, failure to evaluate outcomes may have caused an increase in the behavior the program was designed to prevent.

Secondary Prevention Programs

Secondary prevention programs are designed for youths at risk for developing substance use problems. Most secondary prevention programs are **ecologically based**; that is, they target at-risk youth in certain areas or neighborhoods (Pumariega, Rodriguez, & Kilgus, 2004). Programs are usually designed for middle-school students who are about to make the transition from childhood to early adolescence. Program developers reason that a successful transition from preadolescence to adolescence can protect youths from developing substance use problems.

Ecologically based prevention programs target multiple risk factors simultaneously. First, information is provided to adolescents about substance use and misuse. Adolescents are also taught techniques to avoid substance use with peers. Second, parents are taught about adolescent substance use problems and steps that they can take to decrease the likelihood that their adolescents will use alcohol and other drugs. Many programs emphasize the importance of improving parent-child communication, monitoring children's friends and activities, and setting clear but developmentally appropriate limits on children's behavior. Third, ecologically based programs address the child's larger social system: school, peers, and the community. Some programs offer after-school activities to promote abstinence to entire peer groups. Other programs work with community officials and police to limit adolescents' access to alcohol and other drugs.

Researchers evaluated the effectiveness of 48 secondary prevention programs using a sample of approximately 10,000 adolescents (Sambrano et al., 2005). Roughly half of the sample participated in a prevention program while the remaining adolescents served as controls. Results of the evaluation were disappointing. Overall, adolescents who participated in the prevention programs did not differ in their alcohol and marijuana use compared to controls. However, when researchers looked at the data more carefully, they noticed that the programs that provided high-intensity, comprehensive services reduced substance use more than controls. These findings indicate that all prevention programs are not equal. To be effective, prevention programs must target multiple risk factors in the adolescent's life and teach skills to avoid substances and develop positive relationships with peers.

Psychosocial Treatments

Inpatient Treatment and Twelve-Step Programs

Some adolescents with serious substance use disorders participate in **28-day inpatient treatment** programs. Although inpatient treatment programs vary, most have three goals: (1) to attend to the adolescent's immediate medical needs and to detoxify her body, (2) to help the adolescent recognize the harmful effects of the substance on her health and functioning, and (3) to improve the quality of the adolescent's relationships with others.

To accomplish these goals, nearly all inpatient programs require adolescents to abstain from alcohol and other drug use during treatment. Staff members educate adolescents about the process of substance dependence and the physiological, psychological, and social effects of substance use. Inpatient programs typically provide individual and group therapy to adolescents. Staff members also offer family therapy sessions designed to improve parent-adolescent communication and problem solving. Before the end of treatment, staff members help the adolescent and family members prepare for a return to school and home.

Most inpatient programs incorporate 12-step philosophies into their treatment package. **Twelve-step programs** include Alcoholics Anonymous (AA) and Narcotics Anonymous (NA). Proponents of these programs conceptualize alcohol and other drug use as a disease. From this perspective, substance abuse and dependence is a medical disorder that develops because of genetics; is maintained because of biology and "brain chemistry"; and deleteriously affects the person's social, emotional, and spiritual life. Proponents of 12-step programs argue that individuals must first acknowledge that they have the disease and that they are powerless to overcome its effects.

Participants progress through a series of 12 steps designed to help them cope with their substance use and remain abstinent. At some point in their participation, they must recognize their inability to overcome their substance use problem and they must surrender themselves to a "higher power." Indeed, they are taught to rely on spirituality and support from others to cope with urges to drink or use other drugs. Participants attend group meetings to gain the support of other people struggling with substance use disorders. Each participant also selects a mentor who provides individual support and advice to help her maintain sobriety.

Twelve-step programs are the most frequently used means of treating Substance Abuse and Dependence in the United States. Typically, 12-step programs are initiated during inpatient treatment. After the individual completes inpatient treatment, he or she is encouraged to continue participating in 12-step programs in the community. Very often, individuals participate in 12-step group meetings while simultaneously meeting with an individual therapist.

Twelve-step programs have demonstrated efficacy among adults with substance use problems. However, less information is available regarding the efficacy of 12-step treatment for adolescents (Elliott, Orr, Watson, & Jackson, 2005). Twelve-step programs that are administered as part of inpatient treatment tend to be highly effective, probably because adolescents are living in controlled environments with limited opportunities for substance use. Some participants are able to maintain treatment gains 6 to 12 months after program completion (Winters et al., 2000). However, adolescents released from these inpatient programs usually have high rates of relapse. Approximately 60% relapse within 3 months of discharge and as many as 80% relapse within one year (Kaminer & Bukstein, 2005).

Cognitive-Behavioral Therapies

Cognitive-behavioral therapy (CBT) for substance use disorders has gained considerable popularity in recent years (Waldron & Kaminer, 2004). Practitioners of CBT view problematic substance use as a learned behavior that is acquired and maintained in four ways.

First, people often learn to use alcohol and other drugs through operant conditioning. For example, alcohol can be positively reinforcing to the extent that it gives people a subjective sense of satisfaction and well-being or enhances enjoyment during social interactions. Alcohol can also be negatively reinforcing to the extent that it reduces tension or alleviates pain. Over time, the reinforcing properties of alcohol lead to increased use.

Second, through classical conditioning, people learn to associate substance use with certain situations or mood states. For example, an adolescent might use marijuana with a certain group of friends. He discovers that smoking with these friends allows him to relax and have a good time. Through classical conditioning, he associates this group of friends with marijuana use. In the future, these friends might serve as a trigger or "stimulus cue" for him to use again.

Third, substance use is often maintained through social learning. Specifically, family members sometimes model substance use. Adolescents might view substance use as an acceptable means to cope with stress or facilitate social interactions. Similarly, peers often model and reinforce drug and alcohol use, communicating that to gain social approval, drug and alcohol use is not only acceptable, but expected.

Fourth, adolescents' beliefs mediate the relationship between events that trigger substance use and consumption of alcohol and other drugs (J. S. Beck, Liese, & Najavits, 2005). Strictly speaking, events do not cause people to use substances; rather, people's interpretations and thoughts about events lead to either substance use or abstinence. Adolescents often hold distorted beliefs about situations that prompt their substance use (see Figure 10.9). These distorted beliefs elicit drinking or other drug use.

To understand the way beliefs mediate the relationship between events and behavior, consider the following example. Sam is a shy tenth grader who has been

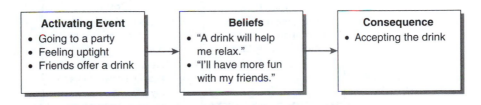

Figure 10.9   Cognitive Model for Adolescent Alcohol Use

Note: Cognitions mediate the relationship between events and people's overt behavior. Adolescents who believe that alcohol will facilitate social interactions or help them have more fun are more likely to drink than adolescents who believe that alcohol will not produce pleasurable effects.

invited to a party. When his friends pick him up to go the party, they offer him some beer to help him relax. Sam's decision to drink or abstain will depend largely on his thoughts about the situation. Beliefs such as "Having a couple of drinks will help me relax and get into a good mood" will increase his likelihood of accepting the drink. Alternatively, beliefs such as "I'll be OK without the drink; Jim isn't having any" may lead him to decline the drink.

The techniques used in CBT target each of the four ways substance use problems develop and are maintained: (1) operant conditioning, (2) classical conditioning, (3) social learning, and (4) ways of thinking. First, the therapist asks the adolescent to monitor her substance use and note environmental factors or mood states that precede substance use. For example, an adolescent might discover that she only drinks when she is nervous before or during a party. With this information, the therapist and adolescent try to find ways for her to avoid feelings of nervousness that trigger alcohol use. The adolescent might decide to ask a friend to go to parties with her so that she does not experience as much anticipatory anxiety.

Second, the therapist encourages the adolescent to consider the consequences of her substance use. Specifically, the therapist and adolescent might conduct a **cost-benefit analysis** of using alcohol or other drugs (see Figure 10.10). For example, the adolescent might list certain benefits of drinking before attending a party: it helps her relax; it allows her to have a good time. However, these benefits might be over-shadowed by potential drawbacks: she drinks too much and gets sick; she feels guilty afterward; her parents become angry.

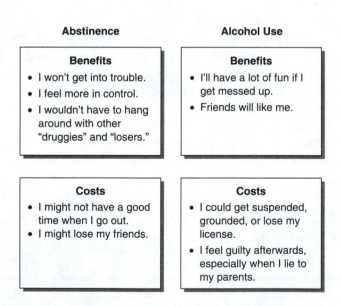

Figure 10.10   Cost-Benefit Analysis of Alcohol Use

Source: Based on J. S. Beck et al. (2005).

Note: Cognitive-behavioral therapists often ask adolescents to consider the pros and cons of (1) abstinence and (2) continued drinking.

Third, to help adolescents avoid substance use, therapists teach their clients specific skills to reduce the reinforcing effects of alcohol. The skills that they teach depend largely on the adolescents' reasons for using. Adolescents who consume alcohol to reduce anxiety before a party might benefit from relaxation or social skills training. If they felt more relaxed or confident before the party, they might experience less desire to drink. Adolescents who drink in order to gain peer acceptance might be taught alcohol refusal skills. During the session, the therapist and adolescent might generate and practice ways to refuse alcohol when peers offer it.

Fourth, most cognitive-behavioral therapists examine the beliefs that adolescents have about substances and challenge distorted cognitions that lead to problematic use. Many adolescents overestimate the benefits of alcohol and dismiss its potentially harmful effects. An adolescent might reason, "It's fun to get wasted with my friends; we always have a great time." The therapist might encourage the adolescent to look at his alcohol use more objectively, by considering the negative consequences of use.

Similarly, an adolescent might overestimate the frequency with which peers use alcohol and other drugs, claiming, "I drink about as much as everybody else." In response, the therapist might share data regarding typical alcohol use among adolescents of the same age and gender. Consider the following transcript of a therapy session:

Therapist:	We've been talking for quite a while and I've noticed that you put a lot of pressure on yourself to drink when you're hanging out.
Adam:	Well, sort of. It's more like the other guys put a lot of pressure on me. I'm fine when I'm with them most of the time. It just gets a little hard when I go to parties or things like that.
Therapist:	So, when you go to one of these parties, what's it like?
Adam:	Well, I usually see a lot of my friends and the other kids from school. They look like they're drinking and having a good time. It's like they expect me to drink too. And I want to have a good time, too—to have fun. I also don't want to let them down and ruin their fun.
Therapist:	You mean if you don't drink, you might be ruining their good time?
Adam:	Yeah, I guess. I just think that they'd think, "What's the matter with him. Doesn't he want to have fun? Does he think he's better than the rest of us?" It makes me nervous.
Therapist:	And *how do you know* that's what's going through their minds? What's the evidence?
Adam:	I don't know. I can just tell, you know. I get real nervous about the situation and I can just tell that's what they're thinking.
Therapist:	It sounds to me like you're reasoning with your emotions, not with your head. This can sometimes get us into a lot of trouble and cause

us to feel nervous. Let's see if we can look at the situation a little more objectively. Was everyone else at the party drinking?

Adam: Yeah, most people.

Therapist: But not everyone?

Adam: No, there were a few guys who weren't drinking.

Therapist: Did the other kids make fun of these other guys?

Adam: No. Everyone was OK with it.

Therapist: And did you think these kids (who didn't drink) were somehow weird or strange or better than you?

Adam: No. I guess I didn't think anything of it. Everyone just wanted to have a good time.

Therapist: So no one at the party was really interested in who drank and who didn't. They were more interested in having fun themselves.

Adam: Yeah. I guess so, now that I think about it.

Within the past 10 years, a number of randomized controlled studies involving adolescents with substance use problems have shown CBT to be efficacious (Patterson & O'Connell, 2003). Adolescents who participate in CBT show greater reductions in substance use than adolescents who receive individual supportive therapy, group therapy, or information about substance use problems alone (Kaminer, Blitz, Burleson, Sussman, & Rounsaville, 1998; Kaminer et al., 2002; Waldron et al., 2001).

Motivational Enhancement Therapy

Another method of treatment involves **motivational enhancement therapy**, sometimes referred to as "motivational interviewing" or "motivational counseling" (Tevyaw & Monti, 2004). The primary goal of motivational enhancement therapy is to increase the adolescent's desire to reduce his alcohol consumption. Practitioners of motivational enhancement therapy recognize that most adolescents are referred to therapy by parents, teachers, or other adults; rarely do adolescents seek treatment themselves. Consequently, adolescents usually have low motivation to participate in treatment and less motivation to change their drinking habits.

Practitioners of motivational enhancement therapy help adolescents increase their willingness to change. Adolescents progress through a series of steps, or **stages of change**, as they move from a state of low motivation to change to a state of high readiness to change (Prochaska, DiClemente, & Norcross, 1992). The stages are precontemplation (not recognizing that their alcohol use is a problem), contemplation (considering the possibility that their alcohol use is problematic), preparation (making initial steps to change, such as making an appointment with a therapist), action (changing behavior), and maintenance (avoiding relapse).

To increase the adolescent's motivation to change, the therapist uses five principles of motivational enhancement (Miller & Rollnick, 2002). First, she approaches the adolescent in an accepting and nonjudgmental way. The therapist *communicates warmth and genuine concern* for the adolescent and avoids signs that she disapproves of the adolescent's alcohol use or disagrees with his attitudes about drinking. Second, she *actively listens* to the adolescent's point of view in order to accurately understand his perspective. The therapist's initial goal is to understand and accept the adolescent, not to persuade him to adopt others' beliefs about drinking. Third, the therapist *highlights discrepancies* between the adolescent's short- and long-term goals and his current alcohol use. For instance, the therapist might surmise that athletic achievement is important to the adolescent. She might ask him whether drinking, which jeopardizes his eligibility to compete, is consistent with his goal to be a star athlete. Fourth, the therapist *rolls with resistance and avoids argumentation*. If the adolescent becomes defensive, angry, or avoidant, the therapist assumes it is because she is not adequately understanding and appreciating the adolescent's perspective. Fifth, the therapist *supports any commitment to change*, no matter how small. The therapist sees herself as being "in the adolescent's corner," that is, supporting and encouraging his decisions regardless of whether they agree with her own. For example, the therapist might support the adolescent's decision to cut back on his drinking, even if this falls short of complete abstinence.

Practitioners of motivational enhancement therapy usually do not see abstinence as the primary goal of therapy. Instead, these practitioners often adopt a **harm reduction** approach to treatment (Miller, Turner, & Marlatt, 2001). According to the harm reduction perspective, the primary goal of therapy is to help adolescents identify and avoid alcohol use that has great potential for harm. For example, the therapist might support the adolescent's decision to drink fewer than four beers at a party, even if this decision might not make the adolescent's parents very happy. Any reduction in alcohol use that decreases risk or harm to the adolescent is viewed as successful.

Many people, especially parents, question the ethics of using a harm reduction approach with adolescents under 18 years of age. After all, is it appropriate for therapists to support an adolescent's decision to engage in an illegal behavior? Although ethical questions like these cannot easily be answered, we should consider three points. First, therapists who adopt a harm reduction perspective must obtain parental consent prior to treatment. Although adolescents have basic rights to autonomy and self-determination, parents have the ultimate responsibility for their children's welfare and development. The therapist cannot ethically proceed with a harm reduction approach to therapy without parental consent. Second, most therapists who adopt a harm reduction perspective would probably argue that abstinence is the *ideal* goal of therapy. To the extent that abstinence has low probability, any reduction in alcohol use can be seen as beneficial. Finally, practitioners need to consider empirical data, in addition to personal beliefs, when they judge the merits of a harm reduction approach to treatment. If harm reduction works and clinicians do not use it, can they defend their practice?[7]

---

[7] The American Academy of Child and Adolescent Psychiatry (2005) identifies abstinence as the primary goal of treatment for adolescent substance abuse. Harm reduction can be an acceptable, implicit method of treatment as long as professionals do not advocate the use of alcohol and other drugs in therapy.

Emerging data indicate that motivational enhancement therapy can be effective for high school students at risk for substance use problems. In two studies, adolescents who presented to an emergency department because of an alcohol-related event were randomly assigned to either one session of motivational enhancement therapy or usual care. At six-month follow-up, adolescents who participated in motivational enhancement therapy showed lower rates of alcohol-related problems and injuries than controls. Furthermore, adolescents with the lowest motivation to change before treatment showed the greatest benefits from their participation in treatment (Monti, Barnett, O'Leary, & Colby, 2001; Monti et al., 1999).

Two additional studies examined the efficacy of motivational enhancement among high school students who frequently used alcohol and marijuana (Grenard, Ames, Wiers, Thush, Stacy, & Sussman, 2007; McCambridge & Strang, 2004). Adolescents received either one session of motivational enhancement therapy or no intervention. Three months later, adolescents who participated in motivational enhancement therapy showed significant reductions in alcohol and marijuana use. Furthermore, reductions were greatest among adolescents who showed the most frequent use before treatment (see Figure 10.11).

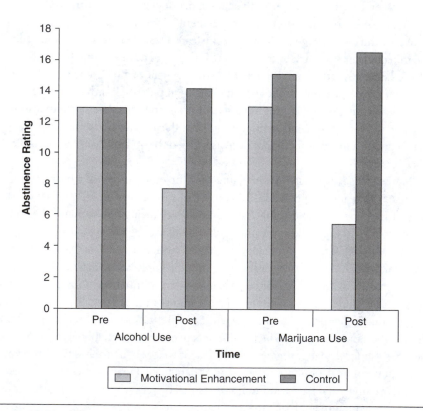

Figure 10.11 Efficacy of Motivational Enhancement Therapy for Adolescents With Alcohol or Marijuana Use Problems

Source: Based on McCambridge and Strang (2004).

Note: Individuals in the treatment group received only one session of motivational enhancement. Three months later, they were less likely to use drugs than adolescents who served as controls.

Family Therapies

The most extensively studied treatment for adolescent substance use problems is **family therapy** (Hogue, Dauber, Samuolis, & Liddle, 2006; Liddle, 2004). Practitioners of family therapy view adolescent substance use as a family problem. The causes of adolescent substance abuse must be understood in light of the adolescent's family and her surrounding social system. Consequently, family therapists are interested in how the adolescent's relationships with parents, home environment, and school/neighborhood influence her substance use. Since all three ecological factors are interconnected, change in any one factor can affect all of the others. For example, increasing parents' involvement in the adolescent's activities could improve the adolescent's commitment and attitude to school. Helping the adolescent manage anger could enhance her relationship with parents and decrease her likelihood of seeking support from deviant peers.

Although the therapeutic tactics used by family therapists vary, they usually share two objectives. One objective is to help parents manage their adolescent's substance use. This component of treatment typically involves education about normal and atypical adolescent development, the causes and consequences of adolescent substance abuse, and the role parents play in their adolescent's alcohol use. Therapists usually stress the importance of placing developmentally appropriate limits on adolescents' behavior, disciplining adolescents in a manner that is fair and consistent, and monitoring adolescents' activities.

The second objective of family therapy is to improve the quality of family functioning. Typically, therapists meet with adolescents and parents together and observe the quality of family interactions. Most therapists are chiefly interested in patterns of communication among family members. For example, some families avoid direct confrontation with each other and rarely talk about topics that make them angry, worried, or upset. Other families show frequent emotional outbursts and criticism toward each other, behaviors that often leave family members feeling isolated or rejected. Therapists often point out these communication patterns and teach family members to use different, more effective strategies (Hogue et al., 2006).

Family therapists are usually interested in the way parents and adolescents solve problems. They want to know how well parents balance the adolescent's needs for autonomy with their desire to direct their adolescent's activities. Some parents adopt authoritarian practices that deny adolescents appropriate self-determination. Excessive parental control can cause adolescents to defy parental commands. Other parents are overly permissive. These parents place too few constraints on their adolescents' activities. Permissive parenting increases adolescents' opportunities to associate with deviant peers (Hogue et al., 2006).

One type of family therapy that has been used for adolescents with substance use problems is **multidimensional family therapy** (MDFT; Liddle, Oakof, Diamond, Parker, Barrett, & Tejeda, 2001). MDFT targets four dimensions of family functioning that are relevant to the adolescent's well-being: (1) the adolescent's substance use, (2) the caregiving practices of the adolescent's parents, (3) the quality of the parent-adolescent relationship, and (4) other social factors that can influence the adolescent's substance use, such as his peer relationships or involvement in school.

MDFT involves a series of individual sessions with the adolescent, individual sessions with the parents, and combined family sessions over the course several months. Individual sessions with the adolescent focus on increasing the adolescent's social skills and involvement with prosocial peers, helping the adolescent recognize and manage negative emotions, and reducing the adolescent's contact with deviant peer groups.

Individual sessions with parents include teaching parents about the causes of adolescent substance use disorders, outlining ways parenting behaviors can contribute to these disorders, and helping parents monitor and discipline adolescent behavior. The therapist also tries to stress the importance of parents' taking an interest in their adolescents' activities.

Family sessions are dedicated primarily to improving dyadic communication and problem-solving skills. Near the end of treatment, family sessions are meant to help maintain treatment gains and develop a plan in case of relapse. Throughout the course of treatment, therapists can help families manage specific problems involving systems outside the family. For example, the therapist might facilitate the adolescent's participation in court-ordered substance counseling or his return to school after suspension.

Family therapy for adolescent substance use problems has been supported by a number of randomized controlled trials. For example, Liddle, Rowe, Dakof, Ungaro, and Henderson (2004) randomly assigned 80 children and adolescents (11–15 years) with marijuana use problems to two treatment conditions: (1) MDFT or (2) traditional group therapy. Outcomes were assessed six weeks into treatment and at termination. Results showed that adolescents in both groups displayed reductions in marijuana use. However, MDFT produced more rapid results and was more effective than group therapy in improving adolescents' social, emotional, behavioral, and academic functioning.

Results of other studies indicate that family therapies are efficacious in reducing the use of alcohol, marijuana, and other drugs relative to controls (Ozechowski & Liddle, 2000). Furthermore, family therapies have been shown to be more efficacious than individual supportive therapy, group supportive therapy, and family-based education about substance use (Liddle, 2004).

Comparison of Treatments

Until recently, little was known about the relative efficacy of treatments for adolescent substance use problems. The most promising treatments, CBT, motivational enhancement therapy, and family systems therapy, had been studied independently. Recently, the Center for Substance Use Treatment conducted the first large-scale comparison study to determine which treatment reduced adolescent substance use in the most time- and cost-effective manner (Dennis et al., 2002). This comparison study, the **Cannabis Youth Treatment Study**, has provided researchers and clinicians with new information about the treatment of adolescent substance use problems.

Dennis and colleagues (2004) conducted two studies administered at four treatment centers across the country. Participants were 600 adolescents with marijuana use problems and their parents. Most adolescents reported daily or weekly marijuana use; almost 20% also reported daily or weekly alcohol use.

In the first study, adolescents were randomly assigned to one of three treatment conditions (Diamond et al., 2002). The first group received five sessions of motivational enhancement therapy and CBT (MET/CBT 5). The second group received 12 sessions of the same treatment (MET/CBT 12). The third group received 12 sessions of motivational enhancement therapy and CBT and an additional 6 sessions of family supportive therapy (MET/CBT 12 + Family Support). The parent/family sessions were designed to improve parents' behavior management skills, improve parent-adolescent communication, and increase parents' involvement in their adolescent's treatment. Researchers assessed adolescent outcomes 12 months after treatment. Results of the first study showed that all three forms of treatment were equally efficacious in reducing adolescent substance use. Five sessions of MET/CBT was the most time- and cost-efficient treatment.

In the second study, adolescents were randomly assigned to one of three treatment conditions (Diamond et al., 2002). The first group received five sessions of MET/CBT. The second group participated in a behaviorally based family therapy program. The third group participated in 15 sessions of MDFT. Results of the second study yielded similar findings. Adolescents in all three treatments showed similar reductions in substance use. In this study, however, MET/CBT 5 and the behaviorally based family therapy program were the most cost-effective interventions.

Results of the Cannabis Youth Treatment Study seem to suggest that five sessions of MET/CBT can be sufficient to treat adolescent substance use disorders (see Figure 10.12). However, other research indicates that family therapy may be an important supplement to motivational enhancement and cognitive-behavioral interventions. Liddle and colleagues (Liddle & Hogue, 2001; Liddle & Rowe, 2006; Waldron et al., 2001) compared CBT with family therapy for adolescents with alcohol use problems. Overall, they found that both CBT and family therapy were efficacious in reducing substance use; however, family therapy sometimes produced more rapid reductions in alcohol use and more lasting abstinence than CBT. The superiority of family therapy over CBT is attributable to its greater emphasis on decreasing family conflict, improving parent-adolescent communication, and strengthening parenting skills (Hogue, Liddle, Dauber, & Samuolis, 2004). Indeed, many professional organizations recommend including families in the treatment of adolescent substance use disorders, even when practicing motivation enhancement therapy and CBT (American Academy of Child and Adolescent Psychiatry, 2005).

Relapse Prevention

Results of the Cannabis Youth Treatment Study highlighted a glaring problem in the treatment of adolescent substance use disorders: Most adolescents who respond to treatment will eventually relapse. In the cannabis study, 66%–83% of adolescents who participated in treatment had either not responded to therapy or had relapsed within 12 months of completing therapy (Diamond et al., 2002). Across other studies of adolescents with alcohol use problems, approximately 50% of youths relapse

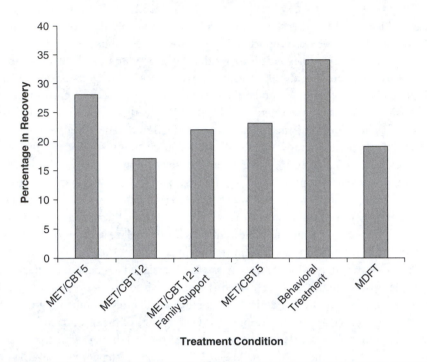

Figure 10.12 The Cannabis Youth Treatment Study

Source: From Dennis et al. (2004). Used with permission.

Note: All groups of adolescents who participated in treatment showed similar rates of recovery. Five sessions of MET/CBT or behavioral treatment were most time- and cost-effective. Notice that only about 20%–30% of youths showed recovery at follow-up.

within three months after treatment, 66% relapse after six months, and as many as 75%–80% relapse after one year (Wagner & Austin, 2006).

Therapists have begun to systematically address the possibility of relapse during the course of therapy. Indeed, Marlatt and Gordon (1985) developed a relapse prevention component to therapy for adults with substance use problems. This approach has subsequently been adapted for use with adolescents (Patterson & O'Connell, 2003).

Relapse prevention is most often used with motivational enhancement and cognitive-behavioral therapy. After the adolescent has shown a decrease in substance use, the therapist begins to discuss the possibility of relapse. The therapist might mention that relapse is likely when the adolescent encounters any high-risk situations. High-risk situations usually involve **stimulus cues** that trigger substance use. Cues might include certain people (e.g., friends who expect the adolescent to drink with them), situations (e.g., parties or being alone), and negative mood states (e.g., feeling depressed or bored). The strongest stimulus cues seem to be exposure to family members and friends who use substances (Latimer, Newcomb, Winters, & Stinchfield, 2000).

Stimulus cues can trigger relapse even if adolescents have been abstinent for long periods of time. Often, adolescents feel shame and guilt after breaking a period of abstinence, an experience referred to as the **abstinence violation effect** (Marlatt & Gordon, 1985). Adolescents may interpret their relapse to internal, stable, and global causes; that is, they blame their relapse on their weak morals, their lack of will power, or their general inability to control their lives. Consequently, many adolescents continue to use, believing that abstinence is impossible.

Adolescents' thoughts about the relapse greatly affect their ability to maintain sobriety. After having one drink, many adolescents show a number of cognitive distortions that make them more likely to continue their alcohol use. For example, many adolescents engage in **catastrophic thinking**; that is, they expect the worst possible consequences from "falling off the wagon." They might reason, "Well, now that I've had one drink, everything is ruined. I'm going to hit rock bottom again, my parents are going to kill me, I'm going to get kicked out of school, and I'm probably not going to graduate." As a result of catastrophic thinking, adolescents conclude, "I guess there's no use; I might as well get drunk."

Therapists who incorporate relapse prevention into their treatment not only help clients develop a plan for responding to a possible relapse, but they also teach youths to learn from the relapse experience. First, the therapist encourages the client to identify stimulus cues that might lead to relapse and generate ways to avoid these cues. Second, the therapist and client might create a concrete strategy for dealing with a relapse. For example, if the adolescent uses alcohol, she might agree to contact the therapist or a support group member immediately, before she has another drink. The therapist or friend might then encourage her to avoid the situation that triggered the relapse and take steps to maintain sobriety. The therapist might help the client to attribute the relapse to external, transient causes (e.g., a stressful day, a lot of pressure from friends) rather than to personal weakness.

Similarly, the therapist might challenge the adolescent's catastrophic thoughts or other cognitive distortions that could increase his likelihood of drinking even more. Consider the following transcript from a therapy session:

Mike: Before I knew it I had had five or six beers at the party and I was doing a lot of stupid stuff. At first, I felt really good. But then I just thought, "What a loser." I'd been so good not drinking for those months and now I just threw that all away.

Therapist: You felt as if all your work had been for nothing?

Mike: Exactly. Like, no matter what I do, I'm going to end up a drunk like my dad. I figure, what's the use?

Therapist: It sounds like you're being a little too hard on yourself. Just because you had a few drinks at the party that night, does that really mean you're going to be a drunk? After all, wasn't there a lot of encouragement from friends to drink that night?

Mike: Well, yeah. I really wanted to have a good time with everybody else.

Therapist: And you didn't get into any serious trouble like last time [when you drove off the road and hit a tree]?

Mike: No, I made it home fine.

Therapist: Then maybe we can look at the situation a little more closely and learn from it. Maybe we can see what triggered your decision to drink and figure out how to avoid these triggers in the future.

As the above narrative suggests, the therapist encourages the adolescent to view the lapse as a possible learning experience rather than a sign of failure. If the adolescent views the lapse as an indicator that she is "back at rock bottom," then she might drink even more heavily. Alternatively, the therapist and client might analyze the antecedents and consequences of the lapse and develop ways to avoid another lapse in the future.

Researchers are only beginning to study factors that affect the likelihood of relapse among junior and senior high school students. Our current knowledge of relapse among adolescents can be summarized as follows. First, adolescents seem to relapse for different reasons than adults. Adolescents are more likely than adults to relapse because of exposure to substance-using peers, pressure or encouragement from friends, and a desire to enhance mood or enjoy the pleasurable effects of the drug. In contrast, adults often relapse when depressed, anxious, or otherwise distressed (McCarthy, Tomlinson, Anderson, Marlatt, & Brown, 2005; Ramo, Anderson, Tate, & Brown, 2005). Second, adolescents' self-efficacy regarding their ability to abstain is inversely related to their likelihood of relapse. Adolescents who are confident that they can resist the pleasurable effects of substances and avoid social pressures to use are more likely to maintain abstinence (Burleson & Kaminer, 2005). Third, adolescents who do not regard their substance use as problematic are far more likely to relapse than adolescents committed to long-term behavior change (Callaghan, Hathaway, Cunningham, Vettese, Wyatt, & Taylor, 2005; Ramo et al., 2005). Since both situational (e.g., peers) and cognitive (e.g., beliefs, readiness to change) factors affect likelihood of relapse, both are targets of relapse prevention.

Update: Erica

Although Erica did not meet diagnostic criteria for Substance Abuse, her drinking was beginning to be problematic. Erica was at particular risk for substance use problems because her friends often encouraged her to drink at parties and her parents did not monitor her behavior.

Randy continued to meet with Erica for 12 sessions of outpatient therapy. He used the principles of motivational enhancement therapy to help Erica increase her readiness to change her drinking behavior. Both Randy and Erica agreed that it was probably unrealistic for her to avoid drinking at parties altogether. However, Randy helped Erica weigh the benefits of drinking (e.g., having fun) with the potential costs of earning lower grades in school and getting arrested.

Erica completed mandated therapy and community service. Several months after termination, Erica called Randy to thank him for being her counselor. Apparently, one of Erica's friends was seriously injured in an alcohol-related car accident. "I suppose that could have just as easily been me," said Erica.

Critical Thinking Exercises

1. Differentiate substance use, substance abuse, and substance dependence. Re-read the account of Erica at the beginning of the chapter. Does she show alcohol use, abuse, or dependence?

2. What physiological changes explain the biphasic effects of alcohol? How can the biphasic effects lead adolescents to binge drink?

3. Many adults use alcohol and marijuana to alleviate anxiety and depression. To what extent does the negative affect model explain adolescent alcohol and drug use?

4. Compare and contrast the 12-step approach to treating adolescent alcohol abuse with cognitive-behavioral therapy. According to these models, (a) what causes alcohol abuse; (b) what is the best way to treat substance abuse problems?

5. Some clinicians who treat adult substance use disorders adopt a "harm reduction" approach. Why is harm reduction controversial when it is used with adolescents? What is the evidence (for or against) using a motivational enhancement/harm reduction approach to treat adolescents with substance use problems?

CHAPTER 11

Depressive Disorders in Children and Adolescents

Hannah

Hannah was a 10-year-old girl who was sent to the emergency department of the hospital following a suicide attempt. The previous evening, Hannah had a fight with her mother, who had asked Hannah to clean her room. After 15 minutes of shouting, Hannah locked herself in the bathroom and swallowed an entire bottle of Tylenol.

Dr. Saunders, the pediatric psychologist at the hospital, interviewed Hannah and her mother. According to her mother, Hannah had showed a gradual deterioration in her mood over the past several months. She had been increasingly irritable and moody. "She just flies off the handle for no apparent reason. I'll ask her to set the table or to turn off the TV and she'll scream, swear, or throw a tantrum. Then she'll run into her room and cry." Her mother was most concerned that Hannah might hurt herself. "Twice, I've had to stop her from banging her head against the wall. She kept crying, 'I want to die. I wish I was dead.'"

Hannah also showed problems with her behavior. In recent months, her appetite greatly decreased and she had problems going to sleep. Hannah used to have many friends at school, but in recent months she stopped playing with peers. She dropped out of the Girl Scouts and the 4-H club, two activities that she formerly enjoyed. "She used to be the perfect child—getting good grades, asking to help around the house, trying to do everything to please us. Now, she deliberately tries to upset us."

Hannah's family life was stressful. Her mother had a history of depression and had attempted suicide on two occasions. Although she took antidepressant medication, she still admitted to periods of intense sadness and loneliness. Hannah's father, a photographer, had longstanding problems with alcohol dependence. According to her mother, "Hannah thinks the world of her dad, and why shouldn't she? He's really fun when he's drunk. Hannah hates me because I'm the one who makes her do her homework, pick up her room, and eat her vegetables."

(Continued)

(Continued)

> Dr. Saunders attempted to interview Hannah. "I feel terrible," said Hannah, whose mouth was covered with charcoal residue. Dr. Saunders explained, "They needed to put that stuff in your stomach to get all the Tylenol out of your system." Hannah explained, "I didn't want to kill myself; I just wanted to show my mom that I'm serious. When I say 'no' I mean 'no.' She just doesn't understand how much my life sucks. No one understands."

What Are Depressive Disorders?

Mood disorders in children and adolescents have only received serious attention from researchers and clinicians in the past few decades. A generation ago, many mental health professionals believed that children were incapable of developing depression. We now know that mood disorders not only exist in children and adolescents, they are actually fairly common. Advances in research and clinical practice are leading to new and exciting developments in how we diagnose and treat childhood mood disorders.

Major Depressive Disorder

In order to be diagnosed with Major Depressive Disorder (MDD), a person must experience a "major depressive episode," that is, a discrete period of dysphoria that lasts for at least two weeks. *DSM-IV-TR* uses specific criteria to differentiate a major depressive episode from transient or minor feelings of sadness. Specifically, people experiencing a major depressive episode must show five out of a possible nine symptoms (see Table 11.1). At least one of these symptoms must be either (1) depressed mood or (2) a diminished interest or pleasure in most activities.

Depressed Mood

People with depression often feel sad, blue, or "down." Most people report these feelings directly. Other people show signs of sadness and emotional pain in their facial expressions and nonverbal behavior. Still others, especially children, express dysphoria through somatic complaints such as headaches and upset stomach. Children and adolescents may show a predominantly irritable mood rather than a more traditional "depressed" mood. For example, children with depression may appear angry, "touchy," easily upset, or annoyed. Parents and other adults may describe these children as crabby or cranky.

Diminished Interest or Pleasure in Most Activities

Most people with depression, regardless of age, also show a marked loss of interest or pleasure in activities they used to enjoy. Children with depression might drop out of sports or clubs. Adolescents with depression might avoid parties and other

Table 11.1   Diagnostic Criteria for Major Depressive Disorder

I. Presence of a Major Depressive Episode
  A. Five (or more) of the following symptoms have been present for at least 2 weeks and represent a change from previous behavior. At least one of the symptoms is (1) depressed mood or (2) loss of interest.
    1. Depressed mood (In children and adolescents, mood can be irritable)
    2. Diminished interest or pleasure in most activities
    3. Significant change in appetite or weight
    4. Significant change in sleep
    5. Psychomotor agitation or retardation
    6. Loss of energy or fatigue
    7. Feelings of worthlessness or guilt
    8. Concentration problems
    9. Recurrent thoughts of death or suicide
  B. Symptoms cause marked distress or impairment in functioning
  C. Symptoms are not caused by alcohol, other drugs, or a medical condition
  D. Symptoms are not better explained by bereavement (i.e., loss of a loved one). If they occur after the loss of a loved one, they must persist longer than 2 months or be characterized by severe impairment in functioning.

II. Symptoms are not better explained by Schizophrenia or another psychotic disorder.

III. Person has never had a Manic Episode, a Hypomanic Episode, or a Mixed Mood Episode (see note).

Source: Reprinted with permission from the *DSM-IV-TR.*

Note: Manic, Hypomanic, and Mixed Mood Episodes are used to diagnose bipolar disorders. If the person has ever had one of these mood episodes, he or she will likely meet diagnostic criteria for a bipolar disorder rather than Major Depressive Disorder. For more information about bipolar disorders, see Chapter 12.

social gatherings. This loss of interest is often referred to as **anhedonia**—literally, a loss of pleasure.

Significant Change in Appetite or Weight

Many people with depression show a marked decrease in appetite. These individuals often report that they "don't feel hungry," and they may need to be reminded and encouraged to eat. Their decreased appetite often leads to weight loss. In adults, a loss of more than 5% body weight in one month indicates significant weight reduction. In children and adolescents, failure to make age-expected weight gains meets this criterion. Some people with depression show increased appetite and weight gain. Increased appetite and weight gain are atypical and are more often seen in adults than in youth.

Significant Change in Sleep

The most common sleep problem among people with depression is **insomnia**. Typically, individuals with depression will wake in the middle of the night or during the early morning hours and be unable to return to sleep. Insomnia is one of the best predictors of mood problems in late childhood and early adolescence. In contrast, **hypersomnia** (i.e., sleeping too much) is more common among adults than among youth (van Lang, Ferdinand, & Verhulst, 2007).

Psychomotor Agitation or Retardation

Psychomotor agitation refers to a noticeable increase in motor activity. Children and adolescents with psychomotor agitation may appear restless, have problems sitting still, pace or wander about the room, or fidget with their hands or clothing. These behaviors seem to have no purpose, and they reflect an increase in children's usual activity level. Agitation must be severe enough to be observable by others. In some cases, individuals with depression show **psychomotor retardation**, that is, a general slowness or sluggishness in movement. Psychomotor retardation is more common in adults than in children and adolescents.

Loss of Energy or Fatigue

Most people with depression experience a loss of energy, tiredness, or fatigue. Adults and adolescents may report that even trivial daily tasks seem to require an enormous amount of energy. An adolescent with depression might have great difficulty getting ready for school or completing a short homework assignment. Children are less likely to report a loss of energy or fatigue than are adolescents and adults. Instead, they may appear unusually resistant or oppositional when asked to perform household chores and participate in activities with family members.

Feelings of Worthlessness or Guilt

Many people with depression are preoccupied by feelings of worthlessness or excessive feelings of guilt. Typically, these individuals ruminate on personal shortcomings or failures and overlook their strengths and successes. For example, a child with depression might get into frequent arguments with parents because of her irritable mood. Then she might feel terribly guilty for having these arguments, believing that she is not worthy of her parents' love and attention. Similarly, an adolescent with depression might fail to complete homework assignments because he believes that he is unintelligent, or he might avoid sports because he believes that he is not athletic.

Concentration Problems

People with depression often report problems with attention and concentration. They may be easily distracted, have problems thinking, or report difficulty making decisions. People with depression often show clouded judgment or lapses in memory. For example, adolescents with depression may have problems performing complex mental activities at school, such as writing a science report or performing a difficult musical arrangement. Children and adolescents with depression show increased difficulty completing homework assignments and may experience a sudden drop in grades.

Recurrent Thoughts of Death or Suicide

Thoughts of death and suicide are common among people with depression, including children and adolescents. Although we commonly think of adolescents and adults committing suicide, prepubescent children also attempt and complete suicide.

The same diagnostic criteria for MDD are used for children, adolescents, and adults. Some people have criticized the *DSM-IV-TR* for its age invariance. However, most research indicates that children and adolescents with depression can be identified using the current *DSM-IV-TR* criteria (Kolvin & Sadowski, 2001). On the other hand, children are less likely than adolescents and adults to show anhedonia, appetite and weight loss, and suicidal ideation (Birmaher et al., 2004; Garber, 2000).

Dysthymic Disorder

Dysthymic Disorder is defined by the presence of chronically depressed mood, occurring most days for at least two years. Adults usually describe their mood as "blah," sad, or "down in the dumps." In children and adolescents, Dysthymic Disorder is characterized by depressed or irritable mood that lasts at least one year (see Table 11.2). Youths with Dysthymic Disorder are often described as touchy, moody, or cranky.

Table 11.2   Diagnostic Criteria for Dysthymic Disorder

A. Depressed mood for most of the day, more days than not, for at least 2 years. In children and adolescents, mood can be irritable and the duration must be at least 1 year.

B. While depressed or irritable, person has at least 2 of the following:

    1. Poor appetite or overeating

    2. Insomnia or hypersomnia

    3. Low energy or fatigue

    4. Low self-esteem

    5. Poor concentration or difficulty making decisions

    6. Feelings of hopelessness

C. During the 2-year period (or 1-year period in children and adolescents), the person has never been without symptoms for more than 2 months at a time

D. The person has not had a Major Depressive Episode during the first 2 years of the disturbance (or 1 year of the disturbance in children and adolescents)

E. Person has never had a Manic Episode, a Hypomanic Episode, or a Mixed Mood Episode, and does not have Cyclothymic Disorder (see note)

F. Symptoms are not better explained by Schizophrenia or another psychotic disorder

G. Symptoms are not caused by alcohol, other drugs, or a medical condition

H. Symptoms cause marked distress or impairment in functioning

Source: Reprinted with permission from the *DSM-IV-TR.*

Note: Manic, Hypomanic, and Mixed Mood Episodes are used to diagnose bipolar disorders. If the person has ever had one of these mood episodes, he or she will likely meet diagnostic criteria for a bipolar disorder rather than Dysthymic Disorder. Cyclothymic Disorder is a specific type of bipolar disorder. For more information about bipolar disorders, see Chapter 12.

Eppy

Elizabeth (Eppy) Andersen was a 15-year-old girl who was referred to our clinic by her mother. According to Mrs. Andersen, Eppy had been experiencing long-term problems with depressed mood and irritability. "For a while now," her mother explained, "Eppy's been withdrawn, touchy, and irritable. Sometimes, she just shuts herself in her room as soon as she gets home from school and we don't see her again until the next morning. At other times, she just mopes around the house, never wanting to do anything with anyone. When we ask her what's wrong, she just snaps at us, 'Nothing! Can't you just leave me alone?'"

Eppy had to deal with multiple psychosocial stressors throughout her childhood. Mrs. Andersen had a history of MDD. Eppy's father abandoned Eppy and her mother when Eppy was in the second grade. Eppy had long-term academic problems. She earned mostly Cs and Ds, even though she studied very hard.

During the course of the interview, Eppy admitted to persistently feeling "not quite right." She admitted to "snapping" at family members and reported that her irritable behavior had caused her to lose friends. Eppy added, "My friends will invite me over to cheer me up. But I always just blow them off or say something stupid to make them mad at me. Afterward I feel terrible. I wonder, 'Why was I so mean to them?' But, you know, I'd just rather be by myself." Eppy admitted to feeling depressed and tired most of the time. She napped approximately two hours each afternoon despite sleeping nine or ten hours every evening. She often felt tired and "run down," as if she never had enough energy to get things done.

Eppy denied suicidal thoughts, but she showed extreme pessimism about the future. "Nothing I do is ever good enough," she explained. "At home, my mom's always nagging me. At school, I work hard and never get anywhere. My friends just don't understand. I'll probably just end up like my mom—a basket case . . . or my dad—an alcoholic." Her therapist asked, "How do you know that?" Eppy responded, "I just know. It's in the genes."

People with Dysthymic Disorder often regard themselves as uninteresting, unlikable, and ineffective. For example, a child with Dysthymic Disorder might not believe that classmates want to play with her or select her to be part of a group activity. An adolescent with the disorder might doubt his ability to make a sports team or to gain admission to college. Youths with Dysthymic Disorder are also prone to self-criticism. They might dwell upon their shortcomings, belittle themselves in front of others, and constantly doubt themselves and their abilities.

Dysthymic Disorder is a long-lasting condition. If we think of MDD as a severe bout of the flu, we might liken Dysthymic Disorder to chronic problems with allergies. The symptoms of Dysthymic Disorder occur for so long that many people with the disorder do not even realize that they have mood problems. Some adults and adolescents with Dysthymic Disorder see the symptoms as part of their personality, claiming, "I've always been this way" or "That's just how I am."

Dysthymic Disorder can be differentiated from MDD in its onset, duration, severity, and (to some extent) its symptoms. Dysthymic Disorder usually begins gradually and slowly over time. In contrast, the onset of MDD is usually rapid. By definition, Dysthymic Disorder is a long-term condition, whereas MDD usually lasts for only a few weeks to a few months. Although MDD and Dysthymic Disorder share some of the same symptoms, symptoms of MDD are more severe. Furthermore, certain symptoms like anhedonia and suicidal ideation are more characteristic of MDD than of Dysthymic Disorder.

Children and adolescents can be diagnosed with both Dysthymic Disorder and MDD. Dysthymic Disorder must be present first and exist for at least two years (one year for children and adolescents) before the onset of MDD. The presence of both Dysthymic Disorder and MDD is sometimes called **double depression**. People with both Dysthymic Disorder and MDD often show very poor functioning and resistance to treatment.

Depression: Categorical or Dimensional?

DSM-IV-TR adopts a categorical approach to diagnosing mood disorders. The categorical approach assumes that depression is a discrete mood state; individuals either have depression or they do not. In contrast, dimensional approaches assume that depression exists along a continuum, ranging from no depressive symptoms to extreme and debilitating depression.

Researchers have examined whether depression is categorical or continuous in adults and adolescents. In general, findings have been mixed. Most studies involving adults have shown that the emotional symptoms of depression (e.g., sadness, anhedonia) are continuous, while the physical symptoms of depression (e.g., sleep and appetite problems) are categorical (Beach & Amir, 2003). On the other hand, research with adolescents suggests that all depressive symptoms fall along a continuum of severity (Hankin, Fraley, Lahey, & Waldman, 2005).

Based on these findings, many professionals view depression in children and adolescents as existing along a continuum in the shape of a positively skewed distribution. Most youths show very few symptoms, some youths show a moderate number of symptoms, and a few youths—those who are diagnosed with MDD—show a great number of symptoms. Youths who show the greatest number of symptoms are qualitatively distinct from other youths; indeed, they are at most risk for lifelong social and emotional problems. However, many youths who do not technically meet *DSM-IV-TR* criteria experience significant emotional suffering.

Some recent research suggests that these subthreshold, dysphoric children show levels of impairment and prognoses similar to those of children who meet all *DSM-IV-TR* diagnostic criteria for MDD (Lewinsohn, Solomon, Seeley, & Zeiss, 2000; Stewart et al., 2002). Some clinicians use the term **Minor Depressive Disorder** to describe youths with subthreshold levels of depression. Gonzalez-Tejera and colleagues (2005) showed that children with minor depression have impairment and comorbidity similar to children with MDD. Furthermore, they are more likely to be referred for psychological treatment than children with MDD and show similarly poor developmental outcomes. The authors argue that children with minor depression should not be dismissed as having transient mood problems. Rather, minor depression (despite its name) should be regarded as a serious disorder that deserves care and attention.

Associated Psychiatric Disorders

Anxiety

Anxiety disorders are highly comorbid with depression. Approximately 40%–50% of adolescents with depression have an anxiety disorder (Kovacs & Devlin, 1998; Lewinsohn, Hops, Roberts, Seeley, & Andrews, 1993). The most common anxiety disorder among children with depression is Social Phobia, a disorder characterized by extreme fear of social situations in which the person might be judged or criticized by others (Treatment for Adolescents With Depression Study Team [TADS], 2005). Both depression and Social Phobia can lead to social withdrawal and avoidance. Youths with both disorders show greater impairment in interpersonal functioning than youths with either disorder alone.

Disruptive Behavior

Childhood depression and conduct problems frequently co-occur; furthermore, the presence of both mood problems and conduct disturbance is associated with high levels of impairment (Angold et al., 1999). The comorbidity of depression and ADHD ranges from 12% to 45% (Biederman et al., 1999; Kennard, Ginsburg, Feeny, Sweeney, & Zagurski, 2005; TADS, 2005). Youths with both disorders show problems with attention and concentration and are easily distractible. They may also have difficulty performing homework assignments and earning high grades in school.

Approximately 23% of depressed youth show ODD or CD (TADS, 2005). When conduct problems and depression co-occur, conduct problems usually precede depression (Biederman, Faraone et al., 1995; Rohde, Lewinsohn, & Seeley, 1991). Capaldi (1992) examined conduct problems and depression in boys from sixth through eighth grades. Approximately 31.5% of boys with conduct problems alone in sixth grade showed comorbid depression by eighth grade. In contrast, only 12.9% of boys with depression alone in sixth grade showed conduct problems by eighth grade. Most experts believe conduct problems lead to conflict with family members and peers. These interpersonal problems, in turn, place children at risk for social isolation, low self-worth, and depression.

Little and Garber (2005) provided support for the notion that peer rejection explains the relationship between conduct problems and depression. In a study of sixth graders, the researchers found that conduct problems predicted interpersonal problems. These interpersonal problems, in turn, predicted depression one year later. However, interpersonal stressors predicted depression only for children who showed high levels of interpersonal orientation (i.e., a strong need for connectedness with others). The authors concluded that children who place great value on interpersonal relationships, yet experience social problems because of their disruptive behavior, may be particularly prone to depression.

Substance Use

Some studies have shown a relationship between adolescent depression and substance use problems (Henry, Feehan, McGee, Stanton, Moffitt, & Silva, 1993). The strength of this relationship seems to depend on the age and gender of the adolescent. Older adolescents with depression are more likely to show substance use problems than younger adolescents and children. Furthermore, boys with depression are somewhat more likely than girls to show substance use problems (Maag & Irvin, 2005). In one study, approximately 33% of boys with depression and 16% of girls with depression also showed signs of problematic alcohol use (Windle & Davies, 1999).

Why are youths with depression at increased risk for substance use problems? In some cases, particularly among older adolescents, depression precedes alcohol use (Costello, Erkanli, Feerman, & Angeld, 1999). These adolescents may use alcohol and other drugs to cope with psychological distress, a practice sometimes called **self-medication**. Alcohol consumption is negatively reinforced by a reduction in depressed mood (Khantzian, 1995).

However, most research suggests that a third variable, peer rejection, predicts both adolescents' likelihood of depression and their likelihood of using alcohol and other drugs. Some children, especially those with disruptive behavior problems, experience conflict with family members, rejection by classmates, and low academic achievement. Peer rejection, in particular, can cause these adolescents to become depressed. At the same time, peer rejection can prompt many of these youths to associate with deviant peers who encourage them to use alcohol and other drugs. These youths, therefore, develop both mood problems and substance use problems as a consequence of peer rejection (S. M. King et al., 2004).

Suicide and Self-Harm

Children and adolescents with depression are at increased risk for suicide. Indeed, suicide is one of the three leading causes of death among adolescents in the United States (World Health Organization, 2001). Suicide kills more children and adolescents than cancer, heart disease, AIDS, birth defects, stroke, and chronic lung disease combined. Approximately 4,000 youths die by suicide annually. Approximately 8% of adolescents attempt suicide every year. Less than 1% of adolescents who attempt suicide are successful (Flisher, Ziervogel, Chalton, Leger, & Robertson, 1993; Pomerantz, 2005).

Mental health professionals assess a person's risk for suicide by examining three criteria:

- whether the person wants to die,
- whether the person has a plan to kill himself or herself, and
- the feasibility of the suicide plan.

Transient thoughts of one's own death are fairly common among children and adolescents; they usually indicate low risk by themselves. For example, it is fairly common for a child to ask, "I wonder if Mom and Dad would miss me if I caught a terrible disease and died?" Recurrent thoughts of suicide, with no specific suicide plan, merit greater concern. For example, a child might admit, "I've thought about killing myself, to make everyone feel bad about being mean to me, but I don't know how I'd do it."

Even more risky are youngsters who report recurrent thoughts of suicide with specific suicide plans. For example, an adolescent with depression might state, "I've thought about killing myself a few times, by shooting myself or taking pills, but I'm not sure whether I could go through with it."

Of greatest concern are children and adolescents who show high motivation to kill themselves and have a well-thought-out suicide plan. For example, an adolescent might want to die, know that a combination of certain medications and alcohol can be lethal, and have access to these substances.

Researchers have identified a number of risk factors for suicide: depression and other mood disorders, low self-esteem, substance use problems, feelings of hopelessness, stressful life events, and family dysfunction (R. A. King et al., 2001; Lewinsohn, Rohde, & Seeley, 1994; Wild, Flisher, & Lombard, 2004; Yoder, 1999). Among these factors, the best predictor of adolescent suicide is depression. In one study of depressed adolescents, 4.4% completed suicide within 10 years after diagnosis.

Although depression is the best predictor of suicide, it is not a reliable predictor. Most youths who are depressed never attempt suicide, and many youths who attempt suicide do not experience depression (Wild et al., 2004). Recently, researchers have examined how combinations of risk factors might best predict suicide. Wild and colleagues (2004) discovered that the combination of depression and low self-esteem regarding one's family predicted both suicidal ideation and suicide attempts among adolescents. These results suggest that adolescents' relationships with family members are important in maintaining their psychological well-being.

In addition to suicide, depressed youths are at risk for self-harm. **Self-harm** refers to deliberate, physical self-injury without intent to kill oneself. The most common forms of self-injury are cutting, burning, hitting, or excessively scratching oneself (Favazza, 1996).

The onset of self-harm is usually middle adolescence (Favazza, 1996). Most research indicates that girls are more likely than boys to deliberately injure themselves. Individuals usually engage in self-harm as a maladaptive way to cope with stress or emotional pain. Indeed, individuals who injure themselves show much higher levels of depression than adolescents who do not harm themselves (Martin, Rozanes, Pearce, & Allison, 1995; Ross & Heath, 2002). Usually, adolescents who injure themselves do not want to kill themselves and do not intend to die from their injuries (Favazza, 1998). In contrast, adolescents who attempt suicide report greater emotional distress and repulsion toward life than adolescents who engage in self-harm (Muehlenkamp & Gutierrez, 2004).

Epidemiology

Prevalence

The prevalence of depression varies by age and gender (Hankin, Abramson, Moffitt, Silva, McGee, & Angell, 1998; Lewinsohn et al., 1993). Most young children show few problems with mood; only 1%–2% experience MDD (P. Cohen et al., 1993; Fleming & Offord, 1990; Keenan, Hipwell, Duax, Stouthamer-Loeber, & Loeber, 2004). In childhood, boys and girls are approximately equally likely to show depression (Costello, Pine, Hammen, John, Plotsky, & Weissman, 2002; Hankin et al., 1998).

In adolescence, the prevalence of depression increases dramatically. At any given time, 3%–7% of adolescents are depressed (Costello et al., 2002; Hankin et al., 1998). Furthermore, as many as 20% of youth may experience MDD at some time during adolescence (Cole et al., 2002; Garber, Keiley, & Martin, 2002; Lewinsohn, Rohde, & Seeley, 1998).

The dramatic increase in the prevalence of depression from late childhood to early adolescence is largely due to a corresponding increase in the number of adolescent girls with depression. Indeed, adolescent girls are twice as likely as adolescent boys to experience a depressive disorder. By age 18, as many as 28% of girls and 14% of boys have experienced either MDD or Dysthymic Disorder. The prevalence of child and adolescent depression *has not* increased over the past several years (Costello, Erkanli, & Angold, 2006).

Gender Differences

Depression is not only more common among adolescent girls, it may also be more impairing. Compared to adolescent boys with depression, girls with depression show a greater number of symptoms, more severe symptoms, and greater likelihood of self-harm. Initial depressive episodes last longer for adolescent girls than boys and are more likely to lead to long-term mood problems (Kovacs, 1997; McCauley, Myers, Mitchell, Calderon, Schloredt, & Treder, 1993).

Keenan and Hipwell (2005) developed a theoretical model to explain gender differences in adolescent depression. According to their model, girls who are at risk for depression have three personality characteristics that predispose them to mood problems.

First, some girls display excessive empathy; that is, they are unusually sensitive to the emotional well-being of others and may assume unwarranted responsibility for others' negative emotions. Consequently, girls may try to solve other people's problems and experience excessive guilt and helplessness when they are unable to alleviate others' distress.

Second, some girls show excessive compliance; that is, they have a strong need to meet others' needs and to gain others' approval. Often, they sacrifice their own well-being and autonomy in order to please others. Excessive compliance can be problematic in two ways. First, depression can occur when girls comply with others' requests in situations when noncompliance might be more appropriate (e.g., a girl giving in to a boy's demands for sex). Second, depression can occur when girls repeatedly remain passive in interpersonal situations to meet the social expectations of others (e.g., a girl reluctant to speak up in class). Excessive compliance can stifle the development of autonomy and individuality and contribute to low self-esteem and depression.

Third, some girls show problems with emotion regulation; that is, they have difficulty modifying and altering negative moods. Keenan and Hipwell (2005) argue that some girls have a limited number of coping strategies to deal with negative emotions. When these strategies are ineffective, they can become either excessively distressed or over-controlled. Rather than displaying negative emotions in open and adaptive ways, these girls hide their feelings and develop mood problems.

A combination of biological and environmental factors can lead to excessive empathy, over-compliance, and emotional over-control in girls. Indeed, young girls are more likely than boys to display higher levels of all three risk factors (Keenan & Hipwell, 2005). These three characteristics limit girls' social and emotional competencies, especially their self-confidence, assertiveness, and emotional expressiveness. When they enter adolescence, they may be unprepared to cope with the biological and psychosocial stressors of puberty (Zahn-Waxler, 2000; Zahn-Waxler, Cole, & Barrett, 1991). Consequently, they may show rates of depression much higher than do boys.

Course

Depression in Childhood

Depression is fairly rare in prepubescent childhood; most young children show few symptoms. Depressive symptoms increase considerably after puberty, with the increase occurring earlier and more dramatically in girls than boys (Birmaher et al., 1996; Lewinsohn et al., 1998). Symptoms tend to be at their greatest during late adolescence, after which they usually decline in a linear fashion into early adulthood (Wight, Sepulveda, & Aneshensel, 2004).

Depressive symptoms also show moderate to high stability over time. If left untreated, the duration of depressive episodes ranges from 8–13 months in children and 3–9 months in adolescents. Approximately 90% of children and 50%–90% of adolescents recover from these episodes. Relapse is fairly common (Birmaher, Arbelaez, & Brent, 2002; Birmaher et al., 2004). Approximately 60% of depressed youth have another depressive episode within two years after recovery, whereas 72% have another depressive episode within five years of recovery (Simons, Rohde, Kennard, & Robins, 2005).

Post, Weiss, Leverich, George, Frye, and Ketter (1996) developed the **kindling hypothesis** to explain the tendency of depressed individuals to have recurrent depressive episodes. According to this hypothesis, early depressive episodes sensitize individuals to stressful life events and depression. After multiple depressive episodes, less severe stressors can trigger major depressive symptoms. Support for the kindling hypothesis has been found in adults, but it remains untested in children.

Depression in Adolescence

In order to investigate the course of depression, researchers have conducted longitudinal studies assessing children's mood symptoms from childhood through adolescence. Based on this longitudinal research, researchers have identified four distinct patterns of mood functioning among youth (Brendgen et al., 2005; see Figure 11.1).

First, 50% of children and adolescents show very low levels of depression across childhood and adolescence. These youngsters are at low risk for developing mood problems. Boys are the overwhelming majority of children in this group.

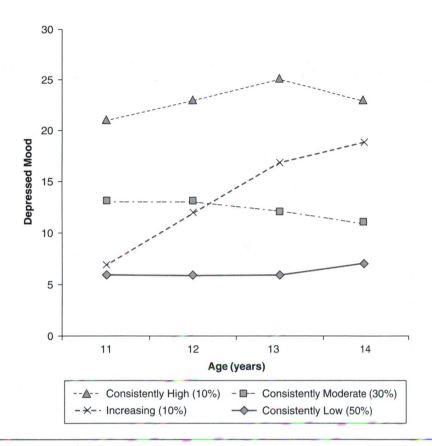

Figure 11.1   Developmental Pathways for Child and Adolescent Mood Disorders

Source: Based on Brendgen et al. (2005).

Note: Most children show either chronically low (50%) or chronically moderate (30%) levels of depressive symptoms and are not at risk for mood disorders. Approximately 10% of youth show chronically high levels of depression through childhood and adolescence. An additional 10% show low levels of depression in childhood but high levels in adolescence.

Second, 30% of youth show consistent but moderate levels of depressive symptoms throughout childhood and adolescence. These youth experience mild dysphoria, but their mood problems usually do not interfere with day-to-day activities. Boys outnumber girls in this group as well.

Third, 10% of youth show chronically high levels of depression, beginning in late childhood and continuing though adolescence. These youngsters are disproportionately girls with histories of early parent-child conflict and difficulties with emotion regulation. These girls often show difficult temperaments that interfere with their social and emotional functioning. They are at risk for long-term problems with mood and behavior.

The remaining 10% of youth show low levels of depressive symptoms in childhood but dramatically higher levels of depression in adolescence. These youngsters also tend to be girls with difficult temperaments and histories of parent-child conflict. However, they frequently experience peer rejection and social alienation during late childhood or early adolescence. It is likely that peer rejection and other psychosocial stressors of puberty exacerbate social and emotional problems in this group of children.

Taken together, these findings indicate that approximately 20% of youth will have mood problems during childhood or adolescence. This is consistent with other longitudinal research that suggests that 20%–25% of youth show moderate to long-term mood problems (Fombonne et al., 2001). Indeed, youths with depression are four times more likely to experience mood disorders in adulthood compared to their non-depressed peers (Harrington, Fudge, Rutter, Pickles, & Hill, 1990).

Etiology

Genetics

MDD in children and adolescents is partially determined by genetics. Research involving adults with MDD has shown a strong genetic component to the disorder. For example, some studies involving adult monozygotic (MZ) twins reared together have yielded concordance rates as high as 70%–85%. Furthermore, adult MZ twins reared apart show approximately 67% concordance for depression. In contrast, dizygotic twins reared together show only about 19% concordance for the disorder. Taken together, these findings indicate that genetic factors place individuals at considerable risk for depression. Having a parent with depression increases one's risk of developing the disorder threefold (Reinecke & Simons, 2005).

Unfortunately, genetic studies of children and adolescents with depression have been plagued by methodological problems. Most studies have relied on extremely small sample sizes. Also, studies have often used different methods to identify depression in youths, making these studies difficult to compare to each other. Furthermore, researchers have often failed to separate the effects of genes from the effects of the environment in their studies of depressed youth. For example, the fact that depression runs in families provides evidence for both genetic and shared environmental causes. Future research that more carefully teases apart the relative effects of genes and environment on children's depression is sorely needed (Reinecke & Simons, 2005).

Neurotransmitters

It is likely that genetic factors contribute to depression by affecting children's neurotransmitter functioning. The **monoamine hypothesis** for depression asserts that two neurotransmitters, in particular, play roles in depressive disorders: serotonin and norepinephrine. These neurotransmitters are monoamines, hence the name of the hypothesis. According to the theory, depression is associated with dysregulation in one or both of these neurotransmitters.

Evidence for the monoamine hypothesis comes primarily from research with adults. The hypothesis is supported by the fact that antidepressant medications, which regulate serotonin and/or norepinephrine, can alleviate depression in adults. Adolescents treated with certain antidepressant medications can also show changes in serotonin functioning; furthermore, the magnitude of these changes is directly associated with the degree of adolescents' symptom reduction (Axelson et al., 2005).

Other evidence for the monoamine hypothesis comes from molecular genetics research. Eley and colleagues (2004) examined genes responsible for serotonergic functioning. They discovered a number of genes that predicted depression in adolescent girls. Furthermore, some of the genes only predicted depression when girls also experienced adverse life events. The authors argued that genes responsible for serotonergic activity play roles in the emergence of depression in youth. However, these genes may require certain adverse environmental conditions to produce their harmful effects.

Temperament

A second mechanism by which genes might contribute to the development of mood problems is through temperament. Recall that temperament refers to the physiological, emotional, and behavioral responses a child typically displays when she encounters environmental stimuli (Rothbart & Bates, 1998). Temperament is largely genetically determined; however, it can be modified by children's early experiences.

Temperament can contribute to the development of mood disorders in at least three ways (Compas, Connor-Smith, & Jaser, 2004). First, difficult temperament can directly contribute to children's depressive symptoms by increasing children's negative emotions. Children with difficult temperament (e.g., excessive irritability, moodiness, difficulty soothing) often overreact to negative life events and have difficulty regulating their emotions. They may simply experience more frequent and intense levels of negative affect than other children their age.

Second, difficult temperament in childhood may elicit negative reactions from caregivers and peers. For example, irritability in early childhood might lead caregivers to adopt more angry, hostile, and coercive parenting tactics. These adverse parenting behaviors can cause parent-child conflict, behavior problems, low self-worth, and depression.

Third, children with difficult temperaments may show greater problems coping with early childhood stressors. These coping problems, in turn, can contribute to mood problems. For example, children with difficult temperaments may become overwhelmed when they encounter stressful life events. When faced with a psychosocial stressor, these children might show high levels of anger, irritability, or moodiness. Alternatively, other children with difficult temperaments may avoid coping with the stressor altogether by emotionally shutting down, withdrawing, or developing anxiety and depression.

HPA Dysregulation

Early childhood stressors can contribute to later mood problems by affecting the body's stress response system. The body's response to stress is regulated by the **hypothalamus-pituitary-adrenal (HPA) axis.** When the child encounters a psychosocial stressor, brain regions that process and regulate emotions (especially the amygdala and hippocampus) activate the HPA axis. When activated, components of the HPA axis release a series of hormones. First, the hypothalamus releases corticotrophin-releasing hormone (CRH). CRH is detected by the pituitary gland, which, in turn, secretes a second hormone, adrenocorticotropin-releasing hormone (ACTH). ACTH, in turn, triggers the release of cortisol from the adrenal cortex. **Cortisol** is the body's main stress hormone; it activates the sympathetic nervous system. Cortisol initiates fight-or-flight behavior and increases feelings of alertness and apprehension.

In typically developing individuals, cortisol flows through the bloodstream and is detected by the hypothalamus, pituitary, and hippocampus. These brain regions shut off production of cortisol, returning the body to a more relaxed state. However, adults with depression often show chronically high levels of cortisol. Furthermore, they often have difficulties stopping cortisol production once it starts. For example, if researchers give adults with depression a synthetic form of cortisol (i.e., dexamethasone), many adults do not show the normal "shutting off" of cortisol production. In fact, as many as 60% of depressed adults do not pass this **dexamethasone suppression test (DST)** and show chronically high levels of cortisol, even when not experiencing an immediate stressor. This dysregulation of the HPA axis is believed to partially explain their depressed mood (Shea, Walsh, MacMillan, & Steiner, 2005).

Depressed youths may also show dysregulation of the HPA axis. First, many depressed youths show elevated cortisol activity, even while at rest (Goodyer, Herbert, Tamplin, & Altham, 2000; Goodyer, Park, & Herbert, 2001). Second, some depressed adolescents show structural abnormalities in parts of the HPA axis. Compared to healthy adolescents, depressed adolescents show smaller amygdalae and hippocampi (MacMaster & Kusumakar, 2004; Rosso, Cintron, Steingard, Renshaw, Young, & Yurgelun-Todd, 2005) and enlarged pituitary (MacMaster & Kusumakar, 2004).

Stress and Coping

Stressful Life Events

Stressful life events are associated with child and adolescent depression. Several studies have shown that major life stressors predict the onset of MDD (Burton, Stice, & Seeley, 2004; Goodyer, Herbert, & Tamplin, 2000; Lewinsohn, Allen, Gotlib, & Seeley, 1999; Luby, Belden, & Spitznagel, 2006). Furthermore, depressed children and adolescents report more frequent and serious stressful life events than their nondepressed peers (Sandberg, McGuinness, Hillary, & Rutter, 1998; Williamson, Birmaher, Frank, Anderson, Matty, & Kupfer, 1998). In fact, children's risk of depression is directly associated with the number of stressful life events that they encounter (Monroe, Rhode, Seeley, & Lewinsohn, 1999; Steinhausen & Metzke, 2000).

The timing of stressful life events may also be important. Events that occur during adolescence seem to be especially problematic. Perhaps stressful life events that occur during adolescence magnify the stress adolescents experience during this developmental period. Stressful events that occur during or shortly after puberty may have especially adverse effects for girls (Ge, Coger, & Elder, 2001). Again, the combination of puberty and the stressful event might be too taxing on girls' coping skills.

Although stressful life events are associated with depression in youth, they are not robust predictors of depression. On average, stressful life events explain only 2% of the variance in adolescents' depressive symptoms (Garber et al., 2002; Lewinsohn, Roberts, Seeley, Rohde, Gotlib, & Hops, 1994). Furthermore, the importance of stressful life events in triggering depressive episodes may diminish over time. Lewinsohn and colleagues (1999) found that adolescents' first depressive episodes were strongly associated with a negative life event. However, later depressive episodes were less closely connected to psychosocial stressors.

Although stressful life events and depression are correlated, stressful life events may not necessarily *cause* adolescents to become depressed. Waaktaar, Borge, Fundingsrud, Christie, and Torgersen (2004) assessed adolescents' depressive symptoms and stressful life events at two times, approximately one year apart. Consistent with previous research, they found a moderate correlation between depressive symptoms and life stressors. Contrary to expectations, however, the researchers discovered that early symptoms of depression predicted *later* stressful life events.

The researchers suggested that the traditional view—that stressful events cause depression—is too simplistic. Instead, the relationship between stressful events and depression may be bi-directional. Of course, stressful events can contribute to depression. However, depressed youths may also elicit stressful events from the environment (Hammen, 1991). For example, children who are rejected by peers may experience depression. Depression, in turn, can lead to social avoidance and increased problems in social interactions.

Coping

Although many youths experience stressful life events, most do not show depression. Stressful events, alone, are often insufficient to explain the emergence of depression. Hammen (1992) has suggested that the effects of stress on children's emotional functioning depend partly on the way children attempt to cope with stress. Stressful life events are not harmful per se; rather, it is the child's ability to cope with these events that determines whether or not he will become depressed (Murberg & Bru, 2005).

Children can cope with stress in two ways (Li, DiGiuseppe, & Froh, 2006). First, children can use **active coping**. Active coping involves taking steps to address the source of psychosocial stress or, at least, to reduce its harmful effects. For example, a child who is bullied at school might actively cope with this stressor by confronting the perpetrator or asking a teacher for help. Most studies have shown that active coping strategies protect children from depression (Vickers et al., 2003).

Alternatively, children can use **avoidance coping** to deal with stress. Children use avoidance coping when they physically or emotionally distance themselves from the stressor. One way to cope with stress, but avoid the stressor, is to act out or show other disruptive behavior problems. For example, a child who is bullied at school might act out in class. Unfortunately, disruptive coping is associated with peer rejection and decreased self-worth (Coie, Dodge, & Kupersmidt, 1990). A second form of avoidance coping is to withdraw from the stress-evoking situation. For example, a child who is bullied might refuse to attend school. Social withdrawal, too, is associated with depression (Li et al., 2006).

A final form of avoidance coping is to mentally disengage from the stressful situation. Children can distract themselves from stressful events by thinking other, more pleasant thoughts or engaging in pleasurable activities. Rather than ruminate about being bullied at school, a child might take his mind off the situation by playing video games or reading a book. In general, mental disengagement has benefits and drawbacks. On the one hand, distraction stops children from dwelling on negative events. On the other hand, excessive use of distraction can interfere with children's use of active coping (Nolen-Hoeksema, 2000).

Cognition

Contemporary models of child and adolescent depression emphasize the role of cognition in the emergence and maintenance of depressive symptoms (Reinecke & Simons, 2005). According to cognitive models, early stressful experiences adversely affect the way children think about themselves and their surroundings. These experiences also color the attributions they make about other people's behavior and the way they interpret events. Cognitions, in turn, can affect children's mood (Mezulis, Hyde, & Abramson, 2006; Spence & Reinecke, 2003).

Beck's Cognitive Theory of Depression

Aaron Beck (1967, 1976) developed a model of depression that focuses primarily on people's cognitions. According to Beck, thoughts, feelings, and actions are intricately connected. The way people think influences the way they feel and act. Beck posited that individuals who are depressed show two characteristic ways of thinking that predispose them to negative emotions and maladaptive behaviors: cognitive biases and cognitive distortions.

First, people with depression often show **cognitive biases**. A bias is a cognitive shift toward looking at the world in a certain way. People with depression show a negative cognitive bias in their view of themselves, the world, and the future. Although these people encounter pleasant and unpleasant experiences every day, they tend to selectively attend to negative experiences while ignoring or dismissing positive aspects about themselves and their surroundings. For example, an adolescent with depression might dwell upon a low grade that she receives on a particular math exam rather than on her otherwise good performance in math class.

Second, people with depression show **cognitive distortions**. A cognitive distortion involves adjusting one's perceptions or interpretations of the world in a manner that is inconsistent with reality (see Table 11.3). Individuals with depression interpret events in an excessively negative light, causing them to feel helpless and hopeless (Brozina & Abela, 2006). For example, after receiving a low grade on a math exam, an adolescent with depression might believe that she is "stupid" and that she will "never get into college." These distortions are untrue; one low math grade is not sufficient evidence that someone is "stupid." Furthermore, one low grade will probably not affect one's chances of gaining college admission. These beliefs reflect distortions of reality that confirm the adolescent's view that she is worthless, that the world is cruel, and that the future is bleak.

Table 11.3   Examples of Cognitive Distortions That May Contribute to Depression

Distortion	Explanation/Examples
Catastrophizing	Overestimating the chances of disaster; expecting something terrible to happen • *What if I go to the party and no one asks me to dance?* • *What if I mess up on the presentation and everyone thinks I'm stupid?*
Overgeneralization	Abstracting a general rule (or coming to a general conclusion) based on a single isolated incident • After breaking up with a boyfriend: *I'll never find anyone as good as him again.* • After failing a test: *I'm just not very smart*
Dichotomous thinking	Categorizing experiences at the extremes (either all good or all bad) • *Unless I make the honor roll, I'm a dummy.* • *If I can't get an A in the class, I just won't even try.*
Mind reading	Making assumptions about other's thoughts, feelings, or behaviors without evidence • *I can tell they hate my clothes.* • *They're probably thinking, "Look how dumb he is."*
Personalization	Taking personal responsibility for something that is not one's fault • *Bill walked by me in the hallway and didn't say hello. I must have said something to make him mad.* • *He didn't ask me out; it must have been my weight.*
Absolute thinking	Beliefs that involve "must," "should," or "have to" • *I must get into college, otherwise I'm a complete failure.* • *My parents have to let me go camping this weekend, otherwise I'll just die.*

Source: Based on J. S. Beck et al. (2005) and A. T. Beck and Weishaar (2005).

According to Beck (1967, 1976), cognitive distortions are especially salient in people's **negative automatic thoughts** about themselves, the world, and the future. Automatic thoughts are transient self-statements or mental images that pop into people's minds immediately after they experience a psychosocial stressor. For example, after missing a game-winning free throw, a child might think to himself, "I'm such a loser" or "Nothing I do ever goes right." Alternatively, he might have a mental image of his friends or family members teasing or ostracizing him for missing the basket. These transient negative thoughts color people's interpretation of events and can contribute to feelings of depression.

Depressed children and adolescents show both cognitive biases and distortions. Furthermore, the number of cognitive biases and distortions shown by youths is associated with the severity of their depressive symptoms (Tems, Stewart, Skinner, Hughes, & Emslie, 1993). Depressed youths typically report more negative automatic thoughts than their emotionally healthy peers (see Figure 11.2). Furthermore, depressed youths tend to dwell upon their negative thoughts and personal failures (Burwell & Shirk, 2007; Wilkinson & Goodyer, 2006). The negative automatic thoughts reported by depressed youths differ from the negative automatic thoughts

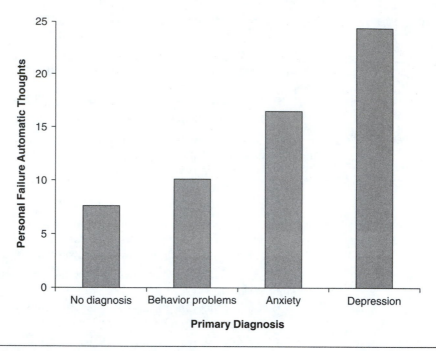

Figure 11.2   Automatic Thoughts Shown by Adolescents With Depression

Source: From Schniering and Rapee (2004b). Used with permission.

Note: Automatic thoughts dealing with personal failure (e.g., "I'm a loser. Nothing I do ever goes as planned") are associated with childhood depression.

reported by youths with other disorders. For example, depressed youths frequently report beliefs characterized by personal loss and failure, whereas anxious youths are more likely to report automatic cognitions about threat and personal vulnerability (Schniering & Rapee, 2004a, 2004b).

Reciprocal Vulnerability

Cognitive theorists argue that ways of thinking, especially negative cognitive biases and distortions, place individuals at risk for depression. However, critics of the traditional cognitive approach argue that depressive symptoms themselves can lead to an increase in negative beliefs and automatic thoughts (Coyne & Whiffen, 1995). Negative beliefs can be a consequence, in addition to a cause, of depression.

Using a large sample of sixth- and seventh-grade girls, Shahar, Blatt, Zuroff, Kuperminc, and Leadbeater (2004) tested the idea that negative self-statements and depressed mood are reciprocally related. By observing adolescents over a one-year period, the research team found that negative automatic thoughts led to increased feelings of depression. This finding supported Beck's (1967, 1976) cognitive theory. However, the researchers also found that feelings of depression led to an increase in self-criticism and other negative automatic thoughts. This finding supported the notion that depression can also affect cognition. In another study involving a large sample of adolescents, depressive symptoms predicted the emergence of cognitive distortions *better* than cognitive distortions predicted later depressive symptoms (Stewart et al., 2004).

Taken together, these results suggest that negative beliefs and depressive symptoms reciprocally affect the emergence of depression in adolescents. Shahar and colleagues (2004) suggest that negative automatic thoughts (especially self-critical statements) and depressive symptoms contribute to a vicious cycle, especially in girls. Girls who set unrealistically high standards and criticize themselves when these standards are not met set themselves up for depression. Their depressed mood, in turn, may interfere with their social and academic functioning, causing them to experience more failure and, consequently, more self-criticism. The reciprocal effects of self-criticism and depression may account for the chronic nature of depression in some adolescent girls (Rice, Leever, Noggle, & Lapsley, 2007).

Learned Helplessness

Martin Seligman (1975) hypothesized that feelings of hopelessness and despair contribute to the emergence of depression. In a now-famous study, Seligman and colleagues attempted to condition fear in dogs by restraining them and administering a mild electrical shock. The researchers expected that when the restraints were removed, the dogs would actively avoid the shock by jumping away. However, to their surprise, the previously restrained dogs passively succumbed to shocks even when they were given the opportunity to escape or avoid them. Seligman believed the dogs learned to helplessly succumb to the shocks. Since the dogs had no control over the shocks, they were unmotivated to avoid the shocks later when given the opportunity.

Seligman proposed that learned helplessness might explain depression in humans (Hiroto & Seligman, 1975). He suggested that people who are exposed to stressful but apparently uncontrollable life events would become passive and depressed. They would not actively cope with stressors but, instead, succumb to feelings of pain and despair.

Reformulated Learned Helplessness Model

Later, Abramson, Seligman, and Teasdale (1978) adjusted the learned helplessness theory of depression to explain *how* negative life events can contribute to depressed mood. They suggested that the **attributions** we make about success and failure in our lives affect our mood. Specifically, depressed individuals attribute *negative* events to internal, stable, and global factors. For example, if an adolescent boys asks a girl for a date and she turns him down, he might attribute his rejection to internal, stable, and global factors. He might reason that he was rejected because he is ugly (internal); he will always be ugly (stable); and no one, no matter how desperate, will ever want to go out with someone as ugly as him (global). This **depressogenic attributional style** can lead to feelings of helplessness, hopelessness, and depression.

Depressed people also tend to attribute *positive* life events to external, unstable, and specific causes. For example, if a child with depression gets an A on an exam, she might attribute her success to the fact that the teacher is an easy grader (external), that she was lucky (unstable), or that she just happened to study the information that was on the exam (specific). These attributions can contribute to her negative mood and low self-regard.

Most research has shown a relationship between depressogenic attributional styles and depressed mood in adults (Sweeney, Anderson, & Bailey, 1986). Similarly, depressed children and adolescents show pessimistic attributions for negative events (Gladstone & Kaslow, 1995; Joiner & Wagner, 1995).

Only recently have researchers looked for the source of children's depressogenic attributions (Stevens & Prinstein, 2005). Available data indicate at least three possible causes. First, negative life events can cause youths to adopt depressogenic attributional styles (Garber & Flynn, 2001; Gibb, Abramson, & Alloy, 2004). For example, children who are physically or sexually abused can erroneously blame themselves for their victimization and view maltreatment as stable and pervasive (Harkness, Bruce, & Lumley, 2006).

Second, depressed mood, itself, might cause depressogenic attributions (Nolen-Hoeksema, Girgus, & Seligman, 1992). When adolescents feel helpless, they may begin to attribute failure to internal, stable, and global causes and attribute success to external, unstable, and specific factors. Depression, therefore, may beget depressogenic thoughts.

Third, and perhaps most interestingly, depressogenic attributions can be acquired though friends. The **peer contagion model** posits that depression, like a cold, can be acquired through close contact with peers. As friends share secrets and talk about stressors in their lives, they may inadvertently model and reinforce depressive symptoms and depressogenic attributions (Rose, 2002). In one large study, sixth to eighth graders often adopted the depressive symptoms and attributional styles of their best friends. Friends maintain each others' depressive symptoms by corroborating depressogenic attributions or avoiding other positive social experiences (Stevens & Prinstein, 2005).

Interactions With Parents

Children's relationship with parents can also affect their likelihood of developing depression. Although a number of parenting variables can place youths at risk for depression or buffer them from the deleterious effects of psychosocial stressors, three of the most important variables are (1) the quality of parent-child attachment, (2) parents' social-emotional health, and (3) conflict in the home (MacPhee & Andrews, 2006).

Parent-Child Attachment

According to the principles of attachment theory, children construct mental representations or **internal working models** of caregivers during the first few years of life (Bowlby, 1969, 1980). These mental representations are based on the quality of parent-child interactions during infancy and childhood. Children whose parents provide sensitive and responsive care during their first few years of life come to expect accessibility and responsiveness from others. Parent-child dyads that develop relationships based on the expectancy of care and sensitivity are said to have developed *secure* attachment relationships. In contrast, children whose parents provide intrusive or unresponsive care come to expect that others will be inaccessible or unavailable in times of stress or crisis. These children are said to have developed *insecure* attachment relationships with their parents.

As children grow, they apply the internal working models developed in infancy and early childhood to other important interpersonal relationships in their lives. Children who develop secure attachment relationships with early caregivers come to expect sensitive and responsive treatment from other adults, teachers, and peers. Alternatively, children who develop insecure relationships in early childhood may anticipate that other adults, teachers, and peers will be dismissive, unavailable, or uncaring. The internal working models, therefore, serve as social-emotional templates for understanding and predicting future relationships. Indeed, these models seem to predict social and emotional competence across childhood.

Attachment theorists have suggested that insecure attachments in infancy and early childhood predispose children to social-emotional problems later in life. Indeed, research has shown a significant correlation between insecure attachment and mood problems among children and adolescents (Essau, 2004; Graham & Easterbrooks, 2000; Muris, Mayer, & Meesters, 2000).

Insecure attachment in infancy and early childhood can place youths at risk for mood problems in one of two ways. First, children and adolescents who hold insecure representations of caregivers also report feelings of low self-worth and low self-confidence (Hankin & Abela, 2005). These youngsters derive self-esteem from their accomplishments and approval of others, rather than from an intrinsic sense of self-worth (Shirk, Gudmundsen, & Burwell, 2005). They need attention and reassurance from caregivers to maintain a sense of worthiness and self-confidence (Joiner, Metalsky, Katz, & Beach, 1999). Youths with insecure attachment histories and feelings of low self-worth are at increased risk for depressive symptoms (Abela, Hankin, Haigh, Adams, Vinokuroff, & Trayhern, 2005; Shirk et al., 2005).

Second, adolescents who hold insecure representations of caregivers do not rely on others for support in times of crisis (Shirk et al., 2005). Although these individuals appear self-reliant under usual circumstances, they may be alone and easily overwhelmed by stress when negative events occur. Children with histories of insecure attachment may be reluctant to seek help from parents or teachers to solve personal problems. Adolescents with insecure attachment histories often under-utilize social support networks in times of crisis (Connor-Smith, Compas, Wadsworth, Thomsen, & Saltzman, 2000). Excessive self-reliance predisposes youths to isolation, failure, and depression.

Maternal Depression

The children of depressed mothers are at risk for depression themselves (Beardslee, Versage, & Gladstone, 1998). As many as 60% of the children of depressed parents show depression by young adulthood. The risk for depression is six times greater for the children of depressed mothers compared to the offspring of non-depressed women (Essau & Merikangas, 1999). The relationship between mother and child depression is complex and not fully understood. However, there are three general approaches to explaining the transmission of depression across generations (Goodman & Gotlib, 1999).

First, some research suggests there might be a genetic component to the relationship between parent and child depression (Goodman & Gotlib, 1999; Gotlib & Sommerfeld, 1999). It is possible that depressed mothers and their offspring share similar genes that predispose them both to mood disorders.

Second, maternal stress during pregnancy might compromise the development of children's neurological and endocrine systems. These developmental problems, in turn, can lead to childhood depression. For example, women's anxiety levels during gestation predict their offspring's ability to regulate cortisol during late childhood (O'Connor, 2003). Maternal stress hormones during pregnancy might adversely affect the development of their children's HPA axis. Furthermore, women's levels of depression shortly after delivery predicted their children's cortisol levels and regulation during childhood and adolescence (Essex, Klein, Cho, & Kalin, 2002; Halligan, Herbert, Goodyer, & Murray, 2004). Being cared for by a depressed parent early in life places considerable stress on infants. This increased stress might lead to dysregulation of the HPA axis and later mood problems.

The **intergenerational interpersonal stress model** of depression offers a third explanation for the relationship between parent and child depression (Hammen, 1991, 2002). According to this model, children of depressed mothers experience two problems. First, they must face many of the same family stressors that their mothers experience (e.g., conflict between parents, economic hardship). Second, the children of depressed mothers are not taught effective problem-solving and social skills to cope with these stressors. Instead, depressed parents often model ineffective problem-solving skills and discipline their children in less-than-optimal ways. Consequently, the children of depressed mothers often display behavior problems and show difficulty in interpersonal relationships themselves. These difficulties, in turn, lead to their own problems with depression and low self-worth (Goodman & Gotlib, 1999).

Several studies have supported the intergenerational interpersonal stress model. For example, longitudinal research shows that maternal depression is associated with more hostile and less responsive parenting behavior. This negative parenting behavior subsequently predicts childhood depression (Bifulco et al., 2002; Burt et al., 2005; Johnson, Cohen, Kasen, Smailes, & Brook, 2001). Furthermore, Hammen, Shih, and Brennan (2004) found the relationship between maternal depression and children's mood problems was explained by mothers' tendencies to use parenting techniques characterized by low warmth and high hostility. Family stress and problematic parenting predicted adolescents' mood problems.

Family Conflict

Parent-child conflict is strongly associated with childhood depression (Marmorstein & Iacono, 2004). Depressed youths often come from families characterized by less cohesion, communication, and responsiveness. Furthermore, parents of depressed youths are often described as antagonistic, punitive, and critical (Kaslow, Deering, & Racusin, 1994; Lewinsohn, Roberts et al., 1994).

Harsh, critical family interactions can lead to the emergence and exacerbation of children's depressive symptoms (Hooley & Gotlib, 2000; MacPhee & Andrews, 2006). Researchers sometimes use the term **expressed emotion** (EE) to refer to caregivers' hostile behavior and criticism directed at family members. Examples of high expressed emotion include belittling children for inappropriate behavior or criticizing adolescents for low grades. High expressed emotion can lower children's self-esteem and deprive them of parental support. High expressed emotion also increases the likelihood of depression and relapse of mood episodes after recovery. Asarnow, Goldstein, Tompson, and Guthrie (1993) showed that 53% of depressed children from low EE families recovered within one year, compared to 0% of depressed children from high EE families.

Interactions With Peers

Friendships

Other researchers have examined the role that peers play in child and adolescent depression. Harry Stack Sullivan (1953) described the importance of peer relationships to the emotional well-being of children. He claimed that children develop the capacity for empathy and emotional autonomy through their friendships in late childhood and adolescence. Through interactions with peers, children learn the emotional give-and-take that characterizes healthy, intimate adult relationships. Through friendships, children also learn about themselves and develop a sense of identity. For example, children compare themselves to peers to determine their strengths and weaknesses. They also derive self-esteem from friends' acceptance of their personality and behavior (Parker, Rubin, Erath, Wojslawosicz, & Buskirk, 2006).

Research has shown that acceptance by peer networks (i.e., "crowds" or "cliques") is important to children's self-concepts and emotional well-being (Klomeck, Marrocco, Kleinman, Schonfeld, & Gould, 2007). Children who are rejected or victimized by peers are more likely to show depressive symptoms. Both physical victimization (e.g., bullying) and relational aggression (e.g., teasing, spreading rumors) are associated with depression in boys and girls (Crick & Bigbee, 1998; Prinstein, Boergers, & Vernberg, 2001). In one study, relational aggression predicted adolescent depression better than physical aggression (LaGreca & Harrison, 2005). This finding contradicts the old saying about "sticks and stones." It also suggests that school-based interventions designed to reduce the harmful effects of bullying must also target relational aggression in order to prevent children's mood problems (LaGreca & Harrison, 2005).

Prinstein and Aikins (2004) showed how the relationship between peer rejection and depressive symptoms is moderated by adolescent cognitions. As expected, peer rejection predicted later depressive symptoms in a sample of tenth graders. However, the relationship was strongest for adolescents who (1) also showed depressogenic attributional styles and (2) placed a great deal of importance on peer acceptance. The researchers suggested that adolescents who attribute peer rejection to internal, stable, and global causes (e.g., "I'm no good") are more likely to become depressed than adolescents who hold less pessimistic attributions for their rejection (e.g., "The other kids are jerks"). Furthermore, adolescents who are rejected, but who desperately want to be accepted by peers, may be especially prone to depression. Prinstein and Aikins's (2004) study is significant because it shows how cognitive factors can moderate the effects of psychosocial stressors on adolescent depression.

Friendships and romantic relationships can also be stressful to adolescents. Friendships characterized by conflict or coercion can negatively affect the emotional well-being of adolescents and contribute to depression (LaGreca & Harrison, 2005). Stressful romantic relationships during adolescence also predict depressive symptoms (Davila, Steinberg, Kachadourian, Cobb, & Fincham, 2004; LaGreca & Harrison, 2005).

What about the possible positive effects of peer relationships? Can peers buffer adolescents from other psychosocial stressors by offering them a source of support? The answer appears to be "no." In their review of the adolescent depression literature, Burton and colleagues (2004) found very little evidence supporting the idea that positive peer relationships protect children from the effects of other psychosocial stress. However, problematic peer relationships did independently predict depression. Although the buffering effect of peer relationships seems intuitive, it may not have much empirical support (LaGreca & Harrison, 2005).

Social Information Processing

In previous chapters, we examined how biases in children's information processing can lead to externalizing behavior problems. Crick and Dodge (1996) found that aggressive boys tend to show hostile attributional biases when solving interpersonal problems. These boys interpret others' benign behavior as malevolent, and they rely on hostile strategies to resolve interpersonal disputes.

Recently, some authors have applied similar information-processing models to explain childhood depression (Prinstein, Cheah, & Guyer, 2005). According to the **social information-processing theory of depression**, children with depression display two types of biases when solving interpersonal problems (see Figure 11.3). First, like aggressive children, depressed children attribute hostile intentions to other people's ambiguous behavior. For example, imagine that a child is playing outside during recess. While playing, a peer kicks a soccer ball and it hits the child in the head. The child might show a hostile attributional bias by attributing hostile intentions to the peer's behavior (e.g., "That kid is picking on me").

Second, children with depression often show internal and stable causal attributions; that is, they attribute social problems or failures to internal and stable causes. For example, the child who is hit by the soccer ball might blame himself for his perceived victimization (e.g., "He hit me in the head because he doesn't like me. I'm no fun to be with").

The social information-processing model of depression suggests that depressed children interpret others' behavior as hostile and attribute others' hostile actions to internal and stable factors (e.g., their own fault). These cognitions can influence children's long-term self-perceptions and social behaviors. Children who adopt these information-processing biases are likely to view themselves negatively and avoid social situations. They are at risk for peer rejection and victimization, which, in turn, can lead to more hostile and depressogenic problem solving (Rubin & Rose-Krasnor, 1992).

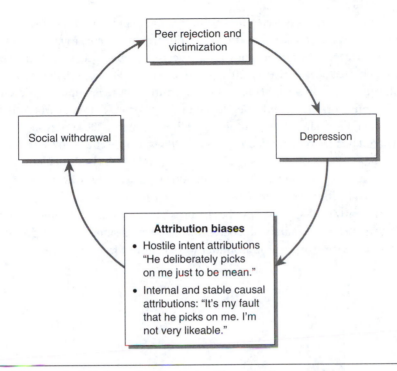

Figure 11.3   Social Information-Processing Theory of Depression

Source: Based on Prinstein et al. (2005).

Note: Children at risk for depression believe that (1) other people have hostile intentions and (2) other people's hostility is their fault. Consequently, these children withdraw from social situations, causing them to experience peer rejection, teasing, and depression.

The social information-processing model of depression is relatively new. A few studies have shown that the combination of hostile and depressogenic attributions leads to decreased self-esteem, loneliness, and depressive symptoms in children and adolescents (Graham & Juvonen, 2001; Prinstein et al., 2005; Suarez & Bell-Dolan, 2001). Perhaps more important, these attributional biases lead children to withdraw from social situations (Prinstein et al., 2005; Quiggle, Garber, Panak, & Dodge, 1992). Social withdrawal, in turn, is associated with peer victimization, which confirms children's belief that they are partially to blame for their own peer problems.

Treatment

Antidepressants

Does Medication Work?

Until the early 1990s, the pharmaceutical treatment of depression in children and adolescents was limited. Most physicians prescribed **tricyclic antidepressants.** These medications, which affect levels of serotonin and norepinephrine, included amitriptyline (Elavil), desipramine (Norpramin), and imipramine (Tofranil).

Tricyclic antidepressants were effective in treating depression in adults. However, two meta-analyses revealed that tricyclic antidepressants were largely ineffective in reducing depressive symptoms in youth, especially prepubescent children (Hazell, O'Connell, Heathcote, & Henry, 2002; see Figure 11.4). This is probably because the serotonin and norepinephrine neurotransmitter systems upon which these medications work are not fully developed until late adolescence or early adulthood (D. Cohen, Gerardin, Mazet, Purper-Ouakil, & Flament, 2004). Researchers also discovered that tricyclic antidepressants caused severe side effects in some children, including cardiac arrhythmia, suicidal behavior, and death (D. Cohen et al., 2004). In one study, 14% of youths taking imipramine reported cardiovascular side effects that caused them to discontinue the medication (Findling, 2005).

In the early 1990s, physicians began prescribing **selective serotonin reuptake inhibitors (SSRIs)** to youths with depression. These medications slow the reuptake of serotonin, allowing the neurotransmitter to remain in the synaptic cleft for longer

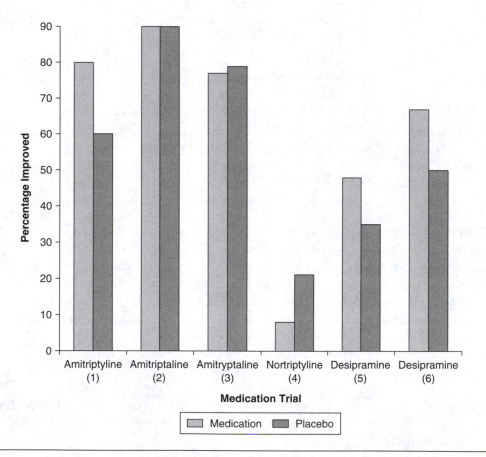

Figure 11.4   Results of Major Randomized Controlled Trials Investigating the Efficacy of Tricyclic Antidepressants on Child and Adolescent Depression

Source: Based on D. Cohen et al. (2004).

Note: In general, tricyclics do not show superiority over placebo. In addition, they can cause dangerous side effects, including death, in some children.

periods of time. The percentage of children taking antidepressant medication, mostly SSRIs, increased markedly from 1.6% in 1998 to 2.4% in 2002 (Delate, Gelenberg, Simmons, & Motheral, 2004). This increase in medication usage occurred despite the fact that the U.S. Food and Drug Administration (FDA) did not approve antidepressant medication for children until 2003.

Currently, the only SSRI that has received FDA approval for the treatment of depression in children is fluoxetine (Prozac). Three published studies of youths with depression have compared fluoxetine to placebo. All three studies have shown fluoxetine to be superior in reducing depressive symptoms with minimal side effects (see Figure 11.5).

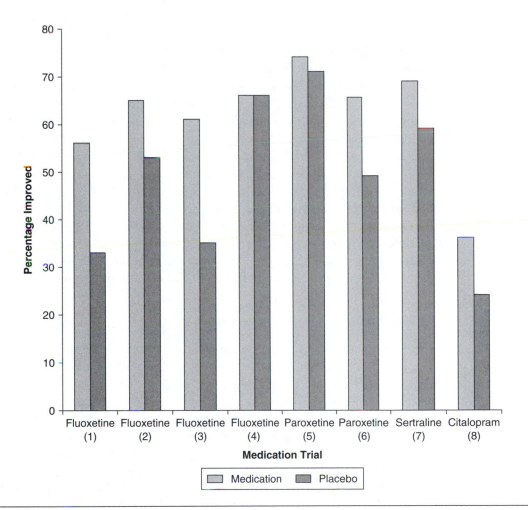

Figure 11.5   Results of Major Randomized Controlled Studies Investigating the Efficacy of SSRIs on Child and Adolescent Depression

Source: Based on (1) Emslie et al. (1997); (2) Emslie et al. (2002); (3) TADS (2004); (4) Simeon, Dinicola, Ferguson, and Copping (1990); (5) Milin, Walker, and Chow (2003); (6) Keller et al. (2001); (7) Wagner et al. (2003); (8) Wagner, Berard et al. (2004).

Note: In general, only fluoxetine (Prozac) is associated with consistent improvement in depressive symptoms with minimal side effects. However, most SSRIs (including fluoxetine) perform only slightly better than placebo.

Despite these results, the efficacy of fluoxetine in children and adolescents has been questioned. First, the magnitude of the difference between youths taking fluoxetine versus placebo is somewhat small. For example, in one study, approximately 65% of youths improved with fluoxetine compared to approximately 52% with placebo. Although fluoxetine decreases children's depressive symptoms, some of its benefits can be attributed to placebo. Second, the superiority of fluoxetine over placebo depends partially on *who* is reporting children's symptoms. In another study, medication was associated with symptom reduction when reported by clinicians, but *not* when reported by parents or children (Emslie et al., 2002). Third, the superiority of fluoxetine over placebo may be largely due to its efficacy in reducing symptoms of comorbid anxiety, not depression per se (Garland, 2004).

Two other SSRIs have also been shown to be superior to placebo in treating pediatric depression. Wagner and colleagues (2003) showed that 69% of depressed children improved after using sertraline (Zoloft) compared to 59% of children receiving placebo. Again, the magnitude of the difference between children receiving the medication versus placebo was small. Wagner, Robb, and colleagues (2004) also showed that citalopram (Celexa) was more effective than placebo in reducing depression among children and adolescents. However, only 36% of the sample responded to citalopram. A second study of citalopram did not demonstrate its superiority over placebo (Wagner, 2005).

Other antidepressant medications have *not* been shown to be superior to placebo in treating child or adolescent depression. Five large, randomized controlled studies of the SSRIs paroxetine (Paxil) and escitalopram (Lexapro) have shown these medications to be no better than placebo in reducing core depressive symptoms. Venlafaxine ER (Effexor), a medication that inhibits the reuptake of both serotonin and norepinephrine, has also been shown in two independent trials to be equivalent to placebo in treating childhood depression (Wagner, 2005).

Are Antidepressant Medications Safe?

In 2003, regulatory agencies in the United States, Great Britain, and Canada issued warnings against prescribing SSRIs to children and adolescents. The warnings followed a series of unpublished studies of two SSRIs frequently used with children: paroxetine (Paxil) and venlafaxine (Effexor). These studies showed that the SSRIs were not effective in reducing depression in children and that they doubled children's likelihood of suicide and aggression (Garland, 2004).

The U.S. Food and Drug Administration (Wagner, 2005) subsequently conducted its own study of nine antidepressant medications for depressed youth and found that the risk of suicidal ideation and behavior was roughly twice for patients on medication (4%) compared to patients receiving placebo (2%). Indeed, 7.5% of mildly depressed adolescents taking paroxetine showed an *increase* in suicidal ideation, suicidal behavior, aggression, or conduct problems that required hospitalization (Keller et al., 2001).

Today, most physicians are extremely cautious when prescribing antidepressant medication to youth. Their caution arises primarily because (1) some of these medications have showed limited effectiveness beyond placebo, and (2) they are

Suicidality in Children and Adolescents

Antidepressants increased the risk of suicidal thinking and behavior (suicidality) in short-term stuidies in children and adolescents with Major Depressive Disorder (MDD) and other psychiatric disorders. Anyone considering the use of [Insert established name] or any other antidepressant in a child or adolescent must balance this risk with the clinical need. Patients who are started on therapy should be observed closely for clinical worsening, suicidality, or unusual changes in behaviour. Families and caregivers whould be advised of the need for close observation and communication with the prescriber. [Insert established name] is not approved for use in pediatric patients. (See Warnings and Precautions: Pediatric Use) *[This sentence would be revised to reflect if a drug were approved for a pediatric indication(s). Such as, [Insert established name] is not approved for use in pediatric patients except for patients with [Insert approved pediatric indications(s)]. (See Warnings and Precautions: Pediatric Use)]*

Pooled analyses of short-term (4 to 16 weeks) placebo-controlled trials of 9 antidepressant drugs (SSRIs and others) in children and adolescents with major depressive disorder (MDD), obsessive compulsive disorder (OCD), or other psychiatric disorders (a total of 24 trials involving over 4400 patients) have revealed a greater risk of adverse events representing suididal thinking or behavior (suididality) during the first few months of treatment in those receiving antidepressants. The average risk of such events in patients receiving antidepressants was 4% twice the placebo risk of 2%. No suicides occurred in these trials.

Image 11.1   "Black Box" Warning on Antidepressant Medication. Although very few children and adolescents experience dangerous side effects associated with SSRI use, this warning appears on antidepressant medication.

Source: Extracted from http://www.fda.gov.

associated with adverse side effects in some studies. Furthermore, the FDA directed pharmaceutical manufacturers to post "black box" warnings on all antidepressant medications, informing caregivers of the apparent increased risk of suicidal ideation and behavior associated with SSRI treatment (Wagner, 2005; see Image 11.1). Professional organizations, such as the American Psychiatric Association and the American Academy of Child and Adolescent Psychiatry, have criticized the FDA's action, claiming that such warnings limit patients' access to pharmaceutical treatment (Whittington et al., 2004; Wohlfarth, Lekkerkerker, & van Zwieten, 2004).

Cognitive-Behavioral Therapy

Although cognitive-behavioral therapy (CBT) for depression is typically offered as a single treatment "package," it actually consists of two separate treatment components (Kazdin & Marciano, 1998). First, cognitive therapy for depression is based on the notion that maladaptive patterns in thinking contribute to people's depressed mood. In cognitive therapy, clients learn more accurate and realistic ways to perceive themselves, others, and the future.

Second, behavior therapy for depression is based on the idea that depression is caused by a lack of **response-contingent reinforcement** (Lewinsohn, 1974). Specifically, people become depressed when they are unable to derive pleasure or satisfaction from their environments. For example, adolescents who lack adequate social or communication skills may frequently argue with parents and isolate themselves from peers. Consequently, they may spend much of their time alone, deriving little satisfaction from interpersonal relationships. Over time, they may become depressed and show even greater social isolation and mood problems. In behavior therapy, therapists try to improve adolescents' social and communication skills, increase their level of social activity, and teach them to reward themselves for their successes and accomplishments.

There are many cognitive-behavioral interventions designed for youths with depression. We will examine two of the best-studied treatments: Stark's cognitive-behavioral therapy (for school-age children) and the Coping With Depression program (for adolescents).

Stark's Cognitive-Behavioral Therapy for Children

One of the first CBT packages developed for depressed children was created by Kevin Stark and colleagues (Stark & Kendall, 1996; Stark, Hoke, Ballatore, Valdez, Scammaca, & Griffin, 2005). The goal of treatment was to change children's problematic ways of thinking and to increase their satisfaction with themselves, others, and their surroundings. To accomplish this task, the therapist teaches children social, emotional, and behavioral skills so that they can effectively cope with negative feelings, solve problems, and interact with others. Treatment is conducted in small groups consisting of school-age children and a therapist. Sessions occur biweekly for 10 weeks.

In Stark's treatment (Stark et al., 2005), the therapist teaches four basic skills: (a) recognizing and understanding emotions, (b) solving social problems, (c) coping with negative feelings, and (d) cognitive restructuring. The first goal of therapy is to help children recognize and label emotions. Many children with depression have difficulty labeling their feelings. For examples, some children can only differentiate "happy" and "sad." The therapist might use emotion flash cards, charades, or role play to teach children to differentiate within these mood states. For example, the facial expressions and physical sensations that accompany the feeling "embarrassed" are different from those that characterize feeling "angry" or "left out."

After children are able to recognize, differentiate, and label emotions, they learn basic problem-solving skills. That is, children must learn what to do when they feel embarrassed, angry, or left out. Many children with depression feel overwhelmed by their negative emotional states and withdraw from family and peers. Other depressed children express their negative emotions directly, through acting out and aggression. The goal of problem-solving training is to help children actively address social problems and the mood states they engender.

In problem-solving training, children are taught to systematically identify a social problem, brainstorm possible solutions, evaluate each solution, select and implement the best course of action, and evaluate outcomes (Crick & Dodge, 1996). In addition, problem-solving training for children with depression has two unique components. First, when children identify the problem, the therapist teaches them to "psych-up" (Stark et al., 2005, p. 249), or direct all of their attention and energy to solving it. "Psyching-up" helps children feel more empowered to confront and solve social problems, and less hopeless. Second, after children evaluate the consequences of their actions, the therapist encourages them to reward their problem-solving efforts. Children are encouraged to praise themselves for their attempts at solving social problems, even if their solutions are not 100% effective.

Cognitive-behavioral therapists also teach coping skills. Many children with depression lack the ability to regulate their emotions. When they feel sad or helpless, they ruminate on their feelings rather than try to cope with them directly. The therapist might help children improve their coping skills in three ways. First, she might teach specific coping strategies, like relaxation. Second, she might ask children to interview their nondepressed peers and find out how these children cope with negative moods and everyday hassles. Third, she might ask children to actively plan pleasurable activities during the week so that they can experience positive emotions. For example, she might encourage children to go to a movie with friends or to a sporting event with family.

Finally, therapists use **cognitive restructuring**; that is, they attempt to challenge and alter the cognitive biases and distortions that maintain children's negative moods. Stark and colleagues (2005) discuss a number of games to help children look at themselves, others, and the future more objectively. In *What's the Evidence,* children must provide empirical support for their negative thinking. If a child is earning a low grade in reading class, she might conclude that she is not very smart. The therapist might challenge her conclusion by asking her for evidence to support her claim and by challenging her to provide evidence to the contrary (i.e., that she *is* smart). Although she may score poorly in reading, she may be extremely talented in art or math.

In another cognitive game, *Alternative Interpretations,* the therapist challenges children's automatic thoughts about ambiguous events by asking them to consider other ways of viewing the event. If a child is ignored by her classmates while walking down the hallway at school, she might conclude that her classmates are upset with her. The therapist might challenge this cognitive distortion and encourage her to consider other possibilities for their behavior: Perhaps her friends were late for class and in a hurry, or perhaps they did not see her.

A third strategy is to use the *What If* technique. Therapists use this technique to combat the high and (sometimes) unreasonable expectations children place on themselves and their tendency to engage in catastrophic thinking. For example, a boy who earns low grades might think, "Oh no. Now I'll never make the honor roll and my parents are going to kill me!" The therapist might ask *what if* he does not make the honor roll; will his parents actually kill him? Will they disown him? Will they stop loving him?

Controlled studies of CBT for children with depression have shown it to be more effective than no treatment or placebo (Butler, Miezitis, Friedman, & Cole, 1980; Rossello & Bernal, 1999; Stark, Reynolds, & Kaslow, 1987; Weisz, Thurber, Sweeney, Proffitt, & LeGagnoux, 1997). It has also been shown to be more effective than other forms of nondirective counseling (Brent et al., 1997; Stark, 1990; Stark, Rouse, & Livingston, 1991).

On the other hand, CBT is equally as effective at reducing depressive symptoms as supportive psychotherapy (Vostanis, Feehan, Grattan, & Bickerton,1996a, 1996b), social skills training (Butler et al., 1980), problem-solving training (Stark et al., 1987), and relaxation training (Kahn, Kehle, Jenson, & Clarke,1990). In some studies, CBT was superior to alternative treatments like relaxation training and supportive therapy in the short term, but treatment groups showed comparable outcomes at long-term follow-up (Birmaher, Brent, & Benson, 2000; Wood, Harrington, & Moore, 1996). Overall, these results indicate that CBT is useful for reducing children's depressive symptoms. However, it is likely that certain components of the CBT package (i.e., problem-solving training, coping skills training) are sufficient to produce these benefits.

Cognitive-Behavioral Group Therapy for Adolescents

The Adolescent Coping With Depression Course (CWD-A; Clarke, Lewinsohn, & Hops, 1990; Lewinsohn, Clarke, Hops, & Andrews, 1990) is a group treatment for older adolescents (14–16 years) with MDD or Dysthymic Disorder. CWD-A was designed to be nonstigmatizing. It is conducted like a class, with the therapist playing the role of teacher. In class, adolescents learn and practice new skills to help them cope with depressive symptoms and daily stressors. Skills are taught using traditional instruction, role play and dialogue, workbook exercises, and quizzes. Adolescents complete homework to help generalize skills to outside the therapy setting.

CWD-A is based heavily on the behavioral theory of depression developed by Lewinsohn and colleagues (Lewinsohn, Youngren, & Grosscup, 1979). According to this theory, adolescents become depressed because of a lack of positive reinforcement and an excess of punishment from their environments. When they succeed, these adolescents do not give themselves credit or enjoy their success. When they fail, they attribute their failure to internal and stable causes (i.e., personal faults) and assign self-blame. Over time, they experience only failure and frustration and perceive themselves as helpless and powerless. They also begin to show certain maladaptive thought patterns that contribute to their depressed mood, such as cognitive biases and distortions.

In CWD-A, adolescents learn new skills to cope with depressive symptoms, increase self-efficacy and pleasure, and change maladaptive thought patterns. Each week, the therapist-teacher introduces a new skill, which is practiced in the session and at home. In the first phase of treatment, the therapist teaches adolescents how to increase their energy levels and degree of positive emotions. First, adolescents learn to monitor their emotions and notice how changes in their behavior can improve their mood. For example, adolescents might notice how riding a bike, playing a sport, or calling a friend on the telephone usually results in greater energy. Later in treatment, the therapist uses social skills training to teach adolescents how to make friends and engage in social activities (Rohde, Lewinsohn, Clarke, Hops, & Seeley, 2005).

Finally, the therapist encourages adolescents to plan pleasurable activities in their daily lives. Specifically, the therapist encourages adolescents to identify activities that they formerly enjoyed and set realistic expectations for engaging in these activities. For example, a girl who formerly enjoyed going to school dances might plan on attending a dance over the weekend. An unrealistic expectation for the dance is that everyone would compliment her on her appearance and that she would be the center of attention. Such an expectation would set the girl up for disappointment.

A more realistic expectation would be to attend the dance and spend some time with friends. The therapist encourages adolescents to deliberately schedule pleasurable events into their weekly routine. As adolescents engage in these pleasurable activities, they may derive greater reinforcement from their environment and improve their mood.

In the second phase of CWD-A, the therapist targets adolescents' negative mood. First, the therapist teaches relaxation techniques, like deep breathing and muscle relaxation, to help adolescents cope with anxiety and other negative moods. Later, the therapist teaches adolescents to recognize cognitive biases and distortions using cartoons and role-play exercises. Adolescents are also taught to modify their thoughts with more realistic cognitions. In fact, the ability to replace negative automatic thoughts with more realistic cognitions may be one of the primary mechanisms by which CWD-A reduces depressive symptoms (Kaufman, Rohde, Seeley, Clarke, & Stice, 2005). Finally, adolescents are taught communication and conflict-resolution skills to help them negotiate interpersonal disputes. Typically, conflict-resolution training involves teaching adolescents how to listen to others with an open mind, avoid critical or accusatory comments, brainstorm possible solutions to interpersonal problems, and select a course of action that everyone can accept.

The efficacy of CWD-A has been examined in a number of randomized controlled studies. The first two studies involved a total of 155 adolescents with MDD or Dysthymic Disorder (Clarke, Rohde, Lewinsohn, Hops, & Seeley, 1999; Lewinsohn et al., 1990). Adolescents were randomly assigned to one of three treatment conditions. The first group participated in CWD-A. The second group participated in CWD-A and their parents also participated in parallel parenting sessions. Adolescents in the third group served as waitlist controls. Adolescents' depressive symptoms were assessed before treatment, immediately after treatment, and two years after treatment. Results showed that adolescents who participated in CWD-A (e.g., the first two groups) showed greater symptom reduction than adolescents on the waitlist. However, the adolescents in the two treatment conditions showed comparable outcomes, indicating that adding the parent group to CWD-A may be desirable, but not necessary.

In a more recent study, Clarke and colleagues (2002) compared the relative efficacy of CWD-A to treatment in the community. Specifically, 88 adolescents with MDD or Dysthymic Disorder were randomly assigned to traditional care alone or traditional care plus CWD-A. Adolescents in both treatment groups showed reductions in depressive symptoms. However, adolescents who also participated in CWD-A did not show better outcomes than adolescents who only participated in traditional care.

Interpersonal Psychotherapy for Adolescents

The underlying premise of interpersonal psychotherapy (IPT) is that depression is best understood as an adverse reaction to interpersonal problems (Mufson & Pollack Dorta, 2003; Mufson, Pollack Dorta, Moreau, & Weissman, 2005). Adolescents with depression have usually experienced disruptions in their interpersonal functioning or high levels of interpersonal stress (Puig-Antich et al., 1993;

Stader & Hokanson, 1998). These interpersonal problems both contribute to and maintain their depressed mood (Hammen, 1999). IPT seeks to improve people's interpersonal functioning by helping them develop more satisfying and meaningful relationships, cope with the separation and loss of loved ones, and alleviate social distress and isolation.

Early in treatment, the adolescent and therapist select one or two problems to be the focus of therapy. These problems usually center on one of the following interpersonal themes: (1) grief and loss, (2) interpersonal role disputes, (3) role transitions, and (4) interpersonal deficits (Young, Mufson, & Davies, 2006).

Some adolescents become depressed following the loss of an important relationship. Adolescents can grieve the death of a family member, the separation from a parent, or the departure of a friend. When a relationship with a loved one is disrupted, adolescents can experience feelings of insecurity and helplessness. From the perspective of attachment theory, these adolescents have lost a secure base from which they derive comfort and interpersonal confidence. As a result, some adolescents become anxious, fearful, or unsure of themselves. Others become withdrawn and lethargic. Still others act out. The interpersonal therapist helps adolescents mourn the loss of the relationship and develop alternative sources of social support (McBride, Atkinson, Quilty, & Bagby, 2006).

Other adolescents become depressed due to interpersonal role disputes. Role disputes are usually between the adolescent and his parents; they typically reflect differences in values. Although parent-child disagreements are common during adolescence, they can become problematic if left unresolved. Adolescents who perceive their parents as unsympathetic or disinterested can feel low self-worth and helplessness. The interpersonal therapist teaches both parents and adolescents more effective communication skills and ways to resolve disagreements—ways that balance the authority of the parent with the autonomy of the adolescent.

Still other adolescents experience depression following a major role transition or psychosocial stressor. Adolescents experience considerable life transitions: entering junior and senior high school, beginning dating and serious romantic relationships, separating from family members, entering the work force. At other times, life transitions are forced upon adolescents through the birth of a new sibling, an unexpected pregnancy, the deployment of a family member in the armed forces, or a chronic illness in the family. The interpersonal therapist helps the adolescent define, accept, and cope with his new social role. Coping may involve grieving the loss of the old role and learning new skills (or adjusting one's lifestyle) to suit new responsibilities.

Finally, adolescents can become depressed because of interpersonal deficits. Adolescents who lack appropriate social skills may have difficulty making friends, dating, and participating in extracurricular activities. Since adolescents' self-concepts are heavily influenced by peers, problems in peer functioning can cause a lack of self-esteem, self-confidence, and social isolation. The therapist teaches social skills, usually through role-play exercises.

Although a number of randomized, controlled studies have supported the efficacy of interpersonal therapy for depression in adults, less research has focused on adolescents. In one study, 48 adolescents with depression were randomly assigned to one of two groups (Mufson, Weissman, Moreau, & Garfinkel, 1999). The first group participated in 12 weeks of IPT. The second group met with a counselor but did not receive any active form of treatment. Results showed that adolescents who participated in IPT were more likely to complete treatment (88%) than adolescents in the control group (46%). Furthermore, adolescents who received IPT showed greater improvement in mood, overall functioning, and social problem-solving skills than controls. A second study (Rossello & Bernal, 2005), using a slightly different version of IPT, showed similar results with Puerto Rican youths.

A more recent study compared the effectiveness of IPT and traditional counseling (Mufson, Pollack Dorta, Wickramaratne, Nomura, Olfson, & Weissman, 2004). Sixty-three adolescents with depression who were attending schools in low-income neighborhoods were randomly assigned to two treatment groups. The first group received 12 sessions of IPT at school. The second group received nondirective counseling at school; in most cases, counseling involved supportive psychotherapy. After treatment, adolescents in both groups showed improvement in depressive symptoms and overall functioning. Clinician ratings indicated that IPT was superior to traditional counseling in improving mood and functioning. Adolescents' self-reports indicated that IPT was superior to traditional counseling in improving social functioning, but not in reducing depressive symptoms. Taken together, these results indicate that IPT is effective in treating adolescent depression, even when it is not administered as part of a university-based research trial. However, IPT may not always be superior to supportive psychotherapy in reducing adolescents' self-reported depressive symptoms.

Combining Medication and Psychotherapy

Many experts recommend combining medication and psychotherapy to treat child and adolescent depression (Birmaher et al., 1998; March & Wells, 2003). The rationale for combined treatment is threefold (Kratochvil et al., 2005). First, combining medication and psychotherapy might provide a greater "dose" of treatment, thereby producing faster symptom reduction and greater treatment response. Second, medication plus psychotherapy might target different symptoms, thus maximizing the range of symptoms that might be improved. For example, medication might target the physical symptoms of depression (e.g., fatigue, sleep/appetite changes), whereas therapy might target cognitive symptoms (e.g., anhedonia, thoughts of death). Third, combined treatment might address a wider range of comorbid problems.

The **Treatment for Adolescents With Depression Study** (TADS, 2004) was designed to investigate the relative merits of medication and psychotherapy in treating adolescent depression. In TADS, researchers compared the efficacy of medication and CBT in adolescents aged 12 to 17 years. Four hundred and thirty-nine adolescents with MDD were randomly assigned to one of four treatment groups: (1) fluoxetine only, (2) CBT only, (3) combined fluoxetine and CBT, and (4) placebo (see Figure 11.6). All treatments were administered for 12 weeks. Researchers measured adolescents' depressive symptoms before and after treatment. They also measured adolescents' self-harm during the course of treatment.

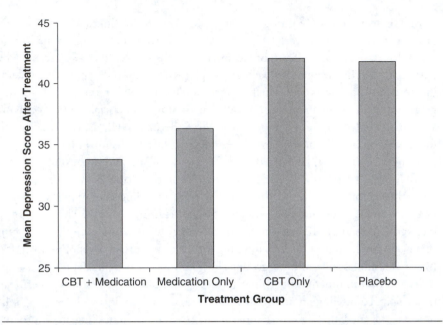

Figure 11.6   Results of the Treatment for Adolescents With Depression Study

Source: Based on TADS (2004).

Note: Adolescents who received medication (either with or without CBT) showed lowest depression scores after treatment. Adding CBT to medication did not produce significantly greater effects than using medication alone. Youths who participated in CBT alone showed similar outcomes as youths who received placebo.

Children in all groups showed reductions in their depressive symptoms, although children in the combined treatment group showed the greatest symptom reduction at the fastest rate. At the end of treatment, the percentage of adolescents who showed significant improvement were 71% (combined treatment), 60.6% (medication only), 43.2% (CBT only), and 34.8% (placebo), respectively.

Follow-up tests revealed three important findings. First, the difference between adolescents who received combined treatment and adolescents who received medication alone was *not* statistically significant. In fact, another study published after TADS showed similar results: Combining psychotherapy with medication yielded no better outcomes than medication alone (Clarke et al., 2005). Second, adolescents who received combined treatment or medication alone showed significantly greater improvement than adolescents who received either CBT alone or placebo. Third, adolescents who received CBT alone and adolescents who received placebo *did not* statistically differ.

The results of TADS have been somewhat controversial. In general, the results of the study indicate that a combination of fluoxetine and CBT should be considered a first-line treatment for adolescent depression. Furthermore, some adolescents may respond to fluoxetine alone (Ginsburg, Albano, Findling, Kratochvil, & Walkup, 2005). CBT alone may be a useful alternative for adolescents and families unwilling to participate in pharmacotherapy, especially in light of recent FDA warnings against SSRIs. However, many youths will not respond to CBT alone. The benefits associated with CBT may be attributable, in part, to placebo (Jensen, 2005).

Some experts have criticized TADS, claiming that methodological problems made CBT appear less efficacious than it actually is (Apter, Kronenberg, & Brent, 2005). First, the form of CBT used in TADS was not identical to other forms of cognitive-behavioral therapy previously shown to be efficacious in treating adolescent depression (Curry & Wells, 2005). In the TADS study, CBT might have yielded better results had researchers administered a more traditional CBT treatment package. Second, critics have argued that the form of CBT used in the TADS study was too structured and rigid (Hollon, Garber, & Shelton, 2005). Such rigidity may have interfered with clinicians' abilities to tailor treatment to the needs of their clients. Despite these criticisms, the TADS study is one of the best-conducted randomized trials for adolescent depression to date. It will likely guide research for years to come.

Update: Eppy

Eppy was diagnosed with Dysthymic Disorder. Although Eppy believed that her mood problems were caused by her genes, her therapist, Nancy, preferred to conceptualize her problems in terms of learning theory. Nancy suggested that Eppy's problems with her mother and struggles at school made her feel hopeless. Feelings of hopelessness, in turn, caused her to adopt negative attributions about herself, others, and the future.

Nancy tried to improve Eppy's mood in three ways. First, she met with Eppy individually to teach her ways to increase her energy and positive emotions. For example, Nancy encouraged Eppy to schedule time each day to do things that she found pleasurable, like journaling, taking a walk, riding a bike, and going shopping with friends. Nancy taught Eppy to notice the correspondence between engaging in these physical and social activities and her improved mood.

Second, Nancy helped Eppy identify and challenge negative automatic thoughts that contributed to her pessimistic attitudes. For example, when Eppy received a D on a math assignment, Eppy said, "I'm just not good at anything." Nancy challenged this distorted belief, "Really? Just because you earn low grades in math, does that mean that you don't have any talents?"

Third, Nancy met with Eppy and her mother to improve the quality of their interactions at home. Specifically, Nancy helped Eppy and her mother develop better communication skills so that they could discuss problems more effectively.

Eppy's mood gradually improved. Eppy spent less time in her room alone and more time with her friends and family. Eppy was especially impressed with her newfound energy. Although Eppy's academic performance did not improve, she discovered that she enjoyed several subjects. Eppy joined the drama club and decided to become a beautician after high school.

Critical Thinking Exercises

1. Imagine that you are a school psychologist. You want to help the teachers in your school recognize the symptoms of depression in middle school students. Create a list of symptoms (with examples) of what teachers should look for to identify students with depression.

2. Only trained professionals should evaluate someone's risk for suicide. However, it is often helpful for parents and paraprofessionals (e.g., teachers, coaches) to know suicide risk factors. What are some risk factors? If you suspected that an adolescent had suicidal thoughts, what would you do?

3. G. Stanley Hall, the first president of the American Psychological Association, described adolescence as a period of "storm and stress." He believed that adolescents typically show parental conflict and mood problems during the teenage years. Evaluate Hall's claim. Is it normal for adolescents to be depressed?

4. Alida is participating in cognitive therapy for depression. During therapy, Alida comments, "I messed up on my math test yesterday and got a D–. I just can't make myself study. I'm just no good at anything." If you were Alida's therapist, how might you use cognitive restructuring to change her ways of thinking?

5. Three treatment options for adolescent depression are (1) medication, (2) psychotherapy, and (3) a combination of medication and psychotherapy. If your adolescent was depressed, what course of treatment would you choose? Why?

CHAPTER 12

Bipolar Disorders in Children and Adolescents

Melody

Melody Gellar was a 16-year-old girl who was referred to our clinic by her parents. Mrs. Gellar said that Melody had been more reclusive, sullen, and moody in recent weeks. Melody was often disrespectful, irritable, and upset. When her mother asked Melody to clean up after dinner, Melody replied, "Why don't you just do it—that's all you're good for around here anyway!" In the previous four weeks, Melody dropped out of two of her favorite activities at school. She also showed decreased appetite and a general sluggishness in her behavior.

Melody reluctantly agreed to a "trial run" of therapy with a clinical social worker, Elise Turner. Elise diagnosed Melody with MDD and began to use interpersonal therapy to improve Melody's mood. However, by the fourth session, Elise noticed a dramatic change in Melody's affect and behavior. Melody arrived at the session in an unusually good mood. She spoke very fast: "I feel great today, Elise, you know, like I can do anything. I think it's because I am in love." As Melody discussed her new boyfriend, Elise noticed that her speech was extremely loud and her train of thought was difficult to follow. "Have you been drinking today?" Elise asked. In a giddy tone of voice, Melody responded, "Not today, I don't feel like I need to."

During the session, Elise noticed how distractible Melody was. Melody fidgeted in her chair, paced about the room, and kept complaining how "boring" it was to sit and talk. Melody admitted to a sudden increase in energy and mood. She said, "You know, I think I'm cured. Maybe we don't have to meet any more." Melody said she slept only about three or four hours in the previous two days, but still did not feel tired. In fact, at 3 a.m. the night before, Melody decided to paint her room. "Thank God for Wal-Mart!" she said, "Do you know they're open 24 hours . . . and they sell paint?"

(Continued)

(Continued)

> After the session, Elise telephoned Mrs. Gellar to express her concern. Mrs. Gellar reported that Elise did, in fact, attempt to paint her bedroom in bright green, but only managed to complete 1½ walls before moving on to another project. Melody also had been in trouble that week for skipping school, staying out all night, and going on a shopping spree with her mother's credit card. Mrs. Gellar stated, "She's been so distractible and flighty lately, I don't know what's gotten into her. Do you think she's just being a crazy teenager?" Elise answered, "No, I don't think so."

What Are Bipolar Mood Disorders?

Bipolar disorders are serious mood disturbances characterized by the presence of mania. **Mania** refers to a discrete period of elevated, expansive, or irritable mood and increased level of energy. Many (but not all) individuals with bipolar disorders show both manic and depressive symptoms. Consequently, these disorders are referred to as "bipolar" mood disorders, in contrast to "unipolar" depression.

Although bipolar disorders in adults have received considerable attention, bipolar disorders in children and adolescents have been relatively neglected until recently. Emil Kraepelin (1921) first raised the possibility that children could develop mania. Indeed, Kraepelin documented several cases of mania in prepubescent children. However, most clinicians who followed Kraepelin doubted whether children and adolescents could even experience depression, much less bipolar disorder (Kanner, 1937). Furthermore, when researchers applied criteria for bipolar disorder (developed for adults) to children, very few children met diagnostic criteria (Anthony & Scott, 1960).

As little as two decades ago, most clinicians dismissed the possibility of children having bipolar disorders. The American Academy of Pediatrics did not publish guidelines for assessing and treating the disorder until 1997. Since that time, the subject of bipolar disorders in children and adolescents has received more attention by researchers, clinicians, parent groups, and the media. Professionals are now beginning to appreciate the extent of these serious mood problems and the best ways to treat them.

DSM-IV-TR identifies four bipolar disorders: Bipolar I Disorder (BP-I), Bipolar II Disorder (BP-II), Cyclothymic Disorder, and Bipolar Disorder Not Otherwise Specified (BP-NOS).

Bipolar I Disorder

To be diagnosed with BP-I, a person must have (or have had) a manic episode (see Table 12.1). By definition, a **manic episode** is characterized by "a discrete period of abnormally and persistently elevated, expansive, or irritable mood" that lasts at least one week (*DSM-IV-TR*, p. 362). During manic episodes, adults usually describe their moods as euphoric, cheerful, high, or elated. Some adults describe feeling powerful or "on top of the world."

Table 12.1   Diagnostic Criteria for Bipolar I Disorder

I. Presence (or history) of at least one Manic Episode or one Mixed Episode.
  A. Criteria for Manic Episode
    1. A distinct period of abnormally and persistently elevated, expansive, or irritable mood, lasting 1 week (or any duration if hospitalization is necessary)
    2. Three or more of the following (four if mood is only irritable):
      a. Inflated self-esteem/grandiosity
      b. Decreased need for sleep
      c. Flight of ideas, racing thoughts
      d. Talkativeness, pressured speech
      e. Distractibility
      f. Increase in goal-directed activity
      g. Excessive involvement in risky, pleasurable activity
    3. Symptoms cause marked impairment in functioning
    4. Symptoms not caused by alcohol, other drugs, or a medical condition
  B. Criteria for Mixed Episode
    1. Person meets criteria for Manic Episode and Major Depressive Episode nearly every day for 1 week
    2. Symptoms cause marked impairment in functioning
    3. Symptoms not caused by alcohol, other drugs, or a medical condition
II. Symptoms are not better explained by Schizophrenia or another psychotic disorder

Source: Reprinted with permission from the *DSM-IV-TR*.

Children and adolescents are also capable of showing elevated or expansive mood, although they display mania somewhat differently than adults. Children with mania may display elevated mood by acting silly, giddy, or unusually happy. Adolescents may display loud, boisterous behavior or labile (i.e., quickly fluctuating) mood (Biederman, Faraone et al., 2005; G. A. Carlson, 2005; Kowatch & Fristad, 2006; Weller, Weller, & Danielyan, 2004).

Only about one-fourth of youths with bipolar disorder show elevated or expansive mood symptoms like adults. Instead, children and adolescents are more likely to show irritable mood during manic episodes. Their mood is often described as "touchy," angry, oppositional, or reactive. Young children with mania can throw hour-long tantrums marked by yelling, crying, throwing objects, and acting physically aggressive toward others. Older children and adolescents sometimes display emotional outbursts or "affective storms." These tantrums, "rages," or "meltdowns" often seem to come out of the blue or arise with little provocation. For example, a child with bipolar disorder may tantrum for hours, destroying toys and furniture, because his father tells him to clean up his room (Kowatch, Fristad, Birmaher, Wagner, Findling, & Hellander, 2005).

In addition to persistently elevated, expansive, or irritable mood, mania is characterized by at least three of the following symptoms (or four, if the person's mood is only irritable): inflated self-esteem and grandiosity; decreased need for sleep; flight of ideas or racing thoughts; excessive talking or pressured speech; distractibility; increased goal-directed activity or psychomotor agitation; and excessive involvement in pleasurable, but possibly dangerous, activities.

Inflated Self-Esteem and Grandiosity

In adults, inflated self-esteem is characterized by unusually high self-confidence, exaggerated self-esteem, and overrated self-importance. Some adults hold erroneous beliefs that they have special abilities, talents, or skills. Youths with mania are also capable of grandiosity and inflated self-esteem. Children may manifest grandiose thinking by claiming that they are special, have superhuman abilities, or hold magical powers. For example, a child with bipolar disorder may try to outrun a train because he thinks that he has superhuman speed, while another child may jump from a window because she believes she can fly. Older children and adolescents might tell their coach how to run the team, or their teacher how to instruct the class, because they believe that they have special talents or intelligence (G. A. Carlson, 2005; Kowatch et al., 2005; Kowatch & Fristad, 2006).

Decreased Need for Sleep

Adults with mania show a marked decreased need for sleep. Some may feel rested after only three hours of sleep, while others go for days without feeling sleepy or fatigued. Youths with mania also show decreased need for sleep. Many youths with mania sleep only four or five hours at night and wake in the early morning feeling full of energy. Some wander the house, play video games, or watch TV during the early morning hours.

Flight of Ideas or Racing Thoughts

Adults with mania often report that their thoughts are "racing" or occurring too fast to articulate to others. One adult with mania described the sensation as watching two or three television programs at once (*DSM-IV-TR*). Racing thoughts are sometimes referred to as a **flight of ideas**. Children and adolescents also report racing thoughts. For example, they may say that their minds are going "100 miles an hour" or report that "there is an Energizer Bunny up there [in my head]" (Kowatch et al., 2005, p. 216).

Excessive Talking or Pressured Speech

Many adults with mania talk rapidly in an attempt to keep up with racing thoughts. Their speech is typically fast, loud, and difficult to understand. Youths with mania may also speak rapidly. Their speech seems pressured; that is, they seem to keep talking in order to avoid periods of silence. Sometimes, their train of thought is difficult to follow as they jump from one topic to the next. Some physicians call this phenomenon "knight's move thinking" because the person jumps from topic to topic like the knight on a chessboard jumps from one square to the next without moving in between.

Distractibility

Adults with mania are easily distracted by irrelevant external stimuli or unimportant details. For example, an adult with mania may find it difficult to converse with another person because he is distracted by the pattern of the other person's tie or events occurring outside the room. Youths with mania almost always show distractibility. They may have problems concentrating on schoolwork or completing chores at home. Teachers and parents may describe them as disorganized or "flighty." These problems with distractibility reflect a marked change in the youth's typical behavior, not a general problem with inattention or hyperactivity-impulsivity (i.e., not due to ADHD).

Increased Goal-Directed Activity or Psychomotor Agitation

Adults with mania often show a marked increase in **goal-directed activity**; that is, they initiate a wide range of new activities and behaviors. For example, some adults with mania may decide to rebuild their car engine, write a novel, or start a new business with little preparation or training. Usually, these goal-directed activities are poorly planned and executed. Youths with mania can also show increased goal-directed activity. For example, children may draw, color, or build elaborate block towers for hours on end. Older adolescents may begin a number of ambitious projects, like taking apart their computer. Youths with mania may also show **psychomotor agitation**; that is, they may appear hyperactive, restless, or impulsive. They often engage in short bursts of frenzied activity that do not seem to have much purpose (Kowatch et al., 2005; Weller et al., 2004).

Excessive Involvement in Pleasurable (But Possibly Dangerous) Activities

Many adults with mania engage in pleasurable activities that are likely to have negative consequences. For example, some adults with mania go on shopping sprees, gambling trips, or risky sexual encounters. Youths with mania may also engage in pleasurable, but reckless, behaviors. Younger children may ride their bikes through dangerous intersections or perform stunts on their skateboards. Older children and adolescents may carelessly spend money, drive recklessly, steal items from a store, or indulge in alcohol and other drugs. Many youths with mania also show **hypersexuality**. Some show increased interest in pornography. Others engage in inappropriate flirtatious and erotic behaviors toward family members and peers. For example, some youths will dance suggestively, attempt to touch others' private parts, or try to open-mouth kiss family members. Youths with mania may show these hypersexual behaviors even if they have never experienced sexual abuse.

Individuals can also be diagnosed with BP-I if they have (or have had) a **mixed mood episode**. A mixed mood episode is defined by the presence of a manic episode and a major depressive episode nearly every day for at least one week. Typically, people experiencing a mixed mood episode show a combination of irritability, agitation, sleep and appetite problems, concentration problems, and thoughts about death and suicide. These mood symptoms cause significant impairment in social, occupational, or academic functioning, or they require that the person be hospitalized to prevent self-harm.

In summary, individuals can be diagnosed with BP-I if they have (or have had) at least one manic episode or at least one mixed mood episode. In most cases, individuals with BP-I also have a history of major depressive episodes. That is why some people refer to BP-I as "manic-depression." Technically speaking, however, depressive episodes are not required for the diagnosis of BP-I; the presence of a manic or mixed mood episode is sufficient.

Bipolar II Disorder

To be diagnosed with BP-II, the person must have (or have had) at least one major depressive episode and at least one **hypomanic episode** (see Table 12.2). By definition, a hypomanic episode is characterized by "a discrete period of persistently elevated, expansive, or irritable mood" that is clearly different from the person's usual mood (*DSM-IV-TR*, p. 368). The features of hypomania are the same as the features of mania: grandiosity, decreased need for sleep, racing thoughts, talkativeness, distractibility, agitation, and risky pleasurable activity. Generally speaking, a hypomanic episode is similar to a manic episode except (1) it lasts at least four days rather than at least one week; (2) it *does not* cause significant impairment in social, occupational, or academic functioning; and (3) it *never* requires the person to be hospitalized.

By definition, a person cannot be diagnosed with BP-II if she has ever had a manic or mixed mood episode. If the person has had a manic or mixed mood episode, she would probably be diagnosed with BP-I. Indeed, many individuals initially diagnosed with BP-II eventually experience a manic or mixed mood episode and are subsequently diagnosed with BP-I.

Table 12.2 Diagnostic Criteria for Bipolar II Disorder

I. Presence (or history) of at least one Major Depressive Episode

II. Presence (or history) of at least one Hypomanic Episode
   A. A distinct period of persistently elevated, expansive, or irritable mood, lasting at least four days, that is clearly different from the person's normal mood

   B. Three or more of the following (four if mood is only irritable):
      1. Inflated self-esteem/grandiosity

      2. Decreased need for sleep

      3. Flight of ideas, racing thoughts

      4. Talkativeness, pressured speech

      5. Distractibility

      6. Increase in goal-directed activity

      7. Excessive involvement in risky, pleasurable activity

   C. Symptoms are a marked change in the person's usual behavior and are observable by others

   D. Symptoms are not severe enough to cause marked impairment in functioning or require hospitalization

   E. Symptoms are not caused by alcohol, other drugs, or a medical condition

III. There has never been a Manic or Mixed Mood Episode

IV. Symptoms are not better explained by Schizophrenia or another psychotic disorder

V. Symptoms cause marked distress or impairment in functioning

Source: Reprinted with permission from the *DSM-IV-TR*.

Cyclothymic Disorder

Cyclothymic Disorder is a rare condition characterized by the presence of significant symptoms of hypomania and significant symptoms of depression (see Table 12.3). To be diagnosed with Cyclothymic Disorder, adults must show numerous periods of hypomanic symptoms and numerous periods of depressive symptoms over a two-year period. Children and adolescents must also show numerous periods of hypomanic symptoms and numerous periods of depressive symptoms, but they only need to show these symptoms over a one-year period to be diagnosed with Cyclothymic Disorder.

By definition, children and adolescents with Cyclothymic Disorder must never have had a manic episode, a mixed mood episode, or a major depressive episode during the timespan of the disorder. If the child has had a manic, mixed, or depressive episode, he or she would likely qualify for the diagnosis of BP-I or BP-II instead (see Figure 12.1).

Table 12.3   Diagnostic Criteria for Cyclothymic Disorder in Children and Adolescents

A. For at least 1 year, the youth has had numerous periods of hypomanic symptoms and numerous periods of depressive symptoms
B. During this 1-year time period, the youth has not been without hypomanic or depressive symptoms for more than 2 months at a time
C. The youth has not had a Manic Episode, Mixed Episode, or Major Depressive Episode during the first year of the disorder
D. Symptoms are not better explained by Schizophrenia or another psychotic disorder
E. Symptoms are not caused by alcohol, other drugs, or a medical condition
F. Symptoms cause marked distress or impairment in functioning

Source: Reprinted with permission from the *DSM-IV-TR.*

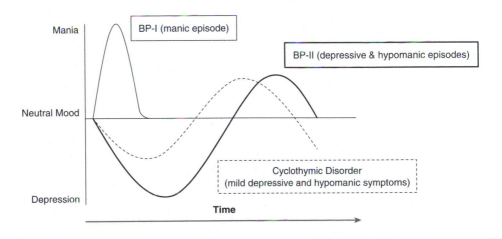

Figure 12.1   Distinguishing Among the Bipolar Disorders

Note: BP-I is defined by at least one manic or mixed episode. BP-II is defined by at least one major depressive episode and at least one hypomanic episode (but no manic episodes). Cyclothymic Disorder is defined by recurrent depressive and hypomanic symptoms (but no major depressive or manic episodes).

Cyclothymia, therefore, is a chronic but low-grade mood disturbance. Youths with Cyclothymic Disorder show significant distress or impairment in their social and/or academic functioning.

Bipolar Disorder Not Otherwise Specified

Many children and adolescents who show bipolar symptoms do not meet full diagnostic criteria for either BP-I, PB-II, or Cyclothymic Disorder. Instead, they are diagnosed with Bipolar Disorder Not Otherwise Specified (BP-NOS). For example, many youths show very rapid alteration between manic symptoms and depressive symptoms over the course of a single day. Consequently, they do not meet the duration requirement to be diagnosed with BP-I (i.e., 1 week) or BP-II (i.e., 4 days). Children and adolescents diagnosed with BP-NOS are a heterogeneous group of youngsters with a wide range of mood problems. Currently, BP-NOS is considered a "working diagnosis" that clinicians and researchers use to classify youths with bipolar symptoms who do not fit neatly into other diagnostic categories. As knowledge about childhood bipolar disorder grows, professionals hope that BP-NOS might be better understood and treated (Kowatch & Fristad, 2006).

My Own Waves

Anonymous Child With Bipolar Disorder, Age 11

I live my life on the beach's waters
riding waves I have to control.
My medicine is my surfboard
my emotions are in my soul.

When the wave is real high
I am the happiest guy
I can do anything,
even fly.

When the wave is low
my mind goes slow
nothing is good
I just don't want to go.

Now I can surf
I use the surfboard
I use what I learned
about changing my thoughts.

In my life there are no more
tidal waves
only me surfing forever
on medium waters.

Bipolar Disorders in Children Versus Adults

The diagnostic criteria for the bipolar disorders are the same for children, adolescents, and adults. However, the manifestation of these disorders differs somewhat, depending on the person's age and level of development (Danielyan, Pathak, Kowatch, Arszman, & Johns, 2007; Masi, Perugi, Millepiedi et al., 2006). Most adults with bipolar disorders show classic, discrete episodes of mania and depression (i.e., BP-I). A typical adult patient has reasonably good functioning before his first mood episode. Then, usually between the age of 18 and 25 years, he experiences a clear manic episode marked by euphoria, inflated self-esteem and grandiosity, decreased need for sleep, racing thoughts and rapid speech, and risk-taking behavior. Following this clear-cut manic episode, which may last for a few weeks, he enters a period of major depression that can persist for weeks or months. Finally, his depression abates and he shows a return to reasonably good functioning until his next mood episode.

Children and adolescents with bipolar disorders rarely show this classic presentation of mania and depression (Biederman, Faraone et al., 2005; G. A. Carlson, 2005; Kowatch et al., 2005). In general, youths with bipolar disorders differ from adults in four ways:

First, youths with bipolar disorders tend to show mixed mood episodes rather than clear-cut episodes of mania and depression. For example, many children with bipolar disorder display a mixed presentation of giddiness, irritability, and grandiosity at the same time. Adolescents with bipolar disorder often describe mood episodes as "meltdowns" or as feeling "tired but wired." It is relatively rare for children, in particular, to have clear-cut manic episodes. In one study of 298 children with bipolar disorders, no child showed clearly demarcated episodes of mania and depression (Biederman, Kwon et al., 2004; Kowatch & Fristad, 2006; Miklowitz et al., 2004).

Second, youths with bipolar disorders cycle from one mood state to another fairly frequently. Family members usually perceive these rapid shifts in emotion as "mood swings" rather than as discrete mood episodes. In one study, 81% of children with bipolar disorders displayed mood shifts from hypomania to normal mood to depression during a single 24-hour period. In another study, approximately one-third of adolescents with bipolar disorders displayed rapid-cycling moods. This "rapid cycling" pattern is extremely rare among adults with bipolar disorder. Instead, most adults experience fewer than four discrete mood episodes per year (Biederman, Kwon et al., 2004; Findling, Gracious, McNamara, Youngstrom, Demeter, & Branicky, 2001; Geller, Zimmerman et al., 2000).

Third, the onset of mood symptoms in children and adolescents is usually insidious; that is, symptoms typically emerge slowly over time. Early symptoms can easily be overlooked or mistaken for hyperactivity or oppositional behavior. In contrast, adults with bipolar disorder often have rapid symptom onset (Lofthouse & Fristad, 2004).

Fourth, children and adolescents with bipolar disorder often show chronic and continuous mood problems. It is not uncommon for youths with bipolar disorder to show long-term mood disturbances, sometimes lasting months or years. In one large study, 82% of children and 83% of adolescents with bipolar disorders showed chronic mood symptoms lasting longer than 12 months. In contrast, adults with bipolar disorder tend to have brief mood episodes with marked recovery in between episodes (Biederman, Faraone et al., 2005; Masi, Perugi, Millepiedi et al., 2006).

Reese

Reese was a nine-year-old African American girl who was referred to the hospital after an apparent suicide attempt. One day, while traveling to school with her mother, Reese began talking and laughing uncontrollably. Then, she unbuckled her seat belt and jumped out of the moving car, seriously injuring herself. After she was treated in the emergency department, Dr. Saunders, a pediatric psychologist at the hospital, interviewed Reese and her mother.

Reese had a longstanding history of behavior problems. Her mother said Reese was a "colicky" infant who never seemed to be able to settle down. As a toddler, Reese would frequently throw tantrums, talk back, and disobey. About the same time, Reese began to show high-rate, disruptive behavior that interfered with her ability to pay attention and follow the rules at home and preschool. Reese would often wake up in the early morning, after sleeping only four or five hours, and watch television or play video games. In kindergarten, Reese's pediatrician diagnosed her with ADHD and ODD. The pediatrician began prescribing stimulant medication to help Reese manage her hyperactivity; however, these medications had little effect on her behavior.

By the time Reese was in first grade, she had been expelled from two schools for throwing violent temper tantrums. During one tantrum, she threw a chair at her teacher; during another tantrum she bit several classmates and stabbed a girl with a pencil. At the time of the interview, Reese was attending a school for children with "emotional disturbance." Reese continued to throw tantrums multiple times each week, at home and at school. These tantrums usually lasted 30 minutes to two hours. During her "meltdowns," Reese would scream, cry, throw furniture, destroy toys, and finally collapse from exhaustion.

Reese also had a history of mood problems. Her mother and father separated when Reese was six years old. Shortly after their separation, Reese became increasingly irritable, spiteful, and "touchy." Around this same time, Reese began to have crying spells in her room, which usually followed her tantrums. On two occasions, her mother overheard Reese crying, "I want to die. Just let me die. Nobody loves me." Her mother also had to stop Reese from banging her head on the bedroom wall during some of these crying spells.

Dr. Saunders asked Reese about her apparent suicide attempt. Reese denied wanting to kill herself. She said, "I thought that if I just ran really fast, I could keep up with the car. Besides, I told my mom I didn't want to go to school and she wouldn't listen."

Because of Reese's behavior and mood problems, Dr. Saunders asked about her family's psychiatric history. Reese's mother was diagnosed with Bipolar I Disorder in her early twenties but had generally managed her mood symptoms with medication. Her mother stated, "I just don't know what to do about Reese. I'm so scared for her and I don't know who to turn to for help. Everybody keeps saying, 'she just needs more discipline,' but I just don't think it's that simple."

Associated Characteristics and Psychiatric Disorders

ADHD and Conduct Problems

The most common comorbid condition among youths with bipolar disorders is ADHD. The prevalence of ADHD among youths with bipolar disorders ranges from 60% to 98% (Evans et al., 2005; Geller et al., 1998; Wozniak et al., 1995). Prevalence tends to be highest in samples of younger children. Conversely, bipolar disorders are present in as many as 22% of youths with ADHD (Butler, Arredondo, & McCloskey, 1995).

Most clinicians have difficulty distinguishing ADHD from bipolar disorders in children and adolescents. Both disorders can be characterized by an increase in behavioral activity, short attention span, distractibility, talkativeness, and impulsive behavior. However, youths with ADHD show these symptoms chronically and in less severe form. In contrast, youths with bipolar disorders show these symptoms more episodically, and they tend to cause serious impairment in functioning. Also, youths with ADHD sometimes show low self-regard, while youths with mania often report increased sense of self-worth and grandiosity (Weller et al., 2004).

Emerging data indicate that the high rate of comorbidity between ADHD and bipolar disorders in children may be due to common genetic causes. For example, studies of adults and children with bipolar disorder indicate that unaffected family members have higher-than-expected likelihoods of having ADHD (Faraone, Biederman, Mennin, & Russel, 1998).

Adolescents with bipolar disorders show high rates of conduct problems. Between 42% and 69% of clinic-referred youths with bipolar disorders also meet diagnostic criteria for CD. Symptoms of CD can sometimes overshadow bipolar symptoms. For example, adolescents with both CD and bipolar disorders sometimes engage in delinquent behavior such as theft, vandalism, and disruptive behaviors at school. However, youths with bipolar disorders usually show disruptive behaviors predominantly during manic and hypomanic episodes (Weller et al., 2004).

Substance Use Problems

Adolescents with bipolar disorders are at risk for developing substance use problems. One prospective study showed that childhood-onset bipolar symptoms predicted later substance use. Furthermore, use of alcohol and other drugs did not seem to depend on extraneous factors, like whether the adolescent had ADHD (Biederman et al., 1997). It is likely that many youths with bipolar disorders use alcohol and other drugs to cope with mood problems. However, other data indicate that substance use problems sometimes predate the emergence of mood symptoms. It is also likely that the use of alcohol and other drugs can elicit a manic episode among youths who are at risk for developing bipolar symptoms (Carlson, Bromet, & Sievers, 2000; Evans et al., 2005).

Anxiety and Suicide

Anxiety disorders are common among youths with bipolar disorder. The prevalence of anxiety disorders ranges from 33% to 76% of youths with bipolar disorders.

The most common anxiety disorders are Separation Anxiety Disorder, Social Phobia, and Specific Phobias (Ahn & Frazier, 2004).

Adolescents with bipolar disorders show increased risk of suicide compared to adolescents with other psychiatric diagnoses. In one large study of children and adolescents with bipolar disorders, 32% of youths reported a history of at least one serious suicide attempt (Goldstein et al., 2005). Youths with bipolar disorders who are at greatest risk for suicide show more severe mood problems, display psychotic symptoms, and have histories of psychiatric hospitalization. At-risk youths also tend to have comorbid substance use disorders, anxiety disorders, histories of nonsuicidal self-injury (e.g., cutting or burning), and family members who attempted suicide. This increased risk of suicide is likely caused by the combination of dysphoria, impulsivity, and comorbid psychiatric conditions. Indeed, bipolar disorders may be one of the most lethal mental disorders in adolescence (see Figure 12.2).

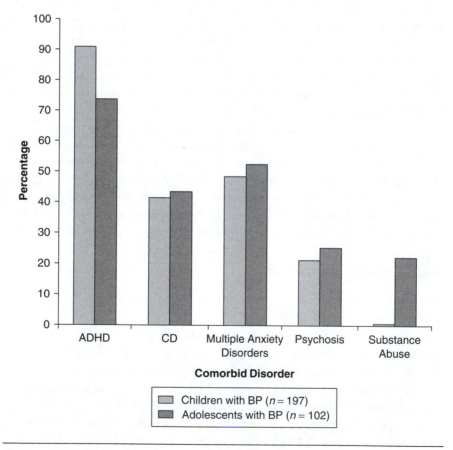

Figure 12.2   Youths With Bipolar Disorders Often Have Comorbid Psychiatric Problems

Source: Based on Biederman, Faraone et al. (2005).

Psychotic Symptoms

Approximately one-third of children and adolescents with bipolar disorder display psychotic symptoms. Psychotic symptoms include delusions, hallucinations, and disorganized thinking. **Delusions** are "erroneous beliefs that usually involve a misinterpretation of perceptions or experiences" (*DSM-IV-TR*, p. 299). These unrealistic beliefs lead to impairment in functioning or otherwise interfere with day-to-day activities.

Most youths with bipolar disorders who have delusions show mood-congruent delusions; that is, their erroneous beliefs are consistent with their elevated mood or grandiosity. For example, a young child with mania might believe that he is a superhero and has extraordinary strength. He may dart into the street, unafraid of passing cars, because he believes that he is impervious to injury. An adolescent with grandiose delusions might refuse to attend school because he believes that he has hidden artistic talents that will make him rich and famous (Biederman, Faraone et al., 2005; Goldstein et al., 2005).

Delusions may also be mood-incongruent; that is, erroneous beliefs may be inconsistent with feelings of euphoria or grandiosity. For example, a small number of adolescents with bipolar disorders show delusions of persecution (e.g., belief that people are out to get them), thought insertion (e.g., belief that others are controlling their thoughts), thought broadcasting (e.g., belief that others can hear their thoughts), or delusions of control (e.g., belief that others are controlling their actions; *DSM-IV-TR*). Mood-incongruent delusions are relatively rare among youths with bipolar disorders and may reflect a more negative prognosis.

Hallucinations are erroneous perceptions that do not correspond to reality. Although hallucinations can occur in any sensory modality, auditory hallucinations are most common. Auditory hallucinations usually involve hearing voices that give commands, comment on the person's actions or thoughts, criticize, threaten, or otherwise impair concentration (*DSM-IV-TR*).

Disorganized thinking involves general problems in reasoning, understanding, and logic. The most common symptom indicative of disorganized thinking is speech disturbance. Youths who show disorganized speech may "slip off track" when discussing topics; fail to give direct or appropriate answers to questions; or speak using incomprehensible, jumbled language. In general, listeners find disorganized speech difficult to follow, tangential, or bizarre (*DSM-IV-TR*).

Studies investigating the prevalence of psychotic symptoms among youths with bipolar disorders have yielded inconsistent results. Between 16% and 75% of youths with bipolar disorders have at least one mood episode marked by psychotic symptoms. Children and adolescents with bipolar disorders and psychotic symptoms tend to have greater impairment, more resistance to medication, and worse prognosis than youths with bipolar disorders alone (Pavuluri, Herbener, & Sweeney, 2004).

Children with bipolar disorders who show psychotic features are often misdiagnosed with **Schizophrenia**, a mental disorder characterized by delusions, hallucinations,

Table 12.4   Differentiating Childhood Schizophrenia and Childhood Bipolar Disorder

Feature	Schizophrenia	Bipolar Disorder
Delusions	• Usually mood incongruent • 11% show grandiose delusions	• Usually mood congruent • 50% show grandiose delusions
Hallucinations	• Relatively common; 80%	• Relatively uncommon; 23%
Disorganized thinking	• Often lose train of thought when talking (i.e., "loose associations")	• Often show rapid, pressured speech
Mood symptoms	• Chronic; marked by depression	• More episodic; marked by irritability, agitation, and depression
Family history	• Relatives may have schizophrenia or mood disorders	• Relatives may have mood disorders

Source: From Pavuluri et al. (2004). Used with permission.

disorganized thinking, disorganized behavior, and limited emotional displays. Although bipolar disorder and schizophrenia have some resemblance, they are distinct disorders. Schizophrenia is predominantly a thought disorder; disorganization of thoughts, perceptions, and language are central to the illness. In contrast, bipolar disorders are mood disorders; disturbance of mood is central to the presentation of bipolar disorders.

Children with bipolar disorders and children with schizophrenia can be differentiated in several ways (see Table 12.4). First, the delusions held by children with bipolar disorders tend to be mood congruent. In contrast, the delusions held by youths with schizophrenia are often mood incongruent. Second, the mood symptoms displayed by youths with bipolar disorder tend to be marked by a mixed presentation of irritability, agitation, and depression. In contrast, the mood symptoms shown by youths with schizophrenia tend to be depressive in nature. Third, family members of youths with bipolar disorder tend to have histories of mood disorders, but not schizophrenia. In contrast, family members of youths with schizophrenia tend to have histories of both mood disorders and schizophrenia (Pavuluri et al., 2004).

Identifying youths who have bipolar disorders with psychotic features is extremely important. These youths often have worse prognoses and are more resistant to medication than youths who have bipolar disorders without psychotic features (see Figure 12.3). Youths with both bipolar disorders and psychosis also show greater likelihood of suicidal ideation and psychiatric hospitalization than youths with bipolar disorders alone or youths with other psychiatric illnesses (Caetano et al., 2006).

Family, School, and Peer Problems

Because of the chronic nature of bipolar disorders, many children and adolescents experience considerable problems at home, at school, and in the community (see Figure 12.4). At home, youths with bipolar disorders often conflict with family members. For example, mothers of children with bipolar disorders are less likely to engage in frequent pleasant activities with their children than mothers of children with either ADHD or no psychiatric diagnosis. Furthermore, mothers of children

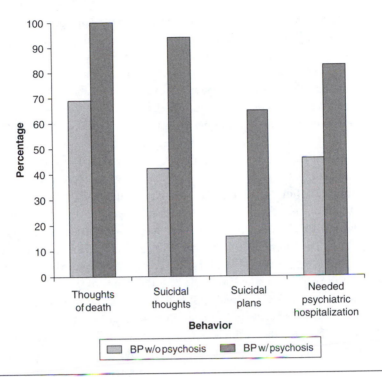

Figure 12.3   Youths With Bipolar Disorders and Psychotic Symptoms Show More Severe and Serious Problems Than Youths With Bipolar Disorders Alone

Source: Based on Caetano et al. (2006).

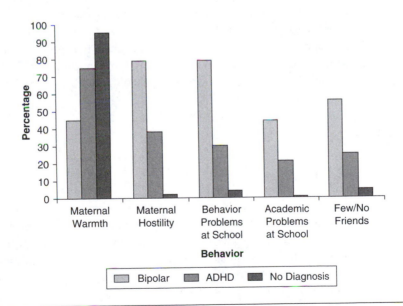

Figure 12.4   Psychosocial Functioning of Youths With Bipolar Disorders, ADHD, and No Psychiatric Diagnosis

Source: Based on Geller, Bolhofner, Craney, Williams, Del, and Gundersen (2000).

Note: Youths with bipolar disorders show more problems with parents, school, and peers than other youths.

with bipolar disorders are more likely to physically punish their children than mothers of children with ADHD or healthy children. Parents of children with bipolar disorder often feel overwhelmed by their caregiving duties. They report considerable worry and frustration, physical illness, financial strain, isolation, stigma, guilt, and self-blame (Hellander, Sisson, & Fristad, 2003; Kowatch & Fristad, 2006).

At school, children with bipolar disorders are more likely to show significant behavior problems and to earn low grades than children with ADHD and children without psychiatric diagnoses. Furthermore, children with bipolar disorders show comparable rates of repeating a grade, being assigned to a remedial class, and being classified as having a learning disability or as children with ADHD. In one large study, one-third of adolescents with bipolar disorders had failed at least one grade in school, and slightly more than one-third were receiving special educational services for academic or behavioral problems (Biederman, Faraone et al., 2005).

Bipolar disorders can interfere with children's school performance in four ways (Kowatch & Fristad, 2006). First, the cognitive symptoms of bipolar disorder, such as the racing thoughts in mania and the concentration problems in depression, can directly affect children's ability to learn. Second, comorbid conditions, such as ADHD, can indirectly affect concentration and learning and contribute to academic failure and disruptive behavior problems. Third, the side effects of medication that children take to manage bipolar disorder can interfere with learning. Finally, children with bipolar disorder can be suspended or expelled from school and, therefore, miss out on learning opportunities.

Children with bipolar disorders often have considerable problems in their peer relationships. In one study, children with bipolar disorders had fewer friends than children with ADHD. Although both children with ADHD and children with bipolar disorders have difficulty making and keeping friends, children with ADHD usually know how they ought to behave toward others. In contrast, youths with bipolar disorders often show social skill deficits. It is likely that peers find the disruptive behavior of children with bipolar disorders to be off-putting, so they shy away from these children (Geller, Zimmerman et al., 2000; Kowatch & Fristad, 2006).

Epidemiology

Prevalence

Very little research has been conducted on the prevalence of bipolar disorders among children and adolescents. In the only published population-based study of bipolar disorders among youths in the United States, Lewinsohn, Klein, and Klein (1995) found that approximately 0.12% of adolescents in the community met diagnostic criteria for BP-I. The prevalence of BP-II and Cyclothymic Disorder was approximately 1%. An additional 5.7% of adolescents showed subthreshold symptoms that might qualify adolescents for the diagnosis of BP-NOS. Other studies conducted in Germany, Holland, and Finland suggest similar prevalence. These findings indicate that the vast majority of adolescents with bipolar symptoms do not show BP-I, the most common bipolar disorder in adults. Instead, adolescents are more likely to show hypomanic and rapid-cycling mood episodes and, consequently, to be diagnosed with BP-II, Cyclothymic Disorder, or BP-NOS.

There are no epidemiological studies of children with bipolar disorders in the community. However, one unpublished study involving 1,285 children and adolescents indicated that 1.2% of children had bipolar disorders (reported in Evans et al., 2005). In another study, 31% of adults with bipolar disorder recalled the onset of their disorder to be during childhood (Lish, Dime-Meenan, Whybrow, Price, & Hirschfeld, 1997). Clearly, more research needs to be conducted to obtain a better estimate of the prevalence of bipolar disorders in both childhood and adolescence.

Gender, SES, and Ethnicity

Data on gender differences in child and adolescent bipolar disorders is sparse. Data from adult samples indicate that men and women are equally likely to develop the disorder. However, symptoms of bipolar disorder differ somewhat in men and women. Men tend to have earlier symptom onset and more frequent manic episodes than women. Women, on the other hand, tend to show higher frequency of mixed episodes and psychotic features than men.

In contrast, adolescent boys and girls with bipolar disorders show few differences in symptom presentation. The prevalence of bipolar disorders among clinic-referred youth is approximately equal for adolescent boys (19%) and girls (17%). Adolescents with bipolar disorders also tend to show chronic mood problems marked by a mixture of irritability, agitation, and grandiosity, regardless of gender. Very few adolescents showed distinct manic or depressive episodes. Boys and girls also showed similar levels of social and educational impairment (Biederman, Kwon et al., 2004; Geller, Zimmerman et al., 2000).

Adolescent boys and girls with bipolar disorder do show slightly different comorbid symptoms. Boys (91%) were somewhat more likely than girls (70%) to have comorbid ADHD. Girls (61%) were more likely than boys (46%) to have comorbid anxiety disorders (Biederman, Kwon et al., 2004).

Very little information is available regarding gender differences in children with bipolar disorders. Some data indicate that the disorder is much more common among prepubescent boys than girls. Approximately 80% of clinic-referred children with the disorder are boys (Ahn & Frazier, 2004; Biederman, Kwon et al., 2005).

Very few studies have investigated differences in pediatric bipolar disorders as a function of SES and ethnicity. Studies involving adults indicate that the prevalence of the disorder is similar regardless of income and education. The prevalence of bipolar disorder among African Americans is similar to the prevalence of the disorder among whites. However, some data indicate that the *presentation* of bipolar disorders may vary across ethnic groups. African American adolescents with bipolar disorders are more likely to show psychotic symptoms, especially auditory hallucinations, than white adolescents with the disorder. Researchers are uncertain what causes these ethnic differences in symptom presentation (Patel, DelBello, Keck, & Strakowski, 2006). Very little information is available regarding the prevalence and presentation of bipolar disorder in other ethnic minority groups. Some data indicate that the disorder is frequently overlooked among

Latinos (Dilsaver & Akiskal, 2005). Clearly, more research needs to be directed in this area.

Course

Bipolar disorders are serious conditions that must be managed across the life-span. Kowatch and Fristad (2006) liken bipolar disorder to diabetes. Both disorders are greatly influenced by the person's genes and biological functioning. However, the severity of these disorders and the extent to which they interfere with people's lives greatly depends on environmental experiences. Children with diabetes must monitor their blood sugar and regulate their diet to remain symptom-free and healthy. Children with bipolar disorders must monitor their mood states and behavior, comply with physician's recommendations regarding medication, and improve the quality of their social-emotional environment in order to avoid mood episodes. There is currently no "cure" for either diabetes or bipolar disorders. However, environmental experiences can determine whether these disorders are manageable or debilitating.

In most cases, bipolar disorders in children and adolescents emerge gradually. Most children display problems with mood and behavior before they develop full-blown mania or depression. **Prodromal symptoms** in young children include anxiety, sleep and appetite disturbance, oppositional behavior, extreme tantrums, and bed wetting (see Table 12.5). Many parents of young children eventually diagnosed with bipolar disorder describe them as "irritable" or "difficult" infants and as having an extreme case of the "terrible twos." In one study, 74% of children with bipolar disorders showed prodromal symptoms before they were three years old (Faedda, Baldessarini, Glovinsky, & Austin, 2004; Kowatch & Fristad, 2006).

Usually, prodromal symptoms gradually worsen until the child can be classified as having a manic, depressive, or (most likely) mixed mood episode. Typically, the first mood episode is depressed or mixed rather than manic (Lewinsohn et al., 1995).

Once children and adolescents experience a full-blown mood episode, symptoms usually persist for some time. The median length of children's initial mood episode is approximately 78 to 79 weeks. Children who are younger and are diagnosed with BP-NOS take longer to recover than children and adolescents who show more "classic" BP-I (Birmaher et al., 2006; Geller, Tillman, Craney, & Bolhofner, 2004).

Table 12.5 Prodromal Symptoms in Childhood-Onset Bipolar Disorder

Symptom	Percentage Showing
Depressed mood	53
Increased energy	47
Tiredness or fatigue	38
Anger, quick temper	38
Irritability	33
Conduct problems	28
Decreased need for sleep	26
Crying	26
Oversensitivity	24

Source: Based on Egeland, Hosteller, Pauls, and Sussex (2000).

After children recover from their initial mood episode, relapse (i.e., experiencing another mood episode) is extremely common (see Figure 12.5). Approximately 56% of youths who recover experience relapse within two years of their first mood episode, while approximately 70% of youths relapse within four years of their initial mood episode. The median time from recovery to relapse is only about 40 to 60 weeks. Therefore, children with bipolar disorders spend the majority of their childhoods experiencing manic, hypomanic, depressive, or mixed mood episodes. Indeed, these youths experience normal mood states only about one-third of the time (Birmaher et al., 2006; Geller et al., 2004).

Two variables seem to delay relapse. First, youths who consistently take mood stabilizing medication have lower relapse rates than youths who are noncompliant with pharmacotherapy. Second, youths whose parents provide warm and supportive care are less likely to relapse than youths whose parents are less responsive (Geller et al., 2004; Jairam, Srinath, Girimaji, & Seshadri, 2004).

Individuals with childhood- and adolescent-onset bipolar disorders may have worse outcomes than individuals whose bipolar symptoms emerge during adulthood (Masi, Perugi, Toni et al., 2006). Carlson and colleagues (2000) compared individuals with early- and adult-onset bipolar disorders on a number of outcome variables. They found that individuals whose symptom onset was during adolescence showed greater frequency of manic symptoms, less remission of symptoms and more relapse over time, and a greater number of psychiatric hospitalizations than individuals whose onset occurred during adulthood. Furthermore, individuals with early-onset bipolar disorder were more likely to have experienced educational, employment, and substance use problems than people whose symptoms emerged during adulthood.

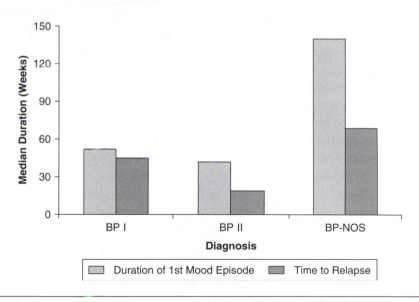

Figure 12.5   Course of Bipolar Disorders in Children and Adolescents

Source: Based on Birmaher et al. (2006).

Note: Most youths with bipolar disorders have mood episodes lasting many months or years. Furthermore, relapse is common.

Bipolar disorders can be debilitating if left untreated. Over time, individuals with bipolar disorders who do not participate in pharmacotherapy are at considerable risk for recurrent episodes of mania and depression, employment and relationship problems, legal problems, periodic hospitalizations, substance abuse, and suicide. These outcomes highlight the importance of identifying and managing bipolar disorders as early as possible (Findling et al., 2001; Lewinsohn, Seeley, & Klein, 2003).

Etiology

Genetics

Behavioral genetic studies involving adults indicate that bipolar disorders are heritable. For BP-I, concordance for monozygotic twins ranges from 50% to 67%, while concordance for dizygotic twins ranges from 17% to 24%. When researchers examine concordance for *any* bipolar disorder, not just BP-I, rates for monozygotic twins and dizygotic twins approach 87% and 37%, respectively (Badner, 2003; Rende et al., 2007).

Bipolar disorders run in families. In the general population, the prevalence of bipolar disorders is approximately 1%–2%. However, the chance of developing a bipolar disorder increases to 5%–10% if a person has a first-degree relative with the illness. If someone has a parent with a bipolar disorder, his or her chance of developing the illness may be as high as 27%. In contrast, the likelihood of a child developing a bipolar disorder if parents and extended family members are unaffected is less than 1% (Chang & Steiner, 2003; Craddock & Jones, 1999).

Despite the genetic evidence, many questions remain. First, researchers do not know whether pediatric bipolar disorders have as strong a genetic component as bipolar disorders displayed by adults. After all, most adults show BP-I while most children are classified with BP-NOS. Second, researchers do not yet know which genes place children at risk for bipolar disorders. It is likely that several genes are involved. Identifying these genes will be necessary in order to understand and possibly prevent the disorder at the genetic level in the future. Third, researchers do not yet know the mechanism by which genes can lead to the development of bipolar disorders in children. Experts presume that genes affect brain structure and neurological development (Pavuluri, Henry, Nadimpalli, O'Connor, & Sweeney, 2006).

Brain Structure and Functioning

Several neuroimaging studies have compared the brains of youths with and without bipolar disorders. One of the most consistent neuroanatomical findings is that youths with bipolar disorders often have smaller brains than unaffected youths. In several studies, adolescents with bipolar disorders showed a 5% reduction in total cerebral volume compared to adolescents without bipolar disorders. These findings suggest that genetic factors may cause irregular neurological development, which results in smaller brain size (Frazier et al., 2005).

Since bipolar disorders are mood disorders, researchers have focused on areas of the brain responsible for emotion processing and regulation. These areas include the prefrontal cortex, the limbic system (especially the amygdala and hippocampus), and the thalamus.

Although the results of neuroimaging studies on youths with bipolar disorders have not been entirely consistent, they indicate that structural abnormalities of the frontal cortex, limbic system, and thalamus may underlie some of the symptoms of the disorder. First, compared to adolescents without psychiatric problems, adolescents with bipolar disorders show significantly more white matter below the cortex. White matter refers to the axons on nerve cells, which appear white in humans due to the myelin that surrounds them. Researchers are not sure how white matter "hyperintensity" might be important to bipolar disorder; however, the same phenomenon is seen in adults with the disorder (Botteron, Vannier, Geller, Todd, & Lee, 1995; Woods, Yurgelun-Todd, Mikulis, & Pillay, 1995).

Second, adolescents with bipolar disorders often show reduced volume in portions of the limbic system, especially the amygdala, hippocampus, and cingulate gyrus, relative to healthy adolescents (Blumberg et al., 2003; DelBello, Zimmerman, Mills, Getz, & Strakowski, 2004; Frazier et al., 2005; Kaur et al., 2005). These findings are noteworthy because these three brain regions are responsible for emotion processing. The **amygdala** is especially important in perceiving, processing, and responding to emotional displays, while the **hippocampus** appears to play a major role in processing emotion-laden memories. The **cingulate gyrus** shows increased activity during episodes of mania. Lithium, the most common medication used to treat mania, is associated with neurochemical changes in the cingulate gyrus in youths with bipolar disorder (Davanzo et al., 2001; DelBello & Kowatch, 2003).

Third, adults and adolescents with bipolar disorders may have reductions in the size of the thalamus. The thalamus is important to emotion processing. It processes sensory information and relays this information to other brain regions, especially the prefrontal cortex. Abnormalities in thalamic structure or functioning could affect emotional responsiveness or expression (Frazier et al., 2005).

Other researchers have focused on the brain functioning of adolescents with bipolar disorders. In two studies, researchers have asked adolescents with bipolar disorders to examine faces of individuals displaying various emotions, such as happiness, sadness, fearfulness, and anger. In one study, researchers discovered underactivity of the right prefrontal cortex and overactivity in the left amygdala among youths with bipolar disorders, especially when they were processing fearful faces. The other study showed increased activity in the thalamus and hippocampus, especially while processing fearful faces (Lawrence et al., 2004; Yurgelun-Todd, Gruber, Kanayama, Baird, & Young, 2000).

Although researchers are not sure how these functional abnormalities might underlie bipolar disorders, they suggest that adolescents with bipolar disorders may have abnormalities in both the frontal lobe and limbic system. In typically developing individuals, the **right prefrontal cortex** plays an important role in organizing, planning, and inhibiting behavior. Underactivity of this brain region might explain the problems with impulsivity and undercontrol evidenced by many youths with bipolar disorders. The **limbic system** (e.g., amygdala, hippocampus, cingulate gyrus, thalamus) is partially responsible for emotion processing and regulation. Overactivity in this area might underlie some of the mood symptoms that characterize the disorder.

Environmental Experiences

Sleep-Wake Cycles

Relatively little is known about the environmental experiences that contribute to pediatric bipolar disorders. One of the best predictors of relapse among adults with bipolar disorder is sleep disturbance. Adults who report disruptions to their sleep-wake cycles or circadian rhythms are more likely to experience a recurrence of manic or depressive episodes compared to adults with the disorder who maintain regular sleep-wake cycles. Indeed, one psychosocial treatment for adults with bipolar disorder is called **social rhythm therapy**. In this form of treatment, the therapist helps the client maintain regular sleep-wake cycles and avoid disruptions in day-to-day routines. For example, adults with bipolar disorder might be taught to avoid changes in work schedules, all-night studying for exams, late-night partying, or social stressors that can cause insomnia. Social rhythm therapy is associated with less frequent relapse among adults with the disorder (Rao, 2003).

Unfortunately, information about the sleep-wake cycles of children and adolescents with bipolar disorders has been largely anecdotal. Clinical reports indicate that disruptions in daily routines and circadian rhythms can trigger manic symptoms in adolescents with bipolar disorders, especially if they have a tendency toward rapid-cycling mood symptoms. Researchers do not yet know how sleep disturbance increases the likelihood of mania in youth. Sleep disruption may affect certain hormones (e.g., thyroid-stimulating hormone, cortisol) and neurotransmitters (e.g., serotonin) that are associated with mood regulation. Most psychosocial treatments for youths with bipolar disorders involve teaching these youths to maintain consistent sleep-wake schedules and avoid psychosocial stressors that could lead to sleep disturbance (Rao, 2003).

Family Conflict

In adults with bipolar disorder, high levels of expressed emotion (EE) in the family predict relapse. Expressed emotion refers to critical, hostile, or judgmental comments by family members. Researchers believe that expressed emotion adds to the experience of subjective distress and, consequently, can trigger a depressive or manic episode. It is possible that reducing family conflict and EE might decrease the likelihood of relapse in adolescents with bipolar disorder, as well.

Low maternal warmth predicts relapse of bipolar symptoms in children (Geller et al., 2003). Researchers have suggested that reducing parenting stress and improving the quality of the parent-child relationship might decrease risk of relapse (see Figure 12.6). Consequently, psychosocial interventions designed for youths with bipolar disorders often focus on improving parent-child communication and the

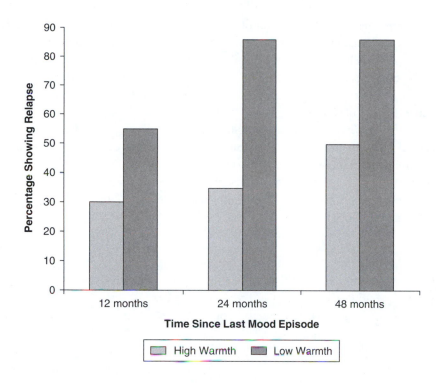

Figure 12.6   Maternal Warmth May Protect Youths With Bipolar Disorders From Relapse

Source: Based on Geller et al. (2004).

Note: Children whose mothers showed high levels of sensitive and responsive care were less likely to relapse over a four-year time period. Helping parents provide sensitive and responsive care and avoid conflict is a key component of most psychosocial treatments for pediatric bipolar disorders.

quality of the dyadic relationship. Dyads are usually taught strategies to cope with stress and negative emotions, to solve interpersonal problems, and to communicate more effectively (Lofthouse & Fristad, 2004).

Stressful Life Events

Stressful events have also been shown to trigger manic and depressive episodes in adults with bipolar disorder. The death of a loved one, the loss of a job, or a crisis at home can lead to relapse. Interestingly, stressful life events do not always have to be negative to trigger relapse. Any life experience that seriously disrupts day-to-day routines can contribute to a change in mood. For example, adults with bipolar disorder who get married, change jobs, move, or have a baby may be at increased risk (Johnson et al., 2000; Malkoff-Schwartz et al., 1998).

Very little research has investigated the impact of stressful life events on youths with bipolar disorders. Some data indicate that children with bipolar disorders experience a greater number of stressful events than children with ADHD or no psychiatric diagnosis. In one study of clinic-referred youths with bipolar disorders, 91% experienced parental divorce and 32% were adopted or placed in foster care. Other research has discovered that children with bipolar disorders are much more likely to have been sexually or physically abused than youths without bipolar disorders. Researchers do not know whether these stressful life events cause or are a consequence of children's bipolar symptoms; however, these stressful experiences seem to interfere with children's ability to cope with their bipolar illness (see Figure 12.7). In one study, the number of stressful life events experienced by children with bipolar disorders was directly related to children's subsequent number of psychiatric hospitalizations. Stressful events also predicted a more negative response to treatment (Marchand, Wirth, & Simon, 2005; Rucklidge, 2006; Tillman et al., 2003).

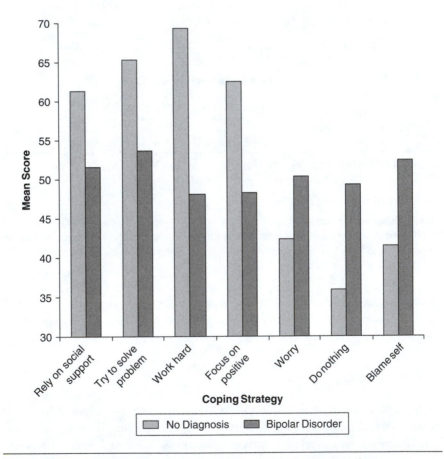

Figure 12.7   Coping Strategies Used by Youths With Bipolar Disorders

Source: Based on Rucklidge (2006).

Note: In general, youths with bipolar disorders not only experience a greater number of stressful life events but also use more ineffective means of coping with these psychosocial stressors than youths without bipolar disorder.

Treatment

Medication

The first-line treatment for child and adolescent bipolar disorders is pharma-cotherapy. Only medication has been shown to be efficacious in reducing the acute symptoms of mania and hypomania that characterize bipolar disorders. Psychoso-cial interventions, such as family therapy, are best used in conjunction with pharma-cotherapy and only after children's moods are stabilized (Findling, 2005).

Considerable research on adults with bipolar disorder has demonstrated the effi-cacy of **lithium** in stabilizing mood. The mechanism by which lithium decreases mania and stabilizes mood is unknown. Lithium seems to reduce the action of the neurotransmitters norepinephrine and serotonin, which play important roles in mood and emotional expression. Currently, lithium is considered the first-line treatment for bipolar disorders in children and adolescents. Indeed, lithium is the only mood-stabilizing medication approved for adolescents by the U.S. Food and Drug Administration (Weller et al., 2004).

Surprisingly little research has investigated the efficacy of lithium with children and adolescents. In one large study, 100 adolescents with bipolar disorders were administered lithium. After four weeks, 63% showed at least *some* reductions in mania and 26% showed *significant* remission of manic symptoms (Kafantaris, Coletti, Dicker, Padula, & Kane, 2003). In another study, researchers randomly assigned 25 adolescents with bipolar disorders to either lithium or placebo. After six weeks, patients receiving lithium showed significantly better outcomes than patients taking placebo (Geller et al., 1998).

Anticonvulsant medications are also frequently used to treat child and adoles-cent bipolar disorders. The two most commonly used anticonvulsants are dival-proex (Depakote) and carbamazepine (Tegretol). These medications are typically used to treat seizure disorders, but they have also been shown to be useful in reduc-ing mania and stabilizing mood in adults with bipolar disorder.

Unfortunately, there are no placebo-controlled studies investigating the efficacy of anticonvulsants with children showing bipolar disorders. However, Kowatch and colleagues (2000) compared the efficacy of lithium, divalproex, and carbamazepine in a sample of 42 children and adolescents with bipolar disorders. After six weeks of treatment, response to the medication was higher for divalproex (53%) than lithium (38%) or carbamazepine (38%). Another study involving children and adolescents with bipolar disorders yielded similar results. In this study, 61% of youths who took divalproex showed significant reductions in manic symptoms (Wagner et al., 2002).

Taken together, results indicate that approximately 30% to 60% of youths with bipolar disorders respond to either lithium or an anticonvulsant medication like divalproex alone (Findling et al., 2003; Kowatch & DelBello, 2005). However, many youths do not respond to these medications and continue to show mood problems.

Very few studies have examined the effectiveness of combining medications to treat bipolar disorders in youth. So far, researchers have examined the effectiveness of combining (1) lithium and divalproex, (2) lithium and the antipsychotic medication risperidone (Risperdal), and (3) divalproex and the antipsychotic medication quetiapine (Seroquel). In general, the combination of medications often results in a greater percentage of youths showing symptom reduction (DelBello, Schwiers, Rosenberg, & Strakowski, 2002; Findling, 2005; Findling et al., 2003; Frazier et al., 1999). For example, DelBello and colleagues (2002) randomly assigned 30 adolescents with mania to two treatment conditions: (1) divalproex plus quetiapine and (2) divalproex plus placebo. Approximately 87% improved taking divalproex plus quetiapine while only 53% improved taking divalproex plus placebo.

Physicians may also use medication to treat comorbid disorders, such as ADHD. Prescribing stimulant medication to youths with bipolar disorders is somewhat risky because stimulants can induce mania and exacerbate bipolar symptoms. However, two studies indicate that when used cautiously, methylphenidate (Ritalin) and amphetamine (Adderall) can effectively treat ADHD symptoms in youths with bipolar disorders after their mood is stabilized (Ahn & Frazier, 2004).

Currently, the American Academy of Child and Adolescent Psychiatry recommends using a single mood stabilizer, such as lithium or divalproex, as a first-line treatment for pediatric bipolar disorders. If the child or adolescent shows bipolar symptoms with psychotic features, then most experts recommend supplementing a mood stabilizer with an antipsychotic medication as a first-line treatment. After the child's or adolescent's mood stabilizes, physicians may prescribe a stimulant medication to address symptoms of ADHD if they are present (Kowatch et al., 2005).

Pharmacotherapy is not without risks. First, many of the aforementioned medications can cause side effects in children and adolescents. For example, the side effects of lithium include nausea; diarrhea; fatigue; and, in rare cases, tremors and cardiovascular problems. Anticonvulsant medications can cause drowsiness, coordination problems, nausea, headache, and concentration problems. Antipsychotic medications, like risperidone, can cause unwanted weight gain. Second, there are reports of some medications like antidepressants and stimulants actually inducing manic episodes in children and adolescents. Third, discontinuation of medications is strongly associated with relapse. Therefore, medication is best seen as a way to manage bipolar symptoms, not as a "cure" for the disorder. Youths who are prescribed these drugs must be monitored closely by their physicians (Biederman, Mick, Spencer, Wilens, & Faraone, 2000; Findling, 2005; Kafantaris, Coletti, Dicker, Padula, & Kane, 2001; Weller et al., 2004).

Psychosocial Treatment

The primary purpose of psychosocial treatment is twofold: (1) to increase the family's compliance with pharmacotherapy and (2) to prevent relapse. To accomplish these goals, psychosocial treatment includes several components. First, treatment involves psychoeducation; children and families are taught about bipolar illnesses and how medication can be used to manage symptoms. Second, psychosocial treatment usually involves some aspect of skill building. Parents and children work with therapists to develop behavioral, emotional, and social skills to help them manage stress and negative emotions that might trigger a relapse. Third, psychosocial treatment provides support to children with bipolar disorders and their families. Support is extremely important because children and family members are often rejected and blamed by others because of the illness.

Cognitive-Behavioral Therapy for Adolescents

CBT is based on the notion that people's mood states are greatly determined by environmental experiences and ways of thinking. Changing children's ways of coping with environmental stressors, or ways of thinking about life, can improve their mood (Feeny, Danielson, Schwartz, Youngstrom, & Findling, 2006).

Researchers at Case Western Reserve University have developed a cognitive-behavioral treatment program for adolescents with bipolar disorders (Danielson, Feeny, Findling, & Youngstrom, 2004). The program consists of 12 sessions of individual therapy for adolescents. Some of the sessions also involve parents. The treatment is designed to be used in conjunction with pharmacotherapy.

In the first session, the adolescent and parents meet with the therapist to discuss the adolescent's mood symptoms and to learn about the cognitive-behavioral approach to treatment. One particularly important element of this first session is to help family members understand that the adolescent's mood and behavior problems are symptoms of bipolar disorder and are not caused by a failure in parenting or a character flaw of the adolescent. By attributing the family's problems to the disorder rather than to the adolescent, the therapist alleviates feelings of guilt and blame that might otherwise be placed on family members.

In most of the other sessions, the therapist meets individually with the adolescent. In each session, the therapist tries to teach the adolescent a new skill or "tool" that he can use to manage his mood symptoms, improve the quality of his interactions with family and peers, and avoid relapse. Five major themes are covered over the 12-week intervention: (1) medication compliance, (2) mood regulation, (3) social problem solving, (4) sleep maintenance, and (5) family communication skills (Danielson et al., 2004).

The first important topic, which is addressed early in treatment, is medication compliance. The therapist and adolescent discuss the importance of taking mood stabilizing medication on a daily basis. Medication compliance is sometimes a problem (see Figure 12.8). Many adolescents forget to take their medication, others avoid medication because they do not like its side effects, and still others refuse to take medication because they resent being ordered to do so by physicians and parents. Some adolescents find manic and hypomanic states to be pleasurable and refuse to take medication because they do not want to miss out on these experiences.

To promote medication compliance, the therapist asks the adolescent to consider the costs and benefits of taking (and not taking) medication. The therapist attempts to show the adolescent how benefits usually outweigh costs. Then, the therapist and adolescent identify obstacles to medication compliance and generate ways to overcome these obstacles. For example, if an adolescent says that he often forgets to take his morning dose because he is usually in a hurry to get to school, the therapist might recommend that he place his medication near his lunch in the refrigerator. When he reaches for his lunch, he will be reminded to take his medication.

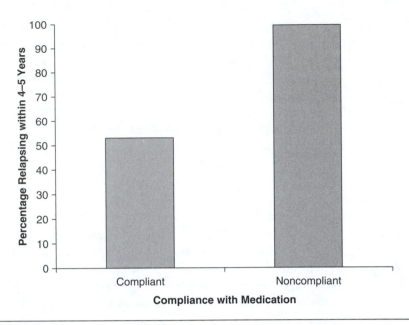

Figure 12.8   Medication Noncompliance Predicts Relapse

Source: Based on Jairam et al. (2004).

Note: Most psychosocial interventions for pediatric bipolar disorder help parents and youths adhere to medication.

A second theme of treatment involves teaching the adolescent how to monitor his mood and cope with negative emotional experiences to avoid relapse. First, the therapist teaches the adolescent to identify and keep track of negative emotions. Then, the therapist helps the adolescent identify environmental events that often trigger these negative feelings. The therapist shows the adolescent that people's beliefs or interpretations of environmental experiences determine their emotional consequences, not the experiences themselves. For example, the adolescent might say that he often feels sad and worthless when his father criticizes his academic performance. If the adolescent thinks, "I've really let my father down; I'm no good at anything," then he will likely feel sad when his father criticizes him. However, if he has a different thought, such as, "My father's such a hypocrite; he calls me 'lazy' but he spends every evening watching TV," he would likely experience a different emotion, such as anger or irritability.

Later, the therapist tries to teach the adolescent how to recognize negative thoughts that often cause him to experience unpleasant emotions. The thought, "I've really let my father down; I'm no good at anything" is an example of a cognitive distortion that can lead to feelings of depression. The therapist tries to show that cognitive distortions are not true; they twist reality and make the adolescent hold negative views of himself and others. The therapist encourages the adolescent to challenge this overly pessimistic world view and to generate an alternative, more realistic self-statement. For example, a more realistic thought might be, "My father's really frustrated with me; maybe I can ask for help."

A third important topic of CBT for bipolar disorder is social problem solving. During the course of treatment, the therapist teaches the adolescent a basic approach to social problem solving. This approach involves solving problems systematically by following a series of steps: (1) identifying the problem, (2) generating as many possible solutions to the problem as possible, (3) evaluating each possible solution, (4) selecting the best solution, and (5) implementing the solution and evaluating its outcome. The therapist and adolescent practice using this social problem-solving strategy on hypothetical situations created by the therapist:

> This upcoming Saturday night is the big homecoming dance at our school. I am really excited because I am going to the dance with a person I really like. I don't know what to do because my date and all of my friends are allowed to stay out until 1:30 a.m. and my parents said that I have to be home by my normal curfew, which is midnight. My parents hate me—they want me to be unpopular! I am going to miss out on the big party after the dance because I have to go home! Everyone is going to think that I am so lame. I am thinking about just staying out and making up an excuse when I get home late. What do you think I should do? (Danielson et al., 2004; used with permission.)

By learning to engage in social problem solving in a methodical way, the adolescent can weigh the strengths and weaknesses of each possible solution to the problem before acting. This can decrease the likelihood that he will act in an impulsive fashion, get into trouble, and experience a negative mood state.

The fourth major goal is to help the adolescent develop regular sleeping habits. As we have seen, disturbance to daily routines, especially sleep schedules, may trigger manic episodes in adolescents with bipolar disorders. Consequently, it is important that adolescents with the disorder avoid disruptions to their daily routines and maintain a consistent sleep schedule. Adolescents' sleep-wake cycles can be upset by stressful life events that cause insomnia (e.g., worry about an upcoming exam), late-night homework assignments, social activities (e.g., sleepovers, parties), and excessive media consumption (e.g., TV, video games). The therapist encourages the adolescent to keep track of his sleep-wake cycle and events that might interfere with these social rhythms. The therapist and adolescent may also work to establish a more regular cycle.

A fifth topic of therapy is the quality of parent-adolescent communication. Recall that high levels of EE predict relapse in adults with bipolar disorder. Furthermore, children with bipolar disorders are more likely to relapse when their parents show low levels of warmth and support. An important goal of therapy, therefore, is to help families develop more effective communication skills. To accomplish this objective, the therapist works individually with the adolescent to teach him how to appropriately express his feelings toward parents and how to resolve family arguments. The therapist might help the adolescent avoid yelling at, blaming, or responding sarcastically to his parents during arguments and teach him how to convey his point of view in an age-appropriate manner. Then the therapist might meet with the adolescent and his parents together to practice these communication skills. Practice might involve role-playing common areas of dispute or discussing topics generated by the family (Danielson et al., 2004).

Family-Focused Treatment for Adolescents

In family-focused treatment, adolescents with bipolar disorders and their parents participate in therapy together. Including parents throughout treatment is important in this form of therapy for several reasons. First, parents play critical roles in helping adolescents adhere to medication. Therapists work with parents to develop strategies to increase the likelihood that youths will take medication and avoid relapse. Second, the quality of parent-child interactions appears to be important to relapse. Therapists can help parents improve the quality of their relationships with their children and reduce family tension. Third, many parents feel blamed by other family members for their adolescents' mood and behavior problems. Some parents feel guilty for passing on "bad genes" to their children. Therapists can help reduce these feelings of guilt and offer empathy and support to parents (Mackinaw-Koons & Fristad, 2004; Perlick et al., 2007).

One family-based approach to treating adolescents with bipolar disorders is Family-Focused Psychoeducational Treatment for Adolescents (FFT-A; Miklowitz et al., 2004; West, Henry, & Pavuluri, 2007). FFT-A is based on the realization that high family conflict and expressed emotion can lead to relapse in people with bipolar disorders. To prevent relapse, the therapist works with family members to help them understand the illness, to recognize the importance of pharmacotherapy, and to improve the quality of communication and problem solving within the family.

FFT-A is designed for adolescents aged 13 to 18 years who have bipolar disorders, their parents, and their siblings. Therapy is divided into three components: (1) psychoeducation, (2) communication enhancement training, and (3) problem-solving skills training. In the first phase of treatment, the therapist and family discuss the symptoms of bipolar disorder, how medication can be used to manage these symptoms, and how stress and the quality of family interactions can increase the likelihood of relapse.

An important component of this first phase of treatment is teaching family members about the **vulnerability/stress model of bipolar disorder**. According to this model, adolescents with bipolar disorder are vulnerable to mood disturbance because of genetic and biological factors beyond their control. However, the frequency and intensity of their mood episodes is greatly influenced by environmental stress. Certain environmental experiences can increase stress and exacerbate aversive mood states, such as disruption of the adolescent's sleep-wake cycle, the discontinuation of medication, and unconstructive family conflict. Other environmental factors, which are within the family's control, can decrease the likelihood or relapse: keeping regular sleep-wake patterns, complying with pharmacotherapy, and improving communication between family members. Adolescents are taught to decrease environmental risks that can lead to relapse and increase environmental factors that can protect them from future mood episodes. Family members are encouraged to assist adolescents in decreasing risks and increasing protective factors.

During the second phase of treatment, the therapist teaches four communication skills. First, family members learn to pay attention to positive aspects of each others' behavior and provide feedback (e.g., praise, gratitude) for these positive behaviors. This step is important because many parents of adolescents with bipolar disorders overlook the positive behaviors and talents of their adolescents and, instead, focus on only the adolescent's disruptive behavior or mood symptoms. Second, the therapist teaches family members active listening skills. Active listening involves accurately understanding family members' verbal and nonverbal messages in an accepting and nonjudgmental way. Active listening can be difficult for high-conflict families because it involves listening to and acknowledging others' points of view instead of dismissing them or becoming defensive. Third, the therapist teaches family members effective ways to make requests. Making effective requests is important because family members often perceive each other as demanding or unreasonable. Fourth, family members learn how to provide constructive feedback. For example, parents can learn that when they correct their adolescent's behavior, they should refer to concrete examples of misbehavior, offer alternative ways of responding, and administer clear and consistent consequences.

During the final phase of treatment, the therapist teaches problem-solving skills. This phase of treatment is analogous to the problem-solving training component of CBT; however, the focus is primarily on how the *family* solves disputes rather than how *individual members* solve problems. The family is taught to use effective communication skills when they encounter a problem or dispute. Then, they are encouraged to use systematic problem-solving steps to solve the problem. These steps involve identifying the problem from each member's perspective, generating possible solutions, evaluating each solution, implementing the best course of action, and monitoring the effectiveness of the problem-solving strategy.

The therapist might also teach family members how to establish behavioral contracts. **Behavioral contracts** are written agreements between family members that indicate (1) what each family member agrees to do to solve a problem and (2) the consequences for failing to live up to the agreement. For example, an adolescent and his parents might create a behavioral contract to help the adolescent comply with pharmacotherapy. The adolescent agrees to take his medication in the morning and at night; if he fails to comply, he loses access to television and video games until his next scheduled dose. His parents agree to reward the adolescent with television and video games only when he remembers to take scheduled doses. Furthermore, if he takes all scheduled doses in a given week, parents agree to drive him someplace he wants to go on the weekend. Behavioral contracts clearly identify the desired behavior for all parties, establish incentives for compliance and consequences for noncompliance, and reduce arguments between family members.

Two randomized controlled trials of FFT for adults with bipolar disorder indicate that it is an efficacious approach to treatment when it is used in conjunction with medication. FFT with adults is associated with better adherence to pharmacotherapy, lower rates of relapse, and less severe mood episodes when they occur. FFT appears to achieve these benefits by improving the communication and problem-solving skills of family members (Miklowitz, George, Richards, Simoneau, & Suddath, 2003; Rea, Tompson, Miklowitz, Goldstein, Hwang, & Mintz, 2003; West et al., 2007).

To date, only one published study has investigated the effectiveness of FFT for adolescents. In this study, 20 adolescents with bipolar disorder participated in FFT-A with their parents. These adolescents also received medication. Mood and behavior was assessed before treatment, periodically during the course of treatment, and

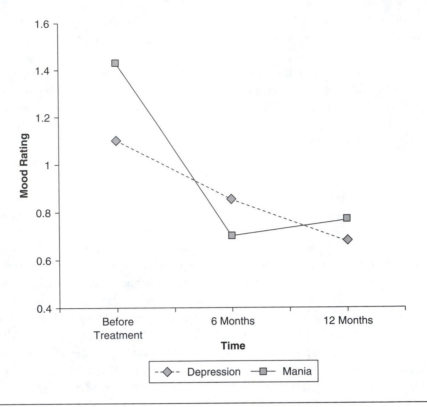

Figure 12.9   Effectiveness of Family-Focused Psychoeducational Treatment for Adolescents (FFT-A)

Source: Based on Miklowitz et al. (2004).

Note: FFT-A seems to reduce manic and depressive symptoms in adolescents when used in conjunction with medication.

one year after beginning the study (see Figure 12.9). Results showed 38% reduction in depressive symptoms, 46% reduction in manic symptoms, and clinically meaningful reductions in overall externalizing and internalizing symptoms, as reported by parents. The main limitation of this study was its small sample size and lack of a control group. A larger, randomized controlled trial of FFT-A is currently underway (Miklowitz et al., 2004).

Multi-Family Psychoeducation Group for Children

A second family-based intervention for children with bipolar disorders is the Multi-Family Psychoeducation Group (MFPG), developed by Mary Fristad and colleagues (Kowatch & Fristad, 2006). MFPG was designed for school-age children and their families. In MFPG, multiple families with children who have mood disorders (including bipolar disorders) meet together for eight 90-minute sessions (see Table 12.6). The purpose of MFPG meetings is to provide families with information about depression and bipolar illnesses and medication, to improve parents' and children's skills

Table 12.6   Components of Multi-Family Psychoeducation Group (MFPG)

1. Parents and children discuss the group's purpose and symptoms of mood disorders.

2. Parents and children are taught about medications used to treat mood disorders, expected benefits, and possible side effects. Parents and children learn to use medication logs to monitor medication effects.

3. Parents learn about systems of care; that is, how professionals at the child's school and clinic can work together to provide comprehensive treatment. Children create a "tool kit" of skills designed to help them cope with negative events and emotions. Coping skills include four areas: creative coping (e.g., dance), physical coping (e.g., sports), social coping (e.g., playing with a friend), and rest/relaxation coping (e.g., mom giving a back rub).

4. Parents learn how children's mood symptoms can cause conflict in family. They participate in the "Naming the Enemy" exercise, in which they differentiate the child from his/her symptoms. This exercise demonstrates that symptoms can cover up the positive aspects and strengths of the child. Children participate in the thinking-feeling-doing exercise to learn the connection between thoughts, feelings, and actions. Therapists demonstrate how thoughts mediate the relationship between events and behavioral responses.

5. Parents and children learn to break down social problems into multiple steps: (1) Stop, (2) Think, (3) Plan, (4) Do, (5) Check.

6. Therapists and parents discuss "helpful" and "hurtful" forms of communication with children. Children learn this distinction through role play.

7. Parents learn specific symptom management skills. Children continue to learn and practice communication skills.

8. Families review what they have learned and receive feedback regarding family/child strengths. They are also given resource material (i.e., books, support groups in the community).

Source: From Kowatch and Fristad (2006). Used with permission.

with respect to behavior management and problem solving, and to give families a source of support for dealing with their children's mood problems. Therapists assume the role of teacher, facilitator, and supporter. They adopt an accepting, non-judgmental attitude and try to appreciate the challenges confronting their clients.

Each session of MFPG begins and ends with children and parents together. In the middle of each session, parents and children participate in separate activities. Initial sessions with parents involve a review of mood disorders and their pharmacological treatment. Then, parents discuss how other professionals (e.g., teachers, school psychologists, physicians) can participate in their children's care. Later sessions are designed to help parents recognize signs of relapse in their children and develop techniques to manage their children's behavior. Since parental behavior partially predicts relapse, therapists spend considerable time helping parents improve their communication and problem-solving skills with their children. Because parents meet together, they can share experiences and provide support to one another.

One important goal of the parent sessions is to help parents appreciate their children's strengths and positive characteristics. This is sometimes difficult because children's emotional and behavioral symptoms often occupy much of parents' attention and energy. Some parents of children with bipolar disorders may have a difficult time "liking" their children because of their children's mood symptoms. Consequently, the therapist helps parents distinguish between their children's emotional and behavioral symptoms and positive aspects about the child. This is accomplished through an activity called Naming the Enemy. The therapist gives each parent a sheet of paper divided into two sections: (1) things I like about my child and (2) my child's symptoms. With the help of the therapist, parents generate examples of the child's behavior for both columns. Then, the paper is folded in half, to demonstrate how mood symptoms can "cover up" the endearing aspects of children's behavior. Parents are encouraged to identify bipolar disorder as their family's enemy and to avoid blaming themselves or their children for their children's symptoms.

Child sessions parallel the sessions offered to parents. Children's sessions include hands-on activities and are designed to be fun. Initial sessions are primarily psychoeducational; they help children understand mood disorders and how medication and other forms of therapy can help manage symptoms. Subsequent sessions teach cognitive-behavioral skills to manage mood and behavior. First children learn about mood states and build a "tool kit" to help them manage their feelings. Then, children perform activities designed to teach them the connection between their feelings, thoughts, and actions. Later sessions focus on problem-solving and communication skills.

A critical component of child therapy is to help children understand the connection between thoughts, feelings, and actions. This connection is introduced through a Thinking-Feeling-Doing Exercise during one of the child sessions (see Image 12.1). Children are shown a picture of a stick person and three boxes reflecting the person's thoughts, feelings, and actions. Each box is divided into two parts that reflect helpful and hurtful behaviors, respectively. Children are first asked to identify common unpleasant (i.e., "hurtful") mood states, such as anger or sadness, and write these in the lower portion of the heart-shaped box. Then, children are asked to generate alternative, positive mood states such as calmness or happiness, and write these feelings in the upper portion of the heart-shaped box (Goldberg-Arnold & Fristad, 2003).

Next, the therapist shifts children's attention to the actions box and asks children to list actions that might be "hurtful" and "helpful" when someone is feeling angry or sad. For example, a child might report that a hurtful response might be to yell or hit someone while a helpful action might be to take a walk or to talk to a friend. Finally, the therapist directs children's attention to the thought bubble. The therapist asks children to list "hurtful" and "helpful" thoughts that might accompany feelings of anger or sadness. For example, a hurtful thought might be "Nothing ever goes my way" while a helpful thought might be "I'm mad right now, but I'll feel better after I let off some steam."

The Thinking-Feeling-Doing Exercise helps children see the connection between thoughts, feelings, and actions. Children with bipolar disorders experience considerable negative emotions. It is unrealistic to expect them to simply "wish" or "will" these emotions away. However, emotions can be changed indirectly by altering one's thoughts and actions. If children learn new ways of thinking and acting, they can better cope with these negative feelings (Goldberg-Arnold & Fristad, 2003).

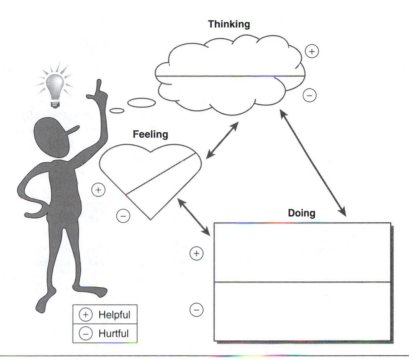

Image 12.1 Thinking-Feeling-Doing Exercise. Children learn the connection between feelings (the heart), thoughts (the cloud), and actions (the box) in this game. Although it is unrealistic for children with mood problems to "wish" bad feelings away, they can change negative emotions by altering their behavior or ways of thinking.

Source: From Goldberg-Arnold and Fristad (2003). Reprinted with permission.

Fristad, Goldberg-Arnold, and Gavazzi (2003) conducted a randomized controlled trial of MFPG with a sample of 7- to 12-year-old children with mood disorders. Participants were assigned to either MFPG or waitlist control conditions. Results showed that the treatment program increased parents' knowledge of mood disorders, improved the quality of parent-child interactions, and strengthened children's perceptions of the support they received from parents. A larger, more comprehensive evaluation of MFGP is currently being conducted.

Update: Melody and Reese

Melody showed discrete episodes of depression and mania and, therefore, would probably have been diagnosed with Bipolar I Disorder. Unfortunately, after leaving the therapy session, Melody and her boyfriend, an unemployed 24-year-old man whom she met over the Internet, disappeared for two days. During their time together, they had a sexual relationship, engaged in excessive use of alcohol and other drugs, and spent a great deal of money taken from Melody's parents. Melody was eventually discovered when she and her boyfriend attempted to withdraw funds at a casino using a stolen credit card.

(Continued)

Reese's outcome was much more positive. After administering several norm-referenced measures of mood and behavior, and after consultation with other professionals, Dr. Saunders diagnosed Reese with BP-NOS. A pediatric psychiatrist prescribed divalproex (Depakote), which significantly reduced the frequency and intensity of Reese's tantrums. Then Reese and her mother were referred to a psychologist for outpatient therapy. In the first few sessions, the psychologist met with Reese's mother to help her learn more about pediatric bipolar disorder and the importance of using medication to manage its symptoms. Then, the therapist used a modified version of behavioral parenting training, to help Reese's mother learn effective ways to increase Reese's compliance at home and to avoid defiance, tantrums, and aggressive outbursts. In later sessions, the psychologist taught Reese coping strategies to manage negative feelings so that she could avoid "meltdowns." Medication and therapy did not eliminate all of Reese's behavioral and emotional problems, but these interventions did lead to significant improvement in Reese's functioning. Reese's mother commented, "It's a good first step, but we have a long road ahead of us. I think we can make it if we work really hard."

Critical Thinking Exercises

1. What is the difference between Bipolar I Disorder, Bipolar II Disorder, and Bipolar Disorder-NOS? Why are most children with bipolar disorder diagnosed with Bipolar Disorder-NOS?

2. Why is it difficult to differentiate ADHD and childhood bipolar disorder? If you were a clinician, how might you determine whether a child has ADHD versus bipolar disorder?

3. Bipolar disorder is usually regarded as a genetic disorder. What is the evidence that genes contribute to the development of child and adolescent bipolar disorder? Do environmental factors play any role in the development of the disorder?

4. Brice is a 16-year-old adolescent with bipolar disorder. Brice and his mother argue frequently because Brice often stays out too late with his friends. These arguments often exacerbate Brice's mood symptoms. If you were a family therapist, how might you use a behavioral contract to decrease the frequency of arguments between Brice and his mother?

5. The treatment for youths with bipolar disorder often involves families. How are families involved in (1) family-focused treatment for adolescents and (2) multi-family psychoeducation group therapy?

CHAPTER 13

Anxiety Disorders in Children and Adolescents

Tammie

Tammie Velazquez was a 12-year-old girl who was referred to the hospital by her parents because she was having difficulty going to sleep at night. "A few months ago," Mrs. Velazquez explained, "Tammie started complaining about having problems falling asleep. We'd put her to bed, but she'd lie awake for several hours. Then, she'd wander out of her room and ask for a drink of water. Sometimes, she's not asleep until 11:30 or midnight and then she's exhausted the next day."

Dr. Baldwin reviewed Tammie's developmental and medical history, her diet, and her habits before bed. However, he couldn't find any explanation for her sleep problems. Tammie's father said, "Tammie's never been a problem. She's very smart and does extremely well in school—a real perfectionist. She's popular with the other kids and has a lot of friends. She's very mature for her age and almost always listens to her mother and me."

Dr. Baldwin interviewed Tammie: "When you're in bed at night, how do you feel?" Tammie replied, "At first I feel good, because I'm so tired. Then, I sort of tense up and feel nervous. I get tingly in my stomach." Dr. Baldwin asked, "Do you think about anything?" Tammie responded, "I start to think about all the things I need to do the next day for school. I worry about my homework, tests the next day, volleyball . . . stuff like that. Then, I get more and more nervous and tingly. I just can't stop. I start to bite my lip or pick at my fingernails until they bleed. When I've had enough, I get out of bed."

Dr. Baldwin continued, "And is there anything you can do to make yourself relax and go to sleep?" Tammie responded, "If my mom or dad give me a hug or talk to me, I can usually stop worrying and think about other things and calm down. Sometimes, though, the worrying starts up again and I know it's going to be a long night."

What Is Child and Adolescent Anxiety?

We all know what it is like to be anxious. Think about how you felt before your last important exam or job interview. You probably experienced physiological symptoms like butterflies in your stomach, a rapid heart beat, or sweaty palms. You might have also shown anxiety through your behavior, by fidgeting with your clothes, pacing about the room, or appearing restless and agitated. You probably also had certain thoughts that accompanied your physiological and behavioral symptoms. These thoughts might have included self-statements like, "I really *need* to do well on the test" or "I *have* to get the job" or "What if I fail?" **Anxiety**, therefore, is a complex state of psychological distress that reflects emotional, behavioral, physiological, and cognitive reactions to threatening stimuli (Barlow, 2002).

Psychologists often differentiate between two types of anxiety: worry and fear (Weems & Watts, 2005). **Fear** is primarily a behavioral and physiological reaction to immediate threat, in which the person responds to imminent danger. People respond to fearful stimuli by confrontation (e.g., fight) or escape (e.g., flight). We might experience fear when we discover that we are poorly prepared for an important exam. As we stare at the test, our pulse quickens, our breathing becomes shallow, and we may become dizzy or light-headed. Subjectively, we might experience a sense of panic or terror and a strong desire to run out of the classroom.

In contrast, **worry** is primarily a cognitive response to threat, in which the person considers and prepares for future danger or misfortune. We might worry about next week's exam, an upcoming job interview, or tomorrow's big game. The subjective experience of worry is a chronic state of psychological distress that can cause uneasiness, apprehension, and tension. Worry is typically accompanied by thoughts and self-statements about the future such as "What is going to be on the exam?" "What should I wear to the interview?" and "What if I make a mistake and lose the game?" (Ramirez, Feeney-Kettler, Flores-Torres, Kratochwill, & Morris, 2006).

In most cases, anxiety is a beneficial emotional state that helps us prepare for future danger or deal with immediate threats to our integrity and welfare. For example, a moderate degree of apprehension before an important exam can motivate us to study. Similarly, moderate symptoms of fear in dangerous or life-threatening situations can protect us from danger.

Maladaptive anxiety can be differentiated from normal, healthy anxiety in at least three ways: (1) by its intensity, (2) by its chronicity, and (3) by its degree of impairment. First, maladaptive anxiety tends to be intense and out of proportion to the threat that triggered the anxiety response. For example, many students experience apprehension about giving an oral report in front of the class. In most cases, moderate anxiety is appropriate and adaptive; it can motivate students to prepare for the presentation. However, apprehension becomes maladaptive when it causes intense feelings of distress or psychological discomfort. For example, the student's mind may "go blank" during the presentation, or she may become physically ill shortly before the presentation because of her anticipatory anxiety (Ramirez et al., 2006).

Second, maladaptive anxiety tends to be chronic. Worry about an upcoming exam is appropriate and adaptive when it motivates individuals to prepare for the exam and terminates after the exam's completion. Chronic worry, however, is often maladaptive. Chronic worriers, who always anticipate disasters on the horizon, tend to experience longstanding agitation and emotional discomfort.

Third, maladaptive anxiety interferes with people's ability to perform daily tasks. For example, most people experience moderate anxiety before a job interview. Anticipatory anxiety becomes maladaptive when people decide to keep their current, low-paying job in order to avoid the anxiety-provoking interview. Similarly, many people experience moderate apprehension before riding in an airplane. This apprehension becomes problematic, however, if the person is unable to attend his best friend's wedding because of his fear of flying.

Anxiety Disorders

Anxiety disorders are among the most frequently diagnosed psychiatric disorders in children and adolescents (Curry, March, & Hervey, 2004). Approximately 20% of individuals will develop an anxiety disorder at some time in their youth (Shaffer et al., 1996). At any given time, 5% of children and adolescents have anxiety disorders (Costello, Egger, & Angold, 2004; see Figure 13.1). The prevalence of anxiety disorders is higher for adolescents than children. The prevalence is also usually higher for girls than boys, but differences are typically not large and not consistent across all anxiety disorders (Costello et al., 2004).

DSM-IV-TR identifies seven anxiety disorders that can be diagnosed in children, adolescents, and adults. These disorders can be loosely grouped into three categories. The first category includes **conditioned fear disorders:** (1) Specific Phobia, (2) Social Phobia, and (3) Posttraumatic Stress Disorder (PTSD). People with these disorders show fear or panic in response to certain situations, events, or objects. For

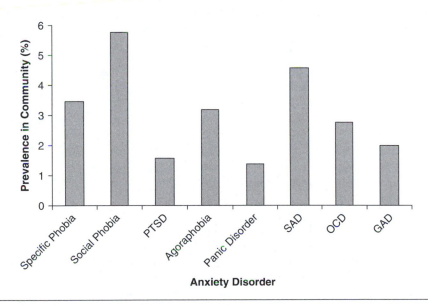

Figure 13.1   Prevalence of Pediatric Anxiety Disorders in the Community

Source: Based on Costello et al. (2004).

Note: At any given time, approximately 5% of children and adolescents have an anxiety disorder.

example, a person with Specific Phobia might fear snakes, a person with Social Phobia might fear attending parties or other social gatherings, and a person with PTSD might fear situations that remind him of a traumatic experience. These disorders are called "conditioned" fear disorders because people usually acquire these fears through classical conditioning or some other form of learning.

The second category of anxiety disorders includes the **unconditioned fear disorders**: (1) Panic Disorder with Agoraphobia, (2) Separation Anxiety Disorder, and (3) Obsessive-Compulsive Disorder (OCD). People with these disorders also show fear when exposed to certain situations, events, or stimuli. For example, a person with Panic Disorder with Agoraphobia might fear crowded buildings, a child with Separation Anxiety Disorder might fear being away from her parents while at school, and a person with OCD might fear touching "dirty" objects like an elevator button or a park bench. These disorders are "unconditioned" fear disorders because they do not clearly arise from classical conditioning or other forms of learning.

The last disorder, Generalized Anxiety Disorder, is unlike the other anxiety disorders because it is characterized by persistent worry, rather than fear. People with Generalized Anxiety Disorder do not fear specific situations, objects, or events; instead, they chronically worry about future misfortune.

Conditioned Fear Disorders

Specific Phobia, Social Phobia, and PTSD are sometimes referred to as conditioned fear disorders. Individuals with these anxiety disorders display fear or panic when confronted with specific objects or situations. Although their etiology cannot always be determined, these disorders are believed to be caused by a combination of genetic and biological diathesis and specific learning experiences. Often, they are acquired through classical conditioning or social learning and maintained through negative reinforcement (Pine & Grun, 1999).

Specific Phobia

Definition

Specific Phobia is defined as a "marked and persistent fear of clearly discernible, circumscribed objects or situations" (*DSM-IV-TR,* p. 443; see Table 13.1). Although people fear a wide range of stimuli, the most common phobias tend to fall into five broad categories:

- Animals—fear of snakes, spiders, dogs, birds
- Natural environment—fear of thunderstorms, heights, water
- Blood, injections, and injuries—fear of receiving an injection, seeing blood
- Specific situations—fear of airplanes, elevators, enclosed places
- Other stimuli—fear of choking, contracting an illness, clowns

Individuals with Specific Phobia immediately experience anxiety symptoms when they encounter a feared situation or object. Sometimes, they may show extreme panic, characterized by racing heart, rapid and shallow breathing, sweaty

Table 13.1   Diagnostic Criteria for Specific Phobia

A. Marked and persistent fear that is excessive or unreasonable, cued by the presence or anticipation of a specific object or situation (e.g., flying, heights, animals, receiving an injection, seeing blood).

B. Exposure to the phobic stimulus almost invariably provokes an immediate anxiety response, which may take the form of a situationally bound or situationally predisposed panic attack. Note: In children, the anxiety may be expressed by crying, tantrums, freezing, or clinging.

C. The person recognizes that the fear is excessive or unreasonable. Note: In children, this feature may be absent.

D. The phobic situation(s) is avoided or else endured with intense anxiety or distress.

E. The avoidance, anxious anticipation, or distress in the feared situation(s) interferes significantly with the person's normal routine, academic functioning, or social activities or relationships, or there is marked distress about having the phobia.

F. In individuals under age 18 years, the duration is at least 6 months.

G. The anxiety, panic attacks, or phobic avoidance associated with the specific object or situation are not better accounted for by another mental disorder, such as Social Phobia (e.g., avoidance of social situations because of fear of abandonment), Posttraumatic Stress Disorder (e.g., avoidance of stimuli associated with a severe stressor), Separation Anxiety Disorder (e.g., avoidance of school), Panic Disorder with Agoraphobia, or Obsessive-Compulsive Disorder (e.g., fear of dirt in someone with an obsession about contamination).

Source: Reprinted with permission from the *DSM-IV-TR*.

Note: Specify types of phobia: Animal Type (e.g., dogs, snakes), Natural Environment Type (e.g., heights, storms, water), Blood-Injection-Injury Type (e.g., immunizations, drawing blood), Situational Type (e.g., airplanes, elevators, enclosed places), Other Type (e.g., fear of choking, loud noises, costumed characters)

palms, dizziness, and other somatic symptoms. Often, individuals with Specific Phobia avoid situations in which they might encounter feared stimuli. For example, a child who is afraid of dogs might plan her route to school in order to avoid encountering a dog. Adults (but not necessarily children) with Specific Phobia recognize that their fears are excessive and unreasonable.

People are only diagnosed with Specific Phobia if (1) their anticipatory anxiety or fears significantly interfere with their day-to-day functioning or (2) their symptoms cause significant distress. An adolescent who fears the sight of blood and avoids watching gory movies might not be diagnosed with Specific Phobia because her fears do not seriously affect her daily activities. However, if her fear of blood affects her career (e.g., she wants to be a doctor but pursues a different career), then the diagnosis of Specific Phobia might be appropriate.

Mary

Mary Valenta was a six-year-old girl who was referred to our clinic because of her intense fear of dogs. Whenever Mary saw a dog, regardless of its size, Mary's body would tense and she would run away. If she was forced to remain near a

(Continued)

(Continued)

> dog, she would cry, tantrum, and even hyperventilate! Mary's fear of dogs began two years ago when she saw a cocker spaniel bite her older brother.
>
> Mrs. Valenta commented, "It seems silly, but Mary's fear of dogs really interferes with our day-to-day lives. We can't visit friends who have dogs as pets; Mary will panic, cry, or tantrum." Mary's phobia became even more salient because her family recently moved next door to a family that owns a Great Dane. Mrs. Valenta reported, "Now, Mary doesn't even want to go outside to play. We need to do something."

Specific Phobia in Childhood and Adolescence

Specific fears are extremely common among children and adolescents, and they generally reflect youngsters' levels of cognitive development. Young children tend to fear concrete objects such as animals and imaginary creatures. Older children tend to fear situations that might result in injury to themselves or others, such as storms and other natural disasters. Adolescents' fears reflect their interest in social interactions and achievement. Common phobias among adolescents include fear of being alone and fear of exams (Warren & Sroufe, 2004).

Feared stimuli activate children's cognitive, physiological, and behavioral responses (N. J. King, Muris, & Ollendick, 2004). With respect to cognition, children make negative self-statements that maximize the danger of the situation (e.g., "That dog is going to bite me") and minimize their ability to cope (e.g., "There's nothing I can do to stop it"). With respect to physiological responses, children show changes in autonomic functioning such as increased heart rate, rapid breathing, sweatiness, dizziness, or upset stomach. Finally, with respect to behavior, children may attempt to flee the situation. If they cannot flee, they may become extremely irritable or throw a tantrum.

Specific phobias are seen in approximately 2%–9% of youth (Ginsburg & Walkup, 2004) and they rarely occur in isolation. Approximately 86% of children with Specific Phobia show at least one other anxiety disorder. The most common comorbid anxiety problems are fears of social situations (Social Phobia), fears of public places (Agoraphobia), and fears of separation from parents (Separation Anxiety Disorder; Costello et al., 2004; Ginsburg & Walkup, 2004). Youths with Specific Phobia may also show other mental health problems. Approximately 36% have depression while 33% show comorbid physical problems caused by stress (Essau, Conradt, & Petermann, 2000).

Phobias can last for at least one to two years and cause considerable distress and impairment if left untreated. Most childhood phobias do not persist into adulthood. However, children's phobias can develop into other anxiety, mood, and somatic problems later in adolescence and adulthood. Consequently, childhood phobias merit clinical attention if they cause significant impairment or distress (Ginsburg & Walkup, 2004; N. J. King et al., 2004).

Etiology

Behavioral genetics research indicates that genes play relatively small roles in the development of most phobias (N. J. King et al., 2004). Fears of specific stimuli (e.g., dogs, clowns) usually do not run in families. Instead, people may inherit a general tendency toward anxiety, which can later develop into a specific fear.

Genetics seems to play a relatively greater role in the development of blood-injection-injury phobias than in other phobias. Individuals with blood-injection-injury phobias become dizzy or faint when confronted with blood, needles, or open wounds. Their reaction may be due to an unusual sensitivity of the **vasovagal response**, a physiological response that involves a rapid increase and sudden decrease in blood pressure. There is a strong relationship between parents' and children's fear of blood and needles, indicating that shared genetic factors could be partially responsible for blood-injection-injury phobias (Dejong & Merckelbach, 1998).

Most other phobias are acquired chiefly through environmental experience. One method of acquisition is **classical conditioning.** Watson and Rayner (1920) demonstrated that fear could be acquired through classical conditioning. In the famous "Little Albert" study, Watson and Rayner conditioned a fear response in an 11-month-old boy by pairing a white rat with a loud sound. Initially, the child was not afraid of the rat (NS), but the loud noise (UCS) produced an intense fear response (UCR). After repeated pairing of the rat and noise, the rat alone (CS) produced a fear response (CR). Classical conditioning might explain some common childhood fears. For example, a child who is bitten by a dog or frightened by a mysterious noise at night might develop phobias of dogs or the dark, respectively.

One brain region, the **median raphe nucleus,** seems to be particularly important in classically conditioned fears (Sweeney & Pine, 2004). Melik, Babar-Melik, Ozgunen, and Binokay (2000) classically conditioned a fear response in rats and then produced lesions in the median raphe nuclei of some of the rats. Although all of the rats initially showed the conditioned fear response, rats with lesions showed a deficit in fear 48 hours after the surgery. Results indicate that conditioned fear responses are partially dependent on the raphe nucleus. Indeed, the raphe nucleus is connected to the hippocampus, another brain structure partially responsible for remembering emotion-laden events.

An alternative means of fear acquisition is through **observational learning.** Children can acquire fears by watching other people respond with fear or avoidance to certain objects, events, or situations. For example, parents who avoid visiting the dentist or show fear while getting a flu shot can convey this anxiety to their children. Mary seemed to develop her fear of dogs after witnessing someone being bit by a dog.

A third way of acquiring fears is through **informational transmission**. Children can learn to fear objects or situations by talking with others or overhearing others' conversations. For example, hearing about a friend's dog bite or reading a story about a child lost in the dark can contribute to the development of phobias.

Children who are genetically susceptible to anxiety can develop specific fears through classical conditioning or social learning. However, classical conditioning and social learning do not explain why children's fears persist over time. Imagine that a child is bitten by a dog and subsequently develops dog phobia. As he encounters more and more friendly dogs, we would expect his fear to decrease over time. However, most children with dog phobia continue to fear dogs for months or years.

Why do phobias persist? According to the **two-factor theory of anxiety**, phobias *develop* though classical conditioning and other forms of social learning, but they are *maintained* through operant conditioning, namely, negative reinforcement (Mowrer, 1960). A child who is bitten by a dog subsequently develops dog phobia. Whenever he encounters a dog, he experiences extreme fear. However, the child discovers that avoiding dogs causes a reduction in his anxiety. Through negative reinforcement, he learns to avoid dogs to manage his anxiety.

Although avoidance offers immediate benefits to the child (e.g., the child avoids anxiety), it interferes with his long-term functioning. For example, the child may not be able to visit friends or family members who have dogs, or he may have to walk home from school using a longer route to avoid dogs. In addition, avoidance of feared stimuli interferes with the child's development of coping strategies to deal with anxiety. If the child never confronts his fear of dogs, he may never be able to learn how to cope with other, similar anxiety-provoking situations.

Social Phobia

Definition

Social Phobia is characterized by a "marked and persistent fear of social or performance situations in which embarrassment might occur" (*DSM-IV-TR*, p. 450; see Table 13.2). Like individuals with specific phobias, people with Social Phobia

Table 13.2   Diagnostic Criteria for Social Phobia

A. A marked and persistent fear of one or more social or performance situations in which the person is exposed to unfamiliar people or to possible scrutiny by others. The individual fears that he or she will act in a way (or show anxiety symptoms) that will be humiliating or embarrassing. Note: In children, there must be evidence of the capacity for age-appropriate social relationships with familiar people and the anxiety must occur in peer settings, not just in interactions with adults.

B. Exposure to the feared social situation almost invariably provokes anxiety, which may take the form of a situationally bound or situationally predisposed panic attack. Note: In children, the anxiety may be expressed by crying, tantrums, freezing, or shrinking from social situations with unfamiliar people.

C. The person recognizes that the fear is excessive or unreasonable. Note: In children, this feature may be absent.

D. The feared social or performance situations are avoided or else endured with intense anxiety or distress.

E. The avoidance, anxious anticipation, or distress in the feared social and performance situation(s) interferes significantly with the person's normal routine, academic functioning, or social activities or relationships, or there is marked distress about having the phobia.

F. In individuals under age 18 years, the duration is at least 6 months.

G. The fear or avoidance is not due to the direct physiological effects of a substance or a general medical condition and is not better accounted for by another mental disorder.

Source: Reprinted with permission from the *DSM-IV-TR*.

show immediate anxiety or panic symptoms when they encounter feared situations. For people with Social Phobia, feared situations involve social settings in which they might be judged, criticized, or negatively evaluated by others. These settings include public speaking, attending a party or social gathering, or performing in front of others. People with social phobia worry that they will be embarrassed in front of others, that others will think they are "crazy" or "stupid," or that others will notice their anxiety symptoms (e.g., shaking hands, sweaty palms). People with Social Phobia often avoid social or performance situations. If forced to attend social gatherings, they endure them with extreme distress. Adults (but not necessarily children) recognize that their social anxiety is excessive or unreasonable.

Erin

I've been dealing with social phobia since I was 10 or 11. I struggled all through middle school, crying every day, feeling like I had no friends, wondering why I couldn't just be normal! Meeting new people without other friends around to make me feel "normal" was extremely difficult. I hated parties, dances, interviews, class presentations, and get-to-know-you type of games. I dreaded any type of social setting.

   I didn't ever want to share my writing in my composition class, even though I was friends with just about everyone in the class. I found that I had trouble being creative. . . . I edited all my ideas as being too "weird" or "stupid." I worried all the time about how I looked. I also worried about calling my friends or asking them to do things with me. I thought that I might be bothering them. I kept a lot of things to myself and never told anyone what I felt. When they asked me what was wrong, I was sure that they would think that I was ridiculous.

Source: Used with permission from www.awarenessequalspwer.com.

Social Phobia in Children and Adolescents

The onset of social phobia is usually in late childhood or early adolescence. Indeed, it is usually not diagnosed before age 10 (Albano, Chorpita, & Barlow, 1996). The two most common situations that are feared by youths with Social Phobia are formal presentations and unstructured social interactions (Beidel, Morris, & Turner, 2004). Most youths with Social Phobia report intense anxiety associated with reading aloud in class, giving a class presentation, or performing for others on stage or at an athletic event. Youths with Social Phobia often experience anxiety initiating conversations with strangers, asking questions, or attending parties (see Table 13.3).

Any situation in which the person might be judged or evaluated negatively by others can potentially be a source of anxiety for a person with Social Phobia. Many children with Social Phobia experience anxiety while taking tests because they fear criticism by teachers. Some children experience anxiety eating in public because they believe others may be watching them and criticizing their diet or etiquette.

Table 13.3   Situations Feared by Children With Social Phobia

Situation	% Endorsing
Reading aloud in front of the class	71
Musical or athletic performances	61
Joining in on a conversation	59
Speaking to adults	59
Starting a conversation	58
Writing on the blackboard	51
Ordering food in a restaurant	50
Attending dances or activity nights	50
Taking tests	48
Parties	47
Answering a question in class	46
Working or playing with other children	45
Asking a teacher for help	44
Physical education class	37
Group or team meetings	36
Having picture taken	32
Using school or public bathrooms	24
Eating in the school cafeteria	23
Walking in the school hallway	16
Answering or talking on the telephone	13
Eating in front of others	10

Source: From Beidel et al. (2004). Used with permission.

Youths with Social Phobia usually experience considerable impairment in their social and emotional functioning (Beidel, Turner, & Morris, 1999). Usually, youths with Social Phobia avoid situations that elicit anxiety. Social avoidance is negatively reinforced by anxiety reduction. For example, by avoiding the school cafeteria, a child with Social Phobia will not experience anxiety associated with interacting with classmates. However, social avoidance also reduces children's contact with peers. Over time, peer avoidance can cause social impairments. Approximately 60% of youths with social phobia show school problems; 53% display serious social withdrawal and lack of friends; and 27% report difficulty engaging in sports, clubs, and other leisure activities (Essau, Conradt, & Petermann, 1999). Children with Social Phobia are at particular risk for depression, social isolation, and loneliness. Adolescents with Social Phobia are at additional risk for substance use problems (Beidel et al., 2004; Chavira, Stein, Bailey, & Stein, 2004).

Most children with Social Phobia do not have the disorder long term. In one study, nearly half of children with Social Phobia did not show the disorder three years after initial diagnosis (Last, Perrin, Hersen, & Kazdin, 1996). In another study, most adolescents with Social Phobia did not continue to meet diagnostic criteria in adulthood (Pine, Cohen, Gurley, Brook, & Ma, 1998). However, most adolescents with histories of Social Phobia develop other mental health problems, especially anxiety and depressive disorders (Albano & Hayward, 2004).

Etiology

Genetic factors seem to underlie children's risk for developing Social Phobia. Twin studies indicate that 50% of the variance in children's symptoms of Social Phobia is attributable to genetics. Family studies indicate that the tendency to experience anxiety in social situations, and the diagnosis of Social Phobia in particular, runs in families (Albano & Hayward, 2004; Hirshfeld-Becker, Biederman, & Rosenbaum, 2004).

Emerging evidence suggests that children inherit a temperamental predisposition toward social anxiety that can develop into Social Phobia later in life (see Figure 13.2). Infants and young children at risk for later anxiety disorders, especially Social Phobia, tend to show temperaments characterized by a high degree of **behavioral inhibition**. Behavioral inhibition was first described by Jerome Kagan and colleagues (Kagan, Reznick, & Snidman, 1988) to describe children's tendency to withdraw when confronted with unfamiliar situations. Children who show high levels of behavioral inhibition are reluctant to explore new settings, are reticent to engage new playmates or enter new peer groups, and are avoidant of novel situations and strangers. Approximately 10%–15% of children show high levels of behavioral inhibition.

Social Phobia also depends on environmental factors, especially classical conditioning and negative reinforcement (Beidel et al., 2004). For example, a child who makes many mistakes when asked to read aloud in front of the class may associate public speaking with humiliation. Consequently, she may experience anxiety when asked to perform in other social settings. Over time, she may learn to avoid social

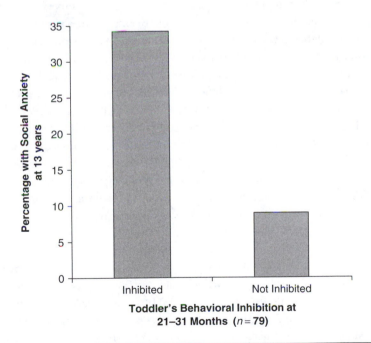

Figure 13.2   Behavioral Inhibition in Toddlerhood Predicts Social Anxiety Symptoms in Adolescence

Source: Based on Schwartz and colleagues (1998).

and performance situations in order to avoid these negative feelings. Indeed, approximately 50% of youths with Social Phobia are able to report a specific humiliating or embarrassing social experience that was associated with the onset of their Social Phobia.

Parent-child interactions can also contribute to the development of Social Phobia. The parents of children with Social Phobia are more likely to have problems with social anxiety themselves (Morris, 2004). Although this suggests a genetic transmission of anxiety from parent to child, it also indicates that anxious parents might teach anxiety responses to their children during parent-child interactions (Biederman et al., 2006).

First, the parents of children with Social Phobia are often described as more controlling than the parents of nonanxious children (Ginsburg, Siqueland, Masia-Warner, & Hedtke, 2004; Morris, 2004). For example, the parents of children with anxiety problems often intrude on their children's behavior and do not allow their children to make decisions for themselves. This highly controlling behavior may stifle the development of children's autonomy. Over-controlling parents may communicate to children that they are not capable of coping with challenges in life (Hudson & Rapee, 2004). As a consequence, children of over-controlling parents may require frequent reassurance from parents when completing tasks or solving problems.

Second, the parents of children with Social Phobia are often described as overprotective; that is, they excessively restrict children's exploration and play because they fear harm befalling their children (Ginsburg, Siqueland et al., 2004). For example, it is reasonable for a mother to prohibit her 14-year-old daughter from attending a party that might involve older boys, a lack of adult supervision, and alcohol consumption. However, it is probably not reasonable for a mother to prohibit her 14-year-old daughter from attending a similar party with same-age peers, responsible adult supervision, and nonalcoholic beverages. Although the world can be a dangerous place, overprotective parents can convey to their children an excessive degree of risk and worry. Children can learn to overestimate the degree of threat in their surroundings and become excessively inhibited (Bogels & van Melick, 2004).

Third, the parents of children with Social Phobia often show high levels of hostile and critical behavior toward their children (Ginsburg, Siqueland et al., 2004). Not only are these parents highly controlling, but they are prone to criticizing and rejecting their children when they do not live up to their high expectations. Such critical behavior may communicate to children that the world is a hostile and dangerous place and that they should not expect sympathy from caregivers if they take risks and fail (Moore, Whaley, & Sigman, 2004).

Fourth, parents of children with Social Phobia may inadvertently teach their children to be anxious in social situations. Specifically, these parents may model anxiety and reinforce their children's anxiety reactions (Barrett, Rapee, Dadds, & Ryan, 1996). Dadds, Barrett, Rapee, and Ryan (1996) observed anxious children and their parents discussing hypothetical, ambiguous social situations. Some of the situations described people experiencing physical ailments, like an upset stomach. Other situations involved ambiguous social situations, like a group of peers laughing and joking. Youths with anxiety problems interpreted these ambiguous situations negatively. For example, they often interpreted the upset stomach as a sign of serious illness or the laughing peers as a sign of teasing or bullying. The parents of these anxious children also interpreted a great deal of hostility and danger in these ambiguous situations. Perhaps more important, the parents often supported children's decisions to overreact or withdraw from these social situations (Creswell, Schniering, & Rapee, 2005).

Fifth, parents can contribute to their children's social anxiety by avoiding emotionally charged discussions. Children's emotional well-being depends greatly on their ability to discuss and think about their feelings. One way children learn to recognize, understand, and discuss their feelings is through interactions with their parents. Parents model emotional expression, teach children how to label emotions, and communicate socially acceptable ways to discuss emotions with others (Eisenberg, Cumberland, & Spinrad, 1998). However, the parents of anxious children often avoid discussions about their children's feelings (Suveg, Zeman, Flannery-Schroeder, & Cassano, 2005). This lack of emotional expressiveness in the family can deprive children of skills and opportunities to label, talk about, and process emotions and, consequently, it can contribute to their social anxiety.

Keep in mind that parent-child interactions are bidirectional (Ginsburg & Schlossberg, 2002). Although parents can contribute to children's anxiety, children's behavior can also cause their parents to be excessively controlling, protective, or critical. For example, young children with high levels of behavioral inhibition often demand considerable reassurance and protection from their parents (Bogels & van Melick, 2004; Moore et al., 2004). Children's behavioral inhibition also seems to elicit harsh, critical, and demanding parenting practices (Chen, Hastings, Rubin, Chen, Cen, & Stewart, 1998; Hirshfeld, Biederman, Brody, Faraone, & Rosenbaum, 1997; Smoller et al., 2005). It is likely that parent and child behaviors mutually influence each other across development and, together, contribute to children's emerging anxiety.

Posttraumatic Stress Disorder

Definition

PTSD is defined by a characteristic set of emotional, physiological, and behavioral symptoms that emerge following exposure to a traumatic event (see Table 13.4). By definition, a traumatic event is a psychosocial stressor that involves actual or threatened death, injury, or harm to a person's physical integrity. To be diagnosed with PTSD, a person must be exposed to a traumatic event in one of three ways: (1) through personal experience, (2) by witnessing the event occurring to another, or (3) by learning about the event from another person (e.g., family member or friend). Individuals with PTSD must respond to the traumatic event with intense fear, helplessness, or horror.

After exposure to the traumatic event, people with PTSD show three characteristic symptoms. First, they persistently re-experience the event, often in the form of recurrent dreams, transient images, unwanted thoughts, or flashbacks. For example, an adolescent involved in an auto accident might have nightmares about the incident or have recurrent images of the accident pop into his mind while attending school.

Table 13.4   Diagnostic Criteria for Posttraumatic Stress Disorder

A. The person has been exposed to a traumatic event in which both of the following were present:
   1. The person experienced, witnessed, or was confronted with an event or events that involved actual or threatened death or serious injury or a threat to the physical integrity of self or others
   2. The person's response involved intense fear, helplessness, or horror. Note: In children this may be expressed instead by disorganized or agitated behavior.

B. The traumatic event is persistently re-experienced in one (or more) of the following ways:
   1. Recurrent and intrusive distressing recollections of the event, including images, thoughts, or perceptions. Note: In young children, repetitive play may occur in which themes or aspects of the trauma are expressed.
   2. Recurrent distressing dreams of the event. Note: In children there may be frightening dreams without recognizable content.
   3. Acting or feeling as if the traumatic event were recurring (includes a sense of reliving the experience, illusions, hallucinations, and dissociative flashback episodes). Note: In young children, trauma-specific reenactment may occur.
   4. Intense psychological distress at exposure to internal or external cues that symbolize or resemble an aspect of the traumatic event
   5. Physiological reactivity on exposure to internal or external cues that symbolize or resemble an aspect of the traumatic event

C. Persistent avoidance of stimuli associated with the trauma and numbing of general responsiveness (not present before the trauma), as indicated by three (or more) of the following:
   1. Efforts to avoid thoughts, feelings, or conversations associated with the trauma
   2. Efforts to avoid activities, places, or people that arouse recollections of the trauma
   3. Inability to recall an important aspect of the trauma
   4. Markedly diminished interest or participation in significant activities
   5. Feelings of detachment or estrangement from others
   6. Restricted range of affect (e.g., unable to have loving feelings)
   7. Sense of foreshortened future (e.g., does not expect to grow up, marry, have a career)

D. Persistent symptoms of increased arousal (not present before the trauma), as indicated by two (or more) of the following:
   1. Difficulty falling or staying asleep
   2. Irritability or outbursts of anger
   3. Difficulty concentrating
   4. Hypervigilance
   5. Exaggerated startle response

E. Duration of the disturbance (symptoms in Criteria B, C, and D) is more than one month

F. The disturbance causes clinically significant distress or impairment in social, academic, or other important areas of functioning

Source: Reprinted with permission from the *DSM-IV-TR*.

Second, people with PTSD persistently avoid stimuli associated with the trauma or experience a numbing of general responsiveness. Avoidance might come in the form of an unwillingness to discuss the traumatic experience or visit people or places associated with the trauma. Numbing might come in the form of a sense of detachment from others or a restricted range of emotions. For example, an adolescent involved in an auto accident might avoid driving and be reluctant to talk with parents and counselors about the experience. He might also appear emotionally withdrawn and distant.

Third, individuals with PTSD show persistent symptoms of physiological arousal. Symptoms might include difficulty sleeping, irritability or anger, concentration problems, and excessive vigilance. Many individuals personally involved in traumatic events show exaggerated startle response. For example, if the adolescent involved in the auto accident hears a loud noise similar to the sound of a crash, he might jump or panic (McKnight, Compton, & March, 2004).

Charna

Charna was a nine-year-old African American girl who was referred to our clinic because of intense fear of thunderstorms. Charna's fear developed after she witnessed the destruction of her home and neighborhood by Hurricane Katrina. After the disaster, Charna was temporarily separated from her mother and two brothers when she moved to her maternal aunt's home in Houston, Texas. While living with her aunt, Charna developed symptoms of PTSD. First, Charna began having nightmares about the storm and persistent fears of danger befalling her family. Charna often insisted on sleeping with her aunt to avoid these bad dreams and recurrent fears. Second, Charna refused to talk about the storm with her aunt or anyone else. Finally, Charna became increasingly agitated, even panicky, during bad weather. Sometimes, when it would rain heavily, Charna became irritable and moody. At other times, before storms, Charna became needy and showed immature behaviors like thumb-sucking and using "baby talk."

PTSD in Children and Adolescents

Exposure to trauma is not uncommon among youth in the United States. Approximately 40% of adolescents in the general population have experienced at least one serious trauma (Giaconia, Reinherz, Silverman, Pakiz, Frost, & Cohen, 1995). The most common traumatic events involving youth include exposure to violent crime, auto accidents, home fires and injuries, natural disasters, domestic violence, physical and sexual abuse, and serious physical illnesses. Exposure to violence is especially common in urban settings. In one study of predominantly African American low-income children, 39% had witnessed a shooting, 35% had seen a stabbing or physical assault, and 24% had observed another person being killed. Nearly one-half of the sample reported being a victim of violent crime (Jenkins & Bell, 1994).

Very young children exposed to traumatic events may not show PTSD in the same way as older children, adolescents, and adults. Because young children often have difficulty articulating their fears, they may display general anxiety or fear of separation from parents. They may also report specific phobias such as fear of the dark or monsters under the bed. Some young children with PTSD show regressive behaviors. For example, they might suck their thumb, refuse to go to bed at night, or tantrum. Some young children reenact traumatic events through their play. For example, a child rescued from a flood might reenact the disaster with action figures or dolls.

Older children typically display a closer correspondence between their PTSD symptoms and the trauma that they experienced. For example, a child involved in a fire at school may subsequently exhibit school refusal. Older children are also more likely to report intrusive thoughts and nightmares associated with the trauma. They sometimes show **omen formation**. Omen formation refers to the belief that warning signs immediately preceded the traumatic event; consequently, the child constantly scans the environment looking for similar signs of impending misfortune. For example, if a certain song was playing on the radio shortly before a serious auto accident, the child may believe that hearing the song again indicates another upcoming disaster. Omen formation is likely formed through classical conditioning. It occurs when the child incorrectly assumes a causal relationship between two stimuli that occur together in time (e.g., the "omen" and the trauma).

Adolescents tend to show PTSD similar to adults. However, unlike adults, adolescents usually do not experience flashbacks. Instead, adolescents are more likely to have intrusive and recurrent thoughts, images, and dreams. Nightmares associated with the trauma are particularly common among older children and adolescents (McKnight et al., 2004).

PTSD interferes with children's emotional well-being. Youths with PTSD often have other anxiety disorders, especially phobias. In most cases, phobias exist before the development of PTSD (LaGreca, Silverman, & Wasserstein, 1998). Consequently, most experts believe that youths with anxiety problems *before* their exposure to trauma are at greatest likelihood of developing PTSD after a traumatic event. Depression and suicidal ideation are also comorbid with PTSD. In one study of adolescents with PTSD, 41% met criteria for MDD (Giaconia et al., 1995). As many as 46% of adolescents with PTSD develop alcohol use problems, while 25% abuse other drugs (Giaconia et al., 1995). Adolescents with PTSD seem to use substances to cope with anxiety and depression associated with the trauma (Chilcoat & Breslau, 1998).

September 11 Terrorist Attacks

Many adults living in New York City after the terrorist attacks on September 11, 2001 displayed psychiatric symptoms. Immediately after the trauma, 7.5% of adults in New York and 20% of adults living close to Ground Zero showed anxiety problems consistent with PTSD (Galea et al., 2002).

Children's reactions to the terrorist attacks were similar. Most studies indicated higher-than-expected rates of anxiety and emotional distress among New York City youth. For example, 87% of New York City children displayed at least one PTSD symptom after the attacks. Almost 25% of children showed intrusive thoughts, concentration problems, *and* sleep disturbance (Aber, Gershoff, Ware, & Kotler, 2004; Schlenger et al., 2002). After the attacks, approximately 27% of youth living in New York City met diagnostic criteria for at least one anxiety or mood disorder. The most common psychiatric disorders were Agoraphobia (12.8%), SAD (12.3%), PTSD (10.6%), GAD (12.3%), Panic Disorder (8.7%) and Major Depressive Disorder (8.1%; Aber et al., 2004; Hoven, Mandell, & Duarte, 2003; Stuber, Galea, Pfefferbaum, Vandivere, Moore, & Fairbrother, 2005).

One of the primary predictors of children's response to the trauma was their degree of exposure to traumatic events. Psychologists distinguish between four types of exposure to trauma: (1) direct exposure, such as immediately experiencing the trauma; (2) indirect exposure, such as witnessing the trauma from a distance; (3) family exposure, such as having a family member injured in the trauma; and (4) distal exposure, such as having one's parents lose their job because of the trauma.

Data collected shortly after 9/11 revealed that many New York City children attending school near Ground Zero received considerable exposure to the trauma (Hoven et al., 2003). Overall, 76% of children were directly exposed to the attack and 3,250 children lost their parents in the disaster. Approximately 67% reported considerable indirect exposure through television, and 7% reported that a family member was in the World Trade Center on the day of the attack. Furthermore, children who were directly exposed to the trauma showed greater likelihood of psychiatric symptoms than children who were indirectly exposed to the attacks.

What about children exposed to the attacks from a distance? At least three studies have investigated the effects of the terrorist attacks on children outside the locale where they occurred. A national telephone survey conducted a few days after the attack showed that 35% of parents across the country reported that their children displayed an increase in anxiety symptoms, including worrying about safety, sleep problems, and difficulty concentrating (Schuster et al., 2001). Investigating PTSD symptoms two to five months after the attacks, Whalen, Henker, King, Jamner, and Levine (2004) found 20% of children showed moderate to severe re-experiencing symptoms while 50% expected the event to recur. Six months after the attacks, as many as 15% of youth in Washington State showed at least one symptom of PTSD (Lengua, Long, Smith, & Meltzoff, 2005). Furthermore, the frequency of children's re-experiencing symptoms was comparable to the symptoms of children who were directly involved in an earthquake a few years earlier (Foa, Johnson, Feeny, & Treadwell, 2001). These findings indicate that even indirect or distal exposure to a trauma (e.g., via television) can have a negative effect on children's emotional functioning.

Text Box Table 13.1 Children's Anxiety Symptoms (%) Following Distal Exposure to 9/11 Attacks Versus Direct Exposure to an Earthquake

Symptom	Children in Seattle, WA After 9/11 Attacks	Children in Northridge, CA After Earthquake
Re-experiencing		
Upsetting thoughts	39	25
Nightmares	12	32
Flashbacks	26	28
Upset by reminders	68	24
Feelings in body	26	23
Avoidance		
Trying not to talk about it	48	39
Avoiding activities	20	24
Can't remember	19	23

(Continued)

(Continued)

Mood/arousal disturbance		
Loss of interest	6	13
Emotional problems	4	19
Restricted affect	14	23
Limited future plans	13	25
Trouble sleeping	19	40
Irritable	22	33
Concentration problems	22	36
Overly careful	36	40
Jumpy	25	48

Source: From Lengua et al. (2005). Used with permission.

Note: Children exposed to the terrorist attacks from a distance showed comparable re-experiencing and avoidance symptoms as, but fewer mood/arousal symptoms than, children who directly experienced an earthquake that rated 6.6 on the Richter scale. These results suggest that children exposed to trauma from a distance can develop significant anxiety symptoms.

Although most children were exposed to the terrorist attacks, either directly or indirectly, only a minority of children developed PTSD symptoms. This observation led researchers to examine risk and protective factors that contribute to the development of PTSD. One fairly consistent finding has been that children's social-emotional functioning *before* the trauma predicted the severity of their posttraumatic symptoms. Several studies have found that children with elevated anxiety and/or depression levels before the terrorist attacks were more likely to develop distress and impairment after the attacks (Gil-Rivas, Holman, & Silver, 2004; Hock, Hart, Kang, & Lutz, 2004; Lengua et al., 2005; Whalen et al., 2004). In one study of New York schoolchildren, the relationship between exposure to the trauma and PTSD symptoms disappeared after researchers controlled for children's pretraumatic psychological functioning (Aber et al., 2004). Similarly, children's emotional functioning *before* hurricane Katrina predicted their likelihood of PTSD, general anxiety, and depression after the hurricane (Weems, Pina, Costa, Watts, Taylor, & Cannon, 2007). Collectively, these findings indicate that children already showing mood or anxiety disorders are most susceptible for developing PTSD following a traumatic event.

A second factor that influenced the likelihood that children would develop PTSD following the 9/11 attacks was their cognitive appraisals of the trauma. Specifically, children who experienced the trauma as personally relevant typically showed more distress than children who cognitively distanced themselves from the attacks. For example, children who knew someone involved in the trauma or who believed that they or their families could be victims of a similar trauma in the future were more likely to develop PTSD symptoms (Pfefferbaum et al., 2000). However, children who believed that it was unlikely that their families would be harmed in subsequent attacks showed relatively few anxiety and mood problems.

Text Box Table 13.2	Children's Reactions to the September 11 Terrorist Attacks

Personalization

- It was scary. If they could do it to the World Trade Center, they could do it to our house. It bothered me because so many people died.
- Yes, I was worried because not far from where I live there are tall buildings. I don't like to go into tall buildings.
- I didn't like it. It was sad and scary. It made me worry about going on planes and living next to a stadium that they might bomb.
- I'm afraid that Dad might get drafted if they lose too many soldiers. My mom is a nurse so I kind of worry about her.
- The week after it happened my dad had to fly to [city name]. That made me scared.
- I was worried something would happen whey they [Mom and Dad] would go someplace alone. I wanted to go, but I couldn't go.

Distancing

- There are a billion people in the world; it would be like a one in a billion chance that something like that would happen to me.
- The school is the safest place I can be—they just have to push buttons to get the cops here.
- I was a little bit scared after the attack, but now I know I'm safe. Here in [city name], what are the odds of someone crashing? There are no big monuments.
- No, I don't think something bad might happen to my parents. My dad doesn't work in a big building, only 20 stories, and my mom only works in a one-story building.
- It made me mad and I wished the U.S.A. could get revenge. It did not really cause me to worry. I've never been on an airplane before.

Source: Adapted from Hock et al. (2004).

Note: Verbatim statements given by school-age children to open-ended questions about the 9/11 attacks. Children's cognitive appraisals of the trauma influenced their emotional reactions. Personalizing traumatic events is associated with more severe anxiety.

A third risk factor for anxiety problems following a major trauma is children's coping strategies immediately following the attack. Researchers found that a small minority of adolescents, who showed emotional numbness immediately after the attacks, displayed the poorest outcomes: increased depression, hopelessness, suicidal ideation, and PTSD symptoms. The researchers suggested that the tendency to respond to trauma with avoidance and emotional numbing might be a useful predictor in identifying youth most in need of treatment.

Finally, maternal support can protect youth from anxiety and mood disorders following a major trauma. Anna Freud first observed that children whose mothers held and reassured them during the air raids over London during World War II

(Continued)

(Continued)

were less likely to develop adverse emotional reactions to the bombings (Freud & Burlingham, 1943). More recently, researchers have noticed that parents' emotional reactions to trauma influence their children's adjustment (Fremont, 2004). Specifically, parents who are able to provide stable and consistent care, to model constructive coping, and to reassure their children of their availability and safety often buffer their children from the adverse effects of the trauma.

What else can parents and teachers do to protect children from the potentially deleterious effects of traumatic events, like terrorist attacks (LaGreca & Silverman, 2006)? First, caregivers must appreciate the sensitivity of children to these traumatic events and take them seriously. Even children living thousands of miles away from the attacks experienced considerable distress. Many children personalized the attack, expecting future attacks in their community. Parents should not underestimate the influence of indirect exposure on children's social-emotional health (LaGreca, Silverman, Vernberg, & Roberts, 2002).

Second, parents can limit children's exposure to traumatic events by regulating access to media images and conversations about the event. For example, researchers have found moderate correlations between children's access to television stories about the terrorist attacks and children's anxiety (Lengua et al., 2005; Schuster et al., 2001). It is particularly important to shield children from extremely distressing images of destruction that could cause them to personalize the attack to their own lives.

Third, it is important for parents to provide consistent, sensitive care to children following trauma and avoid displays of hostility or anxiety. For example, hostile parent-child interactions or displays of parental anxiety predicted children's negative emotional reactions to the 9/11 attacks (Gil-Rivas et al., 2004; Phillips, Prince, & Schiebelhut, 2004). In contrast, children whose parents helped them cope with the trauma in a sensitive and supportive fashion displayed better outcomes. Parents must give children the opportunity to discuss their impressions of the traumatic event in a safe, supportive environment. The nature of these parent-child conversations will depend on the child's age and development, but should always involve reassurance that the parents will provide physical security and emotional support.

Etiology

The likelihood of developing PTSD following exposure to a trauma depends on the type and duration of the traumatic experience. Terr (1991) differentiated sudden traumatic events (Type I traumas) from traumatic events that are chronic (Type II traumas). Examples of Type I traumas include car accidents, natural disasters, and isolated violent crimes. Examples of Type II traumas include living in a war-torn country or being repeatedly physically or sexually abused. Children exposed to Type I traumas are most likely to show characteristic symptoms of PTSD. Children exposed to Type II traumas, especially repeated abuse, tend to show different patterns of emotional and behavioral problems (Goodwin, 1988; Hornstein, 1996).

The likelihood of developing PTSD is also dependent on the child's proximity to the traumatic event (McKnight et al., 2004). For example, a child who is the victim of an automobile accident would be more likely to develop PTSD than a child who witnesses an accident. Similarly, witnessing an accident is more risky than merely hearing another person's account of the accident second-hand (Saigh, 1991).

The amygdala plays a role in the development of PTSD. In healthy people, the amygdala is the starting point for the body's physiological stress response. When a person encounters a stressful event, the amygdala causes the **periventricular nucleus of the hypothalamus** to release a hormone called corticotropin releasing factor (CRF). CRF is detected by a second brain area, the **pituitary**, which releases the hormone corticotropin. Finally, corticotropin triggers the release of cortisol by the **adrenal gland**. Cortisol, the body's primary stress hormone, activates the sympathetic nervous system and prepares the body for confronting or fleeing potential dangers. After the body has produced sufficient levels of cortisol to effectively deal with the stressful situation, the amygdala inhibits further activity by the hypothalamus. Because the three areas of the body that regulate the stress response are the (1) hypothalamus, (2) pituitary, and (3) adrenal regions, this system is usually called the **HPA axis** (J. A. Cohen, Perel, DeBellis, Friedman, & Putnam, 2002).

Traumatic events can cause disruption in the body's stress response system (DeBellis et al., 1994). People with PTSD often show abnormal functioning of the amygdala and, consequently, the hypersecretion of cortisol. These youths may be unusually sensitive to stressful stimuli, show hypervigilance, and display an exaggerated startle response. The amygdala also plays a role in the formation of emotion-laden memories. Overreactivity of the amygdala may be responsible for the unwanted and intrusive memories of traumatic events seen in PTSD (J. A. Cohen et al., 2002).

Unconditioned Fear Disorders

The second group of anxiety disorders consists of unconditioned fear disorders: Panic Disorder, Separation Anxiety Disorder, and Obsessive-Compulsive Disorder. Unconditioned fear disorders usually do not arise from classical conditioning, modeling, or information transfer. Instead, they are largely due to a combination of biogenetic and environmental factors that lead to (1) higher levels of general physiological arousal, (2) unusual sensitivity to threats or danger, and (3) a tendency to engage in catastrophic thinking (Pine & Grun, 1999).

Panic Disorder and Agoraphobia

Definition

Panic Disorder is a serious condition characterized by the presence of recurrent, unexpected panic attacks that cause the person significant distress or impairment in functioning. During a **panic attack**, individuals experience an acute and intense episode of psychological distress. During the panic episode, they experience physiological symptoms that fall into three broad clusters: cognitive symptoms (e.g., thoughts of losing control or going crazy), emotional symptoms (e.g., feelings of unreality or detachment), and somatic symptoms (e.g., heart palpitations, chest pain, dizziness). People who experience panic attacks feel as if they are having a heart attack, believe that they are dying or going crazy, or experience a strong desire to flee the situation. Indeed, panic attacks can be extremely scary because they are so severe and because people seem to have little control over their onset. Panic attacks reach their peak intensity in about 10 minutes and usually last 15–30 minutes.

In order to be diagnosed with Panic Disorder, an individual must have recurrent unexpected panic attacks followed by (1) one month of persistent concern about having another panic attack, (2) worry about the implications of the attacks, or (3) a significant change in daily routines because of the attack. For example, many people who have had a panic attack fear having another one. They might believe that the attacks are a sign of psychosis or serious physical illness. They may also avoid situations where they experienced attacks in the past, in order to prevent their recurrence.

Paul

Paul was a 16-year-old boy who was sent to the emergency department of the hospital after two episodes of "heart problems" in one week. Paul's mother told the emergency room physician that Paul had experienced symptoms of a heart attack after dinner at their home. Specifically, Paul's heart raced and beat very fast, his breathing became shallow, he experienced dizziness, and his skin became clammy to the touch. "It came out of the blue. I felt like my heart was going to explode in my chest. Then, I got a terrible urge to run way, but I couldn't. I was scared and shaking all over."

The physician at the hospital determined that Paul was medically healthy and showed no signs of heart problems. Dr. Dresser, a pediatric psychologist, suggested that Paul may have had a panic attack. She asked Paul and his parents, "Do anxiety problems run in your family?" Paul's father admitted to taking medication for both anxiety and depression. Paul worried, "Do you mean that I'm going to have more of these attacks?" Dr. Dresser replied, "That is a possibility. The important thing is that you learn to cope with them if they recur. Do you want to learn some techniques that can help?"

Panic Disorder in Children and Adolescents

Panic attacks are relatively common among youth. As many as 18% of adolescents have had at least one full-blown panic attack (Essau et al., 1999; Hayward, Killen, Kraemer, & Barr Taylor, 2000). Furthermore, 60% of adolescents may have had subthreshold panic symptoms (Ollendick, Birmaher, & Mattis, 2004). Panic attacks are equally common in boys and girls, but they may be more severe in girls (Ollendick et al., 2004).

Although panic attacks occur relatively frequently, Panic Disorder is relatively uncommon among adolescents and rare in children. The onset of Panic Disorder is usually between the ages of 15 and 19 (Curry et al., 2004). However, there are isolated instances of its onset occurring before puberty (Ollendick, Mattis, & King, 1994). Most cases of Panic Disorder in children and adolescents go undetected. Parents and physicians usually interpret panic symptoms as medical problems. Consequently, youngsters who are eventually diagnosed with panic disorder wait, on average, 12.7 years until their disorder is properly identified and treated (Essau et al., 1999, 2000).

Some, but not all, individuals with Panic Disorder also have Agoraphobia (see Table 13.5). **Agoraphobia** refers to anxiety about being in places or situations from which escape is not possible without considerable effort or embarrassment. Common places are shopping centers, grocery stores, and schools. As many as 30% of adolescents with Panic Disorder eventually develop Agoraphobia (Essau et al., 1999; Hayward et al., 2000). Usually, Agoraphobia develops when adolescents associate certain places or situations with a panic attack, through classical conditioning. For example, an adolescent who experiences a panic attack while shopping might avoid the mall. Similarly, a junior high school student who experiences a panic attack at school might refuse to attend school. Agoraphobic avoidance is maintained though negative reinforcement. By avoiding the mall or school, these adolescents experience anxiety reduction. Consequently, they are more likely to avoid these places in the future.

Youths with Panic Disorder almost always have other anxiety problems. The most commonly occurring anxiety disorder is Generalized Anxiety Disorder, a condition

Table 13.5   Diagnostic Criteria for Panic Disorder With Agoraphobia

A. Both (1) and (2):
  1. Recurrent and unexpected panic attacks (see definition above)
  2. At least one of the attacks has been followed by one month (or more) of one (or more) of the following:
     a. Persistent concern about having additional attacks
     b. Worry about the implications of the attack or its consequences (e.g., losing control, having a heart attack, "going crazy")
     c. A significant change in behavior related to the attacks

B. Presence of Agoraphobia
  1. Anxiety about being in places or situations from which escape might be difficult (or embarrassing) or in which help might not be available in the event of having a panic attack or panic-like symptoms. Agoraphobic fears typically involve characteristic clusters of situations that include being outside the home alone; being in a crowd or standing in a line; being on a bridge; or traveling on an airplane, train, or bus
  2. The situations are avoided or endured with marked distress or anxiety about having a Panic Attack or panic-like symptoms, or the person requires the presence of a companion
  3. The anxiety or avoidance is not better accounted for by another mental disorder such as Specific Phobia (e.g., avoidance limited to a single situation, like elevators), Social Phobia (e.g., avoidance limited to social situations because of fear of embarrassment), Obsessive-Compulsive Disorder (e.g., avoidance of dirt in someone with obsessions about contamination), Posttraumatic Stress Disorder (e.g., avoidance of stimuli associated with a severe stressor), or Separation Anxiety Disorder (e.g., avoidance of leaving relatives or home because of fears of separation or loss)

C. The panic attacks are not due to the direct effects of a substance or a medical condition

D. The panic attacks are not better explained by another mental disorder such as Specific Phobia (e.g., occurring on exposure to a specific phobic object or situation), Social Phobia (e.g., on exposure to feared social situations), Obsessive-Compulsive Disorder (e.g., on exposure to dirt in someone with obsessions about contamination), Posttraumatic Stress Disorder (e.g., in response to stimuli associated with a severe stressor), or Separation Anxiety Disorder (e.g., in response to being away from relatives or home)

Source: Reprinted with permission from the *DSM-IV-TR*.

characterized by persistent psychological tension and worry about the future (Last, Perrin, Hersen, & Kazdin, 1992). Generalized anxiety during childhood might predispose adolescents to experience Panic Disorder in late adolescence (N. J. King, Gullone, Tonge, & Ollendick, 1993). Panic Disorder can also lead to mood problems. Adolescents and young adults with Panic Disorder show increased risk for depression, substance use problems, and suicide (Birmaher & Ollendick, 2004). Panic disorder typically precedes mood and substance use problems, indicating that panic symptoms may cause later emotional impairment. Adolescents sometimes rely on alcohol and marijuana to cope with panic symptoms.

Etiology

The causes of Panic Disorder are complex; no single theory can adequately explain all of the features of this disorder. However, cognitive and behavioral models of Panic Disorder have received the most empirical support from studies involving adolescents (Barlow, 2002; Beck & Emery, 1985; Clark, Salkovskis, & Chalkley, 1985). According to these models, biological, cognitive, and behavioral factors interact to produce recurrent panic attacks and (sometimes) Agoraphobia.

Individuals prone to Panic Disorder may inherit a biological disposition toward anxiety sensitivity (Dehon, Weems, Stickle, Costa, & Berman, 2005; Ollendick et al., 2004; Silverman & Dick-Niederhauser, 2004). **Anxiety sensitivity** refers to the tendency to perceive the symptoms of anxiety as extremely upsetting and aversive. For example, most people experience moderate anxiety before an important exam. A person with low anxiety sensitivity might be able to acknowledge her anxiety, cope with its symptoms (e.g., take deep breaths), and proceed with the exam. In contrast, a person with high anxiety sensitivity might experience pre-exam anxiety as extremely distressing and respond with fear. This unusual sensitivity to the physiological symptoms of anxiety (e.g., shakiness, rapid heartbeat, unusual body sensations) can lead to panic (Hale & Calamari, 2007).

According to the **expectancy theory of panic**, people with high anxiety sensitivity are unusually sensitive to the physiological symptoms of anxious arousal. Specifically, individuals with high anxiety sensitivity pay special attention to the increase in heart rate and shallowness of breathing that characterizes the early signs of anxiety. Additionally, these individuals show characteristic ways of thinking that exacerbate their anxiety symptoms (Weems, Berman, Silverman, & Saavedra, 2001).

First, these individuals tend to personalize negative events; that is, they blame themselves for negative outcomes. For example, an adolescent with high anxiety sensitivity who experiences anxiety during an exam might blame herself for her anxiety: "I didn't study enough—it's my own fault that I'm not prepared." Personalization exacerbates the adolescent's anxiety and interferes with coping.

Second, adolescents with high anxiety sensitivity often engage in catastrophic thinking. When distressed, they anticipate the worst possible outcomes. For example, when an adolescent with high anxiety sensitivity experiences mild anxiety before an exam, she might expect her anxiety to escalate and become uncontrollable. She might think, "Oh no, I'm having one of those attacks again. I'm going to blank out and forget everything I studied! What am I going to do?" Catastrophic thinking is often self-fulfilling; it leads to an escalation of psychological distress.

Anxiety sensitivity, and the tendency to personalize and catastrophize negative events, can trigger a panic attack (Ginsburg, Lambert, & Drake, 2004). Unfortunately, one panic attack can cause adolescents to pay excessive attention to early warning signs of future attacks. Consequently, these adolescents become highly aware of even the mildest symptoms of anxious arousal. Even mild anxiety symptoms can cause them to think, "Oh no! Am I going to have one of those attacks again?"

Separation Anxiety Disorder

Definition

Children and adolescents with Separation Anxiety Disorder (SAD) show excessive anxiety about leaving caregivers and other individuals to whom they are emotionally attached (see Table 13.6). Typically, these youths are preoccupied by fears that misfortune or harm will befall either themselves or their caregivers during the separation period. For example, young children with SAD may believe that monsters might kidnap them while their parents are away. Adolescents might fear that their parents will become injured in a serious accident while at work. Children with SAD usually insist that caregivers remain in close proximity, and they may become angry, distressed, or physically ill upon separation. Many refuse to attend school, summer camps, and activities with friends, in order to avoid separation.

Table 13.6   Diagnostic Criteria for Separation Anxiety Disorder

A. Developmentally inappropriate and excessive anxiety concerning separation from home or from those to whom the individual is attached, as evidenced by three (or more) of the following:

1. Recurrent excessive distress when separation from home or major attachment figures occurs or is anticipated

2. Persistent and excessive worry about losing, or about possible harm befalling, major attachment figures

3. Persistent and excessive worry that an untoward event will lead to the separation from a major attachment figure (e.g., getting lost or kidnapped)

4. Persistent reluctance or refusal to go to school or elsewhere because of fear of separation

5. Persistently and excessively fearful or reluctant to be alone

6. Persistent reluctance or refusal to go to sleep without being near a major attachment figure or to sleep away from home

7. Repeated nightmares involving the theme of separation

8. Repeated complaints of physical symptoms when separation from major attachment figures occurs or is anticipated

B. The duration of the disturbance is at least 4 weeks

C. Onset is before age 18 years

D. The disturbance causes clinically significant distress or impairment in social, academic, or other important areas of functioning

E. The disturbance does not occur exclusively during the course of another disorder and is not better accounted for by Panic Disorder with Agoraphobia

Source: Reprinted with permission from the *DSM-IV-TR*.

Valerie

Valerie was a 14-year-old girl referred to our clinic because she persistently refused to go to school. According to her father, Valerie would feign sickness, lie, tantrum, and do "just about anything" to stay home. He explained, "Last week, she promised me that she would go. I watched her get on the bus, but she never made it to school. She was back home 25 minutes later saying that her stomach hurt."

Valerie's mother added, "It's really getting to be a problem. All she wants to do is stay home. I ask her, 'Don't you want to go to Julie's or shopping with your friends?' but she always prefers to stay home."

Dr. Saunders asked Valerie about her reluctance to go to school. "Did something bad happen at school? Are you having trouble there?" Valerie responded, "No. I get along fine with the other kids and I'm getting good grades. I just like being at home better, near my dad." Dr. Saunders learned that Valerie's school refusal began several months ago, shortly after her father had heart surgery. Valerie was asked to take care of her father as he recovered. Since that time, Valerie's father had worked from his home and Valerie showed especially strong attachment to him.

After several sessions, Dr. Saunders asked, "Are you worried about something bad happening to your father, like maybe he'll have another heart problem?" Valerie responded, "Of course not! The doctors say he's fine." After a long pause, she added, "I just want to make sure."

SAD in Children and Adolescents

Among infants and young children, a certain degree of separation anxiety is adaptive. Older infants and toddlers show moderate levels of separation anxiety as they develop a sense of trust in the availability of their caregivers. Separation anxiety keeps infants in close proximity to caregivers and serves to protect them from harm. Preschoolers and young school-age children require reassurance from caregivers when scared, upset, or unsure. The tendency to seek out caregivers when scared or upset indicates that the young child expects the parent to meet his or her needs for comfort and care.

Periodic concerns about separation are also common among school-age children. Indeed, approximately 70% of school-age children admit to periodic anxiety when separating from parents, and 15% report occasional nightmares about being kidnapped or harm befalling loved ones (Muris, Merckelbach, Mayer, & Meesters, 1998; Muris, Merckelbach, Gadet, & Moulaert, 2000). However, only about 15% of school-age children report persistent fears about separation, and 3%–4% meet diagnostic criteria for SAD (Muris, Merckelbach et al., 2000; Perwien & Bernstein, 2004). SAD is differentiated from developmentally expected fears of separation by the intensity of the fear, its persistence, and the degree to which the fear interferes with the child's overall functioning.

The presentation of SAD varies by age (Fischer, Himle, & Thyer, 1999). Young children with SAD worry about physical harm befalling themselves or their parents, usually through unlikely means. For example, a seven-year-old boy with SAD might worry about being kidnapped on the way to school or his parents being abducted by robbers while at work. Young children with SAD may refuse to attend school and throw tantrums if forced to go. When their parents are home, young children may "shadow" them from room to room or engage in other "clinging" behavior. Parents often regard these children as excessively needy. They may become frustrated with their children's strong desire for reassurance. Young children with SAD often experience nightmares about harm befalling themselves or family members. They may have difficulty going to sleep, insist on a parent staying in their room, or ask to sleep in their parents' bed. If denied, some youths with SAD will sleep outside their parents' bedroom door in order to gain closer proximity.

Older children with SAD often worry about more realistic events that might separate them from parents. For example, a 12-year-old with SAD might worry about her parents contracting a terrible disease or getting into an auto accident. Adolescents with SAD often have diffuse fears of separation. They might report only a vague sense that "something bad will happen" if they are separated from their parents or family.

Older children and adolescents with SAD usually tolerate separation better than younger children; however, older children still experience considerable anxiety and sadness when separated. Some become physically ill if forced to separate from parents. Others show severe social withdrawal, concentration problems, and symptoms of depression. Many older children and adolescents sacrifice time with peers to be near their families. Often, these fears of separation interfere with academic and social functioning (Silverman & Dick-Niederhauser, 2004).

Researchers disagree about the prognosis of children with SAD. Some data indicate that youths with SAD are more likely to recover than youths with other anxiety disorders. In one study, 80% of youths with SAD recovered within an 18-month period. Other data indicate that SAD can persist through adolescence or develop into other psychiatric disorders. Approximately 26%–30% of youths diagnosed with SAD eventually show other anxiety or depressive disorders (Foley, Pickles, Maes, Silberg, & Eaves, 2004; Manicavasager, Silove, Curtis, & Wagner, 2000).

SAD in childhood may predispose youths to Panic Disorder in adolescence and early adulthood. Retrospective studies show that many adults with Panic Disorder experienced SAD in their youth (Perwien & Bernstein, 2004). Unfortunately, prospective longitudinal studies (i.e., following children with SAD into adulthood) have not been conducted (Costello et al., 2004). Consequently, the relationship between childhood SAD and Panic Disorder in adulthood is unclear (Barlow, 2002).

Etiology

Compared to other anxiety disorders, genetic factors play a relatively small role in the development of SAD. Twin studies indicate that nonshared environmental experiences likely account for most of the variance in children's SAD symptoms (Silverman & Dick-Niederhauser, 2004). Genetic factors likely predispose children to SAD by increasing their level of behavioral inhibition. In fact, young children who show high behavioral inhibition are at increased risk for developing SAD. These children show increased autonomic arousal following the presentation of novel stimuli. Consequently, they often demand considerable reassurance and comfort from parents when scared, upset, or unsure of their surroundings (Barlow, 2002).

The quality of parent-child interactions, especially the early attachment relationship, likely plays an important role in the development of anxiety problems, including SAD, among youths with high behavioral inhibition (Manassis, 2001). According to Bowlby (1973), the purpose of **parent-child attachment** is to provide safety and security to the child. Attachment behaviors, such as approaching the parent when scared, are evolutionarily adaptive; they keep children in close proximity to their caregivers and increase the likelihood that they will remain safe and secure.

Insecure attachment relationships in early life predispose individuals to anxiety problems in childhood (Manassis, Bradley, Goldberg, Hood, & Swinson, 1994). Several prospective, longitudinal studies suggest that insecure attachment in infancy predicts anxiety problems during childhood. Furthermore, risk for anxiety is greatest among youths with both high levels of behavioral inhibition and a history of insecure attachment (Manassis, 2001; Warren, Emde, & Sroufe, 2000). Children who show behavioral inhibition in infancy and early childhood are extremely sensitive to psychosocial stressors, and they often demand considerable reassurance and comfort from parents. However, if parents are unable to meet their needs for comfort and security, these infants may experience prolonged and considerable feelings of insecurity and distress.

Insecure attachment in infancy may also predispose youths to anxiety problems in adolescence. Warren, Huston, Egeland, and Sroufe (1997) examined the relationship between the quality the attachment relationship in infancy and the prevalence of anxiety disorders, including SAD, during adolescence. Infants who initially displayed insecure attachment relationships with their mothers at age 12 months were more likely to develop anxiety disorders by late adolescence. Furthermore, a particular pattern of insecure attachment predicted later anxiety. This pattern, called **insecure-ambivalent attachment**, is associated with inconsistent parental care. It is possible that children who receive inconsistent care from parents experience considerable anxiety in times of stress because they do not know when (or if) parents will come to their aid. They seem to lack a secure base from which they can derive comfort and protection.

On the other hand, parents who provide their infants and young children with sensitive and responsive care may prevent the emergence of SAD and other anxiety problems later in childhood. Warren and Simmens (2005) examined the quality of parent-child interactions in families with infants who had difficult temperaments or high levels of behavioral inhibition. The researchers found that infants whose parents provided sensitive and responsive care were less likely to have anxiety problems during toddlerhood.

Parents' own levels of anxiety and insecurity can contribute to the development of SAD in their children (Silverman & Dick-Niederhauser, 2004). The parents of children with SAD often appear overly involved, controlling, and protective of their children's behavior. Rather than encouraging independent play and exploration, these parents may model anxiety and fearfulness to their children and encourage their children to be excessively cautious (Dadds et al., 1996; Hudson & Rapee, 2002). The tendency to parent in a highly controlling, overprotective manner is strongest among mothers with histories of insecure attachment relationships with their own parents (Rapee, 1997).

Obsessive-Compulsive Disorder

Definition

Obsessive-Compulsive Disorder (OCD) is characterized by the presence of recurrent obsessions or compulsions that are extremely time consuming, cause marked distress, or significantly impair daily functioning (see Table 13.7). **Obsessions** are "persistent ideas, thoughts, impulses, or images that are experienced as intrusive and inappropriate and that cause marked anxiety or distress" (*DSM-IV-TR*, p. 257). Common obsessions include thoughts about contamination (e.g., touching "dirty" objects like door handles), repeated doubts (e.g., wondering whether someone left the door unlocked), need for order or symmetry (e.g., towels arranged a certain way), aggressive or horrific impulses (e.g., thoughts about swearing in church), and sexual imagery. Most adults and adolescents with OCD recognize that these unwanted thoughts and images are a product of their own mind. Children may not have this insight.

Table 13.7   Diagnostic Criteria for Obsessive-Compulsive Disorder

A. Either obsessions or compulsions:

    1. Obsessions, as defined by all of the following:

        a. Recurrent and persistent thoughts, impulses, or images that are experienced, at some time during the disturbance, as intrusive and inappropriate and that cause some marked anxiety or distress

        b. The thoughts, impulses, or images are not simply excessive worries about real-life problems

        c. The person attempts to ignore or suppress such thoughts, impulses, or images, or to neutralize them with some other thought or action

        d. The person recognizes that the obsessional thoughts, impulses, or images are a product of his or her own mind

    2. Compulsions, as defined by both of the following:

        a. Repetitive behaviors (e.g., hand washing, ordering, checking) or mental acts (e.g., praying, counting, repeating words silently) that the person feels driven to perform in response to an obsession, or according to rules that must be applied rigidly

        b. The behaviors or mental acts are aimed at preventing or reducing distress or preventing some dreaded event or situation; however, these behaviors or mental acts are not connected in a realistic way with what they are designed to neutralize or prevent or are clearly excessive

B. At some point during the course of the disorder, the person has recognized that the obsessions or compulsions are excessive or unreasonable. Note: This does not apply to children.

C. The obsessions or compulsions cause marked distress, are time consuming (take more than 1 hour a day), or significantly interfere with the person's normal routine, academic/occupational functioning, or usual social activities or relationships

D. If another Axis I disorder is present, the content of the obsessions or compulsions is not restricted to it (e.g., preoccupation with alcohol and other drugs in the presence of Substance Dependence; guilty ruminations in the presence of Major Depressive Disorder)

E. The disturbance is not due to the direct effects of a substance or a general medical condition

Source: Reprinted with permission from the *DSM-IV-TR*.

Most people with OCD attempt to ignore or suppress obsessions. However, ignoring obsessions usually causes an increase in anxiety and subjective distress. To reduce feelings of distress, most people engage in compulsions. **Compulsions** are repetitive behaviors or mental acts that are designed to reduce anxiety or prevent some imaginary dreaded event from occurring. Common compulsions include washing, cleaning, counting, checking, repeating, arranging, and ordering. Compulsions are usually performed in a highly rigid and stereotyped manner, often according to certain idiosyncratic rules. For example, an adolescent with recurrent obsessions involving sexual imagery may feel compelled to pray to alleviate anxiety or guilt. If she makes mistakes in her prayers, she may require herself to repeat them until they are flawlessly recited.

Obsessions and compulsions tend to be time consuming, distressing, and impairing. It is not uncommon for obsessions and compulsions to occupy hours of the individual's time each day (Lin et al., 2007).

Tony

Tony was a 12-year-old boy who was referred to our clinic by his mother after she noticed him repeatedly engaging in "bizarre rituals" around the house. Mrs. Jeffries first became aware of Tony's ritualistic behavior when she noticed his persistent habit of turning lights on and off multiple times before entering or leaving a room. When she asked about this habit, Tony seemed embarrassed and dismissed it as "nothing." Mrs. Jeffries subsequently noticed other rituals. Tony avoided cracks in sidewalks, always entered rooms with his right foot, and always opened doors with his right hand. Mrs. Jeffries confronted Tony about these behaviors. In tears, Tony eventually admitted to being bothered by a persistent need to engage in these compulsive acts.

Dr. Saunders interviewed Tony. "Do you have any thoughts that pop into your mind before you perform these acts?" Tony replied hesitatingly, "Yeah, but they're hard to describe. I sort of feel nervous. I feel like something bad is going to happen to me or to my mom . . . like maybe I'll get an F in school or my mom will lose her job. Then, I just feel like I need to do something in a certain way, like turn the lights on and off three times, or open and close the refrigerator three times, or enter and exit a room three times." Dr. Saunders asked, "Always in threes?" Tony explained, "Yeah, it has to be in threes and just right so that I don't feel nervous anymore."

OCD in Children and Adolescents

Approximately 0.5%–1% of children and adolescents have OCD (March, Franklin, Leonard, & Foa, 2004). The typical age of onset is usually late childhood (March et al., 2004). In childhood, OCD is more common in boys than girls. By adolescence, the gender ratio is approximately equal (Flament et al., 1988).

The most common obsessions among children and adolescents are fear of germs (e.g., contamination), fear of harm befalling self or others, and an overwhelming need for order or symmetry. The most common compulsions are washing and cleaning, checking, counting, repeating, touching, and straightening (March et al., 2004).

Children's obsessions and compulsions differ somewhat from those of adults. First, it is not unusual for children to change obsessions and/or compulsions over time. Second, children's obsessions and compulsions are often more vague, magical, or superstitious than those of adults (Franklin, Rynn, Foa, & March, 2004). Third, many children have difficulty describing their obsessions. For example, they might report fearing "bad things" rather than contamination or asymmetry. Fourth, some children who are able to articulate their obsessions are unwilling to do so because they fear that stating them aloud will make their feared consequences come true.

Technically, individuals can be diagnosed with OCD if they show *either* obsessions *or* compulsions. In reality, most children show both symptoms (March et al., 2004). Sometimes, children appear to display only obsessions because their compulsions involve mental rituals. For example, obsessions regarding harm befalling a loved one might be accompanied by ritualistic counting or praying. These mental acts might be easily overlooked by parents and clinicians, leading them to mistakenly conclude that no compulsions exist. Indeed, the treatment of mental compulsions is more difficult than the treatment of behavioral compulsions because they are difficult to detect and monitor.

Youths with OCD often have other psychiatric disorders. The most commonly co-occurring problems are other anxiety disorders, depression, and tics. Among clinic-referred children, as many as 70% of children with OCD have another anxiety disorder, while approximately 70% of adolescents with OCD have depression (Curry et al., 2004). OCD and tics may have a common genetic etiology. For example, individuals with OCD often have first-degree relatives with tics, while individuals with tics often have first-degree relatives with OCD. Children and adolescents with both OCD and tics tend to show the greatest degree of anxiety and impairment (March et al., 2004).

Childhood OCD is a serious disorder that often results in impaired social, emotional, and academic functioning. Approximately 50% of youths with OCD continue to show the disorder in late adolescence and early adulthood. In most cases, symptom severity decreases with age. In a small minority of youths with OCD, however, symptom severity and impairment gradually increase to debilitating levels (Rasmussen & Eisen, 1990).

Etiology

OCD is moderately heritable. The disorder appears to run in families; individuals with first-degree relatives with OCD are at increased risk for developing OCD. Approximately 10%–25% of youths with OCD have at least one parent with the disorder. Twins studies indicate a 68% concordance for monozygotic twins compared to a 31% concordance for dizygotic twins. Furthermore, concordance for OCD symptoms (as opposed to full-blown OCD) may be as high as 87% (Hanna, 2000).

OCD is best viewed as a neuropsychiatric disorder that is caused by abnormalities in brain structure and functioning. A neural pathway, known as the **cortico-ganglionic-thalamic circuit**, seems to be particularly important in the disorder. This circuit forms a feedback loop involving three brain regions: (1) the orbital-frontal cortex; (2) the caudate, which is part of the basal ganglia; and (3) the thalamus. The orbital-frontal cortex is responsible for detecting abnormalities or irregularities in the environment and initiating a behavioral response to correct these irregularities. For example, the orbital-frontal cortex might be activated when a person notices dirt on his hands. Signals from the orbital-frontal cortex pass through the caudate to the thalamus, which becomes highly active. The thalamus routes the information to various brain regions to initiate a behavioral response (e.g., wash hands) and sends a feedback signal back to the orbital-frontal cortex. In healthy people, the caudate inhibits information from the cortex to the thalamus, thereby regulating the amount of arousal experienced by the thalamus. However, individuals with OCD often show irregularities in the structure and functioning of the caudate. Consequently, the cortico-ganglionic-thalamic circuit is not inhibited. Instead, the orbital-frontal cortex continues to send signals to the thalamus, increasing the person's desire to perform the behavior or ritual (March et al., 2004; Rosenberg & Keshavan, 1998).

Serotonin also likely plays a role in OCD. Medications like fluoxetine (Prozac) that inhibit the reuptake of serotonin reduce OCD symptoms in adolescents with the disorder (Franklin, March, & Gracia, 2007). Furthermore, drugs that artificially increase serotonergic activity often exacerbate symptoms. Consequently, many researchers believe that OCD symptoms are partially caused by excessively high levels of serotonin. Medications may reduce OCD symptoms by decreasing the number or sensitivity of serotonin receptors (March et al., 2004).

Genetic and biological factors might underlie OCD symptoms, but the disorder is probably maintained through learning. Obsessions develop when people associate specific environmental stimuli with anxiety-provoking thoughts or beliefs. For example, a door handle might be paired with anxiety-provoking thoughts of contamination. Later, the individual learns that washing reduces anxiety; consequently, he is more likely to wash his hands in the future. Compulsions, therefore, are negatively reinforced by anxiety reduction.

Cognitive theorists have argued that the way adolescents think can also contribute to the development of OCD (Salkovskis, Forrester, & Richards, 1998). Adolescents with OCD show two ways of thinking that contribute to their symptoms (S. Libby, Reynolds, Derisley, & Clark, 2004). First, adolescents with OCD experience inflated responsibility for misfortune. For example, if the adolescent's mother is fired from her job or the adolescent's father experiences car trouble on the way home, the adolescent might blame herself for their misfortune. She might think, "My mother lost her job because I'm too much of a burden for her. She can't handle me and her job at once" or "My father had car trouble because I was late in getting the oil changed last week. It must be my fault." These appraisals of misfortune contribute to feelings of guilt and self-doubt.

Second, adolescents with OCD often display **thought-action fusion**, the erroneous belief that merely thinking about an event will increase its probability. For example, an adolescent might believe that simply because he thought of his grandfather becoming sick and dying, his grandfather's likelihood of dying actually increased. Because the adolescent believes her thoughts can influence the external world, she attempts to control negative thoughts to prevent future disaster. Thought-action fusion causes adolescents to feel great distress when they experience transient negative thoughts. Whereas most people dismiss such thoughts as "irrational" or "unlikely," an adolescent with OCD might take them seriously because she believes she has the ability to mentally influence outside events.

Worry

Generalized Anxiety Disorder is unlike the other anxiety disorders because it is characterized by persistent worry, rather than fear. People with GAD do not fear specific objects, situations, or sensations; instead, they worry about future misfortune (Pine & Grun, 1999).

Generalized Anxiety Disorder

Definition

The hallmark of Generalized Anxiety Disorder (GAD) is **apprehensive expectation**, that is, excessive anxiety and worry about the future (see Table 13.8). Adults with GAD worry about aspects of everyday life, such as completing tasks at work, managing finances, meeting appointments, and performing household chores.

Table 13.8   Diagnostic Criteria for Generalized Anxiety Disorder

A. Excessive anxiety and worry (apprehensive expectation) occurring more days than not for at least 6 months, about a number of events or activities (such as school performance)

B. The person finds it difficult to control the worry

C. The anxiety and worry are associated with three (or more) of the following six symptoms (with at least some symptoms present for more days than not for the past 6 months). Note: Only one item is required in children.
   1. Restlessness or feeling keyed up or on edge
   2. Being easily fatigued
   3. Difficulty concentrating or mind going blank
   4. Irritability
   5. Muscle tension
   6. Sleep disturbance (difficulty falling asleep or staying asleep, or restless unsatisfying sleep)

D. The focus of the anxiety and worry is not confined to features of an Axis I disorder; e.g., the anxiety or worry is not about having a panic attack (as in Panic Disorder), being embarrassed in public (as in Social Phobia), being contaminated (as in Obsessive-Compulsive Disorder), being away from home or close relatives (as in Separation Anxiety Disorder), and the anxiety and worry do not occur exclusively during Posttraumatic Stress Disorder

E. The anxiety, worry, or physical symptoms cause clinically significant distress or impairment in social, academic, or other important areas of functioning

F. The disturbance is not due to the direct effects of a substance or a general medical condition and does not occur exclusively during a Mood Disorder, a Psychotic Disorder, or a Pervasive Developmental Disorder

Source: Reprinted with permission from the *DSM-IV-TR*.

Children and adolescents with GAD also worry about activities and events in their day-to-day lives, especially performing well on exams, school assignments, athletics, and extracurricular activities. By definition, people with GAD find it extremely difficult to control their worries. They may have other symptoms indicative of chronic anxiety, such as restlessness, sleep problems, fatigue, muscle tension, irritability, and difficulty concentrating. Although all people worry from time to time, the worry shown by individuals with GAD is excessive, prolonged, and difficult to control.

GAD in Children and Adolescents

Worry is generally regarded as a cognitive activity characterized by repeated and increasingly elaborated thoughts about future negative events and their consequences (Borkovec & Inz, 1990). Children might worry about an upcoming exam, the possibility of not studying adequately for the exam, and the repercussions of earning a low grade or gaining the disapproval of teachers and parents. Children begin to show the ability to worry around age four or five years (Muris, Merckelbach et al., 2000). However, the ability to think about and dwell upon negative events in the distant future does not seem to emerge until after age eight (Vasey, Crnic, & Carter, 1994). The onset of GAD is usually after this cognitive capacity for worry develops, that is, between 8 and 10 years of age (Keller, Lavori, Wunder, Beardslee, Schwartz, & Roth, 1992; Last et al., 1992). As children's capacity for worry increases with age, so does the frequency and severity of GAD (Kendall, Pimentel, Rynn, Angelosante, & Webb, 2004).

Children with GAD do not simply worry about an upcoming homework assignment or a school dance; they worry about people and events in almost all areas of their lives. The most common worries among children with GAD include health problems (e.g., getting sick and dying), school problems (e.g., failing, being ridiculed by teachers, not getting admitted to college), disasters (e.g., harm in a thunderstorm, terrorist attacks), and personal harm befalling others (e.g., a loved one hit by a car, a parent losing a job). Children with GAD also have many adult-like worries, such as whether a parent might lose her job or whether the family has enough money (Weems, Silverman, & La Greca, 2000).

The worries shown by children with GAD interfere with their daily functioning (Flannery-Schroeder, 2004; Masi, Millepiedi, Mucci, Poli, Bertini, & Milantoni, 2004; see Figure 13.3). First, worry causes significant distress and consumes significant time and energy. Second, worry interferes with children's abilities to concentrate on important activities, such as listening to parents or completing homework assignments. Third, worry can cause mood problems, frustration, and irritability. Fourth, worry can cause somatic problems, such as headaches, sleep problems, or fatigue. Finally, worry can interfere with the development of more adaptive coping strategies (Shoal, Castaneda, & Giancola, 2005). Children who frequently worry may not learn other ways to deal with anxiety, such as using relaxation or play, expressing negative emotions to parents or peers, or engaging in a sport or hobby.

Children with GAD are often described by parents and teachers as "little adults" (Kendall, Krain, & Treadwell, 1999). These youths are often perfectionist, punctual, and eager to please. They are usually quite self-conscious around others, especially

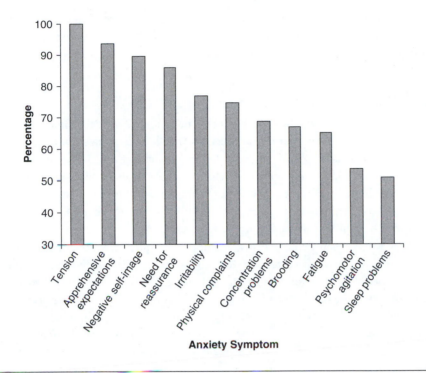

Figure 13.3 Anxiety Symptoms in Youths With GAD

Source: Based on Masi et al. (2004).

Note: Children and adolescents with GAD show a wide range of impairments, including tension, apprehension about the future, and negative self-image.

adults and people in authority. They also tend to be highly conforming to rules and social norms. For these reasons, Kendall and colleagues (1999) suggest that children with GAD create an "illusion of maturity" that makes them appear more emotionally competent than they really are.

Beneath this "illusion of maturity," children with GAD harbor feelings of self-doubt, self-criticism, and uncertainty. They may strive for perfection when completing a homework assignment, preparing for a piano recital, or practicing for an athletic competition. However, they often require excessive reassurance from teachers, tutors, and coaches to make sure that they gain the approval of others. Children with GAD may also refuse to submit homework, play, or compete unless they know their performance will be perfect. They often interpret signs of imperfection (e.g., homework mistakes, misplayed notes, coming in second) as indicators of failure and worthlessness.

Children with GAD are at risk for other anxiety disorders. In one large study, 75% if youths with GAD showed one comorbid anxiety disorder and 38% showed two or more coexisting anxiety disorders (Masi et al., 2004). The most common comorbid anxiety disorders are SAD, Specific Phobia, and Social Phobia (Kashani & Orvaschel, 1990; Masi et al., 2004). It is possible that persistent worry sensitizes children to developing specific fears (e.g., harm to family members, fear of animals, fear of social criticism). GAD in childhood is also associated with depression. Approximately 50% of youths with GAD show MDD (Masi, Favilla, Mucci, & Millepiedi, 2000; Masi et al., 2004).

Etiology

Little is known about the causes of GAD in children (Kendall, Pimentel et al., 2004). Most research has examined the causes of childhood anxiety more generally. Many of the risk factors of anxiety disorders in general apply to GAD. For example, children with difficult temperaments, behavioral inhibition, and less-than-optimal parent-child interactions are probably at risk for GAD, in addition to the other anxiety disorders (Flannery-Schroeder, 2004; Hale, Engels, & Meeus, 2006).

From a behavioral perspective, worrying seems to make little sense. Most people consider worrying to be an aversive activity. Consequently, worrying appears to have no reinforcing properties. However, behavioral theorists suggest that worrying serves a special purpose for children and adolescents with GAD. Namely, worrying helps them avoid emotionally and physically arousing mental images (Borkovec & Inz, 1990; Roemer & Borkovec, 1993). Worry allows people to replace emotion-laden images of imminent danger with more abstract, analytical thoughts about future misfortune. According to the **behavioral hypothesis of GAD**, worry is a form of avoidance and is negatively reinforcing.

To understand how worry can be negatively reinforcing, consider Elsa, a perfectionist 12-year-old with GAD. Elsa's teacher has assigned her to work with three classmates on an important science project. As a group, the students must complete the project, write a poster, and present their findings at the school science fair. Most children would experience moderate anxiety when faced with this assignment; however, Elsa shows great distress. She imagines the group failing miserably in their experiment, making countless mistakes on their poster, and humiliating themselves during the presentation. Furthermore, she foresees chastisement and disapproval from her teacher and parents. To cope with these mental images, Elsa thinks about the situation in more abstract, verbal terms—she worries. She thinks to herself, "What if my classmates don't follow through with their part of the project?" or "I had better double-check our spelling on the poster" or "Maybe I'm not prepared enough for the oral presentation—I should rehearse one more time." These worries occupy Elsa's time and energy. They serve an important function: They allow Elsa to avoid imagining the terrible consequences of failing the project. To the extent that worry allows children like Elsa to avoid or escape distressing images, worry can be negatively reinforcing (Borkovec, Ray, & Stober, 1998).

In fact, children with GAD worry to *avoid* thinking about problems, not to solve them. Most children use worrying to anticipate future problems and generate possible solutions ahead of time. For example, a child worrying about an upcoming exam might reason, "The test is going to be very hard, so I'm going to have to start studying right away—a little bit each night—in order to do well." In this case, worrying serves a positive, problem-solving function. In contrast, children with GAD show very little problem solving while worrying (see Figure 13.4). Instead, these children simply ruminate about the negative event (Szabo & Lovibond, 2004). For

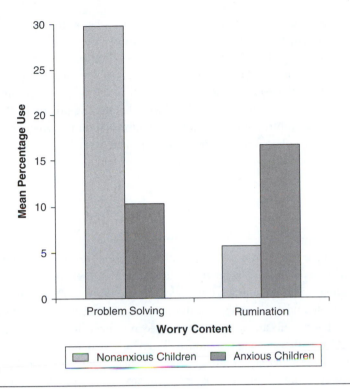

Figure 13.4 How Do You Worry?

Source: Based on Szabo and Lovibond (2004).

Note: Children without anxiety disorders tend to generate solutions to future problems when they worry. In contrast, children with anxiety disorders, like GAD, tend to ruminate about potential trouble in the future.

example, a child with GAD who is worrying about a future exam might think, "The exam is going to be really difficult. What if I fail? What will my mom say?" Because children with GAD are less likely to generate solutions for their worries, their worries persist uncontrollably.

Youths with GAD may show **cognitive distortions** that cause them to worry. Weems and Watts (2005) identified three cognitive distortions seen in children's worries: catastrophizing, overgeneralizing, and personalizing. Catastrophizing occurs when children expect disastrous outcomes from mildly aversive events. For example, a girl with GAD who has an upcoming dance recital might anticipate disaster: She might forget her dance shoes, trip on stage, and humiliate her family. Overgeneralizing occurs when children assume that a single adverse event is an indicator of future misfortune. For example, a child who makes a mistake in her first recital might anticipate mistakes in all subsequent performances. Finally, personalizing occurs when children assume personal responsibility for misfortune. For example, a child who trips during a dance recital might attribute her mistake to her own clumsiness, rather than to a slippery floor (Weems et al., 2001).

Youths with GAD also underestimate their ability to cope with threatening events (Weems & Watts, 2005). Children with anxiety disorders in general, and GAD in particular, often display an **external locus of control**; that is, they believe events and situations are largely determined by external causes (e.g., luck, fate) rather than internal causes (e.g., hard work). Youths with GAD, in particular, often show low self-efficacy (Weems & Watts, 2005). **Self-efficacy** is a concept created by Albert Bandura (1973) to describe a person's appraisal of her ability to accomplish tasks and control her surroundings. When faced with threatening situations, children with GAD are often doubtful of their abilities to confront and overcome their problems. Low self-efficacy, therefore, breeds rumination and worry. In contrast, high self-efficacy fosters confidence about the future.

Treatment

Anxiety disorders in children often go undetected and untreated. As many as 86% of youths with anxiety disorders never see mental health professionals (Costello, 2005). Even among children attending outpatient clinics, almost 70% never receive treatment for their anxiety disorder (Chavira & Stein, 2005). Anxiety disorders are easily overlooked by parents and teachers, the people most likely to refer children for treatment. After all, internalizing symptoms, like anxiety, demand less immediate attention than externalizing symptoms, like physical aggression or hyperactivity. Furthermore, many children recognize their anxiety symptoms are unusual, and they attempt to hide their symptoms from adults. Ethnic minority children and children from lower-SES backgrounds are especially likely to be overlooked (Chavira & Stein, 2005; Costello et al., 2004).

Almost all efficacious psychosocial treatments for childhood anxiety disorders involve exposure therapy (Bouchard, Mendlowitz, Coles, & Franklin, 2004). **Exposure therapy** occurs when the client confronts a feared stimulus for a discrete period of time. Over time, and across multiple confrontations, the client's anxiety gradually decreases. Exposure therapy can occur in many ways. Exposure can occur gradually (i.e., graded exposure) or rapidly (i.e., flooding). The client can confront real objects, people, or situations (i.e., in vivo exposure) or the client can imagine the feared stimulus (i.e., imaginal exposure). Exposure can occur multiple times over a number of weeks (i.e., spaced exposure) or over the course of hours or days (e.g., massed exposure). Although all forms of exposure can be used with children, exposure therapy is usually most effective when it is graded, in vivo, and massed.

Behavior Therapy for Phobias

Behavioral treatments for children's phobias have existed for nearly 80 years. Mary Cover Jones (1924), a student of John Watson, used behavioral techniques to reduce a fear response in a 34-month-old child named Peter, who was afraid of rabbits. Jones used three techniques to reduce Peter's fear. First, she gradually exposed Peter to a rabbit for progressively longer periods of time. Initially, the rabbit remained on the other side of the room and in a cage. In subsequent sessions, assistants brought the rabbit closer to Peter, released it from the cage, and encouraged

Peter to touch it. Second, Peter was provided with candy whenever he tolerated the rabbit's presence; that is, he was positively reinforced for coming into contact with the rabbit and not running away. Third, other children Peter's age, who were not afraid of rabbits, were asked to play with Peter while the rabbit was present. Peter observed these children approach and pet the rabbit without fear. Over the course of several weeks, Peter's fear of the rabbit decreased.

Contingency Management

Behavioral techniques, like the ones used to treat Peter's phobia, are still used today (Ginsburg & Walkup, 2004). Jones's (1924) primary technique is now called **contingency management**. Contingency management is based on the principles of operant conditioning; it involves exposing the child to the feared stimulus and positively reinforcing the child contingent on the exposure. At the same time, the child is *not* allowed to avoid or withdraw from the feared stimulus. Jones progressively exposed Peter to the rabbit and reinforced him with candy. Furthermore, she prohibited him from running away.

Today, a therapist who wants to use contingency management would first meet with parents and the child to establish a **behavioral contract**. The contract specifies exactly what behaviors the child is expected to perform and what reinforcement will be provided when the child follows through with the behavior. Usually, parents and the child rank order the child's behavior in a hierarchical fashion. Behaviors that elicit mild anxiety are introduced first, while behaviors that cause high anxiety are presented last.

The child is required to come into closer and closer contact with the feared stimulus for longer and longer periods of time. When the child successfully completes the required behavior, he is positively reinforced (e.g., given praise, access to toys/games). At the same time, he is not permitted to run away, tantrum, or otherwise avoid the feared stimulus. The child is encouraged to confront the feared stimulus until his anxiety dissipates.

Modeling

A second technique to treat phobias, also used by Jones (1924), involves observational learning or modeling. In modeling, the child watches an adult or another child confront the feared stimulus. For example, a child with dog phobia might watch his therapist approach, pet, and play with a dog during the therapy session. He might also see another child, approximately his age, perform the same behaviors. The child sees that confronting the feared stimulus does not result in punishment (e.g., the model is not bitten by the dog) and often results in positive reinforcement (e.g., the model enjoys playing with the dog). Jones used modeling to extinguish Peter's fear; Peter watched other toddlers approach and play with the rabbit.

Modeling can occur in real life (i.e., in vivo modeling) or by watching video tapes (i.e., videotaped modeling). Some therapists use a third strategy called participant modeling. In **participant modeling**, the therapist first models the behavior for the child and then helps the child perform the behavior himself.

Systematic Desensitization

A third behavioral technique to treat phobias is **systematic desensitization**, a technique based on the principle of classical conditioning. In systematic desensitization, children learn to associate a feared stimulus with a response that is incompatible with fear. Usually, this incompatible response involves relaxation.

First, parents and the child create a hierarchy of feared stimuli, just like in contingency management. The goal is to gradually progress up the fear hierarchy by exposing the child to the feared stimulus for longer periods of time. However, before exposure begins, the child is taught an incompatible response to use when confronting the feared stimulus. Some therapists teach children deep breathing techniques to help them relax. Other therapists teach children how to relax their muscles.

Then, children gradually progress up the fear hierarchy. When they experience anxiety, children use their relaxation skills to produce an incompatible (relaxation) response. Through classical conditioning, children come to associate the previously feared stimulus with the relaxation response.

Efficacy of Behavioral Techniques

Research supports the efficacy of behavior therapy for phobias in children and adolescents (Barrios & O'Dell, 1998; Ollendick & King, 1998). Behavioral techniques have been successfully used to reduce fears that range from the commonplace (e.g., animals, the dark, heights) to the atypical (e.g., menstruation, bowel movements).

Ollendick and King (1998) performed an extensive review and analysis of behavioral treatments of childhood anxiety. Contingency management, modeling, and systematic desensitization all enjoyed at least some support in the treatment literature. The greatest support was found for contingency management and participant modeling. These techniques seem to be superior to no treatment and other, nonbehavioral interventions. Systematic desensitization was also found to be efficacious, especially when it involves in vivo confrontation of the feared stimulus. These results suggest that behavioral techniques that involve direct exposure to the feared stimulus and positive reinforcement contingent on that exposure seem to produce the greatest benefits.

Cognitive-Behavioral Therapy for Social Phobia, SAD, and GAD

Description of CBT

Cognitive-behavioral therapy (CBT) is an effective treatment for many childhood anxiety disorders, especially Social Phobia, GAD, and SAD. The underlying premise of CBT is that there is an interrelationship between a person's thoughts, feelings, and actions. Changes in thinking can affect the way people feel and act. Similarly, changes in overt behavior can influence thought patterns and mood. In CBT, children with anxiety disorders are taught to recognize anxiety (feelings) and use cognitive and behavioral coping strategies to reduce the anxiety until it is more manageable (Beidel & Turner, 2007).

Philip Kendall and colleagues (Kendall, Hudson, Choudhury, Webb, & Pimentel, 2005) have examined the efficacy of a 16-week cognitive-behavioral treatment for children. The program is divided into two phases: education and practice. In the first phase, children learn about the relationship between thoughts, feelings, and actions, and they are taught new ways to cope with anxiety and worry. Therapy is structured around a personalized **FEAR plan**. The steps in the plan are represented by the acronym FEAR: feelings, expectations, attitudes, and results (see Table 13.9). When the child confronts an anxiety-provoking situation, she uses the FEAR steps to manage her anxiety.

First, children learn to identify feelings and somatic sensations associated with anxiety. Children learn to ask themselves, "Am I feeling frightened?" Children are taught to use muscle relaxation when frightened as a way to reduce distress.

Next, children learn to recognize and modify negative thoughts (i.e., self-talk) that contribute to their anxiety. They ask themselves, "Am I expecting bad things to happen?" The therapist uses a workbook, games, and role-playing exercises to show how changes in thoughts can influence changes in feelings and actions. For example, the *Coping Cat Workbook* (Kendall, 1992) consists of a series of exercises designed to teach children to recognize and alter negative self-talk (see Image 13.1).

Therapists help children reduce the frequency of negative self-statements (Kendall et al., 2005). Children with anxiety disorders engage in many more negative self-statements, but the same number of positive self-statements, as nonanxious children (Treadwell & Kendall, 1996). The therapist's goal is not to increase the

Table 13.9   Sample FEAR Plan for a Socially Anxious Child Giving a Class Presentation

Step	Example
F: Feeling frightened	"Well, I have butterflies in my stomach and my palms are kind of sweaty."
E: Expecting bad things to happen	"I will mess up." "The other kids will make fun of me." "I'm going to look stupid and they'll laugh at me."
A: Attitudes and actions that will help	"I can practice beforehand and make sure I know what I'm going to say." "I didn't mess up the last time and the teacher said I did a good job." "Even if I mess up, it's not a big deal anyway because everybody messes up sometimes."
R: Results and rewards	"I was nervous in the beginning, but I felt OK by the end." "Nobody laughed at me." "I think I did a pretty good job and I tried really hard." "My reward is to go to the movies with Mom and Dad this weekend."

Source: Based on Kendall et al. (2005).

Some type of thoughts can help people deal with the situation, while other thoughts might make people feel more nervous or scared. Take a look at this cartoon scene. Circle the cat that would be most frightened. Why do you think he would feel more scared?

Image 13.1 The Coping Cat. Children complete the *Coping Cat Workbook* to help them make connections between their thoughts, feelings, and actions.

Source: From Kendall (1992). Used with permission.

child's positive cognitions, that is, to help the child see the world through "rose-colored glasses." Rather, the therapist focuses on helping the child see the world more realistically, rather than negatively or catastrophically. According to Kendall (1992) the goal of therapy is to teach children the power of "non-negative" thinking. Reductions in negative self-talk predict success in therapy (Treadwell & Kendall, 1996; Wilson & Rapee, 2005).

In subsequent sessions, children learn cognitive problem-solving skills designed to cope with anxiety-provoking situations. They try to develop attitudes that can help. Problem-solving training is designed to help children view the social situations or problems realistically, generate as many solutions to these problems as possible, consider the benefits and costs of each solution, and select the best course of action.

Finally, in the results and rewards component of treatment, children are encouraged to realistically judge the effectiveness of their problem solving and to reward themselves for addressing the feared situations. Since anxious children often place unrealistic expectations on themselves or exaggerate negative events, it is important for them to view outcomes in a realistic light and to take pride in *attempting* to cope with anxiety-provoking situations (Kendall et al., 2005).

After children have mastered the FEAR plan, they begin using it in the community. Use of the FEAR steps in the community involves graded exposure. The type of exposure largely depends on the child's disorder. Children with Social Phobia might be asked to approach a group of children playing a game; adolescents with SAD might be encouraged to separate from their parents for 15 minutes during a shopping trip. Initially, children report intense anxiety following exposure. However, as children habituate to the anxiety-provoking situation, anxiety levels drop. Children learn that exposure does not result in catastrophe.

Several randomized, controlled studies indicate that CBT is efficacious (Barrett, Dadds, & Rapee, 1996; Cobham, Dadds, & Spence, 1998; Kendall, 1994; Kendall, Flannery-Schroeder, Panichelli-Mindel, Southam-Gerow, Henin, & Warman, 1997; Silverman, Kurtines, Ginsburg, Weems, Lumpkin, & Carmichael, 1999; Spence, Donovan, & Brechman-Toussaint, 2000). Research has typically involved children aged 7 to 13 years diagnosed with Social Phobia, SAD, and GAD. CBT is associated with improvements in self-report, parent-report, and behavioral observations of children's anxiety symptoms, compared to control groups. Furthermore, reductions in anxiety tend to be clinically significant; most children who participate in CBT no longer meet diagnostic criteria for anxiety disorders after treatment (Kendall et al., 1997; Kendall, Marrs-Garcia, Nath, & Sheldrick, 1999). Gains are maintained from one to seven years after treatment (Barrett, Duffy, Dadds, & Rapee, 2001; Cobham et al., 1998; Kendall, 1994; Kendall & Southam-Gerow, 1996; Kendall, Safford, Flannery-Schroeder, & Webb, 2004; see Figure 13.5). CBT can also be administered to groups of children at the same time (Flannery-Schroeder & Kendall, 2000; Flannery-Schroeder, Choudhury, & Kendall, 2005).

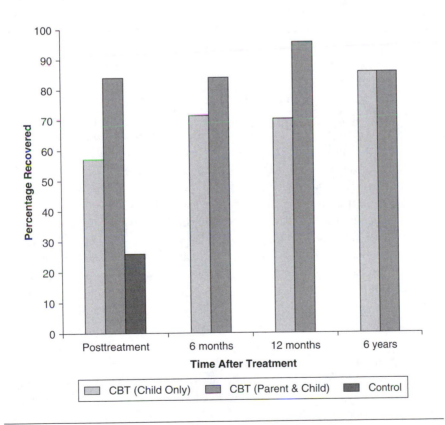

Figure 13.5   Efficacy of CBT for Children With Social Phobia, SAD, and GAD

Source: Based on Barrett, Dadds, et al. (1996) and Barrett et al. (2001).

Note: CBT is more effective than placebo. Furthermore, providing therapy to parents and children may produce faster results than providing treatment only to children. Consequently, involving parents in therapy is usually recommended.

Most recently, CBT treatment packages have been modified so that children and adolescents can participate via the computer. A computer-based CBT program called *Cool Teens* has been developed for youths with Social Phobia, SAD, and GAD (Cunningham, Rapee, & Lyneham, 2007). Similarly, a computer-administered version of the *Coping Cat* workbook has been developed for youths with a wide range of anxiety problems (Khanna, Aschenbrand, & Kendall, 2007). Both programs teach youths the relationship between thoughts, feelings, and actions and encourage them to change their patterns of thinking and behaving to improve their mood. Youths who have tried these computer-based programs report that they are convenient, easy to use, and fun. Computer-based programs might be used to supplement traditional therapy or as an alternative to traditional therapy.

Cognitive-Behavioral Therapy for PTSD

Trauma-Focused CBT

Trauma-focused CBT involves exposing children to memories or stimuli associated with traumatic events and then encouraging them to think about and cope with the trauma in more adaptive ways. Trauma-focused CBT has several important features (Cohen & Mannarino, 2004; McKnight et al., 2004). First, early treatment sessions are used to teach families about PTSD. It is usually helpful for parents and children to know that PTSD symptoms are relatively common among individuals who experience trauma and that treatment can be effective in reducing children's distress.

Second, the therapist teaches the child coping skills to deal with the anxiety associated with the trauma. Most therapists teach relaxation skills such as deep breathing or muscle relaxation. Some therapists also teach children to engage in positive self-talk that is designed to give them greater confidence and security when they encounter memories of the trauma. For example, a child might practice saying to herself, "It's going to be OK" when she experiences distress or "I can do it" when she attempts to use relaxation techniques to combat anxiety.

Third, trauma-focused CBT involves gradually exposing children to stimuli or memories associated with the traumatic event. At a minimum, exposure usually involves the therapist encouraging the child to imagine the traumatic event in the safety and security of the therapy session. The therapist might ask the child to give a play-by-play account of the event, paying attention to sights, sounds, images, and feelings associated with the trauma. The goal is to expose the child to the anxiety-provoking stimuli for progressively longer intervals. Many therapists also ask the child to provide increasingly more detailed narratives of the traumatic event, either orally or in writing. Ideally, the child will eventually feel comfortable enough to share his narrative with others. If possible, some therapists use in vivo exposure to correct avoidance of situations associated with the trauma. For example, a child might avoid recess at school because he witnessed a classmate being severely injured in a car accident in the school parking lot. The therapist, with the help of parents and teachers, might encourage the child to gradually expose himself to the parking lot to overcome his anxiety (J. A. Cohen, 2005).

Fourth, trauma-focused CBT involves identifying and changing children's maladaptive cognitions about the traumatic event (Stallard & Smith, 2007). Many children believe they somehow caused the traumatic event or are to blame for the misery and hardship the event placed on others. For example, an adolescent who is sexually abused might assume blame for her maltreatment because she acquiesced to the demands of her abuser. Another child, whose mother died in an auto accident, might believe that he is to blame because he was arguing with his sister in the car when the accident occurred. The clinician identifies and challenges these maladaptive beliefs. The therapist might ask children to provide evidence for their beliefs. A clinician might say to a sexually abused child, "It is true that you never told anyone about the abuse. However, didn't he threaten to kill you and your mother if you didn't give in to his demands? Were you really free to say 'no'?"

At least three randomized controlled studies have investigated the efficacy of trauma-focused CBT for children with PTSD caused by sexual abuse (Nemeroff et al., 2004). In general, children who participate in trauma-focused CBT showed reductions in PTSD symptoms and increases in social competence greater than youths who receive no treatment or nondirective counseling. Furthermore, in some cases, involving parents in CBT results in reductions in children's depressive symptoms as well. Other studies have demonstrated the efficacy of CBT in reducing PTSD symptoms in children exposed to natural disasters and violence (Chemtob, Nakashima, & Carlson, 2002; Cohen & Mannarino, 2004; Goenjian et al., 1997).

Cognitive-Behavioral Therapy for Panic Disorder

Cognitive-behavioral therapy for adolescents with Panic Disorder involves four components: (1) relaxation training, (2) interoceptive exposure, (3) cognitive restructuring, and (4) graded in vivo exposure (Birmaher & Ollendick, 2004). In **relaxation training**, the adolescent learns ways to reduce physiological arousal when he begins to experience panic. Relaxation training is designed to combat the adolescent's anxiety sensitivity and tendency to overreact to stress. Most therapists teach breathing exercises, muscle relaxation, or calming self-statements to help clients learn to relax.

Interoceptive exposure is a technique unique to the treatment of panic disorder. In interoceptive exposure, the adolescent learns to produce some of the physiological symptoms of panic and then use relaxation techniques to cope with these symptoms. Panic-like symptoms can be intentionally produced by spinning in a chair, hyperventilating into a paper bag, or running in place for 1–2 minutes. Mimicking panic symptoms has at least three benefits. First, adolescents recognize that panic symptoms can be intentionally produced and, therefore, are not always beyond their control. Second, adolescents learn that they will not die or pass out from panic. Although distressing, panic symptoms decrease over time. Third, adolescents learn that relaxation techniques can be used to effectively cope with panic symptoms.

Cognitive restructuring is also used to treat Panic Disorder. Cognitive restructuring techniques generally involve challenging cognitive biases and distortions that lead to panic attacks. The main target of cognitive restructuring is catastrophic thinking. Some therapists play the "detective game" with their adolescent clients to help them critically evaluate the likelihood of catastrophic events occurring as a result of a panic attack. For example, a therapist might challenge her client's distorted beliefs by asking for evidence for and against those beliefs:

Marie: When I start to get those feelings, you know, with my heart beating fast and hyperventilating, I feel like I'm having a heart attack, like I'm going to die!

Therapist: What's the likelihood that you're *actually* going to die when you feel that way?

Marie: Pretty high; at least, it feels that way.

Therapist: Yes, but you've had a number of these attacks before.

Marie: Uh-huh.

Therapist: And you obviously haven't died from them.

Marie: No.

Therapist: And you've never even fainted or lost consciousness before, right?

Marie: No. I never have.

Therapist: So what's the likelihood that you will die, faint, or lose consciousness from an attack in the future?

Marie: I guess pretty low since it's never happened before.

Therapist: You're probably right. You can even tell yourself, when you feel an attack coming on, that you'll be OK, that you're not going to die or faint or pass out.

Marie: Yes. But it sure feels like I will.

Therapist: Yes, it does. But *feeling* like it will happen and *actually* fainting are two different things. Besides, what is the worst possible thing that could happen?

Marie: Well, I could sweat all over and hyperventilate and get all pale and clammy. I'd have to run out of class and go to the bathroom to feel better. The teacher and the other kids in class would think I was crazy.

Therapist: OK. So we agree that you'll probably not die or pass out, right?

Marie: Yeah, but I would probably make a fool out of myself.

Therapist: Well, if you saw another kid in your class suddenly look sweaty and clammy and then run out of class for the bathroom, what would you think?

Marie: I'd think she was sick.

Therapist: Would you think she was crazy?

Marie: No. I'd think she had the flu.

Therapist: Would you tease her after class or talk about her with your friends?

Marie: Of course not. I'd probably ask her if she was feeling OK.

Therapist: Don't you think your teacher and classmates would react the same way if they saw you do the same thing?

Marie: Yes. I suppose they would.

The final component of CBT for Panic Disorder is graded exposure. Graded exposure is primarily used to correct agoraphobic avoidance. The therapist and adolescent create a hierarchy of situations or events that range from moderately distressing to extremely feared. The adolescent is encouraged to face each feared situation until she experiences a reduction in anxiety.

Cognitive-Behavioral Therapy for OCD

CBT is currently the treatment of choice for youths with OCD. Usually, CBT is administered as a treatment package consisting of three basic components: (1) information gathering, (2) exposure and response prevention, and (3) generalization (Grabill, Storch, & Geffken, 2007).

First, the clinician interviews the parents and child to obtain information regarding the family's psychosocial history, the child's symptoms, and the onset and course of the disorder. It is important for the clinician to determine exactly what kinds of obsessions and compulsions the child shows. For example, treating a child's ritualistic actions (e.g., hand washing, checking) would require different methods than addressing a child's mental rituals (e.g., counting, praying silently; Franklin et al., 2007).

The next step is **exposure and response prevention (EX/RP)**. Using information gathered during the interview, the child and clinician develop a hierarchy of feared stimuli. Over several weeks, the child exposes himself to each of the feared stimuli, gradually progressing up the hierarchy. At the same time, the child must not engage in the rituals he feels compelled to do after confronting the feared stimuli.

To illustrate EX/RP, imagine a ten-year-old boy who obsesses about contamination. After he touches certain objects that he considers "dirty," he feels compelled to wash his hands. His obsession is contamination by "dirty" objects; his compulsion is ritualistic washing. The boy and his therapist develop a fear hierarchy, ranging from behaviors that elicit only mild anxiety (e.g., sitting in the therapist's chair) to strong anxiety (e.g., touching a public toilet). During each session, the boy and his therapist confront a different feared stimulus, gradually moving up the hierarchy. The therapist might teach the boy relaxation techniques, like controlled breathing, to help him cope with anxiety during the exposure. The therapist might also use modeling, positive reinforcement, and the strength of their therapeutic relationship to help the boy to successfully confront the stimuli. At the same time, the therapist prohibits the boy from washing.

EX/RP works through the principle of extinction. Initially, exposure produces a rapid surge of anxiety. Over time, however, the child's anxiety gradually decreases and become more manageable.

Older children and adolescents with OCD might benefit from cognitive therapy in addition to EX/RP. Cognitive techniques do not reduce OCD behaviors directly; rather, they help some children engage in the EX/RP exercises. Many therapists use cognitive restructuring to help children view feared situations more realistically, rather than in an excessively negative light. For example, a child might initially think, "That chair is disgusting. It has germs all over it and I'll get sick if I touch it." The therapist might challenge the child's thinking by asking, "Lots of other people have sat in that chair; have they all gotten sick?" Some therapists help children replace self-defeating, negativistic self-statements with more realistic statements. For example, after confronting a feared stimulus, a child might initially say, "I just can't stand it. I have to wash." The therapist might encourage him to say, "It's tough, but I can do it. I just need to hang in there" (Franklin et al., 2007).

The final component of CBT involves **generalization training and relapse prevention**. Parents play an important role in this part of treatment. The therapist teaches parents how to coach their children through the EX/RP tasks and asks parents and children to continue confronting feared stimuli outside the therapy setting. In the final sessions, the therapist, child, and parents discuss what to do in case symptoms return. Most therapists suggest viewing relapses as learning experiences, rather than as signs of failure. If relapses occur, the family can try using EX/RP techniques or they can call the therapist for additional training and support.

The efficacy of CBT for children and adolescents is supported by a number of uncontrolled studies (de Haan, Hoogduin, Buitelaar, & Keijsers, 1998; Franklin et al., 2007; March, 1998; March, Franklin, & Foa, 2005) and some randomized controlled trials (Pediatric OCD Treatment Study Team, 2004). These studies showed reductions in OCD symptoms ranging from 50% to 67% among children who participated in CBT. Furthermore, a few small-scale studies show that treatment gains are maintained at least nine months after therapy (Franklin, Kozak, Cashman, Coles, Rheingold, & Foa, 1998; March, Mulle, & Herbel, 1994). EX/RP seems to be the most important component of treatment (March et al., 2005). Relaxation training and cognitive interventions that are often part of OCD treatment packages may be useful, but they do not seem to be critical to treatment (March et al., 2005; van Oppen, de Haan, van Balkom, Spinhoven, Hoogduin, & van Dyck, 1995).

Pharmacotherapy for Child and Adolescent Anxiety

Exposure-based, psychosocial interventions are the first-line treatment for most pediatric anxiety disorders (Connolly & Bernstein, 2007). However, many children do not respond to exposure-based therapy, or symptom reduction may not occur fast enough to satisfy families. For these children, medication can sometimes be helpful (Stein & Seedat, 2004).

Social Phobia, GAD, and SAD

In several studies, researchers have investigated the efficacy of SSRIs in the treatment of pediatric Social Phobia, SAD, and GAD (Beidel et al., 2004). Trials of fluoxetine (Prozac), sertraline (Zoloft), fluvoxamine (Luvox), and paroxetine (Paxil) indicate that these medications are superior to placebo in treating anxiety problems, especially symptoms of Social Phobia. Across studies, 65% to 90% of youths prescribed these medications show at least moderate improvement (Birmaher et al., 2003; Compton, Grant, Chrisman, Gammon, Brown, & March, 2001; Pappadopulos, Guelzow, Wong, Ortega, & Jensen, 2004; Rynn, Siqueland, & Rickels, 2001; Vitiello, 2006; Wagner, Berard et al., 2004; Walkup et al., 2003).

On the other hand, studies investigating the efficacy of SSRIs have several limitations. First, most of the studies involved only a small number of youths. Second, most did not compare children who received medication to a placebo control group. Third, most of the children who received medication still showed significant anxiety symptoms after treatment. Consequently, SSRIs may be an important component of treatment for child and adolescent anxiety disorders, but they should not be used as a substitute for an exposure-based, psychosocial treatment.

OCD

Both tricyclic antidepressants and SSRIs have demonstrated efficacy in treating children and adolescents with OCD (Franklin et al., 2004). Randomized controlled studies indicate that the tricyclic antidepressant clomipramine (Anafranil; DeVeaugh-Geiss et al., 1992) and the SSRI fluoxetine (Geller et al., 2001; Riddle et al., 1992) reduce OCD symptoms better than placebo. Indeed, approximately 75% of youths with OCD taking these medications show significant improvement. Some evidence suggests the SSRIs fluvoxamine (Riddle et al., 2001) and sertraline (March et al., 1998) may also be efficacious.

In an important study, the Pediatric OCD Treatment Study Team (2004) examined the relative efficacy of medication and CBT for pediatric OCD (see Figure 13.6). Researchers studied 112 children and adolescents (aged 7–12 years) with OCD. Children and adolescents were assigned to one of four groups. The first group received CBT alone. The second group received sertraline, an SSRI. The third group received both CBT and medication. The fourth group received a placebo. Children participated in their respective treatments for 12 weeks.

Results showed the children who received combined CBT and medication showed greater symptom reduction than children who received either CBT or medication alone. Children who received either of the treatments alone showed approximately equal symptom reduction. Furthermore, youths who received either treatment alone showed greater symptom reduction than children who received a placebo. The researchers also examined the percentage of children who no longer showed significant OCD symptoms after treatment in each group. Results showed that 53.6% of children in the combined group, 38.3% in the CBT-only group, 21.4% in the medication-only group, and 3.6% in the placebo group showed significant symptom reduction. These results suggest that both CBT and medication are efficacious at reducing OCD symptoms in children and adolescents. Combining CBT with medication may be more effective than either treatment alone.

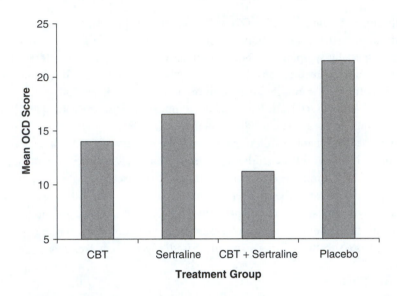

Figure 13.6   Results of the Pediatric OCD Treatment Study

Source: Based on Pediatric OCD Treatment Study Team (2004).

Note: After treatment, youths with OCD who participated in either CBT or pharmacotherapy showed greater improvement than youths who received a placebo. However, combining CBT with medication was associated with greater symptom reduction than either therapy or medication alone.

Other Anxiety Disorders

Few randomized, controlled studies have investigated the efficacy of medication for other pediatric anxiety disorders. SSRIs have been effectively used to treat Specific Phobias, PTSD, and Panic Disorder in children and adolescents. However, studies have tended to rely on small sample sizes and have lacked control groups for comparison. Most experts do not consider medication to be a first-line treatment for these disorders, although they might be helpful as an adjunct to cognitive and behavioral treatments (Birmaher & Ollendick, 2004; N. J. King et al., 2004; J. A. Cohen & Mannarino, 2004; Silverman & Carmichael, 1999).

Update: Tammie

Tammie, the 12-year-old girl who experienced problems falling asleep at night, displayed many symptoms of GAD. Her problems falling asleep seemed connected to her persistent worries about school, sports, and friends. Furthermore, these worries caused her to feel restless and "edgy," interfered with her sleep and caused fatigue, and produced feelings of agitation and tension.

Dr. Baldwin suggested that Tammie participate in cognitive-behavioral group therapy for older children and adolescents with anxiety problems. In the group sessions, Tammie learned to recognize the connection between her patterns of thinking (i.e., worry) and her feelings (i.e., tension, anxiety). Then, she learned how to look at her worries more critically and realistically. For example, when she worried about failing an upcoming test, she learned to ask herself, "What's the chance that I'll actually fail? Isn't it more likely that I'll do OK since I studied hard and have always done fine in the class?" Challenging unrealistic worries helped Tammie gain some control over them.

Tammie also found that she could manage her nighttime worries by writing them down during the day. With the help of her therapist, Tammie kept a list of all the things she worried about. When she began worrying at night, she told herself, "It's OK. I don't need to worry about this now. I have it on my list so that I can think about it tomorrow." Her list seemed to give her permission to worry at appropriate times during the day.

Dr. Baldwin met with Tammie's parents on several occasions to give them information about GAD in children. He encouraged them to be sensitive to Tammie's anxiety and to be ready to listen when she wants to talk about her worries. After approximately 20 weeks of group and individual/family therapy, Tammie was better able to manage her worrying and her sleep improved greatly. "I'm still a worry-wart," Tammie said, "but now I can control myself better than before." As a reward, Tammie and her mother had their nails professionally manicured.

Critical Thinking Exercises

1. Many children fear snakes, although relatively few children have ever been bitten by snakes. If a child has *never* been attacked by a snake, how can she develop snake phobia?

2. Some people believe that children with Social Phobia are simply "extremely shy." How is Social Phobia different from shyness?

3. After the 9/11 terrorist attacks, many children were exposed to traumatic images of violence. However, not all children developed PTSD. Why not?

4. Mallorie is a 16-year-old girl who experienced two panic attacks while at school. Since that time, she has been reluctant to go to school. How might learning theory be used to explain Mallorie's school refusal?

5. What is the evidence that serotonin plays a role in child and adolescent OCD?

6. Christian is a 14-year-old boy with GAD. During an important basketball game, Christian mistakenly passed the ball to an opponent and his team lost the game. After the game, Christian thought, "How could I have been so incredibly stupid? The coach is never going to let me play again! I single-handedly ruined the game." Explain how Christian's thoughts about the event contribute to his negative feelings.

7. How is exposure used to treat most child and adolescent anxiety disorders?

CHAPTER 14

Eating Disorders in Adolescents

Julie

Julie was a 15-year-old girl who was referred to the hospital because of malnourishment and dehydration. Although Julie was 5'5" tall, she weighed only 87 lbs. Her skin had a dry, yellow appearance and her clothes, which were stylish, hung from the frame of her body. Dr. Matyas escorted Julie and her mother to an examination room.

"We were brought to the hospital because Julie passed out after gym class at school," her mother explained. Julie interrupted her mother harshly, "It was nothing. I just felt lightheaded." Her mother interjected, almost in tears, "I'm very worried about her. She doesn't listen to me. She's irritable all the time." Dr. Matyas asked, "Julie, what did you eat for breakfast and lunch today?" Julie replied, "A hard-boiled egg for breakfast . . . and I think that I had some yogurt at lunch."

Dr. Matyas noticed Julie's emaciated body. Her ribs and pelvic bones were clearly visible, extruding from her skin. Her hair was dry and brittle. On her face and arms, Julie had soft, downy hair to protect her from the cold. Dr. Matyas listened to Julie's heart and asked, "Do you have regular periods?" Julie responded, "Yes . . . well I used to, but now I don't."

"Julie," said Dr. Matyas, "do you know that you're underweight?" Julie snapped, "If I was on television or in the movies, I'd be perfectly normal. It's just because I'm in high school that everybody thinks I'm too thin." Dr. Matyas handed Julie her pen. Pointing to the exam table, she said, "I want you to imagine that you're sitting up there. I want you to use my pen to mark the width of your thighs on the exam table." With a sigh, Julie grabbed the pen and made two marks on the butcher-block paper spread out on the examination table. The distance was almost four feet.

What Are Adolescent Eating Disorders?

Anorexia Nervosa

Individuals with Anorexia Nervosa (AN) show four essential features (see Table 14.1). First, people with AN refuse to maintain normal body weight. In general, abnormally low body weight is body weight less than 85% of what might be expected based on the individual's age and height. For example, the average American 16-year-old girl stands approximately 5' 3" tall and weighs approximately 118 lbs. A 16-year-old girl of average height who weighed less than 100 lbs. would be below the 85th percentile (National Center for Health Statistics, 2006). Indeed, only about 10% of 16-year-old girls in the United States weigh 100 lbs. or less. For younger adolescents, failure to make age-appropriate weight gains might indicate abnormally low weight.

Second, individuals with AN show excessive concern over their body shape and weight. Almost all adolescents with AN report that they are afraid of becoming fat. However, it might be more precise to say that they have an intense fear of gaining any weight whatsoever. The self-esteem of these adolescents is closely connected to their abilities to control their weight, appear attractive, and gain the approval and acknowledgment of others. Failure to control weight is seen as a sign of personal weakness and a risk to self-esteem. An adolescent with AN who gains even one pound might see herself on the path to obesity, peer rejection, and worthlessness.

Third, individuals with AN usually deny the seriousness of their low body weight. AN tends to be **ego-syntonic**; that is, people with the disorder usually do not think that their eating is problematic (Stice, Wonderlich, & Wade, 2006).

Table 14.1   Diagnostic Criteria for Anorexia Nervosa

A. Refusal to maintain body weight at or above a minimally normal weight for age and height (e.g., weight loss leading to maintenance of body weight less than 85% of that expected, or failure to make expected weight gain during period of growth, leading to body weight less than 85% of that expected)

B Intense fear of gaining weight or being fat, even though underweight

C. Disturbance in the way in which one's body weight or shape is experienced, undue influence of body weight or shape on self-evaluation, or denial of the seriousness of the current low body weight

D. In postmenarcheal females, amenorrhea, i.e., the absence of at least three consecutive menstrual cycles

E. Specify type:
   1. Restricting Type: During the current episode of Anorexia Nervosa, the person has not regularly engaged in binge eating or purging behavior (i.e., self-induced vomiting or the misuse of laxatives, diuretics, or enemas)
   2. Binge-Eating/Purging Type: During the current episode of Anorexia Nervosa, the person has regularly engaged in binge eating or purging behavior (i.e., self-induced vomiting or the misuse of laxatives, diuretics, or enemas)

Source: Reprinted with permission from the *DSM-IV-TR*.

Instead, most adolescents with AN take pride in their ability to restrict their diet and avoid weight gain. They often derive a certain degree of pleasure from resisting the temptation to eat even though they are severely malnourished. Resisting the temptation to eat is seen as a sign of control; dieting is regarded as a personal accomplishment. Severe dieting is doubly reinforced when other people, like parents or friends, comment on their will power or slim figure. Since their self-esteem is dependent on their ability to avoid weight gain, they are usually resistant to treatment. Treatment, which would involve eating and gaining weight, would represent a loss of control and a reduction in self-worth.

Fourth, by definition, older adolescent girls and women with AN show **amenorrhea**, that is, they have missed at least three consecutive menstrual cycles. Amenorrhea is usually caused by low body fat, a consequence of starvation.

Bulimia Nervosa

The essential feature of Bulimia Nervosa (BN) is recurrent binge eating (see Table 14.2). **Binge eating** occurs when a person (1) consumes an unusually large amount of food in a discrete period of time (e.g., within two hours), and (2) he or she feels out of control while eating. During binge episodes, some people with BN consume 1,000 to 2,000 calories, roughly one-half to one full day's caloric requirements. Most individuals with BN prefer foods that are high in sugar and fat like breads, cakes, ice cream, and other desserts (Stice et al., 2006).

Table 14.2   Diagnostic Criteria for Bulimia Nervosa

A. Recurrent episodes of binge eating. An episode of binge eating is characterized by both of the following:

   1. Eating, in a discrete period of time (e.g., within any 2-hour period), an amount of food that is definitely larger than most people would eat during a similar period of time and under similar circumstances

   2. A sense of lack of control over eating during the episode (e.g., a feeling that one cannot stop eating or control what or how much one is eating)

B. Recurrent inappropriate compensatory behavior in order to prevent weight gain, such as self-induced vomiting; misuse of laxatives, diuretics, enemas, or other medications; fasting; or excessive exercise

C. The binge eating and inappropriate compensatory behaviors both occur, on average, at least twice a week for 3 months

D. Self-evaluation is unduly influenced by body shape and weight

E. The disturbance does not occur exclusively during episodes of Anorexia Nervosa.

F. Specify type:

   1. Purging Type: During the current episode of Bulimia Nervosa, the person has regularly engaged in self-induced vomiting or the misuse of laxatives, diuretics, or enemas

   2. Nonpurging Type: During the current episode of Bulimia Nervosa, the person has used other inappropriate compensatory behaviors, such as fasting or excessive exercise, but has not regularly engaged in self-induced vomiting or the misuse of laxatives, diuretics, or enemas

Source: Reprinted with permission from the *DSM-IV-TR*.

By definition, people with BN also engage in some form of **inappropriate compensatory behavior** to prevent weight gain. Most people with BN purge; that is, they induce vomiting or misuse laxatives, diuretics, or enemas to avoid caloric absorption. Some individuals with BN do not purge. Instead, they avoid weight gain primarily through excessive fasting or exercise. For example, an adolescent who consumes 1,200 calories during a midnight binge might decide to "make up for it" by fasting the next day or running an extra four miles. Individuals with BN binge and use compensatory means of weight control regularly, at least twice each week. In extreme cases, individuals binge and show compensatory behaviors multiple times each day.

Like individuals with AN, people with BN show unusual preoccupation with body shape and weight. Indeed, the self-esteem and mood of individuals with BN is closely connected to their subjective impressions of their appearance. In contrast to AN, BN is usually an **ego-dystonic** disorder (Stice et al., 2006). Individuals with bulimia usually regard their eating behavior as problematic. Indeed, people with BN often binge in private because bingeing produces guilt and shame. Adolescents will often go to great lengths to hide their bingeing and purging from family members, sometimes for months or years. Adolescents with bulimia usually seek treatment for their disorder only after they feel that they can no longer keep their eating habits a secret from loved ones or when they feel a complete lack of control over their behavior.

Distinguishing Anorexia Nervosa From Bulimia Nervosa

Many people believe that AN is defined by excessive dieting while BN is defined by bingeing and purging. In fact, neither disorder is defined in this way. Individuals with AN are classified into two subtypes, based on their symptom presentation. Individuals with **AN-Restricting Type** maintain their low body weight through caloric restriction, that is, through extreme dieting. In contrast, individuals with **AN-Binge Eating/Purging Type** maintain low body weight primarily through binge eating and purging.

Similarly, individuals with BN are classified into two subtypes, based on their symptom presentation. People with **BN-Purging Type** regularly induce vomiting or misuse laxatives, diuretics, or enemas to avoid weight gain. In contrast, people with **BN-Nonpurging Type** use other compensatory behaviors, such as excessive fasting or exercise, to avoid weight gain.

The difference between AN and BN is *not* based on whether the person fasts or purges. In fact, some people with AN binge and purge while some people with BN seldom purge at all.

AN and BN can be differentiated in three ways. First, all individuals with AN show unusually low body weight. In contrast, low body weight is not required for the diagnosis of BN. In fact, most individuals with BN have weight within the normal range, and some people with BN are overweight. Second, all postmenarcheal females with AN show amenorrhea. In contrast, females with BN usually do not show amenorrhea. Third, all individuals with BN show recurrent binge eating. In contrast, not all people with AN binge.

Problems Diagnosing Adolescents

Most experts use *DSM-IV-TR* criteria when studying and treating adolescents with eating disorders. However, the diagnostic criteria are somewhat problematic when they are applied to adolescents. First, most adolescents who have eating disorder symptoms do not actually meet diagnostic criteria for either AN or BN (Clinton & Norring, 2005). Most adolescents have subthreshold symptoms of one or the other disorder. For example, some adolescents show serious malnourishment but have not yet missed three consecutive menstrual periods to warrant the diagnosis of AN. Similarly, many adolescents engage in occasional bingeing and purging, but the frequency of these behaviors does not meet criteria for BN. Adolescents with subthreshold symptoms are frequently diagnosed with **Eating Disorder-Not Otherwise Specified (EDNOS)**. In two recent studies, more than 50% of adolescents with serious eating disorder symptoms were classified with EDNOS rather than with AN or BN (Fairburn & Harrison, 2003; Turner & Bryant-Waugh, 2004).

A second problem with the diagnostic criteria for AN is that establishing amenorrhea in adolescent girls is sometimes difficult. Many healthy adolescent girls do not have regular menstrual cycles, especially in early adolescence. The absence of regular cycles may not necessary be attributable to an eating disorder. Furthermore, adolescents often inaccurately report their menstrual history. It is often difficult for clinicians to gather reliable data regarding adolescents' cycles. Finally, there are no data to show that the presence of amenorrhea is important to the diagnosis of AN. For example, girls who meet all diagnostic criteria for AN except amenorrhea have prognoses similar to those of girls who meet full diagnostic criteria for AN (Evans et al., 2005).

A third problem with the diagnostic criteria concerns the definition of "binge eating" in BN. Experts do not know how much food actually constitutes a "binge." *DSM-IV-TR* provides some guidance: "an amount of food that is definitely larger than most people would eat during a similar period of time and under similar circumstances." However, two people's conceptualizations of a "large" amount of food might differ. A related problem with this definition is that many people with bulimia do not consume an extremely large amount of food when they binge. In one study, approximately one-third of patients with BN consumed fewer than 600 calories per binge, which is approximately one-third of their daily dietary requirement. Most experts believe that the subjective experience of feeling out of control over one's eating is more important to the diagnosis and treatment of BN than exactly how much a person eats during each binge episode. Consequently, some experts use the term **subjective binge** to describe the feeling of being out of control while eating, even if the number of calories consumed is relatively small (Wilson, Becker, & Heffernan, 2003).

Associated Features and Problems

Psychiatric Disorders

Approximately 80% of adolescents with AN or BN meet diagnostic criteria for at least one other disorder. The most common comorbid problems are depression, anxiety, and substance use problems (Evans et al., 2005).

Depression and Suicide

The most common comorbid psychiatric condition among adolescents with eating disorders is MDD (Lucka, 2006). The lifetime prevalence of MDD for individuals with AN or BN is approximately 50%–60%. The prevalence of depression among adolescents with eating disorders is much higher than in the general adolescent population. However, the prevalence of depression among adolescents with eating disorders is similar to rates of depression among other clinic-referred children without eating problems (McDermott, Forbes, Harris, McCormack, & Gibbon, 2006).

Depression seems to emerge after the onset of the eating disorder and often persists after treatment of the eating problem. In one study, nearly 70% of individuals who previously suffered from AN subsequently developed depression (Halmi, Eckert, Marchi, Sampagnaro, Apple, & Cohen, 1991). Depression, therefore, is often a consequence of AN and BN, not a primary cause of these conditions.

Individuals with eating disorders are also at risk for suicide. Overall, approximately 25% of individuals with eating disorders have attempted suicide. Attempts are most common among individuals who purge, as opposed to those people who use dietary restriction or exercise to control their weight (see Figure 14.1). Rates of suicide completion are especially high among people with AN. Approximately 5% of individuals with AN commit suicide every decade that they live with the disorder. Indeed, malnourishment and suicide are the two leading causes of death associated with AN (Milos et al., 2004; Youssef, Plancherel, Laget, Corcos, Flament, & Halfon, 2004).

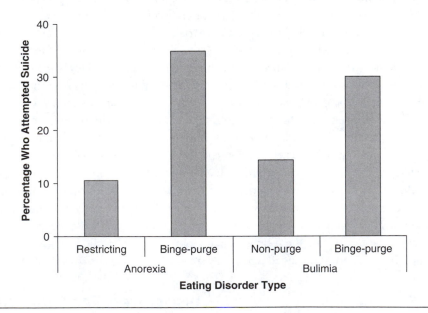

Figure 14.1 Suicide Attempts Among Individuals With Eating Disorders

Source: Based on Milos, Spindler, Hepp, and Schnyder (2004).

Note: Suicide attempts are more common among people who binge and purge, regardless of whether they have AN or BN. Impulsivity might underlie the tendency to binge-purge and attempt self-harm.

Anxiety Disorders

The two most common anxiety disorders seen among adolescents with AN are Social Phobia and OCD (Wilson et al., 2003). Social Phobia affects 30%–50% of females with eating disorders. Social Phobia usually predates the emergence of AN and BN and persists after treatment. Many adolescent girls and women with eating disorders are extremely sensitive to criticism by others and have histories of avoiding situations in which they might be negatively evaluated by others. These individuals also frequently show a high need for approval by peers. Some may use dietary restriction and/or purging to assume physical appearances that meet the approval of others and enhance their social standing. Over time, these behaviors can lead to AN or BN (Atlas, 2004).

Approximately 30%–40% of people with eating disorders show OCD. Most research indicates that perfectionism and OCD symptoms often precede the development of eating problems. Females with eating disorders often have longstanding problems with rigid, obsessive thinking. It is possible that rigid cognitive style places these individuals at risk for eating problems (Halmi et al., 2005).

Common genetic or environmental factors might partially account for the co-occurrence of eating disorders and anxiety disorders. Keel, Klump, Miller, McGue, and Iacono (2005) examined 14 monozygotic twins, aged 16–18 years, discordant for eating disorders; one of the twins had an eating disorder while the other twin did not. Then the researchers examined the prevalence of anxiety disorders among the twins who did not have an eating disorder. They found that these discordant twins were twice as likely to have an anxiety disorder as individuals in the general population. These findings suggest that common factors underlie both eating and anxiety disorders. However, we do not know whether these factors are predominantly genetic, environmental, or (most likely) a combination of the two.

Substance Use Disorders

Substance Abuse and Dependence frequently occurs with eating disorders. The most frequently abused substances among individuals with AN or BN are nicotine, alcohol, marijuana, and cocaine. Overall, 20% to 25% of individuals with eating disorders show comorbid substance use disorders (Evans et al., 2005).

The prevalence of substance use disorders varies, depending on the subtype of eating disorder. Specifically, individuals who frequently engage in binge eating (i.e., AN-Bingeing Type, BN) are three times more likely to show comorbid substance use problems than individuals with eating disorders who do not binge (i.e., AN-Restricting Type). Experts believe that underlying problems with impulsivity account for both the tendency to binge and the tendency to misuse alcohol and other drugs (Bulik et al., 2004). In most cases, Substance Abuse and Dependence emerges during or after the onset of the eating disorder. Consequently, many individuals with eating disorders seem to use alcohol and other drugs to reduce symptoms of anxiety (Bulik et al., 2004).

Personality

A central personality characteristic of AN is perfectionism. More than 30 years ago, Hilde Bruch (1973) described adolescents with AN as excessively compliant, eager to please, and lacking an autonomous sense of self. Subsequent research on adolescents with AN has generally confirmed Bruch's impressions. Even before they meet diagnostic criteria for AN, these adolescents are usually described as perfectionist, driven, and goal-oriented. They are often over-achievers, popular, and academically successful. They tend to be very conscientious about their appearance and the way they present themselves to others. They are often reluctant to take risks because they do not want to make mistakes or lose the approval of family or peers.

A second, related personality characteristic of adolescents with AN is rigidity and over-control (Tozzi et al., 2005). Adolescents with AN often show rigidity in their actions, feelings, and thoughts. With respect to actions, many of these individuals say that they need to have things "their way" in order to feel comfortable. They may become upset when they lack control over situations. Other people describe adolescents with AN as "obsessive" or excessively organized. With respect to their feelings, adolescents with AN are often guarded and emotionally reserved. They are especially reluctant to express sadness, frustration, and anger directly, preferring to keep these feelings hidden or to deny them altogether (Fairburn, Cooper, Doll, & Welch, 1999). Finally, adolescents with AN often show rigidity in their thoughts. Many show **black-or-white thinking**; that is, they view themselves and others as either "good" or "bad." This type of dichotomous thinking causes them to see the world in harsh, concrete, and simplistic ways. For example, if they gain one pound, they might regard themselves as "worthless" or "a complete failure."

Adolescents with BN show many of the same personality features as adolescents with AN (Tozzi et al., 2005). Perhaps the most salient characteristic of adolescents with BN is their tendency toward perfectionism and their generally low self-evaluation. In contrast to adolescents with AN, adolescents with BN tend to be more emotionally labile and impulsive. Adolescents with BN often show problems with temper and acting out. Some engage in self-harm or misuse alcohol and other drugs. Many youths with BN show chronic problems with emotion regulation.

Associated Problems

Health Problems

Eating disorders can cause serious health problems. A frequent and serious medical complication associated with eating disorders is **electrolyte imbalance** (Evans et al., 2005). Electrolytes are minerals found in the body; they include calcium, sodium, and potassium. These minerals help maintain proper fluid levels throughout the body. They also regulate important metabolic functions, such as heart rate and brain activity. Activities that cause the body to lose excessive amounts of water (e.g., vomiting, excessive use of diuretics or laxatives) can lead to electrolyte imbalance.

Electrolyte imbalance can cause cardiac arrhythmias (i.e., irregular heart rate) and death. A serious condition called **hypokalemia**, caused by low potassium levels, can be fatal. People with AN are especially vulnerable to cardiac arrhythmias when they attempt to gain weight during treatment. In fact, physicians use the term **refeeding syndrome** to describe the cardiac and other health-related problems shown by patients with AN during the first 7 to 10 days of treatment. Because of the danger of arrhythmia, refeeding is conducted slowly and under close medical supervision.

Another serious medical complication associated with AN is **osteopenia**, that is, reduced bone mass. In healthy girls, bone density increases during childhood and early adolescence. Approximately 60% of a girl's bone density is acquired during her early adolescent years. However, AN interferes with this increase in bone density. The combination of poor nutrition, decreased estrogen levels caused by amenorrhea, and excessive exercise can lead to significantly lower bone density. Bone density loss is greatest in the spine and hips. Approximately 90% of adolescents and young adults with AN show osteopenia, placing them at risk for osteoporosis and hip fractures later in life. Bone loss may be irreversible.

Other medical complications associated with AN seem to be temporary. AN seems to disrupt hormone and endocrine functioning, which can lead to disturbances in appetite, physical growth, heart rate, and temperature regulation. Lack of body fat sometimes causes the development of fine downy hair (i.e., lanugo) on the trunk, limbs, and face. These soft hairs help conserve body temperature. Hair can become brittle and skin may adopt a yellow color. Malnutrition associated with AN also seems to cause problems with concentration, memory, and problem solving.

Medical complications associated with BN are largely due to bingeing and purging. As mentioned above, hypokalemia is the most serious medical risk factor associated with BN. Frequent vomiting can cause enlargement of the salivary glands, erosion of dental enamel, and damage to the esophagus. Some individuals who use their fingers to induce vomiting show temporary scarring of the skin tissue up to the second or third knuckle. Frequent laxative use can contribute to gastrointestinal problems, especially constipation.

Family Relationships

Research has consistently shown problems in the family functioning of girls with eating disorders. Adolescents with AN often come from highly rigid, overprotective homes. The parents of adolescents with AN typically adopt authoritarian child-rearing strategies: They place high demands on their children's behavior, but they show limited responsiveness to their children's needs. Parents usually assume considerable control over their children's lives and do not allow their adolescents to take much part in decision making.

Adolescents with BN also tend to come from homes that place a premium on obedience and achievement. However, their homes are usually chaotic and stress-filled. These adolescents often report a high degree of family conflict and, sometimes, domestic violence. Adolescents with BN tend to have higher rates of insecure attachment compared to adolescent without eating problems.

Diet, weight, and body shape are given considerable attention in the families of girls with eating disorders (Smolak, 2006). Girls with AN often report that their parents frequently dieted in order to lose weight and made periodic comments about their weight and physical appearance. Indeed, some of these girls reported a history of eating disorders within the immediate family. In contrast, the family members of girls with BN are sometimes obese or overweight. These girls often report considerable tension during mealtime; parents encouraging them to lose weight; or family members teasing them about their weight, shape, or appearance.

Parents' comments about weight and body shape are associated with adolescents' body satisfaction, self-esteem, and eating habits (Field, Camargo, Taylor, Berkey, Robert, & Colditz, 2001; Smolak, Levine, & Schermer, 1999). For example, the frequency of parents' comments about their daughters' body shape and weight is associated with body dissatisfaction in elementary school girls (Smolak, 2006). In one study, 23% of middle school girls said that at least one parent teased them about their appearance (Keery, Boutelle, van den Berg, & Thompson, 2005). Teasing by fathers was associated with body dissatisfaction, dietary restriction, and symptoms of bulimia. Teasing by mothers was associated with depression. Even mothers' comments about *their own* weight were associated with their daughters' body dissatisfaction (Tiggeman & Lynch, 2001). Although these associations do not necessarily mean that parental comments cause girls to feel poorly about their appearance, they suggest that parents' comments about shape and weight are connected with their daughters' feelings about their own bodies.

School and Sports

Adolescents with eating disorders are often overachievers and perfectionists when it comes to school and sports. These adolescents often derive self-esteem from their accomplishments, especially the praise and recognition of others. They tend to earn high grades, excel in sports, and assume leadership roles in extracurricular activities (Fairburn & Harrison, 2003).

On the other hand, adolescents with eating disorders are often unwilling to take risks because they fear that they will fail and lose the approval of others. Because their self-worth is so heavily dependent on their accomplishments, they do not tolerate failure. They often appear driven, perfectionistic, and obsessed about school work, sports, and other extracurricular activities. They may see setbacks in school and extracurricular activities as indicators of personal weakness and worthlessness.

Adolescents experiencing severe malnourishment because of AN usually show some problems in academic and social functioning. Malnourishment leads to fatigue, irritability, and concentration problems that interfere with girls' abilities to perform academically and socially. Adolescents with advanced BN also tend to show academic problems. BN often leads to mood and substance use problems that affect adolescents' school performance (Stice et al., 2006).

Epidemiology

Prevalence

It has been difficult to estimate the prevalence of eating disorders among adolescents, for two reasons. First, most people with eating disorders, especially adolescents, are reluctant to admit their symptoms. Consequently, surveys, even those conducted anonymously, may underestimate prevalence. Second, eating disorders are relatively rare, especially among adolescents. Therefore, researchers need to gather data from large numbers of people in order to obtain a precise estimate of the prevalence of AN and BN. To date, there has been only one study that examined the prevalence of eating disorders using a nationally representative sample of U.S. citizens, and this study was conducted 25 years ago (Evans et al., 2005).

Despite these limitations, researchers have been able to obtain rough estimates for the lifetime prevalence of eating disorders in the United States (Stice et al., 2006). The lifetime prevalence of AN is between 0.5% and 1% for females and less than 0.3% for males. The lifetime prevalence of BN is between 1.5% and 4% in females and less than 0.5% in males. The prevalence of AN and BN among adolescent girls is slightly lower than the prevalence for women (Wilson et al., 2003).

Available data probably underestimate the prevalence of eating problems among adolescents because most adolescents do not meet full diagnostic criteria for either AN or BN. Available data indicate that an additional 1% to 2% of adolescent girls show subthreshold levels of AN, while an additional 2% to 3% of adolescent girls show subthreshold symptoms of BN (Evans et al., 2005). Although full-blown eating disorders are relatively rare among adolescents, subthreshold eating problems (i.e., EDNOS) are more common (see Figure 14.2).

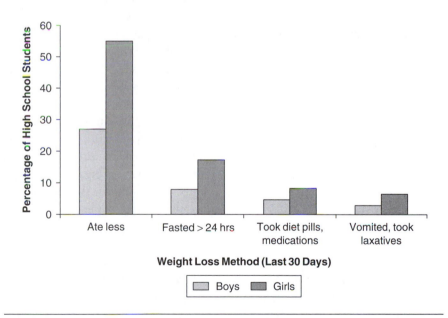

Figure 14.2   Maladaptive Weight Loss Methods Used by High School Students in the Last 30 Days

Source: Based on the Youth Risk Behavior Surveillance System (Centers for Disease Control, 2007).

Note: Data are based on a sample of approximately 14,000 adolescents in ninth through twelfth grades. Although most youth do not have eating disorders, many (especially girls) use risky methods to lose weight.

Eating Problems in Boys

The prevalence of eating disorders differs by gender. Adolescent girls are 10 to 15 times more likely than adolescent boys to develop eating disorders. The prevalence of AN among adolescent boys and young men is less than 0.16%. The prevalence of BN among boys and young men is less than 0.7%. Some researchers indicate that as many as 1% of adolescent boys and young men may have subthreshold eating problems.

Instead of AN and BN, some adolescent boys are at risk for eating problems caused by a desire to *gain* weight, body mass, and muscle. Many boys attempt to gain body mass and muscle in appropriate ways, such as by eating healthy foods and exercising. However, some boys rely on risky strategies such as overeating, excessive exercise, or use of dietary supplements. One-fourth to one-half of adolescent boys admit to using dietary supplements (e.g., protein shakes, creatine, ephedrine) to increase mass. Between 3% and 12% have used anabolic steroids to build muscle. Approximately 5% of adolescent boys exercise more than seven times each week, exercise despite pain and injury, and experience guilt or depression on days they are unable to exercise (McCabe & Ricciardelli, 2001).

Culture and Ethnicity

Eating Disorders Across Countries

For years, experts believed that eating disorders were only found in Western, industrialized countries, predominantly in high socioeconomic groups. Today, researchers have found eating disorders across all cultures and socioeconomic strata that have been studied (Polivy, Herman, Mills, & Wheeler, 2003).

AN and BN appear to be universal phenomena, existing across countries and cultures. For example, eating disorders have been identified in Asia, Africa, the Middle East, the Caribbean, the Pacific Islands, and Eastern Europe, in addition to Western Europe and the United States. However, eating disorders are more prevalent among Western societies and industrialized nations than non-Western and pre-industrialized countries. For example, the prevalence of eating disorders in Eastern Europe, Japan, Singapore, South Africa, and Israel is generally equivalent to the prevalence of these disorders in the United States. In non-Western and pre-industrialized countries like Nigeria and Belize, prevalence is lower (Anderson-Frye & Becker, 2004).

Considerable evidence indicates that globalization has spread eating disorders from industrialized counties to developing nations. For example, eating disorders were largely unknown in the island of Fiji in the south Pacific a generation ago. However, the prevalence of eating disorders rose dramatically after Western culture was introduced to the island by television and other media. Similarly, adolescents who immigrate to the United States from developing countries initially show low rates of eating disorders. However, after years of living in the United States, their likelihood of eating disorders increases dramatically (Anderson-Frye & Becker, 2004; Polivy et al., 2003).

> ## Grace
>
> Grace was a 16-year-old girl who immigrated to the United States with her parents from the African nation of Rwanda following the 1994 genocide that occurred in that country. Although Grace's family was a member of the majority Hutus, her father aided and protected members of the minority Tutsis who were slaughtered by extremist Hutu militia. Fearing retribution, the family fled the country and eventually sought asylum in the United States.
>
> In Africa, Grace was viewed as an intelligent and beautiful girl. In the United States, however, she had difficulty gaining acceptance from her peers because of her appearance. By Western standards, Grace was short and slightly overweight. She was unaccustomed to being teased by other girls at school and ostracized by classmates. Within six months of enrolling in high school, Grace developed symptoms of bulimia. She began to binge and purge multiple times each week.

Experts disagree as to how Western culture or industrialization might contribute to an increase in eating disorders. One popular explanation is that girls and women in non-Western and developing cultures compare themselves to the images of models and actresses portrayed in Western magazines and television. These comparisons cause girls in non-Western and developing countries to become dissatisfied with their bodies, to diet, and to engage in unsafe practices to lose weight (Thompson & Heinberg, 1993).

An alternative hypothesis is that girls and women notice a relationship between the physical attractiveness of Western models and other indicators of wealth, social status, and happiness. In order to enhance their social status, they attempt to emulate these models and actresses by losing weight. For example, shortly after the introduction of Western media in Fiji, many girls expressed a desire to lose weight. They reasoned that if they were more attractive, like the models and actresses on television, they might be able to lead more successful lives (Becker, Burwell, Gilman, Herzog, & Hamburg, 2002). In other developing countries, girls and women most at risk for eating disorders tend to come from upwardly mobile families. For example, in Curacao and Belize, girls and women who had aspirations of achieving wealth and social status, or who had economic ties to Western culture through tourism, showed rates of eating disorders similar to those of females in the United States. Upwardly mobile black females living in South Africa show greater prevalence of eating disorders than their white South African counterparts. For some girls and women, AN and BN may reflect a maladaptive attempt to emulate Western culture in order to share in its social and economic prosperity (Anderson-Frye & Becker, 2004).

Eating Disorders in the United States

Some experts have suggested that ethnic minorities in the United States are less likely to develop eating disorders than white adolescents. These experts argue that because ethnic minority adolescents come from subcultures that place less emphasis on slenderness, they may be less likely to diet and engage in problematic eating (Striegel-Moore, Silberstein, & Rodin, 1986). In fact, Latina and African American adolescent girls tend to be more tolerant than white adolescent girls of a heavier and more curvaceous body shape. Furthermore, Latina and African American girls are often less concerned about weight gain than their white counterparts (McKnight Risk Factor Study, 2003).

However, eating disorders exist across all ethnic groups in the United States, and the culturally specific preferences regarding weight and shape may not protect minority girls from developing eating disorders. Native American adolescents appear to have the highest rates of eating disorders among all ethnic groups in the United States (including whites), while Asian Americans appear to have the lowest rates. Most data indicate that the prevalence of eating disorders among Latina adolescents is comparable to the prevalence among whites.

Data regarding African American girls are mixed; prevalence for African American youth varies depending on the type of eating disorder. Most studies show lower rates of AN among African American adolescents than white adolescents. However, most studies have found no differences in BN between African American and white adolescents (Anderson-Frye & Becker, 2004; Polivy et al., 2003).

Shaw and colleagues (2004) surveyed a large group of adolescent girls and young women to assess behaviors indicative of eating pathology and cognitions that might place them at risk for developing eating disorders. Behavioral indicators of eating problems included amenorrhea, low body mass, bingeing, purging, and fear of gaining weight. Risk factors for eating problems included a history of dieting, anxiety, depression, and a strong desire to be thin. The researchers were especially interested in whether participants' behaviors and risk factors varied as a function of ethnicity. The researchers found almost no differences across four ethnic groups: Asian Americans, African Americans, Latinos, and whites. They concluded that eating pathology is more similar across ethnic groups than previously thought.

Course

AN and BN usually begin during adolescence. Early research indicated a bimodal age of onset for AN; some adolescents develop AN shortly after puberty, whereas other adolescents develop the disorder around age 18 years. More recent longitudinal research indicates that the peak age of onset for AN is between 16 and 19 years (Lewinsohn, Striegel-Moore, & Seeley, 2000; Evans et al., 2005). BN usually emerges at a somewhat later age than AN. The peak age of onset for BN is usually between 18 and 20 years. Although eating disorders can emerge at any age, they are extremely rare among prepubescent children and they usually do not emerge after age 25 years.

The reasons for adolescents' maladaptive eating behaviors vary with age (Evans et al., 2005). Some young adolescents with eating disorders, especially AN, report a fear of physical maturation. Some researchers have speculated that these young adolescents avoid weight gain in order to delay the onset of puberty and retain a childlike appearance and social status. In contrast, older adolescents and adults with eating disorders usually report fear of weight gain or becoming overweight.

The course of AN is variable. Approximately 50% of individuals with AN recover from the disorder, 30% improve but continue to meet diagnostic criteria for either AN or BN, and 10%–20% have chronic symptoms of AN. Individuals with chronic symptoms are most at risk for death, either from malnourishment or suicide. Adolescents with AN who receive treatment shortly after symptom onset have the best chance of recovery (Evans et al., 2005; Wilson et al., 2003).

The prognosis of BN is somewhat better than for AN. In one large study of individuals previously diagnosed with BN, 15% continued to meet diagnostic criteria for the disorder five years later. Unfortunately, 36% of patients continued to show subthreshold eating problems while 41% met diagnostic criteria for MDD, instead. While the chance of recovery is greater for BN than AN, the majority of people diagnosed with either eating disorder continue to show psychiatric problems years later. The mortality rate for BN is approximately 0.5% (Fairburn, Cooper, Doll, Norman, & O'Connor, 2000).

A significant percentage of adolescents with eating problems change diagnostic classification over time, a phenomenon called **diagnostic migration**. For example, individuals might initially meet diagnostic criteria for AN-Restricting Type and later be diagnosed with AN-Binge Eating/Purging Type or BN. In one large study, 36% of patients with AN-Restricting Type later showed BN. Furthermore, 27% of patients with BN later developed AN (Tozzi et al., 2005). Diagnostic migration is especially common among adolescents with eating disorders, and it usually occurs within five years after the initial diagnosis.

Etiology

Genetics

Genes likely play a role in the development of eating disorders (Bulik, 2004). Behavioral geneticists have determined that eating disorders run in families. Females who have a first-degree relative with an eating disorder are 4 to 11 times more likely to develop an eating disorder themselves compared to females with no family history of eating problems (Strober, Freeman, Lampert, Diamond, & Kaye, 2000). This increased genetic risk for eating disorders is not specific to AN or BN. Instead, a family member with BN places other biological relatives at risk for *all* eating disorders, not BN per se. Genes probably predispose individuals to general eating pathology.

Behavioral geneticists have also tried to determine how much of the variance of eating disorders can be explained by genetic versus environmental factors. Twin studies indicate that the heritability of AN is between 48% and 74%, depending on the sample and the definition of AN that the researchers use (Bulik, 2004). Twin studies indicate that the heritability of BN is roughly the same: between 59% and 83%. The remaining variance is largely explained by nonshared environmental factors, that is, events and experiences unique to the adolescent and not her twin (e.g., different friends, teachers, sports, or hobbies). Shared environmental factors (e.g., same parents, house, socioeconomic status) seem to play relatively little role in explaining either AN or BN.

Molecular geneticists have tried to locate specific genes that might be responsible for placing individuals at risk for eating pathology (Bulik, 2004). Unfortunately, this line of research has produced inconsistent results. So far, researchers have been unable to identify a single gene or set of genes that are consistently associated with either AN or BN. Some evidence suggests that chromosome 1 may be involved in the development of AN-Restricting Type as well as in the tendency to obsess over thinness. Other data indicate that chromosome 10 may play a role in the development of purging behavior, especially vomiting. More research is needed.

Serotonin and Cholecystokinin

The neurotransmitter serotonin may be involved in the development of eating disorders, especially AN. In healthy individuals, serotonin is involved in general metabolism, mood, and personality. With respect to metabolism, serotonin plays a crucial role in appetite; it is partially responsible for feelings of satiety. With respect to mood, serotonin plays a major role is emotion regulation. Abnormalities in serotonergic functioning are likely involved in depression. With respect to personality, high levels of serotonin are associated with sensitivity to psychological stress, perfectionism, and a need for order and organization.

Some individuals with eating disorders show a disturbance in serotonin levels. For example, people with AN often show unusually high levels of serotonin, even after they have recovered from the disorder (Kaye, Weltzin, & Hsu, 1993). Similarly, individuals with BN show abnormalities in serotonin levels both during their illness and after recovery (Kaye et al., 1998). Kaye, Bastiani, and Moss (1995) suggest that elevated serotonin may make certain individuals prone to psychological distress, anxiety, and perfectionism. Restrictive dieting can temporarily decrease serotonin levels, causing a reduction in negative affect. Thus, dietary restriction is negatively reinforced and maintained over time.

Serotonin disturbance has also been suggested as a cause for bingeing and purging. In healthy individuals, serotonin plays a role in inhibiting eating. Individuals with BN, however, show low serotonin activity. These low levels of serotonin activity might explain their tendency to binge. Furthermore, individuals who recover from BN often show increased serotonin levels, indicating that recovery is partially dependent on changes in serotonergic activity (Ferguson & Pigott, 2000).

Some people with BN show low levels of a hormone called **cholecystokinin** (**CCK**). In healthy individuals, CCK is produced after eating a large meal. This hormone triggers satiety and regulates the amount of food consumed. However, people with BN produce much less CCK when they eat, perhaps allowing them to binge without experiencing satiety (Polivy et al., 2003).

Studies showing an association between serotonin, CCK, and eating disorders have relied on cross-sectional designs. These studies cannot tell us whether abnormalities in neurotransmitters or hormones are a cause or a consequence of eating disorders. For example, individuals with AN often have elevated levels of another neurotransmitter, norepinephrine. However, recent studies indicate that reductions in norepinephrine are the result of severe weight loss, not a cause of the disorder (Wilson et al., 2003). Although it is tempting to infer causal relationships from correlational data, such inferences can lead to an inaccurate understanding of adolescent eating disorders.

Sexual Development

Puberty

Experts have given considerable attention to the role of puberty in the emergence of eating disorders. Research has consistently shown that eating disorders usually develop sometime during or after puberty, and they rarely emerge before puberty or after age 25.

One explanation for the association between puberty and eating disorders is that the physical changes that characterize puberty are particularly stressful to adolescent girls. Before puberty, girls tend to have slender figures that are relatively low in body fat. Their body weight and shape are relatively close to the socially sanctioned ideal body promoted by Western society. With the onset of puberty, girls gain weight and body fat, making their bodies less compatible with this Western ideal. This increase in weight and change in shape can lead to body dissatisfaction in some girls, causing them to diet in order to regain their prepubescent shape (Smolak, 2006).

A related hypothesis is that the timing of puberty might be important in the development of eating disorders. Specifically, girls who mature earlier may be at particular risk for body dissatisfaction and eating pathology. These girls will not only violate socially sanctioned ideals regarding weight and shape, but they will do so when their peers are not developing in similar ways. Some early-maturing girls may be teased because of their precocious physical development.

Empirical studies have not consistently supported these hypotheses regarding the association between puberty, body dissatisfaction, and eating *problems*. Some studies have shown significant associations between pubertal development, pubertal timing, and body dissatisfaction; however, the strength of these associations has been relatively modest. Other studies have failed to support an association between pubertal development, pubertal timing, and body dissatisfaction altogether. Indeed, the only longitudinal study to test this hypothesis did not support the notion that puberty contributes to later body dissatisfaction (Stice, 2003).

Research investigating the association between pubertal development, pubertal timing, and eating *disorders* has also yielded mixed results. Pubertal development and timing is associated with dieting in some studies, but not others. However, pubertal development and timing tends to be weakly correlated with the likelihood of eating disorders. Taken together, these findings indicate that puberty may be a developmental time frame, during which adolescents are vulnerable to the emergence of body dissatisfaction and eating pathology. However, there is relatively little evidence to suggest that puberty, by itself, *causes* eating problems or eating disorders.

Child Sexual Abuse

Some experts have speculated that a sexual victimization during childhood can lead to the development of eating pathology, especially BN (Kearney-Cooke &

Striegel-Moore, 1994; Mannarino & Cohen, 1996). According to these theorists, the experience of sexual abuse makes girls feel helpless and shameful. Maltreated girls may be disgusted by their bodies or view their bodies as "tainted" by the abusive act. Some girls may express this shame and disgust by harming their bodies through starvation, bingeing, and purging. Other girls attempt to regain a sense of control over their bodies by dieting. In any case, girls place themselves at risk for developing eating disorders as a consequence of their abuse.

There is considerable evidence that child sexual abuse is associated with eating disorders, especially BN (Thompson & Wonderlich, 2004). Studies involving abused children, adolescents with eating disorders, and youth in the community have shown that girls who are sexually maltreated show increased likelihood of developing eating disorders later in life. Furthermore, adolescents and adults with eating disorders often report that their sexual victimization occurred before the onset of their eating disorders.

On the other hand, child sexual abuse seems to place children at risk for a host of psychiatric problems, not eating disorders per se. Fairburn and colleagues (1999) conducted a series of studies involving 102 women with BN, 102 women with other psychiatric disorders (usually depression), and 204 women with no mental health problems. Results showed that women with BN or another psychiatric disorder were more likely to have been sexually abused than women without a current mental illness. However, history of sexual abuse was equally common among women with BN as it was among women with other psychiatric problems (Fairburn et al., 1999; Welch & Fairburn, 1996).

Child sexual abuse seems to lead to BN when individuals show other psychological problems, such as impulsivity, risk-taking behavior, and substance abuse. These findings indicate that child sexual abuse is a risk factor for many psychiatric illnesses, but it is probably not a unique predictor of eating pathology (Thompson & Wonderlich, 2004; Wonderlich et al., 2001).

Cognitive-Behavioral Theory

The cognitive-behavioral conceptualization of eating disorders is based on the notion that thoughts, feelings, and actions are closely connected. Each component of behavior affects the others. Cognitive-behavioral theorists believe eating disorders are caused by a disturbance among these three factors: an *affective* disturbance characterized by low self-esteem; a *cognitive* disturbance characterized by distorted perceptions of weight, shape, and body image; and a *behavioral* disturbance marked by dietary restriction (Pike, Devlin, & Loeb, 2004; Wilson, Fairburn, & Agras, 1997).

At the heart of the cognitive-behavioral model for eating disorders is low self-esteem. Adolescents at risk for AN and BN are believed to have underlying problems with dysphoria and generally low regard for themselves. Although the source of this low self-esteem is unknown, it likely stems from a combination of genetic and environmental factors. For example, individuals at risk for eating disorders tend to have personality dispositions that make them sensitive to psychological distress and highly critical of themselves and others. Furthermore, many youths with eating disorders come from disruptive or stressful family environments that can contribute to their feelings of low self-worth. To compensate for these negative emotions, adolescents may place considerable value on their physical appearance, especially their weight and body shape. They believe that by attaining a certain weight or shape, they can overcome feelings of low self-esteem and self-worth.

Most adolescents diet to attain ideal weight and shape. Severe dieting is negatively reinforced by the reduction of low-self esteem. Adolescents feel temporarily better about themselves and their appearance as they lose weight and receive compliments from others. Unfortunately, severe dieting usually exacerbates adolescents' dysphoria over time. First, adolescents usually hold such unrealistic ideals of weight and shape that no amount of dieting can allow them to reach these ideals. Second, dietary restriction causes feelings of hunger, irritability, and fatigue.

To compensate for feelings of frustration, hunger, and fatigue, many adolescents break their diets and binge. Binges are negatively reinforced by temporary reductions in negative affect. However, binges are quickly followed by more lasting feelings of guilt, disgust, and physical discomfort.

To alleviate guilt and avoid weight gain, some adolescents will engage in inappropriate compensatory behaviors. At first, these behaviors include fasting or extra exercise. Fasting is negatively reinforced by reductions in guilt and anxiety about weight gain. However, fasting also produces long-term feelings of dysphoria and hunger. Other adolescents purge in order to avoid weight gain. Purging is also negatively reinforced by temporary reductions of anxiety. However, purging usually exacerbates feelings of guilt and disgust over time. Furthermore, after purging, adolescents often feel the same sense of emptiness and dysphoria that existed before the binge.

In summary, low self-esteem and dysphoria form the basis for the cognitive-behavioral model of eating disorders. Dietary restriction causes a temporary reduction in dysphoria (negative reinforcement) but long-term feelings of frustration and hunger. Binge eating reduces feelings of hunger (negative reinforcement) but produces guilt and anxiety about weight gain. Fasting and purging can alleviate guilt and fears of weight gain (negative reinforcement) but exacerbate feelings of low self-worth. Eating disorders, therefore, are caused by underlying mood problems and maintained by problematic thoughts and a cycle of negative reinforcement.

Social-Cultural Theories

Dual Pathway Model

Other researchers are interested in how social and cultural factors might contribute to the emergence of eating disorders. Stice (2002) has offered one of the most influential social-cultural models to explain binge eating: the dual pathway model. According to the **dual pathway model**, eating disorders develop through two pathways: (1) dietary restriction and (2) negative affect.

At the center of the dual process model is the notion that society places great demands on adolescent girls to lose weight and appear attractive. Many girls internalize the socially sanctioned **thin ideal** because they are reinforced by others when they conform to this ideal and punished when their appearance violates this standard. For example, adolescent girls often praise peers who lose weight and ostracize peers who are overweight. Praise (positive reinforcement) and teasing or ostracism (punishment) can be powerful motivators.

Idealization of thinness contributes to body dissatisfaction, even in very young girls (Smolak, 2006). When girls are dissatisfied with their bodies, they may engage in dietary restriction to lose weight and achieve their ideal size and shape. Unfortunately, dieting is an ineffective means of long-term weight control. Instead, dieting usually produces feelings of hunger, irritability, and fatigue. Furthermore, failure to lose weight and achieve the thin ideal contributes to low self-esteem, frustration, and negative affect (see Image 14.1).

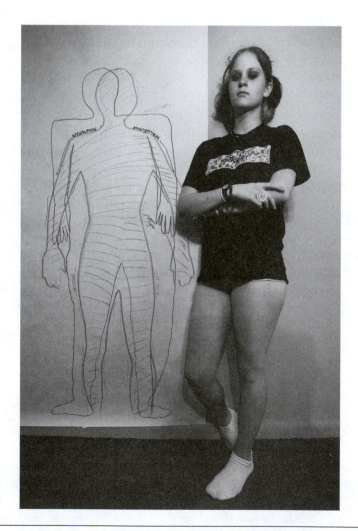

Image 14.1   Distorted Body Image. Brittany stands next to her body tracing during a therapy session for girls with eating disorders. The body tracing exercise allows her to see the distortion between her actual body, traced by the therapist, and her perceived body image.

Source: AP Photo/Mandatory Credit: Lauren Greenfield. Used with permission.

In some girls, dietary restriction and negative affect lead to binge eating. Bingeing causes a temporary reduction in both hunger and negative emotions. Indeed, binge foods tend to be high in fat and carbohydrates—foods we usually call "comfort foods." However, as described by the cognitive-behavioral model of eating disorders, bingeing also elicits increased guilt and the likelihood of purging or other compensatory behaviors.

Tripartite Influence Model

An alternative social-cultural model for the development of eating disorders is the tripartite influence model (Thompson, Coovert, & Stormer, 1999). According to this model, three social-cultural factors influence adolescent girls' eating behavior: peers, parents, and the media (see Figure 14.3).

Peers can influence adolescent girls' eating when they place importance on weight and body shape, tease other girls about their weight or appearance, or diet themselves. Parents affect a girl's eating behavior when they make comments about their own weight, shape, or appearance, when they diet, or when they criticize their daughter's appearance or urge her to lose weight. The media can also affect girls' eating behavior. Models on television, movies, and magazines can convey the importance of physical attractiveness to girls' well-being. Similarly, television and magazines can provide girls with maladaptive ideas about dieting, exercise, and weight loss.

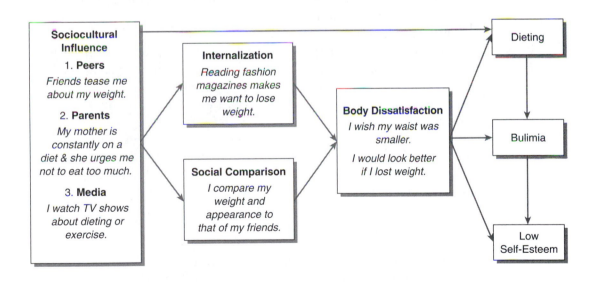

Figure 14.3   Tripartite Influence Model of Eating Disturbance

Source: From Shroff and Thompson (2006). Used with permission.

Note: Social-cultural factors lead to body dissatisfaction and BN in two ways: (1) by causing girls to internalize the thin ideal and (2) by causing girls to compare their appearance to others.

According to the tripartite influence model, these three social-cultural factors (peers, parents, media) can lead to the development of eating problems in three ways. First, they can directly affect eating behavior by motivating a girl to diet. For example, a girl who sees her mother, her best friend, and her favorite television star diet might regard dieting as a developmentally normative and socially expected means of losing weight. She might decide to diet in order to appear more like these significant people in her life. As we have seen before, however, dietary restriction is not an effective, long-term means of weight control. In fact, it often causes negative affect and can lead to binge eating.

Second, the relationship between these three social-cultural factors and girls' eating might be mediated by girls' internalization of the thin ideal. Messages from peers, parents, and the media about body shape, weight, or attractiveness might cause girls to internalize the often unrealistic standards for beauty conveyed in Western culture. For example, girls who read fashion magazines might internalize the often unrealistic standards for body shape and weight conveyed by the models in these magazines. Girls who internalize these standards, in turn, might experience dissatisfaction with their own shape and weight. Such body dissatisfaction can lead to dieting, negative emotions, and bulimic symptoms.

Third, the relationship between these three social-cultural factors and girls' eating might be mediated by girls' tendency to compare their appearance with the appearance of others. For example, peers might make comments about classmates who are exceptionally thin and attractive or overweight and unattractive. Adolescent girls, in turn, might compare their own weight and body shape to these attractive and unattractive classmates. These social comparisons, in turn, might cause girls to feel dissatisfied with their bodies. Body dissatisfaction can contribute to dieting, emotional problems, and eating disorders.

The tripartite influence model is a relatively new model for the development of eating disorders. Initial data with adolescents and adults indicate that the tripartite influence model might be a useful way of explaining the potential influences of peers, parents, and the media on the emergence of dieting and eating pathology (Keery, van den Berg, & Thompson, 2004; Shroff & Thompson, 2006; van den Berg, Thompson, Brandon, & Coovert, 2002). Future research will likely be directed at examining the relative importance of these three social-cultural influences in girls of various ages. For example, older adolescents may be greatly influenced by peers, whereas younger adolescents may be influenced more heavily by parents.

Feminist Theories

Some authors have adopted a feminist perspective to explain the development of eating disorders in adolescent girls (Smolak & Murnen, 2004). Central to the feminist understanding of eating disorders is the notion of gender roles. **Gender role** refers to the degree to which girls adopt masculine and/or feminine behaviors and internalize these gender-relevant attributes into their sense of selves. Traditionally masculine characteristics include assertiveness, dominance, and leadership abilities. Traditionally feminine characteristics include nurturance, empathy, and compassion for others. Some evidence indicates that girls who adopt masculine gender roles may be at lower risk for eating disorders, whereas girls who endorse feminine characteristics may be at slightly greater risk (Smolak, 2005).

Other theorists claim that feminine gender roles place some girls at risk for eating disorders. Carol Gilligan (1982) argues that before puberty, girls are as assertive, outgoing, and self-confident as boys. However, during early adolescence, girls suppress some of their assertiveness and self-reliance while boys maintain these personality characteristics. Gilligan asserts that this difference in social behavior reflects boys' and girls' different values during early adolescence. The primary developmental task facing adolescent boys is establishing a personal identity and sense of self. Boys accomplish this developmental task by trying out a variety of social roles and achieving a sense of autonomy, independent of parents and family. In contrast, adolescent girls value interpersonal relationships more than boys. When girls' bids for autonomy come into conflict with their desire for intimacy in interpersonal relationships, girls sacrifice their autonomy to maintain these relationships. Boys gain self-esteem and recognition from others because of their accomplishments. In contrast, girls gain self-esteem and approval from others when they deny their own wishes and conform to the expectations of others. Gilligan argues that adolescent girls suppress their autonomy and sense of self in order to please parents, family, and friends. She calls this suppression of autonomy a "loss of voice."

Eating disorders reflect girls' "loss of voice" in two ways. First, girls gain social approval when they lose weight and conform to society's expectations regarding weight and body shape. Second, girls with eating disorders assume control over the only area of their lives that they can control: their bodies.

Other feminist theorists have argued that the objectification of women and girls contributes to eating disorders (Fredrickson & Roberts, 1997). Advocates of **objectification theory** assert that Western culture values women primarily for their appearance and sexual identities. Advertising, popular music, television, movies, and other media convey the notion that women are sexual objects whose primarily value is to gratify the needs of men. At an early age, girls learn that appearing attractive brings reinforcement from society while appearing unattractive leads to social rejection. Girls develop body dissatisfaction and eating pathology when they internalize society's standards of beauty and come to see themselves primary as sexual objects to be viewed by others. Their self-esteem becomes dependent on their ability to please others rather than on internal indicators of self-worth.

Although feminist theories for the etiology of eating disorders are popular, they have not been adequately tested. A few studies have provided limited support for the notion that gender roles influence the likelihood of eating disorders (Murnen & Smolak, 1998). On the other hand, Gilligan's (1982) hypothesis that adolescent girls suppress autonomy in order to gain social approval has not been consistently supported by empirical data. Furthermore, Gilligan's concept of "loss of voice" has not been adequately studied with adolescents (Smolak & Murnen, 2004).

Objectification theory is relatively new, but emerging data provide initial support for some of its claims (Smolak, 2005). For example, girls who compare themselves to models in fashion magazines report greater body dissatisfaction and more concern about their weight and appearance than girls who do not make such comparisons (Smolak, 2005). In contrast, girls who actively reject the portrayal of women in the media show greater body satisfaction than girls who internalize these standards of attractiveness (Murnen, Smolak, Mills, & Good, 2003). Objectification theory holds considerable promise as a way of explaining some aspects of eating disorders in adolescents.

Treatment

Inpatient Treatment for Anorexia Nervosa

Behavioral Treatment

Inpatient treatment for AN initially focuses on changing the adolescent's eating behavior, rather than on providing relief for the adolescent's emotional distress. The primary goal of treatment is to monitor the adolescent's physical health and to help her gain weight. Since rapid weight gain is dangerous to severely malnourished patients, physicians monitor the refeeding process. Typically, adolescents with AN are required to consume 1,500 calories per day for the first few days of inpatient treatment. Then, their target caloric intake is increased by about 500 calories every other day until the target reaches 3,500 calories daily (almost twice the amount of daily calories needed for weight maintenance). Consumption of 3,500 calories per day usually results in a gain of 2–4 lbs. per week (Linscheid & Butz, 2003).

Most adolescents with AN are resistant to inpatient treatment because they fear any weight gain, no matter how small. Rigid, black-or-white thinking leads these adolescents to believe that if they gain even one pound, they have lost all control over their eating behavior and are on the road to obesity. Furthermore, adolescents with AN often derive self-worth from their ability to control their weight. To these adolescents, gaining weight means a loss of identity and self-esteem.

To help girls gain weight, the treatment team administers a behavioral protocol that reinforces caloric intake and participation in the treatment program. Usually, this behavioral protocol is based on the notion that girls with AN are afraid of weight gain. In order to overcome this fear, they are required to consume a wide variety of foods during regularly scheduled mealtimes and avoid behaviors designed to limit weight gain (e.g., purging, excessive exercise).

Meal completion is positively reinforced by hospital staff. Upon entering treatment, adolescents are denied most of the privileges they enjoyed at home: watching television and reading magazines; taking telephone calls and visits from friends; and access to makeup, favorite clothes, and accessories. Adolescents can earn these privileges by eating meals and participating in other aspects of the treatment program.

Some inpatient programs require patients to remain in their beds until they meet certain caloric intake goals. For example, hospital staff might explain that if the patient does not consume enough calories, she might be too weak to leave her bed or socialize with others. Under these circumstances, meal completion is negatively reinforced, by allowing patients to escape the confine of their rooms.

Patients are also prohibited from engaging in compensatory behaviors to avoid weight gain. Initially, nursing staff monitor patients to ensure that they do not purge or engage in covert exercise.

Group Therapy

In most inpatient treatment programs, adolescents participate in group therapy (Guarda & Heinberg, 2004). Groups consist of adolescents who are new to the inpatient program as well as adolescents nearing completion. **Supportive confrontation** between patients is encouraged by the group therapist. In supportive confrontation, senior group members are encouraged to challenge the cognitive distortions and food obsessions of newer members. For example, a new group member who complains that the food she is forced to consume will make her fat might be challenged by the other group members to avoid "fat talk" during the session. Attempts to lose weight or outsmart staff are discouraged by the group and lead to peer rejection. The therapist uses peer pressure during the session to promote healthy eating in the same way peer pressure likely contributed to the adolescent's eating problems outside of treatment.

Group therapy is structured along several tasks designed to teach adolescents about eating disorders, manage emotions and cope with low self-esteem, develop social skills, maintain a healthy diet, and recognize and challenge beliefs that lead to problematic eating behavior (see Table 14.3). Individuals with eating disorders

Table 14.3   Group Therapy for Adolescent Eating Disorders

Topic	Description
Psychoeducation	Provides adolescents with information about eating disorders
Behavioral recovery	Teaches adolescents to recognize and challenge cognitive distortions that lead to eating problems; promotes weight gain and healthy eating using supportive confrontation between group members
Relaxation training	Teaches adolescents relaxation and emotion-regulation skills, such as deep breathing, imagery, yoga, and meditation
Nutrition	Teaches adolescents about basic nutrition, the risks associated with dieting, and alternative ways to manage weight and consume healthy foods
Meal planning	Helps adolescents select balanced meals and healthy portions; teaches social skills while eating
Body image	Teaches adolescents to correct maladaptive beliefs about their bodies, to critically evaluate images of women's bodies on TV and in magazines
Self-esteem	Provides adolescents with assertiveness training and communication skills training to improve self-confidence
Family issues	Helps adolescents understand how family relationships can lead to healthy or problematic eating; allows adolescents to develop more healthy patterns of interaction with family
Relapse prevention	Teaches adolescents to recognize and avoid environmental events or mood states that trigger problematic eating; helps adolescents plan for their return to family and school

Source: Based on Guarda and Heinberg (2004).

Note: Most inpatient treatment programs for adolescents with eating disorders require patients to participate in group therapy. Patients at the Johns Hopkins Eating Disorders Program participate in three group sessions daily. Each session covers one of the topics listed above.

often show two types of cognitive distortions. First, many erroneously believe that their self-worth is directly associated with their weight. They think, "If it is good to be thin, then you are the best if you are the thinnest" (Linscheid & Butz, 2003, p. 645). The second distortion involves dichotomous (i.e., black-or-white) thinking. Specifically, they believe that if they start eating, they will be unable to stop (Linscheid & Butz, 2003). Therapists try to teach patients to recognize and critically evaluate these faulty beliefs.

There is little evidence supporting the efficacy of inpatient group therapy for AN. In fact, no randomized controlled trials of group therapy for adolescents with AN have been published. Some researchers believe that individuals with AN are too malnourished to fully participate in group therapy. For example, problems with concentration and problem solving, caused by malnourishment, can interfere with adolescents' abilities to recognize and critically evaluate cognitive distortions (Linscheid & Butz, 2003). Other researchers have suggested that group therapy might even be dangerous, especially if adolescents compete with other members in the group to lose weight or share weight-loss techniques (Maher, 1980).

Partial Hospitalization

Inpatient treatment lasts about three to four weeks; however, some adolescents participate in inpatient treatment for much less time, while other programs routinely keep patients six weeks or longer. Because inpatient treatment is expensive, many hospitals have developed day treatment or **partial hospitalization programs** for patients with eating disorders. After discharge from the hospital, adolescents continue to receive services from hospital staff, but spend evenings with their families in their own homes. Day treatment is a less restrictive and intense form of treatment than inpatient hospitalization, although adolescents spend almost their entire day in the day treatment program. Day treatment can help adolescents transition from the hospital to their homes.

Inpatient treatment programs are efficacious in increasing the weight of patients with AN (Guarda & Heinberg, 2004). Programs that adopt behavioral strategies, like the kinds described above, tend to lead to weight gain of approximately two to four pounds per week. Partial hospitalization programs have also been shown to be effective in helping individuals with AN gain weight. Weight gain tends to be slower than in traditional inpatient treatment, with patients averaging only 0.5 to 1.0 lbs. per week. Unfortunately, 30%–50% of patients with AN who successfully gain weight during inpatient treatment or partial hospitalization relapse within one year (Pike, 1998). Consequently, most clinicians recommend that girls with AN participate in outpatient therapy after they are discharged from a hospital or day treatment program.

Family Therapy for Anorexia Nervosa

Structural Family Therapy

After adolescents with AN gain sufficient weight, most professionals recommend family therapy as the first line of psychosocial treatment (*DSM-IV-TR*). Although many kinds of family therapy are available, the most well-known and widely used approach is structural family therapy, developed by Salvador Minuchin.

Structural family therapy focuses primarily on the quality and patterns of relationships between family members. Therapists place little emphasis on the adolescent's eating behavior, per se. In fact, the adolescent's AN symptoms are believed to serve a diversionary function. As long as family members concentrate their energy and efforts on the adolescent's problematic eating, they do not have to focus on the real source of the problem: family relationships and communication. Family therapists see their "client" as the entire family system, not just the adolescent with the eating disorder.

Minuchin believed that adolescents with AN belong to highly controlling, overprotective families. He used the term **enmeshment** to describe family relationships in which boundaries between parents and children were blurred or diffuse. In enmeshed families, parents control too many aspects of their adolescents' lives and do not allow adolescents to express developmentally appropriate levels of autonomy. For example, parents might place excessive demands on adolescents' choice of after-school activities, show a lack of respect for the adolescents' privacy, and insist on strict obedience to rigid family rules. At the same time, parents of adolescents with AN are overly concerned with the appearance of the family to others. Family members avoid conflict with one another, preferring to ignore family problems rather than discuss them openly. Minuchin believed that adolescents from enmeshed families develop AN as a means to assert autonomy over the only aspect of their lives that they are able to control: their bodies.

Structural family therapists have two main goals. First, they try to open lines of communication among family members. Specifically, therapists help family members realize how their adolescent's eating problems might distract them from other relationship problems in the family, such as a mother's excessive alcohol use or a father's tendency toward anger. Improved communication between family members, especially between parents, will decrease overall tension in the family that can contribute to the adolescent's eating problems.

Second, the therapist helps the family recognize the adolescent's emerging needs for autonomy and find developmentally appropriate ways for her to show self-direction. For example, parents might agree to knock on their adolescent's bedroom door before entering, to avoid snooping through her room when she is not home, or resist listening to her telephone calls without her knowledge. They might also give their daughter more freedom to select classes and extracurricular activities. At the same time, the therapist might help the adolescent express concerns to her parents in direct and mature ways in order to reduce family conflict.

Data on the efficacy of family therapy are extremely limited. Minuchin's idea that adolescents with AN come from highly controlling, enmeshed families has not been adequately tested. Furthermore, structural family therapy has not been adequately evaluated using randomized controlled trials. Uncontrolled trials of structural family therapy indicate that 66% to 86% of adolescents with AN show improvements in weight gain and menstruation following family treatment (Minuchin, Rosman, & Baker, 1978; Stierlin & Weber, 1989). Despite its popularity, more research is needed to establish structural family therapy as an efficacious treatment.

The Maudsley Hospital Approach

Although structural family therapy is a popular form of outpatient treatment for AN, another variant of family therapy developed at Maudsley Hospital in London has received considerably more empirical support. Indeed, several randomized controlled trials have been conducted investigating the Maudsley approach to treatment, making it the best-studied family approach to treating AN (Lock, 2004).

On the surface, the Maudsley approach to family therapy is quite different from traditional structural family therapy. Initially, clinicians using the Maudsley approach target the adolescent's eating disorder symptoms, rather than communication patterns in the family. During the first phase of treatment, the therapist encourages parents to take control of their adolescent's eating behavior and develop a plan for helping her gain weight. The therapist is usually not concerned with the tactics parents use to take control of their adolescent's eating, so long as both parents work together. At the same time, the therapist blames the adolescent's weight loss on the eating disorder itself, not on the parents or family-related problems. The goal of the initial phase of treatment is to help parents feel empowered over the adolescent's eating and to allow the adolescent to gain weight.

Under the surface, the initial phase of the Maudsley approach resembles that of structural family therapy. Both schools of therapy require parents to solidify their relationship and communicate with each other. Structural family therapists make this goal explicit, by focusing on communication patterns between parents. Practitioners of the Maudsley approach keep this goal implicit, by encouraging parents to find ways to "refeed" their adolescent. Accomplishing the refeeding task requires parents to open lines of communication and work together to solve a common problem.

In the second phase of the Maudsley approach, parents are encouraged to gradually shift responsibility for refeeding to their adolescent. Again, it is more important that families work out for themselves how to transfer this responsibility than it is for the therapist to tell families the "right way" to do it. Accomplishing this task requires families to give their adolescent progressively greater freedom and autonomy over her eating behavior.

The third phase of treatment begins when the adolescent has achieved sufficient weight and menstruation has returned. In this phase, treatment focuses less on the adolescent's eating behavior and more on the developing autonomy of the adolescent. Parents and adolescents work together to help adolescents negotiate rights and responsibilities within the family that satisfy all family members.

The Maudsley approach to family therapy takes approximately one year. Randomized controlled trials indicate that the Maudsley approach is efficacious in treating adolescents who show relatively recent onset of AN. Furthermore, the Maudsley approach is associated with more rapid weight gain than individual psychotherapy (Robin, Siegal, Moye, Gilroy, Dennis, & Sikand, 1999).

Outpatient Treatment for Bulimia Nervosa

Cognitive-Behavioral Therapy

Cognitive-behavioral therapy is one of the most frequently used outpatient treatments for BN (Guarda & Heinberg, 2004). Recall that cognitive-behavioral therapists conceptualize BN as reflecting a disturbance in mood, cognition, and eating (Pike et al., 2004; Fairburn, Cooper, & Safran, 2002). All three aspects of functioning (mood, cognitions, and eating behaviors) are interrelated. Adolescents initially diet to achieve a highly idealized and unattainable weight or shape. By acquiring this ideal body, they believe that they will overcome feelings of low self-worth. Unfortunately, dieting often leads to binge eating, which causes adolescents to feel guilty and out of control. Many adolescents engage in further dietary restriction to alleviate these negative feelings, but continued dieting produces only more negative emotions. Other adolescents purge to reduce fears of weight gain, but purging exacerbates guilt and low self-esteem. The bulimic cycle is maintained through negative reinforcement. Binges are negatively reinforced by temporary reductions in hunger, irritability, and fatigue brought on by severe dieting. Purging is negatively reinforced by temporary reductions in guilt and dysphoria brought on by binges.

The goal of CBT is to break this cycle of negative reinforcement by exposing girls to normal amounts of food and prohibiting them from purging or engaging in other maladaptive means of avoiding weight. Clients initially experience considerable discomfort ingesting food and avoiding weight loss strategies; over time, however, anxiety is gradually reduced and compensatory behaviors are no longer negatively reinforced.

CBT for bulimia is typically conducted in 20 weekly sessions (Wilson & Pike, 2001) and is divided into three phases. In the first phase, the therapist introduces the cognitive-behavioral model for BN and shows how the client's emotions, thoughts, and eating behaviors are closely connected. Early in treatment, the therapist asks the adolescent to identify situations or events that do and do not trigger bingeing or purging. Consider the following dialogue:

Therapist: OK. Now I'd like you to complete the following form with me about the times when you binge and the times you make yourself throw up. Tell me about situations that almost always cause you to binge.

Sara: Well, you know, I binge a lot when I'm alone in the house. Like, before my brother gets home from school and my parents get home from work.

Therapist: What do you mean by "a lot?" Do you mean all of the time?

Sara: No, maybe about half of the time. Maybe three or four times each week.

Therapist: OK. Then let's say that being home alone triggers a binge about 50% of the time. What kinds of situations or feelings *almost always* cause you to binge?

Sara:	Feelings?
Therapist:	Yes. Sometimes you might find that certain emotions cause you to binge.
Sara:	Like, whenever I get into an argument with my boyfriend or I feel like he doesn't care about me or is angry with me.
Therapist:	That almost always causes you to binge?
Sara:	All of the time. I feel terrible inside, you know, depressed. And then I eat.
Therapist:	OK. And in what sorts of situations do you *never* binge?
Sara:	Well, I never binge when other people are around, like with my friends or family. I also never binge when I'm having fun with the other kids.
Therapist:	OK. So you never binge when you're with other people, especially when you're having fun with friends?
Sara:	Yeah.
Therapist:	OK. So you see that certain situations and feelings often cause you to binge, like when you're alone or feeling depressed about your boyfriend. When you're in other situations or in a good mood, you never binge. Do you see how situations and feelings can affect your likelihood of binging?
Sara:	Yeah.
Therapist:	Also, do you see your bingeing is not completely out of control? After all, in some situations you never binge, right?
Sara:	Yes. I guess I never thought about it that way.

Another early goal is to increase the adolescent's motivation to change her eating behavior. Although adolescents with BN usually recognize that they have an eating disorder, they may be unwilling to give up bingeing and purging because they fear becoming fat. The therapist might ask the adolescent to complete a cost-benefit analysis (see Figure 14.4). First, the therapist might ask the adolescent to consider the positive and negative consequences of maintaining her present eating habits. A perceived benefit might be to lose weight, while a perceived cost might be feeling that she is out of control. Second, the therapist asks the adolescent to consider the benefits and costs of changing her eating habits. A possible benefit might be to feel less guilty about bingeing and purging. A potential drawback might be that she gains weight and is rejected by her boyfriend.

After the adolescent completes the cost-benefit analysis, the therapist asks the adolescent to critically evaluate perceived benefits of maintaining her present eating habits and perceived costs associated with reducing her bingeing and purging.

Continue Bingeing and Purging	**Change Eating Behavior**
Benefits • I'll lose weight. • I'll get compliments from friends, boyfriend.	**Benefits** • I won't feel guilty about bingeing and purging. • I might feel better about myself—more in control.
Costs • I feel guilty and out of control for bingeing. • I feel guilty (disgusting) after purging. • I don't like lying to my family.	**Costs** • I will gain a lot of weight. • People might criticize me (parents) or make fun of me (friends) if I get heavy.

Figure 14.4   Cost-Benefit Analysis of Bingeing and Purging

Therapist: So, you said that you'd like to stop purging, but purging helps you lose weight. Is that right?

Becca: Yeah. If I stop throwing up or exercising and stuff, I'll probably gain 50 pounds like that.

Therapist: Well, let's look that that belief for a minute. Right now you're bingeing and purging pretty frequently . . . usually once or twice a day. How much weight have you lost over the last month?

Becca: Well, none. But I haven't gained any either.

Therapist: So purging hasn't caused you to lose weight?

Becca: No.

Therapist: Well, let's look at the alternative. If you stopped purging, would you really gain 50 lbs "just like that?"

Becca: Maybe not 50. Maybe 25.

Therapist: If you gained 25 lbs., do you think your friends would reject you?

Becca: I don't know. I worry about that.

Therapist: Well, if your best friend, Marcie, gained that much weight, would you stop being her friend or tease her or do something else mean like that?

Becca: Of course not.

Therapist: So you wouldn't do that to Marcie, but she might do that to you?

Becca: I guess not. I guess my real friends wouldn't do that to me even if I gained the weight.

The cost-benefit analysis often increases adolescents' willingness to participate in therapy. Adolescents can view the cycle of bingeing and purging as the cause of their emotional problem, not the solution.

In the second phase of treatment, therapy focuses primarily on identifying and challenging dysfunctional thoughts that contribute to the adolescent's eating disorder. Adolescents are taught that situations and events do not directly affect behavior. Instead, beliefs mediate the relationship between antecedent events and behavioral consequences. Many therapists teach adolescents the A-B-C approach to analyzing the relationship between antecedent events, beliefs, and emotional and behavioral consequences. Consider the following dialogue:

Therapist: So you said that you binged a lot this week and felt totally out of control?

Heather: Yeah. I was doing real well, you know, on my diet. I went two days eating very little. Just some low-fat yogurt and steamed vegetables and stuff like that. Then, I was so hungry and feeling sort of bored, and I started to eat some potato chips. They tasted real good at first, but then I felt so guilty for breaking my diet. But I just couldn't stop, so I ate the whole bag and I kept on eating until I was stuffed. That was Wednesday, when my parents were out. Afterward I felt terrible, like a pig. I felt, you know, real dirty and bloated. So I threw up. That made me feel even worse because I had been so good lately and then I was hungry again.

Therapist: OK. So let's look at the situation a little more closely. You were hungry and bored so you started eating the potato chips? That was the event that started the binge?

Heather: Yeah. Then I just kept right on eating.

Therapist: Actually, something occurred in between. What was going through your mind when you started eating the chips?

Heather: I don't know . . . nothing.

Therapist: You said you felt so guilty for breaking your diet?

Heather: Yeah. I guess I thought, "Oh well, what the hell, I might as well eat the whole bag and pig out since I broke my diet."

Therapist: That's what I mean. Eating one potato chip didn't cause you to eat the whole bag and all the rest of the food. Your *thought* caused you to binge. You thought, "Well, I'm terrible for breaking my diet so I might as well pig out." That's what caused you to binge.

Heather: I guess so.

Therapist: Well, if you had another thought at the time, a different thought, might have you acted differently? For example, if you thought "Well, I ate a few chips and broke my diet a little, but I was really hungry. Maybe I should eat something healthy now," maybe you wouldn't have binged.

Heather: Yeah. Probably not.

The therapist spends the majority of the second phase of treatment teaching adolescents to recognize and challenge distorted thoughts that lead to bingeing and purging. In the example above, Heather displays a common cognitive distortion called dichotomous thinking. She sees herself in black-and-white terms, either all good or all bad. Therefore, she believes that if she violates her diet, she is a terrible person who is out of control over her eating.

In the final phase of treatment, the therapist and client prepare for termination and plan for the possibility of relapse. Since relapse is common among individuals with BN, the therapist openly talks about the possibility that some time in the future, the adolescent might binge and purge. The therapist encourages the adolescent to anticipate high-risk situations that might trigger relapse. Then, the therapist and client develop strategies to manage those high-risk situations.

Several randomized controlled trials have demonstrated the efficacy of CBT in treating bulimia (Pike et al., 2004). CBT is associated with reductions in bingeing, purging, dietary restraint, and concern over shape and weight. Furthermore, CBT has been shown to cause clinically meaningful reductions in these symptoms; after treatment, many adolescents no longer meet diagnostic criteria for BN (Lundgren, Danoff-Burg, & Anderson, 2004). CBT appears to be most effective in reducing dietary restraint and purging, while it is somewhat less effective in reducing the frequency of bingeing and general concerns about weight and shape (see Figure 14.5).

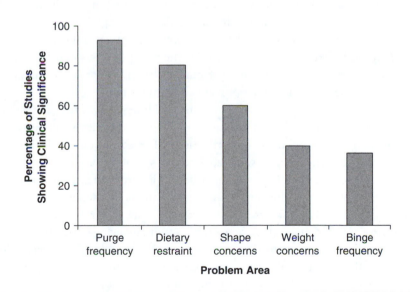

Figure 14.5   Effectiveness of CBT for BN

Source: Based on Lundgren et al. (2004).

Note: CBT is most effective in reducing purging and dietary restraint and least effective at reducing weight concerns and frequency of binges.

Although CBT is currently the treatment of choice for adolescents with bulimia, it is not a panacea (Agras, Crow, Halmi, Mitchell, Wilson, & Kraemer, 2000; Agras, Walsh, Fairburn, Wilson, & Kraemer, 2000). Approximately 20%–30% of individuals who begin CBT withdraw before completion. Among those who complete CBT, 50% are not able to abstain from bingeing and purging after treatment. Finally, most studies have examined the efficacy of CBT with older adolescents and adults. More research is needed to confirm its utility with younger adolescents.

Interpersonal Therapy for BN

Although CBT is currently the treatment of choice for adolescents with BN, not all patients respond to CBT. An alternative treatment is interpersonal therapy (IPT). Interpersonal therapists focus on the number and quality of their client's relationships with others. While they do not necessary believe that interpersonal problems *cause* eating disorders, therapists recognize that eating disorder symptoms are usually closely connected to adolescents' social functioning. Consequently, interpersonal therapists focus primarily on the adolescent's relationships with family members and friends, rather than on her eating disorder symptoms (Tantleff-Dunn, Cokee-LaRose, & Peterson, 2004).

IPT is based on the medical model of psychopathology; that is, clients are told that BN is a medical illness that is interfering with their physical, psychological, and social well-being. Adolescents are allowed to assume the sick role. They are not blamed for having an eating disorder, nor are their symptoms interpreted as indicators of personal weakness. Instead, symptoms are attributed to the medical illness.

The therapist initially teaches the adolescent about BN and demonstrates how interpersonal problems frequently coincide with (and sometimes elicit) maladaptive eating. Indeed, 75% of people with eating disorders experience a significant interpersonal stressor shortly before the onset of their eating problem (Schmidt, Tiller, Blanchard, Andrews, & Treasure, 1997). The therapist offers to help the adolescent improve the quality of her interpersonal relationships so that she might feel better about herself and correct her problematic eating habits.

Interpersonal therapists target one or two areas of interpersonal functioning that are associated with the adolescent's eating disorder. These problems can be loosely classified into four interpersonal problem areas: grief, role transitions, role disputes, and interpersonal deficits. First, some adolescents' symptoms are associated with grief, specifically, the death of a loved one or separation from a family member. For example, an adolescent might show severe depression and moderate symptoms of BN after her mother is sent overseas to serve in the army. In her mother's absence, she may have assumed many of the housekeeping and caregiving duties in the home and is generally not able to process the negative feelings associated with separation from her mother. An interpersonal therapist would help this adolescent grieve the loss (albeit temporary) of her mother's companionship.

Second, many eating disorder symptoms are associated with role transitions in the adolescent's life. Life-changing experiences such as beginning a new school, moving to a new neighborhood, or coping with parental divorce requires adolescents to assume new roles. Often, these roles threaten the adolescent's self-esteem.

For example, an adolescent who begins high school must abandon the old, comfortable roles that she played in junior high and create a new social niche. For some adolescents, this transition can be threatening. The interpersonal therapist helps the adolescent mourn the loss of her old social roles and embrace the challenges of her new surroundings. The therapist acts as a source of support as the adolescent begins to develop new areas of social competence.

Third, adolescent eating disorders are often associated with interpersonal role disputes. Role disputes usually occur when adolescents and their parents have mismatched expectations for each other's behaviors. For example, a 15-year-old adolescent might believe that she is old enough to start dating; however, her parents might believe that she should wait at least one more year, and then only date boys with their approval. The adolescent might view herself as an emerging adult who deserves certain rights and responsibilities. Her parents, however, might still view the adolescent as a child who needs protection and guidance. Role disputes can lead to tension in the home, leaving the adolescent feeling misunderstood and unfairly treated. However, if role disputes are successfully resolved, they can lead to stronger parent-adolescent relationships. The interpersonal therapist's goal is to facilitate parent-adolescent communication so that both parties can achieve a greater understanding of each other's perspectives.

Fourth, eating disorders can be tied to adolescents' interpersonal deficits. Some adolescents lack adequate social skills to make and keep friends. Other adolescents are rejected by peers because they are socially withdrawn or disruptive. For example, an extremely shy adolescent might desperately want friends, but she might be unsure how to join peer groups. She might believe that if she were more attractive, she would gain social standing. Consequently, she might begin dieting and purging to lose weight. An interpersonal therapist might help her develop assertiveness skills so that she might feel more comfortable meeting peers and expanding her social network.

Preliminary evidence indicates that IPT is efficacious in reducing symptoms of BN, especially the frequency of bingeing and purging (Tantleff-Dunn et al., 2004). A large, randomized controlled study directly compared CBT and IPT (Agras, Walsh et al., 2000). In this study, 220 women and adolescent girls with BN received either CBT or IPT over the course of 20 weeks. Outcomes were assessed immediately after treatment and at one year follow-up. Immediately after treatment, clients who participated in CBT showed greater improvement than clients who participated in IPT. At follow-up, however, clients who participated in IPT continued to improve and showed comparable levels of functioning as clients who participated in CBT. These findings indicate that IPT may be a viable alternative for adolescents who do not respond to CBT (see Figure 14.6).

Medication

Pharmacotherapy for AN

The first medications used to treat AN were traditional antipsychotics—medications that influenced the neurotransmitter dopamine. Clinicians reasoned

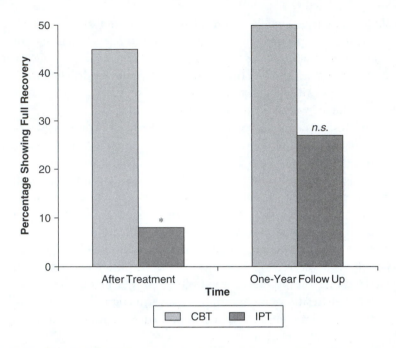

Figure 14.6   Comparison of CBT and IPT in Treating BN

Source: Based on Wilson, Fairburn, Agras, Walsh, and Kraemer (2002).

*p < .05, n.s. = not significant.

Note: Immediately after treatment, more people improved after receiving CBT. One year later, people who received CBT and IPT showed similar outcomes.

that people with AN often had obsessions about their shape and weight that resembled the delusions of patients with psychotic disorders. Several randomized controlled trials of antipsychotic medications showed them to be ineffective.

More recently, clinicians have used newer antipsychotic medications, which affect a wider range of neurotransmitters. Case studies indicate that these novel antipsychotics may work for some patients, but there are not sufficient randomized controlled trials of these medications to support their widespread use (Flament, Furino, & Godart, 2005).

Antidepressant medications have also been used to treat AN. Clinicians have speculated that antidepressant medications may be effective for three reasons. First, there is high comorbidity between eating disorders and depression; as many as 80% of individuals with eating disorders show significant mood problems (Lilenfeld et al., 1998). Second, many people believe low self-esteem and dysphoria underlie eating disorder symptoms. Decreasing dysphoria with medication might alleviate eating disorder symptoms. Third, serotonin is involved in both mood regulation and satiety. Antidepressant medications that affect serotonin might improve mood and eating.

Unfortunately, randomized controlled trials of tricyclic antidepressants and selective serotonin reuptake inhibitors (SSRIs) have shown them to be largely ineffective in treating anorexia. Both medications are generally equivalent to placebo in producing weight gain. One study indicates that the SSRI fluoxetine (Prozac) might be useful in preventing relapse after patients had already gained adequate weight (Kaye et al., 2001). However, another study suggests that patients treated with both

SSRIs and psychotherapy showed poorer outcomes than patients treated with psychotherapy alone (Bergh, Eriksson, Lindberg, & Sodersten, 1996). Consequently, medication is not regarded as a first-line treatment for AN (Flament et al., 2005).

Pharmacotherapy for BN

Antidepressant medications have been shown to be effective in controlling BN (Flament et al., 2005). Two randomized controlled trials, involving more than 700 patients with BN, showed that fluoxetine (Prozac) was superior to placebo in reducing bingeing and purging (Fluoxetine Bulimia Nervosa Study Group, 1992; Goldstein, Wilson, & Thompson, 1995). A second SSRI, fluvoxamine (Luvox), has been shown to prevent relapse in patients who have already recovered from BN (Fichter, Kruger, Rief, Holland, & Dohne, 1996). Unfortunately, the vast majority of patients treated with medication do not stop bingeing or purging. Approximately 75%–80% of patients remain symptomatic even while taking the medication. Medication can reduce, but not eliminate, symptoms (see Figure 14.7).

Furthermore, antidepressants should not replace psychotherapy for BN (Flament et al., 2005). Four randomized controlled studies that have compared CBT to antidepressant medication have found CBT to be superior to medication alone. Some recent data indicate that combining antidepressant medication with psychotherapy, especially CBT, may be slightly more efficacious than providing CBT alone (Bacaltchuk, et al., 2000; Narash-Eisikovits, Dierberger, & Westen, 2002). Consequently, medication is probably used best as an adjunct to CBT or as a means to prevent relapse after treatment.

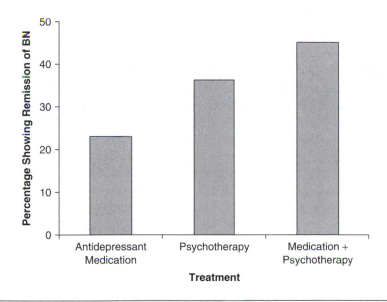

Figure 14.7   Comparison of Medication and Psychotherapy in Treating BN

Source: Based on Bacaltchuk, Trefiglio, Oliveira, Hay, Lima, and Mari (2000).

Note: Combining SSRIs and psychotherapy (especially CBT) was slightly more effective in reducing BN than using therapy alone. Medication alone resulted in poorest outcomes.

Update: Julie

Julie was admitted to the hospital because of malnourishment and dehydration. She participated in a behavioral program in which she was rewarded with privileges (e.g., makeup, telephone calls to friends) for consuming a certain number of calories each day. Julie was extremely resistant to participate in the refeeding program, but she did gain enough weight to be discharged from the hospital. Dr. Matyas referred Julie to a counselor near her home. Julie never visited the counselor.

Critical Thinking Exercises

1. Is it possible for a 14-year-old girl who binges and purges to have AN? Is it possible for a 15-year-old girl to have BN but *never* purge?

2. Many people believe that girls develop eating disorders because of pressure placed on them by society and the media. What is the evidence that society and the media *cause* eating disorders in adolescent girls? Is there any evidence that genetic and biological factors also play some role in the development of eating disorders?

3. What role does (1) culture and (2) ethnicity play in the development of eating disorders among adolescent girls?

4. Compare and contrast Structural Family Therapy and the Maudsley Hospital Approach to treating AN. Which approach appears to have greater empirical support?

5. Ronnie is a 15-year-old girl with early signs of BN. In therapy, she explained to her counselor, "After I ate the pizza, ice cream, and soda, I felt disgusting—like I was an ugly slob with no self-control. I knew the other girls thought so too because they were watching me. So I went into the bathroom and threw it all up." If you were Ronnie's counselor, how might you challenge her ways of thinking?

CHAPTER 15

Child Abuse and Neglect

The Significance of Child Maltreatment

Child maltreatment is a significant problem in the United States. Each year, approximately 2.6 million youths are referred to child protective services for suspected maltreatment. After review and investigation, almost 900,000 of these reported cases are substantiated. These statistics indicate that approximately 1.3% of children and adolescents are abused or neglected in the United States every year. However, this estimate does not include the vast number of maltreated youths who are never reported.

Child maltreatment places considerable financial demands on society. Most obvious are the direct financial costs associated with child maltreatment: the cost of providing medical, mental health, and home placement services to victims; the cost of providing training and rehabilitative services to offending parents; and (in some cases) the cost of prosecuting and incarcerating adult offenders. Less noticeable are the indirect financial costs associated with maltreatment: lower academic and job attainment by victims, lost wages and productivity by parents, and the negative impact on the community caused by antisocial behavior shown by many maltreated youths who do not receive treatment. The estimated annual financial cost of child maltreatment in the United States is approximately $50–$100 billion (Cicchetti, 2004).

Child maltreatment has less tangible, but no less important, emotional costs. Child victims typically experience considerable emotional pain and psychological distress, family members often report increased conflict and reduced quality of life, and perpetrators must face the consequences of their acts, ranging from humiliation, to social ostracism, to imprisonment. Child maltreatment seriously affects victims, families, and society.

Definition

Public policy and research has been limited by a lack of consensus regarding the definition of child maltreatment. Put simply, experts cannot agree what behaviors constitute abuse and neglect. Indeed, definitions of child maltreatment vary from state to state and from professional to professional.

The first general definition of child maltreatment was presented in the Child Abuse Prevention and Treatment Act of 1974 (PL 93-247). This act defined maltreatment as

> The physical or mental injury, sexual abuse, exploitation, negligent treatment, or maltreatment of a child under the age of 18 . . . by a person who is responsible for the child's welfare under circumstances which indicate that the child's health or welfare is harmed or threatened.

Although somewhat vague, this definition is noteworthy because it identifies four types of child maltreatment: (1) physical abuse, (2) sexual abuse, (3) psychological abuse (i.e., "mental injury"), and (4) neglect.

Physical Abuse

Most experts believe that physical abuse includes deliberate behaviors that result in injury, or the serious risk of injury, to a child. Examples of physically abusive behavior include hitting, kicking, shaking, throwing, burning, stabbing, or choking an infant or child. States have different definitions of physical maltreatment. Some states use the **harm standard** to identify cases of physical abuse; that is, the abusive act must result in physical harm to the child. Other states apply the **endangerment standard**, in which the *potential* for harm is sufficient to merit the classification of physical abuse. For example, dangling a small child over a balcony in order to punish him would be considered physical abuse according to the endangerment standard, even if the child did not experience physical injury.

Kaela

My grandmother died when I was 13, and I was alone with my older brother, who is mentally handicapped, and my grandfather. I was beaten daily for almost a year. My grandfather used to scream at me . . . tell me I was worthless, and ugly, and a disappointment, stuff like that. I would take the blame for stuff my brother did just so that he might be spared from the pain I was forced to deal with.

One night, I was alone in my room, crying from the verbal abuse I'd just been subjected to. I picked up a razor blade and just started slicing my arms and wrists. For some reason, it made me feel better. I'd swallow painkillers to try and kill myself. I was hospitalized on one occasion and a man from the local mental health center came to speak with me. I could not answer all his questions truthfully because my grandfather stood right next to me.

Factitious Disorder by Proxy

A rare but dramatic form of child physical abuse is Factitious Disorder by Proxy, sometimes referred to as Munchausen by Proxy Syndrome (Parnell, 2002). In this disorder, the caregiver, usually the child's mother, deliberately fabricates or induces physical symptoms in her child. She then seeks medical care for her child, usually reporting considerable distress and concern for her child's welfare. In most cases, the deliberate feigning of illness in the child satisfies some need for the mother. For example, some mothers seem to enjoy the attention and sympathy given by medical staff. Others enjoy playing the role of "nurse" to their children, believing that if their child has a serious illness, they can keep the child at home. Still other mothers engage in these behaviors as a sign that they need help with parenting. Usually, however, these mothers do not show other psychological disorders.

Factitious Disorder by Proxy usually occurs in the mothers of infants and toddlers. Caregivers usually misreport, exaggerate, and induce symptoms. Indeed, there are cases in which parents have physically injured, poisoned, and drugged young children in order to present physical symptoms to medical professionals. In some instances, victims are older children who are coached by their mothers to provide coherent reports of medical illness. Mothers with Factitious Disorder by Proxy usually have extensive knowledge of medical illnesses and the health care system.

Factitious Disorder by Proxy is extremely difficult to identify. Most medical professionals are confused by children's bizarre symptoms but reluctant to believe that the child's mother is responsible. Usually, the disorder is identified when children present symptoms that are not medically plausible. Sometimes, however, medical staff observe mothers inducing symptoms in their children while their children are at the hospital. The average length of time between onset and identification of the disorder is approximately 15–22 months. During that time, most children experience considerable physical harm.

Sexual Abuse

There is no consensus regarding the definition of child sexual abuse (Bergevin, Bukowski, & Karavasilis, 2003). In fact, experts disagree about the precise meaning of each component of the term: *child, sexual,* and *abuse.*

Experts disagree regarding the age of "child" victims. Some professionals limit their definition of child sexual abuse to sexual acts committed against individuals 14 years of age and younger. Other experts, adopting a more liberal definition, classify all individuals under the age of 18 as "children." Still others consider the age difference between the victim and the perpetrator of the abuse.

Experts also disagree about the types of sexual acts that constitute sexual abuse. Some individuals only consider penetration as sexually abusive. Others believe all sexual activity that involves physical contact merits the definition of sexual abuse (e.g., fondling, open-mouth kissing). Still other experts include sexual acts that do not involve physical touching in their definition of abuse, so long as these acts are directed toward children and intended to sexually gratify the adult. From this perspective, voyeurism, exhibitionism, and the use of children for sexually explicit pictures or videos constitute sexual abuse.

Finally, experts disagree about the exact definition of abuse. Some individuals claim that physical force or coercion is necessary for a sexual act to be considered abusive. Other experts believe that *all* sexual activity toward children and adolescents is abusive, even those acts that are seemingly performed willingly by adolescents.

According to Lucy Berliner (2000), **child sexual abuse** involves any sexual activity with a child in which consent is not or cannot be given. Berliner's definition includes all sexual behavior regardless of whether the interactions are physical or nonphysical. Consequently, both physical contact (e.g., touching, penetration) and nonphysical sexual interactions (e.g., voyeurism, exhibitionism) with children can be considered sexual abuse (Bonner, Logue, & Kees, 2003).

Berliner's definition of sexual abuse also includes all sexual interactions between adults and nonadults (i.e., children and adolescents). Even sexual contact between adults and adolescents can be considered abusive, despite the fact that some adolescents may want to engage in the sexual activity. Adult sexual contact with children and adolescents is *always* abusive because nonadults are incapable of consenting to sexual activity. In order to consent, people must (1) understand all of the implications associated with their sexual behavior and (2) freely decide to engage in the sexual activity without any outside pressure. Of course, most youths are unable to appreciate the full implications of engaging in sexual behavior with an adult. Furthermore, by virtue of their age and developmental status, children and adolescents are always at a power disadvantage in their interactions with adults. Consequently, they can *never* consent to sexual activity without adults influencing their decision.

Of course, there are gray areas in determining what constitutes child sexual abuse. For example, experts disagree how to classify sexual contact between two children or two adolescents. Furthermore, experts disagree whether sexual contact between a minor adolescent (e.g., 16 years) and a young adult (e.g., 19 years) constitutes abuse. In these cases, professionals usually consider the age and developmental status of the two youths, their relationship to each other, and any power differentials that might have led to coercion.

Angela

Angela was a 13-year-old girl who was referred to our clinic because she was sexually abused. Before being placed in foster care, Angela lived with her mother, Mrs. Alosio, her stepfather, Mr. Valenta, and her three younger half-sisters. Angela grew up in a tumultuous home. Angela's biological father had a history of aggressive and antisocial behavior. He was incarcerated for domestic violence at the time of the evaluation. Angela's mother had a history of alcohol and other drug abuse and had been arrested for selling narcotics on two occasions. Mrs. Alosio used alcohol, cocaine, and other drugs during her pregnancy with Angela. Angela was born prematurely and showed cognitive delays.

Angela's mother married Jason Valenta when Angela was six years old. Mr. Valenta appeared to provide a stable home and family life for Angela and her sisters. However, several weeks before Angela's referral, Mrs. Alosio discovered Mr. Valenta engaging in sexual intercourse with Angela. Shocked and repulsed, Mrs. Alosio yelled at both Mr. Valenta and Angela and ordered them to leave the house.

Angela had been repeatedly sexually abused for at least five years. Mr. Valenta eventually admitted to seeking out Mrs. Alosio, whom he described as "emotionally and financially vulnerable," to gain access to her daughters. Mr. Valenta instructed Angela never to tell anyone about the abuse because disclosure would cause his imprisonment, family disunification, and Mrs. Alosio's return to poverty and drug abuse.

In foster care, Angela showed problems with anxiety and depression. She displayed sleep difficulties, fear of the dark, and frequent nightmares associated with the abuse. Angela also had unwanted memories of abuse (e.g., a flashback) while in church. During the sermon, Angela showed extreme panic, ran from the congregation, and repeatedly cried, "I'm so bad!"

Angela preferred to play with the six- and seven-year-old children in her foster home, rather than with girls her own age. She had few friends at school. Angela was reprimanded for kissing several boys during recess because "they asked her to." In foster care and at school, Angela tended to act helpless or to use "baby talk" to get special favors. Most of all, Angela seemed to need constant approval and reassurance from adults. Her foster mother described her as "needy" and "crushed by the slightest reprimand or criticism."

Psychological Abuse

Psychological maltreatment is more difficult to identify and substantiate than physical or sexual abuse. The American Professional Society on the Abuse of Children (APSAC) defines psychological maltreatment as a pattern of caregiver behavior that "conveys to children that they are worthless, flawed, unloved, unwanted, endangered, or only of value in meeting another's needs" (Briere, Berliner, Bulkley, Jenny, & Reid, 1996, p. 2). According to the APSAC definition, psychological maltreatment includes six types of behaviors: (1) spurning, (2) terrorizing, (3) isolating, (4) exploiting/corrupting, (5) denying emotional responsiveness, and (6) neglecting children's health and educational needs (see Table 15.1).

Dee

One Saturday night, I went with my friend to a restaurant. My mother found out and she came to the restaurant and yelled at me in front of my friends. She pulled me home, where she threw me to the floor and started kicking me and slapping me.

The next day, she called me to her bed and gave me a two-hour lecture on how it was my fault that I had forced her to hit me because I wouldn't listen to her. I then had to write a sorry letter to her for forcing her to hit me. It was like that every time after we got hit. She would always make us tell her that we were sorry for forcing her to hit us, and we were forced to thank her for doing it because it was for our own good.

Every night we fell asleep knowing sooner or later we would be awoken for a lecture about something we had done. It would go on for 2–3 hours. And just wanting it to end, we had to agree she was right. She forced us to repeat after her:

"I am a lazy, clumsy girl."

"I am stupid."

"I don't respect my parents enough."

Table 15.1   Six Types of Psychological Abuse

Type of Abuse	Description
Spurning	*Verbal and nonverbal acts that reject or degrade a child:* • Ridiculing a child for showing normal emotions (i.e., crying). • Consistently singling out a specific child for punishment or chores. • Showing extreme favoritism to one child and neglecting another. • Humiliating a child in public.
Terrorizing	*Threatening to hurt or abandon a child or injure/kill a child's loved one:* • Threatening to hurt or kill a child if he/she does not obey. • Allowing the child to witness domestic violence. • Threatening to kill the child's pet if the child does not obey. • Threatening to leave the child.
Isolating	*Denying a child opportunities to interact with peers or adults outside the home:* • Refusing the child's reasonable requests to interact with peers. • Denying the child telephone contact or legal visitation with parent.
Exploiting	*Encouraging a child to adopt inappropriate, maladaptive behaviors:* • Modeling, permitting, or encouraging antisocial acts. • Using the child to sell or transport drugs. • Asking the child to engage in prostitution or pornography.
Denying emotional responsiveness	*Ignoring the child's bids for attention and emotional interactions:* • Remaining emotionally detached, cold, distant from the child. • Rarely showing care, affection, or love toward the child. • Failing to comfort the child when he/she is scared, upset, or unsure.
Health and educational neglect	*Failing to meet a child's medical, mental health, and educational needs:* • Failing to provide medical care to the child when necessary. • Ignoring or refusing to participate in the child's psychological treatment when necessary. • Ignoring or refusing to participate in the treatment of the child's learning problems.

Source: Based on Hart, Brassard, Binggeli, and Davidson (2002).

Psychological maltreatment denies children the respect and dignity that is the inherent right of all human beings. At one extreme, psychological maltreatment involves the repeated and outright rejection of children through seriously hostile, aggressive, or coercive displays. These behaviors are included under the APSAC domains of spurning, terrorizing, isolating, and exploiting children. At the other extreme, psychological maltreatment communicates to children that their needs, interests, emotions, and bids for autonomy lack value. These sentiments are conveyed when parents deny emotional responsiveness or neglect children's health and emotional needs.

One particularly troubling form of psychological maltreatment is exposing children to domestic violence (Graham-Bermann, 2002). In the United States, domestic violence occurs in approximately one-fourth of all marriages, with rates possibly much higher among cohabiting nonmarried couples. No one knows how many children witness acts of domestic violence each year. However, the effects of domestic violence on children are striking. Children exposed to violence in the home show a wide range of internalizing and externalizing behavior problems, especially depression, anxiety, conduct problems, and PTSD. Many adults who physically abuse their spouses also engage in child maltreatment (Appel & Holden, 1998).

Neglect

Neglect occurs when caregivers do not meet children's essential needs and when their negligence harms or threatens children's welfare. There are at least four ways caregivers can neglect children: physically, emotionally, medically, and educationally (Erickson & Egeland, 2002).

Physical neglect occurs when caregivers fail to protect children from danger and provide for their physical needs. Failing to provide food, shelter, and clothing is usually considered neglectful. Physical neglect is, perhaps, the most common form of neglect and the easiest to identify. However, it is sometimes difficult to differentiate parents who physically neglect their children from parents who, because of economic hardship, are unable to provide for their children's needs.

Emotional neglect occurs when caregivers fail to provide for children's social and emotional needs. Erickson and Egeland (2002) describe emotionally neglectful caregivers as "psychologically unavailable" to their children. These caregivers do not provide sensitive and responsive care to their children, ignore their children's bids for comfort and attention, and remain physically and emotionally distant or disconnected. The emotional neglect of infants is associated with **nonorganic failure to thrive syndrome**; that is, the infant shows problems gaining weight and reaching expected developmental milestones. In severe cases, emotional neglect can result in infant mortality.

Medical neglect occurs when children's basic health care needs are unmet (Dubowitz & Black, 2002). Basic health care refers to medical procedures or treatments that, if not administered, would seriously jeopardize the health of the child. Medical neglect might include failing to provide children with necessary immunizations, not taking children for a medical examination when they display serious illness, or refusing to follow doctors' recommendations regarding the treatment or management of a severe illness (e.g., parents not helping a young child with diabetes management).

Educational neglect usually occurs when parents do not enroll their children in school or otherwise provide for their education. Educational neglect might also occur when parents repeatedly allow their children to skip school.

Michael

Michael was a 5-year-, 11-month-old boy who was referred to the hospital by the department of child protective services. Michael and his half-siblings were removed from their grandmother's care because of neglect. The children were discovered living in a dirty apartment with little food and almost nonexistent

---

(Continued)

(Continued)

daytime supervision. They had an inconsistent history of medical care (e.g., immunizations, well-child checks), were malnourished, and were generally unkempt. All of the children were physically sick, and Michael's two-year-old sister had extensive diaper rash that needed medical attention.

Michael displayed below-average social and self-care skills. Upon arriving in foster care, he was unable to wash his face, brush his teeth, bathe, dry, and dress. Michael hoarded food, displayed poor table manners, and did not know how to use utensils. He also showed excessive preoccupation with food. His teeth were decayed.

Michael displayed poor social skills. He refused to share toys, wait his turn, pick up his clothes, or obey other rules of the home. He usually settled interpersonal disputes through physical violence. Ironically, Michael was expelled from Sunday School for punching a classmate. Michael's foster mother said that he intimidated and bullied the other children in the home. "Michael is a needy kid," his foster mother explained. "He demands constant reassurance. He's always acting up and then asking us, 'Am I a good boy?'"

Epidemiology

Prevalence

For several reasons, it is difficult to estimate the prevalence of child maltreatment. First, many instances of child abuse are never identified. For example, many abused children never disclose their victimization because they feel shame, others are intimidated by the adults who victimize them, and still others are simply too young to tell others about their experiences. Similarly, many psychologically abused and neglected children never come to the attention of teachers or neighbors because their maltreatment does not result in a deterioration in their appearance or behavior (Dubowitz et al., 2005).

Second, even when child maltreatment is identified, it is not always reported to authorities. Many parents decide not to report instances of child maltreatment to authorities, believing that they can help their children cope with the experience themselves. Other adults avoid reporting maltreatment in order to avoid the stigma associated with an investigation.

Third, no government agency collects data on all reported cases of child maltreatment. Instead, different government agencies and independently funded researchers collect data from local areas that may or may not be representative of all children across the country.

How common is child maltreatment? In a recent survey of a large, nationally representative sample of youth, Finkelhor, Cross, and Cantor (2005) estimated that 13.8% of children and adolescents have experienced at least one form of maltreatment (see Figure 15.1). This estimate is based on a definition of maltreatment that involves the *potential* for the child to experience serious harm. When researchers limit their definition of maltreatment to include only instances that resulted in *actual* injury, then the estimated prevalence of maltreatment decreases to 12.4%. This percentage reflects approximately 8,000,000 youths in the United States.

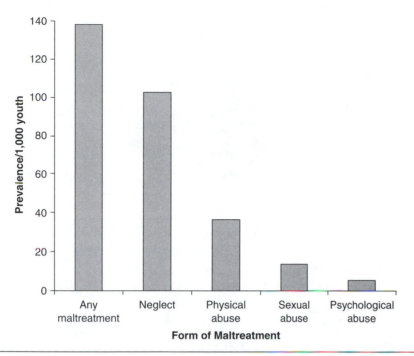

Figure 15.1   Prevalence of Child Maltreatment in the United States

Source: Based on Finkelhor et al. (2005).

If we use the harm standard to identify maltreated youth, the most common form of child maltreatment in the United States is neglect, accounting for 60% of reported cases (Runyon, Kenny, Berry, Deblinger, & Brown, 2006). Approximately 19% of maltreated children experience physical abuse, 10% experience sexual abuse, and 8% experience psychological abuse. The remaining children experience acts of maltreatment that are undifferentiated or difficult to classify. It is important to remember that most children who experience maltreatment are victimized in multiple ways. The statistics provided above reflect children's most frequent or severe experience of maltreatment.

Overall, boys and girls show approximately equal likelihood of experiencing physical abuse, psychological abuse, and neglect. Girls, especially adolescent girls, are more likely than boys to be sexually abused.

Research is mixed regarding the prevalence of child maltreatment as a function of age. Most data indicate that infants, toddlers, and preschoolers are at greater risk for physical abuse and neglect than older children and adolescents (Stevens, Ruggiero, Kilpatrick, Resnick, & Saunders, 2005). Young children may be more susceptible to maltreatment because they depend heavily on the nurturance and protection of adults. However, some research shows that older children and adolescents show greater prevalence of maltreatment than younger children. Older children may be at particular risk for psychological and sexual abuse (Finkelhor et al., 2005).

Most acts of sexual abuse are committed by people whom the child knows (see Figure 15.2). Approximately 85% of sexually maltreated children are victimized by their parents or stepparents. The vast majority of other cases of abuse are committed by other family members, babysitters, teachers, and coaches. Strangers are responsible for only about 2% of cases of sexual abuse.

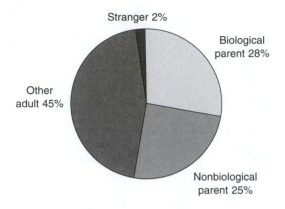

Figure 15.2 Relationship of Sexual Abuse Perpetrator to Victim

Source: Based on Fagan, Wise, Schmidt, and Berlin (2002) and U.S. Department of Health and Human Services (2002).

Note: Strangers account for only about 2% of sexual abuse cases.

Reporting Child Maltreatment

In the United States, medical and mental health professionals are **mandated reporters** of child abuse and neglect. When these individuals suspect child abuse or neglect during the course of their professional practice, they are required by law to notify the police or child protective services.

Laws vary regarding when a professional must contact authorities (Bonner et al., 2003). In most cases, if a professional has reason to *suspect* child maltreatment, a report is warranted. It is not the professional's responsibility to determine whether maltreatment has *actually* occurred. State laws usually protect professionals from civil liability for reporting suspected maltreatment in good faith, even if the maltreatment is not substantiated. However, negligence in reporting child maltreatment can result in both civil and criminal liability.

Reporting child maltreatment is extremely stressful for mental health professionals and families. In most cases, clients have the right to expect that the information they provide to mental health professionals will remain confidential. However, in cases of child abuse, a duty to protect the child supersedes the family's expectation of confidentiality.

Effects of Physical Abuse and Neglect

Physical Health

Child physical abuse and neglect can take its toll on children's physical health. Severely neglected infants can exhibit nonorganic failure to thrive, which can cause long-term health and behavior problems or death. Children who experience physical abuse often suffer bruises, broken bones, burns, and scars. These injuries are sometimes accompanied by neurological damage due to head trauma or abnormally elevated levels of stress hormone. As many as 35% of physically abused children suffer serious injury requiring medical or psychiatric treatment to prevent long-term impairment (Sedlak & Broadhurst, 1996).

The most serious and potentially lethal form of child physical abuse is **shaken baby syndrome** (Johnson, 2002). Shaken baby syndrome occurs when a caregiver vigorously shakes an infant back and forth, causing a rapid acceleration and deceleration of the brain within the skull. This shaking can cause severe damage to brain tissue. The syndrome is characterized by initial drowsiness or sleepiness, failure to respond to outside stimulation, breathing problems, vomiting, seizures, coma, and death. Usually, symptoms are not apparent until hours or days after the damage has been inflicted.

Behavior Problems

Children who experience physical abuse or neglect are at risk for developing disruptive behavior problems. Children with histories of maltreatment are frequently diagnosed with Oppositional Defiant Disorder. At home, they are often spiteful and argumentative toward caregivers. At school, they are frequently disruptive and defiant. Most research indicates that this tendency toward negativistic, disruptive behavior continues throughout childhood and early adolescence. Children exposed to physical abuse or neglect also show increased risk for aggression, especially toward other children. When these children experience interpersonal problems, they are prone to angry outbursts or fits of rage. Physically abused and neglected children tend to use aggression both proactively (i.e., to get what they want) and reactively (i.e., in response to being frustrated by others; Koenig, Cicchetti, & Rogosch, 2004).

Older children and adolescents with histories of physical abuse and neglect are at risk for Conduct Disorder. Abused youth have greater likelihoods of engaging in serious antisocial behavior, especially stealing, cheating, physical assault, and chronic truancy. Underlying deficits in moral reasoning may partially account for these antisocial tendencies. As adolescents, they are twice as likely as nonabused youth to be suspended from school, arrested, or involved in a violent crime. Boys who experience maltreatment show increased likelihood of developing Antisocial Personality Disorder as adults. Girls who experience physical abuse or neglect show increased risk for underemployment and prostitution later in life (Koenig et al., 2004; Luntz & Widom, 1994; Maxfield & Widom, 1996; Widom & Kuhns, 1996).

Why do maltreated children show increased likelihood of disruptive behavior later in life? One explanation is based on **learning theory**. Physically abused children may model the hostile and aggressive behavior of caregivers (Dodge et al., 1997). Indeed, children exposed to child maltreatment often witness other aggressive acts, such as domestic violence, parental antisocial behavior, and violent crime. Children may learn, through their observations, that disruptive and aggressive behavior is an effective way to solve interpersonal problems.

Another explanation for the relationship between early maltreatment and later disruptive behavior problems is based on **social information-processing theory** (Dodge & Pettit, 1990; Rieder & Cicchetti, 1989; Rogosch, Cicchetti, & Abre, 1995).

According to this theory, children solve social problems by engaging in a series of cognitive steps: (1) taking in and interpreting information about the social situation, (2) generating and evaluating a number of possible ways of responding, and (3) selecting and implementing the best plan. Physically abused children show difficulty with all three steps, making them more likely to use hostile and aggressive means to solve interpersonal problems.

First, physically abused children show hostile attributional biases when solving social problems. That is, they expect others to behave in a hostile and aggressive manner toward them. Consequently, they often misinterpret the benign behaviors of others as hostile and aggressive. Second, abused children usually have difficulty generating solutions to social problems; furthermore, the solutions that they are able to generate are usually hostile or aggressive in nature. Third, abused children impulsively select a plan of action; that is, they often do not consider the consequences of their behavior before they act. These social problem-solving deficits increase the likelihood that children will act aggressively in ambiguous social situations (Price & Glad, 2003).

What about neglected youths; how might they develop disruptive and antisocial behaviors? Children who experience neglect often have peer problems and low social functioning. Indeed, many neglected youths have few friends and are actively rejected by classmates. Because neglected children are often ostracized by prosocial peers, they may seek friendships with other rejected children. These rejected peers can introduce them to disruptive and antisocial behaviors such as aggression, delinquency, and substance use. Furthermore, parents who neglect their children usually do not sufficiently monitor their children's activities (Knutson, DeGarmo, Koeppl, & Reid, 2005). Consequently, neglected children are free to engage in antisocial activities with little adult supervision. Association with deviant peer groups and low parental monitoring are primary predictors of conduct problems.

Mood and Anxiety Problems

Many physically abused and neglected children develop mood disorders (Clark, De Bellis, Lynch, Cornelius, & Martin, 2003; Kilpatrick, Ruggiero, Acierno, Saunders, Resnick, & Best, 2003). Comorbid mood problems include MDD, Dysthymic Disorder, and general feelings of hopelessness (Kolko, 2002). Child maltreatment, especially psychological maltreatment, can also lead to more diffuse emotional problems. For example, many psychologically maltreated children report low self-esteem and self-efficacy. These mood problems are especially common in youths who experience multiple types of maltreatment and among girls (Danielson, de Arellano, Kilpatrick, Saunders, & Resnick, 2005).

Maltreated youths are also at risk for developing anxiety disorders. The most common anxiety disorder associated with physical abuse is PTSD. Approximately 16%–36% of youths exposed to physical abuse develop PTSD (Danielson et al., 2005; Famularo, Fenton, Kinscherff, Ayoub, & Barnum, 1994). Furthermore, approximately one-third of children who develop abuse-related PTSD continue to show symptoms two years after the end of their physical maltreatment (Famularo, Fenton, Augustyn, & Zuckerman, 1996).

How does child abuse place children at risk for mood and anxiety disorders? Hart, Brassard, Binggeli, and Davidson (2002) have used **Maslow's hierarchical theory of human needs** to explain the negative effects of child maltreatment on children's social and emotional development. According to Maslow's theory, optimal social-emotional development depends on children's abilities to satisfy certain fundamental needs. These needs are arranged in hierarchical fashion and fall into two general categories. The first category, basic needs, includes the child's physiological needs (e.g., food, shelter, clothing) and psychological needs (e.g., a sense of safety, belongingness, self-esteem). The second category, growth needs, includes the need for knowledge and beauty as well as the tendency toward self-actualization. According to Maslow, **self-actualization** refers to the innate tendency to become fully functioning in all areas of life and is characterized by a sense of high self-efficacy and intrinsic motivation.

From the perspective of human needs theory, child maltreatment interferes with children's attainment of their basic needs. Physical and emotional neglect denies children's physiological needs. Physical and psychological abuse interfere with children's pursuit of psychological needs, especially safety and emotional connectedness with others. Since these basic needs are unsatisfied, high-order needs that promote social and emotional well-being are often left unfulfilled.

Physical abuse, psychological abuse, and neglect also can cause children to adopt negative views of themselves, others, and the future (Runyon & Kenny, 2002; Toth, Cicchetti, Macfie, Maughan, & Vanmeenen, 2000). Compared to nonabused children, maltreated children are more likely to believe that they are inherently unworthy, bad, or flawed (Harter, 1997, 1999). The attributions children make about their maltreatment predict the severity of their internalizing symptoms. Children who blame themselves for their victimization show much greater mood disturbance than children who do not assume responsibility for their maltreatment (Brown & Kolko, 1999).

Quality of Attachment

Abused and neglected children show greater likelihood of developing insecure attachment relationships with parents and other adults responsible for their care. Approximately two-thirds of maltreated children develop insecure attachment relationships with their caregivers, compared to approximately one-third of nonmaltreated children (Cicchetti & Barnett, 1991; Cicchetti, Toth, & Maughan, 2000; Crittenden, 1992).

Insecure attachment might mediate the relationship between child maltreatment and behavioral/emotional problems later in development. That is, child maltreatment can lead children to adopt internal working models of themselves and others that are based on interpersonal mistrust and self-doubt. Although rarely articulated, these working models might include the following beliefs: "The world is dangerous. I cannot trust others. I must rely on myself. I am not worthy of receiving help from others, anyway." These models subsequently color all of the child's future relationships and his self-view. The result could be disruptive behavior, social isolation, and a host of mood and anxiety problems (Erickson & Egeland, 2002).

Some maltreated children display **disorganized patterns of attachment** toward their caregivers (Main, Kaplan, & Cassidy, 1985). Children who form disorganized attachments behave in bizarre, erratic, or unpredictable ways during the Ainsworth strange situation procedure. Some children who are classified as having disorganized attachment show considerable distress when separated from their mothers during the strange situation procedure, but they attempt to flee from their mothers when their mothers re-enter the room. Other children classified as having disorganized attachment also show distress during separation, but when their mothers return, they seek comfort from inanimate objects (e.g., the leg of a table) instead of their mothers. Still other children appear hesitant or fearful of their mothers. Disorganized attachment is most common among children who have experienced physical abuse or neglect. Maltreatment may cause children to expect that their parents will behave in unpredictable or threatening ways (Barnett, Ganiban, & Cicchetti, 1999).

Infants and young children who are severely neglected are at risk for **Reactive Attachment Disorder (RAD).** Infants and toddlers with RAD show marked problems in their interactions with caregivers. These social problems are caused by severe and persistent neglect of their basic physical needs (e.g., food, clothing), denial of basic social-emotional needs (e.g., touch, comfort, affection), or repeated changes in caregivers (e.g., placement in many different foster homes; Chaffin et al., 2006).

Young children can manifest RAD in two ways. Some young children display **RAD-Inhibited Type;** they do not initiate or respond to social interactions in developmentally appropriate ways. For example, a toddler with RAD-Inhibited Type might be reluctant to let his mother hug and comfort him, even when he is scared or upset. His mother might describe him as "distant" or "aloof." Often, young children with RAD-Inhibited Type are fussy and difficult to soothe because they avoid close contact with caregivers. Other youths display **RAD-Disinhibited Type;** these children show indiscriminate sociability. For example, a toddler with RAD-Disinhibited Type might seek comfort or attention from strangers. These children are often described as "needy" and requiring constant attention and reassurance.

In the United States, RAD is a rare condition. However, as many as 5% of foreign-born infants adopted by U.S. families after age six months show features of RAD. RAD is usually seen only among infants with histories of severe neglect. For example, Rene Spitz (1946) and John Bowlby (1953) described features of RAD among orphans in Europe after World War II. More recently, researchers have documented RAD symptoms in Romanian orphans who were exposed to severe psychological neglect during that country's communist regime (Beckett et al., 2006; Rutter et al., 2007). Neglected Romanian orphans who were adopted by loving families after six months of age continued to show cognitive and social deficits, especially disinhibited attachment, ten years later (see Image 15.1).

Cognitive Delays

Physically abused and neglected children are more likely to show cognitive delays than their non-abused peers (Kolko, 2002). Cognitive problems include difficulty with executive functioning, working memory, and language (Eigsti & Cicchetti, 2004). Abused and neglected children often lack impulse control and

Image 15.1   Extreme Neglect. Under the regime of communist leader Nicolae Ceauşescu, Romania's birth rate skyrocketed while poverty became widespread. By 1989, when Ceauşescu was deposed, more than 100,000 infants and children were abandoned to orphanages. Most, like the boy pictured above, were given food and clothing but little attention or comfort. Many developed RAD, autistic-like symptoms, and/or antisocial behavior.

Source: AP Photo/Vadim Ghirda. Used with permission.

have difficulty on a wide range of mental tasks. These cognitive problems tend to be long lasting; they may persist well after the termination of abuse (Claussen & Crittenden, 1991; Crittenden, Claussen, & Sugarman, 1994).

The academic achievement of maltreated youth tends to be less well-developed than the achievement of nonabused children. Academic problems seem to be pervasive; they exist across all major areas of academic functioning (Kolko, 2002). Maltreated children are more likely to repeat a grade, receive special education services for learning problems, and miss school. They are also more likely to show behavior problems at school, to be suspended, and to drop out before graduation. Neglected children tend to show the lowest academic achievement of any group of maltreated youth (Dubowitz et al., 2005).

Effects of Sexual Abuse

Effects on Child Development

Finkelhor and Browne (1985) suggest that childhood sexual abuse traumatizes children in four ways. Specifically, sexual abuse contributes to (1) traumatic sexualization, (2) feelings of betrayal, (3) powerlessness, and (4) stigmatization. Abuse places children on deviant developmental pathways that can lead to impairment.

Traumatic Sexualization

Sexually abused children sometimes show increased levels of sexualized behavior compared to nonabused peers (Kendall-Tackett, Williams, & Finkelhor, 1993). **Sexualized behaviors** are actions that are either not typical for the child's age and development or inappropriate to the social situation. Sexualized behaviors include excessive or public masturbation, preoccupation with sex, sexualized play with dolls, forced sexual activity with playmates, and seductive language and behavior (Heiman & Heard-Davison, 2004).

It is sometimes difficult to differentiate normative and non-normative sexualized behavior during childhood because little research has been conducted on typical sexual activity in children (Friedrich, 1997; Friedrich et al., 2001). Some sexualized behaviors are normative at certain ages. For example, many toddlers engage in self-stimulation, preschoolers try to look at adults while naked or undressing, and school-age children ask parents sex-related questions. However, other sexual behavior is usually never developmentally appropriate, such as sexualized play with dolls, forced sexual behavior, or the insertion of objects into sexual body parts.

Age-inappropriate sexual behavior is *not* a reliable indicator of child sexual abuse (Friedrich, 1997; Johnson & Friend, 1995). Although many sexually abused children show sexualized behavior, most (66%) do not. Even the most problematic sexualized behaviors (e.g., a child forcing sexual activity on a playmate, insertions) differentiate sexually abused and nonabused children with only 75% accuracy. Instead of behavior, emerging data indicate that the presence of **precocious sexual knowledge** might better differentiate sexually abused and nonabused youths (Brilleslijper-Kater, Friedrich, & Corwin, 2004). Young, sexually abused children often have greater knowledge of sexual behavior than their nonabused peers.

Emerging data indicate that child sexual abuse can speed up sexual maturation, especially in girls (Bergevin et al., 2003). In one study, sexually abused girls who experienced vaginal penetration showed menarche approximately one year earlier than their non-abused peers. The mechanism by which child sexual abuse leads to early menarche is unknown, but researchers have suggested that the abuse experience could stimulate hormonal or biochemical (e.g., pheromone) secretions.

Sexually abused girls are at risk for being sexually victimized as adults. A meta-analysis of studies investigating the association between sexual abuse in children and sexual victimization in adults revealed an overall effect size of .59 for women (Roodman & Clum, 2001). Overall, women who were sexually abused as children were two to three times more likely to be sexually assaulted during adulthood than their non-abused peers (Rich, Combs-Lane, Resnick, & Kilpatrick, 2004).

Retrospective studies also indicate that girls who are sexually abused show increased risk for sexual disorders and risky sexual behavior as adults (Koenig & Clark, 2004; Rich et al., 2004). For example, some sexually abused girls show higher rates of sexual arousal problems as adults than their nonabused peers (Laumann, Paik, & Rosen, 1999). Other women with histories of child sexual abuse display hypersexual behavior. Specifically, they are more likely to show sexual promiscuity, engage in unsafe sexual practices such as one-time-only sexual encounters, become involved in prostitution, and contract human immunodeficiency virus (HIV) than their nonabused peers.

The relationship between childhood sexual abuse and sexual re-victimization is less clear for boys. Most research indicates that boys who are sexually abused are not more likely to be sexually assaulted as adults (Purcel, Malow, Dolezal, & Carballo-Dieguez, 2004). However, some data indicate that homosexual men with histories of childhood sexual abuse do show increased risk for adult sexual victimization by other men.

Men with histories of sexual abuse are also more likely to show sexual adjustment problems than their nonabused peers (Heiman & Heard-Davison, 2004; Purcel et al., 2004). Although data are somewhat inconsistent, men with histories of sexual abuse show increased likelihood of sexual dysfunction (e.g., premature ejaculation, erectile dysfunction, low sexual desire), sexually coercive and aggressive behaviors toward their partners, sexual promiscuity, risky sexual behavior, and HIV infection.

Betrayal

Sexual abuse traumatizes children through betrayal. Sexual abuse breeds mistrust, especially when the abuser is a family member or caregiver. Abuse during childhood can also cause mistrust toward adults and authority figures in general. Loss of trust can contribute to feelings of anger, rage, and anxiety in interpersonal relationships (Gold, Sinclair, & Balge, 1999).

Attachment theorists argued that the experience of child sexual abuse contributes to the development of insecure attachment (Howes, Cicchetti, Toth, & Rogosch, 2000). Abused children fail to develop internal working models of caregivers based on trust, security, sensitivity, and support. Instead, the worldview of sexually abused youth is often characterized by insecurity, doubt, and the anticipation of harm. In times of crisis, individuals with histories of abuse may not feel confident in their partner's sensitivity and responsiveness to their needs. Consequently, these individuals may avoid close attachments with others or excessively cling to others because they fear abandonment.

Indeed, many sexually abused children display problems in their adult interpersonal relationships (Finkelhor, Hotaling, Lewis, & Smith, 1989; Gold et al., 1999; Mullen, Martin, Anderson, Romans, & Herbison, 1994). Some women with histories of sexual abuse sacrifice their freedom and autonomy in order to please their partners. Although they describe their partners as overly controlling and unsympathetic to their needs, they remain in these relationships to avoid rejection and abandonment. Other women with abuse histories report a general dissatisfaction in their romantic relationships, pervasive feelings of mistrust and insecurity toward their partners, and an overall lack of emotional intimacy. Both groups of women are more likely to divorce than their non-abused counterparts.

Powerlessness

Sexual abuse victimizes children by making them feel powerless. Children who are abused often feel helpless and unable to cope with the abuse experience or its social-emotional effects. Children who adopt internal, stable, and global attributions for their abuse are especially at risk for feelings of powerlessness and helplessness

(Gold et al., 1999; Sinclair & Gold, 1997). Some maltreated children assume responsibility for their abuse, believe that abuse-related problems will persist, and believe that the effects of abuse will affect many aspects of their lives and day-to-day functioning. Over time, feelings of powerlessness can lead to anxiety and depression, emotional numbing, and hopelessness.

The most common psychological disorder associated with sexual abuse is PTSD (Berliner & Elliott, 2002). Among children referred to psychiatric clinics for sexual abuse, as many as 50% meet diagnostic criteria for PTSD, while another 30% show at least some PTSD symptoms (Ackerman, Newton, McPherson, Jones, & Dykman, 1998; McLeer, Deblinger, Henry, & Orvaschel, 1992). The likelihood of PTSD following sexual abuse is related to the severity of the abuse, especially the degree to which the perpetrator used violence or physical coercion, intimidated the victim, or instilled fear and terror (Chaffin, Silovsky, & Vaughn, 2005; Hanson, Saunders, Kilpatrick, Resnick, Crouch, & Duncan, 2001).

Children can show a host of other internalizing disorders ranging from anxiety, depression, somatic complaints, eating problems, sleep disturbance, and loss of bowel and bladder control. For example, sexually abused children are four times more likely than nonabused youth to develop anxiety disorders. Abused children are at risk for anxiety even if they do not immediately perceive the sexual abuse incident as traumatic (Chaffin et al., 2005).

Stigmatization

Finally, sexual abuse can lead to stigmatization (Browne & Finkelhor, 1986; Feiring & Taska, 2005). Many abused children believe that they are "damaged goods" because of their maltreatment. As a result, abused children may engage in self-destructive behaviors to express their feelings of low self-worth or replace emotional discomfort with physical pain. Self-injury, suicidal behavior, and Substance Dependence can be seen as the outward manifestations of stigmatization.

Although the concept of stigmatization is difficult to measure, adult survivors of child sexual abuse are more likely to display these hypothesized effects of stigmatization than their non-abused peers (Heiman & Heard-Davison, 2004). For example, self-harming behaviors, such as burning and cutting, are two to five times more common among sexually abused adolescent girls and women than among non-abused females (see Figure 15.3). In one study of adolescent girls who recently disclosed their sexual abuse, 62% admitted to some form of self-harm (Cyr, McDuff, Wright, Theriault, & Cinq-Mars, 2005). Child sexual abuse is often seen in the histories of women with Borderline Personality Disorder, a serious disorder characterized by an unstable sense of identity, emotional dysregulation, tumultuous interpersonal relationships, and self-harm.

Sexual abuse also predicts suicidal thoughts and suicide attempts in adolescence and adulthood (Martin, Bergen, Richardson, Roeger, & Allison, 2004; Ystgaard, Hestetun, Loeb, & Mehlum, 2004). Interestingly, the relationship between child sexual abuse and suicidality differs by gender. For girls, child sexual abuse is associated with depression and feelings of hopelessness. These negative emotions, in turn, predict suicidal ideas and plans. For boys, there is a direct relationship between history

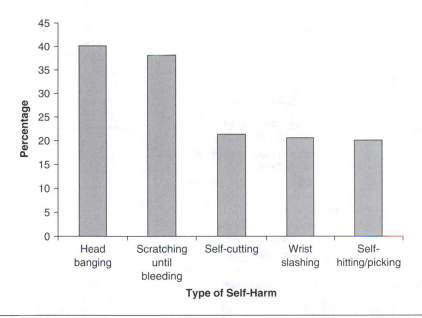

Figure 15.3   Self-Harm Among Youths With Histories of Sexual Abuse

Source: Based on Cyr et al. (2005).

of sexual abuse and later suicidal thoughts and behavior. This direct relationship between abuse and suicide indicates that sexually abused boys may be at risk for suicide even if they do not show depression. Indeed, even after controlling for current levels of depression, adolescent boys with histories of sexual abuse are 15 times more likely than nonabused boys to attempt suicide.

Why Do Adults Physically Abuse and Neglect Children?

Parents' Information Processing

Many parents experience stress when caring for children, especially for youths with difficult temperaments or disruptive behaviors. However, most parents do not engage in child maltreatment. Children's behaviors alone cannot explain their likelihood of victimization. Instead, researchers have suggested that the way parents *think* about their children's behavior greatly influences their actions toward their children.

Joel Milner (1998, 2003) has proposed a general cognitive-behavioral model to describe how parents' cognitions can influence the quality of care they provide their children. The **social information-processing model** of child maltreatment consists of a series of four cognitive stages that describe the processes parents use to deal with their children's misbehavior (see Figure 15.4).

When parents are confronted with problematic child behavior, they rapidly perform a series of four cognitive steps to manage the problem. First, parents encode information about the child's behavior and the situation. For example, a mother

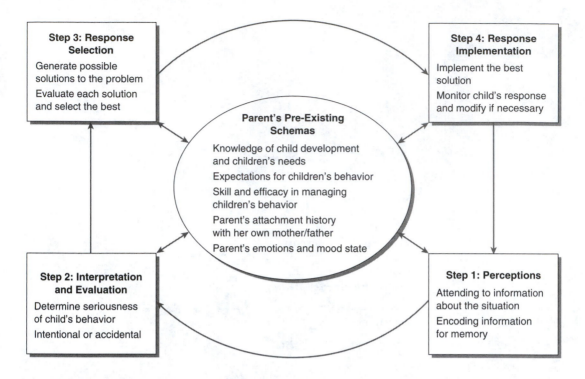

Figure 15.4   Social Information-Processing Model for Child Physical Abuse

Source: Based on Milner (2003).

might discover that her five-year-old daughter spilled juice on her new carpet. She might notice the size of the stain on the carpet, an expression of sadness or remorse on her daughter's face, or some other situational factors that might have influenced her daughter's behavior, such as a dog running away from the situation.

Second, parents must interpret and evaluate the situation using the information they collect. Of course, the way parents interpret the situation will greatly depend on the number and accuracy of the cues they encode (Step 1). For example, if the mother attends to the child's expression of remorse and the dog running away from the situation, she might reason that spilling the juice was accidental. However, if the mother attends only to the large stain on the carpet, she might assign blame to the child.

Third, parents must generate possible solutions to the problem, evaluate each solution, and select the best course of action. The solutions that parents generate will greatly depend on their interpretation of the situation (Step 2). If the parent views the child's behavior as accidental, she might decide to comfort the child and help her clean up the mess. If the parent perceives the child's behavior as purposeful, she might spank or yell at the child.

Finally, parents implement and monitor their solution to the problem. If the solution does not seem to adequately address the problem, parents might modify the solution slightly, performing all of the problem-solving steps again.

At the heart of the social information-processing model is the parent's pre-existing schemas, or mental models, about parenting. These schemas include the parent's knowledge of child development and children's social-emotional needs, her expectations regarding appropriate child behavior, her knowledge of childrearing techniques, and her skills in managing the child's behavior. Some of these schemas include general beliefs about childrearing; they can be applied to all children (e.g., "Children should be seen and not heard"). Other schemas include specific beliefs about children; they apply only to the individual's child (e.g., "It's OK for other kids to act up in public, but not mine"). Pre-existing schemas also include the parent's feelings and emotional states.

Milner's social information-processing model provides a framework for understanding how parents' cognitions can influence their childrearing tactics. Parents who are at risk for physically abusing their children show deficits in their social information-processing skills. For example, physically abusive parents often selectively attend to negative aspects of children's misbehavior (Step 1), attribute child misbehavior to intentional causes (Step 2), and rely heavily on hostile and aggressive disciplinary tactics to solve problems (Step 3). Furthermore, the childrearing histories and negative mood states of physically abusive parents often color their problem solving and interfere with their abilities to parent in a noncoercive, consistent manner.

Parents' Attributions of Child Behavior

Researchers have given special attention to one aspect of parents' social problem solving: the attributions they make about their children's behavior (Dopke, Lundahl, Dunsterville, & Lovejoy, 2003). Parents who physically abuse children often hold a number of biased perceptions of their children's behavior that cause parents to react in hostile and aggressive ways (Dix & Lochman, 1990).

First, parents who physically abuse their children often have unrealistic expectations for their children's behavior (Mammen, Kolko, & Pilkonis, 2003). They believe their children should be more compliant or competent than a typical child of the same age. For example, expecting a two-year-old child to remain quiet and to entertain herself at the Department of Motor Vehicles for two hours would be an unrealistic expectation. Unrealistic expectations can cause parents to become easily annoyed with children's behavior and engage in harsh, physical discipline.

Second, physically abusive parents often show hostile attributional biases. That is, parents attribute children's misbehavior to intentional malice (Dopke & Milner, 2000). For example, if a child spills juice on the carpet, the parent might perceive her child's behavior as "deliberately naughty" instead of accidental. Attributing children's misbehavior to intentional rather than accidental causes increases the likelihood that the parent will respond with anger rather than understanding. Hostile attributions also make parents perceive their children's behavior as excessively problematic (Mash & Johnston, 1990).

Third, parents who engage in physical abuse often see their children as holding considerable power during parent-child interactions. In contrast, these parents see themselves as lacking control over the childrearing situation (Bugental, Ellerson,

Lin, Rainey, Kokotovic, & O'Hara, 2002). Parents who feel powerless over their children can become easily threatened by their children's misbehavior. They may see their children's noncompliance as a deliberate and personal insult to their authority as caregivers. At the same time, they often feel frustrated by their own lack of control over their children's behavior, and they may blame themselves accordingly. These negative thoughts can elicit anger and hostile discipline (Bugental & Johnston, 2000).

Parents' Emotional Health

Parents who are depressed show greater likelihood of abusing or neglecting their children than parents without mood disorders. Depression can interfere with parenting in a number of ways. First, depressed parents often lack the energy and interest to provide their children with sensitive and responsive care in a consistent fashion. Instead, they may be emotionally absent or withdrawn from their children, communicating a sense of disinterest. Second, depressed mood may negatively bias parents' perceptions of their children's behavior. Depressed mothers may view their children's behavior in a manner consistent with their mood state, that is, in an overly negative light. Negative distortions of child behavior may make depressed parents more upset by their children's behavior and more prone to hostile and coercive parenting tactics. Third, maternal depression can interfere with mothers' problem solving during parent-child interactions. Specifically, depressed parents who have difficulty concentrating might be less able to deal with child misbehavior in creative, flexible, and noncoercive ways. Dysphoria can also lead mothers to make hostile attributions for their children's behaviors. Finally, depressed parents may use less effective coping skills to deal with parenting stress. Depressed parents may rely on passive and emotion-focused coping (e.g., reacting to children's misbehavior with frustration or anger) instead of active, problem-focused coping (e.g., taking a time-out from her children in order to manage stress). Ineffective coping mechanisms can exacerbate parents' negative mood and contribute to hostile behavior toward their children (Bugental, Blue, & Lewis, 1990; Cantos, Neale, & O'Leary, 1997).

Parental substance use problems are also associated with child physical abuse and neglect (Kelley, 2002; Kolko, 2002). Approximately 40% of parents who commit physical abuse and 56% of parents who commit child neglect have substance use disorders, compared to approximately 16% of parents who do not mistreat their children (Kelleher, Chaffin, Hollenberg, & Fischer, 1994). Almost 80% of parents whose children were removed from their home display significant substance use problems (Besinger, Garland, Litrownik, & Landsverk, 1999). Parental substance use disorders also predict repeated incidents of child maltreatment (English, Marshall, Brummel, & Orme, 1999).

Substance abuse can have direct effects on children's welfare. First, children who witness their parents' substance use can be confused or distressed by their parents' behavioral responses to alcohol and other drugs. For example, watching a parent become intoxicated, act in an impulsive or violent manner, and pass out on the couch can be extremely distressing to a child or adolescent. Second, children sometimes experience physical harm or impairment after ingesting the substances used by their parents. For example, infants born to women who consumed alcohol during gestation can develop fetal alcohol syndrome. Third, older children and adolescents can model parents' substance use and develop alcohol and other drug use problems themselves.

Parental substance use problems can also have indirect effects on children's development (Kelley, 2002). First, alcohol and other drugs often render parents less motivated to provide their children with sensitive and responsive care. Parents who are dependent on alcohol often show disinterest in their children's activities and whereabouts. In one longitudinal study of high-risk parents, substance use problems were a primary predictor of later child neglect, even after controlling for other sources of stress in parents' lives (Chaffin, Kelleher, & Hollenberg, 1996).

Substance dependence can make parents less able to provide for their children. For example, many parents who become dependent on methamphetamine lose their jobs, sell their homes and belongings, and engage in criminal activity to support their drug use.

The effects of many substances can interfere with parents' judgment and problem solving. Mothers with alcohol and other drug use problems often show reduced empathy for their children, making them more likely to engage in cold and rejecting behavior (Meyers & Battistoni, 2003). Similarly, parents who abuse alcohol often engage in angry and impulsive behaviors toward their children, sometimes resulting in physical and emotional insult.

Parents' Relationship With Their Own Caregivers

Parents' own childhood experiences can influence the care that they give to their children (Stevens et al., 2005). Since children do not come with "owner's manuals," parents often rely on their own socialization experiences to determine their parenting practices. Indeed, people's attitudes toward disciplinary tactics, like spanking, are shaped across childhood and early adolescence and are associated with the disciplinary tactics used by their own parents when they were growing up (Deater-Deckard, Lansford, Dodge, Pettit, & Bates, 2003).

Unfortunately, adults who were mistreated during childhood are at risk for repeating abusive and neglectful behaviors toward their own children. A parent who was physically beaten during childhood might regard harsh physical punishment as a legitimate means of discipline. Similarly, a parent whose mother was emotionally detached might regard distant or aloof parent-child interactions as normative. Approximately 30%–40% of children who experience maltreatment will abuse or neglect their own children (Erickson & Egeland, 2002; Kolko, 2002).

Experts do not agree what perpetuates the **trans-generational cycle of abuse**. One explanation is based on learning theory. Specifically, parents who are exposed to violent and abusive behaviors during childhood might model these behaviors with their own offspring. Modeling is especially likely if hostile and aggressive disciplinary tactics are reinforced by child compliance (Dolz, Cerezo, & Milner, 1997).

Another explanation for the trans-generational transmission of maltreatment is based on attachment theory (Meyers & Battistoni, 2003). From the perspective of attachment theory, adults with histories of maltreatment form mental representations (i.e., working models) of their own parents. These mental representations can interfere with their ability to provide sensitive and supportive care to their children. For example, some adults who were abused by their parents attempt to cope with memories of the abuse by dismissing the importance of parents in their lives or minimizing their parents' contributions to their current functioning. A mother who was repeatedly physically abused by her father might dismiss the significance of this abuse, claiming, "Yes I was mistreated, but I try not to think about it. It has no bearing on my life today." This tendency to dismiss or minimize the importance of early experiences can interfere with the quality of care she affords her own children. Parents who decide that the quality of care that parents give children plays little role in their children's developmental outcomes are not likely to invest a lot of time and energy in parenting.

Other adults are preoccupied by thoughts and negative feelings about their parent-child relationship. Instead of dismissing the importance of their parents' abusive behaviors, these adults may harbor resentment, anger, or confusion about their maltreatment. Their preoccupation with their own socialization history can compromise their ability to provide sensitive and responsive care to their children.

Social-Cultural Theory

Jay Belsky (1993) has developed an influential **social-ecological model for child maltreatment**. His model includes factors that immediately influence the quality of parent-child interactions, such as the characteristics of the child and the thoughts/feelings of parents. However his social-cultural model also posits that parent-child interactions are influenced by more distal environmental factors, such as the family's income, educational background, and culture.

Parent-Child Factors

Environmental risk factors fall along a continuum from proximal (i.e., closely or directly affecting the dyad) to distal (i.e., indirectly influencing the dyad). The most proximal determinants of parent-child interactions are the personal characteristics of the child and parent. We have already considered some of the attributes of parents that place them at risk for child maltreatment. These parental characteristics include problem-solving deficits, psychopathology, and history of abuse and neglect.

Characteristics of the child can also affect the quality of care they receive from parents. Recall that parent-child behaviors are **transactional**. Parent characteristics alone do not fully account for child maltreatment. Children's characteristics, too, play some role in the quality of care that their parents provide. In no way are children responsible for their own maltreatment. However, a complete understanding of maltreatment is dependent on analysis of parent, child, and the surrounding environment.

Infants and toddlers with difficult temperaments may be at greater risk for physical abuse than other infants (see Figure 15.5). Infant crying can cause parents to

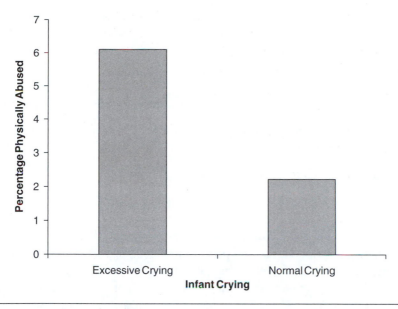

Figure 15.5   Child Temperament Can Increase the Likelihood of Maltreatment

Source: Based on Reijneveld et al. (2004).

Note: Infants who cried excessively were almost three times more likely to be physically maltreated by their caregivers.

feel frustrated, helpless, and irritable. These feelings can compromise parents' problem-solving abilities, making them more likely to mistreat their infants (Reijneveld, van der Wal, Brugman, Sing, & Verloove-Vanhorick, 2004).

Children who display disruptive behavior problems are also at greater risk for child maltreatment than their nondisruptive peers (Kolko, 2002). For example, toddlers who are excessively oppositional and children who show defiant and aggressive behaviors may be more likely to experience physical and emotional maltreatment. These disruptive behaviors can add to parents' levels of stress, decrease their overall tolerance for misbehavior, and increase the likelihood that they will engage in hostile or coercive disciplinary tactics. Abuse is especially likely when harsh discipline is reinforced by child compliance. For example, some parents report using harsh physical discipline or verbal threats because, in their experience, these are the only tactics to which their children respond.

Social Factors

Slightly more distal determinants of child development include interactions between the parent-child dyad and other people within or outside the family. For example, parents who experience marital distress, who are unemployed, or who are dissatisfied with work or other social roles can have difficulty providing sensitive and responsive care to their children. Children who show academic problems at school or social problems with peers can become depressed, irritable, or begin acting out (Davies & Cummings, 2006).

Parents' level of social support can also influence their parenting behavior. **Social support** refers to the emotional, social, informational, and tangible assistance that other people provide to caregivers in order to help them meet their child-rearing responsibilities. The following are examples of social support:

1. Providing empathy to parents who are experiencing stress (emotional support)

2. Engaging in recreational activities with parents to help them alleviate stress (social support)

3. Giving childrearing advice (informational support)

4. Offering to baby-sit or loan money (tangible support)

Parents who believe that they have little social support are at increased risk for child maltreatment. Mothers who perceive a lack of support from their partners, who experience a high degree of marital conflict, or who must parent a child on their own may become overwhelmed by the demands of parenting and other psychosocial stressors. These mothers may act in impulsive and hostile ways toward their children, placing them at risk for physical or psychological abuse. Alternatively, mothers with low social support may experience depression and withdraw from their caregiving responsibilities altogether.

On a more positive note, adequate levels of social support can buffer parents from the deleterious effects of parenting stress. Interestingly, parents' *perceived* level of social support, not the actual support that they receive, predicts their ability to cope with psychosocial stress. Therefore, it is not enough for families and professionals to provide parents with support; parents must also view this support as accessible and helpful.

Socioeconomic and Cultural Factors

Distal factors that can negatively affect child development include all aspects of socioeconomic disadvantage. Belsky (1993) suggested that any environmental factor that makes caregiving unstable, unpredictable, or unavailable can increase the likelihood of child maltreatment.

One risk factor for child maltreatment is low SES (Cadzow, Armstrong, & Fraser, 1999; Sedlak & Broadhurst, 1996). SES generally reflects the family's income, the parents' educational attainment and job status, and the quality of the home environment. Low-SES parents show greatly increased rates of child maltreatment (Stevens et al., 2005). However, it is unclear whether the higher rates of maltreatment among low-SES families reflect an actual increased risk of maltreatment or the increased likelihood of professionals to report acts of abuse in low-income families compared to middle- or high-income families (Berger, 2005).

Community deterioration is also associated with increased child maltreatment. Low-quality day care centers; unsafe or impoverished neighborhoods; and dangerous, high-crime living environments can interfere with the attention and care parents give to their children. Dubowitz, Pitts, and Black (2004) have suggested that children who are exposed to dangerous, impoverished neighborhoods experience a form of environmental neglect that adversely affects their social-emotional development.

Research has not yielded consistent results regarding the relationship between parents' ethnicity and their likelihood of child maltreatment (Miller & Cross, 2006). Some studies have shown a somewhat greater likelihood of child abuse and neglect among ethnic minority families compared to nonminority families. Other studies have failed to find a relationship between ethnicity and child maltreatment. Finkelhor and colleagues (2005) noticed significant associations between ethnic background and some forms of child maltreatment (e.g., emotional abuse) but not other forms of maltreatment (e.g., physical abuse). Since SES is often confounded with ethnicity, SES may be relatively more important than ethnicity in predicting child maltreatment.

Why Do People Sexually Abuse Children?

Men

Researchers have been largely unable to identify personality or behavioral characteristics that differentiate adults who sexually abuse children from non-abusive adults. Clearly, adult sexual offenders are a heterogeneous lot; there is no single "personality type," motive, or reason for child sexual abuse. The only consistently emerging characteristic is that adult sexual abusers tend to be male. Contrary to popular belief, most abusers have no history of criminal behavior or mental illness. Men who sexually abuse children tend to be in their mid- to late 30s; are more likely to be married; and have more prestigious, high-paying jobs than nonabusive adults.

Although researchers have been unable to identify characteristics that differentiate adults who do and no not sexually abuse children, some studies have identified personality features that characterize *some* adult sex offenders. One characteristic of some adults who abuse children is poor social skills (Emmers-Sommer et al., 2004; Nezu, Nezu, Dudek, Peacock, & Stoll, 2005). Some adults victimize children to compensate for inadequate social relationships with other adults. Sexual abuse may be especially likely when poor social functioning is combined with feelings of loneliness and poor attachment relationships (Ward, Hudson, & Marshall, 1996).

A second feature of *some* adult sexual abusers is psychopathy (Firestone, Bradford, McCoy, Greenberg, Larose, & Curry, 1999; Hanson & Bussiere, 1998). **Psychopathy** refers to a persistent pattern of interpersonal functioning marked by emotional detachment and a lack of empathy, callousness, superficial charm, a grandiose view of self, difficulty accepting responsibility and experiencing remorse for one's misdeeds, and general problems with impulsivity and behavioral control. Individuals with psychopathy show blatant disregard for the rights and dignity of others, and they tend to use others to satisfy their own needs and desires. Psychopathy is strongly associated with violent crime and sexual victimization. Indeed, adults who sexually abuse children and who show psychopathy display high rates of recidivism. Furthermore, treatment for these adults may be associated with *increased* recidivism instead of decreased likelihood of reoffending.

Third, some adults who sexually abuse children show substance use problems. Although research has yielded conflicting results, a sizable minority of abuse perpetrators show Alcohol Abuse or Dependence. Approximately 30% report using a substance (usually alcohol) before or during the abusive act. Alcohol and other drugs might be used to cope with feelings of psychological distress, to lower inhibitions against sexual victimization, or to increase the expected pleasurable outcomes associated with the abuse.

Finally, many men who sexually abuse children display Pedophilia (*DSM-IV-TR*; Seto, 2004). **Pedophilia** is a sexual disorder characterized by recurrent sexually arousing fantasies, urges, or behaviors involving sexual activity with prepubescent children. Furthermore, individuals with Pedophilia have either acted upon their sexual desires (i.e., they have abused children) or these feelings cause them considerable distress. Adults with Pedophilia display increased likelihood of abusing children. However, many individuals with Pedophilia never sexually abuse children, and many people who sexually abuse children do not have Pedophilia (i.e., they are not attracted to their victims). Consequently, Pedophilia and child sexual abuse are associated, but are not synonymous, constructs.

Why do men sexually abuse children? One of the most popular explanations is the **victim-to-victimizer hypothesis** (Chaffin, Letourneau, & Silvosky, 2002). According to this explanation, sexually abused children are at risk for sexually abusing other youths later in life. The exact reason why sexually abused children might victimize other children is unknown. Some theorists have argued that sexually abused children achieve a sense of control or mastery by re-enacting their own abuse experiences. Other theorists argue that sexually abused children model the behavior of their abusers. Still other theorists argue that sexual abuse leads to low social competence in children; low social competence, in turn, may contribute to later sexual victimization.

Recently, the victim-to-victimizer hypothesis has been challenged (Chaffin et al., 2002). Carefully conducted prospective studies of sexually abused children indicate that only a minority of victimized children sexually abuse other youths. In one large study of 224 victims of child sexual abuse, 26 (11%) subsequently abused children themselves (Salter et al., 2003). Furthermore, most (70%–80%) adolescents and adults who sexually abuse children *do not* have histories of sexual victimization. Consequently, the victim-to-victimizer hypothesis does not provide an adequate explanation for most instances of sexual abuse.

Women

Less information is known about women who sexually abuse children. Official arrest data indicate that approximately 2%–5% of all sexual abuse perpetrators are female (Tardif, Auclair, Jacob, & Carpentier, 2005). These percentages likely underestimate the prevalence of female sexual abusers. Female perpetrators often go unreported because victims are less likely to disclose abuse perpetrated by women or because investigators view female-perpetrated abuse as less problematic than abuse perpetrated by men.

At least four characteristics of female sexual abusers have been identified (Vandiver & Kercher, 2004). First, female sexual offenders are typically young women between the ages of 22 and 33. The average woman who engages in child sexual abuse is in her late 20s or early 30s. Second, most female sexual abusers have been victims of sexual abuse themselves. In one study, 60% of female offenders had histories of childhood sexual victimization (Tardif et al., 2005). Some authors have suggested that female perpetrators re-enact their own sexual victimization, although empirical data supporting this claim are somewhat lacking (Saradjian & Hanks, 1996). Third, many female sexual abusers have histories of substance use problems, especially Alcohol Dependence. Fourth, most female offenders have histories of mood disorders or other emotional problems, especially Borderline Personality Disorder.

Vandiver and Kercher (2004) reviewed the arrest records of female sexual offenders to identify groups of women who showed similar personality or behavioral characteristics. In their study, the largest cluster of female offenders (30%) consisted of women labeled **heterosexual nurturers**. These women were 25 to 30 years old and without extensive histories of criminal activity. They tended to sexually victimize young adolescent boys. In most instances, these women were placed in positions of power or trust over their victims; they acted as teachers, advisors, or mentors. Even after arrest, these women seldom perceived the sexual activity as abusive. Instead, they often viewed the relationship with their victims as romantic and consensual. These women often sexually abused their adolescent victims to compensate for feelings of emptiness or a lack of intimacy with adults their own age (see Image 15.2).

Adolescents

Approximately 20% of child sexual abuse is perpetrated by adolescents, usually boys (Hanson, 2002). Adolescents who sexually abuse children differ from their adult counterparts in several ways (Chaffin et al., 2002; Miranda & Corcoran, 2000; see Figure 15.6). First, adolescents are more likely to victimize younger children, especially infants, toddlers, and preschoolers. Second, adolescents often engage in fewer abusive behaviors, over shorter periods of times, and with less likelihood of penetration, coercion, or force. Third, adolescents who sexually abuse children do not show the same patterns of deviant sexual arousal as adults who abuse children. For example, adolescent offenders often do not have sexual fantasies toward children.

Adolescents who sexually abuse children are a heterogeneous group of youths, making them difficult to describe and categorize. Like adult sexual offenders, these adolescents tend to have underdeveloped social skills, nonsexual behavior problems, generalized problems with anxiety and depression, poor impulse control, and learning problems (Becker, 1998). The families of juvenile offenders are often disruptive. These adolescents usually have family members suffering from anxiety, depression, substance use problems, or antisocial behavior. Typically, interactions among family members are either extremely chaotic or overly rigid.

Image 15.2   Female Perpetrators. Middle school teacher Debra Lafave (25) pled guilty to two counts of lewd and lascivious battery after she was caught having a sexual relationship with a 14-year-old middle school student.

Source: AP Photo/Chris O'Meara. Used with permission.

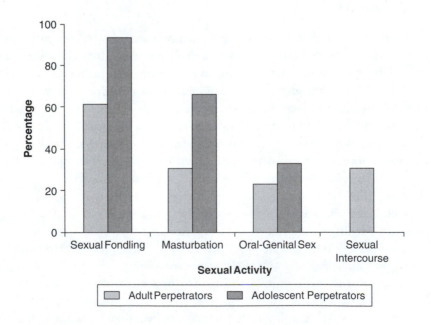

Figure 15.6   Sexual Acts Committed by Adult and Adolescent Offenders

Source: Based on Tardif et al. (2005).

There are at least three causes of child sexual abuse perpetrated by juveniles (Becker, 1998; Becker & Kaplan, 1988). First, some adolescent offenders seem primarily motivated by curiosity and a desire for sexual exploration. These adolescents may have cognitive or social skill deficits that interfere with the development of healthy relationships with peers. Instead, they direct sexual curiosity toward children.

Second, for some adolescent offenders, the sexually abusive act is part of a broader pattern of antisocial behavior. Many adolescent offenders have histories of Conduct Disorder. Furthermore, many adolescents who receive treatment for their sexual offending continue to show symptoms of Conduct Disorder even though their sexual offending desists. For a sizeable group of adolescent sexual offenders, sexually abusive acts are part of a constellation of disruptive behavior problems.

Third, a minority of juvenile sexual offenders may have **emerging Pedophilia**. Approximately 20%–30% of adults with Pedophilia report the onset of their sexual attraction to children during late childhood or adolescence. Some adolescent offenders show patterns of sexual arousal similar to those displayed by adults with Pedophilia. Consequently, a small group of juvenile offenders may be sexually attracted to children. Their sexually abusive behavior could be a manifestation of this attraction.

Treatment for Physical Abuse and Neglect

Supportive Therapy for Children

Most maltreated children do not receive mental health services. Indeed, only about 13% of abused and neglected youths receive any type of treatment after their abuse is discovered (Kolko, Selelyo, & Brown, 1999).

The most common form of treatment given to abused and neglected children is supportive therapy. The primary goal of **supportive therapy** is to help children cope with feelings and memories associated with their maltreatment and to improve their sense of self and relationships with others. William Friedrich (2002) has developed an integrated approach to the treatment of abused and neglected children. In his approach, treatment addresses three core areas of children's functioning: (1) attachment to caregivers, (2) behavioral regulation, and (3) self-perceptions.

Abuse and neglect seriously jeopardize the security of the parent-child attachment relationship (Cassidy & Shaver, 1999). Under optimal conditions, children expect sensitive and responsive care from parents when they are scared, upset, or unsure. However, acts of maltreatment rob children of that security. Physical and emotional neglect communicate to children that parents are not able or willing to provide for their basic material and psychological needs. Furthermore, parents who physically abuse children are, simultaneously, the source of danger and support. The result of maltreatment is an attachment relationship built on mistrust and doubt. In the worst cases, attachment is disorganized, as children learn to fear their caregivers.

Early in therapy, the clinician uses the therapeutic relationship as a source of support, care, and nurturance. The clinician's primary goal is to establish a sense of trust between himself and the maltreated child. Fostering trust is initially a difficult task because maltreated children often expect rejection and abandonment by others. Indeed, children may engage in disruptive behaviors and aversive emotional displays to elicit anger and resentment from the therapist and thereby confirm their expectations that others will reject them.

To establish a sense of trust, clinicians strive to provide a safe, consistent, and accepting therapeutic environment. Therapy sessions are typically used to help children process feelings associated with maltreatment. Some children harbor anger toward parents for their neglectful and abusive behavior. Other children resent the police, child protective services, and foster families for keeping them away from their parents. Still other children blame themselves for their mistreatment, believing they were somehow responsible for their caregivers' actions. Finally, a large number of children deny having problems altogether. The therapist tries to validate children's feelings by listening to them in a supportive, nonjudgmental way.

Later in therapy, the clinician might help children recognize their feelings and understand how these feelings affect their thoughts and actions. For example, feelings of anger and resentment could lead to aggressive outbursts at school and problems with teachers or peers. Peer problems, in turn, could contribute to additional feelings of loneliness, resentment, and hostility. The therapist might teach children more effective ways to cope with negative feelings, in order to avoid long-term emotional and social problems. Some therapists teach children relaxation techniques, others encourage participation in art or sports, while others ask children to keep journals about their memories and experiences.

The clinician hopes that the therapeutic relationship can become a corrective emotional experience for the child, perhaps the first relationship that the child has ever had in which her needs are placed above the needs of others (Friedrich, 2002). Establishing such a corrective relationship is usually quite difficult because many maltreated children are reluctant to trust or confide in another adult who they believe (based on previous experience) will reject, abandon, or mistreat them. By supporting the child, the clinician shows that the child is worthy of receiving care and attention from others. The experience of unconditional positive regard from the therapist can correct self-perceptions of worthlessness or guilt that interfere with the child's self-esteem and self-efficacy.

Parent Training

Description

Most caregivers who physically abuse or neglect children are offered therapy that involves **behavioral parent training**. The primary goal of parenting training is to teach parents more effective ways to socialize children. Specifically, parents are shown how to (1) attend to children's activities and positively reinforce appropriate behavior, (2) give clear and developmentally appropriate commands to maximize children's compliance, (3) ignore inappropriate behaviors and avoid hostile-aggressive displays, and (4) use noncoercive forms of discipline, such as time out (with young children) and response cost (with older children and adolescents).

Parent training can be administered either individually or in group format. Each week, the therapist introduces a new parenting skill and encourages parents to practice the skill at home with their children. The following week, parents provide feedback to the therapist and the therapist offers suggestions on how to tailor the treatment to meet parents' needs. When administered in group format, the therapist might use video demonstrations to elucidate parenting principles and tactics. The therapist might also allow time for parents to discuss their experiences with each other.

Efficacy

Parent training is efficacious in improving the quality of parent-child interactions. Specifically, parent training is associated with improvements in the quality of care parents provide their children, reductions in hostile and coercive parenting behaviors, and a decrease in children's behavior problems. The efficacy of parent training is based primarily on research involving children with disruptive behavior disorders, not abused and neglected children per se (Chaffin & Schmidt, 2006).

A specific parent training program, Parent-Child Interaction Therapy (PCIT), has been effectively used with caregivers who abused their children. Chaffin and colleagues (2004) randomly assigned parents to one of three treatment conditions: (1) PCIT, (2) PCIT plus individual counseling for parents, and (3) a traditional group-based parenting training program. Results showed that PCIT alone (Group 1) was superior to a traditional parenting program (Group 3) in decreasing re-referral to child protective services. These results indicate that the hands-on "coaching" approach used in PCIT may be especially useful to high-risk parents (see Figure 15.7).

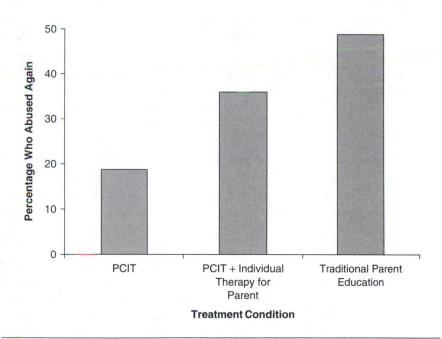

Figure 15.7   Parent-Child Interaction Therapy (PCIT) Is Effective in Preventing Future Abuse

Source: Based on Chaffin and colleagues (2004).

Note: Interestingly, PCIT alone yielded better outcomes than more extensive forms of treatment.

Interestingly, adding individual counseling to PCIT (Group 2) did not increase the efficacy of treatment; in fact, parents who participated in PCIT plus individual therapy showed *greater* likelihood of re-abusing than parents who participated in PCIT alone. The researchers suggest that the addition of individual counseling may have diluted the efficacy of PCIT by decreasing parents' interest in treatment.

Cognitive-Behavioral Family Therapy

Description

Many clinicians use a combination of behavioral parent training and cognitive therapy to help families who have experienced child maltreatment (Azar & Wolfe, 1998; Kolko, 2002). Melissa Runyon and colleagues (Runyon, Deblinger, Ryan, & Thakkar-Kolar, 2004) have developed a combined CBT program for abusive and neglectful parents and their children. Parent-child dyads participate in 16 weekly group therapy sessions, each lasting approximately two hours. Initially, parents and children are separated. Parents receive specific training in the causes and consequences of child maltreatment, child behavior management, stress reduction, and social problem solving.

One important aspect of cognitive therapy is to help parents form more realistic expectations for their children's behavior. Physically abusive parents often set extremely high and developmentally inappropriate expectations for their children. When their children fail to live up to these expectations, parents can become angry and respond with verbal or physical aggression.

Additionally, cognitive interventions for parents often involve challenging caregivers' cognitive distortions that lead up to child maltreatment. For example, a parent might think, "My child is always disrespectful; he never listens to me." The therapist might challenge this distorted belief by asking the parent to provide evidence for and against this claim. In fact, there are probably many instances each day in which the child obeys the parent, but these situations are often overshadowed by acts of noncompliance.

Another cognitive technique is to improve parents' problem-solving skills. Specifically, parents are taught to avoid blaming themselves or their children for children's misbehavior. Instead, parents are encouraged to look for alternative (and more benign) reasons for their children's acting out. For example, if the child becomes disruptive during a shopping trip, the parent might initially blame herself (e.g., "I'm a terrible parent") or the child (e.g., "He's a naughty kid"). Alternatively, the parent might attribute the child's misbehavior to situational factors (e.g., "He missed his nap today" or "He's bored and needs something to do"). Alternative attributions that do not place blame on the parent or child can reduce feelings of guilt, helplessness, or anger and, consequently, the likelihood of maltreatment.

Still another cognitive intervention involves improving parents' coping skills. Since distress, resentment, and anger usually precede child abuse, it is important for parents to learn ways to reduce these emotional states. The techniques that therapists use depend largely on the needs and preferences of parents. Some parents prefer breathing exercises, others respond to muscle relaxation, and still others like journaling. Most therapists also try to increase parents' social support as way to buffer them against the harmful effects of parenting stress.

While parents participate in cognitive group therapy, their children simultaneously participate in group treatment. During the initial sessions, children learn about child abuse and neglect and the possible consequences that child maltreatment can have on children and families. In the early phase of treatment, therapists attempt to normalize children's feelings of anger, sadness, or anxiety. Therapists also help children identify and label their feelings and examine how feelings, thoughts, and actions are connected. This can be accomplished through games, role play, and discussion.

Later, children and therapists develop a **safety plan**. The safety plan is a specific strategy for dealing with future episodes of maltreatment. The safety plan involves (1) learning how to identify signs that abuse might occur (e.g., "Mom gets very angry and starts to threaten me; Dad starts drinking again"), (2) engaging in an immediate behavior to keep the child safe (e.g., leave the house), and (3) going to a trusted person for help (e.g., grandmother, neighbor). Other child therapy sessions are designed to increase children's anger management, social skills, and problem-solving strategies.

After separate parent and child sessions, dyads participate in joint sessions that focus on the quality of parent-child interactions. For most of these combined sessions, parents practice behavior management skills with their children in the room, while they receive coaching from therapists. During some of these combined sessions, therapists encourage parents and children to openly discuss the abuse incident and to talk about ways to prevent it from happening in the future.

Efficacy

CBT for abused and neglected children is promising. Two randomized controlled studies indicate that CBT is efficacious in reducing punitive parenting practices (Whiteman, Fanshel, & Grundy, 1987). An additional study shows that CBT is associated with reductions in maltreated children's PTSD symptoms, anxiety, and anger (Swenson & Brown, 1999).

To date, only one study has examined the efficacy of combined parent-child CBT. Kolko and colleagues (Kolko, 1996; Kolko & Swenson, 2002) randomly assigned families to one of three treatment conditions: (1) family therapy, (2) parent-child CBT, and (3) treatment in the community. Results showed that parents who participated in either family therapy or CBT reported greater reductions in psychological distress, family conflict, and children's behavior problems than parents who received treatment in the community. Additionally, parents who participated in CBT reported lower levels of anger and physical punishment than parents who participated in family therapy (Chaffin & Valle, 2003).

Ecological Approaches to Treatment

Description

Ecological therapists recognize that child maltreatment is multiply determined. Consequently, treatment must address families' needs across multiple levels of functioning. First, the ecological therapist assesses the family's strengths and weaknesses across multiple domains: children's characteristics, parents' characteristics, the family and work environment, peers, school, neighborhood, and the larger community. Then, the therapist and family members set a concrete goal for therapy. Specifically, the therapist and family design a treatment program that acknowledges the family's weaknesses across ecological contexts but capitalizes on the family's strengths (Swenson & Chaffin, 2006).

For example, a single mother might report that she feels tired and depressed because she is working two part-time jobs to support her family. She has no friends or time for herself; consequently, she often feels irritable and emotionally drained. These feelings of depression and social isolation can cause her to lose patience with her children and respond in a hostile and aggressive manner toward them. Her goal for therapy might be to decrease feelings of depression so that she can better avoid these harsh displays. The therapist might refer her to another clinician for individual treatment for depression. At the same time, the therapist might encourage the mother to participate in a support group for single parents in order to decrease her parenting stress and feelings of social isolation.

Ecological treatment does not necessarily mean that therapists will provide *more* treatment services (Swenson & Chaffin, 2006). Instead, an ecological approach to treatment implies that therapists will tailor services to the needs of families. Ecological treatment does not limit therapy to children and parents. Any contextual variable that affects the family is a potential target for treatment. For example, a therapist who adopts an ecological approach might provide marital therapy for a couple experiencing relationship distress, serve as a career counselor to a parent requiring a job change, or act as a liaison between families and school personnel for a child with academic difficulties.

Efficacy

Ecological treatment can be effectively applied to families of abused and neglected children (Swenson & Chaffin, 2006). One treatment program, **Project 12 Ways**, has been developed for families referred to child protective services (Gershater-Molko, Lutzker, & Wesch, 2002; Wesch & Lutzker, 1991). Clinicians administering this program can provide 12 types of services, depending on the needs and resources of the family: parent training, stress reduction training for parents, skills training for children, money management training, parental social support, home safety, behavioral management, health and nutrition, problem solving, marital counseling, alcohol abuse referral, and special services for single parents. All services are provided in the home. Participation in the program is associated with decreased likelihood of future child maltreatment.

Other clinicians have adapted multisystemic therapy (MST) for families referred to child protective services. Recall that MST was originally developed for families with children evidencing disruptive behavior problems. MST typically involves treatment on a number of ecological levels: behavioral parent training and individual therapy for parents, skill and social problem-solving training for children, and school- or community-based treatment. At least one study indicates that MST is superior to parent training alone in reducing child behavior problems in families referred to protective services (Brunk, Henggeler, & Whelan, 1987). A large, randomized controlled trial is currently being conducted to further investigate the effectiveness of MST with physically abused adolescents (Swenson & Chaffin, 2006).

Treatment for Child Sexual Abuse

Trauma-Focused Cognitive-Behavioral Therapy for Children

Description

Trauma-Focused Cognitive-Behavioral Therapy (TF-CBT) incorporates elements of exposure therapy, cognitive restructuring, parent training, and family support into a single treatment package for sexually abused children. The initial goal of TF-CBT is to help children identify and manage negative emotions associated with the traumatic experience. In the first session, children are encouraged to identify positive and negative feelings associated with various social situations and to recognize that negative feelings are acceptable. Then children are encouraged to describe their own traumatic experience and the feelings associated with it. In the second session, children learn stress management techniques such as focused breathing, muscle relaxation, and **thought stopping**. When unwanted and intrusive memories come into the child's mind, the child might mentally say, "Stop! Stop! Stop!" and focus her attention away from the thoughts. The therapist also helps the child identify other stress reduction techniques, such as listening to music, drawing, or playing with friends.

Next, treatment involves exposing the child to memories of the traumatic event and altering the child's thoughts regarding the event. In session three, the therapist teaches the relationship between thoughts, feelings, and actions. Then, children explore how different ways of thinking and feeling change the way they act. In sessions four through six, children gradually disclose more of their traumatic experiences in writing. Children read books written by other youths who were abused. Then, children are encouraged to write their own stories, detailing the events, thoughts, and feelings associated with their abuse. Very young children are encouraged to draw picture books about their abuse experiences (Knell & Ruma, 2003). By session seven, the therapist begins to challenge and reframe children's maladaptive thoughts about the abuse experience. For example, a child might initially think, "It's my fault that I was abused. I let my stepfather do it and I didn't tell anyone." The therapist might reframe this statement as, "It's not my fault; I was scared and couldn't tell anyone."

While children participate in therapy activities, nonoffending parents also meet with the clinician for individual sessions. For the most part, parent sessions mirror the child sessions. For example, both children and parents learn to identify and accept feelings regarding the traumatic experience and to develop coping strategies to deal with negative affect and stress. In addition, parents participate in training designed to improve the support and consistency they give to their children and to teach effective ways of addressing children's problem behavior that might arise after the abuse.

In the final phase of therapy, children and nonoffending parents meet together. Children are encouraged to read their abuse stories to their parents and to discuss their thoughts and feelings about the trauma. Parents are asked to listen with acceptance and understanding and to answer children's questions regarding their abuse. Finally, parents and children develop new strategies to keep children safe. For example, parents might be encouraged to monitor their children more frequently, whereas children might pledge to come to parents immediately if they feel uncomfortable about a person or situation.

Efficacy

The efficacy of TF-CBT has been investigated in a number of randomized controlled studies. For example, J. A. Cohen, Mannarino, and Knudsen (2005) examined 82 children and adolescents (ages 8–15 years) with histories of sexual abuse. Youths were randomly assigned to either TF-CBT or supportive therapy, which involved art, play, and therapists listening to children's feelings. Children's PTSD symptoms, behavior problems, and sexual behavior were assessed before treatment, after treatment, and at 6- and 12-month follow-up. Results showed that both forms of treatment were efficacious in reducing children's mood and anxiety symptoms. However, children were more likely to complete TF-CBT (73%) than nondirective therapy (46%). Furthermore, at 12-month follow-up, children who participated in TF-CBT showed fewer problems with depression, anxiety, inappropriate sexual behaviors, and PTSD symptoms compared to children who received supportive therapy (see Figure 15.8).

Several other randomized controlled trials have yielded similar results (J. A. Cohen, Deblinger, Mannarino, & Steer, 2004; J. A. Cohen et al., 2005; J. A. Cohen & Mannarino, 1996, 1997, 2004; Deblinger, Lippmann, & Steer, 1996; Deblinger, Steer, & Lippmann, 1999a, 1999b). These trials support the use of TF-CBT as a first-line treatment for sexually abused children who display PTSD, other mood and anxiety disorders, and aberrant sexual behaviors (Berliner, 2005).

Cognitive Restructuring With Adolescents

Older children and adolescents who have been sexually abused often report negative thoughts about themselves, others, and the world that contribute to their anxiety and mood problems (J. B. Cohen, Deblinger, Maedel, & Stauffer, 1999; Deblinger & Heflin, 1996). First, sexually abused children often hold negative appraisals of themselves. They may view themselves as worthless, as "damaged

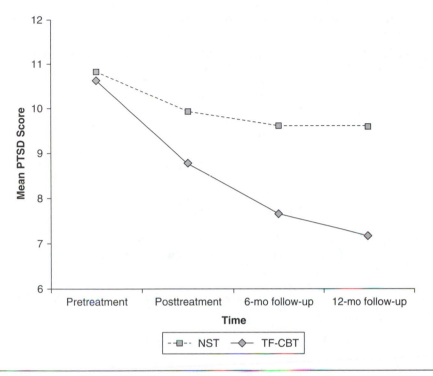

Figure 15.8   Effectiveness of TF-CBT for Sexually Abused Youth

Source: Based on J. A. Cohen et al. (2005).

Note: Both TF-CBT and nondirective supportive therapy (NST) led to reductions in children's symptoms. However, one year after treatment, youth who participated in TF-CBT showed fewer problems with depression, anxiety, inappropriate sexual behaviors, and PTSD.

goods," or as unlovable by others. They may also blame themselves for the abuse, especially if they feel that they were somehow complicit in the sexual act.

Second, sexually abused children often hold negative views of others. They may view other people as untrustworthy, self-centered, and coercive. Consequently, they may be suspicious of others' motives and avoid asking other people for help or support.

Finally, sexually abused children may adopt negative views of the world and the future. Abused children often view the world as a dangerous place. Some children report a pessimistic attitude toward the future and an inability to think about long-term plans.

The way children think about themselves, others, and the world can color their experiences and influence their feelings and actions. A child who believes "No one can be trusted" will likely have difficulty forming attachments with caregivers and friends. An adolescent who believes "I am worthless—even my own father mistreated me" may have problems with low self-esteem and self-efficacy. These negative beliefs, in turn, can cause individuals to distort interpersonal experiences to confirm their pessimistic and mistrustful schemas.

Therapists try to challenge cognitive distortions and help youths find ways to think about their abuse experiences (Heflin & Deblinger, 2003). Consider Michelle, a 14-year-old adolescent who was sexually abused by her father. In the transcript below, the therapist identifies a cognitive distortion that may be contributing to Michelle's guilt. Then, the therapist asks Michelle to critically examine the validity of her distorted belief.

Therapist: When something reminds you of the abuse now, what feelings do you have?

Michelle: I guess I mostly feel bad.

Therapist: I'm not sure what you mean by "bad." Can you tell me a little more about which kind of bad feelings you have?

Michelle: Well, I just feel guilty about all of it.

Therapist: OK, remember how we said sometimes our thoughts influence how we are feeling? Can you tell me what you are thinking about when you feel guilty?

Michelle: I just feel like I must have done something to make my dad decide to do it to me.

Therapist: What do you think you might have done?

Michelle: I don't know. He used to always yell at me for the clothes I wore, so I guess maybe I wore the wrong kind of stuff.

Therapist: What do you think was wrong with your clothes?

Michelle: I don't really know. I dress like all the other kids, but he said I was trying to look too grown up, too sexy. He even said sometimes that I made him do it to me because of the way I walked around in really short shorts and miniskirts.

Therapist: Well, let's think about that carefully. You said that you dress like the other kids?

Michelle: Yeah, pretty much.

Therapist: And so, do you think that dressing like that also caused all of *them* to be sexually abused?

Michelle: Well, not all of them, no. Actually, I don't think this has happened to any of my friends.

Therapist: So, if dressing like that hasn't caused them to be sexually abused, it doesn't make sense that it caused you to be abused, does it?

Michelle: No, I guess not.

Source: From Heflin and Deblinger (2003). Used with permission.

The negative cognitions evidenced by abused children contribute to their psychological and somatic symptoms (Heflin & Deblinger, 2003; Mannarino & Cohen,

1996). Cognitive therapy is designed to challenge these negative cognitions and help children view themselves, others, and the world more realistically.

Update: Angela

Angela, the girl who was sexually abused, needed reassurance that she was safe, that her feelings (even negative ones) were valid and important, and that she would not be betrayed or abandoned by others in the future. Angela's therapist, Lori, saw her primary job as establishing a safe and supportive therapeutic relationship.

Establishing a trusting relationship was slow. However, after several weeks, Lori began to feel the therapeutic bond developing, and Angela began to disclose more of her feelings about day-to-day stressors. Next, Lori began encouraging Angela to talk about aspects of her abuse. She wanted Angela to confront memories and images of the abuse in the safety of therapy so that the negative emotions and physiological reactions associated with the abuse might decrease. Lori explained, "I know it's really hard, but if you talk and think about a bad experience in a safe place, after a while, you don't feel so bad."

Lori used a wide range of techniques to help Angela tell and retell her story. These techniques involved orally discussing aspects of the abuse, drawing pictures of the abuse, telling aspects of the abuse to dolls, keeping a diary, writing a book to help other victims of child abuse recover from their trauma, and sharing the book with her foster mother. With each re-telling of the abuse, Lori tried to highlight aspects of Angela's story that displayed her bravery and resilience rather than her weakness and victimization.

Lori and Angela also found ways to increase Angela's ability to cope with negative emotions in the future. For example, Angela discovered that she could cope with depression, anxiety, and other negative feelings by riding her bike, painting and drawing, and listening to music.

After 24 sessions, Angela showed considerable improvement in her behavioral and emotional functioning. Lori continued to meet with Angela approximately once every other week as she began supervised visits with her mother.

Critical Thinking Exercises

1. What is the difference between using the "harm standard" and using the "endangerment standard" to define child abuse? How do these differing definitions of abuse lead to different estimates for the prevalence of abuse?

2. Maslow's hierarchy of human needs has been used to explain why abused and neglected children often show emotional and behavioral problems. Are there any weaknesses in Maslow's theory? Why might children show resilience *despite* histories of abuse and neglect?

3. Mark was sexually abused by his stepfather during infancy and early childhood. Now a college student, Mark is worried that he will someday sexually abuse

children himself. He visits the counseling center at his university and shares his concerns with the therapist. If you were his therapist, what might you say to Mark?

4. Imagine that your job is to develop a child physical abuse prevention program for a large metropolitan area. In this program, trained volunteers will visit parents who are at risk for physically abusing their children. How might these volunteers teach parents to adopt different *attributions* regarding their children's behavior and, consequently, decrease their likelihood of abuse?

5. What is "supportive therapy" for child abuse? Use attachment theory to explain why establishing a trusting therapeutic relationship is necessary for the treatment of abuse.

6. Discuss the effectiveness of (1) behavioral parent training and (2) cognitive-behavioral family therapy for the treatment of physical abuse and neglect. If you were a therapist, which approach would you use?

References

Abbott, P. J. (2007). Co-morbid alcohol/other drug abuse/dependence and psychiatric disorders in adolescent American Indian and Alaska natives. *Alcoholism Treatment Quarterly, 24,* 3–21.

Abela, J. R. Z., Hankin, B. L., Haigh, E. A. P., Adams, P., Vinokuroff, T., & Trayhern, L. (2005). Interpersonal vulnerability to depression in high-risk children: The role of insecure attachment and reassurance seeking. *Journal of Clinical Child and Adolescent Psychology, 34,* 182–192.

Aber, J. L., Gershoff, E. T., Ware, A., & Kotler, J. A. (2004). Estimating the effects of September 11th and other forms of violence on the mental health and social development of New York City's youth: A matter of context. *Applied Developmental Science, 8,* 111–129.

Abikoff, H., Hechtman, L., Klein, R. G., Gallagher, R., Fleiss, K., Etcovitch, J., et al. (2004a). Social functioning in children with ADHD treated with long-term methylphenidate and multimodal psychosocial treatment. *Journal of the American Academy of Child and Adolescent Psychiatry, 43,* 820–829.

Abikoff, H., Hechtman, L., Klein, R. G., Weiss, G., Fleiss, K., Etcovitch, J., et al. (2004b). Symptomatic improvement in children with ADHD treated with long-term methylphenidate and multimodal psychosocial treatment. *Journal of the American Academy of Child and Adolescent Psychiatry, 43,* 802–811.

Abikoff, H., Jensen, P., Arnold, L. E., Hoza, B., Hechtman, L., Pollack, S., et al. (2002). Observed classroom behavior of children with ADHD: Relationship to gender and comorbidity. *Journal of Abnormal Child Psychology, 30,* 349–359.

Abramson, L. Y., Seligman, M. E., & Teasdale, J. D. (1978). Learned helplessness in humans: Critique and reformulation. *Journal of Abnormal Psychology, 87,* 49–74.

Achenbach, T. M. (1982). Assessment and taxonomy of children's behavior disorders. In B. Lahey & A. E. Kazdin (Eds.), *Advances in clinical child psychology* (pp. 1–38). New York: Plenum.

Achenbach, T. M., Howell, C. T., Quay, H. C., & Conners, C. K. (1991). National survey of problems and competencies among four- to sixteen-year-olds: Parents' reports for normative and clinical samples. *Monographs of the Society for Research in Child Development, 56,* 1–131.

Achenbach, T. M., McConaughy, S. H., & Howell, C. T. (1987). Child/adolescent behavioral and emotional problems: Implications of cross-informant correlations for situational specificity. *Psychological Bulletin, 101,* 213–232.

Ackerman, B. P., Brown, E., & Izard, C. E. (2003). Continuity and change in levels of externalizing behavior in school of children from economically disadvantaged families. *Child Development, 74,* 694–709.

Ackerman, P., Newton, J., McPherson, W. B., Jones, J., & Dykman, R. (1998). Prevalence of posttraumatic stress disorder and other psychiatric diagnoses in three groups of abused children (sexual, physical, and both). *Child Abuse and Neglect, 22,* 759–774.

Adams, G., & Carnine, D. (2003). Direct instruction. In H. L. Swanson, K. R. Harris, & S. Graham (Eds.), *Handbook of learning disabilities* (pp. 403–416). New York: Guilford Press.

Agras, W. S., Crow, S. J., Halmi, K. A., Mitchell, J. E., Wilson, G. T., & Kraemer, H. C. (2000). Outcome predictors for the cognitive behavior treatment of bulimia nervosa: Data from a multisite study. *American Journal of Psychiatry, 757,* 1302–1308.

Agras, W. S., Walsh, B. T., Fairburn, C. G., Wilson, G. T., & Kraemer, C. H. (2000). A multi-center comparison of cognitive-behavioral therapy and interpersonal psychotherapy for bulimia nervosa. *Archives of General Psychiatry, 57,* 459–466.

Ahmann, P., Waltonen, S., Olson, K., Theye, F., Van Erem, A., & LaPlant, R. (1993). Placebo-controlled evaluation of Ritalin side effects. *Pediatrics, 91,* 1101–1106.

Ahn, M. S., & Frazier, A. (2004). Diagnostic and treatment issues in childhood-onset bipolar disorder. *Essential Psychopharmacology, 6,* 25–44.

Ainsworth, M. D. S., Belhar, M. C., Waters, E., & Wall, S. (1978). *Patterns of attachment: A psychological study of the strange situation.* Hillsdale, NJ: Erlbaum.

Alanay, Y., Unal, F., Turanli, G., Alikasifoglu, M., Alehan, D., Akyol, U., et al. (2007). A multidisciplinary approach to the management of individuals with fragile X syndrome. *Journal of Intellectual Disability Research, 51,* 151–161.

Albano, A. M., Chorpita, B. F., & Barlow, D. H. (1996). Childhood anxiety disorders. In E. J. Mash & R. A. Barkley (Eds.), *Child psychopathology* (pp. 196–242). New York: Guilford Press.

Albano, A. M., & Hayward, C. (2004). Social anxiety disorder. In T. H. Ollendick & J. S. March (Eds.), *Phobic and anxiety disorders in children and adolescents* (pp. 198–235). New York: Oxford University Press.

Alloy, L. B., Abramson, L. Y., Raniere, D., & Dyller, I. M. (1999). Research methods in adult psychopathology. In P. C. Kendall, J. N. Butcher, & G. N. Holmbeck (Eds.), *Handbook of research methods in clinical psychology* (pp. 466–498). New York: Wiley.

Aman, M. G., Collier–Crespin, A., & Lindsay, R. (2000). Pharmacotherapy of disorders in mental retardation. *European Child & Adolescent Psychiatry, 9,* 98–107.

Aman, M. G., De Smedt, G., Derivan, A., Lyons, B., Findling, R. L., & Risperidone Disruptive Behavior Study Group. (2002). Double-blind, placebo-controlled study of risperidone for the treatment of disruptive behaviors in children with subaverage intelligence. *American Journal of Psychiatry, 159,* 1337–1346.

American Academy of Child and Adolescent Psychiatry. (2005). Practice parameter for the assessment and treatment of children and adolescents with substance use disorders. *Journal of the American Academy of Child & Adolescent Psychiatry, 44,* 609–621.

American Academy of Pediatrics. (2001). Clinical practice guideline: Treatment of the school-aged child with attention-deficit/hyperactivity disorder. *Pediatrics, 108,* 1033–1044.

American Psychiatric Association. (2000). *Diagnostic and statistical manual of mental disorders* (4th ed., Text Rev.). Washington, DC: Author.

American Psychological Association. (1947). Recommended graduate training program in clinical psychology. *American Psychologist, 2,* 539–558.

American Psychological Association. (1996). Guidelines on effective behavioral treatment for persons with mental retardation and developmental disabilities: A resolution by APA Division 33. In J. W. Jacobson & J. A. Mulick (Eds.), *Manual of diagnosis and professional practice in mental retardation* (pp. 427–430). Washington, DC: Author.

American Psychological Association. (2002). Ethical principles of psychologists and code of conduct. *American Psychologist, 57,* 1060–1073.

Amir, R. E., Van den Veyver, I. B., Wan, M., Tran, C. Q., Francke, U., & Zoghbi, H. Y. (1999). Rett syndrome is caused by mutations in X-linked MECP2, encoding methyl-CpG-binding protein 2. *Nature Genetics, 23,* 185–188.

Amor, L. B., Grizenko, N., Schwartz, G., Lageix, P., Baron, C., Ter-Stepanian, M., et al. (2005). Perinatal complications in children with attention-deficit hyperactivity disorder and their unaffected siblings. *Journal of Psychiatry and Neuroscience, 30,* 120–126.

Anastasi, A., & Urbina, S. (1997). *Psychological testing.* Upper Saddle River, NJ: Prentice Hall.

Anastopoulos, A. D., Shelton, T. L., & Barkley, R. A. (2005). Family-based psychosocial treatments for children and adolescents with attention-deficit/ hyperactivity disorder. In E. D. Hibbs & P. S. Jensen (Eds.), *Psychosocial treatments for child and adolescent disorders: Empirically based strategies for clinical practice* (pp. 327–350). Washington, DC: American Psychological Association.

Anderson, K. G., Ramo, D. E., & Brown, S. A. (2006). Life stress, coping and comorbid youth: An examination of the stress-vulnerability model for substance relapse. *Journal of Psychoactive Drugs, 38,* 255–262.

Anderson, S. R., Avery, D. L., DiPietro, E. K., Edwards, G. L., & Christian, W. P. (1987). Intensive home-based intervention with autistic children. *Education and Treatment of Children, 10,* 352–366.

Anderson-Frye, E. P., & Becker, A. E. (2004). Sociocultural aspects of eating disorders. In J. K. Thompson (Ed.), *Handbook of eating disorders and obesity* (pp. 565–589). Hoboken, NJ: Wiley.

Andrews, J. A. (2005). Substance abuse in girls. In D. J. Bell, S. L. Foster, & E. J. Mash (Eds.), *Handbook of behavioral and emotional problems in girls* (pp. 181–209). New York: Kluwer/Plenum.

Angelman, H. (1965). "Puppet children": A report on three cases. *Developmental Medicine and Child Neurology, 7,* 681–688.

Angold, A., Costello, E. J., & Erkanli, A. (1999). Comorbidity. *Journal of Child Psychology and Psychiatry and Allied Disciplines, 40,* 57–87.

Anthony, J., & Scott, P. (1960). Manic-depressive psychosis in childhood. *Child Psychology and Psychiatry, 4,* 53–72.

Antony, M. M. (2005). Five strategies for bridging the gap between research and clinical practice. *Behavior Therapist, 28,* 162–163.

Appel, A. E., & Holden, W. (1998). The co-occurrence of spouse and physical child abuse: A review and appraisal. *Journal of Family Psychology, 12,* 578–599.

Appleton, R., & Baldwin, T. (2006). *Management of brain injured children* (2nd ed.). New York: Oxford University Press.

Apter, A., Kronenberg, S., & Brent, D. (2005). Turning darkness into light: A new landmark study on the treatment of adolescent depression. Comments on the TADS study. *European Child and Adolescent Psychiatry, 14,* 113–116.

Ardoin, S. P., Witt, J. C., Connell, J. E., & Koenig, J. L. (2005). Application of a three-tiered response to intervention model for instructional planning, decision making, and the identification of children in need of services. *Journal of Psychoeducational Assessment, 23,* 362–380.

Armstrong, D. (2001). Rett syndrome neuropathology. *Brain and Development, 23,* 72–76.

Arnold, L. (1996). Sex differences in ADHD: Conference summary. *Journal of Abnormal Child Psychology, 24,* 555–569.

Asarnow, J. R., Goldstein, M. J., Tompson, M., & Guthrie, D. (1993). One-year outcomes of depressive disorders in child psychiatric in-patients: Evaluation of the prognostic power of a brief measure of expressed emotion. *Journal of Child Psychology and Psychiatry, 34,* 129–137.

Atlas, J. G. (2004). Interpersonal sensitivity, eating disorder symptoms, and eating/thinness expectancies. *Current Psychology: Developmental, Learning, Personality, Social, 22,* 368–378.

Augustyniak, K., Murphy, J., & Phillips, D. K. (2006). Psychological perspectives in assessing mathematics learning needs. *Journal of Instructional Psychology, 32,* 277–286.

Autism Genome Project Consortium. (2007). Mapping autism risk loci using genetic linkage and chromosomal rearrangements. *Nature Genetics, 39,* 319–328.

Axelson, D. A., Perel, J. M., Birmaher, B., Rudolph, G., Nuss, S., Yurasits, L. et al. (2005). Platelet serotonin reuptake inhibition and response to SSRIs in depressed adolescents. *American Journal of Psychiatry, 162,* 802–804.

Aylward, E. H., Richards, T. L., Berninger, V. W., Nagy, W. E., Field, K. M., Grimme, A. C. et al. (2003). Instructional treatment associated with changes in brain activation in children with dyslexia. *Neurology, 61,* 212–219.

Azar, S. T., & Wolfe, D. A. (1998). Child physical abuse and neglect. In E. J. Mash & R. A. Barkley (Eds.), *Treatment of childhood disorders* (pp. 501–544). New York: Guilford.

Bacaltchuk, J., Trefiglio, R. P., Oliveira, I. R., Hay, P., Lima, M. S., & Mari, J. J. (2000). Combination of antidepressants and psychological treatments for bulimia nervosa: A systematic review. *Acta Psychiatrica Scandinavia, 101,* 256–64.

Badner, J. A. (2003). The genetics of bipolar disorder. In B. Geller & M. DelBello (Eds.), *Bipolar disorder in childhood and early adolescence* (pp. 247–254). New York: Guilford Press.

Bagwell, C. L., Molina, B. S. G., Kashdan, T. B., Pelham, W. E., & Hoza, B. (2006). Anxiety and mood disorders in adolescents with childhood attention-deficit/hyperactivity disorder. *Journal of Emotional and Behavioral Disorders, 14,* 178–187.

Baker, D. B., & Benjamin, T. (2000). The affirmation of the scientist-practitioner: A look back at Boulder. *American Psychologist, 55,* 241–247.

Bandura, A. (1973). *Aggression: A social learning theory analysis.* New York: Prentice Hall.

Bandura, A., Ross, D., & Ross, S. A. (1961). Transmission of aggression through imitation of aggressive models. *Journal of Abnormal & Social Psychology, 63,* 575–582.

Barber, B. (2002). *Intrusive parenting: How psychological control affects children and adolescents.* Washington, DC: American Psychological Association.

Bardone, A. M., Moffitt, T. E., Caspi, A., Dickson, N., & Silva, P. A. (1996). Adult mental health and social outcomes of adolescent girls with depression and conduct disorder. *Development and Psychopathology, 8,* 811–829.

Bardone, M. S., Moffitt, T. E., Caspi, A., Dickson, N., Stanton, W. R., & Silva, P. A. (1998). Adult physical health outcomes of adolescent girls with conduct disorder, depression, and anxiety. *Journal of the American Academy of Child and Adolescent Psychiatry, 317,* 594–601.

Barkley, R. A. (1988). The effects of methylphenidate on the interactions of preschool ADHD children with their mothers. *Journal of the American Academy of Child and Adolescent Psychiatry, 27,* 336–341.

Barkley, R. A. (1997a). *ADHD and the nature of self-control.* New York: Guilford Press.

Barkley, R. A. (1997b). *Defiant children: A clinician's manual for assessment and parent training.* New York: Guilford Press.

Barkley, R. A. (1998). *Attention deficit hyperactivity disorder: A handbook for diagnosis and treatment* (2nd ed.). New York: Guilford Press.

Barkley, R. A. (2004a). Adolescents with attention-deficit/hyperactivity disorder: An overview of empirically based treatments. *Journal of Psychiatric Practice, 10,* 39–56.

Barkley, R. A., DuPaul, G. J., & Connor, D. F. (1999). Stimulants. In J. S. Werry & M. G. Aman (Eds.), *Practitioner's guide to psychoactive drugs in children and adolescents* (pp. 213–247). New York: Plenum.

Barkley, R. A., DuPaul, G. J., & McMurray, M. B. (1990). A comprehensive evaluation of attention deficit disorder with and without hyperactivity as defined by research criteria. *Journal of Consulting and Clinical Psychology, 58,* 775–789.

Barkley, R. A., Edwards, G., Laneri, M., Fletcher, K. E., & Metevia, L. (2001). The efficacy of problem-solving communication training alone, behavior management training alone, and their combination for parent-adolescent conflict in teenagers with ADHD and ODD. *Journal of Consulting and Clinical Psychology, 69,* 926–941.

Barkley, R. A., Fischer, M., Edelbrock, C. S., & Smallish, L. (1990). The adolescent outcome of hyperactive children diagnosed by research criteria I: An 8-year prospective follow-up study. *Journal of the American Academy of Child and Adolescent Psychiatry, 29,* 546–557.

Barkley, R. A., Fischer, M., Smallish, L., & Fletcher, K. R. (2002). Persistence of attention deficit hyperactivity disorder into young adulthood as a function of reporting source and definition of disorder. *Journal of Abnormal Psychology, 111,* 279–289.

Barkley, R. A., Shelton, T. L., Crosswait, C., Moorehouse, M., Fletcher, K., Barrett, S., et al. (2000). Multimethod, psycho-educational intervention for preschool children with disruptive behavior: Preliminary results at post-treatment. *Journal of Child Psychology and Psychiatry, 41,* 319–332.

Barlow, D. H. (2002). *Anxiety and its disorders: The nature and treatment of anxiety and panic* (2nd ed.). New York: Guilford Press.

Barnes, G. M., Hoffman, J. H., Welte, J. W., Farrell, M. P., & Dintcheff, B. A. (2006). Effects of parental monitoring and peer deviance on substance use and delinquency. *Journal of Marriage and Family, 68,* 1084–1104.

Barnett, D., Ganiban, J., & Cicchetti, D. (1999). Maltreatment, negative expressivity, and the development of Type D attachments from 12 to 24 months of age. *Monographs of the Society for Research in Child Development, 64,* 97–118.

Barnow, S., Schultz, G., Lucht, M., Ulrich, I., Preuss, U., & Freyberger, H. (2004). Do alcohol expectancies and peer delinquency/substance use mediate the relationship between impulsivity and drinking behaviour in adolescence? *Alcohol and Alcoholism, 39,* 213–219.

Baron, R. M., & Kenny, D. A. (1986). The moderator-mediator variable distinction in social psychological research: Conceptual, strategic, and statistical considerations. *Journal of Personality and Social Psychology, 51,* 1173–1182.

Baron-Cohen, S. (1995). *Mindblindness: An essay on autism and theory of mind.* Boston: MIT Press/Bradford Books.

Baron-Cohen, S. (2005). Autism and the origins of social neuroscience. In A. Easton & N. Emery (Eds.), *The cognitive neuroscience of social behaviour* (pp. 239–255). New York: Psychology Press.

Baron-Cohen, S., Leslie, A. M., & Frith, U. (1985). Does the autistic child have a "theory of mind"? *Cognition, 21,* 37–46.

Baron-Cohen, S., Scahill, V. L., Izaguirre, J., Hornsey, H., & Robertson, M. M. (1999). The prevalence of Gilles de le Tourette syndrome in children and adolescents with autism: A large-scale study. *Psychological Medicine, 29,* 1151–1159.

Barrett, P. M., Dadds, M. R., & Rapee, R. M. (1996). Family treatment of childhood anxiety: A controlled trial. *Journal of Consulting and Clinical Psychology, 64,* 333–342.

Barrett, P. M., Duffy, A. L., Dadds, M. R., & Rapee, R. M. (2001). Cognitive-behavioral treatment of anxiety disorders in children: Long-term (6 year) follow-up. *Journal of Consulting and Clinical Psychology, 69,* 1–7.

Barrett, P. M., Rapee, R. M., Dadds, M. M., & Ryan, S. M. (1996). Family enhancement of cognitive style in anxious and aggressive children. *Journal of Abnormal Child Psychology, 24,* 187–203.

Barrios, A. A., & O'Dell, S. L. (1998). Fears and anxieties. In E. J. Mash & R. A. Barkley (Eds.), *Treatment of childhood disorders* (2nd ed., pp. 249–337). New York: Guilford Press.

Barrouillet, P., Fayol, M., & Lathuliere, E. (1997). Selecting between competitors in multiplication tasks: An explanation of the errors produced by adolescents with learning disabilities. *International Journal of Behavioral Development, 21,* 253–275.

Barry, C. T., Frick, P. J., Grooms, T., McCoy, M. G., Ellis, M. L., & Loney, B. R. (2000). The importance of callous-unemotional traits for extending the concept of psychopathy to children. *Journal of Abnormal Psychology, 109,* 335–340.

Baumeister, A. A., & Bacharach, V. R. (1996). A critical analysis of the Infant Health and Development Program. *Intelligence, 23,* 79–104.

Baumeister, A. A., & Bacharach, V. R. (2000). Early generic educational intervention has no enduring effect on intelligence and does not prevent mental retardation: The Infant Health and Development Program. *Intelligence, 28,* 161–192.

Bauermeister, J. J., Alegria, M., Bird, H., Rubio-Stipec, M. A., & Canino, G. (1992). Are attentional-hyperactivity deficits unidimensional and multidimensional syndromes? Empirical findings from a community survey. *Journal of the American Academy of Child and Adolescent Psychiatry, 31,* 423–431.

Baumrind, D. (1991). The influence of parenting style on adolescent competence and substance use. *Journal of Early Adolescence, 11,* 56–95.

Beach, S. R. H., & Amir, N. (2003). Is depression taxonic, dimensional, or both? *Journal of Abnormal Psychology, 112,* 228–236.

Beardslee, W. R., Versage, E. M., & Gladstone, T. R. (1998). Children of affectively ill parents: A review of the past 10 years. *Journal of the American Academy of Child & Adolescent Psychiatry, 37,* 1134–1141.

Beauchaine, T. P., Webster-Stratton, C., & Reid, M. J. (2005). Mediators, moderators, and predictors of 1-year outcomes among children treated for early-onset conduct problems: A latent growth curve analysis. *Journal of Consulting and Clinical Psychology, 73,* 371–388.

Beck, A. T. (1967). *Depression: Clinical, experimental, and theoretical perspectives.* New York: Harper & Row.

Beck, A. T. (1976). *Cognitive therapy and the emotional disorders.* New York: International Universities Press.

Beck, A. T., & Emery, G. (1985). *Anxiety disorders and phobias: A cognitive perspective.* Philadelphia: Center for Cognitive Therapy.

Beck, A. T., & Weishaar, M. E. (2005). Cognitive therapy. In R. J. Corsini & D. Wedding (Eds.), *Current psychotherapies* (pp. 238–268). Belmont, CA: Brooks/Cole.

Beck, J. S., Liese, B. S., & Najavits, L. M. (2005). Cognitive therapy. In R. J. Frances, S. I. Miller, & A. H. Mack (Eds.), *Clinical textbook of addictive disorders* (3rd ed., pp. 474–501). New York: Guilford Press.

Beck, S. J. (1937). Introduction to the Rorschach method. *American Orthopsychiatric Association Monograph, 1,* 1–278.

Becker, A. E., Burwell, R., Gilman, S. E., Herzog, D., & Hamburg, P. (2002). Eating behaviors and attitudes following prolonged exposure to television among ethnic Fijian adolescent girls. *British Journal of Psychiatry, 180,* 509–514.

Becker, J. V. (1998). What we know about the characteristics and treatment of adolescents who have committed sexual offenses. *Child Maltreatment, 3,* 317–329.

Becker, J. V., & Kaplan, M. S. (1988). The assessment of sexual offenders. *Advances in Behavioral Assessment of Children and Families, 4,* 97–118.

Beckett, C., Maughan, B., Rutter, M., Castle, J., Colvert, E., Groothues, C., et al. (2006). Do the effects of early severe deprivation on cognition persist into early adolescence? Findings from the English and Romanian adoptees study. *Child Development, 77*(3), 696–711.

Beidel, D. C., Morris, T. L., & Turner, M. W. (2004). Social phobia. In T. L. Morris & J. S. March (Eds.), *Anxiety disorders in children and adolescents* (pp. 141–163). New York: Guilford Press.

Beidel, D. C., & Turner, S. M. (2007). Behavioral and cognitive-behavioral treatment of social anxiety disorder in children and adolescents. In D. C. Beidel & S. M. Turner (Eds.), *Shy children, phobic adults: Nature and treatment of social anxiety disorders* (pp. 261–313). Washington, DC: American Psychological Association.

Beidel, D. C., Turner, S. M., & Morris, T. L. (1999). Psychopathology of childhood social phobia. *Journal of the American Academy of Child and Adolescent Psychiatry, 38,* 643–650.

Belsky, J. (1993). Etiology of child maltreatment: A developmental-ecological analysis. *Psychological Bulletin, 114,* 413–434.

Berger, A., Tzur, G., & Posner, M. I. (2006). Infant brains detect arithmetic errors. *Proceedings of the National Academy of Sciences, 103,* 12649–12653.

Berger, L. M. (2005). Income, family characteristics, and physical violence toward children. *Child Abuse & Neglect, 29*(2), 107–133.

Bergevin, T. A., Bukowski, W. M., & Karavasilis, L. (2003). Childhood sexual abuse and pubertal timing: Implications for long-term psychosocial adjustment. In C. Hayward (Ed.), *Gender differences at puberty* (pp. 187–216). New York: Cambridge University Press.

Bergh, C., Eriksson, M., Lindberg, G., & Sodersten, P. (1996). Selective serotonin reuptake inhibitors in anorexia. *Lancet, 348,* 1459.

Berliner, L. (2000). What is sexual abuse? In H. Dubowitz & D. DePanfilis (Eds.), *Handbook for child protection* (pp. 18–22). Thousand Oaks, CA: Sage.

Berliner, L. (2005). The results of randomized clinical trials move the field forward. *Child Abuse & Neglect, 29*(2), 103–105.

Berliner, L., & Elliott, D. M. (2002). Sexual abuse of children. In J. E. B. Myers, L. Berliner, J. Briere, C. T. Hendrix, C. Jenny, & T. A. Reid (Eds.), *The APSAC handbook on child maltreatment* (2nd ed., pp. 55–78). Thousand Oaks, CA: Sage.

Besinger, B., Garland, A. F., Litrownik, A. J., & Landsverk, J. A. (1999). Caregiver substance abuse among maltreated children placed in out-of-home care. *Child Welfare, 78,* 221–239.

Bettelheim, B. (1967). *The empty fortress: Infantile autism and the birth of self.* New York: Free Press.

Beutler, L. E., Zetzer, H. A., & Williams, R. E. (1996). Research applications of prescriptive therapy. In W. Dryden (Ed.), *Research in counselling and psychotherapy: Practical applications* (pp. 25–48). Thousand Oaks, CA: Sage.

Biederman, J., & Faraone, S. V. (2004). The Massachusetts General Hospital studies of gender influences on attention-deficit/hyperactivity disorder in youths and relatives. *Psychiatric Clinics of North America, 27,* 225–232.

Biederman, J., Faraone, S. V., Wozniak, J., Mick, E., Kwon, A., Cayton, G. A., et al. (2005). Clinical correlates of bipolar disorder in a large, referred sample of children and adolescents. *Journal of Psychiatric Research, 39,* 611–622.

Biederman, J., Kwon, A., Aleardi, M., Chouinard, V., Marino, T., Cole, H., et al. (2005). Absence of gender effects on attention deficit hyperactivity disorder: Findings in nonreferred subjects. *American Journal of Psychiatry, 162,* 1083–1089.

Biederman, J., Kwon, A., Wozniak, J., Mick, E., Markowitz, S., Fazio, V., et al. (2004). Absence of gender differences in pediatric bipolar disorder: Findings from a large sample of referred youth. *Journal of Affective Disorders, 83,* 207–214.

Biederman, J., Lopez, F. A., Boellner, S. W., & Chandler, M. C. (2002). A randomized, double-blind, placebo-controlled study of SLI381 (Adderall XR) in children with attention-deficit/hyperactivity disorder. *Pediatrics, 110,* 258–266.

Biederman, J., Mick, E., & Faraone, S. V. (2000). Age-dependent decline of symptoms of attention deficit hyperactivity disorder: Impact of remission definition and symptom type. *American Journal of Psychiatry, 157,* 816–818.

Biederman, J., Mick, E., Faraone, S. V., Braaten, E., Doyle, A., Spencer, T., et al. (2002). Influence of gender on attention deficit hyperactivity disorder in children referred to a psychiatric clinic. *American Journal of Psychiatry, 159,* 36–42.

Biederman, J., Mick, E., Spencer, T., Wilens, T. E., & Faraone, S. V. (2000). Therapeutic dilemmas in the pharmacotherapy of bipolar depression in the young. *Journal of Child and Adolescent Psychopharmacology, 10*(3), 185–192.

Biederman, J., Milberger, S., & Faraone, S. V. (1995). Family-environmental risk factors for attention-deficit hyperactivity disorder. *Archives of General Psychiatry, 52,* 464–470.

Biederman, J., Monuteaux, M. C., Doyle, A. E., Seidman, L. J., Wilens, T. E., Ferrero, F., et al. (2004). Impact of executive functioning deficits and attention-deficit/hyperactivity disorder (ADHD) on academic outcomes in children. *Journal of Consulting and Clinical Psychology, 72,* 757–766.

Biederman, J., Petty, C., Faraone, S. V., Henin, A., Hirshfeld-Becker, D., Pollack, M. H., et al. (2006). Effects of parental anxiety disorders in children at high risk for panic disorder: A controlled study. *Journal of Affective Disorders, 94,* 191–197.

Biederman, J., Wilens, T., Mick, E., & Faraone, S. V. (1997). Is ADHD a risk factor for psychoactive substance use disorders? Findings from a four-year prospective followup study. *Journal of the American Academy of Child & Adolescent Psychiatry, 36,* 21–29.

Biederman, J., Wilens, T., Mick, E., Spencer, T., & Faraone, S. V. (1999). Pharmacotherapy of attention deficit/hyperactivity disorder reduces risk for substance use disorder. *Pediatrics, 104,* 20.

Bifulco, A., Moran, P. M., Ball, C., Jacobs, C., Baines, R., Bunn, A., et al. (2002). Childhood adversity, parental vulnerability and disorder: Examining inter-generational transmission of risk. *Journal of Child Psychology and Psychiatry, 43,* 1075–1086.

Biklen, D. (1993). *Communication unbound.* New York: Teachers College Press.

Binet, A., & Simon, T. (1916). *The development of intelligence in children.* Baltimore, MD: Williams & Wilkins.

Birkeland, S., Murphy-Graham, E., & Weiss, C. (2005). Good reasons for ignoring good evaluation: The case of the drug abuse resistance education (D.A.R.E.) program. *Evaluation and Program Planning, 28,* 247–256.

Birmaher, B., Arbelaez, C., & Brent, D. (2002). Course and outcome of child and adolescent major depressive disorder. *Child and Adolescent Psychiatric Clinics of North America, 11,* 619–637.

Birmaher, B., Axelson, D. A., Monk, K., Kalas, C., Clark, D. B., Ehmann, M., et al. (2003). Fluoxetine for the treatment of childhood anxiety disorders. *Journal of the American Academy of Child and Adolescent Psychiatry, 42,* 415–423.

Birmaher, B., Axelson, D., Strober, M., Gill, M. K., Valeri, S., Chiappetta, L., et al. (2006). Clinical course of children and adolescents with bipolar spectrum disorders. *Archives of General Psychiatry, 63,* 175–183.

Birmaher, B., Brent, D. A., & Benson, R. S. (2000). Summary of the practice parameters for the assessment and treatment of children and adolescents with depressive disorders. *Journal of the American Academy of Child and Adolescent Psychiatry, 37,* 1234–1238.

Birmaher, B., & Ollendick, T. H. (2004). Childhood-onset panic disorder. In T. H. Ollendick & J. S. March (Eds.), *Phobic and anxiety disorders in children and adolescents* (pp. 306–333). New York: Oxford University Press.

Birmaher, B., Ryan, N., Williamson, D., Brent, D., Kaufman, J., Dahl. R., et al. (1996). Childhood and adolescent depression: A review of the past 10 years, Part 1. *Journal of the American Academy of Child and Adolescent Psychiatry, 35,* 1427–1439.

Birmaher, B., Waterman, G. S., Ryan, N. D., Perel, J., McNabb, J., Balach, L., et al. (1998). Randomized, controlled trial of amitriptyline versus placebo for adolescents with treatment-resistant major depression. *Journal of the American Academy of Child and Adolescent Psychiatry, 37,* 527–535.

Birmaher, B., Williamson, D. E., Dahl, R. E., Axelson, D. A., Kaufman, J., Dorn, L. D., et al. (2004). Clinical presentation and course of depression in youth: Does onset in childhood differ from onset in adolescence? *Journal of the American Academy of Child & Adolescent Psychiatry, 43,* 63–70.

Birnbrauer, J. S., & Leach, D. J. (1993). The Murdoch Early Intervention Program after two years. *Behaviour Change, 10,* 63–74.

Black, J. E., Jones, T. A., Nelson, C. A., & Greenough, W. T. (1998). Neuronal plasticity and the developing brain. In N. E. Alessi, J. T. Coyle, S. I. Harrison, & S. Eth (Eds.), *Handbook of child and adolescent psychiatry* (pp. 31–53). New York: Wiley.

Blair, C., & Wahlsten, D. (2002). Why early intervention works: A reply to Baumeister and Bacharach. *Intelligence, 30,* 129–140.

Bloom, B. S. (1956). *Taxonomy of educational objectives.* New York: David McKay.

Blumberg, H. P., Kaufman, J., Martin, A., Whiteman, R., Zhang, J. H., Gore, J. C., et al. (2003). Amygdala and hippocampal volumes in adolescents and adults with bipolar disorder. *Archives of General Psychiatry, 60,* 1201–1208.

Boddaert, N., Chabane, N., Gervais, H., Good, C. D., Bourgeois, M., Plumet, M. H., et al. (2004). Superior temporal sulcus anatomical abnormalities in childhood autism: A voxel-based morphometry MRI study. *Neuroimage, 23,* 364–369.

Bogels, S. M., & van Melick, M. (2004). The relationship between child-report, parent self-report, and partner report of perceived parental rearing behaviors and anxiety in children and parents. *Personality and Individual Differences, 37,* 1583–1596.

Boggs, S. R., Eyberg, S. M., Edwards, D. L., Rayfield, A., Jacobs, J., Bagner, D., et al. (2004). Outcomes of parent-child interaction therapy: A comparison of treatment completers and study dropouts one to three years later. *Child & Family Behavior Therapy, 26,* 1–22.

Bonati, M., & Clavenna, A. (2005). The epidemiology of psychotropic drug use in children and adolescents, *International Review of Psychiatry, 17,* 181–188.

Bond, L., Toumbourou, J. W., Thomas, L., Catalano, R., & Patton, G. C. (2005). Individual, family, school and community risk and protective factors for depressive symptoms in adolescents: A comparison of risk profiles for substance use and depressive symptoms. *Prevention Science, 6,* 73–88.

Bonner, B. L., Logue, M. B., & Kees, M. (2003). Child maltreatment. In M. C. Roberts (Ed.), *Handbook of pediatric psychology* (pp. 652–663). New York: Guilford Press.

Borkovec, T. D., & Inz, J. (1990). The nature of worry in generalized anxiety disorder: A predominance of thought activity. *Behaviour Research and Therapy, 28,* 153–158.

Borkovec, T. D., Ray, W. J., & Stober, J. (1998). Worry: A cognitive phenomenon intimately linked to affective, physiological, and interpersonal behavioral processes. *Cognitive Therapy and Research, 22,* 561–576.

Botteron, K. N., Vannier, M. W., Geller, B., Todd, R. D., & Lee, B. C. (1995). Preliminary study of magnetic resonance imaging characteristics in 8- to 16-year-olds with mania. *Journal of the American Academy of Child and Adolescent Psychiatry, 34,* 742–749.

Bouchard, S., Mendlowitz, S. L., Coles, M. E., & Franklin, M. (2004). Considerations in the use of exposure with children. *Cognitive and Behavioral Practice, 11,* 56–65.

Bowlby, J. (1953). *Child care and the growth of love.* Baltimore, MD: Pelican.

Bowlby, J. (1969). *Attachment and loss: Vol. 1. Attachment.* New York: Basic Books.

Bowlby, J. (1973). *Attachment and loss: Vol. II. Separation: Anxiety and anger.* New York: Basic Books.

Bowlby, J. (1980). *Attachment and loss: Vol. 3. Loss: Sadness and depression.* New York: Basic Books.

Boyle, M. H., & Lipman, E. L. (2002). Do places matter? Socioeconomic disadvantage and behavioral problems of children in Canada. *Journal of Consulting & Clinical Psychology, 70,* 378–389.

Bradley, J. D., & Golden, C. J. (2001). Biological contributions to the presentation and understanding of attention-deficit/hyperactivity disorder: A review. *Clinical Psychology Review, 21,* 907–929.

Brake, W. G., Sullivan, R. M., & Gratton, A. (2000). Perinatal distress leads to lateralized medial prefrontal cortical dopamine hypofunction in adult rats. *Journal of Neuroscience, 20,* 5538–5543.

Bregman, J. D. (2005). Definitions and characteristics of the spectrum. In D. Zager (Ed.), *Autism spectrum disorders: Identification, education, and treatment* (pp. 3–46). Mahwah, NJ: Erlbaum.

Brendgen, M., Wanner, B., Morin, A. J. S., & Vitaro, F. (2005). Relations with parents and with peers, temperament, and trajectories of depressed mood during early adolescence. *Journal of Abnormal Child Psychology, 33,* 579–594.

Brent, D., Holder, D., Kolko, D., Birmaher, B., Baugher, M., Roth, C., et al. (1997). A clinical psychotherapy trial for adolescent depression comparing cognitive, family, and supportive therapy. *Archives of General Psychiatry, 54,* 877–885.

Brereton, A. V., Tonge, B. J., & Einfeld, S. L. (2006). Psychopathology in children and adolescents with autism compared to young people with intellectual disability. *Journal of Autism and Developmental Disorders, 36,* 863–870.

Brestan, E. V., & Eyberg, S. M. (1998). Effective psychosocial treatments of conduct-disordered children and adolescents: 29 years, 82 studies, 5,272 kids. *Journal of Clinical Child Psychology, 27,* 180–189.

Breton, J., Bergeron, L., Valla, J., Berthiaume, C., Gaudet, N., Lambert, J., et al. (1999). Quebec Child Mental Health Survey: Prevalence of DSM-III-R mental health disorders. *Journal of Child Psychology and Psychiatry, 40,* 375–384.

Briere, J., Berliner, L., Bulkley, J., Jenny, C. A., & Reid, T. A. (1996). *The APSAC handbook on child maltreatment.* Thousand Oaks, CA: Sage.

Brilleslijper-Kater, S. N., Friedrich, W. N., & Corwin, D. L. (2004). Sexual knowledge and emotional reaction as indicators of sexual abuse in young children: Theory and research challenges. *Child Abuse & Neglect, 28,* 1007–1017.

British Medical Association. (2006). *Child and adolescent mental health: A guide for healthcare professionals.* London: Author.

Brody, G. H., Ge, X., Conger, R., Gibbons, F. X., McBride Murry, V., Gerrard, M., et al. (2001). The influence of neighborhood disadvantage, collective socialization, and parenting on African American children's affiliation with deviant peers. *Child Development, 72,* 1231–1246.

Bronfenbrenner, U. (1979). *The ecology of human development: Experiments by design and nature.* Cambridge, MA: Harvard University Press.

Bronfenbrenner, U. (2000). Ecological system theory. In A. E. Kazdin (Ed.), *Encyclopedia of psychology* (Vol. 3, pp. 129–133). New York: Oxford University Press.

Bronfenbrenner, U., McClelland, P. D., Wethington, E., Moen, P., & Ceci, S. (1996). *The state of the Americas: This generation and the next.* New York: Free Press.

Bronfenbrenner, U., & Morris, P. A. (1998). The ecology of developmental process. In W. Damon (Ed.), *Handbook of child psychology: Vol. 1. Theory* (pp. 993–1028). New York: Wiley.

Brookes, K., Xu, X., Chen, W., Zhou, K., Neale, B., Lowe, N., et al. (2006). The analysis of 51 genes in DSM-IV combined type attention deficit hyperactivity disorder: Association signals in DRD4, DAT1 and 16 other genes. *Molecular Psychiatry, 11,* 935–953.

Brooks-Gunn, J., & Duncan, G. J. (1997). The effects of poverty on children. *The Future of Children, 7,* 55–71.

Brooks-Gunn, J., Duncan, G. J., Klebanov, P. K., & Sealand, N. (1993). Do neighborhoods influence child and adolescent development? *American Journal of Sociology, 99,* 353–395.

Brown, E. J., & Kolko, J. (1999). Child victims' attributions about being physically abused: An examination of factors associated with symptom severity. *Journal of Abnormal Child Psychology, 27,* 311–322.

Brown, S. A., Myers, M. G., & Stewart, D. G. (1998). Progression from conduct disorder to antisocial personality disorder following treatment for adolescent substance abuse. *American Journal of Psychiatry, 155,* 479–485.

Browne, A., & Finkelhor, D. (1986). Impact of child sexual abuse: A review of the research. *Psychological Bulletin, 99,* 66–77.

Brozina, K., & Abela, Z. (2006). Symptoms of depression and anxiety in children: Specificity of the hopelessness theory. *Journal of Clinical Child and Adolescent Psychology, 35,* 515–527.

Bruch, H. (1973). *Eating disorders: Obesity, anorexia nervosa, and the person within.* New York: Basic Books.

Brunk, M., Henggeler, S. W., & Whelan, J. P. (1987). Comparison of multisystemic therapy and parent training in the brief treatment of child abuse and neglect. *Journal of Consulting and Clinical Psychology, 55,* 171–178.

Buckley, S. (1999). Promoting the cognitive development of children with Down Syndrome: The practical implications of recent psychological research. In J. A. Rondal, J. Perera, & L. Nadel (Eds.), *Down's syndrome: A review of current knowledge* (pp. 99–110). London: Whurr Publishers.

Buckley, S., Dodd, P., Burke, A., Guerin, S., McEvoy, J., & Hillery, J. (2006). Diagnosis and management of attention-deficit hyperactivity disorder in children and adults with and without learning disability. *Psychiatric Bulletin, 30*(7), 251–253.

Bugental, D. B., Blue, J., & Lewis, J. (1990). Caregiver beliefs and dysphoric affect directed to difficult children. *Developmental Psychology, 26,* 631–638.

Bugental, D. B., Ellerson, P. C., Lin, E. K., Rainey, B., Kokotovic, A., & O'Hara, N. (2002). A cognitive approach to child abuse prevention. *Journal of Family Psychology, 16,* 243–258.

Bugental, D. B., & Johnston, C. (2000). Parental and child cognitions in the context of the family. *Annual Review of Psychology, 51,* 315–344.

Bugental, D. B., Johnston, C., New, M., & Silvester, J. (1998). Measuring parental attributions: Conceptual and methodological issues. *Journal of Family Psychology, 12,* 459–480.

Bulik, C. M. (2004). Genetic and biological risk factors. In J. K. Thompson (Ed.), *Handbook of eating disorders and obesity* (p. 3–16). Hoboken, NJ: Wiley.

Bulik, C. M., Klump, K. L., Thornton, L., Kaplan, A. S., Devlin, B., Fichter, M. M., et al. (2004). Alcohol use disorder comorbidity in eating disorders: A multicenter study. *Journal of Clinical Psychiatry, 65,* 1000–1006.

Burke, J. D., Loeber, R., & Lahey, B. B. (2001). Which aspects of ADHD are associated with tobacco use in early adolescence? *Journal of Child Psychology and Psychiatry, 42,* 493–502.

Burleson, J. A., & Kaminer, Y. (2005). Self-efficacy as a predictor of treatment outcome in adolescent substance use disorders. *Addictive Behaviors, 30,* 1751–1764.

Burns, B. J., Costello, E. J., Angold, A., Tweed, D., Stangl, D., Farmer, E. M. Z., et al. (1995). Children's mental health service use across service sectors. *Health Affairs, 14,* 147–159.

Burns, M. K., & Senesac, V. (2005). Comparison of dual discrepancy criteria to assess response to intervention. *Journal of School Psychology, 43,* 393–406.

Burt, S. A., McGue, M., DeMarte, J. A., Krueger, R. F., & Iacono, W. G. (2006). Timing of menarche and the origins of conduct disorder. *Archives of General Psychiatry, 63,* 890–896.

Burt, K. B., Van Dulmen, M. H. M., Carlivati, J., Egeland, B., Sroufe, L. A., Forman, D. R., et al. (2005). Mediating links between maternal depression and offspring psychopathology: The importance of independent data. *Journal of Child Psychology and Psychiatry, 46,* 490–499.

Burton, E., Stice, E., & Seeley, J. R. (2004). A prospective test of the stress-buffering model of depression in adolescent girls: No support once again. *Journal of Consulting and Clinical Psychology, 72,* 689–697.

Burwell, R. A., & Shirk, R. (2007). Subtypes of rumination in adolescence: Associations between brooding, reflection, depressive symptoms, and coping. *Journal of Clinical Child and Adolescent Psychology, 36,* 56–65.

Butcher, J. N., Williams, C. L., Graham, J. R., Archer, R. P., Tellegen, A., Ben-Porath, Y. S., et al. (1992). *MMPI-A: Manual for administration, scoring, and interpretation.* Minneapolis: University of Minnesota Press.

Butler, L., Miezitis, S., Friedman, R., & Cole, E. (1980). The effect of two school-based intervention programs on depressive symptoms in preadolescents. *American Educational Research Journal, 17,* 111–119.

Butler, S. F., Arredondo, D. E., & McCloskey, V. (1995). Affective comorbidity in children and adolescents with attention deficit hyperactivity disorder. *Annals of Clinical Psychiatry, 7,* 51–55.

Butterworth, B. (1999). *The mathematical brain.* London: Macmillan.

Butterworth, B. (2005). Developmental dyscalculia. In J. I. D. Campbell (Ed.), *Handbook of mathematical cognition* (pp. 455–467). New York: Psychology Press.

Button, T. M. M., Hewitt, J. K., Rhee, S. H., Young, S. E., Corley, R. P., & Stalling, M. C. (2006). Examination of the causes of covariation between conduct disorder symptoms and vulnerability to drug dependence. *Twin Research and Human Genetics, 9,* 38–45.

Byrne, B., Olson, R. K., Samuelsson, S., Wadsworth, S., Corley, R., DeFries, J. C., et al. (2006). Genetic and environmental influences on early literacy. *Journal of Research in Reading, 29*, 33–49.

Cadzow, S. P., Armstrong, K. L., & Fraser, J. A. (1999). Stressed parents with infants: Reassessing physical abuse risk factors. *Child Abuse & Neglect, 23*, 845–853.

Caetano, S. C., Olvera, R. L., Hunter, K., Hatch, J. P., Najt, P., Bowden, C., et al. (2006). Association of psychosis with suicidality in pediatric bipolar I, II and bipolar NOS patients. *Journal of Affective Disorders, 91*, 33–37.

Callaghan, R. C., Hathaway, A., Cunningham, J. A., Vettese, L. C., Wyatt, S., & Taylor, L. (2005). Does stage-of-change predict dropout in a culturally diverse sample of adolescents admitted to inpatient substance-abuse treatment? A test of the transtheoretical model. *Addictive Behaviors, 30*, 1834–1847.

Calzada, E. J., Eyberg, S. M., Rich, B., & Querido, J. G. (2004). Parenting disruptive preschoolers: Experiences of mothers and fathers. *Journal of Abnormal Child Psychology, 32*, 203–213.

Cantos, A. L., Neale, J. M., & O'Leary, K. D. (1997). Assessment of coping strategies of child abusing mothers. *Child Abuse & Neglect, 21*, 631–636.

Cao, F., Bitan, T., Chou, T., Burman, D. D., & Booth, J. R. (2006). Deficient orthographic and phonological representations in children with dyslexia revealed by brain activation patterns. *Journal of Child Psychology and Psychiatry, 47*, 1041–1050.

Capaldi, D. M. (1992). Co-occurrence of conduct problems and depressive symptoms in early adolescent boys: II. A 2-year follow-up at grade 8. *Development and Psychopathology, 4*, 125–144.

Caputo, A. A., Frick, P. J., & Brodsky, S. L. (1999). Family violence and juvenile sex offending: Potential mediating roles of psychopathic traits and negative attitudes toward women. *Criminal Justice & Behavior, 26*, 338–356.

Carcani-Rathwell, I., Rabe-Hasketh, S., & Santosh, P. J. (2006). Repetitive and stereotyped behaviours in pervasive developmental disorders. *Journal of Child Psychology and Psychiatry, 47*, 573–581.

Carlson, C. D., & Francis, D. J. (2002). Increasing the reading achievement of at-risk children through direct instruction: Evaluation of the Rodeo Institute for Teacher Excellence (RITE). *Journal of Education for Students Placed at Risk, 7*, 141–166.

Carlson, C. L., & Mann, M. (2002). Sluggish cognitive tempo predicts a different pattern of impairment in the attention deficit hyperactivity disorder predominantly inattentive type. *Journal of Clinical Child and Adolescent Psychology, 31*, 123–129.

Carlson, C. L., Shin, M., & Booth, J. (1999). The case for DSM-IV subtypes in ADHD. *Mental Retardation and Developmental Disabilities Research Reviews, 5*, 199–206.

Carlson, G. A. (2005). Early onset bipolar disorder: Clinical and research considerations. *Journal of Clinical Child and Adolescent Psychology, 34*, 333–343.

Carlson, G. A., Bromet, E. J., & Sievers, S. (2000). Phenomenology and outcome of subjects with early and adult-onset psychotic mania. *American Journal of Psychiatry, 157*, 213–219.

Carpenter, M. (2006). Instrumental, social, and shared goals and interventions in imitation. In S. J. Rogers & J. H. G. Williams (Eds.), *Imitation and the social mind: Autism and typical development* (pp. 48–70). New York: Guilford Press.

Carr, E. G., & Durand, V. M. (1985). Reducing behavior problems through functional communication training. *Journal of Applied Behavior Analysis, 18*, 111–126.

Carr, E. G., Levin, L., McConnachie, G., Carlson, J. I., Kemp, D. C., & Smith, C. E. (1994). *Communication-based intervention for problem behavior: A user's guide for producing positive change.* Baltimore, MD: Paul H. Brooks.

Carrey, N., MacMaster, F. P., Sparkes, S. J., Khan, S. C., & Kusumakar, V. (2002). Glutamatergic changes with treatment in attention deficit hyperactivity disorder: A preliminary case series. *Journal of Child and Adolescent Psychopharmacology, 12*, 331–336.

Carroll, J. B. (1997). Psychometrics, intelligence, and public perception. *Intelligence, 24*, 25–52.

Carter, A. S., Marakovitz, S. E., & Sparrow, S. A. (2006). Comprehensive psychological assessment: A developmental psychopathology approach for clinical and applied research. In D. Cicchetti & D. J. Cohen (Eds.), *Developmental psychopathology, Vol. 1: Theory and method* (2nd ed., pp. 181–210). Hoboken, NJ: Wiley.

Casey, R. J., & Berman, J. S. (1985). The outcome of psychotherapy with children. *Psychological Bulletin, 98*, 388–400.

Caspi, A. (2000). The child is the father of man: Personality continuities from childhood to adulthood. *Journal of Personality and Social Psychology, 78*, 158–172.

Caspi, A., Harrington, H., Moffitt, T. E., & Milne, B. J. (2002). Males on the life-course-persistent and adolescence-limited antisocial pathways: Follow-up at age 26 years. *Development and Psychopathology, 14*, 179–207.

Caspi, A., Lynam, D., Moffitt, T. E., & Silva, P. A. (1993). Unraveling girls' delinquency: Biological, dispositional, and contextual contributions to adolescent misbehavior. *Developmental Psychology, 29,* 19–30.

Caspi, A., Wright, B. R. E., Moffitt, T. E., & Silva, P. A. (1998). Early failure in the labor market: Childhood and adolescent predictors of unemployment in the transition to adulthood. *American Sociological Review, 63,* 424–451.

Cassidy, J., & Shaver, P. R. (1999). *Handbook of attachment.* New York: Guilford Press.

Castellanos, F. X. (2003). Anatomic brain abnormalities in monozygotic twins discordant for attention deficit hyperactivity disorder. *American Journal of Psychiatry, 160,* 1693–1695.

Castellanos, F. X., Giedd, J. N., Berquin, P. C., Walter, J. M., Sharp, W., Tran, T., et al. (2001). Quantitative brain magnetic resonance imaging in girls with attention-deficit/hyperactivity disorder. *Archives of General Psychiatry, 58,* 289–295.

Castellanos, F. X., Giedd, J. N., Eckburg, P., Marsh, W. L., Vaituzis, A. C., Kaysen, D., et al. (1994). Quantitative morphology of the caudate nucleus in attention deficit hyperactivity disorder. *American Journal of Psychiatry, 151,* 1791–1796.

Castellanos, F. X., Giedd, J. N., Marsh, W. L., Hamburger, S. D., Vaituzis, A. C., Dickstein, D. P., et al. (1996). Quantitative brain magnetic resonance imaging in attention deficit hyperactivity disorder. *Archives of General Psychiatry, 53,* 607–616.

Castellanos, F. X., Lee, P. P., Sharp, W., Jeffries, N. O., Greenstein, D. K., Clasen, L. S., et al. (2002). Developmental trajectories of brain volume abnormalities in children and adolescents with attention-deficit/hyperactivity disorder. *Journal of the American Medical Association, 288,* 1740–1748.

Castelli, F., Happe, F., Frith, U., & Frith, C. (2000). Movement and mind: A functional imaging study of perception and interpretation of complex intentional movement patterns. *Neuroimage, 12,* 314–325.

Centers for Disease Control. (2007). *Youth risk behavior surveillance system.* Retrieved June 19, 2007, from http://www.cfoc.org/Info/yrbss.

Centers for Disease Control, Autism and Developmental Disabilities Monitoring Network. (2007a). Prevalence of autism spectrum disorders: Autism and Developmental Disabilities Monitoring Network, six sites, United States, 2000. *Morbidity and Mortality Weekly Report, 56*(SS-1), 1–11.

Centers for Disease Control, Autism and Developmental Disabilities Monitoring Network. (2007b). Prevalence of autism spectrum disorders: Autism and Developmental Disabilities Monitoring Network, 14 sites, United States, 2000. *Morbidity and Mortality Weekly Report, 56*(SS-1), 12–28.

Chaffin, M., Hanson, R., Saunders, B. E., Nichols, T., Barnett, D. Zeanah, C., et al. (2006). Report of the APSAC task force on attachment therapy, reactive attachment disorder, and attachment problems. *Child Maltreatment,* 11, 76–89.

Chaffin, M., Kelleher, K., & Hollenberg, J. (1996). Onset of physical abuse and neglect: Psychiatric, substance abuse, and social risk factors from prospective community data. *Child Abuse & Neglect, 20,* 191–203.

Chaffin, M., Letourneau, E., & Silvosky, J. F. (2002). Adults, adolescents, and children who sexually abuse children: A developmental perspective. In J. E. B. Meyers, L. Berliner, J. Briere, C. T. Hendrix, C. Jenny, & T. A. Reid (Eds.), *The APSAC handbook on child maltreatment* (2nd ed., pp. 205–232). Thousand Oaks, CA: Sage.

Chaffin, M., & Schmidt, S. (2006). An evidence-based perspective on interventions to stop or prevent child abuse. In J. R. Lutzker (Ed.), *Preventing violence: Research and evidence-based intervention strategies* (pp. 49–68). Washington, DC: American Psychological Association.

Chaffin, M., Silovsky, J. F, Funderburk, B., Valle, L. A., Brestan, E. V., Balachova, T., et al. (2004). Parent-child interaction therapy with physically abusive parents: Efficacy for reducing future abuse reports. *Journal of Consulting and Clinical Psychology, 72,* 500–510.

Chaffin, M., Silovsky, J. F., & Vaughn, C. (2005). Temporal concordance of anxiety disorders and child sexual abuse: Implications for direct versus artifactual effects of sexual abuse. *Journal of Clinical Child and Adolescent Psychology, 34,* 210–222.

Chaffin, M., & Valle, L. (2003). Dynamic predictive validity of the child abuse potential inventory. *Child Abuse and Neglect, 27,* 463–482.

Chamberlain, P., Reid, J. B., Ray, J., Capaldi, D. M., & Fisher, P. (1997). Parent inadequate discipline (PID). In T. A. Widiger, A. J. Frances, H. A. Pincus, R. Ross, M. B. First, & W. Davis (Eds.), *DSM-IV sourcebook* (Vol. 3, pp. 569–629). Washington, DC: American Psychiatric Association.

Chang, K., & Steiner, H. (2003). Offspring studies in child and early adolescent bipolar disorder. In B. Geller & M. DelBello (Eds.), *Bipolar disorder in childhood and early adolescence* (pp. 107–129). New York: Guilford Press.

Chapman, J. W., Tunmer, W. E., & Prochnow, J. E. (2001). Does success in the Reading Recovery program depend on developing proficiency in phonological processing skills? A longitudinal study in a whole language instruction context. *Scientific Studies of Reading, 5,* 141–176.

Chard, D. J., Vaughn, S., & Tyler, B. (2003). A synthesis of research on effective interventions for building reading fluency with elementary students with learning disabilities. *Journal of Learning Disabilities, 35,* 386–406.

Charman, T. (2003). Why is joint attention a pivotal skill in autism? In U. Frith & E. Hill (Eds.), *Autism: Mind and brain* (pp. 67–87). New York: Oxford University Press.

Charman, T., & Baron-Cohen, S. (2006). Screening for autism spectrum disorders in populations: Progress, challenges, and questions for future research and practice. In T. Charman & W. Stone (Eds.), *Social and communication development in autism spectrum disorders* (pp. 63–87). New York: Guilford Press.

Chase, C. D., Osinowo, T., & Pary, R. J. (2002). Medical issues in patients with Down syndrome. *Mental Health Aspects of Developmental Disabilities, 5*(2), 34–45.

Chase-Lansdale, P. L., & Gordon, R. A. (1996). Economic hardship and the development of five- and six-year-olds: Neighborhood and regional perspectives. *Child Development, 67,* 338–367.

Chassin, L., Pitts, S. C., & DeLucia, C. (1999). The relation of adolescent substance use to young adult autonomy, positive activity involvement, and perceived competence. *Development and Psychopathology, 11,* 915–932.

Chassin, L., Ritter, J., Trim, R. S., & King, K. M. (2003). Adolescent substance use disorders. In E. J. Mash & R. A. Barkley (Eds.), *Child psychopathology* (pp. 199–230). New York: Guilford Press.

Chavira, D. A., & Stein, M. B. (2005). Childhood social anxiety disorder: From understanding to treatment. *Child and Adolescent Psychiatric Clinics of North America, 14,* 797–818.

Chavira, D. A., Stein, M. B., Bailey, K., & Stein, M. T. (2004). Comorbidity of generalized social anxiety disorder and depression in a pediatric primary care sample. *Journal of Affective Disorders, 80,* 163–171.

Chemtob, C., Nakashima, J., & Carlson, J. (2002). Brief treatment for elementary school children with disaster-related posttraumatic stress disorder: A field study. *Journal of Clinical Psychology, 58,* 99–112.

Chen, X., Hastings, P. D., Rubin, K. H., Chen, H., Cen, G., & Stewart, S. (1998). Child-rearing attitudes and behavioral inhibition in Chinese and Canadian toddlers: A cross-cultural study. *Developmental Psychology, 34,* 677–686.

Chilcoat, H. D., & Breslau, N. (1998). Posttraumatic stress disorder and drug disorders: Testing causal pathways. *Archives of General Psychiatry, 55,* 913–917.

Chronis, A. M., Fabiano, G. A., Gnagy, E. M., Onyango, A. N., Pelham, W. E., Lopez-Williams, A., et al. (2004). An evaluation of the summer treatment program for children with attention-deficit/hyperactivity disorder using a treatment withdrawal design. *Behavior Therapy, 35,* 561–585.

Chronis, A. M., Lahey, B. B., Pelham, W. E., Kipp, H. L., Baumann, B. L. & Lee, S. S. (2003). Psychopathology and substance abuse in parents of young children with attention-deficit/hyperactivity disorder. *Journal of the American Academy of Child and Adolescent Psychiatry, 42,* 1424–1432.

Chronis, A. M., Lahey, B. B., Pelham, W. E., Williams, S. H., Baumann, B. L., Kipp, H., et al. (2007). Maternal depression and early positive parenting predict future conduct problems in young children with attention-deficit/hyperactivity disorder. *Developmental Psychology, 43,* 70–82.

Chung, T., Martin, C. S., Armstrong, T. D., & Labouvie, E. W. (2002). Prevalence of DSM-IV alcohol diagnoses and symptoms in adolescent community and clinical samples. *Journal of the American Academy of Child & Adolescent Psychiatry, 41,* 546–554.

Cicchetti, D. (1990). A historical perspective on the discipline of developmental psychopathology. In J. Rolf, A. Masten, D. Cicchetti, K. Nuechterlein, & S. Weintraub (Eds.), *Risk and protective factors in the development of psychopathology* (pp. 2–28). New York: Cambridge University Press.

Cicchetti, D. (2004). An odyssey of discovery: Lessons learned through three decades of research on child maltreatment. *American Psychologist, 59,* 731–741.

Cicchetti, D. (2006). Developmental psychopathology. In D. Cicchetti & D. J. Cohen (Eds.), *Developmental psychopathology, Vol. 1: Theory and method* (2nd ed., pp. 1–23). Hoboken, NJ: Wiley.

Cicchetti, D., & Aber, J. L. (1998). Contextualism and developmental psychopathology. *Development and Psychopathology, 10,* 137–426.

Cicchetti, D., & Barnett, D. (1991). Toward the development of a scientific nosology of child maltreatment. In D. Cicchetti & W. Grove (Eds.), *Thinking clearly about psychology: Essays in honor of Paul E. Meehl* (pp. 346–377). Minneapolis: University of Minnesota Press.

Cicchetti, D., & Curtis, W. J. (2006). The developing brain and neural plasticity: Implications for normality, psychopathology, and resilience. In D. Cicchetti & D. J. Cohen (Eds.), *Developmental psychopathology, Vol 2: Developmental neuroscience method* (2nd ed., pp. 1–64.). Hoboken, NJ: Wiley.

Cicchetti, D., & Sroufe, L. A. (2000). Reflecting on the past and planning for the future of developmental psychopathology. *Development and Psychopathology, 12,* 255–550.

Cicchetti, D., & Toth, S. L. (1991). The making of a developmental psychopathologist. In J. Cantor, C. Spiker, & L. Lipsitt (Eds.), *Child behavior and development: Training for diversity* (pp. 34–72). Norwood, NJ: Ablex.

Cicchetti, D., & Toth, S. L. (1998). Perspectives on research and practice in developmental psychopathology. In W. Damon (Ed.), *Handbook of child psychology* (Vol. 4, pp. 479–583). New York: Wiley.

Cicchetti, D., Toth, S. L., & Maughan, A. (2000). An ecological-transactional model of child maltreatment. In A. J. Sameroff (Ed.), *Handbook of developmental psychopathology* (pp. 689–722). New York: Kluwer.

Clark, D. B., De Bellis, M. D., Lynch, K. G., Cornelius, J. R., & Martin, C. (2003). Physical and sexual abuse, depression, and alcohol use disorders in adolescents: Onsets and outcomes. *Drug and Alcohol Dependence, 69,* 51–60.

Clark, D. B., Parker, A., & Lynch, K. (1999). Psychopathology and substance-related problems during early adolescence: A survival analysis. *Journal of Clinical Psychology, 28,* 333–341.

Clark, D. B., Vanyukov, M., & Cornelius, J. (2002). Childhood antisocial behavior and adolescent alcohol use disorders. *Alcohol Research and Health, 26,* 109–115.

Clark, D. M., Salkovskis, P. M., & Chalkley, A. J. (1985). Respiratory control as a treatment for panic attacks. *Journal of Behavior Therapy and Experimental Psychiatry, 16,* 23–30.

Clarke, G., Debar, L., Lynch, F., Powell, J., Gale, J., O'Connor, E., et al. (2005). A randomized effectiveness trial of brief cognitive-behavioral therapy for depressed adolescents receiving antidepressant medication. *Journal of the American Academy of Child & Adolescent Psychiatry, 44,* 888–898.

Clarke, G. N., Hornbrook, M. C., Lynch, F. L., Polen, M. R., Gale, J., O'Connor, E., et al. (2002). Group cognitive behavioral treatment for depressed adolescent offspring of depressed parents in an HMO. *Journal of the American Academy of Child and Adolescent Psychiatry, 41,* 305–313.

Clarke, G. N., Lewinsohn, P. M., & Hops, H. (1990). *Instructor's manual for the adolescent coping with depression course.* Retrieved September 6, 2006, from http://www.kpchr.org/public/acwd/acwd.html.

Clarke, G. N., Rohde, P., Lewinsohn, P. M., Hops, H., & Seeley, J. R. (1999). Cognitive-behavioral treatment of adolescent depression: Efficacy of acute group treatment and booster sessions. *Journal of the American Academy of Child and Adolescent Psychiatry, 38,* 272–279.

Claude, D., & Firestone, P. (1995). The development of ADHD in boys: A 12-year follow-up. *Canadian Journal of Behavioural Science, 27,* 226–249.

Claussen, A. H., & Crittenden, P. M. (1991). Physical and psychological maltreatment: Relations among types of maltreatment. *Child Abuse & Neglect, 15,* 5–18.

Clayton, R., Cattarello, A. M., & Johnstone, B. M. (1996). The effectiveness of drug abuse resistance education (project D.A.R.E.): 5-Year follow up results. *Preventative Medicine, 25,* 307–318.

Clayton-Smith, J. (2001). Angelman syndrome: Evolution of the phenotype in adolescents and adults. *Developmental Medicine & Child Neurology, 43,* 476–480.

Clifford, J. J., Tighe, O., Croke, D. T., Sibley, D. R., Drago, J., & Waddington, J. L. (1998). Topographical evaluation of the phenotype of spontaneous behaviour in mice with targeted gene deletion of the D1A dopamine receptor: Paradoxical elevation of grooming syntax. *Neuropharmacology, 37,* 1595–1602.

Clinton, D., & Norring, C. (2005). The comparative utility of statistically derived eating disorder clusters and DSM-IV diagnoses: Relationship to symptomatology and psychiatric comorbidity at intake and follow-up. *Eating Behaviors, 6,* 403–418.

Cobham, V. E., Dadds, M. R., & Spence, S. H. (1998). The role of parental anxiety in the treatment of childhood anxiety. *Journal of Consulting and Clinical Psychology, 66,* 893–905.

Cohen, D., Gerardin, P., Mazet, P., Purper-Ouakil, D., & Flament, M. F. (2004). Pharmacological treatment of adolescent major depression. *Journal of Child and Adolescent Psychopharmacology, 14,* 19–31.

Cohen, J. (1988). *Statistical power analysis for the behavioral sciences* (2nd ed.). Hillsdale, NJ: Erlbaum.

Cohen, J. A. (2005). Treating traumatized children: Current status and future directions. *Journal of Trauma & Dissociation, 6,* 109–121.

Cohen, J. A., Deblinger, E., Mannarino, A. P., & Steer, R. A. (2004). A multisite, randomized controlled trial for children with sexual abuse-related PTSD symptoms. *Journal of the American Academy of Child & Adolescent Psychiatry, 43,* 393–402.

Cohen, J. A., & Mannarino, A. P. (1996). A treatment outcome study for sexually abused preschool children: Initial findings. *Journal of the American Academy of Child and Adolescent Psychiatry, 35,* 42–50.

Cohen, J. A., & Mannarino, A. P. (1997). A treatment study of sexually abused preschool children: Outcome during a one year follow-up. *Journal of the American Academy of Child and Adolescent Psychiatry, 36,* 1229–1235.

Cohen, J. A., & Mannarino, A. P. (2004). Posttraumatic stress disorder. In T. H. Ollendick & J. S. March (Eds.), *Phobic and anxiety disorders in children and adolescents* (pp. 405–432). New York: Oxford University Press.

Cohen, J. A., Mannarino, A. P., & Knudsen, K. (2005). Treating sexually abused children: 1 year follow-up of a randomized controlled trial. *Child Abuse & Neglect, 29,* 135–145.

Cohen, J. A., Perel, J. M., DeBellis, M. D., Friedman, M. J., & Putnam, F. W. (2002). Treating traumatized children: Clinical implications of the psychobiology of posttraumatic stress disorder. *Trauma, Violence, & Abuse, 3,* 91–108.

Cohen, J. B., Deblinger, E., Maedel, A. B., & Stauffer, L. B. (1999). Examining sex-related thoughts and feelings of sexually abused and nonabused children. *Journal of Interpersonal Violence, 14,* 701–712.

Cohen, L., Lehericy, S., Chochon, F., Lemer, C., Rivaud, S., & Dehaene, S. (2002). Language-specific tuning of visual cortex? Functional properties of the Visual Word Form Area. *Brain, 125,* 1054–1069.

Cohen, P., Cohen, J., Kasen, S., Velez, C., Hartmark, C., Johnson, J., et al. (1993). An epidemiological study of childhood disorders in late childhood and adolescence: I. Age and gender-specific prevalence. *Journal of Child Psychology, Psychiatry, and Allied Disciplines, 34,* 851–867.

Cohen, R. J., & Swerdlik, M. E. (2005). *Psychological testing and assessment: An introduction to tests and measurement.* New York: McGraw-Hill.

Coie, J. D., Dodge, K. A., & Kupersmidt, J. B. (1990). Peer group behavior and social status. In S. R. Asher & J. D. Coie (Eds.), *Peer rejection in childhood* (pp. 17–59). New York: Cambridge University Press.

Coie, J. D., Dodge, K. A., Terry, R., & Wright, V. (1991). The role of aggression in peer relations: An analysis of aggression episodes in boys' play groups. *Child Development, 62,* 812–826.

Cole, D. A., Tram, J. M., Martin, J. M., Hoffman, K. B., Ruiz, M. D., Jacquez, F. M., et al. (2002). Individual differences in the emergence of depressive symptoms in children and adolescents: A longitudinal investigation of parent and child reports. *Journal of Abnormal Psychology, 111,* 156–165.

Comery, T. A., Harris, J. B., Willems, P. J., Oostra, B. A. & Greenough, W. T. (1997). Abnormal dendritic spines in fragile X knockout mice: Maturation and pruning deficits. *Proceedings of the National Academy of Sciences, 94,* 5401–5404.

Compas, B. E., Connor-Smith, J., & Jaser, S. S. (2004). Temperament, stress reactivity, and coping: Implications for depression in childhood and adolescence. *Journal of Clinical Child and Adolescent Psychology, 33,* 21–31.

Compton, S. N., Grant, P. J., Chrisman, A. K., Gammon, P. J., Brown, V. L., & March, J. S. (2001). Sertraline in children and adolescents with social anxiety disorder: An open trial. *Journal of the American Academy of Child and Adolescent Psychiatry, 40,* 564–571.

Conger, R. D., Ge, X. J., Elder, G. H., Lorenz, F. O., & Simons, R. L. (1994). Economic stress, coercive family process, and developmental problems of adolescents. *Child Development, 65,* 541–561.

Connolly, S. D., & Bernstein, A. (2007). Practice parameter for the assessment and treatment of children and adolescents with anxiety disorders. *Journal of the American Academy of Child & Adolescent Psychiatry, 46,* 267–283.

Connor, D. F., Steingard, R. J., Cunningham, J. A., Anderson, J. J., & Melloni, R. H. (2004). Proactive and reactive aggression in referred children and adolescents. *American Journal of Orthopsychiatry, 74,* 129–136.

Connor-Smith, J. K., Compas, B. E., Wadsworth, M. E., Thomsen, A. H., & Saltzman, H. (2000). Responses to stress in adolescence: Measurement of coping and involuntary stress responses. *Journal of Consulting and Clinical Psychology, 68,* 976–992.

Constantino, J. N., Chackes, L. M., Wartner, U. G., Gross, M., Brophy, S. L., Vitale, J., et al. (2006). Mental representations of attachment in identical female twins with and without conduct problems. *Child Psychiatry & Human Development, 37,* 65–72.

Coolidge, F. L., Thede, L. L., & Young, S. E. (2000). Heritability of the comorbidity of attention deficit hyperactivity disorder with behavioral disorders and executive function deficits: A preliminary investigation. *Developmental Neuropsychology, 17,* 273–287.

Coppus, A., Evenhuis, H., Verberne, G., Visser, F., van Gool, P., Eikelenboom, P., et al. (2006). Dementia and mortality in persons with Down's syndrome. *Journal of Intellectual Disability Research, 50,* 768–777.

Cornish, K. M., Munir, F., & Cross, G. (1998). The nature of spatial deficit in young females with fragile-X syndrome: A neuropsychological and molecular perspective. *Neuropsychologia, 36,* 1239–1246.

Corsini, R. J. (2005). Introduction to current psychotherapies. In R. J. Corsini & D. Wedding (Eds.), *Current psychotherapies* (7th ed., pp. 1–14). Belmont, CA: Brooks/Cole.

Costantino, G., Malgady, R. G., & Cardalda, E. (2005). TEMAS narrative treatment: An evidence-based culturally competent therapy modality. In E. D. Hibbs & P. S. Jensen (Eds.), *Psychosocial treatments for child and adolescent disorders: Empirically based strategies for clinical practice* (pp. 717–742). Washington, DC: American Psychological Association.

Costello, E. J. (2005). The developmental epidemiology of anxiety disorders: Phenomenology, prevalence, and comorbidity. *Child and Adolescent Psychiatric Clinics of North America, 14,* 631–648.

Costello, E. J., Angold, A., Burns, B., Stangl, D. K., Tweed, D. L., Erkanli, A., et al. (1996). The Great Smoky Mountains Study of Youth: Goals, design, methods, and the prevalence of DSM-III-K disorders. *Archives of General Psychiatry, 53,* 1129–1136.

Costello, E. J., Egger, H. L., & Angold, A. (2004). Developmental epidemiology of anxiety disorders. In T. H. Ollendick & J. S. March (Eds.), *Phobic and anxiety disorders in children and adolescents* (pp. 61–91). New York: Oxford University Press.

Costello, E. J., Erkanli, A., & Angold, A. (2006). Is there an epidemic of child or adolescent depression? *Journal of Child Psychology and Psychiatry, 47,* 1263–1271.

Costello, E. J., Erkanli, A., Feerman, E., & Angeld, A. (1999). Development of psychiatric comorbidity with substance abuse in adolescents: Effects of timing and sex. *Journal of Clinical Child Psychology, 28,* 298–311.

Costello, E. J., Pine, D. S., Hammen, C. M., John, S., Plotsky, P. M., & Weissman, M. (2002). Development and natural history of mood disorders. *Biological Psychiatry, 52,* 529–542.

Cowan, P. A., & Cowan, C. P. (2006). Developmental psychopathology from family systems and family risk factors perspectives. In D. Cicchetti & D. J. Cohen (Eds.), *Developmental psychopathology, Vol 1: Theory and method* (2nd ed., pp. 530–587). Hoboken, NJ: Wiley.

Coyne, J. C., & Whiffen, V. E. (1995). Issues in personality as diathesis for depression: The case of sociotropy-dependency and autonomy-self-criticism. *Psychological Bulletin, 118,* 358–378.

Craddock, N., & Jones, I. (1999). Genetics of bipolar disorder. *Journal of Medical Genetics, 36,* 585–594.

Creswell, C., Schniering, C. A., & Rapee, R. M. (2005). Threat interpretation in anxious children and their mothers: Comparison with nonclinical children and the effects of treatment. *Behaviour Research and Therapy, 43,* 1375–1381.

Crick, N. R. (1995). Relational aggression: The role of intent attributions, feelings of distress, and provocation type. *Development and Psychopathology, 7,* 313–322.

Crick, N. R. (1997). Engagement in gender normative versus non-normative forms of aggression: Links to social-psychological adjustment. *Developmental Psychology, 33,* 610–617.

Crick, N. R., & Bigbee, M. A. (1998). Relational and oven forms of peer victimization: A multi-informant approach. *Journal of Consulting and Clinical Psychology, 66,* 337–347.

Crick, N. R., & Dodge, K. A. (1994). A review and reformulation of social information-processing mechanisms in children's social adjustment. *Psychological Bulletin, 115,* 74–101.

Crick, N. R., & Dodge, K. A. (1996). Social information-processing mechanisms in reactive and proactive aggression. *Child Development, 67,* 993–1002.

Crick, N. R., & Grotpeter, J. K. (1995). Relational aggression, gender, and social-psychological adjustment. *Child Development, 66,* 710–722.

Critchley, H. D., Daly, E. M., Bullmore, E. T., Williams, S. C., Van Amelsvoort, T., Robertson, D. M., et al. (2000). The functional neuroanatomy of social behaviour: Changes in cerebral blood flow when people with autistic disorder process facial expressions. *Brain, 123,* 2203–2212.

Crittenden, P. (1992). Children's strategies for coping with adverse home environments: An interpretation using attachment theory. *Child Abuse & Neglect, 16,* 329–343.

Crittenden, P. M., Claussen, A. H., & Sugarman, D. B. (1994). Physical and psychological maltreatment in middle childhood and adolescence. *Development & Psychopathology, 6,* 145–164.

Crnic, K., & Low, C. (2002). Everyday stresses and parenting. In M. H. Bornstein (Ed.), *Handbook of parenting* (pp. 243–268). Mahwah, NJ: Lawrence Erlbaum.

Crockett, J. L., Fleming, R. K., Doepke, K. J., & Stevens, J. S. (2007). Parent training: Acquisition and generalization of discrete trials teaching skills with parents of children with autism. *Research in Developmental Disabilities, 28,* 23–36.

Crome, I., & Bloor, R. (2005). Substance misuse and psychiatric comorbidity in adolescents. *Current Opinion in Psychiatry, 18,* 435–439.

Cuckle, H. S., Wald, N. J., & Thompson, S. G. (1987). Estimating a woman's risk of having a pregnancy associated with Down's syndrome using her age and serum alpha-fetoprotein level. *British Journal of Obstetrics and Gynecology, 94,* 387–402.

Cunningham, C. E., & Boyle, H. (2002). Preschoolers at risk for attention-deficit hyperactivity disorder and oppositional defiant disorder: Family, parenting, and behavioral correlates. *Journal of Abnormal Child Psychology, 30,* 555–569.

Cunningham, M., Rapee, R., & Lyneham, H. (2007). Overview of the *Cool Teens* CD-ROM for anxiety disorders in adolescents. *The Behavior Therapist, 30,* 15–19.

Curry, J. F., March, J. S., & Hervey, A. S. (2004). Comorbidity of childhood and adolescent anxiety disorders. In T. H. Ollendick & J. S. March (Eds.), *Phobic and anxiety disorders in children and adolescents* (pp. 116–140). New York: Oxford University Press.

Curry, J. F., & Wells, C. (2005). Striving for effectiveness in the treatment of adolescent depression: Cognitive behavior therapy for multisite community intervention. *Cognitive and Behavioral Practice, 12,* 177–185.

Cyr, M., McDuff, P., Wright, J., Theriault, C., & Cinq-Mars, C. (2005). Clinical correlates and repetition of self-harming behaviors among female adolescent victims of sexual abuse. *Journal of Child Sexual Abuse, 14,* 49–68.

Dadds, M. R., Barrett, P. M., Rapee, R. M., & Ryan, A. (1996). Family process and child anxiety and aggression: An observational analysis. *Journal of Abnormal Child Psychology, 24,* 715–734.

Dadds, M. R., Fraser, J., Frost, A., & Hawes, D. J. (2005). Disentangling the underlying dimensions of psychopathy and conduct problems in childhood: A community study. *Journal of Consulting and Clinical Psychology, 73,* 400–410.

Dadds, M. R., & McHugh, A. (1992). Social support and treatment outcome in behavioral family therapy for child conduct problems. *Journal of Consulting and Clinical Psychology, 60,* 252–259.

Dadds, M. R., & Salmon, K. (2003). Learning and temperament as alternate pathways to punishment insensitivity in antisocial children. *Clinical Child and Family Psychology Review, 6,* 69–86.

D'Agostino, J. V., & Murphy, J. A. (2004). A meta-analysis of Reading Recovery in the United States schools. *Educational Evaluation and Policy Analysis, 26,* 23–38.

Danielson, C. K., de Arellano, M. A., Kilpatrick, D. G., Saunders, B. E., & Resnick, H. S. (2005). Child maltreatment in depressed adolescents: Differences in symptomatology based on history of abuse. *Child Maltreatment, 10,* 37–48.

Danielson, C. K., Feeny, N. C., Findling, R. L., & Youngstrom, E. A. (2004). Psychosocial treatment of bipolar disorders in adolescents: A proposed cognitive-behavioral intervention. *Cognitive and Behavioral Practice, 11,* 283–297.

Danielyan, A., Pathak, S., Kowatch, R. A., Arszman, S. P., & Johns, E. S. (2007). Clinical characteristics of bipolar disorder in very young children. *Journal of Affective Disorders, 97,* 51–59.

Darke, S., Ross, J., & Lynskey, M. (2003). The relationship of conduct disorder to attempted suicide and drug use history among methadone maintenance patients. *Drug and Alcohol Review, 22,* 21–25.

Davanzo, P., Thomas, M. A., Yue, K., Oshiro, T., Belin, T., Straber, M., et al. (2001). Decreased anterior cingulate myo-inositol/creatine spectroscopy resonance with lithium treatment in children with bipolar disorder. *Neuropsychopharmacology, 24,* 359–369.

Davidovitch, M., Click, L., Holtzman, G., Tirosh, E., & Safir, M. P. (2000). Developmental regression in autism: Maternal perception. *Journal of Autism and Developmental Disorders, 30,* 113–119.

Davies, P. T., & Cummings, E. M. (2006). Interparental discord, family process, and developmental psychopathology. In D. Cicchetti & D. J. Cohen (Eds.), *Developmental psychopathology, Vol. 3: Risk, disorder, and adaptation* (2nd ed., pp. 86–128). Hoboken, NJ: Wiley.

Davila, J., Steinberg, S. J., Kachadourian, L., Cobb, R., & Fincham, F. (2004). Romantic involvement and depressive symptoms in early and late adolescence: The role of a preoccupied relational style. *Personal Relationships, 11,* 161–178.

Dean, A. J., McDermott, B. M., & Marshall, R. T. (2006). Psychotropic medication utilization in a child and adolescent mental health service. *Journal of Child and Adolescent Psychopharmacology, 16,* 273–285.

Deas, D., Roberts, J. S., & Grindlinger, D. (2005). The utility of DSM-IV criteria in diagnosing substance abuse/dependence in adolescents. *Journal of Substance Use, 10,* 10–21.

Deater-Deckard, K., Dodge, K. A., Bates, J. E., & Pettit, G. S. (1996). Physical discipline among African American and European American mothers: Links to children's externalizing behaviors. *Developmental Psychology, 32,* 1065–1072.

Deater-Deckard, K., Lansford, J. E., Dodge, K. A., Pettit, G. S., & Bates, J. E. (2003). The development of attitudes about physical punishment: An 8-year longitudinal study. *Journal of Family Psychology, 17,* 351–360.

DeBellis, M. D., Chrousos, G. P., Dorn, L. D., Burke, L., Helmers, K., Kling, M. A., et al. (1994). Hypothalamic-pituitary-adrenal axis dysregulation in sexually abused girls. *Journal of Clinical Endocrinology and Metabolism, 78,* 249–255.

Deblinger, E., & Heflin, A. H. (1996). *Cognitive behavioral interventions for treating sexually abused children.* Thousand Oaks, CA: Sage.

Deblinger, E., Lippmann, J., & Steer, R. (1996). Sexually abused children suffering posttraumatic stress symptoms: Initial treatment outcome findings. *Child Maltreatment, 1,* 310–321.

Deblinger, E., Steer, R., & Lippmann, J. (1999a). Maternal factors associated with sexually abused children's psychosocial adjustment. *Child Maltreatment, 4,* 13–20.

Deblinger, E., Steer, R. A., & Lippmann, J. (1999b). Two-year follow-up study of cognitive-behavioral therapy for sexually abused children suffering from post-traumatic stress symptoms. *Child Abuse & Neglect, 23,* 1371–1378.

de Haan, E., Hoogduin, K. A., Buitelaar, J. K., & Keijsers, G. P. (1998). Behavior therapy versus chlomipramine for the treatment of obsessive-compulsive disorder in children and adolescents. *Journal of the American Academy of Child and Adolescent Psychiatry, 37,* 1022–1029.

Dehaene, S., Piazza, M., Pinel, P., & Cohen, L. (2003). Three parietal circuits for number processing. *Cognitive Neuropsychology, 20,* 487–506.

Dehon, C., Weems, C. F., Stickle, T. R., Costa, N. M., & Berman, S. L. (2005). A cross-sectional evaluation of the factorial invariance of anxiety sensitivity in adolescents and young adults. *Behaviour Research and Therapy, 43,* 799–810.

Dejong, P. J., & Merckelbach, H. (1998). Blood-injection-injury phobia and fear of spiders: Domain-specific individual differences in disgust sensitivity. *Personality & Individual Differences, 24,* 153–158.

De La Paz, S., Swanson, P., & Graham, S. (1998). The contribution of executive control to the revising of students with writing and learning difficulties. *Journal of Educational Psychology, 90,* 448–460.

Delate, T., Gelenberg, A. J., Simmons, V. A., & Motheral, B. R. (2004). Trends in the use of antidepressants in a national sample of commercially insured pediatric patients, 1998 to 2002. *Psychiatric Services, 55,* 387–391.

DelBello, M. P., & Kowatch, R. A. (2003). Neuroimaging in pediatric bipolar disorder. In B. Geller & M. DelBello (Eds.), *Bipolar disorder in childhood and early adolescence* (pp. 158–174). New York: Guilford Press.

DelBello, M. P., Schwiers, M. L., Rosenberg, H. L., & Strakowski, S. M. (2002). A double, randomized, placebo-controlled study of quetiapine adjunctive treatment for adolescent mania. *Journal of the American Academy of Child & Adolescent Psychiatry, 41,* 1216–1223.

DelBello, M. P., Zimmerman, M. E., Mills, N. P., Getz, G. E., & Strakowski, S. M. (2004). Magnetic resonance imaging analysis of amygdala and other subcortical brain regions in adolescents with bipolar disorder. *Bipolar Disorders, 6,* 43–52.

Dennis, M., Godley, S. H., Diamond, G., Tims, F. M., Babor, T., Donaldson, J., et al. (2004). The Cannabis Youth Treatment (CYT) Study: Main findings from two randomized trials. *Journal of Substance Abuse Treatment, 27,* 197–213.

Dennis, M. L., Titus, J. C., Diamond, G., Donaldson, J., Godley, S. H., Tims, P., et al. (2002). The Cannabis Youth Treatment (CYT) experiment: Rationale, study design and analysis plans. *Addiction, 97,* 16–34.

DeShazo Barry, T., Lyman, R. D., & Grofer Klinger, L. (2002). Academic underachievement and attention-deficit/hyperactivity disorder: The negative impact of symptom severity on school performance. *Journal of School Psychology, 40,* 259–283.

DeVeaugh-Geiss, J., Moroz, G., Biederman, J., Cantwell, D., Fontaine, R., Greist, J. H., et al. (1992). Clomipramine hydrochloride in childhood and adolescent obsessive-compulsive disorder: A multicenter trial. *Journal of the American Academy of Child and Adolescent Psychiatry, 31,* 45–49.

Diamond, G., Godley, S. H., Liddle, H. A., Sampl, S., Webb, C., Tims, F. M., et al. (2002). Five outpatient treatment models for adolescent marijuana use: A description of the Cannabis Youth Treatment Interventions. *Addiction, 97,* 70–83.

Dick, D., Li, T., Edenberg, H., Hesselbrock, V., Kramer, J., Kuperman, S., et al. (2004). A genome-wide screen for genes influencing conduct disorder. *Molecular Psychiatry, 9,* 81–86.

Dick, D. M., & Todd, R. D. (2006). Genetic contributions. In D. Cicchetti & D. J. Cohen (Eds.), *Developmental psychopathology, Vol. 2: Developmental neuroscience* (pp. 16–28). Hoboken, NJ: Wiley.

Dick, D. M., Viken, R. J., Kaprio, J., Pulkkinen, L., & Rose, R. J. (2005). Understanding the covariation among childhood externalizing symptoms: Genetic and environmental influences on Conduct Disorder, Attention Deficit Hyperactivity Disorder, and Oppositional Defiant Disorder symptoms. *Journal of Abnormal Child Psychology, 33,* 219–229.

Dilsaver, S. C., & Akiskal, S. (2005). High rate of unrecognized bipolar mixed states among destitute Hispanic adolescents referred for "major depressive disorder." *Journal of Affective Disorders, 84,* 179–186.

Dilworth-Bart, J. E., & Moore, F. (2006). Mercy mercy me: Social injustice and the prevention of environmental pollutant exposures among ethnic minority and poor children. *Child Development, 77,* 247–265.

Dimitropoulos, A., Feurer, I. D., Butler, M. G., & Thompson, T. (2001). Emergence of compulsive behavior and tantrums in children with Prader-Willi syndrome. *American Journal on Mental Retardation, 106,* 39–51.

Dishion, T. J., Andrews, D. W., & Crosby, L. (1995). Antisocial boys and their friends in early adolescence: Relationship characteristics, quality and interactional process. *Child Development, 66,* 139–151.

Dishion, T. J., Capaldi, D., Spracklen, K. M., & Li, F. (1995). Peer ecology of male adolescent drug use. *Development and Psychopathology, 7,* 803–824.

Dishion, T. J., Eddy, J. M., Haas, E., Li, F., & Spracklen, K. M. (1997). Friendships and violent behavior during adolescence. *Social Development, 6,* 207–223.

Dishion, T. J., McCord, J., & Poulin, F. (1999). When interventions harm: Peer groups and problem behavior. *American Psychologist, 54,* 755–764.

Dishion, T. J., Spracklen, K. M., Andrews, D. W., & Patterson, G. R. (1996). Deviancy training in male adolescent friendships. *Behavior Therapy, 27,* 373–390.

Dix, T. (1993). Attributing dispositions to children: An interactional analysis of attribution in socialization. *Personality and Social Psychology Bulletin, 19,* 633–643.

Dix, T., & Lochman, J. (1990). Social cognition and negative reactions to children: A comparison of mothers of aggressive and nonaggressive boys. *Journal of Social and Clinical Psychology, 9,* 418–438.

Dodge, K. A. (1993). Social-cognitive mechanisms in the development of conduct disorder and depression. *Annual Review of Psychology, 44,* 559–584.

Dodge, K. A. (2003). Do social information-processing patterns mediate aggressive behavior? In B. B. Lahey, T. E. Moffitt, & A. Caspi (Eds.), *Causes of conduct disorder and juvenile delinquency* (pp. 254–274). New York: Guilford Press.

Dodge, K. A. (2006). Translational science in action: Hostile attributional style and the development of aggressive behavior problems. *Development and Psychopathology, 18,* 791–814.

Dodge, K. A., & Coie, J. D. (1987) Social-information processing factors in reactive and proactive aggression in children's peer groups. *Journal of Personality and Social Psychology, 53,* 1146–1158.

Dodge, K. A., Lansford, J. E., Burks, V. S., Bates, J. E., Pettit, G. S., Fontaine, R., et al. (2003). Peer rejection and social information-processing factors in the development of aggressive behavior problems in children. *Child Development, 74,* 374–393.

Dodge, K. A., & Pettit, G. S. (1990). Mechanisms in the cycle of violence. *Science, 250,* 1678–1683.

Dodge, K. A., & Pettit, G. S. (2003). A biopsychosocial model of the development of chronic conduct problems in adolescence. *Developmental Psychology, 39,* 349–371.

Dodge, K. A., Pettit, G. S., & Bates, J. E. (1997). How the experience of early physical abuse leads children to become chronically aggressive. *Developmental perspectives on trauma: Theory, research and intervention* (pp. 263–288). Rochester, NY: University of Rochester Press.

Dodge, K. A., Pettit, G. S., Bates, J. E., & Valente, E. (1995). Social information-processing patterns partially mediate the effect of early physical abuse on later conduct problems. *Journal of Abnormal Psychology, 104,* 632–643.

Dolan, M., & Rennie, C. (2006). Psychopathy checklist: Youth version and youth psychopathic trait inventory: A comparison study. *Personality and Individual Differences, 41,* 779–789.

Dolz, L., Cerezo, M. A., & Milner, J. S. (1997). Mother-child interactional patterns in high- and low-risk mothers. *Child Abuse & Neglect, 21,* 1149–1158.

Dopke, C. A., Lundahl, B. W., Dunsterville, E., & Lovejoy, M. C. (2003). Interpretations of child compliance in individuals at high and low risk for child physical abuse. *Child Abuse & Neglect, 27,* 285–302.

Dopke, C. A., & Milner, S. (2000). Impact of child noncompliance on stress appraisals, attributions, and disciplinary choices in mothers at high and low risk for child physical abuse. *Child Abuse & Neglect, 24,* 493–504.

Doyle, A. E., Faraone, S. V., DuPre, E. P., & Biederman, J. (2001). Separating attention deficit hyperactivity disorder and learning disabilities in girls: A familial risk analysis. *American Journal of Psychiatry, 158,* 1666–1672.

Drabick, D. A. G., & Goldfried, R. (2000). Training the scientist-practitioner for the 21st century: Putting the bloom back on the rose. *Journal of Clinical Psychology, 56,* 327–340.

Dubowitz, H., & Black, M. (2002). Neglect of children's health. In J. E. B. Meyers, L. Berliner, J. Briere, C. T. Hendrix, C. Jenny, & T. A. Reid (Eds.), *The APSAC handbook on child maltreatment* (2nd ed., pp. 269–292). Thousand Oaks, CA: Sage.

Dubowitz, H., Newton, R. R., Litrownik, A. J., Lewis, T., Briggs, E. C., Thompson, R., et al. (2005). Examination of a conceptual model of child neglect. *Child Maltreatment, 10,* 173–189.

Dubowitz, H., Pitts, S. C., & Black, M. M. (2004). Measurement of three major subtypes of child neglect. *Child Maltreatment, 9,* 344–356.

Dukes, R. L., Stein, J. A., & Ullman, J. B. (1997). Long-term impact of drug abuse resistance education (D.A.R.E.): Results of a 6-year follow-up. *Evaluation Review, 21,* 483–500.

Duncan, G. J., & Brooks-Gunn, J. (2000). Family poverty, welfare reform, and child development. *Child Development, 71,* 188–196.

DuPaul, G. J., & Eckert, T. L. (1997). The effects of school-based interventions for attention deficit hyperactivity disorder: A meta-analysis. *School Psychology Digest, 26,* 5–27.

DuPaul, G. J., & Stoner, G. (2003). *ADHD in the schools* (2nd ed.). New York: Guilford Press.

Durand, V. M. (2005). Past, present, and emerging directions in education. In D. Zager (Ed.), *Autism spectrum disorders: Identification, education, and treatment* (pp. 89–109). Mahwah, NJ: Erlbaum.

Durand, V. M., & Christodulu, K. V. (2006). Mental retardation. In M. Hersen (Ed.), *Clinician's handbook of child behavioral assessment* (pp. 459–475). San Diego, CA: Elsevier.

Dykens, E. M. (1995). Measuring behavioral phenotypes: Provocations from the "new genetics." *American Journal on Mental Retardation, 99,* 522–532.

Dykens, E. M. (2000). Contaminated and unusual food combinations: What do people with Prader-Willi syndrome choose? *Mental Retardation, 38,* 163–171.

Dykens, E. (2001). Introduction to the special issue on behavioral phenotypes. *American Journal on Mental Retardation, 106,* 1–3.

Dykens, E. M. (2003). Anxiety, fears, and phobias in persons with Williams syndrome. *Developmental Neuropsychology, 23,* 291–316.

Dykens, E. M., & Cassidy, S. B. (1999). Prader-Willi syndrome. In S. Goldstein & C. R. Reynolds (Eds.), *Handbook of neurodevelopmental and genetic disorders in children* (pp. 525–554). New York: Guilford Press.

Dykens, E. M., Cassidy, S. B., & King, B. H. (1999). Maladaptive behavior differences in Prader-Willi syndrome due to paternal deletion versus maternal uniparental disomy. *American Journal on Mental Retardation, 104,* 66–77.

Dykens E. M., & Hodapp, R. M. (2001). Research in mental retardation: Toward an etiologic approach. *Journal of Child Psychology and Psychiatry, 42,* 49–71.

Dykens, E. M., Hodapp, R. M., & Evans, D. W. (2006). Profiles and development of adaptive behavior in children with Down syndrome. *Down Syndrome: Research & Practice, 9,* 45–50.

Dykens, E., Hodapp, R. M., & Finucane, B. M. (2000). *Genetics and mental retardation.* Baltimore: Brookes.

Dykens, E. M., & Kasari, C. (1997). Maladaptive behavior in children with Prader-Willi syndrome, Down syndrome, and nonspecific mental retardation. *American Journal on Mental Retardation, 102,* 228–237.

Dykens, E. M., & Shah, B. (2003). Psychiatric disorders in Prader-Willi syndrome. *CNS Drugs, 17,* 167–178.

Egeland, J. A., Hosteller, A. M., Pauls, D. L., & Sussex, J. N. (2000). Prodromal symptoms before onset of manic-depressive disorder suggested by first hospital admission histories. *Journal of the American Academy of Child & Adolescent Psychiatry, 39,* 1245–1252.

Ehrensaft, M. K. (2005). Interpersonal relationships and sex differences in the development of conduct problems. *Clinical Child and Family Psychology Review, 8,* 39–63.

Eigsti, I., & Cicchetti, D. (2004). The impact of child maltreatment on expressive syntax at 60 months. *Developmental Science, 7,* 88–102.

Einfeld, S. L. (2005). Behaviour problems in children with genetic disorders causing intellectual disability. *Educational Psychology, 25,* 341–346.

Einfeld, S. L., Piccinin, A. M., Mackinnon, A., Hofer, S. M., Taffe, J., Gray, K. M., et al. (2006). Psychopathology in young people with intellectual disability. *Journal of the American Medical Association, 296,* 1981–1989.

Eisenberg, N., Cumberland, A., & Spinrad, T. L. (1998). Parental socialization of emotion. *Psychological Inquiry, 9,* 241–273.

Eisenberg, N., Cumberland, A., Spinrad, T. L., Fabes, R. A., Shepard, S. A., Reiser, M., et al. (2001). The relations of regulation and emotionality to children's externalizing and internalizing problem behavior. *Child Development, 72,* 1112–1134.

Eisenberg, N., Fabes, R. A., Guthrie, I. K., & Reiser, M. (2000). Dispositional emotionality and regulation: Their role in predicting quality of social functioning. *Journal of Personality and Social Psychology, 78*, 136–157.

Eisenstadt, T. H., Eyberg, S., McNeil, C. B., Newcomb, K., & Funderburk, B. (1993). Parent-child interaction therapy with behavior problem children: Relative effectiveness of two stages and overall treatment outcome. *Journal of Clinical Child Psychology, 22*, 42–51.

Elbaum, B., Vaughn, S., Hughes, M. T., & Moody, S. W. (2000). How effective are one-to-one tutoring programs in reading for elementary students at risk for reading failure?: A meta-analysis of the intervention research. *Journal of Educational Psychology, 92*, 605–619.

Eley, T. C., Sugden, K., Corsico, A., Gregory, A. M., Sham, P., McGuffin, P., et al. (2004). Gene-environment interaction analysis of serotonin system markers with adolescent depression. *Molecular Psychiatry, 9*, 908–915.

Elkins, I. J., King, S. M., McGue, M., & Iacono, W. G. (2006). Personality traits and the development of nicotine, alcohol, and illicit drug disorders: Prospective links from adolescence to young adulthood. *Journal of Abnormal Psychology, 115*, 26–39.

Elliott, L., Orr, L., Watson, L., & Jackson, A. (2005). Secondary prevention interventions for young drug users: A systematic review of the evidence. *Adolescence, 40*, 1–22.

Ellis, A. (2005). *The myth of self-esteem: How rational emotive behavior therapy can change your life forever.* Amherst, NY: Prometheus Books.

Ellis, A., & Harper, R. A. (1961). *A guide to rational living.* Hollywood, CA: Wilshire Books.

Emmers-Sommer, T. M., Allen, M., Bourhis, J., Sahlstein, E., Laskowski, K., Falato, W. L., et al. (2004). A meta-analysis of the relationship between social skills and sexual offenders. *Communication Reports, 17*, 1–10.

Emslie, G. J., Heiligenstein, J. H., Wagner, K. D., Hoog, S. L., Ernest, D. E., Brown-Nilson, M., et al. (2002). Fluoxetine for acute treatment of depression in children and adolescents: A placebo-controlled, randomized clinical trial. *Journal of the American Academy of Child & Adolescent Psychiatry, 41*, 1205–1215.

Emslie, G. J., Rush, J., Weinberg, W. A., Kovatch, R. A., Hughes, C. W., Carmody, T., et al. (1997). A double-blind, randomized, placebo-controlled trial of fluoxetine in children and adolescents with depression. *Archives of General Psychiatry, 54*, 1031–1037, 1997.

Engelmann, S., & Carnine, D. W. (1975). *DISTAR arithmetic.* Chicago: Science Research Associates.

English, D. J., Marshall, D. B., Brummel, S., & Orme, M. (1999). Characteristics of repeated referrals to child protective services in Washington state. *Child Maltreatment, 4*, 297–307.

Ennett, S. T., Tobler, N. S., Ringwalt, C. L., & Flewelling, R. L. (1994). Resistance education? A meta-analysis of Project D.A.R.E. outcome evaluations. *American Journal of Public Health, 84*, 1394–1401.

Erhardt, D., & Hinshaw, S. P. (1994). Initial sociometric impressions of attention-deficit/hyperactivity disorder and comparison boys: Predictions from social behaviors and from nonbehavioral variables. *Journal of Consulting and Clinical Psychology, 62*, 833–842.

Erickson, M. F., & Egeland, B. (2002). Child neglect. In J. E. B. Meyers, L. Berliner, J. Briere, C. T. Hendrix, C. Jenny, & T. A. Reid (Eds.), *The APSAC handbook on child maltreatment* (pp. 3–20). Thousand Oaks, CA: Sage.

Erikson, E. H. (1963). *Childhood and society.* New York: Norton.

Essau, C. A. (2003). Epidemiology and comorbidity. In C. A. Essau (Ed.), *Conduct and oppositional defiant disorders: Epidemiology, risk factors, and treatment* (pp. 33–59). Mahwah, NJ: Erlbaum.

Essau, C. A. (2004). The association between family factors and depressive disorders in adolescents. *Journal of Youth and Adolescence, 33*, 365–372.

Essau, C. A., Conradt, J., & Petermann, F. (1999). Frequency of panic attacks and panic disorder in adolescents. *Depression and Anxiety, 9*, 19–26.

Essau, C. A., Conradt, J., & Petermann, F. (2000). Frequency, comorbidity, and psychosocial impairment of anxiety disorders in German adolescents. *Journal of Anxiety Disorders, 14*, 263–279.

Essau, C. A., & Merikangas, K. R. (1999). Familial and genetic factors. In C. A. Essau & F. Petermann (Eds.), *Depressive disorders in children and adolescents: Epidemiology, risk factors, and treatment* (p.p. 261–285). Lanham, MD: Aronson.

Essau, C. A., Sasagawa, S., & Frick, P. J. (2006). Callous-unemotional traits in a community sample of adolescents. *Assessment, 13*, 454–469.

Essex, M. J., Klein, M. H., Cho, E., & Kalin, N. H. (2002). Maternal stress beginning in infancy may sensitize children to later stress exposure: Effects on cortisol and behavior. *Biological Psychiatry, 52*, 776–784.

Evans, D. L., Beardslee, W., Biederman, J., Brent, D., Charney, D., Coyle, J., et al. (2005). Depression and bipolar disorder. In D. L. Evans, E. B. Foa, R. E. Gur, H. Hendin, C. P. O'Brien, M. E. P. Seligman, & B. T. Walsh (Eds.), *Treating and preventing adolescent mental health disorders* (pp. 3–74). New York: Oxford University Press.

Exner, J. E. (2003). *The Rorschach: A comprehensive system.* New York: Wiley.

Eyberg, S. M. (2006). Oppositional defiant disorder. In J. E. Fisher & W. T. O'Donohue (Eds.), *Practitioner's guide to evidence-based psychotherapy* (pp. 461–468). New York: Springer.

Eyberg, S. M., Funderburk, B. W., Hembree-Kigin, T. L., McNeil, C. B., Querido, J. G., & Hood, K. K. (2001). Parent-child interaction therapy with behavior problem children: One and two year maintenance of treatment effects in the family. *Child & Family Behavior Therapy, 23,* 1–20.

Eysenck, H. J. (1959). *Behaviour therapy and the neuroses: Readings in modern methods of treatment derived from learning theory.* Oxford, UK: Pergamon Press.

Ezpeleta, L., Domenech, J. M., & Angold, A. (2006). A comparison of pure and comorbid CD/ODD and depression. *Journal of Child Psychology and Psychiatry, 47,* 704–712.

Faedda, G. L., Baldessarini, R. J., Glovinsky, I. P., & Austin, N. B. (2004). Pediatric bipolar disorder: Phenomenology and course of illness. *Bipolar Disorders, 6,* 305–313.

Fagan, P. J., Wise, T. N., Schmidt, C. W., & Berlin, F. S. (2002). Pedophilia. *Journal of the American Medical Association, 288,* 2458–2465.

Fairburn, C. G., Cooper, Z., Doll, H. A., Norman, P., & O'Connor, M. (2000). The natural course of bulimia nervosa and binge eating disorder in young women. *Archives of General Psychiatry, 57,* 659–665.

Fairburn, C. G., Cooper, Z., Doll, H. A., & Welch, S. L. (1999). Risk factors for anorexia nervosa: Three integrated case-control comparisons. *Archives of General Psychiatry, 56,* 468–476.

Fairburn, C. G., Cooper, Z., & Safran, R. (2002). Cognitive behavior therapy for eating disorders: A "transdiagnostic" theory and treatment. *Behavior Research and Therapy, 41,* 509–528.

Fairburn, C. G., & Harrison, P. J. (2003). Eating disorders. *Lancet, 361,* 407–416.

Famularo, R., Fenton, T., Augustyn, M., & Zuckerman, B. (1996). Persistence of pediatric post traumatic stress disorder after 2 years. *Child Abuse & Neglect, 20,* 1245–1248.

Famularo, R., Fenton, T., Kinscherff, R., Ayoub, C., & Barnum, R. (1994). Maternal and child posttraumatic stress disorder in cases of child maltreatment. *Child Abuse & Neglect, 18,* 27–36.

Faraone, S. V., & Biederman, J. (1998). Neurobiology of attention-deficit hyperactivity disorder. *Biological Psychiatry, 44,* 951–958.

Faraone, S. V., Biederman, J., Chen, W. J., Krifcher, B., Keenan, D., Moore, C., et al. (1992). Segregation analysis of attention deficit hyperactivity disorder. *Psychiatric Genetics, 2,* 257–275.

Faraone, S. V., Biederman, J., Mennin, D., & Russel, R. I. (1998). Bipolar and antisocial disorders among relatives of ADHD children: Parsing familial subtypes of illness. *Neuropsychiatric Genetics, 81,* 108–116.

Faraone, S. V., Biederman, J., Weber, W., & Russell, R. L. (1998). Psychiatric, neuropsychological, and psychosocial features of DSM-IV subtypes of attention-deficit/hyperactivity disorder: Results from a clinically referred sample. *Journal of the American Academy of Child and Adolescent Psychiatry, 37,* 185–193.

Farran, D. C. (2000). Another decade of intervention for children who are low income or disabled: What do we know now? In J. P. Shonkoff & S. J. Meisels (Eds.), *Handbook of early childhood intervention* (pp. 510–548). New York: Cambridge University Press.

Farrington, D. P. (1998). Predictors, causes, and correlates of male youth violence. In M. Tonry & M. Moore (Eds.), *Youth violence* (pp. 317–371). Chicago: University of Chicago Press.

Faul, L. A., & Gross, A. M. (2006). Diagnosis and classification. In R. T. Ammerman (Ed.), *Comprehensive handbook of personality and psychopathology* (pp. 3–15). New York: Wiley.

Favazza, A. R. (1996). *Bodies under siege: Self-mutilation and body modification in culture and psychiatry.* Baltimore, MD: Johns Hopkins.

Favazza, A. R. (1998). The coming of age of self-mutilation. *Journal of Nervous & Mental Disease, 186,* 259–268.

Feeley, K. M., & Jones, A. (2006). Addressing challenging behaviour in children with Down syndrome: The use of applied behaviour analysis for assessment and intervention. *Down Syndrome: Research & Practice, 11,* 64–77.

Feeny, N. C., Danielson, C. K., Schwartz, L., Youngstrom, E. A., & Findling, R. L. (2006). Cognitive-behavioral therapy for bipolar disorders in adolescents: A pilot study. *Bipolar Disorders, 8,* 508–515.

Feinberg, D. T. (2006). The cost of over-the-counter substance abuse. *Journal of Child and Adolescent Psychopharmacology, 16,* 801–802.

Feiring, C., & Taska, S. (2005). The persistence of shame following sexual abuse: A longitudinal look at risk and recovery. *Child Maltreatment, 10,* 337–349.

Fenske, E. C., Zalenski, S., Krantz, P. J., & McClannahan, L. E. (1985). Age at intervention and treatment outcome for autistic children in a comprehensive intervention program. *Analysis and Intervention in Developmental Disabilities, 5,* 49–58.

Ferguson, C. P., & Pigott, T. A. (2000). Anorexia and bulimia nervosa: Neurobiology and pharmacotherapy. *Behavior Therapy, 31,* 237–264.

Fergusson, D. M., & Horwood, L. J. (1995). Early disruptive behavior, IQ, and later school achievement and delinquent behavior. *Journal of Abnormal Child Psychology, 23,* 183–199.

Fergusson, D. M., Horwood, L. J., & Nagin, D. S. (2000). Offending trajectories in a New Zealand birth cohort. *Criminology, 38,* 525–552.

Fergusson, D. M., Horwood, L. J., & Ridder, E. M. (2005). Show me the child at seven: The consequences of conduct problems in childhood for psychosocial functioning in adulthood. *Journal of Child Psychology and Psychiatry, 46,* 837–849.

Fergusson, D. M., & Lynskey, M. T. (1998). Conduct problems in childhood and psychosocial outcomes in young adulthood: A prospective study. *Journal of Emotional and Behavioral Disorders, 6,* 2–18.

Fergusson, D. M., Lynskey, M. T., & Horwood, L. J. (1997). Attentional difficulties in middle childhood and psychosocial outcomes in young adulthood. *Journal of Child Psychology and Psychiatry, 38,* 633–644.

Fichter, M. M., Kruger, R., Rief, W., Holland, R., & Dohne, J. (1996). Fluvoxamine in prevention of relapse in bulimia nervosa: Effects on eating-specific psychopathology. *Journal of Clinical Psychopharmacology, 16,* 9–18.

Field, A., Camargo, C., Taylor, C., Berkey, C., Robert, S., & Colditz, G. (2001). Peer, parent, and media influences on the development of weight concerns and frequent dieting among preadolescent girls and boys. *Pediatrics, 107,* 54–60.

Filipek, P. A., Semrud-Clikeman, M., Steingrad, R., Kennedy, D., & Biederman, J. (1997). Volumetric MRI analysis: Comparing subjects having attention-deficit hyperactivity disorder with normal controls. *Neurology, 48,* 589–601.

Finch, A. J., Nelson, W. M., & Hart, K. J. (2006). Conduct disorder: Description, prevalence, and etiology. In W. M. Nelson, A. J. Finch, & K. J. Hart (Eds.), *Conduct disorders: A practitioner's guide to comparative treatments* (pp. 1–13). New York: Springer.

Findling, R. L. (2005). Update on the treatment of bipolar disorder in children and adolescents. *European Psychiatry, 20,* 87–91.

Findling, R. L., Aman, M. G., Eerdekens, M., Derivan, A., Lyons, B., & Risperidone Behavior Study Group. (2004). Long-term, open-label study of risperidone in children with severe disruptive behaviors and below-average IQ. *American Journal of Psychiatry, 161,* 677–684.

Findling, R. L., Gracious, B. L., McNamara, N. K., Youngstrom, E. A., Demeter, C. A., & Branicky, L. A. (2001). Rapid, continuous cycling and psychiatric comorbidity in pediatric bipolar I disorder. *Bipolar Disorders, 3,* 202–210.

Findling, R. L., McNamara, N. K., Gracious, B. L., Youngstrom, E. A., Stansbrey, R. J., Reed, M. D., et al. (2003). Combination lithium and divalproex sodium in pediatric bipolarity. *Journal of the American Academy of Child & Adolescent Psychiatry, 42,* 895–901.

Finkelhor, D., & Browne, A. (1985). The traumatic impact of child sexual abuse: A conceptualization. *American Journal of Orthopsychiatry, 55,* 530–541.

Finkelhor, D., Cross, T. P., & Cantor, E. N. (2005). The justice system for juvenile victims: A comprehensive model of case flow. *Trauma, Violence, & Abuse, 6,* 83–102.

Finkelhor, D., Hotaling, G., Lewis, I., & Smith, C. (1990). Sexual abuse in a national survey of men and women: Prevalence, characteristics, and risk factors. *Child Abuse & Neglect, 14,* 19–28.

Fiorello, C. A., Hale, J. B., & Snyder, L. E. (2006). Cognitive hypothesis testing and response to intervention for children with reading problems. *Psychology in the Schools, 43,* 835–853.

Firestone, P., Bradford, J. M., McCoy, M., Greenberg, D. M., Larose, M. R., & Curry, S. (1999). Prediction of recidivism in incest offenders. *Journal of Interpersonal Violence, 14,* 511–531.

Fischer, D. J., Himle, J. A., & Thyer, B. A. (1999). Separation anxiety disorder. In R. T. Ammerman, M. Hersen, & C. G. Last (Eds.), *Handbook of prescriptive treatments for children and adolescents* (pp. 141–154). Boston: Allyn & Bacon.

Fischer, M., Barkley, R. A., Smallish, L., & Fletcher, K. (2002). Young adult follow-up of hyperactive children: Self-reported psychiatric disorders, comorbidity, and the role of childhood conduct problems. *Journal of Abnormal Child Psychology, 30,* 463–475.

Fischer, M., Barkley, R. A., Smallish, L., & Fletcher, K. (2005). Executive functioning in hyperactive children as young adults: Attention, inhibition, response perseveration, and the impact of comorbidity. *Developmental Neuropsychology, 27,* 107–133.

Flament, M. F., Furino, C., & Godart, N. (2005). Evidence-based pharmacotherapy of eating disorders. In D. J. Stein, B. Lerer, & S. Stahl (Eds.), *Evidence-based psychopharmacology* (pp. 204–254). New York: Cambridge University Press.

Flament, M. F., Whitaker, A., Rapoport, J. L., Davies, M., Berg, C. Z., Kalikow, K., et al. (1988). Obsessive compulsive disorder in adolescence: An epidemiological study. *Journal of the American Academy of Child and Adolescent Psychiatry, 27,* 764–771.

Flannery-Schroeder, E. C. (2004). Generalized anxiety disorder. In T. L. Morris & J. S. March (Eds.), *Anxiety disorders in children and adolescents* (pp. 125–140). New York: Guilford Press.

Flannery-Schroeder, E., Choudhury, M. S., & Kendall, P. C. (2005). Group and individual cognitive-behavioral treatments for youth with anxiety disorders: One-year follow-up. *Cognitive Therapy and Research, 29,* 253–259.

Flannery-Schroeder, E. C., & Kendall, P. C. (2000). Group and individual cognitive-behavioral treatments for youth with anxiety disorders: A randomized clinical trial. *Cognitive Therapy and Research, 24,* 251–278.

Fleischner, J. E., & Manheimer, M. A. (1997). Math interventions for students with learning disabilities: Myths and realities. *School Psychology Review, 26,* 397–413.

Fleming, J., & Offord, D. (1990). Epidemiology of childhood depressive disorders: A critical review. *Journal of the American Academy of Child and Adolescent Psychiatry, 29,* 571–580.

Fletcher, J. M., Lyon, G. R., Barnes, M., Stuebing, K. K., Francis, D. J., Olson, R. K., et al. (2002). Classification of learning disabilities: An evidenced-based evaluation. In R. Bradley, L. Danielson, & D. P. Hallahan (Eds.), *Identification of learning disabilities: Research to policy* (pp. 185–250). Mahwah, NJ: Erlbaum.

Fletcher, J. M., Morris, R. D., & Lyon, G. R. (2003). Classification and definition of learning disabilities: An integrative perspective. In H. L. Swanson, K. R. Harris, & S. Graham (Eds.), *Handbook of learning disabilities* (pp. 30–56). New York: Guilford Press.

Flett, G. L., Hewitt, P. L., Oliver, J. M., & Macdonald, S. (2002). Perfectionism in children and their parents: A developmental analysis. In G. L. Flett & P. L. Hewitt (Eds.), *Perfectionism: Theory, research, and treatment* (pp. 89–132). Washington, DC: American Psychological Association.

Flisher, A. J., Ziervogel, C. F., Chalton, D. O., Leger, P. H., & Robertson, B. A. (1993). Risk-taking behaviour of Cape Peninsula high-school students: Part II. Suicidal behaviour. *South African Medical Journal, 83,* 474–476.

Fluoxetine Bulimia Nervosa Collaborative Study Group. (1992). Fluoxetine in the treatment of bulimia nervosa: A multicenter, placebo-controlled, double-blind trial. *Archives of General Psychiatry, 49,* 139–147.

Foa, E. B., Johnson, K. M., Feeny, N. C., & Treadwell, K. R. H. (2001). The Child PTSD Symptom Scale (CPSS): A preliminary examination of its psychometric properties. *Journal of Community Psychology, 30,* 376–384.

Foley, D. L., Pickles, A., Maes, H. M., Silberg, J. L., & Eaves, L. J. (2004). Course and short-term outcomes of separation anxiety disorder in a community sample of twins. *Journal of the American Academy of Child & Adolescent Psychiatry, 43,* 1107–1114.

Fombonne, E. (2005). Epidemiological studies of pervasive developmental disorders. In F. R. Volkmar, R. Paul, A. Klin, & D. Cohen (Eds.), *Handbook of autism and pervasive developmental disorders, Vol. 1: Diagnosis, development, neurobiology, and behavior* (pp. 42–69). Hoboken, NJ: Wiley.

Fombonne, E., Wostear, G., Cooper, V., Harrington, R., & Rutter, M. (2001). The Maudsley long-term follow-up of child and adolescent depression: 1. Psychiatric outcomes in adulthood. *British Journal of Psychiatry, 179,* 210–217.

Frackowiak, R., Friston, K., Frith, C., Dolan, R., Price, C., Zeki, S., et al. (2004): *Human brain function.* San Diego: Academic Press, Elsevier Science.

Francis, D. J., Fletcher, J. M., Stuebing, K. K., Lyon, G. R., Shaywitz, B. A., & Shaywitz, S. E. (2005). Psychometric approaches to the identification of LD: IQ and achievement scores are not sufficient. *Journal of Learning Disabilities, 38,* 98–108.

Frank, J. D. (1973). *Persuasion and healing.* Baltimore, MD: Johns Hopkins University Press.

Frank, J. D., & Frank, J. (2004). Therapeutic components shared by all psychotherapies. In A. Freeman, M. J. Mahoney, P. DeVito, & D. Martin (Eds.), *Cognition and psychotherapy* (pp. 45–78). New York: Springer.

Franklin, M. E., Kozak, M. J., Cashman, L. A., Coles, M. E., Rheingold, A. A., & Foa, E. B. (1998). Cognitive-behavioral treatment of pediatric obsessive-compulsive disorder: An open clinical trial. *Journal of the Academy of Child and Adolescent Psychiatry, 37*, 412–419.

Franklin, M., March, J. S., & Gracia, A. (2007). Treating obsessive-compulsive disorder in children and adolescents. In M. M. Antony, C. Purdon, & L. J. Summerfeldt (Eds.), *Psychological treatment of obsessive compulsive disorders: Fundamentals and beyond* (pp. 253–266). Washington, DC: American Psychological Association.

Franklin, M. E., Rynn, M. A., Foa, E. B., & March, J. S. (2004). Pediatric obsessive-compulsive disorder. In T. H. Ollendick & J. S. March (Eds.), *Phobic and anxiety disorders in children and adolescents* (pp. 381–404). New York: Oxford University Press.

Frazier, J. A., Chiu, S., Breeze, J. L., Makris, N., Lange, N., Kennedy, D. N., et al. (2005). Structural brain magnetic resonance imaging of limbic and thalamic volumes in pediatric bipolar disorder. *American Journal of Psychiatry, 162*, 1256–1265.

Frazier, J. A., Meyer, M. C., Biederman, J., Wozniak, J., Wilens, T. E., Spencer, T. J., et al. (1999). Risperidone treatment for juvenile bipolar disorder: A retrospective chart review. *Journal of the American Academy of Child & Adolescent Psychiatry, 38*, 960–965.

Fredrickson, B., & Roberts, T. (1997). Objectification theory: Toward understanding women's lived experiences and mental health risks. *Psychology of Women Quarterly, 21*, 173–206.

Freitag, C. M. (2007). The genetics of autistic disorders and its clinical relevance: A review of the literature. *Molecular Psychiatry, 12*, 2–22.

Fremont, W. P. (2004). Childhood reactions to terrorism-induced trauma: A review of the past 10 years. *Journal of the American Academy of Child & Adolescent Psychiatry, 43*, 381–392.

Freud, A. (1936). *The ego and the mechanisms of defense.* New York: International Universities Press.

Freud, A., & Burlingham, D. (1943). *Children in war.* New York: Medical War Books.

Freud, S. (1961). The ego and the id. In J. Strachey (Ed. & Trans.), *The standard edition of the complete psychological works of Sigmund Freud* (Vol. 19). London: Hogarth Press. (Original work published 1923)

Frick, P. J. (2004). Developmental pathways to conduct disorder: Implications for serving youth who show severe aggressive and antisocial behavior. *Psychology in the Schools, 41*, 823–834.

Frick, P. J., Bodin, S. D., & Barry, C. T. (2000). Psychopathic traits and conduct problems in community and clinic-referred samples of children: Further development of the psychopathy screening device. *Psychological Assessment, 12*, 382–393.

Frick, P. J., Cornell, A. H., Barry, C. T., Bodin, S. D., & Dane, H. A. (2003). Callous-unemotional traits and conduct problems in the prediction of conduct problem severity, aggression, and self-report of delinquency. *Journal of Abnormal Child Psychology, 31*, 457–470.

Frick, P. J., Cornell, A. H., Bodin, S. D., Dane, H. A., Barry, C. T., & Loney, B. R. (2003). Callous-unemotional traits and developmental pathways to severe conduct problems. *Developmental Psychology, 39*, 246–260.

Frick, P. J., Lahey, B. B., Applegate, B., Kerdyck, L., Ollendick, T., Hynd, G., et al. (1994). DSM-IV field trials for the disruptive behavior disorders: Symptom utility estimates. *Journal of the American Academy of Child and Adolescent Psychiatry, 33*, 529–539.

Frick, P. J., Lahey, B. B., Christ, M. G., Loeber, R., & Green, S. (1991). History of childhood behavior problems in biological relatives of boys with attention-deficit hyperactivity disorder and conduct disorder. *Journal of Clinical Child Psychology, 20*, 445–451.

Frick, P. J., Lahey, B. B., Loeber, R., Stouthamer-Loeber, M., Christ, M. A., & Hanson, K. (1992). Familial risk factors to oppositional defiant disorder and conduct disorder: Parental psychopathology and maternal parenting. *Journal of Consulting and Clinical Psychology, 60*, 49–55.

Frick, P. J., Lahey, B. B., Loeber, R., Tannenbaum, L. E., Van Horn, Y., Christ, M. A. G., et al. (1993). Oppositional defiant disorder and conduct disorder: A meta-analytic review of factor analyses and cross-validation in a clinic sample. *Clinical Psychology Review, 13*, 319–340.

Frick, P. J., & Loney, B. R. (2002). Understanding the association between parent and child antisocial behavior. In R. J. McMahon & R. De V. Peters (Eds.), *The effects of parental dysfunction on children* (pp. 105–126). New York: Kluwer Academic/Plenum.

Frick, P. J., & Morris, A. S. (2004). Temperament and developmental pathways to conduct problems. *Journal of Clinical Child and Adolescent Psychology, 33*, 54–68.

Frick, P. J., & Munoz, L. (2006). Oppositional defiant disorder and conduct disorder. In C. A. Essau (Ed.), *Child and adolescent psychopathology: Theoretical and clinical implications* (pp. 26–51). New York: Routledge.

Frick, P. J., Stickle, T. R., Dandreaux, D. M., Farrell, J. M., & Kimonis, E. R. (2005). Callous-unemotional traits in predicting the severity and stability of conduct problems and delinquency. *Journal of Abnormal Child Psychology, 33*, 471–487.

Friedrich, W. N. (1997). *Child sexual behavior inventory.* Odessa, FL: Psychological Assessment Resources.

Friedrich, W. N. (2002). An integrated model of psychotherapy for abused children. In J. E. B. Meyers, L. Berliner, J. Briere, C. T. Hendrix, C. Jenny, & T. A. Reid (Eds.), *The APSAC handbook on child maltreatment* (pp. 141–158). Thousand Oaks, CA: Sage.

Friedrich, W. N., Fisher, J. L., Dittner, C. A., Acton, R., Berliner, L., Butler, J., et al. (2001). Child sexual behavior inventory: Normative, psychiatric, and sexual abuse comparisons. *Child Maltreatment, 6,* 37–49.

Fristad, M. A., Goldberg-Arnold, J. S., & Gavazzi, S. M. (2003). Multifamily psychoeducation groups (MFPG) in the treatment of children with mood disorders. *Journal of Marital & Family Therapy, 29,* 491–504.

Frith, C. D., & Frith, U. (1999). Interacting minds: a biological basis. *Science, 286,* 1692–1695.

Fuchs, D., & Young, L. (2006). On the irrelevance of intelligence in predicting responsiveness to reading instruction. *Exceptional Children, 73,* 8–30.

Fulford, K. W. M. (1994). Closet logics: Hidden conceptual elements in the DSM and ICD classification of mental disorders. In J. Z. Sadler, O. P. Wiggins, & M. A. Schwartz (Eds.), *Philosophical perspectives on psychiatric diagnostic classification* (pp. 211–232). Baltimore, MD: Johns Hopkins University Press.

Funderburk, B. W., Eyberg, S. M., Newcomb, K., McNeil, C. B., Hembree-Kigin, T., & Capage, L. (1998). Parent-child interaction therapy with behavior problem children: Maintenance of treatment effects in the school setting. *Child & Family Behavior Therapy, 20,* 17–38.

Galambos, N. L., Barker, E. T., & Almeida, D. M. (2003). Parents do matter: Trajectories of change in externalizing and internalizing problems in early adolescence. *Child Development, 74,* 578–594.

Galea, S., Ahern, J., Resnick, H., Kilpatrick, D., Bucuvalas, M., Gold, J., et al. (2002). Psychological sequelae of the September 11 terrorist attacks in New York City. *New England Journal of Medicine, 346,* 982–987.

Garb, H. N. (1989). Clinical judgment, clinical training, and professional experience. *Psychological Bulletin, 105,* 387–396.

Garb, H. N. (1996). The representativeness and past-behavior heuristics in clinical judgment. *Professional Psychology: Theory and Practice, 27,* 272–277.

Garb, H. N. (2000). Computers will become increasingly important for psychological assessment: Not that there's anything wrong with that! *Psychological Assessment, 12,* 31–39.

Garb, H. N., & Boyle, P. A. (2004). Understanding why some clinicians use pseudoscientific methods. In S. O. Lilienfeld, S. J. Lynn, & J. M. Lohr (Eds.), *Science and pseudoscience in clinical psychology* (pp.17–38). New York: Guilford Press.

Garber, J. (2000). Development and depression. In A. J. Sameroff, M. Lewis, & S. M. Miller (Eds.), *Handbook of developmental psychopathology* (pp. 467–490). New York: Kluwer.

Garber, J., & Flynn, C. (2001). Vulnerability to depression in childhood and adolescence. In R. Ingram & J. Price (Eds.), *Vulnerability to psychopathology: Risk across the lifespan* (pp. 175–225). New York: Guilford Press.

Garber, J., Keiley, M. K., & Martin, N. C. (2002). Developmental trajectories of adolescents' depressive symptoms: Predictors of change. *Journal of Consulting and Clinical Psychology, 70,* 79–95.

Garland, J. (2004). Facing the evidence: Antidepressant treatment in children and adolescents. *Canadian Medical Association Journal, 170,* 489–491.

Gau, S. S. F., Chong, M., Yang, P., Yen, C., Liang, K., & Cheng, A. T. A. (2007). Psychiatric and psychosocial predictors of substance use disorders among adolescents. Longitudinal study. *British Journal of Psychiatry, 190,* 42–48.

Gaub, M., & Carlson, C. L. (1997). Behavioral characteristics of DSM-IV ADHD subtypes in a school-based population. *Journal of Abnormal Child Psychology, 25,* 103–111.

Gaynor, S. T., Baird, S. C., & Nelson-Gray, R. O. (1999). Application of time-series (single-subject) designs in clinical psychology. In P. C. Kendall, J. N. Butcher, & G. N. Holmbeck (Eds.), *Handbook of research methods in clinical psychology* (pp. 297–329). Hoboken, NJ: Wiley.

Ge, X., Coger, R. D., & Elder, G. H. (2001). Pubertal transition, stressful life events, and the emergence of gender differences in adolescent depressive symptoms. *Developmental Psychology, 37,* 404–417.

Geary, D. C., & Hoard, M. K. (2001). Numerical and arithmetical deficits in learning-disabled children: Relation to dyscalculia and dyslexia. *Aphasiology, 15,* 635–647.

Geary, D. C., & Hoard, M. K. (2005). Learning disabilities in arithmetic and mathematics: Theoretical and empirical perspectives. In J. I. D. Campbell (Ed.), *Handbook of mathematical cognition* (pp. 253–267). New York: Psychology Press.

Gelhorn, H. L., Stallings, M. C., Young, S. E., Corley, R. P., Rhee, S. H., & Hewitt, J. K. (2005). Genetic and environmental influences on conduct disorder: Symptom, domain and full-scale analyses. *Journal of Child Psychology and Psychiatry, 46,* 580–591.

Geller, B., Bolhofner, K., Craney, J., Williams, M., Del, B. M., & Gundersen, K. (2000). Psychosocial functioning in a prepubertal and early adolescent bipolar disorder phenotype. *Journal of the American Academy of Child and Adolescent Psychiatry, 39,* 1543–1548.

Geller, B., Cooper, T. B., Sun, K., Zimmerman, B., Frazier, J., Williams, M., et al. (1998). Double-blind and placebo-controlled study of lithium for adolescent bipolar disorders with secondary substance dependency. *Journal of the American Academy of Child and Adolescent Psychiatry, 37,* 171–178.

Geller, B., Craney, J. L., Bolhofner, K., DelBello, M. P., Axelson, D., Luby, J., et al. (2003). Phenomenology and longitudinal course of children with a prepubertal and early adolescent bipolar disorder phenotype. In B. Geller & M. P. DelBello (Eds.), *Bipolar disorder in childhood and early adolescence* (pp. 25–50). New York: Guilford Press.

Geller, B., Tillman, R., Craney, J. L., & Bolhofner, K. (2004). Four-year prospective outcome and natural history of mania in children with a prepubertal and early adolescent bipolar disorder phenotype. *Archives of General Psychiatry, 61,* 459–467.

Geller, B., Zimmerman, B., Williams, M., Bolhofher, K., Craney, J. L., Delbello, M. P., et al. (2000). Diagnostic characteristics of 93 cases of a prepubertal and early adolescent bipolar disorder phenotype by gender, puberty and comorbid attention deficit hyperactivity disorder. *Journal of Child and Adolescent Psychopharmacology, 10,* 157–164.

Geller, D. A., Hoog, S. L., Heiligenstein, J. H., Ricardi, R. K., Tamura, R., Kluszynski, S., et al. (2001). Fluoxetine treatment for obsessive-compulsive disorder in children and adolescents: A placebo-controlled clinical trial. *Journal of the American Academy of Child and Adolescent Psychiatry, 40,* 773–779.

Gelman, R., & Gallistel, C. R. (1978). *The child's understanding of number.* Cambridge, MA: Harvard University Press.

Georgiades, S., Szatmari, P., Zwaigenbaum, L., Duku, E., Bryson, S., Roberts, W., et al. (2007). Structure of the autism symptom phenotype: A proposed multidimensional model. *Journal of the American Academy of Child & Adolescent Psychiatry, 46,* 188–196.

Gershater-Molko, R. M., Lutzker, J. R., & Wesch, D. (2002). Using recidivism data to evaluate Project SafeCare: An ecobehavioral approach to teach "bonding," safety, and health care skills. *Child Maltreatment, 7,* 277–285.

Giaconia, R. M., Reinherz, H. Z., Silverman, A. B., Pakiz, B., Frost, A. K., & Cohen, E. (1995). Traumas and posttraumatic stress disorder in a community population of older adolescents. *Journal of the American Academy of Child and Adolescent Psychiatry, 34,* 1369–1380.

Gibb, B. E., Abramson, L. Y., & Alloy, L. B. (2004). Emotional maltreatment from parents, verbal peer victimization, and cognitive vulnerability to depression. *Cognitive Therapy and Research, 28,* 1–21.

Giedd, J. N., Blumenthal, J., Molloy, E., & Castellanos, F. X. (2001). Brain imaging of attention-deficit/hyperactivity disorder. *Annals of the New York Academy of Sciences, 931,* 33–34.

Giedd, J. M., Shaw, P., Wallace, G., Gogtay, N., & Lenroot, R. K. (2006). Anatomic brain imaging studies of normal and abnormal brain development in children and adolescents. In D. Cicchetti & D. J. Cohen (Eds.), *Developmental psychopathology, Vol 2: Developmental neuroscience* (pp. 127–196). Hoboken, NJ: Wiley.

Gil, A. G., Vega, W. A., & Turner, R. J. (2002). Early and mid-adolescence risk factors for later substance abuse by African-Americans and European Americans. *Public Health Reports, 177,* 15–29.

Gilchrist, A., Green, J., Cox, A., Burton, D., Rutter, M., & Le Couteur, A. (2001). Development and current functioning in adolescents with Asperger syndrome: A comparative study. *Journal of Child Psychology and Psychiatry, 42,* 227–240.

Gilligan, C. (1982). *In a different voice: Psychological theory and women's development.* Cambridge, MA: Harvard University Press.

Gil-Rivas, V., Holman, E. A., & Silver, R. C. (2004). Adolescent vulnerability following the September 11th terrorist attacks: A study of parents and their children. *Applied Developmental Science, 8,* 130–142.

Ginsburg, G. S., Albano, A. M., Findling, R. L., Kratochvil, C., & Walkup, J. (2005). Integrating cognitive behavioral therapy and pharmacotherapy in the treatment of adolescent depression. *Cognitive and Behavioral Practice, 12,* 252–262.

Ginsburg, G. S., Lambert, S. F., & Drake, K. L. (2004). Attributions of control, anxiety sensitivity, and panic symptoms among adolescents. *Cognitive Therapy and Research, 28,* 745–763.

Ginsburg, G. S., & Schlossberg, M. C. (2002). Family-based treatment of childhood anxiety disorders. *International Journal of Psychiatry, 14,* 142–153.

Ginsburg, G. S., Siqueland, L., Masia-Warner, C., & Hedtke, K. A. (2004). Anxiety disorders in children: Family matters. *Cognitive and Behavioral Practice, 11,* 28–43.

Ginsburg, G. S., & Walkup, J. T. (2004). Specific phobia. In T. H. Ollendick & J. S. March (Eds.), *Phobic and anxiety disorders in children and adolescents* (pp. 175–197). New York: Oxford University Press.

Gladstone, T. G., & Kaslow, N. J. (1995). Depression and attributions in children and adolescents: A meta-analytic review. *Journal of Abnormal Child Psychology, 23,* 597–606.

Goenjian, A. K., Karayan, I., Pynoos, R. S., Minassian, D., Najarian, L. M., Steinberg, A. M., et al. (1997). Outcome of psychotherapy among early adolescents after trauma. *American Journal of Psychiatry, 154,* 536–542.

Gold, S. R., Sinclair, B. B., & Balge, K. A. (1999). Risk of sexual revictimization: A theoretical model. *Aggression and Violent Behavior, 4,* 457–470.

Goldberg-Arnold, J. S., & Fristad, M. A. (2003). Psychotherapy for children with bipolar disorder. In B. Geller & M. DelBello (Eds.), *Bipolar disorder in childhood and early adolescence* (pp. 272–294). New York: Guilford Press.

Goldman, S. R. (1989). Strategy instruction in mathematics. *Learning Disability Quarterly, 12,* 43–55.

Goldstein, D. J., Wilson, M. G., & Thompson, V. L. (1995). Long-term fluoxetine treatment of bulimia nervosa. *British Journal of Psychiatry, 166,* 660–667.

Goldstein, S., & Goldstein, M. (1998). *Managing attention deficit hyperactivity disorder in children: A guide for practitioners.* New York: Wiley.

Goldstein, T. R., Birmaher, B., Axelson, D., Ryan, N. D., Strober, M. A., Gill, M. K., et al. (2005). History of suicide attempts in pediatric bipolar disorder: Factors associated with increased risk. *Bipolar Disorders, 7,* 525–535.

Gonzalez-Tejera, G., Canino, G., Ramirez, R., Chavez, L., Shrout, P., Bird, H. et al. (2005). Examining minor and major depression in adolescents. *Journal of Child Psychology and Psychiatry, 46,* 888–899.

Goodman, E., & Capitman, J. (2000). Depressive symptoms and cigarette smoking among teens. *Pediatrics, 706,* 748–755.

Goodman, K. S. (1992). Why whole language is today's agenda in education. *Language Arts, 69,* 354–363.

Goodman, S., & Gotlib, I. (1999). Risk for psychopathology in the children of depressed mothers: A developmental model for understanding mechanisms of transmission. *Psychological Review, 106,* 458–490.

Goodman, Y. M. (1989). Roots of the whole-language movement. *Elementary School Journal, 90,* 113–127.

Goodwin, J. (1988). Posttraumatic stress symptoms in abused children. *Journal of Traumatic Stress, 1,* 475–488.

Goodwin, R. D., Fergusson, D. M., & Horwood, L. J. (2004). Association between anxiety disorders and substance use disorders among young persons: Results of a 21-year longitudinal study. *Journal of Psychiatric Research, 38,* 295–304.

Goodyer, I. M., Herbert, J., & Tamplin, A. (2000). First episode major depression in adolescents: Affective, cognitive and endocrine characteristics of risk status and predictors of onset. *British Journal of Psychiatry, 176,* 142–149.

Goodyer, I. M., Herbert, J., Tamplin, A., & Altham, P. M. (2000). Recent life events, cortisol, dehydroepiandrosterone and the onset of major depression in high-risk adolescents. *British Journal of Psychiatry, 177,* 499–504.

Goodyer, I. M., Park, R. J., & Herbert, J. (2001). Psychosocial and endocrine features of chronic first-episode major depression in 8-16 year olds. *Biological Psychiatry, 50,* 351–357.

Gorman-Smith, D., Tolan, P. H., & Henry, D. B. (2000). A developmental-ecological model of the relation of family functioning to patterns of delinquency. *Journal of Quantitative Criminology, 16,* 169–198.

Gotlib, I. H., & Sommerfeld, B. K. (1999). Cognitive functioning in depressed children and adolescents: A developmental perspective. In C. A. Essau & F. Petermann (Eds.), *Depressive disorders in children and adolescents: Epidemiology, risk factors, and treatment* (pp. 195–236). Lanham, MD: Aronson.

Gottesman, I. I. (1963). Genetic aspects of intelligent behavior. In N. R. Ellis (Ed.), *Handbook of mental deficiency: Psychological theory and research* (pp. 253–296). New York: McGraw-Hill.

Gottlieb, G., & Willoughby, M. T. (2006). Probabilistic epigenesis of psychopathology. In D. Cicchetti & D. J. Cohen (Eds.), *Developmental psychopathology, Vol 1: Theory and method* (pp. 673–700). Hoboken, NJ: Wiley.

Grabill, K., Storch, E. A., & Geffken, G. R. (2007). Intensive cognitive-behavioral therapy of pediatric obsessive-compulsive disorder. *The Behavior Therapist, 30,* 19–21.

Grady, D. L., Chi, H., Ding, Y., Smith, M., Wang, E., Schuck, S., et al. (2003). High prevalence of rare dopamine receptor D4 alleles in children diagnosed with attention-deficit hyperactivity disorder. *Molecular Psychiatry, 8,* 536–545.

Graham, C. A., & Easterbrooks, M. A. (2000). School-aged children's vulnerability to depressive symptomatology: The role of attachment security, maternal depressive symptomatology, and economic risk. *Development and Psychopathology, 12,* 201–213.

Graham, S. (2006). Strategy instruction and the teaching of writing: A meta-analysis. In C. A. MacArthur, S. Graham, & J. Fitzgerald (Eds.), *Handbook of writing research* (pp. 187–207). New York: Guilford Press.

Graham, S., & Harris, K. R. (2000). The role of self-regulation and transcription skills in writing and writing development. *Educational Psychologist, 35,* 3–12.

Graham, S., & Harris, K. R. (2003). Students with learning disabilities and the process of writing: A meta-analysis of SRSD studies. In H. L. Swanson, K. R. Harris, & S. Graham (Eds.), *Handbook of learning disabilities* (pp. 323–344). New York: Guilford Press.

Graham, S., Harris, K. R., & Fink, B. (2000). Is handwriting causally related to learning to write? Treatment of handwriting problems in beginning writers. *Journal of Educational Psychology, 92,* 620–633.

Graham, S., Harris, K. R., & Fink, B. (2002). Contributions of spelling instruction to the spelling, writing, and reading of poor spellers. *Journal of Educational Psychology, 94,* 669–686.

Graham, S., Harris, K. R., & MacArthur, C. (2004). Writing instruction. In B. Y. L. Wong, (Ed.), *Learning about learning disabilities* (pp. 281–313). San Diego: Elsevier Academic Press.

Graham, S., Harris, K. R., MacArthur, C., & Schwartz, S. (1991). Writing and writing instruction with students with learning disabilities: A review of a program of research. *Learning Disability Quarterly, 14,* 89–114.

Graham, S., & Juvonen, J. (2001). An attributional approach to peer victimization. In J. Juvonen & S. Graham (Eds.), *Peer harassment in school* (pp. 49–72). New York: Guilford Press.

Graham-Bermann, S. A. (2002). Child abuse in the context of domestic violence. In J. E. B. Meyers, L. Berliner, J. Briere, C. T. Hendrix, C. Jenny, & T. A. Reid (Eds.), *The APSAC handbook on child maltreatment* (pp. 119–130). Thousand Oaks, CA: Sage.

Gray, J. A. (1982). *The neuropsychology of anxiety: An inquiry into the functions of the septo-hippocampal system.* New York: Oxford University Press.

Gray, J. A. (1987). *The psychology of fear and stress.* New York: Cambridge University Press.

Gray, J. A. (1994). Framework for a taxonomy of psychiatric disorder. In S. H. M. van Goozen, N. E. van de Poll, & J. E. Sergeant (Eds.), *Emotions: Essays on emotion theory* (pp. 29–59). Hillsdale, NJ: Erlbaum.

Greenberg, M., Lengua, L., Coie, J., & Pinderhughes, E. (1999). Predicting developmental outcomes at school entry using a multiple-risk model: Four American communities. *Developmental Psychology, 35,* 403–417.

Greenhill, L. L. (2005). The science of stimulant abuse. *Psychiatric Annals, 35,* 210–214.

Greenhill, L. L., Abikoff, H. B., Arnold, L. E., Cantwell, D. P., Conners, C. K., Elliott, G., et al. (1996). Medication treatment strategies in the MTA study: Relevance to clinicians and researchers. *Journal of the American Academy of Child and Adolescent Psychiatry, 35,* 1304–1313.

Greenhill, L. L., & Ford, R. E. (2002). Childhood attention-deficit hyperactivity disorder: Pharmacological treatments. In P. E. Nathan, & J. M. Gorman (Eds.), *A guide to treatments that work* (pp. 25–55). New York: Oxford University Press.

Greenhill, L. L., Kollins, S., Abikoff, H., McCracken, J., Riddle, M., Swanson, J., et al. (2006). Efficacy and safety of immediate-release methylphenidate treatment for preschoolers with ADHD. *Journal of the American Academy of Child & Adolescent Psychiatry, 45,* 1284–1293.

Greenhill, L. L., Pliszka, S. R., & Dulcan, M. K. (2002). Practice parameter for the use of stimulant medication in the treatment of children, adolescents and adults. *Journal of the American Academy of Child and Adolescent Psychiatry, 41,* 26S–29S.

Grella, C. E., Hser, Y. I., Joshi, V., & Rounds-Bryant, J. (2001). Drug treatment outcomes for adolescents with comorbid mental and substance use disorders. *Journal of Nervous and Mental Disease, 189,* 384–392.

Grenard, J. L., Ames, S. L., Wiers, R. W., Thush, C., Stacy, A. W., & Sussman, S. (2007). Brief intervention for substance use among at-risk adolescents: A pilot study. *Journal of Adolescent Health, 40,* 188–191.

Gresham, F. M. (2006). Response to intervention. In G. B Bear & K. M. Minke (Eds.), *Children's needs III: Development, prevention, and intervention* (pp. 525–540). Bethesda, MD: National Association of School Psychologists.

Grigorenko, E. L. (2001). Developmental dyslexia: An update on genes, brains, and environments. *Journal of Child Psychology and Psychiatry, 42,* 91–125.

Groth-Marnat, G. (2003). *Handbook of psychological assessment.* New York: Wiley.

Grove, W. M., Zald, D. H., Lebow, B. S., Snitz, B. E., & Nelson, C. (2000). Clinical versus mechanical prediction: A meta-analysis. *Psychological Assessment, 12,* 19–30.

Guarda, A. S., & Heinberg, L. J. (2004). Inpatient and partial hospital approaches to the treatment of eating disorders. In J. K. Thompson (Ed.), *Handbook of eating disorders and obesity* (pp. 297–320). Hoboken, NJ: Wiley.

Gurney, J. G., Fritz, M. S., Ness, K. K., Sievers, P., Newschaffer, C. J., & Shapiro, E. G. (2003). Analysis of prevalence trends of autism spectrum disorder in Minnesota. *Archives of Pediatrics and Adolescent Medicine, 157,* 622–627.

Guttmann-Steinmetz, S., & Crowell, A. (2006). Attachment and externalizing disorders: A developmental psychopathology perspective. *Journal of the American Academy of Child & Adolescent Psychiatry, 45*(4), 440–451.

Hale, J. B., Kaufman, A., Naglieri, J. A., & Kavale, K. A. (2006). Implementation of idea: Integrating response to intervention and cognitive assessment methods. *Psychology in the Schools, 43,* 753–770.

Hale, L. R., & Calamari, J. E. (2007). Panic symptoms and disorder in youth: What role does anxiety sensitivity play? In C. M. Velotis (Ed.), *New developments in anxiety disorders research* (pp. 131–162). Hauppauge, NY: Nova Biomedical.

Hale, W. W., Engels, R., & Meeus, W. (2006). Adolescent's perceptions of parenting behaviours and its relationship to adolescent Generalized Anxiety Disorder symptoms. *Journal of Adolescence, 29,* 407–417.

Hallahan, D. P., & Mock, D. R. (2003). A brief history of the field of learning disabilities. In H. L. Swanson, K. R. Harris, & S. Graham (Eds.), *Handbook of learning disabilities* (pp. 16–29). New York: Guilford Press.

Halligan, S. L., Herbert, J., Goodyer, I. M., & Murray, L. (2004). Exposure to postnatal depression predicts elevated cortisol in adolescent offspring. *Biological Psychiatry, 55,* 376–381.

Halmi, K. A., Eckert, E., Marchi, P., Sampagnaro, V., Apple, R., & Cohen, J. (1991). Comorbidity of psychiatric diagnoses in anorexia nervosa. *Archives of General Psychiatry, 48,* 712–718.

Halmi, K. A., Tozzi, F., Thornton, L. M., Crow, S., Fichter, M. M., Kaplan, A. S., et al. (2005). The relation among perfectionism, obsessive compulsive personality disorder and obsessive compulsive disorder in individuals with eating disorders. *International Journal of Eating Disorders, 38,* 371–374.

Hammen, C. L. (1991). *Depression runs in families: The social context of risk and resilience in children of depressed mothers.* New York: Springer-Verlag.

Hammen, C. (1992). Cognitive, life stress, and interpersonal approaches to a developmental psychopathology model of depression. *Development and Psychopathology, 4,* 189–206.

Hammen, C. (1999). The emergence of an interpersonal approach to depression. In T. Joiner & J. Coyne (Eds.), *The interactional nature of depression: Advances in interpersonal approaches* (pp. 22–36). Washington, DC: American Psychological Association.

Hammen, C. (2002). The context of stress in families of children with depressed parents. In S. Goodman & I. Gotlib (Eds.), *Children of depressed parents: Mechanisms of risk and implications for treatment* (pp. 175–199). Washington, DC: American Psychological Association.

Hammen, C., Shih, J. H., & Brennan, P. A. (2004). Intergenerational transmission of depression: Test of an interpersonal stress model in a community sample. *Journal of Consulting and Clinical Psychology, 72,* 511–522.

Han, C., McGue, M. K., & Iacono, W. G. (1999). Lifetime tobacco, alcohol and other substance use in adolescent Minnesota twins: Univariate and multivariate behavioral genetic analyses. *Addiction, 94,* 981–993.

Handen, B. L., & Gilchrist, R. (2006a). Mental retardation. In E. J. Mash & R. A. Barkley (Eds.), *Treatment of childhood disorders* (3rd ed., pp. 411–454). New York: Guilford Press.

Handen, B. L., & Gilchrist, R. (2006b). Practitioner review: Psychopharmacology in children and adolescents with mental retardation. *Journal of Child Psychology and Psychiatry, 47,* 871–882.

Handleman, J. S., Harris, S. L., & Martins, M. P. (2005). Helping children with autism enter the mainstream. In F. R. Volkmar, R. Paul, A. Klin, & D. Cohen (Eds.), *Handbook of autism and pervasive developmental disorders, Vol. 2: Assessment, interventions, and policy* (pp. 1029–1042). New York: Wiley.

Hankin, B. L., & Abela, R. Z. (2005). *Development of psychopathology: A vulnerability-stress perspective.* Thousand Oaks, CA: Sage.

Hankin, B. L., Abramson, L. Y., Moffitt, T. E., Silva, P. A., McGee, R., & Angell, K. E. (1998). Development of depression from preadolescence to young adulthood: Emerging gender differences in a 10-year longitudinal study. *Journal of Abnormal Psychology, 107,* 128–140.

Hankin, B. L., Fraley, R. C., Lahey, B. B., & Waldman, I. D. (2005). Is depression best viewed as a continuum or discrete category? A taxometric analysis of childhood and adolescent depression in a population-based sample. *Journal of Abnormal Psychology, 114,* 96–110.

Hanley, G. P., Iwata, B. A., & McCord, B. E. (2003). Functional analysis of problem behavior: A review. *Journal of Applied Behavior Analysis, 36,* 147–185.

Hanna, G. L. (2000). Clinical and family-genetic studies of childhood obsessive-compulsive disorder. In W. K. Goodman, M. V. Rudorfer, & J. D. Maser (Eds.), *Obsessive-compulsive disorder: Contemporary issues in treatment* (pp. 87–103). Mahwah, NJ: Erlbaum.

Hanson, R. K. (2002). Recidivism and age: Follow-up data from 4,673 sexual offenders. *Journal of Interpersonal Violence, 17,* 1046–1062.

Hanson, R. K., & Bussiere, M. T. (1998). Predicting relapse: A meta-analysis of sexual offender recidivism studies. *Journal of Consulting and Clinical Psychology, 66,* 348–362.

Hanson, R. K., Saunders, B. E., Kilpatrick, D. G., Resnick, H., Crouch, J. A., & Duncan, R. (2001). Impact of childhood rape and aggravated assault on adult mental health. *American Journal of Orthopsychiatry, 71,* 108–119.

Harkness, K. L., Bruce, A. E., & Lumley, M. N. (2006). The role of childhood abuse and neglect in the sensitization to stressful life events in adolescent depression. *Journal of Abnormal Psychology, 115,* 730–741.

Harrington, R., Fudge, H., Rutter, M., Pickles, A., & Hill, J. (1990). Adult outcomes of childhood and adolescent depression: I. Psychiatric status. *Archives of General Psychiatry, 47,* 465–473.

Harris, S., Handleman, J., Gordon, R., Kristoff, B., & Fuentes, F. (1991). Changes in cognitive and language functioning of preschool children with autism. *Journal of Autism and Developmental Disabilities, 21,* 281–290.

Hart, E. L., Lahey, B. B., Loeber, R., Applegate, B., Green, S. M., & Frick, P. J. (1995). Developmental changes in attention-deficit hyperactivity disorder in boys: A four-year longitudinal study. *Journal of Abnormal Child Psychology, 23,* 729–750.

Hart, K. J., Nelson, W. M., & Finch, A. J. (2006). Comparative treatments of conduct disorder: Summary and conclusions. In W. M. Nelson, A. J. Finch, & K. J. Hart (Eds.), *Conduct disorders: A practitioner's guide to comparative treatments* (pp. 321–343). New York: Springer.

Hart, S. N., Brassard, M. R., Binggeli, N. J., & Davidson, H. A. (2002). Psychological maltreatment. In J. E. B. Meyers, L. Berliner, J. Briere, C. T. Hendrix, C. Jenny, & T. A. Reid (Eds.), *The APSAC handbook on child maltreatment* (pp. 79–104). Thousand Oaks, CA: Sage.

Harter, S. (1997). The development of self-representations. In W. Damon (Series Ed.) & N. Eisenberg (Vol. Ed.), *Handbook of child psychology* (5th ed., Vol. III). New York: Wiley.

Harter, S. (1999). *The construction of self: A developmental perspective.* New York: Guilford Press.

Harwood, M. D., & Eyberg, M. (2006). Child-directed interaction: Prediction of change in impaired mother-child functioning. *Journal of Abnormal Child Psychology, 34,* 335–347.

Haselager, G. J. T., Cillessen, A. H. N., Van Lieshout, C. F. M., Riksen-Walraven, J. M. A., & Hartup, W. W. (2002). Heterogeneity among peer-rejected boys across middle childhood: Developmental pathways of social behavior. *Developmental Psychology, 38,* 446–456.

Hawke, J. L., Wadsworth, S. J., & Defries, J. C. (2006). Genetic influences on reading difficulties in boys and girls: The Colorado twin study. *Dyslexia: An International Journal of Research and Practice, 12,* 21–29.

Hayes, J., & Flower, L. (1980). Identifying the organization of writing processes. In L. Gregg & E. Steinberg (Eds.), *Cognitive processes in writing* (pp. 3–30). Hillsdale, NJ: Erlbaum.

Hayward, C., Killen, J. D., Kraemer, H. C., & Barr Taylor, C. (2000). Predictors of panic attacks in adolescents. *Journal of the American Academy of Child and Adolescent Psychiatry, 39,* 207–214.

Hazell, P., O'Connell, D., Heathcote, D., & Henry, D. (2002). Tricyclic drugs for depression in children and adolescents. *Cochrane Systematic Reviews, 2,* 2317.

Hebb, D. O. (1949). *The organization of behavior.* New York : Wiley.

Hechtman, L., Abikoff, H., & Jensen, P. S. (2005). Multimodal therapy and stimulants in the treatment of children with attention-deficit/hyperactivity disorder. In E. D. Hibbs & P. S. Jensen (Eds.), *Psychosocial treatments for child and adolescent disorders: Empirically based strategies for clinical practice* (pp. 411–437). Washington, DC: American Psychological Association.

Hechtman, L., Abikoff, H., Klein, G., Greenfield, B., Etcovitch, J., Cousins, L., et al. (2004a). Children with ADHD treated with long-term methylphenidate and multimodal psychosocial treatment: Impact on parental practices. *Journal of the American Academy of Child and Adolescent Psychiatry, 43,* 830–838.

Hechtman, L., Abikoff, H., Klein, R.G., Weiss, G., Respitz, C., Kouri, J., et al. (2004b). Academic achievement and emotional status of children with ADHD treated with long-term methylphenidate and multimodal psychosocial treatment. *Journal of the American Academy of Child and Adolescent Psychiatry, 43*, 812–819.

Heflin, A. H., & Deblinger, E. (2003). Treatment of a sexually abused adolescent with posttraumatic stress disorder. In M. A. Reinecke, F. M. Dattilio, & A. Freeman (Eds.), *Cognitive therapy with children and adolescents: A casebook for clinical practice* (pp. 214–246). New York: Guilford Press.

Heiman, J. R., & Heard-Davison, A. R. (2004). Child sexual abuse and adult sexual relationships: Review and perspective. In L. J. Koenig, L. S. Doll, A. O'Leary, & W. Pequegnat (Eds.), *From child sexual abuse to adult sexual risk: Trauma, revictimization, and intervention* (pp. 13–47). New York: American Psychological Association.

Hellander, M., Sisson, D. P., & Fristad, M. A. (2003). Internet support for parents of children with early-onset bipolar disorder. In B. Geller & M. P. DelBello (Eds.), *Bipolar disorder in childhood and early adolescence* (pp. 314–329). New York: Guilford Press.

Henggeler, S. W., & Lee, T. (2003). Multisystemic treatment of serious clinical problems. In A. E. Kazdin & J. R. Weisz (Eds.), *Evidence-based psychotherapies for children and adolescents* (pp. 301–322). New York: Guildford Press.

Henggeler, S. W., Pickrel, S. G., Brondino, M. J., & Crouch, J. L. (1996). Eliminating (almost) treatment dropout of substance abusing or dependent delinquents through home-based multisystemic therapy. *American Journal of Psychiatry, 153*, 427–428.

Henker, B., & Whalen, C. K. (1999). The child with attention-deficit/hyperactivity disorder in school and peer settings. In H. C. Quay & A. E. Hogan (Eds.), *Handbook of disruptive behavior disorders* (pp. 157–178). New York: Plenum.

Henry, B., Feehan, M., McGee, R., Stanton, W., Moffitt, T. W., & Silva, P. (1993). The importance of conduct problems and depressive symptoms in predicting adolescent substance use. *Journal of Abnormal Child Psychology, 21*, 469–480.

Herschell, A. D., & McNeil, C. B. (2005). Parent-child interaction therapy for children experiencing externalizing behavior problems. In L. A. Reddy, T. M. Files-Hall & C. E. Schaefer (Eds.), *Empirically based play interventions for children* (pp. 169–190). Washington, DC: American Psychological Association.

Hill, D. E., Yeo, R. A., Campbell, R. A., Hart, B., Vigil, J., & Brooks, W. (2003). Magnetic resonance imaging correlates of attention-deficit/hyperactivity disorder in children. *Neuropsychology, 17*, 498–506.

Hill, J. L. Brooks-Gunn, J., & Waldfogel, J. (2003). Sustained effects of high participation in an early intervention for low-birth-weight premature infants. *Developmental Psychology, 39*, 730–744.

Hinshaw, S. P. (2005). Stigma of mental disorders in children and parents: Developmental issues, family concerns, and research needs. *Journal of Child Psychology and Psychiatry, 36*, 714–734.

Hinshaw, S. P. (2006). Stigma and mental illness: Developmental issues and future prospects. In D. Cicchetti & D. J. Cohen (Eds.), *Developmental psychopathology, Vol. 3: Risk, disorder, and adaptation* (pp. 841–881). New York: Wiley.

Hinshaw, S. P., Klein, R. G., & Abikoff, H. B. (2002). Childhood attention-deficit hyperactivity disorder: Nonpharmacological treatments and their combination with medication. In P. E. Nathan & J. M. Gorman (Eds.), *A guide to treatments that work* (pp. 3–23). New York: Oxford University Press.

Hippler, K., & Klicpera, C. (2003). A retrospective analysis of the clinical case records of "autistic psychopaths" diagnosed by Hans Asperger and his team at the University Children's Hospital, Vienna. In U. Frith & E. Hill (Eds.), *Autism: Mind and brain* (pp. 21–42). New York: Oxford University Press.

Hiroto, D. S., & Seligman, E. (1975). Generality of learned helplessness in man. *Journal of Personality and Social Psychology, 31*, 311–327.

Hirshfeld, D. R., Biederman, J., Brody, L., Faraone, S. V., & Rosenbaum, J. F. (1997). Expressed emotion toward children with and without behavioral inhibition: Associations with maternal anxiety disorders. *Journal of the American Academy of Child and Adolescent Psychiatry, 36*, 910–917.

Hirshfeld-Becker, D. R., Biederman, J., & Rosenbaum, J. F. (2004). Behavioral inhibition. In T. L. Morris & J. S. March (Eds.), *Anxiety disorders in children and adolescents* (pp. 27–58). New York: Guilford Press.

Hock, E., Hart, M., Kang, M. J., & Lutz, W. J. (2004). Predicting children's reactions to terrorist attacks: The importance of self-reports and preexisting characteristics. *American Journal of Orthopsychiatry, 74*, 253–262.

Hocutt, A. M. (1996). Effectiveness of special education: Is placement the critical factor? In D. Terman (Ed.), *The future of children: Special education* (pp. 77–102). Los Altos, CA: David and Lucille Packard Foundation.

Hodapp, R. M., & DesJardin, J. L. (2002). Genetic etiologies of mental retardation: Issues for interventions and interventionists. *Journal of Developmental and Physical Disabilities, 14*, 323–338.

Hodapp, R. M., & Dykens, E. M. (2006). Mental retardation. In K. A. Renninger, I. E. Sigel, W. Damon, & R. M. Lerner (Eds.), *Handbook of child psychology: Vol. 4, Child psychology in practice* (6th ed., pp. 453–496). Hoboken, NJ: Wiley.

Hodapp, R. M., Zakemi, E., Rosner, B. A., & Dykens, E. M. (2006). Mental retardation. In D. A. Wolfe & E. J. Marsh (Eds.), *Behavioral and emotional disorders in adolescents* (pp. 383–409). New York: Guilford Press.

Hogue, A., Dauber, S., Samuolis, J., & Liddle, H. A. (2006). Treatment techniques and outcomes in multidimensional family therapy for adolescent behavior problems. *Journal of Family Psychology, 20,* 535–543.

Hogue, A., Liddle, H. A., Dauber, S., & Samuolis, J. (2004). Linking session focus to treatment outcome in evidence-based treatments for adolescent substance abuse. *Psychotherapy: Theory, Research, Practice, Training, 41,* 83–96.

Holburn, S. (2005). Severe aggressive and self-destructive behavior: Mentalistic attribution. In J. W. Jacobson, R. M. Foxx, & J. A. Mulick (Eds.), *Controversial therapies for developmental disabilities: Fad, fashion and science in professional practice* (pp. 279–293). Mahwah, NJ: Lawrence Erlbaum Associates.

Holden, B., & Gitlesen, P. (2006). A total population study of challenging behaviour in the county of Hedmark, Norway: Prevalence and risk markers. *Research in Developmental Disabilities, 27,* 456–465.

Holdnack, J. A., & Weiss, G. (2006). Idea 2004: Anticipated implications for clinical practice: Integrating assessment and intervention. *Psychology in the Schools, 43,* 871–882.

Hollon, S. D., Garber, J., & Shelton, R. C. (2005). Treatment of depression in adolescents with cognitive behavior therapy and medications: A commentary on the TADS project. *Cognitive and Behavioral Practice, 12,* 149–155.

Hood, K. K., & Eyberg, M. (2003). Outcomes of parent-child interaction therapy: Mothers' reports of maintenance three to six years after treatment. *Journal of Clinical Child and Adolescent Psychology, 32,* 419–429.

Hooley, J. M., & Gotlib, I. H. (2000). A diathesis-stress conceptualization of expressed emotion and clinical outcome. *Applied and Preventive Psychology, 9,* 135–151.

Hornstein, N. L. (1996). Complexities of psychiatric differential diagnosis in children with dissociative symptoms and disorders. In J. Silberg (Ed.), *The dissociative child* (pp. 27–46). Lutherville, MD: Sidran Press.

Horwitz, S. M., Kelleher, K., Boyce, T., Jensen, P., Murphy, M., Perrin, E., et al. (2002). Barriers to health care research for children and youth with psychosocial problems. *Journal of the American Medical Association, 288,* 1508–1512.

Hoskyn, M., & Swanson, L. (2000). Cognitive processing of low achievers and children with reading disabilities: A selective meta-analytic review of the published literature. *School Psychology Review, 29,* 102–119.

Hoven, C. W., Mandell, D. J., & Duarte, C. S. (2003). Mental health of New York City public school children after 9/11: An epidemiologic investigation. In S. W. Coates, J. L. Rosenthal, & D. S. Schechter (Eds.), *September 11: Trauma and human bonds* (pp. 51–74). Hillsdale, NJ: Analytic Press.

Howard, K. I., Kopta, S. M., Krause, M. S., & Orlinsky, D. E. (1986). The dose-effect relationship in psychotherapy. *American Psychologist, 41,* 159–164.

Howes, P. W., Cicchetti, D., Toth, S. L., & Rogosch, F. A. (2000). Affective, organizational, and relational characteristics of maltreating families: A systems perspective. *Journal of Family Psychology, 14,* 95–110.

Howlin, P. (2005). Outcomes in autism spectrum disorders. In F. R. Volkmar, R. Paul, A. Klin, & D. Cohen (Eds.), *Handbook of autism and pervasive developmental disorders, Vol. 1: Diagnosis, development, neurobiology, and behavior* (pp. 201–220). Hoboken, NJ: Wiley.

Howlin, P. (2006). Augmentative and alternative communication systems for children with autism. In T. Charman & W. Stone (Eds.), *Social and communication development in autism spectrum disorders* (pp. 236–266). New York: Guilford Press.

Hoyson, M., Jamieson, B., & Strain, P. S. (1984). Individualized group instruction of normally developing and autistic-like children: A description and evaluation of the LEAP curriculum model. *Journal of the Division of Early Childhood, 8,* 157–181.

Hoza, B., Mrug, S., Gerdes, A. C., Hinshaw, S. P., Bukowski, W. M., Gold, J. A., et al. (2005). What aspects of peer relationships are impaired in children with attention-deficit/hyperactivity disorder? *Journal of Consulting and Clinical Psychology, 73,* 411–423.

Hoza, B., Mrug, S., Pelham, W. E., Greiner, A. R., & Gnagy, E. M. (2003). A friendship intervention for children with attention-deficit/hyperactivity disorder: Preliminary findings. *Journal of Attention Disorders, 6,* 87–98.

Hsieh, S., & Hollister, D. (2004). Examining gender differences in adolescent substance abuse behavior: Comparisons and implications for treatment. *Journal of Child & Adolescent Substance Abuse, 13,* 53–70.

Hudson, J. L., & Rapee, R. M. (2002). Parent-child interactions in clinically anxious children and their siblings. *Journal of Clinical Child and Adolescent Psychology, 31,* 548–555.

Hudson, J., & Rapee, R. (2004). From anxious temperament to disorder: An etiological model of generalized anxiety disorder. In R. G. Heimberg, C. L. Turk, & D. S. Mennin (Eds.), *Generalized anxiety disorder: Advances in research and practice* (pp. 51–76). New York: Guilford Press.

Hudziak, J. J., Heath, A. C., Madden, P. F., Reich, W., Bucholz, K. K., Slutske, W., et al. (1998). Latent class and factor analysis of DSM-IV ADHD: A twin study of female adolescents. *Journal of the American Academy of Child and Adolescent Psychiatry, 36,* 848–857.

Huey, S. J., Henggeler, S. W., Brondino, M. J., & Pickrel, S. G. (2000). Mechanisms of change in multisystemic therapy: Reducing delinquent behavior through therapist adherence and improved family and peer functioning. *Journal of Consulting and Clinical Psychology, 68,* 451–467.

Iacono, W. G., Carlson, S. R., Taylor, J., Elkins, I. J., & McGue, M. (1999). Behavioral disinhibition and the development of substance-use disorders: Findings from the Minnesota Twin Family Study. *Development and Psychopathology, 11,* 869–900.

Ilgin, N., Senol, S., Gucuyener, K., Gokcora, N., & Sener, S. (2001). Is increased D2 receptor availability associated with response to treatment medication in ADHD? *Developmental Medicine and Child Neurology, 43,* 755–760.

Ingoldsby, E. M., & Shaw, D. S. (2002). Neighborhood contextual factors and early-starting antisocial pathways. *Clinical Child & Family Psychology Review, 5,* 21–55.

Jackson, D. M., & Westlind-Danielsson, A. (1994). Dopamine receptors: Molecular biology, biochemistry and behavioural aspects. *Pharmacological Therapy, 64,* 291–370.

Jacobson, J. W., & Mulick, J. A. (1996). *Manual of diagnosis and professional practice in mental retardation.* Washington, DC: American Psychological Association.

Jairam, R., Srinath, S., Girimaji, S. C., & Seshadri, S. P. (2004). A prospective 4–5 year follow-up of juvenile onset bipolar disorder. *Bipolar Disorders, 6,* 386–394.

Jenkins, E. J., & Bell, C. C. (1994). Violence among inner city high school students and post-traumatic stress disorder. In S. Friedman (Ed.), *Anxiety disorders in African Americans* (pp. 76–88). New York: Springer.

Jenkins, R. (1998). Mental health and primary care-implications for policy. *International Review of Psychiatry, 10,* 158–160.

Jensen, P. S. (2005). NIMH's TADS: More than just a tad of progress? *Cognitive and Behavioral Practice, 12,* 156–158.

Jensen, P. S., Hoagwood, K., & Zitner, L. (2006). What's in a name? Problems versus prospects in current diagnostic approaches. In D. Cicchetti & D. J. Cohen (Eds.), *Developmental psychopathology, Vol 1: Theory and method* (pp. 24–40). New York: Wiley.

Johnson, C. F. (2002). Physical abuse: Accidental versus intentional trauma in children. In J. E. B. Meyers, L. Berliner, J. Briere, C. T. Hendrix, C. Jenny, & T. A. Reid (Eds.), *The APSAC handbook on child maltreatment* (pp. 249–268). Thousand Oaks, CA: Sage.

Johnson, J. G., Cohen, P., Kasen, S., Smailes, E., & Brook, J. S. (2001). Association of maladaptive parental behavior with psychiatric disorder among parents and their offspring. *Archives of General Psychiatry, 58,* 453–460.

Johnson, M. H., & de Haan, M. (2006). Typical and atypical human functional brain development. In D. Cicchetti & D. J. Cohen (Eds.), *Developmental psychopathology, Vol 2: Developmental neuroscience* (pp. 197–215). Hoboken, NJ: Wiley.

Johnson, S. L., Sandrow, D., Meyer, B., Winters, R., Miller, I., Solomon, D., et al. (2000). Increases in manic symptoms after life events involving goal attainment. *Journal of Abnormal Psychology, 109,* 721–727.

Johnson, T. C., & Friend, C. (1995). Assessing young children's sexual behaviors in the context of child sexual abuse evaluations. In T. Ney (Ed.), *True and false allegation of child sexual abuse: Assessment and case management* (pp. 49–72). New York: Brunner Mazel.

Johnston, C. (2005). The importance of parental attributions in families of children with attention-deficit/hyperactivity and disruptive behavior disorders. *Clinical Child and Family Psychology Review, 8,* 167–182.

Johnston, C., & Freeman, W. (1997). Attributions for child behavior in parents of children without behavior disorders and children with attention deficit-hyperactivity disorder. *Journal of Consulting and Clinical Psychology, 65,* 636–645.

Johnston, L. D., O'Malley, P. M., Bachman, J. G., & Schulenberg, J. E. (2005). *Monitoring the future national survey results on drug use, 1975–2004. Volume I: Secondary school students* (NIH Publication No. 05-5727). Bethesda, MD: National Institute on Drug Abuse.

Johnston, L. D., O'Malley, P. M., Bachman, J. G., & Schulenberg, J. E. (2006). *Monitoring the future national results on adolescent drug use: Overview of key findings, 2005.* (NIH Publication No. 06–5882). Bethesda, MD: National Institute on Drug Abuse.

Joiner, T. E., Metalsky, G. I., Katz, J., & Beach, S. R. H. (1999). Depression and excessive reassurance-seeking. *Psychological Inquiry, 10,* 269–278.

Joiner, T. E., & Wagner, K. D. (1995). Attribution style and depression in children and adolescents: A meta-analytic review. *Clinical Psychology Review, 15,* 777–798.

Jonas, R., Nguyen, S., Hu, B., Asarnow, R. F., LoPresti, C., Curtiss, S., et al. (2004). Cerebral hemispherectomy: Hospital course, seizure, developmental, language, and motor outcomes. *Neurology, 62,* 1712–1721.

Jones, M. C. (1924). A laboratory study of fear: The case of Peter. *Pedagogical Seminary, 31,* 308–315.

Jordan, N. C., Hanich, L. B., & Kaplan, D. (2003). A longitudinal study of mathematical competencies in children with specific mathematics difficulties versus children with co-morbid mathematics and reading difficulties. *Child Development, 74,* 834–850.

Joshi, S. V. (2004). Psychostimulants, atomoxetine, and alpha-agonists. In H. Steiner (Ed.), *Handbook of mental health interventions in children and adolescents* (pp. 258–287). San Francisco: Jossey-Bass.

Kafantaris, V., Coletti, D. J., Dicker, R., Padula, G., & Kane, J. M. (2001). Adjunctive antipsychotic treatment of adolescents with bipolar psychosis. *Journal of the American Academy of Child & Adolescent Psychiatry, 40,* 1448–1456.

Kafantaris, V., Coletti, D. J., Dicker, R., Padula, G., & Kane, J. M. (2003). Lithium treatment of acute mania in adolescents: A large open trial. *Journal of the American Academy of Child & Adolescent Psychiatry, 42,* 1038–1045.

Kagan, J., Reznick, J. S., & Snidman, N. (1988). Biological bases of childhood shyness. *Science, 240,* 167–171.

Kahn, J. S., Kehle, T. J., Jenson, W. R., & Clarke, E. (1990). Comparison of cognitive-behavioral, relaxation, and self-modeling interventions for depression among middle-school students. *School Psychology Review, 19,* 196–208.

Kahng, S., Iwata, B. A., & Lewin, A. B. (2002). Behavioral treatment of self-injury, 1964 to 2000. *American Journal on Mental Retardation, 107,* 212–221.

Kaminer, Y., Blitz, C., Burleson, J. A., Sussman, J., & Rounsaville, B. J. (1998). Psychotherapies for adolescent substance abusers: treatment outcome. *Journal of Nervous and Mental Disease, 186,* 684–690.

Kaminer, Y., & Bukstein, O. G. (2005). Treating adolescent substance abuse. In R. J. Frances, S. I. Miller, & A. H. Mack (Eds.), *Clinical textbook of addictive disorders* (pp. 559–587). New York: Guilford Press.

Kaminer, Y., Burleson, J. A., & Goldberger, R. (2002). Cognitive-behavioral coping skills and psychoeducation therapies for adolescent substance abuse. *Journal of Nervous and Mental Disease, 190,* 737–745.

Kamphaus, R. W., & Frick, P. J. (2002). *Clinical assessment of child and adolescent personality and behavior.* Boston: Allyn & Bacon.

Kamphaus, R. W., Reynolds, C. R., & Imperato-McCammon, C. (1999). Roles of diagnosis and classification in school psychology. In C. R. Reynolds & T. B. Gutkin (Eds.), *Handbook of school psychology* (pp. 292–306). New York: Wiley.

Kandel, D. B., Yamaguchi, K., & Chen, K. (1992). Stages of progression in drug involvement from adolescence to adulthood: Further evidence for the gateway theory. *Journal of Studies on Alcohol, 53,* 447–457.

Kanner, L. (1937). The development and present status of psychiatry in pediatrics. *Journal of Pediatrics, 11,* 418–435.

Kanner, L. (1943). Autistic disturbances of affective contact. *Nervous Child, 2,* 217–250.

Kashani, J. H., & Orvaschel, H. (1990). A community study of anxiety in children and adolescents. *American Journal of Psychiatry, 147,* 313–318.

Kaslow, N. J., Deering, G. G., & Racusin, G. R. (1994). Depressed children and their families. *Clinical Psychology Review, 14,* 39–59.

Kaslow, N. J., & Thompson, M. P. (1998). Applying the criteria for empirically supported treatments to studies of psychosocial interventions for child and adolescent depression. *Journal of Clinical Child Psychology, 27,* 146–155.

Kates, W. R., Frederikse, M., Mostofsky, S. H., Folley, B. S., Cooper, K., Mazur-Hopkins, P., et al. (2002). MRI parcellation of the frontal lobe in boys with attention deficit hyperactivity disorder or Tourette syndrome. *Psychiatry Research, 116*, 63–81.

Kaufman, N. K., Rohde, P., Seeley, J. R., Clarke, G. N., & Stice, E. (2005). Potential mediators of cognitive-behavioral therapy for adolescents with comorbid major depression and conduct disorder. *Journal of Consulting and Clinical Psychology, 73*, 38–46.

Kaur, S., Sassi, R. B., Axelson, D., Nicoletti, M., Brambilla, P., Monkul, E. S., et al. (2005). Cingulate cortex anatomical abnormalities in children and adolescents with bipolar disorder. *American Journal of Psychiatry, 162*, 1637–1643.

Kaye, W. H., Bastiani, A. M., & Moss, H. (1995). Cognitive style of patients with anorexia nervosa and bulimia nervosa. *International Journal of Eating Disorders, 18*, 287–290.

Kaye, W. H., Greeno, C. G., Moss, H., Fernstrom, J., Fernstrom, M., Lilenfeld, L. R., et al. (1998). Alterations in serotonin activity and psychiatric symptoms after recovery from bulimia nervosa. *Archives of General Psychiatry, 55*, 927–935.

Kaye, W. H., Nagata, T., Weltzin, T. E., Hsu, L. K., Sokol, M. S., McConaha, C., et al. (2001). Double-blind placebo-controlled administration of fluoxetine in restricting and restricting-purging type anorexia nervosa. *Biological Psychiatry, 49*, 644–652.

Kaye, W. H., Weltzin, T., & Hsu, L. G. (1993). Relationship between anorexia nervosa and obsessive and compulsive behaviors. *Psychiatric Annals, 23*, 365–373.

Kazdin, A. E. (1999). Overview of research design issues in clinical psychology. In P. C. Kendall, J. N. Butcher, & G. N. Holmbeck (Eds.), *Handbook of research methods in clinical psychology* (pp. 3–30). New York: Wiley.

Kazdin, A. E. (2003). *Research design in clinical psychology.* Boston: Allyn & Bacon.

Kazdin, A. E. (2005a). Child, parent, and family-based treatment of aggressive and antisocial child behavior. In E. D. Hibbs & P. S. Jensen (Eds.), *Psychosocial treatments for child and adolescent disorders: Empirically based strategies for clinical practice* (pp. 445–476). Washington, DC: American Psychological Association.

Kazdin, A. E. (2005b). *Parent management training: Treatment for oppositional, aggressive, and antisocial behavior in children and adolescents.* New York: Oxford University Press.

Kazdin, A. E., Bass, D., Ayers, W. A., & Rodgers, A. (1990). Empirical and clinical focus of child and adolescent psychotherapy research. *Journal of Consulting and Clinical Psychology, 58*, 729–740.

Kazdin, A. E., & Marciano, P. L. (1998). Childhood and adolescent depression. In E. J. Mash & R. A. Barkley (Eds.), *Treatment of childhood disorders* (pp. 211–248). New York: Guilford Press.

Kazdin, A. E., & Weisz, J. (2003). *Evidence-based psychotherapies for children and adolescents.* New York: Guilford Press.

Kazdin, A. E., & Whitley, K. (2006). Comorbidity, case complexity, and effects of evidence-based treatment for children referred for disruptive behavior. *Journal of Consulting and Clinical Psychology, 74*, 455–467.

Kearney-Cooke, A., & Striegel-Moore, H. (1994). Treatment of childhood sexual abuse in anorexia nervosa and bulimia nervosa: A feminist psychodynamic approach. *International Journal of Eating Disorders, 15*, 305–319.

Keel, P. K., Klump, K. L., Miller, K. B., McGue, M., & Iacono, W. G. (2005). Shared transmission of eating disorders and anxiety disorders. *International Journal of Eating Disorders, 38*, 99–105.

Keenan, K., Gunthorpe, D., & Young, D. (2002). Patterns of cortisol reactivity in African American neonates from low-income environments. *Developmental Psychobiology, 41*, 1–13.

Keenan, K., & Hipwell, A. E. (2005). Preadolescent clues to understanding depression in girls. *Clinical Child and Family Psychology Review, 8*, 89–105.

Keenan, K., Hipwell, A., Duax, J., Stouthamer-Loeber, M., & Loeber, R. (2004). Phenomenology of depression in young girls. *Journal of the American Academy of Child & Adolescent Psychiatry, 43*, 1098–1106.

Keenan, K., Loeber, R., & Green, S. (1999). Conduct disorder in girls: A review of the literature. *Clinical Child & Family Psychology Review, 2*, 3–19.

Keenan, K., & Shaw, D. S. (2003). Starting at the beginning: Exploring the etiology of antisocial behavior in the first years of life. In B. B. Lahey, T. E. Moffitt, & A. Caspi (Eds.), *Causes of conduct disorder and juvenile delinquency* (pp. 153–181). New York: Guilford Press.

Keenan, K., & Wakschlag, S. (2004). Are oppositional defiant and conduct disorder symptoms normative behaviors in preschoolers? A comparison of referred and nonreferred children. *American Journal of Psychiatry, 161*, 356–358.

Keery, H., Boutelle, K., van den Berg, P., & Thompson, J. K. (2005). The impact of appearance-related teasing by family members. *Journal of Adolescent Health, 37*, 120–127.

Keery, H., van den Berg, P., & Thompson, J. K. (2004). An evaluation of the tripartite influence model of body dissatisfaction and eating disturbance with adolescent girls. *Body Image, 1,* 237–251.

Kelleher, K., Chaffin, M., Hollenberg, J., & Fischer, E. (1994). Alcohol and drug disorders among physically abusive and neglectful parents in a community-based sample. *American Journal of Public Health, 84,* 1586–1590.

Keller, M. B., Lavori, P. W., Wunder, J., Beardslee, W. R., Schwartz, C. E., & Roth, J. (1992). Chronic course of anxiety disorders in children and adolescents. *Journal of the American Academy of Child and Adolescent Psychiatry, 31,* 595–599.

Keller, M. B., Ryan, N. D., Strober, M., Klein, R. G., Kutcher, S., Birmaher, B., et al. (2001). Efficacy of paroxetine in the treatment of adolescent major depression: A randomized, controlled trial. *Journal of the American Academy of Child and Adolescent Psychiatry, 40,* 762–772.

Kelley, S. J. (2002). Child maltreatment in the context of substance abuse. In J. E. B. Myers, L. Berliner, J. Briere, C. T. Hendrix, C. Jenny, & T. A. Reid (Eds.), *The APSAC handbook on child maltreatment* (pp. 105–117). Thousand Oaks, CA: Sage.

Kempes, M., Matthys, W., de Vries, H., & van Engeland, H. (2005). Reactive and proactive aggression in children: A review of theory, findings and the relevance for child and adolescent psychiatry. *European Child & Adolescent Psychiatry, 14,* 11–19.

Kempler, D. (2005). *Neurocognitive disorders in aging.* Thousand Oaks, CA: Sage.

Kendall, P. C. (1992). *Coping cat workbook.* Ardmore, PA: Workbook Publishing.

Kendall, P. C. (1994). Treating anxiety disorders in children: Results of a randomized clinical trial. *Journal of Consulting and Clinical Psychology, 62,* 100–110.

Kendall, P. C., Flannery-Schroeder, E. C., & Ford, J. D. (1999). Therapy outcome research methods. In P. C. Kendall, J. N. Butcher, & G. N. Holmbeck (Eds.), *Handbook of research methods in clinical psychology* (pp. 330–363). New York: Wiley.

Kendall, P. C., Flannery-Schroeder, E. C., Panichelli-Mindel, S., Southam-Gerow, M., Henin, A., & Warman, M. (1997). Therapy for youth with anxiety disorders: A second randomized clinical trial. *Journal of Consulting and Clinical Psychology, 65,* 366–380.

Kendall, P. C., Hudson, J. L., Choudhury, M., Webb, A., Pimentel, S. (2005). Cognitive-behavioral treatment for childhood anxiety disorders. In E. D. Hibbs & P. S. Jensen (Eds.), *Psychosocial treatments for child and adolescent disorders: Empirically based strategies for clinical practice* (2nd ed., pp. 47–73). Washington, DC: American Psychological Association.

Kendall, P. C., Krain, A., & Treadwell, K. (1999). Generalized anxiety disorders. In R. T. Ammerman, M. Hersen, & C. G. Last (Eds.), *Handbook of prescriptive treatments for children and adolescents* (pp. 155–171). Needham Heights, MA: Allyn & Bacon.

Kendall, P. C., Marrs-Garcia, A., Nath, S. R., & Sheldrick, R. C. (1999). Normative comparisons for the evaluation of clinical significance. *Journal of Consulting and Clinical Psychology, 67,* 285–299.

Kendall, P. C., Pimentel, S., Rynn, M. A., Angelosante, A., & Webb, A. (2004). Generalized anxiety disorder. In T. H. Ollendick & J. S. March (Eds.), *Phobic and anxiety disorders in children and adolescents* (pp. 334–380). New York: Oxford University Press.

Kendall, P. C., Safford, S., Flannery-Schroeder, E., & Webb, A. (2004). Child anxiety treatment: Outcomes in adolescence and impact on substance use and depression at 7.4-year follow-up. *Journal of Consulting and Clinical Psychology, 72,* 276–287.

Kendall, P. C., & Southam-Gerow, M. (1996). Long-term follow-up of treatment for anxiety-disordered youth. *Journal of Consulting and Clinical Psychology, 65,* 883–888.

Kendall-Tackett, K. A., Williams, L. M., & Finkelhor, D. (1993). Impact of sexual abuse on children: A review and synthesis of recent empirical studies. *Psychological Bulletin, 113,* 164–180.

Kennard, B. D., Ginsburg, G. S., Feeny, N. C., Sweeney, M., & Zagurski, R. (2005). Implementation challenges to TADS cognitive-behavioral therapy. *Cognitive and Behavioral Practice, 12,* 230–239.

Kenney-Benson, G. A., & Pomerantz, M. (2005). The role of mothers' use of control in children's perfectionism: Implications for the development of children's depressive symptoms. *Journal of Personality, 73,* 23–46.

Keogh, B. K., Bernheimer, L. P., & Guthrie, D. (1997). Stability and change over time in cognitive level of children with delays. *American Journal on Mental Retardation, 101,* 365–373.

Kerins, M. (2006). The effects of systematic reading instruction on three classifications of readers. *Reading Research and Instruction, 45,* 243–260.

Kerr, M., & Stattin, H. (2000). What parents know, how they know it, and several forms of adolescent adjustment: Further support for a reinterpretation of monitoring. *Developmental Psychology, 36,* 366–380.

Kessler, R., Berglund, P., Dernier, O., Jin, R., & Walters, E. (2005). Lifetime prevalence and age-of-onset distributions of DSM-IV disorders in the National Co-morbidity Survey replication. *Archives of General Psychiatry, 62,* 593–602.

Khanna, M., Aschenbrand, S. G., & Kendall, P. C. (2007). New frontiers: Computer technology in the treatment of anxious youth. *The Behavior Therapist, 30,* 22–25.

Khantzian, E. J. (1995). Self-regulation vulnerabilities in substance abusers: Treatment implications. In S. Dowling (Ed.), *The psychology and treatment of addictive behavior* (pp. 17–41). Madison, CT: International Universities Press.

Kilpatrick, D. G., Ruggiero, K. J., Acierno, R., Saunders, B. E., Resnick, H. S., & Best, C. (2003). Violence, risk of PTSD, major depression, substance abuse/dependence, and comorbidity: Results from the National Survey of Adolescents. *Journal of Consulting and Clinical Psychology, 71,* 692–700.

Kim, A., Vaughn, S., Wanzek, J., & Wei, S. (2004). Graphic organizers and their effects on the reading comprehension of students with LD: A synthesis of research. *Journal of Learning Disabilities, 37,* 105–118.

Kim, J. A., Szatmari, P., Bryson, S. E., Streiner, D. L., & Wilson, F. J. (2000). The prevalence of anxiety and mood problems among children with autism and Asperger syndrome. *Autism, 4,* 117–132.

Kim, J. E., Hetherington, E. M., & Reiss, D. (1999). Associations among family relationships, antisocial peers, and adolescents' externalizing behaviors: Gender and family type differences. *Child Development, 70,* 1209–1230.

Kim-Cohen, J., Arseneault, L., Caspi, A., Tomas, M. P., Taylor, A., & Moffitt, T. E. (2005). Validity of DSM-IV Conduct Disorder in 4½-5-year-old children: A longitudinal epidemiological study. *American Journal of Psychiatry, 162,* 1108–1117.

King, K. M., & Chassin, L. (2004). Mediating and moderated effects of adolescent behavioral undercontrol and parenting in the prediction of drug use disorders in emerging adulthood. *Psychology of Addictive Behaviors, 18,* 239–249.

King, N. J., Gullone, E., Tonge, B. J., & Ollendick, T. H. (1993). Self-reports of panic attacks and manifest anxiety in adolescents. *Behavior Therapy and Research, 31,* 111–116.

King, N. J., Muris, P., & Ollendick, T. H. (2004). Specific phobia. In T. L. Morris & J. S. March (Eds.), *Anxiety disorders in children and adolescents* (pp. 263–279). New York: Guilford Press.

King, R. A., Schwab-Stone, M., Flisher, A. J., Greenwald, S., Kramer, R. A., Goodman, S. H., et al. (2001). Psychosocial and risk behavior correlates of youth suicide attempts and suicidal ideation. *Journal of the American Academy of Child and Adolescent Psychiatry, 40,* 837–846.

King, S., Waschbusch, D. A., Frankland, B. W., Andrade, B. F., Thurston, C. M., McNutt, L. et al. (2005). Taxonomic examination of ADHD and conduct problem comorbidity in elementary school children using cluster analyses. *Journal of Psychopathology and Behavioral Assessment, 27,* 77–88.

King, S. M., Iacono, W. G., & McGue, M. (2004). Childhood externalizing and internalizing psychopathology in the prediction of early substance use. *Addiction, 99,* 1548–1559.

Kirisci, L., Tarter, R. E., Vanyukov, M., Reynolds, M., & Habeych, M. (2004). Relation between cognitive distortions and neurobehavior disinhibition on the development of substance use during adolescence and substance use disorder by young adulthood: A prospective study. *Drug and Alcohol Dependence, 76,* 125–133.

Kirisci, L., Vanyukov, M., & Tarter, R. (2005). Detection of youth at high risk for substance use disorders: A longitudinal study. *Psychology of Addictive Behaviors, 19,* 243–252.

Kirk, S. A. (1962). *Educating exceptional children.* Oxford, UK: Houghton Mifflin.

Klein, R. G., Abikoff, H., Hechtman, L., & Weiss, G. (2004). Design and rationale of controlled study of long-term methylphenidate and multimodal psychosocial treatment in children with ADHD. *Journal of the American Academy of Child and Adolescent Psychiatry, 43,* 792–801.

Klein, R. G., Abikoff, H., Klass, E., Ganeles, D., Seese, L. M., & Pollack, S. (1997). Clinical efficacy of methylphenidate in conduct disorder with and without attention deficit hyperactivity disorder. *Archives of General Psychiatry, 54,* 1073–1080.

Klerman, G. L., & Weissman, M. M. (1993). Interpersonal psychotherapy for depression: Background and concepts. In G. L. Klerman & M. M. Weissman (Eds.), *New applications of interpersonal psychotherapy* (pp. 3–26). Washington, DC: American Psychiatric Press.

Klimes-Dougan, B., & Kopp, C. B. (1999). Children's conflict tactics with mothers: A longitudinal investigation of the toddler and preschool years. *Merrill-Palmer Quarterly, 45,* 226–241.

Klin, A. (2000). Attributing social meaning to ambiguous visual stimuli in higher functioning autism and Asperger syndrome: The social attribution task. *Journal of Child Psychology, Psychiatry and Allied Disciplines, 33,* 763–769.

Klin, A., Jones, W., Schultz, R. T., & Volkmar, F. R. (2003). The enactive mind: From actions to cognition: Lessons from autism. *Philosophical Transactions of the Royal Society, Biological Sciences, 358*, 345–360.

Klin, A., Jones, W., Schultz, R., Volkmar, F., & Cohen, D. (2002). Visual fixation patterns during viewing of naturalistic social situations as predictors of social competence in individuals with autism. *Archives of General Psychiatry, 59*, 809–816.

Klin, A., McPartland, J., & Volkmar, F. R. (2005). Asperger syndrome. In F. R. Volkmar, R. Paul, A. Klin, & D. Cohen (Eds.), *Handbook of autism and pervasive developmental disorders, Vol. 1: Diagnosis, development, neurobiology, and behavior* (pp. 88–125). Hoboken, NJ: Wiley.

Klinger, L. G., Dawson, G., & Renner, P. (2003). Autistic disorder. In E. J. Mash & R. A. Barkley (Eds.), *Child psychopathology* (pp. 409–454). New York: Guilford Press.

Klomek, A. B., Marrocco, F., Kleinman, M., Schonfeld, I. S., & Gould, M. S. (2007). Bullying, depression, and suicidality in adolescents. *Journal of the American Academy of Child & Adolescent Psychiatry, 46*, 40–49.

Knell, S. M., & Ruma, C. D. (2003). Play therapy with a sexually abused child. In M. A. Reinecke, F. M. Dattilio, & A. Freeman (Eds.), *Cognitive therapy with children and adolescents: A casebook for clinical practice* (pp. 338–368). New York: Guilford Press.

Knutson, J. F., DeGarmo, D., Koeppl, G., & Reid, J. B. (2005). Care neglect, supervisory neglect, and harsh parenting in the development of children's aggression: A replication and extension. *Child Maltreatment, 10*, 92–107.

Kochanska, G., & Aksan, N. (2006). Children's conscience and self-regulation. *Journal of Personality, 74*, 1587–1617.

Koegel, L. K. (1995). Communication and language intervention. In R. L. Koegel & L. K. Koegel (Eds.), *Teaching children with autism: Strategies for initiating positive interaction and improving learning opportunities* (pp. 17–32). Baltimore: Brookes.

Koegel, L. K. (2000). Interventions to facilitate communication in autism. *Journal of Autism and Developmental Disorders, 30*, 383–391.

Koegel, L. K., Carter, C. M., & Koegel, R. L. (2003). Teaching children with autism self-initiations as a pivotal response. *Topics in Language Disorders, 23*, 134–145.

Koegel, L. K., Koegel, R. L., & Brookman, L. I. (2005). Child-initiated interactions that are pivotal in intervention for children with autism. In E. D. Hibbs & P. S. Jensen (Eds.), *Psychosocial treatments for child and adolescent disorders: Empirically based strategies for clinical practice* (pp. 633–657). Washington, DC: American Psychological Association.

Koegel, L. K., Koegel, R. L., Shoshan, Y., & McNerney, E. (1999). Pivotal response intervention II: Preliminary long-term outcome data. *Journal of the Association for Persons With Severe Handicaps, 24*, 186–198.

Koenig, A. L., Cicchetti, D., & Rogosch, F. A. (2004). Moral development: The association between maltreatment and young children's prosocial behaviors and moral transgressions. *Social Development, 13*, 97–106.

Koenig, L. J., & Clark, J. (2004). Sexual abuse of girls and HIV infection among women: Are they related? In L. J. Koenig, L. S. Doll, A. O'Leary, & W. Pequegnat (Eds.), *From child sexual abuse to adult sexual risk: Trauma, revictimization, and intervention* (pp. 69–92). Washington, DC: American Psychological Association.

Koenig, K., & Tsatsanis, K. D. (2005). Pervasive developmental disorders in girls. In D. J. Bell, S. L. Foster, & E. J. Mash (Eds.), *Handbook of behavioral and emotional problems in girls* (pp. 211–237). New York: Kluwer Academic/Plenum Publishers.

Kolko, D. J. (1996). Individual cognitive behavioral treatment and family therapy for physically abused children and their offending parents: A comparison of clinical outcomes. *Child Maltreatment, 1*, 322–342.

Kolko, D. J. (2002). Child physical abuse. In J. E. B. Meyers, L. Berliner, J. Briere, C. T. Hendrix, C. Jenny, & T. A. Reid (Eds.), *The APSAC handbook on child maltreatment* (pp. 21–54). Thousand Oaks, CA: Sage.

Kolko, D. J., Selelyo, J., & Brown, E. J. (1999). The treatment histories and service involvement of physically and sexually abusive families: Description, correspondence, and clinical correlates. *Child Abuse & Neglect, 23*, 459–476.

Kolko, D. J., & Swenson, C. C. (2002). *Assessing and treating physically abused children and their families: A cognitive-behavioral approach.* Thousand Oaks, CA: Sage.

Kolvin, I., & Sadowski, H. (2001). Childhood depression: Clinical phenomenology and classification. In I. M. Goodyer (Ed.), *The depressed child and adolescent: Cambridge child and adolescent psychiatry* (pp. 119–142). New York: Cambridge Press.

Konidaris, J. B. (2005). A sibling's perspective on autism. In F. R. Volkmar, R. Paul, A. Klin, & D. Cohen (Eds.), *Handbook of autism and pervasive developmental disorders, Vol. 2: Assessment, interventions, and policy* (pp. 1265–1275). New York: Wiley.

Koob, G. F., & LeMoal, M. (2006). *Neurobiology of addiction*. Amsterdam: Elsevier.

Kopta, S. M. (2003). The dose-effect relationship in psychotherapy: A defining achievement for Dr. Kenneth Howard. *Journal of Clinical Psychology, 59*, 727–733.

Koskentausta, T., Iivanainen, M., & Almqvist, F. (2007). Risk factors for psychiatric disturbance in children with intellectual disability. *Journal of Intellectual Disability Research, 51*, 43–53.

Kosten, T. R., George, T. P., & Kleber, H. D. (2005). The neurobiology of substance dependence. In R. J. Frances, S. I. Miller, & A. H. Mack (Eds.), *Clinical textbook of addictive disorders* (pp. 3–15). New York: Guilford Press.

Kovacs, M. (1997). Depressive disorders in childhood: An impressionistic landscape. *Journal of Child Psychology and Psychiatry, 38*, 287–298.

Kovacs, M., & Devlin, B. (1998). Internalizing disorders in childhood. *Journal of Child Psychology & Psychiatry & Allied Disciplines, 39*, 47–63.

Kowatch, R. A., & DelBello, P. (2005). Pharmacotherapy of children and adolescents with bipolar disorder. *Psychiatric Clinics of North America, 28*, 385–397.

Kowatch, R. A., & Fristad, M. A. (2006). Bipolar disorders. In R. T. Ammerman (Ed.), *Comprehensive handbook of personality and psychopathology* (pp. 217–232). Hoboken, NJ: Wiley.

Kowatch, R. A., Fristad, M., Birmaher, B., Wagner, K. D., Findling, R. L., & Hellander, M. (2005). Treatment guidelines for children and adolescents with bipolar disorder. *Journal of the American Academy of Child & Adolescent Psychiatry, 44*, 213–235.

Kowatch, R. A., Suppes, T., Carmody, T. J., Bucci, J. P., Hume, J. H., Kromelis, M., et al. (2000). Effect size of lithium, divalproex sodium, and carbamazepine in children and adolescents with bipolar disorder. *Journal of the American Academy of Child & Adolescent Psychiatry, 39*, 713–720.

Kraepelin, E. (1921). *Manic-depressive insanity and paranoia*. Edinburgh: Livingstone.

Kratochvil, C. J., Simons, A., Vitiello, B., Walkup, J., Emslie, G., Rosenberg, D., et al. (2005). A multisite psychotherapy and medication trial for depressed adolescents: Background and benefits. *Cognitive and Behavioral Practice, 12*, 159–165.

Kroesbergen, E. H., & VanLuit, H. (2003). Mathematics interventions for children with special educational needs: A meta-analysis. *Remedial and Special Education, 24*, 97–114.

Kroneman, L., Loeber, R., & Hipwell, A. E. (2004). Is neighborhood context differently related to externalizing problems and delinquency for girls compared with boys? *Clinical Child and Family Psychology Review, 7*, 109–122.

Kruh, I. P., Frick, P. J., & Clements, C. B. (2005). Historical and personality correlates to the violence patterns of juveniles tried as adults. *Criminal Justice and Behavior, 92*, 69–96.

Kuehn, B. M. (2006). Shift seen in patterns of drug use among teens. *Journal of the American Medical Association, 295*, 612–613.

Kuhn, M. R., & Stahl, S. A. (2003). Fluency: A review of developmental and remedial practices. *Journal of Educational Psychology, 95*, 3–21.

Kumin, L. (1994). Intelligibility of speech in children with Down syndrome in natural settings: Parents' perspective. *Perceptual and Motor Skills, 78*, 307–313.

Kupersmidt, J. B., Griesler, P. C., DeRosier, M. E., Patterson, C. J., & Davis, P. W. (1995). Childhood aggression and peer relations in the context of family and neighborhood factors. *Child Development, 66*, 360–375.

Kutcher, S., Aman, M., Brooks, S. J., Buitelaar, J., van Daalen, E., Fegert, J., et al. (2004). International consensus statement on attention-deficit/hyperactivity disorder (ADHD) and disruptive behavior disorders (DBDs): Clinical implications and treatment practice suggestions. *European Neuropsychopharmacology, 14*, 11–28.

Lackaye, T., Margalit, M., Ziv, O., & Ziman, T. (2006). Comparisons of self-efficacy, mood, effort, and hope between students with learning disabilities and their non-LD-matched peers. *Learning Disabilities Research & Practice, 21*, 111–121.

Lacourse, E., Nagin, D. S., Vitaro, F., Cote, S., Arseneault, L., & Tremblay, R. E. (2006). Prediction of early-onset deviant peer group affiliation: A 12-year longitudinal study. *Archives of General Psychiatry, 63*, 562–568.

LaGreca, A. M., & Harrison, M. (2005). Adolescent peer relations, friendships, and romantic relationships: Do they predict social anxiety and depression? *Journal of Clinical Child and Adolescent Psychology, 34*, 49–61.

LaGreca, A. M., & Silverman, W. K. (2006). Treating children and adolescents affected by disasters and terrorism. In P.C. Kendall (Ed.), *Child and adolescent therapy: Cognitive-behavioral procedures* (3rd ed., pp. 356–382). New York: Guilford Press.

LaGreca, A. M., Silverman, W. K., Vernberg, E. M., & Roberts, M. C. (2002). Introduction. In A. M. La Greca, W. K. Silverman, E. M. Vernberg, & M. C. Roberts (Eds.), *Helping children cope with disasters and terrorism* (pp. 3–8). Washington, DC: American Psychological Association.

LaGreca, A. M., Silverman, W. K., & Wasserstein, S. B. (1998). Children's pre-disaster functioning as a predictor of posttraumatic stress following Hurricane Andrew. *Journal of Consulting and Clinical Psychology, 66,* 883–892.

Lahey, B. B., Carlson, C. L., & Frick, P. J. (1997). Attention-deficit disorder without hyperactivity. In T. A. Widiger, A. J. Frances, H. A. Pincus, R. Ross, M. B. First, & W. Davis (Eds.), *DSM-IV sourcebook* (Vol. 3; pp. 163–188). Washington, DC: American Psychiatric Association.

Lahey, B. B., & Loeber, R. (1994). Framework for a developmental model of oppositional defiant disorder and conduct disorder. In D. K. Routh (Ed.), *Disruptive behavior disorders in childhood* (pp. 139–180). New York: Plenum.

Lahey, B. B., Loeber, R., Burke, J. D., & Applegate, B. (2005). Predicting future antisocial personality disorder in males from a clinical assessment in childhood. *Journal of Consulting and Clinical Psychology, 73,* 389–399.

Lahey, B. B., Loeber, R., Quay, H. C., Frick, P. J., & Grimm, J. (1992). Oppositional defiant and conduct disorders: Issues to be resolved for DSM-IV. *Journal of the American Academy of Child & Adolescent Psychiatry, 31,* 539–546.

Lahey, B. B., McBurnett, K., & Loeber, R. (2000). Are attention-deficit/hyperactivity disorder and oppositional defiant disorder developmental precursors to conduct disorder? In A. J. Sameroff, M. Lewis, & S. M. Miller (Eds.), *Handbook of developmental psychopathology* (pp. 431–446). New York: Kluwer Academic/Plenum.

Lahey, B. B., Pelham, W. E., Loney, J., Kipp, H., Ehrhardt, A., Lee, S. S., et al. (2004). Three-year predictive validity of DSM-IV attention deficit hyperactivity disorder in children diagnosed at 4–6 years of age. *American Journal of Psychiatry, 161,* 2014–2020.

Lahey, B. B., Pelham, W. E., Stein, M. A., Loney, J., Trapani, C., Nugent, K., et al. (1998). Validity of DSM-IV attention-deficit/hyperactivity disorder for younger children. *Journal of the American Academy of Child and Adolescent Psychiatry, 37,* 695–702.

Lahey, B. B., Schaughency, E. A., Hynd, G. W., Carlson, C. L., & Piacentini, J. C. (1987). Attention deficit disorder with and without hyperactivity: Comparison of behavioral characteristics of clinic-referred children. *Journal of the American Academy of Child and Adolescent Psychiatry, 26,* 718–723.

Lahey, B. B., & Waldman, I. D. (2003). A developmental propensity model of the origins of conduct problems during childhood and adolescence. In B. B. Lahey, T. E. Moffitt, & A. Caspi (Eds.), *Causes of conduct disorder and juvenile delinquency* (pp. 76–117). New York: Guilford Press.

Lahey, B. B., Waldman, I. D., & McBurnett, K. (1999). The development of antisocial behavior: An integrative causal model. *Journal of Child Psychology and Psychiatry, 40,* 669–682.

Laird, R. D., Pettit, G. S., Dodge, K. A., & Bates, J. E. (2003). Change in parents' monitoring knowledge: Links with parenting, relationship quality, adolescent beliefs, and antisocial behavior. *Social Development, 12,* 401–419.

Lambert, M. J., & Ogles, B. M. (2004). The efficacy and effectiveness of psychotherapy. In M. J. Lambert (Ed.), *Bergin and Garfield's handbook of psychotherapy and behavior change* (pp. 139–193). New York: Wiley.

Langleben, D. D., Austin, G., Krikorian, G., Ridlehuber, H. W., Goris, M. L., & Strauss, H. W. (2001). Interhemispheric asymmetry of regional cerebral blood flow in prepubescent boys with attention deficit hyperactivity disorder. *Nuclear Medicine, 22,* 1333–1340.

Lansford, J. E., Deater-Deckard, K., Dodge, K. A., Bates, J. E., & Pettit, G. S. (2004). Ethnic differences in the link between physical discipline and later adolescent externalizing behaviors. *Journal of Child Psychology and Psychiatry, 45,* 801–812.

Larsson, J., Larsson, H., & Lichtenstein, P. (2004). Genetic and environmental contributions to stability and change of ADHD symptoms between 8 and 13 years of age: A longitudinal twin study. *Journal of the American Academy of Child and Adolescent Psychiatry, 43,* 1267–1275.

Last, C. G., Perrin, S., Hersen, M., & Kazdin, A. E. (1992). DSM-III-R anxiety disorders in children: Sociodemographic and clinical characteristics. *Journal of the American Academy of Child and Adolescent Psychiatry, 31,* 1070–1076.

Last, C. G., Perrin, S., Hersen, M., & Kazdin, A. E. (1996). A prospective study of childhood anxiety disorders. *Journal of the American Academy of Child and Adolescent Psychiatry, 35,* 1502–1510.

Latimer, W. W., Ernst, J., Hennessey, J., Stinchfield, R. D., & Winters, K. C. (2004). Relapse among adolescent drug abusers following treatment: The role of probable ADHD status. *Journal of Child & Adolescent Substance Abuse, 13*, 1–16.

Latimer, W. W., Newcomb, M., Winters, K. C., & Stinchfield, R. D. (2000). Adolescent substance abuse treatment outcome: The role of substance abuse problem severity, psychosocial, and treatment factors. *Journal of Consulting and Clinical Psychology, 68*, 684–696.

Laumann, E. O., Paik, A., & Rosen, R. C. (1999). Sexual dysfunction in the United States: Prevalence and predictors. *Journal of the American Medical Association, 281*, 537–544.

Lawrence, C. J., Lott, I., & Haier, R. J. (2005). Neurobiology of autism, mental retardation, and Down syndrome. In C. Stough (Ed.), *Neurobiology of exceptionality* (pp. 125–142). New York: Kluwer Academic/Plenum.

Lawrence, N. S., Williams, A. M., Surguladze, S., Giampietro, V., Brammer, M. J., Andrew, C., et al. (2004). Subcortical and ventral prefrontal cortical neural responses to facial expressions distinguish patients with bipolar disorder and major depression. *Biological Psychiatry, 55*, 578–587.

Leach, J. M., Scarborough, H. S., & Rescorla, L. (2003). Late-emerging reading disabilities. *Journal of Educational Psychology, 95*, 211–224.

Lee, J. S., Kim, B. N., Kang, E., Lee, D. S., Kim, Y. K., Chung, J., et al. (2004). Regional cerebral blood flow in children with attention deficit hyperactivity disorder: Comparison before and after methylphenidate treatment. *Human Brain Mapping, 24*, 157–164.

Lekhwani, M., Nair, C., Nikhinson, I., & Ambrosini, P. J. (2004). Psychotropic prescription practices in child psychiatric inpatients 9 years old and younger. *Journal of Child and Adolescent Psychopharmacology, 14*, 95–103.

Lengua, L. J., Long, A. C., Smith, K. I., & Meltzoff, A. N. (2005). Pre-attack symptomatology and temperament as predictors of children's responses to the September 11 terrorist attacks. *Journal of Child Psychology and Psychiatry, 46*, 631–645.

Leventhal, T., & Brooks-Gunn, J. (2000). The neighborhoods they live in: The effects of neighborhood residence on child and adolescent outcomes. *Psychological Bulletin, 126*, 309–337.

Levy, F., Hay, D. A., Bennett, K. S., & McStephen, M. (2005). Gender differences in ADHD subtype comorbidity. *Journal of the American Academy of Child and Adolescent Psychiatry, 44*, 368–376.

Lewinsohn, P. M. (1974). A behavioral approach to depression. In R. J. Friedman, & M. M. Katz (Eds.), *The psychology of depression: Contemporary theory and research* (pp. 157–184). Washington, DC: Winston-Wiley.

Lewinsohn, P. M., Allen, N. B., Gotlib, I. H., & Seeley, J. R. (1999). First onset versus recurrence of depression: Differential processes of psychosocial risk. *Journal of Abnormal Psychology, 108*, 483–498.

Lewinsohn, P. M., Clarke, G. N., Hops, H., & Andrews, J. (1990). Cognitive-behavioral group treatment of depression in adolescents. *Behavior Therapy, 21*, 385–401.

Lewinsohn, P. M., Hops, H., Roberts, R. E., Seeley, J. R., & Andrews, J. A. (1993). Adolescent psychopathology: I. Prevalence and incidence of depression and other DSM-IV-III-R disorders in high school students. *Journal of Abnormal Psychology, 102*, 133–144.

Lewinsohn, P. M., Klein, J. R., & Klein, D. N. (1995). Bipolar disorder in a community sample of older adolescents: Prevalence, phenomenology, comorbidity and course. *Journal of the American Academy of Child & Adolescent Psychiatry, 34*, 454–463.

Lewinsohn, P. M., Roberts, R. E., Seeley, J. R., Rohde, P., Gotlib, I. H., & Hops, H. (1994). Adolescent psychopathology: II. Psychosocial risk factors for depression. *Journal of Abnormal Psychology, 103*, 302–315.

Lewinsohn, P. M., Rohde, P., & Seeley, J. R. (1994). Psychosocial risk factors for future adolescent suicide attempts. *Journal of Consulting and Clinical Psychology, 62*, 297–305.

Lewinsohn, P. M., Rohde, P., & Seeley, J. R. (1998). Major depressive disorder in older adolescents: Prevalence, risk factors, and clinical implications. *Clinical Psychology Review, 18*, 765–794.

Lewinsohn, P. M., Seeley, J. R., & Klein, D. N. (2003). Epidemiology and suicidal behavior. In B. Geller & M. P. DelBello (Eds.), *Bipolar disorder in childhood and early adolescence* (pp. 7–24). New York: Guilford Press.

Lewinsohn, P. M., Solomon, A., Seeley, J. R., & Zeiss, A. M. (2000). Clinical implications of "subthreshold" depressive symptoms. *Journal of Abnormal Psychology, 109*, 345–351.

Lewinsohn, P. M., Striegel-Moore, R. H., & Seeley, J. R. (2000). Epidemiology and natural course of eating disorders in young women from adolescence to young adulthood. *Journal of the American Academy of Child and Adolescent Psychiatry, 39*, 1284–1292.

Lewinsohn, P. M., Youngren, M. A., & Grosscup, S. J. (1979). Reinforcement and depression. In R. A. Dupue (Ed.), *The psychobiology of depressive disorders: Implications for the effects of stress* (pp. 291–316). New York: Academic Press.

Li, C. E., DiGiuseppe, R., & Froh, J. (2006). The roles of sex, gender, and coping in adolescent depression. *Adolescence, 41,* 409–415.

Libby, A. M., Orton, H. D., Novins, D. K., Spicer, P., Buchwald, D., Beals, J., et al. (2004). Childhood physical and sexual abuse and subsequent alcohol and drug use disorders in two American-Indian tribes. *Journal of Studies on Alcohol, 65,* 74–83.

Libby, A. M., Orton, H. D., Stover, S. K., & Riggs, P. D. (2005). What came first, major depression or substance use disorder? Clinical characteristics and substance use comparing teens in a treatment cohort. *Addictive Behaviors, 30,* 1649–1662.

Libby, S., Reynolds, S., Derisley, J., & Clark, S. (2004). Cognitive appraisals in young people with obsessive-compulsive disorder. *Journal of Child Psychology and Psychiatry, 45,* 1076–1084.

Liddle, H. A. (2004). Family-based therapies for adolescent alcohol and drug use: Research contributions and future research needs. *Addiction, 99,* 76–92.

Liddle, H. A., & Hogue, A. (2001). Multidimensional family therapy for adolescent substance abuse. In E. F. Wagner & H. B. Waldron (Eds.), *Innovations in adolescent substance abuse interventions* (pp. 229–261). Amsterdam: Pergamon/Elsevier Science.

Liddle, H. A., Oakof, G. A., Diamond, G. S., Parker, G. S., Barrett, K., & Tejeda, M. (2001). Multidimensional family therapy for adolescent substance abuse: Results of a randomized clinical trial. *American Journal of Drug and Alcohol Abuse, 27,* 651–687.

Liddle, H. A., & Rowe, C. L. (2006). *Adolescent substance abuse: Research and clinical advances.* New York: Cambridge University Press.

Liddle, H. A., Rowe, C. L., Dakof, G. A., Ungaro, R. A., & Henderson, C. E. (2004). Early intervention for adolescent substance abuse: Pretreatment to posttreatment outcomes of a randomized clinical trial comparing multidimensional family therapy and peer group treatment. *Journal of Psychoactive Drugs, 36,* 49–63.

Lilenfeld, L. R., Kaye, W. H., Greeno, C. G., Merikangas, K. R., Plotnicov, K., Pollice, C., et al. (1998). A controlled family study of anorexia nervosa and bulimia nervosa: Psychiatric disorders in first-degree relatives and effects of proband comorbidity. *Archives of General Psychiatry, 55,* 603–610.

Lin, H., Katsovich, L., Ghebremichael, M., Findley, D. B., Grantz, H., Lombroso, P. J., et al. (2007). Psychosocial stress predicts future symptom severities in children and adolescents with Tourette syndrome and/or obsessive-compulsive disorder. *Journal of Child Psychology and Psychiatry, 48,* 157–166.

Linnet, K. M., Dalsgaard, S., Obel, C., Wisborg, K., Henriksen, T. B., Rodriguez, A., et al. (2003). Maternal lifestyle factors in pregnancy risk of attention deficit hyperactivity disorder and associated behaviors: Review of the current evidence. *American Journal of Psychiatry, 160,* 1028–1040.

Linscheid, T. R., & Butz, C. (2003). Anorexia nervosa and bulimia nervosa. In M. C. Roberts (Ed.), *Handbook of pediatric psychology* (636–651). New York: Guilford Press.

Lipka, O., & Siegel, L. S. (2006). Learning disabilities. In D. A. Wolfe & E. J. Mash (Eds.), *Behavioral and emotional disorders in adolescents: Nature, assessment, and treatment* (pp. 410–443). New York: Guilford Press.

Lipton, J. S., & Spelke, S. (2003). Origins of number sense: Large-number discrimination in human infants. *Psychological Science, 14,* 396–401.

Lish, J. D., Dime-Meenan, S., Whybrow, P. C., Price, R. A., & Hirschfeld, R. M. (1997). The National Depressive and Manic-Depressive Association (NDMDA) survey of bipolar members. *Journal of Affective Disorders, 31,* 281–294.

Little, S. A., & Garber, J. (2005). The role of social stressors and interpersonal orientation in explaining the longitudinal relation between externalizing and depressive symptoms. *Journal of Abnormal Psychology, 114,* 432–443.

Lock, J. (2004). Family approaches to anorexia nervosa and bulimia nervosa. In J. K. Thompson (Ed.), *Handbook of eating disorders and obesity* (pp. 218–231). Hoboken, NJ: Wiley.

Loeber, R., & Farrington, D. P. (2000). Young children who commit crime: Epidemiology, developmental origins, risk factors, early interventions, and policy implications. *Development & Psychopathology, 12,* 737–762.

Loeber, R., Green, S. M., & Lahey, B. B. (1990). Mental health professionals' perception of the utility of children, mothers, and teachers as informants on childhood psychopathology. *Journal of Clinical Child Psychology, 19,* 136–143.

Loeber, R., & Hay, D. (1997). Key issues in the development of aggression and violence from childhood to early adulthood. *Annual Review of Psychology, 48,* 371–410.

Loeber, R., & Stouthamer-Loeber, M. (1986). Family factors as correlates & predictors of juvenile conduct problems and delinquency. In M. Tonry & N. Morris (Eds.), *Crime and justice: An annual review of research* (pp. 29–149). Chicago: University of Chicago Press.

Loeber, R., & Stouthamer-Loeber, M. (1998). Development of juvenile aggression and violence: Some common misconceptions and controversies. *American Psychologist, 53,* 242–259.

Loesch, D. Z., Bui, Q. M., Grigsby, J., Butler, E., Epstein, J., Huggins, R. M., et al. (2003). Effect of the fragile X status categories and the fragile X mental retardation protein levels on executive functioning in males and females with fragile X. *Neuropsychology, 17,* 646–657.

Lofthouse, N., & Fristad, A. (2004). Psychosocial interventions for children with early-onset bipolar spectrum disorder. *Clinical Child and Family Psychology Review, 7,* 71–88.

Loney, B. R., Frick, P. J., Clements, C. B., Ellis, M. L., & Kerlin, K. (2003). Callous-unemotional traits, impulsivity, and emotional processing in antisocial adolescents. *Journal of Clinical Child and Adolescent Psychology, 32,* 139–152.

Lonigan, C. J., Elbert, J. C., & Johnson, S. B. (1998). Empirically supported psychosocial interventions for children: An overview. *Journal of Clinical Child Psychology, 27,* 138–145.

Loomis, J. W. (2006). Learning disabilities. In R. T. Ammerman, (Ed.) *Comprehensive handbook of personality and psychopathology* (pp. 272–284). Hoboken, NJ: Wiley.

Lord, C., & McGee, J. P. (2001). *Educating children with autism: Committee on Educational Interventions for Children With Autism.* Washington, DC: National Academy Press.

Lord, C., & Richler, J. (2006). Early diagnosis of children with autism spectrum disorders. In T. Charman & W. Stone (Eds.), *Social and communication development in autism spectrum disorders* (pp. 35–59). New York: Guilford Press.

LoTurco, J. J., Wang, Y., & Paramasivam, M. (2006). Neuronal migration and dyslexia susceptibility. In G. D. Rosen (Ed.), *The dyslexic brain: New pathways in neuroscience discovery* (pp. 119–128). Mahwah, NJ: Erlbaum.

Lovaas, O. I. (1987). Behavioral treatment and normal educational and intellectual functioning in young autistic children. *Journal of Consulting and Clinical Psychology, 55,* 3–9.

Lovaas, O. I., Cross, S., & Revlin, S. (2006). Autistic disorder. In J. E. Fisher & W. T. O'Donohue (Eds.). *Practitioner's guide to evidence-based psychotherapies* (pp. 101–114). New York: Springer.

Lovaas, O. I., Koegel, R. L., Simmons, J. Q., & Long, J. S. (1973). Some generalization and follow-up measures on autistic children in behavior therapy. *Journal of Applied Behavior Analysis, 6,* 131–166.

Lovaas, O. I., & Smith, T. (2003). Early and intensive behavioral intervention in autism. In A. E. Kazdin & J. R. Weisz (Eds.), *Evidence-based psychotherapies for children and adolescents* (pp. 325–340). New York: Guilford Press.

Lovejoy, M. C., Graczyk, P. A., O'Hare, E., & Neuman, G. (2000). Maternal depression and parenting behavior: A meta-analytic review. *Clinical Psychology Review, 20,* 561–592.

Lovejoy, M. C., Weis, R., O'Hare, E., & Rubin, E. C. (1999). Development and initial validation of the Parent Behavior Inventory. *Psychological Assessment, 11,* 534–545.

Lovett, M. W., & Barron, R. W. (2002). The search for individual and subtype differences in reading disabled children's response to remediation. In D. L. Molfese & V. J. Molfese (Eds.), *Developmental variations in learning* (pp. 309–338). Mahwah, NJ: Erlbaum.

Luby, J. L., Belden, A. C., & Spitznagel, E. (2006). Risk factors for preschool depression: The mediating role of early stressful life events. *Journal of Child Psychology and Psychiatry, 47,* 1292–1298.

Lucka, I. (2006). Depressive disorders in patients suffering from anorexia nervosa. *Archives of Psychiatry and Psychotherapy, 8*(2), 55–61.

Luckasson, R., Borthwick-Duffy, S., Buntinx, W. H. E., Coulter, D. L., Craig, E. M., Reeve, A., et al. (2002). *Mental retardation: Definition, classification, and systems of support.* Washington, DC: American Association on Mental Retardation.

Lundahl, B., Risser, H. J., & Lovejoy, M. C. (2006). A meta-analysis of parent training: Moderators and follow-up effects. *Clinical Psychology Review, 26,* 86–104.

Lundgren, J. D., Danoff-Burg, S., & Anderson, D. A. (2004). Cognitive-behavioral therapy for bulimia nervosa: An empirical analysis of clinical significance. *International Journal of Eating Disorders, 35,* 262–274.

Luntz, B., & Widom, C. S. (1994). Antisocial personality disorder in abused and neglected children grown up. *American Journal of Psychiatry, 151,* 670–674.

Luthar, S. S. (2006). Resilience in development: A synthesis of research across five decades. In D. Cicchetti & D. J. Cohen (Eds.), *Developmental psychopathology, Vol. 3: Risk, disorder, and adaptation* (pp. 739–795). Hoboken, NJ: Wiley.

Luthar, S. S., & Latendresse, J. (2005). Children of the affluent: Challenges to well-being. *Current Directions in Psychological Science, 14,* 49–53.

Lyon, G. R., Fletcher, J. M., & Barnes, M. C. (2003). Learning disabilities. In E. J. Mash & R. A. Barkley (Eds.), *Child psychopathology* (2nd ed., pp. 520–588). New York: Guilford Press.

Lyon, G. R., Fletcher, J. M., Fuchs, L. S., & Chhabra, V. (2006). Learning disabilities. In E. J. Mash & R. A. Barkley (Eds.), *Treatment of childhood disorders* (pp. 512–591). New York: Guilford Press.

Lyon, G. R., Fletcher, J. M., Shaywitz, S. E., Shaywitz, A. A., Torgesen, J. K., Wood, F. B., et al. (2001). Rethinking learning disabilities. In C. E. Finn, Jr., R. A. J. Rotherham, & C. R. Hokanson, Jr. (Eds.), *Rethinking special education for a new century* (pp. 259–287). Washington, DC: Thomas B. Fordham Foundation and Progressive Policy Institute.

Maag, J. W., & Irvin, M. (2005). Alcohol use and depression among African-American and caucasian adolescents. *Adolescence, 40,* 87–101.

MacArthur, C., Graham, S., & Schwartz, S. (1991). Knowledge of revision and revising behavior among students with learning disabilities. *Learning Disability Quarterly, 14,* 61–74.

Maccoby, E. E., & Martin, J. A. (1983). Socialization in the context of the family: Parent–child interaction. In P. H. Mussen (Ed.) & E. M. Hetherington (Vol. Ed.), *Handbook of child psychology: Vol. 4. Socialization, personality, and social development* (pp. 1–101). New York: Wiley.

Mackinaw-Koons, B., & Fristad, A. (2004). Children with bipolar disorder: How to break down barriers and work effectively together. *Professional Psychology: Research and Practice, 35,* 481–484.

MacMaster, F. P., & Kusumakar, V. (2004). MRI study of the pituitary gland in adolescent depression. *Journal of Psychiatric Research, 38,* 231–236.

MacPhee, A. R., & Andrews, W. (2006). Risk factors for depression in early adolescence. *Adolescence, 41,* 435–466.

Maher, B. S., Marazita, M. L., Ferrell, R. E., Vanyukov, M. M. (2002). Dopamine system genes and attention deficit hyperactivity disorder: A meta-analysis. *Psychiatric Genetics, 12,* 207–215.

Maher, M. S. (1980). Group psychotherapy for anorexia nervosa. In P. S. Powers & R. C. Fernandez (Eds.), *Current treatment for anorexia nervosa and bulimia* (pp. 265–276). Basel, Switzerland: Karger.

Main, M., Kaplan, N., & Cassidy, J. (1985). Security in infancy, childhood, and adulthood: A move to the level of representation. *Monographs of the Society for Research in Child Development, 50,* 66–104.

Malkoff-Schwartz, S., Frank, E., Anderson, B., Sherrill, J. T., Siegel, L., Patterson, D., et al. (1998). Stressful life events and social rhythm disruption in the onset of manic and depressive bipolar episodes: A preliminary investigation. *Archives of General Psychiatry, 55,* 702–707.

Mammen, O., Kolko, D., & Pilkonis, P. (2003). Parental cognitions and satisfaction: Relationship to aggressive parental behavior in child physical abuse. *Child Maltreatment, 8,* 288–301.

Manassis, K. (2001). Child-parent relations: Attachment and anxiety disorders. In W. K. Silverman & P. D. A. Treffers (Eds.), *Anxiety disorders in children and adolescents* (pp. 255–272). New York: Cambridge University Press.

Manassis, K., Bradley, S., Goldberg, S., Hood, J., & Swinson, R. P. (1994). Attachment in mothers with anxiety disorders and their children. *Journal of the American Academy of Child & Adolescent Psychiatry, 33,* 1106–1113.

Mandlawitz, M. R. (2004). Educating children with autism: Current legal issues. In F. R. Volkmar, R. Paul, A. Klin, & D. Cohen (Eds.), *Handbook of autism and pervasive developmental disorders, Vol. 2: Assessment, interventions, and policy* (pp. 1161–1173). New York: Wiley.

Manicavasagar, V., Silove, D., Curtis, J., & Wagner, R. (2000). Continuities of separation anxiety from early life into adulthood. *Journal of Anxiety Disorders, 14,* 1–18.

Mannarino, A., & Cohen, J. (1996). Abuse-related attributions and perceptions, general attributions, and locus of control in sexually abused girls. *Journal of Interpersonal Violence, 11,* 162–180.

Mannuzza, S., Klein, R. G., Abikoff, H., & Moulton, J. L. (2004). Significance of childhood conduct problems to later development of conduct disorder among children with ADHD: A prospective follow-up study. *Journal of Abnormal Child Psychology, 32,* 565–573.

March, J. (1998). Cognitive behavioral psychotherapy for pediatric OCD. In M. Jenike, L. Baer, & W. E. Minichiello (Eds.), *Obsessive-compulsive disorders* (pp. 400–420). Philadelphia: Mosby.

March, J., Biederman, J., Wolkow, R., Safferman, A., Mardekian, J., Cook, E. H., et al. (1998). Sertraline in children and adolescents with obsessive-compulsive disorder: A multicenter randomized controlled trial. *Journal of the American Medical Association, 280,* 1752–1756.

March, J. S., Franklin, M., & Foa, E. (2005). Cognitive-behavioral psychotherapy for pediatric obsessive-compulsive disorder. In E. D. Hibbs & P. S. Jensen (Eds.), *Psychosocial treatments for child and adolescent disorders: Empirically based strategies for clinical practice* (pp. 121–142). Washington, DC: American Psychological Association.

March, J. S., Franklin, M. E., Leonard, H. L., & Foa, E. (2004). Obsessive-compulsive disorder. In T. L. Morris & J. S. March (Eds.), *Anxiety disorders in children and adolescents* (pp. 212–240). New York: Guilford Press.

March, J. S., Mulle, K., & Herbel, B. (1994). Behavioral psychotherapy for children and adolescents with obsessive-compulsive disorder: An open trial of a new protocol-driven treatment package. *Journal of the American Academy of Child and Adolescent Psychiatry, 33,* 333–341.

March, J., & Wells, K. (2003). Combining medication and psychotherapy. In A. Martin, L. Scahill, D. S. Charney, & J. F. Leckman (Eds.), *Pediatric psychopharmacology: Principles and practice* (pp. 326–346). London: Oxford University Press.

Marchand, W. R., Wirth, L., & Simon, C. (2005). Adverse life events and pediatric bipolar disorder in a community mental health setting. *Community Mental Health Journal, 41,* 67–75.

Marino, C., & Molteni, M. (2006). Chromosome 15 and developmental dyslexia. In G. D. Rosen (Ed.), *The dyslexic brain: New pathways in neuroscience discovery* (pp. 107–118). Mahwah, NJ: Erlbaum.

Markie-Dadds, C., & Sanders, R. (2006). Self-directed Triple P (positive parenting program) for mothers with children at risk of developing conduct problems. *Behavioural and Cognitive Psychotherapy, 34,* 259–275.

Marlatt, G. A., & Gordon, J. R. (1985) *Relapse prevention: Maintenance strategies in the treatment of addictive behaviors.* New York: Guilford Press.

Marmorstein, N. R., & Iacono, G. (2004). Major depression and conduct disorder in youth: Associations with parental psychopathology and parent-child conflict. *Journal of Child Psychology and Psychiatry, 45,* 377–386.

Marsh, P. J., & Williams, L. M. (2004). An investigation of individual typologies of attention-deficit hyperactivity disorder using cluster analysis of DSM-IV criteria. *Personality and Individual Differences, 36,* 1187–1195.

Marshal, M. P., Molina, B. S. G., & Pelham, W. E. (2003). Childhood ADHD and adolescent substance use: An examination of deviant peer group affiliation as a risk factor. *Psychology of Addictive Behaviors, 17,* 293–302.

Martin, A., Scahill, L., Klin, A., & Volkmar, F. R. (1999). Higher-functioning pervasive developmental disorders: Rates and pattern of psychotropic drug use. *Journal of the American Academy of Child & Adolescent Psychiatry, 38,* 923–931.

Martin, C. S., Chung, T., Kirisci, L., & Langenbucher, J. W. (2006). Item response theory analysis of diagnostic criteria for alcohol and cannabis use disorders in adolescents: Implications for DSM-V. *Journal of Abnormal Psychology, 115,* 807–814.

Martin, G., Bergen, H. A., Richardson, A. S., Roeger, L., & Allison, S. (2004). Sexual abuse and suicidality: Gender differences in a large community sample of adolescents. *Child Abuse & Neglect, 28,* 491–503.

Martin, G., Rozanes, P., Pearce, C., & Allison, S. (1995). Adolescent suicide, depression, and family dysfunction. *Acta Psychiatrica Scandinavica, 92,* 336–344.

Mash, E. J., & Johnston, C. (1990). Determinants of parenting stress: Illustrations from families of hyperactive children and families of physically abused children. *Journal of Clinical Psychology, 19,* 313–328.

Masi, G., Favilla, L., Mucci, M., & Millepiedi, S. (2000). Depressive comorbidity in children and adolescents with generalized anxiety disorder. *Child Psychiatry and Human Development, 30,* 205–215.

Masi, G., Millepiedi, S., Mucci, M., Poli, P., Bertini, N., & Milantoni, L. (2004). Generalized anxiety disorder in referred children and adolescents. *Journal of the American Academy of Child & Adolescent Psychiatry, 43,* 752–760.

Masi, G., Perugi, G., Millepiedi, S., Mucci, M., Toni, C., Bertini, N., et al. (2006). Development differences according to age at onset in juvenile bipolar disorder. *Journal of Child and Adolescent Psychopharmacology, 16,* 679–685.

Masi, G., Perugi, G., Toni, C., Millepiedi, S., Mucci, M., Bertini, N., et al. (2006). The clinical phenotypes of juvenile bipolar disorder: Toward a validation of the episodic-chronic distinction. *Biological Psychiatry, 59,* 603–610.

Masten, A. S., Burt, K. B., & Coatsworth, J. D. (2006). Competence and psychopathology in development. In D. Cicchetti & D. J. Cohen (Eds.), *Developmental psychopathology, Vol 3: Risk, disorder, and adaptation* (pp. 696–738). Hoboken, NJ: Wiley.

Mather, N., & Schrank, F. A. (2003). Using the Woodcock-Johnson III discrepancy procedures for diagnosing learning disabilities. In F. A. Schrank & D. P. Flanagan (Eds.), *WJ III clinical use and interpretation: Scientist-practitioner perspectives* (pp. 175–198). San Diego, CA: Academic Press.

Maughan, B., Rowe, R., Messer, J., Goodman, R., & Meltzer, H. (2004). Conduct disorder and oppositional defiant disorder in a national sample: Developmental epidemiology. *Journal of Child Psychology and Psychiatry, 45,* 609–621.

Maxfield, M. G., & Widom, C. S. (1996). The cycle of violence: Revisited six years later. *Archives of Pediatrics and Adolescent Medicine, 150,* 390–395.

Mayes, S. D., & Calhoun, L. (2006). Frequency of reading, math, and writing disabilities in children with clinical disorders. *Learning and Individual Differences, 16,* 145–157.

Mayes, S. D., Calhoun, S. L., & Grites, D. L. (2001). Does DSM-IV Asperger's disorder exist? *Journal of Abnormal Child Psychology, 29,* 263–271.

Mazzocco, M. M., & McCloskey, M. (2005). Math performance in girls with Turner or fragile X syndrome. In J. I. D. Campbell (Ed.), *Handbook of mathematical cognition* (pp. 269–297). New York: Psychology Press.

Mazzocco, M. M., Pennington, B. F., & Hagerman, R. J. (1993). The neurocognitive phenotype of female carriers of fragile X: Further evidence for specificity. *Journal of Developmental and Behavioural Pediatrics, 14,* 328–335.

McBride, C., Atkinson, L., Quilty, L. C., & Bagby, R. M. (2006). Attachment as moderator of treatment outcome in major depression: A randomized control trial of interpersonal psychotherapy versus cognitive behavior therapy. *Journal of Consulting and Clinical Psychology, 74,* 1041–1054.

McBurnett, K. (1997). Attention-deficit/hyperactivity disorder: A review of diagnostic issues. In T. A. Widiger, A. J., Frances, H. A. Pincus, R. Ross, M. B. First, & W. Davis (Eds.), *DSM-IV sourcebook* (Vol. 3; pp. 111–143). Washington, DC: American Psychiatric Association.

McBurnett, K., Lahey, B. B., Rathouz, P. J., & Loeber, R. (2000). Low salivary cortisol and persistent aggression in boys referred for disruptive behavior. *Archives of General Psychiatry, 57,* 38–43.

McBurnett, K., Pfiffner, L. J., & Frick, P. J. (2001). Symptom properties as a function of ADHD type: An argument for continued study of the sluggish cognitive tempo. *Journal of Abnormal Child Psychology, 29,* 207–213.

McBurnett, K., Raine, A., Stouthamer-Loeber, M., Loeber, R., Kumar, A. M., Kumar, M., et al. (2005). Mood and hormone responses to psychological challenge in adolescent males with conduct problems. *Biological Psychiatry, 57,* 1109–1116.

McCabe, M. P., & Ricciardelli, A. (2001). Body image and body change techniques among young adolescent boys. *European Eating Disorders Review, 9,* 335–347.

McCambridge, J., & Strang, J. (2004). The efficacy of single-session motivational interviewing in reducing drug consumption and perceptions of drug-related risk and harm among young people: Results from a multi-site cluster randomized trial. *Addiction, 99,* 39–52.

McCandliss, B., Cohen, L., & Dehaene, S. (2003). The visual word form area: Expertise in reading in the fusiform gyrus. *Trends in Cognitive Science, 7,* 293–299.

McCarthy, D. M., Tomlinson, K. L., Anderson, K. G., Marlatt, G. A., & Brown, S. A. (2005). Relapse in alcohol- and drug-disordered adolescents with comorbid psychopathology: Changes in psychiatric symptoms. *Psychology of Addictive Behaviors, 19,* 28–34.

McCauley, E., Myers, K., Mitchell, J., Calderon, R., Schloredt, K., & Treder, R. (1993). Depression in young people: Initial presentation and clinical course. *Journal of the American Academy of Child and Adolescent Psychiatry, 32,* 714–722.

McClead, R. E., Menke, J. A., & Coury, D. L. (1996). Major technological breakthroughs in the diagnosis of mental retardation. In J. W. Jacobson & J. A. Mulick (Eds.), *Manual of diagnosis and professional practice in mental retardation* (pp. 179–190). Washington, DC: American Psychological Association.

McDermott, B., Forbes, D., Harris, C., McCormack, J., & Gibbon, P. (2006). Non-eating disorders psychopathology in children and adolescents with eating disorders: Implications for malnutrition and symptom severity. *Journal of Psychosomatic Research, 60,* 257–261.

McDermott, P. A., Goldberg, M. M., Watkins, M. W., Stanley, J. L., & Glutting, J. J. (2006). A nationwide epidemiologic modeling study of LD: Risk, protection, and unintended impact. *Journal of Learning Disabilities, 39,* 230–251.

McEachin, J. J., Smith, T., & Lovaas, O. I. (1993). Long-term outcome for children with autism who received early intensive behavioral treatment. *American Journal on Mental Retardation, 97,* 359–372.

McFall, R. M. (1991). Manifesto for a science of clinical psychology. *The Clinical Psychologist, 44,* 75–88.

McGoey, K. E., DuPaul, G. J., Eckert, T. L., Volpe, R. J., & van Brakle, J. (2005). Outcomes of a multi-component intervention for preschool children at-risk for attention-deficit/hyperactivity disorder. *Child and Family Behavior Therapy, 27,* 33–56.

McGough, J. J., Biederman, J., Wigal, S. B., Lopez, F. A., McCracken, J. T., Spencer, T., et al. (2005). Long-term tolerability and effectiveness of once-daily mixed amphetamine salts (Adderall XR) in children with ADHD. *Journal of the American Academy of Child and Adolescent Psychiatry, 44,* 530–538.

McGough, J. J., McCracken, J., Swanson, J., Riddle, M., Kollins, S., Greenhill, L., et al. (2006). Pharmacogenetics of methylphenidate response in preschoolers with ADHD. *Journal of the American Academy of Child & Adolescent Psychiatry, 45,* 1314–1322.

McGue, M., Iacono, W. G., Legrand, L. N., & Elkins, I. (2001a). Origins and consequences of age at first drink II. Familial risk and heritability. *Alcoholism: Clinical and Experimental Research, 25,* 1166–1173.

McGue, M., Iacono, W. G., Legrand, L., Malone, S., & Elkins, I. (2001b). Origins and consequences of age at first drink I. Associations with substance-use disorders, disinhibitory behavior and psycho-pathology, and P3 amplitude. *Alcoholism: Clinical and Experimental Research, 25,* 1156–1165.

McGue, M., Pickens, R. W., & Svikis, D. S. (1992). Sex and age effects on the inheritance of alcohol problems: A twin study. *Journal of Abnormal Psychology, 101,* 3–17.

McKee, T. E., Harvey, E., Danforth, J. S., Ulaszek, W. R., & Friedman, J. L. (2004). The relation between parental coping styles and parent-child interactions before and after treatment for children with ADHD and oppositional behavior. *Journal of Clinical Child and Adolescent Psychology, 33,* 158–168.

McKnight, C. D., Compton, S. N., & March, J. S. (2004). Posttraumatic stress disorder. In T. L. Morris & J. S. March (Eds.), *Anxiety disorders in children and adolescents* (pp. 241–262). New York: Guilford Press.

McKnight Risk Factor Study. (2003). Risk factors for the onset of eating disorders in adolescent girls: Results of the McKnight Longitudinal Risk Factor Study. *American Journal of Psychiatry, 160,* 248–254.

McLaren, J., & Bryson, E. (1987). Review of recent epidemiological studies of mental retardation: Prevalence, associated disorders, and etiology. *American Journal on Mental Retardation, 92,* 243–254.

McLeer, S. V., Deblinger, E., Henry, D., & Orvaschel, H. (1992). Sexually abused children at high risk for post-traumatic stress disorder. *Journal of the American Academy of Adolescent and Child Psychiatry, 31,* 875–879.

McLeod, B. D., & Weisz, J. R. (2004). Using dissertations to examine potential bias in child and adolescent clinical trials. *Journal of Consulting and Clinical Psychology, 72,* 235–251.

McLoyd, V. C. (1998). Socioeconomic disadvantage and child development. *American Psychologist, 53,* 185–204.

McLoyd, V. C., Hill, N. E., & Dodge, K. A. (2005). *African American family life: Ecological and cultural diversity.* New York: Guilford Press.

McMahon, R. J., & Frick, J. (2005). Evidence-based assessment of conduct problems in children and adolescents. *Journal of Clinical Child and Adolescent Psychology, 34,* 477–505.

Melik, E., Babar-Melik, E., Ozgunen, T., & Binokay, S. (2000). Median raphe nucleus mediates forming long-term but not short-term contextual fear conditioning in rats. *Behavioural Brain Research, 112,* 145–150.

Meltzer, H., Gatward, R., Goodman, R., & Ford, T. (2003). Mental health of children and adolescents in Great Britain. *International Review of Psychiatry, 15,* 185–187.

Merikangas, K. R. (2005). Vulnerability factors for anxiety disorders in children and adolescents. *Child and Adolescent Psychiatric Clinics of North America, 14,* 649–679.

Mesibov, G. (1997). Formal and informal measures on the effectiveness of the TEACCH program. *Autism, 1,* 25–35.

Mesibov, G. B., & Shea, V. (1996). Full inclusion and students with autism. *Journal of Autism and Developmental Disorders, 26,* 337–346.

Mesibov, G. B., Shea, V., & Schopler, E. (2005). *The TEACCH approach to autism spectrum disorders.* New York: Springer.

Metz, B., Mulick, J. A., & Butter, E. M. (2005). Autism: A late 20th-century fad magnet. In J. W. Jacobson, R. M. Foxx, & J. A. Mulick (Eds.), *Controversial therapies for developmental disabilities: Fad, fashion and science in professional practice* (pp. 237–263). Mahwah, NJ: Erlbaum.

Meyer, J., Rutter, M., Silberg, J., Maes, H., Simonoff, E., Shillady, L., et al. (2000). Familial aggregation for conduct disorder symptomatology: The role of genes, marital discord and family adaptability. *Psychological Medicine, 30,* 759–774.

Meyer, J. S., & Quenzer, L. F. (2005). *Psychopharmacology: Drugs, the brain, and behavior.* Sunderland, MA: Sinauer Associates.

Meyers, S. A., & Battistoni, J. (2003). Proximal and distal correlates of adolescent mothers' parenting attitudes. *Journal of Applied Developmental Psychology, 24,* 33–49.

Mezulis, A. H., Hyde, J. S., & Abramson, L. Y. (2006). The developmental origins of cognitive vulnerability to depression: Temperament, parenting, and negative life events in childhood as contributors to negative cognitive style. *Developmental Psychology, 42,* 1012–1025.

Michelson, D., Allen, A. J., Busner, J. Casat, C., Dunn, D., Kratochvil, C., et al. (2002). Once-daily atomoxetine treatment for children and adolescents with attention-deficit/hyperactivity disorder: A randomized, placebo-controlled study. *American Journal of Psychiatry, 159,* 1896–1901.

Michelson, D., Faries, D. Wernicke, J. Kelsey, D. Kendrick, K., Sallee, F., et al. (2001). Atomoxetine in the treatment of children and adolescents with attention-deficit/hyperactivity disorder: A randomized, placebo-controlled, dose-response study. *Pediatrics, 108,* E83.

Mick, E., Biederman, J., Faraone, S. V., Sayer, J., & Kleinman, S. (2002). Case-control study of attention-deficit hyperactivity disorder and maternal smoking, alcohol use, and drug use during pregnancy. *Journal of the American Academy of Child and Adolescent Psychiatry, 41,* 378–385.

Miklowitz, D. J., George, E. L., Axelson, D. A., Kim, E. Y., Birmaher, B., Schneck, C., et al. (2004). Family-focused treatment for adolescents with bipolar disorder. *Journal of Affective Disorders, 82,* S113–S128.

Miklowitz, D. J., George, E. L., Richards, J. A., Simoneau, T. L., & Suddath, R. L. (2003). A randomized study of family-focused psychoeducation and pharmacotherapy in the outpatient management of bipolar disorder. *Archives of General Psychiatry, 60,* 904–912.

Milberger, S., Biederman, J., Faraone, S. V., Chen, L., & Jones, J. (1997). ADHD is associated with early initiation of cigarette smoking in children and adolescents. *Journal of Academic Child Adolescent Psychiatry, 36,* 37–44.

Milin, R., Walker, S., & Chow, J. (2003). Major depressive disorder in adolescence: A brief review of the recent treatment literature. *Canadian Journal of Psychiatry, 48,* 600–606.

Miller, A. B., & Cross, T. (2006). Ethnicity in child maltreatment research: A replication of Behl et al.'s content analysis. *Child Maltreatment, 11,* 16–26.

Miller, B. A., & Mancuso, F. (2004). Connecting childhood victimization to later alcohol/drug problems: Implications for prevention. *Journal of Primary Prevention, 25,* 149–169.

Miller, E. T., Turner, A. P., & Marlatt, G. A. (2001). The harm reduction approach to the secondary prevention of alcohol problems in adolescents and young adults. In P. Monti, S. M. Colby, & T. A. O'Leary (Eds.), *Adolescents, alcohol, and substance abuse: Reaching teens through brief interventions* (pp. 58–79). New York: Guilford Press.

Miller, W. R., & Rollnick, S. (2002). *Motivational interviewing: Preparing people for change.* New York: Guilford Press.

Milner, J. S. (1998). Individual and family characteristics associated with intrafamilial child physical and sexual abuse. In P. K. Trickett & C. J. Schellenbach (Eds.), *Violence against children in the family and community* (pp. 141–170). Washington, DC: American Psychological Association.

Milner, J. S. (2003). Social information processing in high-risk and physically abusive parents. *Child Abuse & Neglect, 27,* 7–20.

Milos, G., Spindler, A., Hepp, U., & Schnyder, U. (2004). Suicide attempts and suicidal ideation: Links with psychiatric comorbidity in eating disorder subjects. *General Hospital Psychiatry, 26,* 129–135.

Mink, J. K., & Mandelbaum, D. E. (2006). Stereotypies and repetitive behaviors: Clinical assessment and brain basis. In R. Tuchman & I. Rapin (Eds.), *Autism: A neurological disorder of early brain development* (pp. 68–78). London: MacKeith Press.

Minuchin, S. (1974). *Families and family therapy.* Cambridge, MA: Harvard University Press.

Minuchin, S., Rosman, B., & Baker, I. (1978). *Psychosomatic families: Anorexia nervosa in context.* Cambridge, MA: Harvard University Press.

Miranda, A. O., & Corcoran, C. L. (2000). Comparison of perpetration characteristics between male juvenile and adult sexual offenders: Preliminary results. *Sexual Abuse: Journal of Research & Treatment, 12,* 179–188.

Misener, V. L., Luca, P., Azeke, O., Crosbie, J., Waldman, I., Tannock, R., et al. (2004). Linkage of the dopamine receptor D1 gene to attention-deficit/hyperactivity disorder. *Molecular Psychiatry, 9,* 500–509.

Missale, C., Nash, S. R., Robinson, S. W., Jaber, M., & Caron, M. G. (1998). Dopamine receptors: From structure to function. *Physiological Review, 78,* 189–225.

Mix, K. S., Huttenlocher, J., & Levine, S. C. (2002). Multiple cues for quantification in infancy: Is number one of them? *Psychological Bulletin, 128,* 278–294.

Moffitt, T. E. (1993). Adolescence-limited and life-course persistent antisocial behavior: A developmental taxonomy. *Psychological Review, 100,* 674–701.

Moffitt, T. E. (2003). Life-course persistent and adolescence-limited antisocial behavior: A 10-year research review and research agenda. In B. B. Lahey, T. E. Moffitt, & A. Caspi (Eds.), *Causes of conduct disorder and juvenile delinquency* (pp. 49–75). New York: Guilford Press.

Moffitt, T. E., & Caspi, A. (2001). Childhood predictors differentiate life-course persistent and adolescence-limited antisocial pathways in males and females. *Development & Psychopathology, 13,* 355–376.

Moffitt, T. E., Caspi, A., Harrington, H., & Milne, B. (2002). Males on the life-course persistent and adolescence-limited antisocial pathways: Follow-up at age 26. *Development and Psychopathology, 14,* 179–206.

Moffitt, T. E., Caspi, A., Rutter, M., & Silva, P. A. (2001). *Sex differences in antisocial behaviour: Conduct disorder, delinquency, and violence in the Dunedin Longitudinal Study.* Cambridge, UK: Cambridge University Press.

Monroe, B. W., & Troia, A. (2006). Teaching writing strategies to middle school students with disabilities. *Journal of Educational Research, 100,* 21–33.

Monroe, S. M., Rhode, P., Seeley, J. R., & Lewinsohn, P. M. (1999). Life events and depression in adolescence: Relationship loss as a prospective risk factor for the first onset major depressive disorder. *Journal of Abnormal Psychology, 108,* 606–614.

Monti, P. M., Barnett, N. P., O'Leary, T. A., & Colby, S. M. (2001). Motivational enhancement for alcohol-involved adolescents. In P. M. Monti, S. M. Colby, & T. A. O'Leary (Eds.), *Adolescents, alcohol, and substance abuse: Reaching teens through brief interventions* (pp. 145–182). New York: Guilford Press.

Monti, P. M., Colby, S. M., Barnett, N. P., Spirito, A., Rohsenow, D. J., Myers, M., et al. (1999). Brief intervention for harm reduction with alcohol-positive older adolescents in a hospital emergency department. *Journal of Consulting and Clinical Psychology, 67,* 989–994.

Monuteaux, M. C., Fitzmaurice, G., Blacker, D., Buka, S. L., & Biederman, J. (2004). Specificity in the familial aggregation of overt and covert conduct disorder symptoms in a referred attention-deficit hyperactivity disorder sample. *Psychological Medicine, 34,* 1113–1127.

Moore, P. S., Whaley, S. E., & Sigman, M. (2004). Interactions between mothers and children: Impacts of maternal and child anxiety. *Journal of Abnormal Psychology, 113,* 471–476.

Morris, T. L. (2004). Social development. In T. L. Morris & J. S. March (Eds.), *Anxiety disorders in children and adolescents* (pp. 59–70). New York: Guilford Press.

Mostofsky, S., Cooper, K., Kates, W., Denckla, M., & Kaufmann, W. (2002). Smaller prefrontal and premotor volumes in boys with attention-deficit/hyperactivity disorder. *Biological Psychiatry, 52,* 785–794.

Mowrer, O. (1960). *Learning theory and behavior.* New York: Wiley.

MTA Cooperative Group. (1999). A 14-month randomized clinical trial of treatment strategies for attention-deficit/hyperactivity disorder. *Archives of General Psychiatry, 56,* 1073–1086.

Muehlenkamp, J. J., & Gutierrez, M. (2004). An investigation of differences between self-injurious behavior and suicide attempts in a sample of adolescents. *Suicide and Life-Threatening Behavior, 34,* 12–23.

Mufson, L., & Pollack Dorta, K. (2003). Interpersonal psychotherapy for depressed adolescents. In A. E. Kazdin & J. R. Weisz (Eds.), *Evidence-based psychotherapies for children and adolescents* (pp. 148–164). New York: Guildford Press.

Mufson, L., Pollack Dorta, K., Moreau, D., & Weissman, M. M. (2005). Efficacy to effectiveness: Adaptations of interpersonal psychotherapy for adolescent depression. In E. D. Hibbs & P. S. Jensen (Eds.), *Psychosocial treatments for child and adolescent disorders: Empirically based strategies for clinical practice* (pp. 165–186). Washington, DC: American Psychological Association.

Mufson, L., Pollack Dorta, K., Wickramaratne, P., Nomura, Y., Olfson, M., & Weissman, M. M. (2004). A randomized effectiveness trial of interpersonal psychotherapy for depressed adolescents. *Archives of General Psychiatry, 61,* 577–584.

Mufson, L., Weissman, M. M., Moreau, D., & Garfinkel, R. (1999). Efficacy of interpersonal psychotherapy for depressed adolescents. *Archives of General Psychiatry, 56,* 573–579.

Mullen, P. E., Martin, J. L., Anderson, J. C., Romans, S. E., & Herbison, G. P. (1994). The effect of child sexual abuse on social, interpersonal and sexual function in adult life. *British Journal of Psychiatry, 165,* 35–47.

Mundy, P., & Burnette, C. (2005). Joint attention and neurodevelopmental models of autism. In F. R. Volkmar, R. Paul, A. Klin, & D. Cohen (Eds.), *Handbook of autism and pervasive developmental disorders, Vol. 1: Diagnosis, development, neurobiology, and behavior* (pp. 650–681). Hoboken, NJ: Wiley.

Mundy, P., & Thorp, D. (2006). The neural basis of early joint-attention behavior. In T. Charman & W. Stone (Eds.), *Social and communication development in autism spectrum disorders* (pp. 296–336). New York: Guilford Press.

Murberg, T. A., & Bru, E. (2005). The role of coping styles as predictors of depressive symptoms among adolescents: A prospective study. *Scandinavian Journal of Psychology, 46,* 385–393.

Muris, P., Mayer, P., & Meesters, C. (2000). Self-reported attachment style, anxiety, and depression in children. *Social Behavior and Personality, 28,* 157–162.

Muris, P., Merckelbach, H., Gadet, B., & Moulaert, V. (2000). Fears, worries, and scary dreams in 4- to 12-year-old children: Their content, developmental pattern, and origins. *Journal of Clinical Child Psychology, 29,* 43–52.

Muris, P., Merckelbach, H., Mayer, B., & Meesters, C. (1998). Common fears and their relationship to anxiety disorders symptomatology in normal children. *Personality and Individual Differences, 24,* 575–578.

Murnen, S., & Smolak, L. (1998). Femininity, masculinity, and disordered eating: A meta-analytic approach. *International Journal of Eating Disorders, 22,* 231–242.

Murnen, S. K., Smolak, L., Mills, I. A., & Good, L. (2003). Thin, sexy women and strong, muscular men: Grade-school children's responses to objectified images of women and men. *Sex Roles, 49,* 427–437.

Murphy, K. R., & Barkley, R. A. (1996). Prevalence of ADHD and ODD symptoms in a community sample of adult licensed drivers. *Journal of Attention Disorders, 1,* 147–161.

Nace, E. P. (2005). Alcohol. In R. J. Frances, S. I. Miller, & A. H. Mack (Eds.), *Clinical textbook of addictive disorders* (pp. 75–104). New York: Guilford Press.

Nadder, T. S., Rutter, M., Silberg, J. L., Maes, H. H., & Eaves, L. J. (2002). Genetic effects on the variation and covariation of attention deficit-hyperactivity disorder (ADHD) and oppositional-defiant disorder/conduct disorder (ODD/CD) symptomalogies across informant and occasion of measurement. *Psychological Medicine, 32,* 39–53.

Nadel, J., & Aouka, N. (2006). Imitation: Some cues for intervention approaches in autism spectrum disorders. In T. Charman & W. Stone (Eds.), *Social and communication development in autism spectrum disorders* (pp. 219–235). New York: Guilford Press.

Nagaraj, R., Singhi, P., & Malhi, P. (2006). Risperidone in children with autism: Randomized, placebo-controlled, double-blind study. *Journal of Child Neurology, 21,* 450–455.

Najjar, F., Welch, C., Grapentine, W. L., Sachs, H., Siniscalchi, J., & Price, L. H. (2004). Trends in psychotropic drug use in a child psychiatric hospital from 1991-1998. *Journal of Child and Adolescent Psychopharmacology, 14,* 87–93.

Narash-Eisikovits, O., Dierberger, A., & Westen, D. (2002). A multidimensional meta-analysis of pharmacotherapy for bulimia nervosa: Summarizing the range of outcomes in controlled clinical trials. *Harvard Review of Psychiatry, 10,* 193–211.

Nathan, P. E., & Gorman, J. M. (2002) *A guide to treatments that work.* New York: Oxford University Press.

National Center for Educational Statistics. (2003). *National assessment of educational progress: The nation's report card.* Washington, DC: U.S. Department of Education.

National Center for Health Statistics. (2006). *NCHS United States clinical growth charts.* Retrieved December 1, 2006, from http://www.cdc.gov/nchs.

National Institutes of Health. (2000). National Institutes of Health consensus development conference statement: Diagnosis and treatment of attention-deficit/hyperactivity disorder (ADHD). *Journal of the American Academy of Child and Adolescent Psychiatry, 39,* 182–193.

National Reading Panel. (2000). *Report of the National Reading Panel. Teaching children to read: An evidence-based assessment of the scientific research literature on reading and its implications for reading instruction* (NIH Publication No. 00-4754). Washington, DC: U.S. Government Printing Office.

Nemeroff, R., Gipson, P., & Jensen, P. (2004). From efficacy to effectiveness research: What we have learned over the last 10 years. In T. H. Ollendick & J. S. March (Eds.), *Phobic and anxiety disorders in children and adolescents: A clinician's guide to effective psychosocial and pharmacological interventions* (pp. 476–505). New York: Oxford University Press.

Newberger, D. S. (2000). Down syndrome: Prenatal risk assessment and diagnosis. *American Family Physician, 62,* 825–832.

Newcorn, J. H., Halperin, J. M., Jensen, P. S., Abikoff, H. B., Arnold, L. E. Cantwell, D. P., et al. (2001). Symptom profiles in children with ADHD: Effects of comorbidity and gender. *Journal of the American Academy of Child and Adolescent Psychiatry, 40,* 137–146.

Newsom, C., & Hovanitz, C. A. (2005). The nature and value of empirically validated interventions. In J. W. Jacobson, R. M. Foxx, & J. A. Mulick (Eds.), *Controversial therapies for developmental disabilities: Fad, fashion and science in professional practice* (pp. 31–44). Mahwah, NJ: Erlbaum.

Nezu, A. M., & Nezu, C. M. (1993). Identifying and selecting target problems for clinical interventions: A problem-solving model. *Psychological Assessment, 5,* 254–263.

Nezu, C. M., Nezu, A. M., Dudek, J. A., Peacock, M. A., & Stoll, J. G. (2005). Social problem-solving correlates of sexual deviancy and aggression among adult child molesters. *Journal of Sexual Aggression, 11,* 27–36.

Nigg, J. T. (2001). Is ADHD an inhibitory disorder? *Psychological Bulletin, 125,* 571–596.

Nigg, J. T. (2006). Temperament and developmental psychopathology. *Journal of Child Psychology and Psychiatry, 47,* 395–422.

Nigg, J. T., Hinshaw, S. P., & Huang-Pollock, C. (2006). Disorders of attention and impulse regulation. In D. Cicchetti & D. J. Cohen (Eds.), *Developmental psychopathology, Vol. 3: Risk, disorder, and adaptation* (pp. 358–403). Hoboken, NJ: Wiley.

Nixon, R. D. V. (2002). Treatment of behavior problems in preschoolers: A review. *Clinical Psychology Review, 22,* 525–546.

Nixon, R. D. V., Sweeney, L., Erickson, D. B., & Touyz, S. W. (2003). Parent-child interaction therapy: A comparison of standard and abbreviated treatments for oppositional defiant preschoolers. *Journal of Consulting and Clinical Psychology, 71,* 251–260.

Nixon, R. D. V., Sweeney, L., Erickson, D. B., & Touyz, S. W. (2004). Parent-child interaction therapy: One- and two-year follow-up of standard and abbreviated treatments for oppositional preschoolers. *Journal of Abnormal Child Psychology, 32,* 263–271.

Nolen-Hoeksema, S. (2000). The role of rumination in depressive disorders and mixed anxiety/depressive symptoms. *Journal of Abnormal Psychology, 109,* 504–511.

Nolen-Hoeksema, S., Girgus, J. S., & Seligman, M. E. (1992). Predictors and consequences of childhood depressive symptoms: A 5-year longitudinal study. *Journal of Abnormal Psychology, 101,* 405–422.

Nowicki, E. A. (2003). A meta-analysis of the social competence of children with learning disabilities compared to classmates of low and average to high achievement. *Learning Disability Quarterly, 26,* 171–188.

O'Brien, C. P., Anthony, J. C., Carroll, K., Childress, A. R., Dackis, C., Diamond, G., et al. (2005). Substance use disorders. In D. L. Evans, E. B. Foa, R. E. Gur, et al. (Eds.), *Treating and preventing adolescent mental health disorders: What we know and what we don't know: A research agenda for improving the mental health of our youth* (pp. 335–426). New York: Oxford University Press.

O'Connor, T. G. (2003). Early experiences and psychological development: Conceptual questions, empirical illustrations, and implications for intervention. *Development and Psychopathology, 15,* 671–690.

Offord, D. R., Boyle, M. H., Szatmari, P., Rae-Grant, N. I., Links, P. S., Cadman, D. T., et al. (1987). Ontario child health study: II. Six-month prevalence of disorder and rates of service utilization. *Archives of General Psychiatry, 44,* 832–836.

Olfson, M., Gameroff, M. J., Marcus, S. C., & Jensen, P. S. (2003). National trends in the treatment of attention deficit hyperactivity disorder. *American Journal of Psychiatry, 160,* 1071–1077.

Olfson, M., Marcus, S. C., Weissman, M. M., & Jensen, P. S. (2002). National trends in the use of psychotropic medications by children. *Journal of the American Academy of Child & Adolescent Psychiatry, 41,* 514–521.

Ollendick, T. H., Birmaher, B., & Mattis, S. G. (2004). Panic Disorder. In T. L. Morris & J. S. March (Eds.), *Anxiety disorders in children and adolescents* (pp. 189–211). New York: Guilford Press.

Ollendick, T. H., & King, N. J. (1998). Empirically supported treatments for children with phobic and anxiety disorders. *Journal of Clinical Child Psychology, 27,* 156–167.

Ollendick, T. H., Mattis, S. G., & King, N. J. (1994). Panic in children and adolescents: A review. *Journal of Child Psychology and Psychiatry, 35,* 113–134.

Osterling, J., & Dawson, G. (1994). Early recognition of children with autism: A study of first birthday home videotapes. *Journal of Autism and Developmental Disorders, 24,* 247–257.

Overmeyer, S., Bullmore, E. T., Suckling, J., Simmons, A., Williams, S. C., Santosh, P. J., et al. (2001). Distributed grey and white matter deficits in hyperkinetic disorder: MRI evidence for anatomical abnormality in an attentional network. *Psychological Medicine, 31,* 1425–1435.

Owens, J., & Hoza, B. (2003). Diagnostic utility of DSM-IV-TR symptoms in the prediction of DSM-IV-TR ADHD subtypes and ODD. *Journal of Attention Disorders, 7,* 11–27.

Ozechowski, T. J., & Liddle, A. (2000). Family-based therapy for adolescent drug abuse: Knowns and unknowns. *Clinical Child and Family Psychology Review, 3,* 269–298.

Ozonoff, S., & Cathcart, K. (1998). Effectiveness of a home program intervention for young children with autism. *Journal of Autism and Developmental Disorders, 28,* 25–32.

Ozonoff, S., Cook, I., Coon, H., Dawson, G., Joseph, R. M., Klin, A., et al. (2004). Performance on Cambridge Neuropsychological Test automated battery subtests sensitive to frontal lobe function in people with autistic disorder: Evidence from the Collaborative Programs of Excellence in Autism Network. *Journal of Autism and Developmental Disorders, 34,* 139–150.

Ozonoff, S., South, M., & Miller, J. N. (2000). DSM-IV-defined Asperger syndrome: Cognitive, behavioral and early history differentiation from high-functioning autism. *Autism, 4,* 29–46.

Palacios, E. D., & Semrud-Clikeman, M. (2005). Delinquency, hyperactivity, and phonological awareness: A comparison of adolescents with ODD and ADHD. *Applied Neuropsychology, 12,* 94–105.

Pappadopulos, E. A., Guelzow, B. T., Wong, C., Ortega, M., & Jensen, P. S. (2004). A review of the growing evidence base for pediatric psychopharmacology. *Child and Adolescent Psychiatric Clinics of North America, 13,* 817–855.

Pardini, D. A., Lochman, J. E., & Frick, P. J. (2003). Callous/unemotional traits and social cognitive processes in adjudicated youth. *Journal of the American Academic of Child and Adolescent Psychiatry, 42,* 364–371.

Parker, J. G., Rubin, K. H., Erath, S. A., Wojslawosicz, J. C., & Buskirk, A. A. (2006). In D. Cicchetti & D. J. Cohen (Eds.), *Developmental psychopathology, Vol. 1: Theory and method* (2nd ed., pp. 419–493). Hoboken, NJ: Wiley.

Parker, J. S., & Benson, J. (2005). Parent-adolescent relations and adolescent functioning: Self-esteem, substance abuse, and delinquency. *Family Therapy, 32,* 131–142.

Parloff, M. B. (1984). Psychotherapy research and its incredible credibility crisis. *Clinical Psychology Review, 4,* 95–109.

Parnell, T. F. (2002). Munchausen by proxy syndrome. In J. E. B. Meyers, L. Berliner, J. Briere, C. T. Hendrix, C. Jenny, & T. A. Reid (Eds.), *The APSAC handbook on child maltreatment* (pp. 131–138). Thousand Oaks, CA: Sage.

Patel, N. C., DelBello, M. P., Keck, P. E., & Strakowski, S. M. (2006). Phenomenology associated with age at onset in patients with bipolar disorder at their first psychiatric hospitalization. *Bipolar Disorders, 8,* 91–94.

Patterson, G. R., & Capaldi, D. M. (1991). Antisocial parents: Unskilled and vulnerable. In P. A. Cowan & E. M. Hetherington (Eds.), *Family transitions* (pp. 195–218). Hillsdale, NJ: Erlbaum.

Patterson, G. R., DeGarmo, D. S., & Knutson, N. (2000). Hyperactive and antisocial behaviors: Comorbid or two points in the same process? *Development and Psychopathology, 12,* 91–107.

Patterson, G. R., Reid, J. B., & Dishion, T. J. (1992). *Antisocial boys.* Eugene, OR: Castalia.

Patterson, G. R., & Yoerger, K. (2002). A developmental model for early- and late-onset delinquency. In J. B. Reid, G. R. Patterson & J. Snyder (Eds.), *Antisocial behavior in children and adolescents: A developmental analysis and model for intervention* (pp. 147–172). Washington, DC: American Psychological Association.

Patterson, H. O., & O'Connell, D. F. (2003). Recovery maintenance and relapse prevention with chemically dependent adolescents. In M. A. Reinecke, F. M. Dattilio, & A. Freeman (Eds.), *Cognitive therapy with children and adolescents* (pp. 70–94). New York: Guilford Press.

Patterson, T., & Kaslow, F. (2002). *Comprehensive handbook of psychotherapy, Vol. 2: Cognitive/behavioral/functional approaches* (pp. 97–100). New York: Wiley.

Patton, G. C., Coffey, C., Carlin, J. B., Degenhardt, L., Lynskey, M. T., & Hall, W. D. (2002). Cannabis use and mental health in young people: Cohort study. *British Medical Journal, 525,* 1195–1198.

Pavuluri, M. N., Henry, D. B., Nadimpalli, S. S., O'Connor, M. M., & Sweeney, J. A. (2006). Biological risk factors in pediatric bipolar disorder. *Biological Psychiatry, 60,* 936–941.

Pavuluri, M. N., Herbener, E. S., & Sweeney, J. A. (2004). Psychotic symptoms in pediatric bipolar disorder. *Journal of Affective Disorders, 80,* 19–28.

Pearson, M., Sweeting, H., West, P., Young, R., Gordon, J., & Turner, K. (2006). Adolescent substance use in different social and peer contexts: A social network analysis. *Drugs: Education, Prevention & Policy, 13,* 519–536.

Pediatric OCD Treatment Study Team. (2004). Cognitive-behavior therapy, sertraline, and their combination for children and adolescents with obsessive-compulsive disorder. *Journal of the American Medical Association, 292,* 1969–1976.

Pelham, W. E., & Bender, M. E. (1982). Peer relationships in hyperactive children: Description and treatment. In K. Gadow & I. Bailer (Eds.), *Advances in learning and behavioral disabilities* (Vol. 1, pp. 365–436). Greenwich, CT: JAI Press.

Pelham, W. E., Carlson, C., Sams, S. E., Dixon, M. J., & Hoza, B. (1993). Separate and combined effects of methylphenidate and behavior modification on boys with attention-deficit hyperactivity disorder in the classroom. *Journal of Consulting and Clinical Psychology, 61,* 506–515.

Pelham, W. E., Fabiano, G. A., Gnagy, E. M., Greiner, A. R., & Hoza, B. (2005). The role of summer treatment programs in the context of comprehensive treatment for attention-deficit/ hyperactivity disorder. In E. D. Hibbs & P. S. Jensen (Eds.), *Psychosocial treatments for child and adolescent disorders: Empirically based strategies for clinical practice* (pp. 377–409). Washington, DC: American Psychological Association.

Pelham, W. E., Gnagy, E. M., Greiner, A. R., Hoza, B. Hinshaw, S. P., Swanson, J. M., et al. (2000). Behavioral vs. behavioral and pharmacological treatment in ADHD children attending a summer treatment program. *Journal of Abnormal Child Psychology, 28,* 507, 526.

Pelham, W. E., & Hinshaw, S. P. (1992). Behavioral intervention for attention-deficit hyperactivity disorder. In S. M. Turner, K. S. Calhoun, & H. E. Adams (Eds.), *Handbook of clinical behavior therapy* (pp. 259–283). New York: Wiley.

Pelham, W. E., & Hoza, B. (1996). Intensive treatment: A summer treatment program for children with ADHD. In E. D. Hibbs & P. S. Jensen (Eds.), *Psychosocial treatments for child and adolescent disorders: Empirically based strategies for clinical practice* (pp. 311–340). Washington, DC: American Psychological Association.

Pelham, W. E., & Waschbusch, D. A. (1999). Behavioral intervention in attention-deficit/hyperactivity disorder. In H. C. Quay & A. E. Hogan (Eds.), *Handbook of disruptive behavior disorders* (pp. 255–278). Dordrecht, Netherlands: Kluwer.

Pelham, W. E., Wheeler, T., & Chronis, A. (1998). Empirically supported psychosocial treatments for attention deficit hyperactivity disorder. *Journal of Clinical Child Psychology, 27,* 190–205.

Pennington, B. F., & Ozonoff, S. (1996). Executive functions and developmental psychopathology. *Journal of Child Psychology and Psychiatry, 37,* 51–87.

Perham, N., Moore, S. C., Shepherd, J., & Cusens, B. (2007). Identifying drunkenness in the night-time economy. *Addiction, 102,* 377–380.

Perlick, D. A., Miklowitz, D. J., Link, B. G., Struening, E., Kaczynski, R., Gonzalez, J., et al. (2007). Perceived stigma and depression among caregivers of patients with bipolar disorder. *British Journal of Psychiatry, 190,* 535–536.

Perry, C. L., Komro, K. A., Veblen-Mortenson, S., Bosma, L. M., Farbakhsh, K., Muson, K. A., et al. (2003). A randomized controlled trial of the middle and junior high school DARE and DARE Plus programs. *Archives of Pediatrics and Adolescent Medicine, 157,* 178–184.

Perwien, A. R., & Bernstein, G. A. (2004). Separation anxiety disorder. In T. H. Ollendick & J. S. March (Eds.), *Phobic and anxiety disorders in children and adolescents* (pp. 272–305). New York: Oxford University Press.

Petras, H., Schaeffer, C. M., Ialongo, N., Hubbard, S., Muthen, B., Lambert, S. F., et al. (2004). When the course of aggressive behavior in childhood does not predict antisocial outcomes in adolescence and young adulthood: An examination of potential explanatory variables. *Development and Psychopathology, 16,* 919–941.

Pfefferbaum, B., Gurwitch, R. H., McDonald, N. B., Leftwich, M. J., Sconzo, G. M., Messenbaugh, A. K., et al. (2000). Posttraumatic stress among young children after the death of a friend or acquaintance in a terrorist bombing. *Psychiatric Services, 51,* 386–388.

Pfiffner, L. J., & O'Leary, S. G. (1993). School-based psychological treatments. In J. L. Matson (Ed.), *Handbook of hyperactivity in children* (pp. 234–255). Boston: Allyn & Bacon.

Phelps, L. (2005). Health-related issues among ethnic minority and low-income children: Psychoeducational outcomes and prevention models. In C. L. Frisby & C. R. Reynolds (Eds.), *Comprehensive handbook of multicultural school psychology* (pp. 928–944). Hoboken, NJ: Wiley.

Phillips, D., Prince, S., & Schiebelhut, L. (2004). Elementary school children's responses 3 months after the September 11 terrorist attacks: A study in Washington, DC. *American Journal of Orthopsychiatry, 74,* 509–528.

Pianta, R. C. (2006). Schools, schooling, and developmental psychopathology. In D. Cicchetti & D. J. Cohen (Eds.), *Developmental psychopathology, Vol. 1: Theory and method* (2nd ed.; pp. 494–529). Hoboken, NJ: Wiley.

Piazza, M., Giacomini, E., Le Bihan, D., & Dehaene, S. (2003). Single-trial classification of parallel pre-attentive and serial attentive processes using functional magnetic resonance imaging. *Proceedings of the Royal Society, 270,* 1237–1245.

Pickles, A., & Hill, J. (2006). Developmental pathways. In D. Cicchetti & D. J. Cohen (Eds.), *Developmental psychopathology, Vol. 1: Theory and method* (pp. 211–243). Hoboken, NJ: Wiley.

Pidsosny, I. C., & Virani, A. (2006). Pediatric psychopharmacology update: Psychostimulants and tics past, present and future. *Journal of the Canadian Academy of Child and Adolescent Psychiatry, 15,* 84–86.

Pierce, K., Muller, R. A., Ambrose, J., Allen, G., & Courchesne, E. (2001). Face processing occurs outside the fusiform "face area" in autism: evidence from functional MRI. *Brain, 124,* 2059–2073.

Pieretti, M., Zhang, F., Fu, Y. H., Warren, S. T., Oostra, B. A., Caskey, C. T., et al. (1991). Absence of expression of the FMR1 gene in the fragile X syndrome. *Cell, 66,* 817–822.

Pike, K. M. (1998). Long-term course of anorexia nervosa: Response, relapse, remission and recovery. *Clinical Psychology Review, 18,* 447–475.

Pike, K. M., Devlin, M. J., & Loeb, K. L. (2004). Cognitive-behavioral therapy in the treatment of anorexia nervosa, bulimia nervosa, and binge eating disorder. In J. K. Thompson (Ed.), *Handbook of eating disorders and obesity* (pp. 130–162). Hoboken, NJ: Wiley.

Pine, D. S. (2006). A primer on brain imaging in developmental psychopathology: What is it good for? *Journal of Child Psychology and Psychiatry, 47*(10), 983–986.

Pine, D. S., Cohen, P., Gurley, D., Brook, J., & Ma, Y. (1998). The risk for early-adulthood anxiety and depressive disorders in adolescents with anxiety and depressive disorders. *Archives of General Psychiatry, 55,* 56–64.

Pine, D. S., & Grun, J. S. (1999). Childhood anxiety: Integrating developmental psychopathology and affective neuroscience. *Journal of Child and Adolescent Psychopharmacology, 9,* 1–12.

Piquero, A. R., & Brezina, T. (2001). Testing Moffitt's account of adolescence-limited delinquency. *Criminology, 39,* 353–370.

Piven, J., Simon, J., Chase, G., Wzorek, M., Landa, R., Gayle, J., et al. (1993). The etiology of autism: Pre-, peri-, and neonatal factors. *Journal of the American Academy of Child & Adolescent Psychiatry, 32,* 1256–1263.

Pliszka, S. R. (2003a). *Neuroscience for the mental health clinician.* New York: Guilford Press.

Pliszka, S. R. (2003b). Non-stimulant treatment of attention-deficit/hyperactivity disorder. *CNS Spectrums, 8,* 253–258.

Pliszka, S. R., Lancaster, J., Liotti, M., & Semrud-Clikeman, M. (2006). Volumetric MRI differences in treatment-naive vs. chronically treated children with ADHD. *Neurology, 67*(6), 1023–1027.

Plybon, L. E., & Kliewer, W. (2001). Neighborhood types and externalizing behavior in urban school-age children: Tests of direct, mediated, and moderated effects. *Journal of Child & Family Studies, 10,* 419–437.

Polivy, J., Herman, P. C., Mills, J. S., & Wheeler, H. B. (2003). Eating disorders in adolescence. In G. R. Adams & M. D. Berzonsky (Eds.), *Blackwell handbook of adolescence* (pp. 523–549). Malden, MA: Blackwell.

Pomerantz, J. M. (2005). After the black box warning: Treating children and adolescents who have depression. *Drug Benefit Trends, 17,* 183–184.

Pope, H. G., & Yurgelun-Todd, D. (2004). Residual cognitive effects of long-term cannabis use. In D. Castle & R. Murray (Eds.), *Marijuana and madness: Psychiatry and neurobiology* (pp. 198–210). New York: Cambridge University Press.

Post, R., Weiss, S., Leverich, G., George, M., Frye, M., & Ketter, T. (1996). Developmental psychobiology of cyclic affective illness: Implications for early therapeutic intervention. *Development and Psychopathology, 8,* 273–305.

Pottick, K. J., Kirk, S. A., Hsieh, D. K., & Tian, X. (2007). Judging mental disorder in youths: Effects of client, clinician, and contextual differences. *Journal of Consulting and Clinical Psychology, 75,* 1–8.

Power, T. J., Costigan, T. E., Eiraldi, R. B., & Leff, S. S. (2004). Variations in anxiety and depression as a function of ADHD subtypes defined by DSM-IV: Do subtype differences exist or not? *Journal of Abnormal Child Psychology, 32,* 27–37.

President's New Freedom Commission on Mental Health. (2003). *Achieving the promise: Transforming mental health care in America. Final report.* Rockville, MD: U.S. Department of Health and Human Services.

Price, J. M., & Dodge, K. A. (1989a). Peers' contributions to children's social maladjustment: Description and intervention. In T. J. Berndt & G. W. Ladd (Eds.), *Peer relationships and social development* (pp. 341–370). New York: Wiley.

Price, J. M., & Dodge, K. A. (1989b). Reactive and proactive aggression in childhood: Relations to peer status and social context dimensions. *Journal of Abnormal Child Psychology, 17,* 455–471.

Price, J. M., & Glad, K. (2003). Hostile attributional tendencies in maltreated children. *Journal of Abnormal Child Psychology, 31,* 329–343.

Prinstein, M. J., & Aikins, W. (2004). Cognitive moderators of the longitudinal association between peer rejection and adolescent depressive symptoms. *Journal of Abnormal Child Psychology, 32,* 147–158.

Prinstein, M. J., Boergers, J., & Vernberg, E. M. (2001). Overt and relational aggression in adolescents: Social-psychological adjustment of aggressors and victims. *Journal of Clinical Child Psychology, 30,* 479–491.

Prinstein, M. J., Cheah, C. S. L., & Guyer, A. E. (2005). Peer victimization, cue interpretation, and internalizing symptoms: Preliminary concurrent and longitudinal findings for children and adolescents. *Journal of Clinical Child and Adolescent Psychology, 34,* 11–24.

Prochaska, J. O., DiClemente, C. C., & Norcross, J. C. (1992). In search of how people change: Applications to addictive behaviors. *American Psychologist, 47,* 1102–1114.

Prochaska, J. O., & Norcross, J. C. (2003). *Systems of psychotherapy: A transtheoretical analysis* (5th ed.). Belmont, CA: Brooks/Cole.

Puig-Antich, J., Kaufman, J., Ryan, N. D., Williamson, D. E., Dahl, R. E., Lukens, E., et al. (1993). The psychosocial functioning and family environment of depressed adolescents. *Journal of the American Academy of Child and Adolescent Psychiatry, 32,* 244–253.

Pulsifer, M. B., Brandt, J., Salorio, C. F., Vining, E. P. G., Carson, B. S., & Freeman, J. M. (2004). The cognitive outcome of hemispherectomy in 71 children. *Epilepsia, 45,* 243–254.

Pumariega, A. J., Rodriguez, L., & Kilgus, M. D. (2004). Substance abuse among adolescents: Current perspectives. *Addictive Disorders & Their Treatment, 3,* 145–155.

Purcel, D. W., Malow, R. M., Dolezal, C., & Carballo-Dieguez, A. (2004). Sexual abuse of boys: Short- and long-term associations and implications for HIV prevention. In L. J. Koenig, L. S. Doll, A. O'Leary, & W. Pequegnat (Eds.), *From child sexual abuse to adult sexual risk: Trauma, revictimization, and intervention* (pp. 93–114). New York: American Psychological Association.

Quay, H. C. (1997). Inhibition and attention deficit hyperactivity disorder. *Journal of Abnormal Child Psychology, 25,* 7–13.

Querido, J., & Eyberg, S. M. (2005). Parent-child interaction therapy: Maintaining treatment gains of preschoolers with disruptive behavior disorders. In E. D. Hibbs & P. S. Jensen (Eds.), *Psychosocial treatments for child and adolescent disorders: Empirically based strategies for clinical practice* (pp. 575–597). Washington, DC: American Psychological Association.

Querido, J., Eyberg, S. M., & Boggs, S. (2001). Revisiting the accuracy hypothesis in families of young children with conduct problems. *Journal of Clinical Child Psychology, 30,* 253–261.

Quiggle, N. L., Garber, J., Panak, W. E., & Dodge, K. A. (1992). Social information processing in aggressive and depressed children. *Child Development, 63,* 1305–1320.

Quinton, D., & Rutter, M. (1998). *Parenting and breakdown: The making and breaking of intergenerational links.* Aldershot, UK: Avebury.

Raghavan, R., & Small, N. (2004). Cultural diversity and intellectual disability. *Current Opinion in Psychiatry, 17,* 371–375.

Raine, A. (2002). Biosocial studies of antisocial and violent behavior in children and adults: A review. *Journal of Abnormal Child Psychology, 50,* 311–326.

Ramirez, S. Z., Feeney-Kettler, K. A., Flores-Torres, L., Kratochwill, T. R., & Morris, R. J. (2006). Fears and anxiety disorders. In G. G. Bear & K. M. Minke (Eds.), *Children's needs III: Development, prevention, and intervention* (pp. 267–279). Washington, DC: National Association of School Psychologists.

Ramo, D. E., Anderson, K. G., Tate, S. R., & Brown, S. A. (2005). Characteristics of relapse to substance use in comorbid adolescents. *Addictive Behaviors, 30,* 1811–1823.

Ramsay, M. C., Reynolds, C. R., & Kamphaus, R. W. (2002). *Essentials of behavioral assessment.* New York: Wiley.

Ransby, M. J., & Swanson, H. L. (2003). Reading comprehension skills of young adults with childhood diagnosis of dyslexia. *Journal of Learning Disabilities, 36,* 538–555.

Rao, U. (2003). Sleep and other biological rhythms. In B. Geller & M. DelBello (Eds.), *Bipolar disorder in childhood and early adolescence* (pp. 215–246). New York: Guilford Press.

Rao, U., Daley, S. E., & Hammen, C. (2000). Relationship between depression and substance use disorders in adolescent women during the transition to adulthood. *Journal of the American Academy of Child and Adolescent Psychiatry, 39,* 215–222.

Rapee, R. M. (1997). The potential role of childrearing practices in the development of anxiety and depression. *Clinical Psychology Review, 17,* 47–67.

Rapee, R. M., Abbott, M. J., & Lyneham, H. J. (2006). Bibliotherapy for children with anxiety disorders using written materials for parents: A randomized controlled trial. *Journal of Consulting and Clinical Psychology, 74,* 436–444.

Rapport, M. D., Scanlan, S. W., & Denney, C. B. (1999). Attention-deficit/hyperactivity disorder and scholastic achievement: A model of dual developmental pathways. *Journal of Child Psychology and Psychiatry, 40,* 1169–1183.

Rasmussen, S. A., & Eisen, J. L. (1990). Epidemiology of obsessive-compulsive disorder. *Journal of Clinical Psychiatry, 53,* 10–13.

Rayner, K., Foorman, B. R., Perfetti, C. A., Pesetsky, D., & Seidenberg, M. S. (2001). How psychological science informs the teaching of reading. *Psychological Science in the Public Interest, 2,* 31–74.

Rea, M. M., Tompson, M., Miklowitz, D. J., Goldstein, M. J., Hwang, S., & Mintz, J. (2003). Family focused treatment vs. individual treatment for bipolar disorder: Results of a randomized clinical trial. *Journal of Consulting and Clinical Psychology, 71,* 482–492.

Reijneveld, S. A., van der Wal, M. F., Brugman, E., Sing, R. A. H., & Verloove-Vanhorick, S. P. (2004). Infant crying and abuse. *Lancet, 364,* 1340–1342.

Reilly, J., Klima, E. S., & Bellugi, U. (1990). Once more with feeling: Affect and language in atypical populations. *Development and Psychopathology, 2,* 367–391.

Reinecke, M. A. (2006). Cognitive-developmental treatment of conduct disorder. In W. M. Nelson, A. J. Finch, & K. J. Hart (Eds.), *Conduct disorders: A practitioner's guide to comparative treatments* (pp. 99–135). New York: Springer.

Reinecke, M. A., & Simons, A. (2005). Vulnerability to depression among adolescents: Implications for cognitive-behavioral treatment. *Cognitive and Behavioral Practice, 12,* 166–176.

Reiss, A. L., Eliez, S., Smith, J. E., Patwardhan, A. & Haberecht, M. (2000). Brain imaging in neurogenetic conditions: Realizing the potential of behavioural neurogenetic research. *MRDD Research Reviews, 6,* 186–197.

Reiss, S. (1990). Prevalence of dual diagnosis in community-based day programs in the Chicago metropolitan area. *American Journal on Mental Retardation, 94,* 578–585.

Rende, R., Birmaher, B., Axelson, D., Strober, M., Gill, M. K., Valeri, S., et al. (2007). Childhood-onset bipolar disorder: Evidence for increased familial loading of psychiatric illness. *Journal of the American Academy of Child & Adolescent Psychiatry, 46,* 197–204.

Rende, R., & Waldman, I. (2006). Behavioral and molecular genetics and developmental psychopathology. In D. Cicchetti & D. J. Cohen (Eds.), *Developmental psychopathology, Vol. 2: Developmental neuroscience* (pp. 427–464). Hoboken, NJ: Wiley.

Renz, K., Lorch, E. P., Milich, R., Lemberger, C., Bodner, A., Welsh, R. (2003). On-line story representation in boys with attention deficit hyperactivity disorder. *Journal of Abnormal Child Psychology, 31,* 93–104.

Reschly, D. J. (2004). Paradigm shift, outcomes criteria, and behavioral interventions: Foundations for the future of school psychology. *School Psychology Review, 33,* 408–416.

Reschly, D. J. (2006). Legal influences on the identification and treatment of educational disabilities. In I. B. Weiner & A. K. Hess (Eds.), *The handbook of forensic psychology* (pp. 167–189). Hoboken, NJ: Wiley.

Reschly, D. J., Tilly, W. D., & Grimes, J. P. (1999). *Special education in transition: Functional assessment and noncategorical programming.* Longmont, CO: Sopris West.

Reynolds, C. R., & Kamphaus, R. W. (2004). *Behavior assessment system for children* (2nd ed.). Circle Pines, MN: AGS.

Rhee, S. H., & Waldman, D. (2002). Genetic and environmental influences on antisocial behavior: A meta-analysis of twin and adoption studies. *Psychological Bulletin, 128,* 490–529.

Riccio, C. A., Homack, S., Jarratt, K. P., & Wolfe, M. E. (2006). Differences in academic and executive function domains among children with ADHD predominantly inattentive and combined types. *Archives of Clinical Neuropsychology, 21,* 657–667.

Rice, K. G., Leever, B. A., Noggle, C. A., & Lapsley, D. K. (2007). Perfectionism and depressive symptoms in early adolescence. *Psychology in the Schools, 44,* 139–156.

Rich, C. L., Combs-Lane, A. M., Resnick, H. S., & Kilpatrick, D. G. (2004). Child sexual abuse and adult sexual revictimization. In L. J. Koenig, L. S. Doll, A. O'Leary, & W. Pequegnat (Eds.), *From child sexual abuse to adult sexual risk: Trauma, revictimization, and intervention* (pp. 49–68). Washington, DC: American Psychological Association.

Richters, J. E., & Cicchetti, D. (1993). Mark Twain meets DSM–III–R: Conduct disorder, development, and the concept of harmful dysfunction. *Development and Psychopathology, 5,* 5–29.

Riddle, M., Reeve, E., Yaryura-Tobias, J., Yang, H., Claghorn, J., Gaffney, G., et al. (2001). Fluvoxamine for children and adolescents with obsessive-compulsive disorder: A randomized, controlled, multicenter trial. *Journal of the American Academy of Child and Adolescent Psychiatry, 40,* 222–229.

Riddle, M. A., Scahill, L., King, R. A., Hardin, M. T., Anderson, G. M., Ort, S. L., et al. (1992). Double-blind, crossover trial of fluoxetine and placebo in children and adolescents with obsessive-compulsive disorder. *Journal of the American Academy of Child and Adolescent Psychiatry, 31,* 1062–1069.

Rieder, C., & Cicchetti, D. (1989). Organizational perspective on cognitive control functioning and cognitive-affective balance in maltreated children. *Developmental Psychology, 25,* 382–393.

Rimland, B. (1964). *Infantile autism: The syndrome and its implications for a neural theory of behavior.* New York: Appleton-Century-Crofts.

Ringel, J. S., & Sturm, R. (2001). National estimates of mental health utilization and expenditures for children in 1998. *Journal of Behavioral Health and Research, 28,* 319–333.

Rissanen, A., Niemimaa, M., Suonpää, M., Ryynänen, M., & Heinonen, S. (2007). First trimester Downs Syndrome screening shows high detection rate for trisomy 21, but poor performance in structural abnormalities. *Fetal Diagnosis and Therapy, 22,* 45–50.

Robin, A., Siegal, P., Moye, A., Gilroy, M., Dennis, A., & Sikand, A. (1999). A controlled comparison of family versus individual therapy for adolescents with anorexia nervosa. *Journal of the American Academy of Child and Adolescent Psychiatry, 38,* 1482–1489.

Roemer, L., & Borkovec, T. D. (1993). Worry: Unwanted cognitive activity that controls unwanted somatic experience. In D. M. Wegner & J. W. Pennebaker (Eds.), *Handbook of mental control* (pp. 220–238). Englewood Cliffs, NJ: Prentice Hall.

Rohde, P., Lewinsohn, P. M., Clarke, G. N., Hops, H., & Seeley, J. R. (2005). The adolescent coping with depression course: A cognitive-behavioral approach to the treatment of adolescent depression. In E. D. Hibbs & P. S. Jensen (Eds.), *Psychosocial treatments for child and adolescent disorders: Empirically based strategies for clinical practice* (pp. 219–237). Washington, DC: American Psychological Association.

Rogers, C. R. (1957). The necessary and sufficient conditions of therapeutic personality change. *Journal of Consulting Psychology, 21,* 95–103.

Rogers, S. J. (1998). Empirically supported comprehensive treatments for young children with autism. *Journal of Clinical Child Psychology, 27,* 168–179.

Rogers, S. J., & Williams, J. H. G. (2006). Imitation in autism: Findings and controversies. In S. J. Rogers & J. H. G. Williams (Eds.), *Imitation and the social mind: Autism and typical development* (pp. 277–309). New York: Guilford Press.

Rogosch, F., Cicchetti, D., & Abre, J. L. (1995). The role of child maltreatment in early deviations in cognitive and affective processing abilities and later peer relationships problems. *Development & Psychopathology, 7,* 591–609.

Rohde, P., Lewinsohn, P. M., & Seeley, J. R. (1991). Comorbidity of unipolar depression: II. Comorbidity with other mental disorders in adolescents and adults. *Journal of Abnormal Psychology, 100,* 214–222.

Rohrbach, L. A., Sussman, S., Dent, C. W., & Sun, P. (2005). Tobacco, alcohol, and other drug use among high-risk young people: A five-year longitudinal study from adolescence to emerging adulthood. *Journal of Drug Issues, 35,* 333–356.

Rojahn, J., & Esbensen, A. J. (2002). Epidemiology of self-injurious behavior in mental retardation: A review. In S. R. Schroeder, M. L. Oster-Granite, & T. Thompson (Eds.), *Self-injurious behavior: Gene-brain-behavior relationships* (pp. 41–77). Washington, DC: American Psychological Association.

Roodman, A. A., & Clum, G. A. (2001). Revictimization rates and method variance: A meta-analysis. *Clinical Psychology Review, 21,* 183–204.

Root, R. W., Resnick, R. J. (2003). An update on the diagnosis and treatment of attention-deficit/hyperactivity disorder in children. *Professional Psychology: Research and Practice, 34,* 34–41.

Rose, A. J. (2002). Co-rumination in the friendship of girls and boys. *Child Development, 73,* 1830–1843.

Rosenbaum, D. P., Gordon, S., & Hanson, S. (1998). Assessing the effects of school-based drug education: A six-year multilevel analysis of project D.A.R.E. *Journal of Research in Crime and Delinquency, 35,* 381–412.

Rosenberg, D. R., & Keshavan, M. S. (1998). A. E. Bennett Research Award: Toward a neurodevelopmental model of obsessive-compulsive disorder. *Biological Psychiatry, 43,* 623–640.

Rosenshine, B., Meister, C., & Chapman, S. (1996). Teaching students to generate questions: A review of the intervention studies. *Review of Educational Research, 66,* 181–221.

Rosenzweig, S. (1936). Some implicit common factors in diverse methods of psychotherapy. *American Journal of Orthopsychiatry, 6,* 412–415.

Rosner, B. A., Hodapp, R. M., Fidler, D. J., Sagun, J. N., & Dykens, E. M. (2004). Social competence in persons with Prader-Willi, Williams and Down's Syndromes. *Journal of Applied Research in Intellectual Disabilities, 17,* 209–217.

Ross, S., & Heath, N. (2002). A study of the frequency of self-mutilation in a community sample of adolescents. *Journal of Youth & Adolescence, 31,* 67–77.

Rossello, J., & Bernal, G. (1999). The efficacy of cognitive-behavioral and interpersonal treatments for depression in Puerto Rican adolescents. *Journal of Consulting and Clinical Psychology, 67,* 734–745.

Rossello, J., & Bernal, G. (2005). New developments in cognitive-behavioral and interpersonal treatments for depressed Puerto Rican adolescents. In E. D. Hibbs & P. S. Jensen (Eds.), *Psychosocial treatments for child and adolescent disorders: Empirically based strategies for clinical practice* (pp. 187–217). Washington, DC: American Psychological Association.

Rosso, I. M., Cintron, C. M., Steingard, R. J., Renshaw, P. F., Young, A. D., & Yurgelun-Todd, D. A. (2005). Amygdala and hippocampus volumes in pediatric major depression. *Biological Psychiatry, 57,* 21–26.

Rothbart, M. K., & Bates, J. E. (1998). Temperament. In W. Damon (Ed.), *Handbook of child psychology: Vol. 3. Social, emotional, and personality development* (pp. 105–176). New York: Wiley.

Rowe, C. L., Liddle, H. A., Greenbaum, P. E., & Henderson, C. E. (2004). Impact of psychiatric comorbidity on treatment of adolescent drug abusers. *Journal of Substance Abuse Treatment, 26,* 129–140.

Rowe, R., Maughan, B., Pickles, A., Costello, E. J., & Angold, A. (2002). The relationship between DSM-IV oppositional defiant disorder and conduct disorder: Findings from the Great Smoky Mountains Study. *Journal of Child Psychology and Psychiatry, 43,* 365–373.

Rubin, K. H., Bukowski, W., & Parker, J. G. (1998). Peer interactions, relationships, and groups. In W. Damon & N. Eisenberg (Eds.), *Handbook of child psychology: Social, emotional, and personality development* (pp. 619–700). New York: Wiley.

Rubin, K. H., & Rose-Krasnor, L. (1992). Interpersonal problem solving and social competence in children. In V. B. Van Hassett & M. Hersen (Eds.), *Handbook of social development: A life-span perspective* (pp. 283–323). New York: Plenum.

Ruchkin, V. V., Schwab-Stone, M., Koposov, R. A., Vermeiren, R., & King, R. A. (2003). Suicidal ideations and attempts in juvenile delinquents. *Journal of Child Psychology and Psychiatry, 44,* 1058–1066.

Rucklidge, J. J. (2006). Psychosocial functioning of adolescents with and without paediatric bipolar disorder. *Journal of Affective Disorders, 91,* 181–188.

Runyon, M. K., Deblinger, E., Ryan, E. E., & Thakkar-Kolar, R. (2004). An overview of child physical abuse: Developing an integrated parent-child cognitive-behavioral treatment approach. *Trauma, Violence, & Abuse, 5,* 65–85.

Runyon, M. K., & Kenny, M. C. (2002). Relationship of attributional style, depression, and posttrauma distress among children who suffered physical or sexual abuse. *Child Maltreatment, 7,* 254–264.

Runyon, M. K., Kenny, M. C., Berry, E. J., Deblinger, E., & Brown, E. J. (2006). Etiology and surveillance in child maltreatment. In J. R. Lutzker (Ed.), *Preventing violence: Research and evidence-based intervention strategies* (pp. 23–47). Washington, DC: American Psychological Association.

Rutter, M. (2005). Genetic influences and autism. In F. R. Volkmar, R. Paul, A. Klin, & D. Cohen (Eds.), *Handbook of autism and pervasive developmental disorders, Vol. 1: Diagnosis, development, neurobiology, and behavior* (pp. 425–452). Hoboken, NJ: Wiley.

Rutter, M., Colvert, E., Kreppner, J., Beckett, C., Castle, J., Groothues, C., et al. (2007). Early adolescent outcomes for institutionally-deprived and non-deprived adoptees. I: Disinhibited attachment. *Journal of Child Psychology and Psychiatry, 48*(1), 17–30.

Rutter, M., & Sroufe, A. (2000). Developmental psychopathology: Concepts and challenges. *Development and Psychopathology, 12,* 265–296.

Rynn, M. A., Siqueland, L., & Rickels, K. (2001). Placebo-controlled trial of sertraline in the treatment of children with generalized anxiety disorder. *American Journal of Psychiatry, 158,* 2008–2014.

Sadock, B. J., & Sadock, V. A. (2003). *Kaplan and Sadock's synopsis of psychiatry: Behavioral sciences/clinical psychiatry.* Philadelphia, PA: Lippincott Williams & Wilkins.

Saigh, P. A. (1991). The development of posttraumatic stress disorder following four different types of traumatization. *Behaviour Research and Therapy, 29,* 213–216.

Saldana, L., & Henggeler, S. W. (2006). Multisystemic therapy in the treatment of adolescent conduct disorder. In W. M. Nelson, A. J. Finch, & K. J. Hart (Eds.), *Conduct disorders: A practitioner's guide to comparative treatments* (pp. 217–258). New York: Springer.

Salkovskis, P., Forrester, E., & Richards, C. (1998). Cognitive-behavioural approach to understanding obsessional thinking. *British Journal of Psychiatry, 173,* 53–63.

Salter, D., McMillan, D., Richards, M., Talbot, T., Hodges, J., Bentovim, A., et al. (2003). Development of sexually abusive behaviour in sexually victimised males: A longitudinal study. *Lancet, 361,* 471–476.

Salvy, S. J., Mulick, J. A., Butter, E., Bartlett, K. K., & Linscheid, T. R. (2004). Contingent electric shock (SIBIS) and a conditioned punisher eliminate severe head banging in a preschool child. *Behavioral Interventions, 19,* 59–72.

Sambrano, S., Springer, J. F., Sale, E., Kasim, R., & Hermann, J. (2005). Understanding prevention effectiveness in real-world settings: The national cross-site evaluation of high risk youth programs. *American Journal of Drug and Alcohol Abuse, 31,* 491–513.

Sameroff, A. J. (2000). Developmental systems and psychopathology. *Development and Psychopathology, 12,* 297–312.

Sameroff, A. J., Peck, S. C., & Eccles, J. S. (2004). Changing ecological determinants of conduct problems from early adolescence to early adulthood. *Development and Psychopathology, 16,* 873–896.

Samms-Vaughan, M. (2006). Learning disorders. In C. A. Essau (Ed.), *Child and adolescent psychopathology: Theoretical and clinical implications* (pp. 271–289). New York: Routledge.

Sandberg, S., McGuinness, D., Hillary, C., & Rutter, M. (1998). Independence of childhood life events and chronic adversities. *Journal of the American Academy of Child & Adolescent Psychiatry, 37,* 728–735.

Sandman, C. A., Hetrick, W. P., & Taylor, D. V. (1997). Dissociation of POMC peptides after self-injury predicts responses to centrally acting opiate blockers. *American Journal of Mental Retardation, 102,* 182–199.

Sandman, C. A., Spence, M. A., & Smith, M. (1999). Proopiomelanocortin (POMC) dysregulation and response to opiate blockers. *Mental Retardation and Developmental Disabilities Research Review, 5,* 314–321.

Saradjian, J., & Hanks, H. G. I. (1996). *Women who sexually abuse children: From research to clinical practice.* Oxford, UK: Wiley.

Sattler, J. M. (2001). *Assessment of children: Cognitive applications.* San Diego, CA: Jerome M. Sattler.

Sattler, J. M. (2002). *Assessment of children: Behavioral and clinical applications.* San Diego, CA: Jerome M. Sattler.

Sattler, J. M., & Dumont, R. (2004). *Assessment of children: WISC-IV and WPPSI-III supplement.* San Diego, CA; Jerome M. Sattler.

Scarr, S., & McCartney, K. (1983). How people make their own environments: Environment effects. *Child Development, 54,* 424–435.

Schaeffer, C. M., & Borduin, M. (2005). Long-term follow-up to a randomized clinical trial of multisystemic therapy with serious and violent juvenile offenders. *Journal of Consulting and Clinical Psychology, 73,* 445–453.

Schlenger, W. E., Caddell, J. M., Ebert, L., Jordan, B. K., Rourke, K. M., Wilson, D., et al. (2002). Psychological reactions to terrorist attacks: Findings from the National Study of Americans' Reactions to September 11th. *Journal of the American Medical Association, 288,* 581–588.

Schmidt, U., Tiller, J., Blanchard, M., Andrews, D., & Treasure, J. (1997). Is there a specific trauma precipitating anorexia nervosa? *Psychological Medicine, 27,* 523–530.

Schniering, C. A., & Rapee, M. (2004a). The relationship between automatic thoughts and negative emotions in children and adolescents: A test of the cognitive content-specificity hypothesis. *Journal of Abnormal Psychology, 113,* 464–470.

Schniering, C. A., & Rapee, M. (2004b). The structure of negative self-statements in children and adolescents: A confirmatory factor-analytic approach. *Journal of Abnormal Child Psychology, 32,* 95–109.

Schopler, E., Mesibov, G., & Baker, A. (1982). Evaluation of treatment for autistic children and their parents. *Journal of the American Academy of Child Psychiatry, 21,* 262–267.

Schopler, E., Mesibov, G., DeVellis, R., & Short, A. (1981). Treatment outcome for autistic children and their families. In P. Mittler (Ed.), *Frontiers of knowledge in mental retardation* (pp. 293–301). Baltimore, MD: University Park Press.

Schreibman, L., & Koegel, R. L. (2005). Training for parents of children with autism: Pivotal responses, generalization, and individuation of interventions. In E. D. Hibbs & P. S. Jensen (Eds.), *Psychosocial treatments for child and adolescent disorders: Empirically based strategies for clinical practice* (pp. 605–631). Washington, DC: American Psychological Association.

Schroeder, S. R., Oster-Granite, M. L., Berkson, G., Bodfish, J. W., Breese, G. R., Cataldo, M. F., et al. (2001). Self-injurious behavior: Gene-brain-behavior relationships. *Mental Retardation and Developmental Disabilities Research Reviews, 7,* 3–12.

Schuhmann, E. M., Foote, R. C., Eyberg, S. M., Boggs, S. R., & Algina, J. (1998). Efficacy of parent-child interaction therapy: Interim report of a randomized trial with short-term maintenance. *Journal of Clinical Child Psychology, 27,* 34–45.

Schultz, J. R. (2006). Behavioral treatment for youth with conduct disorder. In W. M. Nelson, A. J. Finch, & K. J. Hart (Eds.), *Conduct disorders: A practitioner's guide to comparative treatments* (pp. 137–175). New York: Springer.

Schultz, R. T., Grelotti, D. J., Klin, A., Kleinman, J., Van der Gaag, C, Marois, R., et al. (2003). Autism and movement disturbance. In U. Frith & E. Hill (Eds.), *Autism: Mind and brain* (pp. 267–293). New York: Oxford University Press.

Schultz, R. T., & Robins, D. L. (2005). Functional neuroimaging studies of autism spectrum disorders. In F. R. Volkmar, R. Paul, A. Klin, & D. Cohen (Eds.), *Handbook of autism and pervasive developmental disorders, Vol. 1: Diagnosis, development, neurobiology, and behavior* (pp. 515–533). Hoboken, NJ: Wiley.

Schumann, C. M., & Amaral, G. (2006). Stereological analysis of amygdala neuron number in autism. *Journal of Neuroscience, 26,* 7674–7679.

Schuster, M., Stein, B., Jaycox, L., Collins, R., Marshall, G., Elliot, M., et al. (2001). A national survey of stress reactions after the September 11, 2001 terrorist attacks. *New England Journal of Medicine, 345,* 1507–1512.

Schwartz, D., Dodge, K. A., Coie, J. D., Hubbard, J. A., Cillessen, A. H., Lemerise, E. A., et al. (1998). Social-cognitive and behavioral correlates of aggression and victimization in boys' playgroups. *Journal of Abnormal Child Psychology, 26,* 431–440.

Scott, J., & Baldwin, W. L. (2005). The challenge of early intensive intervention. In D. Zager (Ed.), *Autism spectrum disorders: Identification, education, and treatment* (pp. 173–228). Mahwah, NJ: Erlbaum.

Sedlak, A. J., & Broadhurst, D. D. (1996). *Executive summary of the Third National Incidence Study of Child Abuse and Neglect.* Washington, DC: U.S. Department of Health and Human Services.

Seeman, P., & Madras, B. K. (1998). Anti-hyperactivity medication: Methylphenidate and amphetamine. *Molecular Psychiatry, 3,* 386–396.

Seidman, L. J., Biederman, J., Faraone, S. V., Weber, W., & Ouellette, C. (1997). Toward defining a neuropsychology of attention-deficit/hyperactivity disorder: Performance of children and adolescents from a large clinically referred sample. *Journal of Consulting and Clinical Psychology, 65,* 150–160.

Seidman, L. J., Biederman, J., Monuteaux, M., Weber, W., & Faraone, S. V. (2000). Neuropsychological functioning in nonreferred siblings of children with attention-deficit/hyperactivity disorder. *Journal of Abnormal Psychology, 109,* 252–265.

Seidman, L. J., Biederman, J., Weber, W., Hatch, M., & Faraone, S. V. (1998). Neuropsychological functioning in adults with attention-deficit hyperactivity disorder. *Biological Psychiatry, 44,* 260–268.

Seidman, L. J., Valera, E. M., Makris, N. (2005). Structural brain imaging of attention-deficit/hyperactivity disorder. *Biological Psychiatry, 57,* 1263–1272.

Seligman, M. E. P. (1975). *Helplessness: On depression, development, and death.* San Francisco: Freeman.

Semrud-Clikeman, M. S, & Pliszka, S. R. (2005). Neuroimaging and psychopharmacology. *School Psychology Quarterly, 20,* 172–186.

Seto, M. C. (2004). Pedophilia and sexual offenses against children. *Annual Review of Sex Research, 15,* 321–361.

Shaffer, D., Fisher, P., Dulcan, M. K., Davies, M., Piacentini, J., Schwab-Stone, M. E., et al. (1996). The NIMH diagnostic interview schedule for children version 2. 3 (DISC): Description, acceptability, prevalence rates, and performance in the MECA study. *Journal of the American Academy of Child and Adolescent Psychiatry, 35,* 865–877.

Shaffer, D., Fisher, P., Lucas, C. P., Dulcan, M. K., & Schwab-Stone, M. E. (2000). The NIMH diagnostic interview schedule for children version IV (DISC-IV). *Journal of the American Academy of Child and Adolescent Psychiatry, 39,* 28–38.

Shafritz, K. M., Marchione, K. E., Gore, J. C., Shaywitz, S. E., & Shaywitz, B. A. (2004). The effects of methylphenidate on neural systems of attention in attention deficit hyperactivity disorder. *American Journal of Psychiatry, 161,* 1990–1997.

Shahar, G., Blatt, S. J., Zuroff, D. C., Kuperminc, G. P., & Leadbeater, B. J. (2004). Reciprocal relations between depressive symptoms and self-criticism (but not dependency) among early adolescent girls (but not boys). *Cognitive Therapy and Research, 28,* 85–103.

Shapiro, D. A., & Shapiro, D. (1982). Meta-analysis of comparative therapy outcome studies: A replication and refinement. *Psychological Bulletin, 92,* 581–604.

Shaw, D. S., Gilliom, M., Ingoldsby, E. M., & Nagin, D. (2003). Trajectories leading to school-age conduct problems. *Developmental Psychology, 39,* 189–200.

Shaw, D. S., Lacourse, E., & Nagin, D. S. (2005). Developmental trajectories of conduct problems and hyperactivity from ages 2 to 10. *Journal of Child Psychology and Psychiatry, 46,* 931–942.

Shaw, H., Ramirez, L., Trost, A., Randall, P., & Stice, E. (2004). Body image and eating disturbances across ethnic groups: More similarities than differences. *Psychology of Addictive Behaviors, 18,* 12–18.

Shaywitz, B. A., Holford, T. R., Holahan, J. M., & Fletcher, J. M. (1995). A Matthew effect for IQ but not for reading: Results from a longitudinal study. *Reading Research Quarterly, 30,* 894–906.

Shaywitz, B. A., Shaywitz, S. E., Blachman, B. A., Pugh, K. R., Fulbright, R. K., Skudlarski, P., et al. (2004). Development of left occipitotemporal systems for skilled reading in children after a phonologically-based intervention. *Biological Psychiatry, 55,* 926–933.

Shaywitz, S. E., & Shaywitz, B.A. (2005). Dyslexia (specific reading disability). *Biological Psychiatry, 57,* 1301–1309.

Shea, A., Walsh, C., MacMillan, H., & Steiner, M. (2005). Child maltreatment and HPA axis dysregulation: Relationship to major depressive disorder and posttraumatic stress disorder in females. *Psychoneuroendocrinology, 30,* 162–178.

Sher, K. J. (1991). *Children of alcoholics: A critical appraisal of theory and research.* Chicago: University of Chicago Press.

Sherman, D. K., Iacono, W. G., & McGue, M. K. (1997). Attention-deficit hyperactivity disorder dimensions: A twin study of inattention and impulsivity-hyperactivity. *Journal of the American Academy of Child and Adolescent Psychiatry, 36,* 745–753.

Shirk, S. R., Gudmundsen, G. R., & Burwell, R. A. (2005). Links among attachment-related cognitions and adolescent depressive symptoms. *Journal of Clinical Child and Adolescent Psychology, 34,* 172–181.

Shoal, G. D., Castaneda, J. O., & Giancola, P. R. (2005). Worry moderates the relation between negative affectivity and affect-related substance use in adolescent males: A prospective study of maladaptive emotional self-regulation. *Personality and Individual Differences, 38,* 475–485.

Shroff, H., & Thompson, K. (2006). The tripartite influence model of body image and eating disturbance: A replication with adolescent girls. *Body Image, 3,* 17–23.

Siegel, B., & Ficcaglia, M. (2006). Pervasive developmental disorders. In R. T. Ammerman (Ed.), *Comprehensive handbook of personality and psychopathology* (pp. 254–271). Hoboken, NJ: Wiley.

Siklos, S., & Kerns, A. (2007). Assessing the diagnostic experiences of a small sample of parents of children with autism spectrum disorders. *Research in Developmental Disabilities, 28,* 9–22.

Silver, A. A., & Hagin, R. A. (2002). *Disorders of learning in childhood.* New York: Wiley.

Silverman, W. K., & Carmichael, W. K. (1999). Phobic disorders. In R. T. Ammerman, M. Hersen, & C. L. Last (Eds.), *Handbook of prescriptive treatments for children and adolescents* (pp. 172–192). Boston: Allyn & Bacon.

Silverman, W. K., & Dick-Niederhauser, A. (2004). Separation anxiety disorder. In T. L. Morris & J. S. March (Eds.), *Anxiety disorders in children and adolescents* (pp. 164–188). New York: Guilford Press.

Silverman, W. K., Kurtines, W., Ginsburg, G. S., Weems, C. F., Lumpkin, P. W., & Carmichael, D. H. (1999). Treating anxiety disorders in children with group cognitive-behavioral therapy: A randomized clinical trial. *Journal of Consulting and Clinical Psychology, 67,* 995–1003.

Silverthorn, P., Frick, P. J., & Reynolds, R. (2001). Timing of onset and correlates of severe conduct problems in adjudicated girls and boys. *Journal of Psychopathology and Behavioral Assessment, 23,* 171–181.

Simeon, J. C., Dinicola, V. F., Ferguson, B. H., & Copping, W. (1990). Adolescent depression: A placebo-controlled fluoxetine study and follow-up. *Progress in Neuro-Psychopharmacology & Biological Psychiatry, 14,* 791–795.

Simonoff, E., Pickles, A., Meyer, J. M., Silberg, J. L., Maes, H. H., Loeber, R., et al. (1997). The Virginia Twin Study of Adolescent Behavioral Development: Influence of age, sex, and impairment on rates of disorder. *Archives of General Psychiatry, 54,* 801–808.

Simons, A. D., Rohde, P., Kennard, B. D., & Robins, M. (2005). Relapse and recurrence prevention in the treatment for adolescents with depression study. *Cognitive and Behavioral Practice, 12,* 240–251.

Simos, P. G., Fletcher, J. M., Bergman, E., Breier, J. I., Foorman, B. R., Castillo, E. M., et al. (2002). Dyslexia-specific brain activation profile becomes normal following successful remedial training. *Neurology, 58,* 1203–1213.

Simos, P. G., Fletcher, J. M., Sarkari, S., Billingsley, R. L., Francis, D. J., Castillo, E. M., et al. (2005). Early development of neurophysiological processes involved in normal reading and reading disability: A magnetic source imaging study. *Neuropsychology, 19,* 787–798.

Simpson, R. L., de Boer-Ott, S. R., Griswold, D. E., Myles, B. S., Byrd, S. E. Ganz, J. B., et al. (2005). *Autism spectrum disorders.* Thousand Oaks, CA: Corwin Press.

Sinclair, B. B., & Gold, S. R. (1997). The psychological impact of withholding disclosure of child sexual abuse. *Violence and Victims, 12,* 137–145.

Singh, A. N., Matson, J. L., Cooper, C. L., Dixon, D., & Sturmey, P. (2005). The use of risperidone among individuals with mental retardation: Clinically supported or not? *Research in Developmental Disabilities, 26,* 203–218.

Singh, M. K., DelBello, M. P., Kowatch, R. A., & Strakowski, S. M. (2006). Co-occurrence of bipolar and attention-deficit hyperactivity disorders in children. *Bipolar Disorders, 8,* 710–720.

Singh, N. N., Ellis, C. R., & Wechsler, H. (1997). Psychopharmacoepidemiology of mental retardation: 1966 to 1995. *Journal of Child and Adolescent Psychopharmacology, 7,* 255–266.

Singh, N. N., Osborne, J. G., & Huguenin, N. H. (1996). Applied behavioral interventions. In J. W. Jacobson & J. A. Mulick (Eds.), *Manual of diagnosis and professional practice in mental retardation* (pp. 341–353). Washington, DC: American Psychological Association.

Skinner, B. F. (1974). *About behaviorism.* New York: Knopf.

Smith, M. L., & Glass, G. V. (1977). Meta-analysis of psychotherapy outcome studies. *American Psychologist, 32,* 752–760.

Smith, T., Groen, A. D., & Wynn, J. W. (2000). Randomized trial of intensive early intervention for children with pervasive developmental disorder. *American Journal on Mental Retardation, 105,* 269–285.

Smolak, L. (2005). Eating disorders in girls. In D. J. Bell, S. L. Foster, & E. J. Mash (Eds.), *Handbook of behavioral and emotional problems in girls* (pp. 463–487). New York: Kluwer Academic/Plenum.

Smolak, L. (2006). Body image. In J. Worell & C. D. Goodheart (Eds.), *Handbook of girls' and women's psychological health: Gender and well-being across the lifespan* (pp. 69–76). New York: Oxford University Press.

Smolak, L., Levine, M. P., & Schermer, F. (1999). Parental input and weight concerns among elementary school children. *International Journal of Eating Disorders, 25,* 263–271.

Smolak, L., & Murnen, S. K. (2004). A feminist approach to eating disorders. In J. K. Thompson (Ed.), *Handbook of eating disorders and obesity* (pp. 590–605). Hoboken, NJ: Wiley.

Smoller, J. W., Yamaki, L. H., Fagerness, J. A., Biederman, J., Racette, S., Laird, N. M., et al. (2005). The corticotropin-releasing hormone gene and behavioral inhibition in children at risk for panic disorder. *Biological Psychiatry, 57*, 1485–1492.

Snyder, H. (2000). *Juvenile arrests 1999*. Washington, DC: U.S. Department of Justice, Office of Justice Programs, Office of Juvenile Justice and Delinquency Prevention.

Snyder, H. (2001). Epidemiology of official offending. In R. Loeber & D. P. Farrington (Eds.), *Child delinquents: Development, intervention and service needs* (pp. 25–46). Thousand Oaks, CA: Sage.

Snyder, J., Cramer, A., Afrank, J., & Patterson, G. R. (2005). The contributions of ineffective discipline and parental hostile attributions of child misbehavior to the development of conduct problems at home and school. *Developmental Psychology, 41*, 30–41.

Snyder, J., Reid, J., & Patterson, G. (2003). A social learning model of child and adolescent antisocial behavior. In B. B. Lahey, T. E. Moffitt, & A. Caspi (Eds.), *Causes of conduct disorder and juvenile delinquency* (pp. 27–48). New York: Guilford Press.

Snyder, R., Turgay, A., Aman, M., Binder, C., Fisman, S., Carroll, A., et al. (2002). Effects of risperidone on conduct and disruptive behavior disorders in children with subaverage IQs. *Journal of the American Academy of Child and Adolescent Psychiatry, 41*, 1026–1036.

Snyderman, M., & Rothman, S. (1987). Survey of expert opinion on intelligence and aptitude testing. *American Psychologist, 42*, 137–144.

Solanto, M. V. (1998). Neuropsychopharmacological mechanisms of stimulant drug action in attention-deficit hyperactivity disorder: A review and integration. *Behavioral Brain Research, 94*, 127–152,

Sowell, E. R., Thompson, P. M., Welcome, S. E., Henkenius, A. L., Toga, A. W., & Peterson, B. S. (2003). Cortical abnormalities in children and adolescents with attention-deficit hyperactivity disorder. *Lancet, 362*, 1699–1707.

Spence, S. H., Donovan, C., & Brechman-Toussaint, M. (2000). The treatment of childhood social phobia: The effectiveness of a social skills training-based, cognitive-behavioural intervention, with and without parental involvement. *Journal of Child Psychology and Psychiatry, 41*, 713–726.

Spence, S., & Reinecke, M. (2003). Cognitive approaches to understanding, preventing, and treating child and adolescent depression. In M. Reinecke & D. Clark (Eds.), *Cognitive therapy across the lifespan* (pp. 358–395). Cambridge, UK: Cambridge University Press.

Spencer, T., Biederman, J., Harding, M. Faraone, S., & Wilens, T. (1996). Growth deficits in ADHD children revisited: Evidence for disorder related growth delays. *Journal of the American Academy of Child and Adolescent Psychiatry, 35*, 1460–1467.

Spessot, A. L., & Peterson, B. S. (2006). Tourette's syndrome: A multifactorial, developmental psychopathology. In D. Cicchetti & D. J. Cohen (Eds.), *Developmental psychopathology, Vol. 3: Risk, disorder, and adaptation* (2nd ed., pp. 436–469). Hoboken, NJ: Wiley.

Spitz, R. A. (1946). Hospitalism: A follow-up report. In R. S. Eissler, (Ed.), *The psychoanalytic study of the child* (Vol. II). New York: International Universities Press.

Sroufe, L. A. (1989a). Pathways to adaptation and maladaptation: Psychopathology as developmental deviation. In D. Cicchetti (Ed.), *Rochester symposium on developmental psychopathology: The emergence of a discipline* (pp. 13–40). Hillsdale. NJ: Erlbaum.

Sroufe, L. A. (1989b). Relationships, self and individual adaptation. In A. J. Sameroff & R. N. Emde (Eds.), *Relationship disturbances in early childhood* (pp. 70–94). New York: Basic Books.

Sroufe, L. A. (1997). Psychopathology as an outcome of development. *Development and Psychopathology, 9*, 251–268.

Sroufe, L. A., & Rutter, M. (1984). The domain of developmental psychopathology. *Child Development, 55*, 17–29.

Stader, S., & Hokanson, J. (1998). Psychological antecedents of depressive symptoms: An evaluation using daily experiences methodology. *Journal of Abnormal Psychology, 107*, 17–26.

Stahl, S. A., McKenna, M. C., & Pagnucco, J. R. (1994). The effects of whole-language instruction: An update and a reappraisal. *Educational Psychologist, 29*, 175–185.

Stallard, P., & Smith, E. (2007). Appraisals and cognitive coping styles associated with chronic post-traumatic symptoms in child road traffic accident survivors. *Journal of Child Psychology and Psychiatry, 48*, 194–201.

Stark, J. D., & Kendall, P. C. (1996). *Treating depressed children*. Ardmore, PA: Workbook.

Stark, K. D. (1990). *The treatment of depression during childhood: A school-based program*. New York: Guilford Press.

Stark, K. D., Hoke, J., Ballatore, M., Valdez, C., Scammaca, N., & Griffin, J. (2005). Treatment of child and adolescent depressive disorders. In E. D. Hibbs & P. S. Jensen (Eds.), *Psychosocial treatments for child and adolescent disorders: Empirically based strategies for clinical practice* (pp. 239–265). Washington, DC: American Psychological Association.

Stark, K. D., Reynolds, W. M., & Kaslow, N. J. (1987). A comparison of the relative efficacy of self-control therapy and a behavioral problem-solving therapy for depression in children. *Journal of Abnormal Child Psychology, 15,* 91–113.

Stark, K. D., Rouse, L., & Livingston, R. (1991). Treatment of depression during childhood and adolescence: Cognitive behavioral procedures for the individual and family. In P. C. Kendall (Ed.), *Child and adolescent therapy: Cognitive-behavioral procedures* (pp. 165–208). New York: Guilford Press.

Starkey, P., & Cooper, R. G. (1980). Perception of number by human infants. *Science, 210,* 1033–1035.

Stein, D. J., Keating, J., Zar, H. J., & Hollander, E. (1994). A survey of the phenomenology and pharmacotherapy of compulsive and impulsive-aggressive symptoms in Prader-Willi Syndrome. *Journal of Neuropsychiatry & Clinical Neurosciences, 6,* 23–29.

Stein, M. A., Waldman, I. D., Sarampote, C. S., Seymour, K. E., Robb, A. S., Conlon, C., et al. (2005). Dopamine transporter genotype and methylphenidate dose response in children with ADHD. *Neuropsychopharmacology, 30,* 1374–1382.

Stein, M. B., & Seedat, S. A. (2004). Pharmacotherapy. In T. L. Morris & J. S. March (Eds.), *Anxiety disorders in children and adolescents* (pp. 329–354) New York: Guilford Press.

Steiner, H., & Remsing, L. (2007). Practice parameter for the assessment and treatment of children and adolescents with oppositional defiant disorder. *Journal of the American Academy of Child & Adolescent Psychiatry, 46,* 126–141.

Steinhausen, H. C., & Metzke, C. W. (2000). Adolescent self-rated depressive symptoms in a Swiss epidemiological study. *Journal of Youth & Adolescence, 29,* 421–439.

Stevens, E. A., & Prinstein, J. (2005). Peer contagion of depressogenic attributional styles among adolescents: A longitudinal study. *Journal of Abnormal Child Psychology, 33,* 25–37.

Stevens, T. N., Ruggiero, K. J., Kilpatrick, D. G., Resnick, H. S., & Saunders, B. E. (2005). Variables differentiating singly and multiply victimized youth: Results from the National Survey of Adolescents and implications for secondary prevention. *Child Maltreatment, 10,* 211–223.

Stewart, S. E., Illmann, C., Geller, D. A., Leckman, J. F., King, R., & Pauls, D. L. (2006). A controlled family study of attention-deficit/hyperactivity disorder and Tourette's disorder. *Journal of the American Academy of Child & Adolescent Psychiatry, 45,* 1354–1362.

Stewart, S. M., Kennard, B. D., Lee, P. W. H., Hughes, C. W., Mayes, T. L., Emslie, G. J., et al. (2004). A cross-cultural investigation of cognitions and depressive symptoms in adolescents. *Journal of Abnormal Psychology, 113,* 248–257.

Stewart, S. M., Lewinsohn, P., Lee, P. W. H., Ho, L. M., Kennard, B. D., Hughes, C. W., et al. (2002). Symptom patterns in depression and "subthreshold" depression among adolescents in Hong Kong and the United States. *Journal of Cross Cultural Psychology, 33,* 559–576.

Stice, E. (2002). Risk and maintenance factors for eating pathology: A meta-analytic review. *Psychological Bulletin, 128,* 825–848.

Stice, E. (2003). Puberty and body image. In C. Hayward (Ed.), *Gender differences at puberty* (pp. 61–76). New York: Cambridge University Press.

Stice, E., Kirz, J., & Borbely, C. (2002). Disentangling adolescent substance use and problem use within a clinical sample. *Journal of Adolescent Research, 17,* 122–142.

Stice, E., Wonderlich, S., & Wade, E. (2006). Eating disorders. In R. T. Ammerman (Ed.), *Comprehensive handbook of personality and psychopathology* (pp. 330–347). Hoboken, NJ: Wiley.

Stierlin, H., & Weber, G. (1989). *Unlocking the family door: A systemic approach to the understanding and treatment of anorexia nervosa.* New York: Brunner/Mazel.

Stoolmiller, M. (2001). Synergistic interaction of child manageability problems and parent-discipline tactics in predicting future growth in externalizing behavior for boys. *Developmental Psychology, 37,* 814–825.

Stricker, G., & Trierweiler, J. (2006). The local clinical scientist: A bridge between science and practice. *Training and Education in Professional Psychology, 1,* 37–46.

Striegel-Moore, R. H., Silberstein, L. R., & Rodin, J. (1986). Toward an understanding of risk factors for bulimia. *American Psychologist, 41,* 246–263.

Strober, M., Freeman, R., Lampert, C., Diamond, J., & Kaye, W. (2000). Controlled family study of anorexia nervosa and bulimia nervosa: Evidence of shared liability and transmission of partial syndromes. *American Journal of Psychiatry, 157,* 393–401.

Stromme, P., & Hagberg, G. (2000). Aetiology in severe and mild mental retardation: A population-based study of Norwegian children. *Developmental Medicine & Child Neurology, 42,* 76–86.

Stromme, P., & Magnus, P. (2000). Correlations between socioeconomic status, IQ and aetiology in mental retardation: A population-based study of Norwegian children. *Social Psychiatry and Psychiatric Epidemiology, 35,* 12–18.

Stuber, J., Galea, S., Pfefferbaum, B., Vandivere, S., Moore, K., & Fairbrother, G. (2005). Behavior problems in New York City's children after the September 11, 2001, terrorist attacks. *American Journal of Orthopsychiatry, 75,* 190–200.

Stuebing, K. K., Fletcher, J. M., LeDoux, J. M., Lyon, G. R., Shaywitz, S. E., & Shaywitz, B. A. (2002). Validity of IQ-discrepancy classifications of reading disabilities: A meta-analysis. *American Educational Research Journal, 39,* 469–518.

Suarez, L., & Bell-Dolan, D. (2001). The relationship of child worry to cognitive biases: Threat interpretation and likelihood of event occurrence. *Behavior Therapy, 32,* 425–442.

Sullivan, H. S. (1953). *The interpersonal theory of psychiatry.* New York: Norton.

Sullivan, K., Hooper, S., & Hatton, D. (2007). Behavioural equivalents of anxiety in children with fragile X syndrome: Parent and teacher report. *Journal of Intellectual Disability Research, 51,* 54–65.

Suveg, C., Zeman, J., Flannery-Schroeder, E., & Cassano, M. (2005). Emotion socialization in families of children with an anxiety disorder. *Journal of Abnormal Child Psychology, 33,* 145–155.

Swanson, J., Greenhill, L., Wigal, T., Kollins, S., Stehli, A., Davies, M., et al. (2006). Stimulant-related reductions of growth rates in the PATS. *Journal of the American Academy of Child & Adolescent Psychiatry, 45,* 1304–1313.

Swanson, J. M., Kraemer, H. C., Hinshaw, S. P., Arnold, L. E., Conners, C. K., Abikoff, H. B., et al. (2001). Clinical relevance of the primary findings of the MTA: Success rates based on severity of ADHD and ODD symptoms at the end of treatment. *Journal of the American Academy of Child and Adolescent Psychiatry, 40,* 168–179.

Sweeney, M., & Pine, D. (2004). Etiology of fear and anxiety. In T. H. Ollendick & J. S. March (Eds.), *Phobic and anxiety disorders in children and adolescents* (pp. 34–60). New York: Oxford University Press.

Sweeney, P. D., Anderson, K., & Bailey, S. (1986). Attributional style in depression: A meta-analytic review. *Journal of Personality and Social Psychology, 50,* 974–991.

Swenson, C. C., & Brown, E. J. (1999). Cognitive-behavioral group treatment for physically abused children. *Cognitive & Behavioral Practice, 6,* 212–220.

Swenson, C. C., & Chaffin, M. (2006). Beyond psychotherapy: Treating abused children by changing their social ecology. *Aggression and Violent Behavior, 11,* 120–137.

Szabo, M., & Lovibond, F. (2004). The cognitive content of thought-listed worry episodes in clinic-referred anxious and nonreferred children. *Journal of Clinical Child and Adolescent Psychology, 33,* 613–622.

Szatmari, P., Archer, L., & Fisman, S. (1995). Asperger's syndrome and autism: Difference in behavior, cognition, and adaptive functioning. *Journal of the American Academy of Child and Adolescent Psychiatry, 34,* 1662–1671.

Szatmari, P., Offord, D. R., & Boyle, M. H. (1989). Ontario child health study: Prevalence of attention deficit disorder with hyperactivity. *Journal of Child Psychology and Psychiatry, 30,* 219–230.

Szymanski, L. S., & Kaplan, L. C. (2006). Mental retardation. In M. K. Dulcan & J. M. Weiner (Eds.), *Essentials of child and adolescent psychiatry* (pp. 121–152). Washington, DC: American Psychiatric Publishing.

Tackett, J. L., Krueger, R. F., Iacono, W. G., & McGue, M. (2005). Symptom-based subfactors of DSM-defined conduct disorder: Evidence for etiologic distinctions. *Journal of Abnormal Psychology, 114,* 483–487.

Tackett, J. L., Krueger, R. F., Sawyer, M. G., & Graetz, B. W. (2003). Subfactors of DSM-IV conduct disorder: Evidence and connections with syndromes from the child behavior checklist. *Journal of Abnormal Child Psychology, 31,* 647–654.

Tager-Flusberg, H., Boshart, J., & Baron-Cohen, S. (1998). Reading the windows to the soul: Evidence of domain-specific sparing in Williams syndrome. *Journal of Cognitive Neuroscience, 10,* 631–639.

Tager-Flusberg, H., & Joseph, R. M. (2003). Identifying neurocognitive phenotypes in autism. In U. Frith & E. Hill (Eds.), *Autism: Mind and brain* (pp. 43–66). New York: Oxford University Press.

Tager-Flusberg, H., Paul, R., & Lord, C. (2005). Language and communication in autism. In F. R. Volkmar, R. Paul, A. Klin, & D. Cohen (Eds.), *Handbook of autism and pervasive developmental disorders, Vol. 1: Diagnosis, development, neurobiology, and behavior* (pp. 335–364). Hoboken, NJ: Wiley.

Tamm, L., Menon, V., & Reiss, A. L. (2006). Parietal attentional system aberrations during target detection in adolescents with attention deficit hyperactivity disorder: Event-related fMRI evidence. *American Journal of Psychiatry, 163,* 1033–1043.

Tannock, R. (2000). Attention-deficit/hyperactivity disorder with anxiety disorders. In T. E. Brown (Ed.), *Attention deficit disorders and comorbidities in children, adolescents, and adults* (pp. 125–170). Washington, DC: American Psychiatric Press.

Tantleff-Dunn, S., Cokee-LaRose, J., & Peterson, R. D. (2004). Interpersonal psychotherapy for the treatment of anorexia nervosa, bulimia nervosa, and binge eating disorder. In J. K. Thompson (Ed.), *Handbook of eating disorders and obesity* (pp. 163–185). Hoboken, NJ: Wiley.

Tardif, M., Auclair, N., Jacob, M., & Carpentier, J. (2005). Sexual abuse perpetrated by adult and juvenile females: An ultimate attempt to resolve a conflict associated with maternal identity. *Child Abuse & Neglect, 29,* 153–167.

Tarter, R., Kirisci, L., Habeych, M., Reynolds, M., & Vanyukov, M. (2004). Neurobehavior disinhibition in childhood predisposes to substance use disorder by young adulthood: Direct and mediated etiologic pathway. *Drug and Alcohol Dependence, 73,* 121–132.

Tarter, R. E., Kirisci, L., Mezzich, A., Cornelius, J., Pajer, K., Vanyukov, M., et al. (2003). Neurobehavior disinhibition in childhood predicts early age onset of substance disorder. *American Journal of Psychiatry, 160,* 1078–1085.

Tassone, F., Hagerman, R. J., Ikle, D., Dyer, P. N., Lampe, M. & Willemsen, R. (1999). FMRP expressions as a potential prognostic indicator in fragile X syndrome. *American Journal of Medical Genetics, 84,* 250–261.

Temple, C. M., & Sherwood, S. (2002). Representation and retrieval of arithmetical facts: Developmental difficulties. *Quarterly Journal of Experimental Psychology, 55,* 733–752.

Tems, C. L., Stewart, S. M., Skinner, J. R., Hughes, C. W., & Emslie, G. (1993). Cognitive distortions in depressed children and adolescents: Are they state dependent or traitlike? *Journal of Clinical Child Psychology, 22,* 316–326.

Terr, L. C. (1991). Childhood traumas: An outline and overview. *American Journal of Psychiatry, 148,* 10–20.

Tevyaw, T., & Monti, M. (2004). Motivational enhancement and other brief interventions for adolescent substance abuse: Foundations, applications and evaluations. *Addiction, 99,* 63–75.

Therrien, W. J., Wickstrom, K., & Jones, K. (2006). Effect of a combined repeated reading and question generation intervention on reading achievement. *Learning Disabilities Research & Practice, 21,* 89–97.

Thomas, C. P., Conrad, P., Casler, R., & Goodman, E. (2006). Trends in the use of psychotropic medications among adolescents, 1994 to 2001. *Psychiatric Services, 57,* 63–69.

Thompson, J. K., Coovert, M. D., & Stormer, S. M. (1999). Body image, social comparison, and eating disturbance: A covariance structure modeling investigation. *International Journal of Eating Disorders, 26,* 43–51.

Thompson, J. K., & Heinberg, L. J. (1993). Preliminary test of two hypotheses of body image disturbance. *International Journal of Eating Disorders, 14,* 59–63.

Thompson, K. M., & Wonderlich, S. A. (2004). Child sexual abuse and eating disorders. In J. K. Thompson (Ed.), *Handbook of eating disorders and obesity* (pp. 679–694). Hoboken, NJ: Wiley.

Thompson, T. & Caruso, M. (2002). Self-injury: Knowing what we're looking for. In S. R. Schroeder, M. L. Oster-Granite, & T. Thompson (Eds.), *Self-injurious behavior: Gene-brain-behavior relationships* (pp. 1–21). Washington, DC: American Psychological Association.

Tiet, Q. Q., Wasserman, G. A., Loeber, R., McReynolds, L. S., & Miller, L. S. (2001). Developmental and sex differences in types of conduct problems. *Journal of Child and Family Studies, 10,* 181–197.

Tiggeman, M., & Lynch, J. (2001). Body image across the life span in adult women: The role of self-objectification. *Developmental Psychology, 37,* 243–253.

Tillman, R., Geller, B., Nickelsburg, M. J., Bolhofner, K., Craney, J. L., DelBello, M. P., et al. (2003). Life events in prepubertal and early adolescent bipolar disorder phenotype compared to attention-deficit hyperactive and normal controls. *Journal of Child and Adolescent Psychopharmacology, 13,* 243–251.

Tolan, P. H., & Dodge, A. (2005). Children's mental health as a primary care and concern: A system for comprehensive support and service. *American Psychologist, 60,* 601–614.

Toolan, J. M. (1962). Suicide and suicidal attempts in children and adolescents. *American Journal of Psychiatry, 118,* 719–724.

Toth, S. L., & Cicchetti, D. (1999). Developmental psychopathology and child psychotherapy. In S. Russ & T. Ollendick (Eds.), *Handbook of psychotherapies with children and families* (pp. 15–44). New York: Plenum Press.

Toth, S. L., Cicchetti, D., Macfie, J., Maughan, A., & Vanmeenen, K. (2000). Narrative representations of caregivers and self in maltreated pre-schoolers. *Attachment and Human Development, 2,* 271–305.

Tozzi, F., Thornton, L. M., Klump, K. L., Fichter, M. M., Halmi, K. A., Kaplan, A. S., et al. (2005). Symptom fluctuation in eating disorders: Correlates of diagnostic crossover. *American Journal of Psychiatry, 162,* 732–740.

Treadwell, K. H., & Kendall, P. C. (1996). Self-talk in anxiety-disordered youth: States-of-mind, content specificity, and treatment outcome. *Journal of Consulting and Clinical Psychology, 64*, 941–950.

Treatment for Adolescents With Depression Study Team. (2004). Fluoxetine, cognitive-behavioral therapy, and their combination for adolescents with depression: Treatment for Adolescents With Depression Study (TADS) randomized controlled trial. *Journal of the American Medical Association, 292*, 807–820.

Treatment for Adolescents With Depression Study Team. (2005). Treatment for adolescents with depression study (TADS): Demographic and clinical characteristics. *Journal of American Academy of Child and Adolescent Psychiatry, 44*, 28–40.

Tremblay, R. E. (2003). Why socialization fails: The case of chronic physical aggression. In B. B. Lahey, T. E. Moffitt & A. Caspi (Eds.), *Causes of conduct disorder and juvenile delinquency* (pp. 182–224). New York: Guilford Press.

Tsai, L. Y. (2004a). Autistic disorder. In J. M. Wiener & M. K. Dulcan (Eds.), *The American psychiatric publishing textbook of child and adolescent psychiatry* (pp. 261–315). Washington, DC: American Psychiatric Publishing.

Tsai, L. Y. (2004b). Other pervasive developmental disorders. In J. M. Wiener & M. K. Dulcan (Eds.), *The American psychiatric publishing textbook of child and adolescent psychiatry* (pp. 317–349). Washington, DC: American Psychiatric Publishing.

Tsai, L. Y. (2005). Medical treatment in autism. In D. Zager (Ed.), *Autism spectrum disorders: Identification, education, and treatment* (pp. 395–492). Mahwah, NJ: Erlbaum.

Tsatsanis, K. D. (2005). Neuropsychological characteristics in autism and related conditions. In F. R. Volkmar, R. Paul, A. Klin, & D. Cohen (Eds.), *Handbook of autism and pervasive developmental disorders, Vol. 1: Diagnosis, development, neurobiology, and behavior* (pp. 365–381). Hoboken, NJ: Wiley.

Tucker, J. S., Ellickson, P. L., Orlando, M., Martino, S. C., & Klein, D. J. (2005). Substance use trajectories from early adolescence to emerging adulthood: A comparison of smoking, binge drinking, and marijuana use. *Journal of Drug Issues, 35*, 307–332.

Turkheimer, E., Haley, A., Waldron, M., D'Onofrio, B., & Gottesman, I. I. (2003). Socioeconomic status modifies heritability of IQ in young children. *Psychological Science, 14*, 623–628.

Turner, H., & Bryant-Waugh, R. (2004). Eating disorder not otherwise specified (EDNOS): Profiles of patients presenting at a community eating disorder service. *European Eating Disorders Review, 12*, 18–26.

Urberg, K. A., Luo, Q., Pilgrim, C., & Degirmencioglu, S. M. (2003). A two-stage model of peer influence in adolescent substance use: Individual and relationship-specific differences in susceptibility to influence. *Addictive Behaviors, 28*, 1243–1256.

U.S. Census Bureau. (2006). *Population estimates.* Retrieved November 1, 2006, from http://www .census.gov/popest/estimates.

U.S. Department of Education. (1977). Assistance to states for education of handicapped children: Procedures for evaluating specific LD. *Federal Register, 42*, 65082–65085.

U.S. Department of Education. (2006). Additional procedures for identifying children with specific learning disabilities. *Federal Register, 71*, 46786–46788.

U.S. Department of Health and Human Services. (2002). *Child maltreatment, 2000: Reports from the states for the national child abuse and neglect data systems.* Washington, DC: Government Printing Office.

Vaidya, C. J., Austin, G., Kirkorian, G., Ridlehuber, H. W., Desmond, J. E., Glover, G. H., et al. (1998). Selective effects of methylphenidate in attention deficit hyperactivity disorder: A functional magnetic resonance study. *Proceedings of the National Academy of Sciences, 95*, 14494–14499.

Van Acker, R., Loncola, J. A., & Van Acker, E. Y. (2005). Rett syndrome: A pervasive developmental disorder. In F. R. Volkmar, R. Paul, A. Klin, & D. Cohen (Eds.), *Handbook of autism and pervasive developmental disorders, Vol. 1: Diagnosis, development, neurobiology, and behavior* (pp. 126–164). Hoboken, NJ: Wiley.

van den Berg, P., Thompson, J. K., Brandon, K. O., & Coovert, M. (2002). The tripartite influence model of body image and eating disturbance: A covariance structural modeling investigation testing the mediational role of comparison. *Journal of Psychosomatic Research, 53*, 1007–1020.

Vandiver, D. M., & Kercher, G. (2004). Offender and victim characteristics of registered female sexual offenders in Texas: A proposed typology of female sexual offenders. *Sexual Abuse: Journal of Research and Treatment, 16*, 121–137.

Van Empelen, R., Jennekens-Schinkel, A., Buskens, E., Helders, P. J. M., & Van Nieuwenhuizen, O. (2004). Functional consequences of hemispherectomy. *Brain, 127*, 2071–2079.

van Goozen, S. H. M., Cohen-Kettenis, P. T., Snoek, H., Matthys, W., Swaab-Barneveld, H., & van Engeland, H. (2004). Executive functioning in children: A comparison of hospitalised ODD and ODD/ADHD children and normal controls. *Journal of Child Psychology and Psychiatry, 45*, 284–292.

van Goozen, S. H. M., & Fairchild, G. (2006). Neuroendocrine and neurotransmitter correlates in children with antisocial behavior. *Hormones and Behavior, 50*, 647–654.

van Goozen, S. H. M., Fairchild, G., Snoek, H., & Harold, G. T. (2007). The evidence for a neurobiological model of childhood antisocial behavior. *Psychological Bulletin, 133*, 149–182.

van Kammen, W. B., Loeber, R., & Stouthamer-Loeber, M. (1991). Substance use and its relationship to conduct problems and delinquency in young boys. *Journal of Youth and Adolescence, 20*, 399–413.

van Lang, N. D. J., Ferdinand, R. F., & Verhulst, F. C. (2007). Predictors of future depression in early and late adolescence. *Journal of Affective Disorders, 97*, 137–144.

van Oppen, P., de Haan, E., van Balkom, A. J., Spinhoven, P., Hoogduin, K., & van Dyck, R. (1995). Cognitive therapy and exposure in vivo in the treatment of obsessive-compulsive disorder. *Behavior Research and Therapy, 33*, 379–390.

van Voorst, W., & Quirk, S. (2003). Are relations between parental history of alcohol problems and changes in drinking moderated by positive expectancies? *Alcoholism: Clinical and Experimental Research, 26*, 25–30.

Vanyukov, M. M., & Tarter, R. E. (2000). Genetic studies of substance abuse. *Drug and Alcohol Dependence, 59*, 101–123.

Vasey, M. W., Crnic, K. A., & Carter, W. G. (1994). Worry in childhood: A developmental perspective. *Cognitive Therapy & Research, 18*, 529–549.

Vega, W. A., Gil, A. G., & Wagner, E. (1998). Cultural adjustment and Hispanic adolescent drug use. In H. B. Kaplan, A. E. Gottfried, A. W. Gottfried (Series Eds.), W. A. Vega, & A. G. Gil (Vol. Eds.), *Longitudinal research in the social and behavioral sciences: Vol. 2. Drug use and ethnicity in early adolescence* (pp. 125–148). New York: Plenum Press.

Vellutino, F. R., Scanlon, D. M., & Lyon, G. R. (2000). Differentiating between difficult to remediate and readily remediated poor readers: More evidence against the IQ Achievement discrepancy definition of reading disability. *Journal of Learning Disabilities, 33*, 223–238.

Vellutino, F. R., Scanlon, D. M., Small, S., & Fanuele, D. P. (2006). Response to intervention as a vehicle for distinguishing between children with and without reading disabilities: Evidence for the role of kindergarten and first-grade interventions. *Journal of Learning Disabilities, 39*, 157–169.

Verhoeven, L., & Vermeer, A. (2006). Literacy achievement of children with intellectual disabilities and differing linguistic backgrounds. *Journal of Intellectual Disability Research, 50*, 725–738.

Verkerk, A. J. M. H., Pieretti, M., Sutcliffe, J. S., Fu, Y. H., Kuhl, D. P. A. & Pizzuti, A. (1991). Identification of a gene (FMR-1) containing a CGG repeat coincident with a breakpoint cluster region exhibiting length variation on fragile X syndrome. *Cell, 65*, 905–914.

Vickers, K. S., Patten, C. A., Lane, K., Clark, M. M., Crogan, I. T., Schroeder, D. R., et al. (2003). Depressed versus nondepressed young adult tobacco users: Differences in coping style, weight concerns and exercise level. *Health Psychology, 22*, 498–503.

Viding, E., Blair, J. R., Moffitt, T. E., & Plomin, R. (2004). Evidence for substantial genetic risk for psychopathy in 7 year olds. *Journal of Child Psychology and Psychiatry, 45*, 1–6.

Vig, S. (2005). Classification and labeling. In J. W. Jacobson, R. M. Foxx, & J. A. Mulick (Eds.), *Controversial therapies for developmental disabilities: Fad, fashion, and science in professional practice* (pp. 85–99). Mahwah, NJ: Erlbaum.

Vitiello, B. (2006). An update on publicly funded multisite trials in pediatric psychopharmacology. *Child and Adolescent Psychiatric Clinics of North America, 15*, 1–12.

Volker, M. A., Lopata, C., & Cook-Cottone, C. (2006). Assessment of children with intellectual giftedness and reading disabilities. *Psychology in the Schools, 43*, 855–869.

Volkmar, F. R., Cohen, D. J., & Paul, R. (1986). An evaluation of DSM-III criteria for infantile autism. *Journal of the American Academy of Child and Adolescent Psychiatry, 25*, 190–197.

Volkmar, F. R., & Klin, A. (2000). Diagnostic issues in Asperger syndrome. In A. Klin, F. R. Volkmar, & S. S. Sparrow (Eds.), *Asperger syndrome* (pp. 25–71). New York: Guilford Press.

Volkmar, F. R., Koenig, K., & State, M. (2005). Childhood disintegrative disorder. In F. R. Volkmar, R. Paul, A. Klin, & D. Cohen (Eds.), *Handbook of autism and pervasive developmental disorders, Vol. 1: Diagnosis, development, neurobiology, and behavior* (pp. 70–87). Hoboken, NJ: Wiley.

Volkow, N. D., Wang, G. J., Fowler, J. S., Logan, J., Gerasimov, M., Maynard, L., et al. (2001). Therapeutic doses of oral methylphenidate significantly increase extracellular dopamine in the human brain. *Neuroscience, 21*, 1–5.

Vostanis, P., Feehan, C., Grattan, E., & Bickerton, W. (1996a). A randomized, controlled, out-patient trial of cognitive-behavioural treatment for children and adolescents with depression: 9-month follow-up. *Journal of Affective Disorders, 40,* 105–116.

Vostanis, P., Feehan, C., Grattan, E., & Bickerton, W. (1996b). Treatment for children and adolescents with depression: Lessons from a controlled trial. *Clinical Child Psychology and Psychiatry, 1,* 199–212.

Vygotsky, L. S. (1978). *Mind and society: The development of higher mental processes.* Cambridge, MA: Harvard University Press.

Waaktaar, T., Borge, A. I. H., Fundingsrud, H. P., Christie, H. J., & Torgersen, S. (2004). The role of stressful life events in the development of depressive symptoms in adolescence: A longitudinal community study. *Journal of Adolescence, 27,* 153–163.

Wade, T. J., & Cairney, J. (2006). Sociological contributions. In R. T. Ammerman (Ed.), *Comprehensive handbook of personality and psychopathology* (Vol. 3, pp. 44–63). Hoboken, NJ: Wiley.

Wagner, E. F., & Austin, A. M. (2006). Substance use disorders. In R. T. Ammerman (Ed.), *Comprehensive handbook of personality and psychopathology* (Vol. 3, pp. 348–366). Hoboken, NJ: Wiley.

Wagner, K. D. (2005). Pharmacotherapy for major depression in children and adolescents. *Progress in Neuro-Psychopharmacology & Biological Psychiatry, 29,* 819–826.

Wagner, K. D., Ambrosini, P., Rynn, M., Wohlberg, C., Yang, R., Greenbaum, M. S., et al. (2003). Efficacy of sertraline in the treatment of children and adolescents with major depressive disorder: Two randomized controlled trials. *Journal of the American Medical Association, 290,* 1033–1041.

Wagner, K. D., Berard, R., Stein, M. B., Wetherhold, E., Carpenter, D. J., Perera, P., et al. (2004). A multicenter, randomized, double-blind, placebo-controlled trial of paroxetine in children and adolescents with social anxiety disorder. *Archives of General Psychiatry, 61,* 1153–1162.

Wagner, K. D., Robb, A. S., Findling, R. L., Jin, J., Gutierrez, M., & Heydorn, W. E. (2004). A randomized, placebo-controlled trial of citalopram for the treatment of major depression in children and adolescents. *American Journal of Psychiatry, 161,* 1079–1083.

Wagner, K. D., Weller, E. B., Carlson, G. A., Sachs, G., Biederman, J., Frazier, J. A., et al. (2002). An open-label trial of divalproex in children and adolescents with bipolar disorder. *Journal of the American Academy of Child and Adolescent Psychiatry, 41,* 1224–30.

Wakefield, A. J., Murch, S. H., Anthony, A., Linnell, J., Casson, D. M., Malik, M., et al. (1998). Ileal lymphoid-nodular hyperplasia, non-specific colitis, and pervasive developmental disorder in children. *Lancet, 351,* 637–641.

Wakefield, J. C. (1992). Disorder as harmful dysfunction: A conceptual critique of DSM-III-R's definition of mental disorder. *Psychological Review, 99,* 232–247.

Waldron, H. B., & Kaminer, Y. (2004). On the learning curve: The emerging evidence supporting cognitive-behavioral therapies for adolescent substance abuse. *Addiction, 99,* 93–105.

Waldron, H. B., Slesnick, N., Brody, J. L., Charles W. T., & Thomas R. P. (2001). Treatment outcomes for adolescent substance abuse at 4- and 7-month assessments. *Journal of Consulting and Clinical Psychology, 69,* 802–813.

Walker, D. D., Roffman, R. A., Stephens, R. S., Wakana, K., & Berghuis, J. (2006). Motivational enhancement therapy for adolescent marijuana users: A preliminary randomized controlled trial. *Journal of Consulting and Clinical Psychology, 74,* 628–632.

Walkup, J. T., Labellarte, M. J., Riddle, M. A., Pine, D., Greenhill, L., Klein, R., et al. (2003). Searching for moderators and mediators of pharmacological treatment effects in children and adolescents with anxiety disorders. *Journal of the American Academy of Child & Adolescent Psychiatry, 42,* 13–21.

Wallander, J. L., Dekker, M. C., & Koot, H. M. (2006). Risk factors for psychopathology in children with intellectual disability: A prospective longitudinal population-based study. *Journal of Intellectual Disability Research, 50,* 259–268.

Ward, A., Hudson, S. M., & Marshall, W. L. (1996). Attachment style in sex offenders: A preliminary study. *Journal of Sex Research, 33,* 17–26.

Warner, L. A., Pottick, K. J., & Mukherjee, A. (2004). Use of psychotropic medications by youths with psychiatric diagnoses in the U.S. mental health system. *Psychiatric Services, 55,* 309–311.

Warren, S. L., Emde, R. N., & Sroufe, L. A. (2000). Internal representations: Predicting anxiety from children's play narratives. *Journal of the American Academy of Child and Adolescent Development, 39,* 100–107.

Warren, S. L., Huston, L., Egeland, B., & Sroufe, L. A. (1997). Child and adolescent anxiety disorders and early attachment. *Journal of the American Academy of Child and Adolescent Psychiatry, 36,* 637–644.

Warren, S. L., & Simmens, J. (2005). Predicting toddler anxiety/depressive symptoms: Effects of caregiver sensitivity of temperamentally vulnerable children. *Infant Mental Health Journal, 26,* 40–55.

Warren, S. L., & Sroufe, L. A. (2004). Developmental issues. In T. H. Ollendick & J. S. March (Eds.), *Phobic and anxiety disorders in children and adolescents* (pp. 92–115). New York: Oxford University Press.

Waschbusch, D. A. (2002). A meta-analytic examination of comorbid hyperactive-impulsive-attention problems and conduct problems. *Psychological Bulletin, 128,* 118–150.

Waschbusch, D. A., Willoughby, M. T., & Pelham, W. E. (1998). Criterion validity and the utility of reactive and proactive aggression: Comparisons to attention deficit hyperactivity disorder, oppositional defiant disorder, conduct disorder, and other measures of functioning. *Journal of Clinical Child Psychology, 27,* 396–405.

Wasserman, G. A., & Seracini, A. M. (2000). Family risk factors and family treatments for early-onset offending. In R. Loeber & D. P. Farrington (Eds.), *Child delinquents, development, intervention, and service needs* (pp. 165–189). Thousand Oaks, CA: Sage.

Watson, J. B., & Rayner, R. (1920). Conditioned emotional reactions. *Journal of Experimental Psychology, 3,* 1–14.

Webster-Stratton, C. (1990). Long-term follow-up of families with young conduct problem children: From preschool to grade school. *Journal of Clinical Child Psychology, 19,* 144–149.

Webster-Stratton, C. (2005). The incredible years: A training series for the prevention and treatment of conduct problems in young children. In E. D. Hibbs & P. S. Jensen (Eds.), *Psychosocial treatments for child and adolescent disorders: Empirically based strategies for clinical practice* (pp. 507–555). Washington, DC: American Psychological Association.

Webster-Stratton, C., & Hammond, M. (1990). Predictors of treatment outcome in parent training for families with conduct problem children. *Behavior Therapy, 21,* 319–337.

Webster-Stratton, C., & Hammond, M. (1999). Marital conflict management skills, parenting style, and early-onset conduct problems: Processes and pathways. *Journal of Child Psychology and Psychiatry, 40,* 917–927.

Webster-Stratton, C., & Reid, M. J. (2007). Incredible years parents and teachers training series: A Head Start partnership to promote social competence and prevent conduct problems. In P. Tolan, J. Szapocznik, & S. Sambrano (Eds.), *Preventing youth substance abuse: Science-based programs for children and adolescents* (pp. 67–88). Washington, DC: American Psychological Association.

Webster-Stratton, C., Reid, M. J., & Hammond, M. (2001). Preventing conduct problems, promoting social competence: A parent and teacher training partnership in Head Start. *Journal of Clinical Child Psychology, 30,* 283–302.

Webster-Stratton, C., Reid, M. J., & Hammond, M. (2004). Treating children with early-onset conduct problems: Intervention outcomes for parent, child, and teacher training. *Journal of Clinical Child and Adolescent Psychology, 33,* 105–124.

Wechsler, D. (1958). *The measurement and appraisal of adult intelligence.* Baltimore, MD: Williams & Wilkins.

Wechsler, D. (2003). *Wechsler intelligence scale for Children: Administration and scoring manual* (4th ed.). San Antonio, TX: The Psychological Corporation.

Weems, C. F., Berman, S. L., Silverman, W. K., & Saavedra, L. M. (2001). Cognitive errors in youth with anxiety disorders: The linkages between negative cognitive errors and anxious symptoms. *Cognitive Therapy and Research, 25,* 559–575.

Weems, C. F., Pina, A. A., Costa, N. M., Watts, S. E., Taylor, L. K., & Cannon, M. F. (2007). Predisaster trait anxiety and negative affect predict posttraumatic stress in youths after hurricane Katrina. *Journal of Consulting and Clinical Psychology, 75,* 154–159.

Weems, C. F., Silverman, W. K., & La Greca, A. M. (2000). What do youth referred for anxiety problems worry about? Worry and its relation to anxiety and anxiety disorders in children and adolescents. *Journal of Abnormal Child Psychology, 28,* 63–72.

Weems, C. F., & Watts, S. E. (2005). Cognitive models of childhood anxiety. In C. M. Velotis (Ed.), *Anxiety disorder research* (pp. 205–232). Hauppauge, NY: Nova Science.

Weinfield, N. S., Sroufe, L. A., & Egeland, B. (2000). Attachment from infancy to early adulthood in a high-risk sample: Continuity, discontinuity, and their correlates. *Child Development, 71,* 695–702.

Weiss, L. H., & Schwarz, J. C. (1996). The relationship between parenting types and older adolescents' personality, academic achievement, adjustment, and substance use. *Child Development, 67*(5), 2101–2114.

Weisz, J. R. (1990). Cultural-familial mental retardation: A developmental perspective on cognitive performance and "helpless" behavior. In R. M. Hodapp, J. A. Burack, & E. Zigler (Eds.), *Issues in the developmental approach to mental retardation* (pp. 137–168). New York: Cambridge University Press.

Weisz, J. R., Doss, A. J., & Hawley, K. M. (2005). Youth psychotherapy outcome research: A review and critique of the evidence base. *Annual Review of Psychology, 56,* 337–363.

Weisz, J. R., Jensen, A. L., & McLeod, B. D. (2005). Development and dissemination of child and adolescent psychotherapies: Milestones, methods, and a new deployment-focused model. In E. D. Hibbs & P. S. Jensen (Eds.), *Psychosocial treatments for child and adolescent disorders: Empirically based strategies for clinical practice* (pp. 9–39). Washington, DC: American Psychological Association.

Weisz, J. R., Thurber, C. A., Sweeney, L., Proffitt, V. D., & LeGagnoux, G. L. (1997). Brief treatment of mild-to-moderate child depression using primary and secondary control enhancement training. *Journal of Consulting and Clinical Psychology, 65,* 703–707.

Weisz, J. R., Weiss, B., Alicke, M. D., & Klotz, M. L. (1987). Effectiveness of psychotherapy with children and adolescents: A meta-analysis for clinicians. *Journal of Consulting and Clinical Psychology, 55,* 542–549.

Weisz, J. R., Weiss, B., Han, S. S., Granger, D. A., & Morton, T. (1995). Effects of psychotherapy with children and adolescents revisited: A meta-analysis of treatment outcome studies. *Psychological Bulletin, 117,* 450–468.

Welch, S. L., & Fairburn, C. G. (1996). Childhood sexual and physical abuse as risk factors for the development of bulimia nervosa: A community-based case control study. *Child Abuse and Neglect, 20,* 633–642.

Weller, E. B., Weller, R. A., & Danielyan, A. K. (2004). Mood disorders in prepubertal children and adolescents. In J. M. Wiener & M. K. Dulcan (Eds.), *The American psychiatric publishing textbook of child and adolescent psychiatry* (pp. 411–481). Washington, DC: American Psychiatric Publishing.

Wellington, T. M., Semrud-Clikeman, M., Gregory, A. L., Murphy, J. M., & Lancaster, J. L. (2006). Magnetic resonance imaging volumetric analysis of the putamen in children with ADHD: Combined type versus control. *Journal of Attention Disorders, 10,* 171–180.

Wells, K. C., Pelham, W. E., Kotkin, R. A., Hoza, B., Abikoff, H. B., Abramowitz, A., et al. (2000). Psychosocial treatment strategies in the MTA study: Rationale, methods, and critical issues in design and implementation. *Journal of Abnormal Child Psychology, 28,* 483–505.

Werba, B. E., Eyberg, S. M., Boggs, S. R., & Algina, J. (2006). Predicting outcome in parent-child interaction therapy: Success and attrition. *Behavior Modification, 30,* 618–646.

Wesch, D., & Lutzker, J. R. (1991). A comprehensive 5-year evaluation of project 12-Ways: An ecobehavioral program for treating and preventing child abuse and neglect. *Journal of Family Violence, 6,* 17–35.

West, A. E., Henry, D. B., & Pavuluri, M. N. (2007). Maintenance model of integrated psychosocial treatment in pediatric bipolar disorder: A pilot feasibility study. *Journal of the American Academy of Child & Adolescent Psychiatry, 46,* 205–212.

Westen, D., Novotny, C. M., & Thompson-Brenner, H. (2004). The empirical status of empirically supported psychotherapies: Assumptions, findings, and reporting in controlled clinical trials. *Psychological Bulletin, 130,* 631–663.

Whalen, C. K., Henker, B., King, P. S., Jamner, L. D., & Levine, L. (2004). Adolescents react to the events of September 11, 2001: Focused versus ambient impact. *Journal of Abnormal Child Psychology, 32,* 1–11.

White, H. R., Labouvie, E. W., & Papadaratsakis, V. (2005). Changes in substance use during the transition to adulthood: A comparison of college students and their noncollege age peers. *Journal of Drug Issues, 35,* 281–306.

White, H. R., McMorris, B. J., Catalano, R. F., Fleming, C. B., Haggerty, K. P., & Abbott, R. D. (2006). Increases in alcohol and marijuana use during the transition out of high school into emerging adulthood: The effects of leaving home, going to college, and high school protective factors. *Journal of Studies on Alcohol, 67,* 810–822.

Whiteman, M., Fanshel, D., & Grundy, J. F. (1987). Cognitive-behavioral interventions aimed at anger of parents at risk of child abuse. *Social Work, 32,* 469–474.

Whittinger, N. S., Langley, K., Fowler, T. A., Thomas, H. V., & Thapar, A. (2007). Clinical Precursors of adolescent conduct disorder in children with attention-deficit/hyperactivity disorder. *Journal of the American Academy of Child & Adolescent Psychiatry, 46,* 179–187.

Whittington, C. J., Kendall, T., & Fonagy, P. (2004). Selective serotonin reuptake inhibitors in childhood depression: Systematic review of published versus unpublished data. *Lancet, 363,* 1341–1345.

Widom, C. S., & Kuhns, J. B. (1996). Childhood victimization and subsequent risk for promiscuity, prostitution, and teenage pregnancy: A prospective study. *American Journal of Public Health, 86,* 1607–1612.

Wigal, T., Greenhill, L., Chuang, S., McGough, J., Vitiello, B., Skrobala, A., et al. (2006). Safety and tolerability of methylphenidate in preschool children with ADHD. *Journal of the American Academy of Child & Adolescent Psychiatry, 45,* 1294–1303.

Wight, R. G., Sepulveda, J. E., & Aneshensel, C. S. (2004). Depressive symptoms: How do adolescents compare with adults? *Journal of Adolescent Health, 34,* 314–323.

Wild, L. G., Flisher, A. J., & Lombard, C. (2004). Suicidal ideation and attempts in adolescents: Associations with depression and six domains of self-esteem. *Journal of Adolescence, 27,* 611–624.

Wilens, T. E., Biederman, J., Kwon, A., Ditterline, J., Forkner, P., Moore, H., et al. (2004). Risk of substance use disorders in adolescents with bipolar disorder. *Journal of the American Academy of Child & Adolescent Psychiatry, 43,* 1380–1386.

Wilens, T. E., & Spencer, T. J. (2000). The stimulants revisited. *Child and Adolescent Psychiatric Clinics of North America, 9,* 573–603.

Wilens, T. E., Spencer, T., & Biederman, J. (1996). Attention deficit disorder with substance abuse. In T. E. Brown (Ed.), *Subtypes of attention deficit disorder in children, adolescents, and adults* (pp. 319–339). Washington, DC: American Psychiatric Press.

Wilkinson, P. O., & Goodyer, M. (2006). Attention difficulties and mood-related ruminative response style in adolescents with unipolar depression. *Journal of Child Psychology and Psychiatry, 47,* 1284–1291.

Willcutt, E. G., Pennington, B. F., Olson, R. K., Chhabildas, N., & Hulslander, J. (2005). Neuropsychological analyses of comorbidity between reading disability and attention deficit hyperactivity disorder: In search of the common deficit. *Developmental Neuropsychology, 27,* 35–78.

Williams, C. A. (2005). Neurological aspects of the Angelman syndrome. *Brain & Development, 27,* 88–94.

Williamson, D. E., Birmaher, B., Frank, E., Anderson, B. P., Matty, M. K., & Kupfer, D. J. (1998). Nature of life events and difficulties in depressed adolescents. *Journal of the American Academy of Child & Adolescent Psychiatry, 37,* 1047–1057.

Williamson, P., McLeskey, J., Hoppey, D., & Rentz, T. (2006). Educating students with mental retardation in general education classrooms. *Exceptional Children, 72,* 347–361.

Willoughby, M. T. (2003). Developmental course of ADHD symptomatology during the transition from childhood to adolescence : A review with recommendations. *Journal of Child Psychology and Psychiatry, 4,* 88–106.

Willoughby, M. T., Curran, P. J., Costello, E. J., & Angold, A. (2000). Implications of early versus late onset of attention-deficit/hyperactivity disorder symptoms. *Journal of the American Academy of Child and Adolescent Psychiatry, 39,* 1512–1519.

Wilson, G. T., Becker, C. B., & Heffernan, K. (2003). Eating disorders. In E. J. Mash & R. A. Barkley (Eds.), *Child psychopathology* (pp. 687–715). New York: Guilford Press.

Wilson, G. T., Fairburn, C. G., & Agras, W. S. (1997). Cognitive-behavioral therapy for bulimia nervosa. In D. M. Garner & P. Garfinkel (Eds.), *Handbook of treatment for eating disorders* (pp. 67–93). New York: Guilford Press.

Wilson, G. T., Fairburn, C. C., Agras, W. S., Walsh, B. T., & Kraemer, H. (2002). Cognitive-behavioral therapy for bulimia nervosa: Time course and mechanisms of change. *Journal of Consulting and Clinical Psychology, 70,* 267–274.

Wilson, G. T., & Pike, K. M. (2001). Eating disorders. In D. H. Barlow (Ed.), *Clinical handbook of psychological disorders: A step-by-step treatment manual* (pp. 332–375). New York: Guilford Press.

Wilson, J. J., & Levin, R. (2005). Attention-deficit/hyperactivity disorder and early-onset substance use disorders. *Journal of Child and Adolescent Psychopharmacology, 15,* 751–763.

Wilson, J. K., & Rapee, R. M. (2005). The interpretation of negative social events in social phobia: Changes during treatment and relationship to outcome. *Behaviour Research and Therapy, 43,* 373–389.

Windle, M., & Davies, P. T. (1999). Depression and heavy alcohol use among adolescents: Concurrent and prospective relations. *Development and Psychopathology, 11,* 823–844.

Wing, L. (1981). Asperger's syndrome: A clinical account. *Psychological Medicine, 11,* 115–29.

Wing, L. (2000). Past and future of research on Asperger syndrome. In A. Klin, F. R. Volkmar & S. S. Sparrow (Eds.), *Asperger syndrome* (pp. 418–432). New York: Guilford Press.

Winters, K. C., Stinchfield, R. D., Opland, E., Weller, C., & Latimer, W. W. (2000). The effectiveness of the Minnesota model approach in the treatment of adolescent drug abusers. *Addiction, 95,* 601–612.

Wise, B. K., Cuffe, S. P., & Fischer, T. (2001). Dual diagnosis and successful participation of adolescents in substance abuse treatment. *Journal of Substance Abuse Treatment, 21,* 161–165.

Wohlfarth, T., Lekkerkerker, F., & van Zwieten, B. (2004). Use of selective serotonin reuptake inhibitors in childhood depression. *Lancet, 364,* 659–660.

Wolf, M., & Bowers, P. G. (1999). The double deficit hypothesis for the developmental dyslexias. *Journal of Educational Psychology, 91,* 415–438.

Wolfberg, P. J., & Schuler, A. L. (2006). Promoting social reciprocity and symbolic representation in children with autism spectrum disorders. In T. Charman & W. Stone (Eds.), *Social and communication development in autism spectrum disorders* (pp. 180–218). New York: Guilford Press.

Wolpe, J. (1958). *Psychotherapy by reciprocal inhibition.* Oxford, UK: Stanford University Press.

Wonderlich, S., Crosby, R., Mitchell, J., Thompson, K., Redlin, J., Demuth, G., et al. (2001). Pathways mediating sexual abuse and eating disturbance in children. *International Journal of Eating Disorders, 29,* 270–279.

Wong, B. (1997). Research on genre-specific strategies in enhancing writing in adolescents with learning disabilities. *Learning Disability Quarterly, 20,* 140–159.

Wood, A., Harrington, R., & Moore, A. (1996). Controlled trial of a brief cognitive-behavioural intervention in adolescent patients with depressive disorders. *Journal of Child Psychology and Psychiatry, 37,* 737–746.

Woodcock, R. W., McGrew, K. S., & Mather, N. (2001). *The Woodcock-Johnson III.* Itasca, IL: Riverside.

Woods, B. T., Yurgelun-Todd, D., Mikulis, D., & Pillay, S. S. (1995). Age-related MRI abnormalities in bipolar illness: A clinical study. *Biological Psychiatry, 38,* 846–847.

Woodward, L. J., & Fergusson, D. M. (1999). Early conduct problems and later risk of teenage pregnancy in girls. *Development and Psychopathology, 11,* 127–141.

World Health Organization. (2001). *Mental health: New understanding, new hope.* Geneva: Author.

Wozniak, J., Biederman, J., Kiely, K., Ablon, J. S., Faraone, S. V., Mundy, E., et al. (1995). Mania-like symptoms suggestive of childhood-onset bipolar disorder in clinically referred children. *Journal of the American Academy of Child and Adolescent Psychiatry, 34,* 867–876.

Wu, K. K., Anderson, V., & Castiello, U. (2006). Attention-deficit/hyperactivity disorder and working memory: A task switching paradigm. *Journal of Clinical and Experimental Neuropsychology, 28*(8), 1288–1306.

Wu, P., Hoven, C. W., Liu, X., Cohen, P., Fuller, C. J., & Shaffer, D. (2005). Substance use, suicidal ideation and attempts in children and adolescents. *Suicide and Life-Threatening Behavior, 34,* 408–420.

Wynn, K. (1992). Addition and subtraction by human infants. *Nature, 358,* 749–450.

Yoder, K. A. (1999). Comparing suicide attemptors, suicide ideators, and nonsuicidal homeless and runaway adolescents. *Suicide and Life Threatening Behavior, 29,* 25–36.

Yoder, P. J., & McDuffie, A. S. (2006). Treatment responding to and initiating joint attention. In T. Charman & W. Stone (Eds.), *Social and communication development in autism spectrum disorders* (pp. 117–142). New York: Guilford Press.

Young, A. R. (2005). Learning disorders in girls. In D. J. Bell, S. L. Foster, & E. J. Mash (Eds.), *Handbook of behavioral and emotional problems in girls* (pp. 263–283). New York: Kluwer Academic/Plenum.

Young, J. F., Mufson, L., & Davies, M. (2006). Efficacy of interpersonal psychotherapy-adolescent skills training: An indicated preventive intervention for depression. *Journal of Child Psychology and Psychiatry, 47,* 1254–1262.

Young, S., Stallings, M., Corley, R., Krauter, K., & Hewitt, J. (2000). Genetic and environmental influences on behavioral disinhibition. *American Journal of Medical Genetics, 96,* 684–695.

Youssef, G., Plancherel, B., Laget, J., Corcos, M., Flament, M. F., & Halfon, O. (2004). Personality trait risk factors for attempted suicide among young women with eating disorders. *European Psychiatry, 19,* 131–139.

Ystgaard, M., Hestetun, I., Loeb, M., & Mehlum, L. (2004). Is there a specific relationship between childhood sexual and physical abuse and repeated suicidal behavior? *Child Abuse & Neglect, 28,* 863–875.

Yurgelun-Todd, D., Gruber, S., Kanayama, W., Baird, A., & Young, A. (2000). FMRI during affect discrimination in bipolar affective disorder. *Bipolar Disorders, 2,* 237–248.

Zahn-Waxler, C. (2000). The development of empathy, guilt, and internalization of distress. In R. J. Davidson (Ed.), *Anxiety, depression, and emotion* (pp. 222–265). New York: Oxford University Press.

Zahn-Waxler, C., Cole, P. M., & Barrett, K. C. (1991). Guilt and empathy: Sex differences and implications for the development of depression. In J. Garber & K. A. Dodge (Eds.), *The development of emotion regulation and dysregulation* (pp. 243–272). Cambridge: Cambridge University Press.

Zane, T. (2005). Fads in special education: An overview. In J. W. Jacobson, R. M. Foxx, & J. A. Mulick (Eds.), *Controversial therapies for developmental disabilities: Fad, fashion, and science in professional practice* (pp. 175–173). Mahwah, NJ: Erlbaum.

Zigler, E. (1969). Developmental versus difference theories of mental retardation and the problem of motivation. *American Journal of Mental Deficiency, 73,* 536–556.

Zigler, E., Balla, D., & Hodapp, R. M. (1986). On the definition and classification of mental retardation. *American Journal of Mental Deficiency, 89,* 215–230.

Zigler, E., Hodapp, R. M., & Edison, M. R. (1990). From theory to practice in the care and education of mentally retarded individuals. *American Journal on Mental Retardation, 95,* 1–12.

Zito, J. M., Safer, D. J., dos Reis, S., Gardner, J. F., Boles, M., & Lynch, F. (2000). Trends in the prescribing of psychotropic medications to preschoolers. *Journal of the American Medical Association, 283,* 1025–1030.

Zorzi, M., Priftis, K., & Umilta, C. (2002). Neglect disrupts the mental number line. *Nature, 417,* 138–139.

Zuckerman, M. (2007). Sensation seeking and substance use and abuse: Smoking, drinking, and drugs. In M. Zuckerman (Ed.), *Sensation seeking and risky behavior* (pp. 107–143). Washington, DC: American Psychological Association.

Index

About the Author

Robert Weis earned a B.A. in psychology from the University of Chicago and a Ph.D. in clinical psychology from Northern Illinois University. He completed his predoctoral and postdoctoral work in clinical child and pediatric psychology at Columbus Children's Hospital (Ohio) and Portage County Mental Health Center (Wisconsin). Robert is currently a faculty member in the Department of Psychology at Denison University, a liberal arts college near Columbus, Ohio. He teaches courses in abnormal psychology, assessment and counseling, and research methods. He also supervises an undergraduate internship course in applied psychology. His research interests are in psychometrics, program evaluation, and the quality of parent-child interactions. His work has been published in the *Journal of Abnormal Child and Adolescent Psychology, Journal of Personality and Social Psychology, Psychological Assessment,* and *Psychology in the Schools.* When not working, Robert enjoys spending time with his wife and three children.